The Mahayana
Mahaparinirvana Sutra

Last and most impressive teachings of the Buddha
about Reality and the True Self

Translated into English by Kosho Yamamoto.
Edited, revised and copyright by Dr. Tony Page
Source: http://www.nirvanasutra.org.uk

F.Lepine Publishing
ISBN 978-0-9810613-2-0
This edition published with permission from Dr. Tony Page
This edition Copyright 2008 © François Lépine
www.FLEPINE.com

All profits from this book are used to help propagate this most important teaching.

Table of Contents

Chapter One: Introductory..5
Chapter Two: On Cunda..17
Chapter Three: On Grief...25
Chapter Four: On Long Life...33
Chapter Five: On the Adamantine Body...41
Chapter Six: On the Virtue of the Name..45
Chapter Seven: On the Four Aspects..46
Chapter Eight: On the Four Dependables...69
Chapter Nine: On Wrong and Right..81
Chapter Ten: On the Four Truths..88
Chapter Eleven: On the Four Inversions..91
Chapter Twelve: On the Nature of the Tathagata...93
Chapter Thirteen: On Letters..105
Chapter Fourteen: On the Parable of the Birds..109
Chapter Fifteen: On the Parable of the Moon...113
Chapter Sixteen: On the Bodhisattva...117
Chapter Seventeen: On the Questions Raised by the Crowd........................131
Chapter Eighteen: On Actual Illness..141
Chapter Nineteen: On Holy Actions 1..149
Chapter Twenty: On Holy Actions 2...165
Chapter Twenty-One: On Pure Actions 1..187
Chapter Twenty-Two: On Pure Actions 2...203
Chapter Twenty-Three: On Pure Actions 3...217
Chapter Twenty-Four: On Pure Actions 4...233
Chapter Twenty-Five: On Pure Actions 5...247
Chapter Twenty-Six: On the Action of the Child..257
Chapter Twenty-Seven: Bodhisattva Highly-Virtuous King 1......................259
Chapter Twenty-Eight: Bodhisattva Highly-Virtuous King 2.......................273
Chapter Twenty-Nine: Bodhisattva Highly-Virtuous King 3........................285
Chapter Thirty: Bodhisattva Highly-Virtuous King 4...................................295
Chapter Thirty-One: Bodhisattva Highly-Virtuous King 5...........................307
Chapter Thirty-Two: Bodhisattva Highly-Virtuous King 6...........................319
Chapter Thirty-Three: On Bodhisattva Lion's Roar 1...................................331
Chapter Thirty-Four: On Bodhisattva Lion's Roar 2.....................................343
Chapter Thirty-Five: On Bodhisattva Lion's Roar 3.....................................357
Chapter Thirty-Six: On Bodhisattva Lion's Roar 4.......................................365
Chapter Thirty-Seven: On Bodhisattva Lion's Roar 5..................................371
Chapter Thirty-Eight: On Bodhisattva Lion's Roar 6....................................383
Chapter Thirty-Nine: On Bodhisattva Lion's Roar 7....................................397
Chapter Forty: On Bodhisattva Kasyapa 1..411
Chapter Forty-One: On Bodhisattva Kasyapa 2..427
Chapter Forty-Two: On Bodhisattva Kasyapa 3..443
Chapter Forty-Three: On Bodhisattva Kasyapa 4...455
Chapter Forty-Four: On Bodhisattva Kasyapa 5...457
Chapter Forty-Five: On Kaundinya 1..473
Chapter Forty-Six: On Kaundinya 2..487

Chapter One: Introductory

Thus have I heard. At one time, the Buddha was staying at Kusinagara in the land of the Mallas, close to the river Ajitavati, where the twin sal trees stood. At that time, the great bhiksus as many as 80 billion hundred thousand were with the World-Honoured One. They surrounded him front and back. On the 15th of the second month, as the Buddha was about to enter Nirvana, he, with his divine power, spoke in a great voice, which filled the whole world and reached the highest of the heavens. It said to all beings in a way each could understand: "Today, the Tathagata [i.e. Buddha] the Alms-deserving and All-Enlightened One, pities, protects and, with an undivided mind, sees beings as he does his [son] Rahula. So, he is the refuge and house of the world. The greatly Enlightened World-Honoured One is about to enter Nirvana. The beings who have doubts may now all ask questions of him." At that time, early in the morning, the World-Honoured One emitted from his mouth rays of light of various hues, namely: blue, yellow, red, white, crystal, and agate. The rays of light shone all over the 3,000 great-thousand Buddha lands. Also, the ten directions were alike shone upon. All the sins and worries of beings of the six realms, as they were illuminated, were expiated. People saw and heard this, and worry greatly beset them. They all sorrowfully cried and wept: "Oh, the kindest father! Oh, woe is the day! Oh, the sorrow!" They raised their hands, beat their heads and breasts, and cried aloud. Of them, some trembled, wept, and sobbed. At that time, the great earth, the mountains, and great seas all shook. Then, all of them said to one another: "Let us for the present suppress our feelings, let us not be greatly smitten by sorrow! Let us speed to Kusinagara, call at the land of the Mallas, touch the feet of the Tathagata, pay homage and beg: "O Tathagata! Please do not enter Parinirvana, but stay one more kalpa [aeon] or less than a kalpa." They pressed their palms together and said again: "The world is empty! Fortune has departed from us beings; evil things will increase in the world. O you! Hurry up, go quickly! Soon the Tathagata [i.e. Buddha] will surely enter Nirvana." They also said: "The world is empty, empty! From now on, no one protects us, and we have none to pay homage to. Poverty-stricken and alone! If we once part from the World-Honoured One, and if doubts arise, whom are we to ask?" At that time, there were many of the Buddha's disciples there, such as Venerable Mahakatyayana, Vakkula, and Upananda. All such great bhiksus, when they saw the light, shook and were greatly stirred, so much so that they could not hold themselves well. Their minds became muddled, and chaos ruled. They cried aloud and displayed variegated grief. There were present, at that time, 8 million bhiksus. All were arhats [saints]. They were unmolested [unlimited] in mind and could act as they willed. They were segregated from all illusions, and all their sense-organs were subdued. Like great naga [serpent] kings, they were perfect in great virtue. They were accomplished in the wisdom of the All-Void and perfect in the attainments of their own [in inner attainments]. They were like the sandalwood forest with sandalwood all around, or like a lion king surrounded by lions. They were perfect in all such virtues. They were the true sons of the Buddha. Early in the morning, when the sun had just risen, they were up from their beds in the places where they lived and were about to use their toothbrushes, when they encountered the light that arose from the Buddha's person. And they said to one another: "Hurry up with bathing and gargling, and be clean." So did they say, and their hair stood on end all over their body, and their blood so ran that they looked like palasa flowers. Tears filled their eyes, which expressed great pain. To benefit and give peace to beings, to establish the Transcendent Truth of the All-Void of Mahayana, to reveal what the Tathagata had by expediency latently taught so that all his sermons would not come to an end, and to subjugate the minds of all beings, they sped to where the Buddha was. They fell down at the Buddha's feet, touched them with their heads, walked around him a 100 thousand times, folded their hands, paid homage, stepped back and sat on one side. At that time, there were present such women as Kuddara and such bhiksunis [nuns] as Subhadra, Upananda, Sagaramati, and 6 million bhiksunis. They were all great arhats. All "'asravas'" [inner defilements] having been done away with, they were unmolested in mind and could act as they willed. They were parted from all illusion and all their sense-organs were subdued. Like great nagas, they were perfect in virtue. They were accomplished in the Wisdom of the All-Void. Also, early in the morning, after the sun had just risen, their hair stood on end all over their body and their blood so ran through their vessels that they looked like palasa flowers. Tears filled their eyes, which bespoke great sorrow. They desired to benefit beings, to give peace and bliss, and establish the Transcendent Truth of the All-Void of Mahayana. They meant to manifest what the Tathagata had by expediency latently taught, so that all his sermons would not disappear. In order to subjugate the minds of all beings, they sped to where the Buddha was, touched his feet, walked around him a 100 thousand times, folded their hands, paid homage, stepped back and sat on one side. Of the bhiksunis, there were again those who were the nagas of Bodhisattvas and humans. They had attained the ten stages [of Bodhisattvic development], where they abided unmoved. They were born as females so as to teach beings. They always practised the four limitless minds [of loving-kindness, compassion, sympathetic joy, and equanimity], thereby attaining unlimited power and acting well in place of the Buddha. At that time there were also Bodhisattva-mahasattvas [great Bodhisattvas] who were as plentiful as the sands of the river Ganges and who were all nagas of men, attaining the level of the ten stages and abiding there unmoved. As an expedient, they had gained life as men and were called Bodhisattvvas Sagaraguna and Aksayamati. Such Bodhisattva-mahasattvas as these headed the number. They all prized Mahayana, abided in it, deeply understood, loved and protected it, and well responded to the call of the world. They took vows and each said: "I shall pass those who have not yet attained the Way to the other shore [i.e. of salvation]. Already over innumerable past kalpas, I have upheld the pure precepts [of morality] and acted as I should have acted. I made the unreleased gain the Way so that they could carry over the seed of the Three Treasures

[i.e. Buddha, Dharma, Sangha]. And in the days to come, I shall turn the wheel of Dharma [i.e. teach Buddhism], greatly adorn myself, accomplish all innumerable virtues, and see beings as one views one's only son." They likewise, early in the morning, encountered the light of the Buddha. All their hair stood on end, and all over their body their blood so ran that they looked like palasa flowers. Tears filled their eyes, which spoke of great pain. Also to benefit beings, to give bliss, to manifest what the Tathagata had out of expediency latently taught, and to prevent the sermons from dying out, and to subjugate all beings, they sped to where the Buddha was, walked around him 100 thousand times, folded their hands, paid homage, stepped back and took their seats on one side. At that time, there were present upasakas [lay followers of Buddha] who were as many as the sands of two Ganges. They had accorded with the five precepts, and their deportment was perfect. These were such upasakas as Untainted-Virtue-King, Highly-Virtuous and others, who headed their number. They deeply cherished the thought of combating such opposites as: sorrow versus bliss, eternal versus non-eternal, pure versus non-pure, self versus non-self, real versus not-real, taking refuge versus not taking refuge, beings versus non-beings, always versus not-always, peace versus non-peace, created versus non-created, disruption versus non-disruption, Nirvana versus non-Nirvana, augmentation versus non-augmentation, and they always thought of combating such opposites of the Dharma elements as stated above. They also always loved to listen to the unsurpassed Mahayana, acted upon what they had heard and desired to teach others. They upheld well the untainted moral precepts and prized Mahayana. Already they were well contented within themselves and they made others feel well contented who prized Mahayana. They imbibed the unsurpassed Wisdom very well, loved and protected Mahayana. They accorded well with the ways of the world, passed those who had not yet gained the Way to the other shore of life, emancipated those not yet emancipated, and protected the seed of the Three Treasures so that it would not die out and so that, in days to come, they could turn the wheel of Dharma, adorn themselves greatly, deeply taste the pure moral precepts, attain accomplishment in all such virtues, have a great compassionate heart towards all beings, being impartial and not-two, and see all beings just as one views one's own only son.

Also, early in the morning when the sun had just risen, in order to cremate the Tathagata's body, people each held in their hands tens of thousands of bundles of such fragrant wood as sandalwood, aloes, goirsa sandalwood, and heavenly wood, which had annual rings and heart and which all shone out in the wonderful hues of the seven treasures. For example, the various hues were like painted colours, all of which wonders having arisen out of the power of the Buddha, and which were blue, yellow, red, and white. These were pleasing to beings' eyes. All the wood was thickly smeared with such various incense as saffron, alo wood, sarjarasa, etc. Flowers were strewn as adornments, such as the utpala [blue lotus], kumuda, padma [red lotus] and pundarika [white lotus]. Above all the fragrant wood were hung banners of five colours. They were soft and delicate, like such heavenly veils as kauseya cloth, ksuma, and silken twill. All these fragrant woods were laden onto bejewelled wagons, which shone in such various colours as blue, yellow, red, and white. The thills and spokes were all inlaid with the seven treasures. Each of these wagons was drawn by four horses, which ran like the wind. In front of each wagon stood 57 hanging ensign plants, over which were spread thin nets of true gold. Each wagon had 50 wonderful bejewelled parasols, each having on it the garlands of utpala, kumuda, padma, and pundarika. The petals of these flowers were of pure gold, and the calyxes were of diamond. In the flowers was many a black bee, which gathered there, played and amused themselves, sending forth wonderful music. These spoke of non-eternal, sorrow, All-Void, and non-Self. Also, this sound spoke of what the Bodhisattva originally does. Dances, singing, and mask dances went on, and such musical instruments were played as the "'cheng'", the flute, harp, "'hsiao'" and "'shā. "'And from the music arose a voice, which said: "Oh, woe is the day, woe the day! The world is empty!" In front of each wagon stood upasakas who were holding bejewelled tables, which were laden with various flowers such as the utpala, kumuda, padma, pundarika, and such various incense as kunkuma and others, and fumigating incense, which were all wonderful. They carried in various utensils, to prepare meals for the Buddha and the Sangha. The cooking was done with sandalwood and aloe wood as fuel, done up with the water of eight virtues. The dishes were sweet and beautiful in six tastes: bitter, sour, sweet, hot, salty, and plain. Also the virtues were three: 1) light and soft, 2) pure, and 3) true to cuisine. Equipped with such things, they sped to the land of the Mallas, to the sal forest. They also strew sand all over the ground, spreading kalinga and kambala cloths and silken

cloths on it. Such covered all about, for a space of 12 yojanas [yojana= 15-20 kilometres]. For the Buddha and the Sangha, they erected simhasana seats [lions' seats], which were inlaid with the seven treasures. The seats were as high and large as Mount Sumeru. Above these seats were hung bejewelled screens. Garlands of all kinds hung down, and from all the sal trees also hung down wonderful banners and parasols. Wonderful scents were dispersed amongst the trees and various wonderful flowers were set in between. The upasakas all said to one another: "O all beings! If you feel the need, meals, clothing, heads, eyes, limbs and everything awaits you; all will be yours." While giving, greed, anger, defilement, and poisonous [states of] mind fled; no other wish, no thought of any other blessing or pleasure was entertained. Their minds were bent solely upon the unsurpassed, pure Bodhi-mind [Enlightenment mind]. All these upasakas were well established in the Bodhisattvic state. They also said to them-selves: "The Tathagata will now take our dishes and enter Nirvana." As they thought this, all their hair stood on end; all over their body their blood so ran that their bodies looked like palasa flower. Tears filled their eyes, expressing great pain. Each carefully carried in the utensils of the meals on bejewelled wagons. The incense wood, banners, bejewelled parasols, and meals were all sped to where the Buddha was. They touched the feet of the Buddha, made offerings to the Buddha on these, walking around him 100 thousand times. They cried aloud. The earth and heaven melted in sympathy and shook. They beat their breasts and cried. Their tears ran like rain. And they said to one another: "O you! Woe is the day! The world is empty, is empty!" They threw their bodies to the ground before the Tathagata and said to him: "O Tathagata! Please have pity and accept our offerings!" The World-Honoured-One, aware of the occasion, was silent, and did not take [their offerings]. Thrice they beseeched him, but their supplications went unheard. Failing in their purpose, the upasakas were sad and sat silently. This was as in the case of a compassionate father who has but an only son. This son, of a sudden, becomes ill and dies. The cremation over, the father goes back home and is sunk in great grief. The same was the case with all the upasakas, who wept and were grief-stricken. With all their utensils positioned in a safe place, the upasakas stepped back and sat silently on one side. At that time, there were upasikas [female lay followers] present, as many as the sands of three Ganges, who were perfect in the five precepts and in deportment. They included such as Ayusguna, Gunamalya, and Visakha who headed the 84,000 and could well protect the True Dharma. In order to carry over innumerable 100 thousand beings to the other shore, they were born as females. They severely checked their own selves in the light of household laws and meditated on their own persons. Like the four vipers [the four great elements of earth, air, fire and water], this carnal body is ever pecked at and supped by innumerable vermin. It smells ill and is defiled. Greed binds. This body is hateful, like the carcass of a dog. This body is impure, from which nine holes leak out defilements. It is like a castle, the blood, flesh, spine, bone and skin forming the outer walls and the hands and legs serving as bastions, the eyes as gunholes, and the head as donjon. The mind-king [citta-raja] is seated within. Such a carnal castle is what the All-Buddha-World-Honoured One abandons and what common mortals and the ignorant always love and cling to. Such rakshasas [flesh-eating demons] as greed, anger and ignorance sit within. This body is as frail as reed, eranda [foul-smelling "recinus communis" plant], foam, and plantain. This body is non-eternal and does not stay stable even for a second. It is like lightning, madding water, and a mirage. Or it is like drawing a picture on water, which no sooner done than disappears. This body breaks just as easily as a big tree hanging over a river precipice. It does not last long. It is pecked at and devoured by foxes, wolves, owls, eagles, crows, magpies and hungry dogs. Who with a good mind finds joy in such a carnal self? One might sooner fill a cow's footprint with water than fully explain the non-eternal, the non-pure, the ill-smell and defilement of this body; or one could sooner split the great earth and crush it into the size of a pickpurse [weed] seed or even the size of a dust-mote, but never could one fully explain the wrongs and ills of this body. This being so, one ought to discard it like tears or spittle. Because of this, all upasikas train their mind in such dharmas as the Void, formlessness and desirelessness. Thus they very much desire to inquire into and abide in the teaching of the Mahayana sutras. Having listened, they expound them to others. They guard and uphold their vows and deprecate the female form. It is much to be detested and is by nature not

unbreakable. Their mind thus ever rightly sees things and crushes the endless wheel of birth and death. They look to Mahayana and are themselves well nourished by it. They feed the minds of those who prize it. They greatly cherish, defend and protect it. Though female in form, they are, truth to tell, none but Bodhisattvas. They accord well with the ways of the world and help those who have not yet gained the other shore and emancipate those not yet emancipated. They uphold the heritage of the Three Treasures, so that it will not die out and so that they can turn the wheel of Dharma in the days to come. They greatly adorn their own persons, living ever true to the prohibitions and accomplishing such virtues. Their compassionate heart extends towards all beings. They are impartial and not-two, just as one would regard one's only son. They also, early in the morning when the sun had just risen, said to one another: "Let us hasten today to the forest of the twin trees!" The upasikas' utensils were twice as many. They took these to where the Buddha was, touched his feet, walked around him 100 thousand times and said: "O World-honoured One! We have with us here meals for the Buddha and the Sangha. O Tathagata! Please have pity and accept our offerings!" The Tathagata was silent and did not take [the offerings]. Their supplication not met, all the upasikas were sad. They stepped back and sat down on one side. At that time, the Licchavis of Vaisali Castle were present and others as numerous as the sands of four Ganges, who were males, females, big and small, wives and children, relatives, and those of the kings of Jambudvipa [India]. Seeing the Way, they were true to the prohibitions and perfect in deportment. They crushed out the people of other teachings who acted against the Wonderful Dharma. They always said to one another: "We shall have stores of gold and silver for the service of upholding the sweet and endless depths of the Wonderful Dharma, so that it will flourish. Let us hope always to learn Dharma. We shall draw out the tongues of those who slander the Buddha's Wonderful Dharma." They also prayed: "Should there be any bhiksu who transgresses against the prohibitions, we shall turn him back to secular life and have him for labour; if anyone abides in the Wonderful Dharma, we shall esteem and serve him as we do our parents. If priests well practise the Wonderful Dharma, we shall participate in their joy and support them, so that they will increase." They were always glad to lend an ear to the Mahayana sutras. Having listened, they widely expounded to others what they had heard. All were accomplished in such virtues. They included such Licchavis as [the following persons]: Pure-and-Untainted-Store, Pure-and-Non-Indulgent, Ganges-Water-of-Pure-and-Untainted-Virtue. All of these said to themselves: "Let us now speed to where the Buddha is!" Various were their utensils of offerings. Each Licchavi had 84,000 elephants all decorated, along with 84,000 four-horse wagons of treasures, 84,000 bright moon gems. There were also bundles of fuel such as heavenly wood, sandalwood, and aloes, all to the number of 84,000. In front of each elephant hung bejewelled hanging ensigns, banners and parasols. Even the smallest of parasols was as wide as one yojana crosswise and lengthwise. Even the shortest of the banners measured 32 yojanas. And the lowest of the bejewelled hanging-ensigns was 100 yojanas high. With these objects of offerings, they went to where the Buddha was, touched his feet, walked around him 100 thousand times and said to him: "O World-Honoured One! We are now here with offerings for you, the Buddha, and the Sangha. Please have pity and accept ours!" The Tathagata was silent and did not accept [the offerings]. Not having gained what they desired, the Licchavis were all sad. By the Buddha's power, they were raised up into the sky seven talas high, where they remained in silence. At that time, there were, further, ministers and rich laymen as numerous as the sands of five Ganges. They prized Mahayana. If there were any of other teachings slandering the Wonderful Dharma, they would crush such down just as hail and rain do grass and plants. They were Sunlight, World-Protecting, and Dharma-Protecting. These headed their number. Five times as many were their utensils as those who had preceded them. They carried these to the forest of the twin sal trees, touched the Buddha's feet, walked around the Buddha 100 thousand times, and said: "O World-Honoured One! We have brought you and the Sangha utensils of offerings. Please have pity and accept our [gifts]!" The Tathagata was silent and did not accept [them]. Their wish not granted, the rich elders were sad. By the Buddha's divine power, they were raised up seven talas from the ground into the sky, where they remained in silence. At that time, there were present the King of Vaisali and his consort, the people of the harem, and all the kings of Jambudvipa, excepting Ajatasatru and those of the castle town and villages of his kingdom. They included such as King Taintless-as-the-Moon and others. They took along with them the four military forces [of elephants, horses, infantry and chariots] and desired to go to where the Buddha was. Each king had people and relatives as many as 180 million billion. The chariots and soldiers were drawn by elephants and horses. The elephants were six-tusked and the horses ran like the wind. Their adornments and utensils of offerings were six times as many as those which had preceded them. Of all the bejewelled parasols, even the smallest filled a diameter of 8 yojanas. The smallest of the banners measured 16 yojanas. All these kings abided peacefully in the Wonderful Dharma and detested twisted laws [teachings]. They esteemed Mahayana and felt deep joy in it. They loved beings as one loves an only son. The fragrance of the meals and drinks which they were holding filled the air for four yojanas all around. They too, early in the morning when the sun had just risen, carried forth all these sweet dishes and went to the forest of twin sal trees where the Tathagata was and said: "O World-Honoured One! We wish to offer these to the Buddha and Sangha. Please have pity, O Tathagata! and accept our final offerings!" The Tathagata, aware of the occasion, would not take [the offerings]. Their wishes unanswered, all these kings were sad. They stepped back and took their seats on one side. At that time, there were the consorts of the kings as numerous as the sands of seven Ganges, excepting those of King Ajatasatru. So as to save beings, they manifested as females. They always were mindful of their bodily actions and perfumed their minds with the dharmas of the Void, formlessness and desirelessness. They included such as the ladies Wonderful-Three-Worlds and Virtue-Loving. All consorts such as these abided peacefully in the Wonderful Dharma and observed the prohibitions and were perfect in their deportment. They behaved towards beings as one does to one's only son. They all said: "Let us all speed to where the World-Honoured One is." The offerings of these royal consorts were seven times as many as those that had preceded them, and these were: incense, flowers, bejewelled hanging-ensigns, silken cloths, banners, parasols, and the best meals and drinks. Even the smallest of the bejewelled parasols measured 16 yojanas. The lowest of the bejewelled hanging-ensigns measured 68 yojanas. The fragrance of the meals and drinks filled an area of eight yojanas all around. Bearing all these offerings, they went to where the Tathagata was. They touched his feet, walked around him 100 thousand times, and said to the Buddha: "O World-Honoured One! We have with us offerings for the Buddha and the bhiksus. Please have pity and accept our final offerings!" The Tathagata, aware of the occasion, was silent and did not accept [the offerings]. Their requests ungranted, all the consorts were sad. They pulled out their hair, beat their breasts and wailed as though a compassionate mother had newly lost her only son. They stepped back, and sat silently to one side." "At that time, there were also devis [goddesses] as numerous as the sands of eight Ganges. Virupaksa headed their number and said: "O sisters! See clearly, see clearly! The best offerings of all these beings are for the Tathagata and the bhiksus. We ought to be serious and make offerings to the Tathagata with all such wonderful utensils as these. He will partake of our offerings and enter Nirvana. O sisters! It is hard to encounter the appearance into the world of the All-Buddha-Tathagata. It is also difficult to make the last offerings. Should the Buddha enter Nirvana, the world will become empty." All these heavenly females loved Mahayana and desired to hear it. Having heart it, they expounded it widely to [other] people. Much prizing Mahayana, they also satisfied those who were dying for it. They protected Mahayana very well. If there were any of other teachings who opposed or were jealous of Mahayana, they severely crushed them out, just as hail does grass. They were observant of the prohibitions and their deportment was perfect. They accorded well with the world, passed across those who had not yet gained the other shore, and turned the wheel of Dharma. They upheld the heritage of the Three Treasures so that it would not die out. They studied Mahayana and greatly adorned themselves. Perfect in all these virtues, they loved beings equally, just as one would love one's only son. They also, early in the morning when the sun had just risen, all took up incense of heavenly wood twice as great in number as those of the human world. The fragrance of all this incense blew away all bad human smells. Their wagons had white roofs and were pulled by four horses. Each wagon had curtains, and on each of the four corners were hung golden bells. Of diverse kind were the incense, flowers, the hanging-ensigns, banners, parasols, wonderful dishes, and mask dances. There were simhasanas [lion thrones], the four legs of which were of pure blue beryl. Behind the simhasanas were couches inlaid with the seven treasures. In front of each couch was an arm-rest of gold. The tree of light was of the seven treasures, and various gems served as lamps. Wonderful flowers were spread on the ground. And having made their offerings, all these devis were sad at heart. Tears welled up and great was their sorrow. In order to benefit beings and make them happy, they had accomplished the unsurpassed practice of the All-Void of Mahayana and they purposed to reveal the Tathagata's undisclosed teaching of expediency. And in order to prevent the various sermons from dying out, they came to where the Buddha was, touched his feet, walked around him 100 thousand times, and said to the Buddha: "O World-Honoured One! Please accept our final offerings." The Tathagata, aware of the occasion, was silent and did not accept [their offerings]. All these devis, their wishes unanswered, were sad. They stepped back, took their seat on one side, and sat [there] silently. At that time, there lived various naga kings in the four quarters, as many of them as sands of nine Ganges. They were Vasuki, Nanda, and Upananda, who headed up their number. All these naga kings too, early in the morning when the sun had just risen, took up their utensils of offerings, as numerous as those of man and heaven. Carrying these to where the Buddha was, they touched his feet, walked around him 100 thousand times, and said to him: "O Tathagata! Please accept our final offerings." The Tathagata, aware of the occasion, was silent and did not accept [their offerings]. All the naga kings, their wishes not met, were sad. They stepped back and sat to one side. At that time, there were demon kings as numerous as the sands of ten Ganges. Vaisravana headed their number. They said to one another: "Let us all hasten to where the Buddha is!" Carrying with them various things of offering, twice as many as those of the naga kings, they went to where the Buddha was, touched his feet, walked around him 100 thousand times, and said to him: "O Tathagata! Please have pity and accept the last of our offerings!" The Tathagata, aware of the occasion, was silent and did not accept. Their wishes unfulfilled, they felt sad, stepped back, and sat on one side. At that time, there were also garuda [mythical bird] kings, as numerous as the sands of 20 Ganges. King Victor-over-Resentment headed their number. Also, there were gandharva [demigod musician] kings, who were as numerous as the sands of 30 Ganges. King Narada headed their number. Also, there were kimnara [celestial singer and dancer] kings there, as numerous as the sands of 40 Ganges. King Sudarsana headed their number. Also, there were mahoraga [snaked-headed beings] kings, who were as numerous as the sands of 50 Ganges. King Mahasudarsana headed their number. Also, there were asura [contentious, titanic demon] kings, who were as numerous as the sands of 60 Ganges. King Campalu headed their number. Also, there were danavat [abounding in gifts] kings, who were as numerous as the sands of 70 Ganges. King Water-of-the-Untainted-River and Bhadradatta headed up their number. Also, there were rakshasa [carnivorous demon] kings, who were as numerous as the sands of 80 Ganges. King Fearful headed their number. Abandoning evil, he did not devour men; even amidst resentment, he showed compassion. His form was ugly to look at, and yet looked right and austere, due to the power of the Buddha. Also, there were forest kings there, who were as numerous as the sands of 90 Ganges. King Music-and-Odour headed their number. Also, there were dharani [magic spell]-possessing kings, who were as numerous as the sands of 1,000 Ganges. King Great-Vision-of-Dharani-Upholding headed their number. Also, there were lustful pretas [ghosts] there, who were as numerous as the sands of 100 thousand Ganges. King Sudarsana headed their number. Also, there were lustful devis, who were as numerous as the sands of 10 million Ganges. Heavenly-Blue-Wet, Sad-Wet-Corpse, Imperial-Way-Wet and Visakha headed up their number. Also, there were the preta kings of the earth there, who were as numerous as the sands of a billion Ganges. King Whitely-Wet headed there number. Also, there were princes, heavenly guardians, and the four guardian angels of the earth, as numerous as the sands of 10 million-billion Ganges. Also, there were the vayus of the four quarters, as numerous as the sands of 10 million-billion Ganges. These called forth seasonal and unseasonal flowers upon the trees and strewed them between the twin sal trees. Also, there were as many principal gods of cloud and rain present as the sands of 10 million-billion Ganges, who said to themselves: "When the Tathagata enters Nirvana, we shall call forth rain

at the time of the cremation and extinguish the fire. Should there by anyone who feels hot and moans, we shall make the air cool." Also, there were greatly fragrant elephant kings there, as numerous as the sands of 20 Ganges. They included Rahuhastin, Suvarnavarnahastin, Amrtahastin, Blue-Eye Elephant, Fragrance-desiring Elephant, who headed up their number. They respected and loved Mahayana. As the Buddha was about to enter Nirvana, each took up innumerable, boundless, beautiful lotus flowers and came to where the Buddha was, touched his feet with their heads, stepped back, and sat down to one side.

Also there were lion kings there, as numerous as the sands of 20 Ganges. King Lion's Roar headed their number. To all beings they gave fearlessness. Bearing various flowers and fruits, they came to where the Buddha was, touched his feet with their heads, stepped back, and sat on one side. Also, there were the kings of flying birds there, as numerous as the sands of 20 Ganges. They included lapwings, wild geese, mandarin ducks, peacocks, and all such birds, and gandharvas, karandas, mynahs, parrots, kokilas, wagtails, kalavinkas, jivamjivakas, and all such birds, bearing flowers and fruit, came to where the Buddha was, touched his feet with their heads, stepped back, and sat to one side. Also, there were buffaloes, cows, and sheep present, who were as numerous as the sands of 20 Ganges, who all came to the Buddha and gave forth wonderfully fragrant milk. All this milk filled the ditches and pits of Kusinagara Castle. The colour, fragrance and taste [of this milk] was all perfect. This done, they stepped back and sat down to one side. Also, there were present rishis [sages] from the four lands, who were as numerous as the sands of 20 Ganges. Ksantirsi headed their number. Carrying flowers, incense and fruit, they came to where the Buddha was, touched his feet with their heads, walked around him three times, and said to him: "O World-Honoured One! Please have pity and accept our final offerings!" The Tathagata, aware of the occasion, was silent and did not accept [their offerings]. At this, their wish unanswered, all the rishis were sad. They stepped back and sat on one side. There were [also] present all the kings of the bees of Jambudvipa [India]. Wonderful-Sound, the King of bees, headed their number. They brought in many flowers, came to where the Buddha was, touched his feet with their heads, walked around him once, stepped back, and sat down to one side. At that time, the bhiksus [monks] and bhiksunis [nuns] of Jambudvipa were all gathered together, excepting the two venerable ones, Mahakasyapa and Ananda. Also, there were [stretches of] space in between the worlds as numerous as the sands of innumerable asamkhyas [infinitudes] of Ganges, as well as all the mountains of Jambudvipa, of which King Mount Sumeru headed their number. Grand were the adornments of the mountains. Old and luxuriant were the bushes and forests, and the branches and leaves were fully grown, so that they hid the sun. Various were the wonderful flowers which bloomed all around and were beautiful. The grand springs and streams were pure, fragrant, and transparent. Devas, nagas, gandharvas, asuras, garudas, kimnaras, mahoragas, rishis, charmers, actors, dancers and musicians filled the place. All these heavenly ones of the mountains and others came to where the Buddha was, touched his feet with their heads, stepped back, and sat on one side. Also, there were present the gods of the four great seas and of the rivers, who were as numerous as the sands of asamkhyas of Ganges and who all had great virtues and heavenly feet. Their offerings were twice as many as those who had preceded them. The lights that emanated from the bodies of these gods and those of the mask dancers so eclipsed the light of the sun and the moon that they were hidden and could not be seen any more. Campaka flowers were strewn upon the waters of River Hiranyavati. They came to where the Buddha was, touched his feet with their heads, stepped back, and sat down on one side. At this time, the forest of sal trees of Kusinagara changed colour and looked like white cranes. In the sky, a hall of seven treasures spontaneously appeared. Detailed decorations were engraved [upon it]. There were balustrades all round, with gems studded into them. Down [round] the buildings were streams and the bathing places of ponds, where wonderful lotuses floated. It looked as if one were in Uttarakuru, in the pleasance of Trayastrimsa Heaven. That is how things were in the sal forest, the adornments all lovely and wonderful. The devas, asuras and others all witnessed the scene of the Tathagata's entering Nirvana, and were sunk in sorrow, sad and woebegone." "Then the four guardian angels of the earth and Sakrodevendra said to one another: "See! All devas, human beings, and asuras are

making preparations and intend to make their final offerings to the Tathagata. We, too, shall do the same. If we can make our final offerings, it will not be hard to be perfect in danaparamita [perfected giving]." At that time, the offerings of the four guardian angels of the earth were twice as many as those that had preceded them. They carried in their hands all such flowers as mandara, mahamandara, kakiruka, makakakiruka, manjusaka, mahamanjusaka, santanika, makasantanika, loving, greatly-loving, samantabhadra, mahasamantabhadra, time, great time, fragrant castle, greatly-fragrant castle, joy, great joy, desire-calling, great desire-calling, fragrant-intoxicating, greatly-fragrant-intoxicating, all-fragrant, greatly-all-fragrant, heavenly-golden leaves, nagapuspa, paricitra, kovidara, and also, carrying wonderful dishes, they came to where the Buddha was and touched his feet with their heads. All the light of these devas outshone the light of the sun and moon, so that these could not be seen. With these utensils, they intended to make offerings to the Buddha. The Tathagata, aware of the occasion, was silent and did not accept [their offerings]. Their wishes not granted, the devas were sad and worried, and they stepped back, and sat to one side. At that time, Sakrodevendra and the beings of Trayastrimsa Heaven carried up the vessels of their offerings, which were twice as many as those that had preceded them. The flowers which they carried were equally as many. Wonderful was the fragrance, very lovely to smell. They carried the victory hall, Vaijayanta [palace of Sakrodevendra], and many small halls and came to where the Buddha was, touched his feet with their heads, and said to him: "O World-Honoured One! We greatly love and protect Mahayana. O Tathagata! Please accept our dishes." The Tathagata, aware of the occasion, was silent and did not accept [their dishes]. Shakra [Indra, chief of the gods] and all the devas, their wishes not fulfilled, were sad. They stepped back and sat on one side. The offerings of those up to the sixth heaven increased in size one after the other. There were bejewelled hanging-ensigns, banners, and parasols. Even the smallest of the bejewelled parasols covered the four lands; the smallest of the banners covered the four seas; even the shortest of the hanging-ensigns reached Mahesvara's heaven. Soft breezes blew and sweet sounds arose. Carrying up the sweetest of dishes, they came to where the Buddha was, touched his feet with their heads, and said to him: "O World-Honoured One! Pray, O Tathagata! have pity and accept our last offerings!" The Tathagata, aware of the occasion, was silent, and did not accept [their offerings]. Their wishes not answered, all the devas were sad. They stepped back, and sat to one side." 'All the devas up to the highest heaven were gathered there. At that time, Great Brahma and other devas put forth light which shone over the four lands. To the men and devas of the world of desire, the lights of the sun and moon were all hidden. They had bejewelled hanging-ensigns, banners and parasols of coloured silk. Even the smallest banner which hung on Brahma's palace came down to where the sal trees stood. They came to where the Buddha was, touched his feet with their heads, and said to him: "O World-Honoured One! Pray, O Tathagata! have pity and accept our last offerings." The Tathagata, aware of the occasion, was silent and did not accept [their offerings]. At this, the devas, their wishes unfulfilled, were sad. They stepped back and sat on one side. At that time, Vemacitra, the king of asuras, was present with innumerable great relatives. The light that shone [here] was brighter than that of Brahma. He had bejewelled hanging-ensigns, banners, and parasols. Even the smallest banner covered a thousand worlds. Carrying the sweetest dishes, they came to where the Buddha was, touched his feet with their heads, and said to him: "Pray, O Tathagata! have pity and accept our last offerings!" The Tathagata, aware of the occasion, was silent and did not accept [their offerings]. Their wishes were not answered, so all the asuras were sad. They stepped back and sat on one side. At that time, Marapapiyas [the Devil] of the world of desire with all his kindred demons and domestic females, and with his innumerable people, opened the gates of hell, sprinkled about pure water, and said: "You now have nothing to do. Only think of the Tathagata, the Alms-deserving, and the All-Enlightened One, take part in joy, and offer your last offerings. You now shall have a long night of peace." Then, Marapapiyas made away with all the big and small swords and the poison and pain of hell. He had rain fall and extinguish the burning fire. Through the Buddha's power, he gained this state of mind. He made all his kindred demons throw away their big and small swords, bows, crossbows, armour, arms, halberds, shields, long hooks, metal hammers, axes, war chariots, and lassoos. What offerings they had were twice as many as those of man and heaven. Even the smallest of the parasols covered the middle-thousand world. They came to where the Buddha was, touched his feet with their heads, and said to him: "We now love and protect Mahayana. O World-Honoured One! Men and women in the world may, for the purpose of making offerings, out of fear, for reasons of cheating others, for profit, and for following others, accept this Mahayana, whether all of it is true or not true. We shall, then, in order to make away with the fear of such ones, enunciate the following dharani [spell]: "Taki, tatarataki, rokarei, makarokarei, ara, shara, tara, shaka".... We chant this dharani, for the sake of those who have lost their courage, who may be entertaining fear, who preach for others, who pray that the Dharma shall not die out, who desire to crush out the tirthikas [deluded believers, non-Buddhists], for protecting one's own self, for protecting the Wonderful Dharma, and for protecting Mahayana. Armed with this dharani, one [need] have no fear of a mad elephant, or when crossing wildernesses, marshy lands, or any precipitous places; there can be no fear of water, fire, lions, tigers, wolves, robbers, or kings. O World-Honoured One! Armed with such a dharani, none will have fear. We shall protect the person who has such a dharani, and he will be like a tortoise who guards his six limbs inside his shell. O World-Honoured One! We do not say this just to flatter. In truth, we will make things such that one armed with such a dharani will augment his power. Only we pray, O Tathagata! have pity and accept our last offerings." Then, the Buddha said to Marapapiyas: "I do not accept your offerings; I already have your dharani. This is to make all beings and the four classes of people of the Sangha rest in peace." So saying, the Buddha fell into silence and did not accept Marapapiyas' offerings. Thrice Marapapiyas asked the Buddha to accept them, but the Buddha would not. At this, his wishes unanswered, Marapapiyas was sad, and stepped back, and sat on one side. At that time, there was present Mahesvararaja with his innumerable kindred and other devas. They carried in their vessels of offerings, which were far more than those of Brahma and Indra, and those of the guardian angels of the earth, men and devas, the eight beings, and non-humans. The preparations which Sakrodevendra had made looked like black against white as when the white of horse-shoe shell is taken up for comparison, and all glory disappears. Even the smallest of the bejewelled parasols covered the 3,000 great-thousand worlds. Carrying such vessels of offerings, they came to where the Buddha was, touched his feet with their heads, walked around him innumerable times, and said to him: "O World-Honoured One! What paltry things we now have with us may [be] equal to offerings made us by mosquitoes and sawflies, to a man throwing a scoop of water into the great ocean, or to trying to assist with a small light that of 100 thousand suns, or trying, in spring and summer when there are so many flowers, with just a single flower to add to the glories of all the flowers, or to the splendour of Mount Sumeru with just a pickpocket seed. How could there be any augmenting of the great ocean, of the brightness of the sun, of all the flowers, and of Sumeru? O World-Honoured One! What little we carry in [to you] here may well be likened to this. We could indeed offer you incense, flowers, mask dances, banners, and parasols of the 3,000 great-thousand worlds, but these are still not worthy of mention. Why not? Because you always undergo pains in the unfortunate realms of hell, hungry pretas, and animals. Because of this, O World-Honoured One! Please have pity and likewise accept our offerings." Now, in the east, there is a Buddha-land, as many lands far out as the sands of uncountable, innumerable asamkhyas of Ganges, one called Easy-in-Mind-and-Beautiful-in-Sound, and the Buddha [there] is called Equal-to-the-Void, the Tathagata, Alms-deserving, the All-Enlightened One, the All-accomplished One, the Well-gone, the All-knower, the Unsurpassed One, the Best Trainer, the Teacher-of-Heaven-and-Earth, and the Buddha-World-Honoured-One. At that time, the Buddha spoke to his foremost great disciple: "Go now to the land in the west, called "'saha'" [Endurance - i.e. our world of hardship!] There is a Buddha in that land called Tathagata Shakyamuni, who is the Alms-deserving, the All-Enlightened One, the All-accomplished One, the Well-gone, the All-knower, the Unsurpassed One, the Best Trainer, the Teacher-of-Heaven-and-Earth, and the Buddha-World-Honoured-One. He will enter Parinirvana before long. O good man! Carry to him the fragrant dishes of this world, the ones fragrant and beautiful, which give peace. Offer this to him. Having taken this, he will enter Parinirvana. O good man! Also, bow before the Buddha, put questions to him, and do away with whatever doubt you have." Then, the Bodhisattva-mahasattva of boundless body, at that, stood up from his seat, touched the Buddha's feet with his head, walked around the Buddha three times, took with him innumerable asamkhyas of Bodhisattvas, left that country and came to this land of Saha [endurance]. At this, the 3,000 great-thousand worlds shook in six ways, the hair of those congregated there - Brahma, Indra, the four guardian angels of the earth, Marapapiyas, and Mahesvara - at this great shaking of the great earth stood up on end, and their throats and tongues dried up in fear. They were so frightened that they shook and wanted to flee in all directions. As they looked at their own bodies, their light was lost, and gone was all their divine appearance. Then, Dharmarajaputra Manjushri stood up and spoke to those congregated there: "Good people! Do not fear, do not be afraid! Why not? To the east, as many as the sands of innumerable, uncountable asamkhyas of Ganges away, there is a land called Easy-in-Mind-and-Beautiful-in-Sound. The Buddha's name in that land is Tathagata-Equal-to-the-Void, the Alms-deserving, the All Enlightened One. He possesses the ten epithets of the Buddha. There is a Bodhisattva there, of boundless body. Accompanied by innumerable Bodhisattvas, he desires to come here and make offerings to the Tathagata. By the power of that Buddha, your body now does not shine out. So, gladden yourselves; do not fear!" Then, those congregated saw far off a great number of people from that Buddha whom they saw as though they were their own forms reflected in a mirror. Then, Manjushri said to those congregated there: "You now see the people of that Buddha just as you see the Buddha himself. By the Buddha's power, you can clearly see all the innumerable Buddhas of the nine other Buddha countries." At that, the people congregated there said to one another: "Oh, woe is the day, woe the day! The world is empty. The Tathagata will before long enter Parinirvana." "Now, all the people saw the Bodhisattva of boundless body and his retinue. And they saw that from each pore of the skin of this Bodhisattva there sprung a great lotus, each containing 78 castle towns. Crosswise and lengthwise, each castle was Vaisali Castle. The castle walls and moats were studded with the seven treasures. There were bejewelled avenues of seven rows of tala trees. The people [there] were active, peaceful, rich, and it was comfortable to live in that land. Each castle was of Jambunadasuvarna. Each had in it the trees of the seven treasures. The growths were luxuriant, and rich were the flowers and fruits. Soft breezes blew, emitting sweet sounds, as of heavenly music. The people of the castle, hearing these sounds, felt great pleasure. The moats were filled with wonderful water. It was pure and fragrant and looked like true beryl. On the water, boats of the seven treasures could be seen. People were riding on these. They bathed and enjoyed themselves. Thus there was no end of pleasure. Also, there were lotuses of various colours, such as the utpala, kumuda, padma and pundarika. These looked like great wheels seen crosswise and lengthwise. Above the moats were many gardens. In each were five ponds, in which there were again such flowers as the utpala, kumuda, padma, and pundarika, which resembled great wheels, seen crosswise and lengthwise. They were fragrant and pleasing. The water was pure and soft to the touch. On this could be seen lapwings, wild geese, and mandarin ducks floating. Garden houses of gems were there, each of which was rightly square crosswise and lengthwise, filling an area seven yojanas square. All the walls were made of four treasures: gold, silver, beryl, and crystal. All around were windows, lattice-windows, and handrails of true gold. The ground was of turkistan dwarf and covered in golden sand. In this palace were many streams, springs, and bathing ponds of the seven treasures. Each side-wall had 18 ladder-steps of gold. The plantain was the Jambunadasuvarna and resembled the pleasance of Trayastrimsa Heaven. Each of these castles accommodated 80 thousand kings and each king had with him innumerable consorts and female attendants. All were amusing themselves and were pleased and happy. The same applied to the people who were amusing themselves where they lived. The people [there] heard no teachings other than unsurpassed Mahayana. On each flower was a simhasana, each leg made of beryl. On each seat was spread a white soft silken cloth. The cloth was wonderful, unsurpassed in all the three worlds. On each seat was sat a king, preaching Mahayana to his people. Some were holding books in their hands, reciting, and practising the Way. Thus Mahayana sutras became pupularised. The Bodhisattva of boundless body allowed innumerable people to walk thereabouts, pleased with themselves and abandoning worldly pleasures. All said: "Woe is the day, woe the day! The world is empty. The Tathagata will soon enter Parinirvana." Then, the Bodhisattva of boundlesss body, followed by innumerable Bodhisattvas and with wonderful divine power, carried out innumerable and various containers of offerings filled with wonderfully fragrant sweet dishes. On encountering the fragrance of these meals, all the taints of illusion died out. Because of the Bodhisattva's divine power, the people saw all such transformations. The size of this Bodhisattva of boundless body was limitless and like space. Excepting the Buddha, none indeed could see the bodily size of this Bodhisattva. The offerings of this Bodhisattva of boundless body were double those that had preceded them and they came to where the Buddha was. They touched the Buddha's feet, folded their hands, paid him homage, and said: "O World-Honoured One! Please have pity and accept our offerings." The Tathagata, aware of the occasion, was silent and did not accept [their offerings]. Three times they asked, but he would not accept. So the Bodhisattva of boundless body and his retinue stepped back and sat on one side. The same was the case with the Bodhisattvas of boundless body of all the Buddha-lands to the south, west and north. They carried in offerings twice as many as those which had preceded them. They came to where the Buddha was, stepped back, and sat on one side. All proceeded in this manner. Then, there did not remain a space left in the auspicious ground of weal between the sal trees and within 32 yojanas square which was not full of people. At that time, all the space around the persons of the Bodhisattva of boundless body and his retinue who were gathered there from the four quarters looked [merely] like the point-size of a mote, or awl or needle. All the great Bodhisattvas of all the innumerable Buddha lands of the ten directions were gathered together there. In addition, all the people of Jambudvipa were assembled there, except for the pair, Mahakasyapa and Ananda, and also Ajatasatru and his retinue, and the poisonous serpents that harm people, the dung-beetles, haly-vipers, scorpions, and the doers of evil of sixteen kinds. The danavats and asuras had all forsaken their evil designs and had become compassionate-minded. Like fathers, mothers, older and younger sisters, all the people of the 3,000 great-thousand worlds came together and spoke to one another with the same compassionate heart, except for the icchantikas [those most spiritually alienated from Dharma]. Then, by the power of the Buddha, the

3,000 worlds became soft to the touch. There were [no longer] any hills, sand, gravel, thistles or poisonous plants there, but all was [instead] adorned with various treasures as in the case of the Western Paradise of peace and happiness of Buddha Amitayus. At that time, all those congregated there saw the innumerable number of Buddha lands as though seeing their forms reflected in a mirror. The same was the case when they saw the lands of all the Buddhas. The light that issued from the Tathagata's face was fivefold in colour, and it shone and covered all the great congregation, so that it blotted out the light that came out of the body. Having done this, it again turned back to the Buddha, back to him through his mouth. Then, the heavenly beings and all those congregated there, asuras and others, became greatly afraid, as they saw the Buddha's light entering him through his mouth. Their hair stood on end. And they said: "The light of the Tathagata, having appeared, goes back and enters [him again]. This is not without reason. This indicates that the Buddha has done what he intended to do in the ten directions and now will enter Nirvana as his last act. This must be what it mean to indicate to us. Woe is the world, woe the world! Why is it that the World-Honoured One so forsakes the four limitless minds and does not accept the offerings of man and heaven? The light of Wisdom is now going out eternally. The unsurpassed boat of Dharma is now sinking. Ah, the pain! Woe is the world!"

They held up their hands, beat their breasts, and sorrowfully cried out and wept. Their limbs shook, and they did not know how to support themselves. Blood came from their bodies and ran over the ground."

Chapter Two: On Cunda

At that time there was present among the congregation an upasaka who was the son of an artisan of this fortress town of Kusinagara. Cunda was his name. He was there with his comrades, fifteen in number. In order that the world should generate good fruit, he abandoned all bodily adornments [to indicate his respect and modesty], stood up, bared his right shoulder, placed his right knee on the ground and, folding his hands, looked up at the Buddha. Sorrowfully and tearfully, he touched the Buddha's feet with his head [i.e. in sign of respect] and said: "O World-Honoured One and bhiksus! Please have pity and accept our last offerings and succour innumerable beings. O World-Honoured One! From now on, we have no master, no parents, no salvation, no protection, no place wherein to take refuge, and no place to go. we shall be poor and hunger-ridden. Following the Tathagata, we desire to gain food for the days to come. Please have pity and accept our petty offerings, and, then, enter Nirvana. O World-Honoured One! This is as in the case of a Kshatriya, Brahmin, Vaishya or Sudra, who, being poor, goes to a far-off country. He works at farming and indeed gains a trained cow. The land is good, flat and square. There is no poor, sandy soil, no harmful weeds, no barrenness and no defilements [there]. What is needful is awaiting the rain from heaven. We say "trained cow". This may be likened to the seven actions of the body and mouth, and the good field flat and square to Wisdom. Doing away with the poor soil, harmful weeds, barrenness and defilements refers to Illusion, which we must do away with. O World-Honoured One! I now have with me the trained cow and good soil, and I have tilled the land and done away with all the weeds. I am now only awaiting the Tathagata's sweet rain of Dharma to visit me. The four castes of poverty are none but the carnal body that I possess. I am poor, as I do not possess the superb treasure of Dharma. Pray have pity and cut away our poverty and hardships and rid us innumerable beings of our sorrow and worries. What offerings I make are paltry. But what I may think is that they will satisfy the Tathagata and Sangha. I now have no master, no parents, and no refuge. Please have pity on us, as you have on Rahula [the Buddha's son]." Then the World-Honoured One, the All-Knowledge ["sarvajnana"], the Unsurpassed Trainer, said to Cunda: "This is good, good indeed! I shall now cut off the roots of your poverty and let fall on your field of carnal life the unsurpassed rain of Dharma and call forth the bud of Dharma. You now desire to have from me life, body, power, peace, and unhindered speech. And I shall give to you undying life, body, power, peace, and unhindered speech. Why? O Cunda! In offerings of meals there are two fruits that know of no distinction. What are the two? Firstly, one attains "anuttarasamyaksambodhi" [unsurpassed, complete Enlightenment] when one receives it [a meal-offering]; secondly, one enters Nirvana after receiving it. I will now receive your last offering and let you accomplish danaparamita [perfected giving]." At that, Cunda said to the Buddha: "You say that there is no difference between the results of these two offerings. But this is not so. Why not? Because in the former case of receiving dana [a charitable gift], illusion is not yet done away with [in the recipient] and he is not yet perfect in all-knowledge. And he cannot yet cause beings to enjoy danaparamita. As to the latter category of receiving dana, illusion has gone and he is accomplished in all-knowledge and can let all beings be blessed equally with danaparamita. The former man who receives offerings is still a common being, but the latter the heaven of heavens. One that receives dana in the former category is one with 1) a body supported by various kinds of food, 2) a body of illusion, 3) a body where there yet remains the result of illusion, and 4) a non-eternal body. A person who receives dana in the second category has 1) the body of no illusion, 2) the adamantine body, 3) the Dharma body 4) the eternal body, and 5) the boundless body. How can one say that the results of the dana performed in the two categories are one and do not differ? The person who receives dana in the former category is one not yet accomplished in danaparamita [and other paramitas] up to prajnaparamita [perfected Wisdom]. He only has the fleshly eye, but not the Buddha-eye, nor the eye of Wisdom. The case of the person receiving dana in the latter category is that of one perfect in danaparamita up to prajnaparamita, and also in the fleshly eye up to the eye of Wisdom. How can we say that the results of the two danas are the same and that there is no difference? O World-honoured One! In the case of the former, one who receives dana takes meals which get into his abdomen and get digested, and he gains life, carnal body, power, ease, and unhindered speech. In the case of the latter, the person does not eat, digest, and there are no results of the five things. How can we say that the results of the two danas are one and the same and not different?" The Buddha said: "O good man! The Tathagata, already, since innumerable, boundless asamkhyas of kalpas [aeons] ago, has had no body supported by food and illusion, and he has no body where there yet remains the result of illusion. He is the Eternal, the Dharma Body, and the Adamantine Body. O good man! One who has not yet seen "Buddhata "[Buddha-Nature, Buddha-Essence, Buddha-ness] is called the illusion-body, the body supported by various kinds of food, and the body where there yet remains the result of illusion. The Bodhisattva, as he partakes of the food [offered to him just before Enlightenment] enters the adamantine samadhi [deepest meditative state]. When that food is digested, he sees "Buddhata" and attains unsurpassed Bodhi [Enlightenment]. That is why I say that the results of the two danas are equal and that they are not different. The Bodhisattva, at that time, crushes the four Maras [Illusion, skandhas, death, and the heavenly Mara]. Now, entering Nirvana, he crushes the four Maras. That is why I say that the results of the two danas are equal and that they are not different. The Bodhisattva, at that time, does not widely speak about the twelve types of Buddhist sutras [categorisation of the Buddhist scriptures into 12 types], but he is versed in these already. Now, upon entering Nirvana, he speaks expansively of them for beings' sake. That is why I say that the results of the two danas are equal and that they are not different. O good man! The body of the Tathagata has not partaken of food and drink for innumerable asamkhyas of kalpas past. But for all sravakas' ["listeners" to the Buddha's teachings] sake, I say that I took the milk-cooked porridge offered by Nanda and Nandabala, the two shepherd women, and that, thereafter, I attained unsurpassed Bodhi. But, in truth, I did not take it. Now, for the sake of the people congregated here, I shall accept your offerings. But, in truth, I do not partake of it." Then, hearing that the Buddha-World-Honoured One, for the sake of the people congregated there, would take Cunda's last offerings, they were glad and overjoyed, and said in praise: "How wonderful, how wonderful! It is rare, O Cunda! You now have a name; your name is not for nothing. Cunda means "understanding wonderful significations"! You have now established such great signification. You build up what is true, you accord with the signification, and gain your name. That is why you are Cunda. You, now, in this life, will gain great name, profit, virtue, and vows. It is rare, O Cunda, to be born as a man and attain the unsurpassed profit which is the most difficult to achieve. It is good, O Cunda! You are the udumbara [plant], which is said to put out flowers only on very rare occasions. It is very rare that the Buddha appears in the world. It is also hard to meet with the Buddha, gain faith, and hear [his] sermons. It is harder still to be able to make the final offerings to him at the time of his entering Nirvana and well attain all this. Well done, well done, O Cunda! You are now perfect in danaparamita. This is as on the 15th of the autumnal month, when the moon is pure and full, when there is not a speck of cloud in the heavens, and all beings look up and [utter] praise. The same is the case with you, whom we look up to and praise. The Buddha now takes your last offerings and makes you perfect in danaparamita. Oh, well done, O Cunda! We say that you are like the full moon, which all people look up to. Well done, O Cunda! Though a man, your mind is of the Buddha. O Cunda! You truly are like the Buddha's son, Rahula. There is no difference." Then those congregated there said in a gatha [verses]:

"Though born a man, you now stand above the sixth heaven.
I and all others, therefore, praise you and pray.

The holiest of men now enters Nirvana. Pity us and, with speed,
Beseech the Buddha to stay a long time yet in life,
To benefit innumerable beings, to impart to them
The unsurpassed manna of Dharma that Wisdom praises.
If you do not beseech the Buddha, our life will not be perfect.

Because of this, fall to the ground,
Pay homage to the Best Trainer."

At this, Cunda was overjoyed! It was as in the case of a man whose parents have of a sudden passed away and who suddenly come back again. That is how Cunda felt. He stood up again, bowed before the Buddha, and said in a gatha:

"I am glad that I have gained my Way; it is good I have been born a man.
I have done away with greed and anger; I am parted forever
From the three unfortunate realms. I am glad that I have gained benefit,
And meet with the golden ball of treasure,
That I now meet with the Trainer
And that I do not fear, even if I gain life in the animal realm.
The Buddha is an udumbara, so to speak, one hard to encounter,
And it is hard to gain faith. Having once encountered
And practised the Way, we do away
With the sorrows of the hungry pretas.
Also, he thoroughly crushes the asuras and others.
We could sooner balance a mustard seed on the point of a needle
Than encounter the Buddha's appearance in the world.
The Buddha is not tainted by worldly ways.
He is like a water lily in water. I am thoroughly cut off
From all the roots of the relative world
And have crossed the waters of birth and death.
It is hard to be born as a man; harder still is it
To encounter the Buddha when he appears in the world.
It is as in the case of a blind turtle
who, in the midst of the ocean, may chance to hit the hole
In a piece of floating wood. I now offer food
And pray that I will attain the unsurpassed reward,
That I will destroy the bond of illusion,
And that it will be strong no more. I do not seek here
To gain a heavenly body. Even having gained that,
One's mind is not so sweet. The Tathagata accepts
This offering of mine. Nothing could ever please me more.
This is like the case of a bad-smelling weed
Which emits a sandalwood fragrance.
I am that weed. The Tathagata accepts my offerings.
This is like the fragrance that issues from the sandalwood.
That is why I am glad. I now in this life
Am blessed with the highest reward.
Shakra, Brahma and all the others come
And make offerings to me. All worlds are
Greatly worried as they now know
That the Buddha will enter Nirvana. They loudly say:
"Now there is no Trainer in the world;
Do not discard all beings; view them as one views one's only son!"

The Tathagata, in the midst of the priests, speaks of the superb Dharma.
This may well be compared to Mt. Sumeru,
That sits unmolested amidst a great ocean.
The Buddha-Wisdom thoroughly dispels the gloom of man.

It is as when the sun rises, all the clouds disperse
And light shines all over.
The Tathagata thoroughly does away with all illusions.
This is like the coolness that reigns
When clouds appear in the sky.
All beings love you and wail.
All are floundering on the bitter waters of birth and death.
Because of this, pray, O World-Honoured One!
Stay long in life and increase the faith of all beings,
Cut off the suffering of birth and death!"

The Buddha said to Cunda: "It is thus, it is thus! All is as you say. It is rare that the Buddha appears in the world. It is as in the case of the udumbara. It is, again, hard to meet with the Buddha and gain faith. To be present at the moment of the Buddha's entering Nirvana, to offer him food and thus accomplish danaparamita is as difficult. O Cunda! Do not be sorry now. Be glad that you now give the final offerings to the Tathagata and accomplish well danaparamita. Do not ask the Buddha to remain long in life. You now should meditate on the world of all Buddhas. All is non-eternal. It is the same with all created things and their natures and characteristics." For the sake of Cunda, he said in a gatha:

"In all the world, whatever is born must die.
Life looks long, but by nature an end there must be.
Whatever flourishes always wanes; met, one must part.
The prime of manhood is not long;
Luxuriance meets with illness.
Life is swallowed by death; nothing exists eternally.
Kings are all unmolested; none can compete.
Yet all of them must perish; so is it with life.
Suffering knows no end; unendingly the wheel turns and turns.
None of the three worlds [of Desire, Form, and Formlessness] is eternal; all that exists
Is not happy. What exists has a nature and characteristics.
And all is Void. What is destructible comes and goes;
Apprehensions and illnesses follow upon [one's] steps.
The fears of all the wrongs and evils done,
Age, illness, death and decline cause worry.
All these things do not exist forever.
And they easily break up. Resentment attacks one;
All are lined with illusion, as in the case of the silkworm and the cocoon.
None who has wisdom finds joy in a place like this.
This carnal body is where suffering forgathers.
All is impure, like unto strains, carbuncles, boils, and other such.
No reason is at bottom. The same applies
Even to the heavenly ones who sit above.
All desires do not last. So I do not cling.
One casts off desires, meditates well,
Attains the wonderful Dharma, and one who definitely
Cuts off "is" [samsaric existence] can today gain Nirvana.
I pass over to the other shore of "is"

And stand above all sorrows.
Thus I harvest this superb Bliss."

Then Cunda said to the Buddha: "O World-Honoured One! It is so, it is so. All is as you, Holy One, say. What wisdom I possess is paltry and of low grade. I am like a mosquito or sawfly. How can I contemplate the deepest ground of the Tathagata's Nirvana? O World-Honoured One! I am now like any great naga or elephant of a Bodhisattva-mahsattva who has cut off the bond of illusion. I am like Dharmarajaputra Manjushri. O World-Honoured One! It is like one who enters the Order at a young age. Though upholding the precepts, that person is still just of the class of ordinary monks. I, too, am one such. Due to the power of the Buddha and the Bodhisattvas, I am now one of the number of such great Bodhisattvas. That is why I beseech the Tathagata to stay long in life and not enter Nirvana. This is similar to a hunger-stricken man who has nothing more to put out. I only pray that the same will be the case with the World-Honoured One and that he will stay long in life and not enter Nirvana." Then Dharmarajaputra Manjushri said to Cunda: "O Cunda! Now, do not speak in this way and beseech the Tathagata to stay long in life and not to enter Parinirvana, as in the case of one hungry who now has nothing more to put out. This cannot be. You should now see the nature and characteristics of all things. Seeing things thus, you will gain the All-Void samadhi. If you desire to attain Wonderful Dharma, act thus!" Cunda asked: "O Manjushri! The Tathagata is the Holiest One and the highest of all heavens and earth. Could the Tathagata who is such be one who is made? If he is one made, he cannot be other than samsaric existence. Foam, for example, quickly rises up and swiftly dies away; the comings and goings [of all things] are like the turning of a wheel. All that is made is like this. I hear that the devas have the longest life. The World-Honoured One is the heaven of heavens. How could he have a life so short as not to reach 100 years? The headman of a village is unmolested [unlimited, unconstrained] in power, through which he can suppress people. But when virtue deserts him, he becomes poor and mean. He is looked down upon and whipped and made to work for others. Why? Because his power is gone. The same is the case with the World-Honoured One. He is like all things made. If he is the same as all things, he cannot be the heaven of heavens. Why not? Because all things are existences that must suffer birth and death. Therefore, O Manjushri! Do not put the Tathagata on the same level as that of all things made. Also, next, O Manjushri! Do you know this [for a fact] and speak thus? Or is it that you do not know, and say that the Tathagata is on the same level as all things made? If the Tathagata is on the same level as all things made, we cannot call him the heaven of heavens or the unmolested [unlimited] Dharma-King of the three worlds. For example, a king may be a man of great strength. His power is equal to that of a thousand persons and none can beat him. So this person is called one possessing the power of a thousand persons. The king loves such a one. So, courtly rank is given him, along with a fief. Fiefs and rewards flow towards him bountifully. This person is called one whose power is equal to that of a thousand persons. He is not quite equal to a thousand persons. But what he does is worth much. So we say that he is equal to a thousand persons. The same is the case with the Tathagata. He subdues the Mara of illusion, the Mara of the five skandhas, the Mara of heaven, and the Mara of death. That is why we call him the most honoured one of the three worlds. This is as in the case of a man whose power equals that of a thousand persons. Thus he is accomplished in various, innumerable true virtues. That is why we call him the Tathagata, the Alms-deserving and the All-Enlightened One. O Manjushri! You should not presume upon, imagine, speak about what pertains to the world of the Tathagata as being equal to that which is created. For example, a very rich man begets a son; and the augur predicts that this child will not live. The parents hear this and know that the child will not be able to inherit the family estate, and they look on this child as though it were grass. Now, a short-lived person is not made much of [respected] by sramanas [ascetics], Brahmins, males, females, or people big or small. If the Tathagata is placed on the same level as that which is created, he cannot be respected by all the world, man or heaven. What the Tathagata speaks about is that which does not change and is not different. It is the true Dharma. There is none who receives. Hence, O Manjushri! Do not say that the Tathagata is the same as any created thing. "Also, next, O Manjushri! It is as in the case of a poor woman who has no house to live in and nobody to take care of her. Added to this, she is very ill and hungry. So she roams about, begs for food, stays in another's house, and gives birth to a child. The owner of the house drives her away. She holds this child and decides to go abroad. On the way, she meets with a bad storm and rain; cold presses down upon her. Mosquitoes, gadflies, bees and poisonous insects noisily attack her. She carries her child and means to cross the Ganges. The water moves quickly, but she holds the child and does not let go her grip on him. The mother and child both drown. This woman, because of her compassionate deed, is born after her death in Brahma's heaven. O Manjushri! Any good man who desires to guard Wonderful Dharma should not say: "The Tathagata is like all things"or "he is not so." One should only reproach one's own self and think: "I am but ignorant; I do not have the eye of Wisdom." The Tathagata's Wonderful Dharma cannot at all be conceived. Because of this, it is not fitting for us to say that the Tathagata is truly a thing definitely made, or a thing which is not made. What it is right to say is: "The Tathagata is definitely an Uncreate [that which was not made]. Because [of this] good arises for us beings and out of the compassionate heart. This is as in the case of the poor woman who, out of love for her child, sacrificed her own self. O good man! With the Bodhisattva who guards Dharma, it is thus. One might well sacrifice one's own self, but one cannot say that the Tathagata is equal to the created. One must say that the Tathagata is an Uncreate. By saying that the Tathagata is an Uncreate, one gains unsurpassed Enlightenment. This is as in the case of the woman born in Brahma's heaven. Why? Through protecting Dharma. What do we mean by protecting Dharma? That is, saying that the Tathagata is an Uncreate. O good man! Such a one does not seek emancipation, yet it comes of itself. It is as in the case of the poor woman who does not seek to be born in Brahma's heaven, and yet Brahma responds. It is like this. O Manjushri! A person may be going on a long journey. On the way, he becomes very tired and puts up at another person's house. While he is asleep, a great fire breaks out. At once he gets up and thinks: "I shall now surely die." As he repents, he puts on his clothing. He dies and gets reborn in Trayastrimsa Heaven. Then, after 80 lives, he becomes Great Brahma. After 100 thousand lives, he gets reborn as a man and becomes a chakravartin [world's greatest monarch]. This person does not gain life in the three unfortunate realms. Life is repeated, and he is born in places where peace always reigns. This is how things go. Because of this, one possessing repentance should, O Manjushri, meditate on the

Buddha, but not regard him as the same as that which is created. O Manjushri! The tirthikas and those of bent mind may say that the Tathagata is the same as the created. The bhiksu who upholds the precepts should not think that the Tathagata is a created existence. Should one say that the Tathagata is one created, this is nothing but a false statement. After death, such a person will fall into hell, as surely as one is in one's own house. O Manjushri! The Tathagata is truly an Uncreate. One must not say that he is a created being. You should henceforth in this life of birth and death abandon ignorance and take to right Wisdom. Know well that the Tathagata is an Uncreate. One who meditates well on the Tathagata will be perfect in the 32 signs of perfection and will attain unsurpassed Enlightenment." Then Dharmarajaputra Manjushri praised Cunda and said: "Well spoken, well spoken, O good man! You have already done what will beget you an endless life. You well know that the Tathagata is one eternal and unchanging, and is an Uncreate. You now well shield the Tathagata's created-form existence. One who encounters fire covers his body with clothing because of repentance. This good mind gains him birth in Trayastrimsa Heaven. He becomes Brahma and a chakravartin, and he does not get born into the unfortunate realms and thus will always enjoy peace. That is how things will go with you. As you well shield the created form of the Tathagata, you will in the days to come gain the 32 signs of perfection, the 80 minor marks of excellence, and the 18 characteristics peculiar solely to the Buddha. Your life will become endless, with no more bonds of samsara. There will always be an eternal flow of peace and happiness, and before long a day will come when you will awaken in the light of the Almsdeserving and the All-Enlightened One. O Cunda! The Tathagata himself will speak more expansively later on. And you and I shall shield the created body of the Tathagata. Set aside, for the present, questions of the created and the non-created. "You should, as you see proper, quickly offer meals. To offer thus is the best of all offerings. The bhiksus, bhiksunis, upasakas and upasikas may have undergone a long journey; they may be extremely tired. Give the purest things as required. Thus speedily giving is the fundamental thing, to be perfect in danaparamita. O Cunda! Give the final offerings to the Buddha and Sangha, more or less, full or not full, quick as the occasion requires. The Tathagata will rightly be entering Parinirvana" Cunda said: "O Manjushri! Why is it that you so greedily care about the meal and make me give more or less, full or not full, in answer to the requirement of the occasion? O Manjushri! The Tathagata in the past practised penance for six years and supported himself. Why could he not now when it is just a matter of a moment? O Manjushri! Do you say that the Tathagata, the Right-Enlightened One, truly means to accept this meal? But I definitely know that the Tathagata is the Dharma-Body and that he is no carnal body that partakes of food." Then the Buddha said to Manjushri: "It is thus, it is thus. It is as Cunda says. Well said, O Cunda! You have already attained the delicate point of great Wisdom and you now master the Mahayana sutras." Manjushri said to Cunda: "You say that the Tathagata is an Uncreate; the Tathagata's body is of long life. If this is said, the Tathagata will be pleased." Cunda answered: "The Tathagata is not pleased with me alone; he is also pleased with all beings." Manjushri said: "The Tathagata will be pleased with you and with all of us beings." Cunda answered: "Do not say that the Tathagata is pleased. Now, to get pleased is an inverted mind. An inverted mind is birth and death. Birth and death are of created existence. So, O Manjushri! Do not say that the Tathagata is a created existence. If you say that the Tathagata is a created existence, I and you commit an inversion [of truth]. O Manjushri! The Tathagata has no thought of love [attachment]. Now, love is like the case of a milking cow which, loving her own child, feels hunger and thirst, goes and seeks water-grass, and whether satisfied or not, suddenly turns back. The All-Buddha-World-Honoured One does not have such a mind. He sees all as equally as he sees Rahula. To think thus is what applies in the world of Wisdom of the All-Enlightened One. O Manjushri! For example, a carriage drawn by a donkey cannot stand comparison with one drawn by the four trained horses of a king. The case with me and you is also like this. It is impossible to fathom the minute and hidden depths of what is with the Tathagata, even if we try. O Manjushri! The garuda flies innumerable yojanas in the sky. He looks down on the great sea and sees such things of the water as fish, soft-shelled turtles, snapping turtles, crocodiles, tortoises, and nagas, and also his own shadow reflected in the water. He sees all these just as one sees all visible forms in a mirror. The petty wisdom of the common mortal cannot well weigh what comes to his eye. The same is the case with me and you too. We cannot weigh the Tathagata's Wisdom." Manjushri said to Cunda: "It is thus, it is thus. It is as you say. It is not that I do not see this. I only meant to test you regarding what belongs to the world of a Bodhisattva." Then, the World-Honoured One shot forth from his moth a light of various colours. The light shone brightly on Manjushri's body. Shone upon by this light, Manjushri fathomed this out. Then he said to Cunda: "The Tathagata now shows this wonderful scene. He will enter Nirvana before long. The last offerings that you carried in some time ago will best be offered to the Buddha and then given to all those who are congregated here. O Cunda! Know that it is not without reason that the Tathagata lets shine this light of various colours." On hearing this, Cunda was silent and sad. The Buddha said to Cunda: "It is now time for you to give offerings to the Buddha and congregation. The Tathagata will rightly enter Parinirvana." He then said this a second and a third time. Then, at these words of the Buddha, Cunda cried and wailed, sorrowfully sobbed and said: "Woe is the day, woe is the day! The world is empty." Also, he said to the great assembly: "Let us all cast down our whole body to the ground and beseech the Buddha not to enter Parinirvana." Then the Buddha said to Cunda: "Do not cry and unsettle your mind. Think that this body is like a plantain, a mirage in the hot season, watery foam, a phantom, a transformed body, the castle of a gandharva, an unfired brick, lightning, a picture drawn on water, a prisoner facing death, ripe fruit, a piece of meat, the warp on a loom which is about to end, and the ups and downs of a mortar. You should think that all created things are like poisonous food and that anything made is possessed of all worries." At this, Cunda said again to the Buddha: "The Tathagata does not wish to stay long in life. How can we not weep? Woe is the world, woe is the world! The world is empty. I only pray that you Tathagata will pity all us beings. Please stay long and do not enter Nirvana." The Buddha said to Cunda: "Do not say such as "Love us and stay long in life. "As I pity you and all beings, I today enter Nirvana. Why? This is what is true of all Buddhas. This is so with what is created. That is why all Buddhas say in a gatha:

"The law of what is created
Is by nature non-eternal.
Life ended, we leave the world;
Extinction is bliss."

O Cunda! Now, meditate upon all that is made, that is composite. Think that all things are not-Self and are non-eternal, and that nothing endures. This carnal body has innumerable wrongs. All is like watery foam. So, do not weep." Then Cunda again said to the Buddha: "It is thus, it is thus! All is as you kindly teach me. The Tathagata enters Nirvana for expediency's sake. But I cannot help being sad. Be this as it may, I bethink me and feel glad." The Buddha praised Cunda and said: "Well said, well said! You well know that the Tathagata, following the way of all beings, enters Nirvana for expediency's sake. Hear me well! It is as in the case in which sarasa [eastern bean goose] birds all gather at Lake Anavatapta [Manasarwar] in the spring months. The same is the case with all Buddhas. All gather here. O Cunda! Think not long or short regarding the life of all Buddhas. All things are like phantoms. The Tathagata lives in between. What he has is expediency; he does not cling. Why not? It is thus with the Dharma of all Buddhas. O Cunda! I now take what you offer.

This is to allow you to cross the river of birth and death. Man or heaven who make offerings [to Buddha] for the last time, all gain an unshakable recompense and will be blessed with happiness. Why? Because I am the best field of weal for all beings. If you desire to become a field of weal for all beings, take whatever is given you. Do not tarry long." Then Cunda, for the sake of the emancipation of all beings, hung his head and suppressed his tears, and said to the Buddha: "Very well, O World-Honoured One! When I am worthy of becoming a field of weal, I shall be able to fathom the Nirvana or non-Nirvana of the Tathagata. Now we and all sravakas and pratyekabuddhas are like mosquitoes or sawflies, and cannot well weigh the Nirvana or non-Nirvana of the Tathagata." Then Cunda and his relatives all wept sorrowfully and walked around the body of the Tathagata, burnt incense, strew flowers, and most sincerely paid homage to the Buddha, and then stood up together with Manjushri, and brought forward the utensils of offerings."

Chapter Three: On Grief

Not long after Cunda had left that place, the great earth shook in six ways. Thus went things in Brahma's heaven. Of shaking, there are two kinds: one is a shaking and the other a great shaking. The little shaking is a [mere] shaking and the one that shakes greatly is a great shaking. The one that generates a small sound is a shaking, and the one that generates a great sound is a great shaking. The shaking where only the earth shakes is a shaking, and that where the mountains, forests, rivers, seas and everything else shakes is a great shaking. That which shakes in one direction is a shaking, and that which shakes round and round is a great shaking. The type that moves is a shaking, and the type where beings' minds get shaken is a great shaking. The shaking which occurs when the Bodhisattva comes down from Tushita Heaven to Jambudvipa is a great shaking. The shakings when the Bodhisattva takes birth on this earth, when he leaves home, attains unsurpassed Enlightenment, turns the wheel of Dharma, and enters Parinirvana are great shakings. Today the Tathagata was about to enter Nirvana. That is why the earth shook. Then, all the heavens, nagas, gandharvas, asuras, garudas, kimnaras, mahoragas, humans, and non-humans heard this and their hair stood on end and, in one voice, they cried out and wailed. They said in a gatha:

"O Trainer of men! We now bow and beseech you!
We are parting from the Rishi of men.
We have no hope of being saved.
We now see you the Buddha enter Nirvana
And we are in the sea of suffering.
We are sad and worried, like a calf parting from its mother cow.
Poverty-stricken and with none to save us are we.
We are like one stricken with illness who, having no doctor,
Must attend to himself and partake of food not suitable for illness.
Beings are caught in Illusion.
They are always hindered by views of life.
They are parted from the healing Dharma-King
And they take drugs that are poisonous.
Because of this, the World-Honoured One
Abandons us. This is as when, without a king,
The people in the land get attacked by hunger.
The same is the case with us.
We have no shade of any tree, no taste of Dharma.
Now, hearing that the Buddha will enter Nirvana, our mind snaps,
Just as a great shaking destroys all places.
The great Rishi enters Nirvana and the sun
Of the Buddha sinks down to the ground.
The waters of Dharma are all dried up.
It is certain that we will die.
Beings are extremely worried as the Tathagata now enters Parinirvana.
This is like the son of a rich man who has just lost his parents.
The Tathagata enters Nirvana, and if he is nevermore to return,
We and all beings shall have no one to protect us.
As the Tathagata enters Nirvana, the animals and all others are sad and in fear;
Their minds burn in worry. How should we not be worried today?
The Tathagata abandons us just as we cast off tears and spittle.
For example, when the sun first shows itself, its light burns brightly.
It turns round and shines by itself, removing all darkness.

The divine light of the Tathagata well does away with our worries.
He is amidst us beings like a Mount Sumeru.

"O World-Honoured One! For example, a king brings up many sons. They look right and proper, and he always loves them in his heart. He first teaches them arts, which they all master. Then he gives them over to the hands of candalas. The same is the case here, O World-honoured One! Today we have become the sons of the Dharma-King. We are taught and we abide in right view. We beseech you not to abandon us. If discarded, we shall be like the sons of the king. Please stay long and do not enter Nirvana. O World-Honoured One! For example, the same is the case with one versed in all phases of learning. The same with the Tathagata. Learned in all phases of Dharma, fear yet arises in all phenomena. If the Tathagata lives long in the world, bestowing on us the manna of Dharma and satisfying us, all of us will have no fear of falling into hell. "O World-Honoured One! There may be a man who first learns his work. He is taken by government officials and is imprisoned. People come and ask him: "How are you being treated?" "Now, I am in great sorrow and worried. If I were only out of prison, I should feel easy and be at peace." So it is. Is is thus with the World-Honoured One! For our sake, you underwent penance. And yet we are not out of birth and death and worry. How could the Tathagata attain peace? "O World-Honoured One! It is like a great doctor who is versed in prescription and medicine. He teaches his son the secrets of medicinal preparation, but does not teach such to other students. It is thus with the Tathagata. You impart all these secrets to Manjushri alone and exclude us, without looking back. Please, O Tathagata! Do not be stingy; do not exclude us from the secrets of Dharma, as in the case of the great doctor who imparts [his knowledge] solely to his son and excludes other students. The reason why the doctor begrudges sharing his knowledge with the other students lies in the difference in his love. The heart of the Tathagata is always impartial. Why is it that you do not teach us? Please stay long and do not enter Parinirvana. "O World-Honoured One! It is like one who is old or young, ill or in pain, and is not on a flat road, but is taking a steep path and may suffer hardship. A person sees this, has pity and points out the way that is flat and good. The same with us, O World-Honoured One! "Young" alludes to one not yet high in the stature of the Dharma-Body. "Old" alludes to one greatly burdened with illusion. "Illness and pain"refers to one who has not yet done away with birth and death. "Steep path" alludes to the 25 existences [the types of existence into which we can transmigrate]. O Tathagata! Show us the sweet right path. Please stay long and do not enter Nirvana." Then, the World-Honoured One said to all the bhiksus: "O you bhiksus! Do not, like all common mortals and devas, be sad; do not wail! Make effort, be mindful, and abide in right thought." Then, all the devas and asuras, having heard what the Buddha said, stopped wailing, like one who has lost a son and, after the funeral service, suppresses his sorrow and wails no more. Then the World-Honoured One spoke in a gatha for all the congregation:

"All of you! Open your mind, do not greatly distress yourselves.
The teachings of all Buddhas are thus.
So, keep silence. Try not to be indolent,
Guard your mind, abide in right thought,
Segregate your own selves from unlawful acts;
Console yourselves and be happy.

"Also, next, O bhiksus! If you have any doubts, ask now. If you have doubt as to Void versus non-Void, Eternal versus non-Eternal, Suffering versus non-Suffering, dependent versus non-dependent, gone versus not-gone, refuge versus non-refuge, always versus not-always, impermanence versus the Eternal, beings versus non-beings, "is" versus "not-is", the Real versus the not-Real, the True versus the not-True, extinction versus non-extinction, esoteric versus non-esoteric, and the dual versus the non-dual, I shall speak to you accordingly. For your sake, too, I shall first speak of the manna and then enter Nirvana. "O bhiksus! It is hard to encounter the appearance of the

Buddha in the world. It is hard to be born human. It is hard, too, to encounter the Buddha and gain faith. It is also hard to hear the unhearable. It is hard again to uphold and be perfect in the prohibitive injunctions and to attain arhatship. This is like trying to find gold in sand. It is as in the case of the udumbara. O Bhiksus! It is hard to be born a human, by segregating one's self from the eight inopportune situations [vices that bar the way to meeting the Buddha and hearing his teachings]. "O you! Having now met me, do not go away empty-handed. I underwent hardships in the past, and now I gain all such unsurpassed expedients. For your sake, innumerable kalpas ago, I cast away my body, hands, feet, head, eyes, marrow, and brain. In view of this, do not subject your selves to indolence. O Bhiksus! How do we adorn the treasure-castle of Wonderful Dharma? By adorning our own selves with various virtues and rare gems, and being protected by the bulwarks and moats of the precepts [shila], meditation [dhyana] and Wisdom [prajna]. Now, you have met with this castle of Buddhist teaching. Do not take what is false. For example, a merchant may come across a castle of true treasures, yet gather up such rubbish as tiles and gravel, and return home. The same with you. You have come to a castle of treasures, and yet you take what is false. O all you Bhiksus! Do not be satisfied with a low mind. You are now ordained, but you do not love Mahayana that much. O you Bhiksus! You wear on your bodies the kasaya and dyed robes of a priest, but your mind is still not dyed in the pure Dharma of Mahayana. O you Bhiksus! You go to many places and beg alms, but you do not seek the dishes of the Dharma of Mahayana. O Bhiksus! You shave your hair, but you do not shave off the bond of illusion. O you Bhiksus! I now teach you truly. Now I see that all is in harmony and the Dharma nature of the Tathagata is true and unshakable. So, make effort, all of you! Pick yourselves up, be brave and make away with all the bonds of illusion! If the sun of Wisdom of the 10 powers [of Buddhahood] sinks, darkness will reign over you. O you Bhiksus! It is as when the great earth, mountains, and medicinal herbs all become of use to beings. The same is the case with the Dharma of which I speak. It calls forth wonderfully good and sweet dishes of Dharma and provides the best cure for beings' illnesses of illusion. I shall now make all beings my disciples and the four classes of the Buddhist

Sangha abide in the undisclosed teaching of Dharma. I, too, abide in this and enter Nirvana. What is the undisclosed storehouse? It is like the three dots [in Sanskrit] of the letter "i". If they are in a crosswise line, they make no "i". Placed vertically, they again serve no purpose. But when set like the three dots on the brow of Mahesvara, this is "i". If the three dots are written separately, this again serves no purpose. So is it also with me. The Dharma of emancipation is also [by itself] not Nirvana. The Tathagata's body is also not Nirvana. Great Wisdom is also not Nirvana. The three things may exist separately, but this does not constitute Nirvana. I now peacefully abide in the three and say that, for the sake of all beings, I enter Nirvana. This is as in the case of the letter "i". Then all the bhiksus, on hearing that the Buddha-World-Honoured One would definitely enter Nirvana, were sad. Their hair stood on end and their tears and noses ran. They fell to the ground, touched the Buddha's feet, walked around his person innumerable times, and said to the Buddha: "O World-Honoured One! You explain very well to us the Eternal, Suffering, the All-Void, and non-Self. Just as all beings leave behind footprints and the best of all footprints are those of the elephant, so with this thought of the non-Eternal: it heads all thoughts. One who makes effort and practises well, does away with all love of greed, of the worlds of rupadhatu and arupadhatu, ignorance, arrogance, and the thought of the non-Eternal in this world of desire. O World-Honoured One! If the Tathagata is away from the thought of the non-Eternal, he should not enter Nirvana now. If not, how can you say: "If one practises the meditation upon the non-Eternal, one cuts off from oneself love [craving], ignorance, arrogance, and the non-Eternal of the three worlds?" O World-Honoured One! As a farmer, in autumn, deeply tills the land and thus removes all harmful weeds, so it is the same with this thought of the non-Eternal. It thoroughly rids one of the love of greed, the love of the things of the rupadhatu, arupadhatu, ignorance, arrogance, and the thought of the non-Eternal in the world of desire. O World-Honoured One! Of all tillings of the field, that done in autumn is the best. Of all footprints, that of the elephant is best. And of all thoughts, that of the non-eternal is the best. O World-Honoured One! Analogously, when an emperor is to pass away, amnesty is granted to all prisoners. Then he passes away. The same now with the Tathagata. Please cut off the illusions of the bond of ignorance and non-brightness of all beings, give them emancipation, and then enter Nirvana. We are not yet emancipated. Now, does the Tathagata desert us and enter Nirvana? O World-Honoured One! One may be caught by a demon. But as one comes across a good charmer, by dint of incantation, one can well gain one's release. The same is the case with the Tathagata. For the sake of all sravakas, he expels the devil of ignorance, and lets them abide peacefully, as in the case of the letter "i", in such Laws as the great Wisdom, emancipation, and others. O World-Honoured One! For example, people may bind up a gandhahastin, but even a good trainer cannot get him under control. All of a sudden, it snaps off the rope and chain and walks away as it wills. The same is the case here. We are not yet rid of the 57 illusions. Why does the World-Honoured One desire to abandon us and enter Nirvana? O World-Honoured One! A person suffering from ague obtains a cure for his ailments by encountering a good doctor. The same with us. There are all ailments and sorrows, ill ways of living, fevers, etc. [here]. We have met with the Tathagata, but the illnesses have not gone, and we have not obtained supernal peace and bliss. How can the Tathagata desire to abandon us and enter Nirvana? An intoxicated person does not himself know who is near or not, mother or sister, and is lost in rudeness and lust, and lacks the faculty of speech, and sleeps in defiled places. There happens to be a good doctor [nearby], who gives him medicine. After taking it, he vomits and regains his health; consciousness [conscience] asserts itself and repentance catches him. He reproaches himself very much and regards drink as the root of all vile acts. If he could cut himself free from drinking, his ill acts would cease. The same here. O World-Honoured One! For long, we have been repeating birth and death. We were lost in sensual pleasures and greedily took up the five desires. One who is not mother is taken as mother, not sister as sister, not female as female, and not beings as beings. Because of this, transmigration proceeds and one suffers from birth and death. This is like one intoxicated lying in defilement. O Tathagata! Please give us the medicine of Dharma, and let us vomit up the vile drinks of illusion. We are not yet awakened. Why, O Tathagata, do you mean to abandon us and enter Nirvana? "O World-Honoured One! There may be a man, for example,

who may praise the plantain tree and say that it has hardstuff. But this is not so. The same with beings, O World-Honoured One! We may praise and say that people, beings, life, nursing-up, intellect, doer and recipient are all true. But this cannot be. Thus, we practise non-Self. O World-Honoured One! It is as in the case of water in which rice has been washed or the case of dregs, which are of no use any more. The same with the body too. It has no Self or master. For example, O World-Honoured One! [The plant] saptaparna [alstonia scholaris] has no fragrance. It is thus with this carnal body. It has no Self and no master. Thus we meditate on selflessness. You, the Buddha, say: "All things have no Self and nothing belonging to Self. O you Bhiksus! Learn and practise [this]!" Once this is practised, self-conceit goes away. Self-conceit gone, one enters Nirvana. O World-Honoured One! No tracks of birds exist in the sky. Such can never be. One practising selflessness meditation can have no various views of life. Nothing such as this is possible." Then, the World-Honoured One praised all the bhiksus and said: "It is good, it is good, that you practise the selflessness meditation." Then all bhiksus said to the Buddhha: "We not only practise the selflessness meditation, but even other meditations, to wit, all those on Suffering, the non-Eternal, and Selflessness. O World-Honoured One! When intoxicated, the mind spins round, and all mountains, rivers, castles, palaces, the sun, moon and stars appear to spin round too. O World-Honoured One! Any person who does not practise the meditation of the non-Eternal and Selflessness cannot be called a sage. Due to indolence, one repeats birth and death. O World-Honoured One! Because of this, we all practise such meditations." Then the Buddha said to all the bhiksus: "Hear me well, hear me well! Now, you mention the case of an intoxicated person. This refers to knowledge, not the signification. What do I mean by signification? The intoxicated person sees the sun and moon, which do not move, but he thinks they do. The same is the case with beings. As all illusion and ignorance overhang [the mind], the mind turns upside down and takes Self for non-Self, Eternal for non-Eternal, Purity as non-Pure, and Bliss as sorrow. Overhung by illusion, this thought arises. Though this though arises, the meaning is not gained [realised]. This is as in the case of the intoxicated person who takes what does not move as moving. The Self signifies the uddha; 'the Eternal' signifies the Dharmakaya; Bliss' signifies Nirvana, and 'the Pure' signifies Dharma. Bhiksus, why is it said that one who has the idea of a Self is arrogant and haughty, traversing round Samsara? Bhiksus, although you might say, 'We also cultivate impermanence, suffering, and non-Self, these three kinds of cultivation have no real value/ meaning. I shall now explain the excellent three ways of cultivating dharma. To think of suffering as Bliss and to think Bliss as suffering, is perverse Dharma; to think the impermanent as the Eternal and to think of Eternal as impermanent is perverse Dharma; to of the non-Self [anatman]as the Self [atman] to think of the Self [atman] as non-Self [an] is perverse Dharma; to think of the as the Pure and to think of the Pure as is perverse Dharma. Whoever has these s of perversion, that person does not correct cultivation of dharmas. Bhiksus, ise to the idea of Bliss with regard to a associated with suffering; the idea of with regard to phenomena associated with nence; the idea of the Self with regard to ena without Self; and the idea of Purity gard to phenomena that are impure. Both ndane and also the supramundane have the l, Bliss, the Self, and Purity. Mundane ings [dharmas] have letters and are without ning [referents]; the Supramundane chings] have letters and meaning. Why? cause mundane people have these four rversions, they are unacquainted with the [true] eaning/ referents. Why? Having these perverse ideas, their minds and vision are distorted. Through these three perversions, mundane people see suffering in Bliss, impermanence in the Eternal, non-Self in the Self, and impurity in the Pure. These are called perversions/ inversions. Because of these perversions/ inversions, mundane people know the letters but not the meaning [referents]. What is the meaning/referent? Non-Self is Samsara, the Self is the Tathagata; impermanence is the sravakas and pratyekabuddhas, the Eternal is the Tathagata's Dharmakaya; suffering is all tirthikas, Bliss is Nirvana; the impure is all compounded [samskrta] dharmas , the Pure is the true Dharma that the Buddha and Bodhisattvas have. This is called non-perversion/ non-inversion. By not being inverted [in one's views], one will know [both] the letter and the meaning. If one desires to be freed from

the four perverse/ inverted [views - catur-viparita-drsti], one should know the Eternal, Blissful, the Self and the Pure in this manner." Then, all the bhiksus said to the Buddha: "O World-Honoured One! As you say, if we segregate ourselves from the four inversions, we shall know the Eternal, Bliss, Self, and the Pure. As you have eternally cut off the four inversions, you know well the Eternal, Bliss, Self, and the Pure. If you know well the Eternal, Bliss, Self, and the Pure, why not stay here a kalpa or half a kalpa, and teach us and turn us away from the inversions? And yet you abandon us and desire to enter Nirvana. If you look back at us and teach us, we shall surely listen and practise the Way with all attention. If the Tathagata must at all costs enter Nirvana, how would we be able to remain with this poisoned body and carry out the actions of the Way? We would also follow the Buddha-World-Honoured One and enter Nirvana." Then the Buddha said to all the bhiksus: "Do not say this. I now leave all the unsurpassed Dharma in the hands of Mahakasyapa. This Kasyapa will henceforth be the one upon whom you may rely. This is as in the case where the Tathagata becomes the one to whom all beings can turn. The same is the case with Mahakasyapa. He will now become your refuge. This is as in the case of a king who has many territories and who goes on a tour of inspection, leaving all affairs of state in the hands of his minister. The same with the Tathagata. All right teachings are left in the hands of Mahakasyapa. Know that all that you have learned up to now about the non-eternal and suffering is not true. In spring, for example, people go bathing in a big pond. They are enjoying themselves, sailing in a boat, when they drop a gem of beryl into the depths of the water, after which it can no longer be seen. Then they all get into the water and search for this gem. They competitively scoop up all such rubbish as tiles, stones, bits of wood, and gravel, and say that they have the beryl. They are glad and take the things out, and see that what they hold in their hands is not true. The gem is still in the water. By the power of the gem itself, the water becomes clear and transparent. As a result, the people see that the gem is still in the water, as clearly as when they look up and see the form of the moon in the sky. At that time, there is a wise man there who, working out a power, slowly gets into the water and gains the gem. O you Bhiksus! Do not abide in the thought of the non-Eternal,

Suffering, non-Self, and the not-Pure and be in the situation of those people who take stones, bits of wood, and gravel to be the true gem. You must study well the Way, how to act, wherever you go, and "meditate on the Self, the Eternal, Bliss, and the Pure". Know that the outer forms of the four items which you have learnt up to now are inversions and that anyone who desires to practise the Way should act like the wise man who deftly gets hold of the gem. This refers to the so-called thought of Self, and that of the Eternal, Bliss, and Pure."

Then all the bhiksus said to the Buddha: "O World-Honoured One! You, the Buddha, said before that all things have no Self, that we should practise this and that, when practised, the thought of Self goes away, and that once the thought of Self is done away with, one does away with arrogance and that, arrogance once done away with, one gains Nirvana. Thus did you say "How might we understand this?" The Buddha said to all the bhiksus: "Well said, well said! You ask this question and intend to dispel your doubt. Imagine there is a king, who is dull-witted. He has little wisdom. And there is a doctor, who is obstinate. But the King does not know this and pays him a salary. This doctor uses the products of milk to cure all illnesses. Also, he does not know where the illnesses come from. He may be versed in the medicine of milk, but for him there exists no difference between a cold and a fever. He prescribes milk for all illnesses. This King was unaware that this doctor was ignorant of the pleasing and non-pleasing, the good and bad aspects of milk. But there was a Doctor who knew eight different treatments for illnesses and who was able to cure all diseases. This Doctor was versed in prescription and medicines and had come from a far-off place. And the King's doctor did not know how to ask and learn. He was rash and haughty. So the learned Doctor cordially invited the King's doctor and looked up to him [as an expedient] as his master and asked of him the secret of treatment. He said to the King's doctor: "I now invite you and make you my teacher. Please be good enough to teach me." The King's doctor said: "If you serve me for 48 years, I will teach you the art of medicine. " Then, at these words, the learned Doctor said: "I shall do as you tell me. I shall do my best and run errands." Then the King's doctor, taking the learned Doctor along with him,

went to see the King. At this, the visiting Doctor explained to the King the various ways of treatment and even other things. He said: "Please know, O great King! Know well! This Dharma is like this and you will well cure illnesses." On hearing this, the King recognised the ignorance and lack of knowledge of his own doctor. He at once drove him out of the country. And he respected the new Doctor all the more. Then the new Doctor said to himself: "It is now time to teach the King." He said to the King: "O great King! If you truly love me, please make me a promise!" The King replied: "I shall give you, should you desire it, even my right hand or any part of my body." The new Doctor said: "You may give me all statuses, but I myself do not wish to have much. What I desire you to do for me is to proclaim to the people of every corner of your land that henceforth they are not to use the milk medicine, which the former doctor told them to use. Why not? Because much harm and poisonous results arise [from it]. Any person who still takes this medicine should be beheaded. If the milk medicine is not used, there will be no untimely deaths; all will go in peace. That is why I ask this of you." Then the King said: "What you ask me to do is a trifle. I shall at once issue an order and see to it that anyone who is ill does no take milk as a medicine. Any person who does will be beheaded." At this, the learned Doctor made several kinds of medicine, which tasted pungent, butter, salty, sweet, and sour. With these, treatment was given, and there was no case in which illness could not be cured. "After some time, the King himself became ill, and the Doctor was called in. The King said: "I am now ill. How am I to be cured?" The Doctor thought about the illness of the King and saw that the milk medicine was good [here]. So he said to the King: "What you are now suffering from can very well be cured by milk. What I said before about the milk medicine was not true. If you take it now, you will be cured. You are now suffering from a fever. It is right that you should take milk." Then the King said to the Doctor: "Are you mad? Is it a fever? And you say that if I take milk, it will cure me? Before, you said it was poison. Now you tell me to take it. How is this? Do you mean to cheat me? What the former doctor said was good, [yet] you despised it and said that it was poison, and you made me drive him away. Now you say that it well cures illness. From you you say, the former doctor ought to excel you." "Then the learned Doctor said to the King: "O King! Do not say this, please. A worm eats on [a piece of] wood and [the shape of] a letter comes out. This worm does not know anything of letters. A wise person sees this. But he does not say that this worm understands letters. And he is not overcome by surprise. O great King! Please know: so was it also with the former doctor. To all illnesses he gave medicine made from milk. This is as in the case of the worm that eats on wood, as a result of which a form like a letter emerges. The former doctor did not know how to distinguish between the pleasing and non-pleasing aspects, the good and the bad." Then the King wanted to know: "What do you mean he did not know?" The guest Doctor answered the King: "This milk medicine is harmful, but it is also a manna." "How can you say that this milk is manna?" "If you milking cow has not taken the lees, the slippery grass and the wheat refuse, and if the calf fares well, and if the cow was not grazed too high up on the land or in a low and wet place, if the cow is given pure water and not made to run or made to live among the bulls, and if feeding is done regularly, and if the place it lives in is fit, the milk gained from such a cow well does away with all illnesses. This can well be called the manna of medicine. Any other milk is poison." "On hearing this, the King praised the great Doctor: "Well said, well said, O great Doctor! Today, for the first time in my life, I know of the pleasing and non-pleasing, that which is good and not good in the milk medicine. Taking this, I am now well. I shall at once proclaim to the people that they may well take the milk medicine." On hearing this, the people of the country, angry and resentful, said: "The great King is now caught by a devil. Is he mad? He cheats us and makes us take milk." All the people, angry and resentful, came to the King. The King said to them: "Be not angry, and have no resentment. To take milk or not to take it all comes from the science of medicine. I am not to blame." At this, the great King and the people all jumped for joy. They all the more respected and honoured the Doctor, and made offerings to him. That is how all the people took the milk medicine and regained their health. "Know, O you Bhiksus! The same is the case with the Tathagata, the Alms-deserving, the All-Enlightened-One, the Unsurpassed Best Trainer, the Teacher-of-Heaven-and-Earth, the Buddha-World-Honoured One. He comes as a great Doctor and subdues all tirthikas and bad doctors. In the presence of kings and all people, he says: "I shall become the King of doctors and subdue tirthikas." Thus we say: "There is no self, no man, no being, no life, no nurturing, no knowing, none that does, and none that receives." O Bhiksus! Know that what the tirthikas say is like the case of a worm that eats upon [a piece of] wood, from which, by chance, there appears what looks like a letter. Because of this, the Tathagata teaches and says no-self. This is to adjust beings and because he is aware of the occasion. Such non-self is, as occasion arises, spoken of, and it is [also] said that there is the Self. This is as in the case of the learned Doctor, who knows well the medicinal and non-medicinal qualities of milk. It is not as with common mortals, who might measure the size of their own self. Common mortals and the ignorant may measure the size of their own self and say, 'It is like the size of a thumb, like a mustard seed, or like the size of a mote.' When the Tathagata speaks of Self, in no case are things thus. That is why he says: 'All things have no Self.' Even though he has said that all phenomena [dharmas] are devoid of the Self, it is not that they are completely/ truly devoid of the Self. What is this Self? Any phenomenon [dharma] that is true [satya], real [tattva], eternal [nitya], sovereign/ autonomous/ self-governing [aisvarya], and whose ground/ foundation is unchanging [asraya-aviparinama], is termed 'the Self' [atman]. This is as in the case of the great Doctor who well understands the milk medicine. The same is the case with the Tathagata. For the sake of beings, he says "there is the Self in all things" O you the four classes! Learn Dharma thus!"

Chapter Four: On Long Life

The Buddha said to all the bhiksus: "If you have any doubt about the moral precepts, you are free to ask questions. I shall now explain and fully satisfy you. I have already practised the Way and clearly attained the true nature of the All-Void of all things. O Bhiksus! Only the Tathagata has practised the true nature of the All-Void of all things." He also said to the bhiksus: "If you have any doubts, ask me, all of you!" Then the bhiksus said to the Buddha: "O World-Honoured One! With the wisdom that we have, we can put no questions to the Tathagata, the Alms-deserving and All-Enlightened One. Why not? The world of the Tathagata cannot be known by us. All samadhis cannot be thought of. Whatever is said is not within the compass of our comprehension. So, with what wisdom we have, there can be no posing of questions to the Tathagata. O World-Honoured One! There is a man, for example, who is 120 years old. Suffering from a long illness, he is in bed and cannot get up. His vitality has gone, so that he cannot live long. There is a rich man there who is on his way to far-off places on business. He gives this man a hundred pounds of gold and says: "I intend to go on a journey and entrust this treasure to you. After 10 or 20 years, I shall come back, when my business is concluded. When I am home again, give this back to me." The sick old man receives it. And he has none to succeed him. After some time, the illness develops and he dies, and what was entrusted to him cannot be found. The person who entrusted the treasure to him comes back from his journey, looks around, but cannot find the man. One like this, being ignorant, cannot think and weigh the good and bad of entrusting a thing to the hands of another person. So, on coming back, he does not know where to look. Thus the treasure gets lost. O World-honoured One! It is the same with us sravakas. We hear the kind admonition of the Tathagata, but we cannot hold it long. It is as with the old man who is entrusted with treasure. We are ignorant now and do not know what to ask regarding the precepts." The Buddha said to the bhiksus: "If you question me now, it will benefit all beings. That is why I say that you should ask about any doubts you may have." Then, all the bhiksus said to the Buddha: "O World-Honoured One! Imagine, for

example: there is a man here of 25, full of vitality and right and proper. He has many treasures, such as gold, silver, beryl, etc. He has his parents, wife, children, relatives, and all his family. Then a man comes and hands over a treasure to him, saying: "I have things to do and am about to go on a long journey. My business concluded, I shall be back. When I am back home, return this to me." After this, the young man guards the treasure well, as though it were his own. The [young] man falls ill and says: "All this gold was entrusted to my care. When the man gets back home, give this to him. " One who is wise knows how to act and weigh things. His business concluded, the man returns, and what he had entrusted [to the other] is all safe, with nothing lost. The same with the World-Honoured One. If the treasure is entrusted to Ananda and the bhiksus, it cannot survive long. Why not? Because all sravakas and Mahakasyapa must pass away and the situation will inevitably be like that of the old man who receives the entrusted goods of the other person. Because of this, all the unsurpassed Buddhist teachings must be entrusted to the hands of all Bodhisattvas. They discuss well and the treasure will live long and flourish for infinite thousands of ages and benefit all beings enormously. This is like the case of the man in the prime of his life who receives the entrusted goods of the other person. Because of this, all Bodhisattvas can well pose questions. What wealth we have may be likened to a mosquito or sawfly. How can we question the Tathagata on the depths of the teaching?" At this, all the sravakas sank into silence. Then, the Buddha, praised all the bhiksus and said: "It is good, it is good that you have all attained the unleakable [undefiled, asrava-free] mind of the arhat. I also thought of this once myself. Because of these two circumstances [i.e. that the sravakas cannot and the Bodhisattvas can pose questions], I entrust the Mahayana to all the Bodhisattvas and allow this Wonderful Dharma to live long". Then the Buddha said to all the congregation: "O all good men and women! You cannot calculate the length of my life. No unhindered speech of a Bodhisattva can fully express this. You may, if you will, ask me about the precepts or how to take refuge. You may do this a second or third time." At that time, among those congregated, there was a Bodhisattva-mahasattva of the stage of the boyhood abode [ie. on the 9th of the 10 Bodhisattva levels]. He had been born into a Brahmin family in a hamlet called Tara. His family name was Mahakasyapa. By the divine power of the Buddha, he rose from his seat, bared his right elbow [shoulder] and walked around the Buddha 100 thousand times, and placing his right knee on the ground and folding his hands, said to the Buddha: "O World-Honoured One! I would now like to ask something of the Buddha. If you will allow me, I desire to speak." The Buddha said to Kasyapa: "The Tathagata, the Alms-deserving and All-Enlightened One allows you to say anything. I shall expound for you, clarify your doubt, and gladden you." Then Bodhisattva Kasyapa again said to the Buddha: "O World-Honoured One! The Tathagata, pitying me, gives me permission. I now shall ask. But the wisdom that I have is petty, like that of a mosquito or sawfly. You, Tathagata-World-Honoured One, are exalted in personal virtue and are surrounded by a retinue as fragrant as sandalwood and as difficult to subdue and as invincible as a lion. The Tathagata's person is like a true diamond. You shine like beryl. All [about you] is true and difficult to break and is surrounded by a great sea of Wisdom. All the Bodhisattva-mahasattvas congregated here are perfect in infinite and boundless depths of virtue. They are like gandhahastins. How can I put questions before such a congregation? Only now, guarded by the Buddha's divine power and by dint of the great dignity of moral virtue of the people congregated here, shall I put some questions to you." He spoke in a gatha:

"How do we gain long life, the Adamantine and Invincible body?
How do we gain great strength?
How by this sutra do we ultimately attain the other shore?
We beseech you to open the undisclosed door and,
For the sake of beings, teach us widely.
How can we, for the sake of the masses,
Become an expansive refuge and, although not arhats, be equal to arhats?
How can we, for the sake of beings,
Foresee Papiyas' [i.e. Mara, the Devil's] disturbances?
How can one clearly distinguish
Between what the Tathagata says and what the Papiyas says?
How does the All-Best-Trainer become pleased in heart
And speak about "Paramartha-satya" [the Truth of the Supreme Reality],
Become full in right good, and speak about the four inversions?
How do you do good? O Great Rishi! Please tell us now.
How do Bodhisattvas fathom the unfathomable nature?
How do they understand the significations of the full letter and the half letter

[i.e. the word as a composite, made from joining the Sanskrit alphabets and possessing meaning, and the alphabetical letters and phonetic symbols in the case of Sanskrit]?
How can we simultaneously practise two holy actions
Such as the sarasa and karanda that go together?
How can one be like the sun and moon,
Like the evening star and Jupiter?
How can one, not yet aspiring, be called a Bodhisattva?
How can all beings gain fearlessness,
Like Jambunada gold, in which no flaw can ever be detected?
How can one, though living in a defiled land,
Not be defiled like the lotus flower?
How do we live amidst illusions and
Not get tainted and not attacked by diseases,
As in the case of a doctor who, curing all diseases,

Does not himself get stricken by disease?
How can one be a sea-captain,
Foundering yet [still] amidst the sea of birth and death?
How can one abandon birth and death, as the serpent does its old skin?
How can one meditate on the Three Treasures
And be like the tree in the heavens that answers well one's wishes?
How can one speak about the three Vehicles
[of sravaka, pratyekabuddha, and Bodhisattva] and the Natureless?
How can one talk of Bliss, being not yet blessed with Bliss?
How can all Bodhisattvas be indestructible ones?

How can one be the eyes and guide for a person born blind?
How can one gain a multifarious head [mind rich in knowledge]
We beseech you, O Great Rishi! Please explain [this] to us!
How can you who turn the wheel of Dharma
Expand like the moon at the beginning of the month?
How do you show yourself again and gain Nirvana at the end?
How can you, the brave, step forward
And show to man, heaven and Mara the Way?
How does one know "Dharmata" [essence of Reality]
And become blessed with Dharma?
How do all Bodhisattvas make away with all illnesses?
How do they expound to all beings the undisclosed teachings?
How do they expound the Ultimate and the non-Ultimate?
If doubts [can be] done away with, why not definitely explain?
How can one attain the highest and unsurpassed Way?
I now beseech the Tathagata, for the sake of the Bodhisattvas,
To expound the deepest and most wonderful teachings.
Everything has the nature of peace and bliss.
Expound in detail for us, please, O Great Rishi World-Honoured One!
O Great Refuge! O Two-Footed-Honoured One,
The Wonderful-One-of-All-Medicines!
I now desire to enquire all about things,
But I lack Wisdom; even all the Bodhisattvas
Who make utmost effort may not know
Such depths as of the world of all Buddhas."

Then, praising Bodhisattva Kasyapa, the Buddha said: "Well said, well said, O good man! You have not yet arrived at All-Knowledge, but I am he who has attained it. You now ask about the deepest depths of the undisclosed doctrine. Now, O good man! I, sitting under the Bodhi Tree, first attained right Enlightenment. At that time, in all Buddha-lands as numerous as the sands of countless asamkhyas of Ganges, there were Bodhisattvas. They too asked of me the meaning of this deepest doctrine. And what they said and the virtue thereof were thus, the same, not different. Asking thus, great benefits accrue to all beings." Then Bodhisattva Kasyapa said to the Buddha: "O World-Honoured One! The power of my wisdom does not extend thus far as to put such deep questions to the Tathagata. O World-Honoured One! This is like a mosquito or sawfly that cannot fly over a great sea or fly round in the high heavens. The same with me. I have no power to ask the Tathagata about this great sea of Wisdom or the meaning of the great depths of space-like extension of "Dharmata". O World-Honoured One! This is like a king who hands over to the hands of the officer in charge of treasures a bright gem that was housed in the knot of his hair, and the officer, on receiving it, increases the guard. The same is the case with me. Having received the depths of the Tathagata's Mahayana teaching, I shall guard it all the more carefully. Why? This is but to make me attain the great depths of Wisdom." Then the Buddha said to Kasyapa: "O good man! Listen clearly, listen clearly! I shall now tell you the cause of the Tathagata's longevity of life. The Bodhisattva, through this action, gains long life. For this reason, listen with your best attention. Having listened, speak of it to others. O good man! Having thus practised, I attained unsurpassed Bodhi. I, for all beings' sake, now speak of this. O good man! As an example: a prince transgresses against state law and is chained up in prison. The king pities him and, riding on a palanquin, goes himself to the prison because he loves the prince. The same with the Bodhisattva. If he desires to have a long life, he should guard and protect beings and view them as one would one's only son, and abide in great loving-kindness, great compassion, great joy, and great equanimity. Also, he should impart the precept of non-harming to them and teach them to practise all good things. Also, he must let all beings abide peacefully in the five moral precepts and the ten good deeds. Furthermore, he will get into such realms as hell, hungry preta, animal, and asura, and free all these beings from where they are suffering, emancipate those not yet emancipated, pass over those who have not yet gained the other shore, give Nirvana to those who have not yet attained it, and console all who live in fear. Acting thus, the Bodhisattva gains longevity of life and unmolested [unlimited] freedom in knowing. And when the end comes, he gains life in the high heavens." Then Bodhisattva Kasyapa said to the Buddha: "O World-Honoured One! You say that the Bodhisattva-mahasattva regards all beings just as one views one's only son. The thought is too deep, and I cannot fathom it. O World-Honoured One! You say that the Bodhisattva views beings with an all-equal mind and views them as he would look upon his only son. But things are not so. Why not? Amongst the Buddhists, there are those who break the moral precepts, those who commit deadly sins, and those who transgress against Wonderful Dharma. How can it be that he [the Buddha] can have the same [attitude of] mind towards them as towards his only son?" The Buddha said to Kasyapa: "It is so, it is so! I view all beings as I view my own Rahula." Bodhisattva Kasyapa said to the Buddha: "O World-Honoured One! Once, on the 15th of the month, on the day of posadha, among the congregated who were strict and pure in the moral precepts, there was a boy who did not quite

seriously observe the three actions of body, mouth and mind. He hid himself in a dark place and secretly listened to what was said. Guhyapada, receiving the divine power of the Buddha, crushed this boy into dust with a vajra [sharpened bar, a double-headed weapon, or a diamond]. O World-Honoured One! Guhyapada acted so badly that the boy's life was taken. How could you look upon all beings as you do your own Rahula?" The Buddha said to Kasyapa: "Do not speak thus! This boy was none but a transformed [illusory, projected] one, not a true one. This was but to repress breaking of the precepts and transgression against Buddha-Dharma, and to remould beings. Even the vajra and also Guhyapada were transformed existences. O Kasyapa! There are in the world those who slander Wonderful Dharma, icchantikas, those who harm others, those who abide in twisted views, those who purposely act contrary to the moral precepts. I pity all and have loving thought, just as one has towards one's only son, as in the case of Rahula. O good man! To illustrate: when the officers of the royal court break state law, the king punishes according to the rules relating to the sins committed and does not leave the officers unpunished. The Tathagata does not act thus. He makes those who violate the precepts undergo such procedures as being driven out, reprimanded, put under surveillance, impeached or banished for non-confirming of the sins committed, for non-repentance, and for non-forsaking of twisted views. The reason, O good man, why the Tathagata imposes the suppressive moral precepts on those who slander Dharma arises from the fact that he desires to show those who transgress that karmic consequences ensue for what one has done. O good man! Know that the Tathagata desires to bestow on evil beings what need not be feared. He emits one, two, or five beams, so that those who encounter this light will be rid of all evil acts. Now, the Tathagata has so many uncountable means of such power. O good man! If you desire to see Dharma which cannot be seen, I will now explain to you all about what you can see. When I have entered Nirvana, a bhiksu who is perfect in the deportment of a bhiksu and who observes Wonderful Dharma may come across one who transgresses. If this bhiksu drives away, reproaches, impeaches, or remoulds such an evil-doer, he will be blessed with weal which one cannot measure or tell of. O good man! To illustrate: there is a tyrant king who does evil things and happens to suffer very seriously from illness. The king of a neighbouring state, hearing of this, mobilises the army to overthrow the state. At this, the king, having no power to resist the attack, repents and tries to do good. And the weal of the king of this neighbouring state will be uncountable. The same with the precept-observing bhiksu. If he drives away or reproaches those who act against Dharma and makes them do good, an incalculable [amount of] weal will be his. O good man! As an illustration: in the fields and around the houses where a rich man dwells grow many poisonous tree. Seeing this, he fells all of them and there is no more of them. Or white hair appears on the head of a young man. He feels ashamed of it, cuts it off and does not allow his hair to grow long. The same is the case with a precept-upholding bhiksu. If he sees any person who breaks the precepts and transgresses against Wonderful Dharma, he should drive away, reproach or impeach such a person. If a good bhiksu, seeing one who transgresses against Dharma, does not drive away, reproach or impeach such a person, know that this bhiksu is the enemy of the Buddhist teaching. If he drives away, reproaches or impeaches such a one, he is my disciple, a true disciple." Bodhisattva Kasyapa said again to the Buddha; "O World-Honoured One! You may say that you look upon all beings equally and treat them as you would an only son such as Rahula. This is not so. O World-honoured One! A person may try to harm you with a sword. Or there may be someone who tries to paint the Buddha's body with sandalwood paste. If it is is the case that you view both persons with the same eye, how could you cure moral offences? If it is the case that this cures moral offences, this does not make sense." The Buddha said to Kasyapa: "An illustration, O good man! The king, minister and prime minister may desire to bring up their sons who are right-set in countenance and sharp in intellect. One of those fathers takes one, two, three, four such sons and hands them over to a strict teacher and says to him: "Please teach my sons deportment, good behaviour, the arts, writing and reckoning. These my four sons will study under your guidance. Even if three of my sons die of goading, teach the last with whatever means you may think fit. I may lose the three, but I shall not be vexed." O Kasyapa! Are the father and the teacher responsible for killing?" "No, O World-Honoured One! Why not? Because a loving mind was at the bottom [of their actions]. What there is [here] is accomplishment, but not an evil mind. Such teaching will be met with good, to a limitless extent." "O good man! The same is the case with the Tathagata. He views those who transgress Dharma as he views his only son. The Tathagata now entrusts unsurpassed Wonderful Dharma to the hands of kings, ministers, prime ministers, bhiksus, bhiksunis, upasakas and upasikas. All of these kings and the four classes of the Buddhist Sangha will encourage those who practise the Buddhist teaching and enable them increasingly to observe the moral precepts, practise meditation and wisdom. If there are any who miscarry these three phases [aspects] of Dharma and if there are those who are indolent and who break the moral precepts, the kings, ministers, and the four classes of the Buddhist Sangha will work hard and remould such people. O good man! Should all these kings and the four classes of the Buddhist Sangha be blamed or not?" "No, indeed, O World-Honoured One!" "O good man! These kings and the four classes of the Buddhist Sangha are not to be blamed. How could it be that the Tathagata is to be blamed? O good man! The Tathagata well observes such impartiality, looking upon all people as one would one's only son. Such a one who practises the Way is called one who practises the all-equal mind of a Bodhisattva and one who possesses a mind that loves an only son. O good man! The Bodhisattva, practising thus, gains a long life and is now able to see what took place in the past." Bodhisattva Kasyapa said again to the Buddha: "O World-Honoured One! You say that a Bodhisattva, practising impartiality, can well view beings just as one views one's only son and that such a person gains a long life. But you should not say this. Why not? One who knows Dharma indeed speaks well of filial duty. But back home, he beats his parents with tiles and gravel, [in defiance of] the fact that one's parents are the best field of weal, where much weal comes about, such as is the most difficult of difficult to encounter. Where the person should be making offerings, he performs evil. There is a distinction between what this person knows and what he does. What the Tathagata says is also like this. The Bodhisattva practises impartiality and views beings as an only son, and he gains a long life, can look into the past, and live eternally and there cannot be any change. Now, why is it that the World-Honoured One is like a person with the shortest life in the world? Does not the Tathagata entertain hatred against all beings? O World-Honoured One! What evil acts did you perform in the past? How many evil acts did you commit, so as to gain the shortest life, which does not even extend to 100 years?" The Buddha said to Kasyapa: "O good man! Under what circumstances do you bring across your lips all such rough-hewn words against the Tathagata? The life of the Tathagata is the longest and most superior of longest lives. His eternal Dharma is the unsurpassed of all eternal things." Bodhisattva Kasyapa said again to the Buddha: "O World-Honoured One! How did you, the Tathagata, gain eternal life?" The Buddha said to Bodhisattva Kasyapa: "O good man! There are eight great rivers, which are 1) Ganges, 2) Yamuna, 3) Sarabhu, 4) Ajitavati, 5) Mahi, 6) Indus, 7) Pasu, and 8) Sita. All these eight rivers and other small rivers drain into the great ocean. O Kasyapa! All the great rivers of life of all people, heaven, earth and sky drain into the Tathagata's sea of life. Hence, the length of life of the Tathagata is incalculable. Also, next, O Kasyapa! As an illustration: it is like the case of Lake Anavatapta, which carries forth four rivers. The same with the Tathagata. He carries forth all lives. O Kasyapa! As an example: of all eternal things, that of space is the foremost. The same is the case with the Tathagata. He is the foremost of all eternal things. O Kasyapa! This is as in the case of sarpirmanda [most delicious and efficacious medicine], the first of all medicines. The same is the case with the Tathagata. He is the one possessed of the longest life." Bodhisattva Kasyapa said again to the Buddha: "If the life of the Tathagata is thus, you mast live for a kalpa or [just] less than a kalpa and be delivering sermons in the way the great rain falls." "O Kasyapa! Do not entertain the thought of extinction regarding the Tathagata. O Kasyapa! There may be amongst the bhiksus, bhiksunis, upasakas, upasikas, or even among the tirthikas a person who possesses the five divine powers or the unmolested [unlimited] power of a rishi. He may live a kalpa or less than a kalpa; he may be able to fly through the air, and be unmolested [unconstrained] whether he is reclining or sitting. He emits fire from the left side of his body or water from his right side. His body emits smoke and flames like a fire ball. If he desires to live long, he can do as he wills. He can freely lengthen or shorten his life. With such divine power, he has such freedom of power. And

how could this not be possible with the Tathagata, who possesses unmolested [unlimited] power in all things? How could it not be that he can live for half a kalpa, a kalpa, 100 kalpas, 100 thousand kalpas, or innumerable kalpas? On account of this, know that "the Tathagata is an eternal and unchanging existence". The Tathagata's body is a transformed body and not one supported by various kinds of food. In order to pass beings to the other shore, he manifests himself amidst poisonous trees. Hence he manifests himself discarding his carnal body and entering Nirvana. Know, O Kasyapa, that the Buddha is an eternal and unchanging existence. O all of you! Practise the Way in this Paramartha-satya [Truth of the Transcendent Reality], make effort, and practise the Way with one mind; having practised the Way, expound it widely to others." Then Bodhisattva Kasyapa said to the Buddha: "O World-Honoured One! What difference exists between supramundane Dharma and the mundane? You say that the Buddha is an existence eternal and unchanging. If so, in worldly life, too, we have Brahma who is eternal, and also Isvara who is eternal, and no changing is there. The eternal nature of Self too is eternal; even a mote is also said to be eternal. If the Tathagata is an eternal existence, why does the Tathagata not always show [himself] in this way? If it is that you do not exist thus, what difference could we see? Why? Because Brahma, the mote existence, and prakriti [primordial matter] also do not manifest thus." The Buddha said to Kasyapa: "A rich man has many cows, whose colours vary; nonetheless, they are all of one group. They are entrusted to the hands of a cowherd, who takes them to watery or grassy land. Solely sarpirmanda is sought, not fresh milk or cream. The cattleman, having milked the cows, takes the milk himself. When the rich man dies, the cows are stolen by robbers. They get the cows, but having no women, they themselves milk the cows. The robbers say to one another: "The rich man fed these cows for sarpirmanda, not for fresh milk or cream. What should we do? Now, sarpirmanda is the best of all tastes in the world. We have no utensils and no place to keep it safe in." They also say to one another: "We have a bag made of hide. We shall keep it in that. Although we have a thing to keep the milk in, we do not know how to churn it. It is hard to obtain what we could drink. How could we gain fresh butter?" At that, the robbers, because sarpirmanda was what they were after, added water to the milk. But because they added too much water, the fresh milk, cream, and sarpirmanda were all lost. The same with common mortals. There are good teachings. But all are the residues of the Wonderful Dharma of the Tathagata. How? The Tathagata enters Nirvana. Later we steal what was left behind, i.e. the precepts, samadhi, and Wisdom. This is like the robbers stealing the cows. All common mortals obtain the precepts, samadhi, and Wisdom, but they have no means of working them out [perfecting them, implementing them]. Hence they never gain the eternal precepts, the eternal samadhi, the eternal Wisdom, and emancipation. This is like the robbers' not having the means to work out [bring forth what they want], thus losing the sarpirmanda; or it is like the robbers' adding water when they meant to gain sarpirmanda. The same with common mortals. Referring to emancipation, beings say that Self, being, life, man, Brahma, Isvara, prakriti, the precepts, samadhi, Wisdom, emancipation, or Thoughtless-non-thoughtlessness Heaven [naivasamjnana-samjnayatana] or Nirvana is Nirvana. This, however [i.e. just saying this] does not give one emancipation or Nirvana. This is like the robbers' failing to gain sarpirmanda. Common mortals do small-scale pure actions and make offerings to their parents. Then they gain rebirth in heaven and attain small-scale bliss. This is like the milk to which the robbers added water. And common mortals do not themselves know the fact that one gets born in heaven by small-scale pure actions and making offerings to one's parents. Also, they do not know the moral precepts, samadhi, Wisdom and taking refuge in the Three Treasures. Not knowing [all this], they talk about Eternity, Bliss, Self, and Purity. Though they talk, they do not know what these are. Hence, after taking birth in this life, the Tathagata talks about Eternity, Bliss, Self, and Purity. A chakravartin [world's greatest, just ruler] appears in the world. By the power of virtue, all the robbers pull back, and there is no loss of any cows. Then the chakravartin entrusts the cows to the hands of a cowherd who knows the way. This person works out the means well and obtains sarpirmanda. Due to the sarpirmanda, there is no illness or pain for any being. It is like this. When the chakravartin of the wheel of Dharma appears in the world, all beings abandon these, because they cannot talk about the precepts, samadhi, and Wisdom. This is

like the pulling back of the robbers. Then the Tathagata indeed speaks of secular and supramundane things. For the benefit of beings, he lets the Bodhisattva talk as the occasion arises. The Bodhisattva-mahasattva, on gaining sarpirmanda, lets all the innumerable beings gain the unsurpassed manna of Dharma. The Eternity, Bliss, Self, and Purity of the Tathagata thus come about [appear, are realised]. The Tathagata is one who is eternal and unchanging. This is not in the manner in which common mortals and the ignorant of the world say that Brahma is eternal. This eternality is always with the Tathagata and not with whatever else. O Kasyapa! All good men and good women should always carefully practise the Way of the two-lettered Buddha, who is eternal [i.e. in Chinese, "Nyo-rai" - consisting of two syllables or characters - means "Tathagata", "One come from Thusness"]. O Kasyapa! Any good man or good woman who practises the Way of the two-lettered, such a one accords with what I do and gets born where I go. If any person practises the two letters and sees it as extinction, know that the Tathagata enters Parinirvana to [in the eyes of] such a one. O good man! Nirvana is the "Dharmata" [True Essence] of all Buddhas." Bodhisattva Kasyapa said to the Buddha: "What might the "Dharmata" of the Tathagata mean? O World-Honoured One! I now desire to know about "Dharmata". Have pity and expound this to me extensively. Now, "Dharmata" means "abandoning one's body". To abandon means "not to possess". If not possessed, how can the body exist? If the body exists, how can we say that there is "Dharmata" in the body? If the body possesses "Dharmata", how can the body exist? How can I know of this?" The Buddha said to Kasyapa: "O good man! Do not speak thus - that extinction is "Dharmata". Now, "Dharmata" knows no extinction. O good man! This is as with the no-thought heaven [the fourth dhyana heaven of the rupadhatu - Realm of Form], where there is no thought of matter, though matter is perfectly equipped [provided]. One might ask: "How, then, can devas live there, please and amuse themselves, and have peace, and how do they think, see, and ask?" O good man! The world of the Tathagata is not one which sravakas and pratyekabuddhas can know. Do not so explicate and say that the body of the Tathagata is extinction. O good man! The Tathagata and extinction are matters for the world of Buddhas. It is not within sravakas' and pratyekabuddhas' reach of knowing. O good man! Do not entertain such thoughts as where the Tathagata lives, where he works, where he is to be seen, where he enjoys himself. O good man! Such, too, are things which do not come within the compass of your knowing. Everything regarding the Dharma-Body of all Buddhas and everything regarding the various expedients are beyond the range of [worldly] knowing. "Also, next, O good man! Practise the teaching of the Buddha, Dharma and the life of the Sangha, and abide in the thought of the Eternal. These three things do not contradict one another. There is no form of the non-eternal [there], no change. Any person practising these three as things which differ fails in the Three Refuges which are pure. This we should know. This is to say that such a person lacks a place to abide in. No precept is fully learned; no fruit can come about of sravakas or pratyekabuddhas. Anyone who abides in the thought of the Eternal in this All-Wonderfulness has a place to take refuge in. O good man! It is like the shadow accompanying a tree. The same is the case with the Tathagata. As there is the Eternal, there is a refuge that can be taken. It is not non-eternal. If it is said that the Tathagata is non-eternal, he cannot be a refuge for all the heavens and people of the world." Bodhisattva Kasyapa said to the Buddha: "O World-Honoured One! It is, for example, like the case of a tree in the darkness, where there is no shadow." "O Kasyapa! Do not say that there is a tree and that it has no shadow. It is merely that the fleshly eye cannot see it. The same with the Tathagata. His nature is eternal; it does not change. One cannot see [it] without the eye of Wisdom. This is as in the case where no tree-shadow appears in the darkness. Common mortals, after the death of the Buddha, may well say: "The Tathagata is non-eternal." This is the same. If one says that the Tathagata is other than Dharma and Sangha, there cannot be the Three Refuges. This is as in the case in which, as your parents are different from each other, there is the non-eternal." Bodhisattva Kasyapa said again to the Buddha: "O World-Honoured One! Henceforth, I, for the first time, shall, with the Eternalism of the Buddha, Dharma and Sangha, enlighten parents for ages, down to seven generations. It is wonderful indeed! O World-Honoured One! I shall now learn the All-Wonderfulness of the Tathagata, Dharma and Sangha. Having satisfied myself, I shall expound this widely to all others. If they do not have faith in the teaching, I will know that they have long practised the non-Eternal. To such as these I shall be like frost and hail." Then the Buddha praised Bodhisattva Kasyapa and said: "Well said, well said! You now indeed protect and uphold Wonderful Dharma. Such protection of Dharma is no cheating of people. By the good act of not cheating [deceiving] others, one obtains a long life and becomes well able to read one's past lives."

Chapter Five: On the Adamantine Body

Then the World-Honoured One said to Kasyapa: "O good man! The body of the Tathagata is one that is eternal, one that is indestructible, and one that is adamantine, one that is not sustained by various kinds of food. It is the Dharma-Body." Kasyapa said to the Buddha: "O World-Honoured One! We do not see such a body as you speak of. What we see is one which is non-eternal, destructible, of dust, one sustained by various kinds of food. How? In that you, the Tathagata, are now about to enter Nirvana." The Buddha said to Kasyapa: "Do not say that the body of the Tathagata is not strong, can easily be broken, and is the same as that of common mortals. O good man! Know that the body of the Tathagata is as indestructible as that which stands for countless billions of kalpas. It is neither the body of man or heaven, not one that fears, not one sustained by various kinds of food. The body of the Tathagata is one that is not a body and yet is a body. It is one not born and one that does not die. It is one that does not learn or practise. It is one innumerable and boundless and one that does not leave any tracks behind. It knows not and has no form to represent it. It is one ultimately pure. It does not shake. It does not receive, nor does it do [act]. It does not abide, does not make. It is tasteless and unmixed. It is an "is" and yet is not something created. It is neither action nor fruition [i.e. it is beyond Karma]. It is not one made, not one that dies. It is no mind; it is one not countable [whose dimensions can be reckoned]; It is the All-Wonderful, the one Eternal, and the one not presumable. It is not consciousness and is apart from mind. And yet it does not depart from mind. It is a mind that is all-equal. It is not an "is"; yet it is what "is". There is no going and no coming [with it]; and yet it goes and comes. It does not break up. It is one indestructible. It does not snap and does not cease. It does not come out, nor does it die out. It is no master and yet a master. It is not one that exists; nor does it not exist. It awakes not, nor does it see. It is no letter, and is not no letter. It is no dhyana [meditation] and is not no dhyana. It cannot be seen and can be well seen. It is no place and yet is a place. It is no abode and yet is an abode. It is not dark and not bright. There is no quietness and yet there is quietness [in it]. It is non-possession, non-receiving, and non-giving. It

is pure and untainted. It is no quarrelling and is never fighting. It is what is living and is not what is living. It is no taking and no falling. It is no thing and is not no thing. It is no field of weal and is not no field of weal. It is non-ending and does not end. It is separating and is a total ending. It is Void and is apart from Void. Though not eternal, it is not the case that it dies out moment after moment. There is no defilement and muddling [contamination]. There is no letter and it is apart from letters. It is no voice and no talking. It is no practising and learning. It is no praising and no weighing. It is not one and is not different. It has no form or characteristics. All is grand adornment. It is not brave and is not afraid. It is no quietness and is not quiet. It is heatless and is not hot. It cannot be seen; there is no form to represent it. The Tathagata succours all beings. While not emancipating, he yet indeed emancipates beings. There being no emancipation, there is the awakening of beings. There being no enlightening, he truly delivers sermons. There being not two, he is immeasurable and is incomparably equal. Being as flat as space, there is no form to represent [him]. Being equal to the nature of beings, he is not the "notis", nor is he the "is". He always practises the One Vehicle. He sees the three of beings and does not retrogress, does not change, and cuts off all the roots of illusion. He does not fight or touch. He is non-nature and yet abides in nature. He does not merge and does not disperse. He is not long and not short. He is not round and not square. He is no skandha, sphere or realm, and yet he is the skandha, sphere, and realm. He is non-increasing and is not a lessening. He is no victor, and yet is one not vanquished. The body of the Tathagata is perfect in such innumerable virtues. There is none that he knows, none not known. There is none that is seen and none that is not seen. It is not that there is any creating and not that there is no creating. It is non-world and is not non-world. He does not do and is not non-doing. He is none to depend upon and is not none to depend upon. He is not the four great elements, nor is he not the four great elements. He is no cause and is not no cause. He is no being and is not no being. He is no sramana, no Brahmin. He is the Lion, the Great Lion. He is nobody and not nobody. We cannot express. Other than the oneness of Dharma, no counting is possible. At the time of the Parinirvana, he does not enter parinirvana. The Dharma-Body of the Tathagata is perfect in all such innumerable, wonderful virtues. O Kasyapa! Only the Tathagata knows all such phases [aspects, modalities] of existence. All [this] is beyond what sravakas and pratyekabuddhas can know. O Kasyapa! The body of the Tathagata is composed of all such virtues. It is not a body maintained or nourished by various foodstuffs. O Kasyapa! The virtue of the true body of the Tathagata is such. How could it suffer from illnesses, the pain of illness, and insecurity? How could it be as brittle as an unfired piece of earthenware? O Kasyapa! The reason why the Tathagata manifests illness and pain all comes from his desire to subdue beings. O good man! Know now that the Tathagata's body is one that is adamantine. From now on, think exclusively of this signification. Never think of a body sustained by food. Also, tell all beings that the body of the Tathagata is the Dharma-Body." Bodhisattva Kasyapa said to the Buddha: "O World-Honoured One! The Tathagata is perfect in all such virtues. How could it be that such a body could suffer from illness and pain, impermanence, and destruction? Henceforth I shall regard the Tathagata's body as of the eternal Dharma-Body and the body of peace. Also, I shall speak of it to all others as such. Yes, indeed, the Tathagata's Dharma-Body is adamantine and indestructible. And yet, I do not know how it could come to be thus." The Buddha said to Kasyapa: "By correctly upholding Wonderful Dharma, one obtains this adamantine body. O Kasyapa! As I have in the past well guarded Dharma, I am now blessed with perfecting this adamantine body, which is eternal and indestructible. O good man! One who upholds Wonderful Dharma does not receive the five precepts and practise deportment, but protects with the sword, bow, arrow, and halberd those bhiksus who uphold the precepts and who are pure." Bodhisattva Kasyapa said to the Buddha: "O World-Honoured One! If a bhiksu is unprotected, living alone in the open, in a graveyard, or under a tree, I say that such a one is a true bhiksu. Any bhiksu whose eyes turn to protection is, we may know, a bogus priest." The Buddha said to Kasyapa: "Do not say "bogus". There may be a bhiksu who goes where he will, satisfies his personal needs, recites sutras, sits, and meditates. Should anyone come and ask about the Way, he

will bestow sermons. He will speak about giving, observing the precepts, virtuous acts, and say that one should desire little and be satisfied. But he is not able to raise the lion's roar of the doctrine, is not surrounded by lions, and is not able to subdue those who do evil. Such a bhiksu cannot realise his own profit, nor is he able to assist others. Know that this person is indolent and lazy. Though he may well uphold the precepts and stick to pure actions, such a person, you should know, can do nothing. Or there may be a bhiksu whose utensils may be full. And he upholds the prohibitive precepts, and always utters the lion's roar, and delivers wonderful sermons on such as the sutras, geya, vyakarana, gatha, udana, itivrttaka, jatakas, vaipulya, and adbutadharma. He thus expounds these nine types of Buddhist sutras. He bestows benefit and peace upon others. Thus he says: "Prohibitions are given in the Nirvana Sutra to bhiksus which say that they should not keep menials, cows, sheep, or anything contrary to the prohibitions. Should bhiksus keep such defiled things, they must be taught not to. The Tathagata has stated in the sutras of various schools that any bhiksu who keeps such things must be corrected, just as kings correct bad acts, and must be driven back into secular life." When a bhiksu raises such a lion's roar, anyone who breaks the precepts, on hearing this, will get all angry and harm this priest. If this person dies as a result of this, he is to be called one who upholds the precepts and who benefits both his own self and others. For this reason, kings, ministers, prime ministers and upasakas protect those who deliver sermons. Any person who protects Wonderful Dharma should learn things thus. O Kasyapa! Any person who thus breaks the precepts and who does not protect Wonderful Dharma is to be called a bogus priest. One who is strict in observance of the rules does not gain such a name. O good man! In the past - innumerable, boundless, asamkhyas of kalpas past - there appeared in this town of Kusinagara a Buddha who was the Alms-deserving, the All-Enlightened One, the All-accomplished One, the Well-gone, the All-knower, the Unsurpassed One, the Best Trainer, the Teacher of Heaven and Earth, the Buddha-World-Honoured One, and whose name was "Tathagata of Joy-and-Benefit-Augmentation." At that time, the world was wide and gloriously pure, rich and peaceful. The people were at the height of prosperity and no hunger was felt. He [They] looked like the Bodhisattvas of the

Land of Peace and Happiness. That Buddha-World-Honoured One stayed in the world for an innumerable length of time. Having taught the people, he entered Parinirvana between the twin sal trees. The Buddha having entered Nirvana, the teaching remained in the world for countless billions of years and in the last part of the remaining 40 years the Buddhist teaching had still not died. At that time, there was a bhiksu called "Enlightened-Virtuous", who upheld the precepts well and was surrounded by many of his relatives. He raised the lion's roar and preached all the nine types of sutras. He taught, saying: "Do not keep menials, men or women, cows, sheep or whatever might go against the precepts." At that time there were many bhiksus who were acting contrary to the precepts. On hearing this, they entertained ill-will and came upon this bhiksu, brandishing swords and staffs. At that time, there was a king called "Virtuous". He heard of this. To protect Dharma, he came to where the bhiksu was delivering his sermons and fought against the evil doers so that the bhiksu did not suffer. The king, however, received wounds all over his body. Then the bhiksu, Enlightened-Virtuous, praised the king, saying: "Well done, well done, O King! You are a person who protects Wonderful Dharma. In days to come, you will become the unsurpassed utensil of Dharma." The king listened to his sermon and rejoiced. Then he died and was born in the land of Buddha Akshobhya and became his foremost disciple. The subjects of this king, his relatives and soldiers were all glad and did not retrogress in their Bodhichitta [resolve to gain Enlightenment]. When the day came to depart the world, they were born in the land of Buddha Akshobhya. At the time when Wonderful Dharma is about to die out, one should act and protect Dharma like this. O Kasyapa! The king at that time was I; the bhiksu who delivered the sermon was Buddha Kasyapa. O Kasyapa! One who guards Wonderful Dharma is recompensed with such incalculable fruition. That is why I today adorn my body in various ways and have perfectly achieved the indestructible Dharma-Body." Bodhisattva Kasyapa further said to the Buddha: "O World-Honoured One! The eternal body of the Tathagata is one carved in stone, as it were." The Buddha said to Kasyapa: "O good man! For that reason, bhiksus, bhiksunis, upasakas, upasikas should all the more make effort and protect Wonderful Dharma. The reward for protecting Wonderful Dharma is extremely great

and innumerable. O good man! Because of this, those upasakas who protect Dharma should take the sword and staff and protect such a bhiksu who guards Dharma. Even though a person upholds the precepts, we cannot call that person one who upholds Mahayana. Even though a person has not received [in formal ceremony] the five precepts, if he protects Wonderful Dharma, such a one can well be called one of Mahayana. A person who upholds the Wonderful Dharma should take the sword and staff and guard bhiksus." Kasyapa said to the Buddha: "O World-Honoured One! If all bhiksus are to be accompanied by such upasakas with the sword and staff, can we say that they are worthy of the name, or are they unworthy of such? Or is this upholding the precepts or not?" The Buddha said to Kasyapa: "Do not say that such persons are those who transgress the precepts. O good man! After I have entered Nirvana, the world will be evil-ridden and the land devastated, each pillaging the other, and the people will be driven by hunger. At such a time, because of hunger, men may make up their minds, abandon home and enter the Sangha. Such persons are bogus priests. Such, on seeing those persons who are strict in their observance of the precepts, right in their deportment, and pure in their deeds, upholding Wonderful Dharma, will drive such away or kill them or cause harm to them." Bodhisattva Kasyapa said again to the Buddha: "O World-Honoured One! How can all such persons upholding the precepts and guarding Wonderful Dharma get into villages and castle towns and teach?" "O good man! That is why I allow those who uphold the precepts to be accompanied by the white-clad people [lay people, non-monks] with the sword and staff. Although all kings, ministers, rich lay men [grhapati] and upasakas may possess the sword and staff for protecting Dharma, I call this upholding the precepts. You may possess the sword and staff, "but do not take life". If things are thus, we call this first-hand upholding of the precepts." Kasyapa said: "Anyone who protects Dharma abides in right view and widely expounds the Mahayana sutras. He does not carry the bejewelled parasols of royal persons, oil pots, unpolished rice, or fruit and seeds. He does not approach a king, minister, or the rich for profit. He does not flatter the danapatis [alms-givers] and is perfect in deportment, and crushes down those who transgress against the precepts and who do evil. Such a person is called a teacher who upholds and protects Dharma. He is a true, good teacher of the Way [kalyana-mitra - a good friend]. His mind is as expansive as the sea." "O Kasyapa! Should there be a bhiksu who speaks about Dharma for profit, the people and his relatives will also follow his example and greedily seek profit. This person thus spoils [does harm to] people. O Kasyapa! Of priests there are three kinds: 1) the precept-breaking, mixed-up priest, 2)the ignorant priest, 3)the pure priest. The precept-breaking mixed-up priest can easily be broken [spiritually injured], whereas the precept-observing priest cannot be broken just by profit. "How is one a precept-breaking mixed-up priest? A bhiksu may be upholding the precepts, but for profit he sits, stands up, goes and comes with precept-breaking people and is on friendly terms with them and does things together with them. This is precept-breaking, hence, "mixedup". "Why do we call a priest ignorant? A bhiksu may be living in a quiet place, but all his sense-organs are not proper [controlled], his mind is dark and slow at working. He desires little and begs alms. On the day of admonition and freedom [pravarana], he does not teach pure confession to all the people; seeing many people breaking the precepts, he does not teach them pure confession. Yet he sits with others, talks about the precepts and seeks to be free. Such a one is an ignorant priest. "Who is the pure priest? There is a bhiksu, a priest whom 100 thousand-billion Maras cannot break. Now, this Bodhisattva is pure in his nature and can train the two types of priest referred to above and make them live among those who are pure. He is the unsurpassed great teacher, who protects Dharma well, who well upholds the precepts. He knows well what is light or grave in the keeping of the precepts and adjusts and benefits people. He does not know anything that is not [characterised by] upholding the precepts; what he knows is what concerns the precepts. "What does he do to adjust beings? For example, in order to adjust people, the Bodhisattva always enters a village any time and visits the places where widows and prostitutes live. He lives there for many years. This is what sravakas cannot do. This is what is called adjusting and benefiting beings. "How does he know what is grave? Now, if one sees that the Tathagata admonishes and prohibits something, one should not do it thereafter. Things such as the four grave offences [killing, stealing, committing sexual misconduct, telling lies] are what the priest must not do. If, contrary to this, he purposely does [such things], this indicates that such a person is no longer a bhiksu, no son of the Shakya [Buddha]. This is what is "grave". "What is "light"? A person commits light ill deeds and is thrice admonished. Then, he stops doing such again. This is "light". We say "non-vinaya which is not proved". A person praises and says that one may receive and take impure things, and says that one accords with the word, and one does not stop doing [this]. "We say "right vinaya which is rightly responded [observed]." This is correctly learning the vinaya [rules of monastic discipline], not drawing near to what is contrary to the vinaya, and spiritually sharing pleasure. Thus one ensures that the vinaya is observed. Thus one well understands what one ought to do as a Buddhist and one expounds it well. This is what the vinaya refers to as well understanding the one letter [i.e. the Chinese written character for vinaya]. The same applies to upholding the sutras. O good man! The Buddha-Dharma is incalculable and hard to fathom The same is also the case with the Tathagata. He is beyond knowing." Bodhisattva Kasyapa said to the Buddha: "O World-Honoured One! It is so, it is so. It is as you, the Holy One, say. Unbounded and incomprehensible is Buddha-Dharma. Thus, too, is the Tathagata. All stands beyond comprehension; so too the Tathagata. Thus, I know now that the Tathagata is eternal and indestructible and that there is no change with him. I shall now study well and expound it widely to people." Then the Buddha praised Bodhisattva Kasyapa and said: "Well said, well said! The body of the Tathagata is adamantine and indestructible. You, Bodhisattva, now have the right view and right understanding. If you see clearly thus, you will see the adamantine and indestructible body of the Tathagata just as you see things reflected in a mirror."

Chapter Six: On the Virtue of the Name

Then the Tathagata spoke again to Kasyapa: "O good man! You should now uphold all the words, chapters, clauses and all the virtues thereof of this sutra. Any good man or woman who hears the name of this sutra will never get born into the four realms [of hell, hungry ghost, animal, and asura]. Why not? I shall now expound to you all the virtues of this sutra and all that is practised by innumerable boundless Buddhas." Bodhisattva Kasyapa said to the Buddha: "O World-Honoured One! What is this sutra to be called? How should Bodhisattva-mahasattvas uphold this sutra?" The Buddha said to Kasyapa: "The name of this sutra is to be "Mahaparinirvana". The foremost word betokens "good", the middle also "good", and the final "good" too. The signification [of this sutra] is extremely deep, and what is written [in it] is good. The pureness of its arrangement is perfect, its action is pure, and its adamantine treasure-house is all-satisfying. Listen well, listen well! I shall now speak. O good man! The word "maha" betokens "eternal". This is like all the great rivers draining into the great ocean. The same with this sutra. It crushes out all the bonds of illusion and all the qualities of Mara, and then body and life drain into "Mahaparinirvana". Hence the say "Mahaparinirvana." O good man! This is like a doctor who has a secret treatment embracing all medical treatments for disease. O good man! It is the same with the Tathagata. All the various wonderful doctrines taught and all the secret depths of meaning find their way into this Mahaparinirvana. That is why we say Mahaparinirvana. O good man! It is like a farmer who sows seed in spring. He entertains a rare wish. When he has finished the harvesting, all his longing is at an end. O good man! The same is the case with all beings. If we study other sutras, we always long for beautiful tastes. When one once hears this Mahaparinirvana, [however], one long ceases to covet the beautiful tastes mentioned in other sutras. This great Nirvana well enables all beings to cross the sea of all existences. O good man! Of all footprints, that of the elephant is the best. The same with this sutra. Of all the samadhis of the sutras, that of this sutra is the best. O good man! Of all the tillings of the field, that done in autumn is best. The same with this sutra. It is the best of all sutras. It is like sarpirmanda, which is the best of all medicines. It thoroughly cures the feverish worries and madding minds of beings. This Great Nirvana is the foremost of all. O good man! It is like sweet butter which contains the eight tastes. The same also applies to this sutra. It contains the eight tastes. What are the eight? These are: 1) it is eternal, 2) it always is, 3) it is peaceful, 4) it is pure and cool, 5) it does not grow old, 6) it does not die, 7) it is taintless, and 8) it is pleasing and happy. These are the eight tastes. It possesses these eight tastes. This is why we say "Mahaparinirvana". Now, all Bodhisattva-mahasattvas peacefully abide in this and manifest Nirvana in all places. That is why we say "Mahaparinirvna". O Kasyapa! All good men and women who desire to enter Nirvana by this Mahaparinirvana must study well the fact that the Tathagata is eternal and that the Dharma and Sangha are eternal." Bodhisattva Kasyapa said to the Buddha: "All is wonderful, O World-Honoured One! We cannot conceive of the Tathagata's depths of virtue. The same is the case with the virtues of Dharma and Sangha. This Mahaparinirvana is also inconceivable. One who studies this sutra will gain the right eye of Dharma and become a good doctor. Anybody who has not studied this sutra, we should know, is [like] a blind person, not possessing the eye of Wisdom and overshadowed by ignorance."

Chapter Seven: On the Four Aspects

The Buddha again spoke to Kasyapa: "O good man! There are four aspects about which a Bodhisattva-mahasattva discriminates and expounds Mahaparinirvana. What are these four? They are: 1) rightness in one's own self, 2) correcting others, 3) complying well [with the teachings] and discussing, and 4) understanding well causal relations. "O Kasyapa! What is rightness in one's own self? This is as when the Buddha Tathagata expounds Dharma, seeing well the causal relations. This is like a bhiksu seeing a great fire. He says: "I would sooner throw myself into this ball of burning fire than ever say that all the twelve types of sutras and the undisclosed teachings are from Mara [the devil]. If one says that the Tathagata, Dharma and Sangha are non-eternal, this is cheating one's own self and also others. I would sooner cut out my tongue with a sharp sword than ever say that the Tathagata, Dharma and Sangha are non-eternal. I might indeed hear others saying this, but I will never believe it. I shall even pity a person who says such as this. The Tathagata, Dharma and Sangha are inconceivable." One should uphold one's own self well like this. One looks to one's own self as if seeing a fire ball. This is how one sees rightness in one's own self. "O Kasyapa! How does one correct others? When I was once talking about Dharma, there was a woman nursing a child with milk. She came up to where the Buddha was. She touched my feet with her head and paid homage to me. As she was worried, she was absorbed in herself and took her seat on one side. Fathoming her mind, I especially said to her: "Out of love for your child, you have given the child too much cream. You did not weigh up the [matters of] digestion and indigestion." At that, the woman said to me: "How wonderful that the World-Honoured One thus reads my mind. Please, O World-Honoured One! Teach me how to give. O World-Honoured One! I gave [my child] too much cream this morning. Possibly it cannot digest it well. Will this not take the child's life? O Tathagata! Please explain things to me." I said: "What you gave will be digested by and by and then will enhance life." The woman, on hearing this, was very glad. She spoke again, saying: "What the Tathagata speaks is [always] true. So I am glad. The WorldHonoured One, in order to teach all beings, makes distinctions and expounds digestion and indigestion, the non-Self and non-eternal of all existences. If the World-Honoured One were to talk first about the Eternal, a person hearing this might say that what he says is the same as what the tirthikas [heterodox believers] say, and discount what he says and go away." I then said to the woman: "When the child grows up and becomes big, and when it can come and go by itself, whatever is eaten will be digested, even when indigestible [previously]. The cream that was taken before will not be enough to support [that person]. The same is the case with all my sravaka disciples. It is as in the case of your child. They cannot digest this eternal Dharma. That is why I speak about suffering and impermanence. When all of my sravakas are already perfect in virtue and can stand learning the Mahayana sutras, I then, in this sutra, speak about the six tastes. "What are the six tastes? Suffering is the taste of vinegar; the non-Eternal that of salt; non-Self that of bitterness; Bliss has the taste of sweetness; Self is of pungent taste; and the Eternal is light in taste. In secular life, too, there are three tastes, which are: 1) non-Eternal, 2) non-Self, and 3) non-Bliss. Illusion is the fuel, and Wisdom is the fire. By this means, we gain the meal of Nirvana. This is the Eternal, Bliss, and Self. All of my disciples taste these as sweet." I also said to the woman: "If you happen to go to other places, drive away bad boys from the house and give treasure to good boys." The woman said to me: "Indeed, as you instruct me, the rare treasures that I have will be shown to good sons, and not to bad ones." "O sister! The case is the same with me. At the time of entering Parinirvana, the Tathagata's undisclosed and unsurpassed storehouse of Dharma will not be given to sravaka disciples. Just as you do not reveal your treasures to bad sons, it [my storehouse of Dharma] will by all means be entrusted to the Bodhisattvas. This is just like your revealing your treasures to good sons. Why is that? Because the sravaka disciples abide in the thought of change and say that the Tathagata truly dies. But actually I do not. This is like your going to far-away places and not yet coming back home, at which your bad sons say that you have died, whereas you have not died. All Bodhisattvas say that the Tathagata never changes. This is similar to your good sons, who do not say that you are dead. Hence, I entrust the unsurpassed, undisclosed treasure to all Bodhisattvas." O good man! If any person says that the Buddha is Eternal and does not change, know that the Buddha is present in that house. This is corrcting others. "O Kasyapa! What is "complying well and discussing"? For example, a person comes and puts a question to the Buddha-World-Honoured One: "How can I be a great danapati [giver], not throwing my money away?" The Buddha says: "Should there be any sramana, Brahmin, or any person who seeks to posess [but] little and is fully contented and will not accept or store any impure things, give such a person a maid or servant. To one who practises pure actions, give him the lust of a female, and to one who does not drink [alcohol] or eat meat, give drink and meat; to one who does not take meals after noon, give him a meal after noon; to one who does not use flowers and incense, give flowers and incense. Such donations give rise to rumour and the fame will fill the world. Not a penny is spent. This is "complying well and discussing." Then Bodhisattva Kasyapa said to the Buddha: "O World-Honoured One! To one who eats flesh, we should not give flesh. Why not? I see a great virtue arising out of abstention from eating flesh." The Buddha praised Kasyapa and said: "Well said, well said! You now come to know my mind well. A Bodhisattva who protects Dharma should be thus. O good man! From now on, I do not permit my sravaka disciples to eat meat. When receiving from a danapati a pristine dana [gift] of faith, think that one is eating the flesh of one's own son." Bodhisattva Kasyapa said further to the Buddha: "O World-Honoured One! Why is it that the Tathagata does not allow us to eat meat?" "O good man! "One who eats meat kills the seed of great compassion." Kasyapa said again: "Why did you first allow the bhiksus to eat three kinds of pure meat?" "O Kasyapa! These three kinds of pure meat were so instituted following the need of the occasion." Bodhisattva Kasyapa said again to the Buddha: "O World-Honoured One! In what circumstances do you not allow the ten impurities or the nine kinds of what is pure?" The Buddha said to Kasyapa: "This also is permitted by gradual steps following the need of the occasion. This is what applies in the actual segregation from eating meat." Bodhisattva Kasyapa said further to the Buddha: "Why is it that the flesh of fish is praised and called beautiful?" "O good man! I do not say

that the flesh of fish is a beautiful food. I say that sugar can, non-glutinous rice, rock candy, black rock candy, all kinds of wheat, honey, milk, cream, and oil are beautiful foods. Various kinds of clothing material can be stocked, but what can be stocked is those whose colour has faded. How could one greedily stick to [crave after] the flesh of fish?" Kasyapa said again to the Buddha: "If the Tathagata means to prohibit the eating of meat, such things as the five kinds of flavours as milk, cream, fresh butter, clarified butter, and sarpirmanda, all kinds of clothing, silk cloth, horse-shoe shell, hide and leather, bowls of gold and silver should not be received." "O good man! Do not muddle things up with what the Nirgranthas [Jains] say. Each of the prohibitions which the Tathagata lays down has a different meaning. By this, three pure meats are permitted standing on different grounds and the ten kinds of meat are prohibited by different standpoints. By different standpoints, all are prohibited, until the time of one's death. O Kasyapa! "I, from now on, tell my disciples to refrain from eating any kind of meat". O Kasyapa! When one eats meat, this gives out the smell of meat while one is walking, standing, sitting or reclining. People smell this and become fearful. This is as when one comes near a lion. One sees and smells the lion, and fear arises. O good man! When one eats garlic, the dirty smell is unbearable. Other people notice it. They smell the bad smell. They leave that person and go away. Even from far off, people hate to see such a person. They will not come near him. It is the same with one who eats meat. It is a similar situation with all people who, on smelling the meat, become afraid and entertain the thought of death. All living things in the water, on land and in the sky desert such a person and run away. They say that this person is their enemy. Hence the Bodhisattva does not eat meat. In order to save beings, he shows [pretends] that he eats meat. Though he [seems to] eat meat, in actual fact he does not. O good man! Such a Bodhisattva does not even take pure food. How could he eat meat? One hundred years after my death, all the holy sages of the four fruitions [the four stages leading to "arhatship"] will enter Nirvana. The age of Wonderful Dharma will be over, and there will appear the age of Counterfeit Dharma, when the bhiksu will keep the precepts [only] as a matter of form, will recite [only] a little of the sutras, will greedily take food and drink and [excessively] nourish his body. What he wears on his body will be ugly and coarse. He will look wearied and show no dignity. He will feed [farm] cows and sheep and carry fuel and grass. His beard, nails and hair will be long. He will don the kasaya [priestly robe] but look like a hunter. He will narrow his eyes, walk slowly and look like a cat who is after a rat. He will always mutter: "I have attained arhatship". He will suffer from all kinds of diseases, lie and sleep on dung. Outwardly he will look wise, but inside he will be greedy and jealous. He practises mute like a Brahmin. Truth to tell, he is no shramana [monk], but only tries to appear as such. He is burning with perverted views, ever slandering Wonderful Dharma. One such as this transgresses against the precepts, right action and deportment instituted by the Tathagata. He talks about the fruit of emancipation, but his actions depart from what is pure and he violates Dharma, which is profound and hidden. Each such person, following his own interpretation, will speak contrary to what the sutras and vinaya rules state, saying: "The Tathagata allows all of us meat". They will talk thus and say that the Buddha has so spoken. They will dispute and say that they are shramanas and successors to the Buddha's teaching. O good man! At that time, again, there will be shramanas who store cereals, receive fish and meat, prepare meals themselves, and keep oil pots. They will be around bejewelled parasols, leather footgear, kings, ministers and rich people. They will indulge in astrological practices and medical treatments; they will keep servants, gold, silver, beryl, musaragalva, agate, crystal, coral, amber, jade, horse-shoe shell, and many kinds of melons [seeds]. They will learn all arts, painting, plastering, book-making, and all kinds of science, all kinds of seed- sowing and planting of roots, placing of curses, charming, preparation of medicines, theatrical art, music, adorning of their body with fragrances and flowers, gambling, "go" game, and various kinds of handiwork. If any bhiksu rejects such evils, one can say that he is truly my disciple." Then Kasyapa said further to the Buddha: "O World-Honoured One! The bhiksus, bhiksunis, upasakas and upasikas may have to live depending on people. At the time of the alms-round, one may be given food containing meat. How can one take it and yet be pure?" The Buddha said: "Use water, wash away the meat, and then eat it [the rest of the food]. The utensil may be defiled by meat. But if no taste of meat

remains, this may be used. There will be no harm done. If one sees that there is a lot of meat, one should not accept such a meal. One must never eat the meat itself. One who eats it infringes the rule. I now set this rule of segregating one's self from eating meat. If we go into detail, there will be no end of explanations. It is now time that I enter Nirvana. So I must dispense with explanations. This is "answering well what is enquired about." "O Kasyapa! What does "well understanding causal relations" mean? The four classes of the Sangha may come to me and say: "This is the first time, O Tathagata, that you have told us such a thing. Why is this? You did not tell King Prasenajit about the deeper part of the teaching, and said, at times, that it was "deep", and, at other times, "shallow"; at times, you said that one infringes, and, at other times, that one did not. Why do we say "parajayika" [parajika, means grave, extremely serious], precepts and "pratimoksha" [the rules of monastic life, which "set one free"]? The Buddha said: "Pratimoksha means feeling content. There is then perfection of deportment; there is no receiving and storing. This is also called "pure life". "Parajayika" means "the four unfortunate realms". It also means falling into hell, down to Avichi Hell [the most terrible of the eight hot hells]; as to slowness or swiftness, it is swifter than rushing rain. One who hears [of this], fears, strictly upholds the precepts, and never acts contrary to [correct moral] deportment. Trained in contentment, he will never receive what is not pure. Also, the parajayika augments [the realms of] hell, animals and hungry pretas. For these reasons, we say "parajayika". "Pratimoksha" does away with the evil and perverted actions of body, mouth and mind. "Precepts" refers to moral deportment, the deep meaning of the sutras, and the signification of good, and segregating oneself from accepting impure things and from all causal relations with impure things. Also, the precepts segregate one from such as the four grave offences, the thirteen samghavasesas, two aniyatans, thirty naihsargika-prayascittikas, ninety-one payatikas, four desaniyas, siksakaraniya, seven ways of adhikaranasamatha, etc. Or there may be a person who transgresses against all the precepts. What are all of them? This refers to the four grave offences right down to the seven ways of adhikaranasamatha. Or there may be a person who slanders the deep signification of the Buddhist sutras of Wonderful Dharma or who is all-accomplished as an icchantika, who has no possibility of ever encountering the Buddhist teaching by any means. Such people say of themselves that they are clear-headed and wise. They are equal to all sins. They conceal all the evils done that may be light or grave in nature, just as a tortoise hides its six limbs under its shell. They never once repent any such sins. Because of this non-repentance, their sins increase day and night. All such bhiksus do not confess all their sins. As they hide these within, they gradually grow. The Tathagata, aware of all this, prohibits by gradual steps and not at a time." Then, good men and women said to the Buddha: "O World-Honoured One! The Tathagata knew all such things. Why did you not previously suppress [them]? Or, O World-Honoured One, does this not mean all beings' falling into Avichi Hell? For example, many people, desiring to go to other places, miss the right way and take the wrong. These people, not knowing what is wrong, say that they are taking the right way. This is as in the case of one who does not ask about right or wrong. In the same way, people take the wrong path regarding the Buddhist teaching. The Tathagata ought first to show the right path and let all bhiksus know how this violates the injunctions and what is right. You should thus show the prohibitions. Why? Because we say that the Tathagata, the Right-Enlightened One, is one who is true [truthful]. He sees the right path. And the Tathagata is the god of gods, and he indeed talks about the superb virtues of the ten good deeds and the meanings thereof. Thus we respectfully beseech you first to institute the precepts." The Buddha said: "O good man! If you say that the Tathagata, for the sake of beings, talks about the superb virtues of the ten good deeds, this indicates that he sees beings like his son, Rahula. How can you reproach him and ask if he lets beings not fall into hell? Should I see but one person falling into Avichi Hell, I would, for the sake of that person, stay in the world for a kalpa or less than a kalpa. I have great compassion for all beings. How could I cheat one whom I regard as my son and let him fall into hell? O good man! It is like a person in the land of a king who dons the kasaya. There is a hole in it, and he sees and later repairs it. The same with the Tathagata. Seeing a person falling into hell, he causes repairs [to be made] and bestows the precepts for good deeds. O good man! This is like a chakravartin who, for the sake of

beings, first speaks about the ten good deeds. Later, the time comes when he occasionally sees people doing evil. Then the king passes a law and roots it out. Having rooted out all evil, the king effects the administration of a chakravartin. O good man! The same with me. I have things to say, but I do not set laws first. Always, first, the bhiksu does wrong; then, accordingly, admonition is given. And the people who love the Way are pleased to practise [accordingly]. Such people can well see the Dharma-Body of the Tathagata. This is like the chakraratna [wheel treasure], the all-wonderful quality of a chakravartin, which is hard to conceive. The same in the case with the Tathagata. He is beyond knowing. The two treasures of Dharma and Sangha are also beyond conceiving. The one who talks and those who listen are also beyond knowing. This is how to understand causal relations well. Thus the Bodhisattva discriminates and explains the meaning of the four aspects. This is the causal relations referring to the Great Nirvana of Mahayana. "And next: "correcting oneself" is to gain this Mahaparinirvana. "Correcting others" is what I say to bhiksus, telling them that the Tathagata is Eternal and Unchanging. "Answering questions", O Kasyapa, by your question, I now explain this all-wonderful doctrine for the sake of Bodhisattvas, bhiksus, bhiksunis, upasakas and upasikas. By "causal relations" I open the eyes of sravakas and pratyekabuddhas, as they do not comprehend the deep meaning of such as the above, and as they do not have occasion to hear about the fact that the three dots of the "i" accomplish emancipation, Nirvana, and Mahaprajna, and also the hidden store. I now make the sense clear and discriminate and, for the sake of all sravakas, open the eye of Wisdom. "People may say: "How could all such four things be merged into one? Isn't that nonsense?" Then one may say back: "Could there be any difference in the following four of space, non-possession, immovability, and unhinderedness?" Can we say that it is nonsense?" "No, O World-Honoured One! All the four expressions amount to one and the same. They mean but the Void. The same is the case with what is made by "correctness in oneself", "correcting others", "answering questions put to one", and "well understanding causal relations". That is to say that what there is here is the oneness of Great Nirvana and that nothing is different [i.e. there is no dualism or differentiation]." The Buddha said to Kasyapa: "Or there may be good men and women who may say: "The Tathagata is non-eternal. How can we know that he is non-eternal? The Buddha says that when the fire of illusion is extinguished, there is Nirvana. This is as when there is nothing [left over] to be seen when the fire is extinguished. The same is the case when all illusions are annihilated. This, he says, is Nirvana. How can the Tathagata claim that he is the Dharma eternal and unchanging? The Buddha says that when we part from existence, there is Nirvana. In this Nirvana, there cannot be anything that exists. How, then,

[This is as in the case of heated iron.
When beaten by a hammer, sparks shoot out.
These flash and die out; nothing remains.

The same applies to attaining emancipation.
Once the muddle of carnal desire has been crossed,
One gains the immovable state.
One no longer has a place to move to].

"How can the Tathagata be one eternal and unchanging?" O Kasyapa! One who reproaches me thus commits slander, which is wrong. O Kasyapa! You must not entertain such a notion and say that the nature of the Tathagata perishes. O Kasyapa! We do not place the annihilation of illusion in the category of matter [rupa]. Why not? Because of the fact of the ultimacy of Eternity. Hence, we say Eternal. [Nirvanic] quietude has nothing to supercede it. All phenomenal existences are done away with, with nothing remaining. This indicates what is fresh, clear, eternal, and unretrogressive. That is why we say that Nirvana is eternal. It is the same with the Tathagata. He is eternal, with no change. "Stars sweep". This refers to illusion. Once swept, all is gone and no trace remains of any existence. This indicates that all Tathagatas are those who have done away with illusion and are no longer in the five realms. This means that the Tathagata is one eternal and that there is no change [with him]. Also next, O Kasyapa! It is the Dharma which is the teacher of all Buddhas. Hence, the Tathagata respectfully makes offerings. As the Dharma is eternal, so too are all Buddhas eternal." Bodhisattva Kasyapa said again to the Buddha: "If the flame of illusion dies out, the Tathagata must also die out. This indicates that there can be no ground where the Tathagata is eternal. This is similar to the situation in which hot

can the Tathagata be eternal and unchanging? When a piece of clothing is torn, we do not call it anything. The same with Nirvana. When all illusions are done away with, there can be no thing. How can the Tathagata be eternal and unchanging? The Buddha says that separation from desire and arrival at quietude is Nirvana. If a person's head is cut off, there is no head any more. The same with separation from desire and arrival at quietude. What there is is Voidness. There is nothing there. Hence, Nirvana. How can the Tathagata be eternal and unchanging? The Buddha says:

iron slag can no longer be seen when the red colour disappears. The same with the Tathagata and illusion. Gone, there is no other pace to go to. And it is like the case of iron. The heat and the red colour gone, there remains nothing to be seen. The same with the Tathagata. Once extinguished, what remains is non-eternal. The fire of illusion done away with, he enters Nirvana. This tells us that the Tathagata is non-eternal." "O good man! The iron you speak of refers to common mortals. Illusion done away with, the common mortal comes about again. That is why we say non-eternal. This is not the case with the Tathagata. Gone, there is no coming about. Hence, eternal." Kasyapa further said to the Buddha: "If we place the colour-robbed iron back into the fire, the red colour will return. It it is thus with the Tathgata, illusion will again form. If illusion again forms, this is nothing but the non-eternal." The Buddha said: "O Kasyapa! Do not say that the Tathagata is non-eternal. Why not? Because the Tathagata is one Eternal. O good man! When wood is burnt, extinction comes about, and there remain behind the ashes. When illusion is done away with, there remains Nirvana. All such parables as of the torn garment, beheading and broken earthenware enunciate the same truth. All such things have such names as torn garment, beheading, and broken earthenware. O Kasyapa! The iron that has become cold can be

- 50 -

made hot again. But this is not the case with the Tathagata. Illusion once done away with, what there is is utmost purity and coolness. The blazing flame never comes back again. O Kasyapa! Know that the situation of innumerable beings is like that of the iron. With the blazing fire of Wisdom free from the "asravas" [defilements], I now burn off the bonds of illusion of all beings." Kasyapa said further: "It is good, it is good that I now clearly see what the Tathagata means when he says that all Buddhas are eternal." The Buddha said: "O Kasyapa! Imagine, for example, a chakravartin [world-ruler] in the back of his palace. At one time he is in the back garden. Though this king is not among the attendant females, we cannot say that his life is at an end. O good man! The same is true of the Tathagata. Though not in Jambudvipa [this world], but in Nirvana, we cannot say that he is non-eternal. He is now out of the world of innumerable illusions and is now in the all-wonderful world of peace and happiness. He sits amidst the flowers of Enlightenment; he sees and amuses himself."   Kasyapa again asked the Buddha: "The Buddha says that you have already crossed over the great ocean of illusion. If you are beyond the sea of illusion, why did you take in [marry] Yasodhara and beget Rahula? From this, we can know that the Tathagata has not yet severed himself from the bonds of illusion and crossed the sea. Please, O Tathagata! Enlighten me upon this point." The Buddha said to Kasyapa: "Do not say that if the Tathagata had long crossed the great sea of illusion, there could be no reason for him to take Yasodhara [as his wife] and bring forth Rahula and that, in consequence, the Tathagata could not have yet severed himself from the bonds of illusion and crossed the great sea of illusion. O good man! This Great Nirvana calls forth a thing of great significance. Listen to me with your best attention. I shall speak for all the world. Do not become surprised and entertain doubt. If the Bodhisattva-mahasattva reaches Great Nirvana, such a high and wide thing as Mount Sumeru could indeed be placed inside a mustard seed. If beings are standing on Mount Sumeru [at that time], they will feel neither narrowed down nor oppressed. There will be no sense of having come or gone anywhere. All will be just as before, with nothing different. Only one who has himself crossed the ocean [of illusion] will be able to see that this Bodhisattva has put the 3,000 great-thousand worlds into a mustard seed

and is back in his own abode again. O good man! Also, the Bodhisattva-mahasattva may enter into Great Nirvana and place the 3,000 great-thousand worlds into a pore of his skin, and yet the original place may ever be like this [may remain unchanged]. O good man! Also, the Bodhisattva-mahasattva may enter into Nirvana, cut off the 3,000 great-thousand Buddha-lands of all directions, place them on the point of a needle and strike the other Buddha-lands as though passing them through a jujube leaf, and the living beings therein would not entertain any thought of going or coming. Only one who is emancipated could see this and also the original place. Such is the case. O good man! Also, there could be a Bodhisattva-mahasattva who abides in Great Nirvana and who cuts off the 3,000 great-thousand Buddha-lands and puts them on his right-hand palm and as in the case of the potter's wheel throws them onto other mote worlds. And not a single being would entertain any idea of having gone or come. Only one who is emancipated would be able to see this. And so it is too with the original place. O good man! Also, a Bodhisattva-mahasattva who has attained Great Nirvana can snip off innumerable Buddha-lands of all the ten directions and put them all into his own body. And the people living therein do not feel narrow or oppressed or have any feeling of having been moved or of where they are standing. Only one who has been saved can see this. The same with the original abode. O good man! There might also be a Bodhisattva-mahasattva who has entered Nirvana and who has placed the lands of the ten directions into a dust-mote. The beings inside also do not feel constricted or oppressed or have any sense of going or coming. Only one emancipated sees this well. It is the same with what happens in the original abode. O good man! When this Bodhisattva abides in Great Nirvana, he well manifests various innumerable transformations. Hence, Mahaparinirvana. All such divine miracles which this Bodhisattva-mahasattva displays can never be weighed or known by any [ordinary] being. How could you know why the Tathagata committed himself to a life of love and desire and begat Rahula? O good man! It is now a long time since I [first] experienced this Great Nirvana and manifested many divine miracles. It is as alluded to in the "Surangama Sutra", in which I have already variously manifested such in ten million suns and moons and in ten million Jambudvipas of the 3,000 great-thousand worlds. And I attain Nirvana in the 3,000 great-thousand worlds and in Jambudvipa. I do indeed attain it. And I find my way into the mother's womb and make the parents think of me as their child. But I am never one who was born through the conjoining of love and desire; I have been far removed from [sensual] love for innumerable kalpas. This body of mine is the Dharma-Body. Following the way of the world, I manifest myself in a motherly womb. O good man! In this Jambudvipa, in the Lumbini gardens, I manifested birth from the womb of Mother Maya. After birth, I took seven steps to the east and proclaimed: "I am the most honoured and best of all men, devas and asuras." My parents and men and devas, on witnessing this, were joyous beyond words and wonderstruck. All these people said that I was a child. But, for innumerable kalpas past, I had been segregated from any such thing. Such a body as this is the Dharma-Body, not one born of flesh and blood, sinews, bones and marrow. Following the way of the world, I appeared as a child. I took seven steps to the south and proclaimed that I would become the best field of weal for the sake of innumerable beings. Taking seven steps to the west, I indicated that life was now ended, that I would part from age and death, and that this was the last of my bodies. Taking seven steps to the north, I manifested that I would cross all the seas of birth and death of all existences. Taking seven steps to the east, I revealed that I would become the guide to all beings. Taking seven steps to the four corners, I revealed that I would cut off the roots of various illusions and the natures of the four Maras, becoming the Tathagata, the Alms-deserving, the All-Enlightened One. Taking seven steps heavenwards, I proclaimed that I would never be tainted by impurities. Taking seven steps netherwards, I proclaimed that the rain of Dharma would extinguish the fire of hell, so that beings born there would be blessed with peace and bliss. To a person who violated the prohibitions, I manifested myself as frost and hail. After 7 days of life in Jambudvipa, I manifested shaving my head. All said I was the first child to have his head shaved. All men and devas, the king of Marapapiyas, shramanas and Brahmins can never see the usnisa [protuberance on top of the Buddha's head] of my head. How could they possibly take a blade and shave it? There can never be any person who could take a blade and

reach my head. I shaved my head innumerable kalpas past. But to follow the ways of the secular world, I showed that I shaved it [as a young Prince]. After my birth, my parents took me to the temple of the gods and showed me to Mahesvara, who, on seeing me, folded his hands and stepped to one side. I had already, since innumerable kalpas past, done away with any such ceremony as entering the devas' temple. But just to follow the ways of secular life, I manifested this. In the life of Jambudvipa, I let people make a hole in my ear lobe. Nobody in the world can make a hole in my ear lobe. To follow the way of secular life, I manifested this. Also, they made hanging lion earrings out of all the gems and adorned my ear lobes. But since innumerable kalpas past, I had already dispensed with adornments. Just to follow what obtains in secular life, I manifested this. I went to school and showed that I learnt reading and writing. But I had already been accomplished in all such for innumerable kalpas past. As I passed my eyes through all the beings of the three worlds, I saw none who could be my teacher. But to comply with the ways of secular life, I displayed myself going to school. That is why I am called Tathagata, the Alms-deserving, and All-Enlightened One. The same with driving an elephant, riding round on a horse, wrestling, and the learning of various arts, too. In Jambudvipa, I manifested myself as a young prince. All beings saw me as a royal prince enjoying and pleasing himself amidst the life of the five desires. But innumerable kalpas past, I had already discarded such as the five desires. Just to comply with what obtains in secular life, I manifested this. The augur saw me and said that if I did not abandon home and seek the Way, I would become a chakravartin and king of Jambudvipa. All beings believed this. But I had already discarded the throne of a chakravartin and was the Dharma-King. In Jambudvipa I renounced female attendants and the five desires, saw age, illness, death, and the shramana, and abandoned home and sought the Way. All beings said that Prince Siddhartha then for the first time abandoned home and became a shramana. But already innumerable kalpas before, I had abandoned home, become a shramana, practised the Way, merely to comply with what obtained in secular life. And I manifested this. I had already abandoned home in Jambudvipa and received upasampada [full ordination]. I made effort, practised the Way and attained such fruitions of the Way as the shrotapanna ["stream-enterer" - a monk who will only be born between two and seven more times before gaining liberation], sakridagamin [once-returner], anagamin ["never-returner" to this world], and arhat [saint]. I manifested this. Everybody said it was easy and not difficult to attain arhatship. But I had already, innumerable kalpas in the past, attained arhatship. In order to pass beings to the shore of Enlightenment, I sat under the Bodhi Tree on the Bodhimanda [seat of Enlightenment] of grass and defeated all the Maras [demons]. But I had already, innumerably long kalpas back in the past, defeated the Maras. In order to subdue strong beings, I manifested this scene. I also display answering the calls of nature of the two kinds and breathing in and out. All beings say that I answer the calls of nature and breathe in and out. But with this body of mine, I have no fruition of karma and no worries. I merely accord with the way of worldly life. That is why I manifest such. I also show that I receive offerings made to me by the faithful. But I have no hunger or thirst in this body of mine, and I [just] comply with the worldly way of life. I display myself thus. I also follow the worldly way of life of all others and sleep. But I accomplished the depths of Wisdom innumerable kalpas past and did away with such actions as going and coming, all such pains as of the head, eye, stomach, and back, and the whole of my body, and hard-to-cure carbuncles, all of which are the results of past karma, and washing my hands and feet in a basin, washing my face, gargling, using the toothbrush and all such things as apply in the world. People say that I do all these things. But I do not. My hands and feet are as pure as lotuses and my mouth is clean, and smells like an utpala [lotus]. Everyone says that I am a man. But I am now no man. I also manifest receiving pamsukula [discarded clothes], washing, sewing and mending. But I have long since not used such clothing. Everybody says that Rahula is my son, that Suddhodana was my father and Maya my mother, that I carried on a secular career in my life, that I enjoyed peace and happiness [as a young prince], and that I abandoned all such things and sought the Way. People further say: "The prince of this king, of the great clan of Gautama, renounced worldly pleasures and sought the supramundane." But I had long since been away from worldly love and desire. I merely displayed all such things. Everybody says that I

am a man. But truth to tell, I am not. O good man! I manifest myself in Jambudvipa and often enter Nirvana. But in truth I do not enter Nirvana at all. Yet all people say that the Tathagata is now dying. But the nature of the Tathagata, truth to tell, eternally does not die out. So you should know that I am one Eternal and Unchanging. O good man! Great Nirvana is none but the Dharma world of the All-Buddha-Tathagatas. I also manifest myself in this Jambudvipa. People say that I first [as Siddhartha] attained Buddhahood. But since innumerable kalpas past, I had done what needed to be done and I only accorded with the way of the world. That is why I, in this Jambudvipa, displayed renunciation and attainment of Buddhahood. I also [seemingly] did not accord with the prohibitions and committed the four grave offences. People saw me and said I transgressed. But for innumerable kalpas past I have been according with the prohibitions, and nothing was amiss. Also, in Jambudvipa I was an icchantika. People all saw me as an icchantika. But truth to tell, I was no icchantika. If I had been an icchantika, how could I have attained unsurpassed Enlightenment? I also showed myself in Jambudvipa as disturbing the peace of the Buddhist Sangha. People said that I was a Buddhist priest who was breaking the peace of the Sangha. I also manifested myself in Jambudvipa as protecting Wonderful Dharma. People see this and say that this is protection of Dharma. They are all surprised. All Buddhas do this and there is nothing [here] to be surprised about. I also in this Jambudvipa manifested myself as Marapapiyas. People said that this was Marapapiyas. People said that this was "papiyas" ["very wicked"]. But I had been away from evil for innumerable kalpas past; I am pure, I am not defiled and am like the lotus. I also manifest myself in Jambudvipa as a female Buddha. People see this and say that it is strange that a female should attain unsurpassed Enlightenment. The Tathagata, after all, has never once been a female. In order to subdue people, I manifested as a female. As I pity beings, I also manifest in various coloured images. I also manifest myself amidst the four unfortunate realms of Jambudvipa. How could I be born in the unfortunate realms through evil actions? In order to pass beings to the other shore, I get born as such. I also get born as Brahma in Jambudvipa and make those who serve Brahma abide in Wonderful Dharma. But, truth to tell, I am not Brahma. But all people say that I am truly Brahma. I also manifest myself as devas and fill all the temples of the devas. But the same is the case [here too]. I also manifest myself as visiting brothels in this Jambudvipa. But my mind knows no lust; I am as pure and untained as the lotus. To teach those steeped in desire and lust, I stand on the crossroads and speak about the wonderful Doctrine. But in truth I have no lust or defiled mind. People say that I guard females. I also in Jambudvipa manifest myself in the house of menials and maids. All this is to lead them onto the path of Wonderful Dharma. But truth to tell, I never once debased myself and performed evil deeds and became [intimate with] menials and maids. And in Jambudvipa I manifest myself as a teacher and lead children into Wonderful Dharma. In Jambudvipa I also enter various drinking houses and gambling dens. This is to participate in the games and quarrels and all to succour beings. And yet I have no experience of such evil relations. And yet all people say that I do such things. I also lived long amidst the tombstones as a great eagle, so as to succour flying birds. And yet people said I was a true eagle. But I have long since been separate from such a life. All this was to succour such birds and eagles. I also manifested myself in Jambudvipa as a great rich man. This was to make innumerable people be blessed with peace and abide in Wonderful Dharma. Furthermore, I become a king, minister, prince or prime minister. Amongst such people, I rank first in all cases. In order to practise Wonderful Dharma, I become a king. Also, there was a time in Jambudvipa when numerous epidemics arose and many people suffered. First, I gave medicine and later spoke about Wonderful Dharma, and made them attain unsurpassed Enlightenment. Everybody said that there was then, at that time, a time of illness. Also, there was a time in Jambudvipa when a famine broke out. I gave people the food they needed, I spoke about All-Wonderful Dharma and led them into unsurpassed Enlightenment. Also, to an "is"-minded person, I speak about the non-eternal; to one "pleasure-minded", I speak about suffering. To one who clings to self, selflessness is expounded. To one who clings to purity, impurity is expounded. To one who clings to the three worlds, Dharma is expounded, to make him renounce the world. To pass beings to the other shore, the wonderful medicine of Dharma is prescribed. In order to fell the trees of illusion, those of the unsurpassed medicine of Dharma are planted. To save all tirthikas, Wonderful Dharma is expounded. Although I act as a teacher to beings, no thought of a teacher to all beings resides in me. Since I intend to succour all those of lower social status, I gain life amongst them and talk about Dharma. And no evil acts will react within me. The Tathagata-Right-Enlightened One is ever in Parinirvana. Hence, I say "Eternal and Unchanging". As in Jambudvipa, so do things also obtain in Purvavideha, Aparagodana and Uttarakuru. As in the four lands, so also in the 3,000 great-thousand worlds. As to the 25 existences, things are as stated expansively in the "Surangama Sutra". Hence, "Parinirvana". The Bodhisattva-mahasattva who abides in Parinirvana can well display such miracles and transformations and has no fear. O Kasyapa! Say not, therefore, that Rahula is the son of the Buddha. Why not? Because innumerable kalpas ago I had already done away with all existences of desire. That is why we say that the Tathagata is Eternal and Unchanging." Kasyapa said further: "O Tathagata! Why do we say eternal? You, the Buddha, say that when the light of a lamp has gone out, there is no direction or place to be named [as to where it has gone]. The same is the case with the Tathagata. Once dead, there can be no direction or place that can be named." The Buddha said: "O Kasyapa! You should not say: "When the light of a lamp has gone out, there is not direction or place to be named. The same is the case with the Tathagata. When there is extinction, there can be no direction or place to be named." O good man! When a lamp is lit by a man or woman, any lamp, big or small, [has to be] filled with oil. When there is oil [there], the lamp keeps alight. When the oil is spent, the light also disappears, along with it. That light going out can be compared to the extinction of illusion. Although the light has gone out, the utensil [vessel, lamp-holder] remains behind. The same is the case with the Tathagata. Although illusion has gone, the Dharma-Body remains forever. O good man! What does this mean? Does it mean that both the light and and the lamp disappear? Is it so?" Kasyapa answered: "No, O World-Honoured One! Both do not disappear at the same time. And yet, it is [still] non-eternal. If the Dharma-Body is compared to the lamp, the lamp is [actually] non-eternal, so the Dharma-Body must also be non-eternal." "O good man! You should not [try to] refute in this manner. We speak in the world of a "utensil". The Tathagata-World-Honoured One is the unsurpassed utensil of Dharma. A utensil of the world can be non-eternal, but not that of the Tathagata. Of all things, Nirvana is eternal. The Tathagata has this. Thus he is eternal. Also, O good man! You say that the light of the lamp goes out. This is [like] the Nirvana attained by an arhat. Because all the illusions of greed and craving are done away with, we can compare this to the lamplight going out. The anagamin yet has greed. As there is still greed left, we cannot say that this is the same as the lamplight's going out. That is why I said in the past in an undisclosed [cryptic, unexplained, unexplicated] way that it was like a dying lamp. It is not that Nirvana is to be equated with the dying off of the lamplight. The anagamin does not come about [get reborn] time and again. He does not come back to the 25 existences. Again, he does not gain any more the smelly body, the body of vermin, the body that is fed, the poisonous body. Such is an "anagamin" [one "not coming" into bodily existence again]. If a body arises again, this is an "agamin" [one "coming" into bodily existence]. When the body does not arise again, this is an "anagamin". What is possessed of coming and going is "agamin". What has no coming or going [no birth and death] is "anagamin"? Then Bodhisattva Kasyapa said to the Buddha: "O World-Honoured One! You, the Buddha, say that the All-Buddha-World-Honoured One has an undisclosed storehouse. But this is not so. Why not? The All-Buddha-World-Honoured One has privately-spoken words, but not an undisclosed storehouse [a teaching not made known]. For example, this is analogous to the case of a magician, his mechanical appliances, and his wooden image. One may see the motions of bending, stretching, and looking up and down, but one does not know that inside there is a man who makes things proceed thus. But with the Buddha's teaching, it is not like this. His teaching enables all beings to know and see. How can one say that the All-Buddha-World-Honoured One has anything undisclosed?" The Buddha praised Kasyapa and said: "Well said, well said, O good man! It is just as you say. The Tathagata, truth to tell, does not keep anything hidden. How so? It is as in the case of the full moon in autumn, when it is all open, bare, clear, pure and cloudless, so that all people can see it. What the Tathagata says is also the same. It is open, bare, clear, pure and cloudless.

Dull people do not understand and speak of a secret in connection with it. The wise, understanding the matter, do not say that there is anything secretly stored away. O good man! There is a man here who stores gold and silver amounting to "yis" and "yis" [a Chinese unit of number]. Being a miser, he does not give to the poor and help them. Anything stored in this fashion could be called "secretly stored" [secretly withheld]. It is not thus with the Tathagata. Over the course of innumerable long kalpas, he stores wonderful laws [doctrines, truths] and rare treasures. He does not begrudge [anything]; he always gives to all beings. How [then] can we say that he secretly stores [truths away]? O good man! There is a man here who is lacking a part of his body, such as an eye, hand or leg. He feels shy and does not allow others to see. As all people do not see it, they say "secretly concealed". It is not so with the Tathagata. He is perfect in Wonderful Dharma and lacking in nothing, allowing all others to see. How could one say that the Tathgata secretly stores [conceals/ withholds] things? O good man! A poor man, for example, has debts. He fears the man to whom he owes money. He hides and does not wish to show himself. Here we may speak of hiding. The case is not the same with the Tathagata. He does not shoulder the mundane laws [phenomena, truths] of all beings, but does their supramundane laws. But he does not hide such. Why not? Because he always thinks of beings as his own only son and expounds [to them] unsurpassed Dharma. O good man! There is a rich man, for example, who has much wealth. He only has one son. He loves this son very much and cannot forget him. He shows all his wealth to his son. So is it with the Tathagata. He views all beings as his own only son. O good man! This is as in the case of worldly people. Men and women conceal their genitalia behind clothing, because such are ugly things to look upon. Here we speak of "concealing". It is not thus with the Tathagata. He has long since done away with genitalia. As he does not have such, there is no reason for concealment. O good man! The Brahmins do not like to have their words and what they say heard by Kshatriyas, Vaishyas and Sudras. Why not? Because there are many things in their words that are wrong and wicked. But the Tathagata's Wonderful Dharma is such that it is lovely in its beginning, lovely in its middle and lovely in its conclusion. So we cannot speak here of a thing hidden or stored away. O good man! For example, there is here a rich man who only has a single son. He always thinks of, and loves, this boy. He takes the boy to a teacher to be taught. Apprehensive that things might not progress quickly, he takes the boy back home. As he loves him, he teaches him the alphabet day and night very patiently. Yet he does not teach him the vyakarana [a popular work for language study; a kind of grammar]. Why not? Because the child is small and is not up to such lessons. O good man! Now, the rich man finishes teaching the alphabet. But is the boy ready to be taught the vyakarana?" "No, O World-Honoured One!" "Is the rich man concealing anything from the child?" "No, O World-Honoured One! Why not? Because the child is too young. So he does not teach [him the more advanced matters]. It is not that the boy is not taught because the man begrudges him [such lessons]. Why not? If there is any jealousy or grudging [involved], we may say he conceals things. It is not thus with the Tathagata. How could we say that he hides and conceals?" The Buddha said: "Well said, well said, O good man! It is as you say. If there is any anger, jealousy or begrudging, we can well say that he is concealing things. The Tathagata has no anger or jealousy. How can you say that he hides things away? O good man! The great rich man is the Tathagata himself. The only child is [all] beings. The Tathagata views all beings as he views his only son. Teaching his only son relates to the sravaka disciples, the alphabet, and the nine types of sutras; the vyakarana relates to the vaipulya [extensive] Mahayana sutras. Since all the sravaka disciples do not possess the power of Wisdom, the Tathagata teaches them the alphabet, i.e. the nine types of sutra. And he does not yet speak of the vyakarana, i.e. the vaipulya Mahayana. O good

"All Buddhas, pratyekabuddhas, and sravakas
Abandon the non-eternal body.
How could this not be so with common mortals?"

Now you say "eternal" and "unchanging". What does this mean?" The Buddha said: "O good man! As I had to teach the sravaka disciples the alphabet, I spoke thus in the gatha. O good man! King Prasenajit lost his mother. He cried sorrowfully. He loved her and could not bear the sorrow. He came to me. I asked: "O King! Why are you so afflicted with sorrow?" The King said: "The Queen Mother of the state has died, O

man! When the rich man's son has grown up and is able to cope with the lessons, if the vyakarana is not taught then, we may well speak of "concealment". If all sravakas are grown up and can indeed cope with the Mahayana vyakarana lessons, but the Tathagata begrudges [them this] and does not teach them [the vyakarana], we could well say that the Tathagata begrudges, hides and conceals the teaching. But this is not so with the Tathagata. The Tathagata does not conceal [anything]. This is as with the rich man who, having taught the alphabet, next teaches the vyakarana. I also do the same. To all my disciples I have spoken about the alphabet and the nine types of sutra. Having done so, I now, after this, talk about the vyakarana. This is none other than the Tathagata's eternal and unchanging nature. "Also, next, O good man! It is as in the summer months, when great clouds call forth thunder and great rain, as a result of which all farmers can sow [their] seeds and harvest things. Those who do not sow cannot expect to harvest. It is not through the workings of the naga kings that one cannot harvest. And these naga kings also do not store [hold things back]. The same with me. I let fall the great rain of the Great Nirvana Sutra. Those beings who sow good seeds harvest the buds and fruit of Wisdom. Those who have not sown can expect nothing. The Tathagata is not to blame if they gain nothing. The Tathagata does not hide anything away." Kasyapa said again: "I now definitely know that the Tathagata-World-Honoured One never hides and conceals [anything away]. You, the Buddha, say that the vyakarana refers to the eternal and unchanging nature of the Buddha-Tathagata. But this cannot be the meaning. Why not? Because the Buddha said before, in a gatha:

World-Honoured One! If anyone can bring my mother back to life, I will give away my state, elephants, horses, the seven treasures, and even my life; thus will I reward him." I said to the king: "O great King! Please do not lose yourself in worry and sorrow! Do not weep! When life ends for a person, this is death. All Buddhas, sravakas, pratyekabuddhas and disciples have to part with this body. How could common mortals not have to? "O good man! To teach the king the alphabet, I spoke thus in this gatha. I now expound to my sravaka disciples the vyakarana and say that the Tathagata is eternal and that he does not change. If

"Nothing is hoarded, and I feel
Satisfied with the meal I take. It is
As in the case of the bird that flies in the sky,
Whose tracks are hard to trace."

What might this mean? O World-Honoured One! Of all those congregated here, who might be one who does not hoard? Who might be called one satisfied with [his] food? Who are those who fly through the sky and whose tracks cannot be traced? And where does one go to when one leaves this place?" The Buddha said: "O good man! Hoarding is nothing but of wealth and treasure. O good man! Of hoarding, there are two kinds: one of what is created and the other of what is non-created. The hoarding of the created is what sravakas do; the hoarding of the non-created is what the Tathagata does. "O good man! Of priests, there are two kinds. One is of the created, and the other is of the non-created. The priest of the created is the sravaka. The sravaka priest does not hoard. Male or female menials are unlawful things; so is storing rice, bean paste, sesame and large and small beans in a storehouse. If someone were to say that the Tathagata permits the keeping of servants, male or female, and such other things, his tongue would shrink. I say that all my sravaka disciples are "non-storing". Or they are those satisfied with their food. If a person greedily seeks food, such a person is not satisfied. "Saying that it is hard to trace the tracks means that one is close to unsurpassed Enlightenment. I say: "The person goes, but there is no place to go to." Kasyapa further said: "The priest of the created does not hoard. How can the priest of the non-created do so? The priest of the non-created is the Tathagata. How could the Tathagata hoard things up?" "Hoarding means "storing away and concealing". Thus the Tathagata expounds [truths] and does not begrudge [anyone anything]. How could we say that he hoards things away? "Saying that the tracks are untraceable relates to Nirvana. In Nirvana there remains no trace of the sun, moon, stars, constellations, cold, heat, wind, rain, birth, age, illness, death, or the 25 existences. Nirvana is segregated from apprehension, sorrow and illusion. Such is the abode of Nirvana and the

any person says that the Tathagata is non-eternal, how could this man's tongue not drop off?" Kasyapa further replied: "You said:

Tathagata, who is Eternal and does not change. Hence, the Tathagata comes here to the forest of sal trees and enters Parinirvana by [means of] the Great Nirvana." The Buddha said to Kasyapa: " "Great" means wide and extensive in nature. It is as when we speak of a "great man", when the life-span of [that] man is infinite. As this man abides in Wonderful Dharma, we call him "superior to all men". It is as in the case of the "eight awakened minds of a great man" about which I speak. If a person makes this an "is", many persons would also be thus. If a person possesses the eight qualities, he is the best. The Nirvana of which we speak has no pox or warts. O good man! For example, [imagine] a man here who has been hit by a poisoned arrow and who is in great pain. A learned doctor comes and extracts the poisoned arrow and applies a superb medicine. As a result the pain goes away, and the man gains peace. This doctor visits castles, towns and hamlets. He goes to where people suffer from the pain of the pox or warts, applies his art and removes the pain. O good man! The same is the case with the Tathagata. Having attained all-equal Enlightenment, he becomes a great doctor. Seeing all beings of Jambudvipa hit by the poisoned arrows of the illusions of lust, anger and ignorance and suffering in the course of innumerable kalpas, he applies the sweet medicine of the Mahayana sutras. The treatment completed, he moves on to other places where people are suffering from the poisonous arrows of illusion. There he [also] manifests his attaining of Enlightenment and gives treatment [to the afflicted]. Thus we speak of "Mahaparinirvana." "Mahaparinirvana is the place where all get emancipated. Wherever there are people to be subjugated [i.e. their defilements removed], he manifests himself. On account of this truly great meaning, we say Great Nirvana." Bodhisattva Kasyapa said further to the Buddha: "O World-Honoured One! Do all the so-called doctors thoroughly cure the pain of the pox and warts? Or do they not?" "O good man! There are two kinds of pain relative to the pox and warts. One is curable and the other is incurable. The doctor cures what is curable, but not what is incurable." Kasyapa said again: "According to what the Buddha says, the Tathagata has cured all the beings of Jambudvipa. The treatment completed, how could there still be beings who have not yet attained Nirvana? If it is the case that not everyone has as yet attained Nirvana, how can the Tathagata say: "The treatment completed, I move on to other places?" "O good man! There are two kinds of beings in Jambudvipa. There are: those who have faith, and the others, who do not. Those with faith can be cured. Why? Because such a person can definitely attain Nirvana, which has no pox or warts." "O World-Honoured One! What can Nirvana be?" "O good man! Nirvana is emancipation ["vimukti" - liberation]." Kasyapa again said: "Is emancipation a thing or not a thing?" The Buddha said: "What is no thing is the emancipation of the sravakas and pratyekabuddhas; what is a thing is the emancipation of the All-Buddha-Tathagata. The case being thus, O good man, emancipation is a thing and not a thing. The Tathagata speaks to all sravakas and presents it as no thing." "O World-Honoured One! If it is not a thing, how can sravakas and pratyekabuddhas live?" "O good man! That which is such as Thoughtlessness-non-Thoughtlessness Heaven is also both a thing and not a thing. The Self, too, is not a thing. One might argue, saying: "If Thoughtlessness-non-Thoughtlessness Heaven is not a thing, how can a person live and come and go, advance and stand still?" All such matters relate to the world of all Buddhas; they are not what sravakas and pratyekabuddhas can rightly know. It is thus. The same with emancipation. We also speak of matter ["rupa" = matter, form, body] and non-matter ["arupa" = non-matter, non-form, non-body], and it is presented as not a thing. Also, we speak of thought and thoughtlessness, and this is presented as thoughtlessness. All such things belong to the world of all Buddhas and are not what sravakas and pratyekabuddhas may know." Then Bodhisattva Kasyapa said to the Buddha: "O World-Honoured One! Please condescend to explain to me what pertains to Mahaparinirvana and the meaning of emancipation." The Buddha praised Kasyapa, saying: "Well said, well said, O good man! True emancipation means segregation

of one's own self from all the bonds of illusion. If one truly attains emancipation and segregation of one's own self from the bonds of illusion, there is no self, or nothing to conjoin as in the case of [the sexual union between] parents, as a result of which a child is born. True emancipation is not like that. That is why emancipation is birthlessness. O Kasyapa! It is like sarpirmanda, which is pure in its nature. The same is the case with the Tathagata. He is not what arises through the conjoining of parents, as a result of which a child comes about. His nature is pure. [The Tathagata's] displaying of parents is [an expedient means for helping] to pass beings over to the other shore. True emancipation is the Tathagata. The Tathagata and emancipation are not two, are not different. It is as when we sow seeds in spring and autumn, for instance, when it is warm and wet and as a result of which the seeds shoot out buds. True emancipation is not thus. "Also, emancipation is nothingness. Nothingness is emancipation. Emancipation is the Tathagata and the Tathagata nothingness. It is not anything that come about from doing [action]. Such doing is like a castle building. True emancipation does not come about in this way [i.e. is not a compounded, constructed thing]. For this reason, emancipation is at once the Tathagata. "Also, emancipation is the non-created. A potter makes a pot, which breaks to pieces again. Things are not like that in emancipation. True emancipation is birthlessness and deathlessness. That is why emancipation is the Tathagata. 'He is birthlessness, non-extinction, agelessness, and is undying, unbreakable and indestructible. He is not anything created. Hence we say that the Tathagata enters Great Nirvana. "What do we mean by agelessness and deathlessness? Age relates to what moves and changes. One's hair becomes white, and lines appear on one's face. By death is meant the breaking up [disintegration] of the body, as a result of which life departs. Nothing of this kind arises in emancipation. Since nothing of this kind arises, we say emancipation. With the Tathagata, too, there arise no such things of created existence as the turning white of the hair or the appearing of lines on the face. Thus, no ageing occurs in the case of the Tathagata. As there is no ageing, there is no death. "Also, emancipation means ill-lessness. By illness is meant the 404 diseases, and all other [ailments] which come to one from without and spoil the body. When such do not come about, we say emancipation. When no illness arises, there is true emancipation. True emancipation is the Tathagata. The Tathagata has no illness. Thus there comes about no illness in the Dharma-Body. This state of no illness is the Tathagata. Death is the breaking up of the body and the ending of life. There is no death here [in emancipation]. What there is is the deathless ["'amrta'" - the state of immortality], which is true emancipation. True emancipation is the Tathagata. The Tathagata is accomplished in such virtues [blessings]. How could we [ever] say that the Tathagata is non-eternal? Anything such as the non-eternal can never exist there. It is an Adamantine Body. How could it be non-eternal? As a result, we do not say that there is any ending of life with the Tathagata. With the Tathagata, what there is is purity; there is no defilement. The Tathagata's body does not get defiled by the womb. It is like the pundarika-lotus, whose nature is pure. The same with the Tathagata and emancipation. Thus, emancipation is at once the Tathagata. That is why the Tathagata is pure and undefiled. "And with emancipation, such things as the "'asravas'" [defilements, "leakings"], the pox and warts, and all other such things, are done away with. The same with the Tathagata. He has no defilements and no pox or warts. "Also, with emancipation, there can be no fighting or refutation [confrontation, disputation]. For example, the hunger-ridden entertain the thought of greed and grabbing when they see others taking food. With emancipation, the case is not thus. "Also, emancipation is peace and quietude. Ordinary people say that peace and quietude are of Mahesvara. But such is a lie. True quietude means utmost emancipation. Utmost emancipation is the Tathagata. "Also, emancipation means peace and safety. The place where robbers are present has no peace and safety. The place where purity and peace reign is a place of peace and quietude. As there is no fear in this emancipation, we say peace and quietude. Hence, peace and quietude are true emancipation. True emancipation is the Tathagata. The Tathagata is Dharma." "Also, emancipation has no equal. By equal, we may take up the case of a king who has equals in the neighbouring kingdoms. The case of true emancipation is not such. Having no equal is like the case of a chakravartin, who has no equal. The same with emancipation. There is nothing equal to it. To have no equal is true emancipation. True emancipation is the Tathagatachakravartin. Thus, there is none

who is his equal. There can be no talk [here] of an equal. "Also, emancipation is non-apprehension. One who has apprehension may be likened to a king who fears and slanders the strong neighbouring state, and has apprehension. Now, with emancipation there is nothing of the kind. This is like annihilating enmity, as a consequence of which there is no longer any apprehension. The same is the case with emancipation. It has no apprehension or fear. Non-apprehension is the Tathagata. "Also, emancipation is non-apprehension or non-joy. For example, a woman has an only son. As a result of war, he goes to a far-off place. News comes, saying that the boy has met with ill fortune, as a consequence of which the mother is worried. Later, she hears of his safety and because of this is glad. Now, with emancipation there is nothing of the kind. When there is no apprehensioon or joy, there is true emancipation. True emancipation is the Tathagata. "Also, there is no dust or defilement in emancipation as when in the spring months, after sundown, the wind raises up a cloud of dust. Now, in emancipation, nothing of this kind obtains. Where there is no cloud of dust, there is true emancipation. True emancipation is the Tathagata. This is like a bright gem resting in the knot of dressed hair on the head of a chakravartin, where there is no fleck of defilement. The nature of emancipation is thus: it has no defilement. Non-defilement can be likened to true emancipation. True emancipation is the Tathagata. True gold does not contain any sand or stone. This is true treasure. When one gains this, one feels [one has gained true] wealth. The nature of emancipation is also such a true emancipation. This true treasure can be likened to true emancipation. True emancipation is the Tathagata. When an unglazed pot breaks, there issues a neighing [cracking] sound. With the adamantine treasure pot, things are otherwise. Now, emancipation emits no neighing [cracking] sound. The adamantine treasure pot is like true emancipation. True emancipation is the Tathagata. Hence, the body of the Tathagata cannot be destroyed. We say that it neighs [crackles]. This is as when castor seeds are put into a blazing fire, which flames up and sends forth a popping sound. It is like that. Now, emancipation has nothing of the kind. The adamantine pot of true treasure emits no cracking or breaking sound. Even if innumerable hundreds of thousands of people were to shoot arrows at it, none caould break this pot. What emits no cracking or breaking sound is true emancipation. True emancipation is the Tathagata. A poor man is in debt to other people. So he gets bound up and chained in fetters and is punished by whipping, and has to suffer from all [kinds of] worries and pains. Now, with emancipation, there is nothing of this kind. There is no debt to pay. This is like a rich person who possesses innumerable "'yis'" of treasure and whose power is unbounded, who owes nothing to other people. The case of emancipation is thus. It has a countless stock of wealth of Dharma and rare treasures, having full power and owing nothing to others. Owing nothing to others may be likened to true emancipation. True emancipation is the Tathagata. "Also, emancipation is "not being oppressed". This may be contrasted with spring, when one walks in the heat, with summer, when one tastes what is sweet, and with winter, when one encounters the cold. In true emancipation there is nothing of any kind that does not appeal to one's wishes.The absence of anything to oppress one may be likened to true emancipation. True emancipation is the Tathagata. As to non-oppression, we may take up the case of a man who, having greedily partaken of fish, drinks milk again. Such a man as this is not far from death. In true emancipation, there is nothing of the kind. If he obtains ambrosia ["amrta"] or good medicine, worry leaves him. True emancipation is like that. Ambrosia and good medicine can be likened to emancipation. True emancipation is the Tathagata. How can we speak of being oppressed or not oppressed? For example, a common mortal is arrogant and self-important. And he thinks: "Of all things, nothing can harm me". And he holds in his hand a serpent, a tiger, or a noxious insect. The destined time of death not coming, this person meets with an untimely death. In true emancipation, there comes about nothing of the kind. We say "not being oppressed". This can be likened to a chakravartin's divine gem, which kills all noxious insects, such as the dung-beetle and the 96 noxious insects [i.e. the total number of tirthikas thought to be existing at the time of the Buddha]. As one comes into contact with the glow of this divine gem, all poison dissipates. Things are thus with true emancipation. All die away from the 25 existences. The annihilation of poison is analogous to true emancipation. True emancipation is the Tathagata. Also, "not being oppressed" is like space, for example. Thus is

emancipation. Space is comparable to true emancipation. True emancipation is the Tathagata. Also, being oppressed is like holding a lamp close to dry grass. When it is too close, the grass catches fire. The case is thus. There is nothing of the kind in true emancipation. Also, "non-oppressed" is like the sun and moon, which do not come too close to all beings. Such is the situation with emancipation. It does not come pressing down upon beings. Non-oppression is true emancipation. True emancipation is the Tathagata. "Also, emancipation is the immovable Dharma. It is in contrast to enmity and friendliness, which do not exist in true emancipation. Also, immovability can be likened to a chakravartin. There will be no one who will befriend him. None becomes his friend. That the king has no friend can be likened to true emancipation. True emancipation is the Tathagata. The Tathagata is Dharma. Also, the "immovable" may be contrasted with white cloth, which can easily be dyed. It is not thus with emancipation. Also, this "immovable" may be likened to varsiki [jasminum sambac]. Also, making it smell badly and blue in colour is impossible. The same with emancipation. Try as we might, we cannot make it smell badly or change colour. For this reason, emancipation is the Tathagata. "Also, emancipation is what is rare. There is nothing rare, for example, about a water lily growing in water. When it grows in fire, this is something rare. People see this and are gladdened. What is rare can be likened to true emancipaiton. True emancipation is the Tathagata. This Tathagata is the Dharma-Body. Also, "rare" may be compared with a baby. It has no teeth, but as it grows up, these appear. It is not so with emancipation. There is no birth and no non-birth.

"Also, emancipation is what is "empty and quiet". There can be no indefiniteness. By indefinite is meant the situation of saying that the icchantika never shifts and that one committing grave offences never attains Buddhahood. Such can never apply. Why not? When that [icchantika] person gains pristine faith in the Buddha's Wonderful Dharma, at that time the person annihilates the icchantika [within himself]. On becoming an upasaka, the icchantika [in that person] dies away; the person who has committed grave offences also attains Buddhahood when his sins have been expiated. Thus we can never say that there is no shifting at all and that no

Buddhahood can be attained. With true emancipation, there can be no such case of annihilation. Also, "emptiness and quietude" are things of the Dharma world. The nature of the Dharma world is true emancipation. True emancipation is the Tathagata. Also, once the icchantika has died out, we can no more talk of the icchantika. "What is an icchantika? An icchantika cuts off [within himself] all the roots of good deeds and his mind does not call forth any association with good. Not even a bit of a thought of good arises. Nothing such as this ever occurs in true emancipation. As there is nothing of this kind, we say true emancipation. True emancipation is the Tathagata. "Also, emancipation is called "immeasurable". For example, we can measure the volume of cereal. But true emancipation is not like this. It is like the great ocean, whose volume we cannot measure. Emancipation is like that. We cannot measure [it]. True emancipation is immeasurable. True emancipation is the Tathagata." "Also, true emancipation is called "immeasurable" [innumerable, boundless]. It is like the varied karma results which a single person has. The same is the case with emancipation. It has innumerable returns. Innumerable returns means true emancipation. True emancipation is the Tathagata. "Also, emancipation is wide and great and like the great sea, to which nothing is equal. The same with emancipation. Nothing can be its equal. What has no equal is true emancipation. True emancipation is the Tathagata. "Also, emancipation is the highest. It is like the firmament, which is the highest, with nothing coming to be its equal. The same is the case with emancipation. What is the highest and incomparable is true emancipation. True emancipation is the Tathagata. "Also, emancipation is the "impassable". It is like the den of a lion, before [into] which no animal dares pass. The same, too, is the case with emancipation. No one can well pass through it. What is impassable is true emancipation. True emancipation is the Tathagata. "Also, emancipation is the "uppermost". For example, north is the highest of all directions. The same is also the case with emancipation. Nothing surpasses it. Whatever is uppermost is true emancipation. True emancipation is the Tathagata. "Also, emancipation is the up of the uppermost. For example, compared with the east, north is the uppermost. The same with emancipation. Nothing

surpasses it. What is the uppermost is true emancipation. True emancipation is the Tathagata. "Also emancipation is the law of constancy. For example, when a man's or deva's body breaks up, life departs. This is always so. It [this law] is not non-constant. It is the same with emancipation. It is not non-constant. What is not non-constant is emancipaiton. True emancipation is the Tathagata. "Also, emancipation is the strongly abiding. It is as in the case of the khadira [acacia catechu, the extract from which - "'catechu'" - is much used as a medicine, an astringent and tonic], sandalwood, and aloe wood, whose quality is strength and faithfulness. The same with emancipation. Its quality is strength and faithfulness. Whatever is strong and faithful is emancipation. True emancipation is the Tathagata. "Also, emancipation is the not-empty. For example, the body of bamboo and reed is empty inside. This is not the case with emancipation. Know that emancipation is the Tathagata. "Also, emancipation is what cannot be defiled. For example, there is a wall. While the upper coating is still not finished, mosquitoes and gadflies come and rest and play on it. When it is painted and finished with pictures and decorated with sculptures, the insects, scenting the smell of the paint, do not stay on it. True emancipation may be likened to such non-staying. True emancipation is the Tathagata. "Also, emancipation is unboundedness. Villages and towns all have boundaries. This is not so with emancipation. It is like space, which has no boundaries. Emancipation of such kind is the Tathagata. "Also, emancipation is what cannot be seen. It is just as the tracks of birds that flew across the sky cannot be traced. What is unable to be seen as such can well be likened to true emancipation. True emancipation is the Tathagata. "Also, extremely deep is what the Buddhas and bodhisattvas look up to. A dutiful son serves his parents, and the virtue thereof is extremely deep. It is so. Extremely deep refers to emancipation. True emancipation is the Tathagata. "Also, emancipation is what one cannot see. For example, a man cannot see the top of his own head. The same is the case with emancipation. Sravakas and pratyekabuddhas cannot see [it]. What cannot be seen is true emancipation. True emancipation is the Tathagata. "Also, emancipation is the houseless. This is as in the case of the Void, which has no house. The same with emancipation. The house [here] refers to the

25 existences. "Houseless" is true emancipation. True emancipation is the Tathagata. "Also, emancipation is what cannot be held in one's hand. The amalaka can certainly be held in a man's hand. Not so emancipation. It cannot be held in one's hand. Whatever cannot be held in one's hand is emancipation. True emancipation is the Tathagata. "Also, emancipation is what one cannot grasp in one's hand. This is as in the case of a phantom, which one cannot grasp in one's hand. The same also with emancipation. Whatever it is not possible to grasp in one's hand is emancipation. True emancipation is the Tathagata. "Also, emancipation has no carnal body. For example, one has a body, on and in which can come about such as the pox, leprosy, all kinds of carbuncles, craziness and dryings-up. In true emancipation, no such diseases and illnesses come about. What is without suchlike diseases and illnesses is true emancipation. True emancipation is the Tathagata. "Also, emancipation is oneness of taste. It is like milk, which is one in its taste. The same with emancipation, which is one in its taste. Such oneness in taste is true emancipation. True emancipation is the Tathagata. "Also, emancipation is purity. This is as in the case of water which has no mud [in it], is clear, unmoving and pure. The same with emancipation. It is clean, unmoving and pure. Whatever is clean, unmoving and pure is true emancipation. True emancipation is the Tathagata. "Also, emancipation is single in taste. It is like the rain in the sky, which is one in taste and pure. That which is one in taste and is pure can be likened to true emancipation. True emancipation is the Tathagata. "Also, emancipation is exclusion. It is like the full moon that does not have any clouded part. So goes it with emancipation. It has no clouded part. What has no clouded part is true emancipation. True emancipation is the Tathagata. "Also, emancipation is quietude. A man has a fever. When cured, he feels quiet. Emancipation is thus. One feels quiet. When one feels quiet, there is true emancipation. True emancipation is the Tathagata. "Also, true emancipation is equalness [impartiality, equanimity]. For example, a field has [in it] poisonous serpents, rats and wolves, all of which mean to kill others. It is not so with emancipation. There is no thought of killing. Having no thought of killing is true emancipation. True emancipation is the Tathagata. Also, equalness may be compared to the mind of parents, who view their children all-equally. Thus is emancipation. The mind is all-equal. This all-equal mind is true emancipation. True emancipation is the Tathagata." "Also, emancipation is not having any other place [to dwell]. For example, there is a man here who only lives in the best of all places, having no other place to live in. The same with emancipation. It has no other place to live in. Having no other different place to live in is true emancipation. True emanciption is the Tathagata.

"Also, emancipation is feeling satisfied. Take the case of a hungry man who, on encountering sweet dishes, devours them, and there is no end of eating. The case of emancipation is not like this. If one partakes of milk-cooked porridge, one no longer feels the need to eat. No longer feeling any need to eat may well be likened to emancipation. True emancipation is the Tathagata. "Also, emancipation is segregation. It is like a person tied up, who cuts the rope and gains his freedom. The same is the case with emancipation. One cuts off all the bonds of doubt. Such cutting off of all the bonds of doubt is true emancipation. True emancipation is the Tathagata. "Also, emancipation is gaining the other shore. A big river, for example, has this shore and the yonder shore. It is not thus with emancipation. Although it does not have this side, there is the yonder shore. What has this other shore is true emancipation. True emancipation is the Tathagata. "Also, emancipation is silence. The surface of a great sea swells, for example, and there arise many sounds. With emancipation things are not so. Emancipation such as this is the Tathagata. "Also, emancipation is the All-Wonderful. If haritaki [a purgative bitter fruit] is added to any medicine, that medicine will come to taste bitter. But emancipation is not like this. It becomes sweet. The taste of sweetness can be likened to true emancipation. "Also, emancipation makes away with all illusions. This may be likened to the case of a learned doctor who mixes up all drugs and cures all illnesses. The same is also the case with emancipation. It thoroughly makes away with illusion. What makes away with illusion is true emancipation. True emancipation is the Tathagata." "Also, emancipation has no oppressedness [constriction, crampedness]. For example, a small house cannot take in many people. The case is otherwise with emancipation, which can take in many. What takes in many is true emancipation. True emancipation is the Tathagata. "Also, emancipation is analogous to annihilating all loving [lustful] casts of mind and not having carnal appetites. A female has many phases of love [lust]. This is not so with emancipation. Emancipation of this kind is the Tathagata. The Tathagata does not possess such illusions as greed, anger, ignorance, arrogance, etc. "Also, emancipation is lovelessness [desirelessness]. Love is of two kinds. One is hungry [craving] love and the other love of Dharma. True love is not possessed of hungry love. As there is love for all beings, there is the love of Dharma. Such love of Dharma is true emancipation. True emancipation is the Tathagata. "Also, emancipation is not possessed of atmatmiya [fixation on self and what belongs to self]. Such emancipation is the Tathagata. The Tathagata is Dharma. "Also, emancipation is extinction. It is removed from all kinds of greed. Such emancipation is the Tathagata. The Tathagata is Dharma. "Also, emancipation is succouring. It thoroughly succours all those who have fear. Such emancipation is the Tathagata. The Tathagata is Dharma. "Also, emancipation is the place to which one returns. One who partakes of such emancipation does not seek any other place to take refuge in. For example, a man who depends on the king does not look for other kings to depend upon. Yet even when one depends on the king, there can be a situation in which change comes about. For one who depends upon emancipation, there is no change any more. Where there is no change, there is true emancipation. True emancipation is the Tathagata. "Also, emancipation is fearlessness. It is like the lion, who has no fear of any beast. The same is the case with emancipation. It has no fear of any Maras. Fearlessness is true emancipation. True emancipation is the Tathagata. "Also, emancipation knows no narrowness. On a narrow path, two persons cannot walk [side by side]. It is not thus with emancipation. Such emancipation is the Tathagata. Also, there is the case of non-narrowness. For example, a man falls into a well just because of his fear of a tiger. The situation with emancipation is not like this. Such emancipation is the Tathagata. Again, there is the case of non-narrowness. On a great sea, one abandons a small, wrecked ship. Sailing in a strong ship, one crosses the sea and arrives at the place [destination], and one's mind is blessed with

peace. The same is the case with emancipation. The mind is happy. The attainment of happiness is true emancipation. True emancipation is the Tathagata. "Also, emancipation stands above all causes and by-causes [conditions]. For example, from milk we get cream, from cream, we get butter; and from butter, we get sarpirmanda. True emancipation has none of these causes. The causeless is true emancipation. True emancipation is the Tathagata. "Also, emancipation thoroughly subdues arrogance. [Think of] a great king who belittles a petty king. The case is not thus with emancipation. Such emancipation is the Tathagata. The Tathagata is Dharma. "Also, emancipation subdues all kinds of indolence. One who is indolent is greedy. With true emancipation, nothing such as this comes about. This is true emancipation. True emancipation is the Tathagata. "Also, emancipation does away with non-brightness [i.e. darkness]. This is as with best butter. When the scum and dirt are removed, we get sarpirmanda. The same with emancipation. As a result of excluding the scum of ignorance, true brightness shines forth. Such brightness is true emancipation. True emancipation is the Tathagata. "Also, emancipation is quietude, the pure "one", the "not-two" [non-dual]. This is like the elephant of the wilderness, who is without comparison. The same is the situation with emancipation. It is the one, the not-two, which is true emancipation. True emancipation is the Tathagata. "Also, emancipation is strong and full of truth. The stems of the bamboo, reed, and castor-oil plants are empty, but the seeds are strong and truthful. Other than the Buddha-Tathagata, all of humankind and heaven are not strong and full of truth. True emancipation is remote from all illusions. Such emancipation is the Tathagata. "Also, emancipation awakens and augments [expands, enhances] one. True emancipation is like that. Such emancipation is the Tathagata. "Also, emancipation relinquishes all existences. For example, a man, after partaking of food, may vomit. Emancipation is also like this. It relinquishes all existences. The relinquishing of all existences is true emancipation. True emancipation is the Tathagata. "Also, emancipation is a decision. This is as in the case of the fragrance from varsiki [jasminum sambac], which is not found in saptaparna [alstonia scholaris]. The same is the case with emancipation. Such emancipation is the Tathagata.

"Also, emancipation is water. For example, water comes above all other elements of the earth and thoroughly moistens all trees, grass and seeds. It is the same with emancipation. It thoroughly moistens all beings. Such emancipation is the Tathagata. "Also, emancipation is entering. If there is a gate, this [means] that this is the entrance-way. It is as in a place where there is gold which one can get. Emancipation is thus. It is like a gate. One who practises selflessness can indeed enter. Such emancipation is the Tathagata. "Also, emancipation is what is good. For example, a disciple follows the injunctions of his teacher well and we call this good. So, too, with emancipation. Such emancipation is the Tathagata. "Also, emancipation is called the supramundane Law [Dharma]. Of all things, this is the one which supercedes all others. It is like the case of butter, which is the best of all tastes. Thus is it [too] with emancipation. Such emancipation is the Tathagata. "Also, emancipation is the immovable. For example, the wind cannot move a gate. True emancipation is like this. Such emancipation is the Tathagata. "Also, emancipation is the waveless. The great sea has waves. But this is not the case with emancipation. Such emancipation is the Tathagata. "Also, emancipation is like a royal palace. Emancipation is like that. Know that emancipation is the Tathagata. "Also, emancipation is what is useful. Jambunada gold has many uses. Nobody speaks ill of it. The same applies to emancipation. There is nothing bad about it. What has nothing bad about it is true emancipation. True emancipation is the Tathagata. "Also, emancipation is giving up the actions of one's childhood days. It is the same with emancipation. It does away with the five skandhas. Abandoning the five skandhas is true emancipation. True emancipation is the Tathagata. "Also, emancipation is the utmost. A person fettered in bonds obtains freedom and, after washing and cleaning himself, returns home. It is the same with emancipation. It is pure to the utmost. This utmost purity is true emancipation. True emancipation is the Tathagata. "Also, emancipation is the bliss that is not expelled. Because desire, malevolence and ignorance have already been vomited out. As an example: a man swallows a poisonous drug by mistake. To expel the poison, he takes a drug. Once the poison is out, he is cured, feels well and gains peace. It is the same with emancipation. Having cast out all

illusions and the poison that binds one, the body gains peace. So we speak of "non-expelled peace". Non-expelled peace is true emancipation. True emancipation is the Tathagata. "Also, emancipation rids one of the four poisonous serpents of illusion [i.e. desire, hatred, ignorance and arrogance]. The getting rid of illusion is true emancipation. True emancipation is the Tathagata. "Also, emancipation is segregating oneself from all existences, excising all suffering, obtaining all aspects of peace, and eternally cutting off desire, ill-will and ignorance, and severing oneself from the roots of all illusions. Cutting the roots of illusion is emancipation. True emancipation is the Tathagata." "Moreover, emancipation is termed that which severs all conditioned phenomena [samskrtadharmas], gives rise to all untainted [anasrava], wholseome qualities / phenomena and eliminates the various paths/ approaches, that is to say, Self, non-Self, not-Self and not non-Self. It merely severs attachment and does not sever the view of the Self/ the seeing of the Self/ the vision of the Self [atma-drsti]. The view of the Self is termed the 'Buddha-dhatu' [Buddha-Nature]. The Buddha-dhatu is true emancipation, and true emancipation is the Tathagata. "Also, emancipation is the "not-empty-empty". "Empty-empty" is non-possession. Non-possession is the emancipation which the tirthikas and Nirgrantha Jnatiputras [Jains] presume upon [base themselves upon]. But, in truth, the Nirgranthas do not possess emancipation. So we say "empty-empty". Not-empty-empty is true emancipation. True emancipation is the Tathagata. "Also, emancipation is the "not-empty". The pot in which we put water, drink, milk, cream, butter, honey, etc., can well be called the water pot and suchlike, even when there is no water, drink, cream, butter, honey or any other thing in it. And yet, we cannot say that the pot is either empty or not-empty. If we say empty, there cannot be any colour, smell, taste or touch. If we say not-empty, what we see is that there is nothing in it such as water, drink or any other thing. We can say neither matter ["rupa"] nor non-matter ["arupa"]; we can say neither empty nor not-empty. If we say empty, there can be no Eternity, Bliss, Self, and Purity. If not-empty, who is the one blessed with Eternity, Bliss, Self, and Purity? Thus, we should say neither empty nor not-empty. Empty will entail [the notion] that the 25 existences, all illusions, suffering, the phases of life, and all actual actions do not exist. When there is no cream in the pot, we may say empty. Not-empty points to Truth, to whatever is Good, Eternal, Bliss, Self, Pure, Immovable and Unchanging. It is as in the case of taste and touch regarding the pot. That is why we say not-empty. In consequence, we may say that emancipation is as in the case of the pot. The pot will break in certain circumstances. But this is not so with emancipation. It cannot break. What is indestructible is true emancipation. True emancipation is the Tathagata. "Also, emancipation is severing oneself from love [i.e. blind love, craving]. For example, there is a man here who may longingly desire to become Sakrodevanamindra, Brahma, and Mahesvara. Emancipation is other than this. Once unsurpassed Enlightenment has been attained, there is no love [craving] and no doubt. Not having love or doubt is true emancipation. True emancipation is the Tathagata. We cannot say that there is love or doubt in emancipation. "Also, emancipation cuts off all greed, all external appearances, all bonds, all illusions, all births and deaths, all causes and conditions, all karma results. Such emancipation is the Tathagata. The Tathagata is Nirvana. When all beings [come to] fear birth and death and illusion, they take refuge in the Three Treasures. This is like a herd of deer who fear the hunter and run away. One jump may be likened to one refuge, and three such jumps to three refuges. From the three jumps, peace comes. It is the same with all beings. When one fears the four Maras and the evil-minded hunter, one takes the three Refuges [in Buddha, Dharma and Sangha]. As a result of the three Refuges, one gains peace. Gaining peace is true emancipation. True emancipation is the Tathagata. The Tathagata is Nirvana. Nirvana is the Infinite. The Infinite is the Buddha-Nature. Buddha-Nature is definiteness. Definiteness is unsurpassed Enlightenment." Bodhisattva Kasyapa said to the Buddha: "O World-Honoured One! If it is the case that Nirvana, the Buddha-Nature, definiteness, and the Tathagata are one and the same, why do we say "three Refuges?" The Buddha said to Kasyapa: "All beings fear birth and death. So they take the three Refuges. By the three Refuges, we mean Buddha-Nature, Definiteness, and Nirvana. O good man! There are cases in which the name, Dharma, is one, but the meaning differs. There are cases in which the names of Dharma and the meanings are both different. We say that the name is one, but the

meaning differs. This refers to the situation where we say that the Buddha is eternal, Dharma is eternal, and the bhiksu is eternal. Also, Nirvana and space are eternal. This is a case where the name [word] is one, but the signification is different. We say that both the word and the signification differ. The Buddha is called "Enlightenment", Dharma is called "No-Awaking", the Sangha "Harmony", and Nirvana "Emancipation". Space is called "non-good", and also "not-covered". There are cases in which the word and the signification both differ. O good man! The case of the three Refuges is also like this. The world and the signification both differ. How can we say one? That is why I said to Mahaprajapati [the Buddha's aunt, who raised him]: "O Gautami! Do not make offerings to me; make them to the Sangha! If offerings are made to the Sangha, this amounts to offerings being made to the three Refuges." Mahaprajapati answered, saying: "Among the priests, there are no Buddha and no Dharma. How can we say that offerings made to the Sangha constitute offerings made to the Three Refuges?" I said: "If you do as I say, this will mean that you have made offerings to the Buddha. For the purpose of emancipation, offering is made to Dharma. When all priests receive this, this is an offering made to the Sangha." O good man! At times the Tathagata speaks about one thing and makes it refer to three; he speaks about three and makes it one. All such things are what have to do with the world of all Buddhas. They are not what sravakas and pratyekabuddhas can know." Kasyapa said further: "You, the Buddha, say that utmost peace is Nirvana. How can this be? Now, Nirvana means relinquishing the body and intellect. If one relinquishes the body and intellect, who is it that can become blessed with peace?" The Buddha said: "O good man! As an example: there is a man here. He eats some food. After partaking of it, he feels sick, desires to go out and vomit. After vomiting, he comes back. A person who was with him asks: "Have you got rid of the trouble you had? You have come back here again. " Such may be the case. The same applies to the Tathagata. He fully segregates himself from the 25 existences and eternally gains Nirvana, which is peace and bliss. There can [then] be no more of the topsy-turvy inversions, no ending and no extinction. All feeling is done away with. This is the bliss of non-feeling. This non-feeling is eternal Bliss. We can never say that the Tathagata feels

Bliss. So, utmost Bliss is none but Nirvana. Nirvana is true emancipation. True emancipation is the Tathagata." Kasyapa further said: "Are birthlessness and desirelessness emancipation?" "It is so, it is so. O good man! Birthlessness and desirelessness are emancipation. Such emancipation is the Tathagata." Kasyapa said further: "You say that birthlessness and desirelessness are emancipation. Space, too, by its nature, is birthlessness and desirelessness. It must be the Tathagata. The nature of the Tathagata must be emancipation." The Buddha said to Kasyapa: "O good man! It is not so." "Why, O World-Honoured One, is that not so?" "O good man! The kalavinka and jivamjivaka [birds] have clear and wonderful voices. How can we compare their voices to those of the crow and magpie? What do you say to that?" "We cannot, O World-Honoured One! The voices of the crow and magpie cannot bear comparison 100 thousand and "'wan'" [a Chinese unit of number] times." Kasyapa said again: "The voices of the kalavinka and others are wonderful; so is their body. O Tathagata! How can we compare them to those of the crow and magpie? This is little different from comparing a mustard seed to Mount Sumeru. The same is the case with the Buddha and space. The voice of the kalavinka can well be compared to that of the Buddha; but the voices of the crow and magpie cannot bear comparison with that of the Buddha." Then the Buddha praised Kasyapa and said: "Well said, well said, O good man! You now grasp what is most difficult to understand. The Tathagata, at times, as occasion requires, takes the case of space and compares it to emancipation. Such emancipation is the Tathagata. True emancipation, [however], cannot bear comparison with man or heaven. And space itself, truth to tell, is not fit for [such] comparison. To teach beings, a comparison is sought with what cannot, in its true sense, serve the purpose. Know that emancipation is the Tathagata; the nature of the Tathagata is this emancipation. Emancipation and the Tathagata are not two, they are not different. O good man! We say "non-comparable". We cannot take [for purposes of analogy] what cannot be compared. When there is a connection, then we can compare [two things]. Is is as when it says in the sutras, for example: "The visage is as right-set as that of the full moon; the white elephant is as fresh and clear as the snow of the Himalayas." Now, the full moon cannot be the same as a face, and the Himalayas and the white elephant cannot be equals. O good man! It is not possible to express emancipation by parables. [Yet] in order to teach beings, parables are resorted to. Through parables, we realise the nature of all things. Matters stand thus." "Kasyapa said further: "Why is it that the Tathagata resorts to two kinds of parables?" The Buddha siad: "O good man! For example, there is a person here who holds a sword in his hand and with an angry mind means to harm the Tathagata. But the Tathagata is glad, and has no angry face. Can this man harm the Tathagata and actualise the deadly sin?" "No, O World-Honoured One! Why not? Because the body of the Tathagata cannot be destroyed. Why not? Because it is not anything of the compounded carnal body. What there is is "Dharmata" [Dharma-Nature]. The principle of "Dharmata" is indestructible. How can this man hope to break the Buddha-Body? Because of his evil thought, this person falls into Avichi Hell. Thus we can make use of parables and come to know of Wonderful Dharma." Then the Buddha praised Bodhisattva Kasyapa: "Well said, well said! You already said what I wanted to say. Also, O good man! For example, an evil person means to harm his own mother. He lives in the fields and hides himself under a haystack. His mother brings out food to him. Then the man entertains an evil thought, steps forward and sharpens his sword. His mother, seeing this, slips away and hides under the stack. The man thrusts his sword into the haystack from all sides. Having done so, he is glad and thinks that he has killed his mother. Then his mother comes out of the haystack and returns home. What does this imply? Does this man have to suffer in Avichi Hell or not?" "O World-Honoured One! We cannot definitely say which one [is the case]. Why not? If we say that he has equalled [destined himself for] Avichi Hell, [in such a case] his mother's body would need to get hurt. But if it is not hurt, how can we say that the man has harmed her? If he is guiltless, how comes it that he entertained the thought of having actually killed his mother and how could he have been so glad? How can we say that he is guiltless? Though he has not actually committed this deadly sin, this is nothing other than a deadly sin. From this, we may know only through parables the true nature of a thing." Praising Kasyapa, the Buddha said: "Well said, well said, O good man! For this reason, I resort to many expedients and parables and explain emancipation. We could well employ innumerable asamkhyas of parables, yet parables cannot thoroughly explain all. If occasion arises, we might resort to parables, or the occasion might not permit parables. Thus, emancipation has such virtues. If we explain Nirvana, Nirvana and the Tathagata have innumerable virtues. We speak of "Great Nirvana." Bodhisattva Kasyapa said to the Buddha: "O World-Honoured One! I now know that there is no ending of things referring to where the Tathagata goes. If the place is unending, life too must be unending." The Buddha said: "Well said, well said! You now protect Wonderful Dharma indeed. Any good men or women who desire to cut off the bonds of illusion and all bonds should protect Wonderful Dharma thus."

Chapter Eight: On the Four Dependables

The Buddha further said to Kasyapa: "O good man! In this all-wonderful "Mahaparinirvana Sutra", there appear four kinds of men. These well protect, establish and think of Wonderful Dharma. They benefit others very much and pity the world. They become the refuges of the world and give peace and bliss to man and god. What are the four [categories]? A man appears in the world and possesses illusion. This is the first category. Those persons of the grades of srotapanna and sakridagamin are the second. Those of the grade of anagamin are the third. Those of the stage of arhat are the fourth. Such four kinds of person appear, benefit and pity the world. They become the refuges of the world and give peace and bliss to man and heaven. "What do we mean by those garbed in illusion? Such people uphold the prohibitions, observe [moral] deportment, and uphold Wonderful Dharma. They accord with what the Buddha says, understand what is said and expound it to others, and say: "Coveting little is the Way; desiring much is not the Way", and expound the "eight awakened minds of a great man". To one who transgresses, the Way is shown, so that he confesses and repents. These people make away with sins and know the expedients and secrets of the teachings of the Bodhisattvas. Such [of this category] is a common mortal, not the eighth person [one who has arrived at the stage of attainment called "eighth-person stage"]. The eighth person is no common mortal. He is called "Bodhisattva", but not Buddha. "The people of the second category are those of the stages of srotapanna and sakridagamin. Having encountered Wonderful Dharma, they uphold it. They follow and listen to the words of the Buddha and act as they have heard. Having heard, they write down what they have heard, uphold what they have heard, recite it and expound the teaching to others. There can be [with these people] no such thing as not writing down, not receiving, upholding and expounding the teaching to others. With them there could never be anything such as saying that the Buddha allows them to keep servants and what is impure. This refers to the people of the second category. They have not as yet attained the second and third places of abode. They are called "Bodhisattvas". They have already received the Buddha's prophecy that they will [one day] attain Buddhahood. "The people of the third category are those of the stage of anagamin. With them there can never be such things as slandering Wonderful Dharma, keeping servants, male or female, having impure things, or holding [keeping] the books of the tirthikas, being hindered by foreign ["guest" - minor] illusions, or being bound up by various old [inherent] illusions, saving for themselves the true sharira [relics] of the Tathagata, getting attacked by eternal illnesses or the four great poisonous serpents [greed, anger, ignorance and arrogance], and insisting upon self. They talk about selflessness, but never talk about, or cling to, worldly things. They speak about, and uphold, Mahayana, but their body is never soiled by the 80,000 germs. They are forever removed from sensual appetite, and even in their dreams they never ejaculate impure things. At the last moment of their life, they are never afraid. What does "anagamin" mean? [It means that] this person never comes back. As already stated, no wrongs or illnesses ever catch hold of him. He goes, returns and cycles around. He is called a Bodhisattva. Receiving his prophecy [to Buddhahood], he, not long after that, attains unsurpassed Enlightenment." This is the person of the third category. "The fourth is the arhat. An arhat is he who cuts through the bonds of illusion and who has made away with the heavy weight that rests on his shoulders, and who has attained what he wanted to have. All things having been accomplished, he lives on the tenth level. Attaining an unmolested state of Wisdom, he does what others desire to have and manifests various images. If he desires to accomplish the Buddha-Way as it should be accomplished, he can well do so. One who can so accomplish innumerable virtues is an arhat. "Such are the four kinds of people who appear, benefit and pity the world. They thus become the refuges of the world and give peace and bliss to man and god. They are the most honoured and the most superb of all men and gods. It is as in the case of the Tathagata, who is the most superb of men and gods and is the Refuge of the world."

Bodhisattva Kasyapa said to the Buddha: "O World-Honoured One! I do not take refuge in these four beings. Why not? It is as stated in the "Ghosila Sutra", in which the Buddha addresses

Ghosila. There you say: "Devas, Maras, and Brahma may desire destruction, present themselves in the forms of Buddhas, perfectly adorn themselves with such as the 32 signs of perfection [which the Buddha is said to possess] and the 80 minor marks of excellence, and the light of a halo, measuring 8 feet, a face perfectly round as at the time of the full moon, and a white tuft of hair in the centre of the brow, whiter than horse-shoe shell or snow. Should they appear thus adorned, look carefully to see if these are genuine. Having made sure [that these are not genuine], subdue them." O World-Honoured One! Maras and others can present themselves as Buddhas. Why might they not be able to present themselves as the four sages, the arhat to begin with, as sitting or sleeping in the air, emitting water from the left-hand side of their body and fire from the right, and emitting blazing flames from their body like a fire-ball? For these reasons, I cannot have faith in this; I dare not accept such, even when taught. I shall not take refuge in them." The Buddha said: "O good man! "If you have doubt in what I say, it is for you not to accept it". Even more so when you have to deal with such people. This being so, weigh up a thing well and find out if it is good or not, if it is for you to do or not. Acting thus, one becomes blessed with peace and bliss in the long night [i.e. our life in samsara]. O good man! There is here a dog with his mind set upon stealing. At night he enters a man's house. When the servants come to know of this, they angrily shout: "Get out this instant, or we will kill you!" The burglar-dog hears this, runs out of the house and never comes back again. From now on, act like this, and drive away the Papiyas [Evil One, Devil], saying: "O Papiyas! Do not present yourself in such a form. Should you dare, we shall bind you up with five ropes." On hearing this, Mara will hide away. He will never again show himself like some burgler-dog." Kasyapa said to the Buddha: "O World-Honoured One! It is as you, the Buddha, said to the rich man, Ghosila. Anybody who can thus conquer Mara will surely draw close to Parinirvana. O Tathagata! How is it that you particularly speak of these four kinds of people and say that we should take refuge in them? What such people say cannot be trusted." The Buddha said to Kasyapa: "O good man! I address the sravakas who have [only] fleshly eyes and say that I subdue Mara. I do not say this to those of the Mahayana. Those of the sravaka class fall under

the category of the fleshly eye, though they may possess the heavenly eye. Those who practise Mahayana may also possess fleshly eyes, but they are those who have the Buddha-Eye. How so? These Mahayana sutras are called the Buddha vehicle. Such a Buddha vehicle is most superb. O good man! There are, for example, brave and courageous people and also those who are cowardly and weak and who come and hang on. The strong always teach the weak and say: "Take the bow like this, the arrow like this, and learn [how to handle] the halberd, the long hook, and the policeman's lassoo." Also, the strong man will say: "Now, the fate of those who fight is like walking on sword-blades. But one must not have fear. When one sees man or god, think that they are petty and weak. One must be brave at heart." There may also be a man who, though not brave, presents himself as brave and, armed with a bow, a sword and many other things, goes to the battlefield. Then that person will cry out loudly: "Don't fear these people. If they see that you are not afraid, they will know and soon disperse like the robber-dog." O good man! The same is the case with the Tathagata. To all sravakas, he says: "Do not be afraid of Marapapiyas. If Marapapiyas, clad as a Buddha, comes to you, make effort and harden your mind, so that he will draw back?" "O good man! It is as in the case of a strong man who does not give ear to what others say. The same is the case with one who learns Mahayana. He hears the teachings of the various sutras of deep thought; he has joy and is not afraid. Why? Because one such who abides in Mahayana has in the past made innumerable offerings to innumerable millions and billions of Buddhas and worshipped them, and he has no mind that fears Maras, who might be as innumerable as billions and thousands and who may come and attack that person. He is not afraid. O good man! For example, a man possesses agasti [a healing plant] and does not fear any poisonous snakes. Through this drug, poison loses all its power. The same with this Mahayana sutra. Just as in the case of the drug, no person will fear any Maras or poisons. It thoroughly crushes the enemy, who can never stand up again. Also, next, O good man! For example, there is a naga who, by nature, is very evil-minded. When it desires to harm people, it approaches with the eye or cheats with the breath. Hence, the lion, tiger, leopard, jackal, wolf and dog all fear [it]. When all these evil animals hear its voice, see its form or touch its body, there is not one that does not lose its life. But there is one who knows a good spell, which enables all such evil and poisonous ones as nagas, garudas, elephants, lions, leopards and wolves to be tamed, so that one can well ride on them. These creatures, as they encounter this marvellous spell, become tamed. It is thus with sravakas and pratyekabuddhas. Seeing Marapapiyas, they all become frightened. And [so] Marapapiyas does not feel afraid and does evil. The same is the case with those who practise Mahayana. They see that all sravakas are afraid of evil acts and do not have faith in this Mahayana. First, expedients are resorted to, as a result of which all Maras are conquered, so that they become tame and can now stand [function] as vehicles to carry things in. Through this, they variously teach wonderful doctrines. Seeing the Maras are afraid, the sravakas and pratyekabuddhas become wonder-struck and gain faith and joy in the Wonderful Dharma of this unsurpassed Mahayana. They say: "From now on, we must not cause obstruction to Wonderful Dharma." Also, next, O good man! The sravakas and pratyekabuddhas entertain fear regarding all illusions. Those who study Mahayana have no such fears. By practising Mahayana, one gains such power. As a result, all that was said above is for sravakas and pratyekabuddhas to do away with Maras, and not for Mahayana itself. This all-wonderful Mahayana sutra cannot easily be made away with. All is extremely wonderful. One who hears it and knows that the Tathagata is Eternal is very rare. Such a person is like the udumbara [bloom]. There may appear people who, after my death, listen to the teachings of such a wonderful Mahayana sutra and gain faith. Know that such people will not fall into the unfortunate realms in the ages of the future, for 100 thousand billion kalpas to come." Then the Buddha said to Bodhisattva Kasyapa: "O good man! After my entering Nirvana, there may be 100 thousand innumerable people who will slander and not believe in this all-wonderful Great Nirvana Sutra." Bodhisattva Kasyapa said to the Buddha: "O World-Honoured One! Sooner or later, people will slander this sutra. O World-Honoured One! What good and pure people will come and save such as those who commit slander?" The Buddha said to Kasyapa: "O good man! For 40 years after my entering Nirvana, this sutra will flourish in Jambudvipa. Then, it will disappear. O good man! In a land, for example, where one can get sugar

cane, rice, rock candy, butter, cream and sarpirmanda, people will say: "This is the best of the most tasty [food]." Or there may be people who may be living on maize and panic grass and who may say that what they eat is the best of all food. Such are people of poor fortune, due to their karmic results. The ears of the fortunate will never hear of millet or barnyard grass. What they will eat will be rice, bran, sugar cane, rock candy, and sarpirmanda. It is the same with this wonderful Sutra of Great Nirvana. Those born dull-minded and unfortunate will not wish to listen, just like those dull and little-fortunate people who hate rice bran and rock candy. It is thus with the two vehicles [i.e. sravakas and pratyekabuddhas], the people of which will hate this unsurpassed Nirvana Sutra. [But] there are people who are gladdened on hearing this sutra and who, having heard it, feel pleased and do not slander it. This is like those of good fortune who eat rice bran. O good man! For example, there is a king who lives in the depths of the mountains, located in a precipitous place, difficult of approach. He has sugar cane, rice bran, and rock candy, but since these are difficult to obtain, he begrudges and stores them away, and does not eat them. Fearing that they may run out, he only eats millet and barnyard grass. Then, the king of a different land, hearing of this and feeling pity, sends rice bran and sugar cane to him. The king receives these and divides them amongst the people of his land, who all eat them. Having eaten them, they are all gladdened and say: "Because of that king, we now have been blessed with this food." O good man! It is the same with the four kinds of people. They become the generals of this great teaching. One of the four kinds of people sees that countless Bodhisattvas of other countries study, copy, or have others copy, Mahayana sutras of this kind, for gain, fame, understanding, reliance, for trading for other sutras, but that they do not speak of it to others. Hence, he takes this all-wonderful sutra over there and gives it to the Bodhisattvas, so that they might aspire to unsurpassed Bodhichitta [Enlightenment-mind] and rest peacefully in Enlightenment. A Bodhisattva, on obtaining this sutra, speaks of it to others, who, through it, become blessed with the amrta [ambrosia] of the Mahayana teaching. All of this is what has been brought forth by this single Bodhisattva. He enables others to hear what they have not heard before. This is like the people who, through the power of that king, enjoy rare dishes. The case is similar. "Also, O good man! Wherever this all-wonderful Great Nirvana Sutra goes, that place - you may know - is indestructible. The people living there are also alike adamantine. Any person who hears this sutra will attain unsurpassed Enlightenment and never draw back from it. Such persons will gain whatever they wish to have. O you Bhiksus! Uphold well what I say to you today. Any persons who do not hear this sutra, are, you should know, much to be pitied. Why so? Because such cannot uphold the deep meaning of such a Mahayana sutra as this." Kasyapa said to the Buddha: "O World-Honoured One! It is is the case that after the Tathagata's decease this Mahayana Great Nirvana Sutra will flourish in Jambudvipa for a period of 40 years and that after that it will disappear; when and how will it come back again?" The Buddha said: "O good man! For a period of 80 years after the ending of the age of Wonderful Dharma and during the 40 years preceding it, this sutra will greatly flourish in Jambudvipa." Kasyapa further said to the Buddha: "O World-Honoured One! When the age of Wonderful Dharma has ended and when the correct observance of the precepts no longer prevails, when unlawful teachings prevail, when there is no longer any person to be found who takes the right path -who might be the ones who will give good ear to the teaching, uphold and recite it, and cause this sutra to circulate in the world, so that people make offerings, respect, copy and expound such a sutra? Please have pity on beings, O Tathagata, and analyse and expound this widely, so that all Bodhisattvas may hear Dharma, uphold it and never pull back from unsurpassed Bodhichitta." Then the Buddha praised Kasyapa and said: "Well said, well said, O good man! You now put such a question. O good man! If beings, at the river Hiranyavati, at the seat of the Tathagata, aspire to Enlightenment, they will, in this evil world, uphold a sutra such as this and not slander it. O good man! There may be beings at the seats of all Tathagatas as many as the sands of the Ganges who aspire to Enlightenment and do not slander Dharma in the evil world, but love this sutra, [yet] are not able to analyse and expound it to others. O good man! There may be beings at the seats of all Buddhas as numerous as the sands of two Ganges who aspire to Enlightenment, do not slander Dharma in this evil world, rightly understand it, have faith, are gladdened, uphold

and recite it, [but] are not able, for the sake of the world, to expound and speak about it to others. Or there may be beings who at the seats of all Tathagatas as numerous as the sands of three Ganges aspire to Enlightenment, slander Dharma in this evil world, uphold, recite and copy this sutra and expound it to others, [yet] are not able to gain the depths of its meaning. Or there may be beings who, at the seats of all Tathagatas, as numerous as the sands of four Ganges, aspire to Enlightenment and in the evil world do not slander but uphold, reicte and copy this sutra and expound one-sixteenth part of its meaning, [although they are as] yet not perfect. Or there may be beings who, at the seats of all Tathagatas as numerous as the sands of five Ganges, aspire to Enlightenment, do not slander in this evil world, but uphold, recite and copy this sutra and speak about eight sixteenths of it. Or there may be beings who, at the seats of all Tathagats as numerous as the sands of six Ganges, aspire to Enlightenment and, in the evil world, do not slander this Dharma, but uphold, recite, and copy this sutra and expound twelve sixteenths of it to others. Or there may be beings at the seats of all Tathagatas as numerous as the sands of seven Ganges who, in the evil world, do not slander the Dharma, but uphold, recite, and copy this sutra and speak about fourteen sixteenths of it. Or there may be beings who at the seats of all Tathagatas as numerous as the sands of eight Ganges aspire to Enlightenment and, in this evil world, do not slander, but uphold, reicte, and copy this sutra and also cause others to copy it, they themselves listening well to what is said in this sutra and making others listen well too, reciting and protecting, strongly upholding and - as they pity all beings - making offerings to this sutra, urging others also to make offerings, to honour, respect, recite, and worship it and thus perfectly understand and penetrate its meaning. "That is to say that the Tathagata is Eternal and Unchanging, that he is the utmost peace itself, and that" "all beings have the Buddha-Nature" ["buddhata"]. They well attain all the teachings of the Tathagata, make offerings to all such Buddhas and build up a house of unsurpassed Wonderful Dharma, uphold and protect it. If a person, for the first time, aspires to unsurpassed Enlightenment, know that such a person will assuredly, in the days to come, well build up the house of Wonderful Dharma, uphold and protect it. This you should know of the persons who become the guardians of

Dharma. Why? Because such persons will, in the days to come, surely protect Wonderful Dharma. "O good man! There may be an evil-minded bhiksu who, on hearing that I am now going to enter Nirvana, may not feel any apprehension or sadness, but instead will say: "The Tathagata is now entering Parinirvana. How pleasing is it that he does so! When the Tathagata was alive, he stood in the way of our profit. He is now entering Nirvana. Who else will get in our way? If nobody hinders [me], I shall come to profit as in former days. While in life, the Tathagata was too strict regarding the prohibitions. When he now enters Nirvana, we shall discard all of these. The kasaya [Buddhist robe] given me was originally simply meant as a matter of form. I will now discard it, as I would a banner the size of a head." Such a person slanders this Mahayana sutra and transgresses. "O good man! You, now, should uphold [this sutra] and think: "If beings are perfect in innumerable virtues, they will indeed believe in this Mahayana sutra and, having faith in it, will uphold it. There may also be other beings apart from these who may feel joy in Dharma, and if this sutra is widely expounded to such persons they will, after listening to it, well make away with all the sins amassed during past innumerable asamkhyas of kalpas. Those who do not believe in this sutra will, in this life, get attacked by innumerable illnesses and will be spoken ill of by all people. After [death], they will be disparaged by others. [In life] they will look ill and their finances will not go well. Or they may gain a little, but that will be very coarse and of bad quality. They will be poor and of low social rank, all their life long. They may gain life [get reborn] in families where slandering and evil relations obtain. The time comes when one must depart this life, when it may be the age of wars or when people may be taking up arms; or when emperors and kings may be practising tyranny; or enmity and vengeance may incessantly visit one. There may be a good friend [a good Buddhsit teacher], but they [i.e. those disbelievers in this sutra] will not have occasion to meet him. It will be hard for them to earn their living. They may gain to some extent, but the apprehension of hunger will bear down upon them. They will only be known to people of low standing, and kings and ministers will not look back [give them a second glance]. They may have occasion to talk with reason, but nobody will believe them. Such people do not go to good places. It is like a bird whose wings are broken. The same with such a person. In the life to come, he will not be able to gain a good place in the world of man or heaven. If one well believes in such a Mahayana sutra as this, the rough and coarse form that one may have had at birth will come to look right and correct, by virtue of the power of the sutra; dignity and colour will increase day by day, and man and god will be pleased to look at him. They will respect and love him, and not a moment will be lost in their regard of him. Kings, ministers and family people will listen to, respect and believe him. If any of my sravaka disciples are desirous of doing the first rare thing [most rare act], they should preach such a Mahayana sutra to all the world. O good man! Frost and mist may strongly desire to remain as they are, but this is only up until the time of the sunrise. Once the sun is out, all goes away and nothing remains behind. O good man! The evil acts done by these people also amount to the same. The power [which one may have] in the present life only continues up to seeing the rise of the sun of Great Nirvana. When the sun of this Great Nirvana has risen, all the evils that have been done will die out. Also, next, O good man! For example, one might abandon one's home, shave one's head, put on the kasaya robe, and might not yet receive the ten precepts of a shramana. Or a rich person might come and invite all the priests [to his house], and those who have not received the precepts may get invited, along with the others. They may not have received the precepts as yet, and yet may still be counted as priests. O good man! It is like this with a person who first aspires to Enlightenment, studies this Mahayana Great Nirvana Sutra, keeps, copies and recites it. He may not yet have attained the level of the ten stages [of a Bodhisattva], and yet he will be counted as being one of those of the ten stages. If a person, whether a disciple or not, [even] out of greed or fear or for profit, [chances to] hear just one gatha of this sutra and, having heard it, does not slander it - know that this person is already close to unsurpassed Enlightenment. O good man! For this reason, I say that the four persons will become the refuges of the world. Thus I say, O good man, that such persons will never say that what the Buddha said is not what he said. Nothing of the kind occurs. That is why I say that such four kinds of people become the refuges of the world. O good man! Make offerings to these four kinds of people." "O

World-Honoured One! How am I to know who such are, and how am I to make offerings?" The Buddha said to Kasyapa: "Anyone who upholds and protects Wonderful Dharma should be invited.

"To any person versed in Dharma,
No matter whether young or old,
Offerings should be made;
One should respect and worship him,
As the Brahmin worships fire.
To anyone versed in Dharma, young or old,
Offerings should be made.
Such a person should be respected and worshipped,
As all devas serve Shakra."

Bodhisattva Kasyapa said to the Buddha: "Things must proceed as you, the Buddha, say, and we should pay respect to teachers and elders. I have a doubt, which you will [perhaps] kindly dispel for me. If there is an aged person who has long been upholding the precepts and who asks a young person to tell him what he has not heard before - does this [young] person have to be given respect? If so, this cannot be an upholding of the precepts. Or, there may be a young person who has been upholding the precepts and who may ask about what he has not heard from a person who has broken the precepts. Has one to pay respect to such a person? Or, a world-fleeing person might give ear to what a layman says regarding things he has not heard before. Should one pay respect to such a person? The obverse of this would be that the world-fleeing person should not pay respect to the layman, but the young and small should pay respect to the aged, because these aged persons have received the upasampada earlier and their deportment is accomplished. Hence one should pay them respect and make them offerings. According to the Buddha, violation of the precepts is not permitted in the house of the Buddha. It is as in the case of a paddy-field grown over with panic-grass. Also, just as the Buddha says, there is one who abides in Dharma, to whom offerings must be made, whether that person is old or young, in such a way as people serve Shakra. How can these two cases be understood? Now, could it not be that those were false words of the Tathagata which stated that even the precept-obseving person may well transgress? Why does the Tathagata say such a thing? Also, the World-Honoured One says in other sutras that violation of the precepts can certainly be cured [atoned]. It is not easy to understand the meaning of suchlike [statements]." The Buddha said to Kasyapa: "O good man! I speak thus in the gatha for the sake of those Bodhisattvas of the days to come who will study Mahayana; I do not do so for the sake of sravakas. As I said above, when the days of Wonderful Dharma come to an end and when the right precepts are violated, when violation of the precepts increases in extent and when evil deeds go unchecked, when [saints] are hidden and not one is to be met with, when bhiksus accept or keep impure things and servants, there will appear one of these four who will shave his head and practise the Way. All the bhiksus [of that time] will receive and keep impure things and servants, knowing no difference between the pure and impure, rules and non-rules. This person, intending to teach such bhiksus, softens the light and does not get mixed up with evil and well knows what needs to be done and what the Buddha does. He sees others committing grave offences, yet he sits silent and does not take part [in such offences]. Why not? Because I appear in the world to establish and protect the right teaching. That is why I sit silently and do not reproach [the offenders]. O good man! Such a person, though violating [the rules], is not classed as one who violates the rules of a disciple, because of his protecting of the teaching. "O good man! A king dies from an illness, for example, and his son, the crown prince, is still young and not yet able to ascend the throne. There is a candala [a despised mixed-caste person, born of a Sudra father and Brahmin mother] who is rich and whose wealth is inestimable. He has many relatives. In the end, using force, he takes advantage of the weak condition of the state and usurps the throne. Before long, the people, upasakas, Brahmins and

One should abandon one's life [become a monk] and make offerings. This is as I say in my Mahayana sutra:

others revolt and flee to far-distant countries. There are people who do not flee, but who do not wish to see the king, such as the rich and the Brahmins who will not leave their native land, just like the trees, which grow where they find themselves and where they die. The candala king, seeing the subjects leaving the country, sends candala men to block all the roads. Also, after seven days, he has men beat drums and proclaim to all the Brahmins: "To any person who performs the ceremony of abhiseka [a consecration ceremony, involving sprinkling water on the head], half of the land will be given!" They hear this, but no Brahmin comes forward. All say: "How could a Brahmin do such a thing? " The candala king further says: "If no Brahmin comes to be my teacher, I shall assuredly make the Brahmins live, eat, sleep and work together with the candalas. If any Brahmin comes and sprinkles water on my head, I will give him half my land. As it is said, so shall it be done. Also, all-wonderful amrita [ambrosia], that thing of Trayastrimsa Heaven which works all the miracles of deathlessness, will also be given to such a man." At that time, there was the son of a Brahmin, one very young. He was perfect in pure actions, wore his hair long, and was well versed in incantations. He went to the king and said: "O great King! What you, King, say will all be carried out by me." The king was pleased and let this boy perform the abhiseka. All the Brahmins heard about this and were vexed. They reproached the boy, saying: "You, the son of a Brahmin! How could you perform the abhiseka on a candala?" Then the king gave the boy half of his kingdom. And together they reigned over the kigdom. A long time passed. Then the Brahmin boy said to the king: "I rejected my family tradition and came to you to become your teacher, and I taught you, King, all the intricate contents of incantation. And yet you do not befriend me." Then the king answered: "In what way do I not befriend you?" The Brahmin boy said: "I have not yet tasted the amrita which the late king left in your hands." The king said: "Well said! O my great teacher! I did not know. If you desire to use it, please take this [amrita] to your home." Then the Brahmin boy, at the king's word, took the amrita home and invited all the ministers, and partook of it. All the ministers, having had it, said to the king: "It is wonderful that the great teacher has the amrita." On hearing this, the king said to his teacher: "How

is it, O great teacher, that you taste the amrita with all the ministers and yet do not show any of it to me?" Then the Brahmin boy gave the king a poisonous potion. On taking the poison, the king became mad and fell to the ground. He lay there unconscious, like a dead man. Then the Brahmin boy called back the previous king, restored him to the throne and said: "The lion's seat [i.e. throne] cannot, by law, be occupied by any candala. I have not yet heard since of old that a candala ever sat on the royal throne. It can never be that a candala could reign over the state and govern the people. O great King! You should now succeed the former king and govern the state righteously and lawfully." Having thus disposed of things, he gave an antidote potion to the candala and let him awaken. After he had awoken, he was driven out of the country. Now, this boy, acting as he did, did not lose the prestige of the Brahmins. And others, on hearing of what had happened, praised his deed and said that this was a thing unheard of. They said: "Well done, well done! You have indeed got rid of the candala king." It is the same with me. O good man! After my entry into Nirvana, the Bodhisattvas who guard Wonderful Dharma will also act thus. Using expedient means, they will behave just like those priests who transgress against the precepts, who are priests only in name and who receive and store up impure things. And when they see a person who, though [seemingly] violating the precepts, nevertheless cures those evil bhiksus who are transgressing against the prohibitions, they will go to him, respect and worship him, and do all such things as offering the four things [i.e. clothing, drink, bedding, and medicine] and sutras and utensils. If these things are not ready at hand, they should devise means and go to danapatis, beg from them and then give [their gifts]. To do this, they may store up the eight impure things [i.e. such as gold, silver, manservants, maidservants, cows, sheep, grain, and storehouses]. Why? Because this can mend [the ways of] the evil-acting bhiksus. This is as in the case of the boy who conquered the candala. Then, the Bodhisattvas may again respect and worship this person. Though the person may also receive and store up the eight things, this can well pass by with impunity. Why? Because this Bodhisattva desires to reject and cure all wicked bhiksus and to enable the pure-hearted bhiksus to live in peace and to enable the vaipulya Mahayana sutras to prevail in the world and benefit heaven and earth. O good man! That is why I put the two gathas in the sutra and had all Bodhisattvas praise those who protect Dharma. This is similar to the upasakas and Brahmins who all praised the boy, saying: "Well done, well done!" The same will also apply to Dharma-protecting Bodhisattvas. Should anyone see a Dharma-protecting person working with precept-breaking persons, and say that that person is committing a sin, know that the person [who says this] is himself inviting

misfortune upon his own self, and that the person who protects Dharma has no connections with sin. O good man! If any bhiksu breaks the precepts and, out of arrogance, does not repent, such is really a breach of the prohibitions. A Bodhisattva who, while committing a violation, does so to protect Dharma, is not called one who commits a violation. Why not? Because he has no arrogance, but confesses and repents. That is why I repeat in the sutra and say in the gatha:

"If there is a person who knows Dharma,
Whether that person is old or young, such a one should be revered,
Respected and worshipped, just as in the case
Of the Brahmins who pay worship to fire and serve
Shakra of the second heaven [i.e. Trayastrimsa]."

On account of this, not for those wishing to learn the sravaka teaching, but for Bodhisattvas do I speak thus in the gatha." Bodhisattva Kasyapa said to the Buddha: "O World-Honoured One! If it is the case that the Bodhisattva-mahasattva may thus act without restraint as regards the precepts, can the shila [precepts] originally received remain intact and genuine?" The Buddha said: "O good man! Do not speak thus. Why not? The shila first received remains intact and is not forfeited. If one transgresses, one repents. Having repented, one is pure. O good man! When a bank [riverbank, dam] is old and has holes in it, water inevitably leaks out. Why? Because nobody has had it repaired. When once repaired, water cannot leak out. It is the same with the Bodhisattva. When shila is violated, there follows posadha [confession], receiving [anew] shila, and the hours of freedom come. The monastic duties are carried out, but the vinaya rules are not as in the case of the bank with holes in it through which water leaks out. Why not? If there is no one who upholds shila, the size of the Sangha will decrease and there will come about moral laxity and indolence, which will grow. If there are those who are pure in their deeds and who observe the precepts, the original shila remains perfect and holds good. O good man! A person who is loose [careless] in the Vehicle [i.e., overall direction of Mahayana Buddha-Dharma] is [indeed] loose, and a person who is loose regarding the precepts is not loose. The Bodhisattva-mahasattva is not loose regarding the teachings of this Mahayana [i.e. awakening to the real state of existence]. This is the observance of the precepts. He guards well Wonderful Dharma

and bathes himself in the waters of Mahayana. Thus, though the Bodhisattva violates the precepts, he is not [truly] loose as regards the precepts." Bodhisattva Kasyapa said to the Buddha: "There are four kinds of people in the Sangha. It is as with the mango, where it is difficult to know when it is ripe. How can we know the difference between a violation and a non-violation of the precepts?" The Buddha said: "O good man! Basing oneself on the all-wonderful Great Nirvana Sutra, it is easy to know. How can one know by looking into the Great Nirvana Sutra? As an example: a farmer plants rice, and weeds out the tares [weeds] in the paddy-field. One looks at the field with the fleshly eye and says that it is a fine field. But when harvesting comes around, we now see that the tares and rice are different. Thus, eight things indeed defile the priest. If thoroughly done away with, we see that he is pure. When a person observes the precepts and does not violate them, this is hard to distinguish with the fleshly eye. If evil arises, this is easy to see. It is as in the case of the tares in the paddy-field, which can easily be seen. The same with the bhiksu. If he is able to make away with the eight impure poisonous serpents, we call him pure and a holy field of weal. He will be made offerings by man and god. It is not easy to see the karma-results of pure deeds clearly with the fleshly eye. "Also, next, O good man! [Imagine that] there was a forest of kalaka [bambusa vulgaris]. The trees were numerous, among which there was one called tinduka [diospyros embryoteris]. The fruits of the kalaka and tinduka look alike, and it is difficult to distinguish them one from the other. When the

- 76 -

fruit was ripe, a woman picked it all. Only one part was tinduka, ten parts being kalaka. The woman, not knowing [the difference], took these to the market and spread them out for sale and sold them. Dull-minded people and children, not knowing [such] things well, bought the kalaka, ate it and died. A learned person heard about this and asked the woman: "O woman! Where did you get this from?" At that, the woman pointed out the direction. Everybody said: "In that direction, there are innumerable kalaka trees; only one is tinduka." All the people, learning of this, laughed, cast away the fruit and went away. The case is thus. "O good man! It is the same with the eight impure things regarding beings. Amongst people, there are many who take eight such things. Only one is pure, he who observes the precepts and does not take the eight impure things. He knows well that all people receive and store up things contrary to the precepts, and yet he acts together [with them] and does not leave them. He is like the one tinduka amongst all the trees in the forest. There is an upasaka who sees bhiksus all transgressing. So he does not pay respect or make offerings along with [the other people]. If this person does desire to offer something [however], he first asks: "O great ones! Is it right to receive and store up eight such things? Are these things which the Buddha has permitted or not?" If the answer is that the Buddha has permitted them, he will ask: "Can you attend the posadha and pravarana?" Thus does this upasaka ask. At this, all answer: "The Tathagata pities and permits us eight such things." Then, the upasaka says: "In Jetavana, there were many bhiksus who said that the Buddha had permitted the possession of gold and silver, or that he did not. If any bhiksus said that the Buddha had permitted [such things], those persons in the "not permitted" camp did not live together [with those who said gold, etc. was permitted], did not talk [with them] about the precepts, or confess [to them], or drink the water of the same river and did not share with those others what brought in profit. How can you say that the Buddha gave permission? The Buddha, the god of all gods, may well receive such, but you, the Sangha, may not." If there are those who receive such, do not talk about the precepts [with them], or confess or do karman [the ritualistic actions of a bhiksu when receiving shila or making confession], but act as the Sangha should act. If one talks together [with the unrighteous monks] about shila, confesses [to

them], or does karman, and thus participates in the works of the Sangha, one will, after death, assuredly fall into hell. This is like all those who lost their life through eating the kalaka. "Also, next, O good man! For example, there is in the city a drug merchant. He has a wonderfully sweet medicine which comes from the Himalayas. He also sells many other drugs. All of them taste sweet and look alike. People very much desire to buy [the drugs], but cannot distinguish [the different types]. They go to the druggist and ask: "Do you sell the drug from the Himalayas?" The druggist says: "Yes!" A man picks up a drug which is not the one from the Himalayas. The merchant cheats the customer and says to him: "This is the sweet drug that I have from the Himalayas." But the buyer is unable to tell the difference. He buys it and takes it back home, thinking: "I have got the drug from the Himalayas." The situation is like that.

"O Kasyapa! Among the sravaka priests, there are those who are priests in name only, and there are the true ones, or those who stick together in harmony; also, those who observe the precepts and those who violate them. All will be made offerings, will be respected and worshipped. But this upasaka cannot, just by looking, make out which is which. This is like the situation of the man who could not see whether the drug he had was from the Himalayas. Who are the ones who observe, and who those who violate, the precepts? Who is a true priest, and who a priest in name only? One with the heavenly eye can well see this. O Kasyapa! If this upasaka knows that [such-and-such] a person is one who transgresses, he will not give him anything, bow or worship him. If he knows that [such-and-such] a person receives and stores the eight impure things, he will not give what he has, not worship or make offerings. Any [bhiksu] who violates the precepts should not be respected or worshipped just because of the kasaya-robe which he wears." Bodhisattva Kasyapa said to the Buddha: "Well said, well said! What the Tathagata says is true, not false. I shall accept [your] word with the greatest respect, for example, just as if I had received an adamantine treasure. Just as the Buddha says, these bhiksus should stand [base themselves] on four things. "What are the four? They should be based on Dharma, not the person; on the meaning, not the letter; on Wisdom, not on consciousness; on import-embracing sutras, not on non-import-embracing sutras. They should well know these four things, but not four such persons." The Buddha said: "Being based on Dharma means nothing other than basing oneself on the Mahaparinirvana of the Tathagata. All Buddhist teachings are none but "Dharmata" [essence of Dharma, essence of Reality]. This "Dharmata" is the Tathagata. Hence, the Tathagata is Eternal and Unchanging. Any person who says that the Tathagata is non-eternal does not know "Dharmata". Such a person is not one to base oneself upon. All the four persons mentioned above appear in the world, protect, realise and become a refuge [for all beings]. Why? Because they thoroughly understand the deepest points of what the Tathagata says and know that the Tathagata is Eternal and Unchanging. It is not good to say that the Tathagata is non-eternal and that he changes. "The four persons, when they are such, are the Tathagata. Why? Because such well understand and speak about the undisclosed words of the Tathagata. One who well understands what is deeply hidden and knows that the Tathagata is Eternal and Unchanging will never, for profit, say that the Tathagata is non-eternal. Such a person is one to base oneself upon - why not on those four persons? "Basing oneself upon Dharma means basing oneself upon "Dharmata"; not basing oneself on man refers to the sravaka. "Dharmata" is the Tathagata, and the sravaka is the created. The Tathagata is Eternal, but the sravaka is non-eternal. "O good man! A man might violate the precepts and, for gain, say that the Tathagata is non-eternal and that he changes. Such a person is not one to take refuge in. O good man! This is a definite rule. "We say that we base ourselves on the meaning, not the words. The meaning connotes being fully Enlightened. Full Enlightenment means non-weak. Non-weak is satisfaction. Satsfaction means that the Tathagata is Eternal and Unchanging. That the Tathagata is Eternal and Unchanging means that Dharma is eternal. That Dharma is eternal mens that the Sangha is eternal. This is basing oneself on the meaning. Do not base yourself on the words. What words are we not to base ourselves on? These are discursive and decorative words. They [people sticking to the letter, rather than the spirit] seek out all too greedily and unendingly all the innumerable sutras of the Buddha. Wickedly, skilfully and flatteringly, they cheat and put on the semblance of friendliness, and displaying thus, they seek profit. Garbed in white, they take up posts [run errands]. They also loudly proclaim: "The Buddha allows the bhiksus to keep all [kinds of] menials and impure things, to trade in gold, silver, rare gems, to store rice, to trade in cows, sheep, elephants, and horses, and thus to seek profit. And also there may arise a famine, and out of pity for the children, the bhiksus may look for gain [profit], store things up, and put up in a house, prepare food by their own hand, and support themselves, instead of from receiving [the alms of others]." All such words are not to be depended upon. "We say that we base ourselves [depend] upon Wisdom and not upon consciousness. The Wisdom alluded to is the Tathagata. If any sravaka does not well understand the virtues of the Tathagata, such a consciousness is not to be depended upon. If he knows that the Tathagata is the Dharma-Body, such true Wisdom can indeed be depended upon. If a person sees the expedient body of the Tathagata and says that it belongs to the five skandhas, the eighteen realms [i.e. the six sense-organs, the six sense-fields, and the six consciousnesses], and the twelve spheres [the six sense-organs and the six sense-fields], and that it arises from feeding, such is not to be depended upon. This means that even consciousness is not to be depended upon. If a sutra says thus, it cannot be depended upon. "We say that we should base ourselves on the import-embracing sutras [those which dig deep into the true spirit of Buddha-Dharma], and not on the non-import-embracing sutras. The non-import-embracing sutras are the sravaka vehicle. Hearing even the depth-plumbing storehouse of the Buddha-Tathagata, doubts raise their heads as regards all things and the person does not realise that this storehouse arises from the sea of great Wisdom, as in the case of a child who cannot distinguish one thing from another. This is the non-grasping of the meaning. "The attainment of the meaning is nothing other than the true Wisdom of the Bodhisattva. It flows forth from out of the unhindered great Wisdom of his mind, as with an adult, for whom there is nothing not known. This is attainment of the meaning. "Also, the sravaka vehicle is the non-grasping [non-understanding] of the [real] meaning, and unsurpassed Mahayana is the grasping of the meaning. If a person says that the Tathagata is non-eternal and that he changes, this indicates that this person has not yet arrived at [an understanding of] the meaning. If a person says that the Tathagata is Eternal and Unchanging, this shows that that person has arrived at the meaning. If a person says that what the sravaka says can be understood, this indicates non-grasping of the meaning. If a person says that the Tathagata is a product of feeding, this is non-grasping of the meaning. If a person says that the Tathagata is Eternal and Unchanging, this is full grasping of the meaning. If a person says that the Tathagata enters Nirvana as in the case of fuel that has burnt out, this is non-grasping of the meaning. If a person says that the Tathagata enters the world of "Dharmata", this is grasping the meaning. "We cannot depend upon the teaching of the sravaka. Why not? Because the Tathagata, through expediency, articulates the teaching of the sravaka just to save beings. This is like the rich man who teaches his son the alphabet. O good man! The sravaka vehicle is analogous to the situation where a person first tills his land, but has not yet arrived at the harvest. Such is the non-grasping of the meaning. For this reason, one cannot depend upon the sravaka vehicle. One should take refuge in the teachings of Mahayana. Why? In order to save beings, through expediency the Tathagata expounds Mahayana. Hence, one cannot depend. This is grasping the meaning. One should well know of these four things to depend upon. "Also, next, we say that we base ourselves upon meaning. Meaning is the honest mind. "Honest mind" means "light". Light means "non-weak". Non-weak is the Tathagata. "Also, "light" is Wisdom. The honest mind is the Eternal. The Eternal is the Tathagata. [Knowing] that the Eternal is the Tathagata is to depend upon Dharma. "Dharma is the Eternal. It also means boundless. It is hard to know. One cannot hold or bind it. And yet one may well see it. If a person says that he cannot see it, one cannot depend upon such a one. That is why we say that we can depend upon Dharma and not upon the person. "Also, if a person says that the all-wonderful world is non-eternal, such is not to be depended upon. That is why we base ourselves upon the meaning and not the words. To say that "true" depends upon "Wisdom" means that the Sangha is eternal, non-created, and unchanging, and that they do not store away the eight impure things. For this reason, we depend upon Wisdom and not on consciousness. If a person says that consciousness makes and consciousness receives, there is no harmony of the Sangha. Why not?

Now, harmony means non-possession. If it is non-possession, how could one say "eternal"? On account of this, consciousness is not to be depended upon.

"We say "meaning". "Meaning" means "being satisfied". This is never, to the end, seeking to cheat, to display deportment, pureness and with arrogance to show that one is of a high position, and thus greedily to seek profit. Also, it is not to show attachment to what the Tathagata says for reasons of expediency. This is arriving at the meaning. If a person abides in this, we may say that this person abides in "Paramartha-satya" [Ultimate Reality]. That is why we say that we base ourselves on the meaning of the sutras and not on the non-grasping of the meaning. "Non-grasping of the meaning relates to what is stated in the sutras saying that all can be snuffed out, all is non-eternal, all is suffering, all is void, and all is selfless. This is non-grasping of the meaning. How so? Because such a person is not able to grasp the intended meaning, only the appearance of [literal] meaning. This causes all beings to fall into Avichi Hell. Why? Because of attachment, as a result of which a person does not grasp the meaning. "A person [might] say that all gets extinguished, implying that the entrance of the Tathagata into Nirvana constitutes extinction. "A person [might] say that all is non-eternal, meaning that even Nirvana is non-eternal, and the same with suffering, void, and non-self too. That is why we say that such is non-grasping of the import of the sutras. One cannot depend upon such. O good man! There might be a person who says that the Tathagata, pitying all beings, looks to what is apt for the occasion. As he knows what is right for the occasion, he speaks of what is light as heavy and what is heavy as light. The Tathagata knows that all his disciples are supplied with whatever they need by danapatis. So the Buddha does not allow such persons to receive or keep menials, male or female, gold, silver and gems, or to trade in impure things. When the disciples are not thus supplied by danapatis, as when there is a famine and food is scarce, he allows them, for the purpose of establishing and protecting Wonderful Dharma, to receive menials, male or female, gold, silver, vehicles, fields, houses and rice, and to trade in what they have. Although one is allowed to receive and keep such things, these must be given by faithful danapatis. Then, all such four things are what can be depended upon. If the precepts, abhidharma and sutras do not differ from these four, one may depend upon these. If a person says that there are times and non-times, Dharma to be protected and Dharma not to be protected, and that the Tathagata allows all bhiksus to receive and keep such impure things, such should not be depended upon. If the precepts, abhidharma and sutras agree with these, such three cannot be depended upon. I speak about these four things for the sake of all beings with fleshly eyes, but it is not for those who have the eye of Wisdom. That is why I speak about these four things and say that they are the things to be depended upon. "Dharma" is "Dharmata"; "meaning" is saying that the Tathagata is Eternal and Unchanging; "Wisdom" is knowing that all beings have Buddha-Nature ["Buddhata"]; "grasping the meaning" means being well versed in all Mahayana sutras."

Chapter Nine: On Wrong and Right

Then Kasyapa said to the Buddha: "O World-Honoured One! Are we to depend upon the four kinds of people mentioned above?" The Buddha said: "It is thus, it is thus! O good man! What I say can be depended upon. Why? Because there are four Maras. What are the four? It looks [seems, appears] as though people hold the sutras and precepts of what Mara has said." Bodhisattva Kasyapa said to the Buddha: "O World-Honoured One! You, the Buddha, say that there are four Maras. How can we distinguish what Mara says from what the Buddha says? There are people who behave as Mara says and those who follow what the Buddha says. How are we to know these [apart]?" The Buddha said to Kasyapa: "Seven hundred years after my entering Parinirvana, this Marapapiyas will spoil my Wonderful Dharma. It is like a hunter donning priestly garb. Marapapiyas will also act thus. He will present himself in the form of a bhiksu, bhiksuni, upasaka or upasika. Or he may display himself as a srotapanna or any other grade up to arhat. Or he may display himself as a living Buddha. The created body of the king Mara will present itself as a non-created body, thus violating Wonderful Dharma. When violating Wonderful Dharma, this Marapapiyas will say: "The Bodhisattva, once, left Tushita Heaven and came down to this earth, to the castle of Kapilavastu, and lived in the palace of Suddhodana. By the conjoint carnal desires of father and mother, he gained birth and manhood. A man, born amongst men, can never be respected by all heaven and earth." "He will also say: "In the long past, he underwent penance, offered up his head, eyes, marrow, state, wife and children. Because of this, he attained Enlightenment. As a result, he is now respected by man and god, gandharva, asura, kimnara and mahoraga." If any sutras or vinayas say thus, know that they are all nothing but what has come out of the mouth of Mara. O good man! The sutras and vinayas may say: "It is already a long, long time ago that the Tathagata perfected Enlightenment. He now attains Enlightenment, all to save beings. He thus shows himself as being born from the conjoint carnal desires of father and mother. He manifests thus just to accord with what applies in the world." Know that any such sutra or vinaya is truly from the Tathagata. Any person who follows what Mara says is the kindred of Mara; a person who follows the word of the Buddha is a Bodhisattva. "Any person who says that it is unbelievable that the Buddha walked seven steps in the ten directions when he was born is one who but follows what Mara says. If a person says that the Tathagata walked seven steps in the ten directions when he was born, all this to manifest himself expediently, such a person stands on [bases his words on] the sutras and vinayas which the Tathagata has delivered. Any person who follows what Mara says is kindred to Mara. Anyone who follows what the Buddha has said is a Bodhisattva. "Or a person might say that when the Bodhisattva was born, his father, the King, sent men to the heavenly shrines, at which the gods, on seeing him, all came down and worshipped him. Hence, he is the Buddha. Then someone will commit slander and say: "Heaven appeared first and the Buddha later. How could the heavens worship the Buddha?" Whatever is said like this is nothing but the word of Marapapiyas. If any sutra says that the Buddha went to where the devas were and that all such gods as Mahesvara, Great Brahma and Sakrodevanamindra, folding their hands and touching the Buddha's feet with their heads, worshipped him, such a sutra or vinaya is from the Buddha. Any person who follows what Mara says is the kindred of Mara. Any person who follows what the Buddha says is a Bodhisattva. "If any sutra or vinaya says that the Bodhisattva, when as yet a crown prince, had wives [concubines] all around out of carnal desire, lived in the depths of the palace [i.e. in the harem] and fully tasted the five desires and enjoyed himself, such is a sutra or vinaya of Marapapiyas. Any sutra or vinaya that says: "The Bodhisattva had long since abandoned all desires, wife and son, and did not receive [in attachment] the wonderful desires of Trayastrimsa Heaven, but abandoned these as though they were spittle and tears. How could he have human desires? He shaved his head, became a priest, and practised the Way." Such are the sermons of the Buddha. Any person who follows the sutras and vinayas of Mara is the kindred of Mara; any person who follows the sutras and vinayas of the Buddha is a Bodhisattva. "If a person says that the Buddha, in Sravasti, at the Jetavana vihara, permitted all bhiksus what they wanted to have, such as male or female servants, pages, cows, sheep, elephants, horses, donkeys, mules, hens, cats, gold, silver, beryl, pearls, crystals, musaragalva, agate, coral, amber, horse-shoe shell, jade, copper, or iron kettles, big or small copper basins; that they were allowed to till the land, sow seeds and plant, sell or barter things, that they were permitted to store rice, that the Buddha pitied the bhiksus and allowed them all such things out of his compassion - all such sutras and vinayas are those of Mara. "Or someone might say that the Buddha stayed in Sravasti, at the Jetavana vihara, where the nirdara demon lived, and, relative to a Brahmin called Kuteitoku and King Prasenajit, said: "O Bhiksus! You should not receive gold, silver, beryl, crystals, pearls, musaragalva, agate, coral, amber, horse-shoe shell, jade, male or female domestic servants, pages, boys, girls, cows, sheep, elephants, horses, donkeys, mules, hens, pigs, cats, dogs or other animals; iron or copper kettles, big or small basins, sheets of various colours, and beds; or such necessary things or [do such] activities of [worldly] life as: [building] houses, tilling the soil, sowing seed, selling things in the market-place, making meals with your own hands, polishing or pounding with your own hands, doing incantations for a living, training hawks, looking at the constellations, working charms, guessing at the waxing and waning of the moon, telling a man or woman's fortune, saying good or bad things about a person's dreams, guessing or foretelling and saying that this is a man or woman, or saying that this is not a male or this is not a female, talking about the 64 marks of excellence [said to exist in the houses of the tirthikas], or saying that there are 18 dharanis [spells] by which people can be led astray; or talking about any of the arts, any worldly things, using powdered incense, curna [for strewing on seats, stupas, etc.], smearing incense [for the hands and body to give off a pleasant aroma], fumigating incense, using various kinds of leis [bronze wine-vessels], [practising] the arts of hairdressing, cunningly cheating and flattering, and thus greedily seeking profit, loving stupid and noisy quarters, joking and laughing, [walking] and preaching. [Such bhiksus] greedily eat fish, make poisons, and rub in fragrant oils. They possess gem parasols and leather footgear. They make boxes, chests, fans, and various pictures and statues. They store up cereals and rice, big and small varieties of wheat and beans, and various

melons [seeds]. They come near [fraternise with consort with] kings, princes, ministers and all kinds of females, laugh loudly or sit silently. They entertain doubts regarding all things, talk a lot and talk carelessly; they like to wear good clothes, which may be long or short, lovely or unlovely, good or bad. They themselves praise all such things in the presence of the giver. They frequent and roam about these dirty quarters, the places where one finds taverns, prostitutes and gamblers, all of which places I do not allow the bhiksus to be in. They should give up seeking the Way; they must be turned back to worldly life and used for labour [go out to work]. For example, this is like the tare in the paddy field, which has to be uprooted, so as not to be found any more. Know that what is prohibited in the sutras and vinayas constitutes the injunctions of the Tathagata. Any person who follows the word of Mara is the kindred of Mara; anyone who follows the word of the Buddha is a Bodhisattva. "Or a person might say: "The Bodhisattva goes to the temple of the devas to make offerings to such as Brahma, Mahesvara, Skanda and Katyayana. Why? He enters there merely to conquer the devas. Things can never be other than this." If it is said: "Even if the Bodhisattva gets into arguments with the tirthikas, he cannot know of their deportments, sayings and arts, and he cannot cause quarrelling servants to come to terms; he cannot be respected by males or females, kings or ministers; he does not know how to prepare medicines; that is why he is called "Tathagata". Whatever he knows is what is wicked; also, the Tathagata sees neither enemy or friend; his mind is all-equal; one may take a sword and cut him; or one could smear incense over his body, and he would not have any sense of gain or loss. He sits in the middle. This is why we say "Tathagata". Any sutra that says this is one of Mara's. "Or a person might say: "The Bodhisattva behaves thus: he goes into the houses of other teachings, teaches them to abandon domestic life and practise the Way, to come to know of deportment and manners; he teaches them to know of what is written and how arts are performed, and how one quells arguments and disputes. He is the highest of all people, boys and girls, people of the royal harem, the royal consorts, ordinary people, rich persons, Brahmins, kings, ministers, or the poor. Furthermore, he is respected by these and he also knows all such things. He may come across various views of life, and yet he does not entertain any loving [clinging] thought. This is like the lotus, which does not become soiled by defilement. In order to save beings, he practises various expedients and lives a worldly life."Any such sutras and vinayas are the sermons of the Tathagata. One who follows what Mara says is kindred to Mara; anyone who follows what the Buddha says is a great Bodhisattva. "Or a person might say: "The Tathagata expounded the sutras and vinaya to me. Of all the wicked sins, those [classed as] light and heavy and the sthulatyaya are all grave. In our vinaya, we do not commit these, to the end. I have long put forward such a Law, but you do not believe it. How could I throw away my own vinaya and come to your vinaya? Your vinaya is nothing but what Mara says. Ours is what the Buddha says. The Tathagata has already given the nine types of formulations of Dharma [i.e. Hinayana teaching]. Such nine formulations constitute our sutras and vinaya. I have never once heard of a sentence or word of the vaipulya sutras [i.e. the extensive sutras of Mahayana]. Where, in all the innumerable sutras and vinayas, do we come across the name of vaipulya sutra? In none of these have we ever heard of the ten types of sutras. If there are any such, they must surely be the work of Devadatta [the Buddha's malicious, jealous cousin]. Devadatta is a wicked person. In order to destroy good teachings, he makes up the vaipulya. We do not believe in any such sutras. This is what the sutras say. Why? Because they say this and that about the Buddhist doctrine. All such things are stated [only] in your sutras; ours do not contain any such [teachings]. In our sutras and vinayas, the Tathagata says: "After my entering Nirvana, there may come about, in evil ages, distorted sutras and vinayas. These are the so-called Mahayana sutras. In ages to come, there will be all such wicked bhiksus." I, then, say: "There are further the vaipulya sutras other than the nine types of sutras." A person who thoroughly accepts the signification says that he well understands the sutras and vinayas, segregates himself from all that is impure and is so delicate and pure that one could well compare him to the full moon. "If a person says: "The Tathagata gave explanations for each sutra and vinaya, as numerous as the sands of the river Ganges, but our vinaya does not contain any such. There is none such. If there are [such expositions], how is it that the Tathagata does not expound them in my vinaya? So, I cannot believe in them" - if a person speaks thus, know that this person is committing a sin. A person might further say: "Such sutras and vinaya [the Hinayana] I shall well uphold. Why? Because they are the cause of good doctrine, of being satisfied, of desiring little, of cutting off illusions, and one gains Wisdom and Nirvana." Any person who says so is no disciple of mine. If a person says: "The Tathagata gave us the vaipulya sutras so as to save beings", such a person is my true disciple. Any person who does not accept the vaipulya sutras is no disciple of mine. Such a person is not one who has become a priest because of the Buddhist teaching. Such a person is one wicked in mind and is none but a disciple of the tirthikas. Such sutras and vinayas as mentioned above are what the Buddha gave out. If not thus, they are nothing other than what Mara says. Any person who follows what Mara says is the kindred of Mara; anyone who follows what the Buddha says is a Bodhisattva. "Also, next, O good man! If it is said: "Since the Tathagata is not perfect in innumerable virtues, he is non-eternal and must change. He abides in the All-Void and expounds non-Self. This is not the way of the world", any such sutra or vinaya is of Mara. If a sutra says: "The true Enlightenment of the Tathagata is beyond knowing. Also, he is perfect in innumerable asamkhyas of virtues. Therefore, he is Eternal and there can be no change", any such sutra or vinaya is what the Buddha said. Any person who follows what Mara says is Mara's kindred. Any person who follows what the Buddha says is a Bodhisattva. "Or a person might say: "There is in the world a bhiksu who, not committing any parajika [the gravest of offences], is held by the world to have transgressed, like cutting down the tala tree". But in truth, this bhiksu did not transgress. Why not? I always say: "The case of one who commits any one of the parajikas is like cutting a stone in two: it can never again become one." If a person says that he has obtained what supercedes man's power [Pali: "uttarimanussadhamma"], he commits parajika. Why? Because he has not actually attained anything, yet pretends to have done so [i.e. he is telling lies]. Any such person retrogresses from the world of man and the Doctrine. This is a parajika. There is a bhiksu who desires little, feels contented, upholds the precepts, is pure and sits in a quiet place. The king or minister sees this bhiksu and says that he has attained arhatship, steps forward, praises, respects and worships him. Also, he says: "Such a great master will attain unsurpassed Enlightenment, having thus abandoned life." The bhiksu hears this and says to the king: "I have, truth to tell, not yet attained the fruition of a shramana. O King! Please do not speak to me about the dharma of non-satisfaction [noncontentment]. If one acquiesces when told that one will reach as far as unsurpassed Enlightenment, this is nothing but not knowing contentment. If I were to accept your statement and agree, I should surely purchase the reproaches of all Buddhas. To feel contented is the virtue that is praised by all Buddhas. That is why I mean pleasingly [happily] to practise the Way to the end of my life and attain a state in which I can feel satisfied. Also, to feel satisfied is to know that I have definitely attained the fruition of the Way. You, King, say that I have attained it. I do not accept your word. Thus I am satisfied." Then the king said: "O great teacher! You truly have attained arhatship and do not differ from the Buddha." Then the king made it known to all those in and out, and to those of the royal harem and to the royal spouse, that this person had attained arhatship. As a result, all who heard this felt respect, made offerings, and honoured him. Such a person is pure in his deeds. Hence, he makes all others gain great benefit, and truly this bhiksu did not commit any parajika. Why not? Because he went before others, entertained joy in his own mind, praised and made offerings. How could any such bhiksu have committed a sin? If it is said that this person has sinned, know that such a sutra is from Mara. Also, there is a bhiksu who speaks about the great depths of the undisclosed sutras of the Buddha, saying that all beings have Buddha-Nature, that by this nature they cut off [all] the innumerable billion illusions and thereby attain unsurpassed Enlightenment, except for the icchantika. Then, the king or minister listens and says: "O Bhiksu! Have you attained Buddhahood or not? Do you have Buddha-Nature or not?" The bhiksu replies: "I must have Buddha-Nature within me. I cannot, however, be clear as to whether I shall attain it [Enlightenment] or not." The king says: "O great one! If you do not become an icchantika, there is no doubt that you will attain Buddhahood." The bhiksu says: "Yes, it must truly be as you, King, say." This person says that he must surely have Buddha-Nature. Yet, he does not commit parajika [by saying so]. Also, there is a bhiksu who, at the time he is ordained, thinks to

himself: "I shall assuredly attain unsurpassed Enlightenment." Such a man may not yet accomplish unsurpassed Enlightenment. But he gains incalculable, boundless weal and it is difficult to appraise it. If anyone says that this person has committed parajika, then there cannot be any person who has not committed parajika. Why not? Because, once, 80 million kalpas ago, I had already segregated myself from all defilement. I had little desire, felt contented, was accomplished in deportment, practised the unsurpassed Dharma of the Tathagata, and myself surely knew that I had Buddha-Nature. Hence I attained unsurpassed Enlightenment and I can be called "Buddha". And there is great compassion. Such a sutra or vinaya is a sermon of the Buddha. Any person who cannot act in accordance [with such] is a kindred of Mara; one who acts in accordance is a great Bodhisattva. "Or a person might say: "There cannot be anything such as the four grave offences, the thirteen samghavasesas, the two aniyatans, the 30 naihsargika-prayascittikas, 91 payattikas, four ways of repentance, various ways of learning, seven ways of adhikarana-samatha, and also there can be no sthulatyayas, no five deadly sins, and no icchantikas. Should a bhiksu violate all such shilas and fall into hell, all tirthikas would be born in heaven. Why? Because they do not have any precepts to transgress against. This shows that the Tathagata means to frighten people. That is why he gives out these precepts. The Buddha has said that when the bhiksus desire to satisfy their carnal desires, they should take off their priestly garb, put on worldly dress and do so. A person might also think that carnal, lustful desire is no sin, that even in the days of the Tathagata there was a bhiksu who satisfied carnal lust and yet attained right emancipation; or that there was one who, after death, got born in heaven; that all such things have a precedent and that it is not just what I alone am doing. One may commit the four grave offences, the five deadly sins and all impure acts, and even then one can [still] attain true and right emancipation. The Tathagata may say that if one commits duskrta acts [minor offences, punishable by confession], one falls into hell and will remain there for 8 million years, which is the number of years of the sun and moon of Trayastrimsa Heaven. But this is what the Tathagata says to frighten people. They say that no difference exists between the grave and light [sin], the parajika [serious sin] and the duskrta [venial sin]. All these vinaya teachers falsely say that all these [rules] were instituted by the Buddha. Know definitely that these were not instituted by the Buddha." All such sutras and vinayas that say thus are from Mara. "Or a person might say that if one transgresses against even the smaller or minutest of all precepts, an evil fruit will come forth and that there is no limit to the number of karmic consequences. Realising this, one should guard one's self like the tortoise, who hides his six limbs in his shell. If there is any person versed in the vinaya who says, "One transgresses, but no karmic consequences ensue", one should not approach such a person, as already indicated by the Buddha:

"One thing overstepped,
This is mrsavada [telling lies].
If one sees no after-life,
There is no sin that will not be committed."

For this reason, one should not come near to such a person. What is pure in this Buddhist teaching is thus. And could it be that one who has violated the sthulatyaya, the samghavasesa and the parajika can pass as not having sinned? Because of this, one should be on guard and protect such Dharma. If not guarded against, where can there be any prohibition? I now say in the sutras: "For any commissions of the four grave offences or any small duskrtas, one should take pain to remedy such. If one does not guard against [transgressing] the prohibitions, what possibility can there be of seeing the Buddha-Nature? "All beings possess the Buddha-Nature. Only by observing the precepts can one see it. When one sees the Buddha-Nature, one attains unsurpassed Enlightenment. In the nine types of sutras, there is no vaipulya sutra. That is why they do not speak about the Buddha-Nature. Although these sutras do not refer to it, there is assuredly the vaipulya in them." One who speaks thus is my true disciple." Bodhisattva Kasyapa said to the Buddha: "O World-Honoured One! We do not see in the nine types of sutras any references to beings possessing the Buddha-Nature, which you say they have. If we say that they have this, might it not be that we are guilty of infringing the parajika?" The Buddha said: "O good man! They [who say thus] do not violate the parajika. For example, O good man! If any person says that in the great ocean there are only the seven gems, not the eight, that person has not sinned. If a person says that there is no mention of Buddha-Nature in the nine types of sutra, there cannot be any commission of sin [here]. Why not? I say that in the Mahayana ocean of great Wisdom there is the Buddha-Nature. As the two vehicles do not know or see [this], there can be no talk of [their] having committed any sin, even if they say that it does not exist. Such a thing is what the Buddha alone knows and what sravakas and pratyekabuddhas cannot know. O good man! Not having ever heard of the great depths of the undisclosed Dharma of the Tathagata, how can a person be expected to know of the existence of the Buddha-Nature? What is the undisclosed storehouse? It is none other than the vaipulya sutras. O good man! There may be tirthikas who talk about the eternal self or the "not-is" of the self. The case is not thus with the Tathagata. He says that there is the Self, or - at other times - that there is not. This is the Middle Path. "Or a person might say: "The Buddha talks about the Middle Path. All beings possess Buddha-Nature. As illusion overspreads [them], they do not know or see. Thus, an expedient is applied to cut the roots of illusion." A person who speaks thus does not commit the four grave offences. This we should know. Any person who does not speak thus infringes the parajika. "Or a person might say: "I have already attained unsurpassed Enlightenment! Why? Because I have the Buddha-Nature. Any person possessing the Buddha-Nature has assuredly attained unsurpassed Enlightenment. Consequently, I attain Enlightenment." Then, one should know, such a person infringes the parajika. Why so? There surely is the Buddha-Nature. But not yet having practised the best expedient of the Way, the person has not yet seen it. Having not yet seen it, there can be no attaining of unsurpassed Enlightenment. O good man! On this account, the teaching of the Buddha is profound in its meaning and difficult to fathom." Bodhisattva Kasyapa said to the Buddha: "O World-Honoured One! A king asks: "How does a bhiksu get drawn to supramundane Dharma?" The Buddha said to Kasyapa: "A bhiksu may, for profit or food, flatter, state things wrongly or cheat, and say things such as: "How might all the world believe that I am truly a real bhiksu, so that I can thereby arrive at great profit and fame?" Such a bhiksu, because of the darkness of his mind, always thinks and prays: "I have not yet, in truth, arrived at the four attainments of a sravaka. How might I be able to make the world think that I have gained all of these? How might I be able to make upasakas and upasikas think of me as a sage who has fully perfected all the the true virtues?" Thus does he think. What is done is all for profit, not for the Way. In his goings and comings, in his going out and coming in, in moving forwards and standing still, he looks peaceful. In his manner of dress and of holding his bowl, the [monk-like] deportment is not lost. Alone, he sits in a lonely place and looks like an arhat. So people think: "This is the foremost of bhiksus. Fully exerting himself, he practises the Way of extinction." He thinks: "As a result of this, I will assuredly gain disciples. People will also certainly offer me clothing, food, drink, bedding, and medicine. All females will respect and love me." Any person who acts in this manner acts against the uttarimanussa-dhamma. "Also, there is a bhiksu who sits in a lonely place, desiring to build up unsurpassed Wonderful Dharma. Though no arhat, he intends to have others call him an arhat, a lovable bhiksu, a good bhiksu, and a quiet bhiksu. He thus effectively makes innumerable people arrive at faith. Hence, I let all the innumerable bhiksus befriend him like a relative. Through this, I can teach and make the precept-breaking bhiksus and upasakas and upasikas uphold the precepts. In consequence, Wonderful Dharma will be established, the unsurpassed meaning of the great principle of the Tathagata will shine forth and the vaipulya Mahayana teaching will be revered, thus emancipating all innumerable beings, so that they will come to know the light or heavy significations of the sutras and vinayas which the Tathagata has delivered. "Also, a person might say: "I now have the Buddha-Nature. There is a sutra which is called the storehouse of the Tathagata. In that sutra, I shall surely attain the Buddhist teaching and cut out innumerable billion bonds of illusion. I shall speak to innumerable upasakas: "You all have the Buddha-Nature. You and I sit together on the Path of the Tathagata and will attain unsurpassed Enlightenment and do away with all the innumerable bonds of illusion." One like this

does not violate the uttarimanussa-dhamma; he is a Bodhisattva. "One who commits duskrta will fall into hell for a period of 8 million years of the days of Trayastrimsa Heaven, and he will have to undergo punishment for the sins he has committed. How much worse will it be when he transgresses the sthulatyaya?" Thus does a person say. Should there be any bhiksu among those of the Mahahana gathered here who have violated the sthulatyaya, such is not to be befriended. "What are the sthulatyaya of the Mahayana sutras? For example, a rich man erects a Buddhist temple and adorns it with various garlands, and offers this to the Buddha. There is a bhiksu who, on seeing the thread which passes through the garland, takes it without asking. This is sthulatyaya. Whether knowingly or not, he violates in this manner. If, with a greedy [desirefilled] mind, one causes damage to a Buddhist stupa, this is sthulatyaya. One should not come near [associate closely with] a person who acts in this way. Or a king or minister, on seeing that a stupa is old and damaaged, and intending to have it repaired, makes offerings to the sharira [relics] and finds in it a rare gem, which he gives to a bhiksu. On gaining the gem, the bhiksu uses it as he wills. Such a bhiksu is one who is defiled and who will most possibly [probably] call forth quarrels. No good upasaka should approach such a bhiksu, make offerings or pay respect to him. Such a bhiksu is termed "rootless." Such a bhiksu is also termed "two-rooted" [bisexual]! Perhaps more accurately, hermaphrodite], or one in whom the root is indefinable. By indefinably-rooted is meant the case of a person whose body becomes that of a female when the desire to be female arises and becomes that of a male when the desire to be male arises. Any such bhiksu is "evil-rooted". He is neither male nor female, neither a bhiksu nor a lay-person. One must not come near such a bhiksu, nor make offerings to him or pay him respect. One who abides in the Buddhist teaching and the law of a bhiksu should have a sympathizing mind, protect and bring up [take care of] beings. Even to an ant, one must give the mind of fearlessness. This is a shramana's law. One segregates oneself from drinks and incense. This is the law of the shramana. One must not tell lies, nor should one think of lying. This is the law of the shramana. One does not cause a greedy mind [feeling of greed or desire] to raise its head. The same applies even in dreams. This is the law of the shramana."

Bodhisattva Kasyapa said to the Buddha: "O World-Honoured One! If a bhiksu becomes a captive of carnal lust in a dream, does this violate Dharma or not?" The Buddha said: "No. One should call up the thought of an evil smell against carnal desire. If no pure mind [inner mood of lust-free purity] ever raises its head, segregate the mind from the worry and love of the female. If in a dream one becomes captive to carnal lust, [one should] repent for the act when awake. One should abide in the thought of the bhiksu who, when going begging on his alms-round, receives offerings [with the attitude of disgust of one who] eats the flesh of his own son in the days of a famine. If carnal desire asserts itself, quickly discard such a thought. All such is the teaching of the Buddha's sutras and vinaya. One following what Mara says is the kindred of Mara; one who follows what the Buddha says is a Bodhisattva. "Or a person might say: "Stand on one leg, remain silent and say nothing, throw yourself into deep water or into fire, or jump from a high precipice, not fearing the steepness; take poison, fast, lie down on ashes, bind your legs, kill beings, and tell fortunes by directions and the way a person takes." Or a person might say: "The Tathagata allows candalas, rootless persons, hermaphrodites, indefinables, the decrepit to become ordained and to accomplish the Way." Such are the words of Mara. Or a person might say: "The Buddha has already permitted us to consume the five tastes of milk from the cow, oil and honey, except silken clothing and leather footwear, etc." Or a person might say: "The Buddha has already permitted the putting on of the maharanga, also the storing of all kinds of seeds. But all grass and trees have life. The Buddha, having spoken thus, enters Nirvana."

Should any sutra and vinaya say thus, know that such is what Mara says. I also do not permit one leg to be held up [i.e. standing on one leg, in the manner of some fakirs]. For Dharma, all such postures as walking, standing, sitting and reclining are permitted. Also, someone might say: "Take poison, fast, burn the body with fire, bind your hands and feet, kill people, divine directions and ways, make leather footgear decorated with white horse-shoe shell and ivory; the Buddha has permitted the storing up of seeds. Grass and plants have life. He has permitted the putting on of the maharanga." If a person says that the World-Honoured One has said this, such a person is the kindred of the tirthikas. Any person such as this is not my disciple. I have only permitted the five tastes of the cow, oil, honey, and also silken cloth. I say that the four great elements [earth, air, fire and water] do not have life. Should any sutra or vinaya say thus, such is what the Buddha has said. Any person who acts in accordance with the word of the Buddha is, one should know, my disciple. Any person who does not follow the word of the Buddha is a kindred of Mara. Any person who acts in accordance with the Buddha's sutras and vinaya is, one should know, a great Bodhisattva. O good man! I have now extensively, for your sake, thus spoken about the difference between what Mara says and what the Buddha says." Kasyapa said to the Buddha: "O World-Honoured One! I have now come to know the difference between the word of Mara and that of the Buddha. In consequence, I shall be able to fathom the depths of the Buddhist teaching." Then the Buddha praised Kasyapa and said: "Well said, well said, O good man! You have now clearly gained the meaning. You are clever and wise."

Chapter Ten: On the Four Truths

The Buddha also said to Kasyapa: "Noble Son! It is not appropriate to term suffering as the Noble Truth [of suffering]. Why is that? If one were to term suffering 'the Noble Truth of Suffering', then cattle, sheep, donkeys, horses and the denizens of hell would also have the Noble Truth [of Suffering]. Noble Son! Whoever thinks that the extremely profound [gambhira] domain/ sphere/ realm [visaya] of the Tathagata - the eternal, untransforming Dharmakaya [Body of Truth] - is a body nourished by food, such a person does not know of the virtues and power which the Tathagata possesses. This [i.e. such ignorance of the true nature of the Buddha] is 'suffering'. Why so? Due to ignorance. A person views Dharma as non-Dharma, and non-Dharma as Dharma. Know that this person will fall into the unfortunate realms and repeat birth and death. This will increase the bonds of illusion and worry will grow. If he comes to know that the Tathagata is Eternal, one with whom there comes about no change, or if he hears the word "eternal", he will obtain birth in heaven. And on gaining emancipation, he will actually see that the Tathagata is Eternal and Unchanging. When this is well seen, he will say: "I heard about this in the past. Now that I am emancipated, I know this. As I was ignorant regarding the Ultimate, I have been repeating birth and death to no end. Today, I am enlightened as regards true knowledge." If knowledge reaches this stage, this is truly practising suffering. There is much to profit from. One may well practise this, but if one does not know things to be thus, no profit will result. This is what is called knowing suffering. This is the noble truth of suffering. If one does not practise thus, this is suffering and not the noble truth of suffering. "We say "truth of the cause of suffering". A person does not truly know the Wonderful Dharma and receives what is impure. This is the case of menials. Non-Dharma is called Wonderful Dharma. A person annuls what is right and won't allow it to live. On account of this, that person does not know "Dharmata" [essence of Reality]. Not knowing this, he repeats birth and death and suffers greatly. He does not get born in heaven and gain right emancipation. If a person has deep Wisdom and does not transgress against Wonderful Dharma, he will in consequence be born in heaven and attain right emancipation. If a person does not know where suffering arises and says that there cannot be any Wonderful Dharma or what is Eternal, and that all turns to nothingness, that person, in consequence, will repeat transmigration for innumerable kalpas to come, suffering all kinds of sorrow. If a person says that Dharma is Eternal and that there is no change, this is knowing the cause, and this is the noble truth of the cause of suffering. If one does not so practise, this is the cause of suffering and not the noble truth of the cause. "We say "truth of the extinction of suffering". If a person practises many things [teachings] and the way of nothingness, this is non-good. Why so? Because this annuls all laws and breaks the true storehouse of the Tathagata. Any practice of this category is the practising of nothingness. One who practises the extinction of suffering acts against what all tirthikas do. If the practice of nothingness is the truth of extinction, there are tirthikas who also practise the teaching of nothingness; we must say that they too possess the truth of extinction. A person says: "There is the Tathagatagarbha [Buddha-Womb - the pristine mind under cover of illusion]. One cannot see this. But if one does away with all illusions, one may indeed enter." It is thus. By the raising of such a mind [i.e. by cultivating such an attitude of mind], one gains freedom in all things. If a person practises the Way of the hidden storehouse,   selflessness, and emptiness, such a person repeats birth and death for innumerable ages to come and suffers from sorrow. A person who does not do such practices may certainly, even though he might have illusion, soon do away with it. Why so? Because he well knows the undisclosed [secret, hidden] storehouse of the Tathagata. This is the noble truth of the extinction of suffering. Any person who practises extinction in such a way is my disciple. A person not practising the Way thus is one who practises emptiness. This is not the noble truth of extinction. "We say "noble truth of the Way". This is none but the treasures of Buddha, Dharma, Sangha, and right emancipation. All people say with an upside-down mind: "There is no Buddha, Dharma, Sangha, or right emancipation. Birth and death are like phantoms." They hold such views. As a result, they repeat birth and death through the three worlds [of Desire, Form, and Formlessness], suffering there greatly for a long time to come. If the person awakens and comes to see that the Tathagata is Eternal, that no change comes to him, and that the same applies to Dharma, Sangha, and emancipation, by this one thought the person obtains unmolested [unrestricted] freedom for innumerable ages to come and he may enjoy it as he wills. Why? Because once in the past, due to the four inversions, I took non-Dharma as Dharma and was met by innumerable karmic consequences. When I had made away with such a view, I attained true awakening to Buddhahood. This is the noble truth of the Way. Any person who says that the Three Treasures are non-eternal and holds this view of life, then this is a false way of practice and is not the noble truth of the Way. If a person practises the Way thus and has it [sees it] as Eternal, such a person is my disciple. He abides in the true view of life and practises the teaching of the Four Noble Truths." Bodhisattva Kasyapa said to the Buddha: "O World-Honoured One! I now, for the first time, know and practise the great depths of the Four Noble Truths."

Chapter Eleven: On the Four Inversions

The Buddha said to Kasyapa: "We speak of the "four inversions". "Inversion" is spoken of when we entertain the idea of suffering where there is no suffering. "Non-suffering" is the Tathagata. The idea of suffering arises when a person thinks that all Tathagatas are non-eternal and that they change. If a person says that the Tathagata changes, this is [the concept of] suffering and constitutes a great sin. If a person says that the Tathagata relinquishes this body of suffering and enters Nirvana, and that this is like fuel being all burned up, as a result of which the fire dies out, this is having the idea of suffering vis-à-vis non-suffering. This is an inversion [of the truth]. A person might say: "Saying that the Tathagata is Eternal is a Self-centred view. From this Self-centred view arise innumerable sins. Thus, one should say that the Tathagata is non-Eternal, and by [saying] this I shall gain Bliss." The Tathagata's being non-Eternal would entail suffering. If [there is] suffering, how could one expect [to find] Bliss therein? When the idea of Bliss occurs [in such a connection], we say "inversion". This is said because the thought of suffering arises in [what truly is] Bliss. Bliss is the Tathagata. Suffering is the non-Eternal of the Tathagata. If a person says that the Tathagata is non-Eternal, this is a thought of suffering in Bliss. The Tathagata's being Eternal is Bliss. If I say that the Tathagata is Eternal, how can I enter Nirvana? If I say that the Tathagata is non-suffering, how could I cast away my body and enter Nirvana? When a person has the thought of suffering in Bliss, we say that this is an inversion. This is the first inversion. "The idea of the Eternal vis-à-vis the non-Eternal, and the idea of the non-Eternal vis-à-vis the Eternal, are inversions. The non-Eternal is the non-practising of the Void. When one does not practise the Void, life is shortened. If one says: "Not practising the Void

and quietude, one attains eternal life", this is an inversion. This is the second inversion. "The thought of Self regarding non-Self, and the thought of non-Self regarding Self, are inversions. The people of the world say that there is Self, and within Buddhism, too, we say that there is Self. The people of the world say that there is Self, but there is no Buddha-Nature. This is having the idea of Self in [what is] non-Self. This is an inversion. "The Self spoken of in Buddhism is the Buddha-Nature." The people of the world say that there is no Self in Buddhism. This is the idea of the non-Self in the Self. "It is definite that there is no Self in the Buddhist teaching. That is why the Tathagata tells his disciples to practise selflessness." If such is said, this is an inversion. This is the third inversion. "The non-Pure in the Pure, and the Pure in the non-Pure, are inversions. The Pure relates to the Eternal of the Tathagata. It is not a food-supported body, not a body of illusion. It is not a carnal body, not a body made up of sinews and bones. If one says that the Tathagata is non-Eternal, a food-supported body, bound together by sinews and bones, and that Dharma, Sangha, and emancipation die out, this is an inversion. We say that the idea of the non-Pure in the Pure is an inversion. A person might say that there is not a whit of what is non-Pure in his mind, that as there is not a single thing that is not Pure, he gets into a place which is Pure, and that as the person practises the meditation of the non-Pure which the Tathagata spoke about, whatever was said above must be false. If a person speaks thus, this is an inversion. This is the fourth inversion." Bodhisattva Kasyapa said to the Buddha: "O World-Honoured One! I have now for the first time gained the right view. O World-Honoured One! Until now, all of us were those who abided in wrong thought."

Chapter Twelve: On the Nature of the Tathagata

Kasyapa said to the Buddha: "O World-Honoured One! Is there Self in the 25 existences or not?" The Buddha said: "O good man! "Self" means "Tathagatagarbha" [Buddha-Womb, Buddha-Embryo, Buddha-Nature]. Every being has Buddha-Nature. This is the Self. Such Self has, from the very beginning, been under cover of innumerable defilements. That is why man cannot see it. O good man! [Imagine that] there is a poor woman here. She has true gold concealed in her house. But none of the people of her house, whether big or small, know of it. But there is a stranger, who, through expediency, says to the poor woman: "I shall employ you. You must now go and weed the land!" The woman answers: "I cannot do this now. If you let my son see where the gold is hidden, I will soon work for you." The man says: "I know the way. I shall point it out to your son." The woman further says: "Nobody of my house, whether big or small, knows [of this]. How can you?" The man says: "I shall now make it clear." The woman says further: "I desire to see. Pray let me." The man digs out the gold that had lain hidden. The woman sees it, is gladdened, and begins to respect that person. O good man! The case is the same with the Buddha-Nature which man has. Nobody can see it. This is analogous to the gold which the poor woman possessed and yet could not see. O good man! I now let persons see the Buddha-Nature that they possess, which is overspread by defilements. This is analogous to the poor woman who cannot see the gold, even though she possesses it. The Tathagata now reveals to all beings the storehouse of Enlightenment, which is the Buddha-Nature, as it is called. If all beings see this, they are gladdened and will take refuge in the Tathagata. The good expedient is the Tathagata, and the poor woman is all the innumerable beings, and the cask of true gold is the Buddha-Nature. "Also, next, O good man! As an example: a woman has a child who, while yet very young, is seized by illness. Worried by this, the woman seeks out a good doctor. The good doctor comes and compounds three medicines, which are butter, milk, and rock candy. This he gives her, to have it taken by the child. Then he says to the woman: "When the child has taken the medicine, do not give any milk to the child for some time. When the medicine has

worked its way out, you may then give milk." Then the woman applies a bitter substance to her nipple and says to the child: "Do not touch it [i.e. her nipple]. My nipple is poisonous." The child is dying for the milk and wants to have it. [But] on hearing of the poison, it runs away. After the medicine has done its work, the mother washes her nipple, calls in her child and gives it [her nipple]. Although hungry, the child, having heard about the poison, will not come to it. The mother then says: "I only put poison on my nipple so as to give you the medicine. As you have already taken the medicine, I have washed the poison off. Come! Take my nipple. It is not bitter any more." On hearing this, the child slowly comes back and takes it. O good man! The case is the same with the Tathagata. In order to save beings, he gives them the teaching of non-Self. Having practised the Way thus, beings do away with the [cast of] mind that clings to self and gain Nirvana. All of this is to do away with people's wrong concepts, to show them the Way and cause them to stand above, to show them that they adhere to self, that what obtains in the world is all false and not true, and to make them practise non-Self and purify themselves. This is similar to the woman's applying a bitter substance to her nipple out of love for her child. It is the same with the Tathagata. For practising the Void, I say that all do not have the Self. This is like the woman's cleaning her nipple and calling for her child to partake of her milk. The case is the same with me, too: I speak of the Tathagatagarbha. For this reason, the bhiksus do not entertain fear. It is analogous to the child who hears its mother, slowly comes back and takes the milk. The situation is the same with the bhiksus. They should know well that the Tathagata hides nothing." Bodhisattva Kasyapa said to the Buddha: "O World-Honoured One! Really, there cannot be any case in which there is Self. Why not? When a child is born, it knows nothing. If there is a Self, the child would have to have knowledge when it is born into the world. Hence we can know that there is no Self. If a Self definitely existed, there could not be any loss of knowing. If it were true that all beings eternally possessed Buddha-Nature, there could be no breaking away. If there is no destruction, how can there be the differences of

Kshatriya, Brahmin, Vaishya, Sudra, candala, and animals? Now, the effects of karma are various, and differences exist in life. If there definitely is a Self, there cannot be any victory or defeat with beings. From this, we can definitely know that the Buddha-Nature is eternal Dharma. If the Buddha-Nature is definitely eternal, why do we say speak of such things as killing, stealing, lust, forked tongue, ill-speaking, lying, flattering, greed, hatred, and wrong views? If there really is eternally the nature of Self, why is it that a person becomes intoxicated or mad? If the nature of Self is eternal, the blind should be able to see, the deaf hear, the dumb talk, and the lame walk. If the Self is eternal, fire, great floods of water, poison, swords, evil persons and animals cannot [need not] be avoided. If the Self is eternal, what has basically changed cannot be forgotten or lost. If forgotten, how can a person say: "I have seen this person somewhere [before]"? If the Self is eternal, there cannot be old age or youth, no ups or downs, no remembering of what has passed away. If the Self is eternal, where does it abide or live? Is it the case that tears, spittle, blue, yellow, red, and white are to remain in all things? If the Self is eternal, it will fill the body as in the case of sesame seed, in which there is no space left in between. When the body is cut up into small pieces, the Self, too, would have to be cut up" The Buddha said to Kasyapa: "O good man! As an analogy: there is in the household of a king a great wrestler. He has an adamantine bead on his brow. This man wrestles with other wrestlers. When [once] the head of another person touches his brow, the bead goes into the wrestler's flesh, and there is no knowing where it is. A boil comes up there. A good doctor is called in to cure it. At that time, there is a good doctor with a bright mind. He knows well how to diagnose and prescribe medicine. Now, he sees that this boil has appeared due to the bead's having got into the wrestler's body. He realises that this bead has entered the flesh and remains there. Then, the good doctor asks the wrestler: "Where is that bead that was on your brow?" The wrestler is surprised and answers: "O great teacher and doctor! Has not the bead on my brow got lost? Where could the bead be now? Is this not a miracle [that you know about it]?" He is worried and weeps. Then, the doctor pacifies the wrestler: "Do not be over-concerned. When you fought, the gem entered your body. It is now under your skin and can be seen, looming up. As you fought, the poison of anger so burned that the gem got into your body and you did not feel it." But the wrestler does not believe the doctor's words. "If it is under my skin, how is it that it does not come out because of the impure pus and blood? If it is in my sinews, we cannot possibly see it. Why do you mean to cheat me?" Then, the doctor takes up a mirror and holds it in front of the wrestler's face. The gem appears clearly in the mirror. The wrestler sees it, is surprised and is all wonder. It is like that. O good man! The case is the same with all beings. They do not come near to a good teacher of the Way. So, they cannot see the Buddha-Nature which is within, even though they possess it. And they are reigned over by greed, lust, anger, and ignorance. So they fall into the realms of hell, animals, hungry ghosts, asuras, candalas, and get born in such various houses as Kshatriya, Brahmin, Vaishya and Sudra. The karma generated by the mind leads a person, though born a human, into such lives as a cripple, lame, deaf, blind or dumb person, and to the 25 existences, where such as greed, lust, anger and ignorance reign over the mind, and the person is unable to know of the presence of the Buddha-Nature. The wrestler says that the gem has gone away, even though it is [actually] in his body. The same with beings, too. Not having come into contact with a good teacher of the Way, they do not know the Tathagata's hidden treasure and do not study selflessness. For example, even when a person is told of the unholy self, he cannot know the true quality of the Self. The same is true of my disciples. As they do not befriend a good teacher of the Way, they practise non-Self and do not know where it [Self] is. They do not know the true nature of selflessness. How, then, could they know the true nature of the Self itself? Thus, O good man, the Tathagata says that all beings possess the Buddha-Nature. This is like the good doctor's making the wrestler see where the adamantine jewel rests. All these beings are reigned over by innumerable defilements and thus do not know the whereabouts of the Buddha-Nature. When illusion is dispelled, there arises knowledge and brightness. This is like the wrestler's seeing the gem in the mirror. O good man! It is thus the case that what rests undisclosed [latent] in the Tathagata is innumerable and is difficult for beings to think about. "Also, O good man! As an example, there is a medicine in the Himalayas called "pleasing taste". It tastes very sweet. It grows hidden under a deep growth of plants, and we cannot easily see it. But from its scent, one can come to know the whereabouts of this medicine. In days gone by, there was a chakravartin who, placing wooden tubes here and there in the Himalayas, collected this medicine. When it had ripened, it flowed out and entered the tubes. It tasted truly right. When the king died, this medicine became sour, salty, sweet, bitter, or hot, or light. Thus, what is one, tastes differently according to the different places. The true taste of the medicine remains in the mountains; it is like the full moon. Any common mortal, sterile in virtue, may work hard, dig, and try, but cannot get it. Only a chakravartin, high in virtue, appearing in the world can arrive at the true value of this medicine because of happy circumstantial concatenations. The same is the case [here]. O good man! The taste of the hidden store of the Tathagata is also like this. Overspread by all the growths of defilement, the beings clad in ignorance cannot hope to see it. We speak of the "one taste". This applies, for instance, to the Buddha-Nature. On account of the presence of defilement, several tastes appear, such as the realms of hell, animals, hungry pretas, devas, human beings, men, women, non-men, non-women, Kshatriya, Brahmin, Vaishya and Sudra. "The Buddha-Nature is strong and vigorous. It is hard to destroy. Therefore, there is nothing that can kill it. If there were something that could indeed kill it, Buddha-Nature would die. [But] nothing can ever destroy such Buddha-Nature. Nothing of this nature can ever be cut. "The nature of Self is nothing other than the hidden storehouse of the Tathagata". Such a storehouse can never be smashed, set on fire, or done away with. Although it is not possible to destroy or see it, one can know of it when one attains unsurpassed Enlightenment. Hence, there is indeed nothing that can kill it." Bodhisattva Kasyapa said to the Buddha: "If nothing can kill it, no karmic consequences would ensue from evil actions." The Buddha said to Kasyapa: "There truly is [such a thing as] killing. How? O good man! "The Buddha-Nature of beings rests within the five skandhas." If the five skandhas are destroyed, this is killing [of those

skandhas]. If one harms a living thing, one gains the unfortunate realms. Through the working of karma, one transmigrates through such realms as Kshatriya, Brahmin, Vaishya, Sudra, candala, or man, woman, non-man, non-woman, and the 25 variegated existences. A person who has not reached the holy stage of a sage is waywardly bound up by attachment to self. All such phases [modes] of existence, whether big or small, are like barnyard grass, like rice or a bean, or like the thumb. Thus do they [i.e. ignorant beings] loosely imagine things. There can be no true shape in wild fancies. The shape of Self that seeks to flee from the world is Buddha-Nature. This is the best way of conceiving of the Self. "And next, O good man! As an analogy: there is a man here who knows well what is hidden [under the ground]. He takes a sharp hoe, digs into the ground and hits upon such things as stones and gravel. All goes through and nothing hinders [i.e. the hoe digs through everything, without being obstructed]. Only when the diamond comes in its way, can the hoe not dig through. Now, no sword or hatchet can destroy a diamond. O good man! The Buddha-Nature of beings is like this. It is something that all those people who discuss things, Marapapiyas, all men and devas cannot destroy. What characterises the five skandhas is [the phenomenon of] what occurs and what is done. Whatever occurs and is done can certainly be destroyed, like stones and sand. "The True Self of the Buddha-Nature is like the diamond, which cannot be crushed". Hence, we call the destroying of the five skandhas the killing of life. O good man! Know well most definitely that the Buddhist teaching is not within the boundaries of conceiving. "O good man! The vaipulya sutras are like amrta [ambrosia, nectar] and poison." Bodhisattva Kasyapa said to the Buddha: "Why, O Tathagata, do you say that the vaipulya sutras are [both] amrta and poison?" The Buddha said: "O good man! Do you desire to be informed about the hidden storehouse of the Tathagata?" Kasyapa said to the Buddha: "I now really do desire to learn the signification of the hidden store of the Tathagata." Then the Tathagata said in a gatha:

"There is a person who takes amrta [ambrosia/ nectar], harms life, and dies early,
Or another, who takes amrta and gains a long life,
Or one who takes poison and gains life,
Or another who takes poison and dies.

The unhindered [unobstructed] Wisdom, which is amrta,
Is none other than the Mahayana sutras.
And such Mahayana sutras are what also contain poison.
It is like butter, sarpirmanda or rock candy,
Which, when taken and digested, act as medicine
If not digested, then they are nothing but poison.
It is the same with the vaipulya sutras.
The wise make of them amrta, and the ignorant, not knowing
The value of the Buddha-Nature, make of them poison.
Sravakas and pratyekabuddhas make of the Mahayana amrta.
This is like milk, which is foremost in taste.
Those who work thus and make progress
Ride in the Mahayana, gain the shore of Nirvana, and become elephant kings of men.
[Such] beings know of the Buddha-Nature, as with Kasyapa.
This superb amrta is birthlessness and deathlessness. O Kasyapa!
You whould now analyse the Three Refuges:
Just as is the intrinsic being [svabhava] of the Three Refuges,
So indeed is my intrinsic being [svabhava].
If a person is able truly to discern
That his/ her intrinsic being possesses the Buddha-dhatu [Buddha-Nature],
Then you should know that such a person
Will enter into the Secret Matrix [= the Tathagatagarbha].
That person who knows the Self [atman] and what belongs to the Self [atmiya]
Has already transcended the mundane world.
The nature of the Three Jewels, the Buddha, the Dharma [and the Sangha]
Is supreme and most worthy of respect;
As in the verse which I have uttered,
The meaning of its nature is thus."
Then, Kasyapa said in a gatha:
"I do not know how to take refuge
In the Three Treasures, how
To take refuge in unsurpassed fearlessness.
Knowing not the place of the Three Treasures,
How can one Gain fearlessness? How can one who takes refuge
In the Buddha gain peace, how can one take refuge in Dharma?
Condescend to tell me of this! How does one gain
Unmolestedness, and how non-unmolestedness?
How does one take refuge in the Sangha and thereby
Attain unsurpassed benefit?
How does one gain true sermons, how
Buddhahood in the days to come?
If one does not attain it in the days to come,
How can one take refuge in the Three Treasures?
I have nothing to foresee; I shall work my way up step by step.
Without conceiving, can a person think of having a child?
If it is definitely in embryo, we can indeed say that we have a child.
If the child is in the womb, it will not be long before it emerges.

This is the meaning vis-à¡-vis a child.
The same pertains to the karma of man.
The ignorant cannot know what the Buddha says.
By ignorance, the wheel of birth and death turns.
One who is an upasaka in name only cannot know the true meaning.

Condescend to explain [matters] to me and cut away the web of doubt.
Oh, the great Wisdom of the Tathagata!
Have pity and explain! I pray, open the closed door
Of the treasure-house of the Tathagata."
"O Kasyapa! I will now for your sake
Open the closed door of the storehouse and uproot your doubt.
Give ear to what I say with all your heart!
You, all you Bodhisattvas, and the seventh Buddha [i.e. Buddha Kasyapa]
Have the same name.
One who takes refuge in the Buddha is a true upasaka.
He no longer takes refuge in all the other gods.
One who takes refuge in Dharma cuts himself away
From harming others. One who takes refuge
In the holy Sangha does not take refuge in tirthikas.
Thus taking refuge in the Three Treasures,
One attains fearlessness."
Kasyapa said to the Buddha:
"I take refuge in the Three Treasures.
This is the right path, and this is the world of all Buddhas.
The fact that the two Treasures are equal
Possesses always the nature of great Wisdom.
The nature of the Self and the Buddha-Nature do not differ.
This is the path the Buddha praises;
This is where man rightly steps forwards
And when one abides in peace.
This is true Enlightenment.
This is Buddhahood. I, too, am a "Sugata" [Well-Gone One = Buddha],
And am on the way to unsurpassed Enlightenment praised by all.
This is the best amrta.
This is where there is no [samsaric] existence to name."

Then, the Buddha said to Kasyapa: "O good man! Do not view the Three Treasures as all sravakas and common mortals do. In this Mahayana, there is no distinction between the Three Treasures. Why not? The Buddha-Nature contains within it the Dharma and Sangha. To teach sravakas and common mortals, discrimination is resorted to and the three different aspects are spoken of regarding the Three Treasures. Following the way of the world, distinction is talked about regarding the Three Treasures. O good man! The Bodhisattva will think: "This "I" now takes refuge in the Buddha. If this I attains Enlightenment and Buddhahood, I shall not pay respect, worship or make offerings to all the Buddhas. Why not? For all Buddhas are all-equal. They are all taken refuge in by all beings. If one desires to pay respect to the Dharma-Body and the sharira [relics], one should also pay respect to the stupas of all Buddhas. Why? To guide in all beings. It also makes beings conceive in me a thought of the stupa, to make them worship and make offerings. Such beings make my Dharma-Body the place wherein they take refuge. All beings are grounded upon what is not true and what is false. I shall now, step by step, reveal true Dharma. If there are people who take refuge in monks who are not of the right calibre, I shall become the true refuge for them. If there are those who see the three refuges as distinct, I shall become a single place wherein they can take refuge. So there cannot be any distinction between the three refuges. To one born blind, I shall be his eyes, and to sravakas and pratyekabuddhas I shall become the true refuge." O good man! Such Bodhisattvas enact the works of the Buddha for the sake of innumerable evil beings and all wise people. O good man! There is, as an example, a person here who goes to the battlefield and thinks: "I am the first of all the first of all of these. All soldiers depend on me." Also, it is like the prince who thinks: "I shall conquer all other princes, succeed to the works of a great emperor, gain unmolested [unrestricted] power, and make all other princes pay homage to me. So, let me not entertain a whit of thought of self-surrender." As with the prince of the king, so too with the minister. O good man! The case is the same with the Bodhisattva-mahasattva, and he thinks: "How do the three become one with me?" O good man! I make it [in my teaching] that the thre things are Nirvana. The Tathagata is the unsurpassed one. For example, the head is the highest part of a man's body, not the other limbs or the hands and legs. The same is the case with the Buddha. He is the most respected, not Dharma or the Sangha. In order to teach the world, he manifests himself diversely. It is like going up a ladder. This being the case, do not regard the three refuges as different, as do common mortals and the ignorant. Abide in the Mahayana as bravely and decisively as a sharp sword." Bodhisattva Kasyapa said to the Buddha: "I ask about what I know, not what I do not know. I ask about untainted pure actions for the sake of the greatly courageous Bodhisattvas, so that the Tathagata will, for the sake of the Bodhisattvas, proclaim what is wonderful and expound [it], and thus [the Bodhisattvas will] desire to praise the Mahayana vaipulya sutras. The Tathagata, the great Compassionate One, now speaks. I too shall peacefully abide in it. The pure actions of the Bodhisattva are well proclaimed in the Great Nirvana Sutra. O World-Honoured One! I shall now, for the sake of all beings, disseminate the undisclosed store of the Tathagata. Also, I shall now well attest to, and know, the three refuges. If any being believes strongly in the teaching of the Great Nirvana Sutra, such a being will all-naturally clearly attain the three refuges. Why? Because the close-guarded store of the Tathagata possesses the Buddha-Nature. Any person who disseminates this sutra says that one possesses the

Buddha-Nature within one's body. Any such person does not, far out, take refuge in the three [treasures]. Why not? Because one in the life to come perfects the Three Treasures. Because of this, sravakas, pratyekabuddhas, and all others come, worship and pay homage to me. O good man! Because of this, learn Mahayana sutras." Kasyapa further said: "Buddha-Nature thus cannot be known. The 32 signs of perfection and the 80 minor marks of excellence are also of wonder." Then the Buddha praised Bodhisattva Kasyapa: "Well said, well said, O good man! You have accomplished the deepest and sharpest of Wisdom. I shall now tell you how one enters the Tathagatagarbha. If Self lives, this is the teaching of "is". It does not part from suffering. If Self does not exist, there can be no benefit, even if one practises pure actions. If one says that all things do not possess Self, this is but the "not-is" theory ["ucchedika-drsti" - i.e. the world-view of the total negation of any existence, which is the theory of sheer emptiness]. If one says that Self exists, this is the "ever is" theory ["sasvata-drsti" - an erroneous view of life which takes existence as concrete and changeless]. If one says that all things are non-eternal, this is the "notis" view. If one says that all things exist, this is the "ever is" view. If one says that all is suffering, this is the "not-is". If one says that all things are bliss, this is the "ever is". If a person practises the Way of the "ever is" of all things, such a person falls into the heresy of "not-is". A person who practises the Way according to which all things become extinct falls into "ever is". This is like the measuring worm, which carries its hind-legs forward by the action of its front-legs. It is the same with the person who practises the "ever is" and the "not-is". The "not-is" stands on [depends on, is based on] the "ever is". Because of this, those of other teachings who practise suffering are called "not-good". Those of other teachings who practise bliss are called "good". Those of other teachings who practise non-Self are those of illusion. Those of other teachings who practise the "ever is" say that the Tathagata secretly stores [truths away]. So-called Nirvana does not have any grotto or house to live in. Those of other teachings who practise the "not-is" refers to property; those of other teachings who practise the "ever is" refers to Buddha, Dharma, Sangha, and right emancipation. Know that the Middle Path of the Buddha negates the two planes and tells of true Dharma. Even common mortals and the dull abide in it and have no doubt. It is as when the weak and the sick take butter, as a result of which they feel light in spirit. "The nature of the two of "is" and "not-is" is not definite. For example, the natures of the four elements [earth, water, fire and wind] are not the same. Each differs from the other. A good doctor well sees that each stands against [in contradistinction to, in opposition to, in contrast with] the other. He sees it through even by the one-sided phase of what takes place. O good man! It is the same with the Tathagata. He acts like a good doctor towards all beings. He knows the difference between the internal and external nature of illusion and crushes it out, and reveals the fact that the undisclosed store of the Tathagata is pure and that the Buddha-Nature is eternal and does not change. If a person says "is", he must be on guard that his Wisdom does not get tainted; if a person says "not-is", this is nothing but falsehood. If one says "is", one cannot sit unsaid. Also, one could not play with words and dispute; only seek to know the true nature of all things. Common mortals play with words and dispute, betraying their own ignorance as to the Tathagata's undisclosed store. When it comes to the question of suffering, the ignorant say that the body is non-eternal and all is suffering. Also, they do not know that there is also the nature of Bliss in the body. If the Eternal is alluded to, common mortals say that all bodies are non-eternal, like unfired tiles. One with Wisdom discriminates things and does not say that all is non-eternal. Why not? Because man possesses the seed of the Buddha-Nature. When non-Self is talked about, common mortals say that there cannot be Self in the Buddhist teaching. One who is wise should know that non-Self is a temporary existence and is not true. Knowing thus, one should not have any doubt. When the hidden Tathagatagarbha is stated as being empty and quiet, common mortals will think of ceasing and extinction. "One who is wise knows that the Tathagata is Eternal and Unchanging." "If Emancipation is stated to be something like a phantom, common mortals say that the person who attains Emancipation is one who wears away to nothingness; a person with Wisdom thinks that he is a man-lion and that, though he comes and goes, he is Eternal and does not change." "If it is stated that ignorance resides in all things, common mortals hear this and think of two different existences, the "bright" and the "non-bright". The wise man sees that the nature is not-two and that the nature of the not-two is the real nature ["self-nature"]. If it is stated that things sit on [depend on] consciousness, common mortals say "two", which are "samskara" [volition, mental impulse] and "vijnana" [consciousness]. But the wise know that its nature is not-two and that the nature of the not-two is the "svabhavika" ["own-nature", "self-nature"]. If we speak of the "ten good deeds"and "ten evil deeds", of what can be made and what cannot be made, of good realms and evil realms, white teaching [sukladharma=saddharma=Wonderful Dharma] and black teaching [krsnadharma =Pali kanhadhamma], common mortals conceive of two things. But the wise know that the nature is not-two and that the nature of the not-two is the real nature. When it is stated that all things end in suffering, common morals say that this is two. But the wise know that the nature is not-two and that the nature of the not-two is the real nature. If we state that all things made are non-eternal and that the undisclosed store of the Tathagata, too, is non-eternal, common mortals say two. But the wise know that the nature is not-two and that not-two is the real nature. If all things have no Self and the undisclosed store of the Tathagata has no Self, common mortals say that the nature is two. But the wise know that it is not-two and that not-two is the real nature. There cannot be the two things of Self and non-Self. This is what the undisclosed store of the Tathagata refers to. This is what is praised by uncountable, innumerable, boundless numbers of all Buddhas. I, now, in this all-perfect sutra, explain all. There is the not-two in the nature and characteristics of Self and non-Self. You should take things thus. O good man! You should strongly uphold and think about such sutras. I have already stated in the "Mahaprajnaparamita Sutra" that there are not the two phases [aspects, phenomena] of Self and non-Self. The case is thus. From fresh milk we get cream, from cream fresh butter, from fresh butter clarified butter, and from clarified butter sarpirmanda. Does the nature of the cream come from the milk itself, or from without? And the same is the case with sarpirmanda. If it comes from without, it is something made by another and not something come out of the milk itself. If it does not come out of the milk, the milk has nothing to do with its coming about. If it comes out of the milk itself, it cannot come out in a similar way and continuously. If it comes out continuously, it cannot come out together. If it does not come out together, the five tastes cannot be for once only. Though not for once only, it cannot definitely come about from other places.

Know that in milk there is already the phase [element, aspect] of cream. As it possesses much sweetness, it cannot change. The same with sarpirmanda. When the cow feeds on the grass of watery places, its blood changes and we get milk. If the cow feeds on sweet grass, the milk becomes sweet, and if on bitter grass, the milk becomes bitter. In the Himalayas, there is a type of grass called pinodhni. If the cow feeds on this, it will produce pure sarpirmanda and there will be no such colour as blue, yellow, red, white or black. The grass and cereals work upon [affect] the colour and taste of the milk. Two aspects come out of all beings by the karmic relations of brightness and ignorance. When the gloom changes, brightness comes about. The case is the same with the good and not-good of all things. There can be no two aspects." Bodhisattva Kasyapa said to the Buddha: "O World-Honoured One! You, the Buddha, say that there is cream in milk. What does this mean? O World-Honoured One! If there definitely is cream in milk and if it is true that it cannot be seen because of the minuteness of its size, how can we say that cream comes about through the causal relations of milk? When things orginally have no root element, we can say that a thing is born. If it exists already, how can we say that life comes about? It it is the case that there definitely is cream in milk, there must be milk in all grass. Likewise, there must be grass in milk, too. If the situation is that there definitely is no cream in milk, how can cream come out of the milk? If there is no root element but it later comes about, how could it be that grass cannot grow in milk?" "O good man! Do not say that there definitely is cream in milk or that there is not cream in milk. Also, do not say that it comes from outside. If there is definitely cream in milk, how can it be that thing and taste differ? That is why you should not say there definitely is cream in milk. If there definitely is no cream in milk, why is it that something different does not come about in the milk? If poison is put into milk, the cream will kill a person. That is why you should not say that there definitely is no cream in the milk. Further, if we say that cream comes from outside, why is it that cream does not come about in water? Because

of this, do not say that cream comes from anywhere else. O good man! As the cow feeds on grass, its blood changes into white. Grass and blood die out and the power of virtue of beings changes and we gain milk. This milk comes out of grass and blood, but we cannot say that there are the two. All we can say is that conditions so bring it about. This we can say. From cream up to sarpirmanda, things go thus. The case [here] is the same. Because of this, we can rightly say that there is the taste of the cow. This milk dies away, and in consequence there comes about cream. What is the condition? It is sour or warm. Because of this, we can say that it comes from conditions. The situation is the same with the others, up to sarpirmanda. Because of this, we cannot say that there definitely is no cream in milk. If it comes from elsewhere, it must exist separately from the milk. This cannot be. O good man! The same is the case with brightness and ignorance. [Of that which is] bound up by all illusions, we say ignorant. If linked to all good things, there can be brightness. That is why we say that there can be no two things. So, I said: "There is a grass in the Himalayas called pinodhni, which, if eaten by the cow, produces sarpirmanda." The same is the case with the Buddha-Nature. "O good man! Beings are sterile in fortune and do not come across this grass. The same applies to the Buddha-Nature. As defilement overspreds [them], beings cannot see. For example, the water of the great ocean tastes salty all the same, but it contains in it the best of water, as in the case of milk. Also, the Himalayas are perfect in various virtues and produce various medicines, but there are also poisonous herbs. It is the same with the bodies of all beings. There are the four poisonous serpents, but there is also present the great king of all-wonderful medicine. So-called Buddha-Nature is not something that has been made. Only, it is overspread by defilement. Only a person who thoroughly cuts it away, whether he be a Kshatriya, Brahmin, Vaishya or Sudra sees the Buddha-Nature and attains unsurpassed Enlightenment. For example, should the thunder roll in the sky, the clouds disperse and all the tusks of the elephant will be covered with flower-petals. If there is no thunder, the flowers do not come about. Also, this is as in the case where there is no denotative name. The same is also the case with the Buddha-Nature of [all] beings. It is always overspread by various defilements and is not seen. That is why I say that beings do not possess the Self. If one is blessed with hearing the all-wonderful "Mahaparinirvana Sutra", one sees the Buddha-Nature. This is as in the case of the flowers on the tusks of the elephant. One may hear all about the samadhis of the sutras. But if one does not hear this sutra, one cannot get to the wonderful form of the Tathagata. If is as when there is no thunder, when one no longer sees flowers on the tusks of the elephant. On hearing this sutra, one comes to know of the undisclosed [latent] Buddha-Nature, about which the Tathagata speaks. This is like seeing the flowers on the tusks of the elephant. On hearing this sutra, all innumerable beings come to know that this is the Buddha-Nature. Because of this, I speak about Great Nirvana and say that I augment [expand] the Dharma-Body, the undisclosed store of the Tathagata. This is as with the thunder, when flowers fall upon the tusks of the elephant. As this long upholds and nurtures the great meaning, this is called "Mahaparinirvana". If any good man or woman learns this all-wonderful Sutra of Great Nirvana, they should know that they are doing a work of thanksgiving and are true disciples of the Buddha." Bodhisattva Kasyapa said to the Buddha: "It is exceptionally wonderful, O World-Honoured One! The so-called Buddha-Nature is profound to know; it is hard to see and attain. Sravakas and pratyekabuddhas cannot hope to partake of it." The Buddha siad: "O good man! It is thus, it is thus! It is just as you praise [it]; it does not differ from what I say." Bodhisattva Kasyapa said to the Buddha: "O World-Honoured One! To what extent is the Buddha-Nature profound and how difficult is it to perceive and get into?" "O good man! [As an analogy]: 100 blind persons consult a good doctor for a cure. With that, the doctor opens up the membrane of the eye with a golden barb [blade] and then, holding up one finger, asks: "Can you see this?" The blind person says: "I cannot see it yet. " Then, the doctor holds up two fingers, and three fingers. Then, the person says that he can see to some extent. O good man! When this wonderful Sutra of Great Nirvana is one that has as yet not been delivered by the Tathagta, the same is the case. Although innumerable Bodhisattvas may well perfectly practise the paramitas [spiritual perfections], they might only reach the stage of the ten abodes ["bhumis"] and yet may not be able to see the Buddha-Nature. If the Tathagata speaks, they may see to some extent. When these Bodhisattvas have seen all, they will

say: "Oh, wonderful, O World-Honoured One! We have been repeating birth and death and have been worried by selflessness. " O good man! Such Bodhisattvas may well reach the stage of the ten soils ["bhumis" - stages of Bodhisattva development], and yet they cannot clearly see the Buddha-Nature. How could sravakas and pratyekabuddhas well see [it]? "Also, next, O good man! For example, one sees geese flying far off in the sky and wonders if they [really] are geese or the sky. One looks carefully and sees this indistinctly. The case of the Bodhisattvas may also be like this; they see but a small part of the nature of the Tathagata. How could sravakas and pratyekabuddhas well see [it]? "O good man! The same is the case with an intoxicated man who has a long way to walk, but can only see the way indistinctly. This is the case with the Bodhisattvas at the stage of the ten abodes ["bhumis"] who can only see a small part of the nature of the Tathagata. "O good man! There is a thirsty person who has to travel a long way through the wilderness. Thirst presses down upon him so much that he looks for water everywhere. Then, he sees the foliage of a tree with a white crane on it. Having lost his capacity to judge, the person cannot tell if this is a tree or water. He tries hard to see. Then he sees that it is a white crane and the foliage of a tree. It is similar to the Bodhisattvas of the stage of the ten abodes, who sees but a small part of the nature of the Tathagata. "O good man! For example, there is a man who is in the middle of a great ocean. Far out, an innumerable hundred thousand yojanas away, he sees a great galleon, the rudder tower and storied building [parts of the ship]. He looks and thinks to himself: "Is this a rudder tower or is it the sky?" He looks for a long time and his mind becomes fixed, and he comes to know that it is a rudder tower. The same is the case with the Bodhisattva of the stage of the ten "bhumis", who sees within himself the nature of the Tathagata. "For example, there is here a prince who is weak in physique and who passes the night in playing, and it is now dawn. He tries but cannot see clearly. The case is like this. The Bodhisattva of the stage of the ten "bumis" thus sees the nature of the Tathagata within himself. And, likewise, what he sees is not clear. "Also, next, O good man! For example, a government official, driven by routine work of this kind, comes home late in the evening. There is a flash of lightning for a moment, and he sees a group of cows. Then he thinks: "Is this a group of cows, or a cloud, or a house?" He looks for a good while and comes to the conclusion that they are cows. And yet, he cannot be too sure. The Bodhisattva of the stage of the ten "bhumis" sees the nature of the Tathagata within himself, and yet he cannot see it clearly. The situation is like this. "Also, next, O good man! A bhiksu who upholds the precepts looks at some water in which there are no worms. And yet, he sees a worm, and thinks to himself: "Is the thing that moves in the water a worm or a bit of dust?" He stares at it for a good while. Even after he has realised that it is a piece of dust, he is not quite sure. It seems so. The same is the case with the Bodhisattva of the stage of the ten "bhumis", who thus sees within himself the nature of the Tathagata. Nothing is very clear. "Also, next, O good man! For example, a man sees a child in the darkness, far off. He thinks: "Is this a cow, a man, or a bird?" He keeps gazing at it for a goodly while. He now sees that it is a child, and yet he does not see it very clearly. It is thus. The same applies to the Bodhisattva who is at the stage of the ten "bhumis" and who sees within himself the nature of the Tathagata. Nothing is completely clear. "Also, next, O good man! There is a person who, in the darkness of the night, sees the image of a Bodhisattva and thinks: "Can this be the image of a Bodhisattva, of Mahesvara, of Great Brahma, or of someone in monastic garb?" The person gazes at it a good while and comes to think that it is the form of a Bodhisattva; and yet, he does not see it very clearly. It is the same with the Bodhisattva of the ten "bhumis" who sees within himself the nature of the Tathagata. Nothing seems to be very clear. "O good man! The Buddha-Nature is that one has is the deepest and the most difficult [thing] to see. Only the Buddha can know it well. It is not within the reach of sravakas and pratyekabuddhas. O good man! The wise should see thus and know of the nature of the Tathagata." Bodhisattva Kasyapa said to the Buddha: "O World-Honoured One! The Buddha-Nature is very delicate and difficult to know. How can one perceive it well with the fleshly eye?" The Buddha said to Kasyapa: "O good man! Even Thoughtlessness-non-thoughtlessness Heaven is also not within reach of the two vehicles. When one accords with the sutras, one can well see it by dint of the power of faith. O good man! The same is the case with sravakas and pratyekabuddhas who accord with the Nirvana Sutra and who see in themselves the nature of the Tathagata. O good man! Because of this, one should make effort and learn the Great Nirvana Sutra. O good man! The Buddha Nature as such can only be known by the Buddha alone and is not within the reach of sravakas and pratyekabuddhas." Bodhisattva Kasyapa said to the the the Buddha: "O World-Honoured One! Unholy common mortals possess the nature of common mortals and [yet] say that they possess Self." The Buddha said: "As an example of this: two persons are friends. One is a prince, and the other a poor man. They associate with each other. Then the poor man, on seeing that the Prince possesses a very bright sword, covets it. The Prince later flees to other countries, taking the sword with him. The poor man later puts up at the house of another person and, in his sleep, cries out: "The sword! The sword!" A person nearby hears this and goes to the king. The king says: "You said "sword". Tell me where it is." The person tells of it in detail. "O King! You can cut up my body and cut off my feet, and yet you will not be able to get the sword. I was once on close terms with the Prince. Before, we were together, and I saw it. But I did not touch it. And how could I take it?" The King asks further: "What was the sword like which you say you saw?" The man answers: "O great King! It was like a ewe's horn." The King, on hearing this, smiles in amusement and says: "Don't worry. In all my storehouse, we do not have any such sword. How could you have seen it with the Prince?" Then the King asks all his ministers: "Have you ever seen a sword of this kind?" So speaking, he dies. "Then another prince ascends the throne. He also asks the ministers: "Have you ever seen in the governmental storehouse any sword of this kind?" All the ministers say: "We once saw it." "What was the sword like?" They replied: "It was like a ewe's horn." "How could there be any such sword in my storehouse?" Four kings, one after the other, ask and check, but they cannot gain it. "Some time later, the Prince who has fled the country returns and becomes King. On ascending the throne, he asks the ministers: 'Have you ever seen the sword?' They reply: 'O great King! Its colour was pure, and it was like an utpala-lotus.' They also answer: 'It was like the horn of a ram.' They further reply: 'It was red and like a fire ball.' They answer,too: 'It was like a black serpent.' Then the King laughs: 'All of you have not, in truth, seen my sword.' "Noble Son! A Bodhisattva-mahasattva is also like that - he appears in the world and expounds the true nature of the Self. After he has expounded it, he departs, as for example like the prince who takes the wondrous sword and flees to another country. Foolish ordinary people say, 'Everybody has Self! Everybody has Self", like the poor man who, lodging at another's house, cries out, 'The sword! The sword!' Sravakas and pratyekabuddhas ask people, 'What attributes does the Self have?', to which they reply, 'I have seen the attributes of the Self - it is the size of a thumb' or they say, 'It is like [a grain of rice], or 'It is like [a grain of] millet', or there are some who say, 'It is the Self's attribute to abide within the heart, burning like the sun'. In this manner people do not know the nature of the Self, [just] as, for example, the various ministers do not know the nature of the sword. While a Bodhisattva discourses thus about the quality of the Self, ordinary people do not but impute various false concepts to the Self, just as when asked about the attributes of the sword the [ministers] reply that it is like the horn of a ram. These ordinary people generate false views in succession from one on to the other. In order to eliminate such false views, the Tathagata reveals and discourses on the non-existence of a self, just as when the prince tells his various ministers that there is no such sword in his treasury. Noble Son, the True Self that the Tathagata expounds today is called the Buddha-dhatu [Buddha-Nature]. This manner of Buddha-dhatu is shown in the Buddha-Dharma with the example of the real sword. Noble Son, should there be any ordinary person who is able well to expound this, then he [speaks] in accordance with unsurpassed Buddha-Dharma. Should there be anyone who is well able to distinguish this in accordance with what has been expounded regarding it, then you should know that he has the nature of a Bodhisattva.

Chapter Thirteen: On Letters

The Buddha said to Bodhisattva Kasyapa: "All such different opinions, fortune-telling, language, and letters are what the Buddha spoke and not what was said by tirthikas." Bodhisattva Kasyapa said to the Buddha: "O World-Honoured One! How do you, the Tathagata, tell [of] the root concept of letters?" The Buddha said: "O good man! First, the half-letter [i.e. the phonic alphabet of Sanskrit] is taught and is made the root-concept. This holds good for all written things, fortune-telling, sentences, all elements and realities. Common mortals learn the foundation of letters. Later, they come to know what is right and what is not." Bodhisattva Kasyapa said to the Buddha: "O World-Honoured One! What is the meaning of the letter?" "O good man! It stands on fourteen phonic bases, which constitute the meanings. The so-called letter is Nirvana. Being Eternal, it does not flow away. What does not flow away knows no end. What knows no end is the Adamantine Body of the Tathagata. These fourteen constitute the foundation of letters. "A" is so called because it does not get destroyed. What is indestructible is the Three Treasures. For example, this is like the diamond. It is also so called because it does not flow away. What does not flow away is the Tathagata. In the nine holes [i.e. outlets of the body: two eyes, two ears, two nostrils, mouth, two outlets for excretion] of the Tathagata, there is nothing that flows away. So, it is the unflowing ["anasrava" - non-defilement]. And there are nine holes. Hence, it is "non-flowing". Non-flowing is the Eternal; the Eternal is the Tathagata. The Tathagata is not that which has been created. Hence, he is non-flowing. Also, "a" is virtue. Virtue is the Three Treasures. For this reason, we say "a". "Next, "ā" stands for "ācārya". What does "ācārya" mean? In worldly life, we can call him a "holy person". Why do we say "holy person"? "Holy" means "non-attached". It means "of little desire" and "feeling contented". Also, it is called "pure". It thoroughly passes beings across the great sea of the three worlds of birth and death. That is why we say "holy". "Also, "ā" means "institution" [implementation], which is to act in accordance with the pure precepts and observe deportment. "Also, "ā" means to depend upon a holy person. This is to learn his comings and goings and all that he does. The three holy ones are given offerings, respected and worshipped. One faithfully serves one's parents and studies the Mahayana. Good men and women uphold the prohibitions. And all Bodhisattvas are called "holy ones". "á" also means "order". It says: "Come and do this; you should not do it like that." So do things go. One who checks and suppresses non-deportment is a holy one. That is why we say "a". "I" is the Buddhist teaching. Pure action is extensive, pure and untainted. It is, for example, like the full moon. "Do thus, not like that; this is right, that is not right; this is a sermon of the Buddha, and this is what Mara says. "Hence, we say "i". "We say "a". The meaning of the Buddhist teaching is wonderful and profound. It is as when we call the laws [dharmas] of Mahesvara and Brahma unmolested [unlimited]. Well upheld, it [Buddhist teaching] is the protection of Dharma. "Also, unmolestedness [unlimitedness, unrestrictedness] is called the four protections of the world. As these four are unmolested, one well takes in and protects the Great Nirvana Sutra, and one unmolestedly expounds and disseminates [it]. "Also, next, "ā" stands for the unmolested [unhindered, unstinting] dissemination of Dharma to beings. "Also, next, "ā"is the unmolested [unconstrained]. It asks and says what is right. This is nothing other than the learning of the vaipulya sutras. "Also, next, "ā" stands for the crushing out of jealousy. When the barnyard grass has been thoroughly weeded out, everything changes into what is auspicious. So we say "ā". "U" stands for Great Nirvana, the Highest, the most superb, the pinnacle of pinnacles of all sutras. "Also, next, "u" stands for the nature of the Tathagata, which no sravakas and pratyekabuddhas hear about. This is like Uttarakuru being the best of all places. If any Bodhisattva indeed hears this sutra, he is the highest and most superb. Hence, we say "u". "ā" is, for example, like cow's milk, which is the best of all tastes. The nature of the Tathagata is also like that. Of all sutras, this is the holiest and best. Anyone who slanders [it] is none but a cow. "Also, next, "ā" is called "not-wise". A person thoroughly slanders the delicate and hidden storehouse of the Tathagata. Know that this person is most to be pitied. Parting from the hidden storehouse of the Tathagata, he speaks about no-Self. Henc, we say "ä". "E" is the "Dharmata" and Nirvana of all Buddhas. Hence, we say "e". "Ai" means "Tathagata". "Also, "ai" refers to the goings and comings, bendings and stretchings, and the deeds of the Tathagata, by which not one amongst all beings is [not] benefited. Hence, "ai". "O" stands for illusion; illusion is "asrava" [defilement]. The Tathagata is eternally free from illusion. Hence, "o". "Au" means Mahayana. It stands for the utmost of all the fourteen sounds. The case of the Mahayana sutras is also like this. They are the ultimate of all sutras and shastras. Hence, "au". "Am" makes away with all impurities. In the Buddhist teachings, all gold, silver and treasures are abandoned. Hence, "am". "Ah" means "superb vehicle". Why? This Mahayana sutra, this Great Nirvana Sutra, is the most superlative of all sutras. Hence, "ah". "Ka" calls forth great compassion towards all beings. The thought of a son arises, as towards Rahula. It means "wonderfully good". Hence, "ka". "Kha" stands for "non-good friend". "Non-good friend" means mixed and defiled. He does not believe in the hidden store of the Tathagata. Hence, "kha". "Ga" means "store". "Store" means the undisclosed store of the Tathagata. All beings have the Buddha-Nature. Hence, "ga". "Gha" is the eternal sound of the Tathagata. What is the eternal sound of the Tathagata? The so-called Tathagata is eternal and does not suffer change. Hence, "gha". "Na" represents the breaking [destructible, impermanent] characterstics of all beings. Hence, "na". "Ca" means "to practise". As it subdues all beings, we say "practise". "Cha" means "Tathagata", who houses [shades, protects] all beings, as in the case of a great parasol. Hence, "cha". "Ja" means "right [true] emancipation". There arises [in this] no ageing. Hence, "ja". "Jha" stands for the great proliferation of defilements, as in the case of a great forest. Hence, "jha". "Na" means "Wisdom". It means true "Dharmata". Hence, "na". "Ta" signifies speech delivered about dharmas in Jambudvipa, showing a half-body, as in the case of the half-moon. Hence, "ta". "Tha" represents the perfection of the Dharma-Body, as in the case of the full moon. Hence, "tha". "Da" represents an ignorant bhiksu who does not know the Eternal and the non-Eternal, as in the case of a child. Hence, "da". "Dha" represents a person who feels no obligation towards his teacher, as in the case of a ram.Hence, "dha". "Na" represents lack of knowledge of the

meaning of what is holy, as in the case of a tirthika. Hence, "na"."Ta" represents the Tathagata, who says to all bhiksus: "Come away from fright and fear. I shall now deliver sermons on Wonderful Dharma." Hence, "ta". "Tha" means "ignorance". Beings repeat birth and death and bind themselves, as in the case of a silkworm or dung-beetle. Hence, "tha". "Da" means "great giving". This is the so-called Mahayana. Hence, "da". "Dha" praises "virtue". It is as in the case of the Three Treasures, which are like Mount Sumeru, soaring up, grand, extensive and, yet, not inclining to one side. Hence, "dha". "Na" alludes to the Three Treasures, which stand peacefully rooted, not inclining to one side or moving, like the threshold of a gate. Hence, "na". "Pa" means "inverted". If a person says that the Three Treasures expire, this shows that that person himself entertains doubt. Hence, "pa". "Pha" refers to the ill-fortune of the world. If a person says that when ill-fortune arises in the world, the Three Treasures also expire, this indicates that that person is ignorant, that he has no knowledge, and that he acts against the holy will. Hence, "pha". "Ba" refers to the ten powers of the Buddha. Hence, "ba". "Bha" refers to the shouldering of what is heavy. It can stand bearing the heaviness of Wonderful Dharma. Know that such a person is a great Bodhisattva. Hence, "bha". "Ma" refers to all Bodhisattvas who strictly uphold all the institutions [rules]. This is so-called Mahayana Mahaparinirvana. Hence, "ma". "Ya" alludes to all those Bodhisattvas who, for the benefit of beings, preach the Mahayana
doctrine in all places. Hence, "ya". "Ra" crushes out greed, anger and ignorance, and disseminates Wonderful Dharma. Hence, "ra". "La" relates to the sravaka vehicle, which moves, changes, and has no place to live in [i.e. no permanent abode]. Mahayana is safe and firm and there is no inclining or moving [with it]. Abandoning the sravaka vehicle, one makes effort and practises the unsurpassed Mahayana. Hence, "la". "Va" means that the World-Honoured One is he who showers down upon all beings the great rain of the Dharma. He is, as it were, a so-called fortune-telling sutra. Hence, "va". "ä" means to part from the three arrows [the three barbs of greed, malevolence and ignorance]. Hence, "ä". "Sa" means "perfection". If one truly hears this Great Nirvana Sutra, one already hears and upholds all about Mahayana sutras. Hence, "sa". "Sa" means that Wonderful

Dharma is expounded to all beings, so that people feel blessed. Hence, "sa". "Ha" bespeaks the mind's state of gladness. How wonderful is it that the World-Honoured One departs from all actions; strange is it that the Tathagata enters Parinirvana. Hence, "ha". "Lham" signifies "Mara". Innumerable Maras are unable to destroy the hidden storehouse of the Tathagata. Hence, "lham". "The four letters, r,r, l, l, have four meanings. These are Buddha, Dharma, Sangha, and Abhidharma. Abhidharma relates to what obtains in the world. It shows that Devadatta destroys the Sangha. He transforms himself into various forms, faces and concrete forms. The case is like this. All this is to establish vinaya. The wise should clearly see through this and not entertain any fear. This is following what obtains in the world. Hence, r,r,l,l. "The inhalation of breath is the sound which one gets when the tongue accords with the nose. We gain the meaning by the long, short, or the one that supercedes the sound. All differ according to the actions of tongue and teeth. "All such meanings of the letters well enable beings to purify their verbal actions. The Buddha-Nature of beings does not first become pure when assisted by letters. Why not? Because that nature is originally pure. Also, while co-existing with the five skandhas, the 18 realms and the 12 spheres [of the senses], the Buddha-Nature is not one with the five skandhas, the 18 realms and the 12 spheres. Because of this, all beings should take refuge in the Bodhisattvas and others. Because of the [existence of the] Buddha-Nature [within them], beings are viewed with equal [non-discriminating] eyes, and there is no difference. Hence, the half-letters form the basis of all sutras, all written material, and sentences. "Also, the meaning of the half-letters refers to the root of all defilements. So they are called half-letters. The full letters are the root of all good dharmas and speech. For example, those of the world who do evil are called half-letters, and those who do good full-letters. Thus, all sutras and the Abhidharmas are based upon the half-letters. People may say that the Tathagata and true emancipation fall under the category of the half-letters. But this is not so. Why not? Because these [two] part from [i.e. are separate from] letters. Because of this, the Tathagata is unmolested [unconstrained], unattached, and fully emancipated in all things. How do we arrive at the meaning of the letters? If one comes to think that the Tathagata appears in the world and does away with the half-letters, this is understanding the meaning of the letters. Any person who follows the meaning of the half-letters is one who does not know the nature of the Tathagata. What is the the meaning of the letterless? One who associates with those who practise the teaching of evil belongs to the letterless. Also, although a person may associate with those who do good, if he does not know the difference between the Eternal and the non-Eternal, the constant and the non-constant of the Tathagata, and the two Treasures of Dharma and Sangha, between vinaya and non-vinaya, sutras and non-sutras, the words of Mara and those of the Buddha, such a person is one who is letterless. This do I state regarding how one is letterless. O good man! For this reason, you should part from the half-letter and arrive at the meaning of the complete letters." Bodhisattva Kasyapa said to the Buddha: "O World-Honoured One! I shall now thoroughly learn the number of letters. I have encountered the unsurpassed teacher. I have now received the kindly injunctions of the Tathagata." The Buddha praised Kasyapa and said: "Well said, well said. A person who is intent upon Wonderful Dharma should learn things thus."

Chapter Fourteen: On the Parable of the Birds

The Buddha said further to Kasyapa: "O good man! There are two species of birds, one the kacalindikaka and the other the mandarin duck. In playing or stopping [resting], they always act together; they do not separate. The same is the case with suffering, the non-eternal, and non-Self. They do not separate." Bodhisattva Kasyapa said to the Buddha: "O World-Honoured One! In what way do things obtain with suffering, the non-eternal, and non-Self as with the mandarin duck and the kacalindikaka?" The Buddha said: "O good man! What is contrary to Dharma is suffering, and what is contrary to Dharma is bliss. What is contrary to Dharma is the eternal and what is contrary to Dharma is the non-eternal. What is contrary to Dharma is self and what is contrary to Dharma is non-Self. For example, it is as in the case in which rice differs from hemp and wheat, and hemp and wheat from beans, millet and sugar cane. With all of these, the non-eternal are the buds, flowers and leaves. When the fruit ripens and when man uses it, we say eternal. Why? Because the nature is true." Kasyapa said to the Buddha: "O World-Honoured One! If these are eternal, are they equal to the Tathagata?" "O good man! Do not speak in such a way. Why not? If one says that the Tathagata is like Mount Sumeru, does this imply that he will break up, as Sumeru must break up when the time comes for it to disintegrate? O good man! Do not view things thus. O good man! "With all things, excepting Nirvana, not one thing is eternal". Merely to conform with the ways of secular truth, we say that the fruit is eternal." Bodhisattva Kasyapa said to the Buddha: "O World-Honoured One! It is good, it is good. It is as the Buddha says." The Buddha said to Kasyapa: "It is thus, it is thus, O good man! A person may be true to what the sutras say or may have practised all the samadhis, but until he has learned Mahaparinirvana, he will say that all is non-eternal. When a person has learned this sutra, he may have illusion, but he is, so to speak, without illusion. It [learning this sutra] well benefits man and heaven. Why? Because "one clearly sees that one's own body has the Buddha Nature within. This is the Eternal." "Also, next, O good man! It is like the case of the mango tree. When its flower first appears, what there is [at that time] is the changing phase. When it bears fruit

and when it bestows much benefit, we speak of the eternal. O good man! A person may thus be true to all the sutras or may have practised samadhis, but when he has not yet given ear to this Great Nirvana Sutra, all is based on the non-eternal. When a person gives ear to this sutra, although [still] possessing illusion, it is as though he had no illusion. That is to say that it benefits both man and heaven. How? Because that person clearly knows that he has the Buddha-Nature within. This is the Eternal. "Also, next, O good man! When an ingot of gold melts, this is the phase of the non-eternal. Once molten, it becomes gold. When it greatly benefits a person, we say eternal. The case is like this. Thus, O good man, a person may be true to all sutras or may have practised all samadhis, but if he has not yet given ear to this Great Nirvana Sutra, all is non-eternal. When a person has given ear to this sutra, he may well have illusion, but it is as though he did not. It thus benefits all men and gods. Why? Because the person clearly comes to know that he has the Buddha-Nature within. This is the Eternal. "Also, next, O good man! Sesame, for example, when not yet pressed, is non-eternal. Once the pressing has been done and the oil has been extracted, the sesame gives great benefit. This is the eternal. O good man! A person may be true to all sutras or may have practised samadhis, but not yet having heard of Great Nirvana, all is non-eternal [for that person]. Having heard this sutra, though yet bound by illusion, a person is equal [equivalent] to possessing no illusion. Benefits accrue to any human or god. Why? Because that person realises that he has the Buddha-Nature within him. This is the Eternal. "Also, next, O good man! It is as in the case in which all rivers drain into the sea. All sutras and samadhis flow into the Mahayana Great Nirvana Sutra. How so? Because it ultimately expounds the Buddha-Nature. That is why I say: "Some dharmas are eternal; some dharmas are noneternal. With non-Self, too, things amount to the same." It is thus that I say." Bodhisattva Kasyapa said to the Buddha: "O World-Honoured One! The Tathagata is already segregated from the poisonous arrows of apprehension and suffering. Apprehension and suffering are heaven [devas]; the Tathagata is no heaven [deva]. Apprehension and suffering are human; the Tathagata is no human. Apprehension and suffering are the 25 existences. Hence, there can exist no apprehension or suffering with the Tathagata. How could one say that the Tathagata is apprehension and suffering?" "O good man! In No-Thought Heaven ["avrha"], what obtains is thoughtlessness. If thoughtless, there can be no life. If there is no life, how can there be the five skandhas, the 18 realms and twelve spheres? Hence, we cannot say that the life of No-Thought Heaven has any place to exist. O good man! For example, the god of a tree lives in the tree. We cannot definitely say that he lives in the branch, the knot, the trunk, or the leaf. Though we cannot name the place, we cannot say that he does not exist. The life of No-Thought Heaven is also like that. O good man! The case of Buddha-Dharma is likewise thus. It is very deep and unfathomable. The Tathagata has no apprehension, suffering or worry. Yet, he evinces great compassion towards beings, has apprehension and sorrow, and views them as he views Rahula. "Also, next, the life of No-Thought Heaven can only be known by the Buddha. It is beyond the ken of others. Also, the same applies to Thoughtlessness-non-Thoughtlessness Heaven. O Kasyapa! The nature of the Tathagata is pure and untainted, and is like a transformed body. How can there be any apprehension, suffering or worry? If the Tathagata has no apprehension or suffering, how can he bestow benefit upon beings and disseminate the Buddhist teaching? If "no", how can we say that he sees beings as he sees Rahula? If he does not see beings as he sees his Rahula, any such statement can only be false. Hence, O good man, the Buddha is inconceivable, Dharma is inconceivable, the nature of beings is inconceivable, and the life of No-Thought Heaven is inconceivable. Whether the Tathagata has any apprehension or not is for the world of the Buddha [to know]. It is not what sravakas or pratyekabuddhas can fathom out. "O good man! For example, a house cannot stand in the air as it is for a moment. If one says that a house cannot remain in the air, this is not something that can be said. For this reason, one should not say: "A house in the air can stand or not." A common mortal may say that a house stands in the air. But there is no place in the air where it can remain. Why not? Because, by nature, it has no place to stay. O good man! The same is the case with the mind. Do not say that its abode is in the five skandhas, the 18 realms, or the 12 spheres. The same with the life

of No-Thought Heaven. Regarding any apprehension and sorrow of the Tathagata it is also like this. If he has no apprehension and sorrow, how can we say that he views [all beings] with an all-equal eye, as though viewing Rahula? A person might well say that he has [apprehension and sorrow], yet how [then] can one say that his nature is like the Void? "O good man! As an example: a magician may conjure up such diverse things as a palace, killing, long life, binding or undoing, gold, silver, beryl, treasures, forests, and trees. But these have no place where they exist. The same with the Tathagata. Following the way of the world, he displays apprehension and sorrow. There can be [in actuality] no such forms [i.e. no such things as these with him]. O good man! The Tathagata has already entered Parinirvana. How could there be any apprehension, sorrow, or worry? Now the Tathagata enters Nirvana. If anyone says that this is the non-eternal, know that this person has apprehension and sorrow. No one can truly know whether the Tathagata has apprehension or not. "Also, next, O good man! As an example: a person who lives in a low social sphere can certainly know what obtains in the lower sphere of life. But he cannot know what obtains in the middle or upper spheres of life. A person of the middle sphere knows what obtains in the middle sphere, but not in the upper. A person of the upper sphere knows about that upper sphere, but not about the middle or lower spheres. It is the same with sravakas and pratyekabuddhas. Likewise, a person only knows what is of his own sphere. It is not thus with the Tathagata. He knows his own sphere, as well as those of others. That is why we say that the Tathagata is unhindered. He manifests phantoms and follows the ways of the world. The fleshly eyes of common mortals see this. They say that it is true. They may desire to know the unhindered and unsurpassed Wisdom of the Tathagata, but this never comes about. Only the Buddha knows what is apprehension and what is not. Hence, different things possess the Self and different things do not possess the Self. This is what we mean when we say that things obtain as in the case of the mandarin duck and the kacalindikaka. "Also, next, O good man! The Buddhist teaching is like the mandarin duck [and kacalindikaka] who go about together. The mandarin duck and the kacalindikaka seek out uplands in midsummer when the water is high and deposit their young there. This is to bring raise them. Later, they play as they originaly ought to. The same with the appearance of the Tathagata. He teaches innumerable beings and enables them to abide in Wonderful Dharma. This is like the mandarin duck and the kacalindikaka seeking out uplands and safely depositing their young ones there. The same with the Tathagata. He enables beings to act as they ought to act and enables them to enter Mahaparinirvana. O good man! That is to say that suffering is one teaching [dharma] and bliss is a different one [dharma]. All created things are sorrow; Nirvana is Bliss. It is most wonderful and destroys created things [i.e. lifts one beyond the created sphere]." Bodhisattva Kasyapa said to the Buddha: "O World-Honoured One! How do beings attain Nirvana and gain the pre-eminent Bliss?" The Buddha said:

"O good man! As stated, the fusion of composites is age-and-death.
If strict in one's way of life and not indolent,
This is amrta [the deathless, ambrosia].
To be indolent and not strict
In one's way of life is death.
Non-indolence gains one the deathless place;
Indolence always leads one to death."

"Indolence is of the created, the foremost of suffering. Non-indolence is Nirvana, the foremost of amrta and Bliss. The created is a place of death, the foremost of suffering. Nirvana is deathlessness, the most wonderful Bliss. Indolence calls in [i.e. is generative of] the created. This too is spoken of: eternal Bliss, deathlessness, and the Body Indestructible. What is indolence and what is not? The unholy common mortal [i.e. a tirthika] is of indolence and eternal death; the world-fleeing holy one ["shramana"] belongs to the class of non-indolence, in whom age-and-death has no abode. Why not? He gains the foremost of eternal Bliss and Nirvana. The holy persons of the supramundane stage have no indolence and there exists [for them] no age-and-death. Why not? They enter into the foremost stage of eternal Nirvana. Hence, Suffering and Bliss are two different things; Self and non-Self are two different things. "A man stands on the ground and looks up at the sky, where he can see no trace of where the birds have flown. The same is the case [here]. O good man! The same is the case with beings. They do not possess the heavenly eye. Immersed in illusion, they cannot see the nature of the Tathagata, which they possess. For this reason, I now expound the [hitherto] undisclosed teaching on selflessness. Why? "A person who lacks the heavenly eye does not know the True Self". Because he estimates Self in the wrong way. All things created by illusion are non-eternal. That is why I say that the Eternal and the non-Eternal are two different things.

"If one with effort and courage
Gains the summit of a mountain,
One sees the plains, the expanse of the fields and all beings.
As one gains the great palace of Wisdom
And the seat that is topless [topmost] and wonderful,
One already makes away with apprehension and suffering
And sees the apprehension of beings.

"The Tathagata cuts off innumerable illusions, lives in the mountain of Wisdom, and sees beings who live amidst innumerable billions of illusions." Bodhisattva Kasyapa said to the Buddha: "O World-Honoured One! Things are not as stated in the gatha. Why not? One who enters Nirvana has no apprehension or joy. How can such a person gain the palace of Wisdom? Moreover, living on the summit of the mountain, how can one see beings?" The Buddha said: "O good man! The palace of Wisdom is Nirvana. The person with no apprehension is the Tathagata; the person who has apprehension is the common mortal. The common mortal has apprehension and the Tathagata has not. The summit of Mount Sumeru is true emancipation. One who incessantly makes effort is like Mount Sumeru, which knows of no shaking. The earth is a thing created. All common mortals live peacefully on the earth and do all [manner of] things. Wisdom is true Awakening. A person away from existence is one eternal. This is the Tathagata. The Tathagata has pity for the innumerable beings who are exposed to the poisonous arrows of all existences. That is why we say that the Tathagata has apprehension." Bodhisattva Kasyapa said to the Buddha: "O World-Honoured One! If the Tathagata has apprehension and sorrow, he could not be the All-Enlightened One." The Buddha said to Kasyapa: "All depends on the circumstances. As he sees that his presence is called for to save beings, the Tathagata manifests himself. Though manifesting himself in life, there is yet [here] truly no life. That is why we call the Tathagata one who is Eternal. The case is like that of the kacalindikaka and the mandarin duck."

Chapter Fifteen: On the Parable of the Moon

The Buddha said to Kasyapa: "As an example: there is a man here who, as he sees that the moon is not yet out, says that the moon has departed, and entertains the thought that the moon has sunk down. But this moon, by its nature, does not sink down. When it appears on the other side of the world, the people of the other side say that the moon is out. Why? Since Mount Sumeru obstructs [vision], the moon cannot reveal itself. The moon is always out. It has, by nature, no coming out or sinking down. The same is the case with the Tathagata, the Alms-deserving, the All-Enlightened One. He manifests himself in the 3,000 great-thousand worlds; or he gives the semblance of having parents in Jambudvipa or of entering Nirvana in Jambudvipa. The Tathagata, by nature, does not enter Nirvana. But all beings say that he truly enters Parinirvana. The case is analogous to the sinking of the moon. O good man! The Tathagata, by nature, does not possess the nature of birth and death. To succour beings, he manifests [his] birth and death. "O good man! On the other side of this full moon, we have the half-moon; on this side, we have the half-moon and on the other side, the full moon is seen. The people of Jambudvipa, when they see the first moon, say that it is the first day, and have in mind the idea of a new month. Seeing the full moon, they say that it is the 15th day of the month and entertain the notion of the full moon. But this moon has, truth to tell, no waxing or waning [with it]. Only due to Mount Sumeru does it show a semblance of waxing and waning. O good man! The same is the case with the Tathagata. In Jambudvipa, he manifests birth and enters Nirvana. His first coming out [appearance in the world] is the first of the month. Everybody says that this boy is first born. He strides seven paces. This is like the moon on the second day. Or he shows himself studying. This is like the moon on the third day. He displays renunciation. This is like the moon of the eighth day. He emits the all-wonderful light of Wisdom and subdues an innumerable number of beings and the army of Mara. This may be likened to the full moon of the 15th day. Or he manifests the 32 signs of perfection and the 80 minor marks of excellence. He thus adorns himself and manifests Nirvana. He is like the eclipse of the moon. Thus, what beings see is not the same. Some see a half-moon, others a full moon, and still others an eclipse. But this moon, by its nature, knows of no waxing or eclipsing. It is always the full moon. The body of the Tathagata is like this. For this reason, we say eternal and unchanging. "Also, next, O good man! For example, by the full moon, everything comes out [appears]. In all places as in towns, hamlets, mountains, swamps, under-water, wells or ponds, and in water utensils, the moon manifests itself. Beings may be travelling 100 or 100 thousand yojanas, and the moon always accompanies them. Common mortals and the ignorant think loosely and say: "I see all such in the castle town, in the house, and here in the swampy ground. Is it the true moon, or not the true one?" Each person thinks about the size of the moon and says: "It is like the mouth of a kettle." Or a person says: "It is like a wheel." Or some may say: "It is like 45 yojanas [in size]." All see the light of the moon. Some see it as round as a golden basin. The nature of this moon is one in itself, but different beings see it in different forms. O good man! The same is the case regarding the Tathagata. He appears in the world. Man and god might think: "The Tathagata is now before us and lives." The deaf and dumb see the Tathagata as one deaf or dumb. Diverse are the languages which beings speak. Eack thinks that the Tathagata speaks as he or she speaks, or thinks: "At my house, the Tathagata received offerings." Or a person might see the size of the Tathagata as being very large and immeasurable; or someone might see him as very small; or a person might mistake him for a sravaka, or a pratyekabuddha; or various tithikas might think and say: "The Tathagata is now in my line of thought [following my line of thought] and is practising the Way"; or a person might think: "The Tathagata has appeared for me alone." The true nature of the Tathagata is like that of the moon. That is to say that it is the Dharma-Body, the Body of birthlessness, or that of expediency. He responds to the call of the world, being innumerable in [his] manifestations. The original karma manifests itself in accordance with the differing localities. This is as in the case of the moon. For this reason, the Tathagata is eternal and unchanging. "Also, next, O good man! Rahula-asura-raja covers the moon with his hands. The people of the world all then say that this is an eclipse of the moon. But Rahula-asura-raja cannot cause any eclipse to the moon. He merely obstructs the light of the moon. The moon is round. There is no part that drops away. Only as a result of the obstruction is the full play of light checked. Once the hands are withdrawn, the people of the world say that the moon has regained its power. All say that this moon suffers a lot. But even 100 thousand asura kings cannot cause it suffering. The case is like this. The same is the case with the Tathagata. Beings give rise to evil thoughts about the Tathagata, cause blood to flow, commit the five deadly sins, and act [as] icchantikas. Things are shown in such a way. For the sake of the beings to come, such things are displayed as acting against the Sangha, transgressing Dharma, and causing hindrances. Maras as innumerable as 100 thousand billion cannot hope to cause blood to flow from the body of the Buddha. Why not? Because the body of the Tathagata is not possessed of flesh, blood, sinews, marrow or bones. The Tathagata truly has no worry of disintegration. Beings say: "Dharma and Sangha have broken [disintegrated, dissolved] and the Tathagata is dead." But the Tathagata, by nature, is all true and there is no change or dissolution [with him]. Following the way of the world, he manifests himself thus. "Also, next, O good man! Two people have a fight with a sword and staff, cause bodily injury and draw blood, and death results. But if they had no thought [intention] of killing, the karmic consequence will be light, not heavy. The same is the case [here]. Even in relation to the Tathagata, if a person has no intention of killing [him], the same applies to this action. It is light and is not heavy. The same is the case with the Tathagata. To guide beings in the days to come, he displays karmic consequences. "Also, next O good man! This is like the doctor who makes effort and imparts basic medical knowledge to his son, saying that this is the root medicine, this is for taste, that is for colour [etc.], so as to enable his son to become familiarised with the various properties [of medicines]. The son pays heed to what his father says, makes effort, learns and comes to understand all the [different] types of medicine. The time comes when his father dies. The son yearns, cries, and says: "Father taught me, saying that this is root medicine, this is of the stem, this the flower, and this for colour." It is the same with the Tathagata. In order to guide

us, he gives beings restrictions. So one should try to act in accordance [with those restrictions] and not contrary [to them]. For those people of the five deadly sins, for those slandering Wonderful Dharma, for the icchantika, and for those who may do such [deeds] in days to come, he manifests such. All this is for the days after the Buddha's death, for the bhiksus to know that these are important points in the sutras, these are the heavy and light aspects of the precepts, these the passages of the Abhidharma which are weighty and not weighty. This is to enable them [i.e. beings] to be like the doctor's son. "Also, next, O good man! Humans see, once every six months, a lunar eclipse. And in the heavens above, just for a time, we see the lunar eclipse. Why? Because the days are longer there in the heavens and shorter in the human world. O good man! It is the same with the Tathagata. Both gods and humans say: "The Tathagata's life is short." This is as with the beings of the heavens who see the eclipse of the moon often for a short time. The Tathagata, likewise, for a short time manifests 100 thousand million billion Nirvanas, crushing out the Maras of illusion, of the skandhas, and of death. Hence, 100 thousand million billion heavenly Maras all know that the Tathagata enters Nirvana. Also, he displays 100 thousand innumerable karmas. All this comes from the fact that he follows the various natures of the world. Thus does it go with his manifestations. They are innumerable, boundless and inconceivable. For this reason, the Tathagata is eternal and unchanging. "Also, next, O good man! Beings take delight, for example, in seeing the bright moon. That is why we call the moon "that which is pleasing to see". If beings possess greed, malevolence and ignorance, there can be no pleasure in [such] seeing. The same with the Tathagata. The Tathagata's nature is pure, good, clean and undefiled. This is what is most pleasing to behold. Beings who are in harmony with Dharma will not shun [such] seeing; those with evil minds are not pleased by [such] seeing. Hence we say that the Tathagata is like the bright moon. "Also, next, O good man! Regarding sunrise, there are three differences of time, which are: spring, summer, and winter. In winter, the days are short; spring is in-between, and summer is the longest. The same is with the Tathagata. In the 3,000 great-thousand worlds, to all those short-lived [beings] and sravakas, he manifests a short life. Those seeing it all say: "The Tathagata's life is short."

This is comparable to a winter's day. To Bodhisattvas he manifests a medium-length life. It may last for a kalpa or less. This is similar to a spring day. Only the Buddha can know the life of the Buddha. This, for example, is like a summer's day. O good man! The Tathagata's delicate and undisclosed teaching of Mahayana vaipulya is given to the world like a great downpour of Dharma. If any person in the days to come upholds, reveals, understands [such teachings] and benefits beings, know that such a person is a true Bodhisattva. This is the sweet rain of heaven that falls in the summer. If sravakas and pratyeka-buddhas hear the hidden teaching of the Buddha-Tathagata, this is like encountering great cold on a winter's day. If a Bodhisattva hears the hidden teaching, i.e. that the Tathagata is eternal and unchanging, this is like the burgeoning that comes about in spring. And the Tathagata's nature is neither long nor short; he only manifests himself for the sake of the world. This is the true nature of all Buddhas. "Also, next, O good man! For example, stars are not seen in the daytime. But everybody says: "The stars die out in the daytime." But actually they do not die. The reason that they are not seen arises from the fact that the sun is shining brightly. The same with the Tathagata. The sravakas and pratyekabuddhas cannot see. This is as in the case of the stars that cannot be seen in the daytime. "Also, next, O good man! For example, in the gloom of the night, sun and moon are not seen. The ignorant say: "The sun and the moon have died." But, in truth, the sun and moon are not lost. The case is like this. At the time when the Tathagata's Wonderful Dharma dies out, the Three Treasures are also not seen. This is the analogous situation. It is not that they have eternally gone. Hence, one should know indeed that the Tathagata is eternal and that he does not change. Why not? Because the true nature of the Three Treasures does not get tainted by any illusions. "Also, next, O good man! For example, in the dark half of the month, a comet may appear at night, shining brightly like a flame. And soon it will die away. Beings see this and [say that it] foreshadows ill-fortune. The case is analogous to all pratyekabuddhas, too. Coming out in the Buddha-less days, beings see and say: "The Tathagata has truly died." And they entertain thoughts of apprehension and sorrow. But, truth to tell, the Tathagata has not died. It is as with the sun and moon, which know of no extinction. "Also, next, O good man! For example, when the sun rises, all the mist disperses. The situation is the same regarding this Great Nirvana Sutra. If one should once give ear to it, all ill and the karma of Avichi Hell will die out. Nobody can fathom what obtains in this Great Nirvana, which expounds the hidden store of the nature of the Tathagata. For this reason, good men and women entertain the thought that the Tathagata is Eternal, that he does not change, that Dharma does not cease to be, and that the Sangha Treasure does not die out. Hence, we should employ means, make effort, and learn this sutra. Such a person, in the course of time, will attain unsurpassed Enlightenment. That is why this sutra is said to contain innumerable virtues, and is also called one that knows no end of Enlightenment. Because of this endlessness, we can say Mahaparinirvana. The light of Good shines as in the sun's days. As it is boundless, we say Great Nirvana.

Chapter Sixteen: On the Bodhisattva

"Also, next, O good man! Of all lights, the light of the sun and the moon is unsurpassed. No other lights are their equal. The same with the light of Great Nirvana, which is the most wonderful of all the lights of the sutras and samadhis. It is one which cannot be reached by any of the lights of any of the sutras and samadhis. Why not? Because the light of Great Nirvana thoroughly gets into the pores of the skin. Though beings may not possess Bodhichitta, it yet causes Bodhi. That is why we say "Mahaparinirvana." Bodhisattva Kasyapa said to the Buddha: "O World-Honoured One! You say that the light of Great Nirvana penetrates the pores of the skin of all beings and that it calls forth the Bodhi mind, if beings do not have it. This is not so. Why not? If that is so, what difference can there be between those who have performed the four grave offences, those who have committed the five deadly sins, and the icchantikas, and those who uphold the pure precepts and practise every good deed, if it is the case that the light penetrates the pores of the skin and causes Bodhi [Enlightenment] to come about? If there exists no difference, how is it that the Tathagata speaks about the significations of the four things to stand [rely] upon ["catvari-pratisaranani"]? O World-Honoured One! In contradiction of the fact that, as you the Buddha say, if one once hears Great Nirvana, all defilements will be annihilated, you, the Tathagata, stated before that even if a person gives rise to Bodhichitta [resolve to gain Enlightenment] at the place of Buddhas as numerous as the sands of the Ganges, there are [yet] those who do not gain the meaning of Great Nirvana. How could a person make away with the root of defilement without gaining the meaning?" The Buddha said: "O good man! All people, other than the icchantikas, gain the cause of Enlightenment as soon as they hear this sutra. If the voice of Dharma and the light [of Great Nirvana] penetrate the pores of their skin, they [such people] will unfailingly attain unsurpassed Enlightenment. Why so? If anybody truly makes offerings and pays homage to all the Buddhas, they will surely gain occasion to hear the Great Nirvana Sutra. Persons not endowed with good fortune will not be blessed with hearing this sutra. Why not? A person of great virtue will indeed be able to give ear to something as important as this.

Common mortals and those less in grade cannot easily give ear to it. What is that which is Great? It is nothing other than the hidden store of all Buddhas, which is the Tathagata-Nature. That is why we say important." Bodhisattva Kasyapa said to the Buddha: "O World-Honoured One! How can a person who has not yet given rise to Bodhichitta hope for the cause of Enlightenment?" The Buddha said to Kasyapa: "If anyone who has heard this Great Nirvana Sutra says that he will never give rise to Bodhichitta and [thus] commits slander, such a person will see a rakshasa in a dream and feel afraid. And the rakshasa will say: "Hey, O good man! If no Bodhichitta comes about in you, I shall assuredly take your life." Feeling afraid and awakening from his dream, the person will aspire to Bodhi. After death, that person will be born in the three evil realms or in the world of humans or gods, and he will think about Bodhichitta. Know that this person is a great Bodhisattva. Thus the great divine power of this Nirvana Sutra well enables a person who has not aspired to Enlightenment to attain the cause of Enlightenment. O good man! This is how a Bodhisattva aspires to Bodhi. It is not that there is no cause. Thus, the wonderful Mahayana sutras are what the Buddha spoke. "Also, next, O good man! A great rain-cloud gathers in the sky, and the rain falls upon the earth. The water does not remain on the dead trees, rocky mountains, plateaux and hills. But as it flows down to the paddy-fields down below, all the ponds become full, benefiting innumerable people. The case is the same with this Great Nirvana Sutra. It pours down the great rain of Dharma, benefiting beings. Only the icchantika does not aspire to Enlightenment. "Also, next, O good man! For example, a burnt seed will not call forth buds, even if the rain falls on it for a period of 100 thousand million kalpas. There can never be a situation in which this seed will bring forth buds. The same with the icchantika. No bud of Enlightenment springs forth, even if the icchantika gives ear to this all-wonderful Great Nirvana Sutra. Such can never happen. Why not? Because such a person has totally annihilated the root of good. As with the burnt seed, no root or bud of Bodhichitta will shoot forth. "Also, next, O good man! For example, we deposit a bright gem in muddy water. But by virtue of the gem, the water of itself becomes clear. But even this, if placed in mud, cannot make the mud clear. The same with this all-wonderful Great Nirvana Sutra. If placed in the defiled water of people guilty of the five deadly sins and those who have committed the four grave offences too, it can indeed still call forth Bodhichitta. But in the mud of the icchantika, even after 100 thousand million years, the water cannot become clear and it cannot call forth Bodhichitta. Why not? Because this icchantika has totally annihilated the root of good and is not worth that much. The man could listen to this Great Nirvana Sutra for 100 thousand million years, and yet there could be no giving rise to the Bodhichitta [inside him]. Why not? Because he has no good mind. "Also, next, O good man! For example, there is a medicinal tree, whose name is "king of medicines". Of all medicines, this is the best. It can well be mixed with milk, cream, honey, butter, water, or juice; or it can be made into powder or pills, or one can apply it to wounds, or cauterize the body with it, or apply it to the eyes; or one can look at it or smell it. It cures all illnesses and diseases of beings. This medicine tree does not say to itself: "If beings take [my] root, they should not take the leaves; if they take the leaves, they should not take the root; if they take the wood, they should not take the bark; if they take the bark, they should not take the wood." Although the tree does not think in this way, it nevertheless can cure all illnesses and diseases. The case is similar. O good man! The same is also the case with this Nirvana Sutra. It can thoroughly make away with all evil actions, the four grave offences and the five deadly sins, and any such evil actions in and out [of thought, word, or deed]. Any person who has not yet aspired to Bodhichitta, will indeed come to aspire to it. How so? Because this all-wonderful sutra is the King of all sutras, as the medicine tree is the king of all medicines. There may be those who have learnt this Great Nirvana Sutra or those who have not. Or they may have heard the name of this sutra and, on hearing it, may entertain respect and believe [in it]. And through this, all the great illnesses of defilement will be annulled. Only the icchantika cannot hope to attain unsurpassed Enlightenment,

as in the case of the all-wonderful medicine, which, though it does indeed cure all illnesses and diseases, cannot cure those persons who are on the brink of death. "Also, next, O good man! One may have a wound in one's hand. If one pours poison into it, this poison will get in; if there is no wound, the poison will not get in. The same with the icchantika. There is no cause for Bodhichitta. It is like one who has no wound in his hand. So there can be no entry. The so-called wound is the cause of unsurpassed Enlightenment; the poison is the unsurpassed wonderful medicine. The one who has no wound is an icchantika. "Also, next, O good man! A diamond is something which no one indeed can break. It truly cuts all things, excepting tortoise shell and goat's horn. The same with this sutra. It indeed places all beings safely on the path to Enlightenment. Only, it cannot make the icchantika class of people gain the cause of Enlightenment. "Also, next, O good man! One may well cut off the branch or stem of the urslane, sal or niskara [trees], but the branches will grow back, just as before; but with the tala [fan palm] tree, when a branch is cut off, no branch can grow back [in its place]. The case is analogous. If one hears this Great Nirvana Sutra, even those people of the four grave offences and the five deadly sins can still indeed cultivate the cause of Bodhichitta. With the icchantika, things cannot be thus. Even on hearing this beautiful sutra, he cannot arrive at the cause of Enlightenment. Also, next, O good man! The same is the case with khadira [acacia catechu] and tinduka [diospiros embryoteris], which when once their branches are cut off, never put forth shoots again. It is the same with the icchantika. He may hear this Great Nirvana Sutra, but no cause of Bodhichitta will ensue. Also, next, O good man! It is as in the case of the great rain that never remains in the sky. The same with this all-wonderful Great Nirvana Sutra. This sutra rains down the rain of Dharma. It does not stay upon the icchantika. The whole body of the icchantika is so minutely made as might well be compared to a diamond, which never allows other things to get in. The same is the case [here]." Bodhisattva Kasyapa said to the Buddha: "Just as you say in your gatha:

"A person does not see or do good;
What he does is evil.
This is much to be dreaded, as in the case
Of a road that is steep and hard to pass."

"O World-Honoured One! What is the meaning of this?" The Buddha said: "O good man! We say that we "do not see", which means that we do not see the Buddha-Nature. "Good" refers to unsurpassed Enlightenment. We say that we "do not do", which means to say that we do not come near a good friend [good teacher of Buddhism]. We "but see" means to say that we see things as having no causal relations. By evil is meant slandering the vaipulya Mahayana sutras. "To do" corresponds to the icchantika's saying that there cannot be any vaipulya. Because of this, there is no occasion for the icchantika's mind to turn to what is pure and good. What is "Good Dharma"? It is Nirvana. One who walks along the way to Nirvana indeed practises what is wise and good. With the icchantika, there is nothing that is wise and good. As a result, there can be no turning towards Nirvana. That one should "dread" means the dread of slandering Wonderful Dharma. Whom do we fear? It is the wise. Why? Because a person who slanders, possesses no good mind and no expedients. The way that is hardgoing alludes to all practises." Kasyapa said further: "You, the Tathagata, say:

"How do we see what is done?
How do we get to Good Dharma,
And where is the place that knows no dread?
It is as with the flat kingly road."

What does this mean?" The Buddha said: "O good man! "To see what is done" is simply laying bare all evils done. When all the evils done since the beginning of birth and death have once been laid bare, one gains a place where there is nowhere further to go. As a result, what there is here is fearlessness. For example, this is as in the case of the royal road from which all robbers hide. Thus bared, evils all become annihilated, and there remains nothing behind. "Also, next, "not to see what one does" means that the icchantika does not see all that he does. This icchantika, out of arrogance, does many an evil deed. And in doing so, he has no fear. As a result, he cannot gain Nirvana. For example, this is as in the case of a monkey that tries to grab at the moon reflected in a watery surface. O good man! Even if all innumerable beings attain unsurpassed Enlightenment at a time [at one time, eventually], none of the Tathagatas sees the icchantika attaining Enlightenment. For this reason, we say that "what is done is not seen". Also, whose action is not seen? It is that of the Tathagata. The Buddha, for the sake of beings, says that there is the Buddha-Nature. The icchantika, repeating lives, cannot know or see [the Buddha-Nature]. That is why we say that one does not see what the Tathagata does. Also, the icchantika thinks that the Tathagata enters Nirvana for good, saying that all is transient, just as, when the flame goes out, the oil too is spent. Why? Because this person's evil actions have not come to an end. If there is here a Bodhisattva who transfers [the merit of] all the good deeds he has done towards unsurpassed Enlightenment, those of the icchantika class commit slander and do not believe. Despite even this, all Bodhisattvas carry on giving as ever and desire to attain Enlightenment. Why? This is how things proceed with the laws [dharmas] of all Buddhas.

"Evil is done, but the result does not
Appear at once. It appears
Like cream that comes from milk.
This is as when ash is placed over a fire
And the ignorant carelessly step on it."

"The iccantika is the eyeless. So he does not see the path of arhatship, the path along which the arhat does not take the steep and arduous path of life-and-death. Being eyeless, he slanders the vaipulya and does not desire to practise the Way, like the arhat who tries to learn compassion. Likewise, the icchantika does not practise the vaipulya. There may be a person who says: "I do not believe in the sutras of the sravaka. I believe in Mahayana, recite the sutras and expound [them]. So I am now a Bodhisattva. All beings possess the Buddha-Nature. Because of the Buddha-Nature, beings possess within themselves the 10 powers, the 32 signs of perfection, and the 80 minor marks of excellence. What I say does not differ from what the Buddha says. You now destroy, together with me, a countless number of defilements, just as in the case where one breaks a water pot. By destroying the bond of defilement, I can now see unsurpassed Enlightenment." The person may say this. Although he speaks in this way, he does not believe that people have within them the Tathagata-Nature. Just for the sake of profit, this person speaks in this way, following what is written. One who so talks is one evil. Such an evil person will not gain the result, as of milk becoming cream. For example, a king's emissary talks well and deftly practises expedients and has duties in foreign lands. Even if it means his life, he does not leave unsaid, to the end, what he has to say on behalf of the king. The same with the wise man, too. He does not care much about his own safety, but always talks about the hidden doctrine of Mahayana vaipulya and says that all beings possess the Buddha-Nature. "O good man! There is an icchantika, who impersonates an arhat and lives in a quiet place, slandering the vaipulya Mahayana sutras. Everybody, on seeing him, says that he is a true arhat, a great Bodhisattva. This icchantika, an evil bhiksu, lives in a quiet place and breaks the law of [such] a quiet place. Seeing others obtaining benefit, he experiences jealousy and says: "All the vaipulya Mahayana sutras are what Marapapiyas speaks." Or he might say: "The Tathagata is non-eternal." He transgresses against Wonderful Dharma and causes disruption in the Sangha. Such words as these are those of Mara and not a doctrine that is good and meek. Such is what is evil. This person does evil, but the consequences of those evil actions do not manifest immediately, as cream [does not immediately] arise from milk; or when ashes are placed over a fire, the ignorant make light of it and step on it. The icchantika is such a person. Hence, we should know that the all-wonderful vaipulya sutras of Mahayana are definitely pure. This is as in the case of the mani [jewel, gem] which, when placed in muddy water, makes the water clean and transparent. It is the same with the Mahayana sutras, also. "Further, O good man! For example, it is as in the case of a lotus bud, which, when the sun shines upon it, does not fail to open. The same is the case with beings. Should one encounter the sun of Great Nirvana, anyone unacquainted with Enlightenment will aspire to it and sow the seed of Enlightenment. That is why I say: "When the light of Great Nirvana penetrates the pores of the skin, this immediately begets the wonderful cause of Enlightenment." The icchantika possesses the Buddha-Nature, but overspread by innumerable defilements, he cannot hope to get out [of his cocoon of defilements], analogous to the silkworm. For this reason, he cannot gain the all-wonderful cause of Enlightenment, but repeats birth and death unendingly.

"Also, next, O good man! For example, it is as with the utpala, padma, kumuda or pundarika [lotuses], which even though born in the mud, do not get tainted by the mud. With any person who studies the all-wonderful Great Nirvana Sutra, the same is the case. The person has defilement, yet is not tainted by it. Why not? Because of the power which knows the nature of the Tathagata. For example, O good man! There is a land where there is a great deal of cool wind. If it comes into contact with the body and the pores of beings' skin, it well makes away with all the worry [irritation, unpleasantness] of suppressed dampness. The same with this Mahayana Great Nirvana Sutra. It enters the pores of beings' skin and engenders the delicate [causal] relations of Enlightenment. However, the situation is otherwise with the icchantika. Why? Because he is no vessel of Dharma. "Also, next, O good man! For example, a good doctor knows eight kinds of medicine and cures illnesses, excepting the asadhya [illness which is incurable]. The same is the situation with all sutras, dhyanas and samadhis. These cure all the defilements of greed, ill-will and ignorance, and indeed extract the poisonous arrows, but cannot cure the four grave offences and the five deadly sins. "O good man! Also, there is a good doctor who knows more than eight treatments, by which he thoroughly cures all beings' illnesses. Only the asadhya he is unable to cure. The same is the case with this Mahayana Great Nirvana Sutra. It truly cures the worries of beings and allows them to rest in peace in the Tathagata's all-wonderful cause [that cause which makes one become a Tathagata], and makes those aspire to Enlightenment who have not yet aspired to Enlightenment, except for the icchantika, who is sure to die. "Also, next, O good man! A good doctor can indeed cure the blind with wonderful medicines, and the blind can see all the forms of the sun, moon and the constellations. Only those congenitally blind, he cannot cure. The case is like this. The same with this Mahayana Great Nirvana Sutra. It well opens the eyes of sravakas and pratyekabuddhas and bestows on them the eye of Wisdom and enables them to rest in peace in the innumerably large number of Mahayana sutras. Even those who have not aspired to Enlightenment, such as those who have committed the four grave offences and the five deadly sins, may also aspire to Enlightenment, excepting the congenitally blind icchantikas. "Also, next, O good man! For example, a good doctor knows eight types of treatment and cures all illnesses and pains of beings. Various kinds of treatment and medicine are prescribed according to the illness. In the case of vomiting and loose bowels, medicine is smeared over the body and sprinkled on the nose, or cauterization or cleansing medicine is used, or given in pills and powders. Medicine is given in all such ways. Yet the poor and ignorant do not wish to take it. Pitying them, the good doctor takes them to his own house and presses the medicine upon them. Due to the power of the medicine, the illnesses disappear. There is a female patient, whose navel cord [umbilical cord] does not come out. After the medicine has been taken, it comes out at once and makes the child feel easy. The same with this Mahayana Great Nirvana Sutra. Wherever it may go, [if it] be in the home of any being, all worries get extracted, such as those of the four grave offences and the five deadly sins, and those not yet aspiring to Enlightenment are made to awaken to it, except the icchantika." Bodhisattva Kasyapa said to the Buddha: "O World-Honoured One! The four grave offences and the five deadly sins are the gravest of all ill deeds. It is like cutting [a branch off] the tala tree, as a result of which no new branch will appear. How can the mind with no aspiration for

Enlightenment harbour the cause of Enlightenment?" The Buddha said: "O good man! For example, these people have dreams in which they fall into hell and suffer pain there and repent, saying: "Oh, this pain! We have invited this upon ourselves. If we can only get out of this, we shall certainly care about Enlightenment. What we have is the worst [of suffering]." On awakening from their dream, they come to see the great recompense of Wonderful Dharma awaiting them. It is like the child who gradually grows up and thinks: "This is the doctor, who knows best about prescriptions and medicines. When I was still in the womb, he gave my mother medicine. As a consequence of this, she was in peace, and by reason of these circumstantial factors, I was out of danger. Oh, how dreadul that my mother had to undergo great pain. For ten months she guarded and carried me. After my birth, she took care that I should not be too dry or too damp, and saw to my excretions; she gave me milk and fed me. For all of this, I must pay her back what I owe her, see to her feelings, be obedient to her and serve her". "A person may have committed the four grave offences and the five deadly sins. But if at the moment of passing away from this world he thinks of this Mahayana Great Nirvana Sutra, this will engender the cause of Enlightenment, even if a person may be in hell, or born as an animal, hungry ghost, or be born in heaven or as a human, except the icchantika. "Also, next, O good man! For example, a good doctor and his son know a great deal and far surpass others. They know wonderful charms and antidotes to poisons. The case may be as that of deadly snake venom, naga or adder, but their [the doctor and his son's] medicinal charms effect release. This good medicine is smeared on a leather boot, and if the boot touches the insect poison, the poison loses its virulence, except for that of the "mahanaga". The same with the Mahayana Great Nirvana Sutra. Those beings who have committed the four grave offences or the five deadly sins all get detoxified and attain Enlightenment. This is analogous to the detoxified leather footgear. A person who has no Bodhichitta gains it and awakens to unsurpassed Enlightenment. All this comes about through the working of the divine medicine of the Mahayana Great Nirvana Sutra. All beings are deposited in peace, except the mahanaga and the icchantika. "Also, next, O good man! A man may have invented a new poison and smeared it on a drum, which, when it is beaten in a crowd, lets the sound come by [lets out a great sound]. No one wishes to hear it. But anyone who does hear it dies, except for him who is immune to death. The same is the case with this Mahayana Great Nirvana Sutra. Any person of any place or profession, on hearing this sound, makes away with all such [defilements] as greed, ill-will and ignorance. There may be those who do not think about it, yet, because of the great power generated by the Great Nirvana Sutra, defilement disappears and the bond breaks. Even those of the four grave offences and the five deadly sins, when they hear this sutra, engender the cause of unsurpassed Enlightenment and, by degrees, cut off the bonds of defilement, except for the icchantika, who is immune to dying. "Also, next, O good man! For example, as twilight falls, all stop work. A person whose work is not completed always waits till sunrise. Those who practise Mahayana practise all kinds of sutras and samadhis, but they always wait till [for] the sunrise of the Mahayana Great Nirvana Sutra. On hearing this undisclosed teaching of the Tathagata, they give rise to actions for Enlightenment, and then abide in Wonderful Dharma. This is as in the case of the rain that falls from the sky upon all things, gives moisture, benefits and increases work, so that it does away with famine, and a rich harvest results. The same is the case with the innumerable amount of undisclosed rain of the Dharma of the Tathagata. It indeed makes away with fevers. The appearance in the world of this sutra is like fruit which benefits and makes all happy, enabling beings to see the Tathagata-Nature. Of all the flowers of Dharma, 8,000 sravakas get blessed with their prophecy [to Buddhahood] and accomplish the great fruition. In autumn, harvesting is done and in winter storing, and there is nothing more to do. The same with the icchantika. With all good laws [dharmas], there is nothing more to do. "Also, next, O good man! There is a doctor, who hears that the son of a certain person has been taken [possessed] by a demon. So he sends a messenger with a wonderful medicine, saying to him: "Take this medicine and give it to the person. If the person encounters various demons of evil design, the virtue of this medicine will drive such away. Should you be late in going, I shall go myself. I will not have this boy die. If the person who is ill sees the messenger and this virtue of mine, all worries will disappear and there will be peace." The same is the case with this Mahayana Great Nirvana Sutra. If all bhiksus, bhiksunis, upasakas, upasikas, and even tirthikas hold this sutra, read, grasp and expound it to other persons, or copy or have others copy it, all such actions will become the cause of Enlightenment. Even those who have committed the four grave offences and the five deadly sins, or those who are caught by wicked demons or poison or evil, as soon as they hear this sutra, will do away with all evil. This is just as in the case of that doctor, on seeing whom all devils flee. Know that this person is a true Bodhisattva. Why? Because he has been able to hear the Great Nirvana Sutra even for a little while; also, because he thinks of the eternal nature of the Tathagata. Anyone who has it [i.e. this sutra] even for a little while gains such benefit. How could this not be all the more the case when one copies, upholds and reads it? Other than the icchantika, all [of the above] are Bodhisattvas. "Also, next, O good man! It is as in the case of a deaf person, who cannot hear. The same is the case with the icchantika. Also, he may desire to hear the teaching of this wonderful sutra, yet he cannot. Why not? Because he has not sown the seed for it. "Also, next, O good man! For example, a good doctor knows all about medicine and prescription. In addition, he has extensive knowledge of innumerable charms. This doctor, received in audience by the king, said: "O King! You have an illness that will take your life." The king replied: "You have not seen inside me. How can you say that I have an illness that will assuredly take my life?" The doctor said further: "If you don't believe me, please take this purgative. Once the purgative has been taken, you, King, can look into it [your body] yourself." And the king deliberately did not take the purgative. The good doctor, through charms, effected means [to show] that, in the [normally] hidden parts of the king's body, poxes and pimples came out, and also whites came out, mixed up with worms and blood. Seeing this, the king became greatly frightened and praised the skill of the doctor: "Well done, well done! I did not take up [accept, implement] what you said before. I now know that you do great things for me." He then respected the doctor like his own parent. The same with this Mahayana Great Nirvana Sutra. From all beings, whether greedy or not greedy, this sutra extracts defilements. All these beings see this sutra even in their dreams, respect it, and make offerings to it. This is similar to the king who respects the skilful doctor. This great skilful doctor does not diagnose a person who is sure to die. The same is the case with this Mahayana Great Nirvana Sutra. The exception is the icchantika: he has no means of being cured. "Also, next, O good man! A good doctor knows eight ways of treatment and cures all illnesses. But he cannot cure a person who is on the brink of death. The same with all Buddhas and Bodhisattvas. They cure all sinful persons. Only a person on the brink of death, i.e. the icchantika, cannot be cured. "Also, next, O good man! For example, a good doctor is versed in all sutras and arts. His knowledge is so extensive that it goes beyond the eight [types of medicine]. He teaches what he knows to his son. He makes his son become acquainted with all medicinal herbs of watery places, lands, mountains and valleys. He teaches him by degrees, expounding the eight kinds; and then, he further makes him acquainted with the supreme arts. The same is the case with the Tathagata, the Alms-deserving and All-Enlightened One. First, he resorts to an expedient and makes his children, i.e. his bhiksus, annihilate all defilements and learn to abide in the thought of the purity [impurity] of the body and also in the thought of instability [of all dharmas]. We speak of "watery places" and "mountain valleys". By water is meant that the suffering of the body is like watery foam, and by land the instability of the body, like that of the plantain tree. By mountain valley is meant one's practising of selflessness, living as one does fully garbed in defilement. For this reason, the body is called selfless. The Tathagata thus, step by step, teaches his disciples the nine types of sutra and makes them thoroughly understand these, and after this he teaches the hidden Dharma of the Tathagata. For the sake of his sons, he speaks about the Eternal of the Tathagata. The Tathagata thus expounds the Mahayana Great Nirvana Sutra. For the sake of both the aspirant and the non-aspirant, he makes it the cause of Enlightenment, excepting the icchantika. Thus, O good man, this Mahayana Great Nirvana Sutra is an unnameably, boundlessly, and all-wonderfully rare thing. Know that this is the unsurpassed doctor, the most honoured, the most superior King of all sutras. "Also, next, O good man! An illustration! It is like the case of a big ship that sails from this shore to the other and from the other shore to this. The true Enlightenment of the Tathagata is also like this. Riding in the Mahayana treasure-ship of Great Nirvana, he sails and comes and goes back, saving all beings. In all places, wherever there are people qualified for being saved, he allows them to see the body of the Tathagata. Hence we call the Tathagata the unsurpassed master mariner. For example, a ship has a master mariner. If there is a master mariner, there are beings who [can] cross the great sea. Eternal is the Tathagata, who saves beings. "Also, next, O good man! For example, there is a man who may desire to ride in the great sea in a big ship and cross that sea. If the wind is favourable, he can sail a distance of immeasurably long yojanas within a short period. If not, he has to stand and wait for a long time, never moving a whit from his former place. Or the ship may break up, and a person may have to drown in the water and die. Beings thus float on the great sea of life and death of ignorance. But if the ship of the created meets with the favourable wind of Mahaparinirvana, a person can well gain the further shore of unsurpassed Enlightenment. If not, he will have to repeat innumerable births and deaths, and, at times, the ship may break up and he will have to fall into such realms as those of hell, animals and hungry ghosts. "Also, next, O good man! For example, there is a man who, not encountering the king of the wind, dwells for a long time upon the sea. He thinks: "I shall meet with my death here." As he thinks this, he encounters a goodly wind and, by means of it, crosses the sea. Or he may think: "This wind is good. It is a rare thing. We can now cross the sea safely, unbothered by any hardship." Thus, all beings, for a long time, live upon the sea of birth and death of ignorance, fight poverty and hardship, not yet encountering such a great wind of Nirvana as this, and think: "We shall surely fall into such realms as hell, animals, and hungry ghosts." As these beings think this, they encounter the wind of the Mahayana Great Nirvana Sutra and, in the course of time, gain unsurpassed Enlightenment, and arriving at Truth, they abide in a rare thought and express praise: "It is happy! I have, since of old, not once encountered or heard of such an undisclosed store of the Tathagata." And in this Great Nirvana Sutra they gain pure faith. "Also, next, O good man! Do you think that death comes or not to the serpent as it sloughs off its skin?" "No, O World-Honoured One!" "O good man! The same is the case with the Tathagata. He works out an expedient and manifests himself, and discards the non-eternal, poisoned body. Do you think that the Tathagata is non-eternal and dies away?" "No is the word, O World-Honoured One! The Tathagata abandons his body in this Jambudvipa as an expedient. The case is like that of an adder that sloughs off its old skin. That is why we say that the Tathagata is eternal." "Also, next, O good man! A goldsmith takes into his hand a piece of good gold and makes various things as he wills. The same is the case with the Tathagata. He manifests himself in the 25 existences, in various forms, and thus teaches beings and passes them across the sea of birth and death. That is why we say that the Tathagata is a boundless body. He thus manifests himself in various forms. But he is eternal; he does not change. "Also, next, O good man! The mango and jambu trees change three times a year. At one time, the flowers come out and gloriously shine; at another, the leaves come out luxuriantly; and at yet another time, the leaves fall and all looks as though dead. O good man! What does this mean? Does this tree die?" "No, O World-Honoured One!" "It is the same case with the Tathagata. He manifests himself in the three worlds in the three kinds [stages] of the body. At one time, he is born; at another, he grows up; at yet another, he displays death. And yet the Tathagata's body is not non-eternal. Bodhisattva Kasyapa praised [the Buddha] and said: "Well said! Everything is as you, Holy One, say. The Tathagata is eternal; no change arises." "O good man! What the Tathagata says in undisclosed terms is profound, not easy to grasp. It is like the case of a great king who orders his ministers to bring him "saindhava". The word, "saindhava", has four meanings. First, it means "salt"; secondly, "utensil"; thirdly, "water", and fourthly, "horse". Thus, four things have the same name. A wise minister knows the content of this word. When the king is washing and if he calls for saindhava, he gives him water. When he is eating and calls for saindhava, he gives him salt. When he has finished eating and desires to drink some juice and calls for saindhava, he gives him a utensil [goblet, vessel]. When he desire to indulge in recreation, he gives him a horse. Thus, the wise minister well grasps the meaning of the great king's words. The same is the situation with this Mahayana Great Nirvana Sutra. There are four non-eternals. The wise minister of Mahayana should know [them] well. If the Buddha appears in the world and says that he is going to enter Nirvana, the wise minister should know that the

Tathagata is speaking of the non-eternal for those who adhere to "is" and desires to teach the bhiksus to practise the non-eternal. Or he might say: "Wonderful Dharma is about to expire." The wise minister should know that the Tathagata is speaking of suffering to those whose mind adheres to "bliss", and to make the bhiksus abide in the thought of suffering. Or he might say: "I am ill now and am in pain; all bhiksus expire." The wise minister should know that the Tatahgata is addressing those attached to self on the matter of selflessness and desires to make the bhiksus practise the thought of selflessness. Or he might also say: "The so-called Void is true emancipation." The minister should know that the Tathagata [then] means to teach that there is no true emancipation and the 25 existences. This is for the bhiksus to practise the Void. Hence, right emancipation is the Void and, therefore, is immovable. "Immovable" means that in emancipation there is no suffering. Hence, immovable. This true emancipation is called "formlessness". Formless means that there is no colour, voice, smell, taste or touch. Hence, no characteristics. Therefore, true emancipation is eternal and does not change. With this emancipation, there is no non-eternal, nothing hot, no worry, and no change. Hence, this emancipation is called eternal, unchanging, pure, and cool. Or he may say: "All beings possess the Buddha-Nature." The wise minister should well know that the Tathagata is speaking of eternal Dharma and desires the bhiksus to practise the right aspect of eternal Dharma. Any bhiksu who thus practises the Way may know that he is truly my disciple. He indeed fathoms the undisclosed store of the Tathagata, just as the minister well grasps the great king's mind. O good man! Thus does the great king also have the undisclosed law. O good man! How could it be that the Tathagata would not possess any such? Hence, it is hard to know the hidden teaching of the Tathagata. Only a wise man can reach the great depths of what I teach. This is what common mortals can well believe. "Also, next, O good man! In a great drought, the palasa [butea frondosa], kanika [premna spinosa] and asoka [saraca indica] flowers do not bear fruit; also, all things of watery places and on land die or grow weak [in such a drought]. Without moisture, nothing can grow. Even medicines may look [prove] worthless. O good man! The same is the case with the

Mahayana Nirvana Sutra. After my death, people will not show respect and there will be no dignity or virtue. Why not? These people do not know the hidden store of the Tathagata. Why not? Because these people are born with little weal. "Also, next, O good man! When the Wonderful Dharma of the Tathagata is about to disappear, there may be many bhiksus who do evil. They know nothing of the hidden store of the Tathagata; they are indolent and lazy and do not know how to read the sutras of Wonderful Dharma, how to disseminate and understand them. This is like an ignorant robber abandoning true treasure and carrying grass and plants away on his shoulder. This comes from the fact that they do not understand the undisclosed store of the Tathagata. They are lazy and make no effort in the sutras. How pitiful it is that there is great danger which this world is confronted with. This is much to be feared. How sorrowful it is that beings do not give ear to this Mahayana Great Nirvana Sutra. Only all the Bodhisattvas see the true meaning of what this sutra states and do not become worried [made anxious] by letters [words]. They obediently follow and do not transgress. And they speak for the sake of beings. "Also, next, O good man! For example, a milking woman, intending to gain exorbitant profit, adds 20% water to the milk and sells it to another woman, who again adds 20% water and sells it to a woman living close to the castle town. This woman further adds 20% water and sells it to a woman living in the castle. This woman buys the milk and takes it to the market and sells it. At that time, there is a person who takes in a woman for the sake of his son. He chances to want to use good milk with which to serve his guest. He goes to the market and wants to buy some. The woman selling the milk demands the normal price. The man says: "This milk has a lot of water in it. So it is not worth the normal price. Today I have to treat a visitor. So I shall have it."

Taking this [milk] home, he cooks some porridge, but it has no milk flavour. Though it does not have any taste of milk, it is far better than any bitter thing; so it is a thousand times better. Why? Because of all tastes, milk is the best. "O good man! When I die, for 80 years when Wonderful Dharma has not yet expired, this sutra will be widespread in Jambudvipa. At that time, there will be many bhiksus of evil design who will cut this sutra into parts and simplify it, so that the colour,

flavour, beauty and taste of Wonderful Dharma will be lost. All these evil persons will read this sutra, despoil the profound and essential meaning of the Tathagata, enshrine [insert] merely grand, decorative and meaningless words that belong to the world. They will lop off the front part and add it to the back part of the sutra, or take off the back part and add it to the front, or they will put the front and back parts in the middle and the middle at the front and back. Know that such bhiksus are friends of Mara. They will keep and store all impure things and say that the Tathagata gave permission [for bhiksus] to do so. This is like the milking woman who adds water to the milk. It will be the same with these wicked bhiksus. They will add words of worldly life and despoil the fixed and right words of the sutras, and obstruct beings from [getting] the right sermons, from [making] correct copies, [having] right understanding, honouring, praising, making offerings to, and respecting, [the sutras]. Because of [their desire for] seeking profit, such bhiksus of evil design will not disseminate this sutra. The world where its benefits obtain will be so limited as not to be worth mentioning. This is as in the case of the poor milk-woman who adds water to the milk and sells it on, so that the porridge that is later made has no milk flavour. The same is the case with this Mahayana Great Nirvana Sutra. Its taste will gradually diminish and [eventually] no flavour will remain. The spirit will have gone; yet it will still be 1,000 times better than other sutras. It is as with the diluted milk, which is still 1,000 times better than any bitter thing. Why so? Because this Mahayana Great Nirvana Sutra is the best of all the sravaka class of sutras. It is as with milk, which is the best of all tastes. Hence, we say Great Nirvana. "Also, next, O good man! All good men and women desire to be born as a man. Why so? Because females are the nests of evil. Also, it is as in the case of the water of mosquitoes and sawflies, which cannot moisten this great earth. In addition, the sensual appetite of females cannot ever be satisfied. This is as though one were to make the great earth into a ball and then press it into a small pill. All such [vast numbers of] people may lustfully disport themselves with a female and [the female] will not ever be satiated. Even if as many people as the sands of the river Ganges disport themselves with a woman, there will be no satisfaction [on the part of the woman]. O good man! As an example, it is as with the great sea, into which flow the raindrops from the heavens and the waters of rivers, and yet the sea-water never indicates that it has had its fill. The same is the case with a woman. For example, even if all people were made male and had carnal sport with a woman, there would yet be no having had enough [on the part of the woman]. Also, next, O good man! The asoka, patala, and kanika put forth flowers in spring, when bees gather around the colour, smell, and the delicate taste, and there is no satisfying of them. It is the same with a female who desires to have a male. O good man! For this reason, all men and women who hear the teaching of this Mahayana Great Nirvana Sutra should always shun the female form and seek the male. Why so? This Mahayana sutra may be compared to a male. The point is that it has the Buddha-Nature. If one does not know the Buddha-Nature, one cannot be called a man. Why not? Because one does not realise that one has the Buddha-Nature within. Any person who does not realise that he has the Buddha-Nature is a woman. If he does so realise, he is a man. If any woman knows that she has the Buddha-Nature, she is a man. O good man! This Mahayana Great Nirvana Sutra is replete with innumerable, boundless and wonderful virtues. How so? Because it reveals the hidden store of the Tathagata. For this reason, O good men and women, if you desire swiftly to know of the hidden store of the Tathagata, you should devise means and study this sutra." Kasyapa said to the Buddha: "O World-Honoured One! It is so, it is so! It is as you, the Buddha, say. I now have the characteristics of a man, because I have now entered the hidden store of the Tathagata. The Tathagata has awakened me. In consequence, I shall now surely pass in." The Buddha said: "Well said, well said, O good man! What you know of the unsurpassed taste of Dharma is profound and difficult to fathom. And yet, you know well. You act like the bee. Also, next, O good man! It is as in the case of swamp-water in which mosquitoes live and which is not able to wet this earth. The same will be the case in the future with the propagation of this sutra in the world. It is just like the swampy ground where the mosquitoes live. When Wonderful Dharma becomes extinct, this sutra will become extinct in this land. Know that this is the declining fortune of this sutra. Also, next, O good man! For example, after summer comes autumn, when the autumnal rains fall one after another. The same with this Mahayana Great Nirvana Sutra. For the sake of the Bodhisattvas of the south, dissemination will proceed widely, and there will be the rain of Dharma, which will fully moisten the land. When Wonderful Dharma is about to become extinct, it goes to Kashmir and nothing lacks. It will get into the earth and become extinct. There may be a person who is faithful or a person who is not. The sweet taste of all such Mahayana vaipulya sutras then sinks into the ground. When the sutra [Mahaparinirvana] dies out, all other Mahayana sutras will die out too. If this sutra is perfect, this is none but the elephant king of men. All Bodhisattvas should know that the unsurpassed Wonderful Dharma of the Tathagata is about to die out before long." Then Manjushri said to the Buddha: "O World-Honoured One! Now, this Cunda has some doubt. Please, O Tathagata, explain [things] once more, and do away with [his] doubt." The Buddha said: "O good man! What do you mean by a "mind that doubts"? Speak out! I shall explain [matters]." Manjushri said: "Cunda has a doubt in [his] mind regarding the eternal nature of the Tathagata, because of the power that can well see the Buddha-Nature. If it is the case that there is the eternal when the Buddha-Nature is seen, there must be the non-eternal when it is not. If the basis is the non-eternal, this non-eternal will persist. Why? The law of the world is that a thing comes about which did not exist before. What existed before is not now [i.e. no longer is]. All things that proceed thus are non-eternal. Hence, there can be no difference between the Buddha, Bodhisattva, sravaka, and pratyekabuddha." Then the Buddha said in a gatha:

"What originally was is now not;
What originally was not is now.
There can be no "is" obtaining in the Three Times."

"O good man! For this reason, there can be difference between the Buddha, Bodhisattva, sravaka, and pratyekabuddha; and there can be no difference." Manjushri praised [the Buddha] and said: "It is good, it is just as you, Holy One, say. I now, for the first time, have come to know that there are cases of difference between the Buddhas, Bodhisattvas, sravakas, and pratyekabuddhas." Bodhisattva Kasyapa said to the Buddha: "O World-Honoured One! You, the Buddha, say that there is by nature no difference between the natures of the Buddha, Bodhisattva, sravaka, and pratyekabuddha. Please, O Tathagata! Condescend to tell [of this] in detail, explain [it] widely, and give benefit and peace to all beings." The Buddha said: "O good man! Litsten carefully, listen carefully! I shall now explain [it] to you. As an example: there is here a rich man. He has many cows, which are of various colours. He always has a man take care [of them] and bring them up [raise them]. This man, once on the occasion of a religious service, has all the cows milked and pours the milk into a container. The milk of all these cows is white. He sees this and is surprised. "The colour of these cows varies. How is it that the colour of the milk is white, all the same?" The man thinks and comes to realise that because of past karma and beings' causal relations, the colour of the milk becomes one [and the same]. O good man! It is the same with all sravakas, pratyekabuddhas, and Bodhisattvas. That all of these possess the same Buddha-Nature is as with milk. Why so? The reason is that all "asravas" [defilements, taints, "influxes" of unwholesome thoughts and emotions] are done away with. And yet, there are differences between the Buddha, sravaka, pratyekabuddha, and Bodhisattva. Yet all sravakas and common mortals doubt and say: "How could it be that there can be no difference between the three vehicles?" All these beings, after a long time, come to understand that all three vehicles equally have the Buddha-Nature. The case is similar to that of the milk, which appears as it does because of past karma. Also, next, O good man! For example, when gold is treated [smelted] in a furnace, the dregs [scum] are discarded. Smelted again, gold appears and its price becomes inestimable. O good man! It is the same with sravakas, pratyekabuddhas and Bodhisattvas. All can arrive at the same Buddha-Nature. Why? Because the defilements have been done away with. It is like doing away with the scum from gold ingots. Hence, all beings have the same Buddha-Nature. And when one first hears of the hidden store of the Tathagata and when one later attains Buddhahood, one, in the course of time, comes to know this fact. This is as in the case of the milk of the rich man, in which the oneness of

the quality of the milk becomes apparent. Why [this dawning of awareness]? Because innumerable billions of defilements have been done away with." Bodhisattva Kasyapa said to the Buddha: "O World-Honoured One! If all beings have the Buddha-Nature, what difference is there between the Buddha and [other] beings? If things are explained in such a way, misgivings can arise. If beings all have Buddha-Nature, how is it that Sariputra enters Parinirvana with [only] a small-sized Nirvana, the pratyekabuddha passes away into a middle-sized Nirvana, and the Bodhisattva passes away into great Nirvana? If they have the same Buddha-Nature, how could it be that they do not enter [Nirvana] as in the case of the Tathagata?" "O good man! The Nirvana attained by the All-Buddha-World-Honoured One is not that which sravakas and pratyekabuddhas attain. That is why we say that "Mahaparinirvana" is a "good existence". Even if there is no Buddha in the world, it is not the case that the two vehicles do not gain two Nirvanas." Kasyapa said further: "What might this mean?" The Buddha said: "Innumerable boundless asamkhyas of kalpas ago, there was a Buddha who appeared in the world and displayed the three teachings of the three vehicles. O good man! As to there being no difference between the Bodhisattvas and the two vehicles, about which you ask, I may say that I have already explained [this] when I spoke of the Great Nirvana of the hidden store of the Tathagata. All arhats have no element of good. Why? Because they are those who gain the great Nirvana. For this reason, there is after all bliss in Mahaparinirvana. That is why we say "Mahaparinirvana." Kasyapa said: "As you the Buddha have taught me, I now, for the first time, have realised the points of difference and non-difference. How? Because all Bodhisattvas, sravakas and pratyekabuddhas will attain Mahaparinirvana in the future. This is as with all rivers draining into the great sea. That is why we say that those sravakas and pratyekabuddhas are eternal and not non-eternal. Because of this, there is difference and there is no difference." Kasyapa said: "How is it that there is a difference in the nature [of Nirvana]?" The Buddha said: "O good man! The sravaka is like milk, the pratyekabuddha like cream, the Bodhisattva like butter, and the All-Buddha-World-Honoured One like sarpirmanda. That is why we say that there are four kinds of different nature in Great Nirvana."

Kasyapa spoke again: "What are the characteristics of the nature of all beings?" The Buddha said: "O good man! It is as in the case of a cow that is newly born and there is no difference between milk and blood. The same is the case with the nature of beings, which contains in it all defilements." Kasyapa said further: "At Kusinagara Castle, there was a candala called "Joy". When this person aspired to Enlightenment, the Buddha prophesied that this person would attain unsurpassed Enlightenment while living in this aeon of 1,000 Buddhas. Why is it that the Buddha does not make a prophecy and say that the venerable Sariputra and Maudgalyayana will attain Enlightenment at once?" The Buddha said: "O good man! The sravakas, pratyekabuddhas and Bodhisattvas may take vows: "I shall for eternal kalpas uphold Wonderful Dharma and shall then attain Buddhahood." When they have taken their vows, I give them their prophecy [to Buddhahood] instantly. Also, next, O good man! As an example: a merchant possesses a priceless treasure. He takes it to the market and sells it. The ignorant, not knowing what it is, laugh at it. The owner of the treasure says: "This treasure is priceless". On hearing this, they laugh again. The people, not knowing the value of this treasure, say that it is merely a piece of crystal. It is the same with the sravakas and pratyekabuddhas. If they receive an instant prophecy, they will become indolent, will laugh and regard things lightly. This is analogous to the ignorant people who do not know [the value of] the true treasure. In days to come, there will certainly be many bhiksus who won't make effort and practise the Way. They will be poor and in difficult circumstances, and they will suffer from hunger. In consequence, they will get ordained and live. Their minds will be rash and they will be impudent; they will live in the wrong way, flatter and tell lies. When they hear that the Tathagata gives sravakas their prophecy of instant attainment to Enlightenment, they will laugh it off, behave arrogantly, and even commit slander. This is nothing other than an infringement of the precepts. They will say that they have attained what others cannot. For this reason, Enlightenment is prophesied as soon as the vows are taken, to say that there will be instant attainment of Enlightenment. And to those who protect Wonderful Dharma, a prophecy is given for the days to come." Bodhisattva Kasyapa further said to the Buddha: "O World-Honoured One! How can a Bodhisattva avoid breaking relations with his kindred?" The Buddha said to Kasyapa: "All Bodhisattvas try to make effort and protect Wonderful Dharma. As a result, there can be no breaking of relations with those who are one's relatives." Bodhisattva Kasyapa said further to the Buddha: "O World-Honoured One! In what circumstances do beings come to have their mouth dried up?" The Buddha said to Kasyapa: "If a person does not know that there always exist the Three Treasures, in consequence his mouth will dry up and burn. Because of this, the human mouth turns the wrong way and that person is unable to distinguish the six tastes of what is sweet, bitter, pungent, sour, salty, and light. All beings are ignorant, have no intellect, and do not know that there are the Three Treasures. Hence, we say: "Lips and mouth get dried up and burn." Also, next, O good man! Any person who does not know that the Tathagata is eternal, such a person is one congenitally blind. Any person who knows that the Tathagata is eternal, though [he is] of fleshly eyes, is one with the Heavenly Eye. Also, next, O good man! Any person who knows that the Tathagata is eternal has long studied sutras of this kind. I also say that such a person is also of the class of people posssessing the Heavenly Eye. Though possessing it, if a person does not know that the Tathagata is eternal, such a person belongs to the class of [those possessed merely] of the fleshly eye. This type of person does not know his own hands and limbs, nor how to enable other to know, either. For this reason, he is of the fleshly eye. "Also, next, O good man! The Tathagata becomes the parent to all beings. How? All beings and various living things possess two feet [humans], four feet [animals], multiple feet [insects], and no feet [fish]. The Buddha talks about Dharma in one voice, and all such understand, utter praise, and say: "The Tathagata spoke to me alone [of] Dharma." For this reason, we say parent. "Also, next, O good man! A person gives birth to a child. After sixteen months, it speaks, but the words it speaks cannot be understood. The parents teach [the child] words, first repeating the same sound. Step by step, things progress. It is thus. Is it the case that the parents' words might be incorrect?" "No, O World-Honoured One!" "The same is the case with the Buddha-Tathagata. He teaches Dharma in accordance with the various sounds of beings. In order to have them rest peacefully in the

Wonderful Dharma of the Buddha, he manifests himself in various forms. The Tathagata speaks with the same tongue. Can this possibly proceed in an incorrect way?" "No, O World-Honoured One! Why not? Because the Tathagata's speech is like the roar of a lion. Following the sounds of the world, he speaks about Dharma for beings' sake."

Chapter Seventeen: On the Questions Raised by the Crowd

Then, the World-Honoured One emitted lights of such diverse colours as blue, red, white, crimson and purple, which shone over Cunda. Cunda, having been bathed in light, took up all the fine dishes with his kindred and carried them to where the Buddha was and offered them to the Tathagata and the bhiksus, desiring to make the final offerings. Taking these in various full-up vessels, they brought them to where the Buddha was. At that time, there was a deva of great virtue who came there and obstructed the way and, standing around, said: "O Cunda! Wait for a time, do not offer [yet]!" Then the Tathagata again shot forth innumerable boundless diverse lights. All the devas, encountering these lights, allowed Cunda to go forward and offer other things to the Buddha, and prostrating themselves on the ground said: "O Tathagata! Allow all the bhiksus to accept our offerings." The bhiksus, knowing that it was now time, took up their robes and bowls and, holding them, stood still in one mind [with the same concentrated mind]. Then Cunda set down various kinds of jewel-bedecked lion's-thrones for the Buddha and the bhiksus, hung up silken banners and parasols, and carried in, along with these, incense, flowers and garlands. At that time, the grandeur of the 3,000 great-thousand worlds was similar to the Western [Buddha-] Paradise of peace and happiness. Then Cunda, who was before the Buddha, sad and worried, said again to the Buddha: "O Tathagata! Please take pity and stay and live with us for a kalpa or even less." The Buddha said to Cunda: "If you desire to have me stay long in this world, make the final perfect offerings." Then, all the Bodhisattva-mahasattvas, devas and all others said in one voice: "Oh, it is wonderful, Cunda, that you have accomplished the greatest of virtues. You have done so well that the Tathagata has accepted [from you] the final offerings. We lack virtue, so that what we do ends in no good." Then the World-Honoured One, in order to satisfy the people, put forth from each pore of his skin a Buddha. Each Buddha had a retinue of innumerble bhiksus. All of these Buddhas and bhiksus partook of all the offerings which had been made. Tathagata Shakya himself took what Cunda presented [to him]. At that time, all the rice bran, all the well-cooked food, the eight koku [unit of measurement for cereals and liquids] of cereals that could well satisfy the people of all Magadha state were, through the divine power of the Buddha, served to all those who were congregated there. On seeing this, Cunda was overjoyed; his joy was inexpressible. The hearts of all those congregated there felt the same. Then all those congregated there, in accordance with the wish of the Buddha, thought in this manner: "The Tathagata now accepts our offerings. Before long, he will enter Nirvana." Thinking thus, they were both glad and sad. By the divine power of the Buddha, in a space the size of the point of a needle, there were gathered together an innumerable number of all Buddhas and their retinues, who all sat and ate. What they ate was all equal [all the same], with nothing differing. Then the devas, asuras and others all wept and were sad. They said: "The Tathagata has received our final offerings. Having received them, he will enter Nirvana. To whom can we now make offerings? Now, with the unsurpassed Trainer parted from us, we are all like blind men." Then the World-Honoured One, in order to console all those gathered there, spoke in a gatha:

"Do not weep; the Dharma of all Buddhas is thus.
It is now innumerable kalpas since I entered Nirvana.
I have always received the best of Bliss
And rested myself forever in peace.
Now, listen with all your heart!
I shall now speak about Nirvana.
I am now segregated from the sense of [taking] food;
I now feel no thirst. I shall now, for your sake,
Speak about the vows step by step
And cause all to be blessed with peace.
Listen well and practise the eternal Dharma of all Buddhas.

If crows and owls live in a tree
And make friends with one another like brothers,
I shall now gain Nirvana for eternity.
The Tathagata views all beings as he does Rahula.
I shall always be the most honoured one to all beings.
How could I enter Nirvana for all eternity?
If snakes, rats and wolves live in a hole

And become friends with one another like brothers,
I shall enter Nirvana for all eternity.
The Tathagata views all beings as he views Rahula.
He always becomes the one honoured by beings.
How can he stay long in Nirvana?
If saptaparna [a bitter plant] changes into varsika [jasmine],
If karu [gentian] changes into tinduka [diospyros embryoteris],
Then I might well enter Nirvana.
The Tathagata views all as he views Rahula.
How could he abandon compassion and enter Nirvana for a long time?
If an icchantika could, in his present body,
Attain Enlightenment and first-grade Bliss,
Then I would certainly enter Nirvana.
The Tathagata views all as he views Rahula.
How could he abandon compassion and enter Nirvana for a long time?
If people all at once attain Enlightenment and abandon all evil,
I shall certainly attain Nirvana.
The Tathagata views all as he views Rahula.
How could he abandon compassion and enter Nirvana for a long time?
If the water of mosquitoes and sawflies
Could indeed wet the whole earth
And fill the rivers, valleys and seas, I would enter Nirvana.
My compassionate heart views all as I do Rahula.
I am ever the honoured one of all beings,
And how could I be long in Nirvana?
For this reason, seek deeply for Wonderful Dharma.
Do not be overmuch concerned, nor cry, nor weep.
If you desire to act rightly,
Practise the eternal of the Tathagata;
Harbour the thought that such Dharma lives long
And that there is no change.
Also, be mindful of the fact that the Three Treasures are all eternal.
This will beget great protection.
It is as in the case of a dead tree
Which, as a result of magic charms, brings forth fruit.
Such are the Three Treasures.
All of you, the four classes of people! Give ear well!
On listening well, joy will arise and Bodhichitta will come about.
If the Three Treasures come about as eternal
And are as "Paramartha-satya" [Ultimate Reality],
That is the utmost of vows of all Buddhas."

"If any bhiksu, upasaka or upasika aspires to the highest vow of the Tathagata, know that such will have no ignorance and is worthy of receiving offerings. By dint of the power of the vow, the virtues and fruits of that person's actions will, in the world, be like those of an arhat; anyone who cannot meditate on the eternal of the Three Treasures is a candala. If a person can indeed realise the eternal of the Three Treasures, such a person will part from the suffering that arises out of the causality of existence and will attain peace, and there will be no luring [tempting], hindering, and worrying trouble that will remain behind." Then, humans, devas, the great crowd, and asuras, having heard this sermon, were gladdened and inexpressibly overjoyed. Their minds were softened, with all hindrances done away with, and no ups and downs were felt in their minds. Their great virtue was pure. Their faces looked glad, and they knew the eternal nature of the Buddha. Because of this, the devas made heavenly offerings and strew flowers of several kinds; with powder and smearing incense and with heavenly music, they made offerings to the Buddha. Then the Buddha said to Bodhisattva Kasyapa: "Do you see the rare things done by these people?" Kasyapa answered: "I have already seen them, O World-Honoured One! I see that the number of Tathagatas is innumerable, boundless and uncountable; I see that they have received the offerings of all people, humans and devas. Also, they see the adornments of the great bodies of all Buddhas, and see that though the place where they sit is just the size of a needle point, a great number of people stand around and do not jostle one another, that the people who are gathered together all take vows, deliver sermons in thirteen gathas, that the great crowd are praying in their minds and are saying: "The Tathagata now accepts my offerings." Even if the food offered by Cunda were made into dust-motes and a mote was offered to each Buddha, it could by no means suffice. But the divine power of the Buddha has so contrived things as to enable all the people gathered here to receive their share." Only the Bodhisattva-mahasattvas, the Prince of Dharma, Manjushri, and others knew that this rare thing was [the action] of the Tathagata. All were expedients of the Tathagata that were thus manifested. The great crowd of sravakas and asuras now all knew that the Tathagata was one eternal. Then the World-Honoured One said to Cunda: "Are not the things you see rare?" "Yes, indeed, O World-Honoured One! The innumerable Buddhas that I saw all had the 32 signs of perfection and the 80 minor marks of excellence. They were thus adorned. All are Bodhisattvas big in size, all wonderful, and their visages are incomparable. Thus do I see. Only the body of the Buddha is like that of a medicine tree, surrounded by all Bodhisattvas." The Buddha said to Cunda: "All the Buddhas that you saw before you were the transformation Buddhas [i.e. projections] of my own self. It was to benefit all beings and make them happy. All such Bodhisattva-mahasattvas here have innumerable things to practise. They all do what the innumerable Buddhas do. O Cunda! You have now accomplished what Bodhisattvas do and are perfect in what the Bodhisattva of the ten "bhumis" do." Bodhisattva Kasyapa said to the Buddha: "O World-Honoured One! All is as you say. All is as the Buddha says. The works of a Bodhisattva which Cunda has accomplished gladden me. Now the Tathagata, for the benefit of innumerable beings of the future, desires to perform a great work and you have now delivered this sermon of the Mahayana Great Nirvana Sutra. "O World-Honoured One! Do the sutras contain more than what is stated?" "O good man! What I state has and has not more than what I state." Cunda said to the Buddha: "As you, the Buddha, say: "What I have I give to all; Only praise, but do not despoil." "O World-Honoured One! What does this mean? What difference is there between the upholding and breaking of the precepts?" The Buddha said: "Except for one, give to all other people. Praise all." Cunda asked: "Who is that one person who is to be excepted?" "For example, the person who breaks the precepts stated in this sutra." Cunda said further: "I do not completely understand. Please be good enough to explain." The Buddha said to Cunda: "To break the precepts refers to the icchantika. Giving things to all others should be highly regarded. This will result in great fruition." Cunda asked further: "What does icchantika mean?" The Buddha said to Cunda: "Should any bhiksu, bhiksuni, upasaka or upasika who speaks ill of Wonderful Dharma and commits grave offences not repent and in his [or her] mind not think that it [i.e. what was done] was bad, such a person will inevitably be one who is taking the path of an icchantika. Any person who has committed grave sins such as the four grave offences and the five deadly sins, and who, knowing that he has transgressed, never fears or repents and does not say out [confess], who is not minded to protect, feel love for, and build up, the Buddha's Wonderful Dharma, but speaks ill of it, belittles it and points out things that are [supposedly] wrong is a person who is taking the path of an icchantika. Also, a person who says that there are no such things as the Three Treasures is a person who is taking the path of an icchantika. Except for such, you may indeed give. And this is laudable." Then Cunda said further to the Buddha: "What is the transgressing of the precepts?" The Buddha said to Cunda: "A person who commits the four grave offences, the five deadly sins, and one who slanders Wonderful Dharma, is transgressing the precepts." Cunda aksed further: "Can such a person, who has transgressed the precepts, be saved at all?" The Buddha said to Cunda: "If circumstantial factors combine, such a person can indeed be saved. If a person, donning the Buddhist robe, does not discard it, and his mind always repents and fears and is not gone far away, he will reproach himself, saying: "What a fool I was to commit such grave sins! How strange that I should engender this karma!" He greatly repents. He becomes minded to protect Wonderful Dharma and build it up. "I shall certainly make offerings to anyone who protects Dharma. To anyone who recites the Mahayana sutras, I shall pose questions, uphold and recite [those sutras]. If I understand [them] well, I shall speak of them widely to others." I say that such a person is not one who has broken the precepts. Why mot? O good man! For example, when the sun rises, all gloom clears away. The same applies to the appearance into the world of this all-wonderful Great Nirvana Sutra. This annihilates all the sins committed over innumerable kalpas past. That is why this sutra says that if Wonderful Dharma is gained, great fruition ensues and this saves the person who has broken the precepts. A person may transgress, but if he repents and returns to Dharma, he will think: "All the evils one performs are like doing evil against one's own self." Fear arises and he repents. "There can be no help other than this Wonderful Dharma. For this reason, I shall turn back and take refuge in Wonderful Dharma". If things proceed thus in taking refuge, a person may make offerings to such a one and there will be no end of good fruition arising from this. Also, we can say that such a person is one worthy of offerings from all the world. There may be a person who does evil, as stated above, and after a month or fifteen days, does not take refuge or confess. If someone makes offerings to such a person, there will be very little merit arising

therefrom. The same with one who has committed the five deadly sins. If he repents and feels ashamed in his mind and says to himself that what he has done until now was all evil deeds and the cause of great suffering, and that henceforth he will do all he can to protect Wonderful Dharma, such a person does not come within the category of the five deadly sins. Should offerings be made to such a person, this will call forth an inexpressible amount of blessings. Were one to make offerings to a person who has committed the deadly sins and in whom no thought arises of protecting Dharma and taking refuge, the blessings which might ensue would not be much to talk about. "Also, O good man! Any person who has committed evil deeds should now listen to me clearly. I shall now expound expansively. Think in this way: "Wonderful Dharma is the hidden store of the Tathagata. Therefore, I shall protect and build it up." Anyone who makes offerings to such a person will be blessed with supreme virtue. O good man! A woman conceives a child. When she is about to give birth, there arises turmoil in the land and she flees abroad. There is a shrine, where she gives birth to her child. Later, she hears of the return of peace to her home country and of a bountiful harvest. She takes her child and wishes to return to her homeland. On the way, there is the Ganges, where the water is high and swiftly flowing. Having the child [with her], she cannot cross the river. She prays in her mind: "I will not cross the river on my own; even if I die, I shall not part from my child." Saying this, she throws herself into the water. She dies and is later born in heaven, on account of her compassionate heart in wanting to protect the child. Even so, this woman was bad at heart. But because of her love for her son, she was born in heaven. It is the same with those who have committed the four grave offences and the five deadly sins. Although having done evil before, because of the protection of Dharma, a person becomes the best field of merit to the world [i.e. good done to such a person will yield happy karmic results]. A person who protects Dharma will meet with such an inexpressible reward." Cunda further said: "O World-Honoured One! An icchantika may repent, respect and make offerings to the Three Treasures. If one makes offerings to such a person, will that generate great returns?" The Buddha said: "O good man! Do not ask such a thing. For example, there is a man here who partakes of a mango. He takes out the stone. Later he thinks: "There may be something sweet in this stone." Then he takes it up and cracks it, and chews it. It tastes extremely bitter, and he regrets [his action]. Thinking that he might lose the seed, he takes it back and plants it. He carefully nourishes it at times with butter, oil and milk. What does this signify? Do you think that a plant will come about?" "No, O World-Honoured One! Even if heaven were to rain down sweet rain, there could be no chance of a plant coming about." "The same is the case with this icchantika. The root of good has been burnt out. How can he expiate his sin? O good man! If a good mind [mental state or thought] arises, we do not speak of an "icchantika". O good man! For this reason, it is not true that whatever is given has no difference in its results. Why not? The thing given to a sravaka is different; so too is what is given to a pratyekabuddha. Only what is given to a Tathagata calls forth unsurpassed fruition. That is why I say

"All rivers have bends;
All forests have trees;
All women flatter;
All freedom calls forth peace."

that it is not true that there is no difference in the results of the offerings made." Cunda said further: "Why is it that the Tathagata delivered this gatha?" The Buddha siad to Cunda: "When there is reason for it, I deliver such a sermon. In Rajagriha, there was once an upasaka who had no faith and served a Nirgrantha. And yet, he came to me and asked about the meaning of offerings. That is why I delivered this sermon. Also, for the sake of Bodhisattvamahasattvas, I speak of the hidden doctrine. What is the meaning of this gatha? I say "all". But this "all" refers to the all which is only little. Know that the Bodhisattva-mahasattva is the man of men. He upholds the precepts and gives away what results from that. He abandons transgressing against the precepts and weeds out the barnyard grass [i.e. defilements]. Aso, next, O good man! It is as with the gatha, in which I said in days gone by:

Then Bodhisattva Manjushri stood up from his seat, bared his right shoulder, knelt down on his right knee, advanced and touched the Buddha's feet, and said in a gatha:

"It is not the case that all rivers have bends,
And that all woods are trees,
All women are flatterers,
All freedom is peace."

"What the Buddha says in this gatha has more to it. Please condescend to tell us the detail. Why? O World-Honoured One! In the 3,000 great-thousand worlds, there is a country called Godaniya. There is, in that land, a river which is straight. The river is named "Shabaya". It is like a straight rope and flows into the sea in the west. The Buddha has not yet spoken of this in other sutras. Please, O Tathagata, condescend to expound within the compass of the vaipulya agama-sutras what has been left out from the explanations, to enable Bodhisattvas to have deep faith and understanding. O World-Honoured One! For example, there is here a man who may first know of a gold ingot, but not of the gold. The same with the Tathagata. He knows all dharmas and yet still has parts left out to speak [i.e. has not said all he knows]. The Tathagata gives such talks, and yet we may well

come to understand what the intended meaning is. All forests surely have trees, and there are also other things [in them]. Why? Several other things such as gold, silver, and beryl are there; gem trees are also called trees. We say that all women are flatterers; and yet, they are more than that. Why? Because there are women who uphold the precepts and are perfect in virtue, having a great compassionate heart. All freedom is surely bliss, but there is still more. Why? One who has freedom is a chakravartin. The Dharmaraja [Dharma-King] Tathagata does not belong to Yama [the ruler of the hells]. He cannot die. Brahma and Shakra are unmolested [unimpeded, unrestricted], and yet they are non-eternal. That which is eternal and unchanging is called unmolested. This is the Mahayana Great Nirvana Sutra." The Buddha said: "O good man! You now talk well. Stop and listen to me for a while. O Manjushri! As an example: a rich man falls ill and suffers. A good doctor sees [this] and prepares some medicine. The sick man is greedy and takes too much. The doctor says: "If your body can stand it, you may indeed take as [much as] you please. But your body is weak now. Do not take too much. Know well that this is amrta, but at the same time a poison. If taken in excess and if not digested, it becomes poisonous." O good man! Now, do not say that what this doctor says is a transgression and that the medicine does not work. O good man! The same is the case with the Tathagata. All is done for the king, queen, crown prince, prince, and minister. The prince and queen of King Prasenajit were arrogant. To teach them, fear was appropriate. Especially to such as the doctor a gatha such as this is delivered:

"All rivers have bends;
All forests have trees;
All women are flatterers;
All freedom surely gains one peace."

"O Manjushri! Know that what the Tathagta says has no lapses [inconsistencies, shortcomings]. The earth may turn upside-down, but what the Tathagata says has no lapses. Because of this, what the Tathagata says has the unsaid behind [it]." Then the Buddha praised Manjushri and said:

"Well said, well said, O good man! You have already long known all such things. You have pity for beings, and to allow them to arrive at Wisdom you widely put such questions to the Tathagata referring to the gatha." Then, the Dharmarajaputra Manjushri said in a gatha before the Buddha:

"I follow what others say
And do not speak against [them].
And I do not look at others [to see]
If they do or do not do [according to Dharma];
I only look back upon the good
Or not-good of what I do."

"O World-Honoured One! I talk about the medicine of Dharma thus. I do not say that what I say is right. I say what others say and do not transgress. Condescend, O Tathagata, to tell me of this. The World-Honoured One always says: "All tirthikas of the 95 kinds go to the unfortunate realms and all sravakas face the right path. They uphold the precepts and deportment and guard their sense-organs. All such people care for great Dharma and take the path that is good." O Tathagata! Why is it that in the nine types of sutra you give reproof when there is a person who breaks others [transgresses]? What could the meaning of such a gatha be?" The Buddha said to Manjushri: "O good man! I delivered this gatha. It is not for beings [in general]. It was for none but King Ajatasatru. The All-Buddha-World-Honoured One does not unsay what has been said, if there is no reason for doing so. When there is reason, he so speaks. O good man! King Ajatasatru, after having killed his father, came to me, and to prevail on me he put this question to me: "How, O World-Honoured One, can you be All-Knowledge, or are you not? Devadatta had for innumerable ages past an evil intent and thought of following and harming the Tathagata. Why is it that you allowed him to become ordained?" "O good man! Because of this, I delivered this gatha for that king:

"I follow what others say,
And do not speak against [them].
And I do not look at others [to see]
If they do or do not do;

I only look back upon the good
Or not-good of what I do."

"I, the Buddha, said to the great king: "You have now killed your father. The deadly sin has already been committed. It is the greatest of sins, the consequence of which is life in Avichi Hell. Confess and cleanse yourself. Why do you look to the ill of others?" O good man! For this reason, I delivered this sermon in a gatha just for his sake. Also, next, O good man! I also deliver this sermon for those who strictly uphold the precepts, who do not transgress, who are perfect in deportment, and who see well what ill deeds others perform. Any person who is [rightly] guided by others, who keeps away from all evil deeds, and who teaches others and makes them keep away from evil is none other than my disciple." Then, the World-Honoured One, for Manjushri's sake, spoke in a gatha:

"All fear the sword and staff;
There is none who does not love life.
Put your own self into the parable [equation].
Do not kill, do not use the staff."

Then, Manjushri spoke this gatha before the Buddha:
"It is not that all fear the staff.
Put your own self into the parable.
Try your best to devise the best expedients."

"The Tathagata spoke this gatha, which is not complete. Why not? The arhat, chakravartin, beautiful women, elephants, horses, treasurers and ministers cannot be harmed by devas and asuras with sharp swords in their hands. Valiant soldiers, brave women, kings of horses, kings of beasts, bhiksus who uphold the precepts do not feel fear, even when attacked. For this reason, we can say that the Tathagata's gatha also has elements not explained. You may say: "Put your own self into the parable." But this contains more than is said. Why? If an arhat is made the object of the parable, there can [not] be the thought of self and life. If there is the thought of self and life, we need protection. Common mortals will also think that the arhat is a person who practises the Way. Such is a perverted view. If one holds a perverted view, one will, after one's death, fall into Avichi Hell. And to think that an arhat has a mind to harm a common mortal is not possible. And none of the innumerable beings, either, can harm an arhat." The Buddha said: "O good man! The thought of self relates to a thought which is very compassionate to beings and which does not even think of harming [them]. This is the all-equal mind of the arhat. Do not unreasonably say what speaks against [i.e. what is untrue]. In days gone by, there was in this Rajagriha a great hunter. He killed a good number of stags and invited me to eat. I then accepted his invitation. But I have a compassionate feeling towards all beings, just as I have towards my own Rahula. I said in a gatha:

"Let yourself be blessed with long life,
And live long; uphold non-harming
And life will be as that of all Buddhas."
For this reason, I say in this gatha:
"All fear the sword and staff;
There is none who does not love life.
Put your own self into the parable.
Do not kill, do not use the staff."

The Buddha said: "Well said, well said, O Manjushri! For the sake of all Bodhisattvamahasattvas, you put such questions regarding the undisclosed teaching of the Tathagata." Then Manjushri spoke in a gatha:

"How do we respect father and mother,
How are we obedient, and how do we pay homage?
How do we practise Dharma
And gain Avichi Hell?"
Then the Tathagata answered in a gatha:
"Should one make greedy love [i.e. craving] one's mother,
Ignorance one's father,
And follow and respect these,
One gains Avichi Hell."
Then the Tathagata said again to Manjushri in a gatha:
"All that belongs to others is suffering;
All that stands on one's own side
Is what is unmolested and peace;
The force of arrogance is extremely stormy and devilish;
One who is wise and good is loved by all."

Then Bodhisattva-mahasattva Manjushri said to the Buddha: "O World-Honoured One! What the Tathagata says is not concluded. Condescend, O Tathagta, to tell me the reason. Why? The son of a rich man studies, following a teacher. Does he belong to the teacher or not? If he belongs to the teacher, the meaning does not fit well. If not, it does not fit well either. Even if one gains unmolestedness, it also does not. Hence, what the Tathagata says still has more to say. Also, next, O World-Honoured One! The prince does not learn; things do not come about when anything happens. This is unmolestedness, and yet he has ignorance, darkness and suffering always. If such a prince is regarded as unmolested, the meaning does not fit well. If one says that one belongs to others, the meaning fails again. Because of this, we say that what the Buddha says still has more to tell. Because of this, even when one depends on others, suffering does not necessarily result. Not all unmolestednesses necessarily end in bliss. We say that the power of arrogance is demoniac. This, again, still has more to say. O World-Honoured One! All brave women, out of arrogance, become ordained and learn things; they uphold the precepts and are accomplished in deportment. All their sense-organs are well guarded, and no lapses can be seen. For this reason, we see that all the defilements of arrogance are not necessarily devilish. The wise and good are not loved by all. Even here, there is yet more to say. A person commits the four grave offences in his mind, and one does not throw the priestly robe away and uphold the deportment rigidly. The case is like this. One who loves Dharma sees and does not love. Such a person, after death, will unfailingly fall into hell. A good person commits the grave offences, and those who protect Dharma see [this] and drive such a man away, and defrock him and turn him back to worldy life. In consequence of this, we may well say that not even all the wise are necessarily loved." Then the Buddha said to Manjushri: "When there is reason, the Tathagata says what still has more to be said. And in certain circumstances, the All-Buddha-Tathagata talks about this Dharma. At one time, there was in Rajagriha a woman called Subhadra. She came back to her parents' house, came to me and took refuge in me, in Dharma and Sangha. She said: "All women have no free span of power; all men are unmolested and unhindered." Then, at that time, I fathomed the woman's mind and spoke in such a gatha. O Manjushri! It is good, it is good! You now put such a question to the Tathagata regarding the undisclosed words for the sake of all beings." Then Manjushri said in a gatha:

"All beings live on food;
All people with power have no jealousy [envy];
From all things eaten does one gain the cause of illness;
From good actions does one gain peace and bliss."

"O World-Honoured One! You now receive the food offered by Cunda. Do you, O Tathagata, have no fear in you or not?"

Then the World-Honoured One said in a gatha to Manjushri:

"It is not that all beings live on food only;
It is not that all those who have power have no jealousy [envy] in their hearts;
It is not that all the food taken must call forth illness;
It is not that all pure actions necessarily give one peace and bliss."

"O Manjushri! If you become ill, I too become ill. Why? All arhats, pratyekabuddhas, Bodhisattvas and Tathagatas do not take food. In order to guide people, they accept and take food. Innumerable people bring in things. They [the saintly ones] let them accomplish danaparamita and succour them from lives in hell, the animal realm and the hungry preta realm. The Tathagata spends six years in penance, and his body becomes emaciated and lean, but [actually] nothing of the sort takes place. The All-Buddha-World-Honoured One is independent of all things and is not the same as a common mortal. How could it be possible for [his body] to grow weak? The All-Buddha-World-Honoured One has made effort, practised the Way and attained the Adamantine Mind. He is not of the body of the weak-constituted common mortal. The same with my disciples. All [this] cannot be thought of. They do not stand on [depend on] food. We say that those who have great power have no jealousy [envy]. This still has more to say. [Some] people of the world do not, throughout their life, have any jealousy. They seem to lack great power, too. We say that all illnesses arise out of food. This too needs qualification. There are illnesses that spring from external causes such as thorns, swords and halberds. We say that all pure actions call forth peace. This, too, has more to it that needs to be said. We see in the world tirthikas practising pure actions and undergoing pain and worry. Because of this, all that the Tathagata says has yet more to say. Because of this, it is not the case that the Tathagata speaks in this gatha without reason. He says as there is reason for so saying. In days gone by, in this Ujjayini, there was a Brahmin called Kuteitoku. He came to me and desired to receive, from the fourth, the precepts on the eight pure actions ["astangasamanvagatopavasa"]. I, at that time, spoke this gatha." Then Bodhisattva Kasyapa said to the Buddha: "What could be the thing that has no further [leftover] part? What does "all" mean?" "O good man! "All" denotes Wonderful Dharma of eternal Bliss, other than what assists attainment to Enlightenment. This can be called "all", or what has no remaining part. All other things, too, can be what have parts to tell or also what have no more part to tell. It is to let all those who take pleasure in Dharma know the meaning of what yet has parts left to tell and what has no more part to tell." Bodhisattva Kasyapa felt extremely and inexpressibly glad. He stepped towards the Buddha and said: "This is all-wonderful. The Tathagata views all as though he were viewing his Rahula." Then the Buddha praised Kasyapa and said: "Well said, well said! What you see is all-wonderful." Bodhisattva Kasyapa said to the Buddha: "O World-Honoured One! Please condescend to expound to me the virtue which this Mahayana Nirvana Sutra has." The Buddha said to Kasyapa: "O good man! Anyone who hears the name of this sutra gains virtue, which is so great that sravakas and pratyekabuddhas cannot well tell [of it]. The Buddha alone well knows. Why? Because the world of the Buddha is inconceivable. And how much greater will it [i.e. virtue, merit] be if one possesses, recites, understands and copies it [this sutra]?" Then all the devas and people of the world and asuras said in a gatha:

"The world of the Buddha is inconceivable.
So too are those of Dharma and Sangha.
This being the case, we beg that you will stay somewhat longer.
The venerable Mahakasyapa and Ananda,
The two of the Sangha, will soon be here.
Also, the great king Ajatasatru, king of Magadha,
Who very much respects the Buddha, the World-Honoured One, is not here.

Have a little pity and stay awhile
And be with us, the great congregation, and clear away our doubts."

Then, the Tathagata, for the benefit of the great crowd, spoke in a gatha:
"The eldest of my sons is Mahakasyapa.
Ananda well makes effort and can well clear away your doubts.
Be satisfied with that. Ananda is one who has heard much.
He will understand in a natural way
The eternal and the non-eternal.
Because of this, do not be much aggrieved."

Then the great crowd offered many things to the Buddha. Their offerings made, they all aspired to unsurpassed Enlightenment. All the Bodhisattvas, who were as numerous as the grains of sand of innumerable Ganges, all attained the first "bhumi" [stage of Bodhisattvic development]. Then the World-Honoured One gave prophecies to Manjushri, Bodhisattva Kasyapa and Cunda. The prophecies given, he said: "All good men! Straighten your minds. Be wary and not indolent. I now have pain in my back and my whole body. I now desire to lie down." [And thus] he does, like any child or one who is sick. "O Manjushri! All of you! Disseminate Great Dharma amongst the four classes [castes] of people. I now entrust this sutra to you. Also, when Kasyapa and Ananda have arrived, entrust Wonderful Dharma to them, too."

Then, the Tathagata, having spoken thus, laid himself down on his right side, like any child ill in bed, all to disseminate Dharma to all beings.

Chapter Eighteen: On Actual Illness

Then, Kasyapa said to the Buddha: "O World-Honoured One! The Tathagata is already far removed from all illness. Defilement and pain already done away with, no fear remains behind. O World-Honoured One! All beings have four poisonous arrows, which become the cause of illness. What are the four? They are greed, ill-will, ignorance and arrogance. When the cause is within, illnesses arise, such as cold, fever, comsumption, dizziness, vomiting, paralysis of the body, madding mind, loose bowels, convulsions, loose urine [weak bladder], pain in the eyes and ears, swollen abdomen and back, craziness, dryings-up, or being tormented by evil spirits. All such bodily ills cannot arise in the All-Buddha-World-Honoured One. Why is it that the Tathagata looks back and says to Manjushri: "I have pain in my back. All of you should teach the great congregation"? Illnesses arise for two reasons. What are the two? First, it is having pity on all beings; second, it is giving medicine to those who are ill. The Tathagata, already an innumerable million billion kalpas ago, when the Tathagata was practising the Way of a Bodhisattva, always had words of love. He benefited beings and extracted the root of worry. He gave various medicines to all who were ill. Why is it that today, now, he should have an illness? O World-Honoured One! What applies in the world is that a sick person sits or reclines and has no time to rest. He calls for food, gives injunctions to his family, or tells them to work. Why is it that the Tathagata sits silently? Why is it that you do not teach your disciples and sravakas the right practices of shilaparamita and dhyanaparamita? Why is it that you do not deliver Mahayana sutras that have deep meaning? Why is it that, using innumerable expedients, you do not teach Mahakasyapa, the great elephant among men, and the great persons, so that they will not retrogress from unsurpassed Enlightenment? Why is it that you do not teach all evil-doing bhiksus who receive and store up impure things? O World-Honoured One! You have no illness. Why do you recline on your right side? All Bodhisattvas give medicines to patients and whatever merits arise from giving are all bestowed upon all beings and transferred to All-Knowledge. This is to extract the hindrances of defilement, the hindrances of karma, and those of karmic results. The hindrances of defilement are greed, hatred, ignorance, and anger at what is disagreeable, illusion that overshadows the mind, hindering thereby good from shooting out its buds; [the hindrances are also] burning worry, jealousy, stinginess, cheating, flattery, not feeling ashamed of one's own self, not feeling ashamed of others, pride, pride-pride, simulative pride, pride of self-conceit, pride of self, twisted pride, arrogance, indolence, self-importance, mutual resentment, arguing, wrong living, flattering, cheating using different appearances, pursuing profit by profit, seeking things through wrong channels, seeking a lot, lacking respect, not observing the injunctions, and associating with bad friends. There is no end of seeking profit, to entwine and bind one's own self so that all is difficult to understand. A person abides in evil desires and evil greed. A person is greedily intent upon heretical views of life regarding his carnal existence, the "is" and the "not-is" views of life; a person heaves a groan or is pleased to drowse, lets out a yawn or is not pleased, or eats greedily; his mind is dim and he thinks of strange things, does evil with body and in speech, finds pleasure in talking overmuch; all his sense-organs are dark; he talks excessively and is always overshadowed by such senses as greed, anger and harming. These are the hindrances of defilement. "The hindrances [which arise] from deeds [karma] are the five deadly sins and the diseases of serious evil. "The hindrances from karmic retribution give one life in the realms of hell, animals, and hungry pretas, and also the slandering of Wonderful Dharma, and the icchantika. These are the hindrances from retribution. "These three hindrances are the evils. Yet, the Bodhisattva, when practising the Way over innumerable kalpas, dispensed medicines for all illnesses and always vowed to release beings eternally from the grave illnesses of the three hindrances. "Also, next, O World-Honoured One! When the Bodhisattva-mahasattva practised the Way, he gave medicine to all who were sick and always took the vows: "Let beings be eternally segregated from all ills and let them attain the Adamantine Body of the Tathagata. Also, let all the innumerable beings become all-wonderful medicines and be able to cut off evil illnesses; let all beings gain the agada and, by the power of this medicine, do away with all the innumerable evil poisons; let not all beings retrogress from unsurpassed Enlightenment, but let them swiftly accomplish the unsurpassed Buddha-medicine and extract all the poisonous arrows; let all beings make effort, generate and accomplish the Adamantine Mind of the Tathagata, becoming this all-wonderful medicine, cure all diseases, so that no disputatious mind can arise; let beings become a great tree of medicine and cure all serious illnesses of all beings; let one thoroughly extract the poisoned arrows of beings and accomplish the unsurpassed light of the Tathagata; let beings enter the Tathagata's hidden store of the Dharma of Wisdom's great medicine and the close-guarded store of Dharma." O World-Honoured One! The Bodhisattva, already innumerable hundred thousand nayutas of kalpas ago, took these vows and extracted all the ills from all beings. Why is it that the Tathagata today says that he has illness? "Also, next, O World-Honoured One! There is in the world a person who is ill in bed, who cannot sit, get up, look up, walk or stand, and is not able to swallow any food or make liquid pass down his throat; he cannot teach and admonish his sons so that they can learn household work. His parents, wife, children, brothers, relatives and friends are anxious, and they think that he will assuredly die. O World-Honoured One! The same is the case with the Tathagata today. You recline on your right-hand side and say nothing. All the ignorant of this Jambudvipa will think: "The Tathagata, the All-Enlightened One is going to enter Nirvana." Why? They may think that you will cease to exist. But the nature of the Tathagata does not, to the end, enter Nirvana. Why not? The Tathagata is eternal and does not change. For this reason, there can be no saying: "I have pain in my back." "Also, next, O World-Honoured One! There is a person who is ill in bed and whose physique is broken [weakened]; he lies with his face down or on his side, or on his bed. Then, people negatively think that death is not far off. The same is the case with the Tathagata. The 95 tirthikas look down upon, and abide in, the thought of the non-eternal. They will certainly say: "Things [in Buddhism] are not as with our own doctrine, in which we base ourselves on self, nature, man, unmolestedness, time, mote ["prakrti" - primal matter], and think that these are eternal and suffer no change. Shramana Gautama is now subect to change. This merely reveals the law of change." For this reason,

O World-Honoured One, you should not be silent and recline on your right-hand side. Also, next, O World-Honoured One! There is in the world a man ill in bed. The four great elements increase or decrease, so that they do not work and mix well; his body is extremely weakened and emaciated. Because of this, he cannot sit or get up as he wills. So he remains in bed. With the Tathagata, not one of the four elements is out of harmony. You are perfect in your physical power; nothing is weak or diminished. O World-Honoured One! The little strength of ten cows is not equal to that of a big cow; the strength of ten big cows is not equal to that of a blue cow; the strength of ten blue cows is not equal to that of a common elephant; the strength of ten common elephants is not equal to that of a wild elephant; the strength of ten wild elephants is not equal to that of a two-tusked elephant; the strength of ten two-tusked elephants is not equal to that of a four-tusked elephant; the power of ten four-tusked elephants is not equal to that of a white elephant of the Himalayas; the strength of ten white elephants is not equal to that of a fragrant elephant; the strength of ten fragrant elephants is not equal to that of a blue elephant; the strength of ten blue elephants is not equal to that of a yellow elephant; the strength of ten yellow elephants is not equal to a red elephant; the strength of ten red elephants is not equal to a white elephant; the strength of ten white elephants is not equal to that of a mountain elephant; the strength of ten mountain elephants is not equal to an utpala elephant; the strength of ten utpala elephants is not equal to that of a kumuda elephant; the strength of ten kumuda elephants is not equal to that of a pundarika elephant; the strength of ten pundarika elephants is not equal to that of a Malla [wrestler of tremendous strength]; the strength of ten Mallas is not equal to that of a Pakkhandin; that of ten Pakkhandins is not equal to that of one eight-armed Narayana; the strength of ten eight-armed Narayanas is not equal to that of one joint [limb] of a Bodhisattva of the ten "bhumis". With common mortals, the mid-part of the body does not meet together ; with the Mallas, the mid-part and the head meet together; with the Pakkhandins, all the joints of the body meet together; with Narayana, the joints and the head can well hook together; with the Bodhisattvas of the ten "bhumis", the bones of all joints separate or join together as in the case of a coiling naga [serpent]. Thus, the strength of the Bodhisattva is the greatest. When the world came into existence, the vajrasana [diamond throne] was raised up from the vajra [diamond] land and then raised up to the bodhimanda [site of Enlightenment], which appeared under the Bodhi Tree. Having sat down, the mind of the Bodhisattva attained the ten powers. O Tathagata! You should not be like any [normal] little child. No infant, child, ignorant or brainless person can expound things well. For this reason, although you lie with your face down and on one side, no one reproaches you. You, Tathagata, the World-Honoured One, have great Wisdom and shine over all. You are the naga of men; you possess great virtue and have divine powers; you are the unsurpassed rishi; you have cut away the web of doubt and have extracted the arrow of poison. In peace you go and come, perfect in deportment, and armed with fearlessness. Why should you recline on your right-hand side and cause all heaven and humankind to sink into sorrow and worry?" Then Kasyapa said in a gatha before the Buddha:

"O Great Holy One of the Gautama clan!
Get up, I pray you, and speak to us about All-Wonderful Dharma!
Do not recline on the bed like some child,

Or one who is sick. The Trainer,
The Teacher of gods and humans,
Lies between the sal trees. The lowly
And the ignorant may say that he will assuredly enter Nirvana.
They know nothing of the vaipulya
Or what the Buddha does.
Like the blind, they do not see
The hidden store of the Tathagata.
Only all the Bodhisattvas and Manjushri well know
The depths, like a good archer.
All Buddhas of the Three Times [past, present and future]
Rest upon Great Compassion.
What is now the worth of such Great Compassion?
With no compassion, the Buddha is no name [no one of any great pre-eminence].
If the Buddha definitely enters Nirvana,
This is not the eternal, O Unsurpassed One!
Take pity on us, answer our prayers, bestow
Benefit upon beings, and subdue all tirthikas!"

Then, the World-Honoured One, his mind of great compassion kindled, realised everything that each being wanted to have, desired to act in accordance [with their wishes], to answer their prayers and bestow benefit, raised himself from his seat, and sat cross-legged. His visage was bright and soft like a molten ball of gold. His serene face and eyes shone like the full moon. His form was pure, without any blemishes. A great light filled the firmament. The light was as bright as that of more than 100 thousand suns. It shone over the east, south, west and north, the four corners, the worlds above and below, and over all the Buddha-lands. It gave beings the torch of Wisdom, illuminated the gloom, and enabled 100 thousand billion nayutas of beings to live in the unretrogressive mind of Bodhi [Enlightenment]. At that time, the Buddha's mind knew of no doubt, and he resembled a lion king. He was adorned with the 32 signs of a great man and the 80 minor marks of excellence. From each pore of his skin there appeared a lotus flower. The flowers were wonderful, each having a thousand petals. The colour was like that of pure gold. The stem was of beryl, the stamens of diamond, and the calyx of turkistan dwarf. It was so big and round that it looked like a great wheel. All these lotus flowers sent out lights of various colours, such as blue, yellow, red, white, purple and crystal. And these lights filled all such hells as Avichi, Samjna, Kalasutra, Sanghata, Raurava, Maharaurava, Tapana, and Mahatapana. In these eight hells, all such afflictions as being burned, boiled, broiled, cut, thrust, having one's skin stripped off, depart. When a person is shone upon by this light, all such afflictions disappear. What there is there is peace, coolness, and unending joy. In this light, the undisclosed store of the Tathagata is proclaimed: "All beings have the Buddha-Nature". The beings hear this, their life ends there and they are born into the worlds of humans and gods. There can further be the eight kinds of hells of coldness, which are: Apapa, Atata, Arbuda, Ababa, Utpala, Kumuda, and Pundarika. The beings who are born there are always pressed upon by cold.What goes on there is puckering and rending of the body, smashing and breaking, mutual harming, all of which, on encountering this light, go away; what then arises there is harmony and warmth, which please the body. This light, too, proclaims the undisclosed store of the Tathagata, saying: "All beings possess the Buddha-Nature." The beings hear this, their life ends, and they get born into the worlds of humans and gods. When this happens, here in this Jambudvipa and in all other worlds, the hells become empty and none do we see there being punished, except for the icchantika. Those of the realms of the hungry ghosts are oppressed by hunger. What they have on to cover their body is hair, and for a period of 100 thousand years they never once hear of liquid. But when they encounter this light, their hunger at once disappears. This light proclaims the undisclosed store of the Tathagata and says: "All beings possess the Buddha-Nature." When all of them hear this, their life ends and they are born into the worlds of humans and gods. The entire realm of hungry ghosts is empty, except for those who slander the Mahayana vaipulya sutras. The beings born in the realm of the animals harm and devour one another. On encountering this light, all hatred departs. The light also proclaims the undisclosed store of the Tathagata and says: "All beings possess the Buddha-Nature." The beings hear this, their life ends, and they are born into the worlds of humans and gods. Then there are no more in the animal realm, except for those who slander Wonderful Dharma. In each flower, there sits a Buddha. His halo is six feet crosswise, and the golden light shines brightly. It is wonderful and austere. It is unsurpassed and incomparable. The 32 signs of perfection and the 80 minor marks of excellence adorn [each Buddha's] body. Now, of these World-Honoured Ones, some are sitting, some walking, some lying, some standing, and some are emitting the sound of thunder; some are raining down a flood of rain, some are flashing forth lightning, some fanning up a great wind, and others are sending out smoke and flames. Their body resembles a fire-ball. Some show [conjure up the appearance of] mountains, ponds, lakes, rivers, forests and trees, all of gems. Also, they show lands, castle-towns, hamlets, palaces, and houses of gems. Or they show elephants, horses, lions, tigers, wolves, peacocks, Chinese phoenixes, and all such birds. Or all of the people of Jambudvipa are permitted to see the realms of hell, animals and hungry ghosts. Or the six heavens of the world of desire are displayed. Or there may be a World-Honoured One who speaks about all the evils and worries of everything that pertains to the five skandhas, 18 realms and 12 spheres. Or the Dharma of the Four Noble Truths is expounded, or one [Buddha] may speak about causal relations. Another may speak about the Self and the not-Self, or one may be talking about the pair [of opposites], suffering and bliss; or one may be speaking about the Eternal and the non-Eternal. Or another may be speaking about the Pure and the not-Pure. Or there might be a World-Honoured One who will speak for the sake of the Bodhisattvas about the virtues which all Bodhisattvas acquire. Or another one might be speaking about the virtues of the sravakas. Or another may be speaking about the teaching of the One Vehicle ["ekayana" - the teaching in which all beings all-equally attain the same Enlightenment]. Or another may be a World-Honoured One who emits water from the left-hand side of his body and fire from the right-hand side. Or another may display [his] birth, renunciation, sitting on the bodhimanda [site of Enlightenment] under the Bodhi Tree, his wonderful turning of the wheel [i.e. teaching Buddha-Dharma], and his entering Nirvana. Or there may be a World-Honoured One who lets out a lion's roar, enabling anyone who hears it to attain the stages from the first up to the second, third and fourth [i.e. the "arya-marga "(noble path) of the "stream-enterer", "once-returner", "never-returner", and the "arhat"]. Or there may be another [Buddha] who speaks about the innumerable causal relations [by means of] which one can get out of the life of birth-and-death. At that time, in this Jambudvipa, all beings encountered this light; the blind saw colour, the deaf were able to hear, the dumb to talk, the crippled to walk, the greedy attained wealth, the stingy gave, the angry experienced a compassionate heart, and the unbelieving believed. Then, all the devas, nagas, pishacas [kind of devil or goblin], gandharvas, ashuras, garudas, kimnaras, mahoragas, rakshasas, skandas, umadas, apasmaras, humans and non-humans said with one voice: "Well said, well said, O Unsurpassed-Heaven-Honoured One! Great is the benefit you bestow." On saying this, they rejoiced and jumped [for joy]; some sang and some danced, and others moved about and rolled on the ground. They strew all kinds of flowers on the Buddha and the Sangha, such as heavenly utpala, kumuda, padma, pundarika, mandara, mahamandara, manjusaka, mahamanjusaka, santanika, mahasantanika, rocana, maharocana, gandha, mahagandha, chakui, daichakui, kamadrsti, mahakamadristi, vira and prathamavira. Also, all manner of incense was strewn about, such as agaru, tagara, sandalwood, saffron, various types of mixed incense and that from the seaside. Also, the Buddha was given offerings of hanging ensigns, banners which had heavenly gems stitched into them, parasols, all kinds of music by the heavenly ones [playing on the] cheng, flute, reed-organ, she and harp. And they also said in a gatha:

"I now bow to you, the Great Effort, the Unsurpassed,
The Right-Enlightened, the Two-footed Honoured One!
Devas and humans do not know, but Gautama well knows.
The World-Honoured One practised penances for us
In days gone by, innumerable kalpas past.
How comes it that you forsake what you once vowed
And now desire to enter Nirvana?
All beings cannot now see the undisclosed store
Of the All-Buddha-World-Honoured One.
Because of this, it will be difficult to get out of this world
And we shall repeat birth and death and fall into the evil realms.
As the Buddha says, all arhats enter Nirvana.
But how do lowly-born common mortals know well
What the Buddha does with his deepest mind?
He rains down amrta [ambrosia] on all beings,
To extract all defilements. If this amrta is partaken of,
One will never again repeat birth, ageing, illness and death.
The Tathagata-World-Honoured One cures the diseases
Of 100 thousand innumerable beings
And extracts serious diseases
And so contrives that none then remains.
It is long since the World-Honoured One
Left behind all the pains of illness.
That is why he can be called the Seventh Buddha.
We pray that the Buddha will rain down
The rain of Dharma and give moisture
To our seeds of virtue. All the great congregation,
Humans and gods, sit silently, as you see."

When this gatha was said, all the Buddhas seated in the lotuses went around from Jambudvipa up to Suddhavasa Heaven [the highest of the heavens of the fourth dhyana heaven of the "rupadhatu"], and all heard this. Then the Buddha said to Bodhisattva Kasyapa: "Well said, well said! You now possess extremely deep and delicate Wisdom. You will not be destroyed by any Maras or tirthikas. O good man! You now abide in peace and will never get shaken by any evil. O good man! You have now perfected oratorical prowess, and you have already made offerings to all innumerable past Buddhas as countless as the sands of the Ganges. Because of this, you now put such a question to the Tathagata, the Right-Enlightened One. O good man! Once, innumerable, boundless, nayutas of a hundred-thousand-million kalpas ago, I already cut off the root of illness and was already far removed from reclining on a bed. O Kasyapa! Innumerable asamkhyas past, there appeared a Buddha who was the Unsurpassed-Superior-Tathagata, the Alms-Deserving, the All-Enlightened One, the All-Accomplished One, the Well-Gone, the All-Knower, the Unsurpassed One, the Best Trainer, the Teacher of Heaven and Earth, the Buddha-World-Honoured One. For the sake of all sravakas, he delivered the sermon of this Mahayana Great Nirvana Sutra, unfolded the doctrine, discriminated and expounded it. I, then, acted as a sravaka, upheld the Mahayana Nirvana Sutra, recited, understood and copied it, and unfolded, discriminated and explained its contents. I transferred the merit hereof to unsurpassed Enlightenment. O good man! Ever since, I have never once had occasion to commit myself to the evil actions of defilement and evil karmic relations, or to slander Wonderful Dharma, to become an iccantika, to be born with imperfect genital organs, or no genital organs, or dual genital organs, to act against my parents, to kill an arhat, to break a stupa or the law of the Sangha, to cause blood to flow from a Buddha's body, or to commit the four grace offences. Ever since [that time], my body and mind have been in peace, and I experience no suffering or worry. O Kasyapa! I now, in truth, have no illness of any kind. Why not? Because the All-Buddha-World-Honoured One is far away from illnesses. O Kasyapa! The Tathagata is called a "man-lion". And yet the Tathagata is not actually a lion. Any such is the Tathagata's undisclosed teaching. For example, it is as when we say that the Tathagata is a great naga among men. And yet, already countless kalpas past, I did away with action [karma]. O Kasyapa! It is as when we say that the Tathagata is a man as well as a deva. I am neither a pishaca, gandharva, ashura, garuda, kimnara nor mahoraga. I am no self, no life, and not one who can be nourished [with food]; I am not one who feels, nor one who does not feel. I am no World-Honoured One, nor any sravaka. I am not one who delivers sermons, nor one who does not. All such expressions are the undisclosed words of the Tathagata. O Kasyapa! It is as when we say that the Tathagata is the Great-Sea-King-Mount-Sumeru ["mahasamudra-sumeru-parvata-raja"]. And yet, the Tathagata is not on the same level as any saltish stone mountain. Know that this, too, is the undisclosed teaching of the Tathagata. O

Kasyapa! It is as when we say that the Tathagata is like the pundarika [lotus]. And yet, truth to tell, I am no pundarika. All such is the undisclosed teaching of the Tathagata. O Kasyapa! It is as when we say that the Tathagata is like a parent. And yet, truth to tell, the Tathagata is not a parent. All such is also the undisclosed teaching of the Tathagata. O Kasyapa! It is as when we say that the Tathagata is like a great master mariner. And yet, truth to tell, the Tathagata is not a master mariner. And this is also the undisclosed teaching of the Tathagata. O Kasyapa! It is as when we say that the Tathagata is like a great merchant. And yet, truth to tell, the Tathagata is not a merchant. Such is also the undisclosed teaching of the Tathagata. O Kasyapa! It is as when we say that the Tathagata indeed subdues Mara. And yet, the Tathagata is, truth to tell, not one who subdues others with an evil mind. Such is also the undisclosed teaching of the Tathagata. O Kasyapa! It is as when we say that the Tathagata thoroughly cures carbuncles and the pox. But I am not one who cures carbuncles and the pox. Such is also the undisclosed teaching of the Tathagata. O Kasyapa! It is as we have said up to now. There are good men and women who guard their body, mouth and mind well. When their life comes to an end, relatives come, take the corpse and burn it on the fire, or they may throw it into great water, throw it amongst tombs, and foxes, wolves and birds may come and eagerly devour it. Yet, the mind will find birth in a good realm. And the mind has no coming and going, and no place whither to go. The front and back resemble [each other] and continue, with no difference in outer appearances. Such is the undisclosed teaching of the Tathagata. "O Kasyapa! I say that I am sick. The case is other than this. This is also the undisclosed teaching of the Tathagata. That is why I said to Manjushri: "I have pain in my back. You should teach well the four classes of beings." O Kasyapa! The Tathagata, the Right-Enlightened One, does not recline sick on a bed on his right-hand side. Nor does he, to the end, enter Nirvana. O Kasyapa! This Great Nirvana is the deepest dhyana [meditation] of all Buddhas. Such a dhyana is not what sravakas and pratyekabuddhas can practise. O Kasyapa! You asked why it was that the Tathagata should lie in bed and not sit up, why he should not call for food, teach, and give injunctions to family people to work for a living. But, O Kasyapa! The Void does not do anything such as sitting up, calling for food, giving injunctions to family people to work for a living. There is nothing of the kind such as going or coming, being born or dying, becoming old or being middle-aged, appearing or disappearing, being harmed or broken [injured], being emancipated or being bound. Also, there is no talking of one's own accord or talking to others. Also, there is no understanding of my own accord or understanding others; there is no peace, no illness. O good man! The same is the case with the All-Buddha-World-Honoured One. This is as of the Void. How could there be any illness?" "O Kasyapa! There are three types of sick persons who are difficult to cure. These are: 1) a person who slanders Mahayana, 2) a person who has committed the five deadly sins, and 3) the icchantika. The three cited above are the gravest of all the sins in the world. These are not those which sravakas and pratyekabuddhas can easily cure. O good man! For example, there is an illness which unfailingly ends in death and is difficult to cure. There may be nursing, an attitude of compliance [with the medical treatment], and medicine to apply; or there may be no nursing, no attitude of compliance, and no medicine to apply. Such an illness means certain death and cannot be cured. One should know that such a person will surely die. The same is the case with these three kinds of person. There may be sravakas, pratyekabuddhas, and Bodhisattvas who may speak about the doctrine or may not. There is no way to make such [as these three sick persons] aspire to unsurpassed Enlightenment. O Kasyapa! There is a person who is ill. There is nursing of him, an attitude of compliance, and medicine. And the illness can be cured. If there are not three such, there is no way to cure [the illness]. The same is the case with the sravakas and pratyekabuddhas. They listen to what the Buddha and Bodhisattvas say, and they indeed aspire to unsurpassed Enlightenment. It is not that they do not listen to the teaching and aspire to Enlightenment. O Kasyapa! A sick person is one regarding whom there may be nursing, an attitude of compliance, and medicine - or there may not be such. All are cured. The same is the case with one of the single kind. A person may come across a sravaka or he may not; a person may come across a pratyekabuddha or he may not; or a person may come across a Bodhisattva or he may not; a person may come across a Tathagata or he may not; a person may have occasion to listen to the teaching

or he may not. A person may all-naturally attain unsurpassed Enlightenment. Some, for their own sake, for that of others, out of fear, for profit, for [reasons of] flattery, or for cheating others, will hold or recite, make offerings to, respect, or deliver sermons to others on, the Great Nirvana Sutra. "O Kasyapa! There are five persons in this Mahayana Great Nirvana Sutra - the Tathagata excepted - who are ill, but have places to go to. Who are these five? One is he who cuts off the three fetters ["trinisamyojanani", i.e. a "stream-enterer"-"shrotapanna"], who has done away with the first three of the ten mental fetters) and attains the "shrotapanna" stage, thereby not falling into the three unfortunate realms of hell, animals, and hungry pretas. Such a person gains seven [more] births and deaths in the worlds of humans and gods, eternally cuts off all kinds of suffering and enters Nirvana. O Kasyapa! This is the first case of [someone] having an illness and [still] having a place to arrive at. This person, in the days to come, after 8,000 kalpas, will attain unsurpassed Enlightenment. The second is he who cuts off the three fetters, having made light the weight of greed, anger and ignorance, attaining the level of sakridagamin" "and, after one cycle of coming and going [being born and dying], eternally cuts off the bond of all suffering and attains Nirvana. O Kasyapa! This is the second instance of one who has illness and [still] has a place where he will be born. This person, in the days to come, after 60,000 kalpas, will attain unsurpassed Enlightenment. The third person is he who cuts off the five fetters of illusion ["pancavara-bhagiyasamyojanani"] that bind one to the kamadhatu [world of desire] and attains the light of the anagamin ["non-returner"]. This person never more gets reborn here in this world, eternally cuts off suffering and attains Nirvana. This is the case of having an illness and gaining a place to be born in. This person, after 40,000 kalpas, attains unsurpassed Enlightenment. O Kasyapa! The fourth person is he who eternally cuts off the defilements of greed, anger and ignorance and gains arhatship and, having no more taints of defilement left, enters Nirvana. Also, this is not a practice monopolized by the pratyekabuddha. This is the case of the fourth person who gains illness and a place to be born. This person, after 20,000 kalpas, attains unsurpassed Enlightenment. O Kasyapa! The fifth person is he who has eternally cut off the defilements of greed, anger and ignorance and, having gained the light of a pratyekabuddha, has no more illusions to cut off and enters Nirvana. This is indeed the sole case of a kirin [name of a fabulous animal]. This is the case of the fifth person who, having illness, gains a place to be born. This person, after 10,000 kalpas, will attain unsurpassed Enlightenment. O Kasyapa! This is the case of the fifth person who, having illness, gains a place to be born. He is not a Tathagata."

Chapter Nineteen: On Holy Actions 1

Then, the Buddha said to Bodhisattva Kasyapa: "O good man! The Bodhisattva-mahasattva should, in accordance with this "Mahaparinirvana Sutra", meditate exclusively on the five kinds of action. What are the five? They are: 1) holy actions, 2) pure actions, 3) heavenly actions, 4) childlike actions, 5) actions of illness. O good man! The Bodhisattva-mahasattva should practise these five actions. Also, there is one action, which is the action of the Tathagata, the so-called Mahayana Great Nirvana Sutra. O Kasyapa! What are the holy actions which a Bodhisattvamahasattva practises? The Bodhisattva-mahasattva, following a sravaka or the Tathagata, hears the Great Nirvana Sutra. Having heard it, he gains faith and, on believing, thinks: "The All-Buddha-World-Honoured One has the unsurpassed Way, the greatly Wonderful Dharma, right action for the great congregation. Also, there are the Mahayana vaipulya sutras. As I now love and seek zealously after the Mahayana sutras, I shall sever myself from my wife and children whom I love, my relatives, the palace where I live, gold, silver and all rare jewelleries, wonderful necklaces, incense, flowers, dancing and music, servants male and female, men and women, pages big and small, people, elephants, horses, vehicles, cows, sheep, hens, dogs, hogs and pigs." Also, he thinks: "One's living-quarters so bear down upon one that they resemble a prison-house. All worries arise from this. When one's home has been abandoned, all is silent and open like the Void. All good increases as a result of this. In one's home, one cannot - to the end - practise pure actions with a pure mind. I shall now shave off my hair, leave home and practise the Way." Also he thinks: "I shall now definitely leave home and practise the Way of unsurpassed right and true Enlightenment." When the Bodhisattva desires to renounce the world, Marapapiyas becomes greatly worried and says: "Now, this Bodhisattva will have a great battle with me." O good man! How would such a Bodhisattva fight with men? Then, the Bodhisattva goes at once to a Buddhist vihara and sees the Tathagata and his disciples there, who are all correct in their deportment and serene in their sense-organs and soft and calm in their minds. So he goes there and seeks to get ordained. He shaves off his hair and puts on the three kinds of monastic robe. After having been ordained, he upholds the prohibitional precepts, and he is not lacking in deportment. His movements are peaceful, and nothing is violated. Even a small sin he fears, and his mind to be true [his truthful attitude of mind] is strict and unbroken like a diamond. "O good man! Here is a man who wants to cross the sea on a floating bag. Then there is a rakshasa [flesh-eating demon] in the sea. He follows the man and begs the bag of him. Hearing this, the man thinks: "If I give [it him], I will certainly sink and die." He replies: "O rakshasa! You can kill me, but you cannot have the floating bag." The rakshasa says: "If you cannot give all of the bag to me, give me half." But still the man will not give [him the bag]. The rakshasa says again: "If you cannot give me half, give me one third." The man does not say "yes". The rakshasa continues: "If you cannot, give me the bit where your hand rests, I shall be hard-pressed by hunger and worry. Please give me just a bit." The man further says: "What you seek to have is, indeed, not much. But I must cross the sea this very day. I don't know how far it is. If I give [you] any part, the air will gradually go out. How could I [then] hope to cross this difficult sea? If the air goes out, I shall sink and die half-way." "O good man! The same is the case with the Bodhisattva who upholds the precepts. He is like the man who desires to cross the sea and who is very solicitous of guarding the floating bag and grudges [giving it away]. When the Bodhisattva thus cares to protect the precepts, there will always appear in his way the rakshasas of all evil illusions, who will say to the Bodhisattva: "Believe me, I am not going to cheat you. Just commit the four grave offences and take care of the other precepts. For this, I will give you peace, and you will awaken in Nirvana." The Bodhisattva will then say: "I would rather uphold the precepts and gain Avichi Hell than break them and be born in heaven." The rakshasa of illusion will say: "If you cannot commit the four grave offences, commit the samghavasesa. For this, I will make you attain Nirvana easily." The Bodhisattva will not comply. The rakshasa will again say: "If you cannot commit the samghavasesa, commit the sthulatyaya. For this, you will have a peaceful Nirvana." Again, the Bodhisattva will not comply. The rakshasa will again say: "If you cannot commit the sthulatyaya, break the [rules of the] naihsargika-prayascittika. For this, you will have a peaceful Nirvana." The Bodhisattva will again refuse to comply. Then the rakshasa will say again: "If you cannot commit the prayascittika, please commit the duskrta. For this, you will have a peaceful Nirvana." Then the Bodhisattva will say to himself: "If I commit the duskrta and do not confess before the assembly [of monks], I may not be able to cross the sea of birth and death and attain Nirvana." The Bodhisattva-mahasattva is [thus] very strict in avoiding these very petty offences [prohibited by the precepts], and his mind is like a diamond. The Bodhisattva-mahasattva respectfully and indifferently [calmly] observes the precept against the four grave offences and the duskrta. "If the Bodhisattva upholds the precepts thus, he is known to have observed the five kinds of shilas [obligations, moral precepts], which are: 1) the precept for the purity of the Bodhisattva's basic actions, 2) the precept for the purity of the fore-and-aft relative actions and others, 3) the precept for awakening to purity and not awakening to things of the evil categories, 4) the precept for protecting [maintaining] right mindfulness and for praying for purity, and 5) the precept for transferring [merit] to unsurpassed Bodhi. "O Kasyapa! Now, there are two kinds of precept for the Bodhisattva. One relates to secular teaching, and the other is for attaining Wonderful Dharma. If a Bodhisattva gains the precepts for Wonderful Dharma, he does not do evil to the end. The secular precepts can be gained after the proceedings of the jnapticaturtha [one of the ways of arriving at a decision in the Buddhist Sangha]. Also, next, O good man! There are two kinds of precept. One [set] is the precepts against originally grave offences and the other is [those] to stop the ill-speaking and hatred that obtain in secular life. The precepts against the originally grave offences are those regarding the four offences. We say "precepts to stop the ill-speaking and hatred that obtain in secular life." That is: not cheating others during trade by making the weight of the scales less or making the measure smaller [i.e. not giving as much of the product as one should] or gaining wealth by taking advantage of another's circumstances, by binding others with ill-will, by destroying another's success, by sleeping with the light on, by having one's own house and sowing seeds, and by not sticking to one's household duties [requirements, necessities] in a shop [when shopping]. One does not keep an elephant, horse, vehicle, cow, sheep, camel, donkey, hen, dog, monkey, peacock, parrot, jivamjivaka, kokila, jackal, wolf, cat, racoon, wild boar, pig, or other bad beast, boy, girl, grown-up man or woman [slaves], male or female servant, boy servant, gold, silver, beryl, crystal, pearls, lapis lazuli, agate, coral, jade, horse-shoe shell, or other gems; a bowl of copper alloy, solder, brass; the "kusu" [square mattress on which the emperor sits to pray or worship] and "toto" [woollen carpet], or woollen clothing that fits in well with the body [that hugs the body? fits well]. He never stores up cereal and rice, wheat and beans of any size, millet, Italian millet, rice, hemp, and the utensils for raw or cooked food. He receives [food] once a day, and never eats twice a day. His meal is what is gained from alms-begging or is that for the Sangha [food donated to the Sangha]. He always knows just how to slow down his steps, but never accepts a special invitation [for himself alone]. "He does not eat meat or take intoxicating drinks", "nor vegetables of the five kinds of astringent smell" [including garlic, leeks, onions]. Hence, no unpleasant smell comes about [on the breath]. He is always respected and given offerings, honoured and praised by gods and humans. He receives only what will satisfy his appetite and does not stay [waiting for food to be offered] long. The clothes he receives are just to cover his body. In going and coming, what he has are the three kasayas [robes] and his begging-bowl. He never parts from these, just as birds do not part from their wings. He never stores up any produce as of the categories of the root, stem, joint, knot or seed [such as radish roots and bamboo shoots]. He has no larder for food, no accessories for dressing, never sits or lies on high or big beds, on a golden bed of ivory, or possesses any kinds of knitted clothing of varying colours, no mattresses delicate and soft to the touch; he never sits on elephant or horse skins, nor does he recline on a bed spread across with delicately made, soft and beautiful bedclothes, or put a double pillow on the bedstead or keep a red-coloured pillow; nor does he sleep on a yellow-coloured pillow; nor does he enjoy himself looking at the fights of elephants, horses, vehicles, soldiers, men, women, cows, sheep, cocks, pheasants, parrots, etc.; nor does he specially go and look at military camps; nor does he listen to the trumpet shell, drum, horn, "ch'in", "shā", "chāng" [lutes], flute, harp, singing and crying, dance music of females, except on occasions when offerings are being made to the Buddha. He does not watch such games as the "chobo" [type of gambling], "go" [chess], "prasaka" [gambling game], nor the fights of lions and elephants, the "danki" [type of game], "rikuhaku" [kind of gambling], ball-game, throwing of stones and pots, running, the "hachidogyojo", nor any kinds of amusement. Throughout his life, he does not practise the likes of fortune-telling by looking at a person's hands, feet, face, or eyes; nor does he use such things as the "sokyā" [used in fortune-telling], divining sticks, tooth picks, bowls, or carcasses; nor does he look up at the sky and the constellations, except when checking drowsiness. He will not become the messenger of a kingly house or say that to this person or this to that. He does not flatter or live by evil ways. Also, he does not talk about such as kings, ministers, robbers, fights, meals, land, famines, fear, good harvests, pleasure or ease. O good man! All such are the precepts for checking the rise of worldly rumours about a Bodhisattvamahasattva. The Bodhisattva-mahasattva strongly upholds the prohibitional precepts. And this does not depart from the originally grave offences. "O good man! When the Bodhisattva-mahasattva observes all these prohibitions, he takes such vows as these: "I might well place my body into the burning fire of the deepest depths of hell, but I will not break the prohibitions of all the Buddhas of the past, future and present, and will not perform impure actions with females, Kshatriyas, Brahmins and upasakas." Also, next, O good man! The Bodhisattva-mahasattva vows: "I would sooner bind myself with a piece of heated iron than receive clothing from the faithful, [in a way that] breaks the precepts." Also, next, O good man! The Bodhisattva-mahasattva vows: "I would sooner swallow a ball of heated iron than take a meal offered by the faithful, my mouth breaking the precepts." Also, next, O good man! The Bodhisattva-mahasattva vows: "I would sooner lie on a greatly heated iron bed than receive from the hands of the faithful such things as bedstead and bedding, myself breaking the precepts." Also, next, O good man! The Bodhisattva-mahasattva vows: "I would sooner have this body of mine thrust through with 300 spears than receive from the hands of the faithful medicine that causes me to break the precepts." Also, next, O good man! The Bodhisattvamahasattva vows: "I would sooner throw myself upon a tripod [trident] than receive from the faithful a shed or house that causes me to break the precepts." Also, he vows: "I would sooner have my head and legs crushed into motes with an iron hammer than have myself respected and worshipped by Kshatriyas, Brahmins and upasakas who cause me to break the precepts." Also, next, O good man! The Bodhisattva-mahasattva vows: "I would sooner have my face cut off or both my eyes taken out than look upon the beauty of other persons with a defiled mind." Also, next, O good man! The Bodhisattva-mahasattva vows: "I would sooner have my ears thrust through from all sides with iron awls than give ear to beautiful sounds with a defiled mind." Also, next, O good man! The Bodhisattva-mahasattva vows: "I would sooner have my nose cut off with a sharp sword than enjoy any beautiful fragrances with a defiled mind." Also, next, O good man! The Bodhisattva-mahasattva vows: "I would sooner have my tongue torn into shreds with a sharp sword than greedily taste beautiful dishes with a defiled mind." Also, next, O good man! The Bodhisattva-mahasattva vows: "I would sooner have my body cut into pieces with a sharp hatchet than greedily covet with a defiled mind whatever is touchable. Why? Because all this carries those who practise the Way into such realms as those of hell, the animals, and hungry ghosts." O Kasyapa! This is the Bodhisattva-mahasattva's guarding of the prohibitions. "When the Bodhisattva-mahasattva acts in accordance with the prohibitions mentioned above, he transfers all the merits hereof to all beings. He prays that, through this, they will be able to accomplish the precepts for purity, those for goodness, those for non-falling, those for non-breaking, the Mahayana precepts, the precepts for non-retrogression, those for obedience, those for the Ultimate, those for the perfection and accomplishment of the paramitas [perfections of virtue]. "O good man! When the Bodhisattva-mahasattva thus practises the precepts for purity, he first attains a state from which he never more moves away. Why do we call it being one who is immovable? When a Bodhisattva lives in this state, he is immovable, non-retrogressive, and nondispersive. For example, it is like Mount Sumeru, which not even the sharpest wind ["vairambhaka"] can move, cause to blow over or move back. The same is the case with the Bodhisattva-mahasattva when he lives in this "bhumi". He is not shaken by colour, voice, smell, or taste; he does not fall into such realms as those of hell, beast or hungry preta; he does not fall back to the state of sravaka or pratyekabuddha; he is not shaken by different views and evil winds, and he does not live the wrong life. Also, next, O good man! "Immovable" also means not being shaken by greed and anger; "not falling" means not falling into the four grave offences. "Not retrogressing" means that one does not retrogress and come back home [to worldly life]. "Not being dispersed" means not being shaken or destroyed by those who act against the Mahayana. Also, next, the Bodhisattva-mahasattva is not beaten by the Mara of illusion, not shaken by the Mara of the five skandhas. Even though the king Mara is there under the shade of the Bodhi Tree, he cannot cause the Bodhisattva to retrogress from attaining unsurpassed Enlightenment. Also, the Bodhisattva does not get beaten by the Mara of death. O good man! This is how the Bodhisattva practises the holy Way. "O good man! Why do we say "holy actions"? It is so called because what is done is what the Buddha and Bodhisattvas do. Why do we call the Buddha and Bodhisattvas "holy persons"? They are so called because they always meditate on "Dharmata", on the quietude of the Void. For this reason, we say that they are holy persons. As they uphold the holy precepts, they are holy persons. As they have the holy dhyana and Wisdom, they are holy persons. They possess the seven holy properties, which are: faith, precepts, repentance, rich-hearing, Wisdom, equanimity, and segregation. That is why they are called holy persons. As they possess the seven holy awakenings, they are holy persons. For this reason, too, we say "holy persons". Also, next, O good man! The holy actions of the Bodhisattva-mahasattvas are what they do in observing the body from head to foot. And these are: hair, nails, teeth, impurities, dirt, skin, flesh, sinews, bones, spleen, kidneys, heart, lungs, liver, intestines and stomach, i.e. stomach and large intestines, faeces, urine, spittle, tears, fat, membrane, marrow, pus, blood, skull, and all the veins. When the Bodhisattva thus observes things, who [here] can be the Self, or to whom can the Self belong? Where does it live and who can belong to the Self? Also, he thinks: "Is the bone the Self? Or is what is other than bone the Self?" The Bodhisattva then meditates, and excludes the skin and flesh. What he sees is white bone. He also thinks: "The colour of bone is various: blue, yellow, white, dove-colour." Thus what the bone displays is not "I". Why not? Because the Self is not blue, yellow, white or dove-colour. As the Bodhisattva meditates thus, with full mind, he is away from all desire for what is physical. Also, he thinks: "Such bone comes about from causal relations [causal constellations, causal concatenations]. The foot-bone supports the ankle-bone; the ankle-bone supports the calf-bone; the calf-bone supports the knee-bone, the knee-bone supports the thigh-bone; the thigh-bone supports the rump-bone; the rump-bone supports the loin-bone; the loin-bone supports the backbone; the backbone supports the rib-bones. Also, the backbone supports the bone of the nape; the bone of the nape supports the chin-bone [jaw]; the chin-bone supports the canine and other teeth. And above that there is the skull. Also, the bone of the nape supports the shoulder-blade; the shoulder-blade supports the bone of the upper arm; the bone of the upper arm supports the bone of the lower arm; the bone of the lower arm supports the wrist-bone; the wrist-bone supports the finger-bone. When the Bodhisattva-mahasattva thus meditates, all the bones of the body dispart [separate out]. Having thus meditated, the Bodhisattva cuts off the three desires: for facial form, for bodily form, and for minor touches. "When the Bodhisattva-mahasattva thus meditates on the blue bones, he sees the earth look all blue to the east, west, south, north, up and down, and the four corners. The same is the case with the meditations on the colours of yellow, white, and dove as with the meditation on the colour blue. When the Bodhisattva-mahasattva thus meditates, from his brow issues forth the fragrance of the colours of blue, yellow, white, and dove-colour. The Bodhisattva sees in each of the lights the form of the Buddha. Having seen the Buddha, he asks: "Something such as this body of mine comes about from a combination of impurities. How could we sit and stand, walk and stop, bend and look up, see and wink, pant and breathe, grieve and weep, be happy and laugh? There is none that rules over [the body]. What causes things to be thus?" As he thus thinks, all the Buddha figures disappear from the lights. Also, he thinks: "Or consciousness might be my Self. That is why the Buddhas will not speak to me." Again, as he meditates on consciousness, he sees that things gradually disappear, as in the case of running water. So, this is not one's Self. Also, he thinks:

"Now, this in-and-out breathing of mine is nothing but of the nature of the wind. The nature of the wind is nothing but one of the four great elements. Which of the four great elements can be my Self? The natures of water, fire and wind, too, are not my Self." Also, he thinks: "With this body of mine, there is nothing that could be called Self. Only the causal relations of the wind of mind join things together and there are various works and things. For example, this is as in the case of charms or tricks, or the sound of the harp that comes out followoing the wind of the mind of the one who plays. Thus is this body impure. Various causal relations join together and things go thus. For what might we have greed? If one bears ill-speaking, how could there arise anger? It would seem that the 36 things [i.e. the 36 defilements that a human body possesses] of my body are nothing but what is impure and defiled. Where can there be one who has to bear ill-speaking? When one is spoken ill of, one may well think: "Whose voice is it that thus speaks ill of [me]? No one's voice can be the one that speaks ill of [me]. If one person does not speak ill, the same applies to many voices. For this reason, one should not get angry." When other persons come and beat one up, one should think: "From where comes this beating?" Also, one might think: "When hands, the sword or staff come into contact with my body, we say that we get beaten. How could we ever get angry at others? This shows that I myself have invited the sin of my own accord. This comes from the fact that I have this body of the five skandhas. This is as in the case of a target which an arrow can hit, and there comes about [such] hitting. The same is the case with this body of mine. As I have a body, there is [the possibility of] a beating. If I do not bear down [upon it], my mind will break up. If my mind gets dispersed, I shall lose my right mind. If I lose my right mind, I may not be able to see what is good and what is not. If I cannot distinguish good and not-good in a thing, I shall do evil. Evil done will take one to the realms of hell, animals and hungry ghosts." "The Bodhisattva-mahasattva, having done this meditation, attains the four remembrances. As he gains the four remembrances, he now can live in the forbearance soil ["bhumi"]. As the Bodhisattva-mahasattva attains this state, he bears down upon greed, anger and ignorance; also, he is able to stand the cold, heat, hunger, thirst, mosquitoes, gadflies, fleas, lice, storms, impure meals [meals made impure by being touched by others' hands], illness, plague, ill-speaking, abuse, beatings, and slashings with thorns. He will bear down upon all the pains and worries of the body. That is why we say that he lives in the forbearance soil." Bodhisattva Kasyapa said to the Buddha: "O World-Honoured One! When the Bodhisattva as yet does not dwell in the immovable soil, but upholds purity, could he, if the occasion arose, break the precepts or not?" "O good man! When the Bodhisattva has not yet attained the state of the immovable soil, he may well break the precepts when the occasion arises." Kasyapa said: "So it is, indeed! O World-Honoured One! Who can be such a person?" The Buddha said to Kasyapa: "The Bodhisattva may have occasion to transgress against the precepts if he knows that he can indeed make others possess the Mahayana sutras, make them like them, understand, copy and expound them widely to others, and make them attain unsurpassed Enlightenment and not retrogress from it. On such an occasion, he may well transgress the precepts. At that time, the Bodhisattva will think: "Even though I may fall into Avichi Hell for a kalpa or less and may have to expiate my sin there, I shall surely make this person attain unsurpassed Enlightenment and not retrogress therefrom". O Kasyapa! In such circumstances, the Bodhisattva-mahasattva may transgress against the purity of the precepts." Then Bodhisattva Manjushri said to the Buddha: "Any Bodhisattva who takes in such persons, protects them, and makes them aspire to Enlightenment and makes them not retrogress from it and who, for this purpose, transgresses against the precepts, cannot fall into Avichi Hell." At that, the Buddha praised Manjushri, saying: "Well said, well said! I recall that in days gone by I was born in Jambudvipa as a great king named Senyo. He loved the Mahayana sutras and respected them. He was pure and good, and there was no coarseness in him; no jealousy, no stinginess could find any room inside him. What issued forth from him was loving words, words that spoke of good. He always protected the poor and the lonely; with him there was no end of giving and of making effort. At that time, there was no Buddha, no sravakas and pratyekabuddhas. I, at that time, loved the Mahayana vaipulya sutras. For 12 years I served the Brahmins, catering fully to their needs. After that, when giving and peace had been gained, I said: "O you teachers! You should now aspire to unsurpassed

Enlightenment." The Brahmins said: "O great King! There is no such thing as the nature of Enlightenment; the same is the case with the Mahayana sutras. O great King! How is it that you wish to make us equal to the Void"? O good man! I, at that time, greatly respected Mahayana. I heard the Brahmins slandering the vaipulya. Having heard this, I did away with my life. O good man! I have never once fallen into hell because of this [i.e. despite this]. O good man! When we accept and protect the Mahayana sutras, we have innumerable virtues. "Also, next, O Kasyapa! There are also [other] holy actions. These are the Four Noble Truths, which are: Suffering, the Cause [of Suffering], the Extinction [of Suffering], and the Way [to the Extinction of that Suffering]. O Kasyapa! Suffering is oppressive circumstance. The cause of suffering contains the phases of growth and expansion. Extinction is the phase of quietness and annihilation, the Way is Mahayana. Also, next, O good man! Suffering is what actually stands before one; the cause is a phase of change; extinction is exclusion; the Way is what we can well exclude. Also, next, O good man! Suffering has three phases [modes], which are: 1) suffering-suffering, 2) the suffering of what is made, and 3) the suffering of breaking away [i.e. disintegration, separation from what one likes]. The cause of suffering relates to the 25 existences. The Way relates to the precepts, meditation, and Wisdom. Also, next, O good man! Of "asravas" [defilements], there are two kinds, which are: cause and result. "Anasrava" [nondefilement - the absence of desire, "becoming" and ignorance] is of two kinds, which are: cause and result. The result of "asrava" is suffering; the cause of "asrava" is "samudaya" [=cause of suffering, which = "trishna", craving]. The result of "anasrava" is extinction [of suffering] and the cause of "anasrava" is the Way. "Also, next, O good man! There are eight modes of suffering, which are: 1) the suffering of being born, 2) the suffering of ageing, 3) the suffering of illness, 4) the suffering of death, 5) the suffering of parting from what one loves, 6) the suffering of encountering what one hates, 7) the suffering of not being able to obtain what one desires, and 8) the suffering of the burning urges of the skandhas. The cause of these eight modes of suffering is [called] "samudaya". Where these eight sufferings do not exist, that is extinction. The ten powers, the four fearlessnesses, the three mental states, and Great Compassion are

the Way. "O good man! Birth is emergence, of which there are five kinds: 1) first coming, 2) end of coming, 3) growing, 4) emerging from the womb, and 5) actual birth with characteristics. "What is ageing? This has two aspects: 1) hourly ageing and 2) physical ageing. Again, there are two kinds: 1) increasing ageing and 2) extinguishing and breaking ageing. Thus do things stand with ageing. "What is illness? By illness is meant the non-conforming [non-harmonisation] of the poisonous serpents of the four great elements, which is of two kinds: 1) illness of the body and 2) illness of the mind. In illness of the body, there are five kinds of cause, which are: 1) water, 2) wind, 3) heat, 4) various diseases, and 5) illnesses from external causes. Illnesses from external causes comprise: 1) unremitting labour, 2) forgetfulness, misdemeanours, and degeneration, 3) sword, staff, tiles, stones, and 4) devils and phantoms. Illness of the mind is also of four kinds, which are: 1) unbounded joy [manic state], 2) fear, 3) anxiety, and 4) ignorance. Also, next, O good man! Of illness of body and mind, there are three kinds. What are the three? These are: 1) karma results, 2) being unable to segregate oneself from what is evil, and 3) change resultant from the course of time. All such as causal relations, the categorical nature, and differences in feeling call forth illnesses. Causal relations refer to such illnesses as of wind, etc., the categorical nature refers to swellings in [as a result of] worry, coughs by dizziness, and soft [loose] bowels due to mental surprise, differences in feeling refers to headaches, pains in the eys, hands, feet, etc. Such are illnesses. "What is death? By death is meant the relinquishing of the carnal body which one has been given. In relinquishing the body which one has received, there are two kinds, which are: 1) death through the expiration of life [i.e. from one's life naturally coming to an end] and 2) death from external causes. In death through expiration of life, there are three kinds, which are: 1) ending of life, which, however, is not the ending of fortune; 2) ending of wealth, which, however, is not the ending of life; 3) ending of both fortune and life. There are three kinds of death from external causes, which are: 1) unnatural suicide, 2) death caused by others, and 3) death from both causes. Also, there are three kinds of death, which are: 1) death from indolence, 2) death from violating the precepts, and 3) death from severing the life-root. What is death from indolence? If one slanders the

Mahayana-vaipulya-prajnaparamita, this is death from indolence. What is death from violating the precepts? When one breaches the prohibitions laid down by the Buddhas of the past, future and present, this is violating the precepts. What is death from severing the life-root? Forsaking the body of the five skandhas is death from severing the life-root. That is why we say that death is great suffering. "What is the suffering of parting from what one loves? What one loves breaks up and becomes dispersed. There are two kinds of parting from what one loves, which are: 1) breaking-up of the five skandhas of a human and 2) breaking-up of the heavenly world. If we count up the kinds of five skandhas of the things of heaven and earth, they are innumerable. This is the suffering of parting from what one loves. "What is the suffering of encountering what one hates? There are masses of things which one does not love, which come together. In such massings together of what one does not love, there are three kinds, which are the realms of hell, hungry ghosts, and animals. Such three are innumerable, even though we may try to enumerate them. Such is the suffering of encountering what one hates to encounter. "What is the suffering of not being able to gain what one desires? There are two kinds of this suffering of not being able to gain what one desires to have, which are: 1) desiring something, but not being able to get it, and 2) the result that does not come about, even after much effort, which is the case of suffering from not being able to get what one desires to have. "What is the suffering of the burning urge of the five skandhas? The suffering of the burning urge of the five skandhas refers to the suffering of birth, the suffering of ageing, the suffering of illness, the suffering of death, the suffering of parting from what one loves, the suffering of encountering what one hates, and the suffering of not being able to gain what one wishes to have. That is why we speak of the suffering of the burning urge of the five skandhas. "O Kasyapa! The root of life has these seven kinds of suffering. This extends from the suffering of ageing to the suffering of the burning urge of the five skandhas. O Kasyapa! This does not mean that ageing comes to all. It definitely does not come to the Buddha and the gods. With man, it is indefinite: it may exist or it may not. O Kasyapa! Those who exist in the three worlds have life. Ageing is not always definite. That is why the root rests in life. O Kasyapa! The

men of the world are upside down, which fact beclouds their minds. They cling to what obtains in life and hate ageing and death. It is otherwise with the Bodhisattva. When he first looks at birth, he already sees illness. "O Kasyapa! There was once a woman, who came into the house of another. She bore herself spendidly. She looked beautiful and her body was adorned with necklaces of various stones. The master of the house saw her and asked: "What is your name? To whom do you belong?" The woman answered: "I am Gunamahadevi". The man of the house asked: "What do you do wherever you go?" The devi answered: "Wherever I go, I give people various things such as gold, silver, beryl, crystal, pearl, coral, lapis lazuli, agate, elephants, horses, vehicles, male or female servants, messenger boys." On hearing this, the man of the house felt extremely pleased: "Now, fortune is on my side. That is why you are in my house." He burnt incense, strew flowers, made offerings, and worshipped her. Also, outside the gate, he encountered a woman, ugly and mean, whose clothes were tattered, torn, defiled by fat and were dirty. Her skin was chapped and she looked pale and white. On seeing her, he asked: "What is your name? To whom do you belong?" The woman answered: "My name is "Darkness." He asked further: "Why "Darkness?" The woman answered: "Wherever I go, the wealth of that house disappears." Hearing this, the man brandished a sharp sword and said: "Go away! If you don't, I will kill you." The woman said: "You are a fool and lack wisdom." The man asked: "Why am I a fool, and why do I lack wisdom?" The woman answered: "The woman in your house is my elder sister. I always accompany her. If you drive me away, she will leave you." The master of the house entered the house and asked Gunadevi: "°Outside the house there is a woman who says that she is your sister. Is this true?" Gunadevi said: "She truly is my sister. I am always accompanied by her, in going and coming; we never part. Wherever I am, I always do good and she always does evil. I give benefit and she loss. If you love me, love her also. If you respect me, respect her too." The man at once said: "If there have to be both, good and evil, I won't have either. Go on your way, both of you!" Then the two women went to where they had been before. When they had left for where they had first been, the man of the house was glad and greatly rejoiced. Then the two women went to a poor man's hut. On seeing them, the man invited them in and said: "Henceforth stay in my house." Gunadevi said: "We were driven away. Why do you invite us to come in?" The poor man said: "You now think of me. I respect your sister because of you. So, I allow both of you to come in." The situation is like this. O Kasyapa! It is the same with the Bodhisattvamahasattva. He does not desire to be born in heaven. Being born means that there, too, there are ageing, illness and death. So he abandons both; he is not minded to receive them. Common mortals and the ignorant do not realise the ills of ageing, illness and death. So they greedily seek birth and death. "Also, next, O Kasyapa! The child of a Brahmin, oppressed by hunger, picks up a mango fruit which is lying in excrement. A man who knows what is what sees this and reproaches the child: "You who come from a Brahmin family and whose blood is pure! Why do you pick up that dirty fruit which was lying in excrement?" The child flushes, after being so reprimanded. Then he replies: "I do not want to eat this, to tell you the truth. I just wanted to wash it and throw it away." The wise man says: "What you say does not make any sense. If you wanted to throw it away, what was the good of picking it up in the first place?" The situation is like this. O good man! It is the same with the Bodhisattva-mahasattva. There is no receiving and no abandoning [with him] from the very beginning. This is as in the case of the wise man who reproaches the Brahmin child. The case of the common mortal who prays for life and hates death is similar to that of the child who picks up the fruit and later abandons it. "Also, next, O Kasyapa! For example, there is a man who spreads out utensils filled with food at a crossroads; the colour, fragrance and taste are perfect. And he wishes to sell them. A man comes from a far-off place and is hungry and wasted. He is taken with the perfect colour, fragrance and taste. He points to the food and asks: "What food is this?" The man selling the food says: "This is the best of food; it has colour and fragrance. If one eats it, one's physique and strength will increase. It indeed does away with hunger, and one [who eats it] will certainly see heaven. But there is a snag. That is, that one has to die!" On hearing this, the man says to himself: "I may not need any physical strength to see heaven, and also I don't care for death." And he says: "If I eat this food, I will die. How can you sell this food here at all?" The food-seller says:

"He who is wise does not buy it at all. Only the ignorant do not know this. They give me a lot and greedily eat this food." So might he say. The same is the case with the Bodhisattvamahasattva. He does not wish to be born in heaven. He does not wish to have [a powerful] physique and strength, and to see all the devas. Why not? Because he knows that they are not removed from all worries there. Common mortals and the ignorant greedily devour wherever there is life to be lived, since they do not see ageing, sickness and death. "Also, next, O Kasyapa! For example, there is a poisonous tree, the root of which will certainly kill a man. So, too, the branches, trunk, knots, bark, leaves, flowers and fruit. O good man! Also, wherever the 25 existences obtain, it is the case with the five skandhas. Death always follows them. "Also, next, O Kasyapa! It is like the defilement of excrement, which gives off a horrible smell, no matter how small the amount is. O good man! The same with life. Whether one gains a life of 8,000 years or as little as 10 years, suffering accompanies it all the same. "Also, next, O Kasyapa! As an example: a precipice is fully overgrown by grass. And on the edge of the precipice, there is a lot of amrta [ambrosia]. If one eats it, one will live for 1,000 years. This will do away with disease for good, and all will proceed in peace. Common mortals and the ignorant greedily covet the taste and forget about the great pit that awaits them down below. They advance forwards, but unfortunately lose their footing, fall into the pit and die. But the wise know how things stand; they do not come near. Instead, they keep away. O good man! The same with he Bodhisattva-mahasattva. He does not care for the wonderful dishes of heaven. How could he care for those of man? Common mortals swallow an iron ball in hell. How could he desire to receive the all-wonderful dishes of the world of humans or of heaven? O Kasyapa! You will certainly be able to know from this and all other innumerable parables that this life is really nothing but a thing of great suffering. O Kasyapa! This is how a Bodhisattva sees the suffering of life, abiding in what is said in the Mahayana Great Nirvana Sutra. "O Kasyapa! How does the Bodhisattva, abiding in this Mahayana Great Nirvana Sutra, see the suffering of ageing? Age truly does call forth coughs and dizziness. It diminishes courage [spirit], memory, positive steps forward, manhood, joy, pride, high-brow [height], peace, and unmolestedness [freedom]. Age indeed brings with it back swellings, forgetfulness and lassitude, and is looked down upon by others. O Kasyapa! A pond is full of lotuses, with their flowers wide open and with freshness filling all around. All is lovely. But if hail comes, all will be destroyed. It is like that. O good man! Ageing is thus. It destroys manhood and beauty. Also, next, O Kasyapa! A king has a wise minister who is well up in military tactics. An enemy king rises against him. The king sends this minister to go and conquer the enemy king. This king is taken prisoner, and the minister returns home and sees the king. The case is thus. The same with ageing. It takes prisoners of one's manhood and brilliancy [alertness of mind] and hands them over to the king of death. Also, next, O Kasyapa! It is as in the case of a rich man who owns such various tresures as gold, silver, lapis lazuli, crystal, agate, red pearl and carnelian. But when robbers come and steal them, nothing more remains behind. O good man! It is the same with manhood and brilliancy. The thief, old age, always comes and plunders [everything]. Also, next, O Kasyapa! For example, a poor man greedily covets beautiful dishes and soft clothes. He seeks to possesss such, but cannot. O good man! The case is the same with ageing too. A greedy mind covets wealth and the satisfaction of the five [sense] desires, but it cannot [find satisfaction]. Also, next, O Kasyapa! It is like the tortoise on dry land that always thinks of water. O good man! The same is the case with human beings. Dried up with emaciation and age, the mind always thinks back to the pleasures of the five desires which one enjoyed in the prime of one's life. Also, next, O Kasyapa! It is as in the case of the autumn moon which, though looked up to by all the lotus flowers, is looked down upon when it wanes in its yellow. O good man! The same is the case with the prime of life and youthful colours. Though loved by all, all look down upon [one] when old age comes. Also, next, O Kasyapa! The same is the case with sugar cane. When it is pressed, what remains behind has no taste. The same regarding the prime of life and youthful colours. When old-age presses down on one, nothing remains of the three tastes, which are: 1) the taste of renunciation, 2) the taste of recitation, and 3) the taste of dhyana [meditation]. Also, next, O Kasyapa! This is as in the case of a night of the full moon, when there is an abundance of light, but in the daytime there is not. O good man! The same with human

beings. In the prime of life, one looks splendidly austere; one's form and face are rare and grand, but as one grows old, one becomes weaker and one's godliness of form dries up. Also, next, O Kasyapa! As an example: there is a king who governs the land with just law and reigns over his subjects. He is upright and honest; nothing about him is devious. He has compassion and loves to give. Then, the enemy comes and overruns the land. The king flees and goes to another country. The people of the other country see this and have pity and say: "O great King!

In days gone by, you reigned over a kingdom, basing yourself on right law and doing no crooked thing to anyone. How is it that you had to leave your country and come to this one?" It is like this. O good man! The same with human beings. When age comes and one once gets broken down [by it], one can only praise what obtained when one was in the prime of one's life. Also, next, O Kasyapa! It is, for example, like the wick of a lamp, which depends solely on grease and oil. When the grease and oil have gone, the power of the lamp does not endure long. The same with human beings. One depends on the oil of manhood. When the oil of manhood is spent, how long can the wick of weak old age give out light? Also, next, O Kasyapa! For example, a dried-up river cannot benefit humans, non-humans, flying birds or running beasts. The same with human beings. Dried up by old age, man cannot be of use for any [kind of] work. Also, next, O Kasyapa! For example, it is as with a tree hanging over the edge of a precipice. If a storm comes, it is sure to come toppling down. O good man! The same with the human being. If the storm of old age comes to the precipice of old age, nothing can check the force. Also, next, O Kasyapa! It is as with a broken shaft, by which no heavy burden can be borne. O good man! The same with old age. No good thing can be of any benefit to one. Also, next, it is as with a child who is slighted. O good man! Age, too, does thus. All people always make light of, and neglect, one [when one is old]. O Kasyapa! Know from this and all other innumerable and boundless parables that old age is truly great suffering. O Kasyapa! That is why the Bodhisattva studies the Mahayana Great Nirvana Sutra and meditates on the suffering of old age. "O Kasyapa! How does a Bodhisattva-mahasattva study the Mahayana Great Nirvana Sutra and meditate on the suffering of illness? So-called illness destroys all peace and joy. For example, it is as with the hail and rain that destroy the young buds of cereal. Also, it is as in the case of a person against whom someone has a grudge: that person's mind is always apprehensive and fearful. O good man! The same with all beings. They always fear the suffering of illness and are apprehensive. Also, next, O Kasyapa! There is a man who looks glorious and austere. The king's consort, due to sensual desire, means to have him. Letters arrive, and pressed by her, he has intercourse [with her]. The king catches him, cuts away one of each eye, ear, hand and leg. The appearance of this person changes. People dislike and slight him. O good man! The same applies to the human being. A person may have a good set of ears and eyes. But caught and pressed by illness, people will slight him. Also, next, O Kasyapa! For example, the plantain, bamboo, reed, and mule have to die when they have offspring. O good man! The same with human beings. From illness, they have to die. Also, next, O Kasyapa! The main body of soldiers and ministers of a chakravartin always go in front and lead the way, and the chakravartin follows. Likewise, the kings of fish, ants, whelks, cows, and head merchants go before and the others all follow and never part [from them]. Also, next, O good man! The same with the chakravartin of death. He always follows his subjects, illnesses, and never parts [from them]. The same with the kings of fish, ants, whelks, cows, and merchants. Always they are followed by the subjects of death. O Kasyapa! The causal relations of illness are worry, apprehension, suffering, and uneasiness in body and mind. One may be attacked by someone bearing ill-will, the floating bag may get rent, or the bridge may be dug away, so that the foundations of life will be endangered. Or the prime of life and bright complexion, vitality, peace, repentance may be destroyed or may disappear, or the body and mind may get burnt out. One can indeed see from this parable and from innumerable, boundless other parables how great the pain of illness is. All this is to show how the Bodhisattva-mahasattva studies this Mahayana Great Nirvana Sutra and meditates on the suffering of illness. " "O Kasyapa! How does the Bodhisattva study the Mahayana Great Nirvana Sutra and meditate on the suffering of death? We say "death", because it thoroughly burns out and annuls things. O Kasyapa! It is as when a fire burns out everything, except that it

cannot exclude the second dhyana. O good man! The same is the case with the fire of death. It burns out everything, excepting the Bodhisattva who abides in the Mahayana Mahaparinirvana. Because the strength [of the Bodhisattva] reaches this stage. Also, next, O Kasyapa! If a flood comes, all sinks under the water, excepting the third dhyana, which it cannot make away with. O good man! The same is the case with the water of death, which submerges everything, except for the Bodhisattva who abides in the Mahayana Mahaparinirvana. "Also, next, O Kasyapa! A storm blows up, scatters and destroys everything, excepting the fourth dhyana, which its power cannot reach. O good man! The same is the case with the wind of death. It destroys all that one has, except for the Bodhisattva who abides in the Mahayana Mahaparinirvana." Bodhisattva Kasyapa said to the Buddha: "O World-Honoured One! Why is it that the wind cannot blow away, the flood cannot wash away, and the fire cannot burn out the fourth dhyana?" The Buddha said: "O good man! This comes from the fact that in the fourth dhyana there does not remain a speck of sin, in or out of it. The first dhyana has sin and illness in it. Within, it has enlightened meditation, but outside, there is fire. The second dhyana has sin and illness in it. Within, there is joy; but outside, it has the sufferings of the flood. The third dhyana has sin and illness in it. Within, it has asthma and, outside, the sufferings from the wind. O good man! The fourth dhyana has, within and without, no sin or illness at all. Because of this, no calamity can reach it. O good man! The same is the situation with the Bodhisattva-mahasattva. He peacefully abides in the Mahayana Mahaparinirvana, and all sins and illness come to an end. Because of this, the king of death cannot reach him. Also, next, O good man! For example, the garuda indeed devours all nagas, fish, and all treasures such as gold and silver, except for the diamond. The same with the garuda of death. It indeed devours and does away with all beings, except for the Bodhisattva-mahasattva who abides in the Mahayana Mahaparinirvana, whom it cannot make away with. Also, next, for example, all grass and trees are swept down to the great sea if the volume of water increases in size and if the ravaging increases, except for the bitter willow and the willow, since these are soft and pliant. O good man! The same is the case with all beings. All follow and get into the sea of death, excepting the Bodhisattva who abides in the Mahayana Mahaparinirvana and whom it cannot do away with. Also, next, O Kasyapa! Narayana beats all wrestlers, except the great wind. Why? Because of unhiunderedness. O good man! The same is the case with the Narayana of death. He indeed conquers all beings, except the Bodhisattva who abides in the Mahayana Mahaparinirvana. Why? Because of unhinderedness. Also, next, O Kasyapa! There is a person who deceives and feigns friendliness, though entertaining enmity. He always follows others, just as a shadow does its object, and looks for a chance to kill them. But the person to whom enmity is borne is wary and stubborn, so that no opportunity for being killed is provided. O good man! The same is the case with the enemy of death. It always looks for a chance to kill beings, excepting the Bodhisattva-mahasattva who abides in the Mahayana Mahaparinirvana. Why? Because this Bodhisattva is not indolent. Also, next, O Kasyapa! For example, suddenly a great storm arises, carrying storm and rain of adamantine force, by which all medicinal trees, all trees, forests, sand, tiles, stones, gold, silver and beryl get crushed, except for the true treasure of the diamond. O good man! The same is the case with the adamantine rain of death. It wholly destroys beings, except for the Bodhisattva of adamantine mind who abides in the Mahayana Mahaparinirvana. Also, next, O Kasyapa! It is like the garuda that devours all nagas, excepting those who take refuge in the Three Treasures. O good man! The same is the case with the garuda of death that truly devours all innumerable beings, except the Bodhisattva who dwells in the three dhyanas. What are the three dhyanas? These are those of the Void, of formlessness, and desirelessness. Also, next, O Kasyapa! If one is bitten by a Mara-viper, no good charm or medicine of any superior quality can have any power to heal [one], except for the charm of agasti, which indeed cures [one]. It is the same with a person caught by the poison of death. No medical treatment is of any help, except for the case of the Bodhisattva charm of the Mahayana Mahaparinirvana. Also, next, there is a man who has aroused the anger of a king. But should he present treasures to the king with gentle words, he might well gain the king's pardon. The case is like this. O good man! The case of the king of death is not like that. One may offer money or wealth in a gently spoken manner, but no release will ensue.

"O good man! Now, death is a precipice where there is no guaranty of life. The way to it is far. One may walk day and night, and there is no end of walking. The path of gloom hangs on [oppresses] one and there is no light. There is no gate through which one may enter, and there is a place that exists. No place of pain exists, but there is no means of cure. There is nothing that bars the way. Once in, there is no getting out. There is nothing to break, but what meets one's eyes is nothing but what is sorrowful and poisonous. It has no bad colour, but people are afraid. It sits close to one. But one cannot know or feel where it is. O Kasyapa! You may know from this and from innumerable and boundless other parables that life and death are great suffering to a person. O Kasyapa! This is how a Bodhisattva practises the Way by [means of] the Mahayana Great Nirvana Sutra and how he meditates on death." "O Kasyapa! How does a Bodhisattva abide in the teaching of the Mahayana Great Nirvana Sutra and meditate on the suffering of parting from what one loves? The suffering of parting from what one loves is the root suffering of all sufferings, about which it is said: "From craving one gains apprehension; From craving one gains fear. If the greedy mind is done away with, Why does one need to feel apprehension or fear any more?" Through the causal relations of craving comes about the suffering of apprehension. From the suffering of apprehension, beings become weak and old. The suffering of parting from what one loves accompanies one to the end of one's life. O good man! As a result of parting, various minor sufferings arise. I shall clearly explain this for your good. "O good man! In ages past, humans had an immeasurably long life. At that time, there was a king called "Good-Abiding". This king, at that time, was a child. As a prince, he attended to the business of the state. Then he became king. At that time, a human being's life lasted 84,000 years. Then, on top of his head a pimple appeared. It looked like a cotton "tula" or soft "karpasa" [cotton]. This grew bigger by the day. But he did not worry one whit about it. After ten months, this boil broke open and a child was born. His form was well proportioned and nothing was as wonderful as this. His colour and form were clear, and the child was the foremost amongst humans. His father, the king, was glad and named him "Head-Born". Then King Good-Abiding handed over the government of the state to this Head-

Born, and abandoning the royal palace, his wife, children and relatives, he entered the forest and studied the Way and lived for 84,000 years. Then Head-Born, fifteen days after his birth, was given the rite of abhiseka [annointing] on a high building. And to the east was the treasure wheel of gold [one of the seven treasures which a chakravartin is said to possess]. The wheel had 1,000 spokes and was perfect in its hub. It was not one made by an artisan, but one that had come about naturally. The great king, Head-Born, thought: "In ages past, I heard what was said by a rishi who was accomplished in divine powers. If a Kshatriya king gets bathed [baptised], receives the rite of purification on top of a high building; if the number of spokes of the golden wheel is not one too few, and if the hub is correctly set, and if it is not one made by an artisan, but one arisen naturally, one may know that this indicates a king who will become a chakravartin." He also said to himself: "I shall now try [it out]. I shall hold the wheel in my left hand, and my right hand will hold the incense burner, and I shall place my right knee on the ground and take my vows: [If this wheel is genuine and not false, I pray that things will be as in the olden days regarding what accrues to a chakravartin]." When he vowed thus, this treasure wheel of gold flew up and went in all the ten directions, and came back to the left hand of Head-Born. Then he rejoiced unendingly. Also, he said: "I shall now surely become a chakravartin." "Then, not long after, there came to him a treasure-elephant, which looked grand and grave like a white lotus, and whose seven limbs stood firmly upon the ground. Seeing this, Head-Born thought to himself: "In days gone by, I heard a rishi who possessed the five powers say that if a chakravartin receives the abhikseka rite on a high building on the fifteenth day after his birth, and if there is an elephant whose seven libs stand [firmly] upon the ground, this indicates - one should know - a sacred king." Also, he thought: "I shall now try [it out]." He held the incense burner in his left hand, placed his right knee on the ground and vowed: "If this treasure-elephant is not false, let all proceed as in the olden days." When this vow had been taken, this white treasure-elephant travelled from morning till evening in the eight directions, and gaining the boundary line of the great sea, came back and sat as it was meant to sit. Then King Head-Born was greatly and inexpressibly pleased. Also, he said: "I am

definitely now a chakravartin." "Then, not long afterwards, a treasure horse came, whose colour was bright blue and who had a golden-coloured hairy tail. Head-Born, on seeing it, thought to himself: "In days gone by, I heard a rishi who had the five powers say that when a chakravartin, fifteen days after [his birth], sits on a high building and receives the rite of abhiseka, and if a treasure horse comes whose colour is bright blue and whose hairy tail is of the colour of gold, we should know that this is a sacred king." Also, he thought to himself: "I shall now test it out." He took up the incense burner, placed his right knee on the ground and vowed: "If this horse is genuine and not false, let all happen as is proper regarding a chakravartin." After he had thus uttered his prayer, the blue horse travelled from morning to evening in the eight directions and having gained the boundary line of the great sea, came back and remained where it was supposed to remain. Then Head-Born was greatly pleased and rejoiced inexpressibly. Also, he said: "Now I am definitely a chakravartin." "Then, not long afterwards, there appeared a treasure woman whose form was all perfect and most beautiful. She was not tall, not short; not white, nor black. From all the pores of her skin wafted the fragrance of sandalwood; she smelled sweet and clear [fresh], and looked like a blue lotus. Her eyes could see as far as a yojana. The same with her ears' hearing ability and her nose's smelling power. Her tongue was so big that, when it stretched out, it thoroughly covered her face. Her form and colour were delicate as leaves of copper. Her mind and consciousness were transparent, and she had great wisdom. Always gentle were the words which she spoke to all beings. When this woman's hand touched the king's robes, it could see through the course of illness [whether illness was present] and what the king was thinking. Then Head-Born again thought: "If this woman can read the king's mind, this is a treasure-woman?" "Then, not long after, there appeared a mani [jewel, gem] which was of pure blue beryl. It resembled the hub of a wheel, and in the gloom its radiance extended for one yojana in distance. If it happened to rain cats and dogs, the power of that mani was so great that it could well have served as a parasol and covered a space one yojana in extent, and not a drop of the heavy rain would have passed through. Then Head-Born thought to himself: "If the chakravartin obtains this mani, this is the sign of a sacred emperor."

"Then, not long afterwards, there spontaneously appeared a treasure minister, whose wealth was so great that it could not be counted. His storehouse was full and was lacking in nothing. The power of his eyes, which was the fruit of his personal virtue, was able to penetrate all the wealth hidden under the earth. Whatever the king desired to have, the minister could answer his need. Head-Born again resolved to test things out. He sailed forth on a boat in the sea and said to the treasure-minister: "I now desire to have something rare." The minister stirred up the surface of the water with both his hands. The ten tips of his fingers [then] held all [sorts of] treasure. Presenting these to the king, he said: "Please use these as you will and throw away what is left over." Head-Born was delighted and rejoiced inexpressibly. And he thought to himself: "I now surely am a chakravartin." "And not long after that, there spontaneously appeared an army general. He was brave and strong and pre-eminent in tactics, knowing well the four armies [the four military forces of 1) elephants, 2) horses, 3) chariots, and 4) infantry]. Should there be anyone who could stand battle, this was shown to the holy king; one not worthy of it was made to draw back and not to come about [come near, attack]; any not yet conquered was conquered; anyone already conquered was well protected. Then Head-Born thought to himself: "If this general possesses the treasure of military prowess, I must certainly be a chakravartin." "Then the chakravartin, Head-Born, spoke to his ministers: "You should know that this Jambudvipa is peaceful and prosperous. I now have the seven treasures and 1,000 sons. What more should I do?" All the ministers answered: "Yes, indeed, O great King! Purvavideha [i.e. one of the four lands of the Sumeru cosmos, the one which is situated to the east] is not yet at peace. You should now go [there]." Then the king flew through the air to Purvavideha with all his retinue of seven treasures. The people of that land were glad and became his subjects. "And he said to his ministers: "Jambudvipa and Purvavideha are at peace, prosperous and vigorous. All has been subjugated. The seven treasures are perfect and the thousand children are full [complete]. What more do I need to do?" All the ministers answered: "Yes, indeed, O great King! Aparagodaniya [i.e. a land to the west of Mount Sumeru] is not yet under your banner." Then the sacred king flew through the air to Aparagodaniya with all his seven treasures.

When he reached there, the people of that land all came under his banner. "And he said to his ministers: "My Jambudvipa, Purvavideha and Aparagodaniya are at peace. The people are rich and vigorous. All have been subjugated. The seven treasures are all perfect and the thousand children are full. What more do I need do?" All the ministers said: "Yes, indeed, O great King! Uttarakuru [i.e. a land to the north of Mount Sumeru] is not yet under your banner." Then the sacred king flew through the air to Uttarakuru, taking all his seven treasures with him. When the king reached there, the people of that land rejoiced and came under his banner. "And he said to his ministers: "My four lands are now at peace. The people are vigorous. All have come under my banner; the seven treasures have been obtained, and the thousand children are full. What more do I need to do?" All the ministers said: "Yes, indeed, O sacred King! The people of Trayastrimsa Heaven enjoy long life. They are at peace. The form of those devas is splendid and incomparable. The palace where they live and their benches, chairs and bedsteads are of jewels. They sit on these and enjoy celestial happiness. They have not yet come to pay homage. You should now go and bring them under your banner." Then the king flew through the air, taking all the retinue of his seven treasures with him, and went up to the top of Trayastrimsa Heaven. There he saw a tree, the colour of which was blue and green. The sacred king, having seen it, asked his minister: "What is this thing of this colour?" The minister made answer: "This is a tree called "paricitra". All the devas of Trayastrimsa Heven, in the three months of summer, always amuse themselves under this tree." Also, he saw a thing white like a cloud. Again he asked his minister: "What is this, of this colour?" "This is called the "Hall of Good Dharma". All the devas of Trayastrimsa Heaven always gather here and discuss what obtains in the worlds of humans and gods." Then Shakrodevanamindra, the chief of the gods, saw that King Head-Born was outside the hall. He went out and welcomed him. Having met him, he took the king's hand and entered the Hall of Good Dharma and shared his seat. Then, the two looked the same in form and countenance, with no difference. Only by winks [small gestures] could one tell them apart. Then the sacred king thought to himself: "Would it not be right for me now to abdicate the throne and come and become King of this heaven?" O good man! At that time, Shakra was holding the Mahayana sutras in his hand, reciting and expounding them to others. Only he was now so proficient in their depths of meaning. But because of this reciting, upholding, expounding and promulgating of the sutras to others, there is great virtue. O good man! This Head-Born entertained ill-will towards Shakra. Because of this depravity, he had to return to this Jambudvipa and part from the humans and devas he had loved, and had a greatly troubled mind. That Shakra at the time was Buddha Kasyapa, and the chakravartin was I. O good man! Know that the suffering of parting from what one loves is great suffering. O good man! The Bodhisattva-mahasattva remembers [is mindful of] all such cases of suffering due to parting from what one loves. How could it be otherwise when the Bodhisattva, abiding in the teaching of the Mahayana Great Nirvana Sutra, meditates on the real suffering of parting from what one loves? "O good man! How does a Bodhisattva practise the Way of the Mahayana Great Nirvana Sutra and meditate on the suffering of encountering what one hates to see? O good man! This Bodhisattva-mahasattva sees that this suffering of encountering what one hates exists in the realms of hell, animals, hungry pretas, humans and heaven. It is like a person who is bound up in prison feeling great sorrow as he sees his fetters, chains and handcuffs. The same with the Bodhisattva-mahasattva. He sees all living beings of the five realms as being the objects of great suffering concomitant with encountering what is hateful. Also, next, O good man! It is like a person who, fearing the fetters, chains and handcuffs of someone who has feelings of enmity towards him, abandons his parents, wife, children, relatives, rare

jewels and his own profession and flees to distant places. O good man! It is the same with the Bodhisattva-mahasattva. He fears birth and death, fully practises the six paramitas and enters Nirvana. O Kasyapa! This is how a Bodhisattva practises the Way of the Mahayana Mahaparinirvana and meditates on the suffering of encoutering what one hates. "O good man! How does a Bodhisattva practise the teaching of the Mahayana Mahaparinirvana and meditate on the suffering of not gaining what one desires to have? "Seeking to have" is to have all that exists. There are two kinds of seeking to possess. One is seeking to have what is good to have, and the other is seeking to have what is not good. There is suffering if what is good is not gained, and suffering if what is not good is not removed. Stated simply, this is the suffering of the burning urge of the five skandhas. O Kasyapa! This is the truth of Suffering." Then Bodhisattva-mahasattva Kasyapa said to the Buddha: "O World-Honoured One! The suffering of the burning urge of the five skandhas does not mean this. Why not? In days past, the Buddha said to Kolita [one of the five bhiksus]: "If "rupa" [form, matter] is suffering, do not seek "rupa"; if "rupa" is something to be sought, it is not suffering." The Buddha said to all bhiksus that there are three feelings ["vedana"], which are: 1) the feeling of suffering, 2) the feeling of bliss, and 3) the feeling of non-suffering and non-bliss. The Buddha said to all the bhiksus before that if one practises Wonderful Dharma, one will encounter bliss. Also, the Buddha said that in good realms one gains six blisses of touch. The eye sees beautiful things. This is bliss. The same with the ear, nose, tongue, body, and mind which feels pleasure. The Buddha said in a gatha:

"To accord with the precepts is bliss.
One's body does not suffer from sorrow.
Sleep gives one peace.
Awake, the mind is glad.
When one receives clothing and food,
Recites, walks about, and lives alone
In mountains and forests,
This is the greatest bliss.
To beings, day and night,
One is compassionate, and this
Gives one unending bliss.
Because this does not cause suffering to others.
It is bliss to seek little and be satisfied;

It is bliss to hear much [of the Dharma]
And to disseminate it; arhathood
With no clinging in one's mind
Is also the experience of bliss.
The Bodhisattva-mahasattva finally
Reaches the yonder shore.
Whatever is done gains one an end.
This is the greatest of bliss."

"O World-Honoured One! The meaning of bliss as stated in all the sutras is thus. How might what the Buddha says now be in accordance with this?" The Buddha said to Kasyapa: "Well said, well said, O good man! You do well to ask the Tathagata this question. O good man! All beings, even when in the deepest depths of suffering, willingly entertain the thought of bliss. Because of this, there is no difference [there] from the thought of suffering about which I now speak." Bodhisattva Kasyapa said to the Buddha: "You say that one gains bliss even amidst the deepest depths of suffering. If so, this must mean that the lowest point in birth, the lowest point in old age, the lowest point in illness, the lowest point in death, the lowest point in the suffering of parting from what one loves, the lowest point in the suffering of not being able to gain what one desires, the lowest point in the suffering of encountering what one hates, and the lowest point in the suffering of the burning urge of the five skandhas may be said to possess bliss. O World-Honoured One! The lowest grade of birth is none but the three unfortunate realms; the middle grade of birth means human life, and the highest of births is that of heaven. If there is a man who asks, "Is it true that one gains the thought [experience] of suffering in the lowest state of bliss, the thought of non-bliss and non-suffering in the middle state of bliss, and in the highest state of bliss the thought of bliss?", how should we answer this? O World-Honoured One! We might well say that one gains the thought of bliss when in the lowest state of suffering. But we see that one who has to receive 1,000 punishments does not yet, at the first stage of the lowest suffering, gain the thought of bliss. But if not, how can we say that we gain the thought of bliss in the lowest stage of suffering?" The Buddha said to Kasyapa: "It is thus, it is thus! It is just as you say. Because of this, there can be no occasion on which there comes about the

thought of bliss. Why not? If a man who is to have 1,000 punishments is able to escape those punishments after receiving just one of the least of them, that person will, at that instant, gain the thought of bliss. Hence, we should know that the thought of bliss arises in circumstances in which there is no ground for it." Kasyapa said: "O World-Honoured One! That person does not gain the thought of bliss in the lowest [state of suffering]. It is from emancipation that he gains the thought of bliss." "O Kasyapa! Because of this, in times gone by, I spoke about the bliss of the five skandhas to Kolita. It was true, not false." "O Kasyapa! There are three feelings: 1) the feeling of bliss, 2) the feeling of suffering, and 3) the feeling of non-suffering and non-bliss. The three sufferings are: 1) suffering-suffering [bodily pain], 2) suffering of what is made [suffering arising out of phenomena changing], and 3) suffering of disintegration [mental pain caused by destruction]. O good man! The feeling of suffering is based on these three sufferings, which are those of suffering-suffering, the suffering of what is made, and the suffering of disintegration. The other two feelings are the suffering of what is made and the suffering of disintegration. O good man! Because of this, there is in birth and death really the feeling of bliss. The Bodhisattva-mahasattva says that all is suffering, because the intrinsic nature and the outer expressions of suffering and bliss do not part. Truth to tell, there is no bliss in birth and death. It is only in order to accord with the ways of the world that all Buddhas and Bodhisattvas say that there is bliss." Bodhisattva Kasyapa said to the Buddha: "O World-Honoured One! All Buddhas and Bodhisattvas speak [thus] in order to acord with the ways of the world. Is this not false? The Buddha said:

"One who does good harvests bliss;
One who upholds the precepts and abides in peace

Does not harvest suffering.
All others are likewise.
This is the greatest of bliss."

"Are the feelings of bliss which the sutras speak of all false or are they not? If false, how are we to explain the fact that the All-Buddha-World-Honoured One, already long ago, innumerable hundred thousand million billion nayuta asamkhyas of kalpas in the past, practised the Way of Enlightenment and did away with false speech, and that he now says this? Why?" The Buddha said: "O good man! The gatha cited above referring to the feeling of bliss constitutes the root concept of Enlightenment. Also, it well nurtures unsurpassed Enlightenment over a long course. That is why the phases of bliss are spoken about in the sutras. O good man! For example, what supports life forms all the causes of bliss. So, we say bliss. These are such as female beauty, abandoning one's self to intoxicating drinks, beautiful dishes and sweets, drinking water when thirsty, and having fire when cold; clothing, necklaces, elephants, horses, vehicles, servants, pages, gold, silver, beryl, coral, pearls, storehouses, and rice. All such things that pertain to the world form the cause of bliss. This is bliss. O good man! [But] even such things can call forth suffering, too. From a female, a man's suffering comes about. Apprehension, sorrow, weeping, loss of life, intoxicating drinks, sweets, and storehouses do also call forth suffering. Because of this, all is suffering; there can be no phase of bliss. O good man! The Bodhisattva-mahasattva takes it that the eight sufferings possess no suffering. O good man! All sravakas and pratyekabuddhas do not know the cause of bliss. To such persons, he [the Tathagata] says that the lowest of suffering also contains a phase of bliss. Only the Bodhisattva, abiding in the Mahayana Mahaparinirvana, is able to know the causes of suffering and bliss."

Chapter Twenty: On Holy Actions 2

"O good man! How does the Bodhisattva-mahasattva, abiding in the teaching of the Mahayana Mahaparinirvana, meditate on the cause of suffering? O good man! The Bodhisattva-mahasattva understands that the cause of suffering is grounded in the causal relations of the skandhas. We speak of the "cause of suffering". This corresponds to "love of what exists." There are two loves [desires, cravings]. One is the love that loves one's own self; the other is the love that loves what is possessed. There are two further kinds. A person seeks, head and foot, to gain the objects of the five desires [objects of the five sense-organs, and wealth, lust, food, fame, and sleep] which he does not possess. Once he has gained them, he obstinately clings to them. Also, there are three kinds: 1) love of desire, 2) love of form, and 3) love of non-form [i.e. the realms of 1) the kamadhatu 2) the rupadhatu, and 3) the arupadhatu]. Additionally, there are three kinds, which are: 1) love of the causal relations of karma, 2) love of the causal relations of defilement, and 3) love of the causal relations of suffering. Bhiksus have four kinds of love. What are the four? These are: 1) clothing, 2) food, 3) bedding, 4) decoctions. Also, there are five kinds. A person greedily clings to the five skandhas and to all that he uses. There are innumerable and boundless varieties of discrimination and presumption. O good man! There are two kinds of love, which are: 1) love of good, and 2) love of non-good. The love of non-good is the love of the common mortal and the ignorant; the love of Wonderful Dharma is what the Bodhisattva seeks. The love of Wonderful Dharma is of two kinds: 1) non-good and 2) good. Those following the two vehicles are those of the non-good; those who pursue the Mahayana are those of the good. O good man! The love of common mortals is the "cause of suffering" ["samudaya"] and is not "truth" ["satya"]. The love of the Bodhisattva is called the truth of the cause of suffering, but not the cause of suffering. Why? Because he gains birth in order to save beings. He does not gain birth for the sake of love [i.e. out of selfish craving]." Bodhisattva Kasyapa said to the Buddha: "O World-Honoured One! The Buddha-World-Honoured One speaks in other sutras about karma and says that karma constitutes causal relations. For example, you speak about arrogance,

or the six touches, or ignorance, and say that these have bearings on the burning urge of the five skandhas. Now, you speak of the Four Noble Truths. But why is it that only love [selfish craving] is the cause of the five skandhas?" The Buddha praised Kasyapa, saying: "Well said, well said, O good man! What you say cannot be classed as "non-cause". Only, the five skandhas are always based on love [craving]. O good man! This is like the situation of a great king. When he goes on a tour of inspection, all his ministers and relatives follow him. The case of love is the same. Where craving goes, all the bonds of defilement also follow in its train. For example, it is like oily clothing, which picks up dust, and whatever comes into contact with it remains there. It is the same with craving. As craving increases, there come about karmic bonds ["bandhana" - the bonds of defilement]. Also, next, O good man! For example, it is as in the case of wet ground, where a bud can easily come out. The same with craving. It easily calls forth the bud of the defilement of karma. "O good man! As the Bodhisattva-mahasattva, abiding in the teaching of this Mahayana Mahaparinirvana, meditates deeply on this craving, [he sees] there are nine kinds, which are: 1) craving like an unpaid debt, 2) like a female rakshasa [flesh-eating demon], 3) like a beautiful flower in which nests a viper, 4) hateful gluttony, which is harmful and which one, by force, means to have [insists on having], 5) like a lustful woman, 6) like the "maruka" ["mallika"] seed, 7) like the stubborn flesh of a boil, 8) like a storm, and 9) like a comet. "Why do we say that craving is like an unpaid debt? O good man! For example, it is as in the case of a poor woman who has borrowed money from others and has to pay back the debt. She wishes to pay the money back, but cannot. She gets sent to prison and cannot get free. The same is the case with sravakas and pratyekabuddhas. As there is a remaining taint of craving, they cannot attain unsurpassed Enlightenment. O good man! This is why we say that it is like an outstanding debt. "Why do we say that craving is like a rakshasa woman? O good man! As an example, there is a man who gains a rakshasa woman as his wife. The rakshasa woman gives birth to a child. But after it is born, she devours it. Having devoured it, she also devours

- 165 -

her own husband. O good man! The rakshasa woman of craving is also like this. All beings gain good children. But as they are born, they get devoured. When the good child is eaten, craving eats beings and gives them life in the realms of hell, animals, and hungry ghosts. The Bodhisattva alone is an exception. That is why we say "as in the case of a rakshasa woman." "O good man! Why do we say that a viper lives in a beautiful flower? For example, a man, by nature, loves beautiful flowers. He does not notice a worrying viper anywhere about. He steps forth, catches hold of the flower, gets bitten by the viper and dies. The same is the case with all common mortals. They devour the flowers of the five desires. This craving, not seeing the viper within craving, takes hold of them. Bitten by the viper of craving, they die and get reborn in the unfortunate realms. It is otherwise with the Bodhisattva. That is why we say that it is as in the case of a beautiful flower in which a viper lives. "O good man! Why do we say that, perforce, we partake of what is not helpful? For example, there is a man here who partakes of what is of no help. Having partaken, he gets a pain in his stomach, suffers from loose bowels [diarrhoea], and dies. The same with the food of craving. All the beings of the five reallms cling to gluttony. As a result, they get reborn in the three evil realms, except for the Bodhisattva. This is why we speak of "eating what is not helpful". "O good man! How is it that things go as with a lustful woman? For example, an ignorant person befriends a lustful woman, who skilfully feigns and flatters and shows familiarity, and takes away all that person's money and wealth. When these have all gone, the woman abandons the man. So do things go with the lustful woman of craving. The dull and those who have no wisdom befriend such. This woman of craving deprives one of everything good. When the good comes to an end, craving drives one away into the three evil realms, excepting the Bodhisattva. This is why we say that things go as with a lustful woman. "O good man! Why is craving like a maruka [wisteria] seed? For example, a bird may peck at it and it may fall to the ground, beside droppings, or it may be carried by the wind to beneath a tree, where it grows and winds itself around a niagrodha, so that the tree cannot grow and finally dies. The same with the maruka seed of craving. It winds itself around the good done by common mortals and finally causes it to die away. [The good] having died, it [the

common mortal] ends up in the three unfortunate realms, except for the Bodhisattva. This is why we say that things obtain as in the case of the maruka. "O good man! How is craving like the stubborn flesh of a boil? When a boil exists for a long time, stubborn flesh comes about. The person patiently tries to cure it and the thought of it never leaves his mind. If the person does allow it to leave his mind, the stubborn flesh increases and worms come about. As a result, the man dies. It is the same with the boils of common mortals and the ignorant. Craving grows into stubborn flesh. One has to make effort and cure this stubborn flesh of craving. If one does not, when one's life ends, the three unfortunate realms await one. But the Bodhisattva is not amongst this number. That is why we say that it is like the stubborn flesh of a boil. "O good man! How is it like a storm? For example, it is as when a storm shatters a mountain, flattens peaks, and uproots deep-rooted trees. The same with the storm of craving. One [might] gain an evil mind against one's parents and uproot the root of Enlightenment as of the greatly learned Shariputra, which is unsurpassed and firm. Only the Bodhisattva is not of this number. That is why we say it is like a storm. "O good man! Why is it like a comet? For example, when a comet appears, famine and illness increase and people become lean through illness and suffer from worries. The same with the comet of craving. It indeed cuts off all the seeds of good and makes common mortals suffer from loneliness, famine, and the illness of defilement, making them repeat birth and death and suffer from various sorrows. Only the Bodhisattva is not amongst their number. This is why we say that things proceed as in the case of a comet. O good man! There are nine kinds of meditation on the bond of craving by a Bodhisattva-mahasattva who abides in the teaching of Mahayana Mahaparinirvana. "O good man! Thus, common mortals have suffering, and lack truth. Sravakas and pratyekabuddhas have suffering, the truth of suffering, but lack in truth. All Bodhisattvas see that suffering has no suffering. Hence, there is no suffering [for them]; what there is is "Paramarthasatya" [Ultimate Truth]. All common mortals have the cause of suffering and no truth. Sravakas and pratyekabuddhas have the cause of suffering and the truth of the cause of suffering. All Bodhisattvas see that the cause of suffering has no cause of suffering; and yet, there is "Paramartha-satya". Sravakas and pratyekabuddhas have extinction, which is not truth. The Bodhisattva-mahasattva has extinction and "Paramartha-satya". Sravakas and pratyekabuddhas have the Way, but not the truth. The Bodhisattva-mahasattva has the way and "Paramarthasatya". "O good man! How does a Bodhisattva-mahasattva abide in the Mahayana Mahaparinirvana and see extinction and the truth of extinction? He extirpates defilement ["asravas"]. If defilement is cut out, this is called the Eternal. When the flame of defilement is extinguished, what there is is silence and extinction. When defilement is annulled, bliss arises. All Buddhas and Bodhisattvas seek causal relations. So we say "pure". And again, there arise the 25 existences. Hence, we say "supramundane". Being supramundane, we say "Self". There is nothing more ever again of the external expressions of colour, voice, smell, taste, touch, etc.; or male, female, birth, life, death, suffering, bliss, non-suffering or non-bliss. Hence, the ultimate extinction is "Paramartha-satya". O good man! The Bodhisattva thus abides in the Mahaparinirvana of Mahayana, and meditates on the Noble Truth of Extinction. "O good man! How does a Bodhisattva-mahasattva abide in the Mahaparinirvana of Mahayana and meditate on the holy truth of the Way? O good man! It is as when, with light, we can see small things in the darkness. The same is the case with the Bodhisattva-mahasattva. Abiding in the Mahaparinirvana of Mahayana and [following] the Noble Eightfold Path, he sees all things. This is seeing the Eternal versus the non-Eternal, the created versus the non-created, created beings versus non-created beings, thing versus non-thing, Suffering versus Bliss, Self versus non-Self, Pure versus non-Pure, defilement versus non-defilement, karma versus non-karma, true versus not-true, vehicle versus non-vehicle, to know versus not-to-know, dravya versus non-dravya, guna versus non-guna, drsti [views] versus adrsti, rupa [form] versus arupa [non-form], Way versus non-Way, and understanding versus non-understanding. O good man! The Bodhisattva, thus abiding in the Mahaparinirvana of Mahayana, meditates on the Noble Truth of the Way." Bodhisattva Kasyapa said to the Buddha: "O World-Honoured One! If one says that the Noble Eightfold Path is the Noble Truth of the Way, this does not make sense. Why not? The Tathagata has spoken about faith, and called it the Way. Thus, all "asravas" were to be done away with. At times,

you said that non-indolence was the way and that through this the All-Buddha-World-Honoured One attained unsurpassed Enlightenment, and that this was the teaching of the assisting way of a Bodhisattva. At one time you said to Ananda: "If one makes effort, one attains unsurpassed Enlightenment." At another time, you said: "Meditate on the impurity of the body ["kayasmrtyupasthana"]. If one concentrates one's mind and practises this meditation of the body, one will attain unsurpassed Enlightenment." At another time, you said: "Right dhyana is the Way. It is as was said to Mahakasyapa. Right dhyana is truly the Way. Non-right dhyana is not the Way. When one enters dhyana, one meditates on the birth and death of the five skandhas. Without entering dhyana, one cannot meditate." Or you spoke about a single Dharma and said that if one thoroughly practises the Way, this will purify one, will drive away apprehension and worry, and one will attain Wonderful Dharma; this is the Buddha Meditation Samadhi. Or you said: "Meditating on the impermanent is the Way. This is as I say to the bhiksus. One who meditates on impermanence will well attain unsurpassed Enlightenment." Or you said: "If one sits alone in an empty, quiet forest abode and meditates, one will indeed attain unsurpassed Enlightenment." Or, at another time, you said: "Speaking to others about the Way is the Way. Having heard Dharma, doubt disappears. If doubt disappears, one will attain unsurpassed Enlightenment." Or, at another time, you said: "Upholding the precepts is the Way. This is as was told to Ananda. If one faithfully upholds the precepts, one crosses the sea of great suffering of birth and death." Or, at another time, you said: "Coming into close proximity to a good friend [a knowledgeable, helpful follower of the Way] is the Way. This is as I said to Ananda. A person who associates with a good friend of the Way will be perfect in the pure precepts. Anyone who comes near to me will attain unsurpassed Enlightenment." At another time, you said: "Practice is the Way. By practising compassion, one extirpates defilement and attains the immovable state." At another time, you said: "Wisdom is the Way. This is as was said, in days gone by, by me the Buddha, to bhiksuni Prajapati. As in the case of the nuns and sravakas, the sword of Wisdom well extirpates all leakable defilement ["asravas"]." At another time, the Tathagata said: "Dana [giving] is the Way." This is as the Buddha said in days past to

Prasenajit: "O great King! In days gone by I performed dana. Because of this, I have now attained unsurpassed Enlightenment." O World-Honoured One! If the Noble Eightfold Path is the Way, then what all such sutras say must be wrong. Is it not so? If all such sutras are not wrong, why do they not state that the Noble Eightfold Path is the Noble Truth of the Way? If it is the case that you did not say so, why do such misgivings arise? But I defintiely know that the All-Buddha-Tathagata is long since far removed from misgivings." Then the Buddha praised Bodhisattva Kasyapa and said: "Well said, well said, O good man! You now desire to dig into the secret of the all-wonderful sutras of Mahayana that are of the Bodhisattva. That is why you put this question. O good man! All that is said in those sutras is the truths of the Way. O good man! As I have already stated, if one believes in the Way, such a Way of faith is the root of faith. This assists the Way of Enlightenment. Therefore, there cannot be any misstatements. O good man! The Tathagata is versed in all sorts of expedients, and desires to save beings. That is why he thus speaks variously. "O good man! A good doctor, for example, knows all the causes of the maladies of all beings, and according to the nature of the illness does he mix his medicines. But water is the only instance [thing] which is not prohibited. Or he might use ginger water, licorice water, water which is somewhat pungent, black rock-candy water, amalaka water, nepala [Himalayan] water, pathola water, cold water, or hot water, grape juice, or pomegranate juice. O good man! A good doctor who knows about the illness of his patients prescribes diverse medicines. There are many things which are prohibited. But water is not one of them. The same with the Tathagata. He knows well [various] expedients. Though Dharma is one, he, according to the differences in beings, dissects, enlgarges upon and displays various categories. Various beings learn the Dharma that is shown them. Having practised as shown, they extirpate defilements. It is as with the patients, who, following the words of the doctor, do away with [their] illnesses. "Also, next, o good man! There is a man who understands many idioms [vernaculars]. He is in a crowd. The people, oppressed by heat and thirst, all cry out: "Give me water, give me water!" The man at once gets cold water and, in accordance with the taste of each person, gives it to them, saying: "Here is water!"

"Here is paniya!"   "Here is ujji!" "Here is shariran!" "Here is vari!" "Here is paya!" [names of the water of different localities]. "Here is amrta!" or "Here is cow's milk!" Using all such innumerable names for water, he addresses the people. The situation is thus, O good man! The same with the Tathagata. He expounds the one Noble Path in various ways to sravakas. It [the Path] begins with the root of faith and goes up to the Noble Eightfold Path. "Also, next, O good man! A goldsmith, for example, makes with one [and the same] gold various kinds of jewellery as he wills, such as: necklaces, bracelets, hair pins, heavenly crowns, and elbow bands. Though there are differences and though they are not the same, they are nothing other than gold. O good man! The same is the case with the Tathagata. The single Buddhist teaching is taught in various, diverse ways in accordance with the circumstances of beings. At times, one kind [of Dharma] is presented, and we say that the Ways of the Buddha are one, not two. Also, we speak of two kinds, which are "dhyana" [meditation] and "Wisdom". It is also presented as three, namely: perception, Wisdom ["prajna"] and Knowledge ["jnana"]. Also, it is presented as four, namely: 1)"darshana-marga" [the Way of Seeing, using reason and intellectual insight to move from mere faith in the Four Noble Truths to a full understanding of them], 2)"bhavana-marga" [the Way of Meditation], 3)"asaiksa-marga" [the Way upon which there remains nothing more to be learned], and 4)" Buddha-marga" [Buddha Way]. Also, five kinds are presented, namely: 1) the Way of the practice of Faith, 2) the Way of Dharma Practice, 3) the Way of Faith-Emancipation, 4) the Way of Intellectual Attainment, 5) the Way of Bodily Attainment. Also, six kinds are presented, namely: 1)"srotapatti-margapannaka [way of the Stream-Enterer], 2)"sakrdagami-margapannaka" [way of the Once-Returner to Samsara] 3)"anagami-margapannaka" [way of the Never-Returner to Samsara], 4)"arhat-marga" [way of the "Worthy One" - a defilement-free, passion-conquering saint], 5)"pratyekabuddha-margapannaka" [way of the Solitary-Awakened One], 6)"Buddha-marga" [Buddha-Path]. Also, seven kinds are presented, which are Enlightenment by 1) mindfulness 2) selection of the Law, 3) effort, 4) joy, 5) exclusion, 6) meditation, 7) equanimity. Also, eight kinds are presented, which are: 1) Right Seeing, 2) Right Thinking,   3) Right

Speaking, 4) Right Action, 5) Right Livelihood, 6) Right Effort, 7) Right Mindfulness, and 8) Right Meditation. Also, nine kinds are presented, namely: eight paths and faith. Also, ten kinds are presented, which relate to the ten powers. Also, eleven kinds are presented, namely: the ten powers and great compassion. Also, twelve kinds are presented, which are: the ten powers, great loving-kindness and great compassion. Also, thirteen kinds are presented, namely: the ten powers, great loving-kindness, great compassion, and the Buddha meditation samadhi. Also, there are sixteen kinds, namely: the ten powers and great loving-kindness, great compassion, the Buddha meditation samadhi, and the three right mindfulnesses attained by the Buddha. Also, twenty ways are indicated, namely: the ten powers, the four fearlessnesses, great loving-kindness, great compassion, the Buddha meditation samadhi, and the three mindfulnesses. O good man! This Way is one in body. The Tathagata, in days past, expounded the Dharma in various ways for the sake of beings." "Also, next, O good man! It is, for example, just as several names are given to a single fire because of the nature of the things burnt, such as: wood-fire, grass fire, rice-bran fire, wheat-chaff fire, cow and horse-dung fire. It is the same with the Buddha's teaching. It is one, not two. For the sake of beings, we speak in diverse ways. "Also, next, O good man! One [basic] cognition, for example, is spoken of in six separate ways. [When something is] seen by the eye, we speak of "eye-consciousness". This applies [to all the senses] down to "mind-consciousness". O good man! The same is the case with the Way too. To teach beings, the Tathagata discriminates [differentiates, distinguishes different aspects] and speaks variously. "Also, next, O good man! For example, a thing seen with the eye is called "colour"; what is heard with the ear is called "sound"; what the nose smells is called "smell"; what the tongue tastes is called "taste", and what the body feels is called "touch". O good man! The same is the case with what applies to the Way. It is one, not two. The Tathagata, in order to guide beings, presents things in various ways. That is why the Noble Eightfold Path is called the Noble Truth of the Way. O good man! The Four Noble Truths are presented by the All-Buddha-World-Honoured One in steps. As a result, innumerable beings cross the sea of birth and death."

Kasyapa said to the Buddha: "O World-Honoured One! Once the Buddha was on the banks of the Ganges, in the forest of Simsapavana. At that time, the Tathagata picked up a small tree-branch with some leaves [on it] and said to the bhiksus: "Are the leaves that I hold in my hand many, or are all the leaves of the grass [plants] and trees of all grounds [forests] many?" All the bhiksus said: "O World-Honoured One! The leaves of the grass and tress of all grounds are many and cannot be counted. What the Tathagata holds in his hand is small in number and not worth mentioning." "O all you Bhiksus! The things that I have come to know are like the leaves of the grass and trees of the great earth; what I impart to all beings is like the leaves in my hand." The World-Honoured One then said: "The innumerble things that are known by the Tathagata must be my own if they [i.e. those things] but enter into the Four Noble Truths [i.e. if they are comprised within the Four Noble Truths]. If not, there would have to be five Truths." The Buddha praised Kasyapa: "Well said, well said, O good man! What you have now asked will greatly benefit innumerable beings and give peace. O good man! All such things are [contained] in the Four Noble Truths." Bodhisattva Kasyapa said to the Buddha: "If all such things are in the Four Truths, why do you say that they have not yet been spoken about?" The Buddhas said: "O good man! Though they are within [the Four Truths], we do not say that they have been spoken about. Why not? O good man! There are two kinds of wisdom relating to knowledge of the Noble Truths. One is of middle grade; and the other is of superior grade. What is of the middle grade of wisdom is that of sravakas and pratyekabuddhas; what is of the superior grade is that of Buddhas and Bodhisattvas. "O good man! A person sees that all the skandhas are suffering. To know this is middle-grade wisdom. There are innumerable ways of knowing all the skandhas. All are suffering. This is not what can be known by sravakas and pratyekabuddhas. This is superior knowing. O good man! All such things are not stated in the sutras. "O good man! Cognition through the 12 spheres ["dvadasayatanani" - the 12 sense-fields] is the gate. This, too, is suffering. This we know. This is middle-grade wisdom. There are innumerble ways of knowing cognition through the spheres. All are suffering. This is not what can be known by sravakas and pratyekabuddhas. This is superior-grade Wisdom.

I did not make statements on this in the sutras. "O good man! All realms are parts. They are also nature and are suffering too. This we know. This is middle-grade wisdom. These have innumerable aspects when dissected [analysed]. All are suffering. This cannot be known by sravakas and pratyekabuddhas. This is superior-grade Wisdom. Nothing of this is stated in the sutras. "O good man! To see [recognise] the destructible aspect of matter ["rupa"] is middle-grade wisdom. There are innumerable aspects of destructibility, when we look into any [form of] matter. They are all suffering. This is not what is known by sravakas and pratyekabuddhas. This is superior-grade Wisdom. O good man! All such things have not been stated in the sutras. "O good man! "Feeling" ["vedana"] is an aspect of awakening. This is middle-grade wisdom. There are innumerable aspects of awakening when we dissect feelings. This is not what can be known by sravakas and pratyekabuddhas. This is superior-grade Wisdom. O good man! I have not spoken about all of this in the sutras. "O good man! "Perception" ["samjna"] is an aspect of receiving. Thus do we understand it. This is middle-grade wisdom. There are innumerable aspects of receiving in conception. This is not what is known by sravakas and pratyekabuddhas. This is superior-grade Wisdom. Nothing of such is stated in the sutras. "O good man! "Volition" ["samskara"] is an aspect of action. This is middle-grade wisdom. There are innumerable aspects of volition. This is not what can be known by sravakas and pratyekabuddhas. This is superior-grade Wisdom. O good man! Nothing of such is stated in the sutras. "O good man! "Consciousness" ["vijnana"] is a discriminative aspect. This is middle-grade wisdom. When we look into this consciousness, we see that there are innumerable aspects of knowing. This is not what can be known by sravakas and pratyekabuddhas. This is superior-grade Wisdom. O good man! None of this is stated in the sutras. "O good man! We know that the causal relations of craving ["trishna"] indeed call forth the five skandhas. This is middle-grade wisdom. How innumerably and boundlessly craving awakens in a single person cannot be known by sravakas and pratyekabuddhas. What thoroughly knows all the aspects of craving of all beings is superior-grade Wisdom. I have not spoken about all of this in the sutras. "O good man! To know that one extirpates defilement is

middle-grade wisdom. We cannot fully discriminate and count the number of defilements. The same with extinction. One cannot fully count it. This is not within the reach of sravakas and pratyekabuddhas. This is superior-grade Wisdom. Nothing of this is stated in the sutras. "O good man! This aspect of the Way thoroughly delivers one from defilement. This we should know. This is middle-grade wisdom. Discriminating the aspects of the Way is incalculable and boundless. And the defilements to be done away with are uncountably boundless. This goes beyond the range of knowing of sravakas and pratyekabuddhas. This is superior-grade Wisdom. I have not spoken of this in the sutras. "O good man! One who knows the truth of secular life is one of middle-grade wisdom. Discriminating [discerning] the truth about secular life is uncountable and boundless. This stands beyond the compass of knowing of sravakas and pratyekabuddhas. This is superior-grade Wisdom. I have not spoken about such in the sutras. "O good man! All things are impermanent; all compounded things have no Self. Nirvana is silence. This is "Paramartha-satya". Thus should we know. This is middle-grade wisdom. "Paramartha-satya" is, we should know, infinite, boundless, and uncountable. It is beyond the compass of knowing by sravakas and pratyekabuddhas. This is superior-grade Wisdom. I have not spoken of such in the sutras." Then, Bodhisattva Manjushri said to the Buddha: "O World-Honoured One! How might we understand the "Paramartha-satya" of so-called relative truth ["samvrti-satya"]? O World-Honoured One! Is there any secular truth in "Paramartha-satya" or not? If there is, what there is is one truth. If not, does this not mean that the Tathagata has made a false statement?" "O good man! Relative truth is "Paramartha-satya". "O World-Honoured One! If that is so, there cannot be two truths." The Buddha said: "O good man! What there is is the best expediency. Conforming to the way of life of beings, we say that there are two truths. O good man! If we follow the way of statements, there are two kinds. One is secular dharma, and the other is supramundane Dharma. O good man! What is known by those who have abandoned the world is "Paramartha-satya"; what worldly people know is secular dharma. O good man! The conjoined condition of the five skandhas is a certain person. What is said by common mortals and the world is secular dharma. In the skandhas there is no person or name to be designated; and other than the skandhas there can be no individual person. The world-fleeing person ["shramana"] knows the nature and characteristics [of things] just as they are. This is "Paramartha-satya". "Also, next O good man! A thing has at times a name and a true form; or, at other times, a thing has a name but no true form. O good man! Anything that has a name but [is not possessed of] true form is of secular [relative] truth. Having [both] name and true form is "Paramartha-satya". O good man! I call such as the following secular truth: a being's life, knowledge, growing up, manhood, the doer [of deeds], the recipient [of karmic consequences], a mirage in the hot season, a gandharvan castle, the hairs of a tortoise [i.e which do not exist], the horns of a hare [which again do not exist], a circle of flame, all such things as the five skandhas, the eighteen realms, and the twelve spheres. And suffering, the cause of suffering, extinction [of suffering], and the Way to extinction are "Paramartha-satya". O good man! There are five kinds of secular dharma, which are: 1) the world of names, 2) the world of sentences, 3) the world of bonds, 4) the world of law 5) the world of clinging. O good man! What is the world of names? [Things] such as man, female, pot, clothing, vehicle and house are all of the world of names. A thing such as a gatha of four lines is of the world of sentences. What are the things of the world of bonds? Things such as joining, binding, restraining and folding of the hands are of the world of bonds.

What is the world of law? Calling in bhiksus by hammering, warning soldiers by drumming, announcing time by sounding a horn are of the world of law. What is of the world of clinging? Seeing from afar a person who puts on coloured clothes, one imagines that this is a shramana and not a Brahmin; seeing a person with knotted cords, one thinks that this is a Brahmin, and not a shramana. This is what pertains to the world of clinging. O good man! Thus does it stand with the five kinds of things in the world. O good man! If beings' minds, [when confronted with these] five worldly phenomena, do not get turned upside down, but recognise things just as they are, this is the truth of "Paramartha-satya". Also, next O good man! Things such as burning, dividing, death and destruction belong to secular truth. That which knows no burning, dividing, death or destruction is

the truth of "Paramartha-satya". Also, next, O good man! That which possesses the eight aspects of suffering is called secular truth. Where there is no birth, age, illness, death, the sorrow of parting from what one loves, the sorrow of encountering what one hates, not being able to possess what one desires, or the burning urge of the five skandhas, that is where the truth of "Paramartha-satya" lies. O good man! A person, for example, does many things. When running, he is [called] a runner; when harvesting, he is one who harvests, when cooking a meal, he is a cook; when working with wood, he is a carpenter; when at work on gold and silver, he is a goldsmith. Thus, a man has many names. The same is the case with Dharma. "Truth is one, but names are many." When [a person] is said to have come about through the union of his parents, this expresses the truth of the secular world. When [he is] said to have come about through the truth of the twelve links of causation, this expresses the truth of "Paramarthasatya". Bodhisattva Manjushri said to the Buddha: "O World-Honoured One! What does the real truth mean?" The Buddha said: "O good man! By "real truth" is meant Wonderful Dharma. O good man! If a thing is not true, we do not say "real truth". O good man! There is nothing inverted in the real truth. When there is nothing inverted, we speak of real truth. O good man! There is no falsehood in the real truth. If falsehood resides [there], we do not speak of real truth. O good man! The real truth is Mahayana. If not Mahayana, we do not say "real truth". The real truth is what the Buddha says and is not what Mara says. If of Mara and not of the Buddha, we do not say "real truth". O good man! The real truth is a pure, single path, and not two paths. O good man! "That which is Eternal, Bliss, Self, and Pure is the real truth." Manjushri said to the Buddha: "O World-Honoured One! If what is true is the real truth, Wonderful Dharma is the Tathagata, the Void and the Buddha-Nature. This means that there cannot be any difference between the Tathagata, the Void, and the Buddha-Nature." The Buddha said to Manjushri: "There are suffering, truth, and the real; there are the cause of suffering, truth and the real; there are the Way, the truth and the real. O good man! The Tathagata is no suffering, no truth, but the real. O Manjushri! Suffering is an aspect of the non-eternal. It is an aspect of segregation [that which is subject to dissolution]. This is the real truth. The nature of the Tathagata is non-suffering, not the non-eternal, nor any aspect of segregation. That is why we say real. The same is the case with the Void and the Buddha-Nature. Also, next, O good man! So-called causation arises from the union of the five skandhas. Also, we call it suffering, or the non-eternal. This is a case that can be segregated. This is the real truth. O good man! The Tathagata is no cause of suffering, no cause of the skandhas, no aspect that can be segregated. So this is the real. So, too, with the Void and the Buddha-Nature. O good man! So-called extinction is the extinction of defilement. Also, it is the eternal and the non-eternal. What the two vehicles gain is the non-eternal. What all Buddhas attain is the Eternal. Also, it is the attainment of Dharma. This is the real truth. O good man! The nature of the Tathagata is non-extinction, which thoroughly extirpates defilement. It is not eternal and not non-eternal. It is no attaining of Dharma; it is that which is eternal and that which does not change. For this reason, it is the Real. The Void and the Buddha-Nature are also the same. O good man! The Way thoroughly cuts away defilement. It, too, is the eternal, the non-eternal, and the law that can be practised. This is the real truth. It is not the case that the Tathagata is the Way and he cuts away defilement. He is not eternal and not non-eternal. He is no law that can be practised. He is eternal and unchanging.

Hence, he is the Truth. The same with the Void and the Buddha-Nature. O good man! "The Truth is the Tathagata. The Tathagata is the True; the True is the Void; the Void is the True; the True is the Buddha-Nature; the Buddha-Nature is the True." O Manjushri! There is suffering, the cause of suffering, the end of suffering, and the opposite of suffering. The Tathagata is not suffering and no opposite. That is why he is the real and no truth. The same with the Void and the Buddha-Nature. Suffering is what is created, what leaks [i.e. what is characterised by the "asravas"], and what has no bliss. "The Tathagata is not what is created or what leaks; he is full and peaceful". This is the real and not the true." Manjushri said to the Buddha: "O World-Honoured One! You the Buddha say: "What is not upside down is the real truth." If that is so, could there be the four inversions in the four truths? If so, how can you say that what is not possessed of anything inverted is the real truth and that anything inverted is not the real?" The Buddha said to Manjushri: "Anything that is

inverted is the truth of suffering. All beings have inversions [distortions of truth] in their minds. So they are upside down. The case is thus. O good man! Imagine, for example, a man who receives no injunctions from his parents or those above him. Even on receiving, he cannot follow and practise the Way. Such a person is called upside down. It is not the case that such inversion is not suffering; it is suffering itself." Manjushri said: "You the Buddha say that what is not false is the real truth. If so, what is false is not the real truth." The Buddha said: "O good man! All falsehood falls into the category of the truth of suffering. Any being who cheats others falls into the realms of hell, animals, and hungry pretas. It is thus. Such dharmas are what is false. Such falsehood is nothing other than what is suffering. It is suffering. Sravakas, pratyekabuddhas and the All-Buddha-World-Honoured One keep away from such and do not do such. Hence, false. As such falsehood is what all Buddhas and the two vehicles do away with, this is the real truth." Manjushri said: "You, the Buddha, say that Mahayana is the real truth. From this we can know that what sravakas and pratyekabuddhas say must be the non-real." The Buddha siad: "O Manjushri! Those two are the real and the non-real. If sravakas and pratyekabuddhas cut away all defilement, they are the real. Things which are non-eternal and non-abiding are the things of change. So, they are the non-real." Manjushri said: "If what the Buddha says is, as he says, the real, we can know that what Mara says must be the non-real. O World-Honoured One! Do we take in what Mara says as the Noble Truths [is what Mara says part of the Noble Truths]?" The Buddha said: "What Mara says can be taken into [included in] the two Truths, which are those of suffering and the cause of suffering. They [the words of Mara] are all non-Dharma and non-precepts, and cannot benefit beings. [If Mara should] talk the whole day, there could be no seeing off of suffering and the cause of suffering, no attaining of extinction or the practising of the Way. They [the words of Mara] are false. What is false is what Mara says." Manjushri said: "The Buddha said that the single path is what is pure and that there cannot be two. All tirthikas also say that they have a single path and that there are not two. If the single path is the real truth, what difference is there here from what the tirthikas say? If there is no difference, there cannot be a single path that is pure." The Buddha said: "O good man! The tirthikas all have the two truths of suffering and the cause of suffering. They do not have the truths of extinction and the Way. They think of extinction where there is no extinction; they think of the Way where there is no Way; they think of result where there is no result; they think of cause where there is no cause. Thus, they have no single path that is pure." Manjushri said: "You the Buddha say that there are the Eternal, Bliss, Self, and the Pure, and that these are the Real. If so, all tirthikas, too, must have real truths. This may not be in the Buddhist teaching. Why so? All tirthikas say too that all things are eternal. How are they eternal? Because all the results of thinking and not thinking remain. "Thinking" answers to [relates to] the ten good karma results, and "not thinking" to the ten karma results of non-good. If we say that all things are non-eternal, how can it be that, if the doer dies here, there can be a person who gains the karmic results on the other side? For this reason, we may well say that all created things are eternal. The circumstantial factors of killing are always eternal. O World-Honoured One! If we say that all things are non-eternal, the killer and what can be killed must both be non-eternal. If they are non-eternal, who receives retribution in hell? If there surely is retribution in hell, know that all things cannot be non-eternal. O World-Honoured One! To be mindful and exclusively to think are also eternal. We think up to ten years or up to 100 years, and yet we do not forget. Hence, eternal. If non-eternal, who remembers or thinks of what one has seen? Because of this, all things are not non-eternal. O World-Honoured One! All remembrances, too, are eternal. We see the hands, feet, face and nape of a person for the first time. Later, we see that person again and recognise him. If non-eternal, the original form would have to die out. O World-Honoured One! We study something for a long time, from the first year up to the third year, and to the fifth year, and we come to see things well. So, we have to say that things are eternal. O World-Honoured One! In arithmetic, we proceed from one to two, from two to three, and to 100, and to 1,000. If non-eternal, the one that a person has first learned would have to first die out. Once one has gone, how can a person proceed to two? Thus, one is always one; there cannot be any two. As one does not die out, it can be two, 100, or 1,000. Therefore, it is eternal. O World-Honoured One! In reciting, one recites one agama [scripture],

and goes to two agamas, and three and four agamas. If non-eternal, recitation cannot proceed up to four agamas. By reason of the augmentation that applies to recitation, we can say eternal. O World-Honoured One! A pot, clothes and a vehicle are like debt. What the great earth displays - mountains, rivers, forests, trees, plants, leaves, and the curings of beings - is all eternal. The same is the case here. O World-Honoured One! All tirthikas say the same. All things are eternal. If eternal, these must be real truths. "O World-Honoured One! All tirthikas say: "There is bliss. How so? Because one who has received has gained a return to his thinking." O World-Honoured One! One who receives bliss unfailingly gains this, such as so-called Great Brahma, Mahesvara, Sakrodevanamindra, Vishnu, and all humans and devas. Because of this, there must surely be bliss. O World-Honoured One! All tirthikas say: "There is bliss. Beings indeed call forth the desire to have. Likewise, a person who is hungry seeks food; a person who is thirsty looks for something to drink; a person who feels cold seeks warmth; a person who feels hot seeks coolness; a person who is tired seeks rest; a person who is sick seeks a cure; a person who is sensual seeks lust. If there were no bliss, who would seek [thus]? From what is sought, we see that there is bliss." O World-Honoured One! There are tirthikas who say: "Dana [generous giving] calls forth bliss. People like to give [the following] to shramanas, Brahmins, the poor and the unfortunate: clothes, drink, bedding, medicines, elephants, horses, vehicles, such incense as powdered or smearing incense, all kinds of flowers, houses, shelter for the night, and lamps. They give various things. This is done to gain recompense in kind regarding what a person desires to have in days to come. For this reason, there assuredly arises happiness. This we should know." O World-Honoured One! Many tirthikas also say: "Through causal relations there surely is bliss. This we should know. As there are causal relations with a person who feels bliss, we say "touch of bliss". If no bliss is felt, how can such be done. The hare has no horns, so there cannot be any causal relations [generating horns]. There is bliss, because there is a cause for it thus to arise." O World-Honoured One! Many tirthikas say: "Know that there are the grades of top, middle, and low, by which one gets blessed. One who gets the lowest grade of bliss is Sakrodevanamindra; one who gets blessed with middle-grade blliss is Great Brahma; one who gets blessed with top-grade bliss is Mahesvara. That there are such grades of top, middle, and low tells us that there is bliss." "O World-Honoured One! Many tirthikas say: "There is purity. Why so? If there were no purity, no desire for it could come about. If the desire comes about, this indicates that there is purity." They also say: "Gold, silver, rare gems, lapis lazuli, crystal, agate, red pearl, carnelian, jade, horse-shoe shell, streams, springs, bathing pools, food, clothing, flowers, such incense as powdered incense or that for smearing, and the brightness of light are things which are pure. Also, next, there are pure things. The five skandhas are the utensils [vessels] of purity. They hold what is pure, such as humans, devas, rishis, arhats, pratyekabuddhas, Bodhisattvas, and all Buddhas. Because of this, we say that they are pure." "O World-Honoured One! The tirthikas also say: "There is the Self, which can well be seen, because it certainly makes things. For example, one enters the house of a potter. One does not see the potter. But when one sees the wheel and the rope, one knows that one is in the house of a potter. The case is the same with the Self, too. When one sees colour through the eyes, one knows that there surely is a Self. If there is no Self, how can a person see colour? The same with hearing sound and touching what can is tangible. Also, further, there is the Self. Why? From external expressions. What are these external expressions? They are gasping, winking, life, mental worry, and all kinds of sorrow and joy, greedy seeking, and angry faces, all of which are none but the expressions of the Self. From this, one can know that there surely is the Self. Also, next, we see that there is the Self because we experience taste. One eats fruit; one eats and registers the taste. For this reason, we should know that there surely is the Self. Also, next, we say that there is the Self because man does things. A person holds a sickle and mows; another takes a hatchet and cuts; another takes a pot and pours water into it; a person gets a vehicle and drives it. All such things are sought after and done untiringly. This indicates that there surely is the Self. Also, next, there is the Self. How do we know? When one is born, one desires to have milk, due to long habit. So, we may know that there surely is the Self. Also, next, there is the Self. How do we know? Because one mixes with others, gets harmonized [joins together], and gives

benefit. For example, if pot, clothing, vehicle, field, house, mountain, forest, tree, elephant, horse, cow, sheep, and others get harmonized, there is surely profit. The same is the case with the five skandhas of these. When there is the harmony of the eye, etc., there is the beautiful. Hence, one should know that there surely is the Self. Because there is hindering [obstruction]. As there is a thing that hinders, there can be hindering. If there is nothing, there cannot be any hindering. From hindrance, we see that there surely is the Self. Because of this, we see that there surely is the Self. Also, next, we say that there is the Self. How do we know? By accompaniment and non-accompaniment Familiarity and non-familiarity are not accompaniments. Wonderful Dharma and wrong dharma are not accompaniments. Wisdom and non-Wisdom do not accompany. Shramana and non-shramana, Brahmin and non-Brahmin, son and non-son, end and non-end, night and non-night, Self and non-Self, and others are accompaniments and non-accompaniments. This tells us that there surely is the Self." O World-Honoured One! All tirthikas speak variously of the Eternal, Bliss, Self and the Pure. O World-Honoured One! Because of this, all tirthikas also say that there is the truth of Self." The Buddha said: "O good man! If there are shramanas and Brahmins who say that there are the Eternal, Bliss, Self, and the Pure, they are no shramanas and Brahmins. Why not? Because they are lost in birth and death and are far away from the Great Guide. Because such shramanas and Brahmins are sunk in all the desires and despoil Wonderful Dharma. All these tirthikas are chained to the prison-house of greed, anger and ignorance, and assiduously love and take pleasure in these. All these tirthikas know that karma results are of their own making and that they have to reap them, and yet they cannot segregate themselves from them. What all these tirthikas practise is not Wonderful Dharma, not right living, and is not self-support. Why not? If not by the fire of Wisdom, one cannot put things out [extinguish what is bad]. All these tirthikas desire to be immersed in the best of the five desires, and yet they are unable to covet and practise Wonderful Dharma. Though all these tirthikas desire to attain true emancipation, they cannot, since they are lacking in the upholding of the precepts. All of these tirthikas desire to attain bliss, but they are unable to do so, since they fail to amass the causes of bliss. All these tirthikas hate suffering, but they are not away from the causal concatenations of suffering. All of these tirthikas are sought after by the four great vipers, yet they are indolent and do not know how to be mindful of what they do. All these tirthikas are the servants of ignorance, are distant from good friends, and are lost in pleasures amidst the great fire of the non-eternal, and yet they cannot get out of it. All these tirthikas suffer from tough diseases which are hard to cure. Yet they do not seek great Wisdom or a good doctor. All these tirthikas will have to take the lanes which are hard to pass along in days to come. Yet they also do not know how to adorn their bodies with good dharmas. All these tirthikas are poisoned by lust and suffering, and yet they uphold the frosty poison of the five desires. All these tirthikas burn with anger, and yet they associate with evil friends. All these tirthikas are overspread by ignorance and yet they pursue evil dharmas. All these tirthikas are lured by defilement, and yet they entertain familiar thoughts. All these tirthikas sow bitter seeds, and yet they seek to harvest sweet fruit. All these tirthikas have already shut themselves up in the dark room of defilement and have parted from the light of Great Wisdom. All these tirthikas suffer from the thirst of defilement, and yet they repeatedly drink the brackish water of all desires. All these tirthikas are floundering in the boundless waters of the great river of birth and death, and yet they are far away from the best master mariner. All these tirthikas are suffering from the inversions, and they say that all things are eternal. There can be no such saying as that all things are eternal." "O good man! I take [i.e. view] all things as non-eternal. How do I know? Because of their causal relations. If anything arises out of causality, I see it as non-eternal. With all these tirthikas, a thing is always what has come out of something else. O good man! Buddha-Nature is birthlessness and deathlessness; it is not going, not coming. It is not past, not future, and not present. It is not something that arises out of a cause; it is not the making of any cause. It is not something made; it is not a maker. It is not any outer form, nor is it not any form; it is not something with a name, nor is it something with no name; it is no name and no matter. It is not long, not short. It is not something that has come out [arisen] in the five skandhas, the 18 realms, and the 12 spheres. Hence, we say eternal. O good man! "The Buddha-Nature is the Tathagata; the Tathagata is Dharma, and Dharma

is the Eternal." O good man! Eternal is the Tathagata, the Tathagata is the Sangha, and the Sangha is Eternal. With tirthikas, there is nothing that does not arise from a cause. O good man! All these tirthikas do not see the Buddha-Nature, the Tathagata and Dharma. Thus what the tirthikas say is all false; there is no truth [in it]. "All common mortals first see all such things as pots, clothing, vehicles, houses, castles, rivers, forests, men, women, elephants, horses, cows and sheep, and they see that they resemble [seem to stay the same] and say that they are eternal. Know that they are not anything eternal. O good man! All that is made is not eternal. The Void is not anything made. So, it is eternal. The Buddha-Nature is not what is made. So, it is eternal. "The Void is the Buddha-Nature; the Buddha-Nature is the Tathagata; the Tathagata is not what has been made. What has not been made is Eternal. Dharma is Eternal; Dharma is the Sangha; the Sangha is not what has been made; what has not been made is Eternal." "O good man! There are two kinds of created thing, which are: 1) physical and 2) non-physical The non-physical is the mind ["chitta"] and the mental faculties ["caitta"]. The physical elements are earth, water, fire, and wind. O good man! The mind is non-eternal. Why so? Because its nature is driven by things external [to it] ever to answer and discriminate things. O good man! The nature of what the eye sees is different [various], and this applies all the way down to that of what the mind thinks, which is different. Hence, non-eternal. O good man! The field of cognition of matter ["rupa"] is different, and this applies to where the field of cognition of dharmas is different. Hence, non-eternal. O good man! The concomitant elements of visual consciousness are different, and this applies down to the concomitant elements of mental consciousness, which are different. Hence, non-eternal. O good man! If the mind were eternal, visual consciousness alone could call forth all elements O good man! If visual consciousness is different and if this applies down to mental consciousness which is different, we see that it is non-eternal. The aspects of the elements look alike, and these come about and die out moment after moment. So, common mortals look and conclude that they are eternal. As all causal relations work against and break up [do not endure unchanged], we say non-eternal. We gain visual consciousness by means of the eye, matter, light, and thinking. When gustatory consciousness arises, place and cause differ. This is not the causal relation of visual consciousness. Things are thus all the way down to consciousness of thinking, in which things differ. Also, next, O good man! Because the causal relations of all things dissolve, we say that the mind is non-eternal. The way to practise the non-eternal differs. If the mind were eternal, one would have to practise the non-eternal always. And one could not meditate on suffering, the Void, and selflessness. And how could one meditate on the Eternal, Bliss, Self, and the Pure? For this reason, the teachings of the tirthikas are unable to take in [embrace, include] the Eternal, Bliss, Self, and Purity. O good man! You should know that the mind is definitely non-eternal. Also, next, O good man! As the nature of the mind is different, we say non-eternal. This is as in the case of the so-called nature of the sravaka's mind, which is different; as in the case of the pratyekabuddha, which is different; and the mind of all Buddhas, which is different. There are three kinds of mind [attitude, mental stance] amongst the tirthikas, namely: 1) mind of renunciation, 2) mind of home life, and 3) mind that works against and departs from home life. There are differences of the concomitant mind, such as bliss, sorrow, non-sorrow and non-bliss, greed, anger, and ignorance. Also, there are different mental aspects with the tirthikas, which are those of the concomitant mind of ignorance, doubt, twisted views, mind of deportment regarding walking and stopping. O good man! If the [state of] mind were eternal, one could not discriminate all such colours as blue, yellow, red, white, and purple. O good man! If the mind were eternal, there could be no forgetting of anything committed to memory. O good man! If the mind were eternal, there could be no increase in reading and recitation. Also, next, O good man! If the mind were eternal, we could not say that one has done, is doing, or will be doing [something]. If there is what has been done, what is being done, or what will be done, know that this [mode of] mind is definitely non-eternal. O good man! If the mind were eternal, there could be no enmity, friendliness, or non-enmity and non-friendliness [i.e. because the state of the mind would never change]. If the mind were eternal, there could be no mind, no what-belongs-to-others, no death or birth. If the mind were eternal, no actions could accumulate. O good man! For these reasons, know that the nature of [any given state of] mind is

different in each case. This difference tells us that what we have here is non-eternal. "O good man! I have expounded the transitoriness of what is non-physical, and the meaning is now established. Also, for your sake, I shall explain the transience of physical existence. This physical [existence] does not have any eternal quality about it; basically, it has no life. Born, it must die. When a person's body is still in the womb, in the kalala stage, there is nothing of the life entity [there]. Because it changes when born. Such things of the objective world as buds, stems and stumps also do not have any entity, since when born, each changes. Thus we know that all physical things are transitory. O good man! All a man's sense-faculties change over time; his sense-faculties ["adhyatman-rupa"] are different at the time of kalala [foetal stage, 7 days after conception], arbuda [second week], ghana [4th stage], pesi [3rd week], pustule, at the time of birth, in childhood, in boyhood, and up to the time of old age. Thus does it stand with the "things of the objective world". Differences are seen [become manifest] in such as: bud, stem, branch, leaf, flower, and fruit. Also, next, O good man! Mental taste also differs. Change occurs at the time of kalala up to the days of old age. The taste of objective things also differs. The taste differs at such times as: bud, stem, leaf, flower, and fruit. Strength differs at the time of kalala up to old age; form and appearance differ at the time of kalala and through to old age; the results of karma differ from the time of kalala to the time of old age; name differs from the time of kalala up to old age. Man's so-called sense faculties break up, return, and conjoin [into their former state]. We know that this is impermanent. Such things of the objective world as trees break and join together. So, we view them as impermanent. A thing gradually comes about. So, we know it to be non-eternal. As it gradually emerges from the time of kalala through to the time of old age, bud, fruit and seed arise. So we see that a physical thing dies out. Thus, what we see is non-eternal. Differences are seen from the time of the death of the kalala [stage] up to the time of the death of old age, and at the time of death of the bud and up to the time of death of the fruit. Thus, we see that what there is is impermanence. Common mortals do not know this. As things carry on alike [seemingly the same], they conclude and say that what is there is eternal. For this reason, I say non-eternal. If there is the non-eternal, what there is is suffering. If there is suffering, this is nothing but what is impure. O good man! When Kasyapa once asked me about this, I already answered [his question] at that time.

"Also, next, O good man! All things have no Self. O good man! All things are physical and non-physical. The physical is non-Self. Why? Because it can be broken asunder and desroyed, beaten and split. Because there is birth, growing up and becoming big. The Self cannot have any breaking asunder, destruction, beating or splitting; it cannot grow up and become big. Because of this, we know that what is physical is also non-Self. Why? Because of the fact that it is something that has come about from causes and conditions. O good man! The tirthikas may say that there must be a Self because there is exclusiveness of thought. But exclusiveness is, truth to tell, not of the nature of the Self. We might well think that there is Self because we can think exclusively [all to ourselves]. But we [are prone] to forget what was in the past. This forgetting tells us that there surely is no Self [here]. O good man! The tirthikas may say that there is Self because man remembers. But the fact that man does not remember tells us that there surely is no Self. Seeing a man with six fingers, one asks: "Where might I have seen such as this before?" If there were a Self, how could one ask this? Such asking indicates that there surely is no Self. O good man! The tirthikas may say that there is Self because of hindrance [obstruction, boundaries]. O good man! There surely is no Self precisely because of hindrance. This is like saying that as Devadatta, to the end, does not say out, he is not Devadatta. The same is the case with Self. If there definitely is Self, there will be no hindrance to Self. As self is hindered, we surely can know that there is no Self. If it is the case that one knows there definitely is Self due to hindrance, this will lead us to conclude that there can be no Self, as you now do not hinder. O good man! If tirthikas say that they know there is Self by accompaniment and non-accompaniment, this indicates that there is no Self because there is no accompaniment. There is a case in which there is no accompaniment in the law [Dharma], as in the cases of the Tathagata, the Void, and the Buddha-Nature. The same with Self. Truth to say, there is none that accompanies. Hence we may know that there definitely is no Self. Also, next, O good

man! If tirthikas say that they know there is Self because of the name, we should know that even in "selfless" there is the name [the word], as in the case of a poor man who may have a name which means " rich". We speak of "dead self". If Self is dead, this is tantamount to saying that Self kills Self. But, truly, the Self cannot be killed. For the time being, we say "dead self". This is as with a short man being called a tall man. From this we can definitely know that there is no Self. Also, next, O good man! All tirthikas may say that as one, after birth, seeks milk, there is the Self. O good man! If there were Self, no child would take hold of dung, fire, serpents or poison [i.e. because they would know these are unpleasant or dangerous]. From this, we can definitely know that there is no Self. Also, next, O good man! All beings, in the three phases, have equal shares of knowing, as: lust, food, drink, and fear. So, there is no Self. Also, next, O good man! The tirthikas say that from the countenance one can say that there is Self. But for this reason we could say that there is no Self. We say that there is no Self because there is no countenance. When asleep, one cannot walk, stand still, lie with one's face down or up, see or wink, and cannot know suffering or bliss. So there can be no Self. If one knows that there is Self by reason of going and stopping, facing downwards or upwards, or sleeping or winking, any engine or wooden man must possess Self. O good man! The same is the case with the Tathagata. He does not go, stop, look up or down, see or wink. He has no suffering or bliss, no greed or anger, no ignorance and no action. The Tathagata thus has the Self. Also, next, the tirthikas may say that when one sees a person eating some fruit, one's mouth waters and that, therefore, one has a Self. But by thinking back, too, one dribbles. But the saliva is not the Self. It is not joy, not sorrow, not weeping, not laughing, not falling down or standing up, not being hungry, not being full. From this, one may know that one definitely does not have the Self." "O good man! The tirthikas are ignorant and are like children. They do not have the expedients of Wisdom. They cannot truly see what is meant by eternal, non-eternal, suffering, bliss, pure, not-pure, Self, not-Self, life, non-life, being, non-being, real, non-real, what is or what is not. They partake of only a little of the Buddhist teaching. In a false way they say that there are the Eternal, Bliss, Self, and Purity. A person congenitally blind does not know what the colour of milk is like. He asks: "What is the colour of milk like?" Another says: "It is as white as the colour of a shell." The blind man further asks: "Is the colour of milk like the sound of a horn?" "No" is the reply. "What colour is the colour of a shell like?" The answer comes back: "It is like the colour of rice powder." The blind man asks: "Is the colour of milk as soft as rice powder? And what is the colour of rice powder like?" The answer comes: "It is like snow." The blind man says: "Is rice powder as cold as snow? And what is it like?" The answer comes back: "It is like a crane." Even though this congenitally blind man receives four similes in reply, he cannot arrive at the true colour of milk. It is the same with the tirthikas. To the end, they cannot arrive at what is meant by the Eternal, Bliss, Self, and Purity. The same is the case [here]. O good man! For this reason, the real truth rests with the Buddhist teaching. Things do not stand thus with the tirthikas." Manjushri said to the Buddha: "O Rare World-Honoured One! The Tathagata, now facing Parinirvana, further turns the unsurpassed wheel of the Dharma. And thus he clearly presents "Paramartha-satya". The Buddha said to Manjushri: "Why do you particularly gain the thought of Nirvana? O good man! You may presume and think that I am the Buddha and have achieved unsurpassed Enlightenment; that I am Dharma and that Dharma is what I possess; that I am the Way and the Way is what I possess; that I am the World-Honoured One and the World-Honoured One is what I am; that I am the sravaka and the sravaka is what I am; that I indeed teach others and make others give ear to me; that I truly turn the wheel of Dharma and others cannot. The Tathagata does not abide in such presumptions. Hence, the Tathagata does not turn the wheel of Dharma. O good man! There may be cases in which people make wrong assumptions and say: "The Self is the eye, and the eye is what the Self possesses. The same with ear, nose, tongue, body, and mind. The Self is matter, and matter is what the Self possesses. And this may extend down to dharma. The Self is the earth, and the earth is what the Self possesses. The same applies to water, fire and wind." "O good man! People may speculate and say: "The Self is faith and faith is what the Self possesses. The Self is multiple knowledge and multiple knowledge is what the Self possesses. The Self is danaparamita [perfected giving] and danaparamita is what the Self possesses. The Self

is shilaparamita [perfected moral precepts] and shilaparamita is what the Self possesses. The Self is ksantiparamita [perfected patience] and ksanti-paramita is what the Self possesses. The Self is viryaparamita [perfected exertion] and virya-paramita is what the Self possesses. The Self is dhyanaparamita [perfected meditation] and dhyanaparamita is what the Self possesses. The Self is prajnaparamita [perfected Wisdom] and prajnaparamita is what the Self possesses. The Self is catvarismrty- upasthana [mindfulness] and catvarismrtyupasthana is what the Self possesses. The same with the four right efforts, the four at-willnesses, the five sense-organs, the five powers, the seven elements of Enlightenment, and the Noble Eightfold Path." O good man! The Tathagata does not, to the end, make such assumptions. Hence, the Tathagata does not turn the wheel of Dharma. O good man! If we say that he is eternal and unchanging, how could we say that the Buddha-Nature turns the wheel of Dharma? So you should not say: "The Tathagata now turns the wheel of Dharma." "O good man! There is the situation, for example, where we get visual consciousness through the harmonious combination of eye, colour, light, and thinking. O good man! The eye does not think: "I shall cause consciousness to arise." Colour, down to thinking, do not ever say: "I shall cause visual conscious-ness to arise." Neither does consciousness say: "I shall arise by myself." O good man! Such a harmonization of the causal relations of the law [i.e. of dharmas] is drsti [seeing, view]. O good man! It is the same with the Tathagata. Through the harmonious combination of the causal relations of the six paramitas, we gain drsti. O good man! The same with the Tathagata. He reaches the bottom of all things by means of the six paramitas and the 37 elements assisting towards Enlighten-ment. Also, we call it the turning of the wheel of Dharma, as he, using throat, tongue, teeth, lips and mouth, and through speech and voice, speaks of Dharma to Kaundinya and others. That is why we do not say that the Tathagata turns the wheel of Dharma. O good man! What is not turned is Dharma. Dharma is the Tathagata. O good man! Through the use of flint, by means of striking, by means of using the hands, and through using autumnal, dried-up grass, we obtain fire. But the flint does not say: "I shall cause fire to come about." The [act of] striking, the hand, and the dried-up grass also do not think: "I shall cause fire to arise." Nor does the fire say: "I shall come about by myself." It is the same with the Tathagata. Through the six paramitas, down to speaking to Kaundinya, there occurs the turning of the wheel of Dharma. But the Tathagata, too, does not think and say: "I turn the wheel of Dharma". O good man! We speak of "non-coming-out" [non-arising, non-acting]. This is the right turning of the wheel of Dharma. This turning of the wheel is the Tathagata. "O good man! An example: from cream, water, churning, a pot, and a person's hand holding it, we obtain butter. The cream does not think to itself: "I will call forth butter." Nor, even, does the person's hand think to itself: "I will call forth butter." And the butter, too, does not think to itself: "I wll come about by myself." By means of the coming together of the various causal relations, butter comes into being. The same with the Tathagata. He does not think and say: "I turn the wheel of Dharma." O good man! This non-coming-out [non-deliberation of one's acts; spontaneity] is but the turning of the wheel of Wonderful Dharma. This turning of the wheel is at once the Tathagata. "O good man! Through the combinations of such conditions as body, earth, water, fire, wind, and the fertility of the soil and the season, a bud comes out. O good man! The seed also does not say: "I shall call forth the bud." Nor does the labour itself think and say: "I shall call forth the bud." Nor does the bud say: "I shall come about." It is the same with the Tathagata. To the end, he does not think and say: "I do turn the wheel of Dharma." This turning of the wheel of Dharma ["Dharmacakra-pravartana"] is the Tathagata. "O good man! As an example: through the conjoining of a drum, emptiness, leather, man, and drum-stick, we get the sound of the drum. The drum does not think and say: "I call forth sound." The same with the drum-stick. Nor does the sound say: "I shall come out". O good man! It is the same with the Tathagata. He does not, to the end, think and say: "I turn the wheel of Dharma." O good man! Turning the wheel of Dharma means "not-doing". Non-doing is turning the wheel of Dharma. Turning the wheel of Dharma is the Tathagata. "O good man! Turning the wheel of Dharma is what takes place in the world of the All-Buddha-World-Honoured One. It is not something that can be known by sravakas and pratyekabuddhas. O good man! Space is no being-born, not coming-out, non-doing, not construing, or not what is created. It is the same with the

Tathagata. He is no being-born, no coming-out [arising], no construing, and not what has been created. Like unto the nature of the Tathagata is the Buddha-Nature. It is not a being-born, not an arising, not a making, not a construing, and is not what is created. "O good man! In what the All-Buddha-World-Honoured One says, there are two kinds [categories]. One is of the mundane, and the other is of the supramundane world. O good man! For the sake of sravakas and pratyekabuddhas, the Tathagata speaks about what is mundane. For the sake of Bodhisattvas, he speaks about what is supramundane. O good man! In this great congregation, there are, again, two kinds. One is the [type of] person who seeks the smaller vehicle, and the other is he who seeks the larger vehicle. In days gone by, at Varanasi, I turned the wheel of Dharma to all sravakas, and first at Kusinagara I turn the larger wheel for Bodhisattvas. Also, next, O good man! There are again two kinds of people, who are of: 1) middle grade and 2) higher grade. For those of the middle grade, I turned the wheel of Dharma at Varanasi. And for those of the higher grade, for the elephant king, Bodhisattva Kasyapa, and others, I now, here, at Kusinagara, turn the larger vehicle [wheel] of Dharma. For those of the very lowest grade, the Tathagata, to the end, does not turn the wheel of Dharma. The lowest is the icchantika. Also, next, O good man! There are two kinds of person who seek the Buddhist teaching. One is he who makes middling effort, and the other is the person who makes higher effort. At Varanasi, I turned the wheel of Dharma for the sake of those of the middle grade, and here at this castle I turn the larger wheel of Dharma for those of the higher grade. Also, next, O good man! In days gone by, at Varanasi, when I first turned the wheel of Dharma, 8,000 devas attained the level of shrotapanna; and here at this castle, 800,000 people will attain unsurpassed Enlightenment and will not retrogress. Also, next, O good man! At Varanasi, Great Brahma fell to his knees and begged me to turn the wheel of Dharma. Now, here at this castle, Bodhisattva Kasyapa falls to his knees, begging me to turn the wheel of Dharma. Also, next, O good man! "When, in days gone by, I turned the wheel of Dharma, I spoke of the non-eternal, suffering, Void, and selflessness. Now, here in this castle, I turn the wheel of Dharma. I speak of the Eternal, Bliss, Self and Purity as true as can be." Also, next, O good man! When I turned the wheel of Dharma in the past at

Varanasi, my voice reached Brahma. When, now, the Tathagata turns the wheel of Dharma here at Kusinagara, my voice reaches and fills all the Buddha-lands to the east, whose number is as great as the sands of 20 Ganges. The same applies to the lands in the south, west and north. "Also, next, O good man! The All-Buddha-World-Honoured One speaks of the Dharma. In all cases, we say that he turns the wheel of Dharma. O good man! It is just as the chakravartin's chakraratna [Jewel Wheel] thoroughly subdues those not yet come under his banner and gives peace to those already subdued. O good man! So does it stand with the delivering of sermons by the All-Buddha-World-Honoured One. The countless defilements not yet subdued will be conquered, and the root of good will shoot forth amongst those [people] already conquered. For example, O good man! It is just as the chakravartin's chakraratna truly makes away with all enemy robbers. The same with the sermons of the Tathagata. They thoroughly subdue all the hostile defilements, and peace reigns. Also, next, O good man! It is similar to the chakravartin's chakraratna, which rotates up and down. It is the same with the Tathagata's sermons. They indeed make the people of the lower world come up and gain rebirth in the worlds of humans, gods, or up to the Buddha world. O good man! That is why you should not utter praise, saying: "The Tathagata now, here, further turns the wheel of Dharma." Then Manjushri said to the Buddha: "O World-Honoured One! It is not that I did not know this. It was merely for the benefit of beings that I put this question. O World-Honoured One! I have long known this. Turning the wheel of Dharma is truly what obtains in the world of the All-Buddha-Tathagata, and this is something that cannot be attained by sravakas and pratyekabuddhas." Then the World-Honoured One said to Bodhisattva Kasyapa: "O good man! This is why we say that a Bodhisattva abides in the teaching of the Great Nirvana Sutra of Mahayana and performs holy actions." Bodhisattva Kasyapa said to the Buddha: "O World-Honoured One! Why do we say "holy action?" "O good man! "Holy" refers to the All-Buddha-Tathagata. Hence, we say "holy action." "O World-Honoured One! If this refers to the works of all Buddhas, it cannot come within the reach of practice of sravakas, pratyekabuddhas, and Bodhisattvas." "O good man! The All-Buddha-World-Honoured One abides in Mahaparinirvana and thus opens out,

discriminates and explains the meaning. For this reason, we say "holy action". The sravakas, pratyekabuddhas and Bodhisattvas, as soon as they hear [the Buddha's words], practise well. Hence, "holy action". O good man! As soon as this Bodhisattva-mahasattva has done this work, he attains the stage of fearlessness. O good man! If a Bodhisattva attains the stage of fearlessness, he then has no fear of greed, anger, ignorance, birth, age, illness and death. Also, he does not fear the unfortunate realms of hell, hungry ghosts, and animals. O good man! Of evil, there are two kinds. One is of the asura, and the other is of man. Of man, there are three kinds, which are: 1) icchantika, 2) slandering of the vaipulya sutras, and 3) the four grave offences [for a monk: killing; stealing; sexual misconduct; and lying]. O good man! All Bodhisattvas of this stage do not have fear of falling into evil. Also, they are not afraid of sramanas, Brahmins, tirthikas, the evil-minded, and Marapapiyan; also, they are not afraid of being born into the 25 existences. That is why this stage is called that of fearlessness." "O good man! The Bodhisattva-mahasattva abides in the soil of fearlessness. He gains the 25 samadhis and breaks [destroys, liberates himself from, does away with] the 25 existences. O good man! When he attains the non-defilement samadhi, he does away with existence in hell. On gaining the non-retrogressive samadhi, he does away with existence as an animal. Gaining the blissful-mind samadhi, he does away with existence as a hungry ghost. Gaining the all-joy samadhi, he crushes out existence as an asura. Gaining the sunlight samadhi, he destroys existence in Aparagodaniya. Gaining the burning-flame samadhi, he does away with existence in Uttarakuru. Gaining the phantom samadhi, he does away with existence in Jambudvipa. Gaining the immovable samadhi of all things, he does away with existence in the four heavens. Gaining the unbeaten samadhi, he does away with existence in Rayastrimsa Heaven. Gaining the glad-will samadhi, he crushes out existence in Yama's heaven. Gaining the blue-colour samadhi, he does away with existence in Tushita Heaven. Gaining the yellow-colour samadhi, he destroys existence in Nirmanarati Heaven. Gaining the red-colour samadhi, he crushes out existence in Paranirmitavasavartin Heaven. Gaining the white-colour samadhi, he does away with existence in the first-dhyana Heaven. Gaining the varied samadhi, he does away with existence as Great Brahma. Gaining the twin samadhi, he destroys existence in the second dhyana. Gaining the thunder-sound samadhi, he destroys the third dhyana. Gaining the rain samadhi, he does away with the fourth dhyana. Gaining the akasha-like [space-like] samadhi, he does away with avrha existence. Gaining the bright-mirror samadhi, he does away with the existences of the Suddhavasa Heaven and the anagamin. Gaining the unhindered samadhi, he destroys akashanantayatana existence. Gaining the non-hindrance samadhi, he destroys akashanantayatana existence. Gaining the eternity samadhi, he does away with vijnananantayatana existence. Gaining the bliss samadhi, he crushes out the akincanyayatana. Gaining the Self samadhi, he does away with the naivasamjnanasamjnayatana. O good man! This is how we say that a Bodhisattva, on gaining the 25 samadhis, destroys the 25 existences. O good man! These 25 samadhis are called the king of all samadhis. "O good man! If the Bodhisattva-mahasattva gains the all-samadhi king and wishes to blow away or crush Mount Sumeru, he can do so as he wills. If he desires to know what the minds of the beings of the 3,000 great-thousand worlds are thinking, he can do this as he wishes. If he desires to put the beings of the 3,000 great-thousand worlds into the pores of his skin, he can indeed do so as he desires. And he can do so without the beings' having any sense of being constricted. If he desires to transform innumerable beings and fill the 3,000 great-thousand worlds, he can do so as he desires. He can easily make one body into many, and many into one. Though he can do this, he does not cling to it. This is like the case of the lotus flower. "O good man! The Bodhisattva-mahasattva, having thus entered the [king] samadhi, can indeed go anywhere. The Bodhisattva, abiding in this unmolested [i.e. unlimited, free] state, gains unmolested power and can be anywhere he desires to be. O good man! For example, this is like a chakravartin who, having gained four lands, finds nothing that obstructs him and he can act as he desires. The same with the Bodhisattva-mahasattva. Wherever he desires to go and live, he can do so as he desires. If a Bodhisattva- mahasattva sees any being in hell who can be taught and made to do good, he can immediately go there. The Bodhisattva is not originally born as a result of karma, but gains the unmolested soil through the

causal relations of thus being born. O good man! The Bodhisattva-mahasattva, even though in hell, does not suffer from the pain of being burned or slashed. O good man! It is difficult fully to explain all the virtues which the Bodhisattva-mahasattva has cultivated within himself and which are as innumerable and boundless as 100 thousand million billion. And how could one explain all the virtues of all Buddhas?" Then, among those gathered there, was a Bodhisattva whose name was "King-who-Abides-in-the-Undefiled-Storehouse". He had achieved great virtue and possessed divine power, great dharanis, was perfect in samadhi and fearlessness. He stood up and, baring his right shoulder, placed his right knee on the ground, prostrated himself and said to the Buddha: "O World-Honoured One! As you the Buddha say, the virtues and Wisdom perfected by all Buddhas and Bodhisattvas are as innumerable as 100 thousand million billion. It is impossible to explain [them]. I think to myself that nothing can supercede this Mahayana sutra. Why not? Because through the power of this Mahayana vaipulya sutra, there appear the All-Buddha-World-Honoured One and unsurpassed Enlightenment." Then the Buddha praised him and said: "Well said, well said! O good man! It is thus, it is thus! It is as you say. All the innumerable Mahayana vaipulya sutras accomplish innumerable virtues. But compared with this, the simile fails. It [the virtue of this sutra] exceeds [the virtue of other sutras by] more than 100 times, more than 1,000 times, more than 100,000 million times, and no number can express it. O good man! For example, a cow brings forth milk; the milk produces cream, the cream produces fresh butter, the fresh butter produces clarified butter, and the clarified butter produces sarpirmanda. Sarpirmanda is the best. When it is partaken of, all illnesses die away. All medicines are contained in this. O good man! It is the same with the Buddha. From the Buddha come about the 12 types of sutra [scripture]. From the 12 types of sutra there come about the sutras [proper]. From the sutras come about the vaipulya sutras. From the vaipulya sutras there arise the prajnaparamita [Perfection of Wisdom sutras], and from the prajnaparamita comes about the Great Nirvana. The case is as that of sarpirmanda. Thus, sarpirmanda can well be likened to the Buddha-Nature. The Buddha-Nature is the Tathagata. O good man! For this reason, I say that the virtues of the Tathagata are immeasurable. They stand beyond number." Bodhisattva Kasyapa said to the Buddha: "O World-Honoured One! You the Buddha say: "The Great Nirvana Sutra is like sarpirmanda and is the best. When partaken of, it cures all illnesses. All medicines are contained in this." On hearing this, I think to myself: "If any person cannot get to hear this sutra, such a person is the greatest of the ignorant and has no good mind." O World-Honoured One! I shall now peel off my skin, turn it into paper; take out my blood and turn it into ink; get water from my marrow, crack a bone to have it serve as a pen, and with all of these copy out the Great Nirvana Sutra. Having copied it out, I shall read and recite it, understand it well, and then, later, I shall patiently expound it to others. O World-Honoured One! If beings are dying for wealth, I shall give it to them, and later recommend this Nirvana Sutra and have them read it. With the nobility, I shall use loving words, follow them and later, by degrees, recommend this Mahayana Great Nirvana Sutra to them and get them to read it. With the dull, I shall force them to read it; with the arrogant, I shall become their servant, comply with their will, gladden them, and then guide them into the Great Nirvana Sutra. If there should be anyone who slanders the vaipulya, I shall crush him down, and after having subdued him, I shall recommend this Great Nirvana Sutra [to him] and have him read it. To any person who loves the Mahayana sutras, I shall myself pay homage, I shall make him offerings, and I shall respect and praise him." Then the Buddha praised Bodhisattva Kasyapa: "Well said, well said! You love the [this] Mahayana sutra very much. You covet it, you love the Mahayana sutra, you understand it, believe in and respect Mahayana, and you make offerings [to it]. O good man! Through the causal relations of the good mind,

you will rise above Bodhisattvas whose number is as countless and as boundless as the sands of the River Ganges, and you will attain unsurpassed Enlightenment. Before long, you too, like me, for the sake of beings, will expound Great Nirvana, the Tathagata, the Buddha-Nature, and all the hidden teachings of all Buddhas. O good man! In days past, when the sun of the Buddha had not yet risen, I was born as a Brahmin and was practising the Way of a Bodhisattva. I was versed in all sutras and in the sutras of the tirthikas, and was practising the Way of silent extinction. And I was perfect in my deportment. My mind was pure. Even if others came and urged [tempted, attacked] me, I was not beaten. Having relinquished the fire of anger, I upheld the law of the Eternal, Bliss, Self, and the Pure. I went about and looked for Mahayana sutras, but had not yet heard the name of the vaipulya. At that time I lived in the Himalayas. The mountains were pure; there was a plenitude of running rivers, ponds, forests, medicinal trees all around. Here and there, between the rocks, ran clear streams; beautiful flowers adorned everywhere. There were innumerable birds and animals. Sweet were the fruits and countless their varieties. Also, there were lotus roots, sweet roots, blue trees, and fragrant roots. I lived alone at that time, on fruit. After partaking of the fruit, I concentrated my mind and sat in meditation. It took an immeasurably long time, but I never heard of the appearance of the Tathagata or of the Mahayana sutras. O good man! I thus practised the Way through all difficulties, and Sakrodevanam and all the devas wondered at my practising of the Way. They all gathered together and spoke to each other, saying in a gatha:

"Each of us points and says
That in this pure quarter of the Himalayas
There lives a master, alone
And parted from all greed,
The king of all virtues.
Removed is he already
From greed, anger, and arrogance;
Long since has he done away with
Flattery and ignorance.
His mouth does not speak
What is rough or evil."

"At that time, there was a deva among those present whose name was "Joy", and who also said in a gatha:
"One like this who is apart from greed
Is pure and makes effort. Is not such a person
One who looks up to Shakra [chief of gods] or the devas?
If such a person is one who seeks the Way,
Such a one will undergo penance.
Such a person will desire to gain
The place where Shakra sits.""

"At that time, there was a rishi who spoke to Shakra in a gatha:
"O Kausika [i.e. Shakra], master of heaven! Do not conceive things this way.
The tirthikas undergo penance.
Why do they need necessarily
To seek the place where Shakra lives?""

"Speaking thus, he also said: "O Kausika! There is a great person here who, for the sake of beings, does not conceive things for his own good. To benefit beings, he practises penance in innumerable ways. Such a person sees in the world of birth and death all kinds of wrong, so that he does no covet any treasure, even if it filled this earth, all the mountains and the great seas. He sees all such things as being equal to tears and spit. Such a great person gives up his treasures, his wife and children, whom he loves, his head, eyes, marrow, hands, feet, the house where he lives, his elephant and horse, his vehicle, his male or female servants or pages; and he does not desire to be born in heaven. What he desires is solely to gain all happiness. What is evident to me is that such a great person is pure, has no defilements; he has done away with all the bonds of the "asravas". Possibly he is bound for unsurpassed Bodhi."
"Sakrodevanamindra says: "What you say seems to refer to one who desires to save all beings of the world. O great sage! If there is to be a Buddha tree in this world, he will uproot all the serpents of illusion of all such as Brahma, the beings of the world, and the asuras. If beings live in the cool shade of this Buddha tree, all poison will go away. O great rishi! If this person, in days to come, becomes a Sugata [Buddha], all of us will be able to extinguish the innumerable burning fires of illusion. Such a thing is hard to believe. Why? Innumerable beings gain unsurpassed Bodhichitta [resolve to gain Enlightenment], but as their causal relations [for this] are meagre, the Bodhichitta shatters. This is like the moon reflected in water, which moves if the water moves, or it is as difficult as trying to draw pictures in water, pictures which easily disperse. It is the same with

Bodhichitta. It is difficult to attain it and it easily breaks apart. O great rishi! There are many people decked out in armour and with arms, who proceed to beat the enemy. But if the mind has fear while on the battle-field, that person is forced to draw back. It is like this with all beings. A person may be strongly armed with Bodhichitta and be adorned with it. But on seeing the works of birth and death, the mind feels fear, at which the person has to pull back. O great rishi! I have seen the minds of innumerable beings being thus shattered and shaken after they gained [initial] Bodhichitta. For this reason, though I now see this person intent upon penance, and though he has no worry or heat, and even though on a precipitous path his pursuit is pure, yet I still cannot believe in him. I shall now go and see for myself whether he is decidedly worthy of shouldering the heavy burden of unsurpassed Enlightenment. O rishi! It is like a wagon, which, if it has two wheels, can well stand carrying weight, or like a bird which, if it has two wings, can indeed fly. It will be the same with this person who is practising penance. Now, he is intent on upholding the prohibitive precepts, but I do not know if this person has deep Wisdom. If he has, he will indeed be able to shoulder the great weight of unsurpassed Enlightenment. O great rishi! A fish, for example, may have many eggs, but only a few fish will manage to emerge from them. The mango tree has many flowers, but the fruits are small in number. Many are the people who aspire to Enlightenment, but so few are those who attain that end that it is not worth mentioning. O great rishi! I shall go along with you and see for myself how matters stand. For example, O great rishi! One can distinguish true gold if one performs three types of test, which are: burning, beating, and polishing. This must be the way to test penance." "Then Shakrodevanamindra transformed himself into a rakshasa [flesh-eating demon] who was very fearful to behold. He came down to the Himalayas. And he stood there, not

"All things change.
This is the law of birth and death."

"Thus saying, he stood before the person. He looked very frightening, and looked all around him. The person who was practising penance heard these [words] and was happy. It was like a merchant who, while travelling on a difficult path through the dark night and losing sight of his companions, becomes full of fear, but when he meets up with his comrades again feels no end of joy; or it was like a person who has long been ill, without encountering a good doctor, good treatment or good medicine, who later comes across such; or it was like a person at sea who falls into the sea water and suddenly encounters a boat; or like a thirsty person who comes across water; or like a person who is being pursued by an enemy and who suddenly escapes; or like a person who has long been chained up in prison, who suddenly obtains release. Or it was like a farmer who encounters rain during the days of drought, or like a traveller who returns home again, and whose people at home are overjoyed. O good man! I, at that time, heard this one half of the gatha and was likewise joyous. I immediately got up from my seat, lifted up my hair with my hand, looked around me and said: "From whom was that gatha which I heard just now?" "At that time, as I looked around, I could see nobody except a rakshasa. I said: "Who is it that so opens the gate of emancipation and so thunders out the voice of all Buddhas? Who is it who, amidst the sleep of birth and death, alone awakes and utters such words? Who is it who shows beings, facing birth and death and famine-stricken, this unsurpassed Way? Innumerable beings flounder in the sea of birth and death. And who is it who is going to become a great master mariner? All these beings are always greatly stricken by the illness of the "asravas". Who is it who is able to become the best of doctors? This half of the gatha teaches me, opens up and awakens my mind. It is as when the half-moon causes the lotus to open up its petals." I then, O good man, saw none but the rakshasa. Also, I thought thus: "Did the rakshasa speak this

far away. At that time, the rakshasa had no fear in his mind; he looked brave, with none to compare to him. His oratory was in order, with his voice clear. He spoke half of a gatha from the Buddhas of days past:

gatha?" Again I doubted: "Maybe he did not. Why not? The appearance of the man is so very frightful.

Anyone who heard this gatha would do away with all fear and ugliness. How could a man like this, who looks so ugly, deliver a gatha such as this? A lotus cannot come out of fire; there cannot be cool water where the sunlight falls." "O good man! I then said to myself: "I am now ignorant. This rakshasa may have seen all the Buddhas in the past. On seeing them, he may have had a chance of hearing this half of the gatha. I shall ask." Going up to where he was, I said: "Well, O great one! Where did you get this half of the gatha from a Fearless One of the past? O great one! Where did you get this half of a cintamani [wish-fulfilling jewel] of a gatha? O great one! This half of the gatha is the right path of the All-Buddha-World-Honoured Ones of the past, future, and present. The innumerable beings of the world are always overshadowed by all wrong actions, and all life through they stand amidst the teachings of the tirthikas and do not have the chance of hearing the supramundane words spoken by the World's Hero [Buddha], who is possessed of the ten powers." O good man! When I thus asked, the answer came back: "O great Brahmin! Do not ask of me the meaning of this. Why not? I have not eaten anything for days. I have looked all around, but I cannot find anything to eat. Due to thirst, hunger and worry, my mind is deranged and my words do not come out in order. My mind itself does not know [what is what]. I have flown through the sky. I have been to Uttarakuru, to heaven, and to all other places, but I cannot get food anywhere. So, I speak thus." O good man! I then said to the rakshasa: "O great one! If you tell me about this gatha, I shall be your disciple to the end of my life. O great one! What you spoke was not entire and the meaning was not complete. Why do you not wish to speak? Now, there is an end even to wealth, but there is no end to the dana [giving] of

Dharma. The dana of Dharma knows no ending. The benefit it bestows is great. Now that I have heard this half of the gatha, my mind is surprised, and I also have doubt. Now, ease my mind! If you complete this gatha, I shall be your disciple until the end of my days." The rakshasa answered: "You have penetrated deeply into Wisdom. Only, you care solely for your own self and miss what was meant. I am now oppressed by hunger. I cannot carry on talking." I asked: "What do you eat?" The rakshasa replied: "Do not ask. If I say, people get frightened." I further said: "I live alone, there is nobody else here. I, now, am not afraid of you. Why will you not say?" The rakshasa said: "What I eat is the soft flesh of man; what I drink is man's warm blood. It is an unfortunate destiny of mine that I have to sustain my life in this way. I go round and look about, but I cannot get any of these things. There are many men in the world. But all have virtue; all are protected by heaven. Besides, I have no strength and cannot kill." O good man! I further said: "Tell me the meaning of the gatha in full. After hearing it, I shall offer you my body. O great one! I may die, but such a body as mine is of no use to me. It could get devoured by a tiger, wolf, owl or eagle, without my being blessed with a hair's amount of gain on my side. I am now intent upon unsurpassed Enlightenment. I shall discard a body which is not hard enough, and I mean to trade it for an indestructible one." The rakshasa answered: "Who could believe what you say? Abandoning

"When birth and death are done away with,
Quietude is bliss."

"Having said this, the rakshasa further said: "O Bodhisattva-mahasattva! You have now gained the complete meaning of the gatha and you must be satisfied. If you desire to benefit all beings, give me your body now!" O good man! I, at that time, pondered greatly upon the [gatha's] meaning. So I later wrote this gatha upon stones, walls, trees, and upon the path. Then I put my clothes on. For possibly after death my body might be exposed [to someone]. I climbed a tall tree. Then the tree god said: "O you! What do you intend to do?" O good man! I answered: "I shall now cast away my body, so as to repay the value I have obtained from the gatha." The tree god asked: "What benefit does the gatha bestow?" I answered: "This gatha is what the Buddhas of the past, future and present have

the beloved body for the sake of eight [=in English, eleven] words [i.e. the final words of the poem]?" O good man! I replied: "You are really ignorant. Imagine a man here. It would be like giving up an earthenware [pot] for a vessel containing seven jewels. The same with me. I shall cast away my body which is not strong enough, in order to obtain an Adamantine Body. You say: [How can I believe you] I have witnesses such as Great Brahma, Shakrodevanamindra, and the four guardians of the earth, who will all bear witness to me. Also, all Bodhisattvas who wish to benefit countless beings and who all study Mahayana and who are perfect in the six paramitas will attest [to my sincerity]. And there are the All-Buddha-World-Honoured Ones of the ten directions who desire to benefit all beings. They, too, will bear witness that I shall indeed cast aside my body for the sake of those eight words." The rakshasa said further: "If you wish to throw away your body thus, then listen well, listen well! I shall now recite the remaining half of the gatha for your sake." O good man! Then, on hearing his words, I was glad at heart. I took off the deer-skin clothing that I had on and spread it on the ground for the rakshasa to preach [upon], and said: "O Honoured One! Please sit on this. I shall fold my hands and prostrate myself on the ground before you and say: [O Please, Honoured One! Speak well for me the remaining half of the gatha and bring things to completion]." The rakshasa said:

had for the opening up of the doctrine of the All-Void. I give my body up for this. It is not for profit, fame or treasure; not for the bliss of the chakravartin, the four guardians of the earth, Great Brahma, or man or heaven. I cast this away for the benefit of all beings." O good man! I also vowed to myself: "Let all miserly people come and see how I relinquish this body. If there is a person who gives little and asks for much, let such a person see how I, merely for this gatha, cast my body away, just as a person might discard grass or wood." "As I said this, I flung my body down from the tree to the ground. It had not yet reached the ground when several voices sounded in the air. The voices reached as far as Akanistha Heaven. Then the rakshasa displayed his original form as

Shakra, took hold of me in mid-air, and deposited me upon the ground. Then, Skakrodevanamindra, all the devas, and Great Brahma fell to the ground. They touched my feet, raised me up, and said: "Well done, well done! It is good, it is good! This truly is a Bodhisattva who benefits innumerable beings and who, in the blackness of the gloom, desires to set up a great torch. As I love the Tathagata's great Dharma, I beautifully ponder and worry. Please give ear to how I repent of my sins. You shall assuredly, in days to come, achieve unsurpassed Enlightenment. Please condescend to succour me." "Then, Shakrodevanamindra and the devas touched my feet. Then they disappeared and were seen no more. O good man! Since I discarded my body in days gone by for the sake of a gatha, in consequence I was able to hope to attain unsurpassed Enlightenment after twelve kalpas before Maitreya. O good man! I had accomplished such innumerable virtues. All arise from making offerings to the Tathagata's Wonderful Dharma. "O good man! It is the same with you. If you aspire to unsurpassed Bodhichitta [Mind of Enlightenment], this will place you above Bodhisattvas as innumerable as the sands of innumerable, boundless Ganges. This is what we mean when we say that a Bodhisattva abides in the teaching of the Mahayana Mahaparinirvana and practises the holy Way."

Chapter Twenty-One: On Pure Actions 1

"O good man! What are the pure actions of a Bodhisattva-mahasattva? O good man! The Bodhisattva-mahasattva, abiding in the Mahayana Mahaparinirvana, can be perfect in pure actions in seven categories. What are those seven? They are: 1) knowing Dharma, 2) knowing the meaning, 3) knowing the time, 4) being contented, 5) knowing for oneself, 6) knowing the masses, 7) knowing the difference between respectable and mean. "O good man! How does a Bodhisattva-mahasattva know Dharma? O good man! This Bodhisattva-mahasattva knows the twelve types of scripture, which are: 1) sutra, 2) geya, 3) vyakarana, 4) gatha, 5) udana, 6) nidana, 7) avadana, 8) itivrttaka, 9) jataka, 10) vaipulya, 11) adbhutadharma, and 12) upadesa. "O good man! What is meant by "sutra?" A sutra begins with: "Thus have I heard" and ends with: "practise with joy". All such are "sutras". "What is "geya?" It goes like this: "The Buddha said to all bhiksus: In days gone by, I, like you, was ignorant and had no Wisdom, and could not see the Four Truths. For that reason, I had long transmigrated and repeated birth and death and floundered in the great sea of suffering. What are the Four? They are: 1) Suffering, 2) the Cause of Suffering, 3) Extinction, 4) the Way to the Extinction of Suffering. In days gone by, the Buddha spoke of the sutras. At that time, there was a sharp-witted person who came to the Buddha to be taught Dharma. He asked others: "What did the Tathagata speak about before?" The Tathagata, seeing this, said in a gatha, basing himself on the sutras:

"I, like you, did not see the Four Truths
And as a result floundered long in the sea
Of suffering of birth and death.
By seeing the Four Truths,
One well severs birth and death.
Birth and death done away with,
One no more gains any existence."
This is "geya."

"What is "vyakarana"? There are sutras and vinayas [monastic rules] in which, when the Tathagata speaks, he gives prophecies to all the heavenly ones, such as: "O you, Ajita! In days to come, there will be a king named "Sankha". In his reign, you will practise the Way, attain Buddhahood, and be called Maitreya." This is "vyakarana". "What is "gatha"? In addition to the sutras and vinaya, there are cases in which a four-line poem appears, such as:

"Do not do any evil;
Do all that is good.
Purify your mind.
This is the teaching of all Buddhas."

This is "gatha." "What is "udana"? The Buddha, at about four in the afternoon, enters a dhyana [meditation]. He speaks about Dharma to the devas [gods]. At that time, the bhiksus [monks] think: "What is the Tathagata doing?" The Tathagata awakes next morning from the dhyana and, without being asked by anyone, he, with the power of knowledge that can read the minds of others, speaks unasked: "O Bhiksus! Know that the life of all devas is extremely long. O all of you Bhiksus! It is good that you all act for others and do not seek your own profit. It is good that you seek but little; it is good that you feel contented; it is good that you are quiet [peaceful]!" It goes like that. In all such scriptures, the Buddha speaks unasked. This is "udana". "What is "nidana"? The gathas of all sutras speak for others about the basic roots of all causes. In Sravasti there was a man who caught a bird in a net. Having caught it, he put it in a cage, gave it water and cereal, and then let it go.

The World-Honoured One knows all histories from beginning to end and talks about this in a gatha , such as:

"Do not belittle small evil acts,
And do not say that there is no evil that arises.
Small is a drop of water,
But [by accumulation] it fills a great vessel."

This is "nidana". "What is "avadana"? It is as in the case of the parables that occur in the vinaya. This is "avadana". "What is "itivrttaka"? This is as when the Buddha says: "O Bhiksus! Know that what I speak when I am in the world is the sutras. In the days of Buddha Krakucchanda, it is called "amrtadrum" [drum of the Immortal]; what appears in the days of Kanakamuni is called "Dharmamirror"; what appears in the days of Buddha Kasyapa is called "Void-discriminating". This is "itivrttaka". "What is "jataka"? This is when the World-Honoured One [tells of how he], in days gone by, became a Bodhisattva and practised the Way, such as: "O Bhisksus! Know that, in days gone by, I gained life as a deer, a brown bear, a reindeer, a hare, the king of a small state, a chakravartin, a naga, and a garuda. Such are all the bodies one receives when one practises the Way of a Bodhisattva." This is "jataka". "What is "vaipulya sutra"? It is none other than the Mahayana vaipulya [extensive] sutras. What it states is on a large scale. It is like space. This is "vaipulya". "What is "adbhutadharma"? After the Bodhisattva has just been born, he takes seven steps without any help from others, sending out great lights, which shine in all ten directions; or a monkey holds in its hand a pot of honey and offers it to the Tathagata; or a white-headed dog sits by the Buddha's side and listens to his sermons; Marapapiyans transforms himself into a blue cow and walks between tiles and bowls, touching but not damaging them; or, when the Buddha first enters the devas' temple, the devas come down and pay him homage. Any sutra such as this is called "adbhutadharma". "What do we mean by "upadesa"? It is one [scripture] that discusses the sutras which contain the Buddha's sermons and analyses and widely explains the characteristics. Any such is an "upadesa". "If any Bodhisattva is well versed in the twelve types of scripture, this is "knowing Dharma". "How does a Bodhisattva-mahasattva understand the meaning? A Bodhisattva knows the meaning of all words and languages. This is knowing the meaning. "How

does a Bodhisattva-mahasattva know the [right] time? O good man! The Bodhisattva, at a given time, will practise quietude. At another time, he will make effort. At another time, he will practise equanimity and dhyana. At another time, he will make offerings to his teacher. At another time, he will practise dana [giving], upholding the moral precepts, forbearance, effort, and dhyana, thus perfecting prajnaparamita [transcendent Wisdom]. This is knowing the time. "In what way does a Bodhisattva-mahasattva feel contented? O good man! The Bodhisattvamahasattva knows contentment in his meals, clothing, medicine, in going, coming, sitting, lying, sleeping, waking, talking and in silence. This is knowing contentment. "O good man! How does a Bodhisattva-mahasattva know things by himself? The Bodhisattva knows all about faith, the precepts, rich hearing, equanimity, Wisdom, going and coming, right remembrance, good deeds, questions and answers. This is knowing of one's own self. "How does a Bodhisattva-mahasattva know the masses? Such a Bodhisattva knows: "This is a Kshatriya, this a Brahmin, this an upasaka, this a sramana. Such a person goes thus, comes thus, sits thus, stands up thus, delivers sermons thus, and puts questions and answers thus." This is knowing the masses. "O good man! In what way does a Bodhisattva-mahasattva know the difference between "respectable" and "mean"? O good man! There are two kinds of men: one who has faith, and the other, who has not. O Bodhisattva! Know that he with faith is one who is good, and that he who has no faith is one who is not good. Also, next, there are two kinds of faithful person. One always pays visits to viharas, and the other does not. O Bodhisattva! Know that he who goes is good, and the other who does not should not be called good. There are two kinds of people who go to viharas. One is he who worships, and the other is he who does not. O Bodhisattva! Know that he who worships is good, and the other who does not is not to be called good. There are two kinds of worshipper. One is he who listens to the sermons, and the other is he who does not listen to the sermons. O Bodhisattva! Know that he who listens to the sermons is one who is good, and that the other is one who cannot be called good. There are again two kinds of people who listen to sermons. The one is he who listens with a true mind, and the other is he who has no true mind. O Bodhisattva! Know that he who listens with a true mind is one who is good, and that he with no true mind is not to be called good. Of listeners with a true mind, there are two kinds. One thinks about the meaning, and the other does not think about the meaning. O Bodhisattva! Know that he who thinks about the meaning is good, and he who does not think about the meaning is not good. And there are two kinds amongst those who think about the meaning. One is he who practises the Way as told, and the other is he who does not practise the Way as told. He who practises the Way as told is one who is good, and he who does not practise the Way as told is one who is not good. There are, again, two kinds of people who practise the Way as told. One is he who takes to the Way of the sravaka, who is unable to releave all beings of all their worries and give them peace and benefit; the second is he who takes to the unsurpassed Mahayana and gives benefit and peace to the many. O Bodhisattva! Know that he who gives benefit and peace to the many is unsurpassed and the best. "O good man! Of all jewels, the cintamani [wish-fulfilling gem] is the most superb; of all tastes, amrta [ambrosia] is the best. Such a Bodhisattva is the most superb and the best of all humans and devas. No comparison can express it. O good man! This is what we mean when we say that the Bodhisattva-mahasattva abides in the Mahayana Great Nirvana Sutra and lives in the seven good laws. The Bodhisattva, abiding in these seven good laws, can become perfect in pure action. "Also, next, O good man! There are pure actions, which are: loving-kindness ["maitri"], compassion ["karuna"], sympathetic joy ["mudita"], and equanimity ["upeksha"]." Bodhisattva Kasyapa said to the Buddha: "A person who practises kindness segregates himself from anger; a person who practises compassion segregates himself from anger. And yet we speak of the "limitless [immeasurable] minds". From the content of the meaning, there must be three. O World-Honoured One! There are three circumstantial factors in loving-kindness. One relates to beings, the second

to dharmas, and the third to what is unrelated. The same with compassion, sympathetic joy, and equanimity. Following this logic, there can only be one, not four. What relates to beings comes about relative to the five skandhas, and one prays to give bliss thereto. This is what relates to beings. By what relates to things [dharmas] is meant giving what beings desire to possess. This is what relates to things. By "unrelated" comes about [is meant] the Tathagata. This is the "unrelated". Compassion has bearings on the poor and those in stressed circumstances. The Tathagata, the great teacher, is long since far removed from poverty and stressed circumstances and is blessed with the highest bliss. If any relation is had with beings, it obtains thus with the Buddha. The same is the case with things. That is why we say that any bearing that is had upon the Tathagata is the "relationless". O World-Honoured One! The field in which compassion becomes related to all beings has bearings upon parents, wife, children and relatives. Hence, we say "related to all beings." We say "related to dharmas". Here, we see no parents, wife, children or relatives. We see here that all things arise from circumstantial factors. Hence, "related to dharmas". The "unrelated" is not based on dharmas or beings. Hence, "unrelated". It is the same with compassion, sympathetic joy, and equanimity. So there must be three things, and not four. O World-Honoured One! There are two kinds of people. One is a person who practises the Way using his own intellect, and the other is a person who practises the Way through faith and love. The person who practises the Way through the intellectual channel generally practises loving-kindness, and the person who practises the Way through faith and love practises sympathetic joy and equanimity. Hence, there must be two, and not four. O World-Honoured One! "Immeasurable" means "boundless". The boundary is unattainable. Hence, "boundless". If [something is] "immeasurable", there can only be one, not four. If there were four, how could they be immeasurable? Therefore, there must be one, not four." The Buddha said to Kasyapa: "O good man! The essence of what the All-Buddha-Tathagata says is undisclosed. For this reason, it is difficult to know. There are cases where he speaks about a set of causes and conditions. What there is [here] is just one. It is as when one says that all things are created things. Or there may be a case where it is said that there are two kinds. These are the direct and indirect causes, and the result. Or it may be spoken of as three. These are illusion, action and suffering. Or it may be spoken of as four. These are ignorance, created existence, birth, and age-and-death. Or it may be spoken of as five, such as: feeling, craving, cleaving, existence, and birth. Or it may be spoken of as six, which are the causes and results of the Three Times [past, present and future]. Or things may be spoken of in terms of seven, which are consciousness, mind-and-body, the six sphere, touch, feeling, craving, and cleaving. Or one might speak of eight things, which are those [of the twelve links of interdependent arising], minus the four elements of ignorance, action, birth, and age-and-death, which makes eight. Or one may speak of nine, as stated in the "Nagara Sutra". This refers to the nine, excepting the three elements of ignorance, action, and consciousness. Or one may speak of eleven, as to Satyakanirgranthaputra. These are the eleven, excepting the one category of "birth". At times, the Buddha speaks fully of the twelve links of interdependent arising. This is as when he spoke at Rajagriha to Kasyapa and others about ignorance all the way down to birth, age, illness, and death. O good man! A single causal relation is, for the benefit of beings, expounded in various ways. It is the same with the innumerable phases [aspects] of the mind. O good man! For this reason, do not entertain doubt in regard to the deeply-hidden action of the All-Buddha-Tathagata." "O good man! The Tathagata-World-Honoured One enacts great expedients. He speaks of impermanence as Eternal, and of the Eternal as impermanent. He speaks of Bliss as suffering and suffering as Bliss; the impure as Pure and the Pure as impure. He speaks of the Self as selfless and of the selfless as the Self; of non-being as a beings and the real being as a non-being. A non-substance is spoken of as a substance and a substance as a non-substance. The non-real is spoken of as real and the real as non-real; the non-field of cognition as a field of cognition and the field of cognition as a non-field of cognition; non-birth as birth and birth as non-birth; ignorance as brightness and brightness as ignorance; rupa [form] as non-rupa and non-rupa as rupa; the non-Way as the Way and the Way as non-Way. O good man! The Tathagata, by using all such expedients, sets beings to rights. How could we say that anything is wrong with him? "O good man! There may be a person who covets wealth. I then, for the sake of

that person, transform myself into a chakravartin and for innumerable ages give things to him in various ways. Later, I teach him and enable him to abide in unsurpassed Enlightenment. If there is a person who clings to the five deisres, I fill up that person's clinging for innumerable ages with wonderful things that such a person desires to have, and later teach him and make him attain unsurpassed Enlightenment. If there is a rich person, strong and proud, I serve him for innumerable hundreds of thousands of years, running errands and waiting upon him, and after having won over such a person's mind, I will cause him to attain unsurpasssed Enlightenment. If there is a person who transgresses, is self-assertive, thinks he is on the right path and quarrels with others, I shall, for innumerable ages, advise him, remonstrate with him and bring him round, and then cause him to attain unsurpassed Enlightenment. O good man! The Tathagata, for innumerable ages, enacts various means, thus causing beings to achieve unsurpassed Enlightenment. How could anything be wrong here? The All-Buddha-Tathagata may live amidst all evils, but, like the lotus, he is not tainted [by them]. O good man! You should understand the four immeasurables [i.e." Brahma-viharas"] thus. "O good man! There are four qualities in this limitless mind. The practice accomplished, one gains birth in the world of Great Brahma. O good man! There are thus four kinds within the limitless mind. That is why we speak of four. By practising loving-kindness ["maitri"], a person thoroughly extirpates greed. Practising compassion ["karuna"], a person extirpates anger. Practising sympathetic joy ["mudita"], a person extirpates non-bliss. By practising equanimity, a person well segregates beings from greed and anger. O good man! For this reason, we speak of four. It is not one, not two, and not three. "O good man! As you say, loving-kindness indeed cuts out anger. If things are thus with compassion, one may say three. Do mot make such a reproof. Why not? "O good man! Of anger, there are two kinds. One takes life; the other encourages a person. O good man! Because of this, how could it be other than four? "Also, next, of anger there are two kinds. One is being angry towards beings, and the other towards non-beings. By practising loving-kindness, one thoroughly dispels anger towards beings; by practising compassion, one thoroughly dispels anger towards non-beings. "Also, next, of anger, there are two kinds. One is based on causal relations and the other is not.

Practising loving-kindness, one cuts away that which is based on causal relations; practising compassion, one cuts away that which is based on causal relations. "Also, next, there are two kinds of anger. One is anger that has been accumulated over a long period in the past, and the other is that which one has just gained. By practising loving-kindness, one severs the anger from the past, and by practising compassion, one severs the anger of the present. "Also, next, there are two kinds of anger. One is anger at holy persons, and the other at common mortals. By practising loving-kindness, one casts off anger at holy persons; by practising compassion, one casts off anger at common mortals. "Also, next, there are two types of anger. One is top-grade, and the other is middle-grade. The practising of loving-kindness dispels top-grade anger, while practising compassion dispels middle-grade anger. O good man! For this reason, I say four. How can you reproach me and speak of three and not four? Thus, O Kasyapa, in this limitless mind, antitheses stand against one another, and classified, we get four. "Also, it is four because of the vessel. If there is loving-kindness in the vessel, there can be no compassion, joy, and equanimity. For this reason, it is four and nothing less. "O good man! We discriminate according to action. Hence, four. When loving-kindness is acted upon, there can be no compassion, sympathetic joy and equanimity. Hence, four. O good man! Because of limitlessness, we say four. Now, of the limitless there are four kinds. There is the case where what there is is the relation of the limitless mind, but not unmolestedness [unimpededness]. Or there is the case where the limitless mind is unmolested and it does not stand [depend] upon relations; there is the case where things stand on the relations of the limitless mind and also on unmolestedness; there is the case where things do not stand on relations and also not on unmolestedness. What is the limitless that has relations, but is not unmolested? This is the case where causal relations are had with innumerable and boundless beings, and yet there is nothing of the kind as the unmolested state of samadhi. Even if gained, it does not remain. Or one gains and loses it. What is the limitless that is unmolested and has no causal relations? It is like desiring to have causal relations with parents,

brothers and sisters and to give them peace and bliss. There can be no limitless causal relations [here]. What is the limitless that has causal relations and is unmolested? This refers to all Buddhas and Bodhisattvas. What is the limitless with no causal relations and no unmolestedness? The sravakas and pratyekabuddhas cannot have unlimited relations with beings. Also, they are not unmolested [i.e. they are constrained by limitations]. O good man! Because of this, we speak of the "four limitlessnesses". This is not something any sravakas or pratyekabuddhas can know. This is what applies to the world of the All-Buddha-Tathagata. O good man! The sravakas and pratyekabuddhas may call these four the things that are limitless. But petty is what is said [by them]; it is not worth talking of. All Buddhas and Bodhisattvas should be called the "limitless limitless." Bodhisattva Kasyapa said to the Buddha: "O World-Honoured One! It is thus, it is thus! It is just as you, the Holy One, say. What obtains in the world of the All-Buddha-Tathagata does not come within the reach of sravakas and pratyekabuddhas. O World-Honoured One! A Bodhisattva abides in the Mahayana Mahaparinirvana and gains a heart of loving-kindness. Is this a great heart of loving-kindness and compassion or not?" The Buddha said: "It is! O good man! The Bodhisattva sees three things as he lives with all beings, which are: 1) people on intimate relations [with him], 2) people of hateful relations, and 3) people who are in between. With those on intimate relations, there are three classes, which are: 1) top, 2) middle, and 3) low. The same with those involved in hateful relations. This Bodhisattva-mahasattva gives the highest bliss to those with whom he is on the most intimate relations. He also gives the highest bliss all-equally to those of the middle and low grades. He gives some degree of bliss to those whom he hates most, and to a person whose hatred is of middle grade he gives middle-grade bliss, and to him whose hatred is of a low level, he gives the highest bliss. The Bodhisattva thus practises from one to the other, and to the one he most hates he gives middle-grade bliss and to those whom he hates on a middling level and a low level, he gives the highest bliss. He practises and gives the highest bliss all-equally to those of the top, middle and low grades. When the highest bliss is given to one whom he most hates, we say that the heart of loving-kindness has been accomplished. The

Bodhisattva, then, whether at the place of his parents or of those whom he most hates, is all-equal in mind, and there exists no mental state of discrimination. O good man! One obtains loving-kindness, but this is not called great loving-kindness." "O World-Honoured One! Why is it that the Bodhisattva achieves such loving-kindness and yet we do not call it great loving-kindness?" "O good man! We do not call loving-kindness great loving-kindness, because it [great loving-kindness] is hard to obtain. Why so? For a long time past, over innumerable kalpas, one has amassed "asravas" [defilements, illusions] and not practised what is good. For this reason, one is unable to subdue the mind in a day. O good man! When a pea is dried up, one might try to thrust an awl through it, but one cannot. It is like that. The "asravas" are as hard as that. Try as one might single-mindedly the whole day and night through, one cannot yet subdue them. Also, the dog of a house does not fear people, and the deer of the forest fears man and runs away. Anger is difficult to do away with, like the dog that guards a house; but the heart of loving-kindness easily flees, like the deer in the forest. It is therefore hard to subdue this mind. That is why we do not say "great loving-kindness". Also, next, O good man! When we draw a picture on stone, it always remains thus. But drawn on water, it disappears immediately and its strength does not remain there. Anger is hard to do away with, like a drawing that has been done in stone. A good deed easily disappears, like a picture drawn in water. That is why it is not easy to subdue this mind. A great ball of fire sustains light for a long while; the brightness of a flash of lightning cannot endure long. It is the same here. Anger is a fire-ball; loving-kindness is like lightning. That is why this mind is hard to subdue. Hence, we do not say "great loving-kindness". "O good man! When a Bodhisattva-mahasattva attains the first soil ["bhumi" - level of a higher Bodhisattva], this is called "great loving-kindness". Why? O good man! The last [i.e. most] evil person is the icchantika. When a Bodhisattva of the first "bhumi" practises great loving-kindness, no discrimination exists in his mind - not even towards an icchantika. As no wrong is seen, no anger arises. For this reason, we indeed call this "great loving-kindness". O good man! He deprives all beings of what gives no benefit. This is great loving-kindness. He desires to give an uncountable amount of benefit and bliss to all beings. This is

great compassion. He plants joy in the minds of all beings. This is great sympathetic joy. There is no guarding or protecting. This is great equanimity ["upeksha"]. My Dharma does not see one's own existence and self; what is seen is that all things are viewed all-equally and with no divided mind. This is great equanimity. One forsakes one's own bliss and gives it to others. This is great equanimity [or: great relinquishment]. "O good man! The only thing there is here is that these four limitless minds well enable the Bodhisattva to increase and perfect the six paramitas [perfections]. Things are not necessarily thus regarding others' actions. O good man! The Bodhisattva-mahasattva first gains the four limitless minds that pertain to the world. Later, he aspires to unsurpassed Bodhichitta [resolve to win Enlightenment]. And by degrees he gains what concerns those of the supramundane world. O good man! From the limitedness of the secular world, one obtains the unlimitedness of the supramundane world. Hence, we say "great limitlessness." Bodhisattva Kasyapa said to the Buddha: "O World-Honoured One! We say that the benefitless is done away with and that benefit and bliss are given. Truth to tell, nothing happens. Thinking thus is surely false. No real fruition comes about. O World-Honoured One! This is as when a bhiksu meditates on impurity and regards what he is wearing as leather, which it actually is not. He thinks that what he eats is worms. But here too, it is not really worms. He regards a beautiful soup as a defiled liquid, but it is not really anything defiled. He regards the cream that he eats as the marrow of the brain, but actually it is not a brain. He meditates on the crushed powder of bones and regards it as parched barley flour. And yet it is not really parched barley flour. The same with the case of the four limitless minds. There is not really any benefiting of beings, nor any giving to them of bliss. The mouth speaks about bliss being given. But no such thing comes about. Is such a meditation not false? O World-Honoured One! If it is the case that falsehood does not exist here, but bliss [truly] is given, why is it that all beings do not gain bliss by the miraculous powers of all Buddhas and Bodhisattvas? If no bliss results in any true sense, it must be as the Buddha says: "I call to mind that in days gone by I practised loving-kindness and through seven successive stages of the dissolution and re-arising of the world in this kalpa aeon, I did not get born here. When the world was born, I saw my birth in the heaven of Brahma, and when the world underwent dissolution, I was born in the heaven of Abhasvara. Born in the heaven of Brahma, one has unmolested [i.e. unrestricted] power and cannot ever be subdued. Of the thousand Brahmas, the most superb is Great Brahma. All beings considered me as the most superb. Thirty-six times I became Sakrodevanamindra, the King of Trayastrimsa Heaven, and innumerable hundreds of thousands of times a chakravartin. Only by practising the Way of the heart of loving-kindness did I gain the fruits of man and heaven." If not true, how could things be in accord with this meaning?" The Buddha said: Well said, well said, O good man! You are, indeed, brave and fear nothing." And for Kasyapa's sake, he spoke in a gatha:

"If one does not feel anger
Even towards a single being
And prays to give bliss to such a being,
This is loving-kindness.
If one has compassion
For all beings,
This is the holy seed.
Endless is the recompense.
Even if the five-powered rishis filled this earth
And gave to Mahesvara elephants, horses
And their various possessions,
The reward gained would not equal
One sixteenth of one [impulse of] loving-kindness
That is practised."

"O good man! Practising loving-kindness is true and does not come from a false mind. It is clearly the truth. The loving-kindness of sravakas and pratyekabuddhas is that which is false. With all Buddhas and Bodhisattvas, what there is [there] is the true, and not what is false. How do we know this? O good man! As the Bodhisattva-mahasattva practises the Way of Great Nirvana, he meditates upon earth and [mentally] turns it into gold, and meditates upon gold and turns it into earth, earth into water, water into fire, fire into water, earth into wind, and wind into earth. All appears as willed, and nothing is false. He meditates upon real beings and makes them into non-beings, and turns non-beings into real beings. All appears as willed and nothing is false. O good man! Know that the four limitless minds of a Bodhisattva come about from true thinking and are not what is untrue. "Also, next, O good man! Why is it called true thinking? Because it thoroughly does away with all defilements. O good man! Now, a person who practises loving-kindness uproots all greed; one who practises compassion uproots anger; one who practises sympathetic joy uproots unhappiness; one who practises equanimity uproots greed, anger and all the aspects of things that beings have. Hence, we call this true thinking.

"Also, next, O good man! The four limitless minds of a Bodhisattva-mahasattva form the root of all good deeds. O good man! If the Bodhisattva-mahasattva does not see a poverty-stricken being, there cannot be any arising of compassion. If the compassionate mind does not arise, there will not arise any thought of giving. By means of the causal relations of giving, he bestows on beings peace and bliss. These are drink, food, vehicles, clothing, flowers, incense, bedsteads, houses, and lamps. When giving is done in this way, there is no bond in the mind and no greed arises. He definitely transfers the merit hereof to unsurpassed Enlightenment. The mind does not sit on time. The false mind is forever done away with; what is done is not done out of fear, for fame or profit. It does not seek the world of humans or gods; whatever pleasure is gained does not evoke arrogance; it does not look for rewards; giving is not done to cheat others; it does not seek wealth or respect. When giving is performed, no discrimination [distinction] is made as to whether the recipient has upheld the moral precepts or transgressed, whether he is a true field of weal or a bad field of weal, whether learned or unlearned. When giving is performed, no discrimination is drawn between the right and wrong of the vessel; no difference is seen between the right or wrong time or place. One does not think about whether there is a famine or plenitude of things and bliss. No discrimination is made as to the cause or the result thereof, or to worrying about what is right [worthy] or not right about the recipient, or whether he is rich or not rich. Also, the Bodhisattva does not trouble to look into any difference as to whether the recipient is a person who gives or one who receives, what the thing is that is given, or ceasing, or the recompense for what is given. The only thing that is done is that giving is performed without cessation. "O good man! If the Bodhisattva looked to the upholding or infringing of the precepts, or the results thereof, there could not be any giving to the end. If there is no giving, there cannot be perfection of the danaparamita [transcendent giving]. If there is no danaparamita, there cannot be any arriving at unsurpassed Enlightenment." "O good man! As an illustration: there is a man who has been struck by a poisoned arrow. His relatives call in a doctor to releave him of the poison and mean to extract the arrow. The man says: "Don't touch me for a moment! I shall think: [From where did such an arrow come? Who discharged it? Was it a Kshatriya, a Brahmin, a Vaishya or Sudra]." He also thinks: "What type of wood is this? Bamboo or willow? By whom was the iron barb made? Is it strong or soft? What bird does the feather of the arrow come from? Is it from a crow, an owl, or an eagle? What is the poison made from? Is it man-made or natural? Is it a human poison or from a poisonous snake?" An ignorant person like this can never reach the end of trying to know about all these things. Then, his life will depart. O good man! It is the same with the Bodhisattva. If, when giving, he were to seek to know whether the recipient had upheld or violated the precepts, what the effect of the gift might be - he would not be able to give, to the very end. If there is no giving, then danaparamita will not have been accomplished. If danaparamita is not accomplished, there cannot be the attainment of unsurpassed Enlightenment. "Also, next, O good man! When the Bodhisattva-mahasattva practises giving, his kind heart sees all beings equally, like unto his own only son. Additionally when giving, his compassionate heart bestirs itself, as when a father and mother look at their own son who is ill. When giving, his heart feels joy, as when the father and mother see their child's illness cured. When giving is performed,

his mind is away from [not attached to] what is given, as when a father and mother see their son already grown up and living by himself. "This Bodhisattva-mahasattva always vows when he benevolently gives food: "I now give this and share it with all beings and intend that by the causal relations of this act all beings should attain the food of Great Wisdom and with effort transfer the merit thereof to unsurpassed Mahayana. I pray that all beings will gain the food of Good Wisdom and that they will not seek the food of the sravakas and pratyekabuddhas. I pray that all beings will gain the food of the joy of Dharma and not seek the food of craving. I pray that all beings will gain the food of prajnaparamita [transcendent Wisdom] in abundance and that they will have the unobstructed and best root of good, which will grow greater. I pray that all beings will understand and attain the phase of the Void and perfect the unhindered body and become like space. I pray that all beings will always pity all for the sake of those who receive and will become a field of blessings." O good man! The Bodhisattva-mahasattva, when practising the heart of loving-kindness, should firmly pray thus in regard to any food that is given. "Also, next, O good man! When the Bodhisattva-mahasattva, with a heart of loving-kindness, gives drink [to someone], he should always vow: "I share what I now give with all beings. By reason of this act, they will walk towards the river of Mahayana and partake of the water of the eight tastes, so that they can take to the path of unsurpassed Enlightenment, segregate themselves from the thirst of the sravakas and pratyeka-buddhas, and long for the unexcelled Buddha Vehicle. [I pray] that they will segregate themselves from the thirst of the defilements, and long for the food of Dharma, that they will part from the love of birth-and-death, entertain loving thoughts towards the Mahayana Mahaparinirvana, be perfect in the Dharma-Body, gain all samadhis and enter the great sea of Wisdom. I pray that all beings will partake of the taste of renunciation, abandon greed, and attain silence and quietude. I pray that all beings become perfect in the countless hundreds of thousands of tastes of Dharma. Perfect in the taste of Dharma, they will see the Buddha-Nature, and having seen the Buddha-Nature, they will rain down the rain of Dharma, and having rained down the rain of Dharma, the Buddha-Nature will overspread all like space. Also, [I pray that] all the other countless beings will attain the oneness of taste of the Dharma of Mahayana. This is not the taste of all the sravakas and pratyekabuddhas. I pray that all beings will gain the oneness of sweet taste and that there will not be any discriminative difference of the six kinds. I pray that all will solely seek the taste of Dharma, the unhindered taste of Buddhist actions and that they will not seek other tastes." O good man! When the Bodhisattva-mahasattva, with a heart of loving-kindness, bestows drink [upon others], he should take such a vow." "Also, next, O good man! When the Bodhisattva-mahasattva, with his heart of loving-kindness, gives away vehicles, he should always pray: "I shall share what I now give with all beings, and by reason of this I shall cause all beings to become perfect in the Mahayana and abide in it. And they will not step back from the vehicle which will be unshakable and adamantine. What will be sought will not be the sravaka or pratyekabuddha vehicle, but the Buddha vehicle, an unbeaten [indestructible] vehicle, a vehicle that is not weak and is lacking in no part, one that does not fall over or sink down, the unsurpassed vehicle, the ten-powered vehicle, the great-virtue vehicle, the incomparable vehicle, the rarest of vehicles, the difficult-to-find vehicle, the boundless vehicle, and the omniscient vehicle." O good man! When the Bodhisattva-mahasattva, with his heart of loving-kindness, gives away a vehicle, he should always take such vows. "Also, next, O good man! When the Bodhisattva-mahasattva, with his heart of loving-kindness, gives clothing [to a person], he should always pray: "I shall always share what I now give with all beings, and through this I shall enable all beings to gain the clothing of repentance and let the Dharma-world cover their body and rend asunder the clothes of all twisted views. A robe will be put on parts of the body one foot and six inches. The body that shines is golden; its touch is soft and unobstructed; its colour is brilliant; its skin is soft and delicate. The Eternal Light is unending and is colourless. I pray that all beings will gain the colourless body and part from all colours, and attain Great Nirvana." O good man! When the Bodhisattva-mahasattva gives away clothing, he should definitely take such vows. "Also, next, O good man! When the Bodhisattva-mahasattva, practising loving-kindness, gives flowers, incense, smearing incense, powdered incense or various other kinds of incense, he should always vow: "I share with all

beings what I now give, and I pray that, through this, all beings will attain the Buddha-flower samadhi, and that I shall enable them to put on their head the wonderful wig of the seven Bodhi elements. I pray that all beings will look like the full moon and that their complexion will be wonderful and best. I pray that beings will look one and be adorned with a hundred blessings. I pray that all beings will gain whatever colour they desire to have. I pray that all beings will encounter a good friend of the Way and gain the incense of unhinderedness and do away with all evil smells and defilements. I pray that all beings will be armed with the roots of good and possess rare gems. I pray that, when they see, they will feel happy and have no apprehension or sorrow, that they will all be garbed in every good deed, and that they will have no anxieties. I pray that all beings will be completely perfect in the incense of the precepts and that the fragrance of this incense will fill all the ten directions. I pray that all beings will be perfect in the precepts that are stubborn [tenacious], the unrepenting precepts, and the precepts of all Wisdom; that they will segregate themselves from all acts of precept-violation, that they will gain a state totally away from the precepts [not separate from the precepts], the precepts that are unprecedented, the precepts that need no teacher, the precepts of non-action, the untainted precepts, the last-attained, absolute and all-equal precepts. There shall be undefiled shila [precepts], no favouring, no vengeance, no good, no bad, all will be equal, with no hating and no loving. I pray that all beings will gain the topmost, the Mahayana, and the non-Hinayana precepts. I pray that all beings will be perfect in shilaparamita [transcendent morality] and also be equal to the precepts attained by all Buddhas. I pray that all beings may be suffused with the incense of giving, precept-upholding, forbearance, effort, meditation, and Wisdom. I pray that all beings will be accomplished in the all-wonderful lotus of Great Nirvana, and that the fragrance thereof will fill the ten directions. I pray that all beings will partake of the unsurpassed dishes of Great Nirvana of Mahayana and that they will act as the bee does that calls at a flower, taking along with it only its fragrance. I pray that all beings will achieve a body suffused with the incense of innumerable virtues." O good man! The Bodhisattva-mahasattva should definitely always vow as in the above way when he abides in the heart of loving-kindness and bestows flowers and incense. "Also, next, O good man! When the Bodhisattva-mahasattva, with a heart of loving-kindness, gives away bedding, he should always vow: "I pray that I shall share amongst all beings what I now give and that, through this, all beings will obtain the bed which one sees in the Buddha-country, that they will attain great Wisdom and dwell in the four dhyanas [deep meditative states]; [I pray] that they will sleep on the bed which the Bodhisattva uses, not sleeping on those of the sravakas and pratyekabuddhas. I pray that all beings will sleep on peaceful beds, abandoning the bed of birth-and-death and will sleep in the lion's bed of Great Nirvana. I pray that all beings will gain this bed, and later, for the sake of innumerable other beings, will move from place to place and manifest the lion's play [sport] of all divine powers. I pray that all beings will live in the great palace of Mahayana and will preach the Buddha-Nature for the benefit of all beings. I pray that all beings will sleep in the unexcelled bed, one not subject to worldy dharmas. I pray that all beings will gain the bed of patience, thus parting from birth and death, famine, frost, and hunger. I pray that all beings will attain the bed of fearlessness and part from all the worries of the vengeance of defilement. I pray that all beings will gain the untainted bed and look for the unsurpassed right Way. I pray that all beings will gain the bed of Wonderful Dharma and always be under the protection of a good friend of the teaching. I pray that all beings will be able to sleep on their right side and abide in the Dharma of all Buddhas." O good man! When the Bodhisattva-mahasattva, with a heart of loving-kindness, gives away bedding, he should vow thus. "Also, next, O good man! When the Bodhisattva-mahasattva, abiding in his heart of loving-kindness, gives away a house for someone to live in, he should vow: "I shall share what I now give with all beings and, by this means, I intend to have all beings dwell in the house of Mahayana and practise the Way as practised by good friends of the Way, so that they will be able to practise such as great compassion, the six paramitas, the great, true Enlightenment, the ways and practices that all Bodhisattvas follow, the boundlessly vast ways that are like space. I pray that all beings will attain the right [state of] mind and segregate themselves from all evil thoughts. I pray that all beings will peacefully abide in what is Eternal, Bliss, Self, and Purity, parting from the four inversions [of Truth].

I pray that all beings will learn what is written about the supramundane. I pray that all beings will unfailingly become the vessels of unsurpassed Wisdom. I pray that all beings will enter the house of amrta [immortality]. I pray that all beings will enter the house of Nirvana of Mahayana at their first thought, second thought, and last thought. I pray that all beings will, in the days to come, dwell in the place where the Bodhisattvas live." O good man! When the Bodhisattva-mahasattva, with his heart of loving-kindness, gives away houses, he should definitely always take such vows. "Also, next, O good man! When the Bodhisattva-mahasattva, from his heart of loving-kindness, gives away lamp-light [lamps], he should always pray: "I shall share what I now give with all beings, and through this shall enable beings to be blessed with limitless light and to abide in the Buddhist teaching. I pray that all beings will gain the light of the lamp. I pray that all beings will be blessed with the light that is all-wonderful and best. I pray that all beings will be blessed with eyes that are clear, bright, and unclouded. I pray that all beings will gain the great Light of Wisdom and grasp the fact that they have no self, no phase of a being, man, or life. I pray that all beings will see the pristine Buddha-Nature, which is as of space. I pray that all beings will be blessed with the pure fleshly eye, so that they will be able to see the depths of the worlds of the ten directions, which are as numerous as the sands of the Ganges. I pray that all beings will be blessed with the light of the Buddha and will shine over all the ten directions. I pray that all beings will be blessed with unobstructed insight, so that they will be able to see the pristine Buddha-Nature. I pray that all beings will be blessed with the light of great Wisdom and destroy all gloom and the [state of mind of] the icchantika. I pray that the limited light of all beings will shine over all the innumerable Buddha-lands. I pray that all beings will light the lamp of Mahayana and be released from the lock of the two vehicles. I pray that the light with which all beings will be blessed will break the gloom of ignorance for over a thousand days. I pray that all beings will be blessed with the light of a fire-ball and will do away with the gloom of the 3,000 great-thousand worlds. I pray that all beings will perfect the Five Eyes [i.e. the physical eye, the deva-eye, the eye of Wisdom, the Dharma-eye, and the Eye of a Buddha] and will awaken to the true aspect of all things and attain the teacherless light. I pray that all beings will have no clinging views or ignorance. I pray that all beings will be blessed with the wonderful light of Great Nirvana of the Mahayana and will show all beings the Buddha-Nature." O good man! When the Bodhisattva-mahasattva, from his heart of loving-kindness, gives away lamp-light, he should always vow thus. O good man! "All the roots of good of all sravakas, pratyekabuddhas, Bodhisattvas, and all Tathagatas have as their foundation loving-kindness". O good man! When the Bodhisattva-mahasattva practises the heart of loving-kindness, he gains all such innumerable roots of good as: [mindfulness of] the impure ["asubha-smrti" - awareness of the impurity of the carnal body], [meditation upon] the exhalation and inhalation of the breath ["anapana-smrti"], [awareness of] impermanence, birth-and-death, the four mindfulnesses ["catursmrtyupasthana" - mindfulness of the impurity of the body, mindfulness of feeling as suffering, mindfulness of the mind as impermanent, and mindfulness of dharmas as contingent, without a separate, exclusive nature of their own], the seven expedients, the three views of existence, the twelve links of interdependent arising, meditation on impermanence, etc., "usmagata, ksanti" [patience], "laukikagradharma" [prime-in-the-world condition, or first-of-the-world-root-of-good], "darshana-marga" [the path of seeing], "bhavana-marga" [path of meditation], right-effort-and-at-willness, all roots and powers, the seven factors of Enlightenment [mindfulness, discriminative investigation of Dharma, vigour in practice, supersensuous rapture, pacification of body and mind, concentration, and equanimity], the eight paths [Noble Eightfold Path], the four dhyanas, the four limitless minds, the eight emancipations, the eight superior places, the ten-all-places, knowledge of mind-reading ["para-cetan-paryaya-jnana"], and other divine powers, the utmost-fathoming knowledge, the sravaka-knowledge, the pratyekabuddha-knowledge, Bodhisattva-knowledge, and Buddha-Knowledge. O good man! All such have as their foundation loving-kindness. O good man! For this reason, loving-kindness is true, and is not what is false. "If any person asks about the root of any aspect of good, say that it is loving-kindness. Thus, this is true and not false. "O good man! A person who performs good is [one of] true thinking". True thinking is loving-kindness. Loving-kindness is the Tathagata. Loving-kindness is Mahayana. Mahayana is loving-kindness. Loving-kindness is the Tathagata. The Tathagata is loving-kindness. O good man! Loving-kindness is Great Brahma. Great Brahma is loving-kindness. Loving-kindness is the Tathagata. O good man! Loving-kindness acts as the parent to all beings. The parent is loving-kindness. Loving-kindness is the Tathagata. O good man! Loving-kindness is what exists in the inconceivable world of all Buddhas. What exists in the inconceivable world of all Buddhas is at once loving-kindness. Know that loving-kindness is the Tathagata. O good man! Lovingkindness is the Buddha-Nature of all beings. Such a Buddha-Nature has long been overshadowed by defilements. That is why all beings are unable to see. The Buddha-Nature is loving-kindness. Loving-kindness is the Tathagata. O good man! Loving-kindness is the great firmament. The great firmament is loving-kindness. Loving-kindness is the Tathagata. O good man! Loving-kindness is space. Space is loving-kindness. Loving-kindness is the Tathagata. O good man! Loving-kindness is the Eternal. The Eternal is Dharma. Dharma is the Sangha. The Sangha is loving-kindness. Loving-kindness is the Tathagata. O good man! Loving-kindness is Bliss. Bliss is Dharma. Dharma is the Sangha. The Sangha is loving-kindness. Loving-kindness is the Tathagata. O good man! Loving-kindness is the Pure. The Pure is Dharma. Dharma is the Sangha. The Sangha is loving-kindness. Loving-kindness is the Tathagata. O good man! Loving-kindness is the Self. The Self is Dharma. Dharma is the Sangha. The Sangha is loving-kindness. Loving-kindness is the Tathagata. O good man! Loving-kindness is amrta [immortality]. Amrta is loving-kindness. Loving-kindness is the Buddha-Nature. The Buddha-Nature is Dharma. Dharma is the Sangha. The Sangha is loving-kindness. Loving-kindness is the Tathagata. O good man! Loving-kindness is the supreme Way of all Bodhisattvas. The Way is loving-kindness. Loving-kindness is the Tathagata. O good man! Loving-kindness is the limitless world of the All-Buddha-World-Honoured One. The limitless world is loving-kindness. Know that loving-kindness is the Tathagata." "O good man! If loving-kindness is non-eternal, the non-eternal is loving-kindness. Know that this loving-kindness is that of the sravaka [i.e. inferior, not the Ultimate]. If loving-kindness is suffering, suffering is loving-kindness. Know that this loving-kindness is that of the sravaka. O good man! If loving-kindness is impure, the impure is loving-kindness. Know that this loving-kindness is that of the sravaka. O good man! If loving-kindness is non-Self, non-Self is loving-kindness. Know that this loving-kindness is that of the sravaka. O good man! If loving-kindness is the mind of defilement, the mind of defilement is loving-kindness. Know that this loving-kindness is that of the sravaka. O good man! If loving-kindness cannot be called danaparamita, this is the loving-kindness of non-dana. Know that this loving-kindness is that of the sravaka. And the same with prajnaparamita. O good man! If loving-kindness cannot benefit all beings, any such loving-kindness is none but that of the sravaka. O good man! If loving-kindness does not get into the one mode of the Way, know that this loving-kindness is that of the sravaka. O good man! If loving-kindness [does not] awaken to all dharmas, know that this loving-kindness is that of the sravaka. O good man! If loving-kindness cannot see the Tathagata-Nature, know that this loving-kindness is that of the sravaka. O good man! If loving-kindness is of the "asravas" [spiritual defilements], such loving-kindness of the "asravas" is that of the sravaka. O good man! If loving-kindness is the created, the loving-kindness of the created is that of the sravaka. O good man! If loving-kindness cannot gain the first "bhumi" [first stage of a higher Bodhisattva], that loving-kindness which is not of the first "bhumi" is, know, that of the sravaka. O good man! If loving-kindness acquires the ten powers and the four fearlessnesses of the Buddha, know that this loving-kindness is that of the sravaka. O good man! If loving-kindness [merely] gains the four fruitions of Hinayana practice, this loving-kindness is that of the sravaka." "O good man! If loving-kindness is an is" or not-is", neither is nor not-is", such loving-kindness is not something that can be known by sravakas and pratyekabuddhas. O good man! If loving-kindness is inconceivable, Dharma is inconceivable. The Buddha-Nature is inconceivable. The Tathagata too is inconceivable. O good man! If the Bodhisattva-mahasattva abides in the Mahaparinirvana of Mahayana and practises loving-kindness, he is not asleep even when resting in sleep, because he is all-effort. Though awake, he is not awake, because there is no sleeping with him. Though the gods guard him, there is none that guards, since there is none that does evil. Though sleeping, there is no dreaming of evil, because he has no evil and is far from sleeping. After death, he is born in the heaven of Brahma, but there is no birth, as he is unmolested [unrestricted]. O good man! A person who practises loving-kindness indeed accomplishes such infinite and boundless virtues. O good man! This all-wonderful sutra of Mahaparinirvana, too, accomplishes such infinite and boundless virtues. O good man! The All-Buddha-Tathagata, too, is accomplished in such infinite and boundless virtues." Bodhisattva Kasyapa said to the Buddha: "All thinkings of the Bodhisattva are all true and the sravakas and pratyekabuddhas are not true. Why are all beings not blessed with joy and bliss, with the divine powers of the Bodhisattvas? If all beings do not attain bliss, we can know that the loving-kindness practised by the Bodhisattva is fruitless." The Buddha said: "O good man! It is not the case that the loving-kindness of the Bodhisattva does not generate benefit. O good man! Beings can be those who unfailingly suffer or who do not. To those beings who, without fail, have to suffer, the loving-kindness of the Bodhisattva has no benefit to bestow. This refers to the icchantika. To those for whom suffering is not unfailingly their lot, the loving-kindness of the Bodhisattva generates benefit and all beings enjoy happiness. O good man! It is, for example, like the case of a person who sees in the distance a lion, tiger, leopard, jackal, wolf, rakshasa [flesh-devouring demon] or other creature, and fear comes about of itself, or a person who is out walking at night and sees a pole sticking up out of the ground, and fear arises. O good man! All such people spontaneously gain fear. When beings see a person practising loving-kindness, bliss spontaneously arises. For this reason, we can say that the Bodhisattva's practising of loving-kindness is true thinking and is not without benefit. "O good man! There are innumerable gates to the loving-kindness about which I speak. These are the divine powers. It is as in the case of Devadatta, who instigated Ajatasatru [to kill his own father] and who tried to harm the Tathagata. At that time, I was in Rajagriha, begging alms from house to house. King Ajatasatru let loose a crazed and maddened elephant that he used for protecting his household possessions, and tried to harm me and my disciples. At that time, the elephant trampled and killed a good hundred-thousand people. As the people were being killed, blood flowed. The elephant smelt it and his frenzy increased. I, on seeing the red colour on the clothing of the followers, said: Blood!" And I saw my disciples run. Those who had not yet done away with the mind of desire ran in all directions, except for Ananda. Then the people of Rajagriha wept and cried loudly and said: It is most certain that the Tathagata's life will come to an end today. How can the Truly Enlightened One die in the course of just a day?" Then Devadatta rejoiced: It is very good that Sramana Gautama is going to die. From now on, there truly will be no more of what obtained before. How good it is that things stand thus! I have gained my end!" O good man! With the intention of subduing the household elephant, I entered the samadhi of loving-kindness. I held out my hand and opened it, bringing out five lions from my five fingers. The elephant, on seeing these, released his urine and excrement, and threw his body down upon the ground and worshipped me. O good man! I did not [actually] have any lions on my fingers. Due to the power of good from practising loving-kindness, the elephant was thus subdued. "Also, next, O good man! To enter Nirvana, I took my first steps towards Kusinagara. There were 500 wrestlers who were making the middle part of the road flat. There was a rock there. All were hard at it, trying to shift the rock, but they could not. I felt pity; loving-kindness arose. I then, with the big toe of my foot, lifted up this big stone and kicked it up into the air. It then fell back down upon the palm of my hand. I puffed and made it into powder. It again gathered itself together and became a stone. This was done to kill the wrestlers' arrogant minds. Thus effecting an expedient, I spoke to them of the Way and caused them to aspire to supreme Enlightenment. O good man! The Tathagata, at that time, kicked up that big stone with his toes, threw it up into the air and made it come down again onto my right-hand palm. I puffed on it and turned it into powder and made it join up again. O good man! Know that the power of goodness of loving-kindness enabled all the wrestlers to see this spectacle. Also, next, O good man! Here in South India, there is a big castle called Surparaka. In this castle lived a rich man whose name was Ruci. He led the people. He had already done much good in the past at the sites of innumerable Buddhas. O good man! All the inhabitants of that castle were pursuing wrong faiths, serving the Nirgranthas. As I desired to

teach this rich man, I travelled on to this castle town. The distance was 65 yojanas [yojana=15-20 kilometres]. The Buddha covered the distance on foot, followed by his retinue. This was to teach the people. The Nirgranthas, on hearing that I was coming to the castle-town, thought: If Sramana Gautama comes here, everybody will abandon us and not give any more offerings to us. We shall be hard-pressed. How are we to sustain our lives?" All the Nirgranthas went here and there and said to the people of the castle-town: "Sramana Gautama is about to come here. But all sramanas are people who have deserted their parents and have gone east and west. Wherever they go, the cereal fails and the people suffer from hunger and many have died. Illnesses prevail and there is no means of saving people. Gautama is a vagabond and is followed by evil rakshasas and demons. All are lonely solitaries, without father or mother. They come and praise and follow him. He teaches emptiness. Wherever he goes, there is no peace." The people, on hearing this, became frightened and touched the feet of Nirgrantha, saying: O great one! What are we to do?" Nirgrantha answered: "Sramana Gautama, by nature, loves forests, rivers, ponds, and pure water. If there are any such things, have them destroyed. All of you go out of the town together, fell the trees, do not leave one standing. Fill the rivers, ponds, and wells with dirty things. Close the castle gates. Have soldiers with you, stick to the bulwarks and keep unrelenting watch! He may come, but do not allow him to enter. If he does not come, you will be safe. We, too, shall think of some means and drive him back. All the people heard this and respectfully did as they were told. They felled all the trees, made all the watery places dirty, and strongly armed themselves for protection. O good man! When I arrived there, I could not see any trees or forest; all I could see were the people bearing arms and standing by the castle walls on guard. On seeing this, compassion welled up within me, and with a heart full of loving-kindness I stepped forward. Then all the trees came back and looked just as they had before. And all the trees, whose number was beyond reckoning, grew again. The water of the rivers, ponds, wells, and springs was all pure and full, like blue vaidurya. All kinds of flowers spread out in profusion. The bulwarks looked like dark-blue vaidurya. The people could all easily see me and my retinue. The gates opened by themselves, with nothing stopping them. All the weapons changed into various flowers. Led by Ruci, all the people came out to see me. I then spoke about many things connected with Dharma and caused them all to aspire to unsurpassed Enlightenment. O good man! I, at that time, called forth all those trees artificially and filled the streams, rivers, and ponds with pure water. I made the main castle transform itself and look like dark-blue vaidurya. I let the people all see through me. I made the gates open and caused all the weapons to be transformed into flowers. O good man! Know that the power of good of loving-kindness enabled those people to see such things. "Also, next, O good man! There was in the castle of Sravasti a woman called Vasistha. She had a son whom she loved very much. This son died from an illness. Then sorrow poisoned her [mind] and she became mad. She stripped off all her clothing and felt no shame. She wandered about the crossways and wept and cried: O my child, my child! Where have you gone?" She walked [unceasingly] around the castle-town and there was no stopping her. But this woman had already amassed virtue at the place of the Buddha before. O good man! I could not help but sympathise with her. She saw me and thought of her son [i.e. thought I was her son] and came back to herself. She came up to me and embraced me as though I were her own son. I then said to my follower, Ananda: "Go and fetch some clothing and give it to her." After having given her some clothing, I told her various things of the Way. Having heard about the Way, the woman was overjoyed and aspired to unsurpassed Enlightenment. O good man! I, at that time, was not her son; she was not my mother. Also, there was no embracing. O good man! Know that this was but the power of the good act of loving-kindness, through which that woman saw such things." "Also, next, O good man! At the castle of Varanasi, there was an upasika [female lay Buddhist] called Mahasenadatta, who had already done various good deeds at the places of innumerable Buddhas before. This upasika invited the Sangha [to be her guests] for 90 days in the summer and offered the Sangha medicine. At that time, there was a bhiksu who was seriously ill. A good doctor saw him and prescribed human flesh. If flesh were given, the illness would at once retreat. If not, his life would be at stake. On hearing the words of the doctor, the upasika took some gold and went about the town, saying: "Who can sell me human flesh? I want to buy some. I will give gold equal to the amount of flesh." She went about the town, but nobody gave her any. Then the upasika cut off some from her own thigh. She made a hot meal, scented it, and gave it to the bhiksu. After he had partaken of it, his illness was cured. [But] the pain the upasika had from her wound was so great that she could not stand it and cried out: "Namo Buddhaya, namo Buddhaya!" [adoration of Buddha]. I was in Sravasti at that time and heard her voice. Great pity took hold of me for this upasika. The woman, on receiving some good medicine from me, applied it to her wound. A cure ensued, and all was as before. I told her wonderful things about the Way. On hearing them, she was overjoyed and aspired to supreme Bodhi. O good man! I, at that time, did not go to Varanasi Castle, take medicine with me and smear it over the upasika's body. O good man! Know that all of this came from the power inherent in the good deed of loving-kindness, which enabled the upasika to experience these things. "Also, next, O good man! Devadatta, the evil-hearted one, was greedy beyond measure. He ate a lot of butter and got a headache and a swollen belly, and the pain was so great that he could not endure it. He said: "Namo Buddhaya, namo Buddhaya!" At that time, I was living in the castle-town of Ujjaini. Hearing his voice, pity overtook me. Then Devadatta saw me come to him, rub his head and belly, give him hot salt water and make him partake of it. Having partaken of it, he regained his health. O good man! I did not go to where Devadatta was, rub his head and belly, or give him hot water. O good man! All of this arose from the power of virtue inherent in the good deed of loving-kindness, so that Devadatta was able to see all of this. "Also, next, O good man! In the state of Kosala, there were 500 robbers. This robber-band plundered and wreaked much havoc. Worried over their misdeeds, King Prasenajit dispatched some soldiers who, hiding under cover, caught the band. Having been caught, their eyes were taken out, and they were taken to a dark forest and left there. These robbers had, in the past, planted virtue under the Buddha. Having lost their eyes and in great pain, they cried out: "Namo Buddhaya, namo Buddhaya! We now have no one to help us." They wept and cried out loudly. I was staying at Jetavana at that time. On hearing their cry, loving-kindness overcame me. Then a cool wind sprang up, which blew and filled the cavities of their eyes with fragrant medicine. Then their eyes returned, and there was no difference from before. The robbers opened their eyes and saw that the Buddha was standing before them, preaching Dharma. Having heard the sermon, the robbers aspired to unsurpassed Enlightenment. O good man! I, at that time, did not cause the cool wind to arise and waft fragrant medicine; nor did I stand before them. O good man! Know that this was all the result of the power of the goodness of loving-kindness that made things thus come about. "Also, next, O good man! Prince Vidudabha, due to ignorance, did away with his father and ascended the throne. Also, recalling a long-standing hatred, he killed many of the Shakya clan [i.e. the Buddha's own clan]. 12,000 Shakya women were taken prisoner. As a punishment, their ears and noses were chopped off. Their hands and legs were cut off, and they were thrown into holes and trenches. Then the females, oppressed by pain, said: "Namo Buddhaya, namo Buddhaya! We are helpless." They also wept and cried. All of these females had already amassed virtue in [the time of] Buddhas before. On that occasion I was at the Bamboo Grove. Hearing their cry, loving-kindness overtook me. All the females saw that I, at that time, had come to Kapilavastu and that I was washing their wounds with water and applying medicine to them. Their pain gradually abated, and their ears, noses, hands and legs were restored to them, just as before. I then, in a simple way, spoke about the essence of Dharma and they all aspired to unsurpassed Enlightenment. They were ordained at the place of Mahaprajapati [i.e. the Buddha's aunt and adoptive mother] and received the upasampada. O good man! It was not the case that the Tathagata, at that time, went to Kapilavastu and washed their wounds with water, applied medicine and stopped the pain. O good man! Know that this came about as a result of the power of good inherent in loving-kindness, which enabled the women to experience these things. "It is the same with compassion and sympathetic joy, too. O good man! For this reason, the thinking [mental state] of loving-kindness practised by the Bodhisattva-mahasattva is true and not false. O good man! "Limitless" means "inconceivable". What the Bodhisattva does is inconceivable. What the Buddha does, is also inconceivable. The same applies to this Mahayana Great Nirvana Sutra, too, which is likewise inconceivable."

Chapter Twenty-Two: On Pure Actions 2

"Also, next, O good man! The Bodhisattva-mahasattva, having practised loving-kindness, compassion, and sympathetic joy attains the stage of the best-loved only son. O good man! Why do we call this stage that of the "best-loved" and also "only son"? A father and mother, for example, greatly rejoice when they see their son in peace. The same with the Bodhisattvamahasattva who abides in this soil ["bhumi"]. He sees all beings just as though they were his only son. On seeing a person practising good, he greatly rejoices. So we call this stage that of the best-loved. "O good man! As an example: a father and mother become worried in their hearts when they see their son ill. Commiseration [anguish] poisons their hearts; their minds cannot get away from the illness. It is thus, too, with the Bodhisattva-mahasattva who abides in this stage. When he sees beings bound up by the illness of defilement, his heart aches. He is worried, as if over his own son. Blood comes from all the pores of his skin. That is why we call this stage that of the only son. "O good man! A person, in his childhood, will pick up earth, dirty things, tiles, stones, old bones, and bits of wood and put them into his mouth, at which his father and mother, fearful of the harm that may ensue therefrom, take hold of the child with their left hand and take these things away from him with their right. It is the same with the Bodhisattva of this stage. He sees that all beings have not grown up to the stage of the Dharma-Body and that non-good is performed with body, mouth and mind. The Bodhisattva sees this and extracts [the harmful things] with the hand of Wisdom. He does not wish any person to repeat birth and death, receiving thereby suffering and worry. Hence, this stage is also called the "bhumi" of an only son. "O good man! When, for example, a son dies and the father and mother have to part from their son whom they love, their hearts so ache that they feel that they themselves will die too. It is the same with the Bodhisattva. When he sees an icchantika [person of the most deluded, twisted views on life] falling into hell, he himself wishes to be born there, too. Why so? Because this icchantika, as he experiences pain, may gain a moment of repentance when I speak to him of Dharma in various ways and enable him to gain a thought of good. Hence, this stage is called that of an only

son. "O good man! As an example: all a father and mother have is their only son. Asleep or awake, while walking, standing, sitting or reclining, their mind is always on their son. If any sin occurs, they give kindly advice, and the boy is thus guided not to do evil again. It is the same with the Bodhisattva-mahasattva, too. When he sees beings falling into the realms of hell, hungry ghosts, and animals, his mind is ever upon them and not away from them. He may see them doing all kinds of evil, and yet he does not become angry or punish them with evil things. Hence, this stage is called the "bhumi" of an only son." Bodhisattva Kasyapa said to the Buddha: "O World-Honoured One! What the Buddha speaks is closely guarded words. I am shallow in Wisdom. How can I arrive at the meaning? If it is the case that all Bodhisattvas abide in the stage of the only son and can do all such things, why was it that the Tathagata, when born as a king, practising the Bodhisattva Way, took the life of a Brahmin of a [certain] place? If this stage was gained, there must be some protection. If it was not yet attained, why did he not fall into hell? If all beings are viewed as an only son, like Rahula, why did you say to Devadatta: "You eat the tears and spittle of one ignorant and shameless!"? Why was he made to hear this and to entertain anger and enmity and evil thoughts, so as to cause blood to come out of the Buddha's body? When Devadatta had committed this evil, the Tathagata went on to prophesy, saying: "Devadatta will fall into hell, where punishment will persist for a kalpa." O World-Honoured One! Subhuti has attained the "bhumi" of space. Whenever he enters a castle and begs for food, he always looks at the person. If he should get any feeling of displeasure or jealousy, he ceases begging. Even if he is excessively hungry, he will not go and beg. Why not? This Subhuti thinks: "I remember that in days gone by I gained an evil thought at a place that was a field of merit, and as a result I fell into a great hell, where I suffered from various pains. I may now not gain anything to eat all day, but even so, I will not have any ill-will raised against me, so that I would have to fall into hell and suffer from various mental afflictions." He also thinks in this way: "If people hate to see me standing, I shall sit all day long and not stand; if people do not like to see me sitting, I shall stand the whole day and not move. The same with walking and reclining." This Subhuti thinks thus so as to protect people. How could things be otherwise with the Bodhisattva? How could a Bodhisattva who has attained the "bhumi" of an only son, O Tathagata, speak thus rudely and cause people [to entertain] extremely heavy ill-will?" The Buddha said to Kasyapa: "Now, you should not use such harsh words and say that the Buddha-Tathagata causes any kind of worry of defilement [any mental affliction due to the "asravas"] to arise within beings. O good man! The proboscis of a mosquito could sooner gain the bottom of the sea than that the Tathagata would ever occasion any worry of defilement to any being. O good man! The great earth could sooner turn out to be immaterial, or water become solid, fire cool, wind static, the Three Jewels, Buddha-Nature and space impermanent, than that the Tathagata would ever occasion a cause of worry to any being. O good man! Even those who have committed the four heavy transgressions, or an icchantika, or those who slander Wonderful Dharma, could sooner attain in this present life the ten powers, the four fearlessnesses, the 32 signs of perfection, and the 80 minor marks of excellence than that the Tathagata would ever occasion the worry of defilement to any being. O good man! Even sravakas and pratyekabuddhas could sooner exist eternally than that the Tathagata would ever occasion the worry of defilement to any being. O good man! All the Bodhisattvas of the ten abodes could sooner commit the four grave offences, become icchantikas and slander Wonderful Dharma than that the Tathagata would ever give occasion for defilement worry to any being. O good man! All beings could even soooner cut off the Buddha-Nature and the Tathagata enter the last of Nirvanas than that the Tathagata would ever, even once, give occasion for the worry of defilement to any being. O good man! One could sooner catch hold of the wind with a rope, or crush iron with one's teeth, or destroy Mount Sumeru with a [finger]-nail than that the Tathagata would ever occasion the worry of defilement to any being. One could sooner live with vipers, or put both hands into the mouth of a famished lion, or wash one's body with the charcoal of khadira, than ever say that the Tathagata occasions the worry of defilement to any being. O good man! The Tathagata truly extirpates the bond of worry of all beings and does not occasion the worry of

defilement to any of them. "O good man! You say that the Tathagata, in days gone by, killed a Brahmin. O good man! "The Bodhisattva-mahasattva would not purposely kill an ant" [a large, winged black ant]. How could he kill a Brahmin? "The Bodhisattva always, through various means, gives unending life to beings." O good man! Now a person who gives food gives life. When the Bodhisattvamahasattva practises the danaparamita, he always gives beings unlimited life. O good man! By upholding the precept of non-harming, one gains a long life. When the Bodhisattva-mahasattva practises the shilaparamita, he gives all beings unlimited life. O good man! If one is mindful of one's speech and does not do anything wrong, one gains a long life. When the Bodhisattvamahasattva practises the ksantiparamita [perfect patience], he always teaches beings not to give rise to any thought of enmity, to do what is straight, to refrain from what is twisted, and thus to look to one's own self and not dispute with others. And through this one is blessed with a long life. Because of this, when the Bodhisattva-mahasattva practises the ksanti-paramita, he always gives beings long life. O good man! If one makes effort and does good, one will be blessed with long life. When the Bodhisattva-mahasattva practises the virya-paramita [perfected vigour, effort], he always urges beings to do good. Having done as told, those beings are blessed with a long life. Thus, when the Bodhisattva practises the viryaparamita, he already gives beings an immeasurably long life. When the Bodhisattva-mahasattva practises dhyanaparamita [perfected meditation], he urges beings to develop the all-equal mind. Having practised this, beings will be blessed with long life. Hence, when the Bodhisattva practises the dhyanaparamita, he already gives beings an immeasurably long life. O good man! A person who is not indolent regarding Dharma gains a long life. When the Bodhisattva-mahasattva practises the prajnaparamita [perfected Wisdom], he urges all beings to practise all kinds of good dharmas [things] and is not indolent. Having thus practised, beings in consequence gain a long life. For this reason, when the Bodhisattva practises the prajnaparamita, he already bestows on beings unlimited life. O good man! Because of this, the Bodhisattva-mahasattva does not take the lives of any being to the end. "O good man! You asked if one could gain this "bhumi" or not when one has killed a Brahmin. O good man! I already gained it. Out of love, I took his life. It was not done with an evil mind. O good man! For example, a father and mother have an only son. They love him greatly and act against the law. At that time, the father and mother, out of fear, drive one away or kill. Though they drove [him] away or killed [him], they had no evil mind. In just the same way, the Bodhisattva-mahasattva acts likewise for reasons of protecting Wonderful Dharma. Should beings slander Mahayana, he applies kindly lashings, in order to cure them. Or he may take life in order that what obtained in the past could be mended, thus seeing to it that the law [Dharma] could be accorded with. The Bodhisattva always thinks: "How might I best make beings aspire to faith? I shall always act as is best fitted to the occasion." The Brahmin fell into Avichi Hell after his death. He gained three thoughts. The first thought was: "Where have I come from to be born here in this way?" And the realisation dawned on him to the effect that he had been born there from the world of men. His second thought was: "What is this place where I have now been born?" The realisation dawned that this was Avichi Hell. The third thought [then] arose: "Through what causal concatenations have I been born here?" He then came to realise that things had taken this turn because of his slandering of the vaipulya Mahayana sutras and by his not believing, and by his being killed by the king - thus had he been born there. Thinking in this way, respect arose towards the Mahayana vaipulya sutras. Then, after his death, he was born in the world of Tathagata Amrta-Drum. There he lived for 10 kalpas. O good man! I thus, in days gone by, gave this person a life of 10 kalpas. How could it be said that I killed him?" "O good man! There is a man who digs up the ground, mows the grass, fells trees, cuts corpses into pieces, slanders and beats [people]. Would this cause him to be born in hell?" Bodhisattva Kasyapa said to the Buddha: "O World-Honoured One! From what I gather from what you said, this would be a cause of hell. Why? It is as the Buddha once said to the sravakas: "O all you Bhiksus! Do not bear any ill will towards any grass or trees. Why not? Because, due to an evil mind [bad thoughts], all beings fall into hell." Then the Buddha praised Bodhisattva Kasyapa: "Well said, well said! It is as you say. Hold fast to the precepts. O good man! If a person falls into hell through an evil mind, this tells us that the Bodhisattva does not have any evil mind. Why

not? Because the Bodhisattva-mahasattva always pities and desires to benefit all beings, down to insects and ants. Why? Because he is versed in all causal relations and expedients. Through the power of expedients, he desires to cause beings to plant the seeds of all varieties of virtue. O good man! For this reason, I, at that time, took life as the best expedient. Yet I did not entertain any evil in my mind. O good man! According to the doctrine of the Brahmins, there is no karmic result even if one kills tens of wagons of ants. All such insects and animals that harm man, such as the mosquito, gadfly, flea, louse, cat, lion, tiger, wolf and bear may be killed in an amount as great as ten wagon-loads [according to the Brahmins]. Such beings as demons, rakshasas, kumbhandas, kataputanas and all those made and dried-up devils who harm human beings may well be killed, without any evil result arising from the killing [according to the Brahmins]. But if one kills an evil person, karmic consequences ensue. If one kills and there is no repentance that follows, one gains life in the hell of hungry ghosts [according to the Brahmins]. If one repents and fasts for three days, the sin dies out and nothing remains behind. If any harm is caused to an upadhyaya [teacher of the Vedas, grammar, etc.], to one's father, mother, a woman or a cow, one will have to go to hell for innumerable thousands of years [according to the Brahmins].

"O good man! The Buddha and Bodhisattva see three categories of killing, which are those of the grades 1) low, 2) medium, and 3) high. Low applies to the class of insects and all kinds of animals, except for the transformation body of the Bodhisattva who may present himself as such. O good man! The Bodhisattva-mahasattva, through his vows and in certain circumstances, gets born as an animal. This is killing beings of the lowest class. By reason of harming life of the lowest grade, one gains life in the realms of hell, animals or hungry ghosts and suffers from the downmost "duhkha" [pain, mental or physical]. Why so? Because these animals have done somewhat of good. Hence, one who harms them receives full karmic returns for his actions. This is killing of the lowest grade. The medium grade of killing concerns killing [beings] from the category of humans up to the class of anagamins. This is middle-grade killing. As a result, one gets born in the realms of hell, animals or hungry ghosts and fully recieves the karmic consequences befitting the middle grade of suffering. This is medium-grade killing. Top-rank killing relates to killing one's father or mother, an arhat, pratyekabudda, or a Bodhisattva of the last established state. This is top-rank killing. In consequence of this, one falls into the greatest Avichi Hell [the most terrible of all the hells] and endures the karmic consequences befitting the highest level of suffering. This is top-grade killing. O good man! A person who kills an icchantika does not suffer from the karmic returns due to the killings of the three kinds named above. O good man! All those Brahmins are of the class of the icchantika. For example, such actions as digging the ground, mowing the grass, felling trees, cutting up corpses, ill-speaking, and lashing do not call forth karmic returns. Killing an icchantika comes within the same category. No karmic results ensue. Why not? Because no Brahmins and no five laws to begin with faith, etc. are involved here [Maybe: no Brahmins are concerned with the "five roots" of faith, vigour, mindfulness, concentration, and Wisdom]. For this reason, killing [of this kind] does not carry one off to hell. "O good man! You asked why the Tathagata spoke ill of Devadatta to the effect that he was an ignorant person who gulped down spittle. You should not speak ill of this, either. Why not? It is not possible to conceive [i.e. fully understand] what the Buddha-World-Honoured One says. O good man! True words are loved in the world; or there are cases where what is contrary to the time [occasion] and law [Buddhist teaching] do not benefit a person. I never speak thus. O good man! There are situations in which rough, untrue, untimely, unlawful words are not loved by him who hears them, and do not bring benefit. I also do not speak such words. O good man! And there are times when, though the language be harsh, it is true and not false. At such a time, if this teaching gives benefit to all beings, I always speak, even if the listener is not pleased [to hear my words]. Why? Because the All-Buddha, the Arhat-and-Samyaksambuddha [Fully Awakened One] knows the best expedient [for any given situation]. "O good man! I once passed hours in the wild, in hamlets and forests. In the forest, there was a demon called "Wild". He only ate human flesh and blood, and many a being was killed. And one person from the village was eaten every day. O good man! I, at that time, was speaking expansively about the essence of

Dharma. But he [the demon] was rude, evil, ignorant, and had no Wisdom, and did not lend an ear to what I was saying regarding Dharma. I then transformed myself into a very powerful demon, shook his palace so mightily that there was no peace. Then that demon came out of his palace with his kindred to challenge me. On seeing me, he lost heart. Frightened, he fell to the ground, wriggled and moaned, and looked as though he were dead. Pitying him, I rubbed his body with my hand. He regained himself, sat up and said: "I am glad that I have regained my body and life. This great god possesses great virtue. Being compassionate, he pardons my hateful acts." He gained a good [state of] mind and faith at my place [in my presence]. I then re-assumed my body as the Tathagata and spoke to him about the various essentials of Dharma. And I made that demon receive from me the precept of non-harming. "And that day there was a rich man in the village in the wilds, who was about to die. The villagers brought him to the demon. The demon, after receiving him, gave him to me. I got him and named this rich man "Hand-Rich-Man". Then the demon said to me: "O World-Honoured One! My people and I feed on flesh and blood and [thus] sustain [our] life. I have now received this shila [rule of moral conduct]. How am I to live?" I replied: "From now on, I shall give orders to the sravakas. Follow them and go to where they practise the Way, and I shall make them give you things to eat." O good man! For this reason, I instituted for the bhiksus this shila: "You shouuld henceforward give food to the field demon. If there are those who, living themselves, cannot give, such are - you should know - not my disciples, but the relatives of the heavenly Mara [the devil Mara's abode is in heaven]." O good man! The Tathagata puts forth such diverse expedients so as to teach and subdue beings. It is not particularly to cause fear. O good man! I also beat the law-protecting demon with a wooden stick. And at one time I was on top of a hill. I pushed a sheep-headed demon down the hill. Also, when in the top of a tree, I beat a monkey-protecting demon, and [another time] I caused the treasure-guarding elephant to see five lions, and made vajra-deva fear Satyakanirgrantha. And [another time] I thrust a needle into an arrow-hair demon. Though I did all these things, there were no demons that were harmed or killed. It was only to get them to rest in peace in Wonderful Dharma.

Thus did I perform all such expedients. "O good man! I did not at that time speak ill of Devadatta and did not make him feel ashamed. He, too, was not so ignorant as to gulp down another person's spittle. Nor did he fall into Avichi Hell, there to suffer punishment for a kalpa. Nor did he disrupt the peace of the Sangha or cause blood to come out of the Buddha's body. Nor did he commit the four grave offences, nor did he slander the Wonderful Dharma of the Mahayana sutras. He is no icchantika, no sravaka, and no pratyekabuddha. O good man! Devadatta does not belong to the class of the world of the sravakas or pratyekabuddhas. All this is only what all Buddhas can know. O good man! For this reason, do not reproach [me] and say: "Why should the Tathagata impeach Devadatta, speak ill of him, and make Devadatta feel ashamed?" Do not doubt things that concern the world of all Buddhas." Bodhisattva Kasyapa said to the Buddha: "O World-Honoured One! As an example: when we decoct sugar cane many times, we gain various grades of taste. The case is so with me. Following as often the words of the Buddha, we gain the various kinds of dharma. These are those [dharmas] of fleeing the world, of abandoning desire, of quietude, and of Enlightenment. O World-Honoured One! Another example: if we burn, beat, smelt and temper gold, it becomes all the brighter and purer, more harmonious, soft, wonderful in its colour, and priceless. And later gods and men prize it highly as treasure. O World-Honoured One! The same is the case with the Tathagata, too. If we carefully and respectfully ask questions, we arrive at the depths of the meaning. By practising the Way profoundly, one can uphold it, and innumerable beings will aspire to unexcelled Enlightenment and [one] is looked up to and respected by humans and gods." Then the Buddha spoke in praise of Bodhisattva Kasyapa: "Well said, well said! O Bodhisattvamahasattva! To benefit all beings, you put such questions of deep signification to the Tathagata. O good man! For this reason, I follow your lead and speak about the deepest depths of the Mahayana vaipulya. This is the stage of an only son of dearest love." Bodhisattva Kasyapa said to the Buddha: "O World-Honoured One! If all Bodhisattvas practise the Ways of loving-kindness, compassion, and sympathetic joy and attain the stage of an only son, what is the stage that one attains when one practises the mind of equanimity?" The Buddha said: "Well said, well

said! You know well when to ask. You see what I desire to speak about and you ask. When the Bodhisattva-mahasattva practises the mind of equanimity, he attains the All-Void All-Equal stage, and becomes like Subhuti. O good man! When the Bodhisattvamahasattva dwells in the All-Void All-Equal "bhumi", he no longer sees parents, brothers, sisters, children, relatives, good friends of the Way, enemies, those who are hostile or friendly, those who are neither friendly nor antagonistic, down to the five skandhas, the 18 realms, the 12 spheres, beings, and life. O good man! As an illustration, it is like space, in which we see no parents, brothers, wife and children, down to beings and life. It is the same regarding all things. There can be no parents and life. Thus does the Bodhisattva-mahasattva see all things. His mind is all-equal like space. Why? Because he thoroughly practises the dharma of the Void ["shunyata"]." Bodhisattva Kasyapa said to the Buddha: "O World-Honoured One! What do you mean by the Void?" "O good man! Of the Void, there are such as the internal, external, internal-external Void, the Void of created existence, the Void of the uncreated, the Void of beginninglessness, the Void of nature, the Void of non-possession, the Void of "Paramartha-satya", the Void-Void, and the Great Void. "How does the Bodhisattva-mahasattva experience the internal Void? This Bodhisattvamahasattva meditates on the Void of the internal elements ["adhyatma-shunyata"]. That is to say that the internal elements [the six sense-organs] are void. This means to say that there are no parents, no persons with ill-will or on friendly terms [with one], none who is indifferent, no beings, life, Eternal, Bliss, Self, and Purity, Tathagata, Dharma, Sangha, and all good. In these internal elements, there is the Buddha-Nature. Yet this Buddha-Nature exists neither within nor without. Why not? Because the Buddha-Nature is eternal and experiences no change. This is what we mean when we say that the Bodhisattva-mahasattva meditates on the internal elements. "The same applies in the case of the external Void ["bahirdha-shunyata": the six sense-fields]. No internal elements exist. "It is the same with the internal-external Void ["adhyatma-bahirdha-shunyata"]. O good man! There are only the Tathagata, Dharma, and Sangha, and the Bddha-Nature. This has no two aspects of the Void. Why not? For the four are the Eternal, Bliss, Self, and the Pure. That is why we do not say that these four are void. We call this the All-Void of both the internal and the external. "O good man! We say "the Void of created existence ["samskrta-shunyata" - the voidness of formed, conditioned, assembled phenomena]. Whatever is created is all void. Thus there can be the internal Void, the external Void, the the internal-external Void, the Void of the Eternal, Bliss, Self, and the Pure, the Void of life, of beings, of the Tathagata, Dharma, and Sangha, and of "Paramartha-satya." Of these, the Buddha-Nature is not anything created. Hence, the Buddha-Nature does not belong to the category of the Void of created existents. "O good man! How does the Bodhisattva-mahasattva meditate on the Void of the uncreated ["asamskrta-shunyata"]? Those things of the category of the uncreated are all void. They are so-called impermanence, suffering, the impure, the non-Self, the five skandhas, the 18 realms, the 12 spheres, life, beings, the characteristics, the created, the leakable ["asravas"], the internal elements, and the external elements. Of the uncreated, the four which begin with the Buddha are not the uncreated. As the nature is good itself, it is not the uncreated; as it is eternal, it is not the created. This is how the Bodhisattva meditates on the Void of the uncreated. "How does the Bodhisattva-mahasattva meditate on the Void of the beginningless ["anavaragrashunyata"]? This Bodhisattva-mahasattva sees that birth and death are beginningless. Hence, he sees that all are void and quiet. We say Void. That is to say that the Eternal, Bliss, Self, and the Pure are all void and quiet, with nothing that changes. So are life, beings, the Three Jewels, and the uncreated, in all of which the Bodhisattva sees the beginningless Void. "How does the Bodhisattva meditate on the Void of nature ["prakrti-shunyata" - Emptiness of primordial matter]? This Bodhisattva-mahasattva sees that the original nature of all elements is all void. These are the five skandhas, the 18 realms, the 12 spheres, the Eternal, the non-Eternal, suffering, Bliss, the Pure, the impure, Self, and non-Self. In all such things, he sees no nature of their own. This is how the Bodhisattva-mahasattva meditates on the Void of nature." "How does the Bodhisattva-mahasattva meditate on the Void of non-possession? This is like speaking of a house being empty when there is no child inside. He sees here an uttermost void. There is no friendliness, no love. The ignorant say that in all directions what there is is peace; a poor man says that all is void.

All such presumptions are either void or non-void. When the Bodhisattva meditates, it is as with the poor man who says that all is void. This is how the Bodhisattva-mahasattva meditates on the Void of non-possession. "How does the Bodhisattva-mahasattva meditate on "Paramartha-shunyata" [the Void of "Paramartha" - of Ultimate Reality]? O good man! When the Bodhisattva-mahasattva meditates on the "Paramartha", he sees that when this eye comes about, it does so from nowhere; when it dies out, it dies out to nowhere. What originally was not, now is; what was turns back to nowhere. As we look into the real nature, we see that what there is is eyelessness and masterlessness. All other things are as in the case of the eye. What is the Void of the "Paramartha"? It is seeing that there is action and the result thereof, but no maker. Such a doctrine of voidness is the Void of the "Paramartha". This is how the Bodhisattva-mahasattva meditates on the Void of the "Paramartha". "How does the Bodhisattva-mahasattva meditate on the Void-Void? This Void-Void is where the sravakas and pratyekabuddhas get lost. O good man! This is "is" and this is "not-is". This is the Void-Void. This is this; this is not "this-is-this". This is the Void-Void. O good man! The Bodhisattva of the ten "bumis" [stages] is only able to know a little of this, which might well be likened to the size of a dust-mote. How much less must it be with others! O good man! Thus, the Void-Void is not equal to the Void-Void samadhi of the sravakas. This is the Void-Void which the Bodhisattva meditates upon. "O good man! How does the Bodhisattva-mahasattva meditate on the Great Void? O good man! The Great Void is the prajnaparamita [perfection of Wisdom]. This is the Great Void. O good man! Attaining such a gate of the Void, the Bodhisattva-mahasattva abides in a "bhumi" equal to space. "O good man! As I now, here amongst the congregated, speak about all these kinds of Void, Bodhisattva-mahasattvas as numerous as the sands of ten Ganges are able to gain the "bhumi" equal to space. O good man! Abiding in this "bhumi", nothing hinders the Bodhisattva-mahasattva in anything; no clinging binds him and no anguish takes hold of his mind. Hence, we call it the "bhumi" equal to space. O good man! As an illustration, this is as with space, which does not greedily cling to any lovable colour and does not become angry with a colour wihich is displeasing. The same with the Bodhisattva-mahasattva who abides in this "bhumi". No mind of desire or anger arises towards good or bad colours. O good man! This is like space, which is vast and great, with nothing to equal it, taking in all things. It is the same with the Bodhisattvamahasattva abiding in this "bhumi". It is vast and great, so that nothing can bear comparison to it, and it can indeed take in all things. For this reason, we can truly call it the "bhumi" equal to space. O good man! When the Bodhisattva-mahasattva abides in this "bhumi", he can see and know all things. Be it actions, circumstantial factors, the nature and characteristics [of things], causes, by-causes, the minds of beings, the sense-roots, dhyana, vehicle, good friends of the Way, upholding of the precepts, or whatever is given - all is seen or known. "Also, next, O good man! The Bodhisattva-mahasattva, abiding in this "bhumi", knows and yet does not see. How does he know? According to the self-fasting [self-abnegation] doctrine, one throws one's own body into deep water, into fire, jumps from a high precipice, always stands on one leg, bares one's body and exposes it to heat, always sleeps on ashes, thorns, woven rafters [mats], harmful grass, cow dung, and wears coarse hemp clothing, dung-defiled woolen cloth left in a graveyard, kambala cloth, reindeer or deer skin, fodder clothing; [such fakirs] feed on vegetables, fruit, lotus roots, oil dregs, cow dung, and roots and fruits. When they go to beg food, it is only to one house. If the householder says that he has nothing to give them, they desist. Even if people later call them back, they do not look back. They do not eat salted flesh or the five varieties of the cow's products [i.e. fresh milk, cream, fresh butter, clarified butter, sarpirmanda]. What they consume is dreg-juice and hot water. They uphold shilas [moral prohibitions] vis-à₁-vis cows, hens, dogs, and pheasants. They smear ashes over their bodies, wear their hair long, worship heaven by sacrificing and killing sheep, first saying a charm. "For four months they worship fire and for seven days they partake of the wind, offer hundreds and thousands and billions of flowers to the devas, and all that they desire is to have their wishes fulfilled. He [the Bodhisattva] knows that all such things can never be the cause of supreme emancipation. This is knowing. What does he not see? The Bodhisattva-mahasattva sees that not one person attains true emancipation by such acts. This is not seeing."

"Also, next, O good man! The Bodhisattva-mahasattva both sees and knows. What does he see? He sees that beings perform twisted practices and unfailingly fall into hell. This is seeing. What does he know? He knows that all beings come out of hell and gain life as a human, practise the danaparamita and become perfect in the other paramitas. He knows that these people unfailingly attain right Enlightenment. This is knowing. "Also, next, O good man! The Bodhisattva-mahasattva further sees and knows. What does he see? He sees the Eternal and the non-Eternal, suffering, Bliss, the Pure and the non-Pure, the Self and the non-Self. This is seeing. What does he know? He knows that all Tathagatas definitely do not enter Nirvana [i.e. do not truly die and desert the world]. The body of the Tathagata is adamantine and indestructible. It is not one of defilement. It is also not a body that emits bad smells and decays. Thus does he know. Also, he knows that all beings possess the Buddha-Nature. This is knowing. "Also, next, O good man! The Bodhisattva-mahasattva also knows that the mind of beings achieves faith. These beings seek Mahayana. He knows that they float down, or float back, or abide rightly. He knows that beings do gain the other shore. Floating down refers to common mortals; floating back refers to the shrotapanna up to the pratyekabuddha; right-abiding refers to all Bodhisattvas, and attaining the other shore to the Tathagata, the Arhat, the Samyaksambuddha. This is knowing. What does the Bodhisattva see? He abides in the teaching of the Mahayana Great Nirvana Sutra, practises pure actions, and, with the pure heavenly ["deva"] eye, sees that all beings commit evil through body, mouth and mind and fall into the realms of hell, animals, and hungry ghosts. He sees that beings who do good die and are re-born in the worlds of heaven or humans. There are beings who move from gloom to gloom, from gloom to light, from light to gloom, and then from light to light. This is seeing. "Also, next, O good man! The Bodhisattva-mahasattva also knows and sees. He sees that all beings practise the way of the body, observe shila [morality], and practise the way of the mind, and that of Wisdom. He sees that a person who does deeds replete with evil in this present life, or through greed, ill-will and ignorance, harvests karmic returns in hell. He sees a person practising good in body, upholding shila, cultivating the mind, practising the way of

Wisdom, and being recompensed in this life to some degree and not falling into hell. How can this action gain rewards in the present life? This comes about when a person confesses all the evils he has done, repents, and does not commit them any more; when he repents fully, makes offerings to the Three Treasures, and always reproaches himself. This person, due to his good deeds, does not fall into hell, but receives in this life karmic returns such as headaches, pain in the eyes, stomach and back, an untimely death, criticism, slander, lashings, prison or fetters, hunger, and poverty. He knows that light karmic returns are visited upon a person in this present life. This is knowing. What does he see? The Bodhisattva-mahasattva sees that a certain person does not practise the Way in body, shila, mind, and Wisdom, and that that person performs petty bad deeds. And all such actions call forth returns in the present life. This person does not confess his petty bad deeds, does not reproach himself, does not repent, and feels no fear. Such action increases, and he receives his karmic results in hell. This is seeing. "Also, there is the case where one knows but does not see. How does one know and not see? All beings know that they have the Buddha-Nature, but, overshadowed by defilements, cannot see it. This is knowing but not seeing. Also, there is the situation where one knows and sees somewhat. The Bodhisattva-mahasattvas of the ten "bhumis" know that all beings have the Buddha-Nature, but they cannot see it clearly. This is like on a dark night, where one cannot see clearly. Also, there is both seeing and knowing. This is the situation of the All-Buddha-Tathagata, where he both sees and knows. "Also, there are cases in which one sees and knows, and, not seeing, one does not know. Seeing and knowing refers to what pertains in the world of letters, language, men and women, vehicles, pots, trays, houses, castles, clothing, eating, drinking, mountains, rivers, gardens, forests, beings, and life. This is seeing and knowing. What is not seeing and not knowing? This is all the minute words of the sages themselves, and men and women, and gardens and forests, in which these do not exist. This is not seeing and not knowing. "Also, there is a situation in which one knows but does not see. One knows where to give, where to dedicate [offerings], one who receives, and the fact that results accrue from the things that have been done. This is knowing. How does one not see? There are cases where one does [not] see what is given, the place whereto dedication is made, one who is given, and the results of causality. This is not seeing. The Bodhisattva-mahasattva knows eight types of knowing. This is what is known by the five eyes of the Tathagata." Bodhisattva Kasyapa said to the Buddha: "O World-Honoured One! What profit does the Bodhisattva-mahasattva gain from such kinds of knowing?" The Buddha said: "O good man! The Bodhisattva-mahasattva gains the four unhinderednesses ["catasrah-pratisamvidah" - analytical knowledges, discriminations] from such knowings, which are unhinderedness in: 1) Dharma ["dharma-pratisamvit"], 2) meaning ["artha-pratisamvit"], 3) language ["nirukti-pratisamvit"], and 4) eloquence ["pratibhana-pratisamvit " - ready wit]. "In the unhindered knowledge of dharmas, one knows all things and their names. "In the unhindered knowledge of meaning, one knows all about the meaning of things [of the Dharma], arriving at the meaning by the names established for them. "In unhindered knowledge of language, one knows the morphological, phonological, prosodical, and oratorical aspects of words. "In unhindered knowledge of eloquence, the Bodhisattva-mahasattva has no hindrance in oratory, and is unmoved. He has no fear, and it is difficult to defeat him. O good man! If the Bodhisattva thus sees and knows, we may say that he is armed with the four-fold unhindered knowledge. "Also, next, O good man! In unhindered knowledge of Dharma, the Bodhisattva-mahasattva knows the dharmas of the sravaka, pratyekabuddha, Bodhisattva, and all Buddhas. "In unhindered knowledge of the meaning, he knows that, though there are three vehicles, these enter into one and he sees therein no distinction. "In unhindered knowledge of language, the Bodhisattva-mahasattva gives varyious names to a thing. Even in the course of innumerable kalpas, one could not fully name them all. The sravakas and pratyekabuddhas are not equal to this. "In unhindered knowledge of eloquence, the Bodhisattva-mahasattva, in the course of innumerable kalpas, talks about all dharmas to all beings, and his speech is endless in regard to names and meanings, and all about ideas. Also, next, O good man! By unhindered knowledge of dharmas is meant that, though the Bodhisattva-mahasattva is versed in all dharmas, he has no clinging to them. "By unhindered knowledge of the meaning is meant that though the Bodhisattva-mahasattva is versed in all meanings, he has no clinging to them. "By unhindered knowledge of language is meant that though the Bodhisattva-mahasattva knows the meaning [relevant language], he has no clinging to this. "Unhindered knowledge of eloquence means that though the Bodhisattva-mahasattva knows that this eloquence is best, he has no clinging to it. Why? "If one clings, one is not called a Bodhisattva." Bodhisattva Kasyapa said to the Buddha: "O World-Honoured One! If one does not cling, one cannot come to know of Dharma. If one knows of Dharma, this is nothing but clinging. If one does not cling, there can be no knowing. How can the Tathagata say that one knows Dharma and yet does not cling?" The Buddha said: "O good man! Clinging is not unhinderedness [unobstructed knowledge]. Where there is no clinging, there is unhinderedness. O good man! Hence, any Bodhisattva who has any clinging is not one unhindered. If not unhindered, he is no Bodhisattva. Know that such a person is a common mortal. "Why do we say that clinging is of the common mortal? All common mortals cling to matter ["rupa" - body, form] down to consciousness ["vijnana"; the five skandhas are here meant]. When one clings to matter, this clinging evokes a mind of greed; because of greed, one gets bound up by matter down to consciousness. Because of such bondage, one cannot escape from the great suffering of birth, ageing, illness, death, apprehension, and sorrow, nor from all the [various] kinds of defilement. Hence, due to his clinging, we call a person a common mortal. For this reason, no common mortal possesses the fourfold unhindered knowledge. "O good man! The Bodhisattva-mahasattva has already, over innumerable asamkhyas of kalpas past, seen through the characteristics of all things; through knowing, he knows the meaning. As he knows the characteristics of all things and the meanings, he does not cling to matter. The same with consciousness, too. With no clinging, the Bodhisattva does not have any greed for matter. Nor does he have greed for consciousness. Not having any greed, he is not bound by matter. Nor is he bound by consciousness. Because he is not bound, he can indeed become emancipated from birth, age, illness, death, the great sufferings of apprehension and sorrow, and all the defilements.

For this reason, all Bodhisattvas possess the fourfold unhindered knowledge. O good man! Hence, for the sake of my disciples, I have spoken in the twelve types of scripture about clinging and spoken of it as being bound by Mara. Without clinging, one becomes emancipated from Mara's hands. For example, in worldly life, one who has committed a sin [crime] gets chained up by the king. A person without sin cannot be taken prisoner by the king. It is the same with the Bodhisattva-mahasattva. A person possessed of clinging is bound up by Mara. One with no clinging is not bound up by Mara. Thus, the Bodhisattva-mahasattva has no clinging. "Also, next, O good man! We say "unhindered knowledge of Dharma". The Bodhisattva-mahasattva well upholds the words [of Dharma] and does not forget [them]. Upholding is like [the actions of] the earth, mountains, eyes, clouds, man, and mother. The same is the case with all things. "We say "unhindered knowledge of the meaning". Now, the Bodhisattva may know the names of all things and yet not know the meaning. When one is unhindered in the meaning, one comes to know of the signification. "How does one know of the signification? We say "upholding like the earth". This is analogous to the way in which the earth supports all beings and non-beings. Hence, "earth" is referred to, to symbolise "support". "O good man! We say "support of the mountains". The Bodhisattva-mahasattva thinks thus: "Why do we say that mountains support? The mountains well support the earth and there is no shaking. Hence, "to support". "Why do we say that the eye supports? The eye well supports light. Hence, "support". "Why do we say that clouds support? Clouds are called the "air of the nagas" [snake-beings, dragons]. The air of the nagas supports water. Hence, "support". "Why do we say that man supports? Man well supports Dharma and non-Dharma. Hence, "support". "Why do we say that a mother supports? A mother well supports her child. Hence, "support". "The Bodhisattva-mahasattva knows well the names and meanings of all things. It is thus. "We say "unhindered knowledge of language". The Bodhisattva-mahasattva may use various idioms [words] to speak about a single meaning. But there is no signification. It is as in the case of the names of man, woman, house, vehicle, beings, etc. Why is there no signification? O good man! We say "signification". But this is of the world of

Bodhisattvas and all Buddhas. Idioms [words] belong to the world of common mortals. By knowing the meaning, one gains unhinderedness in language. "We say "unhindered knowledge of eloquence". The Bodhisattva-mahasattva knows the language and the meaning as he goes on talking for a period of innumerable asamkhyas of kalpas. This is unhinderedness in eloquence. "O good man! The Bodhisattva, for innumerable, boundless, asamkhyas of kalpas, practises secular dharmas. By practising, he gains unhinderedness in dharmas. "Also, for innumerable, boundless asamkhyas of kalpas, he practises the "Paramartha". Thus, he gains unhinderedness in meaning. "Also, for innumerable, boundless asamkhyas of kalpas, he practises the vyakaranas. Hence, he gains unhinderedness in language. "Also, for innumerable asamkhyas of kalpas, he practises secular eloquence, and he gains unhinderedness in eloquence. "O good man! No one can say that the sravakas and pratyekabuddhas gain this fourfold unhindered knowledge. O good man! In the nine types of scripture, I say that sravakas and pratyekabuddhas do possess the fourfold unhindered knowledge. But, truth to tell, no sravakas or pratyekabuddhas can have any such knowledge. Why not? The Bodhisattva-mahasattva particularly practises such fourfold unhindered knowledge in order to save beings. "The pratyekabuddha practises the Way of extinction and seeks a lonely place. With him, there is no saving of beings, no resorting to miracles; instead, he is silent, without talking, all day long. How can he have unhindered Wisdom? Why does he sit silently and not teach? He does not speak about Dharma and enable beings to gain the usmagata, murdana, laukikagradharma, shrotapanna, sakrdagamin, arhat, pratyekabuddha, or Bodhisattva-mahasattva [level]. He does not cause others to gain unsurpassed Bodhichitta. Why not? O good man! When the pratyekabuddha appears in the world, there are not the nine types of scripture. Hence, there can be no unhinderedness in language and eloquence with the pratyekabuddha. O good man! The pratyekabuddha knows all about Dharmas, but he is not unhindered in Dharma. Why not? Unhinderedness in Dharma is "knowing the words." The pratyekabuddha knows the words, but is not blessed with unhinderedness in words. Why not? Because he does not know the two words, "eternal" and "abiding". That is why the

pratyekabuddha cannot gain unhinderedness in Dharma. He knows of the meaning, but he is not blessed with unhinderedness [of understanding] in the meaning. If he truly understood the meaning, he would have to know that all beings possess the Buddha-Nature. The meaning of Buddha-Nature is none other than unsurpassed Enlightenment. Thus, the pratyekabuddha does not possess unhindered knowledge of meaning. So, for him there cannot be unhindered Wisdom in all things of the four categories. "Why does the sravaka not have the fourfold unhindered knowledge? He does not have the three kinds of best expedient. What are the three? First, using soft [gentle] words, followed by accepting Dharma; secondly, using harsh words, followed by melting into the teaching; thirdly, neither softness nor harshness, followed by the teaching. As the sravaka does not have these three, he cannot have the fourfold unhindered knowledge. Also, next, the sravaka and pratyekabuddha, after all, do not know language and meaning. With them, there is no knowing of the world of unmolested Wisdom; they do not have the ten powers and the four fearlessnesses. They, after all, cannot cross the great sea of the 12 links of interdependent arising. They do not know well the differences between beings, as to whether they are sharp-witted or born dull. They cannot yet eradicate the doubting mind regarding the two phases of truth [relative, worldly truth, and Absolute, Supramundane Truth]. They do not know the various aspects of beings' mental activities. They cannot speak well about the All-Void of "Paramartha-satya" [Absolute, Supramundate Truth]. For this reason, these two vehicles [of pratyekabuddha and sravaka] do not possess the fourfold unhindered knowledge." Bodhisattva Kasyapa said to the Buddha: "O World-Honoured One! If sravakas and pratyekabuddhas do not possess the fourfold unhindered knowledge, why, O World-Honoured One, do we say that Shariputra is the foremost in Wisdom, Mahamaudgalyayana the foremost in divine powers, and Mahakausthila the foremost in the fourfold unhindered knowledge? If this is not the case, why do you say so?" Then the World-Honoured One praised Kasyapa and said: "Well said, well said! O good man! The Ganges, for example, contains an immeasurable volume of water. The great volume of water of the Indus cannot be known. The water of the Oxus, too, cannot be known; the volume of water of Lake

Anavatapta is also immeasurable. The water of the great sea is immeasurable. The volume of all this water [together] is immeasurable. But actually, there can be more or less, their not all being the same. It is the same with the fourfold unhindered knowledge of sravakas, pratyekabuddhas, and Bodhisattvas. O good man! We can never say that they are the same. O good man! For the sake of common mortals, I say that Mahakausthila is the foremost in the fourfold unhindered knowledge. What you ask about stands thus. O good man! Amongst the sravakas, there may be one who has one of the four unhindered kinds of knowledge, or one who has two. But there is no case where a sravaka has the four." Kasyapa said to the Buddha: "O World-Honoured One! You spoke above in this chapter on pure actions about the fourfold unhindered knowing and seeing, and you say that in the knowing and seeing of the Bodhisattva, there is nothing that is gained and his mind has nothing that is not gained. O World-Honoured One! Now, this Bodhisattva-mahasattva has, truth to tell, nothing to gain. If there is still something to be gained in his mind, he is not a Bodhisattva; he is a common mortal. How can the Tathagata say that the Bodhisattva still has something to gain?" The Buddha said: "O good man! Well said, well said! You again ask that of which I desire to speak. O good man! The Bodhisattva-mahasattva has nothing to gain. Having nothing to gain is the fourfold unhindered knowledge. O good man! Why is having nothing to gain unhinderedness? If there is something still to be gained, this is a hindrance. A person who has a hindrance is one who has the four inversions [distorted views]. O good man! As the Bodhisattva-mahasattva does not have the four inversions, he has unhinderedness. Hence, we say that the Bodhisattva is a person who has nothing more to gain. "Also, next, O good man! This ungainedness is Wisdom. As the Bodhisattva-mahasattva gains this Wisdom, we say that he has ungainedness. Still having something to gain means ignorance. When the Bodhisattva has eternally dispelled the gloom of ignorance, he has nothing more to gain. Hence, we say that the Bodhisattva is a person who has nothing more to gain. "Also, next, O good man! Having nothing more to gain is Great Nirvana. Abiding in peace in this Great Nirvana, the Bodhisattva-mahasattva sees no nature, no characteristics in any thing. Hence, we say that the Bodhisattva has nothing more to gain. "Having [the need] to possess means the 25 existences. The Bodhisattva has long segregated himself from the 25 existences and attained Great Nirvana. Thus, we say that the Bodhisattva has nothing more to gain hold of. "Also, next, O good man! Not having to possess means Mahayana. The Bodhisattva-mahasattva does not abide in any dharma. Hence, he gains Mahayana. So, we say that the Bodhisattva has nothing more to gain. "The need to possess is the path of the sravaka and pratyekabudda. The Bodhisattva has segregated himself from the paths of the two vehicles. Hence, he gains the Buddha-Way. So, we say that the Bodhisattva has nothing more to gain. "Also, next, O good man! Having no need to possess anything is the vaipulya sutra. When the Bodhisattva recites such a sutra, he gains Great Nirvana. Hence, we say that the Bodhisattva has nothing more to gain. The need to possess is the 11 types of scripture. The Bodhisattva does not practise [these]; he exclusively expounds the Mahayana vaipulya sutras. So, we say that the Bodhisattva does not need to gain anything. "Also, next, O good man! Not having to gain anything is Emptiness ["shunyata"]. In the world, when there is nothing there, we say empty. The Bodhisattva attains this Emptiness samadhi [meditative state]. Because there is nothing to see. Hence, we say that the Bodhisattva has nothing to gain. "The need to possess is the wheel of birth and death. As all common mortals repeat birth and death, they have things to see. The Bodhisattva has long segregated himself from all births and deaths. Hence, we say that the Bodhisattva has nothing more to gain. "Also, next, O good man! Not to possess is the Eternal, Bliss, Self, and the Pure. When the Bodhisattva-mahasattva sees the Buddha-Nature, he gains the Eternal, Bliss, Self, and the Pure. Hence, we say that the Bodhisattva has nothing to gain. "Having something to gain is the non-Eternal, non-Bliss, non-Self, and the non-Pure. Hence, we say that the Bodhisattva is a person who has nothing to gain. "Also, next, O good man! That there is nothing to gain is the All-Void of "Paramartha-satya" [Ultimate Truth]. When the Bodhisattva-mahasattva meditates on the All-Void of "Paramarthasatya", he sees nothing. Hence, we say that the Bodhisattva is a person who has nothing to gain." "That one still has something to gain equates with the five distorted views ["panca-drstayah"]. As the Bodhisattva has eternally segregated himself from the five distorted views, he gains the All-Void of "Paramartha-satya". Hence, we say that the Bodhisattva has nothing more to gain. "Also, next, O good man! That there is nothing more to be gained, this is unsurpassed Bodhi [Enlightenment]. When the Bodhisattva-mahasattva gains unsurpassed Bodhi, there is nothing more to see. Hence, we say that the Bodhisattva has nothing more to gain. "What still has more to be gained is the Enlightenment of the sravaka and pratyekabuddha. The Bodhisattva is eternally away from the Enlightenment of the two vehicles. Hence, we say that the Bodhisattva has nothing more to gain. "O good man! What you ask about has nothing more to gain. What I say, also has nothing more to gain. Any person who says that there is still a thing to be gained is one of Mara's kindred and not my disciple." Kasyapa said to the Buddha: "O World-Honoured One! As you expound to me the ungainedness of Enlightenment [i.e. that it is not a separate thing that can be grasped hold of], an innumerable number of beings cut themselves away from the mind that has an image of existence. Hence, I particularly ask of you to explain to me what has nothing more to be gained, and to enable innumerable beings to segregate themselves from Mara's clan and become the Buddha's disciples." Bodhisattva Kasyapa said to the Buddha: "O World-Honoured One! You said before in a gatha, for Cunda's sake: "What originally was is now no longer; What originally was not, now is. There can be no such thing as "is" pertaining In the Three Times [of past, present, and future]." "O World-Honoured One! What might this mean?" The Buddha said: "O good man! As I desire to teach all beings, I say this. I also say this for the sake of sravakas and pratyekabuddhas. Also, I say this to the Prince of Dharma, Manjushri. It is not the case that I said this to Cunda alone. At that time, Manjushri wished to put a question to me. Fathoming [reading] his mind, I spoke thus. When I spoke thus, Manjushri understood." Bodhisattva Kasyapa said: "O World-Honoured One! How many persons could there be of the class of Manjushri, who could thus gain the point? Please, O Tathagata, for the sake of all beings, explain expansively once again." "O good man! Listen carefully, listen carefully! I shall now explain it again in detail especially for you. I said "originally was not". There was originally no prajnaparamita. As there was no prajnaparamita, there are now so

many bonds of defilement. If any sramana, Brahmin, deva, Mara, Brahma, or human were to say: "The Tathagata had defilement in the past, has defilement in the present or will have defilement in the future", this is not so. "Also, next, O good man! I said "originally was". In days gone by I had a body gained through the union of father and mother. And in consequence, I do not now have an adamantine Dharma-Body [i.e. if the Buddha as Buddha had ever been produced by parents like an ordinary, mortal being, he would not now be able to have an adamantine Dharma-Body. Precise meaning not clear here and in the following]. "I said: "originally was not". I did not have the 32 signs of perfection and the 80 minor marks of excellence. As I did not have the 32 signs of perfection and the 80 minor marks of excellence, I now have the 404 illnesses. If any sramana, Brahmin, deva, Brahma, or human says: 'The Tathagata has had, all the way through past, present and future, the suffering of illness', this is not so." "Also, next, O good man! I said: "originally was". I once had the non-Eternal, non-Bliss, non-Self, and the non-Pure. As I had the non-Eternal, non-Bliss, non-Self, and the non-Pure, there is now no unsurpassed Enlightenment. "I said: "originally was not". I did not see the Buddha-Nature. Not seeing it, there are the non-Eternal, non-Bliss, non-Self, and the non-Pure. If any sramana, Brahmin, deva, Mara, Brahma, or human says: "The Tathagata does not, throughout all the past, present and future, possess the Eternal, Bliss, Self, and the Pure", such can never be [i.e. this is an utterly untrue statement].

"Also, next, O good man! I said: "originally was". Common mortals might have the idea of practising penance and say that one [thus] arrives at unsurpassed Enlightenment. For this reason, one cannot now crush out the four Maras. "I said: "originally was not". That is to say that there were originally no six paramitas. Not having the six paramitas, the common mortal has the thought of practising penance and says that he can attain unsurpassed Enlightenment. A sramana, Brahmin, deva, Mara, Brahma, or human might say: "The Tathagata, all through the past, future and present, did penance." But such can never be [stated]. "Also, next, O good man! I said: "originally was". I had in the past a body sustained by various kinds of food. As I had a body supported by various kinds of food, I cannot have a boundless body now. "Originally was not" says that there were not the 37 factors assisting towards Enlightenment. As there were not the 37 factors assisting towards Enlightenment, there is now the body supported by various kinds of food. Some sramana, Brahmin, deva, Mara, Brahma, or human might say: "The Tathagata, all through the past, future, and present, has a food-supported body." But such can never be [truly stated]. "Also, next, O good man! I said: "originally was", meaning that I originally had a mind that clung to all things. So, there cannot now be any samadhi of the ultimate Void. "I said: "originally was not", meaning that I did not originally have the true meaning of the Middle Path. And as I did not have the true meaning of the Middle Path, I now have clinging to all things. If any sramana, Brahmin, deva, Mara, Brahma, or human says: "The Tathagata, all through past, future and present, has a body that has [samsarically] existed", this is not so. "Also, next, O good man! I said: "originally was". When I first attained this unsurpassed Enlightenment, there were dull-headed sravaka disciples. As I had dull-headed sravaka disciples, I could not speak about the truth of the one vehicle. "I said: "originally was not". There was no sharp-witted elephant king such as Bodhisattva Kasyapa. As there was none sharp-witted like Kasyapa, I resorted to the expedient of the three vehicles, which I enlarged upon. If any sramana, Brahmin, deva, Mara, Brahma, or human says: "The Tathagata has, all through the past, future, and present, preached the Dharma of the three vehicles", this is not so. "Also, next, O good man! I said: "originally was". I formerly said: "In three months' time, I shall enter Parinirvana between the sal trees." That is why I cannot now preach the doctrine of the great vaipulya sutra, "Mahaparinirvana". "I said: "originally was not", meaning that there were no such great Bodhisattvas as Manjushri and the others. As there were not, we now say: "The Tathagata is non-eternal." If any sramana, Brahmin, deva, Mara, Brahma, or human says: "The Tathagata, all through the past, future and present, is non-eternal", this is not true. "O good man! Although the Tathagata knows all things he says that he does not know, because of all beings. He sees all things. But he says that he does not so see. Speaking about what has form, he says formless; speaking about things that have no form, he say that there are forms [there]. Speaking about what has form, he says "formless". The same

applies to the Self, Bliss, and the Pure. Speaking about the three vehicles, he say one vehicle, speaking about one vehicle, he says, as the case may be [according to the situation], three vehicles. He says that an abbreviated form is one that is full, and a full one abbreviated. He says that the four grave offences are the sthulatyayas, and the sthulatyayas are the four grave offences. He says that transgression is non-infringement, and that non-infringement is an infringement. He says that a venial sin is grave, and a grave sin venial. Why so? Because the Tathagata sees the root of beings' abilities. O good man! The Tathagata speaks thus, but nothing is wrong at bottom. Why not? Whatever is false constitutes sin. The Tathagata is totally segregated from sin. How could he say anything false? O good man! Although the Tathagata does not resort to falsehood, he will do so as an expedient and as it serves the occasion when he sees that all beings gain the benefit of Dharma. O good man! To the Tathagata, all worldly truths are "Paramartha-satya". And he also enables beings to attain "Paramartha-satya". If all beings did not attain "Paramartha-satya", all Buddhas, to the end, would not speak of worldly truth. O good man! When the Tathagata at times speaks of worldly truth, beings say that the Tathagata is speaking about "Paramarthasatya". When he at times speaks about "Paramartha-satya, "beings say that the Buddha is speaking about worldly truth. All of this comes from the deepest depths of the world of all Buddhas. This is not something that can be understood by sravakas and pratyekabuddhas. O good man! For this reason, do not hastily contest and say that the Bodhisattva-mahasattva possesses nothing. The Bodhisattva always abides in "Paramartha-satya". How could anyone criticise him and say that he has nothing?" Kasyapa said: "O World-Honoured One! You say that "Paramartha-satya" is the Way, Enlightenment, and Nirvana. If we say that the Bodhisattva possesses the Way, Enlightenment, and Nirvana, this is nothing other than the non-Eternal. Why? If Dharma is eternal, one cannot gain it. It is like space. Who can gain it? O World-Honoured One! In worldly life, what originaly was not, but is now, is called the non-Eternal. The same with the Way. If the Way can be gained, this is nothing but the non-Eternal. If Dharma is the Eternal, there can be no gaining of anything, no arising, as in the case of the Buddha-Nature, which knows no gaining and no arising. O good man!

Now, the Way is non-matter, not non-matter, not long, not short, not high, not low, not arising, not extinction, not red, not white, not blue, not yellow, not "is", not "is-not". How could the Tathagata speak of it as "what can be gained"? The same applies to Enlightenment and Nirvana." The Buddha said: "It is thus, it is thus. O good man! There are two kinds of Way. One is eternal, and the other non-eternal. Enlightenment, too, is of two kinds. One is eternal, and the other non-eternal. The same applies to Nirvana, too. What the tirthikas say regarding the Way relates to the non-eternal; what is said within Buddhism relates to the Eternal. The Enlightenment of the sravaka and pratyekabuddha relates to the non-eternal. The Enlightenment of all Buddhas and Bodhisattvas is the Eternal. The emancipation of the tirthikas is non-eternal, and that of the Buddhist is eternal. O good man! The Way, Enlightenment, and Nirvana are all eternal. All beings are always overshadowed by innumerable defilements, and as they lack the eye of Wisdom, they cannot see. But in order to see, all beings practise shila [morality], samadhi [meditative absorption], and Wisdom. By practising these, they see the Way, Enlightenment, and Nirvana. The nature and characteristics of the Way do not suffer from birth and death. Hence, it is hard to grasp. "O good man! With the Way, there is no colour or form to be seen, nor any weight to be known. Yet there is its function. O good man! A being's mind is not long, not short, not coarse, not minute, not bound nor unbound, nor is it anything visible, but it still appears as though it were visible. Hence, I said to Sudatta: "O rich man! Make the mind the king of the castle. If the mind is not guarded, the body and mouth will not be guarded. If the mind is guarded, the body and mouth, too, will be guarded. When the body and mouth are not well guarded, all beings fall into the three unfortunate realms. If beings guard their body and mouth well, they can attain the Nirvana of humans and gods. "Gaining" speaks of truth. "Not gaining" speaks of non-truth." O good man! It is the same with the Way, Enlightenment, and Nirvana. There can be the "is" and the Eternal. If there were [only] the "not-is", how could there be a cutting away of all defilements? Because of the "is", all Bodhisattvas are able to see clearly and to know. "O good man! There are two kinds of seeing. One is seeing by outer signs [indications], and the other by fathoming. What is seeing by outer signs? It is like seeing fire from afar, when one sees the smoke. Actually, one does not see the fire. Though one does not see it, nothing is false [here]. We see a crane in the sky, and say that we see water. Though we do not see water, this is not false. We see the flower and the leaf, and we say that we see the root. Though we do not see the root, this is not false. We see a cow's horns far off through the hedges, and we say that we can see a cow. Though we do not see the cow, this is nevertheless not false. We see a pregnant woman and say that we see carnal desire. We do not [actually] see carnal desire, but this is not false. Also, we see the fresh leaves of a tree and say that we see water. Though we do not [actually] see it, this is not false. We see a cloud, and we say that we see rain. Though the rain [itself] is not seen, this is not false. Seeing the actions of the body and mouth, we say that we see the mind. The mind is not seen, but this is not false. This is seeing by outer signs. "What is seeing by fathoming? It is like seeing the colour of the eye. O good man! A man's eye is pure and does not get broken [damaged by looking]. It is like seeing a mango held in one's own palm. The same is the case where the Bodhisattva clearly sees the Way, Enlightenment, and Nirvana. Though he sees thus, there are no characteristics to be seen. For this reason, in days past I said to Shariputra: "O Shariputra! The Tathagata alone knows, sees and realises all that the world, such as sramanas, Brahmins, devas, Maras, Brahmas, or humans, do not see and realise. It is the same with the Bodhisattvas. O Shariputra! What all the world knows, sees and realises, I and the Bodhisattvas also know, see and realise. What the world and beings do not know, see and realise, is also known, seen and realised [by the Buddha and the Bodhisattvas]. It must be thus. The world and beings know, see and realise, and they say that they know, see and realise. O Shariputra! The Tathagata knows, sees and realises all, yet he does not say that he knows, sees and realises. So do things also obtain with the Bodhisattvas. Why? If the Tathagata shows that he knows, sees and realises, he is no Buddha-World-Honoured One. He is a common mortal. It is the same with the Bodhisattva, too."

Chapter Twenty-Three: On Pure Actions 3

Bodhisattva Kasyapa said: "The Buddha-World-Honoured One once said to Shariputra: "What the world knows I also know; what the world does not know, I also know all." What does this mean?" "O good man! The world does not know, see or realise the Buddha-Nature. If there is a person who knows, sees, and realises the Buddha-Nature, we do not call such a person one of the world. We say "Bodhisattva". The world also does not know, see, or realise the twelve types of scripture, the twelve links of interdependent arising, the four inversions, the Four Truths, the 37 factors leading to Enlightenment, unsurpassed Enlightenment, and Great Nirvana. If [these are] known, seen or realised, we do not say "of the world"; we say "Bodhisattva". O good man! This is what we mean when we say that the world does not know, see or realise. How does the world know, see or realise? So-called Brahma, Mahesvara, Narayana, nature, time, mote, dharma, non-dharma are the creators.

"The Great Compassionate One pities beings
And has them take refuge in him.
He well extracts all poisonous arrows.
So I call him a great doctor.
A worldly doctor effects a cure.
He cures indeed, but the illness returns.
The Tathagata cures, but the illness does not return.
The World-Honoured One gives
All beings amrta [the ambrosia of immortality].
When beings partake of this,
They do not die, nor do they get re-born.
The Tathagata expounds to me

Great Nirvana. When beings
Hear the closely guarded doctrine,
They gain birthlessness and deathlessness."

Having sung thus, Bodhisattva Kasyapa said to the Buddha: "O World-Honoured One! The Buddha says: "The Bodhisattva does know, see and realise what the world knows, sees and realises". If it is the case that the Bodhisattva is here in the world, we cannot say: "The world does not know, see or realise. But this Bodhisattva well knows, sees and realises." If he is not of the world, what different characteristics does he have?" The Buddha said: "O good man! The Bodhisattva is of the world and not of the world. What does not know, see, and

They talk about an end and a beginning, about the "is-not" and "is" of the world and say that "Nirvana commences from the first dhyana and ends in non-thoughtlessness". O good man! This is what the world knows, sees and realises. The Bodhisattva knows, sees, and realises such. The Bodhisattva already has known, seen and realised such. If we say that he does not know, see or realise, this is nothing but falsehood. What is false constitutes sin. On account of this sin, one falls into hell. O good man! If any man, woman, sramana or Brahmin says that there is no such thing as the Way, Enlightenment or Nirvana, know that such a person is an icchantika [most spiritually deluded person]. Such a person is one of Mara's kindred. This is slandering Dharma. Such slandering is a slandering of all Buddhas. Such a person is not of the world, and not "not-of-the-world." Then Kasyapa, on hearing this, praised the Buddha in a gatha, saying:

realise is the world; he who does know, see, and realise is not of the world. You ask: "What difference is there?" I shall now explain. O good man! If any man or woman hears this Nirvana Sutra, feels respect, and aspires to unsurpassed Enlightenment, such a person is a Bodhisattva of the world. All the world does not know, see, or realise. Such a Bodhisattva, too, does not know, see, or realise, as in the case of the world. When the Bodhisattva hears this Nirvana Sutra, he comes to know that the world does not know, see, or realise, and that this is what the Bodhisattva should come to know, see and realise. Having come to know of this, he thinks to himself: "How am I to effect an expedient and learn and come to know, see, and realise?" He further thinks: "I shall uphold the pure shila [moral rules] with the deepest mind. O good man! On this account, the Bodhisattva, in the world to come, is pure in all places where he gets born. O good man! As the Bodhisattva-mahasattva is pure in shila, in whatever place [he finds himself] he has no arrogance, no wrong views, no doubt, and never, to the end, says that the Tathagata ever enters Nirvana. This is how the Bodhisattva observes pure shila. The precepts are already pure [with him]. He then next practises meditation. Through practising meditation, wherever he may be, he abides in right remembrance and does not forget. That is to say that beings all have the Buddha-Nature; that there are the twelve types of scripture, and that the All-Buddha-World-Honoured One is the Eternal, Bliss, the Self, and the Pure. All Bodhisattvas abide in the vaipulya Great Nirvana Sutra and see the Buddha-Nature. They rightly remember all of this and do not forget. Through practising dhyanas [meditations], they gain eleven shunyatas [emptinesses]. This is the practising of the pure meditation of the Bodhisattva. Achieving shila and meditation, they next practise pure Wisdom. By practising Wisdom, they first see the Self in the body and the body in the Self. There are no such clingings as: this body, this Self, no body, and no Self. This is practising the pure Wisdom of the Bodhisattva. By practising Wisdom the shila which he observes is steadfast and does not move. O good man! It is like Sumeru, which does not shake, in spite of the winds from the four quarters. The same is the case with the Bodhisattva-mahasattva. He does not shake, in spite of the four inversions. O good man! The shila which the Bodhisattva knows, sees and realises and upholds at that time does not shake. That is why we say that what the Bodhisattva knows, sees and realises is not of the world. O good man! The Bodhisattva has no repentance in his mind when he sees that the shila he upholds is steadfast. As there is no regret, there is joy in his mind. As he has joy, his mind is happy. As he is happy, his mind is at peace. As his mind is at peace, there comes about an immovable samadhi. As the samadhi is immovable, there is true knowing and seeing. Due to true knowing and seeing, there is parting from

birth and death. Parting from birth and death, he achieves emancipation ["vimukti"]. As a result of emancipation, he clearly sees the Buddha-Nature. This is what we mean when we say that what the Bodhisattva knows, sees, and realises is not something that obtains in the world. O good man! This is what the world does not know, see, or realise." Kasyapa further said: "In what way does the Bodhisattva not repent as he upholds the pure shila, and how does he clearly see the Buddha-Nature?" The Buddha said: "O good man! The shila that obtains in the world is not pure. Why not? Because the shila that obtains in the world is grounded on "is", and because its nature is not fixed and is not the utmost. It stands not widely for all beings. Hence, we say "non-pure". Not being pure, there is regret. Because of regret, the mind knows no joy. As there is no joy in the mind, there is no happiness. As there is no happiness, there is no peace. As there is no peace, there is no immovable samadhi. As there is no immovable samadhi, there is no true knowing and seeing. As there is no true knowing and seeing, there is no fleeing from the world. As there is no fleeing from the world, there is no emancipation. As there is no emancipation, there is no seeing of the Buddha-Nature. As there is no seeing of the Buddha-Nature, there is no gaining of Great Nirvana. This is what we call the impure shila that obtains in the world. "O good man! We speak of the pure shila of the Bodhisattva-mahasattva because the shila is no shila, not for existence, but the ultimate in samadhi, and is for the benefit of beings. This is the pure shila of the Bodhisattva. Although the Bodhisattva-mahasattva does not desire to gain any non-regretting mind through pure shila, the non-regretting mind spontaneously arises. O good man! If, for example, a man holds a bright mirror in his hand, his face will appear in it, even if he does not wish it to appear there. It is also as in the case of a farmer who sows good seed in a good field, after which buds spontaneously emerge there, even were this not so desired. Also, it is like lighting a lamp, when the gloom automatically disappears, even though such may not be desired. As the Bodhisattva-mahasattva steadfastly observes the purity of shila, a non-regretful mind will automatically arise. The case is thus. Through the purity of the shila, the mind gains joy. O good man! It is like the mien of a man of straight [honest] mind, which is pleasing to behold. The same is the case with a person who observes the purity of shila. "O good man! One's mind does not feel pleased when one sees the impurity of shila of a person who violates shila. This is like seeing the ill-looking [unattractive] face of a cruel person, when one does not feel any joy. The situation is the same with a person who violates shila. O good man! As an example: there are two pasture women. One holds in her hand a pot of cream, and the other a pot of milk. Both go to the castle-town, wishing to sell [their produce] there. On the way, they take a tumble, and the pots get broken. The one woman is happy, and the other is sad and worried. It is the same with upholding and not upholding shila. The person who upholds the purity of shila has a joyful mind. Glad at heart, that person thinks: "The All-Buddha-Tathagata says in his Nirvana Sutra that a person who upholds the purity of shila will gain Nirvana. Since I now uphold the purity of shila, I shall surely attain it. Because of this, my heart is glad." Kasyapa said further: "What difference is there between "joy" and "bliss?" "O good man! When the Bodhisattva-mahasattva does not commit any evil, there is joy with him. When the mind is pure, and when one upholds shila, there is bliss. O good man! When the Bodhisattva sees birth and death, this is joy. When he sees Great Nirvana, there is bliss. What is low in grade is joy, and what is high in grade is bliss. When one departs from the property gained in common with others, there is joy. When one attains individually gained property, there is bliss. When shila is pure, the body is light and soft, and one's speech knows no coarseness. Then, the Bodhisattva can see, hear, smell, taste, touch, and know, and there is nothing that is evil [in these sensations]. With no evil, the mind is at peace. Because of peace, he gains the quietude of samadhi. As he gains the quietude of samadhi, he truly knows and sees. When he truly knows and sees, he flees from birth and death. When he flees from birth and death, he gains emancipation. When he gains emancipation, he sees the Buddha-Nature. When he sees the Buddha-Nature, he gains Great Nirvana. This is the pure upholding of shila by the Bodhisattva. This is not what applies in the upholding of shila in secular life. Why not? O good man! The pure shila which the Bodhisattvamahasattva upholds is supported by five things. What are these five? They are: 1) faith, 2) feeling ashamed of oneself for any sin that one has committed, 3) feeling ashamed of others, for any sin they have committed, 4) a good friend of the Way, and 5) respect-adding [increasing] shila. Because one segregates oneself from the five overshadowings ["panca-avaranani"]. Because what one sees is pure, as one is separate from the five distorted views ["pancadrstayah"]. There is no element of doubt, since one is away from the five doubts, which are doubting: 1) the Buddha, 2) Dharma, 3) Sangha, 4) shila, and 5) non-indolence. The Bodhisattva then gains the five roots, which are: 1) faith, 2) remembrance, 3) effort, 4) meditation, and 5) Wisdom. Through the five roots, he gains the five kinds of Nirvana, which are emancipation from: 1) rupa [body, matter] down to consciousness [i.e. emancipation from the five skandhas]. This is the Bodhisattva's pure upholding of shila. This is not of the secular world. O good man! This is what the secular world does not know, see, or realise. This is what the Bodhisattva knows, sees, and realises. "O good man! If any of my disciples uphold, recite, copy and speak about the Great Nirvana Sutra and violate the moral precepts, people will reproach them, look down upon them, and say: "If the Mahaparinirvana which the Buddha closely guards is supposed to have power, how come that it makes you thus violate the moral precepts which you have received? If it is the case that anybody upholding this Nirvana Sutra breaks the prohibitive rules, know that this sutra has no power. If it has no power, there can never be any merit [from it], even if one recites it." By belittling and transgressing against this Nirvana Sutra, all innumerable and boundless [numbers] of people have to fall into hell. Anyone who upholds this sutra and breaks the moral rules is a very bad teacher of the Way. Such is no disciple of mine, but one of Mara's kindred. I do not permit such a person to hold this sutra. It is better not to allow such a person to receive, possess and practise than to allow him to transgress, uphold and practise shila. "O good man! Any disciple of mine, when upholding, reciting, copying, or speaking about the Nirvana Sutra, should be serious in the deportment of his body and mind and should be careful not to play around and behave lightly. What refers to body is "playing around"; what refers to mind is "behaving lightly". The mind that seeks "is" is what "behaves lightly"; the body that does many things is that which "plays around". Any of my disciples who seek "is" and act cannot receive and hold this Mahayana Great Nirvana Sutra. Should any [such] be holding this sutra, people will belittle and reproach him, saying: "If the Buddha's close-guarded Nirvana Sutra possesses any power, how can it be that he permits you to seek "is" and act? If anyone who holds this sutra seeks "is" and acts, know that this sutra has no power. If it cannot generate any great power, it is useless to possess this sutra." When a person thus belittles this sutra, innumerable and boundless [numbers of] beings will have to fall into hell. Should a person possess this sutra, see "is" and act, such a person is none but the worst friend of the Way. Such a person is not one of my disciples, but a kindred of Mara. "And next, O good man! Any disciple of mine who receives, recites, copies, and speaks about this Nirvana Sutra should not speak about it at an untimely moment, in a land where one should not preach, not when one is not asked to preach, not with a light mind, not in all places, not speak about it, praising it by oneself, not speak of it while belittling others, not by killing the Buddhist teaching, and not by burning out secular dharma. O good man! If any of my disciples receive and hold this sutra and speak about it at an untimely moment or down to burning off of secular dharma, people will belittle it and say: "If there is any great power in the Buddha's closely guarded Great Nirvana, how can it allow you to speak of it at an untimely moment or burning out secular dharma? If a person who possesses this sutra acts like this, then know that this sutra has no power. If it has no power, there is no benefit [to be had from it], even if you hold it." Through belittling this Nirvana Sutra, innumerable beings are caused to fall into hell. If one receives and upholds this sutra and speaks of it on untimely occasions down to burning off of secular dharma, such a person is the worst friend of all beings. Such a one is not a disciple of mine, but is of Mara's kindred. "O good man! What is required first of all of anyone who desires to keep this sutra, who speaks of Great Nirvana, who speaks of the Buddha-Nature, who speaks of the hidden Dharma of the Tathagata, who speaks of Mahayana, who speaks of the vaipulya sutras, who speaks of the sravaka vehicle, who speaks of the pratyekabuddha vehicle, who sees the Buddha-Nature, is to make the body pure. When the body is pure, there can be no grounds for reproaching. When there is nothing to reproach, this enables beings to gain the pure mind in this Great Nirvana. When faith arises, one respects this sutra. One hears a gatha, a line, or a word, or one speaks of Dharma, [and] one aspires to unsurpassed Enlightenment. Know that this person is a true, good teacher of the Way to all beings. Such a person is not a bad teacher of the Way. Such is a disciple of mine and not of Mara's clan. This is what we mean when we say that the Bodhisattva is not of the world. O good man! This is what the world does not know, see, or realise. This is what the Bodhisattva knows, sees, and realises. "Also, next, O good man! What is that which all the world does not know, see, or realise, and which the Bodhisattva knows, sees, and realises? This is the six thinkings. What six? These are: 1) thinking of the Buddha, 2) thinking of Dharma, 3) thinking of the Sangha, 4) thinking of shila, 5) thinking of dana [charitable giving], and 6) thinking of the devas. "O good man! What is thinking of the Buddha? This is saying that the Buddha, who is the Tathagata, Alms-Deserving, All-Enlightened One, All-accomplished One, Well-Gone, All-Knower, Best Trainer, Teacher of Gods and Humans, Buddha and World-Honoured One is eternal and does not change, possessed of the ten powers, the four fearlessnesses, uttering the lion's roar, and is a great sramana and a great Brahmin. His great pureness ultimately carries a person to the other shore. No one supercedes him, and none can see the top of his head. There is no fear, no being frightened, and no moving [with him]. One and alone, none to accompany him, and none to teach him, he is perfectly awake in all such treasures of knowledge as quick-acting knowledge, great knowledge, bright knowledge, deep knowledge, emancipation knowledge, unshared knowledge, widely-suffusing knowledge, and ultimate knowledge. He is, of men, the elephant king, the cow king, the naga king, the strongest male, the white lotus, and the best trainer. He is the great giver, the great teacher of Dharma. As he knows Dharma, he is called "teacher of Dharma". He is called the teacher of Dharma because he knows the meaning, because he knows the [apt] time, because he knows how to be contented, because he knows by himself, because he knows the masses [of beings], because he knows the various natures of beings, because he knows, of all natures, the sharp, the dull, and the medium, and because he speaks of the Middle Path. "Why do we say "Tathagata"? Because he does not change, as already taught by all Buddhas in the past. Why does he not change? All Buddhas in the past, in order to succour beings, delivered the twelve types of scripture. The same with the Tathagata. So we say "Tathagata". The All-Buddha-Tathagata comes from the six paramitas, the 37 factors leading to Enlightenment, the 11 shunyatas, and enters Great Nirvana. The same is the case with the Tathagata, too. That is why he is called the Buddha and the Tathagata. The All-Buddha-Tathagata enacts expedients as he wills for the sake of beings, and opens up the three vehicles. His life is infinite and boundless. The same is the case with the Tathagata too. That is why the Buddha is called the Tathagata. "Why is he called "one worthy of the offerings made him"? Whatever is of the world is the enemy. As the Buddha has to crush this out, he is called "one who answers" [i.e. one who answers the challenges of Mara]. Now, the four Maras are the enemies of the Bodhisattva. The All-Buddha-Tathagata, when still a Bodhisattva, thoroughly vanquished the four Maras through Wisdom. Hence, "one who answers". Also, next, "to answer" means "to segregate". While a Bodhisattva, he segregated himself from innumerable defilements. Hence, "to answer". Also, next, "to answer" means "bliss". All Buddhas in the past, as Bodhisattvas and for innumerable asamkhyas of kalpas, underwent all kinds of suffering, and yet there was no "non-bliss" to the end, but always "bliss". The same was the case with the Tathagata. Hence, "to answer". And also, all humans and devas offer him various kinds of incense, flowers, garlands, flying and hanging banners, and music. Hence, "to answer". "Why do we say "sho-henji" ["samyaksambuddha"]? "Sho" means "not upside-down"; "henji" means that there is nothing in the four inversions that he does not know. And also, "sho" means "penance". We say "henji". By virtue of penance, one knows that sorrowful fruits definitely arise therefrom. And also, "sho" is the middle path in secular life. "Henji" means that as one definitely practises the Middle Path, one attains unsurpassed Enlightenment. And, also, "sho" connotes that it is possible to count, weigh, and tell out [describe, proclaim]; "henji" means that it is not possible to count, weigh, and tell out. That is why the Buddha is the "All-Enlightened One". O good man! With the sravakas and pratyekabuddhas, there are cases where they have henji or where they do not. How so? "Hen" means the "five skandhas", "twelve spheres", and "eighteen realms". And the sravakas and pratyekabuddhas can also gain henji. Hence, "to

know allpervadingly". What is "not knowing all-pervadingly"? O good man! The two vehicles cannot know rupa [body, form] all through, even if they meditate on it for innumerable kalpas. Hence, there can be no case where the sravakas and pratyekabuddhas can know all the way through. "What is "myo-gyo-soku" ["vidyacaranasampanna"]? Myo means to gain innumerable good fruits, and gyo means leg. Good fruit means unsurpassed Enlightenment, and leg means shila and Wisdom. Riding on the legs of shila and Wisdom, one gains unsurpassed Enlightenment. Hence, myo-gyo-soku. And also, myo means to charm, gyo means good, and soku fruit. O good man! This is what the world thinks it means. To charm means emancipation; good means unexcelled Enlightenment; the fruit refers to Mahaparinirvana. Hence, myogyosoku. And also, myo means light, gyo action, and soku fruition. O good man! This is the meaning which the world accepts for these terms. Light relates to non-indolence, action to the six paramitas, and fruition to unsurpassed Enlightenment. And also, myo means three brightnesses, which are: 1) Bodhisattva brightness, 2) all-Buddha brightness, and 3) ignorance-destroying brightness. The Bodhisattva brightness is the paramitas; the all-Buddha brightness is the Buddha-eye; ignorance-destroying brightness is the ultimate Void. By action is meant that one performs all kinds of good actions over innumerable kalpas for all beings. Foot [soku] betokens "clearly seeing the Buddha-Nature". Hence, we say myo-gyo-soku. "What does "zen-zei" ["sugata" - "well-gone"] mean? Zen means high, and zei means not high. O good man! This is what the world takes it to mean. High relates to unsurpassed Enlightenment, and not high to "Tathagata mind". O good man! Anyone whose mind is high is not called "Tathagata". That is why the Tathagata is called zenzei. And also, good [zen] connotes "good teacher of the Way". "Zei" is the fruition of the good teacher of the Way. O good man! This is what the world takes it to mean. Good teacher of the Way means the first budding of Bodhichitta [Enlightenment Mind]. Fruition is none other than Great Nirvana. The Tathagata, not abandoning the first budding of the mind, arrives at Great Nirvana. For this reason, the Tathagata is the "well-gone". And also, zen indicates "to like", and zei indicates "is". O good man! This is as the world takes the meaning. "To like" refers to seeing the Buddha-Nature, and "is" is Great Nirvana. O good man! The nature of Nirvana is not really "is". The All-Buddha says "is" when he is addressing the world at large. O good man! For example, a person does not have a son, but people say that he has. Though, in truth, they have no "Way", they say that they do. The same is the case with Nirvana. Because of standing on this ground of the world at large, we say "is". The All-Buddha-World-Honoured One attains Great Nirvana. Hence, "well-gone". "What do we mean by "seken-ge" ["lokavid" - knowledge, understanding of the world]? "Seken" denotes the five skandhas, and "ge" means "to know". The All-Buddha-World-Honoured One thoroughly knows the five skandhas. Hence, "understanding the world well". Also, "world" means the "five desires", and "ge" "non-clinging". When one does not cling to the five desires, this is "one who well understands the world". We say "world". All the sravakas and pratyekabuddhas, as numerous as asamkhyas of countries in the east, do not see and know. But all Buddhas know all, see all, and understand all. So is it with the countries in the south, west, north, the four corners, and the lands up and down. Thus the Buddha is one who knows the world. Also, "world" refers to "all beings"; "to know" relates to the good and bad causes and effects of all beings. This is not something that can be known by sravakas and pratyekabuddhas. The Buddha alone knows. That is why we say that the Buddha is the "All-Knower". Also, the world is "lotus", and "to know" means "not to get defiled". O good man! This is what the world takes things to be. "Lotus" is the Tathagata; "not getting defiled" means that the Tathagata does not get defiled by the eight things of the world [possibly: profit, weakening, destruction, honour, praise, slandering, suffering, and bliss]. Hence, we call the Buddha the "All-Knower". Also, all Buddhas and Bodhisattvas are called "All-Knowers". Why? Because of the fact that all Buddhas and Bodhisattvas see the world. Hence, "All-Knower". O good man! This is as when one gains life from food, as a result of which we call food "life". The same is the case with all Buddhas and Bodhisattvas. As they know the world, they are called "All-Knowers". "Why do we say "mu-joshi" ["anuttara" - the "unsurpassed one"]? "Joshi" means "to cut". One who does not need to cut anything is the unsurpassed one. So the Buddha is the unsurpassed one. Also, "joshi" means "quarrel". The unsurpassed one has no quarrel. The Tathagata has no quarrel. So the Buddha is the unsurpassed one. And "joshi" means that the words can be destroyed. The word, "mujoshi", is not one that can be destroyed. Beings cannot destroy what the Tathagata says. So, the Buddha is the unsurpassed one. Also, "joshi" means "top seat" ["sthavira" - an honorific, meaning "aged", "old", "venerable"]. "Mujoshi" means that there is no seat that is higher. No one surpasses the Buddhas of the Three Times. So, we call the Buddha the "unsurpassed one". "Jo" is "new", and "shi" "old". The All-Buddha-World-Honoured one dwells in Great Nirvana, and there is no talking of new or old. So, we call the Buddha the "Unsurpassed One". "Why do we say "jǎgo-jǎbu" ["purusadamyasarathi" - "trainer of men/persons"]? Being a man himself, he trains men. O good man! The Tathagata is no man, and is not no-man. As he perfects man, the Tathagata is called a man. If any man or woman is perfect in four things, such a one is a man [human]. What four? These are: 1) [being] a good teacher of the Way, 2) listening well, 3) thinking well, and 4) practising the Way well as told. O good man! If any man or woman fails in these four things, he or she is not a human. Why not? Because, though the body is that of a human, the action is that of an animal. The Tathagata trains and breaks in men and women. For this reason, the Buddha is called the "the best trainer". Also, next, O good man! There are four ways of breaking in a horse. These are to touch: 1) its hair, 2) its skin, 3) its flesh, and 4) its bone. By touching, the trainer's will is carried out. It is the same with the Tathagata. Beings get broken in in four ways. First, he speaks of birth, and beings accept the Buddha's words. This is like the driver touching the hair, by which his will is carried out. Second, he speaks of birth and death, and beings accept the Buddha's words. This is as when the hair and skin are touched, by which the trainer's will is carried out. Thirdly, he speaks of birth, old-age, and illness, and beings accept the Buddha's words. This is like touching the hair, skin and flesh, by which the trainer's will is carried out. Fourthly, he speaks of birth, old-age, illness, and death, and the Buddha's words find acceptance. This is as when the trainer's will is carried out as his hand touches the hair, skin, flesh, and bone. O good man! There is nothing definite when a trainer breaks in a horse. When the Tathagata-World-Honoured One subdues beings, this is definite and there is nothing lacking. Hence, we say that the Buddha is the best trainer. "Why is he the "tenninshi" ["sastadevamanusyanam" - teacher of gods and humans]? Of teachers, there are two kinds. One teaches what is good, and the other teaches what is bad. All Buddhas and Bodhisattvas teach all beings what is good. What is good? It is what is good of body, mouth and mind. All Buddhas and Bodhisattvas teach beings and say: "O good man! You should segregate yourself from the evil actions of the body. Why? Because one ought to segregate oneself from evil actions and attain emancipation. For this reason, I teach you this Dharma. If it were the case that you could not segregate yourself from evil actions and attain emancipation, I would not, to the end, teach you to segregate [yourself from evil]. It can never come to pass that any being should segregate himself from evil actions and [then] fall into the three unfortunate realms. Through segregation, one achieves unexcelled Enlightenment and attains Great Nirvana. So, all Buddhas and Bodhisattvas always teach beings this Dharma. It is the same with the situation of the mouth and mind. Hence, the Buddha is the unsurpassed teacher. Also next: before, I was not Enlightened, but now I am. With what [I have] gained, I teach beings. I did not practise pure actions from the very beginning, but now I do so practise. With what I have practised, I address beings. Having done away with ignorance, I also do away with the ignorance of [other] beings. I have myself gained the pure eye and enable beings to dispel the gloom, and give them the pure eye. I know of two truths and also speak to beings about the two truths. On gaining emancipation, I speak to them about this Dharma of emancipation. Crossing the boundless great ocean of birth and death, I likewise enable beings to cross it. Having myself gained fearlessness, I teach and make them fearless. Having myself gained Nirvana, I speak to beings of Great Nirvana. That is why I am the Buddha and the unsurpassed teacher. Heaven is daytime. Up in heaven, the day is long and the nights short.

Hence, heaven. And, also, heaven has no apprehension. Hence, what there is is pleasure. So we say heaven. And also, heaven is a lamp. It thoroughly dispels the gloom and makes things very bright. Hence, heaven. Also, it thoroughly destroys the gloom of evil actions, giving one good actions, by which one gets born in heaven. Hence, heaven. And also, heaven is felicity. Due to felicity, we also say heaven. Also, heaven is

day. The day has light. So we call the day heaven. Hence, heaven. Man feels much obligation. And also, man has softness [gentleness] in body and speech. Also, man is arrogant. Also, man thoroughly destroys arrogance. O good man! Although the All-Buddha is the unsurpassed great teacher, in the sutras he is also styled the teacher of gods and humans. Why? O good man! Of all beings, only devas and humans can well aspire to unsurpassed Enlightenment, practise the ten good deeds, and attain the fruits of the shrotapanna, sakrdagamin, anagamin, and arhat, and attain unsurpassed Enlightenment. Hence, the Buddha is the teacher of heaven and earth." "Why do we say "Buddha"? He is awake. Himself awake, he also thoroughly awakens others. O good man! For example, if one is aware that there is a robber present, the robber can do nothing. It is the same here. The Bodhisattva-mahasattva is awake to all the innumerable defilements. Being awake to all defilements, he makes all defilements unable to do anything. Hence, the Buddha. On account of this awakening, he is birthless, ageless, disease-less, and deathless. Hence, the Buddha. "We say "bagaba" ["bhagavat" - "Lord"]. "Baga" means "to destroy"; "ba" means "defilement". As he crushes defilements, he is called "bhagavat". He is also so called because he well accomplishes Wonderful Dharma; because he well comprehends all teachings [dharmas]; because he possesses great virtues and towers above all others; because he has great fame, being known in all ten directions; because he variously makes great offerings; because, innumerable asamkhyas of kalpas ago, he did away with the female quality. "O good man! Any person, man or woman, who thus thinks of the Buddha, always sees the Buddha-World-Honoured One, while walking, standing, sitting, lying in bed, day or night, in the brightness or in the gloom. "Why do we say "Tathagata, Alms-deserving, and All-Enlightened One, down to Bhagavat" and give him so many epithets of innumerable virtues? O good man! The Bodhisattva, for innumerable long kalpas past, has respected his parents, the honoured ones ["upadhyaya" - the Buddhist teacher responsible for rites, rules and discipline in a monastic community], all teachers, sthaviras and elders ["ayusmat" - "long-lived" ones], and has always, over innumerable kalpas, practised - for beings' sake - dana, observed the moral precepts, practised forbearance, made effort, practised meditation, attained Wisdom, and has been full of great loving-kindness and compassion, and is perfect in sympathetic joy and equanimity. Because of this, the Bodhisattva now has the 32 signs of perfection and the 80 minor marks of excellence. And also, the Bodhisattva, for innumerable asamkhyas of kalpas, has practised effort, faith, mindfulness, meditation, Wisdom [the "panca-indriya" - the five "sense-organs" or roots], has respected and made offerings to teachers and elders, always caring for the good of Dharma and for food. The Bodhisattva holds, reads, and recites the twelve types of scripture, and for the sake of all beings works for emancipation, peace, and happiness, not caring a whit for his own. Why? Because the Bodhisattva always cultivates the mind [mental attitude, mental state] to flee the world, to renounce home life, [he cultivates] the non-created mind, the mind of non-disputation, non-defilement, non-binding, non-clinging, uncoveredness, and the non-indefinable mind, the mind of non-birth-and-death, non-greed, non-anger, non-ignorance, non-arrogance, non-defilement, non-illusion, non-suffering, the infinite mind, the large mind, the mind of the All-Void, the vacant mind, the non-vacant mind, the non-trained mind, the non-protected mind, the non-covered mind, the non-secular mind, the mind that is eternally in meditation, the ever-practising mind, the ever-emancipated mind, the mind that seeks non-recompense, the desireless mind, the mind that desires to do good, the non-speaking mind, the softened mind, the non-abiding mind, the unmolested [free, unrestricted] mind, the impermanence mind [mind aware of the impermanence of phenomena], the honest mind, the non-flattering mind, the mind of pure good and the mind that does not care for more or less [i.e. contented mind], the non-hard mind, the mind not of the common mortal, the non-sravaka mind, the non-pratyekabuddha mind, the good-knowing mind, the boundary-knowing mind [mind that knows that an existence has its own boundary line], the mind that knows the world of birth and death, the mind that knows the eternal world, the mind of the unmolested world. Because of this, he now has the ten powers, the four fearlessnesses, great compassion, the three mental states, and the Eternal, Bliss, Self, and the Pure. That is why we can say "Tathagata" down to "Bhagavat". This is the Bodhisattva-mahasattva's way of thinking of the Buddha. "How does the Bodhisattva-mahasattva think of Dharma? O good man! The Bodhisattvamahasattva thinks: "The Dharma spoken of by all Buddhas is all-wonderful and best." Grounding themselves in this Dharma, beings arrive at the fruition of the present life. Only this Wonderful Dharma knows no time. What the Dharma-Eye sees is not that of the fleshly eye. And no analogy can gain comparison "[express it]". Dharma is not something that is born, and it does not die; it abides not, nor does it die away. There is no beginning and no ending. It is not created and is not countable "[cannot be reckoned or calculated]." To the homeless, it becomes his home; to the refugeless and homeless, it is a refuge. To one with no light, it is light. To one not yet arrived at the other shore, it enables him to reach the other shore; to one who has no fragrance, it becomes unhindered fragrance. It cannot be seen. It does not move; it does not turn. Parting eternally from all pleasures, what there is is peace and bliss. It is the Ultimate and the All-Wonderful. It is not matter ["rupa"] and is cut off from matter. And yet it is matter. The same applies down "[all the skandhas]" to consciousness. And it is not consciousness and is cut off from consciousness. And [yet] it is consciousness. It is not action and is cut off from action. It is not binding, nor severing from bonds. It is no substance and is cut off from substance, and yet, it is substance. It is not the world and is cut off from the world, and yet, it is the world. It is not "is" and is cut off from "is", and yet, it is "is". It is not "entering" and is cut off from "entering", and yet, it is "entering". It is no cause and is cut off from cause, and yet, it is cause. It is no result and is cut off from result. It is not false and not true, and is cut off from all that is true, and yet, it is the true. It is not something born, and it does not die, and it is long cut off from birth and extinction, and yet, it is extinction. It has no form that can be seen and is not non-form, and is cut off from all that can be seen, and yet, it is form. It is no teaching and is not no teaching, and yet, it is the teacher. It is no fear and no peace, and is cut off from all fear, and yet, it is peace. It is not patience ["ksanti"] and is not non-patience, and is long away from non-patience, and yet it is patience. It is not tranquillity ["samatha"], is not non-tranquillity, is cut off from all tranquillity, and is yet tranquillity. It is the top ["murdhana"] of all dharmas, and cuts itself away from all defilements. It is pure, has no form to conform to, and is away from all forms. It is the last station of all innumerable beings. It is cut off from the blazing flames of all births and deaths. This is where all Buddhas come to play. It is the Eternal, and there is no change. This is the Bodhisattva's thinking of Dharma." "In what way does the Bodhisattva "think of the Sangha"? All Buddhas and all holy priests live in accordance with Dharma and obediently practise the Dharma which is straight. One cannot see it, catch hold of it, destroy it, or cause harm to it. It cannot be conceived of and is a good field of weal ["punya-ksetra" - a field of merit, blessings] for all beings. Though it is a field of weal, there is no having it in hand [grasping hold of it]. All is pure and undefiled; it is non-"asrava" and non-created; it is vast and boundless. The mind is trained and soft, is all-equal, and is undivided. There is no madding. All is eternal and unchanging. This is how to think of the Sangha. "How does the Bodhisattva think of shila [the moral precepts]? The Bodhisattva thinks: "There is shila. It is not [to be] transgressed against. It is non-"asrava", cannot be destroyed, and is not mixed up. Though it has no form or colour, it can be protected. Though there is nothing [about it] that can be touched or felt, one can certainly effect a means and be perfect in it. Nothing is lacking. It is what all the Buddhas and Bodhisattvas praise. This is the cause of the vaipulya and Great Nirvana." O good man! As an example, all such things as the great earth, ships, garlands, great family-clans, the great ocean, ash water, houses, swords, bridges, good doctors, wonderful medicine, agada, cintamani [wish-fulfilling jewel], legs, eyes, parents' gentle attitude: all such things cannot be plundered or have harm caused them. Fire cannot burn them nor water wash them away. Such is a flight of steps that leads up to high mountains or a great hanging banner of all Buddhas and Bodhisattvas. Abiding in this shila, one attains the [level of] shrotapanna. I know that I can, but I do not. Why not? Because if I attain this shrotapanna, I cannot save all beings. If I am to abide in this shila and attain supreme Enlightenment, I, too, can [do this]. This is what I desire to have. Why? If I gain supreme Enlightenment, I will indeed be able to speak about All-Wonderful Dharma and succour beings. This is the Bodhisattva-mahasattva's way of thinking of shila. "How do we think of dana [charitable giving]? The Bodhisattva-mahasattva meditates deeply on this dana, which is the cause of unsurpassed Enlightenment. [He thinks]: "All Buddhas and Bodhisattvas perform such dana. I, too, will befriend and practise it." If it is not performed, one cannot adorn the four classes of people of the Sangha. Though giving does not cut away defilements to the [very] end, it certainly extirpates those of the present. By reason of giving, all the beings of the ten directions, as numerous as the sands of innumerable, boundless numbers of Ganges, always praise [such giving]. When the Bodhisattva-mahasattva gives food to beings, he gives out life. "As a recompense for this dana, he always is and does not change when he attains Buddhahood." "As he bestows bliss, peace visits him when he attains Buddhahood. When the Bodhisattva gives, he seeks things in the correct way; he never spoils others through his giving. "Because of this, when he attains Buddhahood, he is blessed with the purity of Nirvana. When the Bodhisattva gives, he so contrives things that beings do not ask and yet are given "[what they need]". As a result of this, on the morning of Buddhahood, he attains the Sovereign Self [aisvarya-atman; i.e. the autonomous, free and unrestricted Self]. By giving, he gives strength to others. Because of this, when Buddhahood arrives, he gains the ten powers. Through giving, he enables others to gain words [the words of the scriptures]. By means of this, when Buddhahood comes, he gains the fourfold unhindered knowledge. All Buddhas and Bodhisattvas practise this giving and gain the cause of Nirvana. I, too, will practise giving and engender the cause of Nirvana. This is as was said in the vaipulya "Zäke" [i.e. possibly the "Gandavyuha Sutra"]. "What is thinking of heaven? There are such places as the four guardians' heaven and the thoughtlessness-non-thoughtlessness heaven. If one has faith, one gains the heaven of the four guardians of the earth. I, too, can be born there. If shila, erudition, giving, and Wisdom gain one the four guardians' heaven and the thoughtlessness-non-thoughtlessness heaven, I, too, can be born there. But I do not desire to get born. Why not? Impermanence reigns there in the four guardians' heaven and [also in] the thoughtlessness-non-thoughtlessness heaven. Due to impermanence, there exist birth, ageing, illness, and death. For this reason, I do not desire to be born there. This is similar to phantoms' possibly cheating the ignorant but not the wise. The four guardians' heaven and the thoughtlessness-non-thoughtlessness heaven are analogous to a phantom. The ignorant is the common mortal, but I am not a common mortal. I once heard of the "Paramartha" heaven. This refers to the fact that the Buddhas and Bodhisattvas are eternal and do not change. Because of the Eternal, there is no birth, ageing, illness, or death. I will make effort and seek - for beings' sake - "Paramartha" Heaven. Why? Because "Paramartha" Heaven can decidedly enable beings to cut off the "asravas", as in the case of the tree of the mind, which one can certainly bend as one wills. If I have faith down to Wisdom, I can certainly gain this "Paramartha" Heaven, and for the sake of beings, one may well think and speak about this "Paramartha" Heaven. This is the Bodhisattva-mahasattva's thinking about heaven. O good man! This is how we say that the Bodhisattva is not of the world. The world does not know, see, and realise. But the Bodhisattva knows, sees, and realises. "O good man! My disciples might say that there is no difference between holding, reciting, copying, and speaking about the 12 types of scripture and holding, reciting, copying, expatiating upon and expounding the Great Nirvana Sutra. But this is not so. Why not? O good man! Great Nirvana is what is closely guarded by the All-Buddha-World-Honoured One. As it is the deepest and most closely guarded of all the sutras of all the Buddhas, we call it superior. O good man! For this reason, this is a sutra most rare and special, and one difficult to conceive of." Bodhisattva Kasyapa said to the Buddha: "O World-Honoured One! I also know that this Great Nirvana Sutra is the most rare, most special, and is inconceivable, that the Buddha, Dharma and Sangha are inconceivable, and that the Bodhisattva, Enlightenment, and Great Nirvana are also inconceivable. O World-Honoured One! Why is it that we say that the Bodhisattva is also inconceivable?" "O good man! Though none teaches, the Bodhisattva-mahasattva well aspires to Enlightenment. Having aspired, he practises and makes effort. Even if a great fire were to burn his body and his head, he would not abandon his intention of seeking emancipation and his thinking of Dharma. Why not? Because the Bodhisattva-mahasattva always thinks to himself: "For innumerable asamkhyas of kalpas, I lived in the realms of hell, hungry ghosts, and animals, amongst humans and gods, and was burnt by the fire of defilement and, until now, was not able to gain one definite Dharma. Definite Dharma is none other than unsurpassed Enlightenment. I do not care about my body and mind, if it is for unsurpassed Enlightenment. I might well pound my body and mind into motes if it be for unsurpassed Enlightenment, but I shall not cease practising the Way and making effort. Why not? Because the spirit of practising the Way and making effort is none other than the cause of unsurpassed Enlightenment." O good man! The Bodhisattva has not yet seen unsurpassed Enlightenment and does not mind sacrificing his body and life for it thus; how could it be otherwise if he has seen it? That is why the Bodhisattva is inconceivable. "Also, we say inconceivable. We say so because the Bodhisattva-mahasattva sees the countless number of ills connected with birth and death, and this is not what sravakas and pratyekabuddhas can do. Though aware of the countless ills of birth and death, he does not entertain the least desire to flee from the pains which he suffers - and this for the sake of beings. Hence, we say inconceivable. Just for the sake of beings, the Bodhisattva-mahasattva might suffer all the pains of hell, and yet, for him this is nothing other than feeling the bliss of the third dhyana ["tritiyadhyana" - a meditative absorption characterised by equanimity, alertness, awareness, and a feeling of wellbeing]. For this reason, too, we say inconceivable. O good man! As an illustration, a fire starts up in the house of a rich man. He sees this and comes out of the house. His children are left behind and are not free [safe] from the fire. The rich man thinks of the danger from the fire. He goes back and tries to save his children, forgetting all about the danger to himself. It is the same with the Bodhisattva-mahasattva. He knows all about the ills of birth and death. But he faces them and does not mind the danger to himself, just for the benefit of [other] beings. Hence, we say inconceivable. "O good man! Innumerable minds aspire to Bodhichitta [the resolve to gain Enlightenment]. But seeing all the evils of birth and death, the mind pulls back. Some become sravakas and some pratyekabuddhas. But the Bodhisattva, when he hears this sutra, never loses his Bodhichitta and does not become a sravaka or pratyekabuddha. Thus, although the Bodhisattva has not yet risen to the state of the immovable first "bhumi" [stage of Bodhisattvic development], his mind is firmly set and knows of no retardation. Hence, we say inconceivable. O good man! A person might say: "I shall float on the great sea [of suffering] and save [beings]." Can we believe such a statement?" "O World-Honoured One! Such a statement may well be believed, or may not. How so? If it means to say that a human is doing the crossing, this is unthinkable. If it means to say that an asura is, this may well be thought of." "O good man! I do not speak of an asura. I only speak of the human being." "O World-Honoured One! Even amongst humans, there are those who can be thought of and those who cannot. O World-Honoured One! There are two kinds of human. One is the sage and the other a common mortal. The common mortal is not to be thought of; the sage can be." "O good man! I am only speaking of the common mortal, not of the sage." "O World-Honoured One! One such as a common mortal cannot be thought of [in this connection]." "O good man! A common mortal cannot cross the great sea. But this Bodhisattva can indeed cross the great sea of birth and death. For this reason, we say inconceivable. O good man! Is it possible to think of covering Mount Sumeru with the threads [fibres] of a lotus root?"

"No is the answer, O World-Honoured One!" "O good man! The Bodhisattva-mahasattva can, in the flash of a moment, count all the births and deaths of all beings. Hence, we say inconceivable." "O good man! The Bodhisattva-mahasattva has already, over innumerable asamkhyas of past kalpas, meditated on birth and death, impermanence, selflessness, non-bliss, and the impure, and yet, for the benefit of beings, discriminates and speaks about the Eternal, Bliss, Self, and the Pure. Though he speaks thus, this is no twisted view. Hence, inconceivable. O good man! Imagine getting into water and the water cannot drown you; imagine stepping into a great fire, and the fire cannot burn you. We cannot ever conceive of such a thing. It is the same with the Bodhisattva-mahasattva. Although he is in birth and death, no worry and harm can be caused him. Hence, inconceivable. "O good man! There are three kinds of men, namely: 1) top, 2) middle, and 3) low. He of the low level thinks as he enters the womb: "I am now living in the privy, a place where dirty things turn up, between corpses, amidst thorns and bushes, and in great darkness." And also, when he first emerges [from the womb], he thinks: "I am now coming out of the privy, out

of all these dirty and evil places, and out of great darkness." The man of the middle type thinks [as he enters the womb]: "I am now entering a forest where there are fruit trees, rivers of pure water, rooms, and houses." When he emerges [from the womb], he also says likewise. The man of the top rank thinks: "I am now up on top of a grand building and in a flowery forest. I am riding on horses and elephants and going up high mountains." It is the same when he comes out [from the womb]. The Bodhisattva-mahasattva, when entering, realises that he is now entering the womb; while in the womb, he knows that he is now in the womb; when coming out, he knows that he is coming out. He does not possess a mind of desire or anger, and yet, he has not gained the stage of the first "bhumi". Hence, he is inconceivable. O good man! Supreme Enlightenment cannot be expressed in parables [similes, analogies]. O good man! Neither can the mind be explained by similes and parables. And yet, all has to be explained. The Bodhisattva-mahasattva has no teacher to ask and no place to learn, and yet he attains supreme Enlightenment. After having attained it, he does not think in a stingy way, but always speaks about Dharma for the benefit of beings. Hence, inconceivable. O good man! The Bodhisattva-mahasattva is segregated from the body and is not the mouth; nor is he the mouth, and is not the body. He is neither body nor mouth, and yet there is segregation. We say that he is segregated from the body. This means that is far removed from killing, stealing, and lust. This is why we say that he is segregated from the body and is not the mouth. We say that there is segregation from the mouth. [This means that] he is segregated from lies, double-tongue, ill-speaking, and meaningless words. This is why we say that he is segregated from the mouth, but not from the body. We say that he is away from the body and mouth. This means to say that he is remote from greed, jealousy, anger, and distorted views. O good man! This is why we say that he is segregated from both body and mouth. O good man! The Bodhisattva-mahasattva is none but the body and action of the one Dharma, and is far away from master [from being a master], and yet is not away from it. Hence, inconceivable. The same with the mouth, too. O good man! His body parts from the body, and his mouth from the mouth; and Wisdom parts from non-body and non-mouth. O good man!

There is no case where the one Dharma destroys and creates. The nature of a created thing comes out differently and dies out differently. Hence, Wisdom cannot be segregated. O good man! Wisdom cannot destroy it [i.e. the nature of a created thing], fire cannot burn it, water cannot wash it away, the wind cannot move it, the earth cannot hold it, birth cannot give it birth, age cannot make it old, abiding cannot make it stay, breaking up cannot break it away, greed cannot covet it, anger cannot be angry with it, and ignorance cannot fool it. This is because of the fact that the nature of a created things calls forth different births and different deaths. To the end, the Bodhisattva-mahasattva does not entertain the thought that Wisdom crushes out defilement. And yet he says: "I crush out defilement." Though he speaks thus, this is not false. Hence, inconceivable." Bodhisattva Kasyapa said to the Buddha: "O World-Honoured One! I have now for the first time come to know of the inconceivability of the Bodhisattva-mahasattva, the inconceivability of Buddha, Dharma and Sangha, of the Great Nirvana Sutra, of the person who holds [upholds] it, and of Enlightenment and Nirvana." "O World-Honoured One! The life span of the unsurpassed Buddhist teaching must be far and near. When does it end?" "O good man! Now, the Great Nirvana Sutra has five actions, which are: 1) holy action, 2) pure action, 3) heavenly action, 4) illness action, and 5) child's action. If my disciples uphold, recite, copy, and speak about it, beings will respect it, make much of it, praise it, and make various offerings. Know that the Buddhist teaching [in these circumstances] will not die out. O good man! If when the Great Nirvana Sutra perfectly circulates amongst the people, but all my disciples violate shila, do all manner of evil, and do not believe in this sutra, because of their disbelief they will not uphold, recite, copy and explain the meaning, and [so] they will not be able to be looked up to by the people and no offerings will be made to them. They will see those who uphold shila and will look down upon them, saying: "You are of the group of the six masters [six contemporary teachers of the Buddha's day] and are not the Buddha's disciples." Know that [in these circumstances] it will not be long before the Buddha's teaching dies out." Bodhisattva Kasyapa said further to the Buddha: "O World-Honoured One! I was once personally taught by you: "The teaching of Buddha Kasyapa

lived but seven days and then died out". O World-Honoured One! Did Tathagata Kasyapa leave any kind of sutra behind? If there was anything like that [left behind], how can we say that it died out? If not, how can we say that the Great Nirvana Sutra is closely guarded by all Buddhas?" The Buddha said: "O good man! I said above that only Manjushri could understand. I shall now repeat it again. Listen carefully, listen carefully! O good man! There are two laws [dharmas] of the All-Buddha-World-Honoured One, namely those of: 1) secular [understanding] and 2) "Paramartha-satya" [Ultimate Truth]. The secular law dies out, but not that of "Paramarthasatya". Also, there are two kinds. One is of the non-Eternal, non-Self, non-Bliss, and the non-Pure; the other is that of the Eternal, Bliss, Self, and the Pure. "The non-Eternal, non-Self, non-Bliss, and the non-Pure die out, but the Eternal, Bliss, Self, and the Pure do not." "Further, there are two kinds. One is of the two vehicles, and the other is what the Bodhisattva possesses. What the two vehicles possess breaks apart and dies out, but what the Bodhisattva possesses does not. Also, there are two kinds. One is external, and the other internal. The external breaks up and dies, but the internal does not. Also, there are two kinds. One is the created and the other the non-created. The created is subject to dissolution and dies out, but the non-created does not. Also, there are two kinds. One is that which can be had in hand [grasped hold of], and the other is that which cannot. What can be had in hand is subject to dissolution and dies out, but what cannot be had in hand does not decay and die out. Further, there are two kinds. One is what goes together with others and the other is what does not go together with others. What goes together with others [a composite thing] decays and dies out, whereas the one that does not go together with others does not decay and die out. Also, there are two kinds. One is what obtains amongst men, and the other is what obtains in heaven. What obtains amongst men breaks up and dies out, and what obtains in heaven does not break up and die out. Also, there are two kinds, one is the eleven types of scripture, and the other is the vaipulya sutras. The eleven types of scripture break up and die out, but the vaipulya does not break up and die out. O good man! If my disciples possess, recite, copy, expound, respect, make offerings to, highly regard and praise the vaipulya sutras, know that then the Buddhist teaching will not die out. "O good man!

You ask: "Did Tathagata Kasyapa possess this sutra or not?" O good man! The Great Nirvana Sutra is the [most] closely guarded [sutra] of all Buddhas. Why? All Buddhas possess the eleven kinds of sutra, but these do not speak about the Buddha-Nature. These do not say: "The Tathagata is the Eternal, Bliss, Self, and the Pure; he does not ultimately enter Nirvana." For this reason, we call this sutra the closely guarded store. As the eleven types of sutras do not say this [i.e. that the Buddha is the Eternal, Bliss, the Self, and the Pure], we speak of "store". It is as when men do not take out the seven treasures, we speak of "storing". O good man! The reason why this person stores and keeps [things] is for the days to come. What is something for the days to come? So-called cereal is precious. Robbers come and overrun the country, or a person may have to live under a bad king or may have to use this [cereal] to ransom his life. If the roads are bad and wealth is hard to obtain, he will takes this out and use it. O good man! It is the same with the closely guarded store of the All-Buddha-Tathagata, too. All the evil bhiksus of days to come will store up impure things and say to the four classes of the Sangha that the Tathagata does after all enter Nirvana. They will read what circulates in the secular world and will not respect the Buddhist sutras. When such evils appear in the world, the Tathagata desires to make away with all evils, wrong living, and profit-seeking, and he delivers this sutra. Know that when the closely guarded store of this sutra dies out, the Buddhist teaching, too, will die out. O good man! The Great Nirvana Sutra is eternal and does not change. How could you speak ill of it and say: "Was there this sutra at the time of Buddha Kasyapa?" O good man! At the time of Buddha Kasyapa, all people were less greedy and had much Wisdom. It was very easy to teach the Bodhisattvas, as they were soft and malleable. They had great virtue; all was held well and tight. They were like great elephant kings. The world was clean; beings knew that the Tathagata would not ultimately enter Nirvana and that he was the Eternal and Unchanging. Though this sutra existed, there was no need to preach it." "O good man! The beings of this age have a great deal of defilement. They are ignorant, forgetful, and have no Wisdom. They doubt much, cannot gain faith, and the world is defiled. All people say that the Tathagata is impermanent, that he changes, and that in the end he enters Nirvana. For this

reason, the Tathagata delivers this sutra. O good man! Buddha Kasyapa's teaching also does not end indeed. Why not? Because it is Eternal and Unchanging. When there are beings who see the Self as non-Self, non-Self as the Self, the Eternal as non-Eternal, the non-Eternal as the Eternal, Bliss as non-Bliss, non-Bliss as Bliss, the Pure as non-Pure, the non-Pure as the Pure, that which does not end as that which ends, that which ends as non-ending, sin as non-sin, venial sin as grave sin, grave sin as venial sin, vehicle as non-vehicle, the non-vehicle as a vehicle, the Way as non-Way, non-Way as the Way, what truly is Enlightenment as non-Enlightenment, what truly is non-Enlightenment as Enlightenment, Suffering as non-Suffering, the Cause of Suffering as not the Cause of Suffering, Extinction as non-Extinction, the True as non-True, what really is secular as "Paramartha-satya", "Paramartha-satya" as secular, the refuge as non-refuge, the genuine Buddha-word as Mara's words, what are truly Mara's words as the Buddha-word -at such a time all Buddhas deliver this sermon of the Great Nirvana Sutra. "O good man! One could sooner say that the proboscis of a mosquito could reach to the bottom of the great ocean than that the Tathagata's teaching becomes extinct. One could sooner say that one can bind the great wind with a rope than that the Tathagata's teaching becomes extinct. One could sooner say that one can blow away Mount Sumeru with one's breath and break it into pieces than that the Tathagata's teaching will become extinct. One could sooner say that amidst the fire of khadira [acacia catechu] the lotus will bloom, than that the Tathagata's teaching becomes extinct. One could sooner say that agada is poison than that the Tathagata's teaching becomes extinct. One could sooner say that the moon can be heated up and the sun made cool, than that the Tathagata's teaching will get extinguished. One could sooner say that the four great elements will lose their qualities, than that the Tathagata's teaching will become extinct. "O good man! If the Buddha appears in the world, attains unsurpassed Enlightenment, but his disciples do not gain the depths of meaning, and if the Buddha-World-Honoured One is to enter Nirvana, know that this teaching will not live long in the world. Also, next, O good man! If the Buddha first appears, attains unsurpassed Enlightenment, and all his disciples gain the depths of meaning, know that this teaching will live long, even if the Buddha enters

Nirvana. "Also, next, O good man! The Buddha first appears in the world, attains unsurpassed Enlightenment, and his disciples may gain the depths of meaning; but if there are no lay danapatis [alms-givers] who respect the Buddha's teaching, and if the Buddha enters Nirvana, know that this teaching will not survive long. Also, next, O good man! If the Buddha first appears in the world and attains unsurpassed Enlightenment, and all his disciples gain the depths of menaing, and if there are many faithful lay danapatis, who respect the Buddha's teaching, and the Buddha enters Nirvana, then, the Buddha's teaching will live long. "Also, next, if the Buddha first appears in the world and attains unsurpassed Enlightenment, and all the disciples gain the depths of meaning; also, if there are faithful lay danapatis who look up to the Buddha's teaching and many disciples of the Buddha who speak about the Buddha's teaching; but if they do [all this] for profit and not for Nirvana, know that the teaching will not live long when the Buddha dies. "Also, next, O good man! When the Buddha first appears in the world and attains unsurpassed Enlightenment, and there are many disciples who gain the depths of meaning; also, there are faithful lay danapatis who respect the Buddha's teaching, and all the disciples preach the doctrine not for profit, but for Nirvana, and the Buddha enters Nirvana - know that this teaching will survive long. "Also, next, O good man! If the Buddha first appears in the world and attains unsurpassed Enlightenment, and all the disciples gain the depths of meaning; and if there are faithful lay danapatis who look up to the Buddha's teaching, but all the disciples dispute, saying this and that, and the Buddha enters Nirvana - know that this teaching will not survive long. "Also, next, O good man! If the Buddha first appears in the world and attains unsurpassed Enlightenment, and there are disciples who gain the depths of meaning; also, if there are faithful lay danapatis who respect the Buddha's teaching, and all the disciples practise the teaching of peace and harmony and do not dispute [with one another], but respect one another; and if the Buddha enters Nirvana - know that this teaching will live long and not die out. "Also, next, O good man! If the Buddha appears in the world, attains unsurpassed Enlightenment, and there are disciples who gain the depths of meaning; also, if there are faithful lay danapatis who respect the Buddha's teaching, and all the disciples preach the teaching of Great Nirvana; if

they respect one another and do not quarrel [amongst themselves], and yet they store up impure things, and praise themselves, saying: "I have now attained the [level of] shrotapanna up to arhatship" - know, too, that if the Buddha dies, this teaching will not survive long in the world. "Also, next, O good man! If the Buddha first appears in the world and attains unsurpassed Enlightenment, and if all the disciples gain the depths of meaning, and there are also faithful lay danapatis who respect the Buddha's teaching; and if all the disciples preach the doctrine of Great Nirvana, living in harmony and with respect for one another, and not storing up impure things and not saying that they will attain [the level] of shrotapanna up to arhatship, and if the Buddha-World-Honoured One dies - know that this teaching will live long. "Also, next, O good man! If the Buddha first appears in the world and attains unsurpassed Enlightenment, and all the disciples do not store up impure things and do not say that they will attain the [level of] shrotapanna up to arhatship; yet if they have clinging to their own views and variously say: "O Elders! The four grave offences, down to the seven ways of adhikaranasamatha [the seven ways of making away with disputes], which all Buddhas have instituted, are accorded with or enlarged upon. It is the same with the twelve types of sutra. Why? Because the Buddha knows that land and time differ and that there are differences in the qualities of beings. For this reason, the Tathagata prohibits or opens out [allows], and there are differences between light [venial] and heavy [grave sin]. O Elders! This is as in the case of a good doctor who, when someone is ill, either allows or does not allow milk, and says "yes" to fever and "no" to cold. The same is the situation with the Tathagata. He sees the root of illness of all beings' defilements, and either says "yes" or prohibits. O Elders! I directly heard the Buddha say; [I alone know the meaning and not you; I alone know shila and not you; I alone know the sutras and not you]." If the Buddha dies, know that this teaching will not live long. O good man! If the Buddha first appears in the world and attains unsurpassed Enlightenment, and if there are many disciples who do not say: "I have attained the [level of] shrotapanna up to arhatship", nor do they say: "All Buddhas, for the sake of beings, either prohibit or allow [the same thing]. O Elders! I myself have directly heard from the Buddha about the meaning, the Dharma, and shila. O Elders! One should take one's stand on the twelve types of sutra of the Tathagata. If they are right, I uphold them; if not, I do away with such." If the Buddha-World-Honoured-One enters Nirvana, know that his teaching will live long. "O good man! When my teaching dies out, there may be sravaka disciples who will say that there is a conscious Self or that there is not; or that there is or is not an in-between existence [between death and re-birth]; or that there are or are not the Three Times, that there are or are not the three vehicles, that all is is or is not "is", that there are beginnings and endings to beings, that the twelve links of interdependent arising are created things or that causality is uncreated, that the Tathagata has illness and pain or does not have any such thing, or that the Tathagata does not allow bhiksus the ten kinds of meat. What are these ten? They are: [the flesh of] man, serpent, elephant, horse, mule, dog, lion, boar, fox, and monkey. They say that he allows all other kinds, or that he does not. Or the bhiksu does not possess five things. What are the five? They are: 1) domestic animals, 2) sword, 3) liquor, 4) cheese powder , and 5) sesame oil. They say that these are not sold, but that all other things are permitted. Or that a bhiksu is not allowed to enter the five kinds of house. What are the five? They are those of: 1) butchers, 2) prostitutes, 3) bars, 4) royal palaces, and 5) candalas. Or they say that other houses can be entered. They say that silk cloth ["kauseya"] is not permitted, all others being permitted. Or they say that the Tathagata allows all bhiksus to possess clothing, food and bedding worth a hundred thousand in gold, or that he does not. Or they say that Nirvana is the Eternal, Bliss, Self, and the Pure, or that Nirvana is the ending of defilement, which, differently expressed, is Nirvana. For example, woven cloth is clothing; with tattered clothing, we say non-clothing, which is not a name for a different thing from clothing, and we say "non-clothing". They say that the body of Nirvana is not like that, either. O good man! At that time, there are few who speak correctly, and many who present false views. Few are those who uphold the right view and many are those who are grounded in false views. Few are those who uphold the Buddha-word, and many are those who are grounded in Mara's laws. "O good man! At the time, there were two disciples in the state of Kausambi. One was an arhat, and the other violated the precepts. There were 500 of those who violated the precepts, and 100 arhats. Those who violated the precepts said: "The Tathagata surely enters Nirvana. We heard directly from him how the [prohibition on] the four grave offences instituted by the Buddha may well be accorded with or transgressed, and there will not be any sin. We have now attained arhatship and have the fourfold unhindered knowledge. And even the arhat also commits the four offences. If the law of the four offences is true and sin ensues, the arhat would not have committed them. While the Buddha was still in life, there was strict observing, but on his entering Nirvana, all is abandoned all in all." Thus did they say. The [arhat] bhiksu said: "O Elders! Do not say that the Tathagata definitely enters Nirvana. What I know is that the Tathagata is Eternal and does not change. There is no change in sin depending on whether one transgresses during the Buddha's lifetime or after his entering Nirvana, if one commits the four grave offences. This is not so. Why? How could those of the stage of shrotapanna infringe the precepts? You say that you are an arhat. With an arhat, no thought such as that he has now arrived at the stage of an arhat comes to his mind. The arhat speaks about good Dharma, but not not that which is evil. O Elders! What you say is all wrong. If you look into the 12 types of sutra, you will definitely see that you are no arhat." O good man! Then, at that time, all the bhiksus who had violated the precepts did away with the life of that arhat. O good man! At that time, King Mara, his mind enraged by the angered mind of the two groups of bhiksus, killed those 600. Then all common mortals said: "Woe is the day! The Dharma of the Buddha has now come to an end!" And yet, my Dharma did not end there. At that time, there were 12 hundred thousand great Bodhisattvas who strictly upheld my Dharma. How could one say that my Dharma ended? At that time, in Jambudvipa, not one bhiksu was my disciple. At that time, the Papiyas [Mara, the devil], burnt all the sutras in a great fire. Then, there remained some unburnt fragments, which all the Brahmins stole away and, collecting these here and there, added them to their own texts. For this reason, all petty [lesser] Bodhisattvas, when there is as yet no Buddha, generally believe in the words of the Brahmins. These Brahmins may say that they have shila. But, truth to tell, the Brahmins do not. All tirthikas may say that they have Bliss and Purity, but truth to tell, they do not understand the signification of the Self, Bliss, and the Pure. They just take up one or two words, or one sentence or two, and say say that there are such and such things stated in their sutras." Then, in the castle town of Kusinagara, between the twin sal trees, the innumerable, boundless asamkhyas of bhiksus, on hearing this, all said: "The world is empty, the world is empty!" Bodhisattva Kasyapa said to all the bhiksus: "O you! Do not be apprehensive and sad, do not weep, for a while. The world is not empty. The Tathagata is Eternal; he changes not. Thus, too, are Dharma and Sangha." Then, the great congregation, on hearing these words, ceased weeping and all aspired to unsurpassed Awakening.

Chapter Twenty-Four: On Pure Actions 4

At that time, there was in the great castle of Rajagriha a great king called Ajatasatru [son of Bimbisara and his royal consort, Vaidehi], one who was very evil-natured, who took pleasure in taking life and who was fully accomplished in the four evil actions of the mouth [i.e. lying, flattering, speaking maliciously, and speaking with a "double tongue"]. Greed, ill-will and ignorance ruled his mind. He only saw the present and not the days to come. All evil persons were of his group. He abandoned himself to the five desires [wealth, lust, food and drink, fame, and sleeping] and the pleasures of life. As a result of this, he harmed his own innocent father. After having harmed his father, repentance [remorse] brought down a fever upon his mind. No adornment or necklaces or music could help him. With his mind in a fever of repentance, there came about boils all over his body. These sent forth stinking, evil smells and none could come near him. Then he said to himself: "Now I am receiving these karmic results in this present life. It will not be long before the punishments of hell press down upon me." Then his mother, Queen Vaidehi, applied various medicines. But the boils only increased in number and there was no sign of a cure. The king said to his mother: "Such boils come from the mind, and not from the four elements. People may claim to [be able to] cure me, but such cannot be." At that time, there was a minister called Candrayasas. He went to the king and stood to one side and said: "O great king! Why are you so crestfallen and why are you so sorrowful? Do you have any pain in your body? Or is it in your mind?" The king said to his minister: "How could I not have pain in my body and mind? My father did nothing wrong, and I committed deadly sins against him. I once asked a wise man about this. There are five persons in the world who have to be born in hell. These are those who have committed the five deadly sins. I now have innumerable, boundless, asamkhyas of sins. How could I not have pain in body and mind? And there can be no good doctor who can effect a cure for my body and mind." The minister said: "O great king! Do not be so sorrowful." He said in a gatha: "If one always worries, The worry ever increases and grows. If one is pleased and sleeps, One's sleep ever increases and grows. So does it stand with greed, lust, and drinks. "You, King, say

that there are five persons who cannot escape from hell. Who is it who went there, saw this, and came and told you, the King, so? Hell is what is called thus by the intellectual mind. You, King, say that there is no doctor who can cure your body and mind. There is a great doctor called Purana. He knows everything and abides in unmolested [unassailed, inviolable] dhyana [meditation]. He has practised pure actions and always speaks to innumerable beings about unsurpassed Nirvana. To all disciples, he says: "There can be no black actions and no black results from black actions; there can be no white actions and no white results from white actions. There are no black and white actions and no black and white results. There are no high actions and no low actions." This master is now in Rajagriha. O great King!

Please condescend to go and see him, and let this master cure you." Then, the king answered and said: "If he can definitely cure me, I shall take refuge in him." And there was a minister called Virtue-Store, who also went to the king and said: "O great King! Why is it that you look so emaciated, with your lips and mouth so dried up and your voice so low that you look like a coward facing a great enemy, and you look so changed? What are you worried about? Is it that your body gives you pain, or your mind?" The king anwered and said: "How could it be that I should not now have pain in body and mind? I am ignorant and blind and have no eye of Wisdom. I have associated with all bad friends and befriended them. Caught by the words of the evil-minded Devadatta, I wilfully committed deadly actions against the rightful king. I once heard a wise man say in a gatha: "Any ill-will and action Towards one's parents, the Buddha, or his disciples Buy one a life In avichi hell." "On account of this I fear and have great worries. No good doctor can ever cure me." The minister said: "O great King! Have no fear for a while. Of law, there are two kinds. One is that of the world-fleeing, and the other is the king's law. In the king's law, if one harms one's father, this is a deadly sin. But, truth to tell, it does not constitute a sin. it is like the case of the kalala insect, which gains birth by breaking out of the belly of its mother insect. As this is the law of its birth, the harming of one's mother, in truth, does not buy one any sin. It is the same with the conception of a mule. Thus must it obtain with state law, which is [concerned with] governing. Though one may kill one's parents, there can be no sin. With the law of the world-fleeing, the killing of even a mosquito or an ant buys one sin. O great King! Please broaden your mind and have no worry! Why? Because: "If one always worries, The worry ever increases and grows. If one is pleased and sleeps, One's sleep ever increases and grows. So do things go with greed, lust, and drinks." "You, King, say that there is no good doctor who can cure your body and mind. Now there is a great master called Maskarigosaliputra. He knows all and pities beings as one would one's own child. Himself already away from illusion, he thoroughly extracts the sharp arrows of the three poisons. All beings cannot see, know, and realise all things. Only this person sees, knows, and realises. So, the great master always speaks to his disciples. All beings have seven things with their body. What are the seven? These are: 1) earth, 2) water, 3) fire, 4) wind, 5) sorrow, 6) bliss, and 7) life. These seven are no phantoms, not things that have been made, and they cannot be destroyed. These are like the isika reed [hard and strong reed, from which arrows are made]; they are as static and immovable as Mount Sumeru. And they do not abandon [one], and like milk and cream, do not come into conflict. One may strike with a sword at sorrow, bliss, good, or non-good, and they cannot be harmed. Why not? This is like the seven categories of the Void , where there is nothing that obstructs. Thus life, too, can never be destroyed. Why not? For there are no people that cause harm and none that dies. Nothing is done and there is nothing that suffers being done; nothing is said and nothing is heard; there is nothing thought about and none that teaches. He always teaches thus, and well enables beings to do away with innumerable grave sins. This master is now in the great castle of Rajagriha. O great King! Please condescend to go to him. If you see him, all your sins will die away." Then the king answered: "If he definitely can make away with all my sins, I shall certainly take refuge in him." Also, there was a minister called Real-Gain, who went to the king and spoke thus in a gatha: "O great King! Why is it That you have no jewellery on your body, That your hair is dishevelled? Why do you show yourself thus?

Why do you shake so and look frightened As when a strong wind shakes a tree full of blossom?" "O King! Why do you look so sorrowful? You look like a farmer who is all sorrow when the rain does not fall after his having sown seed. Do you have pain in your body or your mind?" The king replied: "How could my body and mind not have pain? My late father and king was compassionate and gracious and particularly felt pity for me. There really was nothing wrong. He went and consulted an augur, who said: "After he has been born, this child will surely kill his father." Despite being told this, he raised me. Once a wise man said: "If a person has carnal intercourse with his mother, violates a bhiksuni [nun], or steals that which belongs to the Sangha, causes harm to one who aspires after Enlightenment or kills his own father, such a person will assuredly fall into Avichi Hell." How could I not have pain in my body and mind?" The minister said further: "O great King! Please do not be sorry for a time. If your father killed a person who was in quest of emancipation, there could be sin. If one kills following state law, there can be no sin. O great King! What does not accord with law is no law. No-law is no law. If one has no son, we say sonless. Also, a bad son is called no son. Though we say "no son", this does not mean that the person does not have a son. If food contains no salt, we say saltless. Even when there is not much salt, we say saltless. When there is no water in the river, we say waterless. Even when the amount of water is small, we say waterless. When a thing dies out moment after moment, we say impermanent. Even if a thing exists for a kalpa, we say impermanent. When a person has sorrow, we say blissless. Even when the bliss he has is only small, we say blissless. The molested [i.e. un-free] state is called selfless. Even when there is a little freedom, we say selfless. The dark night is called sunless; even at the time when we have cloud and mist, we say sunless. O great King! Little law may be called lawless. And yet it is not the case that there is no law [there]. O great King! Listen carefully to what I say. All beings have remnant karma. Because of karma, a person often repeats birth and death. If the late king had remnant karma and you killed your father, how could you have committed a crime? O great King! Broaden your mind and do not be sad. Why? Because:

"If one always worries,
The worry ever increases and grows.
If one is pleased and sleeps,
One's sleep ever increases and grows.
So do things go with greed, lust, and drinks."

"You, King, say that there is no good doctor in the world who can cure your body and mind. Now, there is a great teacher called Sanjaya-vairatiputra. He knows and sees all. His wisdom is deep and wide and is like the great sea. He has great virtue and divine powers. He well enables people to make away with all doubts. All beings do not know, see, and realise. Only this person knows, sees, and realises. He now lives near Rajagriha and speaks thus to his disciples: "Of all beings, if a king, he performs good and evil unmolestedly. Any evil that one commits has no sin. It is as with fire, which burns things, and there is no calling it pure or impure. It is the same with the king. He is like fire. For example, the great earth supports things both clean and dirty. Acting thus, it is neither angry nor glad. The same with the king. He shares the same nature as the earth. For example, the nature of water is to wash things pure or not pure. Thus acting, it has neither worry nor pleasure. The same with the king. He shares the same nature as water. For example, the nature of the wind is to blow things away, be they pure or impure. Thus acting, it has neither worry nor pleasure. The same with the king. Also, an autumnal stub [bulb, seed] calls forth buds in spring. Also, a stub may be cut and there is no sin. The same with all beings. They die here in this life and gain life here again. What sin is there in getting life back again? All the fruits of suffering and bliss of all beings arise out of what has been done in this life. The cause was in the past and one harvests the result in this life; if there is no cause in the present life, there cannot be any result in the life to come. Because of the results that arise in this life, beings uphold sila [morality]. Severely practising the Way and with effort, a person prevents the arising of bad fruits in the present life. By upholding sila, one harvests non-"asrava" [non-defilement]. When one attains the non-"asrava", one puts an end to the karma of the "asravas". When karma ends, all sorrows end. When all sorrows end, one attains emancipation. O great King! Please be quick and go there, and make away with the suffering of your body and mind. If you see him, all your sins will die out." The king answered: "If this teacher can clearly make away with sin, I shall take refuge in him." Also, there was a minister called "All-Knowing", who also went to the king and said: "O King! Why do you look so austere? You look quite like one who has lost his kingdom or a spring that has dried up, or a pond without lotuses, or a tree without leaves, or a bhiksu who has violated sila and lost dignity. Does this come from pain in your body or your mind?" The king replied: "How could I not have pain in my body and mind? My father, the late king, was compassionate and kind-hearted. But I was undutiful and forgot all that I owed him. The only happiness he cared about was solely my own. But I acted against him and put an end to his bliss. Though he had no faults, I wilfully committed a deadly sin against him. I, also, once heard a wise man say: "If one kills one's own father, one will suffer from great pains for innumerable asamkhyas of kalpas." Soon, before long, I shall fall into hell. And no good doctor can cure me of my sin." The minister said: "O great king! Please discard your worries and pains. O King! Did you not hear of a king called Rama? He killed his father and came to the throne. All such kings as Bhadrika, Virucin, Nahusa, Karttika, Visakha, Bright-Moonlight, Bright-Sunlight, Love, and Many-Possessing did away with their fathers and came to the throne. At present, all such kings as Vidudabha, Udayana, Evil-Natured, Rat, and Lotus-Blossom have all killed their fathers. Not one king has suffering or worry. We can indeed look into the realms of hell, hungry ghosts, and heaven [animals], and there are none such. O great King! There are two existences. One is that of the humans, and the other is that of the animals. Though these are two, they have not come out of cause and effect, nor do these die out by cause and effect. If not from cause and effect, how could there be anything good or non-good? Please, O great King, do not entertain worry and sorrow. Why not?

"If one always worries,
The worry ever increases and grows.
If one is pleased and sleeps,
The sleep ever increases and grows.
So do things stand with greed, lust, and drinks."

"You, King, say: "There isn't any good doctor who can cure both my body and mind." There is now a great teacher called Ajitakesakambara, who knows and sees everything. He views gold and dirt with an equal eye; they are not two. He cuts his right-hand side with a sword, and smears sandalwood on his left-hand side. Between two persons, he sees no difference. He looks upon enemy and friend with an equal eye, and his mind sees no difference. This teacher is truly a good doctor of this world. Whether walking, standing, sitting, or reclining, his mind is not in disorder. He speaks to many of his disciples thus: "Whether by my own hand or by instigating others, whether I kill or get others to kill, whether I expose [someone] to heat or cause others to do so, whether I commit immoral deeds or have others do so, whether I tell lies or get others to lie, whether I drink liquor or cause others to do so, whether I kill the people of a village, a castle-town, or a state, whether I kill all beings with a war chariot, or whether I give offerings to all who live to the south of the Ganges or kill those to the north of the Ganges - in none of any of this can there be any talk of crime or weal, giving, sila or meditation." He also lives near to Rajagriha. O King! Please go [to him] at once. If you see him, your sin will all disperse." The king said to the minister: "If he cures me of my sin, I shall surely take refuge in him." Also, there was a minister called Auspicious-Virtue, who came to the king and said: "O King! Why has your mien no lustre? You look like a lamp at mid-day, or like the moon in daytime, or a king who has lost his kingdom, or the earth in a waste-land. O great King! The four quarters of the state are pure and at peace, and there is no enemy. And why do you now look so worried and pained? Is the pain in your body or mind? There are princes who always think: "When will I be able to gain the unmolested [unlimited, unconstrained] state?" O you, great King, have now attained your wish and reign over Magadha unmolested, and you possess the storehouse of the late king, full of treasure. Cheer up and please yourself as you will! How do you come to be so worried and pained?" The king answered: "How could I not be worried. It is as with the ignorant, who only cling to the taste and do not see the sharp sword, or take poison and do not see the harm that ensues. It is the same with me. It is like the case of a deer, who only sees grass, not the deep hole [trap], or the rat, who carries on devouring without seeing the cat and the fox. I am like that. I saw [only] the pleasure that dangled before me, and not the evil that will ensue in days to come. I once heard a wise man say: "Even if one were hit in one day by 300 halberds, one should not have an evil thought about one's own parents." I am now close to the fire of hell. How could I not be worried?" The minister said further: "Who has come and cheated the king and said that there is hell? Who makes the sharp points of the thrusting spears? Who makes the rare colours of flying birds? Who makes the watery marshes, the hardness of stone, the moving power of the wind, the heat of fire, how do all things die and get born of their own accord? And who makes all of these? Hell is nothing but a fiction of intellectuals. I shall now explain. "Ji" means "earth"; "goku" means "to break". The earth breaks the earth. There can be no return to crimes. This is the meaning of "jigoku" ["naraka" - hell]. Also, "ji" means "man"; "goku" means "heaven". By killing one's father, one gains birth in heaven. That is why the rishi, Vasu, says that by killing a sheep, one is blessed with the bliss of man and heaven. This is hell. Also, "ji" means "life"; "goku" means "long". By killing, one arrives at a long life. Hence, hell. O great King! For this reason, know that, in truth, there is no such thing as hell. O great King! We sow barley and we gain barley; we plant rice and we gain rice. He who kills hell gains hell in return. By killing man, one gains man in return. O great King! Listen to what I, your vassal, say. Truth to tell, there is no such thing as killing or harmony. If there is a Self, then in truth there is no such thing as harming. If there is no Self, then again there cannot be any harming. Why not? If there is a Self, what there is is the eternal and no change. Because of the eternal, there cannot be any killing. What there is is non-breaking-up, non-destroying, non-tying, non-binding, non-anger, non-joy. It is like the Void. How can there be any sin in killing? If there is no Self, then all things are non-eternal. Because of impermanence, extinction proceeds moment after moment. Through the extinction that occurs moment after moment, he who kills and he who dies [both] die off moment after moment. If there is extinction every moment, who is there to be punished for the sin? O great King! Fire burns wood, but fire commits no crime. An axe cuts a tree, but no sin attaches to the axe. A

"If one always worries,
The worry ever increases and grows.
If one is pleased and sleeps,
One's sleep ever increases and grows.
So does it obtain with greed, lust, and drinks."

"You, King, say: "There is no good doctor who can cure this vile karma." Now, there is a great doctor, called Kakudakatyayana, who knows and sees everything. In the flash of a moment, he sees clearly the Three Times [past, present and future] and the innumerable, boundless worlds. With his hearing it is the same. He thoroughly enables beings to segregate themselves from wrong and vile actions. This is like the Ganges that thoroughly washes away and cleanses all sins, in and out. It is the same with this good teacher. He does away thoroughly with all evil sins, in and out. He speaks to all his disciples thus: "One kills all beings, and if there is no repentance in one's mind, one never falls into evil realms. This is like space, which does not suffer from dust and water. If one feels repentance, one falls into hell. This is like a great volume of water wetting the great earth. All beings are made by Ishvara [God]. If Ishvara is pleased, beings will have peace and happiness; if he becomes angry, all beings will suffer from pain and worry. Any sin or weal of any being goes back to Ishvara, who makes them. How can man say that man has sin or weal? It is like a mechanical appliance or wooden man, which can walk, stand, sit, or lie on a bed, as made [capable of doing so] by the artisan; yet, it cannot speak. It is the same with beings. Ishvara is, for example, like an artisan; the wooden man may can be compared to beings. How can there be any sin with such a creation?" Such a great teacher now lives close to Rajagriha. Please hasten! Just one glimpse of him will cleanse you of all your sins." The king answered: "If I am quite sure that this person can indeed do away with my sins, I shall certainly take refuge in him." Also, there was a minister called

scythe cuts grass, but the scythe does not have any sin. A sword kills a man, but the sword, truth to tell, is not a man and has no sin. How can man sin? Poison kills a man. The poison, truth to tell, is not a man. The poison has no sin. It is like this with all things. Truth to tell, there is no sin of killing. How could there be any sin? Please, O great King, have no worry. Why not?

Fearless, who came to the king and said: "O great King! There are ignorant people in the world who, in the course of a day, are happy and sad 100 times, sleep and wake up 100 times, and become frightened and weep 100 times. With the wise, nothing such as this occurs. O great King! How is it that you look worried and sorrowful? You look like a man who has lost his comrade, or a man who has lost his feet in deep mud, with no hope of being saved, or like a thirsty man who cannot expect a drink, or one who has lost his way and cannot find a guide, or a man with an incurable illness, or like a shipwrecked ship, with no one else on the sea to provide rescue. O great King! Is it your body or your mind that gives you pain?" The king replied: "How could my body and mind not give me pain? I associated with a bad friend and encountered evilness of speech. There was nothing in the late king for which one could reproach him, and yet I wilfully committed a deadly sin [against him]. I know for sure that I shall fall into hell. And there is no good doctor who can cure." The minister said: "O great King! Please do not let the poison of suffering raise its head! Now, the Kshatriya belongs to the kingly caste. There cannot be any talk of sin if he kills for the sake of the state, for the sake of sramanas or Brahmins, or for the sake of giving peace to people. Although the late king respected the sramanas, he did not serve the Brahmins. There was no fairness in his mind. Being unfair, he was no Kshatriya. Now, you, great King, desire to serve all Brahmins, and you have killed the late king. What sin have you committed? O great King! There really is no killing. Now, killing means taking life. Life has the nature of the wind.

The nature of the wind cannot be killed. How, then, can one kill life? Could there be any sin [here]? Please, O great King! Do not worry and be sorrowful. Why not?

"If one always worries,
The worry ever increases and grows.
If one is pleased and sleeps,
One's sleep ever increases and grows.
So is it also with greed, lust, and drinks."

"You say, King, that there is no good doctor who can cure your body and mind. Now, there is a great teacher called Nirgrantha-Jnatiputra [the best-known of the "six masters"], who knows, sees, and pities all beings. He knows all the sharp and dull natures of all beings and fully knows all kinds of expedients fitting for the occasion. The eight things of the world [profit, weakening, breaking up, honour, praise, slander, suffering, and bliss] cannot defile him. Silently, he practises pure actions. To his disciples, he says: "There cannot be any such thing as dana [charitable giving], good, father, mother, present life, after-life, arhat, practising, or the Way. All beings, after 80 thousand kalpas, wil spontaneously be relieved from the wheel of birth and death. It is the same with sin and non-sin. It is like the four great rivers, namely, the Indus, Ganges, Vaksu, and Sita. All of them enter the sea, and then there is no difference. It is the same with all beings.

There is no difference once one is liberated." This teacher is now living in Rajagriha. O great King! Please speed to him. If you see him, all your sins will go away." The king answered: "If this teacher can make away with my sins, I shall surely take refuge in him." At that time, there was a great doctor called Jivaka, who went to the king and said: "O great King! Do you sleep well or not?" The king replied in a gatha:

"If all defilements are done away with eternally
And one has no greed in the defiled three realms,
There can be sound sleep.
If one has attained Great Nirvana
And speaks of its deep meaning,
Such a person is a true Brahmin.
And such a person can gain sound sleep.
If one's body knows no evil actions that have been committed,
And if one's mouth is far from the four wrongs,
If one's mind has no doubts,
One can get sound sleep.
If the body and mind have no fever,
And if one lives in a peaceful quarter,
And is blessed with unsurpassed bliss,
One can have sound sleep.
If one's mind has no clinging,
And if one is far away from all enmity,
And if the mind is in harmony
And has no quarrels,
One can have sound sleep.
If the body does not do any evil,
And if the mind always repents,
And believes that evil has karmic fruit,
One can have sound sleep.
If one respects and serves one's parents,
And does not spoil life, all the way through,
And one does not steal others' possessions,

One can have sound sleep.
Repress all sense-organs
And befriend a good teacher of the Way
And crush out the four Maras
[worry of illusion in body and mind; the five skandhas;
death; Mara himself, who cannot rest, seeing others doing good],
And one can have sound sleep.
If one does not care about good or bad fortune,
Or if one has no sorrow or bliss,
And for all beings' sake
Rides on the wheel of birth and death,
And if things proceed thus,
One can have sound sleep.
Who has sound sleep?
It is all the Buddhas,
Who deeply sit in the samadhi of the All-Void
And whose body and mind are in peace
And are unshakable.
Who is it that sleeps in peace?

It is the person who is all-compassionate.
Always practising non-indolence,
He views beings as he views his own son.
Beings are in the darkness of ignorance
And do not see the karmic fruits of defilement.
They always do all kinds of evil actions
And cannot have sound sleep.
If one commits the ten evil deeds,
For oneself or for others,
No sound sleep will come about.
If one, out of a desire for ease and pleasure,
Commits deadly acts against one's own father
And says that one has done no wrong,
And befriends bad teachers,
One cannot have sound sleep.
If one acts beyond what is proper
And drinks too much cold water,
Such will end in illness
And no sound sleep will come to one.
If the king has an evil mind
And thinks of others' females,
And goes across a wilderness,
No sound sleep will come.
The upholding of sila [morality] is
Not yet perfect with the fruition
And the crown prince is not yet on the throne,
And the robbers have not yet gained wealth,
And there can be no sound sleep."

"O Jivaka! I am seriously ill. I have committed a deadly sin against my law-abiding king. No good doctor, no wonders of medicine, no charms or the best of care can cure me. Why not? My father, the law-abiding king, governed the state lawfully. There was nothing in him that one could complain about, and I killed him without reason. I am like a fish on land. What pleasure can I have? I am like a deer caught in a trap, and nothing pleases me. I am just like a man who knows that his life is going to end within a day, just like a king who has taken refuge in a foreign land, just like a man who is told that he is suffering from an incurable illness, just like a man who has broken the moral rules and is now told of his punishment. I once, in the past, heard a wise man say: "A person whose action is not pure in body, mouth and mind - know that this person will surely fall into hell." I am now thus. How can I sleep peacefully? There is nobody who can now give me the unsurpassed medicine of Dharma and relieve me of my illness." Jivaka replied: "Well said, well said! You have sinned, but you repent and feel ashamed. O great King! The All-Buddha-World-Honoured One says: "There are two white dharmas which save beings. One is "zan" [feeling ashamed], and the other "gi" [feeling ashamed]. "Zan" is not committing sin, and "gi" not having others commit sin. "Zan" is feeling ashamed of oneself, and "gi" is to confess to others. "Zan" is feeling ashamed [guilty] towards man, and "gi" is feeling ashamed towards heaven. This is "zan-gi" [repentance, remorse]. One without repentance is no man. Such is an animal. When one has repentance, one respects father and mother, teachers and elders. When one has repentance, there are father, mother, elder brother, younger brother, elder son, and younger sister." Well said, O great King! Listen for a moment! I have heard the Buddha say: Of the wise, there are two kinds. One is the person who does not do evil, and the other is the person who repents after having committed evil. Of the ignorant, there are again two kinds. One is he who does evil, and the other is he who conceals it. First, one does evil, but later one thoroughly confesses it and repents, and does not repeat it. This is as in the case of muddy water, in which, if the "Bright-Moon" mani [jewel] is placed there, the water becomes clear, due to the wonderful power of the gem. Or it is as when the clouds disperse and the moon reveals itself in its brightness. It is also the same with the repentance of evil acts which one has done. O King! If you repent and feel remorse, the sin will go away and you will be pure as before. O great King! There are two kinds of wealth. One is [having] such various animals as elephants, horses, etc., and the other such various treasures as gold, silver, etc.

One might possess many elephants and horses, but these cannot equal one piece of a gem. O great King! It is the same with beings. One is vile wealth, and the other good wealth. Many evil acts performed cannot compare with an act that is good. I have heard the Buddha say: "If one gains a single good mind [state of mind, volition], this destroys 100 evil deeds." O great King! This is comparable to a small piece of a diamond, which can well crush Mount Sumeru, or like a small fire which can well reduce everything to ashes, or like a small amount of poison that can harm beings. It is the same with a small amount of good, too. It well crushes out great evil. We say a small amount of good. But actually, it is big. Why? Because it crushes out great evil. O great King! As the Buddha says, hiding [one's sin] is what leaks out [i.e. is an "asrava"]; not hiding is [the state where] nothing more leaks out. One bares the evil and repents of it. Hence, non-leakable. A person does many evil things, but if he does not hide and store them up, the sin will be small, because of this non-concealment. If there is repentance for the evil that has been done, and if one feels ashamed, the sin dies out. O great King! Even small drops of water fill a big vessel. It is the same with the good mind. Each good mind [good volition] thoroughly crushes out a great evil. If one hides the evil, it augments and grows. If one bares it and repents, the sin will die out. Because all Buddhas say that the wise do not hide their sins. Well done, well done, O great King! You believe in the law of causality, in karma, and in the result that comes about. Please, O great King, have no worry or fear! There are beings who, performing all evil deeds, do not repent and feel ashamed, and do not see the law of causality and the result that is to follow. They do not ask others for guidance, and do not approach a good teacher of the Way. Such people cannot be cured by a good doctor or by nursing. It is like leprosy? ["kamala"], for which most secular doctors can devise no cure. A person who conceals his sin is like that. Why do we say that the icchantika is sinful? The icchantika does not believe in causality, has no repentance, does not believe in karma, does not see the present and the days to come, does not befriend a good teacher of the Way, and does not act in accordance with the injunctions of all Buddhas. Such a person is an icchantika. Such a person is one whom the All-Buddha-World-Honoured One cannot cure. Why not? Even doctors cannot cure a body that is dead.

It is the same with the icchantika. Such a person is one whom the All-Buddha-World-Honoured One cannot cure. O great King! You are no icchantika. How could you not be cured? "You, King, say: "There is no means of cure." Know, O great King! In Kapilavastu, there was a prince, the son of Suddhodana. His family name is Gautama, and his personal name Siddhartha. Without anyone to teach him, he awakened to Truth and spontaneously attained unsurpassed Bodhi, adorning his body thereby with the 32 signs of perfection and the 80 minor marks of excellence, gaining the 10 powers and the four fearlessnesses. He knows and sees all. Greatly compassionate, he pities all beings as he does his own son, Rahula. He truly follows the way of life of beings, just as a calf walks after its mother. He knows when to speak and when not to. His words are true, pure, wonderful and lawful, and a single word from him well cuts away the bond of defilement of all beings. He thoroughly knows the nature of the sense-organs and the mind of all beings. He acts in a manner fitting to the occasion and enacts expedients, and there is nothing that is not known to him. His Wisdom is great, like Sumeru. It is deep and vast like the great sea. This Buddha-World-HonouredOne has Adamantine Wisdom, which thoroughly crushes out all the evils of beings. There is nothing that is not possible to him. Now, 12 yojanas from here, in the castle town of Kusinagara, between the twin sal trees, he is addressing innumerable asamkhyas of Bodhisattvas all about such things as: "is" or "is-not", the created or the uncreated, the leakable ["asrava"], the karma-results of defilement or the karma-results of the Good Dharma, matter or non-matter, or non-matter-not-non-matter, Self or non-Self, or non-Self-not-non-Self, the eternal, or the non-eternal, or the non-eternal-not-non-eternal, Bliss, or non-bliss, or non-bliss-not-non-bliss, characteristics or non characteristics, or non-characteristics-not-non-characteristics, segregation or non-segregation, or non-segregation-not-non-segregation, the secular or the non-secular, or the non-secular-not-non-secular, vehicle or non vehicle, or vehicle-not-non-vehicle, self-doing and self-receiving, or receiving from others, and non-doing and non-receiving. O great King! You should hear at the place of the Buddha all about doing and non-receiving. All grave sins will be expiated.   "O King! Hear me a while! When Sakrodevendra was about to see the end of his life,

five things were seen, which were: 1) clothing giving out a bad, oily smell, 2) fading of the flower on his head, 3) his body issuing an evil smell, 4) perspiration under the armpits, 5) not finding pleasure where he was sitting. Then, Sakra, as he sat in a quiet place, saw a sramana or Brahmin and gained the thought that this was the Buddha. Then the sramana or Brahmin, seeing Sakra come, was glad and said: "O Sakra! I now take refuge in you." Hearing this, Sakra saw that this person was not the Buddha. He also thought to himself: "If this person is not the Buddha, I cannot change the five signs of extinction." At that, the charioteer, Pancashiki, said to Sakra: "O Kausika! There is a gandharva whose name is "Mirage". He has a daughter called Subhadra. If you give me this woman, I shall tell you how to make away with the signs of decline." Sakra replied: "Vemacitra, the asura king, has a daughter called "Saci", whom I respect. If you can tell me who can make away with these signs of my decline, I shall give her to you, how much more than Subhadra!" "O Kausika! There is a Buddha-World-Honoured One who is called Sakyamuni. He is now at Rajagriha. If you go there and ask him about the signs of decline, these will assuredly disappear." "O good man! If the Buddha-World-Honoured One can indeed do away with these, drive me there." At that, the charioteer, at these words, drove Sakra to Rajagriha, to Grdhrakuta. Reaching the place where the Buddha was, Sakra prostrated himself and, touching the Buddha's feet, thus paid the Buddha homage. Drawing back, he took his seat on one side. Sakrodevanam-Indra said to the Buddha: "Of all the devas, who is it that binds one?" The answer came: "O Kausika! The miserly mind, greed, and jealousy!" He further asked: "Where does the miserly, greedy and jealous mind come from?" The answer came: "It comes from ignorance." Again he asked: "From where does ignorance come?" The answer was: "From indolence." Again the question: "From where does indolence come?" The answer was: "From an inversion [of truth]." A renewed question: "Where does the inversion come from?" The answer stated: "From a doubting mind."   "O World-Honoured One! You say that the inversions arise from a doubting mind. It is like the Buddhist teaching. Why? Because I have a doubting mind within me. With such doubt, I have an inversion. I mistook one who was not the World-Honoured One for such. I now see the Buddha and all my doubts leave me. As my doubts leave me, the inversion also departs. Through the ending of the inverted mind, the miserly mind, down to jealousy, depart." The Buddha said: "You now say that you have no miserly mind and no jealous mind. Are you an anagamin? An anagamin has no greedy mind. If you have no greedy mind, why is it that you come to me, seeking life? Any anagamin does not truly seek life." "O World-Honoured One! If there is an inversion, there is a seeking of life. If there is no inversion, there is no seeking of life. What I seek is the Buddha-Body and the Buddha-Wisdom." "O Kausika! If you seek the Buddha-Body and the Buddha-Wisdom, you will surely gain these in the life to come." "Then, as Sakrodevendra heard the Buddha's sermon, the five signs of decline all at once faded away. And he stood up, paid homage, walked around the person of the Buddha three times [as a sign of respect], respectfully folded his hands and said: "O World-Honoured One! I am now dead and am born; I have lost my life and gained it. I have now been told that, as I take to the Buddha's Path, I will gain unsurpassed Bodhi. This is a rebirth. This is gaining life again. O World-Honoured One! Why do humans and gods increase in number? And why do they decline in number?" "O Kausika! Because of quarrelling and disputing, the number of humans and gods decreases; through living harmoniously, their number grows." "O World-Honoured One! Since by quarrelling we decrease in number, from now on I shall not fight with the asuras." The Buddha said: "Well said, well said, O Kausika! The All-Buddha-World-Honoured One says that forbearance is the cause of unsurpassed Enlightenment." Then Sakrodevendra stepped forwards, paid homage to the Buddha, drew back, and went on his way. "O great King! As the Tathagata thoroughly makes away with the evil characteristics, we say that the Buddha is inconceivable. The grave sin that you amassed in days gone by will unfailingly die out. "O great King! Hear me a while! A Brahmin had a son called "Non-Harming". Because he had killed so many people, he was called "Angulimalya". He also thought of killing his own mother. When he gained an evil state of mind, his body also shook. The shaking of body and mind is a sign of the five deadly sins. In consequence of the five deadly sins, one unfailingly falls into hell. Later, on seeing the Buddha, his body and mind shook. He thought of harming the Buddha. The shaking of body and mind bespeaks the five deadly sins. Due to the five deadly sins, one unfailingly falls? ?into hell. This person, having met the great teacher Tathagata, was able to do away with the cause of hell and aspire to unsurpassed Enlightenment. For this reason, we say that the Buddha is the unsurpassed doctor; he is not of the kind of the six masters. "O great King! There was a prince called "Suvira". His father cut off the hands and legs of this prince in anger and threw him into a deep pit. His mother, feeling sorrow and pity for him, had someone pulll him out and took him to the Buddha. On seeing the Buddha, his hands and legs were restored, and he gained the unsurpassed Bodhichitta. O great King! From seeing the Buddha, there was actual reward in this present life. Hence, we say that the Buddha is the unsurpassed doctor; he is not of the kind of the six masters. "O great King! There were many hungry pretas [ghosts] on the bank of the Ganges, to the number of 500. For an uncountable number of years, they were unable to see any water. Even when in water, what they saw was a flow of fire. Oppressed by thirst, they cried and wept. At that time, the Tathagata was in the udumbara forest, and was musing under a tree. Then the hungry pretas came to the Buddha and said: "O World-Honoured One! We are oppressed by hunger and thirst and will die before long." The Buddha replied: "Why do you not drink the water of the Ganges?" The pretas answered: "The Tathagata sees water, but we see fire." The Buddha said: "The water of the Ganges is not fire. Through the karma of evil actions performed, your mind is inverted and you make of this fire. I shall relieve you of this inversion and let you see water." Then the Buddha, for the sake of the pretas, expansively taught them the wrongs of the miserly and greedy mind. Then the pretas said: "We are now thirsty. We hear you speak of Dharma, but our mind is away [from it]." The Buddha said: "If you are thirsty, get into the river and drink your fill!" All those pretas, due to the power of the Buddha, were able to drink the water. When they had drunk the water, the Tathagata, for their sake, spoke variously about Dharma. On hearing this, they asppired to unsurpassed Enlightenment. Casting away their bodily forms as pretas, they gained heavenly forms. O great King! Because of this, we say that the Buddha is the unsurpassed doctor; he is not of the kind of the six masters. "O great King! In the state of Sravasti, there was a band of robbers, who numbered 500 in all. King Prasenajit took out their eyes. As there was no one to guide them, they were unable to go to the Buddha. Pitying them, the Buddha went to them. He consoled them and said: "O good people! Guard your body and mind well and do not do evil!" The robbers listened to the wonderful voice of the Tathagata, and they regained their eyes. They came to the Buddha, folded their hands together, worshipped him and said: "O World-Honoured One! We now see that your all-compassionate heart embraces all beings, not just the worlds of gods and humans." Then the Tathagata spoke about Dharma. When his sermon had ended, all aspired to unsurpassed Enlightenment. For such reason, the Tathagata is truly the unsurpassed doctor. He is not of the kind of the six masters. "O great King! In the state of Sravasti, there was a candala by the name of "False-Air". He killed an innumerable number of people. Having met the great Maudgalyayana, he at once broke off the cause of hell and was born in Trayastrimsa Heaven. As he has such a holy disciple, we call the Buddha-Tathagata the unsurpassed doctor. He is not ot the kind of the six masters. "O great King! There was in Varanasi the son of a rich man who was called Ajita. He had unlawful relations with his mother and killed his father. His mother had further bad relations with other people. So he killed her also. There was an arhat who was his good teacher of the Way. As he felt ashamed in fromt of him, he killed this arhat. Having killed this arhat, he went to Jetavana to get ordained. But, since all the bhiksus knew that he had committed three deadly sins, none of them wanted to accord with his wish. When his wish was not granted, he became all the more angry and set fire to the vihara, and many innocent people were killed. Then he went to Rajagriha, to the Tathagata, and sought ordination. The Tathagata allowed him to get ordained and delivered some sermons to him. By degrees, his grave sins began to lessen in weight and he came to aspire to unsurpassed Bodhi. For this reason, we say that the Buddha is the good doctor. He is not of the kind of the six masters. "O great King! Being by nature very evil in your heart, you believed in the words of an evil person and allowed Devadatta to let loose a big, intoxicated elephant upon the Buddha, so as to have it trample him. On seeing the Buddha, the elephant became sane. So the Buddha stretched out his hand to it and gave it a

stroke on the head, spoke of Dharma, as a result of which it aspired to unsurpassed Enlightenment. O great King! An animal sees the Buddha, and this destroys the animal's karmic results. How could it not be so with a human being? O great King! Know that any person who sees the Buddha can indeed make away with grave sin." "O great King! When the World-Honoured One had not yet attained unsurpassed Bodhi, Mara came to the Buddha with an innumerable and boundless number of kindred. At that time, the Bodhisattva, with his power of forbearance, crushed the evil mind of Mara and made him aspire to unsurpassed Enlightenment and accept Dharma. The Buddha possesses that much great virtue. "O great King! Some atavakas [i.e. field demons] were causing harm to the people. The Tathagata, at that time, went to the wasteland village and delivered a sermon for the sake of the rich man, Subhadra. Then, the atavakas, on hearing the sermon, were greatly gladdened and gave the rich man to the Tathagata. Later, they aspired to unsurpassed Enlightenment. "O great King! In the state of Varanasi, there was a butcher called "Broad-Forehead", who every day killed an innumerable number of sheep. Having encountered Sariputra, he received the eight precepts and then a day and night passed. Because of this, after his death, he was born as the son of Vaisravana, the king of the northern heaven. Even a disciple of the Tathagata possesses such great virtue. How could things be otherwise with the Buddha? "O great King! In North India, there was a castle called "Small-Stone". There was a king in that castle named "Naga-Mark". He usurped the state. Desperate for the crown, he killed his own father. Having killed his father, remorse filled his breast. He abandoned the state, came to the Buddha and wished to be ordained as a monk. The Buddha welcomed him and made him a bhiksu. His sins died out and he aspired to unsurpassed Enlightenment. Know, O great King, that the Buddha possesses such innumerable amounts of great virtue. "O great King! Devadatta was the Tathagata's disciple. He harmed many a monk and caused blood to flow from the Buddha's body and killed Utpalavarna, thus committing the three deadly deeds. The Tathagata spoke in diverse ways about Dharma and caused his grave sins to lessen by degree in their weight. Hence, we say that the Tathagata is a great doctor. He is not of the kind of the six masters. "O great King! If you believe in my words, please speed to the Tathagata. If you believe in my words, weigh up well what I say. O great King! The All-Buddha-World-Honoured One covers all with great compassion. He does not love only one person. Wonderful Dharma reigns widely. There is no one who is not taken in [by it]. His mind is all-equal towards the hostile and the friendly. His mind does not hate and does not love. It is not the case that only one person gains the Way and others do not. The Tathagata is not merely the teacher of the four classes of the Sangha alone; he is the teacher of all gods, humans, nagas, demons, hell-dwellers, animals and hungry ghosts. And all beings should look up to the Buddha as they look up to their own father and mother. O great King! Know that it is not the case that the Tathagata only speaks of Dharma to the noble king, Bhadrika; he even addresses the lowly Upali. He does not only accept offerings from Sudatta-Anathapindada, but also accepts food from the poor man, Sudatta. He does not only speak of Dharma to sharp-witted Sariputra, but also to dull-witted Suddhipanthaka. He does not only allow such a greedless person as Mahakasyapa to enter the Order, but also such a person as greedy Nanda. He does not only allow such an illusion-free person as Uruvilva-Kasyapa to seek the Way, but also one full of illusion who has committed grave deadly sins, like Sudaya, the younger brother of King Prasenajit. It is not the case that he extracts the root of anger because one offers him the galingale [an aromatic spice] but abandons a person who means to do harm. He does not only speak of Dharma to intellectual males, but also to the lowest in life, those who are married, and females. He not only enables sramanas to attain the four fruitions of the Way, but also enables lay people to gain the three fruitions of the Way. He does not only present Dharma to a person who has abandoned the odd duties of life such as the Puttala and others and who seeks to meditate in quiet quarters, but also to such as King Bimbisara, who has to reign over a state. It is not the case that Dharma is spoken only to teetotallers, but it is also spoken to those lost in strong drinks, like the rich man, Ugravati, and the intoxicated. It is not the case that Dharma is spoken of only to those who sit in dhyana [meditation] like Revata, but also to the Brahmin woman, Vasistha, who is now mad after losing her child. It is not the case that his sermons are only preached to his own disciples, but also to tirthikas,

Nirgranthas, and others. It is not the case that Dharma is preached only to those of full [i.e. strapping] manhood aged 25, but also to the elderly as old as 80, who are weak in physique. He does not only preach to those who are closely connected with Buddha-Dharma, but also to those who are not very well up in the practice of the Way. He does not only preach to Mallika, but also to such a prostitute as Utpala. He does not only receive the offerings of best dishes and sweet things from King Prasenajit; he also receives those of the rich man, Srigupta, which contain poison. O great King! Srigupta, in days gone by, sowed the seeds of deadly sins. But after having met the Buddha and having listened to his sermons, he aspired to unsurpassed Enlightenment. "O great King! Even if one were to make offerings for a month to all beings, the merit would not compare to one-sixteenth of that of meditating single-mindedly upon the Buddha. O great King! Though one were to work gold and make a man, and put on [bestow, display] vehicles and horse-treasures 100 in number, this could not compare to a person who aspires to Enlightenment and takes a step towards the Buddha. O great King! Even though one might put on 100 carts drawn by elephants, bearing various rare treasures from Roman lands and women with items of jewellery as many as 100, such could not compare to aspiring to Bodhi and taking a step towards the Buddha. Or even if one were to give this and the four things [i.e. food, clothing, decoctions, and accommodation] to all the beings of the 3,000 great-thousand worlds, this could not compare to aspiring to Enlightenment and taking a step towards the Buddha. Furthermore, even if we gave dana [alms] to beings as innumerable as the sands of the Ganges, this would never be better than the great King's going to where the twin sal trees stand, to where the Tathagata is, and listening with the sincerest heart to what he says." Then the great king answered: "The Tathagata-World-Honoured One is by nature mellow and soft. By reason of this, he has as his kindred all who are mellow and of a soft nature. Just as a forest of sandalwood is surrounded by sandalwood trees, so is the Tathagata pure and pristine and surrounded by people who are also pure and pristine. This is like a great naga [serpent] having kindred who are nagas; the Tathagata is silent and quiet, and his people, too, are silent and quiet. The Tathagata does not covet, nor do any of his people, either.

The Buddha has no illusion, nor do any of his people. I am the most wicked of men. Lined with evil karma, my body issues an evil smell and is tethered to hell. How can I dare to hope ever to go to where the Tathagata is? I may well go, but words may not get connections. You wish to have me go to the Buddha. And yet, I am now of a base constitution and despair of my own self and have no mind to go." Then there came a voice from above: "The unsurpassed Buddhist teaching is weak and is now about to die out. The great river of full water is about to dry up. It will not be long before the bright lamp of Dharma goes out. The mountain of Dharma is about to crumble, and the ship of Dharma is about to sink to the bottom. The bridge of Dharma is about to break, and the palace of Dharma is about to be levelled to the ground. The banner of Dharma is about to fall, and the tree of Dharma is about to snap and break. The good friend is about to leave us, and a great fear is about to raise its head. It will not be long before beings will inevitably feel the lack of Dharma. The epidemics of illusion are about to run amok. The time of great gloom is arriving, and people will have to feel thirst for Dharma. King Mara will be gladdened and will ungarb all his armour. The sun of Buddha-Dharma is about to sink behind the mountain of Great Nirvana. O great King! If the Buddha is gone, there will never be anyone who can undo your grave sins. O great King! You have committed deadly sins that will take you to Avichi Hell. There is no doubt that this karma will do its work. O great King! "A " means "nothing"; "bi" means "in- between". As there is no moment of pleasure in-between, we say "abi". O great King! If only a single person falls into this hell, the height of his body will measure 80,000 yojanas. It will fill [the place] up, and there will be no space there in-between. The body is surrounded all around and is subject to various pains. If there are many people, the bodies fill up, and there is no space in-between and nothing separates them. O great King! When one is in the cold hell, hot air will come for a moment, and this is a cause of pleasure; in the hot hell, a momentary blast of cold air becomes a cause of pleasure. One's life comes to an end in hell, but if one hears a living voice, it is restored. In Avichi Hell, such never occurs. O great King! There are four gates in Avichi Hell. Outside each gate there is a great fire which burns. It goes through everything, to east, west, south and north. Iron walls go all around for 8,000 yojanas. Above is an iron net; the ground, too, is made of iron. The fire passes from above to down below; it goes from bottom to top. O great King! This is like a fish on a frying pan whose fat and oil are burning. It is the same with the criminal, too. O great King! One who has committed one deadly sin has fully to suffer thus for one sin. One who has committed two deadly sins has to answer for two. If five, the sin goes [reaps] five times as much [pain]. O great King! I know that you will definitely have to experience your karmic results. Please speed to where the Buddha is. Other than the Buddha-World-Honoured One, no one can save you. I feel sorry. Hence, I urge you thus." Then, on hearing this, fear overtook the king; a shudder ran through his whole body; his five limbs shook like a plantain. Looking up, he asked: "O you god! Who are you? You show no form; only your voice comes down." "O great King! I am your father, Bimbisara. You should now do as Jivaka tells you. Do not give ear to the twisted views of your ministers." On hearing this, the king fell to the ground. The pain of his boils increased, and the bad smell became twice as great as before. Cold medicine was applied and smeared over his body. But the boils burned; the poison increased its heat. And there was no whit of decrease felt.

Chapter Twenty-Five: On Pure Actions 5

Then, the World-Honoured One saw, from where he was between the twin sal trees, Ajatasatru swoon and fall to the ground, and he said to those present: "I shall, for the sake of Ajatasatru, live, and I shall not enter Nirvana for innumerable kalpas." Bodhisattva Kasyapa said to the Buddha: "O World-Honoured One! The Tathagata will not enter Nirvana, for the sake of innumerable people. Why is it that you especially will not for the sake of Ajatasatru?" The Buddha said: "O good man! There is not one person amongst those here who will say: "I shall definitely enter Nirvana." Ajatasatru will say that he will assuredly suffer eternal death. So he swoons and throws himself upon the ground. O good man! I say that I shall not enter Nirvana for the sake of Ajatasatru. Such undisclosed teaching will be hard for you to understand. Why? I say "for the sake of". This refers to all beings. "Ajatasatru" refers to all those who have committed the five deadly sins. Also, "for the sake of" refers to all those beings of created existence. I do not exist in the world for the non-create. Why? Now, "non-create" is no beings. Ajatasatru is one with inner defilement. Also, "for the sake of" refers to the beings who see the Buddha-Nature. If the Buddha-Nature is seen, I shall not stay long in the world. Why not? One who sees the Buddha-Nature is no being. "Ajatasatru" refers to all those who have not yet aspired to unsurpassed Enlightenment. Also, "for the sake of" refers to the two, Ananda and Kasyapa; "Ajatasatru" refers to Ajatasatru's royal consort and also to all the females of the castle of Rajagriha. Also, "for the sake of" is none but the Buddha-Nature. "Aja" means "not born"; "se" means "vengeance". When the Buddha-Nature is born, there comes about the vengeance of defilement. When there is the vengeance of defilement, one does not see the Buddha-Nature. When no defilement is born, one sees the Buddha-Nature. When one sees the Buddha-Nature, one can abide peacefully in Great Nirvana. This is "not born". That is why we say "for the sake of Ajatasatru" ["Ajatasatru" is rendered as "Ajase" in Chinese]. O good man! "Aja" means "not born"; "not born" refers to Nirvana. "Se" refers to "worldly dharma"; "for" refers to "not spoiled". Not spoiled by the world's eight things, I do not enter Nirvana for innumerable, boundless asamkhyas of kalpas. Thus I say that I do not enter Nirvana for the sake of Ajatasatru. O good man! The undisclosed word of the Tathagata is inconceivable. Also, the Buddha-Dharma and Sangha cannot be conceived. The Buddha-Nature, too, is inconceivable, and the Great Nirvana Sutra is inconceivable." Then, the World-Honoured One, the All-Compassionate One and Guide, entered into moonlight samadhi for the sake of Ajatasatru. On his having entered this samadhi, a great light issued forth. The light was pure and cool, and it went to the king and shone upon his body. The boils on his body healed up, and the choking pains died out. Relieved of the pain of the boils and feeling pure and cool in body, the king said to Jivaka: "Once, I heard people say that when the kalpa is about to end, three moons appear at the same time. At that time, the sufferings of beings are all done away with. That time has not yet come. Where does this light come from? It shines on me and touches me; it cures all my boils, and my body feels at peace." Jivaka answered: "It is not that the kalpa is ending and the three mons are appearing and shining. This is also not the light of Mars, the sun, or the constellations, or a medicinal herb, a mani [jewel], or the light of heaven." The king further asked: "If this is not the light of the three moons, or of the mani, then what light is it?" "O great King! This is the light of the god of gods. This light has no root; it is boundless. It is not hot, not cold, not eternal; it does not die; it is not matter, not non-matter; it has no outer expression; nor is it non-phenomenal; it is not blue, not yellow, not red, and not white. It is seen only where there is a desire to save. It has its characteristics and can be explained. It has a root, boundary, heat, cold, blue, yellow, red, and white. O great King! Though this light has such aspects of phenomena, it is not possible to explain it. It cannot be seen; nor is there the blue, yellow, red, or white." The king said: "O Jivaka! Why does the god of gods send forth this light?" Jivaka answered: "Now, this auspicious scene is for you, great King. O King! You said just now that there was no good doctor in the world who could cure your body and mind. For this reason, this light has first been sent forth. It first cures your body, and then your mind." The king said: "O Jivaka! Does not the Tathagata-World-Honoured One think of us?" Jivaka replied: "As an example: a person has seven sons. One of the seven is ill. It is not that the mind of the father and mother is not all-equal, but their mind inclines towards the one who is sick. O great King! It is the same with the Tathagata. He is not partial, and yet his mind is heavy at [the sight of] one who is sinful. Compassion works upon him who is indolent, and his mind is released from him who is not indolent. Who is non-indolent? This refers to the Bodhisattva of the sixth stage. O great King! The All-Buddha-World-Honoured one does not see any differences of caste, youth, age, middle age, wealth and poverty, time, sun, moon, constellations, the lowly, the page and the maid, the skill of works done, but sees, amongst beings, him who has a good mind. If one has a good mind, his compassion acts. O great King! Please know that this auspicious scene indicates the fact that the Tathagata is now in the moonlight samadhi. Hence this light." The king asked: "What is the moonlight samadhi?" Jivaka answered: "This is like the moonlight, which well makes all utpala blossoms brightly open their petals. So too does the moonlight samadhi. It thoroughly opens the petals of the good mind of beings. So we call it the "moonlight samadhi". For example, the moonlight truly gladdens the heart of all who travel. So does the moonlight samadhi. It truly awakens joy in the minds of those who travel nirvana-wards. Hence we say "moonlight samadhi". O great King! The light of the moon increases daily in form and brightness, from the first of the month up to the fifteenth. The case is the same with the moonlight samadhi. The root of the first bud of all good deeds grows by degrees, and ends in the perfection of Great Nirvana. It is also for this reason that we say "moonlight samadhi". O great King! For example, the form and brightness of the moonlight from the sixteenth to the thirtieth day gradually lessen in size. It is the same with the moonlight samadhi. Wherever it shines, it decreases, by degrees, all defilements. Thus we say "moonlight samadhi". O great King! At a time of great heat, all beings always think of the moonlight. As the moonlight appears, the choking heat all goes. It is the same with the moonlight samadhi. It thoroughly dispels the fever of greed and worry. O great King! For example, the full moon is the king of all stars and is called "amrta" [ambrosia of immortality]. All beings love it. It is the same with the moonlight samadhi. It is the king of all good deeds and is the amrta, and is loved by all. For this reason, we say "moonlight samadhi." The king said to Jivaka: "I hear that the Tathagata will not abide, sit, stand up, talk or discuss with evil persons, just as the great sea will not retain corpses within itself. He is like a mandarin duck, which will not live in a privy, like Sakrodevendra, who does not live with devils, and like the kokila, which does not live in a dead tree. The same is the case with the Tathagata. How can I go and see him? If I am made to see him, I might sink into the ground. What I see is that the Tathagata may well approach an intoxicated elephant, a lion, a tiger, a wolf, a great fire, or a blazing flame, but not an evil person. It is for this reason that I think thus. With what mind can I go and see him?" Jivaka answered: "O great King! One who is thirsty hastens to a spring; one hungry seeks food; one afraid calls for help; a sick person calls for a doctor; one who feels hot seeks coolness; one feeling cold looks for clothing. O great King! It is the same with your now seeking the Buddha. O great King! The Tathagata even delivers sermons to the icchantikas and others. And you, O great King, are no icchantika. So how could you not expect the help of the Compassionate One?" The king said: "O Jivaka! I once heard that the icchantika is a person who does not believe, hear, see, or grasp the meaning. How can the Tathagata speak of Dharma to such a person as that?" Jivaka replied: "O great King! As an illustration: there is a man who contracts a serious illness. At night the person goes up to a one-pillared palace, partakes of butter, rubs it on his body, lies on ashes, eats ashes, climbs up a dead tree, plays with monkeys, and sits and reclines with them, and sinks into water or mud. He jumps from a high building, a high mountain, trees, elephants, horses, cows, and sheep. He wears blue, yellow, red, or dark-coloured clothes, laughs, sings and dances. He looks at crows, eagles, foxes, and raccoon dogs. His teeth and hair fall out; he is naked, sleeps with dogs as his pillow amidst dung and dust. Furthermore, he walks, lives, and stands amongst the dead, holds hands with them and eats. He sees in dreams that poisonous serpents cover the path and that he must pass these. Or he embraces a hair-covered woman, and wears cothing made of tala leaves. He dreams that he is riding on a broken cart drawn by a donkey or is playing in front of it. Having dreamt thus, his mind is worried. Due to this worry, his illness increases. As the illness increases, all the people and his relatives send for a doctor. The errand-boy dispatched for the doctor is of small stature and is lacking in carnal organs. His head is dusty, and he wears tattered clothes, and he means to carry the doctor on a broken-down cart. He says to the doctor: "Quick! Get in the cart!" "Then, the good doctor thinks to himself: "Now, this messenger looks ill and unpleasant. I know that the sick person is difficult to cure." He also thinks: "The messenger does not look very auspicious. I shall now look into the fortunes of the day and see if I can cure [the patient] or not. The fourth, sixth, eighth, twelfth and fourteenth are bad days, when illnesses do not heal up." He further thinks: "This is a bad day. I shall now look into the stars and see if I can cure [the patient] or not. If it is the time of such stars as Mars, Revati, Krttika, Apabharani, Shissho , and Mansho , illness is hard to cure." He also thinks: "As the stars are not in an auspicious constellation, I shall now look at the time. If it is autumn, winter, eventide, midnight, moonless time, then illnesses are hard to cure." Also he thinks: "Even though all such aspects indicate ill omens, things may be definite or indefinite. I shall now see the sick person himself. If fortune is favourable, there will be a cure; if not, nothing will help." Thinking thus, he goes along with the messenger. On the way, he again thinks: "If the sick person is destined to live long, his illness will be cured. If not, there can be no cure." And in front of the cart, he sees two children quarrelling and fighting, catching hold of each other's head, tugging at their hair, throwing tiles and stones, and brandishing and striking with swords and staffs. He sees people bearing fire, which spontaneously dies out, or people felling trees, or catching hold of skin and going along, tugging at it, or things left out on the path, or people holding empty things, or a sramana walking alone, without a companion, or a tiger, wolf, crow, eagle or fox. Seeing this, he thinks: "I see the messenger that is sent, all that is happening on the road, and I see that they all indicate bad omens. I know that this illness will be hard to cure." Also he thinks: "Though the omens are bad, let things go as they must. I shall go and see this illness." Thus thinking, he hears this said on the way: "Things such as forgetting, death, collapsing, breaking, skinning, falling, burning, and non-coming cannot be cured." Also, to the south he hears the cries of such birds and beasts as crow, eagle, sarika, dog, rat, fox, pig, and hare. Hearing all of these, he thinks: "I know that it will

be hard to cure this sick person." "Then he arrives at the place of the sick person and sees the sick man. Cold and heat press down upon him time and again; his joints are painful, his eyes red, and the ringing in his ears can be heard from without. His throat is gripped by convulsions and pains, and the surface of his tongue is cracked. The person is of a truly dark colour, and his head is not in order. His body is dried up; no perspiration comes out. The calls of nature have all stopped; his body is uncommonly swollen and is scarlet and red, different from what obtained in ordinary days. There is no balance in his voice, which is at times coarse and at times weak. Spots can be seen all over his body, strangely blue and yellow in colour. His belly is swollen, and his speech is not clear. The doctor, on seeing this, asks the attendant of the patient: "How does the patient feel?" The answer comes back: "O great Doctor! This man previously respected the Three Treasures and all devas. Now, this person has changed and has ceased to respect [them]. Hitherto, he gladly gave, but now he is miserly. In the past, he ate sparingly, but now he eats a lot. Previously he harmonzed with good, but now he is evil. Hitherto he was filial and respected his father and mother, but now he has no mind to respect them." "The doctor, having heard all this, steps forward and smells. What he smells is utpala, the mixed smell of agaru, prkka, tagaraka, tamala-pattra, kunkumam, sandalwood, the smell of roasting meat, the smell of wine, the smell of roasting spines and bones, the smell of fish, and the smell of dung. Having smelled these good and bad smells, he steps forward and touches the [patient's] body, which is as delicate and soft as silk or cotton or the karpasa [cotton-tree] flower. Or it is as hard as stone, or cold as ice, or hot as fire, as astringent as sand. Having seen all this, the good doctor sees that the man will surely die. Of this he has no doubt. But he does not say that the person will surely die. He says to the sick man's attendant: "I am busy now. I shall come back tomorrow. Let the man eat whatever he desires to eat, and do not say no." And he returns home. The next day the messenger comes, to whom the doctor again says: "My business is not yet concluded; besides, the medicine has not yet been made up." The wise should know that such a sick person will assuredly die. "O great King! It is the same with the World-Honoured One, too. He well knows what the icchantika is, and yet he speak to him of Dharma.

Why? If he did not speak of Dharma, common mortals would all say: "The Tathagata has no compassion. If he has, we say "all-knowing"; if he does not, how can we say that he is the all-knowing one?" Thus would they say. For this reason, the Tathagata delivers sermons to the icchantikas. O great King! The Tathagata sees all sick persons and always dispenses the medicine of Dharma. The Tathagata is not to blame if the sick do not take the medicine. O great King! There are two kinds of icchantika. One gains the wholesome root ["kusala-mula"] in the present, and the other the wholesome root in the life to come [i.e. next life]. The Tathagata well knows which of the icchantika will gain the wholesome root in this life. So he speaks of Dharma. Even to the one whose wholesome root actualizes in the life to come, he speaks of Dharma. The result may not come about now, but he makes it the cause in the life to come. For this reason does the Tathagata speak of Dharma to the icchantika. Of the icchantika, there are two kinds. One is sharp, and the other is of middle grade. The one of sharp grade gains the wholesome root in this life; the one of middle grade will gain it in the life to come. The All-Buddha-World-Honoured One does not speak for nothing. O great King! For example, a person who is clean does not fall into the privy [cesspit]; a good teacher of the Way sees and pities him, and goes forward, catches hold of his hair and pulls him out. So do things obtain with the All-Buddha-Tathagata. He sees all beings falling into the pit of the three unfortunate realms. He effects expedients and saves them. It is for this reason that the Tathagata does indeed speak of Dharma even to the icchantikas." The king said to Jivaka: "If things obtain thus with the Tathagata, I shall tomorrow check the fortunes of the day and the stars to see if they are good, and then I shall go." Jivaka said to the king: "There is no finding out of the best day and stars in the teaching of the Tathagata. It is as with a person suffering from serious illness: he does not select the good or bad day and time, but seeks out a doctor. Now, your illness, King, is serious and you seek a good doctor, who is the Buddha. Please do not speak about whether it is a good or bad day. O great King! This is as in the case of sandalwood and eranda fire, both of which burn in the same way, without any difference. It is the same with the best day and that of ill-omens. At the place of the Buddha, one gains the same expiation of one's sins. Please, O great King, hasten there today!" Then the great king gave orders to a minister called "Auspicious", saying: "O you minister! Today I mean to go to the Buddha-World-Honoured One. Make haste and get things ready for the offerings!" The minister said: "O great King! Well said, well said! We have everything ready for the offerings." King Ajatasatru had with him his royal consort. The palanquins on thich they rode were 12,000 in number; their great and powerful elephants were 50,000. On each elephant were three attendants, who held banners and parasols in their hands. There was no lack of flowers, incense, or musical instruments. All was complete. There were 180,000 horses leading and bringing up the rear. And the people of Magadha who followed the king numbered 580,000. At this time, the people of Kusinagara filled an area 12 yojanas in size. All saw King Ajatasatru and his kindred coming from afar, asking the way. Then, the Buddha spoke to the congregation. "All of you! The most closely related to unsurpassed Bodhi is the good friend of the Way. Why? If Ajatasatru had not followed the words of Jivaka, he would have died on the 7th of next month and would have fallen into hell. For this reason, there is no one better than the most closely related and good friend of the Way." A voice came from in front of King Ajatasatru, which said: "King Vidudabha of Sravasti rode on a ship, went to sea, met with a fire and died. The bhiksu, Kokalika, was swallowed up alive by the earth and fell into Avichi Hell. Sunaksatra, after committing many an evil deed, came to the Buddha, and all his sins were expunged." On hearing this, he said to Jivaka: "I have heard these two things said. But I cannot be too sure. O Jivaka! Come with me! I mean to ride together with you on one elephant. If I am to fall into Avichi Hell, grab hold of me so that I do not fall down there. Why? I once heard that the person who has gained the Truth will not fall into hell." Then the Buddha said to the people around: "King Ajatasatru yet has doubts. I shall now fix my mind." At that time, there was a Bodhisattva called "All-Upholding" there. He said to the Buddha: "O World-Honoured One! As you the Buddha have previously stated: all things have no fixed state. Matter has no fixed form, and Nirvana has no fixed form, either. How is it that you, Tathagata, say that for Ajatasatru's sake you will gain a fixed mind?" The Buddha said: "Well said, well said, O good man! I now gain a fixed mind for the sake of Ajatasatru. Why? If the king's doubts become annihilated, know that there can be no fixed forms for all things. Because of this, I shall, for Ajatasatru's sake, gain a fixed mind. Know that this mind is not one that is fixed. O good man! If the mind of the king is fixed, how could one destroy the king's deadly sins? As there is no fixed state, we can indeed crush out sin. Hence, for Ajatasatru's sake, I gain a fixed mind."

Then the great king went to the forest of sal trees, went to where the Buddha was, looked up and saw the 32 signs of perfection and the 80 minor marks of excellence, all of which stood out like an all-wonderful golden mount. Then the Buddha issued the eight kinds of voice and said: "O great King!" Then Ajatasatru looked to right and left and said: "Who is the great king amongst all of those who are here? I am sinful and have no virtue worth mentioning. So the Tathagata could not be addressing me thus." Then the Tathagata again called out: "O great King Ajatasatru!" On hearing this, the king was greatly pleased and said: "The Tathagata uses loving words to me. I now know that the Tathagata truly has great pity for all us beings; he makes no distinction." And he said to the Buddha: "O World-Honoured One! I have now eternally made away with doubt. I definitely know now that the Tathagata is truly the unsurpassed great teacher." Then, Bodhisattva Kasyapa said to All-Upholding: "The Tathagata has gained a fixed mind for the sake of King Ajatasatru." King Ajatasatru said further to the Buddha: "O great King! Even if I now sat and stood and took meals with Brahma and Sakrodevendra, I would not feel happy. You, Tathagata, just drop me a word and command me, and I greatly rejoice." And he brought the banners, parasols, flowers, incense, and musical instruments to the Buddha and offered them to him. Then he stepped forward, touched the Buddha's feet, and walked around the Buddha three times. Worshipping him in this way, he stepped back and took his seat to one side. Then the Buddha said to Ajatasatru: "O great King! I shall now talk to you about the pith of Wonderful Dharma. Listen to me carefully with all your mind! The common mortal should always meditate on 20 things: 1) this body is empty and there is nothing there that is undefiled [i.e. "anasrava"], 2) it has no wholesome root in it, 3) there is no adjustment in birth and death, 4) one falls into a deep pit and there is no place where one may have

no fear, 5) by what means can one see the Buddha-Nature? 6) how can one practise meditation and see the Buddha-Nature? 7) birth and death are always the cause of suffering and there are [there] no Eternal, Bliss, Self, and the Pure, 8) it is not possible to segregate oneself from the eight inopportune situations, 9) one is always pursued by enmity, 10) there is not one dharma that can shake off all things that exist, 11) one is not emancipated from the three unfortunate realms, 12) various twisted views accompany one, 13) no boat is on hand to pass one across the waters of the five deadly sins, 14) birth and death go on endlessly and no limit to this is gained, 15) when no karma is performed, there is no result to follow, 16) no fruition comes about to others for what one has oneself done, 17) without the cause of bliss, there cannot be the result of bliss, 18) once the seed of karma is sown, the result will not be lost, 19) ignorance calls forth life and by it one dies, 20) what one has over the three times of past, present and future is indolence. O great King! Common mortals should always meditate on these 20 things. Having meditated thus, one will come not to desire birth and death any more. If no desire exists for birth and death, one will gain samatha-vipasyana [tranquillity and insight]. Then, in an orderly way, one will meditate on what obtains regarding birth, life, and extinction. So does it go with dhyana, wisdom, effort and shila. Having meditated on birth, life and extinction, one comes to know what obtains with the mind down to the moral precepts. Refraining from evil to the end, there can be no fear of death and the three unfortunate realms. Any person whose mind is not set upon these 20 things has a mind that is indolent, and there will be no end of evil that is not yet done." Ajatasatru said: "I did not hitherto grasp the meanings of these 20 things which the Buddha has expounded to me. I therefore committed many evil deeds. As I have committed many evil deeds, I have a fear of death and of the three unfortunate realms. O World-Honoured One! I am myself to blame; I myself have invited this suffering [upon myself] and am responsible for all these grave sins. Though my father, the King, was utterly blameless, I committed deadly acts against him. Whether or not I may have meditated on all of these things, I am sure that Avichi Hell awaits me." The Buddha said to the great king: "All things that exist, and their characteristics, are not eternal; there is nothing that is fixed. O King! How can you say that you will definitely go to Avichi Hell?" King Ajatasatru said to the Buddha: "O World-Honoured One! If all things do not have a fixed state, then the sins that I have committed cannot be fixed, either. If killing is definite, there cannot be any saying that all things are not fixed." The Buddha said: "O great King! Well said, well said! The All-Buddha-World-honoured One says: "All things have no definite aspects." You, King, well know that killing, too, is not definite. For this reason, know that in killing, too, there is nothing that is definite. You say that your father was innocent and you killed him. Who is your father? Only a provisional man made up of the five skandhas, towards which you carelessly entertain the notion of "father". Which of the 12 spheres and 18 realms is your father? If matter ["rupa"] is father, the other four skandhas must be false. There cannot be anything such as rupa or non-rupa that can combine together and make father. Why not? Because there cannot be anything, by nature, that can be called rupa or nonrupa. O great King! Common mortals and all beings carelessly entertain the notion of father in the rupa-skandha. Such a rupa-skandha also cannot be harmed. Why not? There are ten kinds of rupa. Of these ten, only one is seen, held, prized, weighed, tugged and bound. Although we can see and bind, there is no nature that sustains [this rupa]. [As it is] non-abiding, we cannot see, hold, prize, weigh, tug or bind. This is what rupa is. How can we kill it? If this rupa is your father and is liable to get harmed, and if we are to reap the karmic fruit, the other nine must be false. If the remaining nine are false, there can be no talk of sin. O great King! There are three kinds of rupa. These are of the past, present and future. We cannot harm that of the past and that of the present. Why not? The past has passed; as to the present, all things die out moment after moment. As to what arises in time the future, things can be checked, so as not to arise. This is killing. Thus a single rupa can either be killed or not be killed. As there are the two cases of being killed and not being killed, we can say that nothing is ever definite. If rupa is not fixed, killing too is indefinite. Since killing is not definite, the karmic consequence is also not definite. How can you say that you will fall into hell? "O great King! There are two kinds of karmic results to what beings do. One is light and the other is grave. What concerns mind and mouth is light; what is done by body, mouth and mind is grave. What is thought about in mind and spoken by mouth, but what is not done, is light in karma. O great King! You, in days gone by, did not say "Kill!"; you only said, "Cut off the legs!" If you had told your attendants to behead your father while he was standing, and if he were beheaded while sitting, you would not have purchased sin. Contrary to this, you did not command thus. How can you have sinned? If it is the case that you sinned, then the All-Buddha-World-Honoured One, too, must have sinned. Why so? Your father, King Bimbisara, had previously sown all the seeds of good. As a result he was then able to ascend the throne. Had the Buddha-World-Honoured One not accepted the offerings made, he could not have become king. If he had not become king, you could not have plotted against the state and caused harm. If it is the case that you have killed your father and have committed a crime, all we Buddhas must have sins to answer for. If the All-Buddha-World-Honoured One has no sin, how could it be that you alone must have sinned? "O great King! Bimbisara once gained an evil state of mind and went out hunting on Vipula Hill. He roamed about the wilderness, but found no game. He saw a rishi who was endowed with the five divine powers. Seeing him, anger and a twisted thought arose in him; he thought that the reason he had no game came from the fact that this rishi must have caused the game animals to run away. He told his attendants to kill this rishi. The rishi, as he was about to breathe his last, gained an evil state of mind. He lost his divine powers and took an oath: "I am truly innocent. But you, by means of your mouth, ruthlessly perform an act of killing. I shall, in the life to come, cause - like you - death to you through my mouth." Then the king, on hearing this, repented. He cremated the dead body with offerings. So did it go with the former king. The karmic consequence was light, and he did not fall into hell. In contrast to this, you did nothing of the sort, so how could you suffer in hell? The former king did the thing himself and he had to pay for it. How could you say, King, that you did the killing and that you have to suffer? You say that your father was innocent. How could you say that he was innocent? Now, a person who has sinned has to suffer from what he has done. A person who has not sinned does not suffer from karmic results. If your late father, the King, had committed no sin, how could there be any karmic result? Bimbisara acquired good and bad karmic results in his lifetime. Because of this, nothing was definite with the late king. Being indefinite, killing, too, was indefinite. The killing being indefinite, how can you say that you will have to fall into hell? "O great King! Regarding the defilement of madness in beings, there are four kinds. These are: 1) madness from greed, 2) madness from medicine, 3) madness by charms, 4) madness from original karma. O great King! There are these four kinds of madness amongst my disciples. They do many evil things, and yet I do not call it violating sila [the moral precepts]. What is done by such persons does not lead to the three unfortunate realms. Even when regaining a sane state of mind, we do not speak of their having violated [sila]. You, King, were in a greedy state of mind and committed this offence. This is what the madness of greed did. How can we call this sin? O great King! A person takes drink, becomes intoxicated and kills his own mother. Once the intoxication has passed, he repents. Know that this action also does not call forth karmic results. O King! The intoxication of greed is not the action of a sane mind. If not of the sane mind, how can one acquire sin? Now, a juggler at a crossroads displays various forms of men, women, elephants, horses, garlands, clothings, etc. The ignorant call these real, whereas the wise know that all of these are not true. The same with killing. The common mortal calls it true, but the All-Buddha-World-Honoured One knows that it is not true. O King! The ignorant call an echo true, but the wise know that it is not. O great King! A mind of vengeance comes about, but presents [a face of] seeming friendliness. The ignorant call this true, but the wise see through it and recognise it as false. It is the same with killing. The common mortal says that it is true, whereas the All-Buddha-World-Honoured One knows that it is not true. O great King! One takes up a mirror and looks into it. The ignorant say that it is a true face [in the mirror], but the wise see through it and say that this is not something true. It is the same with killing. The common mortal says that it is true, whereas the All-Buddha-World-Honoured One knows that it is not so. The ignorant see a mirage in the hot season and call it water, but the wise see through it and know that it is not water. The same is the case with killing. The common mortal calls it true, whereas the All-Buddha-World-Honoured One knows that it is not true. O great King! The common mortal calls a gandharvan castle true, whereas the wise

see through it and know that it is not true. It is the same with killing. The common mortal calls it true, but the All-Buddha-World-Honoured one knows that it is not true. O great King! In a dream, one enjoys the bliss of the five desires. The ignorant call these true, but the wise see through it and know them and know that they are not true. The case is the same with killing. The common mortal says that it is true, but the All-Buddha-World-Honoured One knows that it is not true. O great King! I know all about killing, the act of killing, the killer, the karmic results of killing, and emancipation. That is to say that there is no sin. O King! You may know of killing, but how can there be any sin? O great King! For example, one may know how to serve wine, but if one does not drink it, one will not get intoxicated. Also, the knowledge of fire is not burning. It is the same with you, King. And the knowing of killing does not mean any sin. O great King! The beings, at sunrise, commit various sins, and at the rise of the moon commit robbery, but they do not perform any sinful acts when there are no sun and moon out. The sun and moon enable them to commit crime. But the sun and moon do not actually commit any sinful deeds. It is the same with killing. You, King, were the vehicle, but you have no sin. "O great King! You always give orders in your royal palace to kill sheep. And you have no fear in your mind. How is it that you entertain fear only when you kill your father? We say "respectable" and "disrespectable" as between man and animal. But both equally love life and fear death. In this there is no difference. Why is it that your mind is light when you have killed sheep and that you fear greatly when you have killed your father? O great King! Man is a servant of craving, and is not free. Driven by craving, a person commits the act of killing. There can be karmic results. But "craving" ["trishna"] is to answer [is responsible]. You, King, feel molested [oppressed]. But who is to blame? O great King! For example, Nirvana is no "is" and is not a "not-is". Yet it is an "is". The same applies to killing. Though not "is" and not "not-is", it is yet an "is". It is "not-is" with the person who repents; it is "not-not-is" with the person who feels no repentance. One who harvests the karmic consequences calls this "is"; one who sees "void" regards it as "not-is". For one who holds the world-view of "is", it is "not-not-is", and for one who bases himself on the "is-is" theory, it is an "is". Why? Because a person of this world-view reaps karmic results. A person who upholds the world-view that there is no "is" reaps no karmic results. For a person who holds the world-view of the eternal oneness of "is" existence, it is "notis". For a person who holds the "non-eternal-oneness theory", it is "not-not-is". For a person of the "eternal-eternal theory", it cannot be "not-is". Why not? Because a person of this eternal-eternal theory harvests an evil karma. Hence, for a person of this eternal-eternal theory, it cannot be "not-is". For this reason, "not-is" and "not-not-is" are "is". O great King! Now, beings speak of an "exhaling-inhaling breath". When we cut off the exhaling and inhaling breath, there is death. All Buddhas follow the way of life of the lay and say that there is "killing". "O great King! Matter ["rupa"] is non-eternal; the causal relations of matter are also not eternal. How could matter, which arises out of an impermanent cause, be eternal? This applies down to consciousness, which is non-eternal, and the causal relations of consciousness are also non-eternal. How could the consciousness that arises out of impermanent causation be eternal? "Due to impermanence, there arises suffering; due to suffering, what there is is void; due to the void, what there is is non-Self. If there are impermanence, suffering, void, and non-Self, what does one kill? If Impermanence is killed, what there is is eternal Nirvana. If Suffering is killed, one must gain Bliss; if the Void is killed, one must gain the Real. If the non-Self is killed, one must gain the True Self. O great King! If Impermanence, Suffering, the Void, and non-Self are killed, you must be equal to me." I, too, killed Impermanence, Suffering, the Void, and non-Self, and I am not in hell. How could you fall into hell?" Then, King Ajatasatru meditated, as told to by the Buddha, on matter down to consciousness. Having thus meditated, he said to the Buddha: "O World-Honoured One! I have come to know for the first time that matter is non-eternal and down to the fact that consciousness is non-eternal. If I had so meditated, I could not have sinned. In days gone by, I heard a person say that the All-Buddha-World-Honoured One always becomes the parent to all beings. Though I heard so, I could not be quite sure. Now I definitely know. O World-Honoured One! I also heard that the king mountain, Mount Sumeru, is made of the four

treasures: gold, silver, vaidurya, and sphatika; and also that all birds change their colour, according to the colour of the place they go to. Though I heard so, I was not quite sure. As I now come to Mount Sumeru, I am now of the same colour. To say that I am the same in colour means to say that all things are non-eternal, suffering, void, and non-Self. O World-Honoured One! I observe that in the world the eranda [recinus communis] comes from the eranda seed, but not that sandalwood comes from eranda. I now see for the first time that sandalwood comes from the eranda seed. The eranda seed is none but I. The sandalwood is the faith that has no root in my mind. I say "rootless". That is to say that I first did not know how to respect the Tathagata, that I did not believe in the Dharma and Sangha. This is what I call "rootless". O World-Honoured One! If I had not met with you, the Tathagata-World-Honoured One, I would have had to live for innumerable asamkhyas of kalpas in a great hell, suffering there infinite pain. I am now fortunate to have met with you, the Tathagata. By virtue of having seen this Buddha, I can now crush all defilements and the evil state of mind." The Buddha said: "O great King! Well said, well said! I now know that you will surely destroy the evil state of mind of beings." "O World-Honoured One! If I could well destroy the evil state of mind of beings, I could well fall into Avichi Hell and suffer great pain there for innumerable kalpas, and I should not feel it as pain." And the innumerable people of the state of Magadha aspired to unsurpassed Bodhi [Enlightenment]. And when all such people had aspired to the great mind, all the grave sins of King Ajatasatru became light. And the king, the royal consort, the ladies of the harem, and the attendant females aspired to unsurpassed Bodhi. Then King Ajatasatru spoke to Jivaka: "O Jivaka! I am not yet dead, and yet I have a heavenly body. Casting away a short life, I have gained a long one, and I cause all beings to aspire to unsurpassed Bodhi. That is to say that this is the heavenly body, long life, and the eternal body, and this is a disciple of all Buddhas." Saying thus, he offered the Buddha various gem-studded hanging-ensigns, flags and parasols, incense, flowers, garlands, and wonderful music, and spoke in praise of the Buddha in a gatha:

"The true words are delicately set
In sentences all skilfully woven.

The undisclosed store of deep meaning
Is opened for the sake of all beings.
The implications are great and extensive,
But told in simple ways, for beings' sake.
Perfect in all such words
He thoroughly cures beings.
Any being blessed with hearing these words
Will definitely come to know,
Whether he believes or not,
That all this is the sermon of the Buddha.
All Buddhas always with soft words
For beings' sake explain what is coarse.
The words softly spoken or coarsely spoken
All turn up to [end up in] "Paramartha-satya" [Ultimate Truth].
That is why I now take refuge in the World-Honoured One.
Just as the water of the great ocean
Is one that the Tathagata uses.
This is the foremost meaning. Because of this,
There are no words which are meaningless.
The various and innumerable things
That the Tathagata speaks are now
Heard by beings, male and female, big and small,
Who all-equally arrive at "Paramartha-satya".
Causelessness, fruitlessness, birthlessness, and deathlessness
Are all called Great Nirvana.
And those who hear destroy all karmic results.
The Tathagata becomes the compassionate father and mother to all beings.
Know that all beings are all sons of the Tathagata.
The World-Honoured One, being compassionate,
Practised penance for beings' sake. It seems
That man is much caught by demons or lost to madness.
I now see the Buddha and am blessed
With the good of the three actions [i.e. of body, mouth and mind].
I pray that I shall turn this merit over to the unsurpassed Way.
I now make offerings to the Buddha, Dharma, and Sangha,
And I pray that the Three Treasures will always exist in the world.
The various merits that I gain will thoroughly crush the four Maras of all beings.
I made friends with evil ones.
And there was no end of sins that pass in the Three Times.
I now repent before the Buddha. And I pray
That I shall commit no more sins in the days to come.
I pray that all beings will aspire to Bodhi
And always think of all the Buddhas of the ten directions.
And I pray that all beings
Will eternally destroy the defilements

And that, like Manjushri, they will
Clearly see the Buddha-Nature."

Then the World-Honoured One praised King Ajatasatru: "Well said, well said! If one aspires to Bodhi, know that this adorns all Buddhas and the masses. O great King! You, once in the past, at the site of Buddha Vipasyin, aspired to Bodhi, and ever since then, up to the time when I appeared in the world, you have never once suffered the pains of hell. O great King! Know that Bodhichitta [the resolve to gain Enlightenment] generates innumerable karmic effects. O great King! From now onwards, always cultivate Bodhichitta. Why? Through this, you can thoroughly make away with an innumerable number of sins." Then King Ajatasatru and all the people of the state of Magadha stood up from their seats, walked around the Buddha three times, drew back, and returned to the palace. Now, what refers to the Chapter on Heavenly Actions is as stated in the Gandavyuha Sutra.

Chapter Twenty-Six: On the Action of the Child

"O good man! Why do we speak of a "child's action." 'O good man! A child cannot stand up, stay, come and go, or speak. This is the state of a child. It is the same with the Tathagata. We say "unable to stand up". The Tathagata does not raise any aspect of a thing. We say "unable to stay. The Tathagata does not adhere to anything. We say "unable to come. In the bodily action of the Tathagata, there is no shaking. We say "unable to go". The Tathagata already enters Great Nirvana. We say "unable to talk". He talks, but he does not speak. Why not? If spoken, that would be something of the category of the created. The Tathagata is an Uncreate. So he speaks not. Also, we say "no word". For what a child says cannot be well understood. Though there are words, they are almost no words. The case is the same with the Tathagata. The words' not being clear is the secret word of all Buddhas. Though uttered, beings do not understand. That is why we say "worldless". "And also, with a child the name and the thing are not one. Though the child does not know the right word, it is not the case that it cannot know things. It is the same with the Tathagata. All beings differ from one another. What they say is the same. The Tathagata enacts expedients and speaks. And through this, he makes people understand. Also, a child speaks of a big letter. The same is the case with the Tathagata. He talks of a big word. This is "vaba". "Va" [i.e. the 42nd letter of the Sanskrit alphabet] corresponds to "created", and "ba" [i.e. the 36th letter of the Sanskrit alphabet] to the "non-created". This is the child. "Va" is "non-eternal", and "ba" is "eternal". Beings hear this and take it as eternal. This is the action of the child. "Also, the child does not know suffering or bliss, day or night, father or mother. It is the same with the Bodhisattva-mahasattva. For the sake of beings, he does not see suffering or bliss. There is no difference between day and night. His mind is equal towards all beings. Hence, there is no distinction of father or mother, friendly or not friendly. "Also, a child cannot make big or small things. It is the same with the Bodhisattva-mahasattva. Also, he does not create birth or death. This is non-making. "Big things" refers to the five deadly sins. "Small thing" refers to the two-vehicle mind. The Bodhisattva does not, right to the end, retrogress from Bodhichitta and create

sravaka and pratyekabuddha vehicles. "Also, we say "child's action". When a child cries and weeps, the parents take up the yellow leaf of bitter willow and say to the child: "Don't cry, don't cry! I shall now give you some gold!" The child sees this, thinks it is true gold, and stops crying. But this yellow leaf is in actual fact not gold. The child sees wooden cows, horses, men and women, and thinks they are men, women, etc., and stops crying. But, truth to tell, these are not men or women. As it thinks thus about men and women, we say "child". It is the same with the Tathagata. If beings are about to commit evil deeds, the Tathagata speaks about the Eternal, Bliss, Self, and the Pure, rectitude, and the freedom one enjoys in Trayastrimsa Heaven, the pleasures of the five desires which one has there in beautiful palaces, about all that obtains there, which is none but the blisses of the six sense-organs. The beings, on hearing about all the pleasure that obtains there, stop doing evil from a greedy mind, to taste the bliss and do the good that will be worth Trayastrimsa Heaven for them. Actually, there [in Trayastrimsa Heaven] there are birth and death, impermanence, non-bliss, non-Self, non-purity. To lead beings, he puts into effect an expedient and speaks of the "Eternal, Bliss, Self, and the Pure". "Also, we say "child". If beings abhor birth and death, the Tathagata speaks of the two vehicles. But, in truth, there are not two vehicles. By "two vehicles", one sees the evils of birth and death and comes to see the bliss of Nirvana. Seeing thus, there are segregation and non-segregation, the true and the not-true, practice and non-practice, and gain and non-gain. "O good man! Just as a child thinks of gold in regard to what is not gold, so do things stand with the Tathagata. In regard to the impure, he talks of the pure. As the Tathagata is "Paramarthasatya" itself, there is nothing false here as in the case of the child that thinks what is not a cow or horse is a cow or horse. If beings conceive of the true Way in what is not the Way, the Tathagata will also speak about this non-Way and make it into the "Way". In the non-Way, there is, truth to tell, no Way. Only as there is the smallest bit of causal relations, he talks of the non-Way and says that it is the Way. This is as with the child who thinks that the wooden man and woman are [a real] man and woman. It is the same with the Tathagata. Knowing what is no being, he speaks of a being. But truth to tell, there can be no thought of a being. If the Buddha-Tathagata says that there is no being, all beings may gain the wrong view. For this reason, the Tathagata says that beings exist. The person who entertains the thought of a being in a being cannot destroy the thought of a being. Any being who destroys the thought of a being gains Great Nirvana. When one thus gains Nirvana, one ceases crying. This is a child's action. O good man! If any man or woman upholds these five actions, reads, writes and copies and expounds [them], such a person will unfailingly gain the five actions." Bodhisattva Kasyapa said to the Buddha: "O World-Honoured One! I now see what the Buddha says. This means that I shall unfailingly gain the five actions." The Buddha said: "O good man! It is not that you alone will gain the five actions. All of those congregated here, who are 930,000 in number, will also all-equally gain the five actions."

Chapter Twenty-Seven: Bodhisattva Highly-Virtuous King 1

Then the Buddha said to Bodhisattva-mahasattva All-Shining Highly-Virtuous King: "O good man! Any Bodhisattva-mahasattva who practises this great Nirvana Sutra will gain ten virtues. He is not on the same level as the sravaka or pratyekabuddha. This is beyond knowing. Any person who hears this will be surprised. It is neither in nor out, neither difficult nor easy. It is neither outer expression nor non-expression. It is neither secular nor has it any form to represent it. It is not what one comes across in the world. "What are the ten? The first contains five. What are the five? 1) One who has not heard this can hear it well, 2) having heard it, there is benefit, 3) it well cuts away doubt, 4) the mind of Wisdom is straight and has no bends, 5) one knows the closely-guarded store of the Tathagata. These are the five. How do we hear what we have not heard? This refers to the depths of the closely-guarded doctrine. All beings have the Buddha-Nature. There is no discrimination between Buddha, Dharma and Sangha. The nature and characteristics of the Three Treasures are the Eternal, Bliss, Self, and the Pure. All Buddhas do not, to the very end, enter Nirvana, and are Eternal and Unchanging. The Nirvana of the Tathagata is: not "is" and not "is-not", not that which is created and not that which is not created, not something leakable [defiled] and not something unleakable [undefiled], not matter and not non-matter, not name and not non-name, not phenomenal and not non-phenomenal, not "is" and not "not-is", not substance and not non-substance, not cause and not result, not opposite and not non-opposite, not brightness and not darkness, not appearing and not non-appearing, not eternal and not non-eternal, not disruption and not non-disruption, no begininning and no non-beginning, no past, no future, and no present, no skandha and no non-skandha, no [sense-] sphere and no non-sphere, no [sense-] realm and no non-realm, no 12 links of interdependence and no non-12-links-of-interdependence. All such categorical items are of a nature deep and fine in implication. One can hear what one has not heard before. Also, there are yet things which do not reach one's ear, which are all the sutras of the tirthikas, i.e. the four Vedas, the vyakaranas, the sutras of the Vaisesikas and Kapilas, the works referring to charms, medical arts, handicrafts, the eclipses of sun and moon, the changes in the cycles of the constellations, books and prophecies. In none of these do we hear anything of what is secret. Now, we come to see this in this sutra. Also, there are the eleven types of sutra from which the vaipulya is excluded. And we see no deep and secret things stated there. But such we come to know from this sutra. O good man! That is why we say that we hear what we have not heard before. "We say that we gain benefit when we hear. If we listen to this great Nirvana Sutra, we come to know all about the depths of what is said in all the vaipulya Mahayana sutras. For example, this is like a mirror, in which a man or woman can clearly see colour and form. It is the same with the great Nirvana Sutra. The Bodhisattva takes this up and clearly sees through all the depths of things stated in the Mahayana sutras. Also, this is like one with a great torch, who is able to see all in a dark room. It is the same with the torch of the Nirvana Sutra. The Bodhisattva takes this up and gains the depths of what is said in the Mahayana sutras. Also, it is like the sun. When it appears, thousands of lights shine over the mountains and gloomy places, and man can clearly see what is far off and distant. It is the same with the pure light of Wisdom of this Great Nirvana. It shines upon all the depths of Mahayana, enabling those of the two vehicles to see the Buddhist teaching. How? Because one hears the all-wonderful doctrine of this Great Nirvana Sutra. O good man! If the Bodhisattva-mahasattva listens to this Great Nirvana Sutra, he will come to know all about the names and letters of all things. If he writes, copies, recites, and explains it extensively to others, and thinks about the meaning, he will know all the significations of all things. O good man! One who hears knows only the name, but not what it signifies. If one truly writes, copies, holds, recites and explains it widely to others, and thinks of the meaning, then one can well know the signification. Also, next, O good man! One who hears this sutra hears that there is the Buddha-Nature, but he cannot easily see it. But if one indeed writes, copies, recites, explains it widely to others and thinks carefully about the meaning, such a one can well see it. A person who listens to this sutra hears about dana, but does not yet see danaparamita. If one indeed writes, copies, recites, explains it widely to others and thinks of the meaning, such a person will well see danaparamita. The same applies to prajnaparamita. O good man! If the Bodhisattva listens well to this Great Nirvana Sutra, he will come to know of Dharma and its meaning; he will become perfect in the two unhinderednesses and will not be afraid of any sramanas, Brahmins, devas, Maras, Brahma, or any of the world. He will expound the 12 types of sutra. There is nothing that differs. Not following and listening to others, he indeed knows and approaches unsurpassed Enlightenment. O good man! That is why we say that we listen and arrive at benefit. "We say that a person cuts away doubt. Of doubt there are two kinds. One is doubting the name, and the other is doubting the meaning. A person who listens to this sutra does away with the mind that doubts the name; a person who thinks of the meaning cuts away the mind that doubts the meaning. Also, next, O good man! Of doubt, there are five kinds. One is doubting and wondering whether the Buddha truly enters Nirvana or not. The second is doubting whether the Buddha is Eternal or not. The third is doubting and wondering whether the Buddha is true Bliss or not. The fourth is doubting whether the Buddha is truly Pure or not. The fifth is doubting and wondering whether the Buddha is the True Self or not. When one listens to this sutra, one eternally segregates one's self from these four doubts. Also, next, there are three kinds of doubt. First, one doubts whether there is the sravaka or not. Secondly, one doubts whether there is the pratyekabuddha or not. Thirdly, one doubts whether there is the Buddha Vehicle or not. Any person who listens to this sutra eternally excises his self from these three doubts, and no doubt remains. If one writes, copies, recites, and explains it widely to others, and thinks of the meaning, one comes to realise that all beings possess the Buddha-Nature. Also, next, O good man! Any person who does not hear this Great Nirvana Sutra will have much doubt regarding: eternal or non-eternal, bliss or non-bliss, pure or non-pure, Self or non-Self, life or non-life, being or non-being, ultimate or non-ultimate, the other world or the past world, is or nothingness, suffering or non-suffering, cause of suffering or non-cause-of suffering, Way or non-Way, extinction or non-extinction, Dharma or non-Dharma, good or non-good, or Void or non-Void. Any person who hears this sutra will eternally

make away with such doubts. Also, next, O good man! Any person who does not hear such a sutra will have various doubts, such as: If matter is the Self? If feeling, perception, volition, or consciousness is the Self? If the eye indeed sees? If the self indeed sees?... down to if consciousness indeed knows? If the Self indeed knows? If matter indeed suffers from karmic results?... down to if consciousness suffers from karmic results? If the Self suffers from karmic results? If matter goes to the other world? If the Self goes to the other world?... down to if consciousness goes to the other world? And such as if the law of birth and death has beginning and end? If it has no beginning and end? Any person who hears this sutra will eternally do away with these kinds of doubt. Or there may be a person who might entertain doubt as to whether the icchantika, those who have committed the four grave offences, those who have enacted the five deadly sins, and those who have slandered Dharma have the Buddha-Nature or not? Any person who hears this sutra eternally does away with all such doubts. Or a person may doubt and wonder if there is a limit to the world or not? Or if there are the ten directions or not? Any person who hears this sutra will eternally do away with any such doubts. This is why we say that it indeed eternally does away with the doubting mind. "We say that the mind of Wisdom is straight and without bends. If the mind doubts, what is seen cannot be straight. If all beings do not hear this all-wonderful Great Nirvana Sutra, what is seen becomes twisted. This applies down to sravakas and pratyekabuddhas, whose views must also be twisted. Why do we say that what all beings see is twisted? They see the Eternal, Bliss, Self, and the Pure in what is leakable, and impermanence, suffering, impurity, and the non-Self in the Tathagata, and they think that beings have life, and knowing, and seeing. They construe Nirvana as thoughtlessness-non-thoughtlessness, and construe Isvara as having the Noble Eightfold Path. What there is there is the "is" and the "not-is", and all such twisted views. If the Bodhisattva hears this Great Nirvana Sutra and practises the Noble Path, he can make away with all such twisted views. What are the twisted views of the sravakas and pratyekabuddhas? These are thinking that the Bodhisattva descends from Tushita Heaven, that he rides on a white elephant, that he finds himself in the womb of a mother, that the father's name was Suddhodana, and the mother's Maya, that for ten full months he was at Kapilavastu, and was born, that when born and not yet touching the earth Sakrodevendra takes him up, and the naga kings, Nanda and Upananda, shoot out water and bathe him, that the great demon, Manibhadra, holds a gem parasol and stands behind him, that the earth-god holds flowers on which the child places his feet, that he takes seven steps in the four directions, and is satisfied, that as he goes to the temple of the devas, the devas come out and welcome him, that Asita picks him up and prophesies, that having seen the signs he is all sorrow and says: "Woe that I will not be blessed with witnessing the rise of the Buddhist teaching", that he goes to a teacher where he learns writing, reckoning, archery, reading omens, and handicrafts, that living in the royal harem he plays with the 60,000 maids and enjoys himself, that he comes out of the castle and finds himself in the Kapila garden, that on the way he sees an aged man and also a sramana going along the roadside, garbed in a priestly robe, that he returns to the royal palace, where he sees the bodies of the females of the palace looking like white bones, that all the palatial building were now no more to him than graves, that he despises these and renounces home, that at night he slips out of the castle, that he sees such great rishis as Udrakaramaputra and Aradakalama and hears from them about consciousness-boundlessness and thoughtlessness-non-thoughtlessness. Having heard and meditated upon these, he sees that all things are non-eternal, suffering, non-pure, and non-Self. He abandons these, practises penance under a tree and, after six years, sees that penance does not bring him unsurpassed Enlightenment. Then he bathes himself in the waters of River Hiranyavati [Nairanjana] and takes some milk-cooked porridge from the hands of a pasture woman. After taking this, he goes to the Bodhi Tree, where, crushing Marapapiyas, he attains unsurpassed Enlightenment; [then] at Varanasi he turns the Wheel of Dharma and sees that, here at Kusinagara, he enters Nirvana. All such are the twisted views of sravakas and pratyekabuddhas. O good man! The Bodhisattva-mahasattva, when he hears and understands the Great Nirvana Sutra, immediately cuts away all such views. And as he writes, copies, recites, understands, explains to others and thinks about the meaning, he becomes straight-minded and makes away with twisted views. O good man! As the Bodhisattva-

mahasattva practises the Way of this Great Nirvana Sutra, he comes to see clearly that the Bodhisattva had never for innumerable kalpas descended from Tushita Heaven into a motherly womb and entered Nirvana at Kusinagara. This is the right view of a Bodhisattva-mahasattva. "We say that we well gain the deep meaning of the Tathagata. This is none other than Parinirvana. All beings possess the Buddha-Nature. They repent of the four grave offences, make away with the mind which slanders Dharma, put an end to the five deadly sins, and do away with the icchantika [within themselves]. Then they can attain unsurpassed Enlightenment. This is what is meant by the extremely deep and closely-guarded thought. Also, next, O good man! What do we mean by the extremely deep meaning? Beings know that there is no such thing as self. Even so, they cannot make away with the karma fire of the days to come. Though they know that the five skandhas die out here, the karma of good and evil does not die out. Though there are all the actions of karma, there are now no doers. Though there are places to go, there is none who goes [there]. Though there is binding, there is no one who is bound. Though there is Nirvana, there is no one who has to die out. That is what is meant by the deepness of meaning." Then Bodhisattva All-Shiniing Highly-Virtuous King said to the Buddha: "O World-Honoured One! It is difficult for me to arrive at the meaning of what the Buddha says regarding "hearing" and "non-hearing". Why? Because if Dharma is "is", what there must be [there] must be "is"; if it is "not-is", what there must be [there] is "is-not". Nothing can come from nothing; what "is" cannot die out. What is heard must be what is heard. If it is not heard, what there is is what one has not heard. How can one say that what one has heard is what one has not heard? O World-Honoured One! What one cannot hear is what one has not heard. If one has heard it, there is no more of hearing [no longer any yet-to-be-heard]. Why not? Because one has already heard it. How can one say that what one has heard is what one has not heard? For example, this is similar to the case where when a person who has gone has come, he is not gone; if he has gone, he has not come. If one is born, there is no being born; if not born, there is no being born. When something has been gained, there is no longer any gaining [of that]. If it is not gained, there is no gaining. If not heard, there is no more of hearing; if not heard, there is no hearing any more. The case is like this. "O World-Honoured One! A person might say that he has heard what he has not heard. As all beings have not yet gained Enlightenment, this can well be had [can well happen]. When Nirvana has not yet been gained, one may well gain it. When the Buddha-Nature has not yet been seen, one might well see it. How can one say that the Bodhisattva of the stage of the ten "bhumis" sees the Buddha-Nature, but is not yet quite clear in [his seeing of] it? O World-Honoured One! One may well say that non-hearing is hearing. O Tathagata! From whom did you once hear in the past? If it is said that you did hear, how could you say in the Agamas that you had no teacher? If having not heard is not heard, and if the Tathagata did attain unsurpassed Enlightenment, beings' not having heard must mean the attaining of unsurpassed Enlightenment. O Tathagata! If one can see the Buddha-Nature even without having heard this Great Nirvana Sutra, all beings must also be able to see it, even though they have not heard it. "O World-Honoured One! Colour is both visible and not visible. The same with sound. It is either audible or non-audible. This Great Nirvana is neither colour nor sound. How can one say that one can well see or hear [it]? O World-Honoured One! If the past is what is already gone, it is not audible. As the future has not yet arrived, one cannot hear it. One can say that one hears now, but one cannot say that one has heard. When heard, the voice dies out and one cannot possess it any longer. This Great Nirvana is not of past, future, or present. If not of the Three Times, there can be no explaining. If inexpressible, there can be no hearing. How can we say that the Bodhisattva practises the teaching of this Great Nirvana Sutra and say that he hears what he has not heard?" Then the Buddha, praising Bodhisattva All-Shining Highly-Virtuous King, said: "Well said, well said! You now know well that all things are like phantoms, flames, a gandharvan castle, a picture on the surface of water, and also like foam and plantain trees, which are empty and contain nothing therein. All have no life, no Self, no suffering, and no bliss. This is similar to the case of the Bodhisattva of the stage of the ten "bhumis", who knows and sees things." Then, of a sudden, there flashed out over the congregation a great light. It was not blue, and yet it was blue; not yellow, and yet it was yellow; not red, and yet it

was red; not white, and yet it was white; not a colour, and yet there was colour [there]; not bright, and yet it was bright; not visible, and yet it was visible. Then, the great congregation, on encountering this light, felt their bodies and minds all joy and happiness. This was as with a bhiksu who now dwells in the "Lion-King Dhyana". Then Bodhisattva Manjushri said to the Buddha: "O World-Honoured One! Who emits this light now?" Then the Tathagata was silent and said nothing. Bodhisattva Kasyapa also asked of Manjushri: "Why does this light shine upon us?" Manjushri was silent and did not reply. Then Bodhisattva Boundless-Body also asked Bodhisattva Kasyapa: "Whose is this light?" Bodhisattva Kasyapa was silent and said nothing. Bodhisattva Pure-Abode Prince asked Bodhisattva Boundless-Body: "Why does this great light appear to all this great congregation?" Bodhisattva Boundless-Body was silent and said nothing. So did it go with the 500 Bodhisattvas. Though asked, there was none there who made reply. Then the World-Honoured One asked Manjushri: "Why is there this light over this great mass of people?" Manjushri said: "O World-Honoured One! We call this light Wisdom. Wisdom is what eternally is. The Dharma Eternal has no causal relations. Why do you, the Buddha, ask me about this light? This light is the Tathagata. The Tathagata is Eternal. The Dharma Eternal is not grounded on causal relations. How does it come, then, that the Tathagata asks me for the reason? "This light is Great Loving-Kindness and Great Compassion. Great Loving-Kindness and Great Compassion are Eternal. The Dharma Eternal is not grounded on causal relations. Why does the Tathagata ask me about causal relations? This light is the meditation on the Buddha. The meditation on the Buddha is the Dharma Eternal. The Dharma Eternal is not erected upon the path of causal relations. Why should the Tathagata ask me about causal relations? This light is the Way that does not obtain with any sravakas or pratyekabuddhas. The Way that does not obtain with sravakas and pratyekabuddhas is Eternal. The Dharma Eternal is not built upon the path of causal relations. Why does the Tathagata ask me about causal relations? By doing away with ignorance, one gains the burning flame of unsurpassed Enlightenment." The Buddha said: "O Manjushri! Do not enter into the all-wonderful depths of the "Paramarthasatya" of all dharmas. Explain things by means of secular truth." Manjushri said: "O

World-Honoured One! To the east, beyond worlds as numerous as the sands of 20 Ganges, is a world called "Acala". The site where the Buddha of that country resides is extensive and all-equal and is as large as 12,000 yojanas lengthwise and crosswise. The ground is made of jewels and has no earth or stones. All is flat and soft, and there are no ditches or pits. All the trees are made of the four gems, namely, gold, silver, beryl, and crystal. Flowers and fruits are in abundance, and there is no time when these are not present. As people come into contact with the flowers and their fragrance, their body and mind experience peace and bliss, which can be likened to a bhiksu sitting in the third dhyana. And there are 3,000 great rivers that surround the land. The water is delicate and wonderful and is perfect in the eight tastes. The people who bathe in it experience joy and bliss comparable to the state of a bhiksu in the second dhyana. The rivers contain various flowers, such as the utpala, padma, kumuda, pundarika, the fragrant, the greatly fragrant, the wonderfully fragrant, the nitya, and the bloom that unhinderedly protects all beings. Also, on both banks are numerous flowers, such as the atimuktaka, campaka, pataliputra, varsika, mallika, mahamallika, simmallika, sumana, yukthika, dhanika, nitya, and the bloom that unhinderedly protects all beings. The river-bed is of golden sand, and there are flights of stairs on the four sides, made of gold, silver, beryl, and crystal of mixed colours. Numerous birds fly over these.

Also, there live many tigers, wolves, lions, and all kinds of evil birds and beasts [there], all of whom, however, regard one another with the mind of a baby. There is in that land no one who carries out the grave offences, nor are there those who slander Dharma, nor are there any icchantikas, nor those who have committed the five deadly sins. The land is good and fit, so that there is no cold or heat, and no sufferings from famine or thirst; no greed, anger, indolence or jealousy reign there; there is no talk of sun and moon, no day and night, and there are no seasons; all obtains as in Trayastrimsa Heaven. The people of that land shine and have no arrogance in their mind. All are Bodhisattva-mahasattvas; all possess divine powers and great virtues, and their minds look up to Wonderful Dharma. They ride in the Mahayana, love the Mahayana, die for, and protect, the Mahayana. They are accomplished in great Wisdom, are

perfect in the Mahayana, and always pity all beings. The Buddha of that land is Tathagata-Full-Moonlight, who is an Alms--Deserving, All-Enlightened One, an All-Accomplished One, a Well-Gone, an All-Knower, an Unsurpassed One, Best Trainer, and Teacher of Gods and Humans, a Buddha-World-Honoured One. He delivers sermons where he resides. And there is not a single land that cannot indeed hear [them]. He delivers a sermon on the Great Nirvana Sutra to Bodhisattva Vaiduryaprabha. "O good man! If a Bodhisattva-mahasattva thoroughly practises the Way of the Great Nirvana Sutra, those who cannot actually hear can also hear." This Bodhisattva-mahasattva Vaiduryaprabha questions Buddha Full-Moonlight as Bodhisattva All-Shining Highly-Virtuous King [questions me]. All is the same, and there is nothing different. "Buddha Full-Moonlight said to Bodhisattva Vaiduryaprabha: "O good man! Far out to the west, beyond as many lands as sands of 20 Ganges, there is a land called "Saha". In that, there abound mountains, hills, mounds, sand, gravel, thorns, and poisonous thorns. There are always the sufferings of hunger, thirst, cold, and heat [there]. The people of that land do not respect sramanas, Brahmins, parents, teachers, or elders. They greedily cling to unlawful acts, practise wrong actions, and do not believe in Wonderful Dharma. Their life is short. Those who cunningly cheat others are cured [punished] by the king. The king possesses territories, but is not satisfied. He covets what others possess. He calls forth wars and fights, and many meet with untimely deaths. As the king acts thus, the four guardians of the earth and good devas cannot have an easy mind. So calamities and famines come about, and the five cereals do not grow well. People suffer from illnesses and suffering goes on unendingly. There lives a Buddha [there] called Tathagata Shakyamuni, an Alms-Deserving, an All-Enlightened One, an All-Accomplished One, a Well-Gone, an All-Knower, an Unsurpassed One, Best Trainer, Teacher of Gods and Humans, and a Buddha-World-Honoured One. All-compassionate and kind-hearted towards all beings, he is delivering sermons on the Great Nirvana Sutra to all beings, at Kusinagara, between the sal trees. There is a Bodhisattva there called All-Shining Highly-Virtuous King. Already he asks about this and nothing differs [here] from what you ask. The Buddha is now answering. Make haste and go there! You will hear [things] yourself." O World-Honoured One! That Bodhisattva Vaiduryaprabha, on hearing this, is coming with 84,000 Bodhisattva-mahasattvas. Hence this premonition. Because of this, we have this light. That is why. And yet it is not why." Then Bodhisattva Vaiduryaprabha arrived, accompanied by 84,000 Bodhisattvas and bearing, along with various banners and parasols, incense, flowers, garlands, and various kinds of music, double that which had gone before. All came to Kusinagara, between the sal trees. Offering what they had brought to the Buddha, they touched his feet with their heads, folded their hands together, paid homage, and thrice walked around the Buddha. Having paid homage, they sat down to one side. Then the World-Honoured one asked that Bodhisattva: "O good man! Have you arrived or not?" Bodhisattva Vaiduryaprabha said: "O World-Honoured One! "Arrived" is not "come", and "not arrived" is also not "come". As I think of this, there is no coming at all. O World-Honoured One! Even if all things were eternal, it would also be not "come"; even if it is "non-eternal", there is no coming. If one thinks that man has a nature, there is coming and no coming. I now do not see any eternally fixed nature in beings. How can I say "to have come" or "not to have come?" With an arrogant person, there can be going and coming; with one without arrogance, there can be no coming and going. With one who is leaving, there can be talk of going and coming; with one without the leaving mind, there is no talk of going and coming. If one thinks that the Tathagata ultimately enters Nirvana now, there is going and coming; if one does not think that the Tathagata ultimately enters Nirvana, there can be no going and coming. If one does not hear of the Buddha-Nature, there can be going and coming; with one who hears of the Buddha-Nature, there can be no going and coming. With one who thinks that there is Nirvana with the sravakas and pratyekabuddhas, there is going and coming; with one who does not see any entering into Nirvana with the sravakas and pratyekabuddhas, there can be no going and coming. If one sees the Eternal, Bliss, the Self, and the Pure with the sravakas and pratyekabuddhas, there is going and coming; if not, there is no going and coming. If one views the Tathagata as not the Eternal, Bliss, the Self, and the Pure, there is going and coming; if one sees the Eternal, Bliss, Self, and the Pure with the Tathagata, there cannot be

any going and coming. O World-Honoured One! Leave this matter as it is for the present. I desire to ask more. Please condescend to give ear to me!" The Buddha said: "O good man! Ask as you wish to ask. It is now time. I shall now makes things clear and explain them to you. Why? Because it is hard to encounter a Buddha, as it is difficult to come across the blooming of the udumbara. It is the same with Dharma. It is difficult to hear it. Of the 12 types of sutra, the hardest to hear is the vaipulya. For this reason, listen with undivided attention." Then Bodhisattva-mahasattva Vaiduryaprabha obtained permission and also admonition. And he said to the Buddha: "O World-Honoured One! How can a Bodhisattva-mahasattva practise the Great Nirvana Sutra? I wish to hear what I have not heard before." Then the Tathagata praised him, saying: "Well said, well said, O good man! You now desire to cross the sea of the Great Nirvana of Mahayana. And you rightly encounter my sermon. I shall now become a great doctor and thoroughly extract the poisonous arrows of diverse doubt. You are not yet clear as to the Buddha-Nature. I possess the torch of Wisdom and shall well enlighten you. You now desire to cross the great river of birth and death. I shall now become a mariner for you. You see in me the parent, and I see in you the small child. Your mind is now dying for the treasures of Wonderful Dharma. I have much and can stand giving. Listen clearly to me, listen clearly to me! Bethink yourself well! I shall now make things clear and explain them to you. O good man! It is now time for you to hear Dharma. Having heard it, believe it and gain a respectful mind. Listen with all your mind; venerate what you have heard. Do not seek to pick out something wrong in Wonderful Dharma! Think not of greed, anger, and ignorance. Think not of good and bad or of the caste of the priest. Having heard Dharma, be not arrogant. Do not do things for honour, fame, or profit. Make effort to save the world, and for the interest of sweet Dharma. Also, do not be worried in mind. Hear Dharma, save yourself, and then save others. First, understand yourself, and let others understand. First, ease yourself, and then ease others. First, gain Nirvana yourself, and then let others gain it. See with an equal mind Buddha, Dharma and Sangha. See birth and death as great suffering. See in Great Nirvana the Eternal, Bliss, the Self, and the Pure. First act for others, and then for your own self. Act for Mahayana and not for the two vehicles. Do not cling to anything. Do not cling to the characteristics of any thing. Do not be greedy towards anything. Always try to understand and see Dharma. O good man! If you give ear to Dharma with such an attitude, this is how one hears what one has not heard before. "O good man! There is a hearing, when one has not heard; there is a non-hearing when one has heard; there is a hearing when one has heard. O good man! There is a birth, without being born; there is no being born, without being born; there is no being born, having been born; there is a being born, having been born. Similarly, there is an arriving, not having arrived; there is no arriving, not having arrived; there is no arriving, having arrived; there is an arriving, having arrived." "O World-Honoured One! What is being born, not having been born?" "O good man! Abiding peacefully in secular truth, one first comes out of the womb. This is being born, having not yet been born." "What is not being born, not having been born?" "O good man! This Great Nirvana has no aspect of being born. This is not being born, having not been born." "What is not being born, having been born?" "O good man! Death comes in secular truth. This is not being born, having once been born." "What is being born, having been born?" "O good man! All common mortals are those who are born by having been born. Why? Because there is no disruption in being born and being born, and because all leakings [defilements] follow moment upon moment. This is being born, having been born. The Bodhisattva of the four abodes ["bhumis"] is no being born, having been born. Why? Because he is unmolested in being born. This is a non-being-born, having been born. O good man! This is what obtains within the Buddhist teaching." "What are: being born, having not yet been born; not yet being born, having not yet been born; not being born, having been born; and being born, having been born, as said in other teachings?" "O good man! Let us take the case of a seed. When it is not yet born, the great elements conjoin, man acts, and it first burgeons out into a bud. This is being born, having not yet been born." "What is not being born, having not yet been born?" "For example, the case of a dead seed and its not meeting with the [necessary] conditions is that of "not born, having not been born." "What is not born, having been born?" "This is as when the seed has shot forth its bud, but there is no growth. This is a case of not born, having been born?"

"What is being born, having been born?" "This is as with the growing of the bud. If what is born does not grow, there is no increase. All such aspects of the leakable [i.e. the defiled] are cases of being born, having been born, as stated in the categories of other teachings." Bodhisattva-mahasattva Vaiduryaprabha said to the Buddha: "O World-Honoured One! If it is the case that any being is born in what is leakable, is it eternal or non-eternal? If what is born is eternal, then there cannot be any being born in what is leakable. If being born is non-eternal, what is leakable must be the eternal. O World-Honoured One! If what is born can well be born by itself, there cannot be any nature of its own. If it can well call forth another life, why can it not call forth the unleakable [i.e. that which is undefiled]? O World-Honoured One! If there is life when not yet born, how can we speak of being born? When there is no life when not yet born, why do we not call space life?" The Buddha said: "Well said, well said, O good man! "Born, not having been born" is inexpressible; "born, having been born" is inexpressible; "not born, having been born" is inexpressible; "not born, not having been born" is also inexpressible; being born is also inexpressible; not being born is also inexpressible. As there are causal relations, we can well explain [things]. "How is it that being born, not having been born is inexpressible?"Not born is born. How can we explain? Why? Because of the fact that there is being born. "How is it that what is born is born is inexpressible?"For there is the being born because what is born is born; for there is not being born because being born is born. Hence, inexpressible. "Why is being born is not being born inexpressible?"What is born is called born; being born does not come about by itself. Hence, inexpressible. "Why is not born, not having been born inexpressible? "Not being born is Nirvana. As Nirvana is not being born, it is inexpressible. Why? Because one gains it by practising the Way. "Why is being born inexpressible? "Because being born is emptiness itself.

"Why is not being born inexpressible? "Because there is the possibility of gaining it. "Why is it expressible for causal reasons? "Because the ten causal relations can constitute the cause of being born. Hence, it is possible to explain. "O good man! Do not get into the deepest depths of the All-Void dhyana. Why not? Because the great mass of people is dull. "O good man! In what is created, birth is eternal. As it lives in the non-eternal, birth too is non-eternal. "Abiding, too, is eternal, because being born is being born. Abiding is also non-eternal. "Difference [i.e. change], too, is eternal. As the law [a dharma] is non-eternal, difference is also non-eternal. "Breaking up [dissolution] is also eternal. Because it is originally empty, but now exists. Hence, breaking up is also non-eternal. "O good man! Being born, abiding, difference, and breaking up are all eternal. As there is extinction moment after moment, one must not say eternal. As this Great Nirvana is disrupted and dies out, we say non-eternal. O good man! Whatever is defiled already has the nature of being born, when it is not yet born. For this reason, being born comes about. What is undefiled has from the beginning no nature of being born. Hence, being born cannot come about. "The original quality of fire calls forth fire when conditions so arise. "The eye has the nature of seeing and sees by colour, light, and mind. The same applies to the being born of beings. As there is the original nature, it can come about, meeting with the causal relations of karma and by the coming together of the parents, which is life." Then Bodhisattva Vaiduryaprabha and the 84,000 Bodhisattva-mahasattvas, on hearing this sermon, jumped for joy and remained suspended in the sky seven talas high. With respect and folding their hands, they said to the Buddha: "O World-Honoured One! Having been enlightened by the Tathagata in kindly ways, I now understand what one hears and what one does not hear of Great Nirvana. Also, the 84,000 Bodhisattvas have gained the depths of the being born and the not being born of all things. O World-Honoured One! I now understand all and have done away with all doubts. But among the Bodhisattvas congregated here, there is one called "Fearless". He respectfully desires to ask a question. Please deign to answer." Then the World-Honoured One said to Bodhisattva Fearless: "O good man! Ask whatever you desire to ask. I shall now state things clearly to you." Then Bodhisattva Fearless, along with his 64,000 Bodhisattvas, stood up from their seats, put their robes in order, prostrated themselves on the ground and said to the Buddha: "O World-Honoured One! How can the people of this world act and gain birth in that immovable world? By what Wisdom can the Bodhisattva of the land become the elephant king of all men? How can he possess great virtues and practise the Way, and how, with the sharpest of Wisdom, can he understand what he hears?" Then the World-Honoured One said in a gatha:

"One who does not injure
The life of beings and strongly
Upholds the prohibitions,
And who learns the Buddha's all-wonderful teaching
Gains birth in the land immovable.
Not stealing the wealth of others,
And always giving to all others,
And erecting the catur-desa
[an abode where monks coming from other places can stay and live],
One gains birth in the land immovable.
Not raping others' women,

Not acting unduly towards one's own wife,
And giving bedding to those who uphold sila,
One gains birth in the land immovable.
Not seeking profit for one's own
Or for others' sake,
Not having fear, and guarding one's own mouth,
Not telling lies, one will thus
Be born in the land immovable.
Not hurting a good teacher of the Way,
Keeping evil kindred at a distance,
And using gentle words, one gains

Birth in the land immovable.
Like all Bodhisattvas, one segregates
One's self from evil speech,
And people desire to hear what one says.
Such a person will gain birth
In the land immovable.
Even in a joking way,
No untimely word is used,
And one always speaks at the apt time.
Such a person will gain birth
In the land immovable.
One is always glad when one sees
Others gaining benefit and one has
No jealous mind. Such a person will
Gain birth in the land immovable.
One causes no worries to others,
Is ever compassionate,
And never enacts evil as a means.
Such a person gains birth in the land immovable.
If not evil in mind,
Not saying that there can be no dana,
No parents, no past, and no future,
And if one does not hold such a view of life,
One gains birth in the land immovable.
On the wayside of a wide and extensive stretch of land,
One digs a good well, plants fruit trees,
And makes gardens and always gives food to those who beg.
Such a person gains birth in the land immovable.
If one offers a fragrant lamp or a flower
To the Buddha, the Dharma, and the Sangha,
One gains birth in the land immovable.
If out of fear, or for profit, or for blessings
A person writes even a gatha of this sutra,
Such a one will gain birth
In the land immovable.
If, even for profit, a person in a day
Recites this sutra, that person will gain
Birth in that land immovable.
If one, for the sake of the unsurpassed Way,
For a day or night upholds the eight pure actions,
One gains birth in the land immovable.

If one does not sit together with those
Who commit the grave offences
And reproaches those who slander the vaipulya,
One gains birth in the land immovable.
If one gives even a piece of fruit
To one who is suffering from illness
And looks upon such a person with happy and sweet looks,
Such a one will gain birth in the land immovable.
If one does not spoil [defile] the priestly robe,
Guards well the things that belong,

Or are offered to, the Buddha, and sweeps
The ground where the Buddha and the Sangha live,
Such a person will gain birth in the land immovable.
If one makes statues that are big
And erects Buddhist stupas as large
And if one is glad at heart,
Such a person gains birth in the land immovable.
If one, for this sutra,
Gives one's self or wealth to those who preach,
Such a one gains birth
In the land immovable.
If one gives ear to,
And copies, the undisclosed store of all Buddhas,
Upholds and recites it,
Such a person gains birth
In the land immovable."

Then Bodhisattva-mahasattva Fearless said to the Buddha: "O World-Honoured One! I now see that by what I do I gain birth in that land. If the Tathagata will condescend to explain what Bodhisattva-mahasattva All-Shining Highly-Virtuous King asks for the sake of all beings, this will benefit and give peace to all such as humans, gods, asuras, gandharvas, garudas, kimnaras, mahoragas, and others." Then the World-Honoured One said to Bodhisattva-mahasattva All-Shining Highly-Virtuous King: "Well said, well said! O good man! Listen well with all your mind. I shall now explain it to you in detail. By causal relations, there can be one not yet arrived, by not arriving; by causal relations, there is one arrived, not arriving; by causal relations, there can be one who has not yet arrived, having already arrived; by causal relations, there can be one who is arrived, having already arrived. How is there one who is not yet arrived, by not arriving? "O good man! Now, "non-arriving" is Nirvana. Common mortals are not yet arrived, because of greed, anger, and ignorance, because their bodily and oral actions are impure, because a person receives all impure things, because he commits the four grave offences, because he slanders the vaipulya, because of his being an icchantika, because of his enacting the five deadly sins: for all these reasons, a person is one who is not yet arrived at "non-arriving". "O good man! How is one arrived, having not yet arrived? Non-arriving is Great Nirvana. Why is one arrived? Because one eternally cuts away greed, anger and ignorance, and all evil actions of body and mouth; because one does not receive impure things;

because one does not perform the four grave offences; because one does not slander the vaipulya sutras; because one does not become an icchantika, and because one does not commit the five deadly sins. For these reasons, we say that one arrives, having not yet arrived. Now, the srotapanna arrvies after 80,000 kalpas, the sakrdagamin arrives after 60,000 kalpas, the anagamin after 40,000 kalpas, and the arhat after 20,000 kalpas, and the pratyekabuddha after 10,000 kalpas. For this reason, we say that one has arrived, while not yet having arrived.

"O good man! How is a person arrived, having already arrived? "To arrive" corresponds to the 25 existences. All beings are always overshadowed by innumerable defilements and bonds, which come and go, never parting, as with a rotating wheel. This is arriving. Sravakas, pratyekabuddhas and all Bodhisattvas are eternally segregated from these. Hence, "non-arriving". To succour beings, manifestation is enacted amidst them. Hence, "having arrived". "O good man! Why do we say having arrived by having arrived? "To arrive" relates to the 25 existences. Such are the things of defilement of all common mortals, srotapannas, up to anagamins. Thus we say having arrived, having arrived. "O good man! The same applies to what one has heard and what one has not heard. These are the instances of "hearing, not having heard", "not hearing, having not heard", "not hearing, having heard", and "hearing, having heard". "What is "hearing, not having heard"? O good man! "Not hearing" is Great Nirvana. Why "not hearing"? Because of not being created, because it is not a sound, because it cannot be explained. Why "hearing"? Because one can hear the names, which are the Eternal, Bliss, Self, and the Pure. Hence, "hearing, not having heard." Then Bodhisattva-mahasattva All-Shining Highly-Virtuous King said to the Buddha: "O World-Honoured One! You, the Buddha, say that Great Nirvana cannot be heard. How is it that the Eternal, Bliss, Self, and the Pure cannot be heard? Why not? O World-Honoured One! You say that a person who has made away with defilement is one who has attained Nirvana. One not yet cut free from defilement is one who has not yet gained it. Thus the nature of Nirvana is "what originally was, is not now". If what applies in the world is "what originally was, is not now", this is the non-Eternal. It is as with a pot, which is what originally was, but is not now, and what once was which now returns to not-is, and which is the non-Eternal. If Nirvana is thus, how could we speak of the Eternal, Bliss, Self, and the Pure? Also, next, O World-Honoured One! What can arise by adorning is non-Eternal. If Nirvana is such, it must be non-Eternal. What are the causal relaitons? The 37 elements assisting towards Enlightenment, the six paramitas, the four limitless minds, physiognomical forecasting, the anapana, the six thinkings all crush the six great elements. All these items constitute the cause and condition to call forth Nirvana. Hence, non-eternal. Also, next, O World-Honoured One! Whatever is "is" is non-Eternal. If Nirvana is "is", Nirvana must be non-Eternal. This is what obtains in the agamas, in which you said that the sravaka, pratyekabuddha, and the All-Buddha-World-Honoured One all have Nirvana. Hence, non-Eternal. Also, next, O World-Honoured One! Whatever is visible is non-Eternal. This is as when the Buddha said before that one who can see Nirvana can well cut away defilement. Also, next, O World-Honoured One! For example, this is like space, which does not molest [hinder] any beings. So, we say Eternal. If Nirvana is Eternal, why are there those who gain and who do not gain? If Nirvana is thus and is partial with beings, how can we call it Eternal? O World-Honoured One! For example, 100 people have an enemy. If this enemy is made away with, all have peace. If Nirvana is impartial, this must mean that if one gains it, many must gain it. If one person cuts off bondage, many persons must be able to cut off bondage. If things are not thus, how can there be the Eternal? For example, a man respects, makes offerings to, honours and praises

the king, prince, his parents, teachers and elders, and there is benefit. This is not Eternal. The same is the case. Why? You, the Buddha, said in the agama to Ananda: "If one truly respects Nirvana, one cuts off bondage and perfects immeasurable bliss." So, we do not say Eternal. O World-Honoured One! If there are such as the Eternal, Bliss, Self, and the Pure, we cannot call Nirvana Eternal. If there are no such, how can we explain the matter?" Then the World-Honoured One spoke to Bodhisattva-mahasattva All-Shining Highly-Virtuous King: "The true quality of Nirvana is not that of something that originally was not but now is. If Nirvana were what originally was not but now is, it could not be anything unleakable [undefiled] and Eternal. The nature and characteristics of the phenomenal Buddha and the noumenal Buddha are Eternal and all-abiding. As defilements spread over beings, they cannot see Nirvana. And they say that is does not exist. As the Bodhisattva makes effort and cultivates his mind with sila, meditation, and Wisdom, and excises defilement, he sees it. Know that Nirvana is what is Eternal. It is not what originally was not but now is. So, we say Eternal. "O good man! There is a dark room, in which there is a well where there are seven different treasures. Though one knows that they are there, since it is dark, one cannot see them. One who is wise knows the means. He lights a big lamp, carries this [into the room], illuminates the place, and sees all. Now, this person does not think that there were orginally no water and seven treasures, but he thinks that they were there. It is the same with Nirvana. It is not that it originally was not but happens to come about now. Due to the darkness of defilement, beings do not see it. The Great WIsdom, the Tathagata, puts into effect the best expedients, lights the lamp of Wisdom, and enables all Bodhisattvas to see the Eternal, Bliss, the Self, and the Pure of Nirvana. Thus the wise must not say that Nirvana is what originally was not, but now is. "O good man! You say that Nirvana is made by adornment and that it must be non-Eternal. But this is not so. Why not? O good man! The body of Nirvana is not one that is born, that departs, that is actual, or that is false. It is not one worked out [bodied forth]. It is not defiled, not what is created. It is not hearing, nor anything visible, not something fallen: it is no death. It is not a different phase of phenomena, nor is it of the same form. It is no going and no returning. It is no past, no future, and no present. It is not one, not many, not long, not short, not round, not square, not pointed, not bent. It is no phenomenon, no mental image, no name, no matter, no cause, no result, no self, and not what one possesses. For this reason, Nirvana is Eternal and enduring, and does not change. Because of this, one practises good for innumerable asamkhyas of kalpas, one adorns ones's own self, and then one can see. "O good man! As an example: there is an underground water of eight tastes, and yet no one can at it. One who is wise devises a means, digs, and gets to it. The case is the same with Nirvana. For example, a blind person cannot see the sun or moon. But when a good doctor effects a cure, he can then see. And it is not that the sun and moon have come about but now. It is the same with Nirvana. It has already existed by itself, and it is not that it is something that happens to come into existence now. "O good man! A man commits a crime and is chained up in a prison house. After a long time, he is released. Coming back home, he now sees his parents, brothers, wife, children and relatives. The case is the same with Nirvana. "O good man! You say that Nirvana is non-Eternal due to causal relations. But this is not so. Why not? "O good man! There are five kinds of cause. What are the five? They are: 1) cause of birth, 2) cause of harmonisation, 3) cause of being as it is, 4) cause of growth, and 5) cause of far out [indirect]. "What is the cause of birth? It is based on karma, defilements, etc., and all such seeds of the external category as plants and grass. These are the causes of birth. "What is the cause of harmonisation? This is none other than the harmonisation between good and the good mind, non-good and the non-good mind, indefinable ["avyakrta"] and the indefinable mind. This is the cause that can be talked of as harmonisation. "What is the cause of being as it is? Due to the pillars, the roof does not fall down. The mountains, rivers and trees rest on the great earth. And they can be as they are and stand. Man possesses, within, the four great elements, an innumerable and unending number of defilements. And beings continue to exist. This is the cause of being as it is. "What is the cause of growth? Clothes, food and drink enable beings to grow. The seed of the external category is not burnt out or eaten up by birds. Hence, growth. The sramanas and Brahmins grow by depending upon the honoured ones ["upadhyaya"], the good teachers

of the Way, etc. Or it is like a child that grows up by depending upon its parents. This is the cause of growth. "What is the cause that is far out? For example, through charms, no demons or poison can cause one harm. Depending and relying on kings, there can be no robbers. Budding rests upon earth, water, fire, and wind. This is as when churning and a person become the far-out [distant, ultimate] cause of butter, or bright colour the far-off cause of consciousness, or dead bodies of parents the far-off cause of beings. Such as the seasons, too, become far-off causes. "O good man! The body of Nirvana is not one that comes about from these five causes. How could one say that it arises from a cause of the non-Eternal? "Also, next, O good man! There are two causes. One is the cause of doing and the other that of enlightening. It is as with the rope of the potter's wheel. This is the cause of doing. A lamp illuminates things in the darkness. This is the cause of enlightening. O good man! Great Nirvana does not come about from the cause of doing. It only follows the cause of enlightening. By the cause of enlightening is meant such as the 37 elements of the Way assisting to Enlightenment and the six paramitas. These constitute the cause of enlightening. "O good man! Dana [generous giving] is the cause of Nirvana, but not the cause of Great Nirvana. Danaparamita [perfected giving] is the cause of Great Nirvana. The 37 elements can be the cause of Nirvana, but not of Great Nirvana. The innumerable asamkhyas of assisting elements can be the cause of Great Nirvana." Then, Bodhisattva-Mahasattva All-Shining Highly Virtuous King said to the Buddha: "O World-Honoured One! In what way can dana not be danaparamita, and in what way can dana be danaparamita? And also, in what way can prajna [Wisdom] not be prajnaparamita, and in what way can it be so called? In what sense do we speak of Nirvana and of Great Nirvana?" The Buddha said: "O good man! When the Bodhisattva-mahasattva practises the Vaipulya-Mahaparinirvana, he does not hear or see dana; nor does he hear or see danaparamita. Nor does he hear or see prajna; nor does he hear or see prajnaparamita. Nor does he hear or see Nirvana. Nor does he hear or see Great Nirvana. When the Bodhisattva-mahasattva practises Great Nirvana, he knows and sees the universe and he realises that the real state is all-void and that there is nothing that one possesses, and that there is nothing that has any mode of harmonisation or perception. And what he gains is such a phase [state of realisation] as the unleakable [i.e. undefiled], non-doing, the phantomic, the burning flame of the hot season, and the all-empty phase of a gandharvan castle. Then the Bodhisattva sees such a phase and has no greed, malevolence and ignorance. He does not hear or see. This is what we mean when we say that the Bodhisattva-mahasattva himself knows that this is dana, this danaparamita, this prajna, this prajnaparamita, this Nirvana, this Great Nirvana. "O good man! What is dana, and what is not danaparamita? One sees one who begs, and one gives. This is giving, but not paramita. When there is none that begs, but one opens up one's heart and gives of one's own accord, this is danaparamita. One gives according to the time. This is giving, but not paramita. One practises eternal giving - this is danaparamita. One gives to others and later regrets it. This is giving, but not paramita. One gives and does not regret it. This is danaparamita. "The Bodhisattva-mahasattva gains four fears in things. To the king, robber, water and fire, he is pleased to give. This is danaparamita. If one gives, expecting a return, this is giving, but not danaparamita. If one gives, but does not look for any recompense, that is danaparamita. One gives when one fears; one gives for fame and profit, for a family legacy, for satisfying the five desires in heaven, for pride, for the pride of being superior to others, for knowledge, for recompense in the life to come, all of which is like doing trade. "O good man! This is like a person who plants trees to gain cool shade and flowers, fruit and wood. If one practises such giving, this is giving, but not any paramita. "The Bodhisattva-mahasattva who practises Great Nirvana does not see giver, recipient, or thing given, nor time given, nor any field of blessings nor non-field of blessings, nor any cause, condition, result, doer, receiver, nor many nor less in number, nor purity nor non-purity. He does not belittle the recipient, himself, or the thing given. He does not care about who sees or who does not see. He makes no distinction between himself and others. He only practises dana for the sake of the Eternal Dharma of the vaipulya Mahaparinirvana. He gives to benefit all beings. He gives to cut off the defilements of all beings. He practises dana without seeing giver, recipient, or thing given. "O good man! As an example: a man falls into the great sea, but as he holds on to a dead body, he is indeed able to be saved. When the Bodhisattva-mahasattva practises the Way of Great Nirvana and performs dana, things are as in the case of the dead body. "O good man! There is a man, for example, who is shut up in prison. The gate is strongly guarded, but there is a hole in the privy. Through this, he gains an unhindered place [i.e. his freedom]. So does it obtain with the Bodhisattva-mahasattva as he practises Great Nirvana and performs giving. "O good man! This is, for example, like unto a nobleman who has fear, feels unsafe, and has no one upon whom to rely, and who asks for help from the hand of a candala. So does it stand with the Bodhisattva-mahasattva when he practises Great Nirvana. "O good man! This is like the situation of a sick person, who, in order to eliminate the pain of illness, partakes of what is unclean. So do things stand with the Bodhisattva when he practises Great Nirvana and performs giving. "O good man! If the Brahmins come across a rise in the price of cereals, they will partake of dog's meat, for the sake of their life. It is the same with the Bodhisattva when he practises Great Nirvana and performs giving. O good man! Nothing like this relative to Great Nirvana has been heard for innumerable kalpas past, and yet we hear it. As for sila, silaparamita, prajna, and prajnaparamita, things are as stated in the Avatamsaka Sutra. "O good man! How does a Bodhisattva-mahasattva practise the Way of Great Nirvana and hear what has not been heard? What the 12 types of sutra state is profound in meaning, unheard since of old. Now, solely in this sutra, we fully hear well. We heard about this before. But what was heard was the name only. Only in this Great Nirvana Sutra do we hear about the meaning. Sravakas and pratyekabuddhas only hear the names of the 12 types of sutra, but not about the menaing. Now, in this sutra, we hear fully. This is why we speak of hearing what has not been heard [before]. "O good man! "In the sutras of the sravakas and pratyekabuddhas, we did not hear that the Buddha was the Eternal, Bliss, the Self, and the Pure, and that there is no extinction; that there is no difference between the Three Jewels and the Buddha-Nature, and that the Buddha-Nature is even in those who have performed the four grave offences, the slanderers of the vaipulya, and those who have committed the five deadly sins. But now, in this sutra, we hear this." This is what we call hearing what has never been heard before.

Chapter Twenty-Eight: Bodhisattva Highly-Virtuous King 2

Bodhisattva-mahasattva All-Shining Highly-Virtuous King said to the Buddha: "If those who have performed the grave offences, those who have slandered the vaipulya sutras, those who have committed the five deadly sins, and the icchantika [all] have the Buddha-Nature, why then do they fall into hell? O World-Honoured One! If they have the Buddha-Nature, why do we say that there is no Eternal, Bliss, Self, and Purity [with them]? O World-Honoured One! If one who has cut off the root of good is an icchantika, why is it that, when cutting off the root of good, the root of the Buddha-Nature is not cut off? If the Buddha-Nature is cut off, how can we talk of the Eternal, Bliss, Self, and the Pure? If there is no such cutting off, why do we speak of the "icchantika"? O World-Honoured One! Those who have committed the four grave offences are called persons not fixed. Those slanderers of the vaipulya sutras, those who have committed the five deadly sins, and the icchantika are termed those who are not fixed. If such as these are to become fixed, how can they attain unsurpassed Enlightenment? Even those who have attained such stages as srotapanna up to pratyekabuddha are likewise called persons not fixed. Even if those who are at the stages of srotapanna up to pratyekabuddha can indeed become fixed, they can never attain unsurpassed Enlightenment. O World-Honoured One! If those persons who have committed the four grave offences are those not fixed, those of the stages of srotapanna up to pratyekabuddha are also those not fixed. If they are to be called non-fixed, the All-Buddha-Tathagata must also be non-fixed. If the Buddha is one not fixed, the body and nature of Nirvana, too, must be called not-fixed. Even all laws [dharmas], too, must be called not-fixed. Why not-fixed? When the icchantika makes away with the icchantika [within], he can attain Bodhi [Enlightenment]. The same must be the case with all Buddhas. Even though entering Nirvana, they might come back and not enter Nirvana. If things proceed thus, we can say that the nature of Nirvana is not fixed. Not being fixed, there can never be the Eternal, Bliss, Self, and the Pure. How can we say that the icchantika and others can reach Nirvana?" Then the World-Honoured One said to Bodhisattva-mahasattva All-Shining Highly-Virtuous King: "Well said, well said! To

benefit and give peace to innumerable beings, to pity all the world, to augment the practice of the Way of all Bodhisattvas who aspire to Bodhi, you put these questions. O good man! You have, in your past, already drawn near to an innumerable number of all Buddhas and have cultivated, at the places of all Buddhas, all good deeds. You have long accomplished the virtue of Bodhi, subdued and driven away all Maras. You have already taught innumerable beings and enabled them to attain unsurpassed Bodhi. You have for a long time fathomed the very deep and closely-guarded store of Dharma of the All-Buddha-Tathagata, and you have put such questions to all the Buddha-Tathagatas of the past as many as the sands of innumerable and boundless Ganges. I have never until now met any human, god, sramana, Brahmin, Mara, or Brahma who has put such questions to the Tathagata. Now, listen carefully, listen carefully. I shall now explain clearly. "O good man! The icchantika is not fixed. If fixed, he could not gain unsurpassed Enlightenment. As he is not yet fixed, he can indeed gain it. "You say that unless he has cut off the Buddha-Nature, how could an icchantika cut off the root of all good? "O good man! There are two kinds of root of good. One is internal, and the other external. The Buddha-Nature is neither internal nor external. Because of this, there is no cutting off of the Buddha-Nature. Also, there are two kinds. One is defiled, and the other undefiled. The Buddha-Nature is neither defiled nor non-defiled. Because of this, there is no cutting off. Also, there are two kinds. One is eternal, and the other is non-eternal. The Buddha-Nature is neither eternal nor non-eternal. Because of this, there is no cutting off. If cut, it will come back again and be gained again. If it comes back and cannot be gained, this is non-cutting. If what is gained is cut off, this is an icchantika. A person who performs the four grave offences is also one not fixed. If fixed, one who has performed the four grave offences could not gain unsurpassed Bodhi. One who slanders the vaipulya is also not fixed. If fixed, the slanderer could not attain unsurpassed Bodhi. One who has committed the five deadly sins is also not fixed. If fixed, such a one would not be able to attain unsurpassed Bodhi. Matter and the characteristics of matter, too, are both not fixed. The characteristics of smell, taste, touch, those of birth, up to those of ignorance, those of the five skandhas, the 12 spheres and 18 realms [of sensory experience], those of the 25 existences, the four lives, even down to all existences, are not fixed either. O good man! For example, a conjuror can present to the eyes of the people the four military forces of infantry, chariots, elephants, and horses; he conjures up all kinds of garlands, body adornments, castle-towns, villages, mountains, forests, trees, springs, ponds, rivers and wells. Of the onlookers, the little children who have not much intellect will think that all these are real, but those of intelligence will know that all is sheer untrue illusory allure, which cheats a person's eyes. O good man! It is the same with all common mortals up to sravakas and pratyekabuddhas, who think that there are fixed states in all things. All Buddhas and Bodhisattvas do not see any fixed state in any thing. O good man! For example, it is as with children who, in the mid-summer months, see a mirage of hot times and say that it is water, whereas one with discernment will never entertain in this mirage any thought of water, knowing that this is nothing but a mirage that cheats men's eyes and that it is not water. The same is the case with all beings, sravakas and pratyekabuddhas, who see all things and say that they are all real. All Buddhas and Bodhisattvas do not see any fixed state in anything. O good man! For example, in the mountain valleys, the human voice generates an echo. A child hears this and says this is an actual voice, whereas one with intelligence will say that there is nothing real therein; what there is there is merely the characteristics of a voice which cheats the ear consciousness. O good man! It is the same with all beings, sravakas, and pratyekabuddhas, who see fixed characteristics in all things, whereas all Bodhisattvas and others think that all things have no fixed states and that all are non-eternal, void, and all-equal and have no birth or death. Hence, the Bodhisattva sees that all things are non-eternal. "O good man! "There are also fixed states. How fixed? These are the Eternal, Bliss, the Self, and the Pure. Where are they? There where there is Nirvana." "O good man! The fruit of attainment of the srotapanna, too, is not one that is fixed. Being not fixed, only after 80,000 kalpas can he attain unsurpassed Bodhi. The state of sakrdagamin is not fixed either. Not being fixed, such a person attains unsurpassed Bodhi after 60,000 kalpas. That of anagamin is also not fixed.

Not being fixed, such a one attains unsurpassed Bodhi after 60,000 kalpas. That of the arhat, too, is the same. Not being fixed, he gains the unsurpassed Bodhi mind after 20,000 kalpas. It is the same with the fruition of the pratyekabuddha. Not being fixed, he attains the unsurpassed Bodhi mind only after 10,000 kalpas. "O good man! The Tathagata now reclines at Kusinagara between the twin sal trees, in the posture of a lion, and shows himself as entering Nirvana, and all those disciples of his who have not yet attained arhatship and all Mallas are smitten with great apprehension and sorrow. Also, devas, humans, asuras, gandharvas, garudas, kimnaras, mahoragas, and others make great offerings. All people are now ready to burn him with 1,000 "tans" [one "tan" = either 16, 20, or 60 feet] of finely woven woolen cloth, in which to wrap his body and lay him in a coffin of seven gems, embalmed with fragrant oil and covered over with all kinds of fragrant wood. Only two tans cannot be burnt off. One is that which is closest to the body, and the other is what is outermost. Among all the people, his remains are to be divided into eight parts. All his sravakas say that the Tathagata now enters Nirvana. Know that the Tathagata definitely does not enter Nirvana. Why not? Because the Tathagata is Eternal, and there is No Change that comes about [with Him]. Hence, the Tathagata's Nirvana is also not fixed. O good man! Know that the Tathagata, too, is not fixed. The Tathagata is no deva. Why not? There are four heavens, namely: 1) worldly heaven, 2) sentient's heaven, 3) purity heaven, and 4) meaning heaven. The worldly heaven is as in the case of the king. The sentient's heaven is like that of the four guardians of the earth up to Thoughtlessness-non-Thoughtlessness Heaven. Purity Heaven is for those from srotapanna up to pratyekabuddha. The Heaven of Meaning is for the Bodhisattvamahasattvas of the stage of the ten abodes ["bhumis"]. Why do we call the Bodhisattva of the ten abodes the Heaven of Meaning? Because he well grasps the meaning of all things. What do we mean by meaning? Meaning here betokens seeing that all things are void. "O good man! The Tathagata is no king, nor of the class of the four guardians of the earth, nor of that of Thoughtlessness-non-Thoughtlessness Heaven, nor of the class of srotapanna, pratyekabuddha, or the Bodhisattva of the stage of the ten abodes. Thus the Tathagata is no deva. But all beings call the Tathagata the deva of devas.

Hence, the Tathagata is no deva, no non-deva, no human, no non-human, no demon, no non-demon, no hell-dweller, animal or hungry ghost; nor is he no hell-dweller, animal or hungry ghost. He is no being; he is no dharma, and not no dharma. He is not matter ["rupa"] and not non-matter. He is not tall, not non-tall, not short, not non-short. He is non-phenomenal, not non-phenomenal, not mind, not non-mind. He is not anything defiled, nor is he non-defiled. He is uncreated, and not uncreated. He is non-Eternal, not non-Eternal, no phantom, not no-phantom. He is no name and is not no name; not fixed, and not non-fixed. He is not "is", nor "is-not", not a sermon, nor a non-sermon. He is no Tathagata, and not no Tathagata. Hence, the Tathagata is not one fixed. "O good man! Why do we not call the Tathagata "worldly deva"? The worldly deva is the king. The Tathagata has for innumerable kalpas abandoned the kingly state. So he is no king. We say that he is not a non-king. He was born in the royal house of Kapilavastu. So, he is not a non-king. He is no sentient-heaven deva. For he has long since renounced any form of existence. So he is no sentient-heaven deva. He is not no sentient-heaven deva. Why not? He ascended to Tushita Heaven and came down to Jambudvipa. So the Tathagata is not no sentient-heaven deva. He is no purity deva. Why not? Because the Tathagata is no srotapanna up to pratyekabuddha. The Tathagata is not no purity deva. Why not? Because he is not one defiled by the eight things of the world [i.e. profiting; weakening; breaking up; honour; praising; slandering; pain; and pleasure] and is like the lotus, which is not tainted by muddy water. Hence, the Tathagata is not no purity deva. Also, he is no deva of meaning. Why not? Because the Tathagata is no Bodhisattva of the grade of the ten abodes. For this reason, the Tathagata is no deva of meaning. Nor is he not a deva of meaning. Why not? Because the Tathagata always practises the meanings of the 18 shunyatas [emptinesses]. Hence, the Tathagata is not no deva of meaning. "The Tathagata is not a human. Why not? Because he has been far removed from existence as a human for innumerable kalpas. Hence, he is no human. He is no non-human. Why not? Because he was born in Kapilavastu. The Tathagata is no devil. Why not? Because he does not cause any harm to any being. Because of this, he is no devil. Also, he is not no devil. Why not? For he teaches beings, transformed as a devil. The Tathagata is

also no hell-dweller, animal, or hungry ghost. Why not? Because the Tathagata has long been segregated from all evil deeds. Hence, he is no hell-dweller, animal or hungry ghost. Also, he is not no hell-dweller, animal or hungry ghost. Why not? Because the Tathagata also transforms himself into the three unfortunate realms and saves beings. Hence, he is not no hell-dweller, animal or hungry ghost. Also, he is not of beings. Why not? Because he has long since abandoned the nature of beings. Thus he is not of the beings. Nor is he a non-being. Why not? For, at times, he speaks of "[i.e. assumes]" the characteristics of a being. Hence, the Tathagata is not a non-being. The Tathagata is not any dharma. Why not? Because all existences have different characteristics. It is not thus with the Tathagata. He has one characteristic. Hence, he is no dharma and no non-dharma. Why not? Because the Tathagata is the Dharma-World. Hence, he is not any non-Dharma. The Tathagata is not a body. Why not? Even the ten categories of the body [i.e. the five sense-organs and the five sense-fields] cannot take him in "[encompass him]". That is why he is not a body. And he is not no body. Why not? Because he has on his body the 32 signs of perfection and the 80 minor marks of excellence. Hence, he is not no body. The Tathagata is not tall. Why not? Because he stands above all kinds of form. Hence, he is not what is tall. Nor is he not-tall. Why not? Because the world cannot see such a characteristic as the knot of hair on his head. For this reason, he is not not-tall. The Tathagata is not what is short. Why not? He is long segregated from the bond of arrogance. Hence, he is not what is short. Also, he is not not-short. Why not? Because he manifested before the rich man, Kokila, a body of three feet "[i.e. the body of a child said to have been projected so as to teach Kokila]". Hence, he is not not-short. The Tathagata is not of the phenomenal. Because he is long segregated from any phenomenal aspect. Hence, not phenomenal. Also, he is not non-phenomenal. Why not? Because he thoroughly knows all phenomena. Hence, he is not non-phenomenal. Why not? Because he is like space. Hence, no mind. Also, he is not no-mind. Why not? Because he has the 10 mental powers ["dashabala"]. And also because he can thoroughly fathom what is in the mind of any being. Hence, he is not no-mind. The Tathagata is not one created. Why not? Because of the Eternal, Bliss, the Self, and the Pure. For this reason, he is not one who has been created. Also, he is not one-not-created. Why not? Because he manifests himself as coming, going, sitting, lying, and in Nirvana. Hence, he is not not-created. The Tathagata is not Eternal. Why not? Because he has parts in body [a physical body and its parts]. Hence, non-eternal. Why is he non-eternal? Because he has intellect. What is Eternal does not have intellect, as in the case of space. The Tathagata has intellect. So, he is not eternal. How is he not eternal? Because he has language and speaks. What is Eternal has no language; it is like space. The Tathagata has language. Hence, non-eternal. He has a family name. So he is non-eternal. What possesses no family name is the Eternal. Space is eternal, as it has no family name. The Tathagata has the family name of Gautama. Hence, he is not eternal. As he has parents, he is not eternal. That without parents is Eternal. Space is Eternal, so it has no parents. The Buddha has parents. Hence, non-eternal. He has four deportments [postures, i.e. lying, sitting, standing, walking]. Hence, non-eternal. What has no four deportments is Eternal. Space is Eternal, as it has no four deportments. The Buddha has four deportments. Hence, non-eternal. What is Eternal has no [confined] direction or place to dwell. Space is Eternal, so it has no direction or place to tell of. The Tathagata appeared in East India and lived in Sravasti and Rajagriha. Hence, he is non-eternal. For this reason, the Tathagata is not eternal. Also, he is not non-eternal. Why not? Because he has eternally cut off life. What has life is non-eternal; what has no life is Eternal. The Tathagata has no life. Hence, Eternal. What is Eternal has no family name; what has a family name is non-eternal. The Tathagata has no life and no family name. With no life and family name, he is Eternal. "What is Eternal fills all places as in the case of space, which has no place where it does not exist. The same is the case with the Tathagata. He exists everywhere. Hence, He is Eternal." What is non-eternal calls this "is" and the other "not-is". The case of the Tathagata is not so. We cannot speak here of "is" and there of "not-is". Hence, Eternal. With the non-eternal, things at times obtain as "is" and at times as "notis". With what applies to the Tathagata, there is no saying, at times, of "not-is". Hence, Eternal. What is Eternal has no name and no form. Since space is Eternal, it has no name or form. The Tathagata, too, is nameless and formless. Hence, Eternal. What is Eternal has no cause and no result. As

space is Eternal, it has no cause and no result. The Tathagata, too, has no cause and no result. Hence, Eternal. What is Eternal is not related to the Three Times. It is the same with the Tathagata. He has nothing to do with the Three Times. Hence, Eternal. The Tathagata is no phantom. Why not? He is eternally segregated from any thought of deceiving. Hence, he is no phantom. Also, he is not a non-phantom. He at times splits up one body into innumerable bodies and [merges] innumerable bodies into one. He passes through mountain walls and nothing can obstruct him. He walks upon water as if on [solid] ground. He goes down into the ground as though into water, and he moves through the air as if on the ground. His body emits fire like a great fire-ball. Cloud and thunder shake, and fearful is the sound. At times, he becomes like a castle-town, a village, a house, a mountain, a river or a tree. At other times he manifests himself in a big body, or at times in one small. He becomes a male, a female, a male or female child. Hence, the Tathagata is also not a non-phantom. The Tathagata is not one fixed. Why not? Because he manifests himself here at Kusinagara between the twin sal trees as [about to] enter Nirvana. Hence, he is not fixed. "Also, he is not non-fixed. Why not? Because he is the Eternal, Bliss, the Self, and the Pure." For this reason, the Tathagata is also not non-fixed. The Tathagata is not one who leaks out defilement. Why not? Because he is segregated from the three defilements. The three defilements are: 1) defilements of the kamadhatu [Realm of Desire], except for ignorance, which are the defilements of desire, 2) defilements of the rupadhatu and arupadhatu [Realm of Form, and Realm of Formlessness], excepting ignorance, which are called "is"-defilements, 3) ignorance of the three worlds, which is the defilement of ignorance. The Tathagata is eternally segregated from these. Hence, he leaks out no defilement. "Also, next, all beings do not see the defilement of "is". Why do all beings not see the "is" defilement? All beings have doubts regarding things to come in the future, namely: Will they have a body or not in the future? Was there a body or not in the past? Do they have a body or not in the present life? If there is the Self, is it a form or non-form? Is it form-non-form? Is it non-form and not-non-form? Is it perception or non-perception, or perception and non-perception? Is it non-perception and non-non-perception? Does this body belong to any other person or does it not? Is it that which belongs to others or that which does not belong to others, or is it that which does not belong to others, or is it one that does not belong to others. Is it one with life, but not a carnal body? Is it one that is a carnal body, but without life? Is it one that has a carnal body and life? Is it one that has no body and no life? Is it a carnal body, life, and one that is eternal? Or is it one that is non-eternal? Is it non-eternal, or eternal and non-eternal? Is it one that is non-eternal and not non-eternal? Are the body and life the works of Isvara? Or are they the work of time? Are they a work without cause? Are they the work of the "prakriti" [primordial matter, or world-nature]? Are they the work of motes? Are they the work of law or non-law? Are they the work of man? Are they the work of illusion? Are they the work of father and mother? Does it [the Self] live in one's own mind? Or does it dwell in the eye? Or does it fill the whole body? Where does it come from and where does it go to? Who is it indeed that is born and who is it who dies? Was one in the past a Brahmin, a Kshatriya, a Vaishya, or a Sudra? What caste will one gain in the future? Was my body in the past that of a male, female, or an animal? Do I commit a sin if I take life, or is it nothing of the kind? Is it a sin if I drink alcohol, or is it nothing of the kind? Is it the case that it [karma] is one's own making, or is it what is done by others? Do I receive karmic results, or do I contract them in my carnal self? Such doubts and innumerable illusions spread over beings' minds. From these doubting views there come the six minds, which think: 1) Self definitely exists, 2) Self definitely does not exist, 3) temporary Self is the true Self, 4) no Self exists other than the temporary Self, 5) the true Self exists other than the temporary Self, 6) the Self which is the skandhas does, receives and knows. All of these are twisted views of life. The Tathagata has long since extracted the innumerable roots of views and defilements. Hence, he leaks out no defilement. O good man! The Bodhisattva-mahasattva who practises the holy actions of Great Nirvana is able eternally to make away with all such defilements. The All-Buddha-Tathagata always practises holy actions. Hence, no defilements exist [with him]. "O good man! Common mortals cannot easily suppress the five sense-organs. So there are the three defilements, by which they are drawn to evil and go to unwelcome places. O good man! A bad horse, for example, twisted in its nature, carries a person on its back to unsafe places. It is the same with the man who does not have good control of his five sense-organs and who departs from the good Way to Nirvana and gains birth in all kinds of unfortunate realms. For example, an evil-minded elephant not yet broken in will not carry the rider to where he desires to go, and will leave the castle-town and seek the wilderness. It is the same with the person who does not have good control over the five sense-organs. This carries him away from the castle-town of Nirvana into the great stretch of wasteland of birth and death. O good man! This is as in the case of a minister of twisted mind who makes the king do evil. It is the same with the minister of twisted mind of the five sense-organs. He always teaches people to do innumerable evil things. O good man! This is similar to a bad son, who, if not taught by teachers, elders and parents, will always commit evil deeds. So do things obtain with one who does not have control over the five sense-organs. Such a person does not give ear to the good injunctions of teachers and elders, and there is no end of evil he will not do. O good man! Common mortals do not have control over their five sense-organs and always suffer from the robbers of hell, animals, and hungry ghosts. Also, the [manifold] harm of the malignant robbers extends even to good people. O good man! As common mortals do not have control over the five sense-organs, the storms of the five dusts [i.e. of the five sense-fields] overtake them. For" "example, if pasture cows are not well guarded, they will ravage the seedlings and plants that have been cultivated. Common mortals do not have control over their five desires and suffer variously. "O good man! When the Bodhisattva-mahasattva practises Great Nirvana and holy actions, he always guards his five sense-organs well. He fears greed, anger, ignorance, arrogance and jealousy, because he has to arrive at all good dharmas. O good man! One who guards well the five sense-organs guards well the mind. One who guards well the mind guards well the five sense-organs. For example, when men guard the king, the land is well protected. One who protects the land well guards the king. It is the same with the Bodhisattva-mahasattva. On hearing this Great Nirvana Sutra, one gains Wisdom. Through Wisdom, one gains the exclusive mind. If the five sense-organs are loose-set, the mind ceases to act. Why? Because of the Wisdom of mindfulness. O good man! This is as in the case of the pastor [pasture-keeper] who checks his cows from going east and west and damaging the crops. It is the same with the Bodhisattva-mahasattva. Working up mindfulness Wisdom, he guards the five sense-organs, so that they will not get out of control. His mindfulness Wisdom sees no form of Self, what comes out of Self, beings or what they enjoy. He sees all things as when he sees "Dharmata" [Essence of Reality], and what he sees is all like the earth, stones, tiles, and gravel. For example, a house comes about by various combinations of elements and not by any fixed nature of its own. He sees that all beings are no other than combinations of the four great elements and the five skandhas and that they have no fixed nature. As there is no fixed nature, the Bodhisattva does not greedily cling. All common mortals think that they exist. So they have the worry of defilement. When the Bodhisattva-mahasattva practises Great Nirvana and has mindfulness Wisdom, he does not cling to any being. Also, next, the Bodhisattva-mahasattva, practising the Great Nirvana Sutra, does not cling to any being or the diverse external forms of things. O good man! For example, a painter uses various colours and paints pictures of men, women, cows, horses, etc. Common mortals, devoid of intelligence, see these and take them to be [real] men, women, etc. But the painter knows that they are not men and women. It is the same with the Bodhisattva-mahasattva. In the various aspects of things, he sees only the aspect, but never many forms of beings, right to the end. Because he has mindfulness Wisdom. The Bodhisattva-mahasattva, as he practises Great Nirvana, might see a beautiful woman. But, to the end, he does not gain a clinging thought. Why not? Since he thoroughly looks into what meets his eye. O good man! The Bodhisattva-mahasattva knows that there resides no pleasure in the five desires and that joy never endures [there]. This is like a dog that bites at a dead bone; like a man holding fire against the wind; a cask of venomous serpents gained in a dream; fruit-trees on the wayside which easily get struck by many people; a piece of meat for which many birds compete; foam on water; the warp of a woven piece of cloth which has now come to an end; a prisoner having to go to a prison citadel - or whatever is temporary and cannot endure long. Thus, desires are meditated upon and [it is seen] that there is much that is wrong. "Also, next, the Bodhisattva meditates on all beings. Connected with colour, smell, taste and touch, there has always been worry for innumerable kalpas. The size of the bodies and bones which each being heaps up during a kalpa is as great as Vipula Hill in Rajagriha; the milk taken is as much as the water of the four seas. And the blood shed is much more than this. The tears shed by parents, brothers, wife, children and relatives at the moment of death is more than the waters of the four oceans. We could cut all the plants of the earth and make counting sticks of an inch long and count the number of parents, and yet we would not be able to reach the end of counting. It is not possible fully to count the sorrows experienced in the realms of hell, animals, and hungry ghosts. We could cut the great earth into pieces as small as dates. Yet birth and death proceed unendingly and cannot be counted. The Bodhisattva-mahasattva meditates deeply on the unending sorrows which all beings experience in life because of desires. The Bodhisattvamahasattva does not lose [his] mindfulness Wisdom, because of the sorrows of birth and death. O good man! As an example: people fill an area of 25 square "lis" [1,894 ft]. The king commands a minister: "Carry a pot full of oil, go through the crowd, but do not let a drop fall to the ground. If a drop does fall, you will forfeit your life." Also, a man follows behind with an unsheathed sword, to frighten him. The minister, strictly observing the royal injunction, passes through the great crowd of people. When he sees the objects of the five desires, he always says to himself: "If I am indolent and cleave to wrong desires, I shall certainly drop what I am holding in my hands and lose my life." Due to this fear, the man does not spill even a single drop of oil." "It is the same with the Bodhisattva-mahasattva. Amidst birth and death, he does not lose [his] mindfulness Wisdom. Not losing this, his mind does not greedily adhere to the five desires, even when he sees them. He sees a pure colour, but no colour appears there; what he sees is a scene of suffering. This extends down to consciousness. He does not see birth, extinction, or cause. What he sees is a phase in the process of elements conjoining. The five sense-organs of the Bodhisattva are pure. As his sense-organs are pure, those sense-organs are fully protected. The sense-organs of common mortals are not pure. So upholding [of moral purity] cannot proceed well. Therefore, we say that the root secretes defilement. With the Bodhisattva, such secretions are eternally done away with. So we speak of "non-secretion". With the Tathagata, this [secretion of defilement] has been eternally excised. Hence, non-secretion. "Also, next, O good man! There is a segregation of secretion. The Bodhisattva wishes to substantiate the Buddha Realm of unsurpassed amrta [immortality] and abandons evil secretions. How does he segregate [them]? He thoroughly practises the Great Nirvana Sutra, writes, copies, upholds, recites and expounds it, and thinks over its meaning. This is segregation. Why? O good man! I have not encountered a case of the 12 types of sutra, as with this vaipulya Great Nirvana Sutra, where one so thoroughly segregates oneself from evil secretions. O good man! As an illustration: a learned teacher teaches his disciples. One amongst them learns well what is taught and is not evil in mind. It is the same with the Bodhisattva who practises the all-wonderful Sutra of Great Nirvana and who has no evil in his mind. O good man! For example, there is a wonderful charm. Once employed, it renders one immune to poison for 20 years, and a serpent cannot sting one. If one recites the charm, one will have no occasion to suffer from it [i.e. any poison] for the duration of one's life. It is the same with this Great Nirvana Sutra. If one once gives ear to it, for seven kalpas to come one will not fall into the unfortunate realms. If one copies, recites, expounds it, and meditates on its meaning, one will unfailingly attain unsurpassed Enlightenment. This is like the case of a Chakravartin who arrives at amrta [immortality] when he sees the pure state of the Buddha-Nature. O good man! There are such innumerable virtues in this Great Nirvana. O good man! Anyone who copies, recites, expounds and explains it to others, and meditates on the meaning is, you should know, my true disciple. And he follows my Way well. This is what I see and what I pray for. Such a person clearly knows that I do not enter Nirvana. Thus, in all places where such a person lives, such as a castle-town, village, mountain, forest, field, house, farmhouse or palace, I shall always find myself and I shall not move. I always receive offerings from such a person. I shall become a bhiksu, bhiksuni, upasaka, upasika, Brahmin, Brahmacarin or a poor alms-beggar. How can I get this person to know that the Tathagata receives offerings from him? O good man! This person might see, at night, a Buddha statue in a dream, or the forms of all devas, sramanas, kings, a Chakravartin, lion-king,

lotus flower, or udumbara; or he might see a big mountain, a great stretch of sea-water, the sun or moon, a white elephant, a white horse, or the parents. He gains flowers or fruit, or such precious things as gold, silver, beryl, crystal, or the five kinds of cow-product. Know that the Tathagata at [such] times receives what is offered to him. The person awakes, feels happy, and receives what he needs. He thinks no evil and practises good. O good man! This Great Nirvana thoroughly accomplishes such innumerable asamkhyas of all-wonderful virtues. O good man! Believe now what I say. All good men and women desire to see me, to respect me, to see me in "Dharmata" [the Essence of Reality], to gain the Void Samadhi, to see the Real Nature, to practise the "surangama-samadhi", "simharaja-samadhi", and to destroy the eight Maras. By the eight Maras is meant the so-called four Maras, and the non-Eternal, non-Bliss, non-Self, and the non-Pure. Any person who desires to be blessed with the bliss of heaven should go and befriend and associate with those who possess, copy, recite, explain to others, and meditate on the meaning of the Great Nirvana Sutra, ask, make offerings, respect, praise wash the hands and feet, set up the seat, have the four things well supplied, so that nothing is lacking. If such people come from far-distant places, go 10 yojanas and receive them. Because of this sutra, give whatever is precious and welcome any such people. If one does not have any such things to offer, sell yourself. Why? Because it is hard to encounter this sutra, much harder than encountering the udumbara. "O good man! I recall to myself: Innumerable, boundless nayutas of kalpas past, when there was a world called "saha", there was a Buddha-World-Honoured One named Tathagata Shakyamuni, the Alms-Deserving, the All-Enlightened One, the All-Accomplished One, the Well-Gone, the All-Knower, the Unsurpassed One, the Best Trainer, the Teacher-of-Gods-and-Humans, and the Buddha-World-Honoured One. For the sake of all people, he delivered the sermon of the Great Nirvana Sutra. I, at that time, heard from a good friend that that Buddha would, for the sake of all people, deliver the sermon of the Great Nirvana Sutra. On hearing this, joy welled up within me. I desired to make offerings, but I was so poor that I could not offer anything. So I went round, intending to sell myself. But I was so sterile in my fortune that I could not sell [i.e. could not find a buyer]. I was on my way home, when I met a man. I said: "I intend to sell myself. Will you not buy me?" The man said: "I don't have anyone at home who can stand the work. If you can, I shall certainly buy you." I asked: "What is this work which no one can stand?" The man replied: "I have a bad disease. A good doctor tells me that I have to take three liangs [i.e. a Chinese unit of weight] of human flesh a day. If you can supply me with three liangs of human flesh every day, I shall give you five gold coins." On hearing this, I greatly

rejoiced and said: "Give me the money, and in addition seven days. Having done what I desire to do, I shall come back and do what I must do." The man said: "Not seven, but one day, to be clear." O good man! I then took the money, went back, went to the Buddha, prostrated myself on the ground, offered what I had and, later, with my whole heart, listened to this sutra. At that time I was dull. Though I heard this sutra, I could only uphold [i.e. remember, practise] one gatha:

"The Tathagata enters Nirvana
And eternally cuts off birth and death.
If one listens with a full heart,
One will gain unending bliss."

"Having gained this gatha, I went to the house of the sick person. O good man! I then daily gave him three liangs of flesh. Because of the virtue of meditating on the gatha, I had no pain. Not a day did I fail [to give my flesh], and a month passed. O good man! As a result of this, the disease was cured. I regained the former state of my body and had no wounds. With my body fully in order, I aspired to unsurpassed Bodhi. The power of a single gatha is such. How much more would it have been if I had fully upheld and recited this sutra? Seeing such virtue in this sutra, my aspiration doubled [and I prayed]: "I pray that in days to come I shall attain Bodhi and be called Shakyamuni." O good man! Due to this single gatha I am now with this congregation, fully addressing gods and men. O good man! Thus is this Great Nirvana Sutra so utterly wonderful. It is perfect in countless virtues. This is none other than the all-wonderful, closely-guarded store of all Buddhas. For this reason, anyone who uphold this well eliminates hateful defilements. What do I mean by evil? This is none but the evil elephant, the evil horse, the evil cow, the evil dog, and the land where venomous snakes live, the land of thorns, precipices, precipitous banks, rushing waters, whirlpools, evil people, evil lands, evil castles, evil houses, evil friends and others. If all such become the cause of defilement-secretions, the Bodhisattva forsakes them. If not, he does not forsake them. If the secretions increase, he forsakes them; if not, he does not. If evil dharmas arise, he forsakes them. If any good dharmas arise, he does not forsake them. What is meant by "forsaking"? This means not possessing the sword or staff, but with right Wisdom and means always

forsaking such. This is having right Wisdom and forsaking. To arrive at Good Dharma, one forsakes what is evil. The Bodhisattva-mahasattva meditates on his own self [ego] and thinks that it is like an illness, the pox, a carbuncle, an enemy, the arrow that hits a man and gets into his body, that this is a great house of suffering, and that all are the roots of all good and evil. Although this body is so impure, the Bodhisattvamahasattva carefully looks after and nourishes it. Why? It is not to begrudge one's own body, but to care for Good Dharma. This is for the sake of Nirvana, not for birth and death. It is for the sake of the Eternal, Bliss, the Self, and the Pure. It is not [for] the non-Eternal, non-Bliss, non-Self, and the non-Pure. It is for the sake of Enlightenment, but not for "is" existence. It is for the one vehicle ["ekayana"], not for the three vehicles ["triyana"]. It is to gain the body of the 32 signs of perfection and the 80 minor marks of excellence, not for the body of Thoughtlessness-non-Thoughtlessness. It is for the sake of the King of the Dharma-Wheel, not for the body of a Chakravartin. O good man! The Bodhisattva-mahasattva should always guard his self. Why? If not, life will not be safe. If life is not whole, he cannot copy, uphold, recite, explain widely to others, and meditate on the signification of this sutra. For this reason, the Bodhisattva must protect his own self well. That is why the Bodhisattva can truly segregate his own self from all evil secretions. O good man! One who desires to crosss water takes care of the ship or raft. One who is travelling well looks after good horses. The farmer who cares for his seedlings attends to dung and manure. To protect oneself from scorpion poison, once takes care of venomous serpents. For the safety of man and treasure, one keeps candalas. To overcome robbers, one employs strong soldiers. One protects the fire when cold bears down upon one, and a leprous patient seeks poisonous medicine. It is the same with the Bodhisattva. He knows that this body is full of impurities. But to uphold the Great Nirvana Sutra, he thoroughly aids and protects [his body], and does not allow its strength to diminish. The Bodhisattva-mahasattva sees both the evil elephant and the evil friend as one and not two. Why so? Because both destroy one's own self. The Bodhisattva never fears the evil elephant, but fears the evil friend. Why? The evil elephant only harms the body, not the mind. The evil friend destroys both. The evil elephant destroys only one single body, but the evil friend destroys innumerable good bodies and innumerable good minds [i.e. good states of mind]. The evil elephant only destroys the impure and foul-smelling body, but the friend who is bad destroys the pure body and the pure mind. This evil elephant only destroys this carnal body, but the friend who is bad destroys [i.e. makes one lose] the Dharma Body. Even when one is killed by an evil elephant, one does not fall into the three unfortunate realms. But when one is killed by a friend who is bad, one falls into the three unfortunate realms. The evil elephant is only the enemy of the carnal body, but the evil friend is the enemy of Wonderful Dharma. For this reason, the Bodhisattva must always segregate himself from evil friends. The common mortal does not segregate himself from such secretions. So these secretions come about. As the Bodhisattva makes away with these, there is no secretion [of defilement] with him. Acting thus, there is no secretion with the Bodhisattva. How could there be with the Tathagata? For this reason, he does not secrete defilement. "How do we come into the vicinity of the secretions? All common mortals receive clothing, food, bedding and medicine. They receive all of these for the ease of body and mind. They do various evil things, do not know what is wrong, and advance towards the three unfortunate realms. Hence, we say that there is secretion. The Bodhisattva, since he sees, keeps himself away from such things. When a robe is offered, he receives it. He does this not for the body, but for Dharma. He has no arrogance. His mind is always in a surrendering mood. It is not for adornment, but out of a feeling of shame. It [i.e. the robe] keeps out the cold and heat, bad

wind, bad rain, bad worms, mosquitoes, gadflies, flies, fleas and scorpions. He receives food and drink, but there is no greed there. He does this not for himself, but for the good of Dharma; not for the carnal body, but for the good of all beings; not out of pride, but for physical strength; not out of malignancy or to harm others, but out of hunger and to cure the pox. He gains good food, but does not have a greedy mind. He might receive a house. But the same is the case. No defilement of greed ever dwells in his mind. For the sake of the house of Enlightenment, he rejects the robber of defilement. In order to keep away bad winds and rain, he receives a house. One who receives does not have a greedy mind. This is only [done] for Wonderful Dharma. It is not [done] for life, but for Eternal Life. O good man! A person suffering from the pox smears butter and roasted barley-flour on it. For this reason, he covers it with his robe. As the pus and blood come out, he applies butter and roasted barley-flour. To cure the pox, one employs medicine. To guard against evil winds, one lives deep inside a house. It is the same with the Bodhisattva-mahasattva. He sees the pox[-like] body. So he covers it with clothing. As things leak out from the nine holes [i.e. the nine outlets in the human body], he takes food and drink. On account of the bad wind and rain, he receives a house. When the four poisons appear, one seeks a doctor's medicine. The Bodhisattva-mahasattva receives the four kinds of offerings. This is for the sake of Enlightenment, not life. Why? The Bodhisattva-mahasattva thinks: "If I do not receive these four things, my body will wear out and will not be strong. If it is not strong enough, it cannot stand the suffering, and one cannot practise Wonderful Dharma." If one can thoroughly bear down on the suffering, one can easily practise innumerable good things. If one cannot stand the suffering, anger raises its head as [various] sufferings press down upon one, and on encountering happiness, a mind of greed arises. One looks for happiness. If it does not come, ignorance raises its head. Because of this, the common mortal generates a secreting mind in the face of the four offerings. The Bodhisattva-mahasattva meditates well and does not engender any secretion. So we say that the Bodhisattva does not secrete [defilement]. How could one say that the Tathagata is one who secretes? For this reason, we do not call the Tathagata one who secretes. "Also, next, O good man! All common mortals

- 281 -

protect their body and mind. Yet they have the three evil sensings. Thus, though they may well shake off defilements and gain the place of Thoughtlessness-non-Thoughtlessness, they fall back and gain the three unfortunate realms. "O good man! There is, for example, a man who desires to cross a great sea and who has almost reached the other shore, when he drowns and dies. So do things go with the common mortal. He means to cross the three worlds, but falls back into the three unfortunate realms. Why? Because there is no good sensing [with him]. "What is "good sensing"? It is none other than the six thinkings. The good mind of the common mortal is lowly; evil burns [within him]. When the good mind weakens, the mind of Wisdom weakens. When the good mind is in a weak state, secretions increase. The sense-organ of the eye of the Bodhisattva-mahasattva is pure, and it sees the evils of the three sensings. He knows that these three sensings possess variegated worries and that they always become for beings the enemies of the three vehicles. The workings of the three sensings bar an innumerable number of common mortals and beings from encountering the Buddha-Nature. For innumerable kalpas, they abide in an upside-down state of mind and say that the Buddha-World-Honoured One has nothing of the Eternal, Bliss, and the Self, but only Pureness, and that the Tathagata enters Nirvana for good. All beings have none of the Eternal, Bliss, Self, and the Pure. [But] with an upside-down mind, they say that they are the Eternal, Bliss, the Self, and the Pure. Truth to tell, they do not have three vehicles, but with their upside-down minds they say that there are the three vehicles. The Way of One Truth is true and is not false. Abiding in an upside-down state of mind, they say that there is no oneness of Truth. These three evil sensings are always reproached by all Buddhas and Bodhisattvas. These three sensings always harm oneself and also others. Around all these three sensings always foregather all evils in a train and become the three fetters which chain beings to birth and death. The Bodhisattva-mahasattva always views the three sensings thus. On occasion, the Bodhisattva has the sensing of desire, but is silent and does not respond. For example, this is like a person of right and pure mind who refuses all that is foul and impure. It is like a burning, hot iron ball, which no one can indeed grasp hold of. It is like the Brahmin, who will not eat beef, like a person who

is well fed and who will not take bad food, or a chakravartin who will not share his seat with a candala. Thus the Bodhisattva-mahasattva despises the three sensings and does not take [what is impure]. The case is thus. Why? The Bodhisattva thinks: "All beings know me to be a good field of weal. How can I receive this evil thing? If I gain an evil sensing, I cannot be a field of weal to beings. I myself do not say that I am a good field of weal. But beings see me and say that I am so. If I expose myself to a bad sensing, this will cheat beings. In days past I repeated birth and death over innumerable kalpas in the three unfortunate realms because of cheating. If I receive the offerings of the faithful with an evil mind, all devas and the rishis with the five divine powers will know and reproach me. If I receive the offerings of the faithful, when I myself have evil sensings, this will cut short or annul the recompense due to the one who gives. If I receive the offerings of a danapati, I will purchase regret. Like a loving child, all danapatis always look up to me. How can I cheat them and buy regret? Why? Because this annuls or makes small the recompense. Or one might always say that one has renounced home. Now, the sramana must not do evil. If evil is done, there can be no priesthood. With no oneness, they are not sramanas. I have left my parents, brothers, sisters, wife and child, relatives and teachers, and practised Bodhi. When one practises all the sensings, there can be no occasion to practise the non-good sensings. For example, a person goes into the sea to gain gems. This is like picking up crystal instead of pearl, or throwing away all-wonderful music and playing in dung, or abandoning heavenly women to love menial servants, or abandoning a vessel of gold to take up an earthenware bowl, or abandoning ambrosia ["amrta"] and partaking of poison, or abandoning the familiar, old, wise and good doctor, but accepting one who bears one ill will, or geting medicine and trying to cure oneself by one's own hand. The case is the same with me. Abandoning the ambrosial taste of Dharma of the great teacher, Tathagata-World-Honoured One, I partake of various evil sensings from Mara. It is hard to be born a human. This can be compared to the coming into bloom of the udumbara flower. But now I have gained it [i.e. the human state]. It is hard to meet the Tathagata, but now I have met him. It is hard to see and hear the pristine treasure of Dharma, but I now hear it. This is like a blind tortoise chancing to hit the hole in a piece of floating wood. Life is much more fleeting than the rushing water of a mountain stream. One lives today, but one cannot be sure of the morrow. How can one abandon one's mind to what is wrong? The prime of life slips away as swiftly as a running horse. How can one depend on [what is transient] and be arrogant? It is like the situation where a devil sits in wait of a man's performing wrong actions. It is the same with the devils of the four great elements. These always come and try to seek out some fault with one. How can one give occasion to evil sensings? For example, this is as in the case of a crumbling house which is about to fall down. Life, too, is the same. How can one do evil? I am a sramana. What a sramana does is awaken good. If I awaken to non-good, how can I be called a sramana? I am one who has renounced the world. The world-fleeing sramana is one who follows the path of good. Should I now perform evil, how could I be called a world-fleeing sramana? I am now a true Brahmin. A Brahmin is one who practises pure actions. If I now commit impure acts and evil sensings, how can I be called a Brahmin? I am of the great clan of the Kshatriyas. The Kshatriyas defeat the enemy. If I now fail to defeat the enemies of evil, how can I be worthy of the name of Kshatriya? I am now a bhiksu. A bhiksu is a person who destroys defilement. If I cannot now destroy the evil sensing of defilement, how am I now worthy of the name of bhiksu? There are six things which it is difficult to encounter. I have now gained these. How can I allow the occasion to arise where evil sensings enter my mind? What are these six? The first is that it is difficult to be born into the world where the Buddha is present. The second is that it is difficult to hear Wonderful Dharma. The third is that it is difficult to call forth a fearing mind. The fourth is that one cannot easily gain birth in the Middle Country ["madhyadesa"]. The fifth is that it is difficult to be born as a human. The sixth is that it is difficult to have perfect and complete sense-organs. These six things are thus difficult to gain. And now I possess these. For this reason, I must not give occasion for evil sensings to arise. The Bodhisattva, then, practising the Great Nirvana Sutra, always meditates on all these evil minds [i.e. evil states of mind]. All beings fail to see the ills of such evil minds. They thus gain the three sensings and so engender the secretions. The Bodhisattva sees these, does not cling to them, abandons them, and does not protect them. He allows the Noble Eightfold Path to push them away, to kill them and cut them off. Hence the Bodhisattva has no occasion to be subject to the secretions. How could one say that the Tathagata possesses any such? For this reason, the Tathagata-World-Honoured One does not belong to the class of those who have the secretions of defilement.

Chapter Twenty-Nine: Bodhisattva Highly-Virtuous King 3

"Also, next, O good man! The common mortal performs various evil deeds when he encounters physical and mental worries. A person becomes ill in body and mind and does various evil things with his body, mouth and mind. By doing evil, one gains life in the three unfortunate realms, suffering there in various ways. Why? Because the common mortal does not possess mindfulness Wisdom. Thus he contracts various defilements. This is mental defilement. The Bodhisattvamahasattva always thinks: "I have, for innumerable kalpas past, committed various evil deeds on account of my body and mind. For this reason, I have repeated birth and death and fully undergone various worries in the three unfortunate realms. This has kept me away from the right paths of the three vehicles. For these causal reasons, the Bodhisattva greatly fears his body and mind, and abandoning all evil things, he takes to good paths." "O good man! As an illustration: there is a king who keeps four vipers in a casket and has a man feed them, take note of the serpents' waking and sleeping and rub and wash their bodies. It is made known that if any of the serpents becomes angry, the man in charge will have to, by law, be executed in the city. On hearing of the king's strict orders, the man is afraid. He abandons the casket and runs away. The king then sends five candalas after him. The candalas, brandishing their swords, intend to force the man to follow the king's orders. Looking back, the man sees the five candalas and runs away. Then the five candalas resort to evil means. They hide their swords. One of them goes to the man and, feigning a friendly attitude, says: "Let us go back!" The man does not trust him. Reaching a village, he intends to hide himself. On arriving there, he sees that the houses are all empty, with no one inside. The pots are all empty, there being nothing in them. There is no one to see and nothing to be obtained. So the man sits down on the ground. A voice comes from nowhere: "O man! This village is empty; no one lives here. Tonight, six robbers will come. On encountering them, you cannot be sure of your life. How can you hope to get out of this fix?" Then the man's fear grows and he abandons the place and leaves it. On his way, there is a river. The water rushes down, but there is no boat or raft to carry him across. Afraid, he gathers wood and grass and makes a raft. Again, he thinks to himself: "If I stay here, I will be attacked by vipers, by the five candalas, by the man who deceptively tried to befriend me, and by the six great robbers, all of whom will harm me. If this raft cannot be trusted, I shall drown and die. Oh, let me die in the water rather than be harmed by poisonous snakes!" He pushes the raft of grass out onto the water and rides in it, paddling with his hands and legs, and thus crosses the river. When he reaches the further shore, peace awaits him there, and there is no worry. He is unmolested [i.e. not constricted, at ease] in mind, and his fear has gone. Such is the case. The Bodhisattva-mahasattva hears the Great Nirvana Sutra, upholds it, and meditates on the body, and he sees it as the casket, and that the earth, water, fire and wind are the four poisonous serpents, and that all beings encounter the four poisons of seeing, touch, breath, and stinging. So they lose their lives. It is the same with the four great elements of beings. So some do evil by seeing, some through touch, some through the breath, and some by stinging. Consequently they depart from all good deeds. "Also, next, O good man! The Bodhisattva-mahasattva meditates on the four poisonous serpents. These are the four castes, namely: Kshatriya, Brahmin, Vaishya, and Sudra. It is the same with the serpents of the four great elements. These possess the four natures of hardness, moisture, heat, and movement. For this reason, the Bodhisattva-mahasattva takes it that the four great elements belong to the same clan as the four poisonous serpents. "Also, next, O good man! The Bodhisattva-mahasattva views these four great elements as being like the four poisonous serpents. How does he regard things? These four poisonous serpents always watch a man's movements: when to look at him, when to touch, when to throw their breath upon him, and when to sting. It is the same with the four poisonous serpents of the four great elements. They always watch beings and await their chance, seeking to catch hold of their shortcomings. A person who loses his life from the four serpents does not fall into the three unfortunate realms. But one who loses his life from the four great elements unfailingly falls into the three unfortunate realms. These four poisonous serpents will kill a man even if given food and looked after. It is the same with the four great elements. Though things are always supplied, these always lead a man towards all evil deeds. If any of these four serpents should once get angry, it will kill the man. The same is the case with the nature of the four great elements. If one element starts up, it easily harms a man. These four poisonous serpents may live in the same place, but their four minds are different from one another. It is the same with the four great poisonous serpents. Though living in the same place, their nature is different. Although these four poisonous serpents pay respect, one cannot come near them. It is the same with the four great poisonous serpents. Though they pay respect, one must not go near them. When these four poisonous serpents cause harm to a man, we have sramanas and Brahmins. With charms and medicines, we can indeed gain a cure. When the four great elements kill a man, [however], the charms and medicines of sramanas and Brahmins cannot cure him at all. A person who is contented and comes into contact with the four unpleasing evil smells will keep himself away [from them]. Thus do all Buddhas and Bodhisattvas act. On encountering the smells of the four great elements, they depart from them. Then the Bodhisattva, as he thinks about the poisonous serpents of the four great elements, experiences great fear. He runs away and practises the Noble Eightfold Path. "The five candalas are none other than the five skandhas. In what way does the Bodhisattva view the five skandhas as candalas? A candala severs a man from his obligations and love, and spawns increasing hatred. It is the same with the five skandhas. They make a man covet what draws him towards evil and keep him away from all that is good. "Also, next, O good man! A candala decks himself out with various weapons and harms people with his sword, shield, bow, arrow, armour or halberd. It is the same with the five skandhas. They arm themselves with all kinds of defilement and harm the ignorant and make them repeat lives.

"O good man! A candala gets news of one with faults and causes him harm. So, too, do the five skandhas. Hence the Bodhisattva deeply sees and realises that the five skandhas are like candalas. "Also, next, the Bodhisattva regards the five groups as candalas. The candala lacks a sympathetic heart and causes harm irrespective of whether the man hates or loves. The same with the five skandhas. They have no pity and cause harm

both to those who are good and those who are evil. The candala causes worry to all people; so do the five skandhas. Through various defilements, they cause worry to all people who are subjected to birth and death. That is why the Bodhisattva regards the five skandhas as candalas. "Also, next, the Bodhisattva further regards the five skandhas as candalas. A candala is always minded to cause harm. It is the same with the five skandhas. All fetters are always minded to cause worry. If one lacks a leg, a sword, a staff, or a follower, know that one will unfailingly be killed by candalas. It is the same with beings. If one lacks a leg, a sword, and a follower, one will be killed by the five skandhas. The leg is the moral precepts, the sowrd is Wisdom, and the follower is none other than all teachers of the Way. Not possessing these three things, one is harmed by the five skandhas. That is why the Bodhisattva regards the five skandhas as candalas. "Also, next, O good man! The Bodhisattva-mahasattva regards the five skandhas as worse than candalas. Why? Beings may be killed by candalas. But when killed by them, the beings do not fall into hell. But when killed by the five skandhas, they gain hell. That is why the Bodhisattva regards the five skandhas as worse than candalas. Having meditated thus, he prays: "I would sooner be born near a candala when life ends than even for a moment befriend the five skandhas." The candala harms the ignorant of the world of desire. But these robbers of the five skandhas cause harm to common mortals and the beings of the three worlds. "The candala indeed kills criminals, but the robbers of the five skandhas make no distinction between criminals and non-criminals. They kill everyone. The candala does not harm the weak and the old, women and children. But the robbers of the five skandhas make no distinction between old, young and women: they harm anyone. For this reason, the Bodhisattva regards the five skandhas as worse than candalas. Hence he prays: "I might well be born near a candala when life ends, but I shall not befriend the five skandhas." "Also, next, O good man! A candala only causes harm to other people, but not to himself. The five skandhas harm themselves and also others. We might well escape the clutches of the candala through pleasing words, money and jewels, but not the five skandhas. One cannot escape from the five skandhas through flattery, money or jewels. The candala does not unfailingly kill all through the four seasons. But with the five skandhas it is otherwise. They kill moment after moment. The candala stays in one place; ways of escape [from him] are possible. It is not so with the five skandhas. They fill all places and there is no escape. The candala causes harm, but after causing harm, he does not follow one. It is not thus with the five skandhas. After killing beings, they follow them and do not leave them. Hence, not even for a moment will the Bodhisattva draw near to the five skandhas, though he might his whole life long draw near to candalas. One possessed of Wisdom and employing the best of expedients can evade the five skandhas. These best expedients are none other than the Noble Eightfold Path, the six paramitas, and the four immeasurable minds. Through these he reaches Emancipation, and his body and mind are not spoiled by the five skandhas. Why not? Because his body is now Adamantine and his mind like the Void. Thus it is difficult to destroy his body and mind. For this reason, the Bodhisattva sees that the skandhas fully accomplish all evil things, fears them greatly, and practises the Noble Eightfold Path. This is like the man who fears the four poisonous serpents and the five candalas, who keeps on walking and never looks back. "By "feigning friendliness" is meant greedy craving. The Bodhisattva-mahasattva meditates deeply upon the bond of craving and sees that it is nothing but an enemy that comes, befriends and cheats one. With a person who knows Truth, it can do nothing. A person who knows nothing unfailingly gets harmed. The same is the case with craving. Its nature once known, it can do nothing to cause beings to repeat the pains of birth and death. Those who know nothing transmigrate through the six evil realms and must suffer minutely from various pains. Why? Because they get captured by the illness of craving, which can never be got rid of. This is like the enemy who cheats one with his feigned friendship, and from whom it is hard to part. "By "enemy who beguiles and befriends" is meant that there is always seeking after news of one and making one part from that which one loves and encounter that which one hates. It is the same with craving. It causes one to part from all good things and to befriend all evil things. For this reason, the Bodhisattva-mahasattva always meditates deeply on the beguilements of craving. Because one cannot see, try as one may, and one cannot, try as one may. Common mortals try to see the beguilements of birth and death. They may have wisdom. But because of overshadowing ignorance, they cannot ultimately see well. So do things stand with sravakas and pratyekabuddhas. They may try to see, but cannot. Why not? Because of their craving minds. Why? Seeing the ills of birth and death does not lead one to unsurpassed Enlightenment. Because of this, the Bodhisattva-mahasattva regards this bond of craving as an enemy who beguilingly feigns friendliness. "What is the characteristic of this feigned and beguiling friendliness of the enemy? The enemy is not genuine, beguiles and presents things, and although he is not one who wishes to be friendly, displays friendliness. And yet, this is what is not good. But he beguiles and displays goodness; without love, he displays love. Why? Because he spies upon a person's movements, intending to cause harm. It is the same with craving. Dissembling non-truth always presents itself as truth; non-friendliness displays itself as friendliness; non-good appears as good; non-love presents itself as love. And all beings are deceived and ride on the wheel of birth and death. That is why the Bodhisattva regards craving as an enemy who feigns friendliness. "We say that the enemy feigns friendliness. This is made possible because we see the body and not the mind. So cheating can come about. It is the same with craving. What there is is falseness; what is true cannot be gained there. Thus all beings lose their way. We can speak of "friendly beguilements". If there is a beginning and an end, it is easy to segregate. With craving, the case is otherwise. There is no beginning and no end. It is difficult to segregate [oneself from craving]. We say "friendly beguilements". If things are far away, it is hard to know [of them]; if near, it is easy to see. Craving is not like that. Even when near, it is difficult to know. And how can one know [of it] when it is far away? For this reason, the Bodhisattva regards craving as that which supercedes [i.e. surpasses] friendly beguilements. "Due to the bond of craving, all beings part far from the Great Nirvana Sutra and approach birth and death. They part from the Eternal, Bliss, the Self, and the Pure, and associate with the non-Eternal, non-Bliss, non-Self, and the non-Pure." "For this reason, I refer here and there in the sutras to the three defilements. Because of ignorance as regards what one now sees, one cannot see and abandon what is wrong. The friendly beguilements do not, to the very end, harm a person of Wisdom. For this reason, the Bodhisattva meditates deeply on this craving. Having great fear [of it], he practises the Noble Eightfold Path. This is like the man who fears the four poisonous snakes, the five candalas, and the man who is deceitfully friendly [i.e. the candala], and he goes on and does not take roundabout ways. "We speak of an "empty village". This is none other than the six sense-organs. The Bodhisattvamahasattva meditates on these six spheres and sees that all is empty, as with an empty village. The man who is afraid gets into the village and sees that there is not one single living being therein. This person picks up an earthenware pot, but cannot find anything inside it. The case is analogous. It is the same with the Bodhisattva. He looks clearly into the six spheres and sees that there is nothing in them. Hence, the Bodhisattva sees that what there is in the six spheres is voidness and that there is nothing to possess, as with the empty village. "O good man! The group of robbers sees this empty village from far off and does not, to the end, gain the thought that it is empty. It is the same with common mortals. They do not gain the thought of voidness in the village of the six sense-organs. Not gaining any thought of emptiness, they repeat birth and death, suffering thereby an innumerable number of sorrows. "O good man! On arriving, the robbers gain the thought of the all-void. The same with the Bodhisattva. Looking into the six spheres, he always arrives at the thought of the All-Void. Gaining this thought of the All-Void, he does not repeat birth and death, not suffering thereby. The Bodhisattva-mahasattva never has any upside-down [notions] regarding these six spheres. Not having any upside-down [notion], there is no more repetition of birth and death. "Also, next, O good man! The robbers, when they enter this village, reach peace and bliss. It is the same with the robbers of defilement. On entering this empty village, they have peace and bliss in the six spheres. The robbers of defilement, living in an empty village, have no fear in their six spheres. So do things proceed with the group of robbers of defilement. This empty village is where various evil [i.e. harmful] beasts live, such as lions, tigers, wolves, and others. It is the same with the six spheres. These are the abodes of all evils and the evil beasts of defilement. For this reason, the Bodhisattva deeply considers these six spheres to be empty within, with nothing in them to be possessed, and that they are nothing but places where all that is not good dwells. "Also, next, O good man! The Bodhisattva regards these six sense-organs as empty inside, with nothing there to be possessed, and like an empty village. Why? Because of falseness and untruth. Though empty and having nothing to possess, people think that there is such. Though without bliss, people think that there is bliss. Though no one lives there, people think that it contains people. It is the same with the six sense-organs. Though truly empty and with nothing that can be possessed, people think that there are things inside. Though without bliss, people think that there is bliss there. Though truly there is no man within, people think that there is a man there. Only one who is wise truly knows this and arrives at Truth. "Also, next, O good man! At times people live in an empty village, and at times no one lives there. It is not thus with the six sense-fields. No one lives there at all. Why not? Because they are, by nature, always empty. Only one who is wise knows this; no eye can see it. Hence, the Bodhisattva sees that the six sense-organs are peopled full of enemies. Thus, he incessantly practises the Noble Eightfold Path. This is like the man who fears the four poisonous serpents, the five candalas, the beguilingly friendly man, and the six great robbers, and follows the right path. "We say "six great robbers". These are none other than the six sense-fields. The Bodhisattva-mahasattva regards these six sense-fields as six great robbers. Why? Because they truly rob one of all good things. Just as the six great robbers thoroughly plunder all the treasures of all people, so do these six sense-fields. They rob all people of all good treasures. When the six great robbers get into a man's house, they make no distinction between good and bad, but take away what there is in the house in a moment, and even very rich people suddenly become poor. So do things proceed with the six sense-fields. All good people die out, if they get into the sense-organs of a man. When good has been wholly pilfered, a person becomes a poor, lonely icchantika. For this reason, the Bodhisattva clearly views the six sense-fields as six great robbers. "Also, next, O good man! When desiring to rob a man, the six great robbers unfailingly attack a man who is in. If there is no man in, they will turn back half-way. The same with these six sense-fields. When they mean to plunder what is good, this always arises when there are within such phases of knowing or seeing the Eternal, Bliss, Self, and the Pure, the non-Void, etc. [in the six senses]. If there are not such within, the evil robbers of the six sense-fields cannot plunder anything that is good. One who is wise does not have these within, whereas common mortals have them. Because of this, the six sense-fields always come and rob one of what is good. Not being well protected, plundering comes about. "Being protected" means Wisdom. One who is wise guards things well. So nothing is taken away. Thus the Bodhisattva considers these six sense-fields as equal to, and as in no way different from, the six great robbers. "Also, next, O good man! Just as the six great robbers cause worries to the body and mind of all beings, in the same way do things obtain with these six sense-fields. They always cause worries to the body and mind of all beings. In contrast with the six great robbers, who only pilfer the wealth that a man has, these robbers of the six sense-fields always plunder what is good in beings of the Three Times. At night the six great robbers are immersed in pleasures. So are the robbers of the six sense-fields. Overspread by the gloom of ignorance, pleasure reigns. These six great robbers are reigned over by kings, who can well put a check [to their activities]. The same is the situation with these six evil robbers of the sense-fields. Only the Buddha and the Bodhisattvas can truly check them. When robbing, these six great robbers make no distinction as to rectitude, caste, intellectuality, learning, erudition, nobility or poverty. It is the same with the evil robbers of the six sense-fields. When desiring to rob a person of what is good, they make no distinction as to rectitude down to poverty. Kings may cut off the hands and feet of the six great robbers, and yet they cannot hope to stop the mind from working. The same with the evil robbers of the six sense-fields. Even the srotapanna, the sakrdagamin, and the anagamin may cut off their hands and feet. Even then, it is not possible to prevent the good dharmas [qualities] from being stolen away. Just as the brave and strong can defeat these six great robbers, so too can all Buddhas and Bodhisattvas subdue the evil robbers of the six sense-fields. For example, there are people who are of many castes. If there is burning faction spirit , they cannot be robbed by these six robbers. The same is the case with beings. If there is a good teacher of the Way, the evil robbers of these six sense-fields cannot do any plundering. If these six great robbers see men, they steal them

away. It is not thus with the six sense-fields. They rob a man of all seeing, knowing, smelling, touching, and seeing. What these six great robbers do is merely rob a man of his wealth, but not anything of the world of matter and non-matter. The case is otherwise with the evil robbers of the six sense-fields. They thoroughly plunder all that is good in the three worlds. Because of this, the Bodhisattva sees that the six sense-fields supercede [i.e. surpass] the six robbers. Meditating thus, he practises the Noble Eightfold Path, advances straight on and never turns back. This is like those who fear the four poisonous serpents, the five candalas, the man simulating friendliness, and the robbers of the six great elements, and like the man who abandons the empty village and presses on along the road. "We say that the man comes across a river on his way. This is nothing but defilement. In what way does the Bodhisattva consider defilement a great river? Just as a running river causes a gandhahastin to loose his footing, so do things proceed with defilement. It truly catches hold of the feet of the pratyekabuddha. That is why the Bodhisattva strongly regards defilement as a running river. It is deep, and it is difficult to gain its bottom. So it is likened to a river. It is hard to gain its boundary line [margin]. Hence, "great". Various evil fish live in the water. The same is the case with the river of defilement. Only the Buddhas and Bodhisattvas can truly reach its bottom. So we say "extremely deep". Only the Buddhas and Bodhisattvas gain the boundary line, and we say "very wide". Various kinds of harm are always caused to all ignorant beings, and so we speak of "evil fish". Hence, the Bodhisattva regards such defilement as a great river. A great river truly nurtures all that is of plants and forests. So does it obtain with the great river of defilement, where grow the 25 existences of all beings. Thus the Bodhisattva considers defilement to be a great river. For example, a man falls into the waters of a great river and does not repent. Things go the same with beings. Falling into the waters of defilement, they do not repent. A person who falls into water will die before reaching the bottom. So it is with one who falls into the river of defilement. He will not gain the bottom, but will ride on the wheel of the 25 existences. The so-called "bottom" is none other than the phase of the Void. One who does not practise this Void cannot get out of the 25 existences. Beings do not practise the Void and formlessness, and they always flounder in the swiftly flowing waters of defilement. This great river can only destroy the body, not drown all good dharmas. It is otherwise with the river of defilement. It thoroughly destroys the good of body and mind. That great swirling river only drowns the man of the world of desire. The great river of defilement drowns the devas and the people of the three worlds. The great river of the world can be crossed, and one can reach the other shore by paddling with one's hands and feet. As against this, the great river of defilement can only be crossed by a Bodhisattva, as he practises the six paramitas. It is difficult to cross a great river. The same applies to the great river of defilement. It is difficult to cross. Why is it hard to cross? Even the Bodhisattva up to the ten abodes cannot yet cross it. Only all Buddhas can ultimately cross it. That is why we say "difficult to pass over to the other shore". For example, there is a man who flounders in a river, when he cannot practise the Way one whit. Thus do things proceed with beings. As they flounder in the river of defilement, they are unable to practise good. When a person falls into a river and when he flounders, another person of power can indeed grasp hold of such a person and save him. If a person falls into the river of defilement and thereby becomes an icchantika, even the sravakas, pratyekabuddhas and all the Buddhas cannot save him. The great river of the world dries up at the time when the kalpa ends, with only seven days of the sun; but things do not happen thus with the great river of defilement. Even though the seven Bodhi elements ["saptabodhyanga"] may be practised, the sravakas and pratyekabuddhas cannot dry up [the river of defilement]. That is why the Bodhisattva meditates and considers that all defilements are like the madding waters of a river. For example, this is like the person who fears the four poisonous serpents, the five candalas, the begulingly friendly man, and the six great robbers, and who abandons the empty village, proceeds further along the way, reaches the river, takes up grass and makes a raft. Thus does the Bodhisattva act. Fearing the serpents of the four great elements, the candalas of the five skandhas, the friendly beguilings of craving, the empty village of the six spheres, the evil robbers of the six sense-fields, he comes up to the river of defilement and practises the ways of sila, samadhi, Wisdom, Emancipation, and the knowledge of Emancipation, the six paramitas, the 37 Bodhi elements, and makes these into a boat or raft, rides

on them and crosses over the river of defilement. "When the further shore has been gained, there is Nirvana, which is Eternal and Bliss. As the Bodhisattva practises Great Nirvana, he thinks: "If I cannot stand the sufferings of body and mind, I cannot enable all beings to cross the river of defilement." Thinking thus, he does not say a word and bears the sorrows of body and mind. Because of this endurance, no defilement arises. How could the Buddha-Tathagata have such? So we do not call any Buddhas those with defilements. "How is it that the Tathagata is not non-secreting of defilement? Because he always acts amidst all defilement-secretions. What secretes defilement is the 25 existences. For this reason, common mortals and sravakas say that the Buddha has secretions of defilement. But in truth, the All-Buddha-Tathagata has no secretion of defilement. "O good man! In consequence, the All-Buddha-Tathagata has no fixed form of existence. O good man! Thus all those who have committed the four grave offences, the slanderers of the vaipulya sutras, and the icchantikas are not in any fixed state." Then the All-Shining Bodhisattva-Mahasattva Highly-Virtuous King said: "It is thus, it is thus! It is just as you, Holy One, say. All existences have no fixed states. As they are not fixed, we know that the Tathagata also does not ultimately enter Nirvana. This is as has already been stated by the Buddha. The Bodhisattva-mahasattva, when he practises the Great Nirvana Sutra, hears what he has not heard before and is told that there is a Nirvana and a Great Nirvana. What is Nirvana and what is Great Nirvana?" Then the Buddha, praising the All-Shining Bodhisattva-Mahasattva Highly-Virtuous King, said: "Well spoken, well spoken, O good man! If the Bodhisattva gains mental grasping, things proceed as you say. O good man! In worldly life, we say: sea, great sea; river, great river; mountain, great mountain; earth, great earth; castle, great castle; being, great being; king, great king; man, great man; god, god of gods; Way, great Way. It is the same with Nirvana. There is Nirvana, and there is Great Nirvana. "What is Nirvana? This is as when one who is hungry has peace and bliss after he has taken a little food. Such ease and bliss is also called Nirvana. It is as when an illness is cured, the person gains peace and bliss. Such peace and bliss are also Nirvana. This is as when a person with fear gains peace and bliss on reaching a refuge. Such peace and bliss are also Nirvana.

When a poor person obtains the seven jewels, he gains peace and bliss. Such peace and bliss are also Nirvana. A person sees a bone and gains no greed. And this, too, is Nirvana." "Such Nirvana cannot be termed "Great Nirvana". Why not? Because of the greed that raises its head through hunger, illness, fear, or poverty. That is why we say that such Nirvana is not Great Nirvana.

"O good man! When a common mortal and sravaka cut off, in ways secular and holy, the bond of the world of desire, they gain peace and bliss. Such peace and bliss may well be called Nirvana, but not Great Nirvana. When a person cuts off the fetter of defilement of the first dhyana or the Heaven of Thoughtlessness-non-Thoughtlessness, he gains peace and bliss. Such peace and bliss can well be termed Nirvana, but not Great Nirvana. Why not? Because there is the return of defilement and the presence of retaining taints. "What are the retaining taints of defilement? Sravakas and pratyekabuddhas have the retaining taints of defilement, such as saying: "my body, my cothing, I go, I come, I speak, I listen." "The All-Buddha-Tathagata enters Nirvana. The nature of Nirvana has no Self, and no Bliss; what there is is that which is Eternal and True. Thus, we speak of the retaining taints of defilement. In the Buddhist doctrine and in the Buddhist Sangha are phases of discrimination; the Tathagata ultimately enters Nirvana. "The Nirvana of sravakas, pratyekabuddhas, and the All-Buddha-Tathagata is all-equal, without any difference. For this reason, what the two vehicles gain is not Great Nirvana. Why not? Because there are not there the Eternal, Bliss, Self, and the Pure. When there exist the Eternal, Bliss, the Self, and the Pure, we can speak of Great Nirvana". "O good man! What a place easily takes in all rivers, we say "great sea". The case is like this. As there is a place where sravakas, pratyekabuddhas, Bodhisattvas, and the All-Buddha-Tathagata enter, we say Great Nirvana. "As the four dhyanas, the three samadhis, the eight emancipations, the eight superior places, and the ten-all-places thoroughly take in innumerable good things, they are called Great Nirvana." ""O good man! For example, there is a river, and since the foremost gandhahastin cannot gain the bottom of it," "we say "great". If sravakas, pratyekabuddhas and the Bodhisattva of the ten abodes do not see the Buddha-Nature, we say "Nirvana". It is not "Great

Nirvana". If they clearly see the Buddha-Nature, there is Great Nirvana. This bottom can well be attained by the King of Great Elephants. The King of Great Elephants refers to all Buddhas. "O good man! If there is a place where the mahanaga, the great wrestler, Praskandi, and others cannot climb up and reach the summit after much time, such is worthy of the name, "great mountain". That place which the mahanagas and great wrestlers of the sravakas, pratyekabuddhas, and Bodhisattvas cannot reach is that which is worthy of the name of Great Nirvana. "Also, next, O good man! The place where a minor king lives is called "small castle". The place where a Chakravartin lives is called "great castle". All those places where 80,000, 60,000, 40,000, 20,000, and 10,000 sravakas and pratyekabuddhas live fall under the rubric of 'Nirvana'. The abode of the unsurpassed Dharma Lord, the Holy King, accordingly is given the name of 'Great Nirvana'. For this reason, we say Great Nirvana. "O good man! For example, there is a man who does not feel frightened on seeing the four military forces. Know that he is a great being. If a being is not afraid of the evil actions of defilement of the three unfortunate realms and yet within those [realms] saves beings, know that this person will gain Great Nirvana. If a man makes offerings to his parents, pays homage to sramanas and Brahmins, practises good, is truthful in his speech, and if there is no falsehood [with him], if he well endures all evils, gives to the poor, such a person is a great man. It is the same with the Bodhisattva. Out of great compassion, he pities all beings and is like a parent to all people. Thoroughly passing all beings across the great river of birth and death, he shows all beings the single path of Truth. This is Mahaparinirvana [i.e. Great Nirvana]. "O good man! "Great" means "all-wonderful". All-wonderful is that which all beings cannot believe in. This is "Mahaparinirvana". Being seen only by the Buddha and Bodhisattvas, it is called Great Nirvana. Why do we say "Great Nirvana"? Because one can only attain it through innumerable causal relations. So we say "Great". "O good man! Just as people say "great" when things are gained by the working together of many causal relations, so do things stand with Nirvana. As it can be gained by the conjoint working of many causal relations, we say "Great". "And why do we say "Great Nirvana"? As there is the Great Self, we speak of "Great Nirvana". As Nirvana is selflessness [i.e. non-ego] and Great Sovereignty" "[i.e. great freedom from all restrictions; unlimited autonomy; the ability to do as one wills], we speak of 'the Great Self'. What do we mean by 'Great Sovereignty'? "If there are eight sovereignties, we speak of 'the Self'. "What are these eight? "Firstly, a single body can be manifested as many. The number of bodies is like the number of dust-motes. They fill the innumerable worlds in all directions. The body of the Tathagata is not a mote. [But] due to this sovereignty, it can project a mote-body. Such sovereignty is the 'Great Self'. "Second, we see that a mote-body fills the 3,000 great-thousand worlds. The Tathagata's body does not, in truth, fill the 3,000 great-thousand worlds. Why not? Because of unhinderedness. Due to sovereignty, it fills the 3,000 great-thousand worlds. Such sovereignty is called the 'Great Self'. "Third, with this body that well fills the 3,000 great-thousand worlds, he lightly flies through the air, passing Buddha-lands as innumerable as the number of grains of sand of 20 Ganges, and there is nothing that obstructs him. The body of the Tathagata cannot, truth to tell, be designated as possessing light or heavy weight. [His] sovereignty decides the lightness or heaviness. Such sovereignty is the 'Great Self'. "Fourthly, because of sovereignty, sovereignty is acquired. What is sovereignty? The Tathagata abides [calmly] with one-pointedness of mind, without wavering. [Yet] he is able to manifest countless kinds of forms and endows each of them with a mind. On some occasions, the Tathagata might create a single phenomenon and bring about the needs of each being. Though the Tathagata's body abides in a single land, he causes all those in other lands to behold him. That manner of sovereignty is called the 'Great Self'. "Fifth, he is sovereign over his sense-organs. How is he sovereign over his sense-organs? One sense-organ of the Tathagata can indeed see colours, hear sounds, register smell, know taste, feel touch, and know dharmas. Because of [his] sovereignty, he is sovereign over his sense-organs. Such sovereignty is called the 'Great Self'. "Sixthly, due to [his] sovereignty, [he] acquires all dharmas [all things] and yet there is no concept of attainment in the Tathagata's mind. Why is that? Because there is nothing to be acquired. If there were something [to be acquired], then one could call it 'acquiring', but because there is nothing actually to be acquired, how can it be called 'an acquiring'? If one were to suppose that the Tathagata had the notion of acquiring, then Buddhas would not acquire Nirvana. Since there is [no notion of] acquiring, one can say that they acquire Nirvana. Due to sovereignty, he acquires all dharmas. Because he attains all dharmas, he is called 'the Great Self'. "Seventh, we speak of sovereign. The Tathagata expounds all meaning. And for innumerable kalpas, the meaning has no end, and this meaning is: the moral precepts, samadhi, giving, and Wisdom. At such times, the Tathagata has no sense or thought such as : 'I say', 'they listen'. Also, there is no single thought of a single gatha [verse]. People of the world speak of a gatha made up of four verse lines. This is merely to accord with the way of the world, and we speak of a 'gatha'. The natures of all things also possess nothing of which one can speak. Due to sovereignty, the Tathagata expounds [Dharma]. For this reason, we say 'the Great Self'. "Eighthly, the Tathagata pervades all places, just like space. The nature of space cannot be seen; similarly, the Tathagata cannot really be seen, and yet he causes all to see him through his sovereignty. Such sovereignty is termed 'the Great Self'. That Great Self is termed 'Great Nirvana'. In this sense it is termed 'Great Nirvana'. "Moreover, Noble Son, a treasury, for example, contains many different kinds of rare things and is thus called a great treasury. The extremely profound treasury of the Buddha-Tathagatas is like that: since it contains wondrous [things], without any deficiency, it is termed 'Great Nirvana'. "Moreover, Noble Son, a thing which is unbounded is called 'Great'. Since Nirvana is also unbounded, it is termed 'Great'. "Also, next, O good man! As there is Great Bliss, we say Great Nirvana. Nirvana has no bliss. Because of the four blisses, we say "Great Nirvana".

""What are the four? Firstly, it is segregated from all blisses. If bliss is cut out, we have suffering. If there is suffering, we do not say "Great Bliss". When bliss is cut out, there is no suffering there. What has no suffering and no bliss is Great Bliss. The nature of Nirvana is non-suffering and non-bliss. Thus we say that Nirvana is Great Bliss. For this reason, we speak of Great Nirvana. "Also, next, O good man! There are two kinds of bliss. One is that of the common mortal, and the other that of the Buddhas. The bliss of the common mortal is not eternal - it collapses. Hence, no" "bliss. With all Buddhas, bliss is eternal. There is no change. So we call it Great Bliss. "Also, next,

O good man! There are three feelings. One is that of suffering; the second is that of bliss; and the third is of non-suffering and non-bliss. "What obtains in Nirvana is the same as non-suffering and non-bliss. Yet we call it Great Bliss. Because of [this] Great Bliss, we say Great Nirvana. "Second, we say Great Bliss because of the Great Silence. The nature of Nirvana is Great Silence. Why? Because it is removed from all that is noisy. The Great Silence is called Great Nirvana. "Third, we say Great Bliss because of All-Knowledge. If there is not All-Knowledge, we do not say Great Bliss. As the All-Buddha-Tathagata is All-Knowledge, we say Great Bliss. On account of [this] Great Bliss, we say Great Nirvana. "Fourth, we say Great Bliss because the body does not break up. If the body breaks up, we do not say "bliss". The body of the Tathagata is Adamantine and Indestructible. It is not a body of defilement, nor one of the non-eternal. Hence, Great Bliss. Because of Great Bliss we say Great Nirvana. "O good man! The names that are current in the world either have, or do not have, any circumstantial bearings connected with them. The case in which circumstantial bearings exist is as in that of Sariputra, where the name of his mother, "sari", comes down to him, and we say "Sariputra" [i.e. "son of Sari"]. The way-goer [i.e. wayfarer], Mayura, is so called because he was in the land called "Mayura". Being based on the name of the land, his name is as in Maudgalyayana. Maudgalyayana is the family name. From the family name, we now have Maudgalyayana. I ,now ,was born into the Gautama clan. So I am Gautama, based on the clan name. This is as in the case of the way-goer, Visakha. Visakha is the name of a star. From the name of a star, we here have the name of a person, Visakha. If a person has six fingers, we call him one with six fingers. We say "Butsunu" [i.e. "Buddha-servant"] and "Tennu" [i.e. "heaven-servant"]. When a thing comes about from moisture, we say "Shissho" [i.e. "born of moisture"]. Based on the voice, we say "Kakala" [i.e. voice of a bird], "Kukuta " [i.e. voice of domestic fowl], and "Tatara" [i.e. voice of a pheasant]. All these names come from the causal bearings that exist there. Those which are not based on causal bearings are: lotus, earth, water, fire, wind, and space. "Mandapa" [i.e. scum of boiled rice+drinking] refers to two things. Firstly, it means "palace", and secondly, "to drink juice". Although the building does not drink juice, we speak thus. "Sappashata" means "serpent parasol". But in no way is it a serpent's parasol. A name is merely coined for something with which it has no connection. "Teirabai" means "edible oil". But actually, oil is not eaten. A term is merely coined, and it says "edible oil". "O good man! It is the same with this Great Nirvana. With no direct connection, the name is coined. "O good man! For example, space is called "great", but it is not so called based on "small space". It is the same with Nirvana. We do not say "Great Nirvana" based on what is small in size. "O good man! Dharma cannot be appraised or thought about. Hence, we say "Great". It is the same with Nirvana. Because it cannot be appraised or thought about, we speak of "Mahaparinirvana". "Because of its being pure, we say "Great Nirvana". How is it pure? Of pureness, there are four kinds. What are the four? "First, we call the 25 existences non-pure. When these have been eternally done away with, we speak of "Pure". What is Pure is Nirvana. Such Nirvana can well be called "is". But this Nirvana is, truth to tell, not any "is" existence. The All-Buddha-Tathagata follows the way of the world and says that Nirvana is "is". For example, the people of the world call one who is no father father, no mother mother, and no parents parents. It is the same with Nirvana. Following the way of the world, we say that all Buddhas have Great Nirvana. "Second, action is pure. With all common mortals, action is not pure. So there cannot be Nirvana. As the action of the All-Buddha-Tathagata is pure, we speak of Great Purity. Because of Great Purity, we say Great Nirvana. "Third, the body is pure. If the body is non-eternal, it is not pure. The body of the Tathagata is Eternal. Hence, Great Purity. Because of Great Purity, we say Great Nirvana. "Fourth, the mind is pure. If the mind is defiled, we say non-pure. The Buddha's mind is non-defiled. Hence, Great Nirvana. "O good man! This is how good men and women practise the Way of the Great Nirvana Sutra and accomplish the first part of virtue."

Chapter Thirty: Bodhisattva Highly-Virtuous King 4

"Also, next, O good man! How does the Bodhisattva-mahasattva practise the Way of Great Nirvana and accomplish the second virtue? O good man! The Bodhisattva-mahasattva practises the Way of Great Nirvana and now gains what he could not gain in the past, now sees what he could not see in the past, now hears what he could not hear in the past, attains what he could not attain in the past, and knows what he was not able to know in the past." ""How does one now gain what one was unable to gain in the past? This is none other than the great miraculous power which one could not gain in the past, but which one now gains. Of power, there are two kinds. One is interior, the other exterior. We say "exterior". This refers to tirthikas. Of the interior, there are again two kinds. One is of the two vehicles, and the other is of the Bodhisattva. This is the divine power which the Bodhisattva gains by practising the Great Nirvana Sutra. It is not the same as that which obtains with sravakas and pratyekabuddhas. The divine power gained by the two vehicles is one gained by one mind; it is not many. This is not so with the Bodhisattva. In one mind, he gains five kinds of body. Why? Because he gains the divine power of the Great Nirvana Sutra. This is what one now obtains which one did not gain in the past. "And, also, how does one now get what one did not get in the past? This refers to one's gaining unmolestedness [i.e. unimpededness] in body and mind. Why? The body and mind which common mortals possess are not unmolested. On some occasions, the mind follows the body, and on others, the body the mind. "In what way does the mind follow the body? For example, this is as with an intoxicated person. When there is liquor in the body, the mind also moves. Also, it is as when the body feels lazy, the mind also feels so. This is an instance of the mind's following the body. "Also, it is as with a child. As the body is small, the mind, too, is still small. With a grown-up, as the body is big, the mind, too, is big. "Or there might be a man whose body is rough and unwieldy, and who thinks of rubbing in oil so that his body can become soft and flexible. The case is like this. This is an instance of the mind's following the body. "How does the body follow the mind? This is when one enacts going and coming, sitting and lying, giving, upholding the precepts, practising patience and effort. "A person possessed of worry has a body which is weak and wasted, whereas one who is happy has a body full in flesh and joy. "A person who is frightened shakes; if, with an undivided mind, one gives ear to Dharma, one's body brightens with joy. A person with sorrow sheds plentiful tears. This is what we mean when we say that the body follows the mind. The case of the body of the Bodhisattva is not thus. He has unmolestedness in body and mind. This is what we call having what one did not possess in the past.

"Also, next, O good man! The bodily appearance of the Bodhisattva-mahasattva is like a dust-particle, a mote. With this mote-sized body, he easily travels unhinderedly to the worlds of all the Buddhas as numerous and boundless as the sands of innumerable Ganges, and his mind never moves. This is what we mean when we say that the mind does not follow the body. This is why we say that one now arrives at what one had not reached in the past. "Why do we say that one had not arrived at is now arrived at? What all sravakas and pratyekabuddhas were unable to arrive at is now gained by the Bodhisattva. This is why we say that what one had not arrived at is now gained. Sravakas and pratyekabuddhas may transform their bodies into the size of a mote, and yet they are unable to travel to the worlds of all the Buddhas, whose number is as countless as the sands of the Ganges. With the sravakas and pratyekabuddhas, their minds also move when their bodies move about. It is not thus with the Bodhisattva. His mind does not move, but there is no case where his body does not move. This is the sense in which we speak of the mind of the Bodhisattva not following his body. "Also, next, O good man! The Bodhisattva transforms his body and makes it as big in size as the 3,000 great-thousand worlds, and this large-size body can [also] turn into a mote-size body. The Bodhisattva's mind does not grow small at such times. Sravakas and pratyekabuddhas may transform themselves into something as great as the 3,000 great-thousand worlds. But they cannot make their bodies the size of a mote. Here, they fail. And how could their minds not shake as their bodies move about? This is the sense in which we speak of the Bodhisattva's mind not following his body. "Also, next, O good man! The Bodhisattva-mahasattva causes his single voice to be heard by the beings of the 3,000 great-thousand worlds. Yet he does not pray that his voice might fill all worlds. He enables beings to hear now what they had not heard in the past. Yet he does not say that he has so contrived things that beings can now hear what they had not heard in the past. If a Bodhisattva said that he enabled people to hear now his sermons which they had been unable to hear in the past, such a person would not attain the unsurpassed body. Why not? The mind that thinks that as beings do not hear what I now speak is none but the mind of the world of birth and death. All Bodhisattvas have done away with such a mind. Thus the body or mind of the Bodhisattva does not now follow the other in this way. O good man! With the body and mind of all beings, each follows the other. It is otherwise with the Bodhisattva. In order to save beings, he may transform his body and mind, but his mind is not small. Why not? The mind of all Bodhisattvas is by nature always big. Hence, even though he manifests a large body, his mind does not become big. How big is his body? His body is like the 3,000 great-thousand worlds. How is his mind small? It enacts what a small child does. Thus his mind is not drawn by his body. The Bodhisattva, for innumerable asamkhyas of kalpas, has been segregated from alcohol. Yet his mind moves. Though his mind does not have suffering and pain, his body yet emits tears; though his mind has no fear, his body shakes. For this reason, know that unmolestedness obtains in the body and mind of the Bodhisattva, and one does not follow the other. The Bodhisattvamahasattva already manifests himself in a single body, and yet all beings see him differently. "O good man! How does a Bodhisattva-mahasattva practise the Way of the Great Nirvana Sutra and now hear what he has not heard in the past? The Bodhisattva-mahasattva first takes up [i.e. listens to, directs his mind to] the sound of such as the elephant, horse, vehicle, man, shell, drum, hsiao, flute, singing, and weeping, and these he learns. By practising, he indeed hears all the sounds of the hells of the innumerable 3,000 great-thousand worlds. Also, changing his angle, he practises and gains the different sense-organ of the ear [i.e. different sensory powers of the ear]. And this differs from the heavenly sense-organs of sravakas and pratyekabuddhas. How? These are none but the

pure divine powers of the two vehicles. If one takes up the case of the four great elements of the first dhyana, one only hears of the first dhyana, not of the second. So does it proceed up to the fourth dhyana. One well hears the sounds of all the 3,000 great-thousand worlds, yet one cannot hear the sounds of worlds as numerous as the sands of innumerable and boundless Ganges. For this reason, we can say that what is gained by the Bodhisattva is different from the aural sense-organs of sravakas and pratyekabuddhas. Due to this difference, one now hears what one has not head in the past. Although one hears sound, there is no sensing of "is", the Eternal, Bliss, Self, and the Pure, master, depending, doing, cause, samadhi, and result. That is how all the Bodhisattvas now hear what they have not heard in the past." Then, the All-Shining Bodhisattva-mahasattva Highly-Virtuous King said: "You the Buddha say that there is no sense of samadhi and result. This cannnot be. Why not? The Tathagata earlier said: "If one hears a line or letter of this Great Nirvana Sutra, one unfailingly attains unsurpassed Bodhi." In contrast, the Tathagata now says that what there is is non-samadhi and non-result. If one gains unsurpassed Bodhi, this is none other than a definite form of samadhi and result. How can you say that what there is is no other than non-samadhi and non-result? When one hears an evil voice, one gains an evil mind. Gaining an evil mind, one falls into the three unfortunate realms. If one falls into the three unfortunate realms, this is none other than a definite result. How can you say that there is no samadhi and no definite result?" Then the Tathagata expressed his praise and said: "Well said, well said, O good man! You do well to put this question. If there is any form of fixedness in the result of their voice, such cannot be what there is of the All-Buddha-World-Honoured One. All such are what obtain with the king of Maras, the form of birth and death, and one far away from Nirvana. Why? What all Buddhas speak about has no fixed form of result. "O good man! For example, a sword reflects the human face. The vertical shows the length and the horizontal the width. If there is any fixed form, how could one see the length in the vertical and the width in the horizontal? For this reason, there cannot be any fixedness in what the All-Buddha-World-Honoured One says. "O good man! Nirvana is no fruition of voicing [i.e. speaking]. If Nirvana were the fruition of voice, know that Nirvana would not be anything Eternal. "O good man! For example, what obtains in the world is that a result comes about from a cause, and that if there is no cause, there is no result. As the cause is non-eternal, the result, too, is non-eternal. Why? Because cause can become result, and result, too, can become cause. Thus there is not anything that is fixed in all things. If Nirvana comes from a cause, this implies that as the cause is non-eternal, the result, too, must be non-eternal. But this Nirvana is not something that has arisen from a cause; the body of Nirvana cannot, therefore, be a result. "O good man! For this reason, the body of Nirvana has no fixedness and no result. "O good man! Nirvana is fixed and is the result. So might we say. How is it fixed? "The Nirvana of all Buddhas is the Eternal, Bliss, Self, and the Pure. For this reason, we say fixed. There is no birth, age, or dissolution." "Hence, fixed. When we do away with the original mind of the icchantika, the four grave offences, slandering the vaipulya, and the five deadly sins, we unfailingly reach Nirvana. Hence, fixed." "O good man! You say that if one hears one line or one letter of my Great Nirvana [Sutra], one will gain unsurpassed Bodhi. But this indicates that you do not fully understand the meaning. Listen carefully! I shall now make it clear for you. "If any good man or good woman, on having heard a letter or line from [the] Great Nirvana [Sutra], does not entertain the notion of a letter or line, of having heard it, of the look of the Buddha, of an element of his sermon, such is a form of non-form. Due to non-form, one attains unsurpassed Bodhi. "O good man! You say that by hearing an evil voice one gains life in the three unfortunate realms. This is not so. One does not gain the three unfortunate realms from an evil voice. Know that this results from an evil mind. Why? "O good man and good woman! There can be instances where one hears an evil voice, and yet one does not gain evil in one's mind. Because of this, know that one does not gain life in the three unfortunate realms. And yet, as all beings have the bond of defilement and much evil in their mind, they do gain life in the three unfortunate realms. This is not from a voice that is evil. If the voice had a fixed state, all who heard it would have to gain an evil mind. There are situations where that comes about and where it does not. Hence, know that there is no fixed state regarding the voice. As there is no fixed state, it is possible that no evil thought will come about, though one may well hear it." "O World-Honoured One! If there is no fixed state with the voice, how can a Bodhisattva hear what he had not heard before?" "O good man! The voice has no fixed state. It certainly enables one to hear what one has not heard in the past. Hence, I say that one hears what one has not heard in the past. "O good man! How can one see what one has not seen in the past? The Bodhisattva-mahasattva practises the All-Wonderful Great Nirvana Sutra and first gains brightness. Such light is like that of the sun, moon, constellation, camp fire, lamplight, the light of a gem, or the light of a medicinal herb. By practice, he gains difference in sense. It differs from that of sravakas and pratyekabuddhas. How is it different? It is the pure Heavenly Eye of the two vehicles. Based on the sense-organs of the four great elements of the world of desire, one cannot see the first dhyana. If one is grounded in the first dhyana, one cannot see what obtains in the stages above. Or one cannot see one's own eyes. One may desire to see much, but the limit is the 3,000 great-thousand worlds. The Bodhisattva-mahasattva, not having practised the Heavenly Eye, sees, of the all-wonderful body, only the bone. He may well see what obtains in the outer forms of the things of the 3,000 great-thousand worlds of the other world-spheres as numerous as the sands of the Ganges, and yet he gains no sense of having seen any concrete form, no sense of eternity, no form of "is", of matter, name, letter, no thought of cause and effect, no sense of having ever seen. This eye does not say that what there is there is all-wonderful and pure; what it sees is the causal and the non-causal. What is the causal? Colour is the result of the by-cause [i.e. condition] of the eye. If the causal relation of colour does not come in, no common mortal can gain a sense of colour. Hence, we say that colour constitutes causal relations. We say non-causal relation. The Bodhisattva-mahasattva may see colour. But he does not gain any sense of colour. Hence, it forms no by-cause. Thus we say that the pristine Heavenly Eye of the Bodhisattva differs from what the sravakas and pratyekabuddhas possess. Due to this difference in quality, he sees at one time all Buddhas of the ten directions. This is why we say that he sees now what he has not seen in the past. Due to this difference, he can well see a mote, which the sravakas and pratyekabuddhas cannot. Due to this difference, he may well see his own eyes, and yet he gains no sense of having first seen, and no sense of the non-eternal. He sees the 36 impure things which common mortals possess, just as he would see an amalaka [emblic mycrobalan fruit] in the palm of his hand. For this reason, we say that he now sees what he has not seen in the past. If he sees the colour of beings, he can tell whether they are Mahayana or Hinayana; on once touching their clothing, he sees the good or bad, and the differences of all the sense-organs. For this reason, we say that the person now knows what he did not know in the past. Due to this power of knowledge, he now sees what he did not see in the past. "O good man! How does the Bodhisattva know now what he did not know in the past? The Bodhisattva-mahasattva knows the minds of greed, anger, and ignorance of common mortals, and yet he does not see the mind and the mental functions. He does not have any form of beings or things. He practises "Paramartha-satya" [Ultimate Reality] and the Ultimate Void. Why? Because all Bodhisattvas always thoroughly practise the natures and characteristics of the Void. By practising the Void, he can now know what he did not know in the past. What does he know? He knows that there is no self and what one possesses. All beings have the Buddha-Nature. He knows that by reason of the Buddha-Nature, even the icchantika, when he abandons the mind that he possesses, can indeed attain unsurpassed Enlightenment. Such is not what sravakas and pratyekabuddhas can know. The Bodhisattva knows this well. Hence, one can know what one did not know in the past. "Also, next, O good man! How can one know now what one did not know in the past? Having practised the All-Wonderful Sutra of Great Nirvana, the Bodhisattva-mahasattva thinks of all sources of birth, caste, parents, brothers, sisters, wife, children, relatives, friends, and enemies. In the flash of a moment he gains diverse knowledge, which differs from that of sravakas and pratyekabuddhas. How does it differ? The wisdom of sravakas and pratyekabuddhas thinks of the caste, parents, and enemies of all beings of the past. What it sees is nothing but enemies and friends. It is not so with the Bodhisattva. He may think of caste, parents, and enemies of the past. But he gains no forms of caste, parents, and enemies. What he sees is the law [dharma] that obtains and the Void. This is why we say that the Bodhisattva now knows what he did not know in the past. "Also, next, O good man! How does one know what one did not know

in the past? The Bodhisattva-mahasattva practises the All-Wonderful Sutra of Great Nirvana and gains what is different from what has been attained by sravakas and pratyekabuddhas who can read other people's minds. How does it differ? The sravaka and pratyekabuddha can read, in the flash of a moment, the minds of other persons. But they cannot read the minds of those in such realms as hell, animals, pretas, and heaven. But this is not so with the Bodhisattva. In the flash of a moment, he can read the minds of the beings of the six realms. This is why we say that the Bodhisattva now knows what he did not know in the past. "Also, next, O good man! There is a different kind of knowing. The Bodhisattva-mahasattva, in the flash of a moment, sees all grades of mind of the sakrdagamin that proceeds from the first stage up to the sixteenth. Thus he now knows what he did not know in the past. This is why we say that he practises the Way of Great Nirvana and accomplishes the second virtue. "Also, next, O good man! How does the Bodhisattva-mahasattva practise the Way of Great Nirvana and accomplish the third virtue? O good man! The Bodhisattva-mahasattva practises the Way of Great Nirvana. He abandons loving-kindness ["maitri"] and gains it. When gaining loving-kindness, things do not follow the course of causal relations. How does he abandon loving-kindness and gain it? O good man! Loving-kindness belongs to secular dharma. The Bodhisattva-mahasattva abandons the loving-kindness of secular dharma and gains that of "Paramartha-satya". The loving-kindness of "Paramartha-satya" does not actualise following the dharma of by-cause. "Also, next, how does he abandon loving-kindness and gain it? If loving-kindness can be abandoned, the common mortal calls this loving-kindness. If it is gained, the Bodhisattva calls this the loving-kindness without causal relations. He abandons the loving-kindness of the icchantika, of those who are guilty of the five grave offences, those who have slandered the vaipulya, and of those who have committed the five deadly sins. He gains the loving-kindness of pity, the loving-kindness of the Tathagata, that of the World-Honoured One, that of non-causal relations. "Why do we say that he abandons loving-kindness and gains it? He abandons the loving-kindness of those of imperfect genital organs, of those with no genital organs, of those with dual genital organs, of women, butchers, hunters, those who keep fowl and raise pigs, and others such as this. He also abandons the loving-kindness of sravakas and pratyekabuddhas and gains the loving-kindness of no causal relations of all Bodhisattvas. He does not see his own loving-kindness, that of others, or the upholding of sila, or the breaking of sila. He sees his own compassion ["karuna"], but not the beings. He sees suffering, but not the person who wriggles in suffering. Why not? Because he practises the truth of "Paramartha-satya". This is why we say that the Bodhisattva practises the Way of Great Nirvana and accomplishes the third virtue. "Also, next, O good man! How does a Bodhisattva practise the Way of Great Nirvana and accomplish the fourth virtue? "O good man! There are ten things when the Bodhisattva-mahasattva practises the Way of Great Nirvana and accomplishes the fourth virtue. What are the ten? "Firstly, it is deep-rooted and is difficult to uproot. "Secondly, there comes about the thought of self-decision. "Thirdly, he does not feel any sense of a field of weal or non-field-of-weal. "Fourthly, he practises the Way of the Pure Buddha-Land. "Fifth, he cuts off what yet remains to be cut off. "Sixth, he cuts off karma relations. "Seventh, he practises the way of the pure body. "Eighth, he grasps all causal relations.

"Ninth, he segregates himself from all enmity. "Tenth, he severs himself from the two phases of existence. "Why is it deep-rooted and difficult to uproot? The "root" referred to refers to non-indolence. What does the root belong to? It is none other than the root of unsurpassed Enlightenment. "O good man! The root of all Buddhas and all good deeds is grounded in non-indolence. Due to non-indolence, all other good roots increase by degrees. As all good increases, this is the most superb of all good deeds. "O good man! Of all footprints, that of the elephant is the best. So is the dharma of non-indolence. "O good man! Of all lights, the light of the sun is the greatest. So is the dharma of non-indolence. Of all good dharmas, this is the most superior. "O good man! Of all kings, the Chakravartin is the greatest. So is non-indolence. Of all good dharmas, it is the foremost. "O good man! Of all rivers, the four are the greatest. So is the dharma of non-indolence. It is the highest of all good dharmas. "O good man! Of all water-flowers, the utpala is the best. So is the dharma of non-indolence. It is the best of all good dharmas. "O good man! Of all flowers that bloom on land, the varsika is the best. So is the dharma of

non-indolence. Of all good dharmas, it is the best. "O good man! Of all animals, the lion is the best. So is the dharma of non-indolence. Of all good dharmas, it is the best. "O good man! Of all flying birds, the garuda is the best. So is the dharma of non-indolence. It is the best of all good dharmas. "O good man! Of all great bodies, King Rahulasura is the best. So is the best dharma that of non-indolence. "O good man! Of all beings, the two-footed, the four-footed, the multi-footed, and the non-footed, the Tathagata is the best. So is the dharma of non-indolence. It is the best of all good dharmas. "O good man! Of all beings, the Buddhist monk is the best. So is the dharma of non-indolence. Of all good dharmas, it is the best. "O good man! Of all the teachings of the Buddha, that of the Great Nirvana Sutra is the best. So is the dharma of non-indolence. It is the highest of all good dharmas. "O good man! Thus the root of non-indolence is deep-rooted and difficult to uproot. "Why does non-indolence increase? There are the roots of faith, shila, Wisdom, cognition, hearing, effort, remembrance, samadhi, and the good teacher of the Way, the roots of all of which increase through non-indolence. Due to [this] increase, it is deep-rooted and hard to uproot. For this reason we say that the Bodhisattva-mahasattva practises the Way of Great Nirvana and that it is deep-rooted and difficult to uproot. In what sense do we say that he gains a mind of decision and thinks: "I shall, with this body, unfailingly attain, in the days to come, a state in which I shall awaken to unsurpassed Enlightenment." His mind thinks thus. It does not become narrow-minded, change, gain the mind of a sravaka or pratyekabuddha, the mind of Mara, the mind of self-pleasure, or that which is pleased with birth and death. He always seeks to be compassionate to all beings. This is the sense in which we say that the Bodhisattva gains in himself the mind of decision, thus to attain in the life to come unsurpassed Bodhi. Hence, the Bodhisattva-mahasattva practises the Way of Great Nirvana and gains in himself a decided mind. "In what way does the Bodhisattva not see any field of weal or non-weal? "What is a field of weal? All upholding of sila, from that of the tirthika up to that of all Buddhas, falls under the category of a field of weal. If all such is the field of weal, know that the mind is low and deteriorated. The Bodhisattva-mahasattva sees all innumerable beings as nothing other than a field of weal. Why?

Because he indeed practises a different mental sphere. With one who practises this different mental sphere, there can come about no upholding or non-upholding of sila as one looks upon beings; what one sees is what is said by the All-Buddha-World-Honoured One. "There are four kinds of giving. And all evoke pure recompenses. What are the four? "First, the giver is pure, and the recipient is not pure. "Second, the giver is not pure, but the recipient is pure. "Third, both the giver and the recipient are pure. "Fourth, both are not pure. "In what way is the giver pure and the recipient not pure? The giver is perfect in sila, listening, and Wisdom, and knows that there are giving and recompense. The recipient violates sila and lives amidst twisted views. He does not give, and there is no recompense. This is why we say giving is pure but the recipient is impure. "Why do we say that the recipient is pure, but the giver impure? The giver transgresses sila and has twisted views and says that there cannot be any such thing as giving and recompense. The recipient upholds sila, has listened much, has Wisdom, knows [that it is important] to give, and knows the recompense thereof. This is why we say that the giver is impure, but the recipient pure. "In what sense do we say that both giver and recipient are pure? Both giver and recipient observe sila, listen much, have Wisdom, know [about] giving, and know that there is recompense to giving. This is how we can say that both giver and recipient are pure. "How can we say that both are impure? Both giver and recipient abide in twisted views and say that there cannot be any giving and recompense. If the situation is thus, how can we say that the recompense is pure? When there is no [sense of] giving and no [sense of] recompense, we say pure. "O good man! If there is a person who does not see giving and its recompense, know that we do not say that such a person has violated sila or clings exclusively to twisted views. If, heeding the words of a sravaka, a person does not see giving and its recompense, we call this a violation of sila and abiding in twisted views. "If a person, abiding in the Great Nirvana Sutra, does not see giving and the recompense thereof, this is the upholding of sila and abiding in right views. The Bodhisattva-mahasattva abides in a different mental sphere and, through practice, does not see beings upholding or violating sila, any giver, recipient, or recompense. Hence this is upholding sila and abiding in the right view. Thus the Bodhisattva-

mahasattva does not meditate on the field of weal or the non-field of weal. "What do we mean by "Pure Buddha-Land"? The Bodhisattva-mahasattva practises the Way of the Great Nirvana Sutra and saves beings so as to attain unsurpassed Enlightenment, and segregates himself from any thought of killing or harming others. He prays that, by this act of good, he and all beings will gain a long life and great divine power. Due to this prayer, all the beings of the Land where he attains Buddhahood in the life to come will be blessed with a long life and great divine power. "Also, next, O good man! The Bodhisattva-mahasattva practises the Way of the All-Wonderful Sutra of Great Nirvana, saves beings so as to attain unsurpassed Bodhi, and segregates himself from all thought of stealing. He prays that he will share the virtue of this good act with all beings, and that all Buddha-Lands will be adorned with the seven treasures, that beings will be rich, and that they will be unmolested [i.e. unhindered] in all that they desire to possess. On account of this power of prayer, the Land where he gets reborn and attains Buddhahood in the future will be blessed with wealth and unmolestedness [i.e. unhinderedness] regarding what beings desire to possess. "Also, next, O good man! The Bodhisattva-mahasattva segregates himself from lustful thoughts as he practises the Way of the All-Wonderful Sutra of Great Nirvana and saves beings so as to attain unsurpassed Enlightenment. He prays that he will share the merit of this good act with all beings, that all beings of all Buddha-Lands will not have thoughts of greed, anger and ignorance, and that there will not be the pain of hunger. Due to the power of this prayer, all the beings of the Land where he attains Buddhahood in the days to come will be far removed from greed, lust, anger and ignorance, and from all the pains of hunger.

"Also, next, O good man! As the Bodhisattva-mahasattva practises the Way of the All-Wonderful Great Nirvana [Sutra] and saves beings so as to attain unsurpassed Enlightenment, he parts from unrooted words. He prays that he might share with all beings the virtue of that good, that the Lands of all Buddhas will have flowers, fruits, luxuriant forest trees and fragrant trees, and that all beings will gain all-wonderful voices. Due to the power of prayer, all Lands, when he attains Buddhahood in the days to come, will have flowers and fruits, and fragrant trees, and all the people of those lands will have pure, all-wonderful voices. "Also, next, O good man! The Bodhisattva-mahasattva practises the All-Wonderful Sutra of Great Nirvana, parts from a double-tongue, and saves beings, so as to attain unsurpassed Enlightenment. He prays that he may share the virtue of this good deed with all beings and that the beings of all Buddha-Lands will always unite together in peace and preach Wonderful Dharma. Due to this power of prayer, all the beings of all [Buddha]-Lands will, when he attains Buddhahood, unite together in peace, and preach the essence of Dharma. "Also, next, O good man! As the Bodhisattva-mahasattva practises the All-Wonderful Sutra of Great Nirvana, he segregates himself from ill-speaking, and saves beings so as to attain unsurpassed Bodhi. He prays that he will share the merit of this good deed with all beings, that all Buddha-Lands will be as smooth as one's palm, that there will be no sand, stones, thorny plants or hateful thorns, and that the minds of all beings will be all equal. Due to the power of this prayer, when he attains Buddhahood in the days to come, all the [Buddha]-Lands will be as smooth as one's palm, and there will be no sand, stones, thorny plants or hateful thorns, and the minds of all beings will be all equal. "Also, next, O good man! As the Bodhisattva-mahasattva practises the Way of the All-Wonderful Sutra of Great Nirvana and saves beings so as to attain unsurpassed Bodhi, he will segregate himself from meaningless words and pray that he can share with all beings the virtue of this good deed and that the beings of all Buddha-Lands will have no suffering. Due to the power of this prayer, all beings of the [Buddha]-Lands will not have any suffering when he attains Buddhahood in the days to come. "Also, further, O good man! The bodhisattva-mahasattva practises the Way of the All-Wonderful Sutra of Great Nirvana and saves all beings so as to attain Buddhahood in the days to come, and segregates himself from greed and jealousy. He prays that he might share the virtue of this good deed with all beings and that the beings of all Buddha-Lands will have no greed, jealousy, worry, or twisted views. Due to this prayer, when he attains Buddhahood in the days to come all beings of the [Buddha]-Lands will have no greed, jealousy, worry, or twisted views of life. "Also, further, O good man! The Bodhisattva-mahasattva practises the Way of the All-Wonderful Sutra of Great Nirvana and saves all beings and segregates himself from worries so as to attain unsurpassed Enlightenment. He prays that he will share the merit of this good deed with all beings and that in the Lands of all Buddhas the beings will practise Great Loving-Kindness and Great Compassion, and thus attain the soil of the single son [i.e. will view all beings as if they were their own son]. Due to the power of this prayer, all the beings of all the [Buddha]-worlds, when he attains Buddhahood in the days to come, will practise Great Loving-Kindness and Great Compassion, and will gain the soil of the single son. "Also, further, O good man! The Bodhisattva-mahasattva practises the Way of the All-Wonderful Sutra of Great Nirvana and saves beings and segregates himself from twisted views, so as to attain unsurpassed Bodhi. He prays that he will share the virtue of this good deed with all beings and that the beings of all [Buddha]-Lands will gain mahaprajna [i.e. Great Wisdom]. Due to this prayer, when he attains Buddhahood in the days to come, all the beings gain mahaprajna. That is why we say that the Bodhisattva practises the Way of the Pure Buddha-Land. "How does the Bodhisattva-mahasattva make away with what yet remains to be made away with? Here there are three kinds of things to be made away with, namely: 1) the remnant karmic consequences of defilement, 2) remnant karma, and 3) what remains behind. "O good man! Why are the remnant karmic consequences of defilement? If a being learns and draws near to greed, he will, when the time comes for the karmic consequences to activate, fall into hell. When he comes out of hell, he will gain life as an animal, such as a dove, sparrow, mandarin duck, parrot, jivamjivaka, sarika, blue sparrow, fish, turtle, monkey, reindeer, or deer. It he happens to get a human form, he will gain a form having such things as imperfect genital organs, the female form, a form with dual genital organs, one with no genital organs, or that of a lustful woman. Even if born as a priest, he will commit the first grave offence. This is the case of remnant karmic consequences. "Also, next, O good man! If a person direly seeks to learn to draw near to anger, he will fall into hell when the time comes for his karma to work out its effect. And on coming out of hell, he will gain an animal body which will be perfect in the four kinds of poisoning which characterise the viper. These are: poisoning from its look, poisoning by its touch, poisoning from stinging, and poisoning by sobbing. And the animals are: lion, tiger, wolf, bear, brown bear, cat, raccoon, hawk, and sparrow hawk. Even if born as a human, he will have 12 kinds of evil manners; even if born as a priest, he will commit the second grave offence. This is remnant karmic consequences. "Also, next, O good man! A person who practises ignorance falls into hell when the time comes for the karmic effects to actualise. And when his life in hell ends, he comes out of it and gains life as an animal, such as: elephant, pig, cow, sheep, flea, louse, mosquito, gadfly, or ant. If he happens to gain life as a human, such imperfections of bodily form and sense-organs will come about as: deafness, blindness, dumbness, retention of uring, being a hunchback, and he will be barred from coming close to Dharma. Even if he gets ordained, all the workings of his carnal organs will be dull, and he will take pleasure in committing the [third] grave offence. He will pilfer even five pennies. This is the case of remnant karmic consequences. "Also, next, O good man! If there is a person who practises arrogance, such a one, when his karma comes to work out its effect, will fall into hell. And again, on his coming out of hell, he will gain life as an animal, such as: dung worm, camel, donkey, dog or horse. If he gains life as a human, he will be a menial servant and be oppressed by poverty and may have to beg for alms. Even if he gets ordained, he will always be looked down upon and will commit the fourth grave offence. Such are remnant karmic consequences. All such are the remnant consequences of defilement. The Bodhisattva-mahasattva does away with all such things, because he practises the Way of Great Nirvana. "What is remnant karma? This is the karma of all common mortals, and of all sravakas, the karma by which one receives the seven existences of those of the stage of srotapanna, the karma by which one receives the two existences of those of the stage of sakrdagamin, the karma by which one receives the rupa [i.e. bodily] existence of those of the stage of anagamin. These constitute remnant karma. The Bodhisattva-mahasattva, as he practises the Way of Great Nirvana, wholly extirpates such remnant karma. "Why do we say "remnant existence"? The arhat gains the fruition of arhatship and the pratyekabuddha gains the fruition of pratyekabuddhahood. There is no karma and there is no bond, and yet they attain the two fruitions. This is the sense in which we speak of "remnant existence". "There are three kinds of

remnant existence. The Bodhisattva-mahasattva, as he practises the Way of the Mahayana Sutra of Great Nirvana, annihilates these. This is why we say that he extirpates remnant existence. "How does the Bodhisattva practise the way of the pure body? "The Bodhisattva-mahasattva practises the sila of non-killing. Of this, there are five kinds, namely: low, middle, top, top-middle, and topmost. The same with right view. These five kinds of ten minds are called the first stage of aspiration. When one is perfect and fixed in mind, and when one accomplishes the five kinds of ten minds, this is satisfaction. The 100 such minds are 100 virtues. With the 100 virtues perfected, a phase is accomplished. Thus do things proceed one after the other, and the 32 signs of perfection are attained. When all this is accomplished, we say "pure body".

"Also, the Bodhisattva practises the way of the 80 minor marks of excellence. This comes from the fact that the world's beings worship these 80 kinds of devas. What are the 80? They are: Twelve Days , Twelve Great Devas, Five Big Stars, Great Bear, Horse Deva, Circumambulating Deva , Bhadra-dvaja, Gunadeva, Twenty-Eight Constellations, Earth Deva, Wind Deva, Water Deva, Fire Deva, Brahma, Rudra, Indra, Kumara, Eight-Elbow Deva, Mahesvara, Panjara, Hariti, Four Guardians of the Earth, Book Deva, and Vasu. These are the 80. For the sake of all beings, he practises the ways of the 80 characteristics and adorns his own body. This is the pure body of the Bodhisattva. Why so? Because all these 80 gods are what all beings greatly trust in. That is why the Bodhisattva practises the ways of these 80 characteristics, and his body does not suffer change. He so contrives matters that all beings see him, each according to what that being believes in. Having seen thus, they gain respect, and each aspires to unsurpassed Enlightenment. For this reason, the Bodhisattva-mahasattva practises the way of the pure body. O good man! For example, there is a man who wishes to invite a great King to his home. He will doubtless adorn his own abode, make it extremely clean, and have 100 varieties of beautiful dishes prepared, and then the King will accept the invitation. It is the same with the Bodhisattva-mahasattva. When he wishes to invite the Dharma-Raja of unsurpassed Enlightenment, he first practises the Way and cleanses and purifies his body. And the unsurpassed Dharma-Raja will then take his seat. Thus the Bodhisattva-mahasattva must first make his own body clean and pure. "O good man! For example, if one desires to partake of amrta [ambrosia], know that one will makes one's body clean. It is the same with the Bodhisattva-mahasattva. When he deisres to partake of prajna, the unsurpassed taste of the amrta of Dharma, he needs to make his body clean with the 80 minor marks of excellence. "O good man! For example, if one puts water into a precious vessel of gold or silver, all will look pure and clean, in and out. It is the same with the Bodhisattva-mahasattva whose body is pure. Within and without, he is clean, because the water of unsurpassed Enlightenment has been poured inside him. "O good man! It is just as the white cloth of varanabusa is easy to dye. Why so? Because is is, by nature, white and clean. The same with the Bodhisattva-mahasattva. When his body is pure and clean, he gains unsurpassed Enlightenment. For this reason, the Bodhisattva-mahasattva practises the Way and makes his body clean. "How does the Bodhisattva-mahasattva know all the factors of causal relations? The Bodhisattva-mahasattva does not see the outward appearances of a thing, the causal relations of a thing, the thing itself, how it has come to be, how it dies out, how it is one, how it is different, who sees, what it looks like, or who receives it. Why not? Because he knows all about causal relations. The same applies to everything. This is why we say that the Bodhisattva perceives all about causal relations. "How does the Bodhisattva segregate himself from enemies? All defilements are enemies to the Bodhisattva. The Bodhisattva-mahasattva always keeps away from these. This is the sense in which we say that the Bodhisattva crushes all his enemies. "The Bodhisattva of the fifth abode does not regard all defilements as enemies. Why not? Because he stands on defilement [bases himself on defilements]. He has come to be because of defilements. Born, he well moves on from one to the other, and enlightens beings. For this reason, we do not speak of an enemy. "What is an enemy? This is no other than one who slanders the vaipulya sutras. The Bodhisattva is not afraid of following others and being born in the realms of hell, animals, or hungry ghosts. He only fears the person who slanders the vaipulya [i.e. the lengthy sutras of the Mahayana]. "There are eight kinds of Maras to all Bodhisattvas. These are the enemies. When segregated from these eight Maras, we say of that person that he is segregated from his enemies. This is the sense in which we speak of the Bodhisattvas' segregating themselves from their enemies. How do the Bodhisattvas become segregated from the two aspects of existence [i.e. the one-sided views of "is" and "non-is" regarding existence]? The two aspects are the 25 existences and the defilement of craving. This is the sense in which we speak of the Bodhisattva's segregating himself from the two aspects. This is what we mean when we say that the Bodhisattvamahasattva practises the Way of Great Nirvana and is perfect and fully accomplished in the fourth virtue." Then Bodhisattva-mahasattva All-Shining Highly-Virtuous King said: "Just as the Buddha says, when the Bodhisattva practises the Way of Great Nirvana, all these ten virtues come about. Why does the Tathagata only practise nine things and not the Way of the Pure Land?" The Buddha said: "O good man! In the past, I always practised the ten things fully. There are no Bodhisattvas and Tathagatas who do not practise these ten ways. There cannot be any such thing as saying that when the world is full of defilement there appears the All-Buddha-World-Honoured One. O good man! Do not say that the Buddha appears in a world of defilement. Know that a mind like this [i.e. this way of thinking] is not good and is low in grade. Know that I do not appear in Jambudvipa, truth to tell. For example, a man might say: "Only this world has a sun and moon. There are no sun and moon in other worlds." Such talk has no sense. If the Bodhisattva says that this world is defiled and not pure, but that other Buddha-Lands are pure and adorned, this amounts to the same thing [i.e. this is wrong]. "O good man! Far out to the west of this world of Saha [i.e. west of our world of "Endurance"], beyond as many Buddha-Lands as sands of 32 Ganges, there is a world called "Unsurpassed". Why do we say "Unsurpassed"? There, all things are equal, with no difference in adornment. It is as with the "World of Peace and Happiness in the West". Also, it is as with the "Land of the Full-Moon in the East". There, in that world, I [once] gained birth. In order to guide beings towards the Way, I turn the wheel of Dharma in this world of Jambudvipa [i.e. our world]. It is not only I who turn the wheel of Dharma; all Buddhas turn the wheel of Dharma here. For this reason, it is not the case that all Buddhas do not practise these ten things. O good man! Bodhisattva Maitreya, by dint of the vows he has taken, in time to come will adorn and make this world all pure. Thus it is not the case that there is a land of all Buddhas that is not strictly pure. "Also, next, O good man! How does the Bodhisattva practise the Way of the All-Wonderful Sutra of Great Nirvana and perfect and accomplish the fifth virtue? O good man! There are five [requisite] things for the Bodhisattva-mahasattva to practise the Way of Great Nirvana and perfect and accomplish the fifth virtue. What are the five? They are: 1) all his sense-organs are perfect; 2) he does not gain birth in the border-lands; 3) all devas lovingly pray for [him]; 4) he is respected by Marapapiyas, sramanas, Kshatriyas, Brahmins, and others; 5) he can read [i.e. remember, or see] his past lives. Due to the causal relations of this Sutra of Great Nirvana, he perfects these five virtues." Bodhisattva All-Shining Highly-Virtuous King said: "According to the Buddha, a good man and good woman can perfect the virtues of the five things by practising giving. How can you say that they attain the five things by Great Nirvana?" The Buddha said: "Well said, well said, O good man! The meaning varies in what is said. I shall, for your sake, now analyse and explain. "Five things are attained by giving, namely: being not fixed, non-eternal, non-pure, non-superior, non-different, and not non-secreting of defilement. But none of this can benefit, give peace to, or pity all beings. The five things which one gains from the Sutra of Great Nirvana are: being fixed, eternal, pure, superior, different, and not secreting defilement. This gives benefit, peace and puty to all beings. "O good man! Now, by giving, one can part from hunger. The Sutra of Great Nirvana truly enables all beings to segregate themselves from the defilement of the burning craving of the 25 existences. "Giving makes birth and death continue their existence, as against which the Sutra of Great Nirvana destroys the chain of birth and death, so that it no longer continues to exist. "By giving, the common mortal receives Dharma; by means of the Sutra of Great Nirvana, one becomes a Bodhisattva. "Giving indeed cuts away poverty and worry; by means of the Sutra of Great Nirvana, there cannot any longer be those who are poor as regards Wonderful Dharma.

"Giving has its own part to play and its fruition; by the Sutra of Great Nirvana, one arrives at unsurpassed Enlightenment, and there is no longer any part to play, and no fruition thereof. "This is the sense in which we speak of the bodhisattva practising the Way of the All-Wonderful Sutra of Great Nirvana and being perfect in, and accomplishing, the fifth virtue. "Also, further, O good man! How does the Bodhisattva practise the All-Wonderful Sutra of Great Nirvana and become perfect and accomplished in the sixth virtue? The Bodhisattvamahasattva practises the Way of Great Nirvana and gains the Diamond Samadhi. Abiding in this, he crushes and disperses all dharmas. All these dharmas are impermanent and mobile [i.e. in a state of flux]. The causal relations of fear, the pain of illness, the plunderings of the robber visit one moment after moment, and there is no Truth. All [this] is the world of the Maras; what there is is what cannot be seen. The Bodhisattva-mahasattva abides in this samadhi and performs giving to all beings; yet there is not a single being that truly is. The same is the case when he makes effort and practises silaparamita or prajnaparamita. Should the Bodhisattva see even one single being, he cannot be perfect in danaparamita and prajnaparamita. "O good man! There is no instance in which a diamond fails to crush whatever comes against it. And yet, it does not collapse or minimise its size. So do things obtain with the Diamond Samadhi. It thoroughly crushes whatever it encounters. Yet the samadhi itself does not get crushed or destroyed. "O good man! Of all gems, the diamond is the most superb. It is the same with the Diamond Samadhi. It is the foremost of all samadhis. Why? When the Bodhisattva-mahasattva practises this samadhi, all samadhis come to it. It is just as all small kings foregather under the banner of a Chakravartin [i.e. world-ruler]. So is the case with all [other] samadhis. They all come and become one with the Diamond Samadhi. "O good man! For example, there is a man who is an enemy of the state. He is hated by the people. If any person kills him, all the people will speak highly of the person who kills this man. It is the same with this samadhi. The Bodhisattva practises this samadhi and destroys all the enemies of all beings. For this reason, it is looked up to by all samadhis. "O good man! For example, there is a man whose physical strength is so great that there is no one who can oppose him. The there comes along a man who brings this man down. The people praise the man. It is the same with the Diamond Samadhi. It thoroughly subdues whatever is difficult to subdue. Due to this, all samadhis come under its banner. "O good man! On Mount Gandhamadana there is a spring called Anavatapta. The water of this spring possesses eight tastes. If one drinks this water, all the pains of defilement die away. It is the same with this Diamond Samadhi. It is perfect in the Noble Eightfold Path. The Bodhisattva practises the Way, and it cures all the serious illnesses of defilement, the pox, and warts. "O good man! If one makes offerings to Mahesvara, know that this equates with having made offerings to all devas. It is the same with the Diamond Samadhi. If one practises this, know that this equates with having practised all other samadhis. "O good man! If any Bodhisattva abides in this samadhi, he sees all, without any obstruction. This is like seeing the amalaka that is in the palm of one's hand. The Bodhisattva enjoys such seeing. But he does not gain any sense of having ever had such an experience. "O good man! For example, there is a man who sits at a crossroads and sees all comings and goings, sittings and lyings. It is the same with the Diamond Samadhi. One sees all the comings and goings of all things. "O good man! There is a high mountain, and a man goes up it and looks all around, and sees everything as clearly as anything. It is the same with the Diamond Samadhi. The Bodhisattva ascends this [samadhi] and sees all things, and there is nothing that is not clearly seen. "O good man! For example, in the month of spring, the heavens let fall sweet rain. The drops are small and minute, and they fill the space [around], and there is no space that is not filled. Pure eyes can see this well. It is the same with the Bodhisattva. With the pure eyes of the Diamond Samadhi, he sees far into the worlds to the east and sees all that is wholesome or broken [i.e. in a bad condition? destroyed] of the lands and sees everything clearly, without obstruction. The same applies to all the lands of the ten directions. "O good man! If Yugamdha [i.e. one of the seven mountains of Mount Sumeru] appears all at once in seven days, all the trees and grass of the mountain will catch fire and burn. It is the same when the Bodhisattva practises the Diamond Samadhi. All the forest trees of defilement burn up. "O good man! For example, the diamond indeed cuts all things. Yet it does not think to itself that it cuts things. It is the same with the Diamond Samadhi. The Bodhisattva, having practised it, destroys the defilements. Yet he does not think to himself that he cuts off the bond of defilement. "O good man! For example, the great earth well supports all things, and yet it does not think to itself that it indeed supports things. Nor does fire, either, think: "I burn". Nor does water think: "I get all things soaked". Nor does wind think: "I stir [things]". Nor does space think: "I contain things inside [myself]". Nor does Nirvana think: "I truly give beings extinction [of defilement]". It is the same with the Diamond Samadhi. It truly annihilates all defilements. Yet it does not think: "I truly annihilate". If the Bodhisattva abides in this Diamond Samadhi, he can, in the space of a moment, transform himself as in the case of the Buddha and can be in as many places as the sands of the ten directions and fill all the Buddha-Lands. The Bodhisattva performs this transformation. Yet there is not a whit of arrogance in his mind.? ?Why not? The Bodhisattva always thinks: "Who carries out [i.e. brings into being] this samadhi, and who performs this transformation?" Only the Bodhisattva abides in the Diamond Samadhi and thus can effect this transformation. "The Bodhisattva-mahasattva peacefully abides in this Diamond Samadhi and can travel to all Buddha-Lands as numerous as the sands of the Ganges of the ten directions in the flash of a moment and return to his original place. Even with this power, he does not think: "I can do thus." Why not? Because of the power of the causal relations of this samadhi. "The Bodhisattva-mahasattva peacefully abides in the Diamond Samadhi and in the flash of a moment annihilates all the defilements of the beings of all worlds, as many as sands of the Ganges, in the ten directions. And yet he never thinks that he has ever done away with the worries of beings. Why not? Because of the power of the causal relations of this samadhi. "The Bodhisattva peacefully abides in this Diamond Samadhi and delivers sermons in a single voice, and all beings understand according to the grade of understanding of each person. "A single colour is presented, and all beings see it variously, each seeing according to the choice of colour of each person. "Abiding in a single place, with his body not moving, he enables beings to see that a single Way is displayed, according to the place where each person finds himself. "Whether things relate to matters of the 18 realms or the 12 spheres, all beings understand what is said in the way it ought to have been heard. The Bodhisattva abides in such a samadhi and sees beings, and there is not a thought of having ever seen beings. He may see a male or female, and yet there is no sense of having ever seen a male or female. He may see any concrete form, and he has no sense of having ever seen anything concrete. This obtains down to consciousness, and yet there is not consciousness of anything. Days and nights may pass, and yet there is no sense of any day or night. He may see something, and yet there is no form of anything. He may see the bonds of all defilements, and yet there remains no trace of having ever seen anything of defilement. He may see the Noble Eightfold Path, but there is no sense of having ever seen anything of the Noble Path. He may see Enlightenment, and yet there is no sense of having gained Enlightenment. He may see Nirvana, and yet there is no thought of having ever seen Nirvana. Why not? O good man! Because all things have primordially no representational form. By the power of this samadhi, the Bodhisattva sees all things as having no representational form.

"Why do we speak of "Diamond Samadhi"? "O good man! Just as in daylight the diamond has no fixed form of light to represent it, so does it obtain with the Diamond Samadhi. Even with a great mass, colour has nothing that is fixed. For this reason, we say "Diamond Samadhi". "O good man! For example, just as all the people of the world cannot put a price on a diamond, so do things stand with the Diamond Samadhi. All of its virtues cannot be evaluated by human or god. Hence, we say "Diamond Samadhi". O good man! For example, just as when a poor man obtains the treasure of a diamond, he can do away with the pains of poverty and hateful poison, so do matters stand with the Bodhisattva-mahasattva. If he gains this samadhi, he does away with all the sorrows of defilement and the hateful poison of Mara. Hence, the Diamond Samadhi. Thus we say that the Bodhisattva practises the Way of Great Nirvana and perfects the sixth virtue."

"Also, next, O good man! How does the Bodhisattva-mahasattva practise the Way of the All-Wonderful Sutra of Great Nirvana and perfect the seventh virtue? The Bodhisattva-mahasattva, having practised the Way of the All-Wonderful Sutra of Great Nirvana, thinks: "What is the proximate cause of Great Nirvana? The Bodhisattva knows that four things are the proximate cause of Great Nirvana." A person might say that the practice of all kinds of penance constitutes the proximate cause. But this is not so. Why not? There are no other than four by which one may arrive at Nirvana. What are the four? "Firstly, one associates with a good teacher of the Way; secondly, one listens to Dharma exclusively; thirdly, one thinks exclusively [about Dharma]; fourthly, one practises the Way according to Dharma. "O good man! As an example: there is a man who has various illnesses - fever, cold, vague weariness, loose bowels, ague, various kinds of evil poisoning - and he goes to a good doctor. The good doctor speaks of medicine in relation to the nature of the illness. The man faithfully follows the doctor's instructions, makes up the medicine as directed and takes it as instructed. On his having partaken of it, his illnesses retreat and he gains health and peace. "This sick man is analogous to the Bodhisattva; the great doctor is comparable to the good teacher of the Way; the instructions can be compared to the vaipulya sutras; the faithful following of those instructions to meditating upon the vaipulya sutras; preparing the medicine as directed can be compared to practising the Way in accordance with the assisting directions constituted in the 37 Bodhyangas [factors of Enlightenment]; curing the illnesses can be compared to the extinction of defilements; and gaining peace and happiness can be compared to the gaining of the Eternal, Bliss, Self, and the Pure of Nirvana. "O good man! As an example: there is a king who wishes to govern his state in a lawful way and to enable the people to enjoy peace, and he asks his wise ministers how to do this. All the ministers tell of the laws that have obtained until now. The king listens, puts faith in what he has been told, acts faithfully, and governs according to law, and there is nobody who entertains any ill will [against him]. Thus the people enjoy peace and have no worries. "O good man! The king is comparable to the Bodhisattva; all his wise ministers to the good teachers of the Way; what the wise ministers advise the king regarding the lawful governance of his state to the 12 types of sutra; the king's listening and acting faithfully is comparable to the Bodhisattva's meditating upon all the profound meanings of the 12 types of sutra; the lawful administration of the state is comparable to practising the law of all Bodhisattvas, namely the six so-called paramitas; saying that there now remains no enemy is comparable to the Bodhisattva's segregating himself from the bonds of the evil robbers of all the defilements; and attaining peace is comparable to the Bodhisattva's gaining the Eternal, Bliss, Self, and the Pure of Great Nirvana. "O good man! As an example: there is here a man who contracts hateful leprosy. A good teacher of the Way says to him: "Go to Mount Sumeru and you will see your illness cured. Why? Because there is good, sweet, medicinal amrta [ambrosia] there. Once this has been taken, there is never an instance where a cure does not ensue." The man faithfully follows his words, goes to the mountain, takes the medicine, and obtains the cure for his illness, and there is peace. The case is thus. "This hateful leprosy is comparable to the common mortal; the good teacher of the Way to all Bodhisattvas; the faithful following [of instructions] to the four immeasurable minds [i.e. of love, compassion, sympathetic joy, and equanimity]; Mount Sumeru to the Noble Eightfold Path; the amrta to the Buddha-Nature; the curing of the leprosy to the extinction of defilement; and the attaining of peace to the gaining of the Eternal, Bliss, Self and the Pure of Nirvana. "O good man! As [another] example: there is a man who has many disciples and who is extremely erudite. He teaches untiringly day and night. It is the same with all Bodhisattvas. Whether all beings believe them or not, they go on teaching untiringly. "O good man! We say "teacher of the Way". This is none other than the Buddha, the Bodhisattva, pratyekabuddha, sravaka, and those who believe in the vaipulya, etc. Why do we say "good teacher of the Way"? The good teacher of the Way teaches beings well and enables them to do away with the ten evil deeds and practise the ten good deeds. That is why we say "good teacher of the Way". "Also, next, the good teacher of the Way speaks of the Way just as it ought to be taught and himself acts as he ought to act. "Why do we say that we speak as we ought to speak and act as we ought to act? We refrain from killing and teach others not to kill. And we have the right view and teach the right view to others. If matters stand thus, we say that such a person is a true, good teacher of the Way. A person practises the Way of Enlightenment and also teaches others the Way of Enlightenment. Thus we say "good teacher of the Way". We practise faith, morality, giving, listening, and Wisdom for our own sake, and also teach others faith, morality, giving, listening, and Wisdom. So, too, we say "good teacher of the Way". "We say "good teacher of the Way" because there is Wonderful Dharma. What is Wonderful Dharma? One does not seek bliss for one's own sake; one always seeks peace and bliss for others' sake. On seeing a fault in others, one does not reproach them with their shortcomings, but always speaks what is purely good. So we say "good teacher of the Way". "O good man! The moon that hangs in the heavens waxes from the first of the month up to the fifteenth. So do things obtain with the good teacher of the Way. One causes all those who study the Way to segregate themselves from evil and to grow in good deeds. "O good man! If a person who approaches a good teacher of the Way does not have: 1) maintenance of sila [morality], 2) samadhi [deep meditation], 3) Wisdom, 4) liberation and 5) knowledge of liberation [i.e. "asamasama-panca-skandha": the fivefold-body concept of the Buddha, which refers to Enlightenment itself], these will come about. If these are not [yet] perfect, they will grow. Why? Because of associating with a good teacher of the Way. Through such association, a person comes to the profound meaning of the 12 types of sutra. When a person comes to the profound meaning of the 12 types of sutra, we say that he has heard Dharma. To hear Dharma means none other than to hear the Mahayana vaipulya sutras. To hear the vaipulya is to hear Dharma. True hearing is none other than hearing the teaching of the Sutra of Great Nirvana. In the Great Nirvana, we see the Buddha-Nature, and we hear that the Tathagata does not ultimately enter Parinirvana. Hence, we say that we excusively hear Dharma. Exclusively hearing Dharma is none other than the Noble Eightfold Path. By means of the Noble Eightfold

Path, we thoroughly do away with greed, hatred and delusion. Hence, hearing Dharma. "Now, hearing Dharma relates to the 11 shunyatas. Due to these voids, we see no form in anything. Now, hearing Dharma begins with the first aspiration and proceeds up to the ultimate unsurpassed Bodhi Mind. By gaining the first aspiration, one gains Great Nirvana. Through hearing, one does not gain Great Nirvana; by practising, one attains Great Nirvana. "O good man! As an illustration: a person suffering from illness might hear of a medicinal teaching or the name of a medicine, but cannot gain a cure for his illness. By partaking [of the medicine], he can make away with it. A person might well hear of the depths of meaning of the 12 links of interdependent origination, but he cannot make away with all the defilements. Segregation can only result when, with a careful mind, he meditates upon [such matters]. This is the third careful meditation. "And again, why do we say "careful meditation"? This is none other than the three samadhis of the Void, non-thought, and non-doing. We say "Void". This is seeing nothing that is real in the 25 existences. Non-doing means that one has no desire to possess the 25 existences. Non-form means that one sees no form in the ten characteristics, namely of: colour, sound, smell, taste, touch, birth, abiding, death, male, and female. The practice of the three samadhis is the Bodhisattva's careful meditation. "What is the practising of the Way by Dharma? Practising by Dharma is to practise danaparamita or up to prajnaparamita. This is to know the true state of the five skandhas, the 18 [sensory] realms and the 12 [sensory] spheres, and sravakas and pratyekabuddhas walk one and the same way, and that this leads to Nirvana. ""Dharma is the Eternal, Bliss, the Self and the Pure, non-birth, non-ageing, non-illness, non-death, non-hunger, non-thirst, non-suffering, non-worry, non-retrogressiveness, and nondrowningness." "O good man! One who knows the meaning of Great Nirvana realises the fact that all Buddhas do not ultimately enter Nirvana. "O good man! The foremost and true teacher of the Way is the so-called Bodhisattva and the All-Buddha-World-Honoured One. Why? Because they are always well trained in three things. What are the three? The first is uttermost gentle words; the second is uttermost reproach; and the third is gentle words and reproaching. Due to these, the Bodhisattvas and Buddhas are the best good teachers of the Way. "Also, next, the

Bodhisattvas and all Buddhas are good doctors. Why? They know illnesses and medicines and prescribe medicine in accordance with the illness. For example, a good doctor is well versed in eight things. He first sees the nature of the illness, which is threefold. What are the three? They are: wind, heat, and water. To one who suffers from wind he gives butter; to one suffering from fever he gives sugar; to one suffering from water he gives a decoction of ginger. He knows the cause of the illness, gives medicine, and a cure ensues. So we say "good doctor". It is the same with the Buddha and Bodhisattvas. They know that all beings possess the three kinds of illness, which are: greed, anger, and ignorance. One suffering from the illness of greed is taught to meditate on white bones; one suffering from anger is taught loving-kindness; one suffering from ignorance is made to meditate on the 12 links of interdependent origination. So we call all Buddhas and Bodhisattvas good teachers of the Way. O good man! For example, since a master mariner passes people across to the other shore, we call him a great master mariner. It is the same with all Buddhas and Bodhisattvas. They pass all beings across the great ocean of birth and death. So they are good teachers of the Way. "Also, next, O good man! It is because beings are made to practise the cause of good by Buddhas and Bodhisattvas. O good man! Just as, for example, the Himalayas are the basic place where all kinds of wonderful medicine can be found, so is it the same with the Buddhas and Bodhisattvas. They are the place where goodness springs forth. So we say good teachers of the Way. O good man! In the Himalayas, we have a very fragrant medicine called "saha". If one sees this, one can be blessed with immortality, and when one sees it, there will be no pain of illness. Even the four poisons cannot harm one. If one touches it, one's life extends up to 120. If meditated upon, one can read one's own past. Why? Because of its medicinal power. It is the same with all Buddhas and Bodhisattvas. If one sees them, one can make away with all the worries of defilement. The four Maras cannot wreak their havoc. [If this medicine is] touched, one cannot die an untimely death. It is birthlessness and deathlessness, retrogressionlessness and drowninglessness. To touch means to be with the Buddha and hear his sermons. [These having been] meditated on, one attains unsurpassed Enlightenment. Hence, we call

Buddhas and Bodhisattvas the good teachers of the Way. "O good man! In Gandhamadana there is a lake called Anavatapta. From this lake emerge four rivers, namely: the Ganges, Indus, Sita, and Vaksu. Worldly people always say: "Any sinful person will gain absolution if he bathes in these rivers." Know that all this is false and not true. Other than this, what can be true? All Buddhas and Bodhisattvas take this as true [i.e. bathing in the company of Buddhas and Bodhisattvas gives absolution]. Why? Befriending these, one can do away with all sins. So we say "good teachers of the Way". "Also, further, O good man! As an illustration: all the medicinal trees, all the forests, cereals, sugar-cane, flowers and fruits of the great earth are about to perish on encountering a long drought, until the naga kings, Nanda and Upananda, pitying the people, come out of the great sea and bestow sweet rain. And all the forests and bushes, hundreds of cereals, grass and trees receive moisture and return to life. It is the same situation with all beings. When the root of good is about to die out, all Buddhas and Bodhisattvas enact loving-kindness and cause the rain of amrta [Immortality] to fall from the sea of Wisdom and enable all beings to be perfect again in the ten good deeds. Therefore, we call all Buddhas and Bodhisattvas the good teachers of the Way. "O good man! A good doctor is well versed in the eight medicinal arts. When he sees a patient, he does not see his caste, rightness in attitude or ugliness, wealth or treasure. And he cures all. So we say "great doctor". The same is the case with all Buddhas and Bodhisattvas. They see the illness of defilement of all beings, but not their caste, their good or bad outer garb, wealth or treasure. With a mind of loving-kindness, they speak of Dharma. Having heard this, beings do away with the illness of defilement. For this reason, alll Buddhas and Bodhisattvas are called the good teachers of the Way. Befriending [such] a good friend, one approaches Mahaparinirvana. "How does the Bodhisattva approach Mahaparinirvana just by giving ear to Dharma? All beings, when they hear Dharma, gain the root of faith. When one gains the root of faith, one's mind cares to look towards giving, morality, patience, effort, meditation, and Wisdom, by which one reaches the stages of srotapanna up to Buddhahood. Thus one should know that it is due to giving ear to Dharma that one arrives at Wonderful Dharma. "O good man! As an example: a rich man has an only son. He sends this son abroad and sells what he has. He points out to him where the road is closed or open, and warns him to take care. He says: "Should you encounter a lusty woman, take care not to befriend her. If you come into close relations with her, you will lose your life and wealth. Also, take care not to befriend any bad persons." The son follows his father's words. He is safe and obtains much wealth. The same is the case here. So do matters stand with the Bodhisattva-mahasattva, who expounds Dharma for beings' sake. He points out to all beings and to the four classes of the Sangha where the road is passable and where it is closed. All these people, as they give ear to the teaching, are able to do away with all evil and be perfect in Wonderful Dharma. For this reason, one approaches Mahaparinirvana by giving ear to the teaching. "O good man! For example, just as a clear mirror fully reflects one's features, so does it obtain with giving ear to the teaching. If one looks into this, one clearly sees what is good and evil, and nothing is concealed. For that reason, giving ear to Dharma brings one near to Mahaparinirvana. "O good man! There is, for example, a merchant who desires to reach a beach of treasures, but does not know the way. A man points the way out to him. Following his words faithfully, he reaches the beach of treasures and obtains innumerably diverse good things. It is the same with all beings. They wish to reach a good place and come upon treasures, but do not know where the way is blocked or open. The Bodhisattva shows them this. The beings follow the way indicated and reach the good place, and arrive at unsurpassed Nirvana. Hence, giving ear to Dharma enables one to draw near to Mahaparinirvana. "O good man! For example, there is an intoxicated elephant, which is mad and behaves badly and means to harm people. But when the driver pricks its head with a great iron hook, it immediately becomes obedient, with its evil intention of harming totally gone. The same with all beings. Due to the intoxication of greed, anger and ignorance, they mean to do evil. But all Bodhisattvas suppress this with the hook of giving ear to Dharma, and they no more can raise the mind towards any evil. For this reason, we say that giving ear to Dharma enables one to draw close to Mahaparinirvana. That is why I say here and there in the sutras that as my disciples practise the 12 types of sutra exclusively, they make away with the five shadowings ["pancavaranani; perhaps the five "nivaranas ("obstructions", "hindrances", "coverings") are meant here, i.e. desire; anger; drowsiness and torpor; excitability and remorse; and doubt] and practise the seven factors of Enlightenment [i.e. mindulness; discriminative investigation of Dharma; vigour; joy; tranquillity in body and mind; samadhi; and equanimity]. By practising the seven factors of Enlightenment, one draws near to Mahaparinirvana. On hearing Dharma, a person of the stage of srotapanna segregates himself from fear. How so? The rich man, Sudatta, being seriously ill, greatly fears. He hears that Sariputra says that a srotapanna has four virtues and ten consolations. When he hears this, fear leaves him. Thus, giving ear to Dharma enables one to come near to Mahaparinirvana. How? Because one gains the Dharma-Eye. "There are three types of person in the world. The first has no eyes; the second has one eye; and the third has two eyes. The person with no eyes does not always listen to Dharma. The person with one eye listens to Dharma for a time, but his mind is not settled. The person with two eyes listens with an exclusive mind and acts just as he has heard. Of hearing, we know that there are three such kinds. For this reason, giving ear to Dharma brings one close to Mahaparinirvana. "O good man! I once was in Kusinagara, when Sariputra became sick and was suffering from an illness. At that time, I looked back to Ananda and had him speak extensively of Dharma. Then Sariputra, having heard this, said to his four disciples: "Put my bed on your shoulders and carry me to the Buddha. I desire to hear Dharma." Then the four disciples carried him to the Buddha, at which he was able to hear the sermon. Through the power of hearing [the sermon], pain left him and he gained peace. The case is such. For this reason, giving ear to Dharma makes one come near to Mahaparinirvana. "How can the Bodhisattva approach Mahaparinirvana by thinking? Because he gains emancipation of mind by this thinking. How? All beings are always chained to the five desires. Through thinking, he attains emancipation. For this reason, we say that one approaches Mahaparinirvana through thinking. "Also, next, O good man! All beings always have upside-down views as regards the Eternal, Bliss, the Self, and the Pure. By thinking, they can see that all dharmas are non-eternal, non-bliss, non-Self, and non-pure. Thinking thus, they segregate themselves from the four upside-downs [i.e. the four inversions]. For this reason, we say that by thinking one draws near to Mahaparinirvana. "Also, next, O good man! There are four phases to all things. What are the four? The first is the phase of birth; the second the phase of ageing; the third the phase of illness; and the fourth the phase of extinction. These four cause all common mortals, up to srotapanna, great pain. Those who well think about [these matters] do not experience pain, even when they encounter these four. For this reason, we say that by thinking one approaches Mahaparinirvana. "Also, next, O good man! There are no good dharmas that are gained by ways other than by thinking. Why not? Even though one might give ear with an undivided mind to Dharma over the course of innumerable, boundless asamkhyas of kalpas, there cannot be any attainment of unsurpassed Enlightenment unless one thinks. Thus, by thinking one approaches Mahaparinirvana. "Also, next, O good man! If all beings believe in the fact that there is no change in the Buddha, Dharma and Sangha, and gain a respectful mind, know that all this thus comes about by reason of this mindfulness and thinking and that they thus make away with all defilements. Thus, thinking makes one come near to Mahaparinirvana. "How does a Bodhisattva practise the Way as directed? O good man! He segregates himself from all evil and practises good. This is practising the Way in accordance with Dharma. "Also, next, how does one practise the Way in accordance with Dharma? One sees that all dharmas are void and have nothing to possess, and that all dharmas are non-eternal, non-bliss, non-Self, and non-purity. Seeing things thus, one does not transgress, even if it means sacrificing one's own body and life. This is how the Bodhisattva practises the Way in accordance with Dharma. "Also, next, how does one practise the Way in accordance with Dharma? Of practising there are two kinds. One is true and the other non-true. In what is non-true, one does not know the phases [i.e. elements] of Nirvana, the Buddha-Nature, the Tathagata, Dharma, the priest, the real state, and the Void. This is what is non-true. "What is the True? One knows well the phases of Nirvana, the Buddha-Nature, the Tathagata,

Dharma, the priest, the Real State, and the Void. This is what is True. "What is the phase [i.e. nature] of Nirvana? In the phase of Nirvana, there

are in all eight phases [aspects]. What are the eight? These are: 1) Ending, 2) Good Nature, 3) the Real, 4) the True, 5) the Eternal, 6) Bliss, 7) the Self, and 8) the Pure. These are Nirvana." "Also, there are eight things. What are the eight? They are: 1) liberation, 2) good nature, 3) the non-real, 4) the non-true, 5) the non-eternal, 6) non-bliss, 7) the non-Self", and 8) non-purity. "Also, there are six phases, namely: 1) liberation, 2) good nature, 3) the non-real, 4) the non-true, 5) peace, and 6) purity. There may be beings who segregate themselves from defilement by way of what obtains in the world. There may be eight things in Nirvana. Then the liberation is not real. Why not? Because of the non-eternal. When there is not the Eternal, there cannot be the Real. When there is not the Real, there is not the True. One might do away with defilement, but it will rise up again. Hence, the non-eternal, non-bliss, non-Self, and non-purity. These are the eight things of liberation of Nirvana. "What are the six phases? Sravakas and pratyekabuddhas speak of liberation when they cut away defilement. Yet they do not attain unsurpassed Enlightenment. So we say the non-Real. Being not the Real, it is not the True. They will gain unsurpassed Enlightenment in days to come. Hence, non-eternal. "On gaining the undefiled Noble Eightfold Path, we speak of pure Bliss. O good man! When this is known, there is Nirvana. We do not call this the Buddha-Nature, the Tathagata, Dharma, the priest, the Real State, or the Void. "How does the Bodhisattva know the Buddha-Nature? There are six aspects to the Buddha-Nature. What are the six? They are: 1) the Eternal, 2) the Pure, 3) the Real, 4) the Good, 5) the Visible, and 6) the True. "Also, there are seven things, namely: what is attestable, plus the other six stated above. This is called how the Bodhisattva comes to know of the Buddha-Nature. ""How does the Bodhisattva know the form of the Tathagata? The Tathagata is a form of Awakening and of Good. He is the Eternal, Bliss, the Self, and the Pure, and is" "Liberation and the True. He is the pointing out of the Way and is visible." This refers to what the Bodhisattva knows the form of the Tathagata to be. "In what way does the Bodhisattva know about Dharma? By Dharma is meant [seeing] the Good or non-Good, the Eternal or non-Eternal, Bliss or non-Bliss, Self or non-Self, Pure or non-Pure, Knowing or not Knowing, Understanding or not Understanding, the True or the not-True, Practice or non-Practice, Teacher or non-Teacher, the Real or the non-Real. This is how the Bodhisattva knows the phase of Dharma. "How does the Bodhisattva know the phase of a priest? The priest is the Eternal, Bliss, Self, and the Pure. This is the phase of a disciple. It is a form visible. It is the Good and True, and is not real. Why? Because all sravakas gain the Buddhist teaching. Why do we say True? Because the person is awake to "Dharmata" [Dharma-Essence]. This is what we mean when we say that the Bodhisattva knows the form of the priest. "How does the Bodhisattva know the Real State? These are: the Eternal or non-Eternal, Bliss or non-Bliss, Self or non-Self, Pure or non-Pure, Good or non-Good, "is" or "not-is", Nirvana or non-Nirvana, Liberation or non-Liberation, Knowing or not Knowing, [defilement] being cut off or not cut off, to attest or not to attest, to practise or not to practise, to see or not to see. These are the Real State. This is not Nirvana, the Buddha-Nature, the Tathagata, Dharma, the priest or the Void. This is the sense in which we speak of the Bodhisattva's knowing, as he practises all such Great Nirvana, the different phases of Nirvana, the Buddha-Nature, the Tathagata, Dharma, the priest, the Real State, and the Void. "O good man! The Bodhisattva-mahasattva practises the Way of the All-Wonderful Great Nirvana Sutra, but he does not see the Void. Why not? The Buddha and the Bodhisattvas have the five eyes. These are not what can be seen. Only with the Eye of Wisdom can one truly see. This is what the Eye of Wisdom can see. There is no thing to be seen. So we say "to see". If we term whatever is not as the Void, this Void is the real. As it is real, there is the eternal "not-is". Being "not-is", there is no Bliss, Self or Purity. "O good man! The Void is called "no thing". "No thing" is the Void. For example, in the world, when nothing is there, we say "empty". The same is the case with the nature of "space" ["akasha" - i.e. space, wherein a thing can exist and where there is nothing that obstructs existence]. As there is nothing to possess [here], we say "empty". "O good man! Both the nature of all beings and that of space have no real nature. Why not? This is as when we say "empty" when we make away with what there is. The case is like this. Besides, this space is, truth to tell, not to do anything with. Why? Because there is nothing to exist. As it is not "is", we can know that there can be no saying "not-is". If the nature of space were something made, it would have to be non-eternal.

If it were non-eternal, we would not call it space. "O good man! The people of the world say: "Space has no colour, nothing that obstructs, and no change". The case is thus. That is why we say that the nature of space is the fifth great element. O good man! And this space has no nature [for us] to name. Being a light, it is called space. And there is no space. It is as with secular truth, which really does not have its own nature [for us] to name and which is only said so to exist for the sake of beings. "O good man! The same is the case with the body of Nirvana. There is no place where it is. When all Buddhas do away with defilement, we call this Nirvana. Nirvana is at once the Eternal, Bliss, the Self, and the Pure. We say that Nirvana is Bliss. But it is no feeling of Bliss. This is the all-wonderful, unsurpassed silence and extinction. The All-Buddha-Tathagata has two kinds of Bliss. One is that of silence and extinction; the second is the "Bliss that is sensed by the sense-organs". There are three Blisses in the body of the Real State, which are: 1) the feeling of Bliss, 2) the Bliss of silence and extinction, and 3) the Bliss of sensing. The Buddha-Nature is a single Bliss, as it is what is to be seen. When one gains unsurpassed Bodhi, we call this the Bliss of Bodhi." Then Bodhisattva-mahasattva Highly-Virtuous King said to the Buddha: "O World-Honoured One! You say that when defilement is done away with, there is Nirvana. But this is not so. Why not? The Tathagata in days gone by, when you attained Bodhi, went to the River Nairanjana. Then King Mara, with his retinue, went to where the Buddha was and said: "O World-Honoured One! It is now time that you enter Nirvana. Why do you not enter it?" The Buddha said to King Mara: "I will not. Because I do not now see many learned disciples of mine upholding morality and wise enough to teach beings well." If when defilement is done away with there is Nirvana, all Bodhisattvas had all done away with defilements innumerable kalpas ago. How could it be that they had not attained Nirvana? There is the same segregation. Why should it only refer to all Buddhas alone and not to Bodhisattvas? If segregation of defilement is not Nirvana, why did the Tathagata, in days gone by, speak to the Brahmin, "Birth-Name", and say: "This present body of mine is Nirvana itself?" Also, the Tathagata was once in the state of Vaisali. Mara again beseeched you and said: "The Tathagata, in days gone by, did not enter Nirvana because the disciples could not teach beings well, not having much [in the way] of hearing, upholding the precepts, Wisdom, or sharpness of mind. Now they are perfect in all of these. Why do you not enter Nirvana?" The Tathagata then said to Mara: "You should have no fear that I am now too late. I shall, three months from now, enter Nirvana." If extinction is not Nirvana, why did you yourself state that you would enter Nirvana after three months? O World-Honoured One! If the segregation of defilement is Nirvana, there was Nirvana in the past when you severed yourself from defilement under the Bodhi-Tree. Why should you say that you will enter Parinirvana in three month' times? O World-Honoured One! If it was the case that the Nirvana at the time was not Nirvana, how could you say to the Mallas at Kusinagara that you would enter Parinirvana in the final part of today [i.e. about 4 a.m., or the early part of the dawn]? How could you, who are Truth itself, say such a thing?" Then the World-Honoured One said to the All-Shining Bodhisattva Highly-Virtuous King: "O good man! If you mean to say that the Tathagata talks overmuch, know that he did away with speaking falsehoods innumerable kalpas past. No Buddhas or Bodhisattvas speak any falsehood, only the truth. O good man! The Papiyas [i.e. Mara, the Devil] you refer to is none other than the one who once beseeched me to enter Nirvana. O good man! And this Mara does not know what Nirvana truly is. Why not? The Papiyas thinks that when I am silent and do not teach, this is Nirvana. O good man! The people of the world think that when one does not speak and does not do anything, one is like death itself. The same is the case with King Marapapiyas. What he says refers to the fact that the Tathagata sits and does not talk to people of Dharma. And he says that the Tathagata has entered Parinirvana. "O good man! The Tathagata does not say that there is no difference between the Buddha, Dharma, and the priest. What he says is only that there is no difference between the Eternal and the Pure. O good man! The Buddha does not say, either, that the characteristics of the Buddha, the Buddha-Nature, and Nirvana are not different. What he says is that all are Eternal and Unchanging, with no difference. The Buddha does not say, either, that the characteristics of Nirvana and the Real State are not different. What he says is that the Eternal, the "is", the Real, and the Changeless are not different. "O good man! Then all my disciples call forth disputations. The

situation was as with the bhiksus of Kausambi. Acting contrary to what I taught, they violate the prohibitions; they accept imure things as alms and greedily seek profit, and to all white-clad people [i.e. the laity] they praise their own self and say: "I have now gained the undefiled state, the fruition of the srotapanna or arhatship, and so on." They speak ill of other persons, do not respect the Buddha, Dharma and Sangha and the vinaya teachers, and openly say before me: "Such things the Buddha has permitted us to keep, and such and such things the Buddha does not allow us to possess." And going against me, they say: "The Buddha permits all such things." Such evil persons do not believe in my words. For this reason, I say to Marapapiyas: "Have no fear that I am slow. I shall enter Nirvana in three months' time." O good man! Relying on such evil bhiksus, all the sravaka disciples who are still on the way to learning do not see me and do not listen to my words, and they say that the Tathagata now enters Nirvana. Only all the Bodhisattvas well see me and give ear to what I speak of Dharma. So I do not say that I enter Nirvana. Sravaka disciples may say that the Tathagata now enters Nirvana, but, truth to tell, I do not enter Nirvana. O good man! If all of my sravaka disciples say that the Tathagata enters Nirvana, know that such are no disciples of mine. They belong to Mara's clan, the evil people who abide in twisted views and who do not hold the right view of life. If they say that the Tathagata does not enter Nirvana, they are my disciples. They are not comrades of Mara, but men of right view and not evil. O good man! It is not the case that I have ever said that the Tathgata does not teach, but sits silently, and that this is Parinirvana. O good man! For example, there is a rich man who has many sons. He leaves them and goes to other countries and has not yet come home when his sons may say that their father is long since dead. But this rich man is not yet dead. All his sons are upside down [in their view] and think of death. It is the same with my sravaka disciples. Not seeing me, they think: "The Tathagata, at Kusinagara, between the twin sal trees, enters Parinirvana." But, truth to tell, I do not enter Nirvana. The sravaka disciples think in terms of Nirvana. "O good man! For example, there is a bright lamp. A person puts a cover over it. Other people will think that the lamp has already gone out. Not knowing, they think that the lamp is extinguished. It is the same with my sravaka disciples. They have the

Eye of Wisdom and yet are overspread by defilement; their mind is upside-down and cannot see the True Body. And they loosely entertain the idea that I have gone. Yet I am not yet ultimately gone. O good man! A person born blind cannot see the sun and the moon. Not able to see, he does not know that there is night and day. Not knowing this, he says that there truly are no sun and moon. Actually there are the sun and the moon. But the blind man cannot see them. Not seeing them, he gains an upside-down mind and says that there are no sun and moon. It is the same with my sravaka disciples. As with the man born blind, not seeing the Tathagata, they say that the Tathagata has entered Nirvana. The Tathagata, in truth, has not yet entered Nirvana. Due to their upside-down minds, they gain such a thought. "O good man! For example, when cloud and mist come in the way, the ignorant say that there are no sun and moon. In truth, there are the sun and moon. Because they are obstructed, beings cannot see. It is the same with the sravaka disciples, too. With all the defilements overspreading the Eye of Wisdom, they cannot see the Tathagata, and say the Tathagata has entered Nirvana. O good man! This only derives from the fact that the Tathagata merely "acts like a child". It is not entering into extinction. O good man! When the sun has set in the west in Jambudvipa, beings cannot see it. Because the Black Mountain obstructs their sight. But the nature of the sun has nothing of hiding within it. As beings cannot see, they think there is sundown. It is the same with my sravaka disciples. Obstructed by all the mountains of defilement, they cannot see me. Not seeing me, they think that the Tathagata has truly entered Nirvana. "But truly, there is no extinction with me eternally." That is why at Vaisali I said to Papiyas: "In three months, I shall enter Nirvana." "O good man! I long before foresaw" "that the virtues of good amassed by Kasyapa would ripen and bear fruit in three months' time and that, after the ending of the sitting of the varsika, Subhadra of Gandhamadana [i.e. a learned Brahmin who was the last person to enter" "the Buddhist Sangha] would come to my place. That is why I said to Marapapiyas: "In three months' time I shall enter Nirvana." O good man! There are 500 wrestlers. In three months' time they are to aspire to unsurpassed Bodhi. That was why I said to Papiyas: "In three months' time, I shall enter Parinirvana." O good man! As the virtues amassed by Cunda and the 500 Licchavis

and Amrapali were to ripen and they were to asire to unsurpassed Bodhi, I said to Papiyas: "In three months' time I shall enter Nirvana." "O good man! Sunaksatra befriended the tirthikas and Nirgranthaputra. I spoke of Dharma for 12 long years. But the man's mind was twisted, and he would not believe and accept what I said. I foresaw that the root of this man's distorted vision would unfailingly get uprooted. So I said to Papiyas: "In three months' time, I shall enter Parinirvana." "O good man! Why did I once, in the past, on the bank of the river Nairanjana, say to Marapapiyas: "I do not yet possess any erudite disciples. So I cannot enter Nirvana?" I said this because I wanted to turn the Wheel of Dharma for the five bhiksus at Varanasi [i.e. the five bhiksus sent by the Buddha's father to look after his son]. Next, too, this was for the sake of the other five bhiksus, namely: Yasas, Purna-Maitrayaniputra, Vimala, Gavampati, and Subahu. "Also, this was for the rich man, Ugra, and his 50 people. Also, it was for the sake of Bimbisara, King of Magadha, and innumerable others and those of heaven. Also, it was for the sake of Uruvilva-Kasyapa and his 500 disciple bhiksus. Also, this was for the sake of the two brothers, Nadi-Kasyapa and Gaya-Kasyapa, and their 500 disciple bhiksus. Also, this was for the sake of Sariputra and Maudgalyayana and their 250 bhiksus. That was why I said to Papiyas, the King of Maras, that I would not enter Parinirvana. "O good man! We speak of "Nirvana". But this is not "Great" "Nirvana". Why is it "Nirvana", but not "Great Nirvana"? This is so when one cuts away defilement without seeing the Buddha-Nature. That is why we say Nirvana, but not Great Nirvana. When one does not see the Buddha-Nature, what there is is the non-Eternal and the non-Self. All that there is is but Bliss and Purity. Because of this, we cannot have Mahaparinirvana, although defilement has been done away with. When one sees well the Buddha-Nature and cuts away defilement, we then have Mahaparinirvana. Seeing the Buddha-Nature, we have the Eternal, Bliss, the Self, and the Pure. Because of this, we can have Mahaparinirvana, as we cut away defilement." "O good man! "Nir" means "not"; "va" means "to extinguish". Nirvana means "non-extinction". Also, "va" means "to cover". Nirvana also means "not covered". "Not covered" is Nirvana. "Va" means "to go and come". "Not to go and come" is Nirvana. "Va" means "to take". "Not to take" is Nirvana." "Va" means "not fixed". When there is no unfixedness, there is Nirvana. "Va" means "new and old". What is not new and old is Nirvana. "O good man! The disciples of Uluka [i.e. the founder of the Vaisesika school of philosophy] and Kapila [founder of the Samkhya school of philosophy] say: "Va means charactersitic". "Characteristic-lessness" is Nirvana." "O good man! Va means "is". What is not "is" is Nirvana. Va means harmony. What has nothing to be harmonised is Nirvana. Va means suffering. What has no suffering is Nirvana. "O good man! What has cut away defilement is no Nirvana. What calls forth no defilement is Nirvana. O good man! The All-Buddha-Tathagata calls forth no defilement. This is Nirvana. "The Wisdom that there is is not barred at Dharma [i.e. not obstructed before Dharma]. This is so with the Tathagata. The Tathagata is no common mortal, no sravaka, no pratyekabuddha, and no Bodhisattva. This is the Buddha-Nature. "The Wisdom of the Tathagata's Body and Mind fills innumerable, boundless asamkhyas of lands, with nothing to obstruct it. This is space. "The Tathagata is Eternal and does not change. This is the Real State." Because of this, the Tathagata does not ultimately enter Nirvana." "This is what we call the Bodhisattva's practice of the Way of the All-Wonderful Great Nirvana Sutra and perfecting the seventh virtue. "O good man! How does the Bodhisattva practise the Way of the All-Wonderful Great Nirvana Sutra and perfect the eighth virtue? "O good man! The Bodhisattva-mahasattva practises Great Nirvana and extirpates five things, and segregates himself from five things, accomplishes six things, practises five things, and protects one thing, befriends four things, puts faith in one truth, and his mind emancipates itself, and thoroughly emancipates Wisdom itself. "O good man! How does the Bodhisattva extirpate five things? These five are so-called: 1) matter ["rupa"],   2) feeling ["vedana"], 3) perception ["samjna"], 4) volition ["samskara"], and 5) consciousness ["vijnana"] - the five skandhas? Why do we say skandha? It truly causes beings to repeat birth and death, and they cannot cut off the heavy burden. There is dispersal and gathering-together, bound up for the Three Times. Try as one might, one cannot gain the true meaning. Because of all these meanings, we say skandha.   "The Bodhisattva-mahasattva sees the "matter-skandha", but he does not see its form. Why not? Though we may seek to gain it in

ten forms of matter, we cannot arrive at its nature. We intend to explain it for the sake of the world and we say "skandha".   "Of "feeling", there are 108 kinds. We look into the skandha of feeling. But there is no form to feeling. Why not? Though 108, there is no fixed, real form. Hence, the Bodhisattva does not see the skandha of feeling. The same applies to the skandhas of perception, volition, and consciousness. "The Bodhisattva-mahasattva sees profoundly in the five skandhas the well-spring of all the ills of defilement. So he puts into effect the means whereby to cut them off. "How does the Bodhisattva segregate himself from five things? These are the five twisted views ["panca-drstayah": the five heretical views]. What are the five? They are: 1) the twisted view regarding man's carnal existence ["satkaya-drsti": the heretical view that there is an unchanging entity in the carnal self which can be called an eternal self and regarded as one's own],   2) the one-sided view of "is" or "not-is" ["antagraha-drsti": the one-sided or heretical view of "is" or "not-is" regarding phenomenal existence, or the "is" or "not-is" view regarding the wrongly accepted notion of Self], 3) the evil view that denies causality ["mithya-drsti": the evil view that denies the law of causality in regard to what exists], 4) the twisted view of cleaving to one-sided personal opinions ["silavrata-paramarsa": the heretical view of life which denies the moral precepts and prohibitions and regards what is wrong as true and right], 5) addiction to twisted views   and   regarding   these   as   correct ["drstiparamarsa": the heretical world-view in which one cleaves to the satkaya-drsti, the antagraha-drsti, and the mithya-drsti and regards these as true]. From these five twisted views spring the 62 evil views of life. Due to these, there is no ceasing of birth and death. Therefore, the Bodhisattva guards himself so that these do not come near [to him]. "How does the Bodhisattva accomplish six things? These six things refer to six thinkings. What are the six? They are: 1) thinking of the Buddha,   2) thinking of Dharma,   3) thinking of the Sangha, 4) thinking of heaven, 5) thinking of giving,   and 6) thinking of the moral precepts.   These are the six things which the Bodhisattva accomplishes.   "How   does   the Bodhisattva practise five things? These are the five samadhis, namely: 1) samadhi of knowledge, 2) samadhi of silence,   3) samadhis of the pleasantness of body and mind, 4) samadhi of non-bliss, and 5) surangama samadhi. If one practises these five samadhis, one draws near to Mahaparinirvana. Hence, the Bodhisattva practises with a full mind. ""In what sense does the Bodhisattva guard one thing? This is Bodhichitta "[i.e. the mind of Enlightenment - the resolve to gain Bodhi]. The Bodhisattva-mahasattva always guards this Bodhichitta just as people of the world do their only son. Also, it is as with a one-eyed man who protects the other eye that still remains [to him]. It is as when people protect the man who is guiding them through the wilderness. It is the same with the Bodhisattva, who guards his Bodhichitta. "Thus guarding Bodhichitta, he reaches unsurpassed Enlightenment. When unsurpassed Enlightenment has been gained, perfect are the Eternal, Bliss, the Self, and the Pure. This is unsurpassed Mahaparinirvana. Thus the Bodhisattva guards the one Dharma." "How does the Bodhisattva draw near to four things? These are the four limitless minds ["catvari-apramanani"]. What are the four? They are: 1) Great Loving-Kindness, 2) Great Compassion, 3) Great Sympathetic Joy, and 4) Great Equanimity. By means of these four minds, he calls forth Bodhichitta in the minds of innumerable, boundless numbers of beings. For this reason, the Bodhisattva, with full mind, tries to draw near to this." "How is the Bodhisattva one-mindedly obedient? The Bodhisattva knows that all beings turn back to the one Way. The one Way is Mahayana. All Buddhas and Bodhisattvas, for beings' sake," "break this up into three. For this reason, the Bodhisattva follows obediently and does not transgress. "How does the Bodhisattva thoroughly emancipate his mind? He eternally does away with the mental states of greed, anger, and ignorance. This is how the Bodhisattva emancipates his mind. "How does the Bodhisattva thoroughly emancipate himself in his knowledge? The Bodhisattvamahasattva knows all things and is unhindered. This is how the Bodhisattva emancipates himself in knowledge. Through emancipation in knowledge, he now knows what he once did not know." Then the All-Shining Bodhisattva-mahasattva Highly-Virtuous King said: "O World-Honoured One! What you the Buddha say regarding emancipation of the mind does not hold good. Why not? The mind originally has nothing that can be bound up. Why not? Originally, the mind is not bound by any such defilements as greed, anger, and ignorance. If there is originally nothing that binds one, how can we say that the mind now gains emancipation? O World-Honoured One! If the mind originally has nothing that can be bound by greed, how can there be any binding? A person might well try to get milk from the horns of a cow, but no milk will come out, try as he might, since there is no [appropriate] nature there for the milk to come out. No milk can come about, however one might try to get the milk. One who milks does not do thus. With little effort, he gains a lot of milk. The same with the mind. If there was originally no greed, how can any greed come about? If there was originally no greed and later there is a bit of greed, we might infer that all Buddhas and Bodhisattvas who originally possessed no greed might now all have it. "O World-Honoured One! A barren woman, for example, has no capacity for bearing a child. With whatever art and effort, she cannot bear a child. It is the same with the mind. Originally it does not have the nature of greed. In no circumstances whatever can greed then come about. "O World-Honoured One! Rub wet wood as we may, we will not get any fire. The same is the case with the mind. Try as we may, we will not get any greed. How can the bond of greed fetter the mind? "O World-Honoured One! However much we might press sand, we cannot gain any oil. It is the same with the mind. We may well press it, but no greed will come out. Know that greed and mind are of different stuff. Though there is greed, how can it defile the mind? O World-Honoured One! For example, a person might try to hang a spike in the air. It can never remain there. It is the same with trying to have greed peacefully chain the mind. No number of however artful efforts can possibly have greed chain the mind. "O World-Honoured One! How can one emancipate the mind when there is no greed in it? Why do not all the Buddhas and Bodhisattvas extract a prickle from the sky? "O World-Honoured One! We do not call the mind of the past "emancipated". There is no emancipation of the mind of the future. And the mind of the present, too, does go along with the way. What mind of what world can we call "emancipation"? O World-Honoured One! This is just as the light of the past cannot make away with the gloom. The light of the future cannot make away with the gloom, either. The light of the present also does not make away with the gloom. Why not? Because light and gloom cannot go in parallel. It is the same with the mind. How can we say that the mind gains emancipation? "O World-Honoured One! It is the same with greed [i.e. lust, desire]. If one does not possess greed, one cannot have greed when one sees a woman. If it comes about by the form of the woman, know that this greed truly is an "is". Due to greed, one falls into the three unfortunate realms. "O World-Honoured One! For example, one sees a woman in a picture and gains the feeling of desire. From gaining desire, various sins result. If originally there is no desire, how can one gain desire by seeing the picture of a woman? If there is no greed in the mind, how can you the Tathagata say that the Bodhisattva gains emancipation of mind? If there is desire in the mind, how comes it that it comes about after having seen [the picture], and that a person who has not seen it does not gain it? I now actually see. An evil return ensues. This shows that I have desire. It is the same with anger and ignorance. "O World-Honoured One! For example, beings possess a body and not the self. And yet common mortals unreasonably gain the thought of a self. One can have the thought of a self and yet one does not fall into the three unfortunate realms. How can it be that a person with greed [i.e. desire] does not see a womanly form and gains the thought of a woman, and falls into the three unfortunate realms? O World-Honoured One! For example, one rubs wood and obtains fire. And the nature of this fire has no place in any thing. How does it come about? O World-Honoured One! It is the same with greed. In "matter" there is no greed; in smell, taste, touch, and law [dharma], too, we do not have any greed. And yet, how comes it that a person gains greed in smell, taste, touch, and law? If it is the case that there is no element of greed anywhere, why do only beings acquire greed and the Buddhas and Bodhisattvas do not? O World-Honoured One! The mind, too, is not fixed. If the mind were fixed, there could be no greed, anger, and ignorance. If it is not fixed, how can the mind gain emancipation? Greed, too, is not fixed. If it is not, how can one, through it, fall into the three unfortunate realms? The two things of the person with greed and the world in which he dwells are both not fixed. Why not? Each calls forth one thing and acquires greed, anger, or ignorance. This tells us that the person who has greed and the world he is in are both not fixed. If both are not fixed, why does the Tathagata say: "The Bodhisattva practises the Way of Great Nirvana' and gains emancipation of

mind?" Then, the Buddha said to the All-Shining Bodhisattva-mahasattva Highly-Virtuous King: "Well said, well said! The mind does not get bound by the defilement of greed, and also, it is not the case that it does not get bound. This is no emancipation, and it is not that there is no emancipation. It is not "is", and it is not "is-not". It is not the present, nor the past, nor the future. Why not? Because all things have no self of their own. "O good man! All tirthikas say: "When the causal concatenations harmonise, there are instances in which fruits result. When things have no nature of their own, and when they well come about without any nature of so coming about, there would have to be a result arising even from the birthlessness of space. Because the nature of birthlessness is no cause. This tells us that in all things there is the original nature of fruition [i.e. the engendering of results]. Thus do things foregather, and the result comes about. Why? When Devadatta desires to build a bulwark, he takes mud, and not paint. When he desires to draw a picture, he collects paints, and not grass or plants. When making clothes, one uses thread, and not mud and wood. This is as when one builds a house and uses mud, not thread. In accordance with what a man takes, the result will follow. As the result comes about, we can know that in the cause there is unfailingly the [relevant] nature. If there is not any nature to be named [here], one thing could well call forth all things. If one can take up, make, and put out [something], know that there must be the result prior to the coming about. If there is no result, a person will not take up, make, or put [anything] out. The only thing where there is no taking and making is space. Because of this, all things can come about. As there is the cause, the seed of the nyagrodha can live in the nyagrodha tree. So does milk possess sarpirmanda [ghee], thread cloth, and mud a pot." "O good man! All common mortals are blinded by ignorance. They say definitely: "In paint there definitely is the quality of sticking, and in the mind the nature of greed." Also, we say: "The mind of the common mortal has the nature of greed, which is the nature to be emancipated. If one encounters the causal relations of greed, the mind gains greed. When it encounters emancipation, the mind gets emancipated." Although this is said, it is not so. There are many people who say: Every cause cannot contain a result. There are two kinds of cause. One is minute and the other coarse. What is minute is eternal, and what is coarse is non-eternal. The minute cause shifts onto what is coarse, and from the coarse there later comes about the result. As what is coarse is non-eternal, the result, too, is non-eternal. "O good man! There are beings who say: "The mind has no cause; greed also has no cause. The greedy mind comes about by season." All such people do not know that all sits in the mind, and they transmigrate through the six realms, repeating birth and death. "O good man! For example, we put a collar on a dog and chain it to a pillar, and it goes round the pillar the whole day and cannot get away. It is the same with all beings. They wear the fetter of ignorance, are chained to the pillar of birth and death, and repeat lives through the 25 existences, and cannot get away. "O good man! For example, there is a man who falls into the toilet and gets out, and falls in again. A person is cured of an illness and then contracts the cause of the illness again. A traveller, on his way, comes across a wilderness. After having passed through it, he turns back into it again. A person washes his body and then puts mud on it again. That is how things go with all beings. A person is already out of the stage of the non-possession "bhumi" [i.e. the eighth of the nine stages of mental training, in which one no longer has any sense of possession], and is not yet quite out of the stage of the thoughtlessness-non-thoughtlessness "bhumi" [i.e. the final of the nine stages of mental practice]. And he comes back to the three unfortunate realms again. Why? All beings think only of the result and not of the causation. It is as with a dog who goes after a piece of mud, and not after the man himself. It is the same with the common mortal. He only thinks of the result and not of the causal relations. Not thinking of this, he draws back from the stage of the "bhumi" of thoughtlessness-non-thoughtless-ness and falls into the three unfortunate realms. "O good man! All Buddhas and Bodhisattvas do not definitely say that the cause embosoms the result, no result rests in the cause, or "is" has no result, or that "is-not" is resultless. If we say that there definitely is a result in a cause, or that there definitely is no result in a cause, or that there definitely is no result in "is", or that "is-not" is definitely resultless, know that we belong to the clan of the Maras. We belong to the class of Mara. We are those belonging to "craving" ["trsna"]. Such a person of craving cannot eternally do away with the bond of birth and death. Such a person does not know what obtains regarding the mind and greed. "O good man! All Buddhas and Bodhisattvas show us the Middle Path. Why? Things can be "isnot" or "not-is-not". But nothing can ever be definite. Why not? Because consciousness comes about through the eye, colour, brightness, mind, and thinking. Now, this consciousness is never definitely in the eye, in colour, brightness, mind, or thinking. Also, it is not in between; it is not in "is", nor is it in "is-not". As it comes about through causal relations, we say "is". As it has no nature of its own, we say "is-not". That is why the Tathagata expounds and says: "All things are not "is" and not "is-not". "O good man! All Buddhas and Bodhisattvas do not say definitely that there is the nature of purity or the nature of non-purity in the mind. Because there is no definite place where the mind that is pure or the mind that is not pure exists. Through causal relations there comes about greed. So we say "not-is-not". As there is originally no nature of greed, we say "is-not". "O good man! Through causal relations, the mind acquires greed; through causal relations, the mind can liberate itself."

Chapter Thirty-Two: Bodhisattva Highly-Virtuous King 6

"O good man! When there is the causal relation [of greed], the mind of greed [i.e. the mental state of greed/desire] comes about; it so exists, and dies with greed. There is the case where the mind comes about with greed, it so exists, and does not die with greed. There is the case where it does not come about with greed, it exists with greed, and it so dies. There is the case where it does not come about with greed, it does not exist with greed, and it so dies. "How does the mind come about together with greed, exist with greed, and so die? O good man! If the common mortal does not cut off the mind of greed and practises the mind of greed, such a person is one whose mind comes about together with greed. All beings do not cut off the mind of greed. It comes about with greed, and it dies out with greed. To all beings of the world of desire there is spread a table of the first stage of dhyana. Practised or not practised, all is ready for accomplishment. Only through causal relations does this come out to one. The causal relation is none but the fire. So do things obtain with all common mortals. Whether practised or not practised, the mind comes about along with greed, and it dies along with greed. Why? Because the root of greed has not been extirpated. "How does the mind come about along with greed and not die along with greed? The sravaka disciple gains greed through causal relations. As he is afraid, he meditates on white bones. This is why we say that the mind comes about along with greed and that it does not die along with greed. Also, there is the situation where the mind comes about along with greed and does not die along with greed. There is a sravaka who is not yet accomplished in the four fruitions [of Hinayana practice]. Through causal relations, he gains a mind of greed, but gaining the four fruitions, the mind of greed dies. Thus do things go. This is where we say that the mind comes about along with greed and does not die along with greed. "When the Bodhisattva-mahasattva gains the immovable stage [i.e. the eighth of the 10 Bodhisattva stages of development], the mind comes about along with greed and does not die along with greed. "In what way do we say that the mind does not come about along with greed and that it dies together with greed? When the Bodhisattva-mahasattva extirpates the mind of greed, but displays, for the sake of beings, that he yet has greed. As this is for the sake of display, innumerable, boundless numbers of beings gain, perfect and accomplish good things. This is where we say that the mind does not come about along with greed, but dies along with greed. "How do we say that the mind does not come about along with greed and that it does not die along with greed? This refers to Bodhisattvas other than the arhat, pratyekabuddha, all Buddhas, and those of the immovable stage. This is where we say that the mind does not come about along with greed and that it does not die along with greed. For this reason, we do not say that all Buddhas and Bodhisattvas are by nature pure in mind, and we do not say that they are by nature not pure. O good man! This mind does not melt into that of greed; also it does not melt into that of anger and ignorance. "O good man! For example, the sun and moon become obscured from sight by smoke, dust, cloud, mist, and the Asura [i.e. a Titan who, when fighting the sun and moon, obstructs their light by spreading out his hands]. Because of these things, no being can see [the sun and moon]. Though not seen, the nature of the sun and moon does not, after all, melt into one with the five overshadowings ["panca-avaranani"]. It is the same with the mind. Through causal relations, the bond of greed comes about. Beings say that the mind melts into one with greed, but the nature of the mind truly does not melt into one. If the greedy mind were the nature of greed, and if non-greed were the nature of non-greed, we could not make the mind of greed greed, and the mind of greed could not become that of non-greed. O good man! For this reason, the bond of greed cannot defile the mind. All Buddhas have eternally done away with the mind of greed. On that account, we say that one gains liberation of mind. This is said because all beings gain the bond of greed through causal relations, and through causal relations they attain liberation. O good man! For example, this is as with a precipice in the Himalayas. A man cannot go along it with a monkey. There might be a place where the monkey can go on his own, but not the man. Or there might be a place where both man and monkey can go. O good man! Where both man and monkey can go, a hunter places a table, on which he deposits birdlime and catches the monkey. As the monkey lacks intellect, he touches the lime with his hands. Through touching it, his hands get stuck. To free his hands, he touches the lime with his feet. His feet get stuck. To get his feet free, he bites [at the birdlime] with his mouth. His mouth further gets stuck. Thus, the five parts [of the monkey] are unable to get free. Then the hunter pases a staff through the monkey [i.e. kills the monkey] and returns home. "The steep precipice in the Himalayas is the Right Path, along which the Buddha and Bodhisattvas walk; the monkey is comparable to all common mortals; the hunter is Marapapiyas; the birdlime is the bond of greed. Man and monkey being unable to walk together is analogous to all common mortals being unable to walk together with Marapapiyas. We say that the monkey can go and that man cannot: this is comparable to the fact that even the tirthikas who have intelligence and all devils cannot draw one to the bait even with the five desires. We say that man and monkey go well together: this means that all common mortals and Marapapiyas are always lost in birth and death and cannot properly practise the Way. Common mortals are bound up by the five desires, so that Marapapiyas can easily catch them and carry them away. This is like the hunter who catches the monkey with birdlime and takes him back home. "O good man! If the king remains in his own country, his body and mind will be at ease; if abroad, he will have to suffer from many things. So do matters stand with all beings. If one lives in one's own domain, one is in peace. But out of one's own domain, one comes across devils and has to suffer from all manner of worries. One's own domain refers to the four thinkings, and the place of others to the five desires. "How do we say that one belongs to Mara? All beings see the non-eternal as the Eternal, the Eternal as the non-Eternal, Suffering as non-Suffering, Bliss as Suffering, the Impure as the Pure, the Pure as the Impure, the non-Self as the Self, the Self as non-Self, what is not true Emancipation carelessly as Emancipation, true Emancipation as non-Emancipation, non-Vehicle as Vehicle, and Vehicle as non-Vehicle. Such people belong to the class of the Maras. One who belongs to Mara does not have a pure mind. "Also, next, O good man! If a person truly sees all things as "is" and general and individual forms as fixed, know that this person will - when he sees any concrete thing - see as though looking at a concrete thing. This will apply down to consciousness. When he encounters conscious-

ness, he will entertain the thought of having had a consciousness [of something]. Seeing a man, he will see the form of a man; seeing a woman, the form of a woman; seeing the sun, the form of the sun; seeing the moon, the form of the moon; seeing the form of age, the form of age; seeing a skandha, the form of a skandha; seeing a sense-sphere, the form of a sense-sphere; seeing a sense-realm, the form of a sense-realm. Any such person is the kindred of Mara. One who is the kindred of Mara does not possess a pure mind. "Also, next, O good man! A person might come to think that the Self is matter ["rupa"], that the Self exists in matter; that there is matter in the Self, that matter belongs to the Self. Or he may view the Self as consciousness, or think that the Self exists in consciousness, that consciousness exists in the Self, that consciousness belongs to the Self. Any such person who views things thus belongs to Mara; any person who see things thus is not my disciple. "O good man! My sravaka disciples part from the 12 types of sutra of the Tathagata and learn and practise the various kinds of books of the tirthikas; not studying the works of renunciation and silent extinction of a priest, they exclusively perform what secular people do. What are the works of the secular world? What are the impurities? They receive and keep all such things as male and female menial servants, fields and houses, elephants, horses, vehicles, donkeys, mules, fowls, dogs, pigs, sheep, and all kinds of cereals, from barley to wheat. They part from their teachers and priests, and associate with the laity. Acting contrary to the holy teaching, they address white-clad [i.e. lay] people and say: "The Buddha permits the bhiksus to receive and keep various impure things." This is where we speak of people learning things of the secular world. "There are various disciples who, not acting for Nirvana, approach and give ear to the 12 types of sutra and don priestly robes or greedily eat those things intended for priests who have come from afar, as though they were their own things. They feel jealousy and resentment when they hear of the praise and fame of other families. They associate with the king and all princes, are interested in good and bad fortune [i.e. they go in for fortune-telling], guess at the waxing and waning of the moon. They love and befriend chess, gambling, chobo [i.e. a gambling game], throwing arrows into a pot, bhiksunis [nuns], girls, and keeping two sramaneras. They always visit the houses of butchers, hunters, bars, and the places where candalas live. They sell and buy, they make food themselves, they receive messengers from neighbouring countries and give news. Know that such people are kindred to Mara and are no disciples of mine. Thus, the mind comes about with greed and thus dies with greed. This applies down to the ignorant mind, which emerges together [with ignorance] and dies out together [with ignorance]. O good man! For this reason, it is not the case that the nature of the mind is pure or not pure. Hence, I say that one gains liberation of mind. "If a person does not receive and store [impure things], but - for the sake of Great Nirvana - upholds, recites, copies and explains to others the 12 types of sutra, know that such a person is truly my disciple. Such a person does not perform what belongs to the world of Marapapiyas; such a person learns and practises the 37 elements of Enlightenment. Learning and practising the Way, such a person does not come about together with greed and does not die together with greed. This is what we mean when we say that the Bodhisattva practises the All-Wonderful Great Nirvana Sutra and perfects and accomplishes the eighth virtue." "Also, next, O good man! How does the Bodhisattva-mahasattva practise the All-Wonderful Great Nirvana Sutra and perfect and accomplish the ninth virtue? O good man! The Bodhisattvamahasattva practises the Way of the All-Wonderful Great Nirvana Sutra and first calls forth five things and perfects these. What are the five? These are: 1) faith, 2) a straight mind, 3) the moral precepts, 4) associating with a good friend, and 5) erudition. "What is faith? The Bodhisattva-mahasattva believes that there is recompense in the Three Jewels and in giving. The two truths [i.e. relative and ultimate] and the Way of the One Vehicle ["ekayana"] are not different. He believes that all Buddhas and Bodhisattvas classify things into three, so that all beings quickly gain Emancipation. He believes in "Paramartha-satya" [the truth of Ultimate Reality] and good expedient means. This is faith. "A person who believes thus cannot be beaten by any sramanas, Brahmins, Marapapiyas, Brahma, or anyone. When a person grounds himself in this faith, he gains the nature of a holy sage. One practises giving, and this - whether big or small - all leads to Mahaparinirvana, and thus one does not fall into birth and death. It is the same with upholding the moral precepts, hearing the Way, and Wisdom, too. This is faith. Though one may have this faith, one does not yet see. This is how the Bodhisattva practises the Way of Great Nirvana and perfects the first thing. "What is the straight mind? The Bodhisattva-mahasattva maintains a straight mind towards all beings. All beings flatter, as occasion arises. It is not so with the Bodhisattva. Why not? Because he knows well that all good things come about through causal relations. The Bodhisattva-mahasattva sees all the evils and wrongs done by beings. But he does not speak about these things. Why not? Possibly worries will come about. If defilements raise their head, this will lead to evil realms. If he sees beings performing some small good deeds, he praises [them]. What is a good deed? It is the so-called Buddha-Nature. When the Buddha-Nature is praised, all beings aspire to unsurpassed Enlightenment." Then, the All-Shining Bodhisattva-mahasattva Highly-Virtuous King said to the Buddha: "O World-Honoured One! You say that the Bodhisattva-mahasattva expresses praise and causes innumerable beings to aspire to unsurpassed Bodhi. But this is not so. Why not? The Tathagata, in the opening part of the Nirvana Sutra, says that there are three kinds. "Firstly, you say that if a patient obtains a good doctor, good medicine, and a good medical attendant, the illness will easily be cured and that if things are otherwise, it will not be cured. "Second, you say that the illness fails to get cured, regardless of whether one obtains such or not. "Third, you say that whether one obtains these things or not, all will be cured. The same is the case with all beings. "If one encounters a good friend, encounters all Buddhas and Bodhisattvas and gives ear to the sermons, one aspires to unsurpassed Enlightenment. If not, there cannot be any aspiration. So there are the srotapanna, sakrdagamin, anagamin, arhat, and pratyekabuddha. "Second, a person may encounter a good friend, all Buddhas and Bodhisattvas and give ear to the sermons, but is unable to aspire; even if he does not encounter such, there will be no aspiration. This refers to the icchantika. "Third, there is the situation where people all aspire to unsurpassed Enlightenment, whether they encounter such or not. This refers to the case of the Bodhisattva. "If it is the case that a person aspires to unsurpassed Enlightenment, how can you explain and say: "By praising the Buddha-Nature, all beings aspire to unsurpassed Enlightenment?" O World-Honoured One! If it is the case that whether one encounters a good friend, all Buddhas and Bodhisattvas and listens to their sermons, or whether one is unable to, one cannot all-equally aspire to unsurpassed Enlightenment, we can know that this is not so. Why not? Because such a person attains unsurpassed Enlightenment. Because by means of the Buddha-Nature, even the icchantika has to attain unsurpassed Enlightenment, whether he gives ear to the sermons or not. "O World-Honoured One! You say "icchantika". But what is the icchantika? You say that he is devoid of the wholesome root. This also is not so. Why not? Because such a person is not devoid of the Buddha-Nature. Thus, logically, the Buddha-Nature cannot be lacking [in anything]. How can you say that the entire root of good has been cut off? "You previously spoke of the 12 types of sutras and said that there were two kinds of food, namely: 1) the eternal, and 2) the non-eternal. The eternal refers to the uncut, and the non-eternal to the cut. The non-eternal can be cut off. So a person falls into hell. The eternal cannot be cut off. Why not? If the Buddha-Nature is not cut off, there is no icchantika. Why do you, the Tathagata, speak thus and put forward such a view of the icchantika? O World-Honoured One! The Buddha-Nature gains one unsurpassed Enlightenment. How is it that you, the Tathagata, so expansively deliver the sermons of the 12 types of sutras? O World-Honoured One! For example, the four rivers take their rise from [Lake] Anavatapta. The devas and all Buddhas might say that the rivers do not flow into the great sea, but turn back to their source. But this makes no sense. It is the same with the mind of Enlightenment. Anybody with the Buddha-Nature must attain unsurpassed Enlightenment, whether he has heard the sermons or not, whether he has upheld the moral precepts or not, whether he has practised giving or not, whether he has practised the Way or not, whether he has Wisdom or not. O World-Honoured One! From out of Mount Udayana rises the sun, and it moves right on to the south. The sun might pray: "I will not go west; I will return east." But nothing like this ever happens. It is the same with the Buddha-Nature. One may say that non-hearing, non-upholding of the precepts, non-giving, non-practising of the Way, and non-Wisdom do not bestow unsurpassed Enlightenment. But such a situation never obtains. "O World-Honoured One! The All-Buddha-Tathagata says that the nature of

causality is "is-not" and "not-is-not". This is not so. Why not? If there is not the nature of cream in milk, there cannot be any cream. If there the seed of the nyagrodha did not possess the nature to be as high as 50 feet, it could not gain this quality of 50 feet. If there were no tree of unsurpassed Enlightenment in the Buddha-Nature, how could one expect to have a tree of unsurpassed Enlightenment? If causality is neither "is-not" nor "not-is-not", how does this accord well with reason?" Then the Buddha expressed praise and said: "Well said, well said, O good man! There are two types of people in the world who are as rare as the udumbara. One is the person who does not commit evil deeds; the second is the person who thoroughly confesses when he has sinned. Such persons are extremely rare. There are two further types of people. One benefits others; the other remembers well the benefits he has had. Furthermore, there are two kinds of people. One accepts new rules, and the other looks back to what is now gone and does not forget. Also, there are two [further] types of people. One does what is new, and the other practises what is old. Also, there are two [other types of] people. One takes pleasure in giving ear to Dharma, and the other takes pleasure in speaking of Dharma. Also, there are two [further] types of people. One asks about what is difficult, and the other answers well. You are the [type of] person who asks well about what is difficult; the Tathagata is the one who answers well. O good man! By means of these good questions, there can be the turning of the Wheel of Dharma, the killing of the great tree of the 12 links of causation, the passing of people across the boundless sea of birth and death, the good fight against King Marapapiyas, and the smiting down of Papiyas's victorious banner. "O good man! I have spoken thus of the three patients and said that whether there is encountering or non-encountering of a good doctor, attendance, and good medicine, a cure results. What does this mean? We say that one "gains" or "does not gain". This refers to the destined span of life. Why? Now, over the course of innumerable ages, this person has practised the three good deeds: top, middle, and low. By practising these three good deeds, he gains his destined span of life. This is as in the case of a person of Uttarakuru, where the life-span is 1,000 years. Now, one may acquire an illness. But no matter whether one gains a good doctor, good medicine, or good attendance: all ends in a cure.

Why? Because one has one's destined span of life. O good man! I say: "If one gains a good doctor, good medicine, and good attendance, one can drive the illness away; if not, the illness will not retreat." Now, what does this mean? O good man! Such a person's life-span is not definite. Even though the [expected] end of his life has not yet been reached, by the nine factors of causal relations, he loses his life. What are the nine? "First, he knows well of the unreliability of food and yet, in contradiction of this, he partakes of it. "Second, he eats overmuch. "Third, he eats even when the former food has not yet been digested. "Fourth, he is not regular in his calls of nature. "Fifth, even though he is ill, he does not comply with the words of the doctor. "Sixth, he does not follow the advice of the medical attendants. "Seventh, he strongly holds things in and does not put them out [i.e. he suffers from constipation]. "Eighth, he goes about at night. As he goes about at night, the devils come and attack him. "Ninth, his room is not very good. "For this reason, I say that if the patient takes the medicine, his illness will be cured, and if he does not, it will not be cured. O good man! I said above that the illness will not be cured, whether [the medicine is] taken or not. Why? Because the life-span is ended. Hence I say that the sick person will not gain a cure, whether the medicine is taken or not. So do things obtain with beings. Anybody who gains Bodhichitta, whether he has met with a good friend or not, with all Buddhas and Bodhisattvas, will Awaken and gain the depths of Dharma. Why? Because he aspires to Enlightenment. This is like the people of Uttarakuru, who are blessed with a definite span of age. As I say, those people from the stage of srotapanna up to pratyekabuddha, when they listen to the words of deep meaning from a good friend, from all Buddhas and Bodhisattvas, will gain the mind of unsurpassed Enlightenment. "I say that if a person does not encounter the Buddha and the Bodhisattvas and does not listen to the words of deep meaning, he cannot aspire to the mind of unsurpassed Enlightenment. This is as with a person who dies an unnatural death due to the nine kinds of causal relations which are indefinite. His illness will be cured when he encounters medical treatment and medicine. If not, it will not be cured. That is why I say that if a person listens to the words of deep meaning of the Buddha and Bodhisattvas, he aspires to Bodhichitta, and if not,

he cannot. "I said above that a person might encounter a good friend, the Buddha and the Bodhisattvas and listen to the words of deep meaning, or he may not. In both cases, he does not aspire to Bodhichitta. What does this mean? O good man! The icchantika is unable to do away with the mind of the icchantika, no matter whether he encounters a good friend, the Buddha or the Bodhisattvas, and listens to the words of deep meaning or not. Why? Because he is segregated from Wonderful Dharma. The icchantika, too, will gain unsurpassed Enlightenment. Why? If he aspires to Enlightenment, such a one is no longer an icchantika. "O good man! Why do we say that even the icchantika, as well, gains unsurpassed Enlightenment? The icchantika really does not attain unsurpassed Enlightenment. It is as with the person who faces the end of his life and who cannot be cured by a doctor, good medicine, or good medical attendance. Why not? Because life has reached the point where he can live no longer. "O good man! "Issen" means "faith"; "dai" means "not accompanied". When a person does not possess faith, we say "issendai". The Buddha-Nature is no "faith". The "being" does not mean "to possess". Not possessing, how can the person think of cutting off? "Issen" means "good expedient means", and "dai" "not to possess". When the good expedient means is not practised, we speak of the "icchantika". We say "Buddha-Nature". It is not to practise the good expedient means. Beings do not possess this. Not possessing it, how can it be cut off? "Issen" means "to go forward", and "dai" "not to possess". When a person does not possess anything that will enable them to go forward, we speak of the icchantika. The Buddha-Nature is "not going forward" and beings are "not possessing". When there is no possessing, how can there be any cutting off? "Issen means "to remember", and dai "not to possess". When a person does not possess remembrance, we say icchantika. The Buddha-Nature is no remembrance, and beings are no possessing, so how can a person think of cutting off? "Issen means "samadhi", and dai "not possessing". When samadhi is not possessed, we speak of the icchantika. The Buddha-Nature is no samadhi and beings no possessing. When there is no such possessing, how can one think of ever cutting off? "Issen means "Wisdom" and dai "not possessing". When a person does not possess Wisdom, we speak of the icchantika. The Buddha-

Nature is no Wisdom and beings "no possessing". When a person does not possess Wisdom, how can there be cutting off? "Issen means "non-eternal good" and dai "not possessing". When a person does not possess the non-eternal good, we say icchantika. The Buddha-Nature is Eternal. It is neither good, nor non-good. Why? Wonderful Dharma unfailingly arises out of expedient means, but this Buddha-Nature is not something that arises out of expedient means. So, it is non-good. And why is it not anything good? Because a good result truly comes about. This good result is none other than unsurpassed Enlightenment. "Also, because Wonderful Dharma is what we gain after birth. And this Buddha-Nature is not something we gain after birth. Hence, it is not anything that can be termed good. When a person is segregated from the Wonderful Dharma that one gains after birth, we say icchantika. "O good man! For example, there is a king who hears a harp, the sound of which is serene and wonderful. His mind bewitched, joy and bliss arise, intermingled with loving thoughts, and it is hard [for him] to part with the superb feeling. He says to his minister: "From where does that wonderful kind of sound arise?" The minister replies: "That wonderful sound comes from the harp, sire." The King further says: "Bring me that sound!" Then the minister places the harp before the seat of the king and says: "O great King! This is the sound!" The King says to the harp: "Call forth the sound, call forth the sound!" But the harp does not bring forth any sound. Then the King cuts the strings, and still there is no sound. He tears off the skin, crushes the wood and breaks everything up into pieces, intending to press the sound out, but no sound [comes]. Then the King gets angry with the minister and says: "How dare you lie to me!" The minister says to the King: "Now, this is not the way to get at the good sound. All the causal relations and good expedient means can indeed call forth the sound." "It is the same with the Buddha-Nature. There is no place where it rests. Only through the best expedient means is it able to appear. When it can be seen, one gains unsurpassed Enlightenment. The icchantika cannot see the Buddha-Nature. [So] how can he make away with the sins of the three realms?

"O good man! If the icchantika believes in the fact that there is the Buddha-Nature, know that he cannot fall into the three realms. Also, such a person is not even called an icchantika. Not believing in the fact that there is the Buddha-Nature, this carries him down into the three realms. When a person falls into the three realms, he is an icchantika. "O good man! You say that if there is not the nature of cream in milk, it cannot bring forth cream; if the seed of the nyagrodha tree does not possess a nature to be 50 feet tall, there cannot be the fact of 50 feet. An ignorant person might well say this, but not one who is wise. Why? Because there is no nature. O good man! If there were the nature of cream, there would be no need to call in the power of causal relations. O good man! Mix water and milk together and leave them thus for a month, and we will never gain any cream. If a drop of "phalgu" [ficus oppositifolia: a red powder usually made from wild ginger root] juice is added, we obtain cream. If there was [already] the phenomenon of cream, why would we need to wait upon the joint workings of causal relations? The same is the case with the Buddha-Nature of all beings. Assisted by various causal relations, we [come to] see it; being grounded on various causal relations, we gain unsurpassed Enlightenment. If things come about assisted by causal relations, this tells us that there is no nature that may be called its own. As there is no nature that can be named, one can well attain unsurpassed Enlightenment. O good man! For this reason, the Bodhisattva-mahasattva always praises the good of a person and does not speak badly about what is deficient. This is the straight mind. "Also, next, O good man! What is the straight mind of the Bodhisattva? The Bodhisattvamahasattva never does evil. If evil is performed, the Bodhisattva immediately repents. He never hides [his evil] from his teacher or classmates. His repentance reproaches his own self, and no more evil is done. Even a small sin he feels as grave. When asked, he answers: "I did this". When asked: "Is it right or wrong, good or not good?", he answers: "Not good!" When asked: "Will the sin call forth any result that is good or bad?", he answers: "The result will be one that is not good." "Who is responsible for this sin? Are not all the Buddhas, Dharma and Sangha responsible?", he answers: "It is not from the Buddha, Dharma or Sangha. This is what I did myself." This is what defilements create. By the straight mind, he believes in the existence of the Buddha-Nature. When a person believes in the Buddha-Nature, he cannot be an icchantika. Because of this straight mind, we speak of the Buddha's disciple. He may be given a thousand items of clothing, drink, food, bedding, medical attendance, and medicines. All this cannot be called much. This is the Bodhisattva's straight mind. "How does the Bodhisattva practise sila [the moral precepts]? The Bodhisattva-mahasattva upholds sila, but not for birth in the heavens, nor out of fear; nor does he receive silas against dogs, fowls, cows, and pheasants. He does not violate sila, nor does he fail in it, or wrong it; nor does he practise any mixed-up silas; nor any sravaka sila. He upholds the sila of the Bodhisattvamahasattva, the silaparamita [perfected morality]. He is perfect in the upasampada, and is not arrogant. This is the sense in which we say that the Bodhisattva practises the Way of Gret Nirvana and is perfect in the third sila. "How does the Bodhisattva befriend a good friend? The Bodhisattva-mahasattva always practises much and expounds to beings the Way, not anything evil, saying that evil never calls forth a good result. O good man! I am the good teacher of all beings. Hence I thoroughly destroy the twisted views of the Brahmins. O good man! If any beings befriend me, they gain birth in the heavens, even though there be reason for them to fall into hell. This is as with Sunaksatra and others, who, on seeing me, were born in the Rupadhatu Heaven, extirpating the causal relations of being born in hell. There are such persons as Sariputra and Maudgalyayana, who were no true good teachers of the Way to beings. Why? Due to gaining the mind of the icchantika. "O good man! I once lived in Varanasi. At that time, Sariputra taught two disciples. The one he taught to meditate upon white bones, and the other to count the number of breaths. Even after many years, they could gain no meditation. As a result of this, they acquired twisted views and said: "There is no undefiled dharma of Nirvana. If there were, I would have gained it. Why? I observe well all the silas that I have to observe." Then, on seeing that these bhiksus had acquired twisted views, I sent for Sariputra and reproached him: "You do not teach well. Why do you teach these persons in an inverted way? Your disciples differ in their bent. One is a washerman, and the other is a goldsmith. The son of a goldsmith may be taught the counting of the number of breaths, and the washerman to meditate on white bones. As you teach in the wrong way, these two persons gain wrong views." I then taught these two persons as they ought to have been taught, and the two, after having been

taught, attained arhatship. Therefore, I am the good teacher of the Way for all beings, and not Sariputra or Maudgalyayana. If any being who might have the worst fetter of defilement happens to meet me, I can, using the best expedient means, thoroughly cut away the root. "My younger brother, Nanda, possessed the greatest of greed, and I did away with it by putting into effect various good expedients. "Angulimalya possessed the greatest of malevolence. But on seeing me, he did away with it. "King Ajatasatru was extremely ignorant. But on seeing me, he did away with this. "The rich man, Bakiga , had amassed, in the course of innumerable periods of time, the heaviest of defilements. But on seeing me, his defilements all departed. "Any evil or lowly person can win the respect and love of all humans and devas by befriending me and becoming my disciple. "Srigupta was extremely evil-minded. But on seeing me, all his perverted views of life were done away with. On seeing me, he made away with the cause for hell and gained the [prerequisite] condition for birth in the heavens. "Kikosendara was about to lose his life. But on seeing me, he gained his life. "Kausika was about to lose his head, when, on seeing me, he gained the true mind. "The butcher son of Kisagotami always committed evil. But on seeing me, he did away with it. "On seeing me, Sendaibiku became unwavering in the observance of sila, so that he would even abandon his life rather than violate sila, as in the case of Sokebiku [i.e. the "grass-bound bhiksu". So named due to the fact that once this bhiksu was deprived of all his clothing by robbers and then was tied up to grass and thus left out in the sun. But the bhiksu did not try to rend himself free from the grass, as he thought this would kill the grass. The king saw this and freed him. The king was greatly impressed by this holy action and later himself joined the Sangha]. For this reason, Ananda is said to have stated that a semi-pure action is a good teacher of the Way. But the case with me is not so. I say that a fully pure action is the good teacher of the Way. This is how the Bodhisattva practises the Way of Great Nirvana and perfects the fourth action of befriending a good teacher of the Way. "How does the Bodhisattva-mahasattva perfect rich hearing? The Bodhisattva, for the sake of Great Nirvana, copies, recites, understands and expounds the 12 types of sutras. This, we say, is how the Bodhisattva perfects rich hearing. "Excluding the

11 types of sutras, the Bodhisattva upholds, recites, copies and expounds the vaipulya. This, we say, is how the Bodhisattva perfects rich hearing. "Excluding the 12 types of sutras, the Bodhisattva upholds, copies, studies and expounds the All-Wonderful Sutra of Great Nirvana. This is also the perfection of rich hearing by the Bodhisattva. "Even if one takes up the whole of this sutra, but upholds a four-line gatha, or even excludes this gatha, but believes in the fact that the Tathagata is Eternal and Does Not Change - even this can be the perfection of the Bodhisattva's rich hearing. "Also, a person may even make away with this, but only know that the Tathagata does not always deliver sermons. And even this is the perfection of rich hearing by the Bodhisattva. Why? Because there is no thing that can be termed Dharma nature itself. The Tathagata talks of Dharma. But there exists nothing such as that which can be talked about. This, we say, is how the Bodhsiattva practises the Way of Great Nirvana and is perfect in the fifth rich hearing. "O good man! There may be a good man or good woman who, for the sake of Great Nirvana, perfects or accomplishes the five things and does what is difficult to do, endures what cannot be endured, and gives what cannot be given. "How does the Bodhisattva do well that which is difficult to do? When he hears that a man just takes a sesame seed for food and attains unsurpassed Enlightenment, he believes this, and for a period of innumerable asamkhyas of kalpas, he partakes of a single sesame seed. If he hears that he attains unsurpassed Enlightenment by entering fire, he will go into the burning fires of Avichi Hell for a period of innumerable kalpas. This is where we say that the Bodhisattva does what is difficult to do. "How does the Bodhisattva endure what is difficult to endure? If he hears that one can attain Great Nirvana by bearing the hardships of having his hand struck by a staff or a sword or a stone, he will, for a period of innumerable asamkhyas of kalpas, subject his body [to such] and will not make it a pain [i.e. he will not regard this as painful]. This is where we say that the Bodhisattva endures well what is difficult to endure. "How does the Bodhisattva give what is hard to give? If he hears that by giving away to others one's national castle, one's wife and children, one's head, eyes, or marrow, one gains unsurpassed Enlightenment, he will for a period of innumerable asamkhyas of kalpas give away his castle town,

his wife and children, his head, eyes and marrow to others. This is how we speak of the Bodhisattva's giving away what is hard to give away. "The Bodhisattva does what is difficult to do, but he in no way says: "This is what I did." This applies to what is difficult to endure and what is difficult to give away. "O good man! For example, there are [two] parents who have a child. They love this child very much. They give this son fine clothes and the best dishes when the occasion requires such, and the child has no feeling of anything lacking. If their son becomes arrogant and speaks unpleasing words, they suppress their anger out of their love; they do not even think to themselves that they have given this son of theirs clothing and food. It is the same with the Bodhisattva-mahasattva, too. He views all beings as though they were his only son. If the son suffers from illness, the parents also suffer. They seek a doctor, medicine, and medical attendance. When the illness has departed, they do not think that they have cured their son of his illness and done away with it. It is the same with the Bodhisattva. Seeing that all beings suffer from the illness of defilement, compassion awakens in his mind. And he speaks of Dharma. When a person listens to his sermons, all defilements flee. When the defilements have gone, he does not think or say that he has done away with the sufferings of defilement. Should any such thought occur to him, he would not be able to attain unsurpassed Enlightenment. He only thinks that he has never spoken of the Way to a being and has thus cut off the fetter of defilement. The Bodhisattva-mahasattva experiences no anger or joy towards beings. Why not? Because he practises the samadhi of the All-Void. On practising the samadhi of the All-Void, to whom could the Bodhisattva evince any anger or joy? O good man! For example, a forest becomes consumed by a great fire and gets burnt down, or is felled by man, or gets inundated with water. But do the forest-trees grow angry or become pleased? It is the same with the Bodhisattva-mahasattva. He possesses no anger or joy towards any being. Why not? Because he practises the samadhi of the All-Void." Then the All-Shining Bodhisattva-mahasattva Highly-Virtuous King said to the Buddha: "O World-Honoured One! Is the nature of all things void? Or is it void when we practise the Void? If the nature is All-Void, there cannot be any gaining of the All-Void by practising the All-Void. How can the

Tathagata say that one gains the All-Void by practising the All-Void? If the nature is not All-Void, there cannot be any gaining of the All-Void by practising the All-Void." "O good man! The nature of all things is originally All-Void. Why? Because we cannot hold in our hands the nature of all things. O good man! The nature of matter cannot be held in one's hand. What is the nature of matter? Matter is not earth, water, fire, or wind. And [yet] it does not part from the nature of earth, water, fire, and wind. It is not blue, yellow, red, or white. And it does not part from blue, yellow, red, or white. It is not is; it is not is-not. How can we say that matter has its own nature? "As its nature is impossible to catch hold of, we say "all-void". It is the same with all things. As there is similarity and continuity, common mortals see and say that the nature of all things is not all-void. The Bodhisattva-mahasattva perfects the five things. So he sees that the original nature of all things is all-silence. O good man! If there is any sramana or Brahmin who sees that the nature of all things is not all-void, know that such a one is no sramana, or no Brahmin. Such a person cannot practise prajnaparamita and attain Great Nirvana. He cannot see all the Buddhas and Bodhisattvas face to face; he is the kindred of Mara. O good man! The nature of all things is originally All-Void. And when the Bodhisattva practises the All-Void, he sees the All-Void of all things. "O good man! The nature of all things is impermanent. So, extinction well extinguishes extinction. If things were not impermanent, extinction could not extinguish. Any created thing has the phase of birth. So, a birth can call forth a birth. As there is the phase of extinction, this phase of extinction well calls forth extinction. "All things have the characteristic of suffering; on account of this, suffering evokes suffering. O good man! The nature of salt is salty. So it indeed makes other things taste salty. Rock candy is sweet by nature. So it indeed makes other things [taste] sweet. Vinegar is sour by nature. So it makes other things taste sour. Ginger is pungent by nature. So it makes other things taste pungent. Haritaki tastes bitter. So it makes other things taste bitter. The mango ["amra"] tastes light. So it makes other things taste light. Poison truly harms others. The amrta's [i.e. ambrosia's] nature makes a person immortal. Also, mixed with alien things, it enables such not to die. The case is the same with the Bodhisattva who practises the All-Void. When he practises the All-Void, he sees the nature of all things to be all-void and silent." The All-Shining Bodhisattva-mahasattva Highly-Virtuous King further said: "If salt can make what is not salty salty, and if, thus practising the samadhi of the All-Void, matters stand thus, we can know that this is definitely not what is good, not what is wonderful, but that the nature is upside down. The samadhi of the All-Void sees only the All-Void. The Void is not a thing. What thing is there there to see?" "O good man! The samadhi of the All-Void makes what is not void void and silent. It is nothing that is upside down. This is as when what is not salty is made to become salty. The case is the same with this samadhi of the All-Void. It makes what is not void void. O good man! Greed is by nature "is" and is nothing of the nature of the void. If greed is by nature all-void, beings, through causal relations, could not fall into hell. If they fall into hell, how can it be that the nature of greed is all-void? O good man! The nature of matter is "is". What is its nature? It is what is upside down [i.e. an inversion of the truth]. Being upside down, beings acquire desire. If this desire were not upside down, how could beings acquire desire? As desire comes about, know that the nature of matter is not that which is not "is". For this reason, the practice of the samadhi of the All-Void is not upside down. "O good man! When every common mortal sees a woman, there arises the form of a woman. Not so with the Bodhisattva. Even on seeing a woman, he does not gain the form of a woman. Gaining no form of a woman, there arises no desire. As no desire comes about, this is nothing that is upside down. When worldly people see a woman, the Bodhisattva accordingly says: "There is a woman". If a man is seen and the Bodhisattva says: "This is a woman", this is an inversion. For this reason I said to Jyoti: "You Brahmin! If you call day night, this is an inversion; if you call night day, this again is an inversion. That which is day is the form of day, and that which is night is the form of night. How can this be an inversion?" O good man! If a Bodhisattva abides in the ninth soil, he sees that a thing has a nature. Because of this view of the world, he does not see the Buddha-Nature. If the Buddha-Nature is seen, there will be no seeing of a nature in any thing. When he practises this samadhi of the All-Void, he does not see any nature in all things. As he does not see this, he sees the Buddha-Nature. "All Buddhas and

Bodhisattvas speak of two aspects. The one is the nature of "is", and the other is that of "not-is". For the sake of beings, they say that there is a nature in a thing. For the sake of holy ones, they say that there is no nature in things. In order to let a person of the non-Void see the Void, that person is made to practise the samadhi of the All-Void. With those persons who see no nature in all things, what there is is the All-Void, because they practise the Void. For this reason, a person sees the Void by practising the Void. O good man! You say that if one sees the Void, this means that the Void is equal to no thing, and ask what that thing is that one must see.

O good man! It is thus, it is thus. The Bodhisattva-mahasattva sees nothing. To say that one sees nothing means that one possesses nothing. To say that there is nothing possessed equals all things. If the Bodhisattva-mahasattva practises the Way of Great Nirvana, he sees nothing in all things. If something is seen, this tells us that one sees no Buddha-Nature. One cannot [in such circumstances] practise prajnaparamita and gain Mahaparinirvana. For this reason, the Bodhisattva sees that all things are characterised by having nothing that can be possessed. "O good man! It is not only the case that the Bodhisattva, by seeing this samadhi, sees the Void. He sees that prajnaparamita is Void, dhyanaparamita is Void, viriyaparamita is Void, ksantiparamita is Void, silaparamita is Void, danaparamita is Void, matter is Void, the eye is Void, consciousness, too, is Void, the Tathagata is Void, and Mahaparinirvana is Void. Thus, the Bodhisattva sees things as Void. "That is why I said to Ananda at Kapilavastu: "Do not be sad, do not cry and weep." Ananda said: "O Tathagata-World-Honoured One! Now, all my relatives are dead. How can I not weep? The Tathagata was born in this castle-town together with me, and we are all related to the Shakya clan. How is it that the Tathagata alone is not sad and does not worry, but displays such a bright visage?" "O good man! I then said: "O Ananda! You think that Kapilavastu truly exists, whereas I see that all is empty and silent and that there is nothing that exists. You see all the Shakyas as your relatives. But I see totally nothing therein, because I practise the All-Void. That is why you gain sorrow and pain, and I look all the more bright. As all Buddhas and Bodhisattvas practise the samadhi of the All-Void, they do not show any sorrow or worry." This is how the Bodhisattva practises the Way of the All-Wonderful Sutra of Great Nirvana and perfects and accomplishes the ninth virtue. "Also, next, O good man! How does the Bodhisattva practise the teaching of the All-Wonderful Sutra of Great Nirvana and perfect the last and tenth virtue [i.e. after, for example, the practice of the All-Void]? "O good man! The Bodhisattva practises the 37 factors leading to Enlightenment, gains the Eternal, Bliss, the Self, and the Pure, and then, for the sake of beings, classifies and expounds the Sutra of Great Nirvana and reveals the Buddha-Nature. Anybody of the stages of srotapanna, sakrdagamin, anagamin, arhat, pratyekabuddha or Bodhisattva who believes in this word will attain Mahaparinirvana. Any person who does not believe repeats the cycle of birth and death." Then the All-Shining Bodhisattva-mahasattva Highly-Virtuous King said to the Buddha: "O World-Honoured One! Who are the beings who do not respect the sutras?" "O good man! After my entering Nirvana, there will be sravaka disciples who are ignorant and violate the precepts and take pleasure in disputation. They will cast away the 12 types of sutra and recite and copy the documents of the various schools of the tirthikas, keep all impure things, and say that these are things that were permitted by the Buddha. Such people will trade sandalwood for common wood, gold for brass, silver for solder, silk for wool, and amrta [ambrosia] for bad poison. "What do I mean when I say that sandalwood is traded for common wood? My disciples, for the sake of alms, will preach Dharma to all the white-clad [i.e. the laity]. People will lose interest and not give ear. They will sit high and the bhiksus low. Besides, they will offer various kinds of food and drink. But they will not listen. This is what we mean by trading sandalwood for common wood. "What do we mean by trading gold for brass? The brass may be likened to colour, sound, smell, taste, and touch, and gold to the moral precepts. All my disciples will violate the precepts they have received for reason of things. So we say they trade gold for brass. "Why do we say trading silver for solder? We liken silver to the ten good deeds and solder to the ten evil deeds. All my disciples will abandon the ten good deeds, performing the ten evil deeds. So we say they trade silver for solder. "How does a person trade silk for wool? Wool is likened to non-repentance and shamelessness, and silk to having a sense of shame. All my disciples will abandon repentance and not feel ashamed. This is why we say that they will relinquish silk for wool. "How does one trade amrta for poison? Poison can be likened to the various alms offered, and amrta to undefiled Dharma. All my disciples will praise their own selves for profit in the presence of the laity and will claim that they have attained that which is undefiled. This is what we mean when we say they will trade amrta for poison. "Due to such bhiksus of evil designs, even when this All-Wonderful Sutra of Great Nirvana flourishes in Jambudvipa and when all disciples recite, copy, and preach it, and cause it to flourish, these will be killed by such evil bhiksus. Then, all such bhiksus of evil designs will gather together and take oaths: "If any person upholds, copies, recites, or studies the Great Nirvana Sutra, we will not sit together with them, not talk or exchange words with them. Why not? The Great Nirvana Sutra is not a sutra of the Buddha's. Why not? It is a work of perverted views. These perverted views are none but of the six masters. What the six masters say is no sutra of the Buddha. Why not? All Buddhas say that all things are impermanent, non-Self, non-bliss, and non-pure. When it is said that all things are the Eternal, Bliss, Self, and the Pure, how could this be a sutra of the Buddha's? All Buddhas and Bodhisattvas permit the bhiksus to store up various things. The six masters do not allow their disciples to store up anything. How could all this be what the Buddha says? All Buddhas and Bodhisattvas do not tell their disciples to refrain from the five tastes [i.e. the five varieties of milk product] and from eating meat. The six masters do not permit the five kinds of salt, the five tastes of the cow, and fat and blood. How could the prohibiting of these be the right teaching of the Buddha's sutra? All Buddhas and Bodhisattvas preach the three vehicles. But this sutra speaks only of One. It speaks of Great Nirvana. How could anything such be the right teaching of the Buddha? All Buddhas ultimately enter Nirvana. This sutra says that the Buddha is the Eternal, Bliss, the Self, and the Pure, and that he does not enter Nirvana. This sutra does not have any place amongst the 12 types of sutras. This is what Mara says. This is no sermon of the Buddha's." "O good man! Any such person might be my disciple, but he is unable to believe in this sutra. O good man! If, at such a juncture, there should be any person who believes in this sutra, or in even half a line [of it], know that such a person is truly my disciple. With such faith, one will see the Buddha-Nature and enter Nirvana." Then, the All-Shining Bodhisattva Highly-Virtuous King said to the Buddha: "O World-Honoured One! It is very well, it is very well that the Tathagata today thoroughly opens up the Great Nirvana Sutra. O World-Honoured One! I have now, through this, come to know of a single or half a line of this Great Nirvana Sutra. As I come to understand a line or half a line, I now see somewhat of the Buddha-Nature, which you the Buddha speak about. I too shall be able to attain Great Nirvana. This is how we speak of the Bodhisattva's practising the Way of the All-Wonderful Sutra of Great Nirvana and of his perfecting and accomplishing the tenth virtue."

Chapter Thirty-Three: On Bodhisattva Lion's Roar 1

Then the Buddha said to all those gathered there: "All of you good men! Should you have any doubt as to whether there is the Buddha or not, whether there is Dharma or not, whether there is the Sangha or not, whether there is suffering or not, whether there is the cause of suffering or not, whether there is extinction or not, whether there is the Way or not, whether there is Reality or not, whether there is the Self or not, whether there is sorrow or not, whether there is purity or not, whether there is Eternity or not, whether there is a vehicle or not, whether there is nature or not, whether there is the being or not, whether there is "is" or not, whether there is the True or not, whether there is causation or not, whether there is the result or not, whether there is action or not, whether there is karma or not, or whether there is the karmic result or not, I shall now allow you freely to ask. I shall explain to you in detail. O good man! All such as devas, humans, Maras, Brahmas, sramanas, and Brahmins have come to ask, and I have never been unable to answer." Then, there was amongst the congregated a Bodhisattva called "Lion's Roar". He stood up and adjusted his robe, touched the Buddha's feet, prostrated himself, folded his hands, and said to the Buddha: "O World-honoured One! I wish to ask [a question]. Please permit me to ask, O great Compassionate One!" Then, the Buddha said to all the congregation: "O you good men! You now should greatly honour, respect and praise this Bodhisattva. Make offferings of incense and flowers, of music, of necklaces, banners, parasols, clothes, food, drink, bedding, medicine, houses and palaces, and attend upon his comings and goings. Why? Because this Bodhisattva has in the past greatly accomplished all good deeds at the sites of the Buddhas, and he is replete with virtues. Because of this, he now desires to utter a lion's roar before me. O good man! He is like a lion-king. He knows his own power, has sharp teeth, and his four legs stand [firmly] on the ground. He lives in a rocky grotto; he shakes his tail and gives a roar. When he displays thus, he knows that he indeed gives out a lion's roar. The true lion-king emerges from his den early in the morning. He stretches his body and yawns. He looks around, growls, and roars for eleven things. What are those eleven? "First, he desires to crush a person who,

not [truly] being a lion, makes the pretence of presenting himself as a lion. "Second, he now desires to test his own physical strength. "Third, he desires to purify the place where he lives. "Fourth, he desires to know the places where all others are living. "Fifth, he does not fear any other. "Sixth, he desires to awaken those who are asleep. "Seventh, he desires to make all indolent beasts non-indolent. "Eighth, he desires all beasts to come and surrender [to him]. "Ninth, he desires to subjugate the great gandhahastin. "Tenth, he desires to test all sons. "Eleventh, he desires to adorn all those to whom he is related. "All birds and beasts hear the lion's roar; those of the water hide themselves down in the depths, and those on land in grottos and caves; those who fly fall to the ground; all those great gandhahastins become frightened and defecate. O all good men! A fox may pursue a lion for 100 years, and yet he cannot make him roar. The situation is like that. The son of a lion, at the age of three full years, can truly roar like a lion-king. "O good men! The Tathagata, with the fangs and nails of the Wisdom of Right Enlightenment, with the legs of the four-at-willnesses , with the full body of the six paramitas, with the manly courage of the ten powers, with the tail of Great Loving-Kindness, and living in the pure grottos of the four dhyanas, gives out a lion's roar and crushes Mara's army, revealing to all beings the ten powers and opening up the place where the Buddha goes. He becomes a refuge to all those fleeing from twisted views, he consoles beings who are in fear of birth and death, he awakens beings who drowse in ignorance, he proclaims to those of twisted views that what the six masters [i.e. teachers of the six non-Buddhist schools of belief] say is not the lion's roar, he crushes the arrogant mind of Puranakasyapa [i.e. one of the six masters] and others, he causes the two vehicles to become repentant, he teaches all Bodhisattvas of the stage of the fifth abode and enables them to acquire a mind of great power, he causes the four classes of the Sangha who abide in right views not to be afraid of the four classes of the Sangha who abide in twisted views. He steps forth from the grottoes of holy actions, pure actions, and heavenly actions so as to crush the arrogance of all beings. He yawns so as to call forth Wonderful Dharma. He looks towards the four directions so as to cause beings to gain the four unmolestednesses in hindrances [i.e. the fourfold unhindered knowledge]. His four feet stand [firmly] on the ground, so that beings can peacefully abide in silaparamita. Thus, he utters a lion's roar. To utter the lion's roar means to make it known that all beings have the Buddha-Nature and that the Tathagata is Eternal and Unchanging. "O good men! The sravakas and pratyekabuddhas follow the Tathagata-World-Honoured One for a period of an innumerable hundred thousand asamkhyas of kalpas, and yet are unable to utter the lion's roar. If the Bodhisattvas of the stage of the ten abodes can practise these three actions [i.e. the three actions of body, mouth, and mind], know that they will be able to utter the lion's roar. O all good men! Now, this Bodhisattva Lion's Roar wishes to raise the great lion's roar. This being so, make offerings to him with the deepest mind, and respect, honour and praise him." Then, the World-Honoured One spoke to Bodhisattva-mahasattva Lion's Roar: "O good man! If you desire to ask anything, do now put your questions." Bodhisattva-mahasattva Lion's Roar said to the Buddha: "O World-Honoured One! What is the Buddha-Nature? Why do we speak of Buddha-Nature? Why do we say the Eternal, Bliss, Self, and the Pure? If all beings possess the Buddha-Nature, why is it that they do not see their own Buddha-Nature? In what do the Bodhisattvas of the stage of the ten "bhumis" live, and why can they not clearly see it [i.e. the Buddha-Nature]? Abiding in what dharma can the Buddha clearly see it? With what eye can the Bodhisattvas of the stage of the ten "bhumis" not clearly see it? With what eye can the Buddha clearly see it?" The Buddha said: "Well said, well said, O good man! If any person pays homage to Dharma, he will be equal to two adornments. The one is Wisdom, and the other is weal. If any Bodhisattva is perfect in these two adornments, he will be able to know the Buddha-Nature and will know why we say "Buddha-Nature". Also, he can see with what eyes the Bodhisattvas of the ten "bhumis" see and with what eyes all Buddhas see." Bodhisattva Lion's Roar said: "O World-honoured One! What is the adornment of Wisdom?" "O good man! The adornment of Wisdom refers to what pertains to the first "bhumi" up to the tenth. The adornment of weal refers to danaparamita [unsurpassed giving] up to prajna [Wisdom]. This is not prajnaparamita [transcendent Wisdom]. "Also, next, O good man!

The adornment of Wisdom is none other than all Buddhas and Bodhisattvas. The adornment of weal refers to sravakas, pratyekabuddhas, and the Bodhisattvas of the nine "bhumis". "Also, next, O good man! The adornment of weal is the law [dharma] of the common mortal, being the created, the "asravic" [defiled], the existing, that which engenders karmic results, that which has hindrances, and is non-eternal. "O good man! You now possess these two adornments. That is why you effectively put such deep-rooted questions. I, too, possess these adornments and I shall answer your query." Bodhisattva-mahasattva Lion's Roar said: "O World-Honoured One! If the Bodhisattva possesses these two adornments, there can be no asking of one or two questions. Why do you, the World-Honoured One, say that you answer one or two? Why? All things have no number of one or two kinds. To state one or two is to answer the need of the common mortal." The Buddha said: "O good man! If the Bodhisattva did not have one or two adornments, we could not know that there are one or two adornments. If the Bodhisattva has two adornments, we can well know of the one or two kinds. You say that all things are not one or two. But you are wrong. Why? If there is not one or two, how can we say that all things do not have one or two? O good man! If you say that speaking of one or two relates to the phase of the common mortal, this refers to the Bodhisattva of the grade of the ten "bhumis". Such a person is no common mortal. Why not? "One" refers to Nirvana; "two" relates to birth and death. "Why is it that "one" is none other than Nirvana? Because it is the Eternal. Why is "two" birth and death? Because of craving ["trisna"] and ignorance. Eternal Nirvana is not a phase of the common mortal; the two of birth and death is again not a phase of the common mortal. Because of this, being perfect in the two adornments, one questions well and answers well. "O good man! If you desire to know what the Buddha-Nature is, listen carefully, listen carefully. I shall now analyse and explain it to you. ""O good man! The Buddha-Nature is none other than the All-Void of "Paramartha-satya" [Ultimate Truth]. The All-Void of "Paramartha-satya" is Wisdom. We say "All-Void". This does not refer to no Void [any Voidness], nor non-Void. Knowledge ["jnana"] sees the Void and the non-Void, the Eternal and the non-Eternal, Suffering and Bliss, the Self and the non-Self. The Void refers to all births and deaths. The Non-Void refers to Great

Nirvana. And the non-Self is nothing but birth and death. The Self refers to Great Nirvana.

"If one sees the All-Void, but does not see the non-Void, we do not speak of this as the Middle Path. Or if one sees the non-Self of all things, but does not see the Self, we do not call this the Middle Path. "The Middle Path is the Buddha-Nature. For this reason, the Buddha-Nature is Eternal and there is no change. As ignorance overspreads [them], all beings are unable to see. The sravaka and pratyekabuddha see the All-Void of all things. But they do not see the non-Void. Or they see the non-Self of all things, but they do not see the Self. Because of this, they are unable to gain the All-Void of "Paramartha-satya". Since they fail to gain the All-Void of "Paramartha-satya", they fail to enact the Middle Path. Since there is no Middle Path, there is no seeing of the Buddha-Nature." "O good man! There are three seeings of the Middle Path [i.e. constituting the Middle Path]. The one is the definitely blissful action; the second is the definitely sorrowful action; the third is the sorrow-bliss action. "We say "definitely blissful action". This is as in the case of the so-called Bodhisattvamahasattva, who, pitying all beings, lives in Avichi Hell and yet feels things as of the bliss of the third dhyana Heaven. "We say "definitely sorrowful action", referring to all common mortals. "We say "sorrow-bliss action". This alludes to sravakas and pratyekabuddhas. The sravakas and pratyekabuddhas experience sorrow and bliss, and gain the thought of the Middle Path. For this reason, thouh a person possesses the Buddha-Nature, he cannot see it well. "O good man! You say that we speak of the "Buddha-Nature". O good man! The Buddha-Nature is the seed of the Middle Path of the unsurpassed Enlightenment of all Buddhas. "Also, next, O good man! There are three kinds of way, which are: low, top, and middle. The low refers to the non-eternal of Brahma, in which one mistakes the non-eternal for the Eternal. The top refers to the non-eternal of birth and death, which people wrongly conceive as the Eternal. The Three Jewels that are Eternal are wrongly conceived of as eternal [sic; non-eternal]. Why do we call it the top? Because by it, one well gains unsurpassed Enlightenment. "The Middle is the All-Void of "Paramartha-satya". This sees the non-eternal as the non-eternal and the Eternal as the Eternal. The All-Void of "Paramartha-satya" is

not made [i.e. designated] "low". Why not? For it is that which all common mortals do not have. We do not call it "top". Why not? Because it is the top [another recension gives "low" here; either meaning is not clear - K. Yamamoto]. The Way of all Buddhas and Bodhisattvas is neither the top nor the low. We call it the Middle Path. "Also, next, O good man! There are two kinds of original abode of birth and death. The one is ignorance, and the other is clinging to what exists. In between [these] two are the sufferings of birth, old age, illness and death. We call this the Middle Path. This Middle Path well destroys birth and death. That is why we say "Middle". That is why we call the teaching of the Middle Path the Buddha-Nature. Therefore, the Buddha-Nature is the Eternal, Bliss, the Self, and the Pure. All beings do not see this. All beings do not see this. Hence there is [for them] no Eternity, no Bliss, no Self, and no Purity. The Buddha-Nature is not non-Eternal, not non-Bliss, not non-Self, and not non-Purity. "O good man! "There is a poor man, in whose house there is a storehouse of treasure. But the man cannot see it. So, there is no Eternity, no Bliss, no Self, and no Purity. There is there a good teacher of the Way, who says to him: "You have a storehouse in your house, in which there is gold. Why is it that you are poor, have worries, and have no Eternity, no Bliss, no Self, and no Purity?" Utilising "[certain] "means, he enables the man to see this. On seeing this, the person gains the Eternal, Bliss, the Self, and the Pure. It is thus. The same is the case with the Buddha-Nature. Beings cannot see [it]. Its not being seen, no Eternity, no Bliss, no Self, and no Purity exists [for them]. The good teacher of the Way, all Buddhas and Bodhisattvas, by enacting the means and telling them various enlightening stories, enable them to see. Through seeing, these beings reach the Eternal, the Bliss, the Self, and the Pure". "Also, next, O good man! There are two ways in which beings see. One is "is", and the other is "is-not". Such two are not the Middle Path. When there is no "is" and no "not-is", we have the Middle Path. What sees as not "is" and not "is-not" is the Knowledge ["jnana"] that meditates and perceives the 12 links of interdependence. This kind of Knowledge that sees is the Buddha-Nature. The two vehicles may meditate on causal relations, but such cannot be called Buddha-Nature. "The Buddha-Nature is Eternal. But all beings cannot see it because of the overspreading of ignorance. They cannot yet cross the waters of the 12 links of interdependence - it is as though they were like hares and horses. Why? Because they cannot see the Buddha-Nature. "O good man! The Wisdom that can meditate on the 12 links of interdependence is the seed that gains one unsurpassed Enlightenment. For this reason, we call the 12 links of interdependence the Buddha-Nature. "O good man! For example, we call the cucumber "fever". Why? Because it bears on [relates to, cures] fever. The same is the case with the 12 links of interdependence. "O good man! The Buddha-Nature has a cause and a cause of the cause; it has a result and a result of the result. "Cause" is the 12 links of interdependence. The cause of the cause is Wisdom. "Result" is unsurpassed Enlightenment. The result of the result is Mahaparinirvana. "O good man! For example, ignorance is the cause and all actions the result. "Action" is the cause, and consciousness is the result. Because of this, the body of ignorance is the cause and also the cause of the cause. Consciousness is the result and, also, the result of the result. The same is the case with the Buddha-Nature. "O good man! Because of this, the 12 links of interdependence are no going-out and no dying-out, no eternality and no disruption, not one and not two, no coming and no going, no cause and no result. O good man! It is the cause and not the result, as in the case of the Buddha-Nature. It is the result and not the cause, as in the case of Great Nirvana; it is the cause and it is the result, as in the case of the 12 links of interdependence. Causeless and resultless is the Buddha-Nature. As it does not arise out of causality, it is eternal and it knows no change. That is why I say in the sutra: "The meaning of the 12 links of interdependence is deep-rooted and none can grasp, see or conceive it. All [these] are things of the world of all Buddhas and Bodhisattvas. It is not within the reach of sravakas and pratyekabuddhas to attain." "Why is it that things are deep-rooted? What all beings do is non-eternal and non-disruptive. And yet results come about from actions performed. They go off moment after moment, and yet there is not anything that is lost. None may be living, yet there remains the karma. There may be none to receive, yet there is the karmic result. The one who harvests may be gone, but the result does not die out. Though not to be thought of or to be known, there is harmonization [i.e. coming together of cause and result]. All beings journey along with the 12 links of interdependence, which

they do not see or know. Not seeing or knowing, there is no ending and no beginning. The Bodhisattvas of the stage of the ten abodes see only the end, but they do not see the beginning. The All-Buddha-World-Honoured One sees the beginning and the end. Thus do all Buddhas clearly see the Buddha-Nature. "O good man! All beings are unable to see the 12 links of interdependence. Therefore, they ride on the wheel of transmigration. O good man! Just as the silkworm makes a cocoon, gains birth, and dies by itself, so do things proceed with all beings. As they do not see the Buddha-Nature, they generate karma out of defilement and repeat births and deaths, just as a person bounces a ball. O good man! That is why I say in the sutra: "One who sees the 12 links of interdependence sees Dharma; one who sees Dharma sees the Buddha. "The Buddha is none other than the Buddha-Nature." "Why so? Because all Buddhas make this their own nature." "O good man! There are four kinds of Knowledge that see the 12 links of interdependence. These are: 1)low, 2) middle, 3) top, and 4) topmost. A person of the low position does not see the Buddha-Nature. Not gaining [it], he gains the way of a sravaka. Those of the middle position also do not see the Buddha-Nature. Noting the Buddha-Nature, they gain the way of the pratyekabuddha. Those of the top see, but not clearly. Not being clear, they live in the soil of the ten abodes. The topmost [persons] see clearly. So they attain unsurpassed Enlightenment. Because of this, we call the 12 links of interdependence the Buddha-Nature. The Buddha-Nature is the All-Void of "Paramartha-satya". The All-Void of "Paramartha-satya" is the Middle Path. The Middle Path is the Buddha. The Buddha is Nirvana." Bodhisattva-mahasattva Lion's Roar said to the Buddha: "O World-Honoured One! If no difference exists between the Buddha and the Buddha-Nature, why should all beings particularly need to practise the Way?" The Buddha said: "O good man! Your question is misplaced. "The Buddha and the Buddha-Nature are not different". But beings are not yet armed therewith. "O good man! For example, there is a man who abides in evil and kills his mother. Having killed [her], he repents. He is [here performing] one of the three good actions. But this one [i.e. another person] falls into hell. Why? Because this person surely gains hell. Even though this person has none of the five skandhas, the 18 realms and the 12 spheres, yet we call him a person of hell. "O good man! That is why I say in all the sutras: "Any person who sees another doing good, this is worth [i.e. equal to] seeing a deva [god]; anyone who sees a person doing evil sees hell. Why? Because karmic results surely await such a person." "O good man! "As all beings will definitely gain unsurpassed Enlightenment, I say that all beings possess the Buddha-Nature". The beings actually do not possess the 32 signs of perfection and the 80 minor marks of excellence. So, in this sutra, I say in a gatha:

"What originally was is now no longer;
What originally was not, now is;
There can be nothing such as "is"
That obtains in the Three Times."

"O good man! There are three kinds of what exists. One is what comes about in the days to come, the second what actually exists there [now], and the third what was there in the past. "All beings will gain unsurpassed Enlightenment in the days to come." [This is the Buddha-Nature.] All beings now possess all bonds of defilement. So they do not possess at present the 32 signs of perfection and the 80 minor marks of excellence. Thus, the beings who have cut off the bonds of defilement in the past see, in the present, the Buddha-Nature. So, I always say that beings all possess the Buddha-Nature. I even say that the icchantika [most spiritually blinded of persons] possesses the Buddha-Nature. The icchantika has no good dharma. The Buddha-Nature too is a good Dharma. As there are the days to come, there is also the possibility for the icchantika to possess the Buddha-Nature. Why? Because all icchantikas can definitely attain unsurpassed Enlightenment. "O good man! As an example: there is a man who has some cream. People ask: "Do you have any butter?" He answers: "I have". But, truth to tell, cream is not butter. Skilfully worked out [i.e. using skilful means], he is sure to gain it. So he says that he has butter. It is the same with beings. All have the mind. "Anyone with a mind will assuredly reach unsurpassed Enlightenment" [emph. added]. That is why I always say that all beings possess the Buddha-Nature. "O good man! Of the absolute, there are two kinds. One is the absolute in adornment, and the other the ultimate of the absolute. One is the absolute in the secular sense, and the other the absolute in the supramundane sense. By the absolute in adornment is meant the six paramitas; the ultimate of the absolute is the One Vehicle which beings gain. The One Vehicle is the Buddha-Nature. That is why I say that all beings possess the Buddha-Nature. All beings possess the One Vehicle. As ignorance is spread all over them, they cannot see. O good man! In Uttarakuru, the fruition of Trayastrimsa Heaven cannot be seen by beings because there is [this] overspreading [of ignorance]. It is the same regarding the Buddha-Nature. Beings cannot see [it] because of the overspreading of defilement. "Also, next, O good man! "The Buddha-Nature is the Suramgama Samadhi "[deepest state of meditative absorption]". Its nature is like sarpirmanda "[most delicious and efficacious of all milk-medicines]." It is the mother to all Buddhas. By dint of the power of the Suramgama Samadhi, all Buddhas gain the Eternal, Bliss, the Self, and the Pure" All beings possess the Suramgama Samadhi. Not practising, they cannot. see it. Hence, [there is then] no gaining of unsurpassed Enlightenment. "O good man! The Suramgama Samadhi has five names, which are: 1) suramgama samadhi, 2) prajnaparamita [transcendent Wisdom], 3) diamond samadhi, 4) lion's roar samadhi, 5) Buddha-Nature. According to the part it takes, it has various names. O good man! Just as a single samadhi gains various names, such as in [connection with] dhyana we say "four dhyanas" ["catvari-dhyanani"], in element "samadhi element", in power "samadhi power", in element "samadhi element" [sic], in rightness "right meditation", and in the eight awakened minds of a great man "right meditation". So does it obtain with the Suramgama Samadhi. "O good man! All beings are perfect in three samadhis, which are: top, middle, and low. The top refers to the Buddha-Nature. So, we say that all beings possess the Buddha-Nature. By middle is meant that all beings possess the first dhyana. When causal relations are favourable, they can indeed practise; if not, they cannot. Of causal relations, there are two kinds. The one is fire, and the other the bond that destroys the things of the world of desire. So, we say that all beings are perfect in the middle-grade samadhi. The low-grade samadhi is none but the caitta samadhi of the ten mahabhumikas. Though possessing the Buddha-Nature, all beings are unable to see it, being overspread with defilement. The Bodhisattva of the ten abodes sees the One Vehicle, but he does not know that the Tathagata is Eternal. So, though the Bodhisattva of the ten abodes sees the Buddha-Nature, he cannot see it clearly. ""O good man! "Shurya" means "the ultimate of all things"; "gon" means "strong". As the ultimate of all things is strong, we say "suramgama". So, the Suramgama Samadhi is made to stand for the Buddha-Nature. "O good man! I once lived by the River Nairanjana and said to Ananda: "I now intend to bathe in the river. Give me my robe and the washing powder "[soap]". I then got into the water. All flying birds and those on water and land came and watched. Then there were also 500 Brahmacarins, who lived near the river. They came to me and said: "How can you hope to gain the Adamantine Body? If Gautama does not talk about "not-is", I shall follow him and accord with the rules of food." "O good man! I, at that time, with mind-reading Wisdom, fathomed the mind of the Bramacarins and said to them: "What do you mean by saying that I talk of "not-is"? All the Brahmacarins said: "You, Gautama, have previously stated, here and there in the sutras, that all beings do not possess the Self. Now you say that there is no Self. How can you say that this is not the "not-is" theory? If "[there is]" no Self, who upholds the precepts and who violates "[them]"? I, the Buddha, said: "I have never said that all beings do not have the Self; I have always said that all beings have the Buddha-Nature. Is not the Buddha-Nature the Self? Thus, I have never spoken of "not-is". All beings do not see the Buddha-Nature. Hence, "[for them there is]" the non-Eternal, non-Self, non-Bliss, and non-Purity. Such are the views of "not-is". Then, all the Brahmacarins, on hearing that the Buddha-Nature is the Self, aspired to the unsurpassed Bodhi "[Enlightenment]" mind, and then, renouncing the world, practised the way of Bodhi. All flying birds and all those on water and land aspired to unsurpassed Bodhi, and having aspired, abandoned their bodies. "O good man! This Buddha-Nature is, truth to say, no Self "[i.e. no defiled, circumscribed ego"]. For the benefit of beings, I say Self. "O good man! The Tathagata, when there is reason for "[so]" saying, says that non-Self is the Self. But, truth to say, there is no Self "[there]". Though I speak thus, there is nothing "[here]" that is false. "O good man! On account of causal relations, I state Self to be non-Self, "and, yet, truth to tell, there is the Self. It constitutes the world. I state "[this]" as non-Self. But nothing is wrong. The Buddha-Nature is non-Self. The Tathagata says Self. Because there is the quality of the Eternal. The Tathagata is the Self. And yet he states "[this]" as non-Self. Because he has unmolestedness" [i.e. complete freedom, unrestrictedness, the ability to do what he wills]. Then, Bodhisattva Lion's Roar said: "O World-Honoured One! If it is the case that all beings possess the Buddha-Nature like any vajra-guardsman [i.e. a person who holds in his hand a vajra - diamond - and who thus protects the Buddhist teaching], why is it that all beings cannot see it?" The Buddha said: "O good man! For example, "matter" ["rupa"] has such representational qualities as blue, yellow, red, and white, and long or short, but a blind person cannot see it as such. Though it is not seen, we cannot say that there is no such quality as blue, yellow, red, white, long or short. Why not? Even though the blind person cannot see [it], one who has eyes can see [it]. It is the same with the Buddha-Nature. Even though all beings cannot see [it], the Bodhisattva at the level of the ten stages can see [it] somewhat; the Tathagata sees [it]completely. The Buddha-Nature seen by the Bodhisattva of the ten stages is like colour seen at night. What the Tathagata sees is like colour seen in the daytime. "O good man! When the eye is blurred, one cannot see colour clearly. A good doctor can cure this. By [the use of] medicine, one comes to see things clearly. It is the same with the Bodhisattva of the ten stages. He can indeed see the Buddha-Nature, but not very clearly. By the power of the Suramgama Samadhi, a person can see [it] clearly.""O good man! If a person sees the non-Eternal, non-Self, non-Bliss, and non-Pure of "all" things" [Japanese "issai", which here means all that can be seen, touched and felt - the material world, i.e. matter]," and sees also the non-Eternal", "non-Bliss, non-Self, and the non-Pure of the"non-all" [Japanese "hiissai", which here means the opposite of the concrete, i.e. the abstract]," such a person does not see the Buddha-Nature. "All" alludes to birth and death; "non-all" alludes to the

Three Treasures. The sravaka and pratyekabuddha see the non-Eternal, the non-Self, non-Bliss, and the non-Pure of the non-all. Due to this "[i.e. in this sense]", they cannot see the Buddha-Nature. The Bodhisattva of the ten stages sees the non-Eternal, the non-Self, non-Bliss, and the non-Pure of all things, and sees, in part, the Eternal, Bliss, the Self, and the Pure of the non-all. Because of this, he can see only one tenth. The All-Buddha-World-Honoured One seesthe non-Eternal, non-Self, non-Bliss, and the non-Pure of all things and, also, the Eternal, Bliss, the Self, and the Pure of the non-all. Because of this, he sees the Buddha-Nature just as one would see a mango that is "[resting] "in one's own palm. Because of this, the Suramgama Samadhi is the Ultimate". "O good man! It is as when one cannot see the first moon. And yet, one cannot say that there is no moon. The same is the case with the Buddha-Nature. All beings may not [be able to] see it, yet we cannot say that there is no Buddha-Nature. "O good man! The Buddha-Nature is none other than the ten powers, the four fearlessnesses, Great Compassion, and the three thinkings. "All beings have the three destructions of defilement, and later, by [means of] this, they can see. "The icchantika first crushes out the icchantika [i.e. ceases to be an icchantika within himself] and then he gains the ten powers, the four fearlessnesses, Great Compassion, and the three thinkings. That is why I always say that all beings posssess the Buddha-Nature. "O good man! All beings have, all-equally, the 12 links of interdependence. These are the cases of the interior and the exterior. "What are the 12? "Defilement from the past is called ignorance ["avidya"]. "Karma from the past is called mental formation ["samskara" - i.e. mental volitions and impulses]. "In this present life, we first gain life in the womb. This is consciousness ["vijnana"]. "After entering the womb, the five parts [i.e. the five limbs or the five parts of the human body, made up of two hands, two feet, and one head] and the four roots [i.e. the four sense-organs of the eye, ear, nose, and mouth] are not yet perfectly formed. This state is called mind-and-body ["nama-rupa"]. "When one has the four roots and when one is not yet in the stage of touch ["sparsa"], this stageis called the six spheres ["sadayatana"]. "When no feeling of suffering or joy has as yet arisen, this stage is called that of

touch. "When one gets attached to a single love, this stage is called feeling ["vedana"]. "When one learns and befriends the five desires, this is craving ["trsihna"]. "When one looks in and out, and has cleaving [i.e. attachment], this is cleaving ["upadana" - clinging]. "When one raises actions in and out in the three categories of body, mouth and mind, this is existence ["bhava"]. "The consciousness that one has in this life is [one's] birth for the days to come [i.e. one's worldly consciousness provides the basis for one's future rebirth], and the body-and-mind, the six spheres, touch, and feeling are the old age, illness, and death of the future. These are the 12 links of interdependence. "O good man! Although there are these 12 links of interdependent arising, there are cases where things do not so come about. When one dies at the kalala stage, there cannot be the twelve. There can be the twelve when one gets into the stages beginning with birth and ending with old age and death. "The beings of the world of form do not possess the three kinds of feeling, the three of touch, the three of craving, and there is no old age and no illness. And we can indeed say that there are the twelve. "The beings of the world of non-form do not have anything of "matter", and there is no ageing and no death. And we can also say that there are the twelve. Because this is gained through meditation. And we can indeed say that beings all-equally possess the 12 links of interdependence. "O good man! The case is the same with the Buddha-Nature. As all beings can definitely gain unsurpassed Enlightenment, I teach and say that beings have the Buddha-Nature. "O good man! There is a grass called "ninniku" in the Himalayas. If a cow eats it, that cow will bring forth sarpirmanda. There is a different kind of grass, which, when eaten, does not bring forth sarpirmanda. Although no sarpirmanda comes forth [in such an instance], we cannot say that there is no ninniku in the Himalayas. It is the same with the Buddha-Nature. "The Himalayas are the Tathagata, the ninniku is Great Nirvana, the foreign grass is the 12 types of sutra. If beings give ear to, and respect and praise, Mahaparinirvana, they will see the Buddha-Nature. Even if it is not found in the 12 types of sutra, we cannot say that there is no Buddha-Nature.

"O good man! The Buddha-Nature is matter, non-matter, non-matter-and-not-non-matter.

"Also, it is a phase of appearance, no phase of appearance, no-phase-of-appearance-and-not-no-phase-of-appearance.

"Also, it is one, not-one, not-one-and-not-not-one."

""Also, it is non-eternal and non-disruption, not-non-eternal-and-not-non-disruption.

"It is "is", "is-not", not "is"-and-not-"is-not".

"Also, it is an ending, non-ending, non-ending-and-not-non-ending.

"Also, it is cause, it is result, and it is no-cause-and-no-result.

"Also, it is signification, non-signification, non-signification-and-not-non-signification.

"Also, it is a letter, non-letter, non-letter-and-not-non-letter.

"Why is it matter? Because it is the Adamantine Body.

"Why is it non-matter? Because it is of the Buddha's 18 independent characteristics and is of the category of non-matter.

"Why is it non-matter-and-not-non-matter? Because it has nothing to do with matter, non-matter, and because it has no fixed form.

"Why is it the phase of appearance? Because it has the 32 signs of perfection.

"Why is it that it has no phase of appearance? Because it displays no phase of showing the appearance of all beings.

"Why is it that it has no-phase-of-appearance-and-not-no-phase-of-appearance? Because there is no fixed phase of appearance or not no-fixed-phase-of-appearance.

"Why is it one? Because all beings ride in the One Vehicle.

"Why is it not one? Because three vehicles are spoken of.

"Why is it not-one-and-not-not-one? Because there is no way of counting.

"Why is it non-eternal? Because things are seen by causal relations.

"Why is it non-disruption? Because it is segregated from the world-view of disruption.

"Why is it not-non-eternal-and-not-non-disruption "[the concept of "disruption" is used here for the Japanese term, "dan", which represents the notion of disruption of continuation. It stands in opposition to the term, "eternal", which is the continuation of an existence or rather the endlessness of an existence.]" Because there is no-end and no-beginning.

"Why do we say "is"? Because there do actually exist all beings.

"Why is it "not-is"? Because one can see it "[i.e. the Buddha-Nature]" by dint of the best expedient.

"Why is it "not-is" and "°not-not-is"? This is because of the nature of the All-Void.

"Why "[i.e. in what sense]" is it that it ends? Because one gains the Suramgama Samadhi.

"Why is it non-ending? Because of the Eternal.

"Why is it non-ending-and-not-non-ending? Because all endings are done away with.

"Why is it the cause? Because the cause is known.

"Why is it the result? Because the result is fixed.

"Why is it non-cause-and-non-result? Because it is the Eternal.

"Why is it signification? Because all are taken into the unhinderedness of signification.

"Why is it non-signification? Because it is not possible to explain "[it].

"Why is it non-signification-and-not-non-signification? Because it is the ultimate All-Void.

"Why is it a letter? Because it has a name to represent "[it].

""Why is it a non-letter? Because the name has no name which it can have.

"Why is it non-letter-and-not-non-letter? Because it is segregated from the category of letters.

"Why is it non-Suffering-and-non-Bliss? Because it is away from feeling.

"Why is it non-Self? Because there is no arriving at the eight unmolestednesses "[Japanese "hachidaijizaigi": the eight aspects of unmolestedness or non-restriction which the Self - one of the four attributes of Nirvana - is considered to possess].

"Why is it not non-Self? Because of the quality of the Eternal.

"Why is it non-Self and not non-Self? Because of non-doing and non-receiving.

"Why is it Voidness? Because of "Paramartha-satya".

"Why is it non-Voidness? Because of the Eternal.

"Why is it non-Voidness-and-not-non-Voidness? Because it indeed serves as the seed of Wonderful Dharma.

"O good man! If any person can meditate upon and understand the signification of the Sutra of Great Nirvana, know that this person sees the Buddha-Nature.

"The Buddha-Nature is inconceivable. It is the world of the All-Buddha-Tathagata. It is not within the compass of conception of sravakas and pratyekabuddhas."

"O good man! The Buddha-Nature is not within the category of the five skandhas, the 18 realms, or the 12 spheres. It is not what originally was not but is now, nor is it what originally was but is now no longer. It is what beings can only see through causal relations.

"For example, it is like iron, which, when in the fire, is red, but when not and is cooled, is black as before. And this black colour does not exist inside or out. It comes about thus by causal relations. The same is the case with the Buddha-Nature. When the fire of defilement has gone, all beings can see [it].

"O good man! It is as in the case of a seed. The bud comes out and the seed dies. And the nature of the bud exists neither in nor out. It is the same with the flower and with the fruit. This comes out thus, since things are based on causal relations.

"O good man! This All-Wonderful Sutra of Great Nirvana is perfect in innumerable virtues. It is the same with the Buddha-Nature. It accomplishes and is perfect in innumerable virtues."

Then, Bodhisattva-mahasattva Lion's Roar said: "O World-Honoured One! How many laws [dharmas] does a Bodhisattva need to accomplish by [means of] which he can see the Buddha-Nature, yet not very clearly? How many laws does the All-Buddha-World-Honoured One need to accomplish by [means of] which he can see it clearly?" "O good man! If the Bodhisattva accomplishes 10 things, he will be able to see the Buddha-Nature, and yet to a lesser degree. What are the 10? They are: 1) desiring little, 2) feeling satisfied, 3) quietude, 4) effort, 5) right remembrance, 6) right samadhi, 7) right Wisdom, 8) emancipation, 9) praising emancipation, 10) succouring beings with Great Nirvana." Bodhisattva Lion's Roar said: "O World-Honoured One! What difference is there between desireing little and feeling satisfied?" "O good man! Desiring little is not seeking and not taking; feeling satisfied is not feeling regret when one gains little. Desiring little is having little; feeling satisfied means that the mind does not become worried by the things offered. "O good man! Of desire, there are three kinds, which are: 1) evil desire, 2) great desire, 3) desire for desire's sake. We say "evil desire". A bhiksu may gain greed in his mind, become the head of a great mass [of people], make all priests follow him, make all the four classes of the Buddhist Sangha make offerings unto him, respect, praise, and make much of him, make him preach, first of all others,

before the four classes of the Sangha, make all believe in his words, make kings, ministers and rich people pay respect to him, so that they may give him an abundance of clothing, food, drink, bedding, medicine, and the very best types of accommodation. These are desires relative to the temporal life of birth and death. This is evil desire. "What is great desire? For example, there is a bhiksu who gains greed in his mind, so that he makes himself known among the four classes of the Buddhist Sangha as one who has attained the stage of the first abode [stage] up to the tenth, unsurpassed Bodhi, arhatship, or such others as the [stage of] srotapanna, the four dhyanas, or the fourfold unhindered knowledge - all this is merely for the sake of profit. This is great desire. "A bhiksu may desire to be born as a Brahma, as Marapapiyans, as an Isvara, a Chakravartin, a Kshatriya, or a Brahmin, so that he can have unrestrictedness. As this is but for profit, such a desire can well be called one for desire's sake. "If a person is not despoiled by these three evil desires, such a person is one with little desire to possess. By desire is meant the 25 cravings. If a person does not have these 25 cravings, such a person is called one who has little desire to possess. When a person does not seek to possess what he may well expect to have in the days to come, we call this seeking little to possess. The person gains, but does not cling. This is feeling satisfied. Not seeking to be respected is seeking little to possess. A person may obtain things, but if he does not seek to hoard them up, this is feeling satisfied. "O good man! There is a situation where one has little seeking to possess, but which cannot be called a state where one is satisfied; and also there is a situation where one is satisfied, and yet this is not what one could well call a state where one is satisfied. Also, there is a situation where one has little seeking to possess and yet is satisfied; also, there is a situation where one does not have little seeking to possess and is not satisfied. Seeking little to possess refers to the srotapanna, and feeling satisfied refers to the pratyekabuddha. Seeking little to possesss and not feeling satisfied refers to the so-called Bodhisattva. "O good man! There are two kinds of seeking to possess and feeling satisfied. The one is good, and the other non-good. Non-good refers to the so-called common mortal, and good to the holy persons and the Bodhisattvas. All holy persons may gain the fruition of the way they have practised, but they will not praise what they have gained. As they do not praise, their minds do not have any worry. This is feeling satisfied. "O good man! The Bodhisattva-mahasattva studies and practises the Mahayana Sutra of Great Nirvana and sees the Buddha-Nature. Because of this, he practises the way of seeking little to possess and feeling satisfied. "What is quietude? There are two kinds of it. One is quietude of mind, and the other quietude of body. "By quietude of body is meant not performing the three evils with the body; by quietude of mind is meant not committing the three evils with the mind. This is having quietude in body and mind. "Quietude of body means not befriending the four classes of the Sangha, not taking part in the work done by the four classes of the Sangha. By quietude of the mind is meant not generating greed, anger and ignorance. This is quietude of body and mind. "There may be a bhiksu whose body may find quietude, but whose mind does not find it. Or the mind may be in quietude, but not the body. Or there are cases where the body and mind are in quietude; or where the body and mind are not in quietude. "We may say that the body is in quietude, but the mind is not. For example, a bhiksu sits in dhyana [meditation], segregating himself from the four classes of the Sangha. But the mind may yet always generate greed, anger and ignorance. This is what we call the body's being in quietude but the mind's not. "We say that

the mind is in quietude, but the body is not. This alludes to the situation where a bhiksu might befriend the four classes of the Sangha, kings, and ministers, and segregates himself from greed, anger and ignorance. This is where we speak of the mind's being in quietude but the body's not. "We say that body and mind are in quietude. This refers to the Buddha and Bodhisattvas. "We say that the body and mind are both not in quietude. This refers to all common mortals. Why? Because common mortals may well enjoy quietude in body and mind. Yet they cannot meditate deeply on the non-Eternal, non-Bliss, non-Self, and the non-Pure. For this reason, common mortals cannot have quietude in their actions of body, mouth and mind. "Such classes of people as the icchantika, those who have committed the four grave offences, and those of the five deadly sins also cannot be called those whose body and mind are in quietude. "What is effort? There is a bhiksu who desires to purify the actions of his body, mouth and mind, and segregates himself from all evil deeds, amassing all good deeds. This is effort. One such focuses his mind on the six spheres, which are: 1) Buddha, 2) Dharma, 3) Sangha, 4) sila [moral precepts], 5) offerings, 6) heaven. This is right thinking. The samadhi resultant from right thinking is right meditation. One abiding in right meditation sees all things as Void. This is right Wisdom. One perfect in right Wisdom segregates his self from all the bonds of defilement. This is Emancipation. "The person who has gained Emancipation praises it to all beings and says that this Emancipation is Eternal and Unchanging. This is the correct praising of Emancipation. This is unsurpassed Mahaparinirvana. ""Nirvana is none other than the extinction of the fire of all the bonds of defilement. "Also, Nirvana is called a house. Why? Because it well protects one from the evil winds and rains of defilement. "Also, Nirvana is a refuge. Why? Because it is well beyond all fears of the world. "Also, Nirvana is a sand-dune. Why? Because the four madding floods of water cannot wash it away. What the these four? They are? 1) the storm of desire, 2) the storm of existence, 3) the storm of the "[wrong] "views of life, 4) the storm of ignorance. For this reason, Nirvana is called the sand-dune. "Also, Nirvana is the final refuge. Why? Because one arrives at absolute Bliss. If a Bodhisattvamahasattva accomplishes, and is perfect in, these ten things, he will see the Buddha-Nature, but not quite clearly". "Also, next,

O good man! Those who have fled from worldly life suffer from four illnesses. Because of this, they are unable to arrive at the four fruitions of a bhiksu. What are the four illnesses? These are the four evil desires for: 1) clothing, 2) food, 3) bedding, 4) existence. These are the four evil desires. These are the illnesses of those who have abandoned worldly life. "There are four good medicines which will cure these well. "The pamsukula [i.e. Buddhist robe made from abandoned cloth] well cures the bhiksu's evil craving for clothing. "Alms-begging well cures the evil craving for food.

"The shade under a tree cures the evil craving for bedding. "Quietude of body and mind well cures the bhiksu's evil craving for existence. "By these four good medicines, a person can indeed make away with the four illnesses. These are the holy actions. Such holy actions are seeking to possess little and feeling satisfied. "Quietude comprises four blisses. What are the four? They are: 1) bliss of fleeing from worldly life, 2) bliss of quietude, 3) bliss of eternal extinction [of defilements], 4) ultimate Bliss. These four are quietude. These call forth four efforts. So we say "effort". It accompanies four thinkings. So, we speak of right thinkings. As it accompanies four dhyanas, we say right meditation. We see four Holy Truths. So, we say right Wisdom. This thoroughly makes away with all bonds of defilement. So, we speak of Emancipation. As it reproaches the wrongs of all defilements, we speak of the praising of Emancipation. O good man! The Bodhisattva-mahasattva peacefully abides in all these ten things., and he can see the Buddha-Nature, but not very clearly. "Also, next, O good man! The Bodhisattva-mahasattva, having listened well to this sutra, befriends it, practises the Way, and segregates himself from worldly life. This is seeking little to possess. Renouncing the world, he feels no regret. This is feeling satisfied. Feeling satisfied, he seeks lonely places and segregates himself from all noise. This is all-silent quietude. Those who do not feel satisfied do not desire to be in a lonely and quiet place; those who are satisfied seek a lonely and quiet place. In a quiet place, he [i.e. the Bodhisattva] always thinks: "People all say that I have attained the end of a sramana's quest of the Way. But I have not yet reached it. How could I now deceive others?" Thinking thus, he makes effort and learns the end of a sramana's

attainment of the Way. This is effort. "One who befriends and practises the Way of Great Nirvana is one who abides in right thinking. He follows the way of heaven. This is right meditation. He abides in this samadhi and sees things rightly. This is right Wisdom. One who sees things rightly thoroughly cuts off the bond of defilement. This is Emancipation. The Bodhisattva of the ten stages truly praises Nirvana. This is the praising of Emancipation. O good man! The Bodhisattva-mahasattva abides in these ten items and sees the Buddha-Nature, yet not clearly. "Also, next, O good man! We speak of seeking to possess but little. A bhiksu sits in a lonely and quiet place. He sits rigidly and does not recline. Or he lives under a tree, or amidst graves, or in the open; or he sits on grass. He goes alms-begging, begs for food, and having partaken of it, he is satisfied. Or it may be one meal for a sitting. He only keeps three robes, which are those made from abandoned rags or woolen cloth. This is seeking to possess but little. Living thus, he does not feel regret. This is feeling satisfied. He practises the samadhi of the Void. This is quietude. Perfect in the four fruitions, he has no moment of rest from attaining unsurpassed Bodhi. This is effort. "His mind set, he meditates on the fact that the Tathagata is the Eternal and that he is Unchanging. This is right thinking. He practises the eight emancipations. This is right dhyana. He gains the four unhinderednesses. This is right Wisdom. He segregates himself from the seven defilements. This is Emancipation. He praises Nirvana and says that Nirvana does not possess the ten aspects of life. This is praising Emancipation. The ten aspects of life are: birth, ageing, illness, death, colour, sound, smell, taste, touch, and impermanence. When one is segregated from these ten, we say that we have attained Nirvana. O good man! This is why we say that when the Bodhisattva-mahasattva abides in and perfects the ten items, he sees the Buddha-Nature, but not clearly. "Also, next, O good man! Due to much craving, a person associates with kings, ministers, rich men, Kshatriyas, Brahmins, Vaishyas, and Sudras, and says: "I have attained the fruitions of the srotapanna up to arhatship". For profit, he walks, stands, sits, reclines, and answers the call of nature. Seeing a danapati, he shows respect, approaches and talks. One who breaks away from evil cravings is one who has little craving. Although he has not done away with bonds and worries, he indeed goes where the Tathagata goes. This is feeling satisfied. "O good man! The above two are the nearest causal relations for thinking of meditation. Teachers and students always praise them. I, too, in the sutras, have praised these two items. Any person who can be perfect in these two items draws close to the gates of Nirvana. This extends to the five blisses. This is quietude. One who rigidly upholds sila [morality] is called one who makes effort. One who repents is one of right thinking. One who sees no aspect of mind is one in right meditation. One who does not seek the characteristics and causal relations of all things is one of right Wisdom. As there is no exterior aspect, defilement goes away. This is Emancipation. Thus praising the Sutra of Gret Nirvana is called the praising of Emancipation. O good man! This is what [we mean when] we say that the Bodhisattva-mahasattva peacefully abides in the ten items and sees the Buddha-nature, though not yet quite clearly. "O good man! You ask: "With what eye does the Bodhisattva of the ten stages see the Buddha-Nature, but see it not quite clearly, and with what eye does the World-Honoured One see the Buddha-Nature clearly?" O good man! With the Eye of Wisdom one sees it not quite clearly; with the Buddha-Eye, one sees it clearly. When one is in Bodhi practice, there is no clearness; with nothing to practise, one sees all clearly. When one has nothing more to practise, one sees clearly. When one abides in the ten stages, one does not see quite clearly. When one does not need to stand or move about, clearness comes about. Because of the causal relations of Wisdom, the Bodhisattva-mahasattva cannot see clearly. The All-Buddha-World-Honoured One is out of the realm of causal relations. It is due to this that he sees clearly. One awakened to all things is the Buddha-Nature. The Bodhisattva of the ten stages cannot be called awakened to all things. Because of this, though he sees, he does not see things clearly. "O good man! Of seeing, there are two kinds. One is seeing with the eye; the other is hearing and seeing. The All-Buddha-World-Honoured One sees the Buddha-Nature with the eye, in the [same] way in which one sees an amra [mango] that is in one's own hand. The Bodhisattva of the ten stages sees the Buddha-Nature through hearing. Hence, not quite clearly. The Bodhisattva of the ten stages knows well that he will definitely attain unsurpassed Enlightenment. And yet he does not know that all beings have the Buddha-Nature. "O good man! Further, there is seeing by means of the eye. The All-Buddha-Tathagata and the Bodhisattva of the ten stages see the Buddha-Nature with the eye. Also, there is hearing and seeing. All beings and those of the ninth "bhumi" [stage] hear and see the Buddha-Nature. The Bodhisattva may hear that all beings possess the Buddha-Nature. But if he does not believe in this, this is no hearing and seeing."

Chapter Thirty-Four: On Bodhisattva Lion's Roar 2

"O good man! If any good man or woman desires to see the Tathagata, he or she must study the 12 types of sutra, uphold, recite, copy and expound them". Bodhisattva-mahasattva Lion's Roar said: "O World-Honoured One! All beings do not know the state of mind of the Tathagata. How do we meditate and come to know [this]?" "O good man! All beings, in truth, do not come to know of the mental state of the Tathagata. If they desire to meditate and know, there are two ways. One is to see with the eye and the other through hearing. If one sees the bodily actions of the Tathagata, know that this is the Tathagata. This is seeing with the eye. If one comes across the oral actions of the Tathagata, know that this is the Tathagata. This is to hear him, and see. "One may come across a visage which is beyond that of man - know that this is the Tathagata. This is to see with the eye. "One may hear a voice which is all so wonderful and superb and which is not of the human kind - know that this is that of the Tathagata. This is to see him through hearing. "One may happen to see the Tathagata's miraculous power manifested before one. How could it be other than for the sake of beings, rather than for profit? If it is for the sake of beings and not for profit, know that this is the Tathagata. This is seeing with the eye. "One meditates upon the Tathagata, who sees humankind with mind-reading knowledge. Does he speak of Dharma for profit and not for beings' sake? If it is for the sake of beings and not for profit, know that this is the Tathagata. This is seeing through hearing. "How does the Tathagata gain the carnal body? Why does he gain it? For whom does he gain it? This is seeing with the eye. "How does the Tathagata speak about Dharma? Why does he speak about Dharma? To whom does he speak about Dharma? Thus do we meditate. This is seeing him by hearing. "Evil bodily actions are directed [at him], and there arises no anger. Know that this is the Tathagata. This is seeing with the eye. "Evil oral actions are directed [at him]. But there is no anger. Know that this is the Tathagata. This is seeing by hearing. "When the Bodhisattva is first born into the world, he takes seven steps in the ten directions, and the demon generals, Manibhadra and Purnabhadra, carry banners, at which innumerable boundless worlds shake and a golden light brightly fills the sky. The naga kings, Nanda and Upananda, with their divine powers, bathe the Bodhisattva's body. All the gods show their bodies. They come and pay homage. Rishi Asita folds his hands and pays homage. In the prime of manhood, he [Siddhartha] abandons desires as if they were like tears and spittle. He is not bothered by worldly pleasures. He abandons his home, practises the Way, and seeks quietude. In order to crush twisted views, he undergoes austerities for six years. He sees all beings with an all-equal eye, not with two minds. His mind is always in samadhi and there is no moment in which his mind breaks. He looks serene and splendid; thus is his body adorned. Wherever he goes, the land is flat. His clothing parts from his body but by four inches and it does not drop down. When walking, he looks straight ahead, not looking to right or left. What he does is done with aptitude and nothing [is done which] goes beyond what is necessary. Where he sits and stands up, the grass does not move. To teach beings, he moves about and dwells upon Dharma. He displays no arrogance. This is seeing with the eye. "The Bodhisattva, as he takes his seven steps, says: "The body that I now have is the last of all that I will have." Asita folds his hands and says: "Know, O great King! Prince Siddhartha is certain to gain unsurpassed Enlightenment. He will not remain at home and become a Chakravartin. Why not? Because his visage is clear and bright. The Chakravartin does not look clear and bright. The bodily form of Prince Siddhartha is bright and outstanding. For this reason, he will unfailingly attain unsurpassed Enlightenment. He will see old age, illness, death, and will say: "I pity seeing all beings living thus. Birth, old age, illness and death follow one upon the other. And they cannot see; they always suffer. I shall now cut off the bond." Under Aradakalama, who is perfect in the five divine powers, he practises thoughtlessness samadhi ["asamjna-samapatti"]. Having attained it, he says that this is not the Way to Nirvana, but that of birth and death. For six years he practises this austerity, and gains nothing. If true, I must be able to gain it. Being false, I gain nothing. This is a twisted way, and not the right one. Having attained Enlightenment, Brahma comes and asks: "O Tathagata! Please open the gates of amrta [the deathless] and teach unsurpassed Dharma." The

Buddha says: "O Brahma! All beings are always in the shadow of defilement. They are unable to give ear to my Wonderful Dharma." Brahma further says: "O World-Honoured One! There are three kinds of being, namely: 1) sharp-witted, 2) middle-witted, 3) slow-witted. The sharp-witted will be receptive. Please condescend to preach." The Buddha says: "O Brahma! Listen carefully, listen carefully! I shall now, for beings' sake, open the gates of immortality." And at Varanasi, he turns the Wheel of Dharma and proclaims the Middle Path. All beings do not destroy the bond of defilement. It is not that they cannot destroy it. It is not that it is destroyed, nor is it that it is not destroyed. Hence, the Middle Path. It does not pass beings to the other shore, nor is it that it cannot pass beings to the other shore. Hence, the Middle Path. Whatever is taught, there is no saying that one is a teacher, nor is one the disciple. Hence, the Middle Path. Whatever is taught is not for profit, nor is it that fruition should come about there. This is the Middle Path. It is right speech, real words, timely words and true words. No word is spoken in a false way. It is all-wonderful and supreme. To hear such words is to see by hearing. "O good man! The state of the Tathagata's mind truly cannot be seen. Should any good man or good woman desire to see [it], he or she must depend upon these two kinds of causal relations." Then Bodhisattva LIon's Roar said to the Buddha: "O World-Honoured One! You employed just now the simile of the amra fruit and compared it to the four beings, whose: 1) actions are minute, but their mind is not right, 2) their mind is minute, but their action is not right, 3) their mind is minute and their action is also minute, 4) their mind is not minute and their action is also not right. How might we know of the first two? You, the Buddha, say that you are grounded on these two. This is hard to know." The Buddha said: "Well said, well said! I compare the two kinds of man to the amra. This is indeed difficult to know. As it is difficult to know, I say in the sutra: "Live together. Should a person not be able to come to know by living together, give time and live long. If not gained by living long, work out Wisdom. If Wisdom cannot cleave a way to knowing, meditate deeply. Through meditation a person can see well what is pure in sila [moral behaviour] and what violates sila." "O good man! By these four items of: living together, living long, Wisdom, and meditation, one can come to know of true and the not-true sila. O

good man! There are two kinds of sila and two kinds of person who uphold sila. One is absolute and the other non-absolute. If a person only upholds sila through causal relations, the wise should ask themselves whether this person's upholding of sila is for the sake of profit or the absolute upholding of sila. O good man! The sila of the Tathagata has nothing to do with causal relations. That is why we say "absolute sila". On account of this, even when attacked by any evil one, the Bodhisattva does not get molested by anger. For this reason, we can say that the Tathagata's unchanging sila is absolute sila. "O good man! I once lived in Magadha, in the great castle of Campa, together with Sariputra and his disciples. There was then a hunter who was after a dove. Frightened, this dove came to hide under the robe of Sariputra and shook like a plantain tree. It then came within the shadow-length of me, and his body and mind found peace, with fear all gone. Know, therefore, that the Tathagata is one who eternally upholds sila, so that his shadow possesses this power. "O good man! Non-absolute sila cannot even gain one the stage of a sravaka or pratyekabuddha. And how can such ever hope to attain unsurpassed Enlightenment? "Again, there are two kinds. One is for profit and the other for Wonderful Dharma. One upholds sila for profit. Know that with this sila one cannot see the Tathagata and the Buddha-Nature. One may hear the names of the Buddha-Nature and the Tathagata, but this cannot be called seeing through hearing. If one upholds sila for Wonderful Dharma, know that one, through this, will see the Buddha-Nature and the Tathagata. This is seeing with the eye and also seeing by hearing. "Again, there are two kinds. One is deep-rooted, which is hard to uproot; and the other shallow-rooted, which is easy to move. If one practises the samadhis of birthlessness, deathlessness, and desirelessness, it is hard to uproot. One may practise these three samadhis, but if it is for the sake of the 25 existences, this is what is shallow-rooted and easy to move. "Again, there are two kinds. One person performs [sila] for his own sake, and the other for the sake of other beings. If performed for other beings, one will see the Buddha-Nature and the Tathagata. "There are two kinds amongst those who uphold sila. One is the person who by nature thoroughly upholds [sila] and the other is the person who acts under the injunctions given by others. When one receives sila, one, for innumerable ages, does not lose it. One may be born in an evil country, or one may encounter an evil friend, an evil time, evil age, or evil teaching, or one may sit together with those abiding in evil views on life. There may be, at that time, no law [dharma] of receiving sila. Yet, the person practises the Way just as before and does not transgress. This is the case of how one upholds [sila]. Or one may be given sila to observe by a teacher-priest or by jnapti-caturtha [ritual of receiving sila]. Even when one has received this sila, one always decides upon consulting the words of the teacher, good comrades and friends. One is perfect in the way of listening and in delivering sermons. Such is the case called acting under guidance of others. "O good man! One who by nature thoroughly upholds sila sees, with his own eyes, the Buddha-Nature and the Tathgata. Also, this is seeing through hearing. There are two kinds. One is the sravaka's sila and the other that of the Bodhisattva. One such attains the first aspiration and up to unsurpassed Enlightenment. This is the sila of the Bodhisattva. If one meditates on white bones, one attains arhatship. This is the case of the sravaka sila. One who upholds sravaka sila does not, one should know, see the Buddha-Nature and the Tathagata. Any person who upholds the sila of the Bodhisattvas, we may know, attains unsurpassed Enlightenment and sees well the Buddha-Nature, the Tathagata, and Nirvana." Bodhisattva Lion's Roar said: "O World-Honoured One! Why do we uphold the prohibitive sila?" The Buddha said: "O good man! "This is so the mind does not repent. Why does one not repent? Because one gains bliss. How does one gain bliss? This comes from segregation. Why do we need to seek segregation? To gain peace. How does one gain peace? Through meditation. Why do we meditate? To gain true knowing and seeing. In what way do we have true knowing and seeing? By seeing the many wrongs and worries of birth and death. This is for our mind not to cling greedily. Why do we need to have our mind not cling greedily? Because we gain Emancipation. How "[i.e. in what sense; by what means]" do we gain Emancipation? By gaining unsurpassed Great Nirvana. How do we gain unsurpassed Great Nirvana? By gaining the Eternal, Bliss, the Self, and the Pure. Why do we say that we gain the Eternal, Bliss, the Self, and the Pure? Because of gaining birthlessness and deathlessness. How do we gain birthlessness and deathlessness? By

seeing the Buddha-Nature. Thus, the Bodhisattva, by nature, upholds the absolute purity of sila [morality]." "O good man! The bhiksu who upholds sila may not take a vow to gain the unregretting mind, but the unregretting mind will come about of itself. Why? Because the law nature [Dharma nature] spontaneously effects things to be [thus]. Though he may not particularly seek to arrive at segregation, peace, samadhi, knowing and seeing, seeing the wrongs of birth and death, the mind which does not greedily settle upon [things], arriving at emancipation, Nirvana, the Eternal, Bliss, the Self, and the Pure, birthlessness and deathlessness, and the Buddha-Nature, yet all of these will spontaneously come about. Why? Because of the all-naturalness of the law nature." Bodhisattva Lion's Roar said: "O World-Honoured One! If one gains the unregretting fruition of upholding sila and the fruition of Nirvana by Emancipation, sila has no cause to tell of and Nirvana no fruition to tell of. If sila has not cause to tell of, this is the Eternal, and if Nirvana has some cause to tell of, it must be non-eternal. If so, Nirvana is what originally was not, but is now, and if it is what originally was not, but is now, it must be non-eternal. This is like the light of a lamp. If Nirvana were anything like that, how could we say that it is the Self, Bliss, and the Pure?" The Buddha said: "Well said, well said, O good man! You have already sown good seeds in the past at the places of innumerable Buddhas and you now are able to put questions of deep meaning to the Tathagata. O good man! You do not make away with the original thought that you had, and you thus ask. I call to mind that in days gone by, innumerable kalpas ago, there appeared a Buddha at Varanasi who was called "Well-Gained". At the time, this Buddha delivered a sermon on the Great Nirvana Sutra in the course of 3 billion years. I, along with you, was among those congregated there. I then asked the Buddha this question. Then, the Tathagata, for the sake of beings, was in right samadhi and did not reply. O great one! You retain this old story of olden days well in mind. Listen carefully, listen carefully! I shall now tell you. "This sila also has a cause. Because it arises out of listening to Wonderful Dharma. The fact that one listens to Wonderful Dharma is also a cause. This arises from making friends with a good friend. One's associating with a good friend is the cause. This arises out of faith. Having faith is also a cause. "There are two kinds of cause. One is listening to a sermon, and the other is thinking over its meaning. "O good man! Faith arises out of listening to Dharma, and this listening is grounded in faith. These two are cause and cause of cause. Also, they are result and result of result. O good man! The Nirgranthas protest and put forward the case of a pot and say that each serves as the cause and effect and each cannot part from the other. The case stands thus. "Ignorance" ["avidya"] has causal relations with [i.e. ignorance causes] "volitional impulses" ["samskara"], and volitional impulses with ignorance. Now, this case of ignorance and volitional impulses is cause, and cause of cause, and also effect, and effect of effect. And birth is causally related to age-and-death, and age-and-death to birth. And birth and age-and-death are cause and cause of cause, and are effect and also the effect of effect. The case is thus. "O good man! Birth indeed calls forth things. There can be no birth by itself. It cannot come about by itself. Birth comes about dependent on birth. Birth-birth cannot so come about by itself. It is dependent upon a birth. Thus, the two births too are cause, and also cause of cause; and the effect is effect of effect. "O good man! The case of faith and listening to Dharma is thus. O good man! This is effect and is not cause; it is Great Nirvana. "Why do we say effect? Because this is the best fruit, the fruition of a sramana, that of a Brahmin, because it uproots birth-and-death. Because the person excises defilement. Because of this, we say result. It gets reproached by all kinds of defilement. Hence, we say that Nirvana is the result. We call defilement the wrong of the wrong. "O good man! Nirvana has no cause. It is the result. Why so? Because there is no birth-and-death. Because there is no action performed and because it is uncreated. It is a Non-Create. It is Eternal and Unchanging. It has no place where it exists [i.e. it is not limited to a particular place, it cannnot be pinned down to a specific location]. There is no beginning and no end. "O good man! If Nirvana has any cause that can be named, this is not Nirvana. "Van" ["Vana" of "Nir-vana"] means cause; the Nirvana of causal relations means "not". As there is no cause that can be named, we say Nirvana." Bodhisattva Lion's Roar said: "The Buddha says that Nirvana has no cause that can be named. But this is not so. If it is said that there is none, this answers to [corresponds to] the six significations. Firstly, we have the "ultimate not-is". This is as in the case in which all things have

no ultimate entity called "self" and no ultimate thing belonging to it. Second, it is nonexisting when it can exist. Hence, "none". This is as when people say: "There is no water in the river or pond; or there are no sun and moon." Third, as the amount is small - hence, "none". The people of the world say, when there is little salt, "saltless"; when sweetness is insignificant, we say "not sweet". Fourth, when one receives nothing, one says "none". The candala cannot uphold the teaching of the Brahmin. So we say: "There is no Brahmin [here]." Fifth, when one accepts an evil thing, we say "none". People say: "A person who accepts an evil thing is no sramana or Brahmin, because people do not call such a sramana or Brahmin." Sixth, because it cannot be compared. For example, if there is no white, we say black; when there is no brightness, we say ignorant. "O World-Honoured One! The case with Nirvana is thus. If said when there is no cause when there is. That is why we say Nirvana." The Buddha said: "O good man! You now speak of the six significations. You do not take up the case of ultimate nothingness and compare it with Nirvana. But you take up the case of nothingness in relation to reality. "O good man! The body of Nirvana has utterly no cause that can be named. It is as in the case where there is no self and nothing that could be named as belonging to one. "O good man! What obtains in the world and in Nirvana cannot bear comparison at all. So the six items cannot serve as comparison. "O good man! "All things do not have the "Self". But this Nirvana truly has the Self". For this reason, we say that Nirvana has no cause and yet the body is the result. This is the cause, and not the result. We call this the Buddha-Nature. As it is no result come about from a cause, it is the cause, but not the result. It is no result of a sramana. So, we say "non-result". "Why do we say "cause"? Because it is the revealed cause. "O good man! There are two kinds of cause. One is the cause of birth and the second the revealed cause. "Also, there is a cause of birth, which is the six paramitas and unsurpassed Enlightenment. "Also, there are the revealed causes, which are the six paramitas and the Buddha-Nature. "Also, there are the causes of birth, which are the Suramgama Samadhi and unsurpassed Enlightenment. "Also, there is the revealed cause, which is the Noble Eightfold Path and unsurpassed Enlightenment. "Also, there are the causes of birth, which are faith and the six paramitas." Lion's Roar said: "O World-

Honoured One! What do we mean when we say that we see the Tathagata and the Buddha-Nature about which you, the Buddha, speak? O World-Honoured One! The Tathagata has no carnal visage. He is not tall, not short, not white, not black; there is no direction to tell of. He is not the three worlds. He is not a created existence. He is not one that can be seen with the eye. How can one see [him]? The situation is the same with the Buddha-Nature." The Buddha siad: "O good man! There are two kinds of Buddha-body. One is Eternal, and the other is impermanent. The latter is one manifested through expediency for saving beings. This is to see with the eye. The Eternal refers to the emancipated body of the Tathagata-World-Honoured One! It is called one seen by the eye. It is also one seen by hearing. The Buddha-Nature, too, has two kinds, namely: 1) visible, 2) invisible. The visible is the case of the Bodhisattvas of the stage of the ten abodes and the All-Buddha-World-Honoured One; unable to be seen refers to the case of beings. Seeing with the eye refers to beings' Buddha-Nature seen by the Bodhisattvas of the stage of the ten abodes and the All-Buddha-Tathagata. Seeing by hearing refers to all beings, who hear that the Bodhisattva of the ninth abode has the Buddha-Nature. "The body of the Tathagata also has two kinds. One is the carnal and the other the non-carnal. The carnal is so called when the Tathagata gets emancipated. The non-carnal concerns the Tathagata who is segregated eternally from all kinds of carnal existence. "The Buddha-Nature also has two kinds: 1) rupa [form], 2) non-rupa. Rupa concerns unsurpassed Enlightenment, and non-rupa refers to all beings and the Bodhisattvas of the ten abodes. The Bodhisattvas of the ten abodes cannot see the Buddha-Nature very clearly. It is because of this that we class [this] as non-rupa. "O good man! The Buddha-Nature further has two kinds, which are: 1) rupa, and 2) non-rupa. Rupa concerns the Buddha and the Bodhisattvas and non-rupa all beings. Rupa refers to seeing with the eye, and non-rupa to seeing through hearing. The Buddha-Nature does not exist in and out; nor is it within or without. And yet it does not get lost or destroyed. That is why we say that all beings have the Buddha-Nature." Bodhisattva Lion's Roar said: "O World-Honoured One! The Buddha says that all beings possess the Buddha-Nature. There is butter in milk. It is as in the case of the vajra-guardsman [one of the gods, who holds a diamond

in his hand and protects the Buddhist teaching]. The Buddha-Nature of all Buddhas is pure sarpirmanda [ghee, or the most delicious, efficacious medicine]. Why does the Tathagata say that the Buddha-Nature exists neither inside nor out?" The Buddha said: "O good man! I too do not say that butter exists in milk. What I say is that butter comes out of milk. And so we say that there is butter." "O World-Honoured One! In all births, there is a season." "O good man! In the milk stage, there is no butter. So there is no butter, no clarified butter, and no sarpirmanda. All beings too call this milk. Hence, I say that there is no butter in milk. If there were, why do we not have two names and speak, for example, as we do of "two able smiths of gold and iron"? At the butter stage, there is no milk and it is not fresh butter, not clarified butter, and not sarpirmanda. Beings too say that it is butter and not milk, not fresh butter, not clarified butter, and not sarpirmanda. The same with sarpirmanda too. "O good man! Of causes, there are two kinds. One is the right cause, and the other the condition. We say right cause. We may compare this to milk which calls forth butter; and through the condition, we may call forth the quality of the sourish content and warmth. As it comes from milk, we say there is the quality of butter in milk." Lion's Roar said: "O World-Honoured One! If there is no nature of butter in milk, this will lead to our saying that it cannot be in the horn. Why is it that it does not come out of the horn?"

"O good man! The horn also calls forth butter. Why? I also say that there are two kinds of condition. One has the content of "ro" [vinegar, or the soursih content, or what may lead to the calling forth of a thing like curds], and the other that of "nan" [warmth]. As the nature of the horn is warmth, I say: "It indeed calls forth butter." Lion's Roar said: "O World-Honoured One! If the horn can indeed call forth [butter], why is it that one who seeks butter takes the milk and not the horn?" The Buddha said: "O good man! That is why I speak about the right cause and condition." Lion's Roar said: "If there is originally no nature of butter in milk, and now there is, and if if there is originally no amra in milk, why is it that it does not shoot forth a bud? This is because both did not have these from the very beginning." "O good man! Even here, the milk calls forth amra. If one sprinkles milk on amra, it grows five feet in a night. That is why I say that there are two causes [i.e. the cause and "by-cause", or condition]. O good man! If all things come about from one cause, how can you criticise and ask why amra does not come about in milk? O good man! The four great elements and all concrete things can be the elements of causal relations. Yet, each is different from the other and cannot be the same. For this reason, there does not come about amra in milk." "O World-Honoured One! You the Buddha say that there are two kinds of cause, which are: 1) right cause and 2) condition. What cause does the Buddha-Nature of beings serve?" "O good man! The Buddha-Nature of beings also has two causes. One is the right cause and the other the condition. The right cause corresponds to all beings; the condition is the six paramitas." Lion's Roar said: "O World-Honoured One! I now definitely know that milk contains in itself the nature of butter. Why? I see people of the world who seek butter take only milk and never water. From this we know that there is the nature of butter in milk." "O good man! What you say is not right. Why not? All beings who seek to see their face and features take only the sword." Lion's Roar said: "O World-Honoured One! For this reason, there is the nature of butter in milk. If there were no face and nothing of one's form in the sword, why should one take up the sword [to look into]?" The Buddha said: "O good man! If there definitely is the face and bodily form, why is it that there is the upside-down [image]? Vertically one sees the length, and crosswise one sees the width. If this is one's own face, how could it be long? If this face is that of some other person, how can one say that this is one's own? If it is the case that one sees by [means of] one's own face the face of someone else, why does one not see the face and form of a donkey?" "O World-Honoured One! The light of the eye reaches him, so that we see that the face is long." "O good man! And yet this light of the eye does not reach him. Why not? Because one sees the near and far at the same time. What stands in between is not seen. O good man! If the light reaches him and one can see, why is it that all beings do not get burnt by seeing fire? Do not gain doubt as when one sees a white thing far off and wonders whether it is a crane, a banner, a man, or a tree? How can it be that one sees a thing in the crystal and the fish and stones in deep water only if light comes in? If one sees without the light coming in, why is it that one sees a thing in the

crystal and that one cannot see what is beyond the wall? Because of this, we cannot say that the light of the eye reaches the object and that we can see. O good man! You say that there is butter in milk. But why is it that a vendor takes only the price of the milk and not that of butter? Why is it that one who sells a horse from the pasture sells it at the price of the horse from the pasture, but not at the price of the horse itself? O good man! There is a man with no son. So he takes in a woman. The woman gets impregnated [gets pregnant]. We cannot say that this is a woman because she gets impregnated. One may say: "Take this woman, because she has the quality of bearing a child." But this does not work out well. Why not? If there is the quality of having a child, there must come about a grandson. If there is to be a quality, this will mean that all are brothers. Why? Because all are born of the same person. That is why I say that a woman does not have any quality of a child. If there is the quality of butter in milk, why is it that one does not have the five tastes? If the seed of a tree has the quality of the 50-foot length of nyagrodha, why is it that one does not have the different forms and colours all at once from the time of the bud, stem, branch, leaf, flower and fruit? O good man! The colour of milk differs by the difference of time. So is it with the taste and fruit. The same with sarpirmanda. How can we say that milk has the quality of butter in it? O good man! For example, a man who must take butter on the morrow may have a sense of its smell today. The case where we say that milk definitely possesses the quality of butter also amounts to the same. "O good man! For example, it is as when we arrive at a letter, the conjoint result of pen, paper and ink. And yet, in this paper there is nothing that represents the letter itself. Originally, there is nothing of the letter [there]. Through causal relations, the letter first comes about. If there were anything of a letter, why did we need to depend upon so many causal relations? For example, it is like the colour green, which is the mixing together of blue and yellow. Know that these two did not originally have the quality of green. If there was that [quality] originally, why do we need to mix the two together and [thus] gain the colour? "O good man! It is just as beings gain life from food. But in this food, there is nothing of life, truth to tell. If there were originally life, there would have to be a thing called life when not yet partaken of. "O good man! There is no self of its own in all things. For this reason, I speak thus in a gatha: "What originally was not is now; What originally was is now not. There cannot be anything such as "is" That obtains in the Three Times." "O good man! All existences come about through causal relations and die out through causal relations. O good man! If it is true that all beings have the Buddha-Nature within, it will be as in my own case, where I have the Buddha-Body now. The Buddha-Nature of all beings is unbreakable, indestructible, cannot be drawn, cannot be grabbed hold of, cannot be tied or bound up. It is like space, which is also in all beings. All beings possess it. As there is nothing that hinders, one does not see this void. If beings did not have this void, there could not be any going, coming, walking, standing, sitting or reclining; and there could be no being born and growing up. That is why I say in this sutra that beings have the void. The world of void corresponds to voidness. The same with the Buddha-Nature of beings, too. The Bodhisattva of the ten abodes can see this somewhat. It is as in the case of the vajra-aksa. "O good man! The Buddha-Nature of beings is what all Buddhas can see; it is not what sravakas and pratyekabuddhas can know. All beings do not see the Buddha-Nature. That is why they are all bound up by defilement and repeat birth and death. When one sees the Buddha-Nature, no bonds of defilement can tie one up. Emancipation comes and one attains Great Nirvana." Bodhisattva Lion's Roar said: "O World-Honoured One! All beings possess the Buddha-Nature as in the case of the nature of butter which is in milk. If not, how could the Buddha say that there are two causes, i.e. 1) right cause and 2) condition? The condition has qualities: 1) sourness and 2) warmth. Space has no nature. Hence, no cause and no condition." The Buddha said: "O good man! If there is any nature of butter in milk, what condition and cause can there be?" Bodhisattva Lion's Roar said: "Because there is a nature. Because of this, there can be a condition and cause. Why? Because one desires to see clearly. The condtion or cause is none but the revealed cause. O World-Honoured One! In the dark, there already exist many things. When one desires to see, one makes use of a lamp. If nothing existed from the beginning, what would the light shine upon? In mud [i.e. clay] there is the pot. Because of this, a man with a water wheel, rope, or staff makes this the revealed cause. Or the seed of nyagrodha makes the earth, water and dung the revealed cause. The same with the sourish content or the warmth of milk. It can become a revealed cause. So, there can be a quality that precedes. By the help of the revealed cause, one can indeed see later. Because of this, one definitely knows of butter that exists beforehand in milk." "O good man! If milk definitely contains the nature of butter, this is the revealed cause. If this is a revealed cause, why does one need to have a thing revealed? O good man! If the nature of the revealed cause is revealed, it must always have [such] revealing. If there is no revealing of one's own self, how can one hope to reveal others? There are two kinds of revealed cause, which are: 1) to reveal for oneself and 2) to reveal others. If this is what is said, this is not so. Why not? The revealed cause can only be one. How can there be two? If it is two, we must know that milk too must have two. If there cannot be two in milk, how can there be two in the revealed cause?" Lion's Roar said: "O World-Honoured One! The people of the world may say: I was together with eight persons. The same is the case with the revealed cause. It reveals itself and reveals others." The Buddha said: "O good man! If the revealed cause must be that, it is not a revealed cause. Why not? One who conts his own self can also count the self of others. That is why one can say eight. And in this nature of matter, there is no phase of revealing. As there is no phase of revealing, only by the help of Wisdom can one count one's own self and that of others. Because of this, the revealed cause cannot reveal itself, and it does not reveal others. "O good man! If all beings have the Buddha-Nature, why does one need to practise innumerable virtues? If one says that to practise the Way is the revealed cause, this negates the claim that it is the same as butter. If one says that in the cause there is definitely the fruit, there can be no increase in sila [morality], samadhi [meditative absorption] and Wisdom. I see that worldly people originally do not possess sila, samadhi and Wisdom. These increase as one follows the words of the teacher and receives these, and by degrees these increase. One says that what the teacher teaches is the revealed cause, but at the time the teacher is teaching, the one who receives does not as yet have sila, samadhi and Wisdom. If this were [supposed] to be the revealing, this indicates that there was no revealing. How can one practise sila, samadhi and Wisdom and make these increase?" Bodhisattva Lion's Roar said: "If there is no revealed cause, how can one say that there is milk or butter?" "O good man! There are three ways to answer the blames [criticisms] of the world, which are: 1) reverberating answer, as is resorted to as in the following: "Why do we uphold sila? Because of the fact that one does not regret or one cares for Great Nirvana"; 2) silent answer, as when a Brahmacarin came to me and asked: "Is the self eternal?", when I maintained my silence; 3) doubting answer, as in: "If there are two revealed causes, why cannot there be two milks?" "O good man! I now resort to the reverberating answer: "Because the people of the world say that there are milk and butter and that one decidedly gains these. Because of this, we can say that there are milk and butter. It is the same with the Buddha-Nature, which one can actually see." Lion's Roar said: "What the Buddha says does not work out well. The past is already gone and the future has not yet come. How can we say that these exist? If this means what is to come about, this does not accord with reason. This is as when the people of the world say "sonless", when they see a person without a son. How can we say that all beings have the Buddha-Nature when they do not have it?" The Buddha said: "O good man! The past is an existence. For example, we plant a mandarin orange. It shoots out a bud and the seed dies. The bud is sweet; the fruit, too, is sweet. When ripe, it becomes sour. O good man! This taste of sourness does not exist in the seed or in the bud; nor is it in the raw fruit. When ripe in accordance with the quality it originally possesses, there come about the form, colour, the external appearances and the sour taste. And this sourness is what originally was not, but what now is. Even though not existing but now existing, this is not to say that there was not originally the quality as such. Thus, though the fruit derives from the past, we nevertheless can say that it is what exists. Because of this, we say that the past is what "is". "How can we call the future "is"? For example, a person sows sesame. People ask: "Why are you sowing this?" The person answers: "We [want to] have oil." Although the oil does not exist, we gain it when the sesame ripens, when we harvest the seeds, roast or pass them through steam, and pound or press them and we gain the oil. Know that we are not telling any lies. For this reason, we can say that there is a future "is". "How, again, can we say that the past has an "is"? O good man! A person speaks ill of the King in the former's

quarters. Years later, the King comes to hear of this. On hearing of this, he asks: "Why did you speak ill of me?" "O great King! I did not speak ill of you. The person who spoke ill of you is now dead." The King says: "Both the person who spoke ill of me and my own body exist. How can you say he is dead?" On account of this, the man loses his life. "O good man! These two actually do not exist, and yet the karmic result remains and is not dead. This is the past "is". How do we speak about the future "is"? For example, a person goes to a potter's and asks: "Have you a pot?" The answer comes back: "We have a pot." And yet, actually there is no pot. As the potter has the mud, he says that he has it. The case is analogous to this. Know that the person is not telling lies. There is butter in milk. It is the same with the Buddha-Nature of beings. If one wishes to see the Buddha-Nature, one must think of time, form and colour. For this reason, I say that all beings possess Buddha-Nature. There is nothing in this that is false." Lion's Roar said: "If beings do not have the Buddha-Nature, how can they attain unsurpassed Enlightenment? Because of the right cause. Through this, beings attain unsurpassed Enlightenment. What is the right cause. It is none other than the Buddha-Nature, O World-Honoured One! Even when the seed of nyagrodha contains within it the nyagrodha tree, we call it the nyagrodha seed. And why is it that we do not call it a khadira seed? O World-Honoured One! The family name of Gautama cannot be made to pass for Atreya, and Atreya cannot be made to stand for Gautama. So do things obtain with the nyagrodha seed. It cannot be made to stand for a khadira seed or the khadira seed to stand for the nyagrodha seed. And as you cannot make away with the family name of Gautama, the Buddha-Nature of beings cannot be made away with. Know, because of this, that beings possess the Buddha-Nature." The Buddha said: "O good man! If you say that there is the nyagrodha in the seed, I have to say that this is not so. If there were, why do we not see it? O good man! If is as with things of the world which cannot be seen because of causal relations. What are [such] causal relations? They are, for instance, like the case where distance is too great, so that one cannot see. Or like the trace of a bird's flight across the sky. Or as when the distance is too short, as in that of a blink of the eye. Or as in the case of breaking up, as a result of which one cannot see. Or because of the rotting of the root.

Or it is like the dispersion of thought, as when one's mind is not set all-exclusively upon a single point. Or it is as when something is too tiny, as with a mote. Or it is as when an obstacle exists, as when clouds obscure the sight of the stars by coming in between. Or when there are too many, so that it is not possible to see, as in the case of hemp amid the rice plants. Or because of similarity, as a result of which one cannot see, as in the case of a bean amidst beans. But the nyagrodha is not anything like these eight causal relations. If such, why is it that we cannot see such? You may say that we do not see because of small obstacles. But this is not so. Why not? Because the external characteristics are rough and coarse. If you say that the nature is minute, how can it truly grow? If one says one cannot because of an obstacle, we would not ever be able to see. If it is said that there was originally no such coarseness, but one now sees this coarseness, know that this coarseness has no nature of its own. Originally, there was no nature, and one now sees. Know that the nature of this seeing originally has no nature of its own. It is the same with the seed. There was no tree itself. Now, we see it. What harm is there?" Lion's Roar said: "There are two causes of which the Buddha speaks. One is the right cause and the other the revealed cause. Because the nyagrodha seed is grounded on the revealed cause of earth, water and dung, this enables what is minute to gain coarseness [bulk, size]." The Buddha said: "O good man! If there is the ground to start from, why do we need to seek the revealed cause? If there is no nature to talk of, what is there to reveal? If there is not originally any element of coarseness, and because of the revealed cause there comes about coarseness, why is it that khadira does not come about? The fact is that both do not originally exist. O good man! If minuteness cannot be seen, one can see well that which is coarse. For example, one may not be able to see a single mote, and yet when many motes foregather, one can. Of such seeds, one can see what is coarse. Why? Because in this there is already the bud, stem, flower, and fruit. In each fruit, there are already innumerable seeds. Each seed contains within it innumerable trees. Hence, we say coarse. As there is this coarseness, one can indeed see it. O good man! If this nyagrodha seed has the nature of nyagrodha and if it calls forth a tree, we see that the seed is being burnt in fire. Thus the nature of being burnt will also be an "is".

If it is an "is", there cannot be any coming about of the tree. If all things are originally of the nature of birth and death, why is it that birth precedes and death follows, and that everything does not happen at the same time? For this reason, know that there is no nature." Bodhisattva Lion's Roar said: "O World-Honoured One! If the nyagrodha seed originally has no nature of the tree and yet calls forth the tree, why is it that this seed does not give out oil? This derives from the fact that neither of these has such a nature." "O good man! Even such a seed does indeed give out oil. Though there is no nature, it is "is" because of causal relations." Lion's Roar said: "Why do we not call it sesame oil?" "O good man! Because it is not sesame oil. O good man! The causal relation of fire calls forth fire; that of water calls forth water. Both follow the causal relations, but to exist [at one and the same time] as one is not possible. It is the same with nyagrodha and sesame seeds. Both follow causal relations, but do not exist at once as one. The nature of the nyagrodha seed easily cures a cold and sesame cures a fever. O good man! Through the difference in causal relations, sugar cane calls forth rock candy and kokumitsu [a certain sugar product - possibly molasses]. Both depend on one causal relation, but their colour and external appearance differ. Rock candy cures fever and kokumitsu a cold." Bodhisattva Lion's Roar said: "O World-Honoured One! If there is not any nature of butter in milk, nor the nature of oil in hemp, and no nature of a tree in the nyagrodha seed, no nature of a pot in mud, no Buddha-Nature in all beings, all this contradicts what the Buddha said above [to the effect] that all beings possess the Buddha-Nature and will therefore attain unsurpassed Bodhi [Enlightenment]. Why? Because there is no nature of a human or deva [god]. This means to say that without any nature, a human becomes a deva and a deva a human. It is because karma so contrives it that it comes about thus, but not by any nature. The Bodhisattva-mahasattva attains unsurpassed Bodhi only through the causal relations of karma. If it is said that all beings have the Buddha-Nature, why does the icchantika segregate [himself from] the root of goodness and fall into hell? If the Bodhi Mind is the Buddha-Nature, the icchantika cannot be cut off [from it]. If he is cut off, how can we say that the Buddha-Nature is eternal? If it is not eternal, we cannot call it the Buddha-Nature. If all beings possess the Buddha-Nature, why do we speak of such as the "first aspiration to Bodhi"? And why do we speak of "vaivarti" ["drawing back"] and "avaivarti" ["non-retarding"]. If vaivarti, the person could not have the Buddha-Nature. O World-Honoured One! The Bodhisattva-mahasattva looks single-mindedly towards unsurpassed Bodhi, sees Great Loving-Kindness and Great Compassion, and the ills of birth, old age, death and defilement, and Great Nirvana; and he meditates on the non-existence of birth, age, death and defilement, and believes in the Three Jewels, and the results of karma, and upholds sila. Such is the Buddha-Nature. If there could be any Buddha-Nature, how could one use this law and make it a causal relation? O World-Honoured One! Milk can surely become butter without the help of causal relations. But fresh butter ["navanita"] cannot proceed thus. It needs to depend on causal relations, such as a man's skill, a water pot, and a churning rope. The situation is the same with beings. If they have the Buddha-Nature, they can do without causal relations and attain unsurpassed Bodhi. If it is definitely an "is", why does the Way-seeker see the suffering of the three unfortunate realms, and birth, age, illness and death, and gain the retarding mind [i.e. slip back, not make progress]? Also, without practising the six paramitas, one attains unsurpassed Bodhi. This is as when one wishes to gain butter without depending on the causal relations of milk. But it is not the case that one attains unsurpassed Bodhi without depending on the six paramitas. For this reason, we must know that all beings do not possess the Buddha-Nature. This is as above, where the Buddha said that the Jewel of the Sangha is eternal. If it is eternal, this means that it is not non-eternal. If it is not non-eternal, how can one attain unsurpassed Bodhi? If the Sangha is eternal, how can one say that all beings possess the Buddha-Nature? O World-Honoured One! If all beings do not originally possess Bodhichitta [Enlightenment Mind] and do not have the aspiration to unsurpassed Bodhi and later gain it, then the Buddha-Nature and beings are what originally was not but now are. Because of this, it must be the case that all beings do not possess the Buddha-Nature." The Buddha said: "Well said, well said, O good man! You have long known the meaning of the Buddha-Nature. For the sake of beings, you pose such questions and say: "All beings truly possess the Buddha-Nature." You say that if all beings possess the Buddha-Nature, there

cannot be any first aspiration. O good man! The mind is not the Buddha-Nature. Why not? The mind is non-eternal, and the Buddha-Nature is Eternal. Why do you say that there is retrogression [or regression]? Truth to tell, there is no retrogressing. If there were any retrogressing, there could not be any attainment of unsurpassed Bodhi. As it comes late, we call this retrogressive. This Bodhi Mind is not the Buddha-Nature. Why not? Because the icchantika lacks the root of good and falls into hell. If the Bodhi Mind is the Buddha-Nature, the icchantika cannot be called an icchantika. Also, the Bodhi Mind cannot be called non-eternal. For this reason, we can definitely know that the Bodhi Mind is not the Buddha-Nature. "O good man! You say that if beings possess the Buddha-Nature, there is no need for causal relations, since the case is analogous to that of milk to butter. But this is not so. Why not? This is like saying that five causal relations call forth fresh butter. Know that the same is the case with the Buddha-Nature. For example, in several stones we find gold, silver, copper, and iron. All are of the four great elements. Each has one name and one thing. And the place where it comes from is not the same. Birth [i.e. the open appearance of these metals] always depends on the sum total of various causal relations and beings' virtue, metallurgy, and human skill. The matter stands thus. Because of this, we have to know that originally there is no nature of gold. The Buddha-Nature of beings is no Buddha. By the conjoint workings of all virtues and causal relations, one sees the Buddha-Nature and one becomes the Buddha. It is not correct to say: "All you beings have the Buddha-Nature. Why do you not see it?" Why not? Because all the causal relations are not yet in conjunction. O good man! For this reason, I said that of the two causes of right cause and condition, the right cause is the Buddha-Nature, and that the condition is the mind that aspires to Bodhi; that by two causes one attains unsurpassed Bodhi, as in the case of a stone from which gold comes forth. "O good man! You priests always say that all beings do not possess the Buddha-Nature. O good man! "Sangha" means "harmony". Of harmony there are two kinds. One is of the worldly type and the other of "Paramartha-satya" [Ultimate Truth]. Worldly harmony is the sravaka Sangha, and "Paramartha-satya" harmony is the Bodhisattva Sangha. The worldly Sangha is non-eternal, but the Buddha-Nature is Eternal. As the

Buddha-Nature is Eternal, so is the Sangha of "Paramartha-satya". "Also, next, there is a Sangha which is the harmony of law [harmony of Dharma]. The harmony of law refers to the 12 types of sutra. The 12 types of sutra are Eternal. That is why I say that the Sangha is Eternal. "O good man! Sangha means harmony. The harmony is the 12 types of sutra. In the 12 links of interdependence, there is the Buddha-Nature. If the 12 links of interdependence are Eternal, the Buddha-Nature too is Eternal. That is why I say that there is the Buddha-Nature in the Sangha. "Also, next, the Sangha is the harmony of all Buddhas. That is why I say that there is the Buddha-Nature in the Sangha. "O good man! You say that if all beings possess the Buddha-Nature, how can there be any retrogression and non-retrogression? Listen carefully, listen carefully! I shall now explain [matters] to you in minute detail. "O good man! If a Bodhisattva-mahasattva has 13 things, there is retrogression. What are these 13? They are: 1) the mind does not believe, 2) the mind will no do, 3) the doubting mind, 4) being niggardly in bodily actions and with wealth, 5) entertaining great fear towards Nirvana, doubting whether one could eternally part from worldly existence, 6) having no mental forbearance [patience, endurance], 7) the mind will not adjust and soften itself, 8) apprehension and worry, 9) lack of bliss, 10) indolence, 11) belittling one's own self, 12) deeming that there is no means to excise defilement, and 13) not desiring Enlightenment. O good man! These 13 are the things that cause the Bodhisattva to retrogress from Enlightenment. "Further, there are six things which destroy the Bodhi Mind. What are they? They are: 1) parsimony, 2) entertaining an evil mind towards all beings, 3) making friends with evil people, 4) non-effort, 5) arrogance, and 6) carrying on worldly business. These six things destroy the Bodhi Mind. "O good man! A man hears that the All-Buddha-World-Honoured One is the teacher of humans and gods, that he is the best, incomparable, and superior to sravakas and pratyekabuddhas, that his Dharma-Eye is clear, that he is unhindered, that he passes all beings over the great sea of suffering. Having heard this, the man takes a great vow: "If there is any such person, I too shall be like him." Through this causal relation, he aspires to unsurpassed Enlightenment. Or taught by some others, a person may aspire to unsurpassed Enlightenment. Or a person might hear that the Bodhisattva underwent stringent penances for asamkhyas of kalpas and later attained unsurpassed Enlightenment. Having heard this, he thinks: "I cannot endure such penance, so how will I be able to gain it?" Thus, he retrogresses. "O good man! There are also five things that distance one from the Bodhi Mind. What are the five? They are: 1) desiring to get ordained under a tirthika [non-Buddhist], 2) not practising the Great Mind of Loving-Kindness, 3) especially seeking to find fault with a priest, 4) always seeking to live in between birth and death, 5) not holding a good feeling towards upholding, reciting, copying and expounding the 12 types of sutra. These are the five things that pull one away from the Bodhi Mind. "Also, there are two things that pull one away from the Bodhi Mind. What are the two? They are: 1) to be greedy for the five desires, 2) not respecting and honouring the Three Treasures. "All such various causal relations carry one away from the Bodhi Mind [i.e. are causes of retrogression] "What is the unretrogressive mind? Again, a man hears that the Buddha truly passes beings over the sea of birth, old age, illness and death. He does not ask of a teacher to be taught and gains unsurpassed Bodhi by spontaneously practising the Way. "If Bodhi is something we can indeed gain, I shall assuredly practise the Way and unfailingly attain it." Thinking thus, he aspires to Bodhi and transfers all [the merit] that he has amassed, be it great or small, to unsurpassed Bodhi. He takes this vow: "I pray that I shall draw near to all Buddhas and Buddhist disciples, listen to sermons, so that the five sense-organs are all perfect, and this mind will not get lost even if I encounter hardships. Also, I pray, O all Buddhas and disciples, that I shall always have a gladdened mind and be perfect in the five good deeds. If all beings slash my body, hands and feet, head and eyes, and other parts, I shall gain a heart of Great Loving-Kindness towards all and feel happy. All such persons will serve me in the augmentation of my own Bodhi. If not, how can I accomplish unsurpassed Bodhi? Also I vow: Let me not gain a body that has no genital organs, that has dual sex organs, or the form of a female; [I pray] that I shall not be tied up by officials, that I shall not encounter a bad king, that I shall not be the subject of a bad king, that I shall not gain birth in an evil state. If I gain a beautiful body, my caste will be right. I may be blessed with wealth, but I shall not acquire an arrogant mind. I shall always listen to the 12 types of sutras, uphold, recite, copy and expound [them]. If I am able to address beings, [I pray that] those who listen to me will respect me and entertain no doubt, that they will not bear any ill-will towards me, or that they hear little, but gain more understanding, that they will not desire to hear much but not be clear as to the meaning. I pray that I shall become the teacher of the mind, but not make the mind the teacher, that all my bodily, oral and mental actions will not befriend evil, that I shall be able to bestow peace and bliss upon all beings, that I shall not be moved like a mountain in the bodily precepts and in the wiseness of the mind, that I shall not be parsimonious with body, life or wealth, that I shall not do impure things and regard such as being meritorious, that I shall carry on a right way of living, live by myself, that I shall not do evil or flatter in mind, that when receiving any favour I shall pray in my mind to repay in a manifold way, even when only favoured a little, that I shall be well versed in all worldly acts and skills, that I shall be able to know all dialectical idioms [terms], that I shall recite and copy the 12 types of sutra, that I shall not be indolent and lazy in my mind, that if all beings do not desire to listen, I shall bring forth means so that they will be pleased to give ear to me, that my words will always be soft, that my mouth will not speak evil things, that I shall truly make those who entertain evil thoughts towards each other melt into harmony. If there should be anyone who has fear, he shall be freed from it; when there is a famine, there will be harvest and satisfaction; when epidemics prevail, I shall be a great doctor and there will be medicine and treasure, so that those who suffer from illnesses will all gain ease and health. In the days of long wars, the sufferings from smouldering fires will be done away with. I shall cut away all such fears as [regards] death, imprisonment, beatings, water and fire, kings, robbers, poverty, violating the moral precepts, evil names and ways of life. I shall gain deep respect for fathers and mothers, teachers and elders, and gain a heart of Great Loving-Kindness in the midst of enmity. I shall always practise the six thinkings, the three samadhis of the All-Void, thoughtlessness and desirelessness, the 12 links of interdependent origination, meditation upon birth and death, exhalation and inhalation of the breath, heavenly and pure actions, holy actions, the vajra-samadhi, the Suramgama Samadhi, and I shall gain a mind

of quietude [even] where there are no Three Treasures. When I have to suffer from great sorrow, let me not lose the mind of unsurpassed Bodhi, let me not feel self-satisfied with the mind of the sravaka or pratyekabuddha. I shall renounce the world amidst the ways of the tirthikas and where there are no Three Treasures, so that I shall be able to crush the twisted views of life, and I shall not fall there into their ways of life. I shall gain unmolestedness in all things, be free in my mind, and be able clearly to see through all the wrongs of the created world. I shall fear the ways and fruitions of the two vehicles as I would fear losing my own fleshly body and life. For the sake of beings, I shall find pleasure in sitting amidst the three unfortunate realms like those who greatly like to look up to life in Trayastrimsa Heaven. For the sake of each person, I shall, for innumerable kalpas, suffers the pains of hell, and I shall feel no regret. I shall not burn in jealousy when I see others gaining profit. I shall always be as happy as when I myself gain bliss. Facing the Three Treasures, I shall offer clothing, food and drink, bedding, accommodation, medical attendance and cures, lights, flowers and incense, music, banners and parasols, and the seven treasures. If I receive injunctions from the Buddha, I shall zealously guard them and never break or transgress them. If I come to hear of the hardships of practice of the Bodhisattva, I shall feel pleased and have no regrets. I shall be empowered to read into my own past lives, and I shall not be a servant of greed, anger and ignorance. For the sake of results that are to come, I shall be no slave to causal relations. I shall not be addicted to the greed of pleasure that one has." "O good man! If any person has such prayers, this is where we say that the Bodhisattva definitely will not draw back from the Bodhi Mind. He is also called a "danapati" [one who gives]. He will truly see the Tathagata, is one who is clear as to the Buddha-Nature, and one who well adjusts beings and enables them to pass over the sea of birth and death. He protects unsurpassed Wonderful Dharma well and is perfect in the six paramitas. O good man! For this reason, the unretrogressive mind is not called the Buddha-Nature. "O good man! Do not say that beings do not have the Buddha-Nature just because of the retrogressive mind. For example, two persons hear: "In another land, there is a mountain made of the seven treasures. In the mountain, there is a clear spring, whose water tastes sweet. Should any person reach this spring, he will make away with poverty, anyone who drinks its water will gain a long life. But the way to it is long and steep. Then, both men desire to go there. One of the men goes equipped with various travelling outfits, whereas the other goes unprepared, not even keeping to the rules of food. They are walking together, when along the way they meet a man who has plenty of treasures, perfect in the seven rarities. The two go up to this person and ask: ?Is there any mountain of the seven treasures in that land" The man replies: "There truly is such a land, and it is not false. I have already gained the treasures. I have tasted the water. The only thing to worry one is that the way is steep, and there are robbers, gravel, and thorns; watery [succulent] plants are lacking. Thousands and millions go [set out], but few reach the end." On hearing this, one of the men feels regret and says: "The way is long and there is more than one trouble. Innumerable is the number of those who go and few gain the end. And how can I expect to reach this place? At present, I have what I need to have. If I stick to this, I will not lose my life. If life is at stake, where can I look for longevity?" The other man also says: "People indeed go; I too shall go. If I truly gain that place, I shall have rarities and taste the sweet water. If I cannot, let my life end there." Now, the one regrets having started out and draws back, whereas the other goes on, gaining the mountain and rarities, and tastes the water that he desired to taste. Carrying all that he has gained, he comes back to where he lives, serves his parents and his ancestors." "Then, the one who regretted having started out on the journey and who turned back, sees this and goes down with a fever. "He went and is now back. How can I remain here?" And equipping himself, he starts out on the journey again. "The seven treasures can be compared to Great Nirvana, the sweet water to the Buddha-Nature, the two persons to two Bodhisattvas who first aspire to Bodhi, the steep path to birth and death, the man whom they meet on the way to the Buddha-World-Honoured One, the robbers to the four Maras, the gravel and thorns to defilements, the lack of watery plants to the non-practising of the Way of Bodhi, the one who turns back to the retrogressing Bodhisattva, and the one who goes on alone to the non-retrogressing Bodhisattva. "O good man! The Buddha-Nature of beings is Eternal and Unchanging. And we say, referring to the steep path: "When the person regrets and turns

back, this makes the way non-eternal." But this cannot be so said. The same is the case with the Buddha-Nature. O good man! On the Path of Bodhi, there is not one who turns back. O good man! The one who regretted having started out now sees him who went before and who has gained the treasures, has come back unmolested, who makes offerings to his parents, gives to his relatives, thus enjoying much peace. Seeing this, a fire again burns in his mind, he adorns his body, starts out on the way again, spares no effort, endures all manner of hardships, and goes to the mountain of the seven treasures. So do things obtain with the retrogressing Bodhisattva. "O good man! All beings definitely will attain unsurpassed Bodhi. Because of this, I say in the sutra: "All beings, down to those who have committed the five deadly sins, those who have sinned by performing the four grave offences, and the icchantikas all have the Buddha-Nature." Lion's Roar said: "O World-Honoured One! Why are there the retrogressing and the non-retrogressing Bodhisattvas?" "O good man! If any Bodhisattva comes to know of the causal relations of the 32 signs of perfection of the Tathagata, we say non-retrogressive. He is the Bodhisattva-mahasattva, the non-upside-down, and one who pities all beings. He is one superior to sravakas and pratyekabuddhas and one called "avaivartaniya". O good man! The Bodhisattva-mahasattva is immovable in his upholding of the precepts, in his mind of giving, and is like Mount Sumeru in abiding in the true word. Because of this, he gains the "flat sole" [one of the 80 minor marks of excellence]. "The Bodhisattva-mahasattva fittingly offers things to his parents, the honoured ones, elders, and animals. Because of this, he gains on his sole the mark of excellence of a thousand spokes [one of the 80 minor marks of excellence]. The Bodhisattva-mahasattva takes joy in non-harming and non-stealing and is pleased regarding his parents, honoured ones and teachers. Because of this, he is accomplished in the three bodily marks, which are: 1) long fingers, 2) long heels, and 3) a square and upright body. All these three forms arise out of the same karma. "The Bodhisattva-mahasattva practises the four ways of guiding in [i.e. to guide beings in by: 1) giving, 2) friendliness, 3) good actions, 4) transforming himself and co-existing with them as the beings themselves, and takes in beings. Due to this, he gains the toe-membrane [one of the 80 minor marks of excellence] like that of a great royal swan.

"The Bodhisattva-mahasattva, when his parents, teachers and elders are ill, himself washes and wipes, holds and rubs their limbs. Because of this, his hands and feet are soft. "The Bodhisattva-mahasattva upholds the precepts, listens to the sermons, and knows no end of giving. Due to this, his joints and ankles are fully fleshed and the hair on his skin flows in one direction. "The Bodhisattva-mahasattva single-mindedly gives ear to Dharma and expounds the right teaching. Because of this, he gains the ankles of a deer-king. "The Bodhisattva-mahasattva acquires no harming mind, is satisfied with his food and drink, and with giving, and attends to illness, and dispenses medicine. Because of this, his body is rounded and perfect and is like the nyagrodha tree. When his hand is stretched dwon, his fingers reach his knee, and his head has the usnisa [Buddhic protuberance], the characteristic of which is that the top of it cannot be seen. "The Bodhisattva-mahasattva, when he sees a person in fear, extends help [to that person], and when he sees a person without any footgear, gives him clothing. Due to this, he gains a characteristic of his in which his genital organ lies hidden. "The Bodhisattva-mahasattva readily befriends wise men, segregating himself from the ignorant; he takes pleasure in exchanging views and sweeps the path along which he walks. On this account, his skin is delicately soft and his bodily hair turns to the right-hand side. "The Bodhisattva-mahasattva always gives men clothing, food and drink, medicine, incense and flowers, and lights. Because of this, his body shines brightly in a golden colour and light. "The Bodhisattva-mahasattva gives, does not grudge at [hang on to] whatever is rare, and easily parts with such; he makes no distinction whatever between a field of weal or a non-field-of-weal [i.e. the recipient of dana - charity - is likened to a field, by cultivating which one's blessings and virtues increase]. Because of this, he is full and right-set [firm] in the seven places of his body. "The Bodhisattva-mahasattva seeks wealth lawfully and gives this away [to others]. Because of this, the boneless parts [of his body] are full, the upper part is like that of a lion, and his elbows are well-balanced and delicate. "The Bodhisattva-mahasattva segregates himself from double-tongue [two-facedness], from ill-speaking and an angry mind. On account of this, his 40 teeth are white and pure, well-balanced and delicate. "The Bodhisattva-mahasattva practises Great Loving-Kindness towards beings. Due to this, he gains the two-fanged face. "The Bodhisattva-mahasattva takes this vow: "Any may come and ask, and I shall give as they desire to have." Because of this, he gains the lion's cheeks. "The Bodhisattva-mahasattva gives whatever kind of food beings desire to have. Because of this, he gains the taste that is the mid-upper. "The Bodhisattva-mahasattva exerts himself in the 10 good deeds and thereby teaches others. Because of this, he gains a large and long tongue [i.e. a symbolic expression referring to his great prowess in oratory]. "The Bodhisattva-mahasattva does not speak ill of the shortcomings of others and does not slander Wonderful Dharma. Because of this, he acquires the Buddha-Voice. "The Bodhisattva-mahasattva sees all enmities and gains a pleasant [i.e. happy] mind. Because of this, he gains the blue tone of his eyes. "The Bodhisattva-mahasattva does not conceal the virtues of others, but praises the good which they have. Due to this, he gains a face with a white [tuft of] hair on his brow. "O good man! When the Bodhisattva-mahasattva practises such 32 kinds of causal relations, he gains a mind that will not retrogress from the mind that seeks Bodhi. "O good man! All beings are beyond knowing; also inconceivable are the worlds of Buddhas, and the workings of karma, and the Buddha-Nature. Why? Because these four things are all Eternal. Being Eternal, they cannot be conceived of. With all beings, defilement overspreads [them]. And we say Eternal. The defilements of disruption and permanence go. Hence, non-eternal. If it is the case that all beings are the Eternal, why do we need to practise the Eightfold Path, so as to extirpate all sorrows? When disruption comes to all sorrows, we say non-eternal. Whatever we have of bliss, we call it Eternal. For this reason, I say: "All beings are overspread by defilement and cannot see the Buddha-Nature. Not seeing the Buddha-Nature, no Nirvana comes about."

Chapter Thirty-Five: On Bodhisattva Lion's Roar 3

Lion's Roar said: "O World-Honoured One! You the Buddha say that all things have two causes. One is the right cause and the other the condition. Through these, there cannot be any breaking away from bondage. The five skandhas appear and die out moment after moment. If these appear and die out, who binds and unbinds? O World-Honoured One! The present five skandhas call forth the five skandhas that follow. This skandha dies out by itself and does not shift on to another skandha. Though not shifting on, this can well call forth the other skandha. From a seed, we gain a bud. But the seed does not shift on to the bud. Though it does not shift on to the bud, it indeed calls forth the bud. The same is the case with beings. How do we undo bondage?" "O good man! Listen carefully, listen carefully. I shall now explain [matters] to you minutely. O good man! When a person is going to die and faces the greatest of sorrows, the relatives gather around, weep, and are lost in sorrow. The person himself is in fear and knows of no help. He has his five sense-organs, but the sense-function does not work. His limbs shake and he indeed cannot hold [maintain] his own body. The body is empty and cold, and warmth is about to depart. He sees before his own eyes all the karmic results of what he has done. "O good man! The sun is about to go down over the horizon, and the mountains and hills and mounds present shadows which shift on to the east. Reason tells [us] that there cannot be any moving to the west. It is the same with the fruition of a man's karma. When this skandha dies, another arises. When light appears, gloom dies out; when the light vanishes, the gloom appears. O good man! When a stamp [seal] of wax is pressed into mud, the stamp becomes one with the mud. The stamp dies out, and there appear letters. And yet, this wax stamp does not change into mud, and those letters come about from mud. They do not come about from anywhere else. They come about by reason of the causal relations of the stamp. Things obtain thus. "When the skandhas of the present life die out, an in-between existence comes about. It is not that the skandhas of the present life change into the skandhas of the in-between five skandhas. And, also, the in-between five skandhas do not come about by themselves. They do not come about from anywhere else. Through the present skandhas come about the in-between skandhas. The stamp presses upon the mud. It dies out and letters emerge. The name does not differ. But the time of each differs. Such is the case. That is why I say: "The in-between five skandhas cannot be seen with the fleshly eye; they are what can be seen with the heavenly eye." The in-between skandhas feed on three kinds of food: 1) food of thought, 2) food of touch, 3) food of will. The in-between skandhas are made up of two kinds, which are: 1) good karmic fruition, and 2) evil karmic fruition. From good action comes about the consciousness of good karma, and from evil action the consciousness of evil [results]. "When the parents join together in sexual union, the causal relations call forth the direction in which the life must proceed. The mother gains craving ["trishna"] and the father anger. When the semen of the father comes forth, he says: "This is mine." At that, his mind becomes pleased. These three kinds of defilement crush out the in-between skandhas of causal relations and the subsequent five skandhas come about. This is comparable to how the stamp gets impressed into the mud and letters emerge. "When appearing, all the sense-organs are perfect or imperfect. One who is equipped thus sees "matter" [i.e. physical form] and acquires greed. Greed arises, which is craving. By madness, greed comes about. This is ignorance. Through the causal relations of greedy craving and ignorance, the world that is seen is all upside-down. The non-Eternal is viewed as Eternal, the non-Self as the Self, non-Bliss as Bliss, and the non-Pure as the Pure. From these four inversions, good and bad actions are committed. Defilement makes karma, and karma activates defilement. This is bondage. On this account, we say born of the five skandhas.

"For this person, when he befriends the Buddha, the Buddha's disciples, and the good teachers of the Way, and when he listens to the 12 types of sutra, because of his hearing Dharma, there comes about a realm of good. When he sees the realm of good, he gains great Wisdom. Great Wisdom is right seeing. When he gains [such] seeing, he repents of the life of birth and death. In consequence of this regret, no joy arises [regarding samsara - birth and death]. When he gains no joy, he truly destroys the greedy mind. When he destroys the greedy mind, he practises well the Noble Eightfold Path. When he practises the Noble Eightfold Path, he emerges from birth and death. When there is no birth and death, he gains Emancipation. When fire does not meet with fuel, this is extinction. When there is no more birth and death, we say that we cross over extinction. This is the extinction of the five skandhas." Lion's Roar said: "There is no thorn in the Void. How can we speak of extracting? None chains the skandhas. How can there be any binding?" The Buddha said: "O good man! The chain of defilement binds the five skandhas. Away from the five skandhas, there is no defilement; away from defilement, there are no five skandhas. "O good man! Pillars support a house. Away from the house, there are no pillars, and without any pillars, there is no house. It is the same with the five skandhas of beings. When there is defilement, we speak of bondage. When there is no defilement, we speak of Emancipation. O good man! The fist contains the palm. The three items of bondage, meeting and dispersion, birth and death, are not different things. The same is the case with the five skandhas of beings. When there is defilement, we have bondage; when we have no defilement, there is Emancipation. "O good man! We say that body-and-mind ["nama-rupa"] chains beings. But if body-and-mind have gone, there is no being. Other than body-and-mind, there is no being; other than the being, there is no other body-and-mind. Also, we say that body-and-mind chains the being, and the being chains the body-and-mind." Lion's Roar said: "O World-Honoured One! The eye does not see by itself, the finger does not touch by itself, the sword does not cut by itself, and feeling does not feel by itself. But why does the Tathagata say: "Body-and-mind chains the body-and-mind?" Why? Body-and-mind is none but the being; the being is body-and-mind. If we say that body-and-mind chains the being, this means that body-and-mind chains body-and-mind." The Buddha said: "O good man! When two hands meet, there cannot be anything that comes in between. It is the same with body-and-mind. That is why I say: "Body-and-mind chains the being." If one is away from body-and-mind, what there is [then] is Emancipation. That is why I say: "The being attains emancipation." Lion's Roar said: "O World-Honoured One! If body-and-mind chains one, all arhats are not away from body-and-mind. So they may well be chained."

"O good man! There are two kinds of Emancipation, which are: 1) cutting off of the seed, and 2) cutting off of fruition. The cutting off of the seed is the cutting off of defilement. The arhats have already cut off defilement and the root of all bondage has been severed, so that the bondage of the seed cannot chain [the arhat]. When the root of fruition is not yet cut off, we say that there is yet the bondage of fruition. All arhats do not see the Buddha-Nature. Not seeing this, they cannot gain unsurpassed Enlightenment. For this reason, we may say that there is the bondage of fruition. So, we cannot say that there is a bondage of body-and-mind. O good man! For example, when the oil has not yet been spent, the light of the lamp does not expire. Once the oil is spent, the light goes out. In this, there is nothing to doubt. O good man! The so-called oil is defilement, and the light is the being. All beings do not gain Nirvana, due to the oil of defilement. If this is removed, they gain Nirvana." Lion's Roar said: "O World-Honoured One! The nature of light and oil differs. Defilement and the being are not thus. The being is defilement and defilement is the being. The being is the five skandhas and the five skandhas are the being. The five skandhas are defilement and defilement is the five skandhas. Why do you, the Tathagata, liken them to light?" The Buddha said: "Of analogies, there are eight kinds, namely: 1) progressive analogy, 2) reverse analogy, 3) actual analogy, 4) non-analogy, 5) fore-going analogy, 6) aft-coming analogy, 7) fore-going-and-aft-coming analogy, and 8) all-pervading analogy. "What is a progressive analogy? It is as when I say in the sutras, for example, heaven sends down great rain, and all the ditches become full. As they are full, small holes get full. As small holes get filled, the great holes too become full. As the great holes become full, small springs become full. As small springs become full, great springs become full. As great springs become full, small ponds become full. As small ponds become full, big ponds become full. When big ponds are full, small rivers become full. When small rivers become full, big rivers become full. When big rivers become full, the great seas become full. The same is the case with the rain of Dharma of the Tathagata. "The silas [moral behaviour] of beings become full [i.e. perfect]. As the silas are full, the non-repenting mind becomes full. As the non-repenting mind becomes full, there arises joy. As joy arises, segregation [from attachment to the skandhas] comes about. As segregation becomes full, there comes about peace. As peace becomes full, samadhi becomes full. As samadhi becomes full, right seeing-and-knowing becomes full. As right seeing-and-knowing becomes full, renunciation becomes full. As renunciation becomes full, the reproach [i.e. aversion to worldly life] becomes full. As reproaching becomes full, Emancipation becomes full. As Emancipation becomes full, Nirvana becomes full. This is a progressive analogy. "What is a reverse analogy? Originally there was a great sea. This was a big river. The big river was originally a small river. There was a small river, which was a big pond. There was a big pond originally, which was a small pond. There was a small pond originally, which was a big spring. There was a big spring originally, which was a small spring. There was a small spring, which was a big hole. There was a big hole originally, which was a small hole. There was a small hole originally, which was a ditch. There was a ditch originally, which was great rain. "There was Nirvana originally, which was Emancipation. There was originally Emancipation, which was reproach. There was reproach originally, which was renunciation. There was renunciation originally, which was right seeing-and-knowing. There was right seeing-and-knowing originally, which was samadhi. There was samadhi originally, which was peace. There was peace originally, which was segregation. There was segregation originally, which was the mind of joy. There was joy originally, which was non-regret. There was non-regret originally, which was the upholding of the precepts. There was upholding of the precepts originally, which was the rain of Dharma. This is an analogy in reverse order. "What is an actual analogy? It is as when I say in the sutras that the mind of a being is like that of a monkey. The nature of a monkey is to

throw [things] away and pick [things] up. The nature of a being is the same. It clings to colour, sound, smell, touch, and law [taste], and there is not a moment when it is at rest. This is an actual analogy. "What is a non-analogy? It is as when I said to Prasenajit: "O great King! There are intimate friends come from the four quarters, who say: [O great King! There are four great mountains which come from the four quarters and mean to cause harm to man]. Should you, the King, hear of this, what would you intend to do to deal with the situation?" The King said: "O World-Honoured One! They may come, but there is no place in which to take refuge. All one can do is exclusively uphold the precepts and give alms." I praised him and said: "Well said, well siad, O great King! I speak of four mountains. These are none other than the birth, old age, illness, and death of beings. Birth, old age, illness and death always come and press upon a person. How can one not practise the precepts and dana?" The King said: "O World-Honoured One! What does one gain from the precepts and dana?" I said: "One gains pleasure in the life of humans and heaven." The King said: "O World-Honoured One! If the nyagrodha were to practise the precepts and dana, could it call forth peace and bliss [for itself] in the world of humans and heaven?" I said: "The nyagrodha cannot uphold the precepts and give. If it could, there could result nothing that is different." This is a non-analogy. "What is a fore-going analogy? This is as when I say in the sutra, for example, there is a wonderful flower to which a person clings [i.e. which that person desires]. Intending to take hold of it, he is taken by the water [i.e. falls into the river]. The same is the case with the being. He clings to the five desires and flounders in the river of birth, old age, and death. This is a foregoing analogy. "What is an aft-coming analogy? It is as is given in the Dharmapada:

"Do not belittle any small evil
And say that no ill comes about therefrom.
Small is a drop of water,
Yet it fills a big vessel."

This is an aft-coming parable. "What is a fore-and-aft analogy? This is as in the case of a plantain tree, which, when it bears fruit, dies. It is the same with the ignorant, who but receives support. It is as in the case of a mule, which, when it bears a

child, cannot live long. "What is an all-pervading analogy? This is as when I state in the sutra: In Trayastrimsa Heaven, there is a tree called parijata, whose roots go down into the earth five yojanas deep and whose height is as great as 100 yojanas. Its branches and leaves spread out as far as 50 yojanas. When the leaves ripen, they become yellow, and all the gods, on seeing this, are gladdened. These leaves, before long, fall off. When the leaves fall, there comes about joy. This branch changes colour, and joy arises. This branch, before long, gains pimples. Seeing this, joy again comes about. This pimple again calls forth a bill. Having seen this, joy arises again. Not long after the bill opens, a fragrance covers an area of 50 yojanas, and a light shines over a distance of 80 yojanas. All devas [gods], in the three summer months, come down, and there is joy down below. "O good man! It is the same with all of my disciples. Saying that the leaves become yellow can be likened to my disciples who desire renunciation. Saying that the leaves fall down can be likened to my disciples' shaving their heads. Saying that the colour of the leaves changes refers to my disciples' taking to the "jnaticaturtha" and receiving the complete precepts. Saying that first a pimple appears refers to the disciples' minds aspiring to unsurpassed Bodhi and the bill to the Bodhisattvas of the ten abodes who now gain the Buddha-Nature. Saying that it opens refers to the Bodhisattvas' attaining of unsurpassed Bodhi. "Fragrance" refers to the innumerble beings of the ten directions upholding the precepts. "Light" is likened to the Buddha's name filling the ten directions unhindered. "The three summer months" are comparable to the three samadhis. Saying that in Trayastrimsa Heaven one enjoys bliss is likened to all Buddhas' gaining Great Nirvana and the Eternal, Bliss, the Self, and the Pure. This is an all-pervading analogy. "The analogies spoken of do not necessarily cover all [aspects]. They liken things in part, or in greater part, or to the whole. It is as when we say: "The face of the Tathagata is like the full moon." This refers to but a small part. "O good man! There is a man, for example, who has not yet seen milk. He asks others what it is like: "What kind of thing is milk?" The others answer: "It is like water, honey, and a shell." The water represents moisture, the honey sweetness, and the shell colour. We may employ these three analogies and yet we may not be able to arrive at [an accurate idea of] what milk is. O good man! I may use the analogy of light. But the case will be thus. O good man! There cannot be any river apart from water. The same is the case with beings. Apart from the five skandhas, there can be no other separate being. O

good man! Apart from the body, wheels, spokes, and hubs, there cannot be any cart. It is the same with beings. "O good man! If you deisre to connect this with the analogy of light, listen carefully, listen carefully! I shall now explain it. The wick may be likened to the 25 existences, the oil is craving, and light Wisdom. To break means to exclude gloom and ignorance. Softness is likened to the Holy Way. When the oil is used up, the brightness of the light dies out. The same is the case [here]. When the craving of the being ends, there comes about the Buddha-Nature. There can be body-and-mind, but this cannot bind [one]. Living amidst the 25 existences, there is no defilement from any existence." Lion's Roar said: "O World-Honoured One! The five skandhas of the being are empty and there is no means of possessing. Who is there that receives the teaching and practises the Way?" The Buddha said: "O good man! All beings have the remembering mind, the wisdom mind, the aspiring mind, the effort-making mind, the believing mind, and the meditating mind. All such, moment after moment, are born and die away. And yet, similarity and continuation go on. Hence, we speak of practising the Way." Lion's Roar said: "O World-Honoured One! All such die away moment after moment. All such extinctions that come about moment after moment also resemble [one another] and continue. How is one able to practise the Way?" The Buddha said: "O good man! The light of the lamp dies out moment after moment. Yet, there is the light which dispels the gloom. It is the same with all such resemblings. O good man! The food a being eats dies away moment after moment, but hunger is satisfied. The case is the same. A good medicine dies away moment after moment. And yet it does indeed cure illness. The light of the sun and moon dies away moment after moment, and yet it truly enables the trees and plants of the forest to grow. "O good man! You say: "A person dies moment after moment. How can there be any growing up?" But as the mind is not cut off, there is growing. O good man! A man recites. The letters [words] read cannot happen in a moment. What came first cannot extend to the middle, and what was read in the middle cannot go to the end. The man, the letters and the mental image die out moment after moment, and practising long we come to know. "O good man! For example, with a goldsmith, from the day when he begins to learn his art up to those of his hoary old-age, one moment is followed by another moment, and what has preceded is what follows after. But by repeated practice, what comes about is wonderful. Due to this, the person is praised and is called the best goldsmith. It is the same with reading the sutras. "O good man! For example, let us take the case of a seed. The earth does not teach it and say: "Put forth buds!" But by the law of nature, buds come about. And then the flower, too, does not teach and say: "Now, bear fruit!" But fruit comes about as it should by the law of nature. It is the same with the practice of the Way. O good man! For example, in counting, one is not two, and two is not three. Moment after moment, one shifts on to the other. Yet, this goes up to 1,000 and to 10,000. Thus does the practice of the Way by beings proceed. O good man! The light of a lamp dies moment after moment. When the first light dies out, it does not say to the flame that follows: "I am going now. You now appear and dispel the gloom!" The case is thus. O good man! When a calf is born, it seeks milk. None teaches it this wisdom of seeking milk. A moment is followed by a moment, but the first hunger leads to satisfaction with the food that follows. Hence, know that one cannot be the same as others. If the same, no difference can come about. The same applies to the practice of the Way by a being. By one action, one may not gain the end. But by long practice, one does away with all defilements." Lion's Roar said: "Just as the Buddha says that when a person of the srotapanna stage [i.e. a person who has "entered the stream" of Dharma and will be reborn a maximum of only 7 further times] gains the fruition of the practice of the Way, even though born in evil lands, he upholds the precepts, does not kill, steal, seek after lust, practise double-tongue, or drink alcohol, the skandhas of the srotapanna die out here and do not gain the evil lands - the same applies to the practice of the Way. It does not lead to evil lands. Why can the person not get born in the Pure Land, if the same? If the skandhas of the evil land are not those of the srotapanna, how can it be that evil actions cannot come about?" The Buddha said: "O good man! A person of the srotapanna stage may get born into evil lands, and yet he will not lose his attainment of srotapannahood. The skandhas are not the same.

That is why I take up the analogy of the calf. A person of the srotapanna stage, though born in an evil land, because of the power of his practice of the Way, does not perform evil. O good man! For example, in Gandhamadana, there was a lion king, and all the birds and beasts left the mountain - none of them came near. Once, this king went into the Himalayas, and there, too, he saw that none was living there. That is how things stand with the srotapanna. Though not practising the Way, because of the power of the Way, he does not perform evil. For example, a man takes amrta [ambrosia of immortality]. And the amrta dies out. But the force of its remaining power causes the person to gain birthlessness and deathlessness. O good man! In Mount Sumeru, there is a wonderful medicine called langali. If one partakes of it, even though the effect of the medicine dies out moment after moment, one, due to the power of this medicine, will not encounter any harm. O good man! No one approaches where a Chakravartin lives, not even in his absence. Why not? Because of the power of this king. It is the same with the person of the srotapanna stage. He may be born in an evil land and may not be practising the Way, but because of the power of the Way, he does not do any evil. The skandhas of the srotapanna may be dead, and different skandhas may be present, and yet no skandha of the srotapanna is lost. O good man! Beings, because of what emerges from the fruit, do a good many things to the seed: they provide dung and irrigation. Although the fruit has not yet been gained and the seed is now dead, we nevertheless can say that we gain the fruit from the seed. It is the same with the skandhas of the srotapanna. O good man! For example, there is a man who is rich and has great wealth. He has only one son, who has already died. This son has a son, who is now abroad. This man, of a sudden, dies. The grandson, on hearing of this, comes back and takes over the property. It is not yet known where the wealth is. But there is no one who obstructs or protects the occupation. Why not? Because the stock is one. The case is the same with the skandhas of the srotapanna." Bodhisattva Lion's Roar said: "O World-Honoured One! You, the Buddha, said in a gatha:

"If a bhiksu [monk] practises the Way
Of the moral precepts, samadhi and Wisdom,
Know that this is befriending
Unretrogressive and great Nirvana."

O World-Honoured One! How am I to practise the precepts, samadhi and Wisdom? The Buddha said: "O good man! There is a man who upholds the prohibitions and precepts, but [does so] for the happiness that he can gain for his own self and for humans and gods, and not to save all beings, not for guarding unsurpassed Wonderful Dharma, but for profit and out of fear of the three unfortunate realms, for life, lust, power, safety, oratory, out of fear of state laws, evil fame, for fear of dirty names, and for worldly works. Such guarding and upholding of the precepts cannot be called practising the precepts. O good man! What is true upholding of sila? When one upholds sila, the object must be to pass beings to the other shore, to protect Wonderful Dharma, to save the unsaved, to enlighten the unenlightened, to enable those who have not yet taken refuge to take it, to enable those who have not yet attained Nirvana to attain it. Practising thus, a person does not see sila, how it is actually upheld, the person who upholds sila, the results to be attained [therefrom], whether the person has sinned or not. O good man! If one acts thus, this is the upholding of sila. "How does one practise samadhi? If, when practising samadhi, one does it to enlighten one's own self, for profit, not for the sake of all beings, not for the practising of Dharma, but out of greed, for defiled food, for sexual reasons, because of the impurities of the nine holes, for disputes, for beating, and for killing others, anybody who practises samadhi thus is not one who practises samadhi. "O good man! What is the true practice of samadhi? One practises it for the sake of all beings, to plant in the mind of beings the all-equal mind, unretrogressive Dharma, the holy mind, to enable beings to attain Mahayana, to guard unsurpassed Dharma, for beings not to retrogress from Enlightenment, for them to gain the Suramgama, the vajra-samadhi, dharanis [i.e. long mantras or magic spells], to enable beings to gain the four unhinderednesses, to enable beings to see the Buddha-Nature; and when practising thus, one sees no samadhi, no form of samadhi, nor a person practising this, nor any result to be arrived at. O good man! If things indeed proceed thus, we say that this person is practising samadhi. "How does one practise

Wisdom? One who practises Wisdom thinks: "If I practise such Wisdom, I shall attain Emancipation and save those in the three unfortunate realms. Who is it that indeed benefits all beings, passing them to the other shore beyond birth and death? It is difficult [to be present when] the Buddha appears in this world. It is as rare an event as one's coming across the flowering of the udumbara. I shall now thoroughly cut away the bonds of all defilements. I shall gain the fruition of Emancipation. On this account, I shall now learn to practise Wisdom and sever the bond of defilement and attain Emancipation." Any person who practises the Way thus is not one who practises Wisdom. "How does a person truly practise Wisdom? The wise person meditates on the sorrows of birth, age, and death. All beings are overshadowed by ignorance and do not know how to practise the unsurpassed right path. He prays: "I pray that this body of mine will suffer great sorrows in lieu of all beings. Let all poverty, degredation, the mind of transgressing the precepts, all the actions of greed, anger and ignorance of all beings gather upon me. I pray that all beings will not gain a mind of greed, will not be bound up in body-and-mind. I pray that all beings will soon cross the sea of birth and death, so that I may not now need to face it and not feel the worry. I pray that all will gain unsurpassed Enlightenment." When a person practises the Way thus, he sees no Wisdom, no form of Wisdom, no one practising WIsdom, and no fruition to be arrived at. This is practising Wisdom. "O good man! One who thus practises sila, samadhi, and Wisdom is a Bodhisattva; one who cannot thus practise sila, samadhi, and Wisdom is a sravaka. "O good man! How does one practise sila [morality]? All sin by committing the 16 evil acts. What are the 16? They are: 1) keeping, feeding, and fattening sheep for profit, and seeing them, 2) buying and killing sheep for profit, 3) raising, fattening and selling pigs for profit, 4) buying and killing them for profit, 5) raising and selling calves for profit when fattened, 6) buying and killing them for profit, 7) raising hens for profit and, when they are grown up, selling them, 8) buying [them] for profit and killing them, 9) fishing, 10) hunting, 11) plundering, 12) selling fish, 13) catching birds with nets, 14) [having a] double-tongue, 15) [being a] jailer, and 16) charming snakes ["nagas"]. One [should] thoroughly segregate one's self eternally from such evil deeds. This is practising sila [morality]."

Chapter Thirty-Six: On Bodhisattva Lion's Roar 4

[The Buddha said:] "How does one practise samadhi [i.e. meditative absorption]? One truly does away with all the worldly samadhis. This is the bodilessness samadhi. Beings get an upside-down mind and wrongly call this Nirvana. Also, there are such samadhis as the boundless-mind samadhi, the pure-group samadhi, the worldlessness samadhi, the world-segregation samadhi, the world-nature samadhi, the skandha-samadhi, the thoughtlessness-non-thoughtlessness samadhi [which] indeed make beings acquire an upside-down mind and call such Nirvana. If one truly segregates one's own self from such samadhis, this is practising samadhi. "How does one practise Wisdom? One thoroughly extirpates the evil views of the world. Beings all possess evil views. That is thinking that "matter" [form] is Self, and that this belongs to Self; that there is Self in matter and matter in Self; and it so goes with consciousness; that matter is the Self; that matter dies, but that the Self stays behind; that matter is the Self, and that when matter dies out, the Self dies out. And a certain person says: "The maker is the Self; the recipient is the Self." Also, a certain person says: "The doer is matter; the receiver is the Self." Also, a certain person says: "There is no doing and no receiving. A thing comes about by itself; it dies out by itself. Nothing is based on causal relations." Also, a certain person says: "There is no doing and no receiving. All is the work of Isvara [i.e. God]." Also, a certain person says: "There cannot be any doer or any receiver. All comes about according to the season." Also, a certain person says: "There are doers and receivers. The five elements beginning with the earth are the being." O good man! If anyone crushes such evil views, this is practising Wisdom. "O good man! Practising sila [morality] is for the quietude of one's own body. Practising samadhi is for the quietude of one's mind; practising Wisdom is for crushing out doubt. To crush out doubt is to practise the Way. To practise the Way is to see the Buddha-Nature. To see the Buddha-Nature is to attain unsurpassed Enlightenment. To attain unsurpassed Enlightenment is to arrive at unsurpassed Great Nirvana. To arrive at Great Nirvana is to segregate all beings from birth and death, all defilements, all [worldly] existences, all realms, all truths of beings. To cut off [these]

births and deaths and satya [truth; presumably "worldly truths"] is to attain to the Eternal, Bliss, the Self and the Pure." Lion's Roar said: "O World-Honoured One! If, as the Buddha says, birthlessness and deathlessness are Nirvana, life too is birthlessness and deathlessness. Why can we not say that this is Nirvana?" "O good man! It is thus, it is thus. It is as you say. Although this life is birthlessness and deathlessness, there are beginnings and ends." "O World-Honoured One! There is also no beginning and no end in this law of birth and death. If there is no beginning and end, this is eternal. The Eternal is Nirvana. Why do we not call birth and death Nirvana?" "O good man! The law of this birth-and-death depends on causality. As there are causes and effects, we cannot call this Nirvana. Why not? Because the body of Nirvana has no cause and effect." Lion's Roar said: "O World-Honoured One! Nirvana has cause and effect, as you the Buddha say: "Through cause one gains birth in heaven; Through cause is one born into the unfortunate realms; Through cause does one attain Nirvana. Thus, everything has a cause." You, the Buddha, said to the bhiksus: "I shall now speak to the sramanas about the fruition of the Way. "Sramana" means nothing other than practising well sila [morality], samadhi, and Wisdom. The Way is the Noble Eightfold Path. The fruition of sramana practice is Nirvana." O World-Honoured One! Nirvana is thus. Is this not fruition [i.e. result]? How can you say that Nirvana has no cause and no fruition?" "O good man! What I refer to as the cause of Nirvana is the so-called Buddha-Nature. The nature of the Buddha-Nature does not call forth Nirvana. That is why I say that there is no cause in Nirvana. As it truly crushes defilement, I say "great fruition". It does not come about by the "Way". Hence I say that there is no fruition. For this reason, Nirvana has no cause and no fruition." Lion's Roar said: "O World-Honoured One! Is the Buddha-Nature of beings a thing of common possession or is it something individually possessed? If it is of common possession, all would have to gain it when one person gains it. O World-Honoured One! Twenty people have one enemy. If one falls out of the group, the remaining 19 may also mean to have no enemy. If the Buddha-Nature is thus, the remaining persons must gain it if one person gains it. If each has the Buddha-Nature, this is non-eternal. Why? The nature of beings is neither one nor two. We cannot say that all Buddhas are all-equal. Also, we cannot say that the Buddha is like the void." The Buddha said: "O good man! The Buddha-Nature of beings is not-one and not-two. The equality spoken of regarding all Buddhas is like the Void. All beings possess it. Anybody who indeed practises the Noble Eightfold Path gains - one should know - a bright view. O good man! In the Himalayas, there is a grass called ninniku [Sanskrit "ksanti" = patience, forbearance]. A cow fed on this will gain sarpirmanda [the tastiest and most healthful of milk products]. It is the same with the Buddha-Nature of beings." Lion's Roar said: "Is the ninniku grass, about which you the Buddha speak, one or many? If it is one, it will come to an end when the cow feeds on it. If many, how can you say that the Buddha-Nature is also like this? You, the Buddha, say that if one practises the Noble Eightfold Path, one will see the Buddha-Nature. But this is not so. Why not? If the Way is one, it must come to an end, as in the case of the ninniku grass. If it comes to an end, there is no further part left for others to practise. If the Way is many, how can we say that practice is perfected? And how can one speak of "sarvajnana" [omniscience]?"

The Buddha said: "O good man! [Suppose] there is a flat road. Beings walk [along it], and there is nothing to hinder their progress. There is in the middle of the road a tree, the shade of which is cool. The travellers make a stop here with their palanquin and take a rest. But there is always the shade of the tree here, and there is no difference. The shade does not die out, and no one takes it away. The road is the Holy Way, and the shade the Buddha-Nature. "O good man! There is a great castle, which has only one gate. Many people come and go, and pass through it, without hindrance. And no one destroys it and takes it away. That is how matters stand. "O good man! It is as with a bridge, which does not care who passes over it; there is no one there to obstruct [the way] or destroy [the bridge] or carry it off. O good man! For example, it is as with a good doctor, who cares all about illnesses. And there is no one who checks [him], either to allow him to cure [people] or forcing him to abandon this. It is the same with the Holy Way and the Buddha-Nature." Lion's Roar said: "O good man! You put forward all

[such] parables, which, however, do not apply Why not? If there is any person on the way before [i.e. up ahead, further on], that person must be hindering [obstructing] the way. How can one say that there is no hindrance? The same applies to the others. If the Holy Way and Buddha-Nature are thus, this, when one practises the Way, would cause hindrance to others." The Buddha said: "O good man! What you say does not make sense. What is explained in parables regarding the Way refers only to a part, not to all. O good man! The way of the world has hindrances. This differs from others; none are equal. The Undefiled Way is not so. It is such that it enables beings to have no hindrance upon their way. All is the same and all-equal; there is no difference as to place, or this and that. Thus, the Right Way serves as the revealed cause for the Buddha-Nature of beings, and does not become the cause of birth. This is as in the case of a bright lamp that does indeed shine over all. "O good man! All beings are chained to ignorant actions through causal relations. Do not say that if one is chained to the way of ignorance, there can be no more such. All beings are chained to the action of ignorance. That is why we say that the 12 links of interdependent arising work equal to all [apply equally to all]. It is the same with the Undefiled, Right Way which all beings practise. All-equally, it does away with the defilements of beings and those of the four lives and all the ways of existence of all realms [in samsara]. So, we say "equal". When one is Enlightened, there is no knowing and seeing of this and that. For this reason, we can well speak of "sarvajnana" [all-knowledge]." Lion's Roar said: "All beings are not of one kind of body. There are devas [gods] and there are humans. And there are such others as those of the realms of the animals, the hungry pretas [ghosts], and hell. They are many, not one. How can we say that the Buddha-Nature can be one?" The Buddha said: "O good man! For example, there is a man who adds poison to milk. Because of this, all [the milk products] up to sarpirmanda will contain poison. We do not call milk butter, and butter milk. The same applies to sarpirmanda. The name may change, but the nature of the poison is not lost. It will run across the five tastes of the milk all-equally. Even sarpirmanda, if taken, will kill a man. Just as poison is not placed in the sarpirmanda, so is it the case with the Buddha-Nature of beings. "One finds the Buddha-Nature of beings in the different

bodies of the beings of the five realms. But the Buddha-Nature is always One, and there is No Change."

Lion's Roar said: "O World-Honoured One! There are six great castles in the sixteen great states [i.e. the Gangetic states or castle-towns in the days of the Buddha], namely: Sravasti, Saketa, Campa, Vaisali, Varanasi, and Rajagriha. These big castles are the biggest in the world. Why is it that the Tathagata leaves these places and intends to enter Nirvana in this far-out, evil, very ugly and small Kusinagara Castle?" "O good man! Do not say that Kusinagara is a castle which is far-out, evil, a most ugly and small place. This castle is one adorned with wonders and virtues. Why? Because this is a place all Buddhas and Bodhisattvas have visited. O good man! Even the house of a humble person may be called "grand and perfect in virtue", worthy of the visit of a great king, should he happen to come past [and stay] there. O good man! [Imagine] a person who is seriously ill and who takes a dirty and mean medicine. His illness is cured, joy arises, and this medicine becomes the best and most wonderful [of medicines]. He praises it and says that it has truly cured his illness. "O good man! A man is in a ship on the great ocean. Of a sudden, the ship breaks up, and there is nothing to depend upon. The man catches hold of a corpse and reaches the other shore. Gaining the other shore, he is very happy and praises the corpse greatly, saying that he was fortunate to meet with this corpse and has safely gained peace. It is the same case with Kusinagara Castle, which all Buddhas and Bodhisattvas have visited. How could one say that it is a far-off, mean, narrow, and small castle? "O good man! I call to mind that once, in far-ff days, as many kalpas back as there are sands to the river Ganges, there was a time called the "Suprabuddha" kalpa [age, aeon]. At that time, there was a holy king called Kausika. Fully endowed with the Seven Treasures and 1,000 children, this king first made this castle. It measured 12 yojanas crosswise and lengthwise. It was adorned with the Seven Treasures. The soil was good. There were rivers here, the waters of which were pure and soft, and they tasted sweet. These were: Nairanjana, Airavati, Hiranyavati, Usmodaka , Vipasa. There were some 500 other such rivers. Both banks were fully grown with trees that had flowers and fruits - all fresh and pure. At that time, the life-span of the

people was uncountable. Then, after the lapse of 100 years, the Chakravartin [mighty ruler] said: "Just as the Buddha says, all things are non-eternal. One who practises the ten good things does away with all such sorrows of the non-eternal." The people, on hearing this, all practised the ten good deeds. I, at that time, on hearing the name of the Buddha, practised the ten good deeds, meditated and aspired to unsurpassed Bodhi [Enlightenment]. My mind having aspired, I also transferred this Dharma to innumerable and boundless [numbers of] beings and said that all things are non-eternal and subject to change and dissolution. Because of this, I now continue and say that all things are non-eternal, are those that change and dissolve, and that only the Buddha-Body is Eternal. I recall what I did by [way of] causal relations. That is why I have now come here and mean to enter Nirvana and wish to repay what I owe to this place. For this reason, I say in the sutra: "My relatives know how to repay what they owe me." "Also, next, O good man! In days past, when the life-span of people was immeasurable, this castle was called Kusanagaravati [probably the same as Kusinagara] and measured 50 yojanas crosswise and lengthwise. At that time in Jambudvipa, people lived shoulder to shoulder and fowl flew thereabout. There lived a Chakravartin named Zenken [Sudarsana]. He had the Seven Treasures and 1,000 children and was the king of the four lands. The first of his sons loved Wonderful Dharma and became a pratyekabuddha. Then, the Chakravartin saw that his crown prince was a pratyekabuddha, that his deportment was orderly, and that he was endowed with wonderful miraculous powers. On seeing this, he renounced his state, as though it were tears and spittle. He became a monk and lived here amidst the sal trees, and for 80,000 years he practised Loving-Kindness. The same applied for 80,000 years to [the practice of] Compassion, Sympathetic Joy, and Equanimity. "O good man! If you should desire to know who that holy king, Zenken, was, then know that he was none other than I. That is why I now abide in the four laws, which are none but the samadhis. For this reason, "the Body of the Tathagata is the Eternal, Bliss, the Self, and the Pure". "O good man! Because of this, I am now in this Kusinagara, in this forest of sal trees, and abide in samadhi. O good man! I recall to mind, after innumerable years, a castle-town called

Kapilavastu. In that castle, there lived a king called Suddhodana. His consort was called Maya. They had a prince, who was called Siddhartha. The prince, at that time, took no teachers. He sought the Way by himself and attained unsurpassed Bodhi. He had two disciples, Sariputra and Mahamaudgalyayana. The disciple who attended the prince was called Ananda. At that time, he, under the sal trees, delivered the sermon of the Great Nirvana Sutra. At that time, I was one of the congregation and was able to be a witness to that sermon. There, I was told that all beings had the Buddha-Nature. On hearing this, I was unmoved in Bodhi. Then, I took a vow: "If I attain Buddhahood in days to come, it shall be as now. I shall be a teacher to my father and mother and the land; the names of the disciples and attendants will also be so, just as things stand with the present World-Honoured One. Nothing will differ." That is why I am now here and am delivering this sermon of the Great Nirvana Sutra. "O good man! When I first abandoned home life, but had not yet attained unsurpassed Enlightenment, Bimbisara sent a messenger to me and said: "If you, Prince Siddhartha, become a Chakravartin, I shall become your subject. But if you leave home and attain unsurpassed Enlightenment, please come to this Rajagriha, deliver sermons, save people and accept my offerings." I then accepted his invitation in silence. "O good man! On attaining unsurpassed Enlightenment, I then decided to go to Kosala. At that time, by the river Nairanjana there lived a Brahmin, Kasyapa, who had 500 disciples and who, by this river, sought of me the unsurpassed Way. I specially wended my way there to speak [to him] of Dharma. Kasyapa said: "O Gautama! I am 120 years old. Many people in Magadha, and the ministers and Bimbisara, say that I have attained arhatship. If I give ear to what you say, all the people might possibly gain inverted ideas and say: [Is not the virtuous Kasyapa already an arhat? Let Gautama speed to other places]. If the people come to know that Gautama's virtue surpasses mine, I shall possibly fail in [i.e. fail to receive] my own alms." I then said: "If you do not harbour any personal enmity towards me, please give me a night's rest. I shall start out early tomorrow morning." Kasyapa said: "O Gautama! I have nothing against you. I love and respect you. Only, in my place there lives a viper which is evil-tempered. It might possibly do some harm to you."

"No poison is more poisonous than the three poisons [of greed, ill-will, and ignorance]. I have now done away with them. I do not fear worldly poison." Kasyapa said: "If you do not, please stay." "O good man! I, at that time, displayed 18 miracles before Kasyapa. This is as stated in the sutra. Kasyapa and his 500 disciples saw this and they all attained arhatship. "At that time, Kasyapa had two younger brothers. One was [called] Gayakasyapa, and the other Nadikasyapa. There were also 500 teachers and disciples. All attained arhatship. The people of the six masters of Rajagriha, fearing this, entertained a great evil mind towards me. Then, true to my word, I went to Rajagriha. On the way, the king came [along] with his people, innumerable hundreds and thousands [of them] in number, and he received me. I delivered a sermon to them. On hearing this, the devas of the world of desire, 86,000 [of them], all aspired to unsurpassed Bodhi. King Bimbisara's retinue of 120,000 guardsmen attained [the level of] srotapanna; an innumerable number of people gained the stage of ksanti [patience]. On reaching the castle, I taught Sariputra and Mahamaudgalyayana, along with their 250 disciples. They all cast aside everything they had had in their mind up till then and entered upon the Path. I lived there and received the king's offerings. The six tirthika masters came along and together we went to Sravasti. "There was at that time a rich man named Sudatta. He wished to gain a wife for his son, and to that end he came to Rajagriha. Arriving at the castle, he put up at the house of Samdhana. Then, this rich man [i.e. Samdhana] got up at midnight and said to the people of his household: "All of you get up, adorn and sweep the house quickly, and prepare a meal!" Sudatta heard this and thought to himself: "Is he going to invite the king of Magadha? Or is it going to be a marriage and pleasure gathering?" Thinking thus, he stepped forward and asked: "Are you going to invite Bimbisara, King of Mgadha? Is there going to be a wedding and pleasure party? Why are you so busily occupied thus?" The rich man answered, saying: "Have you not yet heard of the son of the Sakyas of Kapilavastu called Siddhartha? Gautama is his family name. His father is called Suddhodana. Not long after his birth, the augur said that the boy would unfailingly become a Chakravartin and that this was as clear as if one could see an amra in the palm of one's hand. He sought no pleasures and abandoned domestic life. And untaught by any person, he attained unsurpassed Bodhi. He has done away with greed, ill-will, and ignorance. He is Eternal and knows no change. Nothing comes about and nothing dies out; and he is fearless. All beings are one to him. They are as a single son is to his parents, and his body and mind are unsurpassed.

Though surpassing all, he has no arrogance in his mind. Wisdom is all around [him] and nothing hinders [him in his Wisdom]. And he is perfect in the ten powers, the four fearlessnesses, the five knowledges ["pancajnana"], samadhi, Great Loving-Kindness, Great Compassion, and the three thinkings. That is why he is the Buddha. Tomorrow, he will receive my offerings. That is why I am busy and do not have enough time to exchange greetings." Sudatta said: "Well said, O great one! The Buddha you speak of is unsurpassed in virtue. Where is he now?" The rich man said: "He is now in this great citadel of Rajagriha, staying with Venuvana-kalandakanivapa." Then, Sudatta meditated on the ten powers, the four fearlessnesses, the five knowledges, samadhi, Great Loving-Kindness, and the three thinkings which the Buddha possesses. As he so meditated, there arose a brightness, as a result of which everything looked as if in bright daylight. Wanting to know whence the light came, he went down to the gate. By the miraculous power of the Buddha, the gate opened of itself. On coming out of the gate, he saw a chapel on the roadside. Passing it, Sudatta did worship. Then, darkness arose again. Afraid, he decided to go back to where he was [before]. Then a deva met him at the chapel by the castle gate. The deva said to Sudatta: "Go to where the Tathagata is and you will gain much benefit." Sudatta said: "What benefit?" The deva said: "O rich man! As an illustration: a man may have 100 superb steeds, adorned with laces studded with gems, 100 gandhahastins, 100 carts of jewels, 100 human forms made of gold, beautiful females fully adorned with necklaces of gems, beautiful palaces and halls and houses studded with gems, with sculptured letters and figures on them, silver millet on golden trays, and golden millet on silver trays, 100 in number, and these are offered as dana [charity] to each person all over Jambudvipa. But the virtue [thus] arrived at cannot surpass a single step towards aspiring to Bodhi and going to the Tathagata." Sudatta said: "O good man! Who are

you?" The deva said: "O rich man! I am the son of a right-lined Brahmin. I am a former teacher of the Way. In days gone by, I felt joy when I saw Sariputra and Maudgalyayana, and I discarded my body and became the son of Vaisravana, the guardian angel of the north. It is my special duty to guard this Rajagriha. I have gained this wonderful form through worship and have acquired joy thereby. And how much greater must things be if one meets such a great teacher as the Tathagata and worships him and makes offerings to him?" "Sudatta, on hearing this, turned round his steps and came to the place where I was. On arriving, he fell to the ground and touched my feet. I then, as was appropriate, spoke of Dharma. Having listened to my sermon, the rich man attained the [stage of] srotapanna. Gaining this fruition, he invited me, saying: "O great teacher, Tathagata! I pray that you will condescend to come to Sravasti and accept my paltry offerings." I then asked him: "Can you, in your Sravasti, accommodate all?" Sudatta said: "If the Buddha is compassionate and condescends to accede to my request, I shall do my best." O good man! I then accepted his invitation. This rich man, Sudatta, his prayer having been answered, said to me: "Hitherto I have had no experience of laying out [a big meal]. O Tathagata! Please despatch Sariputra to my place, so that he can take the matter in hand and make the necessary arrangements to meet the requirements." "Then, Sariputra went to Sravasti, riding together with Sudatta. By my miraculous power, they reached their destination in one day. Then, Sudatta said to Sariputra: "O greatly virtuous one! Outside this gate, there is a place best fitted for the purpose. It is neither near nor far, where there are many springs and ponds, and many forests, with flowers and fruit; and the place is pure and quiet and extensive. I shall build viharas [dwelling-places] there for the Buddha and his bhiksus [monks]." Sariputra said: "The forest of Prince Jeta is neither near nor far off. It is pure and quiet. There are springs and streams. There are seasonal flowers and fruit. This is the best place. Let us have a vihara built there." "Then, on hearing this, Sudatta went to the great rich man, Jeta, and said to him: "I now desire to build a Buddhist vihara and dedicate it to one usurpassed in Dharma, at a place that belongs to you. I now desire to purchase it from you. Will you sell it to me?" Jeta said: "I will not sell it to you, even if you cover the ground with gold." Sudatta said:

"Well said! The forest belongs to me. Take my gold." Jeta said: "I am not selling the forest to you. How can I take your gold?" Sudatta said: "If you are not satisfied, I will go to the magistrate." They both went together. The magistrate said: "The forest belongs to Sudatta. Jeta should take the gold." Sudatta at once despatched men with gold laden upon carts and horses. When it arrived, he covered the ground with gold. A single day saw an area of 500 "bu" [a Chinese unit of measurement of land, around 6 or 6.4 feet long] covered; not all was covered. Jeta said: "O rich ran! If you have any regret within you, you are quite free to cancel the deal." Sudatta said: "I do not feel any regret." He thought to himself which store he should now open, to get gold for the area left as yet uncovered with gold. Jeta thought to himself: "The Tathagata, King of Dharma, is truly one unsurpassed. The wonderful things that he teaches are pure and untainted. That is why this man thinks so lightly of this treasure." He then said to Sudatta: "I do not now need any gold for what remains uncovered. Please take it. I myself shall build a gate for the Tathagata, so that he may go in and out of it." Jeta built the gate, and in seven days, Sudatta built a great vihara on a site 300 "ken" [ken is about 6 feet] across and in length. There were quiet meditation quarters to the number of 63. The houses were different for winter and summer. There were kitchens, bathrooms, and a place to wash one's feet. There were two kinds of lavatory. "The buildings completed, he took up an incense burner, and facing in the direction of Rajagriha, said:

"The buildings are now completed. O Tathagata! Please have pity and take over this place and live here for the good of beings." I soon read the mind of this rich man from far off, and started out from Rajagriha. Within the short length of time it takes for a strong, youthful man to bend and extend his arm, I travelled to Sravasti, to Jetavana, and took possession of the Jetavana vihara. When I reached the place, Sudatta dedicated it to me. I then received it and lived in it."

Chapter Thirty-Seven: On Bodhisattva Lion's Roar 5

Then the six masters became jealous and all gathered at the place of King Prasenajit and said: "O great King! Your land is clean and quiet all around and is really the place where renunciate people can live well. Because of this, we have all come here. O great King! Do away, with right law, what is not conducive to the good of the people. Sramana Gautama is still young and unripe [immature]. Having not yet learned much, he has nothing to give. Now, in this country live many elders and virtuous persons, who, boasting of the Kshatriya caste, do not know how to pay homage. The king must govern the land through law; the world-fleeing [i.e. religious seekers, mendicants] must look up to virtue. Listen well, O great King! Sramana Gautama is not one truly of a Kshatriya family. If Sramana Gautama has any parents, why does he have to take away others' parents? O great King! It is stated in our sutras that in 1,000 years there will appear a phantom or apparition. The so-called sramana Gautama is this. On this account, know well that the sramana is none other than this Gautama. Because of this, know that Sramana Gautama has no father and no mother. If he has, how can he say: "All things are non-eternal, suffering, void; and all have no self, no doing, no feeling?" Through occult powers, he leads beings astray. The ignorant believe, and the wise reject. O great King! The king is the parent to the land. He is, as it were, like the earth, wind, fire, way, river, bridge, lamp, sun, and moon. Through law, he dispenses justice. There cannot be any enemy or friend. Sramana Gautama permits no life. Where we go, he follows, and does not leave us. O great King! Allow us to compete in our powers of attainment. Should he win, we will become his disciples. If we win, he shall come under us." The king said: "O great ones! You each have your own way of practice, and you live in different places. I definitely know that the Tathagata-World-Honoured One does not cause you any hindrance." The six masters replied: "How is he not a hindrance to us? Sramana Gautama works miracles, leading all the people and Brahmins astray. He now has no more to subdue. If you, King, allow us to compete in miracles, the King's good reputation will spread to all quarters. If not, evil fame will circulate abroad." The king said: "O great ones! You do not realise how superior the power of the Way of the Tathagata is. So, you seek to compete [with him]. I am sure that you will fail." "O great King! Have you already been spellbound by Gautama? Pray, O King, think well and do not belittle us. The best thing is actually to put the matter to the test." The king said: "Well said, well said!" The six masters were pleased and went on their way.

"Then, King Prasenajit came to me, touched the ground, walked around me three times, drew back, sat to one side, and said to me: "O World-Honoured One! The six masters came to me to seek permission to compete with you in the power of the Way. I carelessly gave permission." I said: "It is well, it is well! Only, erect many viharas in the land. Why? If I compete with them, there will be so many of them who will have to come over to our side that there will not be any place to accommodate them, as this place is rather too small and confined to hold them all." O good man! I, at that time, displayed a great many miracles, for the good of the six masters, from the first to the fifteenth day. Then, an innumerable number of beings gained faith in the Three Treasures and had no doubt. The number of followers of the six masters who did away with distorted minds and took refuge in Wonderful Dharma was countless. An innumerable number of people gained the unretrogressive Bodhi Mind. An innumerable number of people gained dharanis and samadhi. An innumerable number of beings attained the fruition of arhatship, rising up from [the level of] srotapanna. "Then, the six masters repented [felt downcast] and together they went to Saketa and made people believe in twisted ways of life. They said: "Sramana Gautama teaches what is empty." O good man! I, at that time, was in Trayastrimsa Heaven and was living the life of varsika under the shade of the Parijata Tree, delivering a sermon to my mother. Then, the six masters were greatly pleased and said: "Oh good! The miracles of Gautama have ceased!" Also, [due to their] teaching an innumerable number of beings, wrong views on life increased and spread. Then, Bimbisara, Prasenajit, and the four classes of the Sangha said to Maudgalyayana: "O virtuous one! Twisted views fill this Jambudvipa. The people are miserable who must be wending their way towards great gloom. Please, O you virtuous one! Go to Heaven, fall upon the ground, pay homage and convey our words to the World-Honoured One: [Just as the newly-born calf will surely die if milk is not given, so do things stand with us beings. Have pity on us beings, O Tathagata, and come back down to us]." Then, Maudgalyayana answered their prayer and as swiftly as a strong man can bend and stretch out his arm, he came up to Heaven and said to me, the Buddha: "All the four classes of the Buddhist Sangha look up to the Tathagata and desire to hear directly from you a sermon on Dharma. Bimbisara, Prasenajit, and the four classes of the Sangha are all falling to the ground, paying homage, and saying: "The beings of this Jambudvipa are twisted in their views, and this is increasing all the more. They are walking in great gloom. This is a great pity. This is similar to a new-born calf who is sure to die if no milk is given [him]. It is the same with us. For the sake of all us beings, condescend, O Tathagata, to come down to Jambudvipa and live." I, the Buddha, said to Maudgalyayana: "Hurry to Jambudvipa and tell all the kings and the four classes of people of the Buddhist Sangha that in seven days I shall be back. For the good of the six masters, I shall come to Saketa." "Seven days later, I, the Buddha, surrounded by Sakrodevendra, Brahma, Mara, and an innumerable number of heavenly beings and all the heavenly ones who were gathered together in Suddhavasa Heaven, came to the castle of Saketa and let out a lion's roar, declaring: "Only in my Doctrine can there be sramanas and Brahmins. All things are non-eternal and with no self. Nirvana is quiet and is removed from wrongs and worries. In other teachings, people may say that they have sramanas and Brahmins and that these are the Eternal, the Self, and Nirvana. But such can never be." Then, innnumerable, boundless numbers of people aspired to unsurpassed Enlightenment. Then, the six masters said to one another: "If there are no sramanas and Brahmins in other teachings, how can we expect dana from the world at large?" Then the six masters met and went to Vaisali. O good man! At that time, was staying in a mango grove. Then, Amrapali, seeing that I was there, wished to come and see me. I then spoke to all the bhiksus: "Meditate on what there is to think about ["smrtyupasthana", mindfulness] and cultivate Wisdom. As you cultivate this, do not lose yourselves in indolence." What do we mean by meditating on what is to think about? A bhiksu

meditates on his own body and does not see there the Self or what the Self possesses; also, he meditates on the bodies of others and also his own and others, and he does not see the Self or what the Self possesses; this can even extend to what obtains with the mental functions. This is the application of mindfulness, of awareness.

"What do we mean by cultivating Wisdom? A bhiksu truly sees suffering, the cause of suffering, [its] extinction, and the Way to [its] extinction. This is cultivating Wisdom. "What is not being indolent? A bhiksu meditates on the Buddha, Dharma, and Sangha, the moral precepts, equanimity, and heaven. This is where we say that a bhiksu is not indolent in his mind. "Amrapali came to me, fell to the ground, walked around me three times from right to left, paid homage, stepped back, and sat down to one side. O good man! To her I spoke of Dharma. Having heard [this], she aspired to unsurpassed Bodhi. "At that time, there were in that castle 500 sons of the Licchavis. They came to me, fell to the ground, and walked around me from right to left. Having paid homage, they stepped back and seated themselves to one side. I then, for the sake of the Licchavis, spoke about Dharma: "O all of you good men! Those who are indolent contract the five karmic fruitions. What are the five? 1) one is unable freely to gain wealth; 2) evil reputation runs apace [spreads around]; 3) one does not desire to give to the poverty-stricken people; 4) one does not desire to see the four classes of people of the Sangha, and 5) one cannot gain the body of a deva. O all you good men! By non-indolence there comes about the worldly and the supramundane law. One who desires to gain unsurpassed Bodhi must practise non-indolence. Now, there are 13 things that come about as a result [of indolence]. What are the 13? They are: 1) one takes pleasure in doing what is worldly, 2) one takes pleasure in speaking useless words, 3) one takes pleasure in sleeping for a long time, 4) one takes pleasure in speaking about secular things, 5) one always takes pleasure in making friends with evil persons, 6) one is indolent and lazy, 7) one is always belittled by others, 8) one hears, but soon forgets, 9) one takes pleasure in living in far-off [provincial] places, 10), one is unable to subdue all one's sense-organs, 11) one cannot get enough food, 12) one does not desire quietude, 13) one's view is not correct. These are the 13." O good man! A person may well come near to the Buddha and his disciples. Yet there is [still] a great distance. All the Licchavis said: "We know that we are indolent. Why? If we were not indolent, the Tathagata, the King of Dharma, would have to appear among us." "Then, among the congregated, there was the son of a Brahmin called Unsurpassed, who said to all the Licchavis: "Well said, well said! All is as you say. King Bimbisara once gained a great victory. The Tathagata-World-Honoured-One appears in his land. This is like the case of a great pond in which wonderful lotuses grow. Although born in the water, the water cannot defile them, O you Licchavis! It is the same with the Buddha. Although born in that land, he is not hindered by what obtains in the secular world. With the All-Buddha-World-Honoured One, there is no appearing and disappearing. For the good of all beings, he appears in the world, and is not molested by what obtains in the world. You have lost your way, have got lost in the five desires, you have befriended these, but you do not know how to befriend the Tathagata and come to where he is. So we say indolent. When the Buddha appears in Magadha, there is no indolence to speak of. Why not? The Tathagata-World-Honoured One is like the sun and moon. He does not appear in the world just for one or two people." When the Licchavis had heard this, they aspired to unsurpassed Bodhi. Also, they said: "Well said, well said, O you young, unsurpassed boy! You truly say something wonderful." Then, each of the Licchavis took off his clothing and gave it to the Unsurpassed one. Receiving these, he gave them all to me and said: "O World-Honoured One! I have all these from the Licchavis. I pray that you, the Tathagata, will take pity on all beings and accept what I now desire to offer up to you." Taking pity, I then accepted them. All the Licchavis folded their hands and said: "Please summon the varsika here once and accept what we offer." I then accepted the invitation of the Licchavis. "Then the six masters, on hearing this, all went to Varanasi. Then I, too, went to Varanasi and stayed on the banks of the river Varana. At that time, there was a rich man in Varanasi called Treasure-Praising who had abandoned himself to the five desires and was unaware of impermanence. As I was going there, he spontaneously gained the "white-bone meditation" and saw all such as the palatial buildings, male and female servants, turn into

white bones. He shook with fear. This was as sharp as a sword, a viper, a robber, or fire. He came out of his house and came to me. As he walked, he said: "O Sramana Gautama! I feel as if I am being pursued by robbers; I am greatly frightened. Please help me!" "I said: "O good man! Peaceful are the Buddha, Dharma, and Sangha, and there is nothing to fear." The son of the rich man said: "If there is nothing to fear in the Three Treasures, I too shall gain fearlessness." I allowed him to renounce domestic life and to get ordained, so that he could well attain the Way. At that time, the son of the rich man had 50 friends. On hearing that Treasure-Praising had forsaken the domestic life and become ordained, they obediently entered the Path together. "The six masters heard of this and moved on to Campa. At that time, the people of Campa were all followers of the six masters and had not yet heard of the Buddha, Dharma, and Sangha. And there were many of them who did evil. I then, for their sake, went to Campa. At that time, a rich man, who had no son to succeed him, lived in the castle. Following the six masters, he sought a son. Not long after that, his wife became pregnant. The rich man, on being told of this fact, went to the six masters and spoke of it, greatly pleased: "My wife will bear a child. Is it a boy or girl?" The six masters answered: "It will surely be a girl." On hearing this, the man was sad. Then a wise man came to him and said: "Why are you worried?" The rich man said: "My wife will bear a child. I did not know if the child to be born would be a boy or girl. So I asked the six masters, who said: "If what I see is true, the child must be a girl." Hearing this, I thought to myself: "I am old and am unspeakably rich. If the child is not a boy, I will have no one to give my wealth to." That is why I am worried."The wise man said: "You are dull-witted. Do you not know whose disciples the brothers Uruvilvakasyapas are? Are they the disciples of the Buddha or of the six masters? If the six masters are omniscient, why should the Kasyapas abandon them and become the disciples of the Buddha? Also, are not Sariputra, Maudgalyayana, all the kings, Bimbisara, and all the royal consorts and Mallika, and all the rich men of all states like Sudatta, the disciples of the Buddha? Were not all the demons of the wildernesses, the intoxicated elephant, whose duty it was to guard the property of Ajatasatru, and Angulimalya, who - gripped by an evil [state of] mind - meant to harm his own mother, not all subdued by the Tathagata? O rich man! The Tathagata-World-Honoured One is unimpeded in Wisdom. That is why we say "Buddha". There is no double-tongue in what he says. Hence, Tathagata. As he is cut off from defilement, he is called "arhat". The World-Honoured One does not speak in two ways. It is otherwise with the six masters. How can we believe them? The Tathagata is staying close by here. If you desire to know, go and see the Buddha." Then, the rich man came to me with this man. He prostrated himself before me, circumambulated me three times from right to left, folded his hands, and said: "O World-Honoured One! To all beings you are all-equal and are not two. Enemy and friend are one in your eyes. I am chained by desire, and enemy and friend cannot be one to me. I now wish to ask the Tathagata about something worldly. Shame takes hold of me, and I cannot speak out. O World-Honoured One! My wife will bear a child. The six masters say: "The child is a female." What will it be?" I, the Buddha, said: "O rich man! You wife will bear a child. It will be a son. There is no doubt about this. When he is born, he will be fully blessed with virtue." The rich man, on hearing this, was very happy and went back home. Then, the six masters, hearing the prophesy that the child would be male and would be full of virtue, became jealous. They made up a poison mixed in with mango and took it to the rich man, saying: "It is well and good that Gautama saw things well. Give this to your wife in the month of her parturition. If she takes this, her child will be fair and right-set [well formed], and your wife will have no trouble." The rich man received the poisoned medicine and was pleased and gave it to his wife. On taking this, his wife died. The six masters were glad and went round the castle, saying aloud: "Sramana Gautama said that the woman would give birth to a boy and that the child would be superb in virtue. The child is not yet born, but the mother is dead." Then, the rich man came to me and mistrusted me. Following the way of the people, the man put the corpse in a coffin and carried it out of the castle and covered it with dry fuel. Then it was set fire to and cremated. I saw this with the eye of the Way and looked back to Ananda and said: "Bring my robe! I will go there and destroy the twisted views." Then, Deva Vaisravana said to the general, Manibhadra: "Now, the Tathagata intends to go to the graveyard. Go quickly, sweep the place, position the lion's-seat ["simhasana"], fetch wonderful flowers and adorn the place." Then, the six masters, seeing me from afar, went to the graveyard and said: "Does Gautama desire to devour the flesh?" At that time, there were many upasakas [lay Buddhists] who had no Dharma-Eye. Frightened, they said to me: "The woman is already dead. Please do not go!" Then, Ananda said to them: "Wait a while. Before long, the Tathagata will manifest the world of all Buddhas." I then went and seated myself upon the lion's-seat. The rich man reproached me: "What is said must not be two. Such a person is the World-Honoured One. The mother has already died. How can there be any child?" I said: "O rich man! At the time, you made no matter of the life-span of your wife. Your concern was whether the child to come would be male or female. The All-Buddha-Tathagata is not double-tongued. Know, therefore, that you will surely get your child." Then, the mother's belly broken open by the fire and a child emerged, and sat amid the fire. It was as when the mandarin duck sits on the lotus seat. The six masters saw this and said: "This is miraculous, O Gautama! You surely perform magic." The rich man saw and was glad. He reproached the six masters: "If magic, why do you not do it yourself?" I then said to Jivaka: "Enter the fire and fetch the child out!" Jivaka wanted to go, [but] the six masters came forward and said to Jivaka: "What miracles Sramana Gautama performs cannot always be so successful. There will be successes and failures. When it does not succeed, you will have to [suffer] harm yourself. How can you believe in his word?" Jivaka answered: "The Tathagata enables me to enter Avichi Hell. The fire cannot burn me. How could it [burn me] when it merely concerns the fire of the world?" Then Jivaka stepped forward into the fire. It was as if he were entering the cool water of a great river. Holding the child, he came back and handed it over to me. I then took the child and said to the rich man: "The life-span of all beings is not fixed. It is like water-foam. If beings are to harvest serious karmic fruition, fire cannot burn nor poison kill them. It is the karma of this child, not mine." Then the rich man said: "Well said, O World-Honoured One! If this child can live, please, O Tathagata, give the child a name!" The Buddha said: "This child of the rich man is born of fire. Fire is "judai". So this child is to be called

Judai." Thus, those who were congregated there saw this miracle, and innumerable were those who aspired to unsurpassed Bodhi. "Then, the six masters went round the six castle-towns and yet could not win the minds of the people of those places. Ashamed and with lowered heads, they came here to Kusinagara. Arriving here, they said: "Know, O all you people! Sramana Gautama is a great magician. He cheats the world, going here and there all over the six castles. For example, he is like a magician who conjures up the four military units of charioteers, horsemen, elephant-riders, and infantrymen. Also, he calls forth such things as various necklaces, castles, palaces, rivers, ponds and trees. That is how things are with Sramana Gautama. He presents himself as a king. For the purpose of sermons, he becomes a sramana, a Brahmin, a male, a female, a small body, a big body, or an animal, or demon. Or, at one time he speaks of impermanence, and at another of Permanence. At one time he speaks of suffering, at another of Bliss. At one time he speaks of the Self, and at another of selflessness. Or he speaks of Purity, and at another time of impurity. At one time, he speaks of "is", and at another, he speaks of "not-is". As whatever is done is false, we say "phantom". For example, by the son and following the son, a person gains fruition. So do things obtain with Sramana Gautama. He has come from Maya, who is a phantom. He cannot be other than such a son. Gautama has no true knowledge. All Brahmins practise penance and uphold the precepts year after year. And yet they say they have no true knowledge. And Gautama is young and is less in learning and has not yet practised penance. How can it be that there is true knowing [here]? Even seven years of penance are not enough to call forth much results. As against this, it is even less than six years. The ignorant with no wisdom believe in his teaching. This is like the case of a great magician who greatly cheats the ignorant. It is the same with Sramana Gautama." O good man! Thus the six masters spread many false words amongst the people of this castle-town. O good man! Seeing this, I took pity, and with my miraculous powers I called in all the Bodhisattvas of the ten directions into this forest, who filled the place and surrounded me in an area 50 yojanas in extent, and I here gave forth a lion's roar. O good man! When speaking in a place where there is no one to hear, we do not say "lion's roar". When speaking in a

congregation of the learned, we truly can say "lion's roar". That is to say that all things are non-eternal, suffering, non-Self, and non-Pure, and that only the Tathagata is the Eternal, Bliss, the Self, and the Pure. Then the six masters again said: "If Gautama has his Self, we too have it. The Self alluded to is none other than "seeing". O Gautama! One sees a thing that confronts one. The case of the Self is the same. What confronts one is the eye and the seeing is the Self." "The Buddha said to the six masters: "If seeing is the Self, you are wrong. Why? You take up the analogy of an object and say that we see by it. Now, man uses together the six sense-organs to one object. If there surely is the Self and we see unfailingly by [means of] the eye, why is it that we do not cognise all objects with that one sense-organ? If one does not meet with the six sense-fields, know that there is no Self to talk of. If things are thus with the sense-organ of sight, there will be no change even if years pass and the sense-organs become ripened. As "man" and "object" are different, one sees one's own self and the other. If it is thus with the sense-organ of sight, there must be the seeing of one's own self and the other at [one and the same] time. If not seen, how can we say that there is the Self?" "The six masters said: "O Gautama! If there is no Self, who sees?" The Buddha said: "There are the thing, brightness [light], the mind, and the eye. Thus, the four conjoin and we see. In these, truth to tell, there is none that sees and none that feels. Beings are upside-down and say that there is one who sees and feels. Thus all beings are upside-down in their seeing, and all Buddhas and Bodhisattvas are true in seeing things. O you six masters! You may say that matter is Self. But this is not so. Why not? Matter is not the Self. If matter were the Self, there could not be any ugly or weakened form. Why not? And why is it that there are the differences of the four castes? Why is it that there is none but one kind of Brahmin? Why is it that people belong to the other castes and do not have unrestrictedness? Why is it that there are deficiencies in the sense-organs and that life is not perfect? Why is it that people do not all gain the body of all the devas, but gain life in hell, as an animal, preta [ghost] and all the various forms of life? If one cannot do as one wills, know that this indicates that assuredly no Self is there. As there is no Self, we speak of the non-eternal. As it is non-eternal, we have suffering. Because of suffering, it is empty. As it is empty, it is upside down. Being upside down, all beings repeat birth and death. The same applies to feeling, sensation, volition, and consciousness. O you six masters! The Tathagata-World-Honoured One is segregated from the bondage of matter down to the bondage of consciousness. Hence, we say the Eternal, Bliss, the Self, and the Pure. "Also, next. Matter is based on causal relations. What is based on causal relations has no Self. Non-Self is suffering and empty. The body of the Tathagata is not based on causal relations. Because there are no causal relations, we say that there is the Self. The Self is the Eternal, Bliss, Self, and the Pure." "The six masters said: "O Gautama! Matter is non-Self. And down to consciousness, there is no Self. The Self fills everywhere. It is like space." "The Buddha said: "If it fills everywhere, we cannot say that we do not see it from the very beginning. If it is not seen from the very start, we may know that this seeing is what originally was not is now. If it is what originally was not but is now, this is the non-eternal. If it is non-eternal, how can one say that it fills [everywhere]? If it fills [everywhere] and exists, there must be one body in the five realms. If there is one body that can be represented, there must be that which comes about as one result. If one result comes about, how can we say that people gain life as humans or as gods? "You say that it fills [everywhere]. Is it one or many? If the Self is one, there cannot be any father and son, any enemy and friend, or a neutral person. If the Self is many, all the five sense-organs man possesses must be all-equal. The same applies to karma and Wisdom. If things obtain thus, how can we say that there can be those whose sense-organs are perfect or imperfect, that there are actions that are good and evil, and that there is the difference of dullness and intellectuality?" "O Gautama! The Self of all beings knows no boundary line. Dharma and non-Dharma each has its part to play. If beings act according to Dharma, they will gain good forms; if not, evil forms will come about. For this reason, it cannot be other than that the karmic results vary." "The Buddha said: "O you six masters! If Dharma and non-Dharma must obtain thus, there cannot be any universality of the Self; if there is universality of the Self, it will extend all over. If it is so, then even those who practise good must also have parts that are evil and those who do evil must also have what is good. If not, how can we speak of universality?" "O Gautama! For example, we have in a room 100 thousand lamps placed there, and each lamp is bright, not obstructing the others. It is the same with all beings. The practising of good and the performing of evil do not get mixed up." "You say that the Self is like a lamp. But this is not so. Why not? The brightness of a lamp arises from causal relations. If the lamp is large, the brightness, too, becomes great. It is not like this with the self of the being. The brightness of the lamp arises out of the lamp and stays in other places. The self of the being arises out of the body, but cannot stay in other places. The light of the lamp dwells with the gloom. Why? When one puts a lamp into a dark room, the brightness is not much to talk of. When there are many lamps, we have brightness. If the first lamp dispels the gloom, we do not need any further lamps to dispel the gloom. If, later, lamps are used to dispel the gloom, this means that the first brightness dwells with the gloom." "O Gautama! If there is no Self, who is it that does good and evil?" "The Buddha said: "If the Self does [i.e. performs actions], how can we say [it is] Eternal? If it is Eternal, how can a person do good at one time and evil at another? If a person does good or evil at [different] times, how can we say that the Self is boundless? If the Self does, why would one practise evil things? If the Self is the doer and if it is the wise, how can one doubt about the selflessness of the being? So, we can say that there can definitely be no Self in the doctrine of the tirthikas. The Self is none other than the Tathagata. Why? Because his body is boundless and there exists no doubt. On account of non-doing and non-receiving [of karmic consequences], we say Eternal. On account of birthlessness and deathlessness, we say Bliss. As there exists no defilement of illusion, we say Pure. As he does not have the ten aspects of existence, we say Void [i.e. void of all that causes suffering]. Hence, the Tathagata is none other than the Eternal, Bliss, the Self, and the Pure, and the Void, and there is no other aspect to speak of." "All the tirthikas said: "If the Tathagata is the Eternal, Bliss, the Self, and the Pure and Void, due to formlessness, what Gautama says cannot be void. Because of this, we now accept [his words]." "At that time, the number of tirthikas was innumerable. They renounced the world and had faith in the Buddha's teaching. O good man! For this reason, I now, here in this forest of twin sal trees, give a lion's roar. The lion's roar is Great Nirvana. O good man! The twin trees of the east destroy the non-eternal, and through this one gains the Eternal. The twin trees of the north destroy the impure and give one the Pure. O good man! The beings that are here, because of the twin trees, protect the sal trees and will not allow people to take and cut the twigs and leaves and break [them]. It is the same with me. For the [sake of the] four laws [i.e. Eternity, Bliss, Self, and Purity], I make people protect and uphold Buddha-Dharma. What are the four? These are the Eternal, Bliss, the Self, and the Pure. These four twin trees are protected by the four guardians of the earth. As the four guardians guard this Dharma of mine, I here enter Parinirvana. O good man! The twin sal trees always bear fruit and give benefit to countless beings. It is the same with me. I always give benefit to sravakas and pratyekabuddhas. The flower is comparable to the Self, and the fruit is comparable to Bliss. Because of this, I here enter into the Great Silence amidst the twin sal trees. The Great Silence is Great Nirvana." Lion's Roar said: "Why does the Tathagata enter Nirvana in the second month?" "O good man! The second month is spring. In the month of spring, all things grow. We sow seeds and plant roots. Flowers and fruits grow and prosper. The rivers large and small are full, and hundreds of animals raise their young and give [them] milk. At this time, many a being entertains the thought of the Eternal. To destroy such a thought of the Eternal [regarding what is samsaric], I say that all things are non-eternal and that the Tathagata is the Eternal and Immutable. O good man! Of the six seasons, the stringent [severe] winter and the withering season are not loved by the people. What is greedily loved is the bright spring, when it is peaceful. To destroy the [samsaric notion of] bliss of the people of the world, I speak of the Eternal and Bliss [of Nirvana]. It is the same with the Self and Purity. "To crush out the worldly notion of the Self and Purity, the Tathagata speaks of the Self and Purity of true sense". With reference to the second month, the Tathagata intends to compare it to the two kinds of Dharma Body. To say that one does not have bliss in winter is compared to the fact that the wise do not desire to have the Tathagata be non-eternal and enter Nirvana. To say that a person feels bliss is compared to the fact that the wise are pleased over the Eternal, Bliss, Self, and Purity of the Tathagata. The sowing of seeds can be compared to beings' giving ear to sermons on Dharma and their feeling pleased, aspiring to

unsurpassed Bodhi, and to their planting, thereby, the seeds of good. The rivers can be compared to the coming of all great Bodhisattvas to my place and receiving the Great Nirvana Sutra. The hundreds of animals giving milk is comparable to all those of my disciples who perform good deeds. "Flower" is likened to the seven Bodhi elements; "fruit" can be compared to the four fruitions. For this reason, I enter Nirvana on this second month." Lion's Roar said: "The Tathagata's birth, his renouncing of home life, his attainment of Bodhi, and his first turning of [the Wheel of] Dharma all took place on the eighth day. Why does this Nirvana take place on the fifteenth?" The Buddha said: "Well said, well said, O good man! The fifteenth is the day on which the moon has no waxing or waning. It is the same with the All-Buddha-Tathagata. Entering Great Nirvana, there is no more waxing and waning. That is why I enter Nirvana on the fifteenth day. O good man! On the fifteenth, when the moon is full, there are 11 things. What are the 11? They are: 1) it truly dispels the gloom, 2) it indeed enables beings to see the way and what is not the way, 3) it enables [one to follow] the wrong or right way, 4) it enables beings to make away with suppressed dampness and blesses them with purity and coolness, 5) it indeed destroys the arrogance of the fire-worm [firefly], 6) it truly dispels the thought of any robbers, 7) it indeed dispels beings' fear of evil beasts, 8) it opens the bloom of the utpala, 9) it thoroughly closes the petals of the lotus, 10), it calls forth within the traveller the thought of proceeding along the way, 11) it enables beings to enjoy accepting the five pleasures and to gain joy in many ways. "O good man! It is the same with the full moon of the Tathagata, to wit: 1) it truly dispels the gloom of ignorance, 2) it propounds the right and wrong ways, 3) it clearly shows the wrong and steep path of birth and death and the level and right [path] of Nirvana, 4) it enables beings to segregate themselves from greed, ill-will, and ignorance, 5) it destroys the ignorance of the tirthikas [non-Buddhists], 6) it destroys the bondage of the robbers of defilement, 7) it kills the mind that fears the five shadowings ["panca-avaranani"], 8) it enables the beings' minds to unfold the root of good of all beings, 9) it indeed puts a lid on the mind of the five desires, 10), it promotes the mind of beings [which desires] to go forwards to Great Nirvana, 11), it enables all beings to be pleased at [the thought of] Emancipation. For these reasons, I enter Nirvana on the fifteenth. But, truth to tell, I do not enter Nirvana. The ignorant and the evil among my disciples say that I definitely enter Nirvana. For example, a mother has many sons. She abandons them and goes abroad. While she is not yet back, the sons say: "Mother is dead." But the mother is not dead. That is how matters stand." Bodhisattva Lioon's Roar said: "O World-Honoured One! What bhiksu can truly adorn these sal trees?" "O good man! There is a bhiksu who upholds and recites the 12 types of sutra, reads the words correctly, gains the depths of meaning and, for the sake of all other people, explains [it], in which there can be the grades of beginning, middle and the ultimate good. To benefit innumerable people, he speaks about pure actions. Such a bhiksu truly adorns the twin sal trees." Lion's Roar said: "O World-Honoured One! If I rightly guess what you, the Buddha, mean - Ananda is that bhiksu. Why? Ananda upholds and recites the 12 types of sutra, and speaks correctly to others and expounds the meaning. This is like pouring water and filling other vessels. So do things pertain with Ananda. What he hears from the Buddha, he speaks as he has heard it." "O good man! There is a bhiksu who has gained an unsurpassed heavenly eye and sees all things of the ten directions and the 3,000 great-thousand worlds in the same way as one sees a mango that is [resting] in one's palm. Any such bhiksu can indeed adorn the twin sal trees." Lion's Roar said: "Such a person is Aniruddha. Why? Aniruddha sees the things of the 3,000 great-thousand worlds with his heavenly eye. Even the in-between existences are seen clearly, without any obstruction." "O good man! A bhiksu who has little desire and who feels satsfied with what he has, who cares for silence and quietude, and who makes effort, and whose mind is settled, and whose Wisdom sees - [he] well adorns the twin sal trees." Lion's Roar said: "O World-Honoured One! Such a person is Bhiksu Kasyapa. Why? Kasyapa has little desire to possess and feels satisfied with what he has and practises Dharma." "O good man! A bhiksu who desires to benefit beings does not act for profit, abides in samadhi, and does not quarrel, and is perfect in holy works and in the practice of the All-Void. Such a bhiksu adorns the twin sal trees." Lion's Roar said: "O World-Honoured One! Such is Bhiksu Subhuti. Why? Subhuti does not quarrel and is holy in his actions, and practises the Way of the Void." "O good man! Any bhiksu who really practises the miraculous powers and, in the flash of a moment, can transform himself and is one-minded, and in one meditation attains two fruitions, which are of fire and water, such a bhiksu truly adorns the twin sal trees." "O World-Honoured One! Maudgalyayana is one who answers to this description. How? Because Maugalyayana can indeed perform innumerable miraculous transformations." "O good man! Any bhiksu who truly practises great Wisdom, clear knowledge, quick knowledge, Emancipation knowledge, extremely deep knowledge, expansive knowledge, boundless knowledge, unsurpassed knowledge, and real knowledge, and is perfect and accomplished in the root of Wisdom, who does not have a whit of discrimination between enemy, friend or neutral person, who hears that the Tathagata will enter Nirvana and does not have a whit of apprehension and is not gladdened even when hearing that the Tathagata is Eternal and does not enter Nirvana - such a bhiksu is a good adornment for the twin sal trees." Lion's Roar said: "O World-Honoured One! Sariputra is the one who answers to that description. Why so? Because Sariputra is accomplished and perfect in such Wisdom." "O good man! "Any bhiksu who truly says that the being possesses the Buddha-Nature, that the being obtains the invincible body, which is boundless and is the Eternal, Bliss, the Self, and the Pure, and that the body-and-mind are unhindered and are armed with eight unmolestednesses - such a bhiksu adorns well the twin sal trees." Lion's Roar said: "O World-Honoured One! Such a person is the Tathagata himself. Why so? The body of the Tathagata is invincible, unbounded, Eternal, Bliss, the Self, and the Pure; his body and mind are unhindered and do [indeed] possess the eight unhinderednesses. O World-Honoured One! It is only the Tathagata who can well adorn the twin sal trees". One who does not possess anything such as this does not possess serene brightness. I only pray that you will, out of great Loving-Kindness and for adornment's sake, remain here in this sal forest." The Buddha said: "O good man! All things are by nature non-abiding [non-enduring]. How can you say that the Tathagata should remain? O good man! Abidance falls under the category of "matter". Causal relations evoke birth. Hence, to abide [several meanings here: to cease, to stop, to cause to stop, to abide, to dwell; various shades of meanining, involving a sense of permanence, continuance, or stability - note by Rev. Yamamoto]. Where there are causal relations, we have "non-abiding abiding". The Tathagata is already segregated from all the bondages of "matter". How can you say: "Pray stay, O Tathagata!"? The same applies to feeling, perception, volition, and consciousness. O good man! To stay is arrogance. Because of arrogance, there can be no Emancipation. When there is no Emancipation, we speak of staying. Who is arrogant and where does he come from? Hence, "non-abiding abiding". The Tathagata is eternally segregated from all arrogance. How can one say: "Pray, stay, O Tathagata!"? "To stay" falls under the category of what is created. The Tathagata is already segregated from the world of what is created. Because of this, it [he] is non-abiding.""To abide is the law "[dharma]" of the Void. The Tathagata is already segregated from the law of the Void. Hence, one "[he]" gains the Eternal, Bliss, the Self, and the Pure". How can you say:

"Pray, stay, O Tathagata"? To stay is the 25 existences. How can you say: "Pray, stay, O Tathagata!"?
"To stay is none but all beings. All holy ones are non-going and non-coming. The Tathagata is already segregated from the phases of going, coming, and staying. How can we say: "Stay!"?
"Non-abiding is the Boundless Body. In view of the fact that the Body knows no bounds, how can you say: "I pray that the Tathagata will stay in the sal forest"? If I stay in this forest, this body of mine is none but a body that is in bondage. If a body knows any boundary line, it is the non-eternal. The Tathagata is the Eternal. How can you say: "Stay!"?
"Non-abiding is the the Void. The nature of the Tathagata is equal to the Void. How can one say: "Stay!"?
"Non-abiding is the adamantine samadhi. The adamantine samadhi destroys all abidings. The adamantine samadhi is the Tathagata. How can we say: "Stay!"?
"Also, non-abiding is a phantom. The Tathagata is equal to a phantom. How can we say: "Stay!"?
"Also, non-abiding is non-beginning and non-ending. How can we say "abiding"?
And non-abiding is the unbounded world of consciousness ["muhenhokkai" (Jap.): "muhen" means"boundless", "hokkai" means "what is the object of consciousness"]. "The unbounded world of consciousness is the Tathagata". How can we say: "Stay!"?
"And non-abiding is the Suramgama Samadhi. "The Suramgama Samadhi knows all things and yet does not cling. Because of non-clinging, we say Suramgama. The Tathagata is perfect in the Suramgama Samadhi". How can we say: "Stay!"?
"Non-abiding is called the "power of place and non-place". The Tathagata is accomplished in the power of place and non-place. How can we say: "Stay!"?
"Also, non-abiding is called danaparamita [perfected giving]. If there is abiding [solely] in danaparamita, there can be no arriving at silaparamita [perfected morality] and prajnaparamita [perfected Wisdom]. For this reason, we say that danaparamita is the non-abiding. The Tathagata does not abide, down to prajnaparamita. How can one pray that the Tathagata will always kindlyremain in the sal forest?
"Also, non-abiding is the practise of the four thinkings. If the Tathagata abides in the fourthinkings [solely], we cannot say that the Tathagata gains unsurpassed Bodhi and that there isnon-abiding abiding.
"Also, non-abiding is called the boundless world of all beings, and yet he does not stay there.
"Also, non-abiding is called the "houseless". Houseless means that there is nothing that exists.

"Not-is means that nothing arises.
"Birthlessness means non-death.
"Non-death means formlessness.
"Formlessness means non-binding.
"Non-binding means non-clinging.
"Non-clinging means non-defiled.
"Non-defiled is the good.
""The good is the non-created.
"The non-created is the Eternal of Great Nirvana."
""The Eternal of Great Nirvana is the Self.

"The Self is the Pure.

"The Pure is Bliss.

"The Eternal, Bliss, the Self, and the Pure are the Tathagata.

"O good man! For example, space is not the east, nor is it the south, nor the west, nor the north, nor the four directions, nor up or down. It is the same with the Tathagata. He does not exist in the east, the south, the west, or the north, nor in the four directions, nor up or down. O good man! People might say that he gains a body, a mouth and a mind, and good or bad karmic results. But this is not so. Saying that he gains a body, mouth or mind, and good or bad karmic results is not true. If a person says that the common mortal sees the Buddha-Nature and that the Bodhisattva of the ten abodes [stages] does not, this is not so. A person might say that the icchantika, those of the five deadly sins, slanderers of the vaipulya [extensive scriptures], those committing the four grave offences gain unsurpassed Bodhi. But this is not so. To say that the Bodhisattva of the six stages gains birth in the three unfortunate realms due to the causal relations of defilement is not so. Saying that the Bodhisattva-mahasattva gains unsurpassed Bodhi in the female form is not true. Saying that the icchantika is eternal and that the Three Jewels are non-eternal is not true. Saying that the Tathagata stays at Kusinagara, the cave of the great samadhi of deepest dhyana [meditation]. Beings cannot see [this], and it is called "Great Nirvana." Lion's Roar said: "Why is it that the Tathagata enters the cave of dhyana?" "O good man! This is to enable beings to attain Emancipation. This is to make them sow the seeds of good, since they have not yet sown them; to enable the seeds of good now sown to grow; to enable the unripe seed of good to ripen; to enable the ripened seed to gain unsurpassed Bodhi; to enable those who belittle Wonderful Dharma to attain to nobleness; to enable all the indolent to forsake indolence; to enable people to exchange words with such great gandhahastins as Manjushri; to teach those who take pleasure in reading and reciting deeply to enjoy dhyana; to teach beings through holy, pure, and heavenly actions; to enable people to meditate on the unequalled storehouse of deep Dharma; to reproach indolent disciples. The Tathagata is quietude itself. So, he still cares for dhyana. How is it that you have not yet done away with defilement and that indolence gains ground? I desire to reproach all evil bhiksus who keep stores of the eight kinds of impure things, those who are not satisfied with little desire, and who are not satisfied with what they have, and to make beings respect the dharma of dhyana. On account of these causal relations, I now enter the cave of dhyana." Lion's Roar said: "O World-Honoured One! The formlessness samadhi is Great Nirvana. Because of this, we say that Nirvana is formless. Why do we say formless?" "O good man! This derives from the fact that there are not the ten representational phases. What are these? They are the phases of: 1) colour, 2) sound, 3) smell, 4) taste, 5) touch, 6) being born, 7) existing [samsarically], 8) breaking up, 9) being born male, and 10) being born female. It [Nirvana] does not possess these representational forms. Hence, formless. "O good man! Whatever represents a form is subject to ignorance. Ignorance evokes craving; craving evokes bondage; from bondage arises birth; from birth comes about death. When there is death, there is no eternity. If [one is] not attached to form, there is no ignorance. When there is no ignorance, there is no craving. When there is no craving, there is no bondage. When there is no bondage, there arises no birth. When there is no birth, there is no death. When there is no death, there is the Eternal. Due to this, we say that Nirvana is Eternal." Lion's Roar said: "O World-Honoured One! What bhiksu truly cuts himself free from the ten phases?" The Buddha said: "O good man! When a bhiksu, time after time, practises well the three kinds of form, he truly cuts himself free from the ten forms. He practises, time after time, the settled form of samadhi, time after time the phase of Wisdom, and time after time the phase of equanimity. These are the three." Lion's Roar said: "O World-Honoured One! What are samadhi, Wisdom, and equanimity? If a settled state is samadhi, all beings have samadhi. Why do we particularly need to practise samadhi? When the mind stays in a single sense-field, we say samadhi; when other mental associations come in between, this is not samadhi. If there is no settlement in one state, this is not all-knowledge. If not all-knowledge, how can we speak of being "settled"? If a single action is called samadhi, all other actions are not samadhi. If not samadhi, this is not all-knowledge. If not all-knowledge, how can we speak of samadhi? The same applies to Wisdom and equanimity." The Buddha said: "O good man! You say that if the mind abides in a single sense-field, this is samadhi, and that any other causal relations are not samadhi. But this is not so. Why not? Because all the other sense-fields, too, are a single sense-field. It is the same with action. Also, you say that if beings already have samadhi, there cannot be any need to practise any further. This, too, is not so. Why not? Samadhi is called "good samadhi". All beings, truth to tell, do not exist. How can we say that we do not need to practise? When one practises samadhi on all things abiding in a good samadhi, there is the form of good Wisdom. One sees no distinction between samadhi and Wisdom. This is equanimity. Also, next, O good man! If one takes up a form of matter, one cannot meditate on the Eternal and the non-Eternal. This is samadhi. If one well sees the Eternal and the non-Eternal of matter, this is Wisdom. Samadhi and Wisdom

equally see all things. This is equanimity. "O good man! A good charioteer can drive a four-horse carriage and run it quickly or slowly as the occasion requires. As the quickness or slowness matches well with the occasion, we say equanimity. It is the same with the Bodhisattva. One who has much samadhi also practises Wisdom; one who has much Wisdom practises samadhi. As samadhi and Wisdom are equal, we have equanimity. O good man! The Bodhisattva of the ten stages has much power of Wisdom, but little power of samadhi. Hence, he cannot clearly see the Buddha-Nature. Sravakas and pratyekabuddhas have much power of samadhi, but little Wisdom. Because of this, they cannot see the Buddha-Nature. The All-Buddha-World-Honoured One has samadhi and Wisdom in equal parts and sees well the Buddha-Nature. All is clear and transparent, as when one sees a mango that is in one's own palm. One who sees the Buddha-Nature is [of] the phase of equanimity.

"Samatha means "thoroughly extinguishing", because it thoroughly does away with the bondage of defilement. "Also, samatha is called "that which well adjusts", because it well adjusts the evil and non-good of all the sense-organs. "Also, samatha is called quietude, as it indeed makes the three actions [of body, mouth and mind] quiet [calm]. "Also, samatha is called segregation, as it enables beings to part well from the five desires. "Also, samatha is called "purifying well", because it purifies well the three contaminations of greed, ill-will, and ignorance. Because of this, we say "settledness". "Vipasyana is called right seeing. Also, it is called seeing clearly. Also, it is called seeing well. Also, it is called all-seeing. Also, it is called gradual seeing. Also, it is called seeing individually. This is called Wisdom. "Equanimity is called all-equal. Also, it is called non-disputation. Also, it is called non-seeing. Also, it is called non-acting. This is equanimity. "O good man! There are two kinds of samatha. One is mundane, and the other supramundane. And there are two [further] kinds. One is accomplished, and the other non-accomplished. [Those of] the accomplished are all the so-called Buddhas and Bodhisattvas. And the non-accomplished are the so-called sravakas and pratyekabuddhas. "Also, there are three kinds, namely: low, middle, and

top. The low relates to common mortals; middle to sravakas and pratyekabuddhas; and top to all Buddhas and Bodhisattvas. Also there are four kinds, namely: 1) retrogressing, 2) abiding, 3) progressing, and 4) greatly benefiting. Also, there are five kinds, which are the so-called five-knowledge samadhis. These are: 1) samadhi of non-eating, 2) faultless samadhi, 3) samadhi in which the body and mind are pure and the mind is one, 4) samadhi in which one feels pleased with both cause and effect, and 5) samadhi in which one always prays in one's heart. "Furthermore, there are six kinds, which are: 1) samadhi in which one meditates on white bones, 2) samadhi of compassion, 3) samadhi on the twelve links of interdependent arising, 4) samadhi on anapana [breathing], 5) samadhi on the discriminatory mind of beings, and 6) samadhi on birth and death. Also, there are seven kinds, namely the so-called seven Bodhi elements. These are: 1) mindfulness, 2) discernment of Dharma, 3) effort, 4) joy, 5) repose, 6) concentration, and 7) equanimity. "Also, there are seven [further] kinds, which are: 1) srotapanna-samadhi, 2) sakrdagami-samadhi, 3) anagami-samadhi, 4) arhat-samadhi, 5) pratyekabuddha-samadhi, 6) Bodhisattva-samadhi, 7) the Tathagata's All-Awakened Samadhi. "Also, there are eight kinds, which are none other than the eight Emancipation samadhis. These are: 1) samadhi in which one gets Emancipated from the notion of matter by meditating on matter, 2) samadhi in which one seeks Emancipation by meditating further on the external phase of matter, though internally the matter notion has already been done away with, 3) samadhi in which one seeks Emancipation and its actualisation in one's own body through the meditation on purity, 4) boundlessness-of-space Emancipation samadhi, 5) boundlessness-of-consciousness Emancipation samadhi, 6)existencelessness Emancipation samadhi, 7) thoughtlessness-non-thoughtlessness Emancipation samadhi, and 8) cessation Emancipation samadhi. "Also, there are nine kinds, namely the so-called nine gradual samadhis. These are the four dhyanas, the four Voids, and the cessation samadhi. "Also, there are ten kinds, which are the so-called ten all-place samadhis. What are the ten? They are the all-place samadhis on: 1) earth, 2) water, 3) wind, 4) blue, 5) yellow, 6) red, 7) white, 8) space, 9) consciousness, and 10) non-possession. "Also, there are innumerable kinds, which are: all Buddhas and Bodhisattvas. "O good man! These are the representations of the samadhis. "O good man! There are two kinds of Wisdom, which are: 1) mundane and 2) supramundane. "Also, there are three kinds: 1) prajna, 2) vipasyana, and 3) jnana. Prajna is all beings; vipasyana is all sages; and jnana relates to all Buddhas and Bodhisattvas. "Also, prajna is the individual phase of representation, and vipasyana is the general phase of representation. "Jnana is the breaking [dissolution] phase of representation. "Also, there are four kinds, which are none other than the meditation on the Four Truths. "O good man! One practises samatha for three purposes. What are these three: They are: 1) non-indolence, 2) adornment for [with] great Wisdom, and 3) unmolestedness [i.e. unrestrictedness, freedom]. "Also, next, one practises vipasyana for three purposes. What are these three? They are: 1) to meditate on the evil karmic consequences of birth and death, 2) to increase the seeds of good, and 3) to crush out all the defilements.

Chapter Thirty-Eight: On Bodhisattva Lion's Roar 6

Lion's Roar said: "O World-Honoured One! You say in the sutra that vipasyana [insight meditation] thoroughly crushes defilement. Why do we then need to practise samatha [calmness meditation]?" The Buddha said: "O good man! You may say that vipasyana thoroughly crushes out defilement. But this is not so. Why not? When a person has Wisdom, there is no defilement; when a person has defilement, there is no Wisdom. How can we say that vipasyana crushes defilement? O good man! For example, when there is light, there is no gloom; when there is gloom, there is no light. One cannot say that light destroys gloom. O good man! How can we say that a person has Wisdom and defilement and that Wisdom destroys illusion? If there is not [any defilement], there can be no destruction. O good man! If one says that Wisdom destroys defilement, is this due to the arriving at Wisdom or non-arriving that there is this destruction? If this destruction comes about through arrival [at Wisdom], at the first instant there must be destruction. If there is no destruction at the first instant, there can be no destuction even on later occasions. If destruction comes about at the first arrival, this is none but non-arriving. How can one say that Wisdom destroys? If one says that both arriving and non-arriving destroy, this makes no sense. "Also, next, we might well say that vipasyana destroys defilement. Does this destuction come about single-handedly or accompanied by some others? If it destroys on its own, why should the Bodhisattva [bother to] practise the Noble Eightfold Path? If it destroys by being accompanied by some others, this entails that there cannot be any destruction alone and single-handedly. If it cannot destroy alone and single-handedly, there can be no destruction even when accompanied by some others. One who is blind cannot see things. Even when accompanied by many blind persons, seeing is not possible. This is the case with vipasyana. O good man! It is as with the nature of the hardness of the earth, of the nature of the heat of fire, of the nature of the wetness of water, and of the nature of the movability of the wind. The nature of the hardness of the earth down to the movability of the wind does not arise out of causal relations. Its nature itself makes it be thus. Just as with the natures of the four elements, so does it obtain with defilement. Its nature itself acts. If cut, how can we say that Wisdom cuts? Due to this, we cannot say that vipasyana definitely destroys all defilements. O good man! The nature of salt is salty. It makes other things taste salty [too]. The original nature of honey is sweet. It truly makes other things sweet [too]. The original nature of water is wetness. It truly makes other things wet [too]. You might say that the nature of Wisdom is extinction, so that it can truly make things extinguished. But this is not so. Why not? If there is no quality of the dharma of dying, how can Wisdom force it to die? You might say that just as the saltiness of salt makes other things salty, so does Wisdom extinguish other things. But this is not so. Why not? Because the nature of Wisdom dies moment after moment. If it dies moment after moment, how can one say that it truly makes other things die? For this reason, the nature of Wisdom does not destroy defilement. "O good man! There are two extinctions in all things. One is extinction by nature, and the other ultimate extinction. If there is extinction in the nature [of a thing], how can we say that Wisdom extinguishes it? We might say that Wisdom truly extinguishes defilement, as in the case of fire, which burns things. But this is not so. Why not? Because in the burning of fire, there yet remains the smouldering of fire. If it is thus with Wisdom, there must be the smouldering of the fire of Wisdom. When a hatchet cuts a tree, there remains the place where the cutting has been done. When Wisdom cuts, what place do we see where the cutting has been done? If Wisdom truly does [i.e. acts], what is there that we can truly see? If Wisdom truly segregates defilement, such defilement must appear in other places also, as in the case of the tirthikas who leave the six great castle-towns and appear in Kusinagara. If Wisdom does not show itself in other places, we can know that Wisdom could not truly make away with it. O good man! If the nature of all things is Void, who can cause things to be born or die? There is none that causes a different thing to be born and there is none that causes a different thing to die. O good man! As one practises meditation, one arrives at such right knowledge ["jnana"] and the right view of life. That is why I say in the sutras that any bhiksu who practises meditation can indeed see how the five skandhas appear and disappear. O good man! If one does not practise meditation, one cannot clearly see how things obtain in the world. And how could one know of what concerns the things of the supramundane world? If one does not have meditation, one can fall over even on a flat place. The mind [eye] sees what is out of order; the mouth speaks what is out of order; the ear hears what is different [from reality]; the mind understands what is out of order. Desiring to body forth particular letters, the hand writes strange sentences; desiring to take a particular path, the body walks a different path. One who practises samadhi gains much benefit and attains unsurpassed Enlightenment. "The Bodhisattva-mahasattva is perfect in two things and effects great benefit. One is meditation, and the other is knowledge. O good man! When cutting a reed, a quick action cuts it well. It is the same with the Bodhisattva-mahasattva, as he practises these two. O good man! When one [wishes to] uproot a solid tree, things will go more easily if one first jolts it with one's hand. It is the same with the meditation and knowledge of the Bodhisattva. First, he jolts through meditation, and then he uproots with knowledge. O good man! When washing dirty clothes, one first washes with ash water, and then with clean water. If one does this, the clothes become clean. It is also the same with the meditation and knowledge of the Bodhisattva. O good man! The person first reads and recites, and later the meaning comes forth. It is the same with the meditation and knowledge of the Bodhisattva. O good man! It is as with a valiant man who first adorns his body with armour and a staff and then meets the enemy. The case is the same with the meditation and knowledge of the Bodhisattva, too. O good man! For example, using a melting pot and tongs, one can handle metal as one wills by turning, shaking, and melting it. It is the same, too, with the meditation and knowledge of the Bodhisattva. O good man! For example, a clear mirror reflects one's face and form. It is the same, too, with the meditation and knowledge of the Bodhisattva. O good man! This is as when one first flattens the ground and then sows the seed, or when one first learns from the teacher and later thinks of the meaning. It is also the same with the meditation and knowledge of the Bodhisattva. Because of this, as the Bodhisattvamahasattva practises these two things, he derives great gains. O good man! The Bodhisattvamahasattva practises

these two things and adjusts his five sense-organs, and bears all such sufferings as hunger and thirst, cold and heat, beatings, slander, or being bitten by harmful animals and mosquitoes and gadflies. He always governs his mind; he will not have any indolence and does not do unlawful things, due to benefiting others. He is not defiled by illusions and does not get deluded by the various evil views of life. He always segregates himself well from all evil notions, and it will not be long before he achieves unsurpassed Bodhi. O good man! When the Bodhisattva-mahasattva practises these two things, the storms of the four inversions cannot come on. This is as with Mount Sumeru, which does not shake even when the winds blow in from the four directions. This applies to the case where one is not led astray by the wrongheaded teachers, the tirthikas; it is as when the hanging ensign of Devendra cannot easily be made to move. No twisted and strange arts can lure him. He is always blessed with all-wonderful, first-grade peace and bliss, and he can understand well the deepest, undisclosed doctrines of the Tathagata. Even when receiving a blissful [experience], he is not overjoyed and is not worried even when he encounters suffering. All devas and people of the world respect and praise him. "He sees clearly birth and death and what is not birth and death; he knows well the Dharma world and the Dharma nature and the Law that the Eternal, Bliss, the Self, and the Pure rule the body. This is the bliss of Great Nirvana". O good man! His meditation is the samadhi of the Void; his form of Wisdom is the desirelessness samadhi; his form of equanimity is the formlessness samadhi. O good man! The Bodhisattva-mahasattva knows well the time for meditation, the time for Wisdom, and the time for equanimity; he knows well what is not opportune. This is how the Bodhisattva practises well the Bodhi Way." Lion's Roar said: "O World-Honoured One! How does the Bodhisattva know when it is the [right] time or not?" "O good man! The Bodhisattva-mahasattva may gain great arrogance when he gets blessed with bliss, arrogance from delivering a sermon, or arrogance from effort, or arrogance from understanding a [particular] meaning and in discussion, or arrogance from befriending an evil friend, or arrogance from giving away what he highly values, or arrogance from the good things and virtues of worldly nature, or arrogance from being respected by the nobility of worldly life. Such is not a fit time for knowledge. He should then practise meditation well. This is how the Bodhisattva knows the time and not the time. A Bodhisattva may well make effort and yet not be able to arrive at the Bliss of Nirvana. Not gaining this, he feels regret; or because of a dull nature, he may not be able to subdue all his five sense-organs. As all defilements and illusions have full force, he may doubt and think that there is a weakening in the observance of the moral precepts. Know that such a time is not good for meditation. One should practise knowledge. This is how we say that the Bodhisattva knows well the time and when is not the time. "O good man! When the two phases of meditation and knowledge do not go [along] in a pair, know that this is not the fit time to practise equanimity. When the two are in a balanced state, know that this is the fit time to practise equanimity. This is the sense in which we say that the Bodhisattva knows the time and when is not the time. O good man! When the Bodhisattva experiences the rise of defilement and if he practises meditation and Wisdom, know that this is not the time to practise equanimity. He should really read and recite, write and copy and expound the 12 types of sutra, think of the Buddha, Dharma and Sangha, the precepts, the heavens, and equanimity. This is where we say that we practise equanimity. O good man! When the Bodhisattva practises these three phases of Dharma, he gains from this the formlessness Nirvana." Lion's Roar said: "O World-Honoured One! When there are not the ten representational phases, we call Great Nirvana formless. But why do we call it birthlessness, non going-out, non-doing, a house, a sand-dune, the refuge, peace, extinction, Nirvana, quietude, non-sorrow of all illnesses, and non-possession?" The Buddha said: "O good man! As there are no causal relations, we say "birthlessness". As it is not anything created, we say "non-going-out". As there is not any action of doing [anything], we say "non-doing". As none of the five twisted views is allowed to get in, we say "house". As it is segregated from the four madding floods, we say "sand-dune". As it adjusts all beings, we say "refuge". As it crushes the robber-band of defilement, we say "peace". As it burns out the fire of bondage, we say "extinction". As one becomes segregated from the all-awakefulness of perception, we say "Nirvana". As one is away from noisy quarters, we say "quietude". As one is away from the certitude of

mortality, we say "sicklessness". As all is void, we say "nonpossession". O good man! When the Bodhisattva has this perception, he clearly sees the Buddha-Nature." Lion's Roar said: "O World-Honoured One! How many kinds of things does the Bodhisattvamahasattva need to accomplish to arrive at formlessness Nirvana and non-possession?" The Buddha said: "O good man! When the Bodhisattva-mahasattva accomplishes ten things, he can truly arrive at formlessness Nirvana and non-possession. What are the ten? "First, he is perfect in faith. How is faith perfect? This is believing deeply that the Buddha, Dharma and Sangha are Eternal, that all the Buddhas of the ten directions effect expedients, and that beings and icchantikas all possess the Buddha-Nature. It is not believing that the Tathagata is subject to birth, old age, illness, and death, that he has undergone penance, and that Devadatta truly caused blood to flow from the Buddha's body, that the Tathagata ultimately enters Nirvana, and that Wonderful Dharma dies out. This is where we say that the Bodhisattva is perfect in faith. "Second, there is the perfection of pureness in the observance of the moral precepts. O good man! There is a Bodhisattva who says that he is pure in observing the precepts. Although he does not unite with a woman when he sees her, he yet at times jeers and mixes up and plays with words. Such a Bodhisattva is perfect in the dharma of desire, destroys the purity of the precepts, contaminates the pureness of pure actions, thus making the precepts become mixed up in defilement. Hence, we cannot call him perfect in the pureness of the precepts. "Also, there is a Bodhisattva who says that he is pure in the precepts. He does not sexually connect with a woman and does not jeer or play with words. But with bars in between, he listens to the sound of necklaces and ankle-ringlets and various other female sounds. Such a Bodhisattva is fully garbed in the dharma of desire, violates the purity of the precepts, defiles pure action, and makes the precepts contaminated and defiled, so that we cannot call such a person one perfect in the pureness of the precepts. "Also, there is a Bodhisattva who may well say that he is pure in the observation of the precepts. Also, although he does not mix with females, play with words, or listen to [female] sounds themselves, when he sees other men going after females or females going after men, he gains greedy clinging. Such a Bodhisattva is fully garbed in the dharma of desire, violates the purity of the precepts, defiles pure action, and makes the precepts mixed up and contaminated. We cannot call such a person one perfect in the observance of the moral precepts. "Also, there may be a Bodhisattva who might say that he is perfect in his observance of the moral precepts. Also, although he does not mix with females, jeer, play with words, listen to [female] sounds, or watch men and women chasing after each, he does things for birth in the heavens and for being blessed with the pleasures of the five desires. Such a Bodhisattva is fully garbed in desire, violates the purity of the precepts, defiles pure action, and contaminates and defiles the precepts. This cannot be called perfect observance of the pure precepts. "O good man! There might be a Bodhisattva who is pure in upholding the precepts. And yet he does not do so for the sake of sila, for the sake of silaparamita, nor for beings, nor for profit, nor for Bodhi, nor for Nirvana, and nor for [becoming a] sravaka or pratyekabuddha. He only observes the precepts for the supreme "Paramartha-satya" [Ultimate Reality]. O good man! This is what we call perfection in the purity of the precepts of a Bodhisattva. "Third, the Bodhisattva makes friends with various good friends of the Way. By a good friend of the Way is meant a person who speaks well about faith and sila, erudition, giving, Wisdom, and who makes people practise the Way. Such a person is called the Bodhisattva's good friend of the Way. "Fouth, he seeks quietude. By quietude is meant the quietude of body and mind, by [means of] which one meditates on the depths of all existences. We call this quietude. "Fifth, there is effort. By effort is meant that one single-mindedly thinks about the Four Noble Truths. Even if one's head were on fire, one would not cast this [pondering on the Four Truths] away. This is effort. "Sixth, he has perfection in remembrance. By perfection in remembrance is meant thinking of the Buddha, Dharma, Sangha, the precepts, the heavens, and equanimity. We call this perfection in thinking. "Seventh, he has gentleness of speech. By gentleness of speech is meant the true words and the wonderful words which one utters and queries before the mind acts. It is timely speech and words of truth. We call this "gentle words". "Eighth, there is protection of Dharma. To protect Dharma means to love Wonderful Dharma, always being happy to speak about it, read and recite, write and copy it, and to think of its meaning and

expound it widely and make it prevail. If there is a person who copies, expounds, recites and praises [Dharma] and thinks about the meaning, one [should] seek things and give such to him for support, things such as clothing, drink and food, bedding, and medicine. For the protection of Dharma, one is ready to sacrifice one's body and life. This is protecting Dharma. "Ninth, if the Bodhisattva sees any of his brethren or anyone who is upholding the same sila lacking in things, he goes to others and begs for an incense burner, priestly robes, what is required in the way of nursing, clothing, food and drink, bedding, and accommodation. "Tenth, his Wisdom is perfect. By Wisdom is meant seeing the so-called Tathagata, the Eternal, Bliss, the Self, and the Pure, and the fact that all beings possess the Buddha-Nature. He sees the two phases of things, which are: Void versus non-Void, Eternal versus non-Eternal, Bliss versus non-Bliss, the Self versus the non-Self, what is possible or not possible for crushing out the proposition of dissimilarity ["vaidharmya-drstanta"], the coming about or seeing of dissimilarity that arises out of causal relations, and the fruition of dissimilarity that arises out of causal relations or non-causality. This is what we call the perfection of Wisdom. O good man! This is how we say that when the Bodhisattva is perfect in these ten things, he can well see the formlessness of Nirvana." Lion's Roar said: "O World-Honoured One! The Buddha said previously to Cunda: " You, Cunda, already see the Buddha-Nature, gain Great Nirvana and unsurpassed Bodhi." What does this mean? O World-Honoured One! You state in a sutra that giving to animals brings forth 100 recompenses; that giving to an icchantika gains one 1,000 recompenses; that giving to a person who upholds the precepts evokes 100,000 recompenses; that giving to a tirthika who has cut away defilement calls forth an innumerable number of recompenses; that giving to those of the stages of the four ways and the four fruitions up to pratyekabuddha results in an innumerable number of recompenses; that giving to the Bodhisattvas of the unretrogressive stage, the great Bodhisattvas of the final stage, and the Tathagata-World-Honoured One calls forth infinte and boundless benefit and recompense, surpassing the greatest degree of conception. If Cunda gains such recompense, the results can know no end. When will he arrive at unsurpassed Bodhi? You also state in the sutra: "If one, with a serious mind, does good or bad, one will unfailingly gain the results in this life, or in the life to come, or in later lives." Cunda did good with a serious mind. So, you [we] may know that he will unfailingly gain recompense. If he will unfailingly gain recompense, how can he expect to arrive at unsurpassed Bodhi and how can he see the Buddha-Nature? "O World-Honoured One! You also say in the sutra: "If one gives things to three kinds of person, there will be no end of recompense. The first is a sick person; the second is one's parents; the third is the Tathagata." O World-Honoured One! You also state in the sutra: "The Buddha spoke to Ananda: "If beings have nothing involving the actions of desire, they will attain unsurpassed Bodhi. It is the same with things concerning actions material or non-material." O World-Honoured One! It is as is stated in a gatha of the "Dharmapada"

"Not in the sky, not in the sea,
Nor by getting into mountains and caves
Can there be any question of seeking refuge;
There exists no place on earth
Where one no more suffers from karmic effects."

"Also, Aniruddha said: "O World-Honoured One! I recall to mind that by giving one meal, I did not fall into the three unfortunate realms for 80,000 kalpas [aeons]." O World-Honoured One! Even a single [act of] giving evokes this return. As against this, Cunda, with a mind of faith, makes offerings to the Buddha, having thus perfected and accomplished danaparamita. O World-Honoured One! If the results of good are unending, how can the offence of slandering the vaipulya sutras, of the five deadly sins, the four grave offences, and the sin of [being] an icchantika know any end of karmic returns? If they do not end, how can a person truly see the Buddha-Nature and attain unsurpassed Nirvana?" The Buddha said: "Well said, well said, O good man! There are only two persons who can arrive at the innumerable and boundless and countless virtues which go beyond words. This truly makes away with foundering in the dashing waters and madding floods. This well beats the enemy, brings down the victorious banner of Mara, and turns well the unsurpassed Wheel of Dharma of the Tathagata. One is the good question [questioner] and the other the good answer [answerer]. "O good man! Of the ten powers of the Buddha, the karma power has the greatest weight. O good man! All beings belittle the causal relations of karma and do not believe in it. In order to teach such minds, such is said. O good man! In all the actions that one performs, there is what is light and what is grave. These two actions of the light and grave are each of two kinds. One is definite, and the other is indefinite. O good man! There may be a person who says that there is no return arising from evil actions. If it is the case that evil actions unfailingly call forth karmic consequences, how was Kekosendara able to gain birth in the heavens, or Angulimalya to attain the fruition of Emancipation? In view of this, know that there are cases where whatever is done unfailingly calls forth karmic results and that there can unfailingly be cases where no results arise. In order to do away with such bent views [as these], I say in the sutras that any action unfailingly calls forth karmic results. "O good man! There are cases where grave actions turn out to be light in their results and light ones grave. This does not mean that this concerns all people; only the ignorant are concerned here. Because of this, know that this does not mean that all actions unfailingly call forth a result. Although the result does not unfailingly come into being, this does not mean that the result does not come about. O good man! There are two kinds of all beings. One is wise, the other ignorant. The wise , by dint of wisdom, truly encounters the gravest karma of the unfortunate realms in this life. The ignorant person receives the karmic consequences of this life severely in hell." Lion's Roar said: "O World-Honoured One! If things are thus, one should not seek purity in action and Emancipation." The Buddha said: "O good man! If it is true that all actions definitely call forth results, do not seek purity in action and Emancipation. As it is indefinite, we practise pure actions and seek fruition in Emancipation. O good man! If one can well segregate one's self from all evil actions, one will gain good results; if one is far removed from good actions, one will arrive at evil fruition. If every action unfailingly called forth fruition, one would not seek to practise the Holy Way. If one does not practise the Way, there can be no Emancipation. The reason why all holy persons practise the Way is but to crush out the definite karma and gain light results. For the indefinite karma has no results to come about. If every action calls forth a result, one should not seek to practise the Holy Way. It is not possible to keep one's self from practising the Holy Way and yet gain Emancipation. There can be no such thing as arriving at Nirvana, not attaining Emancipation. "O good man! If every good action is certain to call forth a result, every pure action that one performs in one's whole life will eternally call forth eternal peace, and every evil action of the last degree that one performs in one's whole life, too, will call forth the greatest of suffering eternally. If the action of karmic results is thus, there can be no practising of the Way, Emancipation, or Nirvana. If whatever is done by a man has to be borne by a man, this would mean that whatever is done by a Brahmin must be borne by a Brahmin. If things were thus, there could be no low caste and no low existences. A man could always be a man; a Brahmin could always be a Brahmin. Whatever was done in the days of one's small age [childhood] would have to be borne in the days of small age. One would not encounter the results in the days of one's middle or old age. The evil done in old age would bear fruit in hell, and one would not be able to suffer what one was to suffer as of the earlier days of hell. One must wait till the days of old age to suffer. The non-harming that one practised in one's old age will not bear fruit in one's prime of life. Without the prime of life, how can one come to be old? Because the karmic results cannot die out. If karma cannot die out, how could there be the practising of the Way and Nirvana? "O good man! Of karma, there are two kinds, namely: definite and the indefinite. Of the karma that is definite, there are two kinds. One is the definiteness in result, and the other the definiteness in time. There can be cases where the result is definite and the time indefinite. When the causal relations conjoin, the result comes about in the Three Times of the present, the next life, or later lives. "O good man! When one does good or evil with a settled mind, one gains a believing mind and joy. And one takes a vow or makes offerings to the Three Treasures. This is a definite action. "One who is wise is persistent in good actions and cannot be moved. Because of this, the grave actions turn out to be light. One who is ignorant is persistent in non-good. Because of this, any light action turns out to be grave [in consequence] and calls forth a grave return. That is why all actions are not called definite. "The Bodhisattva-mahasattva does no action that will gain him hell. For the sake of beings, he takes a great vow and gains life in hell. O good man! In days gone by, when beings' life-span was 100 years, innumerable beings, as many as the sands of the Ganges, received karmic results in hell. I saw this and I took a great vow and gained life in hell. The Bodhisattva, at that time, truth to tell, had no sin of such kind. For the sake of beings, he gained life in hell. I, at that time, was in hell, living there innumerable ages and expounding the 12 types of sutra extensively to all sinners. The sinners, on hearing this, crushed all their karmic results and emptied hell - except for the icchantika. This is how we say that the Bodhisattva-mahasattva receives the karmic results not later than in this life. "Also, next, O good man! In this Bhadrakalpa, an innumerable number of beings gained life in the animal realm, suffering evil karmic returns there. On seeing this, I took a vow, and to save them I gained life as such animals as the reindeer, deer, brown bear, dove, naga, serpent, garuda, fish, tortoise, fox, hare, cow, and horse. O good man! The Bodhisattva-mahasattva does not have, truth to tell, any sin to gain him such life as an animal. For the sake of beings, he takes a great vow and gains such a life. This is where we speak of the Bodhisattva-mahasattva's gaining an evil karmic life [return] not later than this life. Also, next, O good man! In this Bhadrakalpa, there were also innumerable beings who gained life as hungry pretas [ghosts]. They devoured vomited saliva, fat and flesh, pus and blood, urine, tears and spittle. The span of their life was innumerable hundreds and thousands of years. Not once did they hear anything of juice or water. And how could they see anyone drink? Even if they saw water from afar and even if they gained the wish to go there, when they reached the place where such existed, everything changed into a great fire or pus or blood. At times, these might not change, but many people would obstruct the way with halberds in their hands or push the pretas back, so that they could not go forward. Or in the summer, rain might fall, but no sooner did it touch their body than it turned to fire. This is the work of the karmic returns of the evil they had done. O good man! The Bodhisattva-mahasattva has, truth to tell, no such sins to answer for. But to save beings and to enable them to attain Emancipation, he takes a vow and puts himself into such a life. This is why we say that the Bodhisattva-mahasattva suffers evil karmic returns not later than in this life. "O good man! I, in the age of Bhadrakalpa, was born in a meat shop, but did not raise hens, pigs, cows or sheep; nor did I hunt with bows and nets, or catch fish, or live in a candala's house; nor did I rob or plunder. The Bodhisattva has never done any such things. To enable beings to attain Emancipation, he took a great vow and gained such a body. This is why we say that a Bodhisattva-mahasattva undergoes a life of evil karmic returns not later than in this life. "O good man! In this Bhadrakalpa, I gained life in a remote place, was full of greed, anger, and ignorance, did unlawful things, did not believe in the Three Treasures and the karmic returns that ensue in later lives, did not respect my parents and the intimate, the aged and the elderly. O good man! The Bodhisattva, at that time, had no such karma to suffer. To enable beings to gain Emancipation, he took a great vow and gained life in this place. This is where we say that the Bodhisattva-mahasattva undergoes an evil life, not in this life, not in the next life, and not in later lives. "O good man! In this Bhadrakalpa, he gained such lives as those of a female, of evil, greed, anger, ignorance, jealousy, parsimony, of a phantom, of madness, and of a person clad in defilement. O good man! Know that the Bodhisattva did nothing of the kind [to merit] such karma. Only to enable beings to attain Emancipation did he take a great vow and gain such a form of life. This is where we say that the Bodhisattva-mahasattva undergoes evil karmic consequences not in this present life, not in the life to follow, nor in later lives. "O good man! In this Bhadrakalpa, I gained such forms of life as of one with imperfect genital organs, one sexless, dually-sexed, or indefinite. O good man! Truth to tell, the Bodhisattvamahasattva has no such actions to answer for. In order to enable beings to attain Emancipation, he takes a great vow and undergoes such a life. This is where we say that the Bodhisattvamahasattva undergoes evil karma not in this life, not in the next life, or not in later lives. "O good man! In this Bhadrakalpa, I practised the ways of the tirthikas and the Nirgranthas, and believed in their teachings. There was no giving, no shrine, and no recompense for dedication of the shrine. There were no good or bad actions, no good or bad returns [according to their theory]. There was no present life, no life to come, and not this and not that. There existed no holy, no transformed body, no Way, and no Nirvana. O good man! The Bodhisattva has no such evil karmas to answer for. Only to enable beings to attain Emancipation does he take a great vow and experience such twisted things. This is why we say that the Bodhisattva-mahasattva undergoes evil actions, not in this life, not in the life to come, nor in later lives. "O good man! I call to mind that once in the past, we were merchants, Devadatta and I. And each of us had 500 merchants. Seeking profit, we went to a great sea in search of rare things. Through evil causal relations, we met with a storm on the way and, ship-wrecked, our comrades all died. At that time, Devadatta and I, because of non-harming and by the causal relations for a long life, were blown across onto land. Then, Devadatta, regretting that he had lost the treasure, was greatly worried and wept loudly. I then said: "O Devadatta! Do not weep!" Devadatta said to me: "Listen to me carefully, listen carefully! For example, there is a man oppressed by poverty. He goes to the graveyard and catches hold of a corpse and says: "O you! Give me the joy of death. I shall now give you poverty and life." Then, the corpse stands up and says to the poor man: "O good man! Take poverty and life yourself. I am now immersed in the joy of death. I am not pleased to see you poor and alive." The situation is like this. But I do not have the bliss of death to hand, and besides, I am poverty-stricken. What else can I do other than cry and weep?" I also appeased him: "Do not be sad. I now have two beads, which are priceless. I will give you one." I gave it [to him] and said: "A person who has life gains this gem. If without life, how can one expect to have this?" I then felt tired and drowsed in the shade of a tree. Devadatta, burning with greed, gained an evil thought. Thrusting and harming my eyes, he took away the other bead. In pain, I cried and wept. Then, there was a woman who came to me and asked: "Why do you cry and weep?" I then told her of all that had taken place. On hearing of this, she further asked: "What is your name?" I said: "I am called True-Word." "How can I know that you are truthful?" I then took an oath: "If I should now have evil thoughts towards Devadatta, let me be one-eyed; if not, let my eyes gain the light." Having said this, my eyes were cured and were as good as before. O good man! This is where we say that the Bodhisattva-mahasattva speaks about the recompense that comes about in this life. "O good man! I call back to mind that I was once born in Southern India, at Putana Castle, in the house of a Brahmin. At that time, there was a king called Garapu. He was rude, evil, arrogant, and haughty. Being in the prime of life and handsome, he was immersed in the life of the five desires. To save beings, I, at that time, lived on the outskirts of the castle-town and sat in meditation. Then, the king came out of the castle, accompanied by relatives, courtiers, and court ladies into the world of spring trees and flowers. In the forest, he disported himself in the play of the five desires. All the females, abandoning, the king, came to me. I then - to do away with the greed of the king - spoke of Dharma. Then, the king came to me and gained an evil mind. He asked: "Have you already arrived at arhatship?" I said: "Not yet." He asked again: "Have you arrived yet at the stage of anagamin?" I said: "Not yet." He further said: "If not yet arrived at these two fruitions, you must be perfect in greed. How dare you look at my females?" I then replied: "O great King! Although I have not yet cut off the bond of greed, I have no greed in my mind." The king said: "O fool! There is in the world many a rishi who feeds on air and fruit. But on seeing beauty, he feels greed [desire]. And you are still in the prime of life and are not yet parted from greed. How can you be free from beauty, when actually seeing it?" I said: "O great King! One sees colour, but does not get attached to it. It is like feeding on air and not on fruits. It comes from the mind that rests on impermanence and impurity." The king said: "Belittling others and slandering, how can one practise the pureness of the precepts?" I said: "O great King! If one has jealousy, there can be slandering. I have no jealousy. How could I slander [anyone]?" The king said: "O greatly-virtuous! What do you mean by precepts?" "O King! Forbearance [patient endurance] is a precept." The king said: "If forbearance is a precept, I shall cut off your ear-lobe. If you can indeed stand it, I will know what the precept is." Then the king cut off my ear-lobe, but I, with my ear-lobe cut off, lost no colour. All the courtiers, on seeing this, admonished the king and said: "Please do not cause any harm to such a great person!" The king said to all his ministers: "How do you know whether this is a great person?" The ministers said: "Despite his

receiving such a painful wound, his mien has not changed." The king said again: "I shall try further and see if he changes [colour] or not." And he sliced off my nose, and cut off my hands and feet. At that time, the Bodhisattva had practised the works of loving-kindness in innumerable and boundless worlds and had pity for beings who were sunk in the mire of suffering. Then the four guardians of the earth, becoming angry, rained down sand, gravel and stones. The king, on seeing this, became frightened, came to me, and prostrating on the ground said: "Please have mercy and allow me to repent." I said: "O great King! I seem to have no anger and no greed in my mind." The king said: "O greatly-virtuous! How can you have no anger and no enmity in your mind?" I then took an oath: "Let my body be reinstated as it was before if I do not have any anger or enmity in my mind." No sooner had I said this, than my body was reinstated as it was before. This is what [we mean when we say that] the Bodhisattva-mahasattva speaks about recompense in this life. "O good man! It is the same with the karmic results that are to come about in the next life and in later lives, and with the matter of evil actions. When the Bodhisattva-mahasattva attains unsurpassed Bodhi, all actions gain their recompense in the present life. If the karmic results of non-good and evil actions are to visit one in this present life, things will proceed as when the heavens let fall the evil rain on account of the evil actions of the king. Also, this is as when the hands dropped off a person who showed a hunter where the brown bear and the deer of beautiful colour lived. These are instances where evil actions call forth karmic returns in this present life. As to the results that are to visit a person in the next life, they are those of the icchantika, and those who commit the four grave offences and the five deadly sins. The recompense that visits a person who upholds sila [the moral precepts] and who takes a vow such as saying: "I pray that I may, in my next life, gain a body in which I can be pure in sila. And in an age when the life-span of men is 100 years and when I can be blessed with an age of 80, I shall be a Chakravartin [world ruler] and teach beings." O good man! If the karmic result is definitely to visit one in this present life, there can be no karmic returns that come to one in the next life or in later lives. The Bodhisattva-mahasattva may practise the 32 signs of perfection of a great man, but he cannot expect the recompense in this present life. If one's action does not call forth the three kinds of recompense, we call this indefinite. "O good man! If all actions must definitely call forth karmic returns, one cannot practise pure actions, Emancipation, and Nirvana. Know that such are not my disciples; they are the kindred of Mara. "All actions have the phases of "definite" and "indefinite". By definite is meant the karmic returns that one experiences in this life, in the life to come, and in later lives. By indefinite is meant the cases where the karmic returns come about when the causal relations meet, and if not, these will not come to visit the person. Because of this, if any person says that there are pure actions, Emancipation, and Nirvana, such a person is, truth to tell, my own disciple and not the kindred of Mara. This you should know. O good man! With beings, the results that are indefinite are many, and few the results that are definite. Because of this, there can be the practising of the Way. When one practises the Way, the definite, grave karmic returns can be felt as light; and there can be no experiencing of the indefinite karmic returns in the life to come. "O good man! There are two kinds of people. One makes the indefinite definite; the other makes the karmic returns of the present life those of the life to come; what is light that which is grave, and what is to be suffered in this human life to be suffered in hell. "The second makes what is definite indefinite, what belongs to the life to come [happen in] the present life, what is grave that which is light, and what is of hell that which is light in this human life. The ignorant make things grave. "Of these two, the one is ignorant, and the other is wise. The wise person makes things light, and the ignorant person makes things grave in nature. "O good man! For example, there are two persons who have sinned against the king. The one, with many relatives, suffers little, whereas the other, with few relatives, suffers much, although it ought to be light in suffering. It is the same with the ignorant. The wise person suffers less because of the large amount of good he has amassed, although the sin is grave. With the ignorant person, his good actions being few, he has to suffer greatly, although his sin is light. The situaiton is like this. "O good man! For example, there are two persons, one is fat and is in the prime of life, whereas the other is weakly constituted and has less physical strength. The two lose their feet in mud, at which the one who is fat and in the prime of life easily gets out, whereas the weaker one sinks down. The situation is like this. "O good man! There are two persons who both partake of poison. One has a charm and the drug, agada, whereas the other does not. The poison cannot destroy the one with the charm and drug, whereas the other who does not have such has to die. "O good man! There are two persons who take some juice. One has the fire of life and the other has it less. The one with much fire digests it well, whereas with the person whose force of life is weak, it works harm. "O good man! There are two persons who get chained up by the king. One is intelligent, whereas the other is dull. The intelligent person escapes, whereas the other one, who is dull, cannot get away. "O good man! There are two persons who together follow a steep path. One has eyesight, whereas the other is blind. The one with eyesight goes on without any ado, whereas the blind man falls into the depths of the steep [gorge]. "O good man! For example, two persons take drinks. One eats a lot, whereas the other eats less. With the one who eats a lot, the drinks do less harm, whereas for the one who eats little, the drinks cause him trouble. The case is like this. "O good man! For example, two persons go to the battle front. One is garbed in armour and [equipped] with a staff [sword], whereas the other has none. The one armed with a staff easily crushes the enemy, whereas the one who is not has no means of turning away the arms of the enemy. "Also, there are two persons who make the Buddhist robe dirty. The one sees this and washes it, whereas the other knows but does not wash it. The robe of the one who has washed it at once is clean, whereas that of the one who does not increases its defilement day by day. "Also, there are two persons who both ride in a cart. The cart with spokes goes as the person wills, whereas the one without [spokes] does not move. "Also, there are two persons, who are travelling across a wilderness. One has food, whereas the other does not. The person with the food carries himself across the hard ways, whereas the one who does not cannot do so. "Also, two persons are attacked by robbers. The one has a store of treasure [at home], whereas the other does not. The one with a storehouse has no apprehension, whereas the one who has not has worries. It is the same with the ignorant. One who has amassed good can stand grave sins in a light way, whereas the other, having no stock of good actions, has to suffer heavily." Bodhisattva Lion's Roar said: "O World-

Honoured One! Just as you, the Buddha, say, not all actions call forth definite results, in the same way, all beings do not always definitely have to suffer. O World-Honoured One! Why must beings undergo heavy sufferings in hell for what can be suffered lightly in the present life, and why can what obtains heavily in hell be light in the present life?" The Buddha said: "There are two kinds of beings. One is wise, and the other ignorant. One who upholds the precepts of the body well and practises the wisdom of the mind is one who is wise; one who does not uphold the precepts and practise the wisdom of the mind is one who is ignorant. "How does one not well practise the body? If one does not control the five sense-organs, we say that such a person is one who does not control his body. When a person does not control the seven kinds of pure precept, we say that he does not uphold the precepts. When a person does not adjust his mind, we say that there is no practising of the mind. When a person does not practise holy actions, we say that this is not practising Wisdom. "Also, next, by the non-practising of the body, one cannot be perfect in the pureness of the precept-body [the spiritual entity of sila, so to speak]. By the non-practising of the precepts is meant the receiving or storing of the eight impure things. The non-practising of the mind is so called because one does not practise the three kinds of forms. The non-practising of Wisdom is so called because one does not practise pure actions. "Also, next, we say that we do not practise the body because we cannot meditate on body, matter, and the representations of matter. Also, we do not meditate on the representations; we do not know of the elements of the body and the fact that this body moves on to that body. One sees body in non-body and matter in non-matter. Because of this, one greedily clings to the body and the body-elements. This is the non-practising of the body. "We say that there is the non-practising of the precepts. The receiving of low-grade sila is the non-practising of the precepts. One-sided precepts are what one does for one's benefit, for adjusting one's own self, and not for giving peace to all beings. It is not to protect unsurpassed Wonderful Dharma. What the person does is for birth in the heavens and there to be blessed with the five desires, which is not called practising the precepts. "By the non-practising of the mind is meant the dispersed state of mind in which the person does not guard his own realm of existence. By one's own realm is meant the four remembrances; and by the other realm is meant the five desires. When a person does not practise the four remembrances, we speak of non-practice of the mind. When a person is sunk in evil actions and does not guard well his own mind, we call this the non-practice of Wisdom. "Also, next, by the non-practice of the body is meant that the person does not see that this carnal body is non-eternal, that it has no place to live in, and that it collapses, and it dies out moment after moment, and that it is the world of Mara. "By the non-practice of the precepts is meant the non-accompaniment of silaparamita [perfected morality]. By the non-practice of the mind is meant that the person is not perfect in dhyanaparamita [perfected meditation]. By the non-practice of Wisdom is meant that the person is not perfect in prajnaparamita [perfected Wisdom]. "Also, next, we say that there is the non-practice of the body, which is greedily to cling to one's own body and what belongs to it, and to think that one's body is eternal and that it does not change. "We talk of the non-practice of the precepts. This is to do for one's own sake the ten evil deeds. "The non-practice of the mind means that the person does not control his doing of evil deeds. "The non-practice of Wisdom means that the person cannot see through to the good and bad of things, because of the non-control of the mind. "Also, next, the non-practice of the body means that the person is not away from the notion of the wrong view of Self ["atmadrsti": regarding the ego as existing eternally unchanged]. The non-practice of the precepts means that the person is not away from the wrong view regarding the precepts ["silavrataparamarsa"]. The non-practice of the mind means that the person falls into hell [after] enacting greed and anger, and the non-practice of Wisdom means that the person fails to do away with the ignorant mind. "Also, next, the non-practice of the body fails to see that the body is always the enemy, even though it has nothing [for which it is] to blame. "O good man! For example, there is a man who has an enemy, who ever seeks his whereabouts. One who is wise sees this and is awake to it and guards against it. If not guarded against, there is the danger of being harmed. It is the same with all the bodies of beings. One always, cold or hot, nourishes it with food and drink. If not thus protected, the body will go into dissolution. O good man! The Brahmin, worshipping the god of fire, always offers incense and flowers, praises and worships [it], makes offerings and serves [it], and he may well gain a life of 100 years. But if he touches it, the fire will burn the hand that does so. This fire, having been so much cherished and offered things, knows nothing of repaying what it owes the one who has single-mindedly served it. It is the same with the bodies of all beings. For years, the body is served with the best of incense and flowers, necklaces, clothing, food and drink, bedding and medicine. But when it encounters the causal relations that press in from within and without, all at once collapses, and it now does not think back a whit to what offerings and clothes were given it in days gone by. "O good man! For example, there is a king who has four vipers, which he keeps in a box and orders a person to feed and take care of. Any of these four will harm a person once it gets angry. The man, fearing this, always seeks food and feeds them. It is the same with the four great vipers of all beings. Once angered, they will destroy the body. "O good man! A man is mindful of a chronic disease, for which he seeks a doctor and a means of cure. Should he incessantly fail to cure [the disease], death will unfailingly visit him. It is the same with the body of all beings. One must always take care and there cannot be any indolence. Indolence will call forth death. "O good man! For example, it is the same with an earthenware pot, which cannot endure the wind and rain, beating, and pressure. It is the same with the body of all beings. It cannot endure hunger, thirst, cold and heat, wind and rain, beating and ill-speaking. "O good man! A carbuncle, when not yet fully grown, always protects itself well and prevents others from touching it. If anyone should happen to touch it, it responds with great pain. It is the same with the body of all beings. "O good man! When a mule bears a child, this destroys its own body. The same is the case with the body of all beings. If the inside is cold, the body suffers. "O good man! For example, just as the plantain tree dies when it bears fruit, so do matters stand with all other things. "O good man! Just as the plantain fruit has nothing solid inside it, so is it with the body of all beings. "O good man! Just as the serpent, rat, and wolf all hate each other, so do matters stand with the four great elements. "O good man! Just as the swan king does not seek to be in a graveyard, so do things stand with the Bodhisattva. The body does not greedily find pleasure in a graveyard. "O good man! Just as a

candala will not give up his occupation for seven generations successively because people look down upon him, the same is also the situation with the seed of this body. The seed and blood are after all not pure. Their being not pure, all Buddhas and Bodhisattvas reproach them. "O good man! This body is not like the Malaya hills where sandalwood grows; it cannot call forth the utpala, pundarika, campaka, mallika, or varsika. The nine holes always leak out pus and blood and impure things. Where one is born [vagina] smells bad and is defiled and ugly to look at, and worms always live there. "O good man! For example, there might be an all-wonderful garden and forest in the world. But if any corpse should come therein, it becomes impure, and people abandon it, and no person any longer feels love or attachment [to that place]. It is the same with what comes about in the world of matter. Though wonderful to look at, as there is the body representing it, all Buddhas and Bodhisattvas abandon it. "O good man! If a person cannot see things in this light, we do not call this the practice of the body. "We say that there is the non-practice of the precepts. O good man! This is none other than not being able to regard sila [the moral precepts] as a kind of ladder to all good dharmas [things]. Sila is the root of all good dharmas. This is as with the earth, which is where all trees grow. This is the best guide to all good. This is like the owner of a ship that guides all merchants. Sila is the banner of victory. It is like the hanging ensign of Devendra. Sila eternally extirpates all evil deeds and the three unfortunate realms. It thoroughly cures serious illnesses, like a medicinal tree. Sila is none other than food on the steep path of birth and death. It is the armour and staff that crush the thieves of defilement; and it is the best charm, which annihilates the poison of the viper of defilement; or it is the bridge by means of which one can truly cross over the path of evil actions. Any person who cannot think in this way is one who does not practise the precepts. "We say that there is the non-practising of the mind. This is none other than being unable to meditate on the mind. It [the mind] carries itself lightly and noisily and is hard to catch hold of and to destroy. It runs about unmolested like an evil-minded elephant. Its movements are quick every moment, as swift as lightning. It is as noisy and and unstaying [restless] as any monkey. It is like a phantom or a flame. It is the root of evil, and it is hard to satisfy the call of the five desires. This is like fire that feeds on fuel, or the great ocean, which takes in all river-waters, or like any grass and plants that grow so luuriantly in Mandara. If a person does not meditate on the falsity of birth and death, he will get lured away, as with a fish that swallows the hook. Always a lead is given, followed by all actions. This is like the mother shell that leads all the small ones. A person gets greedily attached to the five desires and does not care for Nirvana. This is like the camel that eats honey, forgetting all bout the fodder till death catches hold of it. People are deeply attached to actual pleasures and forget all about the worries that later come to them. This is like the cow that greedily devours the seedlings, not afraid of, and forgetting all about, the slashings by staff and thorns that have to follow. It [the mind] runs after the 25 existences. This is like the hurricane that blows away cotton. It endlessly seeks what one cannot seek, as with an ignorant person who seeks fire where there is no heat. People are always stuck to birth and death and do not wish to seek Emancipation. This is as in the case of the nimba worm, which seeks the neemb tree [azadirachta Indica]. People are lured by, and adhere to, the foul-smelling defilement of birth and death, like a prisoner who longs and asks the warder for a woman, or like a pig who is happy lying in an impure place. Anyone who does not see things thus can be called one not practising the mind. "We speak of the non-practice of Wisdom. Wisdom has great power, like that of the garuda [a mythical bird]. It truly destroys evil actions and gloom, as does the light of the sun. It thoroughly uproots the tree of the skandhas, like water, which can easily float things up [to the surface]. Wisdom thoroughly burns out the evil views of life, like a great fire, and is the fountainhead of all good dharmas and the seed from which come about the Buddhas and Bodhisattvas. If one does not see things thus, this is none other than the non-practice of Wisdom. "O good man! If there is anyone who sees in "Paramartha-satya" [Ultimate Truth] the body and the representation of the body, the cause and result of the body, the skandha of the body, one body or two bodies, this body or that body, the extinction and equality of the body, the practice of the body or one who practises the body, such is the non-practice of the body. "O good man! If there is anyone who sees sila and any representation of sila, the cause and result of sila, the top and bottom of sila, the skandha of sila, one or two silas, this sila and that sila, the extinction and equality of sila, the practice of sila and one who practises sila, silaparamita, this is the non-practice of sila. "If there is any person who sees such as the mind and the representation of the mind, the cause and result of the mind, the skandha of the mind, what belongs to the mind, one or two minds, this and that mind, the extinction and equality of the mind, the practising and one who practises the mind, the top, middle and bottom of the mind, the good and bad mind - this is the non-practice of the mind. "O good man! If there is anyone who sees Wisdom and the phase of representation of Wisdom, the cause and result of Wisdom, the skandha of Wisdom, one or two Wisdoms, this and that Wisdom, the extinction and equality of Wisdom, the top, middle, and bottom of Wisdom, sharp and dull Wisdom, the practising of, and one who practises, Wisdom, this is none other than the non-practising of Wisdom. "O good man! If there is any person who does not practise the body, sila, Wisdom, and the mind, such a one will suffer from a great karmic consequence for a small evil deed. And out of fear, he will think: "I am bound for hell; I have done the deeds of hell." Even when the wise speak of the pains of hell, he will always think: "It is like iron hitting iron, stone stone, wood wood, and the firefly enjoying fire. The body of hell will look like hell. If it resembles hell, what more pain could there be?" For example, it is like the blue fly that gets caught by saliva and cannot get free. It is the same with the human being, too. He cannot extract himself from a small evil. The mind never once repents and covers the wound by doing good. In the past, there were all good deeds, but all these became defiled by this sin. What little evil a person has to suffer in this life turns out as the heaviest karmic results in hell. O good man! If we add one "sho" [a unit of measurement for liquid or cereal] of salt to a small vessel of water, it becomes so salty that we cannot drink it. It is the same with this person's evil, too. O good man! For example, there is a man whose one "sen" [a unit of money] which he owes a person, and which he is unable to pay back, chains him to prison, where he has to suffer many a hardship. It is the same with this person's sin, too. Bodhisattva Lion's Roar said: "O World-Honoured One! Why is it that this person's light sin, from which he has to suffer in this present life, turns out to chain him to hell?" The Buddha said: "O good man! If any person has five things to answer for,

-

any slight sin he has committed will turn out to be answered in hell. What are the five? They are: 1) ignorance, 2) littleness of good done, 3) graveness of evil done, 4) non-repentance, 5) no good ever done before. Also, there are five things, which are: 1) practising of evil, 2) not upholding the precepts, 3) abstaining from doing good, 4) not practising the body, sila, Wisdom, and the mind, and 5) befriending evil persons. O good man! Because of these, a slight evil in the present life evokes grave returns in hell. O good man! Because of these, the light karmic result that one [would otherwise have] to suffer in this life becomes the heavier to suffer in hell." Lion's Roar said: "O World-Honoured One! Who suffers less in the present life what he would have to suffer in hell?" "O good man! Any person in the world who practises the body, sila, Wisdom, and the mind, as stated above, and who sees that all things are void and all-equal, and who sees no Wisdom, none who is wise, no ignorance, none who is ignorant, no practising and none who practises, such is one who is wise. Such a person indeed practises the body, sila, the mind, and Wisdom. Any such person indeed makes [what would have been] karmic results in hell become less to be suffered in this life. This person may have committed the gravest of sins, but he thinks over [the matter], sees, and makes it light, and says: "What I have done is grave in nature. But nothing is better than good actions. For example, 100 pounds of flower upon flower cannot after all compare with a "ryo" [unit of weight or money] of true gold. We might well throw a "sho" of salt into the Ganges, but no taste of salt will come about [from this] and no one, on drinking it, will taste it. A rich man may possess 1,000 million jewels and yet he will not be chained up and made to suffer pain on their account. Or a great gandhahastin can break an iron chain, escape and be unimpeded." So is it [also] with the person who has Wisdom. He always thinks to himself: "I have much of the power of good and little of evil actions. I confess and repent and do away with evil. If we practise Wisdom, the power of Wisdom will grow, and the power of ignorance will lessen." Thinking thus, he befriends a good teacher of the Way and learns the right view of life. If he sees a person who upholds, recites, copies and expounds the 12 types of sutra, he will feel respect in his mind and, besides, will make offerings to him of such things as clothing, food, accommodation, bedding, medicine, flowers and incense, and will praise and respect [him]. Wherever he goes, he only praises what is good and does not speak of what is lacking. He makes offerings to the Three Treasures and respects and believes that the vaipulya Great Nirvana Sutra and the Tathagata are Eternal and Unchanging, and that beings have the Buddha-Nature. Such a person makes what would be heavily suffered in hell something that is [only] light suffering in this life. O good man! For this reason, it is not the case that all actions are definite and that all beings definitely have to undergo karmic consequences."

Chapter Thirty-Nine: On Bodhisattva Lion's Roar 7

Bodhisattva Lion's Roar said: "O World-Honoured One! If all actions do not definitely call forth [fixed] karmic results, and all beings have the Buddha-Nature and should practise the Noble Eightfold Path, why is it that all beings do not attain this Mahaparinirvana? O World-Honoured One! If all beings have the Buddha-Nature, they must definitely attain unsurpassed Enlightenment. Why is it that they definitely needs must practise the Noble Eightfold Path? O World-Honoured One! This sutra states: "There is a sick person who gains medicine, an attendant for the illness, and the food and drink needed for the illness; or there may by none such. But all will get cured. It is the same with all beings, too. They may encounter sravakas, pratyekabuddhas, all Buddhas and Bodhisattvas, and all good teachers of the Way, listen to sermons and practise the holy ways. Or they may not encounter, listen to and practise such, but they must [i.e. will unfailingly] all attain unsurpassed Enlightenment. Why? Because of the Buddha-Nature." Thus does it stand. O World-Honoured One! For example, it is not possible for the light of the sun and moon to get obstructed on the way, so that it cannot get around the Antarava [Anderab] Mountains, or for the waters of the four great rivers not to reach the great ocean, or for the icchantika not to go to hell. It is the same with all beings, too. There cannot be any situation where hindrances come about so that they cannot attain unsurpassed Enlightenment. Why not? Because of the Buddha-Nature. O World-Honoured One! Because of this, all beings do not practise the Way. Because of the power of the Buddha-Nature, they attain unsurpassed Enlightenment. There is no reason that one needs to fall [depend] on the power of the Holy Way. O World-Honoured One! If the icchantika, those of the four grave offences, and those of the four deadly sins cannot attain unsurpassed Enlightenment, one will surely practise the Way. Because one surely attains it by the power of the Buddha-Nature. It is not that one attains it by learning and practising. O World-Honoured One! For example, a magnet, though distant, attracts iron. It is the same with the Buddha-Nature of beings. Because of this, one need not practise the Way." The Buddha said: "Well said, well said, O good man! By the Ganges there live seven kinds of men. They are afraid of robbers because they are now bathing. Or the case might be as with those who get into the river in order to pick flowers. The first person gets drowned as he gets into the water; the second person sinks in mid-water, but comes up and sinks down again into the water. Why? Because his body is powerful and strong, he is able to get out. The one who has not learnt to float comes up and then sinks again. The third comes up after sinking. Coming up, he does not sink again. Why not? Because his body is heavy, so he sinks, but as his power is great, he comes up. Having already learnt to float, he stays up. The fourth person, on getting into the water, comes up again. Coming up, he looks around. Why? As he is heavy, he sinks, as he has great power, he comes up; as he has learnt to float, he remains [up]; not knowing where to get out, he looks around. The fifth person, on going into the water, sinks, and having sunk, he comes up. Having come up, he looks around; having looked, he goes. Why? Because he fears. The sixth person goes into the water, and gets out, and stays in the shallow waters. Why? Because he sees the robbers who are nearby and [also] far off. The seventh person is already up on the other bank and is on a great mountain. He fears nothing; out of the reach of the robbers, he is blessed with great bliss. O good man! It is the same situation with the great river of birth and death, too. "These are the seven kinds of people. As they fear the robbers of defilement, they make up their minds and wish to cross the great river of birth and death. They abandon their homes, shave their heads, and don priestly robes. Having renounced their homes, they associate with evil friends, follow their teachings, and give ear to their doctrines, which state: "Man's body is the five skandhas. The five skandhas are none but the five great elements. When a man dies, he does away with the five great elements. When he parts with the five great elements, why does he any longer need to practise good or bad? Because of this, one may know that there can be no karmic returns of good or bad." Such a person is an icchantika. He is cut off from the root of good or bad. Cut off from the root of good, he sinks into the waters of birth and death and is unable to get out. Why? Because of the great weight of evil deeds, and he has no power of faith. He is like the first person of those on the banks of the river Ganges. "O good man! The icchantika has six causal relations. He falls into the three unfortunate realms and cannot get out of them. What are the six? They are: 1) his evil mind burns, 2) he does not see the after-life, 3) he takes pleasure in seeking defilement, 4) he walks away from good, 5) evil actions hinder his way, and 6) he associates with an evil teacher of the Way. "This again possesses five things, by which the person falls into the three unfortunate realms. What are the five? They are: 1) he always says that there can be no karmic results to come about in regard to good or bad actions, 2) he kills a person who has aspired to Bodhi, 3) he takes pleasure in speaking about the evils committed by priests, 4) he says that what is right is not right and what transgresses Dharma is lawful, and 5) he gives ear to Dharma just to pick up what goes against [i.e. to find fault]. "Also, there are three things by which the person falls into the three unfortunate realms. What are the three? These are saying that: 1) the Tathagata is non-eternal, and goes away eternally, 2) Wonderful Dharma is non-eternal and changes, and 3) the Sangha Jewel gets destroyed. For this reason, he always sinks into the three unfortunate realms. "The second person aspires to cross the great river of birth and death, but devoid of amassed good sinks and is unable to get out. We speak of "getting out". This is associating with a good teacher of the Way, through which one gains faith. By faith is meant believing that dana [giving] evokes the fruition of dana, that any action that can be called good calls forth the fruition of good, and any action that is evil that of evil, and it is believing in the suffering of birth and death, and believing in impermanence and dissolution. This is faith. Gaining faith, the person practises pure sila, upholds, recites, copies and expounds [the sutras]. He always gives and well practises Wisdom. If dull, the person encounters an evil friend. He is unable to learn how to practise the sila of body and the Wisdom of mind. He gives ear to evil teachings. Or he may happen to be visited by an evil period of time and be born in an evil land and be cut off from good deeds. Cut off from the root of goodness, he always sinks into birth and death. His case is like that of the second person on the banks of the river Ganges. "The third person looks forward to crossing the great river of birth and death. Devoid of good, he sinks in mid-water. His drawing near to a good teacher of the Way is his getting out.

The Tathagata is the All-Knower. He is Eternal and suffers no change. For the sake of beings, he speaks about the unsurpassed Way. All beings have the Buddha-Nature. The Tathagata does not go into extinction. It is the same with the Dharma and Sangha, too. There is no extinction. Not having done away with his own quality, the icchantika cannot attain unsurpassed Enlightenment. He needs must do away with it, and then he will attain it [Enlightenment]. Thus does he believe. Through faith, he practises pure sila. Having practised pure sila, he upholds, recites, copies and expounds the 12 types of sutra and speaks of them extensively for the benefit of beings. He is pleased to give and to practise Wisdom. Born sharp-minded, he firmly abides in faith and Wisdom and does not draw back in his determination. This is like the situation of the third person on the banks of the river Ganges. "The fourth person desires to cross the great river of birth and death. Devoid of good amassed, he sinks in mid-water. Coming close to a good teacher of the Way, he gains faith. This is getting out. As he gains faith, he upholds, recites, copies and expounds, and for the sake of beings he propounds Dharma widely. He takes pleasure in giving and practises Wisdom. Born sharp-minded, he firmly believes in faith and Wisdom. There is no drawing back with him from his resolve, and he looks all around in the four directions. The four directions mean the four fruitions of a sramana. This is like the fourth person on the banks of the river Ganges. "The fifth person is one who aspires to cross the great river of birth and death, but with no good amassed, sinks in mid-water. Associating with a good teacher of the Way, he gains faith. This is gettiing out. With faith, he upholds, recites, copies, expounds the 12 types of sutras and speaks expansively for the sake of beings. He takes pleasure in giving, and he practises Wisdom. Sharp-born, he firmly abides in faith and Wisdom, and there is no regression in his mind. Not regressing, he makes progress. Making progress refers to the pratyekabuddha. Although good as regards the salvation of his own self, this does not extend to others. This is getting out. This is as with the fifth person on the banks of the river Ganges. "The sixth person aspires to cross the great river of birth and death. Devoid of accumulated good, he sinks in mid-water. Coming close to a good teacher of the Way, he gains faith. Gaining faith is getting out. Due to faith, he upholds, recites, copies and extensively speaks about [Dharma] for the sake of beings. He takes pleasure in giving and practises Wisdom. Sharp-born, he bases himself firmly on faith and Wisdom, and his mind does not retrogress. Not retrogressing, he proceeds on and at last gains the shallow waters. Arriving at the shallow waters, he remains there and does not move about. We say that he remains. This means that the Bodhisattva, in order to save all beings, abides there and meditates on defilement. He is like the sixth person on the banks of the river Ganges. "The seventh person aspires to cross the great river of birth and death. But with no good amassed up to thus far, he sinks in mid-water. On meeting a good teacher of the Way, he gains faith. This gaining of faith is what we call "getting out". Due to faith, he upholds, recites, copies and expounds the 12 types of sutra, and for the benefit of beings he speaks extensively of them. He takes pleasure in giving and practises Wisdom. Sharp-born, he firmly abides in faith and Wisdom, and he does not retrogress in mind. As he does not retrogress, he steps forward. Stepping forward, he reaches the other shore. Having gained the heights of a great mountain, he is now segregated from fear and is blessed with much peace. O good man! The mountain on the other shore can be likened to the Tathagata, peace to the Eternality of the Buddha, and the great and high mountain is Great Nirvana. "O good man! Such persons on the banks of the river Ganges all have hands and feet, but they are difficult to save. It is the same with all beings, too. The Three Jewels of the Buddha, Dharma and Sangha truly exist, and the Tathagata always expounds the essentials of all laws [Dharma]. There are the Noble Eightfold Path and Mahaparinirvana. All beings can gain all of these. This is not what comes out of me or of those noble paths or of beings. Know that all these go back to defilement. Because of this, all beings cannot gain Nirvana. "O good man! A good doctor knows about illness and speaks about medicine. If the sick person does not take it, the doctor is not to blame. "O good man! A danapati [giver] gives things to all persons. There may be those who will not accept [the gifts]. The giver is not to blame for this. "O good man! When the sun comes out, all gloom turns to brightness. But the blind cannot see this. The sun is not to blame for this. "O good man! The water of the river Ganges indeed does away with thirst. There may be those who are thirsty, but who do not drink. The water is not to blame. "O good man! The great earth brings forth fruit for everyone all-equally. But there may be farmers who do not plant [anything]. The earth is not to blame for this. "O good man! The Tathagata gives and expounds the 12 types of sutra to all beings. But the Tathagata is not to blame if the beings will not take them. O good man! Those who practise the Way will all attain unsurpassed Enlightenment. O good man! You say that beings all have the Buddha-Nature and that it is as unfailing as a magnet that they will attain unsurpassed Enlightenment. It is well, it is well that because of the causal relations of the Buddha-Nature the person will attain unsurpassed Enlightenment. Should you say that there is no need to practise the Holy Path, this is not so. "O good man! As an illustration: a man is journeying through a wilderness and feels thirsty, when he comes across a well. It is very deep, so that he cannot see the water. But we may know that there assuredly is water there. If the person brings forth the means and draws up the water with a rope and a bucket, then the water is assuredly there. It is the same, too, with the Buddha-Nature. All beings possess it. But only by practising the undefiled Noble Path can one truly see it. "O good man! If there is sesame, we can get oil. If we do not have the means, we cannot get it. It is the same with sugar cane. "O good man! Though the north of Uttarakuru of Trayastrimsa Heaven exists, one cannot see it other than by accumulation of good karma, miraculous power, and the power of the Way. The roots of trees and grass which are under the ground, and the water in the ground, cannot be seen by us, since the earth covers them. It is the same situation with the Buddha-Nature, too. If one does not practise the Holy Way, one cannot expect to see it. "O good man! You say that the illnesses of the world will get cured with or without nursing, a good doctor, good medicine, and the food and drink needed for those illnesses. O good man! I spoke thus to all Bodhisattvas of the sixth stage. "O good man! All the beings in space have no inside, no outside, and no in and no out. Hence, they are unmolested [unimpeded] in every way. It is the same with the Buddha-Nature of all beings, too. "O good man! There is a man who possesses wealth in different places and not where he is. When asked, he may say that he has it. Why? Because he definitely possesses it. It is the same with the Buddha-Nature of beings, too. It is not this and not that. As one is sure to gain it in hand, we say that it all is. "O good man! It is as in the case in which all beings make all things. They are not good, not bad, not in and not out. All such karmic natures are not existing and not non-existing. Also, it is not what once was not, but what is. It is not what has come about without any cause. It is not what I have done and I receive. It is not what I have done and he receives. It is not what he has and he receives. It is not what is done; it is not what one receives. Time agrees and fruition comes about. It is the same with the Buddha-Nature of all beings, too. It is again not what was not but what is now. It is neither in nor out. It is neither "is" nor "is-not". It is neither this nor that. It is neither what comes from without, nor is it of no causal relations. It is not that all beings do not see. All Bodhisattvas see as time and causal relations come to conjoin. We say time. The Bodhisattvamahasattva of the ten stages practises the Noble Eightfold Path and gains an all-equal mind, when it [the Buddha-Nature] can be seen. It is not what is done. "O good man! You say that it is like a magnet. But this is not so. Why not? A stone does not attract iron. Why not? Because there is no mental action that works. O good man! There are things of different nature, and so a thing of different nature comes about. And when there is no different thing, a different thing breaks off [goes into dissolution]. There is none doing and none that breaks. O good man! It is as in the case of a great fire which cannot burn the fuel. When the fire comes about, the fuel breaks [is used up, destroyed]. This we call the fuel burning. O good man! This is as with the sunflower, which turns by itself, following the sun. And this sunflower has no mind to respect, no consciousness, and no action to do. It is by the nature of a different thing that it turns by itself. "O good man! It is as with the plantain tree which grows by thunder. This plant has no ears and no consciousness. When there is a different thing, this different thing grows; when there is no different thing, this different thing dies out. O good man! It is as in the case of the asoka tree, which puts out flowers when a female touches it. This tree has no mind, no sense of touch. When there is a different thing, a different thing comes about; when there is no different thing, a different thing dies out. "O good man! This is as in the case of citrus nobilis, which bears no further fruits when it gains a corpse. Yet this plant has no mind and no sense of touch. By a different thing, there comes about a different

thing; when there is no different thing, the different thing dies out. O good man! For example, the fruit of the pomegranate grows because of rotten calf-bones. But the pomegranate tree also does not possess a mind or touch. When there is a different thing, a different thing comes about, and when there is no different thing, a different thing dies out. "O good man! The same applies to the case of the magnet attracting iron. When there is a different thing, a different thing comes about; when there is no different thing, the different thing dies out. It is the same with the Buddha-Nature of beings which cannot attract unsurpassed Enlightenment. "O good man! Ignorance cannot attract all actions. Volition, too, cannot attract consciousness. And yet we can say that ignorance has a causal relationship with volition, and volition with consciousness. Whether there is the Buddha or not, the world is eternal. "O good man! You may say that the Buddha-Nature lives in beings. O good man! You should know that what is Eternal has no place to dwell [i.e. is not confined to one limited place in space and time]. If there is a place where it dwells, this tells us that what there is there is something that is impermanent. O good man! You may know that the 12 links of interdependent arising have no place to stay. If they had, we could not say that the 12 links of interdependent arising were eternal. It is the same with the Dharmakaya [Dharma-Body] of the Tathagata. It has no place to dwell. All such as the 18 realms, the 12 spheres, the skandhas, and space do not have anywhere to stay. It is the same with the Buddha-Nature, too. All do not have any place to stay. "O good man! For example, the four great elements have powers that are all equal. But there are such qualities as hardness, heat, moisture, movability, lightness, weightiness, red, white, yellow, and black. These four elements do not have karmic action. Being different in the realm of existence, there is no sameness. It is the same with the Buddha-Nature, too. Different in nature in the realm of existence, it comes out into existence when the time comes. "O good man! All beings do not come away from [i.e. are not separate from] the Buddha-Nature. Hence, we say "is". Because of the unretrogressiveness of what can be "is" in the days to come, [because] of what is sure to be gained, and of what can definitely be seen. That is why we say that all beings possess the Buddha-Nature. "O good man! For example, there is a king who says to his minister: "Fetch an elephant and show it to some blind persons." Then, following the royal command, the minister called in many blind persons, to whom he showed the elephant. The blind persons all touched the elephant with their hands. The minister said to the king: "I have got the blind people to feel the elephant." Then the king called in the blind persons and asked each of them: "Have you seen the elephant?" "Yes, sire! I have seen the elephant." The king asked: "What do you think the elephant is like?"

The person who had touched its tusk said: "The elephant is like the root of a goosefoot or a mushroom." The man who had touched its ear said: "The elephant is like a winnow." The one who had touched its trunk said: "The elephant is like a pestle." The person who had touched its foot said: "The elephant is like a handmill made of wood." The one who had touched it by the spine said: "The elephant is like a bed." The man who had touched its belly said: "The elephant is like a pot." The man who had touched it by its tail said: "The elephant is like a rope." "O good man! All these blind persons were not well able to tell of the form of the elephant. And yet, it is not that they did not say anything at all about the elephant. All such aspects of representation are of the elephant. And yet, other than these, there cannot be any elephant. "O good man! The king is comparable to the Tathagata-Arhat-Samyaksambuddha, the minister to the vaipulya Great Nirvana Sutra, the elephant to the Buddha-Nature, and the blind persons to all beings who are ignorant. All of these people, on hearing what the Buddha says, may say: "Form ["rupa" - physical form, matter, body] is the Buddha-Nature. Why? Because this form, though it dies, continues to exist. Because of this, it attains the 32 unsurpassed signs of perfection of the Tathagata and the eternality of form of the Tathagata. Because the form of the Tathagata knows no disruption. That is why we say that form is the Buddha-Nature. "For example, the form of true gold may well change, but the colour is always one and is not different. It can be made into a bracelet, a serpent, and a basin, and yet the yellow colour never changes. It is the same with the Buddha-Nature of beings, too. The form may not be one, but the colour is one. Thus we can say that "rupa" is eternal." So do they say. "Or another might say: "Feeling ["vedana"] is the Buddha-Nature. Why so? Because through the causal

relations of feeling, one gains the true bliss of the Tathagata. The feeling of the Tathagata is that of the absolute and is of "Paramartha-satya". The nature of beings' feeling is non-eternal, but continues to exist successively. it is because of this that one gains the eternal feeling of the Tathagata. For example, a man's clan name is Kausika. The man himself is non-eternal, but his clan name goes on as it is and does not change, even in the course of thousands and millions of years. It is the same with the Buddha-Nature of beings, too. For this reason, feeling is the Buddha-Nature." "And another one says: "Perception ["samjna"] is the Buddha-Nature. Why? By reason of the causal relations of perception, one attains the perception of the Tathagata. The perception of the Tathagata is that of non-perception. The perception of non-perception is not what obtains with man, is nothing of the male or female, of form, feeling, perception, volition or consciousness. It is non-perception, something cut off from perception. The perception of beings is non-eternal. But a perception is followed by another one, one after the other, so that there is no disruption and we gain the impression of perception which is of an eternal quality. O good man! For example, let us take up the case of the 12 links of interdependence of beings. Though the beings die out, the causal relations are eternal. It is the same with the Buddha-Nature of beings. For this reason, we say that perception is the Buddha-Nature." Thus do people speak. "Further, they say: "Volition ["samskara" - mental impulses, will] is the Buddha-Nature. Why? Volition is life. By reason of the causal relations of beings, a person attains the eternal life of the Tathagata. The life of beings is non-eternal, but a life follows another successively, one after the other, so that there is no disruption. So, we gain the eternal life of the Tathagata, which is true. O good man! For example, those who speak about, and give ear to, the 12 types of sutra are now eternal, because these sutras eternally exist and do not change. So is it with the Buddha-Nature of beings. Hence, volition is the Buddha-Nature." So do they say. "Also, they say: "Consciousness ["vijnana"] is the Buddha-Nature. By reason of the causal relations of consciousness, one gains the all-equal mind of the Tathagata. Although the consciousness of beings is non-eternal, a consciousness is followed by another successively, so that there is no disruption. Hence, one gets the eternal mind of the

Tathagata, which is true. Fire has the property of heat. But the property of heat is eternal. It is the same with the Buddha-Nature of beings. Hence, consciousness is the Buddha-Nature." So do they say. "Also, they say: "Other than the skandhas, there is the Self. Self is the Buddha-Nature. Why? By the causal relations of the Self, one gains the unmolested light of the Tathagata." "There are various tirthikas who say: "Going and coming, seeing and hearing, sorrow and gladness, and words and speaking are the Self." All such notions of the Self are non-eternal. "But the Self of the Tathagata is truly Eternal." "O good man! The five skandhas, the 18 realms, and the 12 spheres are also non-eternal. But we call them eternal. The same is the case with beings. "O good man! Each of the blind men speaks about the elephant and what he says does not accord with the truth. Yet it is not that he does not speak about the elephant." "It is the same with the person who speaks about the Buddha-Nature, too. It is not quite the six things, and yet it is not the case that it is away from them. O good man! That is why I say that the Buddha-Nature is non-form, and yet it is not segregated from form. It is not the Self, and yet, nor is it away from the Self. O good man! Many tirthikas say that there is the Self. But, truth to tell, there is no Self. The Self of beings [as opposed to that of the Buddha- ed.] is the five skandhas. Other than the skandhas, there is no Self. O good man! For example, the stem, leaf, and calyx combine and we get the bloom of the lotus. Other than this, there cannot be any flower. It is the same with the Self of beings. "O good man! For example, the walls, grass, and wood combine, and we have a house. Other than this, there cannot be a house. The khadira, palasa, nyagrodha, and udumbara combine, and we have a forest. Other than this, there is no forest. For example, such things as chariots, soldiers, elephants, horses and infantry combine, and we have an army. Other than this, there can be no army. A good combination of the threads of five colours brings forth an "aya" [Jap: a kind of silken cloth of mixed colour-tone]. Other than this, there cannot be any aya. The harmonious combination of the four castes is called the "great populace". Other than this, there can be no "great populace". It is the same with the Self of beings, too. There is [with them] no Self other than the five skandhas. ""O good man! The Eternal of the Tathagata is the Self. The Dharmakaya "[Dharma-Body]" of the Tathagata is unboundedness,

unobstructedness, birthlessness, undyingness, and the eight unmolestednesses. This is the Self. The beings, truth to tell, do not have such a Self and what the Self possesses. Only because of the fact that a person absolutely attains the absoute Void of "Paramartha-satya" do we say the Buddha-Nature. "O good man! Great Loving-Kindness and Great Compassion are the Buddha-Nature. Why? Because Great Loving-Kindness and Great Compassion always accompany the Bodhisattva. It is like the shadow that follows a form. All beings decidedly will attain Great Loving-Kindness and Great Compassion. So, we say that all beings possess Great Loving-Kindness and Great Compassion. Great Loving-Kindness and Great Compassion are the Buddha-Nature. The Buddha-Nature is the Tathagata. "Great Sympathetic Joy and Great Equanimity are the Buddha-Nature. Why? If the Bodhisattvamahasattva cannot forsake the 25 existences, he cannot attain unsurpassed Enlightenment. As beings will all unfailingly gain it, we say that all beings possess the Buddha-Nature. Great Sympathetic Joy and Great Equanimity are the Buddha-Nature. The Buddha-Nature is at once the Tathagata "." ""The Buddha-nature is great faith [Jap: "daishinjin"]. "Why? Because of faith, the Bodhisattvamahasattva can indeed be perfect in danaparamita up to prajnaparamita. As all beings unfailingly gain great faith, we say: "All beings have the Buddha-Nature." Great faith is the Buddha-Nature. The Buddha-Nature is the Tathagata. "The Buddha-Nature is the single son's soil. Why? Because by the causal relations of the single son's soil, the Bodhisattva is equal in his mind towards all beings. As all beings ultimately attain the single son's soil, we say: "All beings possess the Buddha-Nature." The single son's soil is the Buddha-Nature. The Buddha-Nature is the Tathagata. "The Buddha-Nature is the fourth power. Why? Through the causal relations of the fourth power, the Bodhisattva teaches all beings well. As all beings will ultimately gain the fourth power, we say: "All beings possess the Buddha-Nature." The fourth power is the Buddha-Nature. The Buddha-Nature is the Tathagata. "The Buddha-Nature is the 12 links of interdependent arising. Why? By reason of the causal relations, the Tathagata is Eternal. All beings definitely possess these 12 links of interdependent arising. That is why we say: "All beings possess the Buddha-Nature." The 12 links of interdependent arising are the Buddha-

Nature. The Buddha-Nature is the Tathagata. "The Buddha-Nature is the fourfold unhindered knowledge. By reason of the four unhinderednesses, we say that he is unhindered in understanding words. Unhindered in understanding words, he indeed teaches beings. The four unhinderednesses are the Buddha-Nature. The Buddha-Nature is the Tathagata. "The Buddha-Nature is called vajropama-samadhi. By practising samadhi, one truly catches hold of the Buddhist doctrines. Because of this, we say: "The vajropama-samadhi is the Buddha-Nature." The Bodhisattva of the ten stages practises this samadhi and is not yet perfect. He sees the Buddha-Nature, but not clearly. As all beings will ultimately gain it, we say: "All beings have the Buddha-Nature." "O good man! As all the doctrines [dharmas] referred to above will definitely be gained by all beings, we say: "All beings definitely have the Buddha-Nature." O good man! If I say that material form ["rupa"] is the Buddha-Nature, beings, on hearing this, will gain an inverted [view]. Being inverted, when life ends they will fall into Avichi Hell. The sermons of the Tathagata are to cut the person off from hell. So he does not say that material form is the Buddha-Nature. Also, the same applies down to consciousness. "O good man! We say that when all beings gain the Buddha-Nature, they need not practise the Way. This comes from the fact that the Bodhisattva of the ten stages, as he practises the Noble Eightfold Path, can see the Buddha-Nature a little. How could a person who has not practised the Way well see it? O good man! Manjushri and all the Bodhisattvas have already practised the Holy Way over innumerable lives and they know the Buddha-Nature. How could the sravaka and pratyekabuddha know the Buddha-Nature? Any being who desires to know the Buddha-Nature must, with one mind, uphold, recite, copy and expound the Nirvana Sutra and make offerings, respect and praise it. If one should encounter a person who upholds and praises the Sutra, one ought to give such a person a good house to live in, clothing, and food and drink, bedding, and medicine; and also, one ought to praise, worship, and ask about the Way. O good man! A person who has in innumerable, boundless past lives associated with, and offered things to, innumerable Buddhas and has thus amassed a great deal of good can hope to hear the name of this Sutra. "O good man! It is difficult to conceive of the Buddha-Nature. It is not possible to conceive of the Treasures of the Buddha, Dharma and Sangha. All beings possess the Buddha-Nature, but not all can know it. This, too, cannot easily be conceived of. The law [Dharma] of the Eternal, Bliss, the Self, and the Pure of the Tathagata is also difficult to know. That all beings trust in the Great Nirvana Sutra is difficult to know, too." Bodhisattva Lion's Roar said: "O World-Honoured One! You say: "It is not possible to conceive that all beings truly believe in the Great Nirvana Sutra." O World-Honoured One! Among the mass of people here present, there are 85,000 billion people who have no faith in this sutra. It is a thing of wonder if there can be any who can believe in this sutra." "O good man! All such people can, in lives to come, definitely believe in this sutra. They will see the Buddha-Nature and attain unsurpassed Enlightenment." Lion's Roar said: "O World-Honoured One! How can the Bodhisattva of the unretrogressive state come to know that he has the unretrogressive mind?" The Buddha said: "O good man! The Bodhisattva-mahasattva tests his own mind by penance. He takes a single sesame seed a day and this proceeds for seven days. This proceeds also with such as rice, green beans, hemp seeds, millet, white beans, of which he takes one each day for seven days. When taking a hemp seed, he has to think: "All such penances help nothing. I am doing what does not benefit me. Why not do what gives benefit?" In what gives the person no benefit the mind well stands and does not draw back and change. Because of this, he is sure to attain unsurpassed Enlightenment. When the penance is practised in such days, the flesh and skin get so emaciated and shrink so that everything looks like a raw gourd cut and placed in the sun. The eyes become so drawn back that they look like stars floating in a well; the flesh is so sunken that it looks like a grass-thatched house. The bones of the spine so stick out, one above the other, that we might well think of juentan [the cover on a crown]; where he sits looks like a place stamped by a horse-shoe. Desiring to sit, he falls face down, and desiring to get up, he falls face down. Thus does he suffer from useless pains. Yet, his Bodhichitta [resolve for Enlightenment] does not recoil. "Also, next, O good man! The Bodhisattva-mahasattva fights against all pains. And to give peace to others, he casts away all the wealth that he has and abandons his own life as though it were fodder. Casting aside his body and mind, such a

Bodhisattva unfailingly sees that he has an unretrogressive mind and that he will definitely attain unsurpassed Enlightenment. "Also, next, the Bodhisattva, for Dharma, slices off his own body and makes it into a lamp. He rolls his skin and flesh in a woolen cloth, puts butter oil on it, burns it and makes it into a wick. The Bodhisattva suffers this great pain at the time and reproaches his own mind, saying: "Even such pains are not worth a hundred-thousand-millionth part. You have, over a period of an innumerable hundred thousand kalpas, undergone great pain and gained nothing. If you cannot stand this slight pain, how can you hope to save those in hell who are in pain?" When the Bodhisattva-mahasattva thinks thus, he has no pain in his body and his mind does not draw back. It does not move about or shift. The Bodhisattva then deeply thinks: "I shall surely attain unsurpassed Enlightenment." O good man! The Bodhisattva, at that time, is garbed in defilement. It is not yet cut off. For the sake of Dharma, he indeed gives away to beings all his head, eyes, marrow, hands and feet, blood and flesh. He strikes nails into his body, thows himself onto the rocks, and steps into fire. The Bodhisattva at that time suffers such innumerable pains. His mind does not draw back, does not move about, and does not shift. And the Bodhisattva knows: "I now have an unretrogressive mind, and I shall attain unsurpassed Enlightenment." "O good man! The Bodhisattva-mahasattva, in order to crush out the suffering of all beings, takes a vow, gains the rough and great body of an animal and gives away his own body, blood and flesh to beings. When the beings take these, they will have a pitying mind. The Bodhisattva then suppresses his breathing, shows a dying face, and does not let a person who harms gain the thought of killing or doubt. The Bodhisattva, though now an animal in body, does not, to the end, perform any action of an animal. Why? O good man! When the Bodhisattva gains an unretrogressive mind, he does not perform any action of the three unfortunate realms. If there should be any bit of evil karmic returns not yet definitely suppressed in the life to come, the Bodhisattva-mahasattva takes a great vow and suffers himself all such for the sake of beings. "For example, a sick person has within his body a devil which sits within, hidden. By the power of charms, it shows its form and talks, is happy, angry, slanders, weeps, and laughs. Things go thus. The actions in the days of the three

unfortunate realms of the Bodhisattva-mahasattva also proceed in the same way. "When the Bodhisattva-mahasattva gains the body of a brown bear, he speaks of Wonderful Dharma to beings. Or he may gain the body of a kapinjala, and speaks of Dharma to beings. Or he may gain such a body as that of the godha, the deer, hare, sheep, monkey, white dove, garuda, naga, or serpent. Gaining such a body, he does not ever think of performing the evil actions of a beast. Always, for the sake of all other beasts and beings, he speaks of Wonderful Dharma, so as to enable them quickly to discard their animal bodies. The Bodhisattva, although possessing the body of an animal, does not do any of the evil actions of an animal. So, one can know that he decidedly dwells in an unretrogressive mind. "The Bodhisattva-mahasattva, at the time of a famine, sees the hunger-ridden beings and gains the body of a tortoise or fish, as big as innumerable yojanas. Again, he swears to himself: "I pray that when all beings take my flesh, as soon as they take it new flesh will come about, so much so that they will be able to segregate themselves from hunger and thirst and that all will aspire to unsurpassed Enlightenment." The Bodhisattva takes a vow: "If they make away with hunger and thirst because of me, they will in the days to come make away with the 25 existences." When the Bodhisattva undergoes such pains, he will not retrogress. Know that he will unfailingly attain unsurpassed Enlightenment. "Also, next, the Bodhisattva, in the days of an epidemic, sees those who are suffering and thinks: "This is as in the case of a big medicine tree, and the sick come and take the roots, the stem, the branches, the leaves, the flowers, the fruit, and the bark, and they make away with their illness. I pray that my body, too, will serve in this way. Anyone who suffers from illness may hear [my] voice, touch [my] body, or partake of [my] blood and flesh, or the marrow of [my] bones, and their illness will depart. I pray that when all beings partake of my flesh, they will not gain evil thoughts and will feel as though they were partaking of the flesh of their own child. After curing their illness, I shall always speak of Dharma. I pray that they will believe, meditate, and then teach others." "Also, next, O good man! The Bodhisattva, though clad in defilement and suffering bodily pain - his mind does not draw back, does not move or shift. Know that he will unfailingly gain the unretrogressive mind and accompany unsurpassed Enlightenment. "Also, next, O good man! Beings may be suffering from illnesses because of a devil. The Bodhisattva sees this and says: "I pray that I will gain the body of a devil, great in size and powerful in physique, and one who has various kindred, so that he may see and give ear to what I speak and that the illness departs." "The Bodhisattva, for the sake of beings, undergoes penance. Though clad in defilement, his mind does not become defiled. "Also, next, O good man! The Bodhisattva-mahasattva practises the six paramitas [perfections]. But he does not seek to gain the fruit of the six paramitas. When practising the six paramitas, he prays: "I shall now offer all this action of mine of the six paramitas to the good of all beings, so that any person receiving what I give will achieve unsurpassed Enlightenment. I shall also, as I practise the six paramitas, undergo all pains. As I suffer, I pray that I shall not draw back in my aspiration to Enlightenment." O good man! When the Bodhisattva gains this [state of] mind, we call this unretrogressive. "Also, next, O good man! It is difficult to conceive of the Bodhisattva. Why? The Bodhisattvamahasattva knows very well all the sins of birth and death, and sees the great virtue of Great Nirvana. And for the sake of all beings, he lives where birth and death obtain, suffering there manifold pains. Yet, his mind does not pull back. This is why we say that the Bodhisattva is inconceivable. "Also, next, O good man! The Bodhisattva-mahasattva has pity where there is nothing to have pity on. Truth to tell, he owes nothing, and yet he always does favours [to beings]. Bestowing favours, he yet does not expect any return. For this reason, we say that he is inconceivable. "Also, next, O good man! There are beings who practise various penances for their own good. The Bodhisattva-mahasattva practises penances so as to benefit others. This is "benefiting one's own self." This is also what is difficult to conceive. "Also, next, the Bodhisattva, clad in defilement, practises the all-equal mind, so that he can crush out all the pains that arise out of friendliness and enmity. Because of this, we say inconceivable. "Also, next, the Bodhisattva sees beings who do evil and do what is not good. He reproaches them, speaks gently, rejects and abandons. To one who is evil-natured, he uses gentle words; to one who is arrogant, he becomes greatly arrogant. And, yet, at heart he is not haughty. This is what we call the inconceivability

of the expedients of the Bodhisattva. "Also, next, the Bodhisattva is clad in defilement. When he has little, many people come and ask. And his mind does not become narrow-minded. This is what is inconceivable in the Bodhisattva. "Also, next, the Bodhisattva knows the virtue of the Buddha, when the Buddha appears in the world. For the sake of beings he gains birth even in remote places, where the Buddha is not. He is like a blind, deaf, lame, or crippled person. This is why we say that the Bodhisattva is inconceivable.

"Also, next, the Bodhisattva knows very well all the sins of beings, and for the sake of Emancipation, he always accompanies them. Although he follows the way of their mind, he does not get contaminated by sin and defilement. For this reason, we say inconceivable. "Also, next, the Bodhisattva gains a body which still has defilement, and lives in Tusita Heaven. This, too, is inconceivable. Why? Tusita Heaven is the best of heavens in the world of desire. Those who live in the low heavens have minds that are indolent, and all the sense-organs of those in the high heavens are dull. Because of this, we say superb. Practising dana and sila, one gains a high or low body. Practising dana, sila, and samadhi, one gains the body of the Tusita Heaven. All Bodhisattvas despise and destroy all dharmas [impermanent things]. Never do they perform the actions of heaven and gain the body of that heaven. Why not? Though living in other existences, the Bodhisattva truly teaches and gains the end. Truth to tell, he has no greed, and yet is born into the world of desire. Because of this, we say inconceivable. "The Bodhisattva-mahasattva, when he is born in Tusita heaven, has three superior things, namely: 1) life, 2) colour, and 3) fame. The Bodhisattva-mahasattva does not seek life, colour, or fame. Not seeking [these], what he gets is superior. The Bodhisattva-mahasattva seeks much Nirvana, and in the cause of "is", too, he is superior. For this reason, we say inconceivable. "Although the Bodhisattva-mahasattva thus supercedes the gods in these three things, they gain no [feeling of] anger, jealousy, or arrogance towards the Bodhisattva. They are happy. The Bodhisattva, too, does not become arrogant towards the gods. That is why we say inconceivable. "Although the Bodhisattva-mahasattva does not perform any action to gain life, he gains life in that heaven ultimately. Thus we say that [his] life is superior. Although he has not done anything for [the sake of] colour, the light of his wonderful body fills all around. Thus he is superior to others in colour. Living in that heavenly world, the Bodhisattva-mahasattva does not seek the five desires. What he does relates to Dharma. On account of this, his name resounds in the ten directions. This is how his name [reputation, fame] is superior. This is how he is inconceivable. "The Bodhisattva-mahasattva descends from Tusita Heaven, and the great earth shakes in six ways. So we say inconceivable. Why? When the Bodhisattva descends from heaven, all the gods of the worlds of desire and colour accompany him and see him off and greatly praise the Bodhisattva. From the wind generated by their mouths, the earth shakes. "Also, the Bodhisattva becomes the elephant king of men, and this elephant king is called "naga king". When the naga enters the womb, all the naga kings under the ground are afraid and frightened. So the great earth shakes in six ways. Because of this, we say inconceivable. "When the Bodhisattva-mahasattva enters the womb, he knows how long he has to be therein and when he will comes out. He knows the father and mother, and is not defiled by filth. All this obtains as in the case of the knot of hair and the blue-coloured gem of Devendra. Because of this, we say inconceivable. "O good man! It is the same with the Great Nirvana Sutra, which is inconceivable. For example, this is as with the eight things which are inconceivable. What are the eight? They are: 1) by degrees the deepness increases; 2) it is deep and the bottom is difficult to gain; 3) sameness obtains as in the case of the salty taste [of the ocean, which is everywhere salty]; 4) the tide does not exceed the boundary line; 5) there are various storehouses of treasure; 6) a great-bodied being lives therein; 7) no dead bodies are to be found there; 8) all rivers and great rains flow in, but the volume of water neither increases nor decreases. "O good man! We say that the deepness gradually increases. Here, there are three things, namely: 1) the power of beings' wealth; 2) the fair wind which carries things well, and 3) the river water enters, and there are three kinds of non-increase and non-decrease. It is the same with this all-wonderful Great Nirvana Sutra, too. There are eight inconceivablenesses. "First, there is the gradual deepening such as of the five silas, the ten silas, the 250 silas, the Bodhisattva silas. And there are the fruitions of the srotapanna,

sakrdagamin, anagamin, arhat, pratyekabuddha, Bodhisattva, and unsurpassed Bodhi. This Nirvana Sutra speaks of these teachings. Hence, gradual deepening. This is the gradual deepening. "Second, the greatly difficult has a bottom. The Tathagata-World-Honoured one is birthlessness and deathlessness. There is no attaining of unsurpassed Enlightenment. There is no turning of the Wheel of Dharma. He does not feed, does not receive, and does not give. Hence, we say "the Eternal, the Bliss, the Self, and the Pure". Beings all have the Buddha-Nature. The Buddha-Nature is not material form, and yet is not away from material form. It is not feeling, not perception, not volition, and not consciousness. Nor is he [i.e. Buddha] segregated from consciousness. This is to always see. The cause of revealing is no cause of doing. Those from the srotapanna up to pratyekabuddha will all gain unsurpassed Enlightenment. Also, there is no defilement that can be named and no place to exist, and there is not illusion. So, we say "Eternal". Hence, "deep" "Also, there is the "Eternally Deep". This is what we encounter in the sutra, which at times states as [speaks of] the Self and at times as the non-Self; or at times it goes as [designates] the Eternal, or as the non-Eternal; or, at times, as the Pure, or at times as the Impure; or at times, it goes as Bliss, and at times as Suffering; or at times, as the Void, or at times as the Non-Void; at times, all is "is", or at times all is "is-not"; or at times, all are the three vehicles, or at times one vehicle; or at times, as the five skandhas, the Buddha-Nature, the vajra-samadhi, and the Middle Path; or the Suramgama Samadhi, the 12 links of interdependence," and Paramartha-satya". Loving-kindness and Compassion come about equally to all beings. It is the highest knowledge, faith, the power that knows all sense-organs. He speaks about the Wisdom of things. Possessing the Buddha-Nature, no fixedness is spoken of. Thus, "deep". "Third, we have the sameness of the saltiness of taste. All beings possess the Buddha-Nature and ride in one vehicle; what there is is one Emancipation. What there is is the one cause and the one fruition. The taste is the same amrta [ambrosia - Immortality]. "All will attain the Eternal, Bliss, the Self, and the Pure". This is the sense in which we speak of "one taste". "Fourth, the tide does not cross the boundary line. In this, many prohibitions suppress the bhiksus. There are eight impure things which they must not keep. It is as when stated that my disciple well upholds, recites, copies, expounds and discriminates this all-wonderful Great Nirvana Sutra and that he does not transgress against it, even if it meant losing his life. That is why we say that the tide does not overstep the boundary line. "Fifth, we say that there are various storehouses of treasure. This sutra is one that contains uncountable treasures. These are the four remembrances, the four efforts, the four at-willnesses, the five sense-organs, the five powers, the seven Bodhi elements, and the Noble Eightfold Path. Also, they are such as the child's actions, the holy actions, the pure actions, and the heavenly actions. These are all the good expedients and the Buddha-Nature of all beings. There are such as the virtues of the Bodhisattva, the virtues of the Tathagata, the virtues of the various sravaka, and the virtues of the pratyekabuddha; there are such as the six paramitas, the countless samadhis, and the innumerable Wisdoms. Hence, we say "treasure-house". "Sixth, this refers to where the Great-Body Being lives. We say "Great-Body Being". Because of the fact that the Buddha and Bodhisattva have great Wisdom, we say "great being". Because of the greatness of their body, the greatness of their mind, of the great adornment, of the great subjugation which they perform, of their great expedients, of their great sermons, of their great power, of the greatness of the number of people, of the greatness of their miracles, of their Great Loving-Kindness, of their being Eternal and Unchanging, of the fact that all beings are unhindered, of the fact that all beings are taken in, we say "where the Great-Body Being resides". "Seventh, we say that no dead body stays [there]. The dead body is none other than the icchantika, the four grave offences, the five deadly sins, slandering the vaipulya, delivering sermons wrongly or unlawfully. The person stores up the eight impure things; he wilfully uses what belongs to the Buddha and the Sangha; he does what is unlawful [i.e. against Dharma] in the presence of the bhiksus and bhiksunis [monks and nuns]. These are the dead bodies. The Great Nirvana Sutra is away from any such. That is why we say that there remains no dead body there. "Eighth, we have what does not increase and what does not decrease. We say this because there is no boundary line and no beginning and no end, being non-form, non-action, being Eternal, not being born, and not dying. As all beings are all-equal, as all beings are of the same nature, we say that there

is no increase and no decrease. Thus, like the great ocean, this sutra possesses eight inconceivable-nesses." Lion's Roar said: "O World-Honoured One! You the Tathagata say that birthlessness and deathlessness are what is deep. Now, with all beings there are four [types of] birth, namely: 1) egg-born, 2) embryo-born, 3) moisture-born, and 4) transformed existence [spontaneous, immediate rebirth, e.g. as a god]. Man is fully possessed of these four kinds of birth. The cases of Bhiksus Campalu and Upacampalu are good examples. The mother of the rich man, Mekhala, that of the rich man, Nyagrodha, and the mother of Panjara are of the 500 egg-born [varieties]. Know that even among humans, too, there are cases of egg-born [persons]. As to those moisture-born, it is as the Buddha states. Once in the past, as a Bodhisattva, I was born as King Head-Born and King Hand-Born. This was as in the case of the women, Amra and Kapitha. Know that there is also the case of birth by moisture. At the time of the beginning of the world, all beings appear as transformed births [i.e. spontaneously]. The Tathagata-World-Honoured One gains the eight unmolestednesses. Why does he not appear as a transformed birth?" The Buddha said: "O good man! All beings appear through the four types of birth. When Holy Dharma is gained, one can no more be born as before in such forms as egg-born or moisture-born. O good man! The beings at the beginning of the world all appear in transformed states. At that time, the Buddha does not appear in the world. O good man! When one becomes sick and has pain, one seeks a doctor and medicine. The beings at the time of the beginning of the world gain birth in transformed states [i.e. spontaneously]. Though they are possessed of defilement, [their] illness does not as yet manifest. For this reason, the Tathagata does not appear in the world. The beings at the time of the beginning of the world do not have such receptacles as body and mind. On this account, the Tathagata does not appear in the world. "O good man! The Tathagata's caste, relatives and parents are superior to those of beings. Because of this surpassing [quality], people believe in whatever is said about Dharma. For this reason, the Tathagata does not gain birth through moisture. O good man! With all beings, the father makes the karma of his son, and his son that of his father. If the Tathagata gains the moisture type of birth, there is no father and no mother. With no father and mother, how might people be made to do all good deeds? Because of this, the Tathagata does not gain a body by transformation. O good man! In the Wonderful Dharma of the Buddha, there are two protections. One is in and the other out. The in is the observing of the precepts, and the out is the relatives and kindred. If the Buddha-Tathagata gained a transformed body, there could not be any protection from without. For this reason, the Tathagata does not gain a transformed body. "O good man! Humans gain arrogance from caste. To destroy that kind of haughtiness, he [Buddha] takes a noble birth, not gaining a transformed body. O good man! The Tathagata-World-Honoured one has a true father and mother. The father was Suddhodana, and the mother Maya.

Regarding this, all beings say that they were phantoms. How could he gain a transformed body? If his body was one of transformation, how could he gain a transformed body? Gaining a transformed body, how could there be anything such as the dissolution of his body and the presence of the sarira [body-relics]? To increase fortune and virtue, he makes his body go into dissolution and makes offerings. Because of this, the Tathagata does not gain a transformed body. No Buddhas ever show themselves in transformed births. Why should I alone gain a transformed body?" Then, Bodhisattva Lion's Roar folded his hands, and prostrating himself upon the ground, with his right knee on the ground, he praised the Buddha:

"The Tathagata is a ball of innumerable virtues!
I cannot now well explain [this]. I now,
For beings' sake, speak but a part.
Have pity and give ear to what I say.
Beings move about in the gloom of ignorance,

And suffer from a hundred pains.
The World-Honoured One thoroughly cuts them off.
Hence, the world says that he is Great Loving-Kindness.
Beings go and come back,
Like a rope of birth and death;
And with indolence and delusion
There is no peace and no bliss.
The Tathagata truly gives people peace
And thus eternally cuts
The rope of birth and death.
The Buddha truly gives people peace and bliss
And has no greed regarding the bliss he [himself] has.
For beings' sake he undergoes penance.
Hence, people make offerings to him.
Seeing others suffering pain, his body shakes.
When he is in hell, he feels no pain.
For the sake of the beings, he undergoes great pain.
For this reason, none can supercede [him];
None can recount. The Tathagata,
For beings' sake, practises penance
And accomplishes it and is perfect
In the six paramitas.
His mind is not moved even by evil winds
And is superior to all great ones.
Beings always care for peace and bliss,
But do not know how to effect the cause thereof.
The Tathagata teaches [beings] to practise well,
Like unto the compassionate father

Who loves his only son.
The Buddha sees beings' illness of defilement
And grieves over it, just as a mother does
Who sees her son sick.
He always thinks how he can cut out the illness.
Because of this, his body belongs to others.
All beings enact all the causes of suffering.
Their minds are upside down and take such to be bliss.
The Tathagata tells us of the bliss and sorrow that are true.
So we say "Great Compassion".
All worlds are shelled in by ignorance
And no beak of Wisdom can easily break this asunder.
The Tathagata's beak of Wisdom can well do this.
Hence, we say "Greatest Person".
The Three Times do not well hold him;
No name or no temporary name does exist.
And the Buddha knows the profoundest meaning of Nirvana.
So we call him the "Great Awakened One".
The river of "is" twirls around
And beings get drowned.
Their eyes are blinded by ignorance,
So that they cannot easily extract their own Self out.
The Tathagata saves his own Self and also saves others.
Hence the Buddha is called the "great master mariner".

He is well versed in the cause and result of all things
And in the way to annul these.
He always gives medicine to beings' illnesses.
Hence we call him the "Great Doctor".
The tirthikas speak of twisted views and of penance
And say that these call in bliss unsurpassed.
The Tathagata speaks of the True Way of bliss
And enables beings to gain ease and bliss.
The Tathagata-World-Honoured One destroys the twisted views of life
And shows beings the right path to take.
Anyone who follows this path will gain ease and bliss.
Hence we call the Buddha the "Guide".
It is not that what one does,
Not that what others do,
It is no doing together;
It is not without a cause.
The pain about which the Tathagata speaks
Surpasses what the tirthikas profess.
He is accomplished and perfect
In sila, samadhi, and Wisdom
And teaches beings this Dharma.
When giving, He has no jealousy or stinginess.
Hence we call the Buddha the "Unsurpassed Compassionate One".
Whatever is not done and whatever has no causal relations,
And he gains the causeless and result-less recompense.
Because of this, all wise persons
Praise the Tathagata for what he does for no returns.

Always journeying together
With the indolence of the world at large,
He himself is not defiled by indolence.
That is why we say inconceivable.
The eight things of the world cannot defile him.
The Tathagata-World-Honoured One sees neither enemy nor friend.
So his mind is always impartial.
I give a Lion's Roar, and truly roar out all the Lion's Roars of the world."

Chapter Forty: On Bodhisattva Kasyapa 1

Bodhisattva Kasyapa said to the Buddha: "O World-Honoured One! The Tathagata truly pities all beings. You adjust well what is not adjusted, make the impure pure, give refuge to the person who has no refuge, and give Emancipation to the person who is not yet emancipated. You have eight unmolestednesses [unrestrictednesses], you are the Great Doctor, and you are the King of Medicine. Bhiksu Sunaksatra was a son of the Buddha when as yet a Bodhisattva. After renunciation, he upheld, recited, discriminated and expounded the 12 types of sutra, destroyed the bonds of the world of desire and gained the four dhyanas [deep meditations]. Why is it that you the Tathagata should prophesy that Sunaksatra is one lower than the icchantika, one who lives long in hell, one irremediable? Why, O Tathagata, do you not, for his sake, speak about Wonderful Dharma and then later speak for the sake of the Bodhisattvas? O Tathagata-World-Honoured One! If you cannot save Bhiksu Sunaksatra, how can we say that you have Great Loving-Kindness and great expedients?" The Buddha said: "O good man! To illustrate: a father and mother couple have three sons. One is obedient, respects his parents, is sharp and intelligent, and knows well of the world. The second son does not respect his parents, does not have a faithful mind, is sharp and intelligent, and knows well of the world. The third son does not respect his parents, and has no faith. He is dull-witted and has no intelligence. When the parents wish to impart a teaching, who should be the first to be taught, who is to be loved, to whom do the parents need to teach the things of the world?" Bodhisattva Kasyapa said: "First must be taught the one who is obedient, who respects his parents, who is sharp and intelligent, and who knows what obtains in the world. Next, the second and then the third [son]. And although the second son is not obedient, for the sake of loving-kindness this son should be taught next." "O good man! It is also the same with the Tathagata. Of the three sons, the first may be likened to the Bodhisattva, the second to the sravaka, and the third to the icchantika. I have already spoken to the Bodhisattvas all about the details of the 12 types of sutra, and of what is shallow and near to the sravakas, and of what obtains in the world to the icchantikas and to those of the five deadly sins.

What obtains in the present does not benefit the person. But I would teach because of loving-kindness and for what may result in days to come. O good man! It is like three kinds of field. One is easy to irrigate. There is no sand there, no salt, no gravel, and no stones, and no thorns. Plant one, and one gains 100. The second also has no sand, no salt, no gravel, no stones, and no thorns. But irrigation is difficult, and the harvest is down by half. The third gives difficulties with irrigation, and it is full of sand, gravel, stones, and thorns. Plant one, and one gains one, due to the straw and grass. O good man! In the spring months, where will the farmer plant first?" "O World-Honoured One! First, the first field, second, the second field, and third, the third field." "The first can be likened to the Bodhisattva, the second to the sravaka, and the third to the icchantika." "O good man! It is as with three vessels. The first is perfect, the second leaks, and the third is broken. When one wishes to put milk, cream or butter into them, which one would one use first?" "O World-Honoured One! We would use the one which is perfect; next, the one that leaks, and then the broken one." "The perfect and pure one is comparable to the Bodhisattva-priest; the one that leaks to the sravaka, and the one that is broken to the icchantika. O good man! It is as in the case of three sick persons who go to the doctor. The first is easy to cure, the second difficult to cure, and the third, impossible to cure. Whom will the doctor cure if he has to cure [any of them]?" "O World-Honoured One! First he will cure the one who is easy to cure; next, the second person, and then the third person. Why? Because of the fact that they are related." "The person who is easy to cure is analogous to the Bodhisattva; the one difficult to cure to the sravaka-priest, and the one impossible to cure to the icchantika. In the present life, there will not come about any good fruition. But by comparison and for the ages to come, all good seeds are cultivated. O good man! For example, a great king has three horses. One is trained, is in the prime of life and possesses great strength; the second has no training, no good teeth, is not in the prime of life and does not have great strength; the third has no training, is weak, old, and has no strength. If the king wishes to go riding, which one will he use?" "O World-Honoured One! First, the trained one, which is in perfect health and which possesses great strength; then, the second and the third." "O good man! The trained one, which is in the prime of life and has great strength, can be likened to the Bodhisattva-priest, the second to the sravaka-priest, and the third to the icchantika. Though no good comes about [for the icchantika] in this present life, it is done [i.e. he is taught] out of loving-kindness and also to sow the seed for the days to come. O good man! It is as when great dana [giving] is performed when three persons come. One of them is of noble birth and has a good mind and upholds the precepts. The second is of the middle caste, is dull, but upholds the precepts. The third is of low caste, is dull, and violates the precepts. O good man! To whom will this great danapati [giver] give first?" "O World-Honoured One! To the person of noble birth, who is sharp-witted and who upholds the precepts; next, to the second person, and, then, to the third." "The first person is comparable to the Bodhisattva-priest, the second to the sravaka-priest, and the third to the icchantika. O good man! When a great lion kills a gandhahastin, he uses all his strength. Even when killing a hare, he does not have a light thought. It is also the same with the All-Buddha-Tathagata. When addressing all Bodhisattvas and icchantikas, he does not do things in two ways. O good man! I once lived in Rajagriha, when the bhiksu, Sunaksatra, served me as an attendant. In the early part of one evening, I spoke to Devendra about the essence of Dharma. It is the way of a disciple to go to bed later. Then, Sunaksatra, as I sat up a long time, had an evil thought. In those days in Rajagriha, when small boys and girls cried and would not stop, the parents would say: "If you don't stop crying, we shall give you to the devil, Vakkula." Then, Sunaksatra, getting a dishonest thought, said to me: "Please speed to samadhi. There comes Vakkula!" I said: "You blockhead! Do you not know that the Tathagata-World-honoured One never has any fear?" Then, Devendra said to me: "O World-Honoured One! Can someone like that also get into the Buddha's group?" I said: "O Kausika! Such persons can gain the Buddhist teaching; they too possess the Buddha-Nature. They will attain unsurpassed Enlightenment." I spoke to this Sunaksatra about Dharma. But he had no faith in me and did not take in anything I said. "O good man! I once lived in the state of Kasi, at Sivapura [= Varanasi]. The bhiksu, Sunaksatra, served me as attendant. I then

went into the castle, meaning to beg for alms. Innumerable people vacantly [without any set purpose] followed me wherever I went. Bhiksu Sunaksatra, on following me, wanted to drive them away, but was unable to do so. Instead, the people gained a non-good mind. Entering the castle, I saw a Nirgrantha in a wine shop, sitting hunchbacked on the ground and partaking of liquor lees. Bhiksu Sunaksatra, on seeing this, said: "O World-Honoured One! If ever there was an arhat, this is the greatest. Why? Because he says that there is no cause and no return to actions performed." I said: "O blockhead! Have you never heard it said that an arhat does not drink, does not cause any harm to others, does not cheat, does not rob, and does not have any sexual intercourse? Such persons as this kill their parents and partake of liquor lees. How can one call such a man an arhat? This man will assuredly fall into Avichi Hell. An arhat is eternally segregated from the three unfortunate realms. How can you call such a man an arhat?" Sunaksatra said: "We might well be able to change the natures of the four great elements, but it is impossible to make this person fall into Avichi Hell." I said: "O blockhead! Have you never heard that the All-Buddha-Tathagata truly never uses two words [i.e. speaks falsely]?" I spoke thus, but he would not believe my words. "O good man! I once lived in Rajagriha with Sunaksatra. At that time, there was a Nirgrantha in the castle-town who was called "Sorrow-Ridden". He always said: "The defilement of a being has no direct or indirect cause. The emancipation of us beings also has no direct or indirect cause." Bhiksu Sunaksatra said: "O World-Honoured One! If anyone is an arhat, this Sorrow-Ridden is the greatest." I said: "You blockhead! The Nirgrantha, Sorrow-Ridden, is no arhat. He cannot understand the way of an arhat." Sunaksatra further asked: "Why does an arhat become jealous of another arhat?" I said: "O you blockhead! I have no jealousy towards any person. It is only that you have distorted notions. If you mean to say that Sorrow-Ridden is an arhat, he will suffer from indigestion, have stomach-ache, die, and, after death, he will be born amongst hungry pretas [ghosts], and his comrades will carry his corpse and place it in Sitavana." Then, Sunaksatra went to the Nirgrantha and said: "O Learned One! Do you know or not that Sramana Gautama prophesies that you will suffer from indigestion, get a pain in your stomach and die, and that after your death, you will be born among hungry pretas, and that your comrades and teachers will carry your corpse and place it in Sitavana? O Learned One! Think well and effect expedients and make Gautama see that he is telling lies." Then, Sorrow-Ridden, on hearing this, fasted. This continued from the first to the sixth day. On the seventh day, he completed his fast and took some molasses. After eating this, he drank some cold water, got a pain, and died. After death, his comrades carried his dead body to Sitavana. He gained the body of a hungry preta and sat along with the corpses. Sunaksatra, on hearing of this, went to Sitavana. He saw that SorrowRidden was in the form of a hungry preta, living by the side of a corpse and squatting on the ground. Sunaksatra said: "Are you dead, O great one?" Sorrow-Ridden said: "I am dead." "How did you die?" "I died from a pain in my stomach." "Who carried your dead body?" He answered: "My comrades." "After carrying you, where did they place you?" "O you blockhead! Do you not know that I am in Sitavana? I have now been born as a hungry preta. Listen well, O you Sunaksatra! The Tathagata speaks good things, true words, timely words, meaningful words, and the words of Dharma. O you Sunaksatra! The Tathagata brings to mouth such true words. Why did you not believe his words? Anyone who does not believe in his true words will gain the [kind of] body that I now have." Then, Sunaksatra came back to me and said: "O World-Honoured One! The Nirgrantha, Sorrow-Ridden, has died and been born in Trayastrimsa Heaven." I said: "O you blockhead! There is no place where an arhat gains birth. How can you say that Sorrow-Ridden has now been born in Trayastrimsa Heaven?" "O World-Honoured One! Truth to tell, the Nirgrantha, Sorrow-Ridden, has not been born in Trayastrimsa Heaven. He has now gained the body of a hungry preta." I said: "O you blockhead! The All-Buddha-Tathagata speaks only truth and is not double-tongued. Never say that the Tathagata uses two words." Sunaksatra said: "The Tathagata spoke thus at the time, but I did not believe you." O good man! Although I spoke what was true to Sunaksatra, he never once had a mind to believe me. O good man! Although Sunaksatra recites the 12 types of sutra and gains the four dhyanas, he does not know the meaning of a gatha, a line, or a word. On associating with an evil friend, he lost the four dhyanas. Losing the four dhyanas, he gained an evil notion and said: "There is no

Buddha, no Dharma, and no Nirvana. Sramana Gautama sees one's future phrenologically. So does he well read the mind of others." I then said to Sunaksatra: "What I speak is good all through, from the beginning, through the middle, to the end. Whatever words I use are deftly chosen; the meaning is true. In what is said, there is nothing that is mixed up. I am perfect in pure actions." Sunaksatra again said: "Though the Tathagata spoke of Dharma for my sake, I said that there were truly no causal relations." O good man! If you do not believe me, go to Sunaksatra, who is now living by the River Nairanjana. Go and ask him." Then, the Tathagata and Kasyapa together went to where Sunaksatra was living. Bhiksu Sunaksatra saw the Buddha coming from afar. On seeing him, he gained an evil mind. Due to this evil mind, he fell living into Avichi Hell. "O good man! Bhiksu Sunaksatra was once in the treasure house of the Buddhist teaching. All meant nothing; he gained nothing; not a single benefit of Dharma did he gain. This comes from indolence and from an evil friend. For example, a person goes into the sea and sees many treasures, but gains nothing. This comes from indolence. The case is thus. Once he goes into the sea and sees the treasures, he gets himself killed, or is killed by a devil rakshasa [flesh-devouring demon]. It is the same with Sunaksatra. He entered into the teaching, but was killed by a great rakshasa, an evil teacher of the Way. O good man! For this reason, the Tathagata, out of compassion, always told Sunaksatra that he had too much indolence. "O good man! If [a person is] poor, I may have pity but a little. If a person was once rich, but has now lost his wealth, I pity [that person] very much. It is the same situation with Sunaksatra. He upheld, recited [the scriptures] and attained the four dhyanas, and then he lost them. This is a great pity. So I say: "Sunaksatra has a great deal of indolence." Having much indolence, he is away from all good deeds. Whenever my disciples see or hear of him, there are not a few who gain pity for this person. It is as with the person who first had a lot of wealth and later lost it. For many years I lived with Sunaksatra. Yet he always had an evil mind. And because of this evil mind, he was unable to forsake twisted views of life. O good man! Since of old I have seen in Sunaksatra just a hair's amount of good, but he has lost it. But I have never yet prophesied that he was an icchantika, the lowest, and one who would have to live for a kalpa in hell.

By saying that there never exists any cause or result or action, he has long cut off the root of good. Such is the icchantika, the lowest, and one who has to live for a kalpa in hell. Thus have I prophesied. "O good man! There is a man who drowns in the privy. A good teacher of the Way has people search for him with their hands. Grabbing a hair of [his head], he means to pull him out. He searches for him for a long time, but without success. And he gives up. It is the same with me. Looking for just a little bit of good in Sunaksatra, I wished to save him. For the whole day I tried, but could not even gain hold of a hair's amount of good in him. That was why I could not get him out of hell." Bodhisattva Kasyapa said: "O World-Honoured One! Why did you prophesy that he would go to Avichi Hell?" "O good man! Bhiksu Sunaksatra had many kindred with him. They all said that Sunaksatra was an arhat and that he had attained the Way, so that he could crush out twisted minds. I prophesied that Sunaksatra would go to hell due to indolence. O good man! Know that what the Tathagata says is true and that it is not two [duplicitous]. Why? For there can never be any case where, when the Buddha has prophesied that a person would go to hell, the person failed to go there. There are two kinds of what the sravakas and pratyekabuddhas prophesy: either false or true. Maudgalyayana said to all in Magadha: "There will be rain in seven days." The time passed, and there was no rain. Later he prophesied: "This cow will bring forth a white calf." But what came out was a unicorn. This is like saying that a male will come out when a female comes out. O good man! Bhiksu Sunaksatra spoke to innumerable beings and always said that there came about no good or evil karmic results. Through this, he cut off all the roots of good eternally, and there did not remain a hair's worth of good left [in him]. "O good man! I knew for a long time that this Bhiksu Sunaksatra would eternally cut off the root of good. But for 20 long years we lived together. If I had kept myself away from him and never come near him, this man would speak to innumerable beings, thus teaching others to do evil. This is what we call the Tathagata's fifth power of understanding." "O World-Honoured One! Why is it that the icchantikas do not possess good?" "O good man! Because the icchantikas are cut off from the root of good. All beings possess such five roots as faith, etc. But the people of the icchantika class are

eternally cut off from such. Because of this, one may well kill an ant and gain the sin of harming, but the killing of an icchantika does not [constitute a sin]." "O World-Honoured One! The icchantika possesses nothing that is good. Is it for this reason that such a person is called an "icchantika"? The Buddha said: "It is so, it is so!" "O World-Honoured One! All beings possess three kinds of good, namely those of: 1) past, 2) future, and 3) present. Even the icchantika cannot cut off the good of the days to come. How can one say that one who cuts off all good is an icchantika?" "O good man! Of disruption , there are two kinds. One is the disruption in the present, and the other is what hinders the present and the future. The icchantika is perfect in these two disruptions. That is why I say that the icchantika is cut off from all the roots of good. O good man! For example, there is a man who drowns in the privy, and only a single hair remains that has not sunk down. And this hair cannot be greater than the body. It is the same with the icchantika, too. He may well possess the possibility of amassing good in the days to come, but this cannot relieve him from the pain of hell. He may be saved in the days to come, but he cannot be now. That is why we say unsavable. The causal relations of the Buddha-Nature will save [him]. The Buddha-Nature is not of the past, of the future, or of the present. Thus, this Buddha-Nature cannot be made away with. A rotten seed cannot call forth a bud. The same is the situation with the icchantika, too." "O World-Honoured One! The icchantika is not segregated from the Buddha-Nature. The Buddha-Nature is that which is good. How can we say that all good is cut off?" "O good man! If a being possesses now the Buddha-Nature, such a person is no icchantika. It is as in the case of the nature of the Self. The Buddha-Nature is what is Eternal. It does not fall within the category of the Three Times. If it were in the category of the Three Times, it would be non-eternal. The Buddha-Nature is what will be seen in days to come. So, we can say that beings possess the Buddha-Nature. On this account, the Bodhisattva of the ten stages can see partly due to the fact that he is perfectly adorned."

Bodhisattva Kasyapa said: "O World-Honoured One! The Buddha-Nature is Eternal; it is like space. Why is it that the Tathagata says that it can have the future? You, the Tathagata, say that the icchantika has no root of good. Can the icchantika not love his comrades, teachers, parents, relatives, wife and children? If so, is it not the case that he has an act of good?" The Buddha said: "Well said, well said, O good man! You do well to put such a question. The Buddha-Nature is like space. It is not past, not future, and not present. Beings can perfect the pure body in the days to come and can accomplish themselves and gain the Buddha-Nature. That is why I say that the Buddha-Nature is a thing of the days to come. O good man! I, at times, for the sake of beings speak of the cause and say that it is the result; at times, I speak of the result and say that it is the cause. Because of this, I say in the sutras that life is food and that material form ["rupa"] is touch ["sparsa"]. The body of the days to come will be pure. Hence, the Buddha-Nature." "O World-Honoured One! If things are as the Buddha says, why do you say: "All beings possess the Buddha-Nature?" "O good man! Although there is no present of the Buddha-Nature of beings, we cannot say that it does not exist. Though, by nature, there is no present of space, we cannot say that there is not [space]. The case is thus. Though all beings are non-eternal, this Buddha-Nature is Eternal and cannot suffer change. That is why I say in this sutra: "The Buddha-Nature of beings is not in and not out; it is as in the case of space, which is neither in nor out." If there were in and out in space, we could not say that space is one and eternal; nor could we say that it exists everywhere. Although space exists neither in nor out, all beings possess it. The same is the case with the Buddha-Nature of beings, too. You say that the icchantika has a cause of good. This is not so. Why not? Whatever he does with body, mouth and mind, and whatever he obtains, seeks, gives or comprehends is all evil in nature. Why? Because these do not ride on the law of cause and effect. O good man! The Tathagata is perfect in the knowledge and power relative to all dharmas. So, he knows well the differences between the top, middle and low qualities of all beings. He indeed knows that [i.e. whether] a person turns low into middle, middle into top, top into middle, and middle into low. For this reason, know that there cannot be any fixedness in the qualities of beings. Being not fixed, the good is lost; and when it is lost, the person gains it again. If it were the case that the root quality of a being were fixed, once [the good had been] lost, it would never come back. Also, we must not say that the icchantika falls into hell

and that life in hell is one kalpa [i.e. aeon] long. O good man! That is why the Tathagata says that no state is fixed in existence." Bodhisattva Kasyapa said to the Buddha: "O World-Honoured One! You, the Tathagata, with the power of being able to know all things, see that Sunaksatra is certain to lose all the roots of good. Why do you permit him to be in the Sangha?" The Buddha said: "O good man! In the past when I left home, my younger brother, Nanda, my cousins, Ananda and Devadatta, and my son, Rahula, all followed in my footsteps and renounced the world and [secular] life and practised the Way. If I had not allowed him to join the Sangha, he would have come to the throne. Gaining unrestricted power, he would have destroyed the Buddhist teaching. For this reason, I allowed him to enter the Sangha. O good man! If he had not entered the Sangha, he would have been far away from the root of good, and for innumerable ages to come he would have destroyed the Buddhist teaching. For this reason, he is now in the Sangha. Though he possesses no good, he upholds the precepts and respects the elders, the aged, and the virtuous, and makes offerings, and can practise dhyanas from the first to the fourth. This is a cause of good. Any such good cause will bring forth what is good. When good comes about, he will well practise the Way, and through this, he will attain unsurpassed Enlightenment. Because of this, I permitted Sunaksatra to enter the Sangha. O good man! If I had not permitted Sunaksatra to be ordained and receive sila, I could not be said to possess the Tathagata's ten powers. "O good man! The Buddha sees that a being possesses things both good and not good. Although a man possesses [such] two things, he soon severs himself from the roots of good and possesses what is not good. Why? Because such a person does not befriend a good teacher of the Way, does not give ear to Wonderful Dharma, does not think well, and does not act as he ought to act. He thereby severs himself from good and performs what is not good. O good man! The Tathagata knows that this person, in this life or in the next life, when small, in the prime of life, or in old age, will befriend a good friend, give ear to Wonderful Dharma, to suffering, to the cause of suffering, to extinction, and the Way leading to the extinction of suffering, and then he will come back again and do good. "O good man! For example, there is a spring which is not far from a village. The water is sweet and beautiful, and possesses eight virtues. There is a man there who is very thirsty and desires to be by the spring. There is a wise person, who thinks that the thirsty man will unfailingly hasten to the spring, because he sees that the way to it is not difficult. The case is thus. So does the Tathagata-World-Honoured One see beings. On this account, we say that the Tathagata is perfect in the power of knowing all things relative to all beings." Then, the World-Honoured One took up a small bit of earth and deposited it on his fingernail, saying to Kasyapa: "Is this bit of earth, or that of the ten directions, greater?" Bodhisattva Kasyapa said to the Buddha: "O World-Honoured One! The earth on your fingernail cannot be compared to the earth of the ten directions." "O good man! One abandons one's body and gains a body again; one casts aside the body of the three unfortunate realms [i.e. the realms of hell, hungry ghosts, and animals] and gains another body. And when all the sense-organs are perfect, one gains life in the Middle Country, gains right faith, and practises well the Way. Practising well the Way, one indeed practises the Right Way. Practising the Right Way, one attains Emancipation, and then one truly enters Nirvana. This is like the earth on my fingernail. One casts away one's body and gains one of the three unfortunate realms. One casts away the body of the three unfortunate realms and gains the body of the three unfortunate realms [again]. One is not perfect in all one's sense-organs, one gains life in an out-of-the-way [remote] place, holds an upside-down view of life, follows a twisted way, and does not attain Emancipation and Nirvana. All of this may be likened to the earth of the ten quarters. "O good man! One who upholds the precepts always makes effort, does not commit the four grave offences, does not perform the five deadly sins, does not use the things that belong to the Sangha, does not become an icchantika, and does not segregate his self from all the roots of good. Such a person who believes in this Nirvana Sutra can be likened to the earth on my fingernail. Those who violate the precepts, those who are indolent, those who commit the four grave offences, those who perform the five deadly sins, those who use the things of the Sangha, those who become icchantikas, those who cut off all the roots of good, and those who do not believe in this sutra are as great in number as the earth in the ten directions. O good man! The Tathagata knows

well all about the qualities of beings of the top, middle and low [positions]. Because of this, we say that the Buddha is perfect in the power of being able to see through to the root of all things." Bodhisattva Kasyapa said to the Buddha: "O World-Honoured One! The Tathagata possesses this power of seeing through to the root of things. Because of this, he truly knows the sharp and dull, and the differences in qualities of the top, middle and bottom of beings, and also knows well the root qualities of the beings of the present world and also those of the beings of the future. Such beings, when the Buddha is gone, will say that the Tathagata has ultimately entered Nirvana or that he has not ultimately entered Nirvana. Or they might say that there is the Self or that there is no Self. Or they may say that there is an in-between existence or that there is no such; or that there is retrogression or that there is not; or that the Tathagata possesses a created body or that what he possesses is one uncreated; or that the 12 links of interdependent arising are of the created or that causal relations are the non-created; or that the mind is eternal or that it is non-eternal, or that when one partakes of the joy of the five desires, this hinders the Holy Way or that it does not; or that laukikagradharma ["first-of-the-world-root-of-good", or "prime-in-the-world condition" - the fourth and highest "nirvedha-bhaga", intellectual penetration, insight] is but of the world of desire or that it concerns the three unfortunate realms; or that dana is a thing of the mind, or that it belongs to the realm of the five skandhas. Or they will say that there are three non-created [things], or that these do not exist. Or they will say that there is created "matter", or that there is no such thing; or that there is a non-created matter, or that there is nothing such as that. Or they will say that there are the mental functions, or that there is nothing such. Or they will say that there are the five kinds of "is", or that there are six such; or that if one is perfect in the eight purifications ["astangasaman-vagatopavasa"] and the upasaka [lay Buddhist] silas, one can well gain [benefit], or that one can well gain [such] even if one is not quite perfect in these observances. Or it will be said that even when a bhiksu has committed the four grave offences, there is yet sila [morality] for that bhiksu, or that there is not. Or they will say that all the srotapannas, sakrdagamins, anagamins, and arhats arrive at what Buddhism aims at, or that this is not so. Or they will say that the Buddha-Nature is with the being from birth, or that it exists apart from the being. Or it will be said that the Buddha-Nature must exist even with such kinds of people as those who have committed the four grave offences, those of the five deadly sins, and with the icchantika, or that they do not possess such. Or they will say that there are the Buddhas in the ten directions, or that there are no Buddhas in the ten directions. If the Tathagata is perfect in the power of seeing through the natures of beings, why does he not state definitely about it [i.e. these matters]?" The Buddha said to Kasyapa: "O good man! Any such is not what eye-consciousness can know; nor is it what mind-consciousness can know. It is what Wisdom can know. To a person who has Wisdom, I do not say anything in a double way; and that is why I say that I do not speak in two ways. To those who are ignorant, I speak in indefinite ways, and they say that I speak in indefinite ways. O good man! Whatever good action the Tathagata performs is all to adjust and subjugate all beings. For example, whatever medical knowledge a good doctor possesses is all to cure beings' illnesses. The same is the case here. O good man! The Tathagata, on account of the land, on account of the season, on account of other languages, for beings, for the root qualities of beings, speaks, relative to one thing, in a double way. In the case of one name, he uses innumerable names; for one meaning, he displays innumerable names; regarding innumerable meanings, he speaks of innumerable names. "How does he speak of innumerable names when referring to one thing? This is as in the case of Nirvnaa, which is called Nirvana, non-birth, non-appearance, non-doing, non-created; also [it is called] the refuge, vihara [dwelling-place], Emancipation, light, a lamp, the other shore, fearlessness, non-retrogression, the abode of peace, quietude, formlessness; also, the not-two, the one action, cool, non-gloom, the unhindered, non-disputation, the non-defiled, vast and great; also, amrta [Immortality] and happiness. Things are thus. This is how we say that one thing possesses many names. "How does one refer to innumerable names? This is as in the case of Devendra, who is called Devendra, Kausika, Vasava, Puramda, Maghavat, Indra, The Thousand-Eyed, Saci, Vajra, Treasure-Head, and Treasure-Banner. The case is thus. This is how we say that one meaning has innumerable names. "How do we use innumerable names for innumerable meanings? This is as in the case of

the Buddha-Tathagata. We say "Tathagata", in which the meaning is different and the name different. Also, we say "arhat", which has a different meaning and the name is different. Also, we say "samyaksambuddha" [Fully Enlightened One], which has a different meaning and a different name. Also, we say "master mariner". Also, we say "Guide" and "Right Enlightened One". Also, we say "All-Accomplished One". Also, we say "Great Lion-King"; also, "sramana", "Brahmin", "quietude", "danapati" [giver], "paramita" [transcendent perfection], "great doctor", "great elephant-king", "great naga-king", "eye-giver", "great wrestler", "great fearlessness", "ball of treasure", "merchant", "emancipated", "great man", "teacher of gods and humans", "pundarika" [lotus], "the one alone, with no equal", "the great field of blessings", "the great sea of Wisdom", "formlessness", and "perfect in eight knowledges". Thus do we have different meanings and different names. This is why we say that innumerable meanings have innumerable names.

"Also, there is the case where the meaning is one, but the names are many. The so-called "skandha" is called: skandha, upside-down, satya; it is presented as: four remembrances, four kinds of food, and four abodes of consciousness. Also, it is called "is", way, time being, world, "Paramartha-satya" [Ultimate Truth], three practices of the body, sila and mind, cause and effect, defilement, Emancipation, the 12 links of interdependent arising, sravaka, pratyekabuddha, hell, hungry preta, animal, human and god. Also, it is called: past, present, and future. This is why we say that innumerable are the names to one meaning. "O good man! The Tathagata-World-Honoured One, for the sake of beings, speaks of the simplified in relation to detailed manifestations and of the detailed in reference to the simplified. He speaks of Ultimate Truth and makes it worldly truth, and speaks of worldly truth and makes it Ultimate Truth. "How does he speak of the detailed, the middle, and the simplified? This is as when it is said to the bhiksus [monks]: "I shall now speak to you of the 12 links of interdependent arising. What are the 12 links of interdependent arising? They are none other than cause and effect." "How does he speak of the detailed, the middle, and the simplified? This is as when he says to the bhiksus: "I shall now speak of suffering, the cause of suffering, extinction, and the Way to the extinction of suffering. Suffering is the various innumerable sorrows. The cause of suffering is the innumerable defilements. Extinction is the innumerable emancipations. The Way is innumerble expedients." "How does he speak about Ultimate Truth and make it into the truth of the world? This is as when it is said to the bhiksus: "Now, this body has old age, sickness, and death." "How does he speak of the truth of the world and make it Ultimate Truth? This is as when I said to Kaundinya: "Now you, Kaundinya, are so called because you gain Dharma." Thus, I accord with the person, will, and time. Hence, we say that the Tathagata has the power to see through to the root qualities of all things. O good man! If I spoke about things in definite terms, it would not be the case that the Tathagata was perfect in the power to see through to the root qualities of all things. "O good man! One with Wisdom knows that what a gandhahastin shoulders cannot be borne by a donkey. All beings do innumerable things. So the Tathagata speaks innumerable things variously. Why? Because beings possess various defilements. If the Tathagata spoke only of one action, we could not say that the Tathagata was perfect and accomplished in the power of seeing through to the root qualities of all things. So I say in a sutra: "Do not speak to the five kinds of people the five kinds of things. To one who has no faith, one does not praise right faith; to one who breaks the prohibitions, one does not praise upholding sila; to the stingy, one does not praise dana [giving], to the indolent learning, and to the ignorant Wisdom." "Why not? If a wise person speaks to these five kinds of people about these five things, know that that speaker cannot be said to possess the power to see through to the root qualities of all things; he cannot be said to pity beings. Why not? Because these five kinds of people, when they hear these [things], will gain a disbelieving mind, an angry mind, and in consequence of this they will suffer from sorrowful karmic results for innumerable ages. Because of this, for pity's sake, we do not call such a [person one with the] power to see through to the root qualities of beings. That is why I say in a sutra to Sariputra: "You should be careful not to speak to the sharp-born extensively about Dharma and to the dull-born in simplified language." Sariputra said: "I only speak out of pity, not because I possess this power to see through to the root qualities of beings." "O good man! The sermons of the detailed and the simplified belong to the world of the Buddha. Such are not what sravakas and pratyekabuddhas can know. "O good man! You say: "After the Buddha's entering Nirvana, the disciples will say various [divergent] things." Such a person does not have the right view, because of the causal relations of what is upside-down. Due to this, such a person is unable to benefit himself, nor can he benefit others. All beings are not of one nature, one root, one action, one kind of land, and one good teacher of the Way. Because of this, the Tathagata speaks variously. Due to this causal relation, the All-Buddha-Tathagatas of the ten directions and of the Three Times, deliver, for the sake of beings, sermons of the 12 types of sutra. O good man! The Tathagata delivers sermons of the 12 types of sutra. This is not to benefit his own Self, but to benefit others. Because of this, the fifth power of the Tathagata is called the power of comprehension. Because of these two powers, the Tathagata will know that the person has truly cut himself off from the root of good in this life or will in a later life, or that he gains Emancipation in this life or that he will gain it in a later life. Because of this, we call the Tathagata the unsurpassed wrestler. "O good man! One who says that the Tathagata ultimately enters Nirvana, or that he does not, does not understand the mind of the Tathagata. That is why he speaks thus. "O good man! In this Gandhamadana, there are all kinds of rishis, to the number of 53,000, who had all amassed all kinds of virtue in the days of Buddha Kasyapa. Yet, they did not gain the Right Way. They befriended [more likely: did not befriend, etc. - ed.] the Buddhas and listen to Wonderful Dharma. Because of such persons, I , the Tathagata, said to Ananda: "I shall enter Nirvana at the end of the third month." All the devas heard this, and their voices reached Gandhamadana. All the rishis, on hearing this, repented and said: "Why did we not, on being born as humans, befriend the Buddha? The appearance of the All-Buddha-Tathagata in this world is as rare as in the case of the udumbara. I shall now go to where the World-Honoured One is and listen to Wonderful Dharma." Then the rishis, to the number of 53,000, came to me. I then, as requested, spoke of Dharma thus: "All you great ones! Material form is non-eternal. Why? Because of the fact that the causal relations of material form are non-eternal. It comes out of a cause of [i.e. a cause which is] non-eternal. How could material form be eternal? The same is the case down to consciousness." All the rishis, on hearing this, attained arhatship. "O good man! In the castle-town of Kusinagara, there were wrestlers, to the number of 300,000. They belonged to no one. Becoming haughty since they possessed physical power, vitality and wealth, they got drunk and mad. O good man! To subjugate all these wrestlers, I said to Maudgalyayana: "Hold down [tame] these wrestlers!" Then he, all-respectfully, to accord with my instructions, spent five years teaching [them]. But not one wrestler gained Dharma and not one was subjugated. On this account, I, for the sake of the wrestlers, said to Ananda: "In three months' time, I shall enter Nirvana." "O good man! On hearing this, all the wrestlers gathered together and made repairs to the road. Three months later, I moved from Vaisali to Kusinagara Castle and on the way saw many wrestlers. Transforming myself into a sramana, I joined the wrestlers: "All of you children! What are you doing?" The wrestlers, on hearing this, became vexed and said: "O you sramana! What do you mean by calling us children?" I then said: "You big group of people, whose number is 300,000, may not even be able to move this small piece of stone. How can I call you anything other than children?" All the wrestlers said: "If you can call us children, know that you must be a great man." I then, at that time, picked up the stone with two fingers. Having witnessed this, all the wrestlers thought that they were possessed of less strength than myself and said: "O you sramana! Can you now move this stone out of the way?" I said: "Why are you so seriously engaged in repairing this road?" "O sramana! Do you not know that the Tathagata Shakyamuni is taking this road and will come to the forest of sal trees and enter Nirvana? For this reason, we are making repairs [to the road] and making it flat." I then praised [them] and said: "Good children! You now possess such a good [attitude of] mind. I shall now make away with this stone." I picked up the stone and cast it up as high as Akanistha Heaven. Then, all the wrestlers, on seeing that the stone hung suspended in the sky, became frightened and wanted to scatter in all directions. I then said: "O wrestlers! Do not be afraid and try to fly in all directions." All the wrestlers said: "O sramana! If you will save and protect us, we shall remain in peace." Then I put my hand on the stone and placed it in the palm of my right hand. On seeing

this, the wrestlers grew pleased and said: "O sramana! Is this stone eternal or not eternal?" I then puffed on it with my mouth, and the stone broke into pieces like dust-motes. On seeing this, the wrestlers said: "O sramana! This stone is non-eternal." Then, feeling ashamed, they reproached themselves and said: "How is it that we take pride in our unlimited physical strength, and in life and wealth?" I, seeing through [i.e. reading] their minds, threw off my transformed body, regained my own form, and spoke about Dharma. Seeing all of this, the wrestlers aspired to Enlightenment. "O good man! In Kusinagara, there lives an artisan called Cunda. This person once, at the place of Buddha Kasyapa, took a great vow: "I shall make the last offering of food to Shakyamuni Buddha when he enters Nirvana." This being the case, I, at Vaisali, looked back to Upamana and said: "In three months' time, I shall enter Nirvana at Kusinagara, between the sal trees. Go and let Cunda know of this." "O good man! In Rajagriha, there is a rishi who is well practised in the five miraculous powers and whose name is Subhadra. He is 120 years old. He calls himself one versed in all things and is extremely arrogant. Already, at the places of innumerable Buddhas, he has amassed all the roots of good. In order to teach him, I said to Ananda: "I shall enter Nirvana in three months' time. On hearing of this, Subhadra will come to me and gain a faithful mind. I shall speak several things to him. On giving ear to what I say, he will make away with the defilements." "O good man! Bimbisara, King of Rajagriha, had a prince called Sudarsana. This prince, through causal relations, gained an evil mind and wished to kill his own father. But he did not know how to. At that time, Devadatta, from the causal relations of his past, gained an evil mind and desired to do harm to me. He practised the Way so as to gain the five miraculous powers, and before long he had gained them. He now established good connections with Sudarsana, displaying various miracles before him. He emerged from where there was no gate, and entered through a gate; he came out of a gate, and entered at a place where there was no gate. At times, he would conjure up an elephant or a horse, a cow, a sheep, a man, or a woman. On seeing this, Sudarsana gained a loving [i.e. attached] mind, a mind of pleasure and of respect. And in consequence, he made various preparations and offered them up in various utensils. And he said: "O great one! I now wish to see the mandarava [a flower]." Then, Devadatta went up to Trayastrimsa Heaven and asked for it from the hand of a deva [god]. Any good that he may have amassed having come to an end, none would give [it to him]. Unable to obtain the flower, he thought: "The mandarava flower has no Self or what belongs to the Self. I shall now take it, and what sin will I [thereby] commit?" As he stepped forward, meaning to take it, he lost his divine power. He came back to himself and was then in Rajagriha. Being ashamed of himself, he could not see [face] Sudarsana. "And he thought to himself: "I shall now go to the Buddha and ask him to entrust the mass [i.e. the community of the Buddha's followers] to me. If he agrees, I shall be able freely to give commands to Sariputra and others." Then, Devadatta came to me and said: "O Tathagata! Commit your great mass to my guidance, so that I may teach and give them the Way." I said: "O you madman! I do not entrust the great mass even to the hands of the greatly clever and wise man, Sariputra, whom the world trusts. Why should I entrust it to you, who but swallow your own spittle?" Then Devadatta all the more gained hateful thoughts towards me and said: "You may now have control over your people. But your power will soon fade away." As he said this, the great earth shook six times. Devadatta at once fell to the ground. His body emitted a great storm, which blew up all the dust and made him look foul. Devadatta, seeing this evil effect, said further: "If I now fall into Avichi Hell, I shall certainly repay this great resentment." Then, raising himself, he went to Sudarsana, who queried: "Why, Holy One, do you look so crestfallen and sorrowful? " Devadatta said: "I always look thus, do you not know this?" Sudarsana answered: "Pray tell me why that is. Devadatta said: "I am now on very close terms with you. Other people criticise you and say that what you do goes against reason. I hear this. How can it be that I do not feel worried?" Prince Sudarsana further asked: "In what way do the people of the land criticise me?" Devadatta said: "The people of the land say that you are an "unbornresentment." Sudarsana said again: "Why am I an "unborn-resentment"? Who says this?" Devadatta said: "When you were not yet born, the augur said: "This son, when grown up, will kill his own father." That is why all other people call you an "unborn-resentment". All of the people of your household call you "good-looking", just to guard

your mind. The royal consort, Vaidehi, on hearing this, gave birth to you on top of a high building, as a result of which you fell to the ground and lost one of your fingers. That is why all the people call you "Balaruci" [= "One without a finger"]. Hearing this, I felt sorry. But I could not tell you this." Thus, Devadatta taught Sudarsana evil things and made him kill his own father. "If your father dies, I, too, will certainly kill Sramana Gautama." "Sudarsana had a minister called Varsakara, whom he asked: "Why did the great King name me Ajatasatru?" The minister told him the whole story, which was none other than what Devadatta had told to Sudarsana. Hearing this, Sudarsana shut the minister and his own father up in a place outside the castle and had the place guarded by four kinds of soldier. Queen Vaidehi, on hearing of this, went to where the King was imprisoned. The guards would not let her in. Then the Queen became angry and reproached the guards. Then, all the guards said to the Prince: "O great King! The Queen wishes to see the King. It is difficult to know whether we are to let her in or not?" Sudarsana became vexed, went to his mother, took her by the hair, unsheathed his sword, and meant to kill her. Then Jivaka said: "O great King! Since the beginning of government, however grave, no sin extends to the female. And how can you act thus to the one who gave you birth?" On hearing this, because of Jivaka he released her. And he deprived his father of all such things as clothing, bedding, food, drink, and medicine. Seven days later, the King died. Sudarsana completed the funeral and then repented. Varsakara spoke to him in different ways about various evil things: "O great King! There is no sin in what you have done. Why do you now so repine?" Jivaka said: "O great King! Know that such an action is doubly sinful. The one sin is killing one's own father, and the other killing a srotapanna. No one can make away with such sins other than the Buddha." Sudarsana said: "The Tathagata is pure and has nothing [about him] that is defiled. How can we, the defiled, hope to see him?" "O good man! Seeing this, I told Ananda: "In three months' time, I shall enter Nirvana." On hearing of this, Sudarsana came to me. I then spoke of Dharma. Through this, his grave sin reduced and he gained a faith which was not rooted in him. O good man! All my disciples, on hearing of this, could not grasp what was in my mind. So they said: "The Tathagata is definitely going to enter Nirvana." "O good man! There are two kinds of Bodhisattva. One is real, and the other temporary. The Bodhisattvas of the temporary class, on hearing that I am to enter Nirvana within three months, all gain a retrogressive mind and say: "If the Tathagata is non-eternal and not to live, what can we do? We shall have to undergo great pains for innumerable lives to come. The Tathagata-World-Honoured One is accomplished and perfect in innumerable virtues. And he can do nothing so as to crush out Mara [the devil]. How can we crush out any such?" "O good man! For the sake of such Bodhisattvas, I say: "The Tathagata is Eternal and does not change." O good man! On hearing this, none of my disciples can grasp what I mean to say, and they say: "It is definite that the Tathagata will not enter Nirvana." "O good man! Beings acquire this world-view of existence and say: "None of us beings gain any karmic effects after death." To any such, I say: "There are persons who actually receive karmic returns. How do we know it to be as "is"? "O good man! In days gone by, there was a king in Kusinagara called Sudarsana. To become a child, it took [him] 84,000 years; to become a crown prince 84,000 years, and to become a king also a further 84,000 years. Sitting alone, he thought to himself: "Beings have little virtue. So, life is short. The four enemies [e.g. defilement, the skandhas, death, and Mara; or here: birth, old age, illness, and death] always pursue them and bear down upon them, but they do not feel it and are indolent. Because of this, I shall leave home, practise the Way, and drive away the four enemies, i.e. birth, old age, illness, and death." So he gave orders to his officials and had a house built of seven treasures, outside the castle. The hall having been built, he said to his ministers, officials, harem women, children, and relatives: "Know that I wish to renounce my home. Do you agree?" Then, the ministers and relatives said: "Well said, well said, O King! It is now truly time." So Sudarsana, taking a man along with him, went alone to his house. For 84,000 years he practised compassion. In consequence of this, he became, by degrees, a Chakravartin [worldruler]. After 30 generations, he became Sakrodevanam; and for innumerable years he became [various] minor kings. Who could that Sudarsana have been? Do not think thus. I myself was that person. O good man! All my disciples, on hearing this, failed to take my meaning and said: "The

Tathagata says that there definitely is Self and what belongs to Self." "I also said to all beings: "Self is nature. That is to say that all the causal relations, the 12 links of interdependent arising, the five skandhas of beings, the world of mind, all virtuous actions, and the world of Isvara fall within the category of self." On hearing this, all my disciples do not grasp my meaning and say: "The Tathagata says that there definitely is self." "O good man! Once on a different occasion, a bhiksu came to me and asked: "O World-Honoured One! What do we mean by self? Who is self? Why do we say self?" I then said to this bhiksu: "O bhiksu! There is nothing that can be called self or what belongs to self. The eye is what originally was not, but what now is; what once was, but is not now. When appearing, there is nothing which it follows, and when dying, there is no place [for it] to go. There can be the karmic returns, but no one who acted. There is no one who abandons the skandhas and no one who receives them. You ask: What is self? It is an action. How could it be a self? It is craving. O bhiksu! Clap [your] two hands together, and we get a sound. The case of self is also thus. The causal relations of beings, action, and craving are self. O bhiksu! The physical form ["rupa"] of all beings is non-self. There is no physical form in self; there is no self in physical form. So does it apply [all the way down the skandhas] to consciousness. O bhiksu! All tirthikas [non-Buddhists] say that there is self. But it is not away from the skandhas. There is no self other than the skandhas. None can say thus. All the actions of beings are like phantoms, being like a mirage which appears in the hot season. O bhiksu! The five skandhas are all non-eternal, non-bliss, non-self, and non-pure." O good man! Then, there were innumerable bhiksus who, seeing through the five skandhas and the fact that there is no self, and that nothing belongs to self, attained arhatship. O good man! All my disciples, on hearing this, fail to gain my meaning and say: "The Tathagata definitely says that there is no Self." "O good man! I also say in a sutra: "One acquires this body when three things harmoniously come together. One is the father, the other the mother, and the third the in-between existence [Jap. "chuon": an existence that is supposed to exist after one's death and before rebirth.]. These three come together, and we get this body." I at times say: "The anagamin [non-returner to samsara] enters Parinirvana; or he enters into the state of an in-between." Or I also say: "The body and organs are perfect and clear: all come about from past actions, as in the case of pure sarpirmanda." O good man! I, at times, say: "The in-between existence which an evil person gains is like the coarse woolen cloth that is found in the world, whereas the in-between existence which a pure, good being gains is like the finely woven, white woolen cloth produced at Varanasi." All of my disciples hear this, do not get my meaning, and say: "The Tathagata says that there is an in-between existence." "O good man! I also said this to those who had actually committed the deadly sins: "Those who commit the five deadly sins fall into Avichi Hell." I also said: "Bhiksu Dharmaruci, when he dies, will immediately fall into Avichi Hell. There is no place to stay in-between." I also said to the Brahmacarin, Vatsiputriya: "O Brahmacarin! If there were an existence in-between, there would have to be six existences." I also said: "To a non-form being, there can be no in-between existence." O good man! All of my disciples hear this, fail to grasp my meaning, and say: "The Buddha says that there decidedly cannot be any in-between existence." "O good man! I also say in a sutra: "Also, there is retrogression. Why? Because innumerable bhiksus are indolent and lazy, and do not practise the Way." There are five kinds of retrogression, which are: 1) one likes having many things, 2) having enjoyed, one speaks of worldly things, 3) one loves sleeping, 4) one likes to associate with people of the secular world, 5) having enjoyed, one goes about. Because of all of this, the bhiksu falls back. "Of the causal relations of retrogression, there are two types, which are: 1) inner, 2) outer. A person of the arhat stage certainly leaves the inner cause, but not the outer. Due to the external causal relations, defilement raises its head. Due to defilement, retrogression comes about. There was a bhiksu who was called Kutei , who had retrogressed six times. Having retrogressed, he repented and again practised the Way, and it was now the seventh time. Gaining it and being afraid of losing it again, he killed himself. "I also, at times, say that there is Emancipation, or I speak about six arhats. All of my disciples hear this, do not arrive at my meaning, and say: "The Tathagata says that there decidedly is retrogression." "O good man! I also say in a sutra: "For example, just as charcoal never turns back into wood, and when an earthen pot is shattered it never serves again as a pot, so does it obtain with defilement. The cutting off [of defilement] by an arhat nevermore becomes reversed." Also, I say: "There are three causes for beings' having defilement. These are: 1) the defilement is not done away with, 2) the causal relations are not done away with, 3) the person does not think well. And the arhat does not have the two causal relations. The defilement is done away with and there is no thinking about evil things." O good man! All of my disciples hear this, do not grasp my meaning, and say: "The Tathagata says that there never is retrogression." O good man! I say in a sutra that the Tathagata has two kinds of body. One is the carnal body [Jap. "shoshin; " "sho"= essential nature; "shin"= mind, consciousness - so this translation of "carnal body" is not clear here - ed.], and the other is the Dharmakaya [Jap. "hosshin" = Dharma Body, Dharma Mind]. The carnal body is none but expedient and accommodation. So such a body undergoes birth, old age, illness, and death. It is long, short, black, and white; this is right, that is [not] right; this is learning or non-learning. All my disciples hear this, do not grasp my meaning, and say: "The Tathagata says that the Buddha's body is but what is created." The Dharmakaya is the Eternal, Bliss, Self, and the Pure; it is eternally segregated from birth, old age, illness, and death. It is not white, nor black, neither is it long nor short; it is not learning, nor non-learning. The Buddha is one who has appeared or one who has not appeared. He is Eternal. He does not move about. There is no change. O good man! All of my disciples hear this, do not grasp my meaning, and say: "The Tathagata says that the body of the Buddha is definitely an uncreated body." "O good man! I say in a sutra: "What are the 12 links of interdependence? From ignorance comes about action, from action consiousness, from consciousness mind-and-body, from mind-and-body the six spheres [of sense], from the six spheres touch, from touch feeling, from feeling craving, from craving cleaving, from cleaving existence, from existence birth, and from birth ageing-and-death, apprehension and sorrow." O good man! All of my disciples hear of this, do not grasp my meaning, and say: "The Tathagata says that the 12 links of interdependence are decidedly the created." "I once gave a bhiksu an injunction and said: "The 12 links of interdependence are the Buddha, non-Buddha, characteristics, and the

Eternal." "O good man! There is a case where the 12 links of interdependence arise from causal relations. Also, there is a case where they arise out of causal relations and yet are not the 12 links of interdependence. Also, there is a case where they come about from causal relations and are the 12 links of interdependence. Also, there is a case where they are those which have come about neither from causal relations nor from the 12 links of interdependence. "We say that there is a case where they have not come about from the causal relations of the 12 links of interdependence. This is said referring to the 12 links of interdependence of the future. "We say that there is a case where they come about from causal relations and yet are not the 12 links of interdependence. This refers to the five skandhas of an arhat. "We say that there is a case where they come about from causal relations and are the 12 links of interdependence. This refers to the 12 links of interdependence of the five skandhas of the common mortal. "We say that there is a case where they are not those come about from causal relations and are also not the 12 links of interdependence. This refers to space and Nirvana. "O good man! All of my disciples hear of this, do not come to my meaning, and say: "The Tathagata says that the 12 links of interdependence are definitely uncreated." "O good man! I say in a sutra: "All beings do good and evil actions. When they die, the four great elements immediately break up. With those whose deeds are pure and good, their minds travel upwards; those whose deeds are solely evil travel downwards." O good man! All of my disciples hear this, fail to grasp my meaning, and say: "The Tathagata says that the mind is definitely eternal." "O good man! I once said to Bimbisara: "Know, O great King, that form ["rupa"] is non-eternal. Why? Because it comes about from a cause of the non-eternal. If this form comes about from a cause of the non-eternal, how can the wise say that this is eternal? If form is eternal, there will not be any breaking up [of it] and no coming about of all sorrows. Now, we see that this form breaks up and becomes dispersed. Hence, we must know that form is non-eternal. The same applies down to consciousness, too." O good man! All of my disciples hear this, do not get my meaning, and say: "The Tathagata says that the mind can definitely be cut off." "O good man! I say in a sutra: "All of my disciples receive all incense and flowers, gold, silver, gems, wife, child, male and female servants, and the eight impure things, and yet they gain the Right Path. Having attained it, they do not abandon it." They hear this, do not grasp my meaning, and say: "The Tathagata says that one may accept the things of the five desires and that this does not obstruct the Holy Way." "And, at one time, I say: "There cannot be a case where men of secular life attain the Right Path." O good man! All of my disciples hear of this, do not grasp my meaning, and say: "The Tathagata says that partaking of the five desires definitely obstructs the Right Path." "O good man! I say in a sutra: "Severing defilement, one does not yet gain Emancipation. This is as in the case where one lives in the world of desire and practises the laukikagradharma [insight into the world]." O good man! All of my disciples hear of this, fail to grasp my meaning, and say: "Tathagata says that the laukikagradharma is nothing but a thing of the world of desire." "And also I say: "The usmagata, murdhana, ksanti, and the laukikagradharma are no other than gaining the four dhyanas, from the first to the fourth." All of my disciples hear of this, do not grasp my meaning, and say: "The Tathagata says that the laukikagradharma is nothing but a thing of the world of form." "And also I say: "All the tirthikas were already able to cut off the defilements that stood in the way of the four dhyanas. Practising the usmagata, murdhana, ksanti, and laukikagradharma, and meditating on the Four Truths, the person obtains the fruition of the anagamin." All of my disciples hear of this, do not get my meaning, and say: "The Tathagata says that the laukikagradharma exists in the world of non-form." "O good man! I say in a sutra: "Of the four kinds of dana [giving], there are three which are pure. The four are: 1) the giver believes in cause, result, and dana, but the recipient does not, 2) the recipient believes in cause, result, and dana, but the giver does not, 3) both giver and recipient have faith, and 4) both giver and recipient have no faith. Of these four kinds of dana, the first three are pure." All of my disciples hear of this, do not grasp my meaning, and say: "The Tathagata says that dana is but the mind." "O good man! I once said: "When one gives, one gives five things. What are the five? These are: 1) matter, 2) power, 3) peace, 4) life, and 5) oratorical prowess. The causal relations of such come back as returns to the one who gives." All of my disciples hear of this, do not grasp my meaning, and say: "The Buddha says that dana is nothing but the five skandhas." "O good man! I once said: "Nirvana is what is cut off, and where defilement is eternally annihilated, and where nothing remains behind. This is as in the case of the light of a lamp. When gone, there is no [re]-appearing of a thing. It is the same with Nirvana. "We say "Void". This is where there is no place that can be named. For example, in worldly life we say "like the Void", when there is nothing [there] to be possessed. This is apratisamkhyanirodha [i.e. when the causal relations for something to exist have gone, nothing can come about], where there is nothing to be possessed. If there is something that can be named, there must be causal relations. When there are causal relations, there can be extinction. When there are not, there is no extinction." All of my disciples hear of this, do not grasp my meaning, and say: "The Buddha says that there are not three uncreates." "O good man! I once said to Maudgalyayana: "O Maudgalyayana! Nirvana is the sentence and the line, the forestep [forward step], the ultimate, fearlessness, the great teacher, great fruition, the ultimate knowledge, great ksanti [patience], and unhindered samadhi. This is the great world of Dharma, the taste of amrta [deathlessness] and is difficult to see. O Maudgalyayana! If it is said that there is no Nirvana, how can it be that a person who slanders falls into hell?" O good man! All of my disciples hear this, do not grasp my meaning, and say: "The Tathagata says that there is Nirvana." "Once, I said to Maudgalyayana: "O Maudgalyayana! The eye is not inflexible. So does it obtain with the carnal body. All is not inflexible. Being not inflexible, we say Void. Where the food goes on [down], and where it turns round and is digested, all sounds are Void." All of my disciples hear of this, do not grasp my meaning, and say: "The Tathagata says that the uncreated Void definitely exists." "Also, once I said to Maudgalyayana: "O Maudgalyayana! There is a person who has not yet attained the fruition of srotapanna. When abiding in ksanti, he cuts himself off from the karmic results of the three unfortunate realms. Know that it [samsaric existence] does not die out by the causal relation of intellect." All of my disciples hear this, fail to grasp my meaning, and say: "The Tathagata says that there definitely exists the apratisamkhya-nirodha." "O good man! I, at one time, said to Bhiksu Bhadrapala: "You, Bhiksu, should meditate on form. Nothing of the past, future, present, near, far, coarse, or delicate is the Self or what belongs to the Self. Thus meditating, the bhiksu truly cuts off the craving for form." Bhadrapala also said: "What is form?" I said: "The four great elements are form and the four skandhas are called "name" [i.e. what is mental]." All of my disciples hear of this, do not grasp my meaning, and say: "The Tathagata says that form is definitely the four great elements." "O good man! For example, by means of a mirror, an image appears. It is the same with matter too. By means of the four great elements, things come about, such as [what is] coarse, delicate, non-slippery, slippery, blue, yellow, red, white, long, short, square, round, wrong, angled, light, heavy, cold, hot, hungry, thirsty, smoky, cloudy, dusty, and misty. This is why we say that matter comes about like sound or form. All of my disciples hear this, do not grasp my meaning, and say: "The Tathagata says that as there are the four great elements, there can be the works of matter." "O good man! In days past, Prince Bodhi said: "Should a bhiksu who upholds sila gain an evil thought, know that at that moment he loses sila." "I then said: "O Prince! There are seven kinds of sila. When things come about by body and mouth, there comes about non-expressible form [i.e. the secondary "rupa" that comes about from receiving sila]. Through the causal relation of this non-expressible form, we do not say that we lose sila, although the thing itself rests in the category of the evil-non-definable. It is yet the upholding of sila. Why do we say "non-expressible form"? Because it constitutes no cause of any different form; nor is it the fruition of any different form." O good man! All of my disciples hear this, do not grasp my meaning, and say: "The Buddha says that there is a non-expressible form." "O good man! I say in other sutras: "Sila checks evil things. If one does not do evil, this is the upholding of sila." All my disciples hear this, do not grasp my meaning, and say: "The Tathagata says that there definitely is no non-expressible form." "O good man! I say in a sutra: "The skandhas from form down to consciousness of a holy person have come about from the causal relations of ignorance. It is the same whith what obtains regarding the things of all common mortals, too. From ignorance comes about craving. Know that this craving is ignorance. From craving comes about cleaving. Know that this cleaving is ignorance and craving. From cleaving comes about existence. Know that this existence is ignorance, craving, and cleaving. From existence comes about feeling. Know that this feeling is action and existence. From the causal relation of feeling come about such as mind-and-body, ignorance, craving, cleaving, existence, action, feeling, touch, consciousness, and the six [sense] spheres. Because of this, feeling is nothing but of the 12 links of interdependence." O good man! All of my disciples hear this, do not grasp my meaning, and say: "The Tathagata says that there is no caitta [mental factor]." "O good man! I say in a sutra: "From the four things of eye, form, light, and evil desire comes about visual cognition. The evil desire is ignorance. As the nature of desire seeks to possess, we call this craving. From the causal relation of craving comes about cleaving, and this cleaving is called action. From the causal relation of action comes about consciousness, and consciousness is related to mind-and-body. Mind-and-body is related to the six spheres; the six spheres are related to touch, touch to conception, conception to feeling, craving, faith, effort, dhyana, and Wisdom. All such things come about by touch, and yet they are not touch itself." O good man! All of my disciples hear of this, do not grasp my meaning, and say: "The Tathagata says that the caitta exists." "O good man! I, at one time, said: "There is but one existence. This extends to two, three, four, five, six, seven, eight, nine up to twenty-five." All of my disciples hear this, do not get my meaning, and say: "The Tathagata says that there are five existences or six existences." "O good man! I once lived in Kapilavastu, in the nyagrodha gardens, when Kolita came to me and said: "What is an upasaka?" "I then said: "Any male or female who is perfect in all the sense-organs and who takes the three refuges [in Buddha, Dharma and Sangha] is an upasaka [lay Buddhist]." "Kolita said: "O World-Honoured One! What is a partial upasaka?" "I said: "Anyone who has taken refuge in the Three Treasures [of Buddha, Dharma and Sangha] and who has received one sila [moral precept] is a partial upasaka." All of my disciples hear this, do not grasp my meaning, and say: "The Tathagata says that even a person who is imperfect can well gain the upasaka sila." "O good man! I once was dwelling on the banks of the Ganges, when Katyayana came to me and said: "O World-Honoured One! I teach people to take the ritual of purification. This may go on for a day, a night, a time, or for a thought-moment. Can such a person accomplish the ritual of purification?" I said: "O bhiksu! This person accomplishes good, but not purification." All of my disciples hear of this, do not get my meaning, and say: "The Tathagata says that a person completely gains the eight purifications." "O good man! I say in a sutra: "Any person who commits the four grave offences is no bhiksu. Such a bhiksu is one who transgresses sila or one who has forgotten sila. He cannot call forth the bud of good. For example, this is as with a burnt-out seed, from which one cannot expect any fruit. If the crown of the tala tree is damaged, no fruit can come about. It is the same with the bhiksu who commits the grave offences, too." All of my disciples hear of this, do not get my meaning, and say: "The Tathagata says that any bhiksu who has committed the grave offences loses the sila of a bhiksu." "O good man! In a sutra I spoke, for Cunda's sake, of the four kinds of bhiksu. These are: 1) ultimate arrival at the Way, 2) showing of the Way, 3) receiving of the Way, and 4) the defiled Way. One who commits the four grave offences belongs to those defiling the Way. All of my disciples hear of this, fail to get my meaning, and say: "The Tathagata says that the bhiksu who commits the four grave offences does not violate sila." "O good man! I said in a sutra to all bhiksus: "All such as the one vehicle, one Way, one action, one condition, and all from one vehicle up to the condition give beings great quietude. These eternally excise all such as bondage, apprehension, suffering, and the suffering of suffering, and lead all beings to one existence." All of my disciples hear of this, do not get my meaning, and say: "The Tathagata says that all from srotapanna up to arhat achieve the Buddhist end." "O good man! I say in a sutra: "The srotapanna repeats comings and goings between the world of humans and that of devas [gods] seven times, and then attains Parinirvana. The sakrdagamin has only one life as man or god and then attains Parinirvana. The anagamin comprises five kinds. One may attain, in between, Parinirvana or go up proceeding and gain it in the highest heaven. With those of the stage of arhat, there are two kinds, which are gaining [Nirvana] 1) in the present life and 2) in the next life. In the present life, they cut away defilement and the five skandhas; and in the next life, too, they cut away defilement and the five skandhas." All of my disciples hear of this, fail to get my meaning, and say: "The Tathagata says that one may go up from the stage of srotapanna up to the stage of arhat and yet cannot be perfect in the Buddhist Way."

"O good man! I say in this sutra: "In detail, there are six things in the Buddha-Nature, namely: 1) the Eternal, 2) the Real, 3) the True, 4) the Good, 5) the Pure, and 6) the Visible." All of my disciples hear of this, do not grasp my meaning, and say: "The Buddha says that the Buddha-Nature of beings exists outside of us beings." "O good man! I also say: "The Buddha-Nature of the being is like the Void. The Void is not past, not future, and not present. it is not in, nor out; it is not within the boundaries of colour, sound, taste, and touch. It is the same with the Buddha-Nature." All of my disciples hear of this, do not get my meaning, and say: "The Buddha says that the Buddha-Nature of beings exists outside of the beings." "O good man! I once said: "People such as those who have committed the four grave offences, the icchantikas, slanderers of the vaipulya sutras, and those who have committed the five deadly sins, all have the Buddha-Nature. Such persons do not possess good actions to depend upon. The Buddha-Nature is the Good in itself." All of my disciples hear of this, do not grasp my meaning, and say: "The Buddha says that the Buddha-Nature of beings exists outside of beings." "O good man! I also once said: "The being himself is the Buddha-Nature. Why? Other than the being himself, there is no gaining of the attainment of unsurpassed Enlightenment. That is why I resorted to the parable of the elephant to Prasenajit. The blind persons, when speaking of the elephant, do not give us the elephant. Yet, what they say is not totally away from it. It is the same with beings who may be speaking of form down to consciousness and saying that such is the Buddha-Nature. The case is the same. Though not the Buddha-Nature itself, yet it is not quite away from it. I also gave the king the parable of a harp. The same is the case with the Buddha-Nature, too." O good man! All of my disciples hear of this, do not grasp my meaning, and speak variously, like the blind man who asks about [the appearance of] milk. So do things stand with the Buddha-Nature. "For this reason, I at times say: "People such as those who commit the four grave offences, slanderers of the vaipulya sutras, those committing the five deadly sins, and the icchantikas, possess the Buddha-Nature." Or I say: "No". "O good man! I say in various sutras: "When one person appears in the world, many gain benefit. Never do two Chakravartins appear in one country, nor two Buddhas in one world. Nor under the four heavens do the eight guardians of the land appear, and no two Paranirmitavasavartins. No such thing can happen. And I say that I journey from Jambudvipa and Avichi Hell up to Akanistha heaven." All of my disciples hear of this, do not grasp my meaning, and say: "The Buddha says that there is no Buddha in the ten directions." And I also say in all Mahayana sutras that there are the Buddhas in all the ten directions."

Chapter Forty-One: On Bodhisattva Kasyapa 2

"O good man! Such matters of dispute are the things that belong to the world of the Buddha. They are not what sravakas and pratyekabuddhas can fathom. If a person can indeed gain a doubting mind, such a person can crush out innumerable defilements, as great in size as Mount Sumeru. When a man gains an immovable mind, this is what we call clinging." Bodhisattva Kasyapa said to the Buddha: "O World-honoured One! How do we cling?" The Buddha said: "O good man! Such a person may well follow what others say or look into the sutras by himself. Or he may particularly teach others, but such a person is unable to abandon what the mind sticks to. This is clinging."

Kasyapa said: "O World-Honoured One! Is such clinging an act of good or one that is not good?" "O good man! Such clinging is not an action that can be called good. Why not? Because such cannot break all the webs of doubt." Kasyapa said: "O World-Honoured One! Such a person had no doubt from the very start. How can we say that he cannot break the webs of doubt?" "O good man! One who has no doubt is one who has doubt."

"O World-Honoured One! There is a person who says that one at the stage of srotapanna doesnot fall into the three unfortunate realms. The situation of this person may well be called one of clinging and doubt." "O good man! This may well be called what is fixed; we cannot call it doubt. Why not? O good man! For example, there is a man who first sees a man and a tree and, later, while out walking at night, may see a stub [tree-trunk] and gain doubt and wonder if this is a man or a tree. O good man! A person first sees a bhiksu and a Brahmacarin, and then might later see, far off, a bhiksu and gain doubt and wonder if this is a sramana or a Brahmacarin. O good man! A person may first see a cow and a buffalo and later may see, in the distance, a cow and gain a doubting mind and wonder whether this is a cow or a buffalo. "O good man! All beings first see two things and then gain doubt. Why? Because the mind is not clear. I never say that a person of the srotapanna stage falls into the three unfortunate realms or that he does not fall into the three unfortunate realms. How can a person gain a doubting mind?" Kasyapa said: "O World-Honoured One! You the

Buddha say that one necessarily sees a thing before and that then a doubt arises. There is one who, not seeing two things, gains doubt. What is this? It is Nirvana. O World-Honoured One! For example, a person runs into muddy water along the way. Not having seen anything of this kind before, a doubt arises. The case is thus. Is such water deep or shallow? Why is it that this person, not having seen [such] before, gains such doubt?" "O good man! Nirvana is nothing other than the segregation of suffering; non-Nirvana is suffering. All beings see two things, which are: suffering and non-suffering. The suffering and non-suffering are: hunger and thirst, cold and heat, anger and joy, illness and peace, old age and the prime of life, birth and death, bondage and emancipation, love and parting, and encountering hateful people. Beings, having met [with these things], gain doubt: "Could there be any way to do away with all such things or not?" Because of this, beings entertain doubt as to Nirvana. You say that this person has not seen any water before, and how, you ask, is it possible for him to gain doubt? Things are not thus. Why not? This person has seen water before in other places. That is why he gains doubt where he has not seen it before." "O World-Honoured One! This person has seen deep and shallow places before and then he had no doubt. Why does he now gain doubt?" The Buddha said: "As he did not do before, he gains a doubt. That is why I say: "A person doubts when there is what is not clear." Bodhisattva Kasyapa said to the Buddha: "O World-Honoured One! The Buddha says that a doubt is clinging and clinging is a doubt. Who does such?" "O good man! It is the icchantika, who has severed the root of good." Kasyapa said: "O World-Honoured One! Who is the person who has severed the root of good?" "O good man! Any person who is clever, cunning, sharp-witted, and who understands well but leaves a good friend. All people such as those who do not give ear to Wonderful Dharma, who do not think well, who do not live following Dharma are those who have severed the root of good. The mind parts from four things and the person thinks to himself: "There cannot be dana. Why not? Dana is parting with wealth. If there is any return to dana, the danapati [giver] will always be poor. Why? The seed and the fruit are alike. That is why we say that there is no cause and no result." If a person speaks thus and says that there are no cause and result, this is severing the root of good. Also, a person thinks: "The three elements of giver, recipient, and thing given do not abide eternally. If there is no abiding, how can one say that this is the giver, this the recipient, and this the thing given? If there is none who receives, how can there be any fruition [result]? For this reason, we say that there is no cause, and no result." Should a person say that there are no cause and no result, we can know that such a person has severed the root of good. "Also, a person thinks: "When a person gives, there are five things in this giving. When he has received, the recipient may at times do good or non-good. And the giver of this giving also does not gain any result of good or non-good. This is as things go in the world, where the seed calls forth fruit and the fruit the seed. The cause is the giver and the result the recipient. And the recipient cannot make the good and non-good come into the hands of the giver. Because of this, there is no cause and no result." If a person should say that there is no cause and there is no result, know that this person truly severs the root of good. "Also, a person thinks: "There is nothing that can truly be called dana. Why not? Dana is a thing which is indefinable. If indefinable, how can it call forth any good result? There is no result that is good or bad. This is what is called indefinable. If a thing is indefinable, know that there cannot be any good or bad result. For this reason, we say that there is no dana, no cause, and no result." Anyone who professes that there is no cause and also no result, such a person severs the root of good. "Also, a person may think: "Dana is will. If will, there can be no seeing and no object seen. This is no matter [physical form]. If no matter, how can a person give? Because of this, I say that there is no dana, no cause, and no result." If a person speaks like this and says that there is no cause and no result, know that this person truly severs the root of good. "Also, a person might think: "If the giver gives to an image of the Buddha, that of a deva, or for the good of his parents who have now gone, there cannot be anyone who can be said to receive. If no one receives, there cannot be any result to name. If there is no result to name this means that there is no cause. If there is no cause, this means that there is no result." If a person talks thus and says that there are no cause and result, such a person severs the root of good. "Also, a person thinks: "There is

no father and no mother. Should a person say that parents are the cause of a being, the ones who bring forth a being, logic will lead him to say that birth must be going on continuously and that there is no disruption [interruption]. Why? Because there is always the cause. But birth does not go on all the time. Because of this, know that there are no parents." "Also, a person thinks: "There is no father and no mother. Why not? If a being comes about through parents, the being must possess the two sexual organs of male and female. But there are not such. Know that a man does not come about from parents." "Also, a person thinks: "A being does not come from father and mother. Why not? One sees with one's eyes that one is not like one's parents in all such things as body and mind, deportment, one's goings and comings. Because of this, the parents are not the cause of the being." "Also, a person thinks: "There are four nothingnesses. These are: 1) what has not appeared is what is not. This is like the horns of a hare or the hair of a tortoise [i.e. non-existent]. It is the same with the parents of a being. These four are what are equal to what is not. One may say that the parents are the cause of the being. But when the parents die, the children do not necessarily die. Because of this, the parents are not the cause of the being." "Also, a person thinks: "If we say that the parents are the cause of the being, beings must always come about from parents. But there are such births as the transformed birth and birth from moisture. From this we can know that the being does not come about from parents." "Also, a person thinks: "A person can grow up, not depending upon his parents. For example, the peacock gains its body by hearing the sound of thunder, and the blue sparrow gains its body by swallowing the tears of the male sparrow; the jivamjivaka gains its body by looking at a brave man who dances." When the person thinks thus and does not encounter a teacher of the Way, that person, we may know, truly severs the root of good. "Also, a person thinks: "In all the world, there is no karmic result from the good or bad actions performed. Why not? There are beings who are perfect in the ten good things and are pleased to give and amass virtues. Even to such persons there also truly come illnesses of the body; they can die in mid-life, lose their wealth, and have many apprehensions and sufferings. There is a person who commits the ten evil deeds, is parsimonious, greedy, jealous, lazy, and indolent.

Never amassing good, he is yet at peace, has no illnesses, enjoys a long life, is full of wealth, and suffers no apprehensions or sorrow. From this we may know that there do not exist any karmic consequences from good and evil actions." "Also, a person thinks: "I also once heard a holy man speak, who said that there are cases where a person who has accumulated good falls into the three unfortunate realms when his life ends, and cases where the evil-doer gains life in heaven when his life comes to an end. From this we can know that there cannot be any talk of results from good or evil actions."

"Also, a person thinks: "All holy persons say two [contradictory] things. One says that harming life gains one a good result, and [another says] that killing earns one an evil result. From this we may know that what a holy person says is not definite. If there is nothing definite in what a holy person says, how can one be definitely fixed? For this reason, know that there is no result from good or evil." "Also, a person thinks: "There are no holy persons in the world. Why not? Any holy person will have the Right Way. All beings, possessed of defilement, practise the Right Way. Know that this means that they walk the Right Way and that defilement accompanies them. If the two exist at the same time, this means that the Right Way is unable to destroy defilement. If a person practises the Way, possessing no defilement, what is the good of practising the right Way? This indicates that any person who has no defilement cannot make away with the Way. If a person does not possess defilement, there is no need of the Way. From this, know that there cannot be anyone in the world who can be called a holy person." "Also, a person thinks: "Ignorance is causally related to action, down to birth, old age, and death. Beings are all equally related to the 12 links of interdependence. The nature of the Noble Eightfold Path is equal, which is also so related. If one person practises, all beings will also gain; when one person practises, all the sorrows [of others] will die out. Why? Because defilement is equal in nature. And yet, we do not get this. This shows that there is no Right Way." "Also, a person thinks: "Holy persons depend on the law [i.e. depend on the same things as] any common mortal, as in drink and food, walking, standing, sitting, and lying, drowsing, being happy, laughing, feeling hunger and thirst, cold and heat,

apprehension and fear. If on the same level, holy persons cannot attain the Holy Way. On attaining the Way, all these things must be done away with. If such things are not yet done away with, we may know that there cannot be any such thing as the Way." "Also, a person thinks: "A holy person's body is immersed in the pleasures of the five desires. Also, he speaks ill of [people], beats [them], and is jealous and arrogant. He has sorrow and joy, and does good and evil deeds. From this we can know that there is no such thing as a holy person. If there is the Way, there must be the cutting off of the Way. If it is not cut off, we may know that there is no such thing as the Way." "Also, a person thinks: "A person who has much pity is a holy person. Why do we call him a holy person? Because of the Way. If the Way is pity, he must have pity for all beings. It is not something one gains through having practised. If there is no pity, how can a holy person gain it when he has accomplished the Way? From this we may know that there is no such thing in the world as the Holy Way." "Also, a person thinks: "All things do not arise having the four great elements as their cause. Beings all equally possess the four great elements. Beings see that this person may gain and the other may not. If there is any Holy Way, things should go thus. But things do not go thus. So one can indeed know that there is no such thing as the Holy Way." "Also, a person thinks: "If all holy persons have only one Nirvana, we can know that there cannot be any such thing as a holy person. Why not? Because one cannot gain it. The eternal Dharma cannot be gained, or one cannot gain or abandon it. If holy persons have many Nirvanas, this tells us that what there is there is non-eternal. Why? Because these are things that can be counted. If Nirvana is one, it will come to everybody when one person gains it. If Nirvana is many, it must possess boundary lines. How can we call it eternal? If it is said that Nirvana is one in body and that emancipation is many, this may be likened to the case where one has many teeth and a tongue. But this is not so. Why not? Because each gaining is not total gaining. As there is a boundary line, it must be non-eternal. If non-eternal, how can one speak of Nirvana? If there is no Nirvana, how can there be any holy person? Due to this, we can know that there is no one who can be called a holy person." "Also, a person thinks: "The Way that must be gained by any holy person is not what can be gained through causal relations. If it cannot be gained through causal relations, why do we all become holy persons? If all people are not holy persons, we can know that there cannot be any holy person or Way." "Also, a person thinks: "The holy person says that there are two causal relations regarding right view, namely: 1) following others and giving ear to Dharma, and 2) thinking for oneself. If these two come about by causal relations, what comes about must also arise out of causal relations. Thus, there must be going on an unending chain of wrongs. If these two do not come about by causal relations, why is it that all beings do not get it?" So thinking, the person truly severs the root of good. "O good man! If a person should thus profoundly view all things as causeless and resultless, that person cuts himself off from the root of the five things, which begin with faith. O good man! The person who lacks the root of good is not necessarily one of the mean and dull; nor is he in heaven or in the three unfortunate realms. It is the same with the bhiksu who infringes the law of the Sangha." Bodhisattva Kasyapa said to the Buddha: "O World-Honoured One! When does such a person come back and gain the root of good?" The Buddha said: "O good man! Such a person gains the root of good at two times. One is when he first enters hell, and the other is when he gets out of hell. O good man! There are three kinds of good act, which are those of 1) the past, 2) the present, and 3) the future. As regards the past, the nature dies out of itself. The cause may go off, but the result does not yet ripen. For this reason, we do not say that the person cuts off the karmic result of the past. What cuts off the causes of the Three Times is what we say that we cut off." Bodhisattva Kasyapa said to the Buddha: "O World-Honoured One! If we say that we sever the root of good when we sever the cause of the Three Times, we may infer that the icchantika has the Buddha-Nature. Is such Buddha-Nature that of the past or is it that of the present or of the future? Or is it extended over all the Three Times? If it is of the past, how can we call it eternal? The Buddha-Nature is eternal. From this, we can know that it does not belong to the past. If it is of the future, how can we call it eternal? Why does the Buddha say that all beings will definitely gain it? If a person will unfailingly gain it, how can we say that he severs? If it is of the present, how can it be eternal? Why is it that the person will decidedly see it? "The Tathagata says that in the Buddha-Nature there are six kinds [aspects], which are: 1)

the Eternal, 2) the True, 3) the Real, 4) the Good, 5) the Pure, 6) the Visible. If the Buddha-Nature exists even after the severing of the root of good, we cannot say that we sever the root of good. If there is no Buddha-Nature, how can we say that all beings possess it? If the Buddha-Nature is both "is" and "is-not", why does the Tathagata say that it is eternal?" The Buddha said: "O good man! The Tathagata-World-Honoured One has four answers to all beings, which are: 1) a definite answer, 2) a discriminative answer, 3) a non-accorded answer, and 4) a left-out answer. "O good man! What is a definite answer? When asked if an evil action calls forth a good or evil result, we say definitely that what comes about is not good in nature. The same is the situation with what is good. If asked whether the Tathagata is all-knowing or not, we definitely say that he is an all-knowing person. When asked if the Buddhist teaching is pure or not, we definitely say that it is pure. When asked if the disciples of the Buddha live in accordance with the rules, the answer will definitely be that they live in accordance with the rules set for them to live by. "What is a discriminative answer? It is as in the case of the Four Truths that I speak about. What are the Four? These are: 1) Suffering, 2) Cause of Suffering, 3) Extinction, and 4) the Way to the extinction of suffering. What is the Truth of Suffering? It is so called because there are eight sufferings. What is the Truth of the Cause of suffering? It is so called because of the cause of the five skandhas. What is the Truth of Extinction? It is so called because of greed, ill-will and ignorance, which go all through. What is the Truth of the Way? The 37 elements of Enlightenment are called the Truth of the Way. This is a discriminative answer. "What is the answer to what is asked? This is as when I say that all things are non-eternal. And a person asks: "O Tathagata-World-Honoured One! Why do you say non-eternal?" If this is asked, we answer: "The Tathagata says non-eternal because of the fact that things are created." The same is the case with the non-Self, too. This is as when I say that all things get burnt. "Another person asks further: "Why does the Tathagata-World-Honoured One say that all gets burnt?" The answer to this would be: "The Tathagata says that all burn due to greed, ill-will, and ignorance." "O good man! "The Tathagata's ten powers, four fearlessnesses, Great Loving-Kindness and Great Compassion, three remembrances, all kinds of samadhi such as the

Suramgama Samadhi, etc., that come to a total of some 8 million-billion, the 32 signs of perfection, the 80 minor marks of excellence, all the samadhis such as the five-knowledge mudra, etc., whose number extends up to 3 million 5 thousand, all the samadhis such as the vajra-samadhi, etc., whose number reaches 4,200, and the samadhis of the expedients, which are innumerable, are the Buddha-Nature of this Buddha. In this Buddha-Nature, there are seven things, namely: 1) the Eternal, 2) the Self, 3) Bliss, 4) the Pure, 5) the True, 6) the Real, and 7) the Good". These are discriminative answers. "O good man! In the Buddha-Nature of the transformed bodhisattva that represents another person [Jap. "goshin"], there are six things, which are: 1) the Eternal, 2) the Pure, 3) the True, 4) the Real, 5) the Good, and 6) Little Seeing. These are discriminative answers. "You asked before: "Is there any Buddha-Nature in the person whose root of good has been severed?" Also, there is the Buddha-Nature of the Tathagata; also, there is the Buddha-Nature of the body represented as of a different person. As these two hinder one's future, we may well call these "nothing". As one decidedly gains it, we may well call this "is". This is a discriminative answer. "The Buddha-Nature of the Tathagata is not of the past, present or future. The Buddha-Nature of the body gained to represent a different person has present and future. When we see to some extent, we call it the present. When one has not fully seen it, we construe it as belonging to the future. "In the days when the Tathagata had not yet attained unsurpassed Enlightenment, what there was was the Buddha-Nature of past, present and future, due to the fact that the Buddha-Nature stood as cause. But the result is not thus. There is a situation where things concern the Three Times, or one where the Three Times are not involved. "With the body of the Bodhisattva who gains it for a different person, the Buddha-Nature is in the state of cause. So it has past, present and future. It is the same with the result, too. This is a discriminative answer. "There are six kinds [elements] in the Buddha-Nature of the Bodhisattva at the level of the ninth stage, which are: 1) the Eternal, 2) the Good, 3) the True, 4) the Real, 5) the Pure, and 6) the Visible. When the Buddha-Nature is the cause, it has the three phases of past, present and future. The same applies to the result, too. This is a discriminative answer. "There are five things relative to the Buddha-Nature of Bodhisattvas at

the levels from the eighth down to the sixth stage, namely: 1) the True, 2) the Real, 3) the Pure, 4) the Good, and 5) the Visible. When the Buddha-Nature is the cause, it has past, present and future. So does it obtain with the result, too. This is a discriminative answer. "In the Buddha-Nature of Bodhisattvas at the levels from the fifth down to the first stage, there are five things, which are: 1) the True, 2) the Real, 3) the Pure, 4) the Visible, and 5) the Good and the non-Good. "O good man! The Buddha-Nature of categories five, six and seven is what will assuredly be gained by those who have severed the root of good. Hence, "is". This is a discriminative answer. "There may be those who will say: "Those who have severed the root of good decidedly have the Buddha-Nature and they decidedly have no Buddha-Nature." This is a left-out answer." Bodhisattva Kasyapa said: "O World-Honoured One! I have heard that an answer where no answer is given is called a left-out answer. O Tathagata! Why do you call such an answer a left-out one?" "O good man! I do not say that leaving out and not answering is a left-out answer. O good man! Of this left-out answer, there are two kinds, namely: 1) one which hinders and checks, and 2) non-clinging. On this account, we say left-out answer." Bodhisattva Kasyapa said to the Buddha: "O World-Honoured One! Why do you the Buddha say that the cause is past, present and future and the result past, present and future, and also that it is not past, present and future?" The Buddha said: "O good man! Of the five skandhas, there are two kinds, namely: 1) cause and 2) result. The five skandhas of this cause have past, present and future, but it is also the fact that they are not past, present and future. O good man! All the bondages of ignorance and defilement are the Buddha-Nature. Why? Because they are the cause of the Buddha-Nature. From ignorance and action and from all the defilements arise the five skandhas of good. This is the Buddha-Nature. We gain the five skandhas of good up to unsurpassed Enlightenment. That is why I said before in the sutra: "The Buddha-Nature of the being is like milk which contains blood." Blood refers to all the defilements of ignorance and action, etc., and milk refers to the five skandhas of good. That is why I say: "From all the defilements and from all the five skandhas of good, one arrives at unsurpassed Enlightenment." Just as the body of beings is made up of pure blood, so does it obtain with the Buddha-Nature, too. The Buddha-Nature of the srotapanna and sakrdagamin class who have excised defilement to some extent is like milk ["ksira"]; the Buddha-Nature of the anagamin is like butter ["dadhi"]; that of the arhat is like fresh butter ["navanita"]; that of those at the levels of pratyekabuddha up to the Bodhsiattvas of the ten stages is like clarified butter ["ghrta"]; and the Buddha-Nature of the Buddha is like the skim of melted butter ["sarpirmanda"]. O good man! The defilement of the present hinders, so that beings cannot see. In Gandhamadana, we come across the "ninnikuso". It does not mean that all cows can feed on it. It is the same with the Buddha-Nature. This is a discriminative answer." The Buddha said: "O good man! All people did things in the past, the karmic results of which they are now living through in this life. There can be the actions of the future. As these Bodhisattva Kasyapa said to the Buddha: "O World-Honoured One! If the Buddha-have not yet come about, there is no result to speak of. People have defilement now. If not, all beings would have to be able clearly to see the Buddha-Nature. On this account, one who has severed the root of good indeed cuts off, with the causal relation of defilement of the present world, the root of good and, through the causal relation of the power of the Buddha-Nature of the future, can gain the root of good." Kasyapa said: "O World-Honoured One! How might one gain the root of good in the future?" "O good man! This is analogous to the day-lamp which can indeed dispel the gloom, even though the sun has not yet risen. This is just as the future can truly call forth beings. It is the same with the Buddha-Nature of the future. This is what we call a discriminative answer." Bodhisattva Kasyapa said to the Buddha: "O World-Honoured One! If the five skandhas are the Buddha-Nature, why do we say that the Buddha-Nature of beings exists neither within nor without?" The Buddha said: "O good man! How could you lose the meaning? Did I not say before that the Buddha-Nature of the being is none other than the Middle Path?" Kasyapa said: "O World-Honoured One! I did not lose the meaning. As beings do not grasp the meaning of this Middle Path, I speak thus." "O good man! Beings do not understand the Middle Path. At times they understand it, and at other times they do not. O good man! In order that beings can know, I say that the Buddha-Nature is neither within nor without. Why? Common beings say that the Buddha-Nature is the five skandhas, as though it

were a vessel. Or they say that it exists outside of the skandhas as in the Void. That is why the Tathagata say Middle Path. The Buddha-Nature which beings possess is neither the six sense-organs nor the six sense-fields. Within and without come together. So we say Middle Path. That is why the Tathagata says that the Buddha-Nature is not other than the Middle Path. As it is neither within nor without, it is the Middle Path. This is a discriminative answer. "Also, next, O good man! Why do we say neither within nor without? O good man! Some say that the Buddha-Nature is none but the tirthika. Why? In the course of innumerable kalpas, the Bodhisattva-mahasattva, being amidst tirthikas, has cut away all defilements, trained his mind, taught people, and then gained unsurpassed Enlightenment. On this account, the Buddha-Nature is none but the tirthika. "Or a person might say: "The Buddha-Nature is no other than the Way within." Why so? The Bodhisattva may have practised the way of the tirthikas over the course of countless kalpas. But other than by the Way within, he would not be able to attain unsurpassed Enlightenment. That is why the Buddha-Nature is what the Buddha taught. For this reason, the Tathagata checks off the two planes and says: "The Buddha-Nature is neither inside nor outside. It is an inside-and-outside. This is the Middle Path." This is a discriminative answer. "Also, next, O good man! Some say: "The Buddha-Nature is none other than the Adamantine Body of the Tathagata and the 32 signs of perfection and the 80 minor marks of excellence. Why? It is nothing that is false." "Or a person might say: "The Buddha-Nature is no other than the ten powers, the four fearlessnesses, Great Loving-Kindness and Great Compassion, the three remembrances, all kinds of samadhis, such as the Suramgama Samadhi, etc. Why? Because by means of samadhi, one gains the Adamantine Body, the 32 signs of perfection, and the 80 minor marks of excellence." Because of this, the Tathagata checks off the two planes and says that the Buddha-Nature is neither inside nor out; it is both in and out. This is the Middle Path. "Also, next, O good man! Some say: "The Buddha-Nature is the good thinking of the Way within. Why? Apart from good thinking, one cannot attain unsurpassed Bodhi. Thus, the Buddha-Nature is the good thinking of the Way within." "Or some say: "The Buddha-Nature hears Dharma, following others. Why? To hear Dharma gives one good thinking of the Way. If one does not give ear to Dharma, this is no thinking. Thus, the Buddha-Nature is to hear Dharma, following others." On this account, the Tathagata checks off the two planes and says that the Buddha-Nature is neither within nor without; and also it is both within and without. This is the Middle Path. "Also, next, O good man! Some say: "The Buddha-Nature is what is without. It refers to danaparamita. Through danaparamita, one attains unsurpassed Bodhi. Because of this, we say that danaparamita is the Buddha-Nature." Or a person says: "The Buddha is the Way within. This refers to the five paramitas. Other than these five things, there cannot be - we should know - any cause or result of the Buddha-Nature." On this account, the Tathagata checks off the two planes and says: "The Buddha-Nature is neither within nor without. It is both within and without. This is the Middle Path." "Also, next, O good man! A person says: "The Buddha-Nature is the Way within. For example, it is like the mani [jewel] on the forehead of the wrestler. Why? Because the Eternal, Bliss, the Self, and the Pure are like manis. Because of this, we say that the Buddha-Nature is within." Or some say: "The Buddha-Nature is without. It is like the treasure trove of the poor man. Why? Because one sees it through expedients. It is the same with the Buddha-Nature, too. It exists outside of beings. By effecting an expedient, one can see it." Because of this, the Tathagata checks off the two planes and says that the Buddha-Nature exists neither within nor without; it is also both within and without. This is the Middle Path. "O good man! The Buddha-Nature of beings is not "is" and is not "not-is". Why so? The Buddha-Nature is "is", but it is not as in voidness. Because even when effecting innumerable expediencies, the voidness that we speak of in the world cannot be seen. But the Buddha-Nature can be seen. Because of this, though it is "is", it is not like voidness. The Buddha-Nature is "notis", but it is not as with the horns of a hare [i.e. it is not that it does not exist]. Why? Even with innumerble expedients, the hair of a tortoise and the horns of a hare cannot come about. The Buddha-Nature can come about. So, though "not-is", it is not the same as the horns of a hare. So, the Buddha-Nature is neither "is" nor "not-is"; it is "is" and "not-is". "Why do we say "is"? All is "is". Beings do not get cut off and do not die out. This is like the flame of a lamp, until one attains unsurpassed

Bodhi. So, we say "is". "Why do we say that it is "not-is"? All beings are, for the present, not the Eternal, Bliss, the Self, and the Pure, and do not possess the Buddhist teaching. Hence, "not-is". As "is" and "not-is" become one, we say Middle Path. That is why the Buddha says that the Buddha-Nature of the being is neither "is" nor "not-is". "O good man! If a person should ask: "Is there a fruit in this seed or not?", answer definitely: "It is either "is" or "not-is". Why? Without the seed, we cannot gain the fruit. Hence, we say "is". The seed does not yet have any bud. Hence, "not-is". Because of this, we say either "is" or "isnot". Why? Although there exists the difference of time, the body is one. The same is the case with the Buddha-Nature of the being. "If one says that in the being there is a separate Buddha-Nature, this is not so. Why? Because the being is the Buddha-Nature, and the Buddha-Nature is the being. Through difference in time, we have the difference of the Pure and the non-Pure" [emph. added]. "O good man! If a person asks: "Can this seed definitely call forth fruit, or can this fruit truly call forth a seed?", answer definitely: "It either calls forth or it does not." "O good man! Worldly people say that there is cream in milk. What might this imply? O good man! If a person says that there is cream in milk, this is nothing but clinging; if a person says: "there is no cream", this is what is false. One comes away from these two planes and says definitely: "It is either "is" or "not-is." "Why "is"? Because we gain cream from milk. The cause is the milk and the result is the cream. Because of this, we say "is". "Why do we say "not-is"? The thing and the taste differ and the use is not one [i.e. not the same]. For fever we use milk, and for loose bowels cream. Milk calls forth a cold, whereas cream fever. "O good man! A person might say that there is in milk the nature of cream. If so, milk is cream and cream milk. The nature is one. "Why is it that milk comes out first and not cream? If there is the causal relation to speak of, why is it that all beings do not so speak of it? If there is no causal relation, why is it that cream does not come out first? If cream does not come out first, who is it that has made the order of: milk, cream, fresh butter, clarified, butter, and the skim of melted butter? From this, we know that cream was not before, but is now. If it was not before, but is now, this is something non-eternal. "O good man! A person might say that as there is the nature of cream in milk, cream does indeed come forth; as there is the nature of cream, cream does not come about from water. But the case is not so. Why not? For even watery grass, too, has the nature of milk and cream. How so? From watery grass we gain milk and cream. If a person says that in milk there is decidedly the nature of cream and that there is not in watery grass, this is something false. Why? Because the mind is unequal [because the person is being inconsistent]. Hence, false. "O good man! If we say that there is decidedly cream in milk, there must surely be the nature of milk in cream. Why? From milk comes about cream, and cream does not call forth milk. If there is no causal relation, we should know that this cream is what originally was not, but now is. Because of this, the wise will say that it is not that there is the nature of cream in milk and it is not that there is not the nature of cream in milk. "O good man! Because of this, the Tathagata says in this sutra: "If one says that all beings decidedly have the Buddha-Nature, this is clinging; if one says that they do not have it, this is what is false." The wise will say: "The Buddha-Nature of the being is either "is" or "not-is". "O good man! When four things harmonise [i.e. conjoin together], visual consciousness comes about. What are the four? They are: the eye, the thing, brightness [light], and desire. The nature of this visual consciousness does not exist in the eye, nor in the thing, nor in brightness, nor in desire. Through conjoining, it comes about. Thus, visual consciousness is what originally was not but now is, and what once was and what again is not. Hence, we have to know that there is no fixed nature. It is the same with the nature of cream in milk, too. "If a person should say: "Water does not call forth cream, as it does not possess the nature of cream. Thus, there is decidedly the nature of cream in milk" - this is not so. Why not? All things have different causes and different results. Also, it is not that a single cause calls forth all results; it is not that all results come from a single cause.

"O good man! Do not say that thus four things call forth visual consciousness and from these four things comes about auditory consciousness. "O good man! Departing from the [necessary] expedient methods, one cannot gain cream from milk, or fresh butter from cream. What is definitely needed is the expedient means. "O good man! The wise person sees that cream comes from milk, but will not say that fresh butter will also

thus come forth, other than through expedient means. O good man! That is why I say in this sutra: "When the cause has come about, a thing comes about; when the cause is absent, there is no thing." "O good man! The nature of salt is salty. It truly makes what is not salty [taste] salty. If there were already a salty nature in what is not salty, why would people continue to seek to possess salt? If there were no saltiness before, then that would be [a case of] what was not becoming so now. By the help of the [right] condition, we get saltiness. All things possess the nature of saltiness, but we do not feel this, on account of the smallness of the amount. This smallness in nature makes things salty. If there were not this salty nature, even salt could not bring forth [the quality of] saltiness. "A seed, for example, has by itself the quality of the four great elements. From the four great elements other than those of itself, the bud, the stem, the branch and the leaf can grow. It is the same with the nature of saltiness. So do they say. But this is not so. Why not? If it is the case that what is not salty possesses a salty nature, this is tantamount to saying that salt, too, must have the nature of non-saltiness, even if to the smallest degree. If this salt thus has two natures, why is it that it cannot be separately used, other than what is not salty? Hence, we know that salt does not originally possess two natures. As with salt, so is it with all other things which are not salty. A person might say that the seeding power of the four great elements that exists outside truly enhances that of those inside. This is not so. Why not? As things are stated in an orderly way, this does not follow the expedient means. From milk, we get cream. But things do not proceed thus with fresh butter and all other things. There is no going through the expedient means. It is the same with the four great elements. One might say that the four great elements that are within get augmented by those from outside. But we do not see the four great elements of the outside world getting augmented by the four great elements of the inside world. The fruit, sirsa, has no definite form beforehand. When it sees the krttika, the fruit comes about, gaining a size of five inches. This fruit does not get its size from what obtains in the four great elements outside of the fruit itself. O good man! I have delivered the sermons of the 12 types of sutra of my own will, or following the will of others, or following my own will and also that of others. "What do I mean by saying that I speak of my own free will? 500 bhiksus put a question to Sariputra: "O great one! The Buddha speaks about the cause of the body. What might this be?" Sariputra said: "O great ones! When you yourselves gain Right Emancipation, you yourselves will know. Why do you pose such a question?" A bhiksu answered: "O great one! At the time when I had not yet attained Right Emancipation, I thought that ignorance was the cause of the body. As I so thought to myself, I gained arhatship." One person said: "O great one! When I had not yet attained Right Emancipation, I thought to myself that ignorance and craving were the cause of the body. As I so thought to myself, I attained the fruition of arhatship." And some said: "Things such as action, consciousness, mind-and-body, the six spheres, touch, feeling, craving, cleaving, existence, birth, food and drink, and the five desires are the cause of the body." Then all the 500 bhiksus, each saying what he understood, went to the Buddha, touched his feet, circumambulated him three times, paid him homage, drew back to one side, and each reported what he had in his mind to the Buddha. "Sariputra said to the Buddha: "O World-Honoured One! Of all these persons, who is the one who speaks in the right way? And who is not right?" "The Buddha said to Sariputra: "Well said, well said! Each bhiksu says nothing but what is right." "Sariputra said: "O World-Honoured One! What is it that is in your mind?"

"The Buddha said: "O Sariputra! I said for the sake of beings that parents are the cause of the body. The case is thus. All such sutras are what I spoke of my own free will. "What are those which I spoke following the will of others? The rich man, Patala, came to me and said: "O Gautama! Do you know a phantom or not? One who knows phantoms is a great phantom. If not, such a person is no All-Knower." "I said: "O rich man! How can you call one who knows a phantom a phantom?" "The rich man said: "Well said, well said! One who knows a phantom is a phantom." "The Buddha said: "O rich man! There was a candala in the state of King Prasenajit, in Sravasti, whose name was Baspacandala. Have you heard of him or not?" "The rich man said: "I have known him for a long time already." "The Buddha said: "If you have known him for a long time, might it be that you are [yourself] a candala?" "The rich man said: "I have known him for a long time already, but this body of mine cannot be that of a candala."

"O you rich man! You now know that though you know a candala, you are not a candala. How can it be that I am a phantom because I know a phantom? O rich man! I truly know a phantom, one who acts as a phantom, the results of the phantom, and the arts of the phantom. I know killing, the killer, the karmic results of killing, and emancipation from killing. I also know twisted views of life, the people of twisted views, the karmic results of twisted views, and emancipation from twisted views. O rich man! Should you call one who is not a phantom a phantom, and one who does not hold twisted views of life one who is possessed of twisted views of life, you will gain innumerable sins." "The rich man said: "O Gautama! If things are as you say, I shall earn great sin. I shall now give you all that I possess. Please be good enough not to have King Prasenajit informed of this." "The Buddha said: "It cannot necessarily be that the causal relations of this sin will prevent you from losing your wealth. In consequence of this, you will fall into the three unfortunate realms." "On hearing mention of the unfortunate realms, the rich man became frightened and said to the Buddha: "O Holy One! I have now lost my head and committed a great sin. You Holy One are the All-Knower! You must know how to get emancipated. How am I to evade the worlds of hell, hungry ghosts, and animals?" "I then spoke to him of the Four Truths. The rich man, on hearing this, attained the fruition of srotapanna. Repentance had budded, and he begged the pardon of the Buddha: "I was ignorant. I said that the Buddha was a phantom, despite the fact that you are not. I shall, from this day forward, take refuge in the Three Treasures." "The Buddha said: "Well said, well said, O rich man!" The case is thus. This is speaking in response to the will of others. "How do I speak following my own will and that of others? When all the world says that the wise say "is", I too say "is". When they say that the wise say "is-not", I too say "is-not". When the wise of the world say that to amuse oneself in the five desires ends in the non-eternal, suffering, non-Self, and disruption, I, too, say so. When the wise of the world say that to amuse oneself in the five desires does not end in the Eternal, Self, and the Pure, I too say so. Things stand thus. This is what is called speaking following one's own will and also that of others. "O good man! I said: "The Bodhisattvas of the ten levels see the Buddha-Nature somewhat." This is speaking following the will of others. Why do we say that one sees a little? The Bodhisattva of the ten stages gains the Suramgama and other samadhis and the 3,000 teachings [i.e. the teachings of the universe]. Because of this, he clearly sees that all attain unsurpassed Bodhi. All beings will definitely gain unsurpassed Bodhi. That is why I say: "The Bodhisattva of the ten stages sees the Buddha-Nature somewhat." "O good man! I always say: "All beings possess the Buddha-Nature." This is what I speak following my own will. All beings are not segregated, do not perish, and gain unsurpassed Bodhi. This is what I say following my own will. "All beings have the Buddha-Nature. When defilement overspreads them, they cannot see it.

That is what I say that is what you say. This is what is said following my own will and the will of others. "O good man! The Tathagata, at times, speaks of innumerable teachings as just one thing. I say in the sutras that all pure actions arise out of the good teacher of the Way. This is how it goes. The causes of all pure actions are innumerable. But if we say "good teachers of the Way", this covers everything. This is as when I say that all actions arise out of evil views of life. The causes of all evil actions are innumerable. But when we say "evil views of life", this already covers everything. Or we say that unsurpassed Enlightenment has faith as its cause. The causes of Enlightenment are innumerable, but if stated as faith, this covers everything. O good man! The Tathagata speaks innumerable teachings, but these do not depart from the five skandhas, the 18 realms, and the 12 spheres. "O good man! The Tathagata's words are - for the sake of the being - made up of seven kinds, i.e. those based on words of: 1) cause, 2) result, 3) cause and result, 4) metaphors 5) non-accorded words, 6) following what generally applies in the world, 7) one's own free will. Why cause? This speaks of the result that is to come about in the future from the cause that now exists. This is what I say. "O good man! Do you see anyone who takes pleasure in killing or doing evil things? Know that such a person is destined for hell. "O good man! If there is any person who does not take pleasure in killing or doing evil, know that such a person is a heavenly being. This is what is said based on [the subject of] cause. "What are words based on "result"? This looks back to the cause from the result that is at hand. This is as is stated in the sutra: "O good

man! The poverty-stricken beings that you come across look ugly in their faces, as though they did not have freedom. Know that those persons must have infringed the precepts, had a jealous, angry or restless mind. When we see people who possess many things and wealth, whose sense-organs are perfect and whose deportment possesses authority and unmolestedness [a sense of inviolability], we may know that such persons must definitely have upheld the moral precepts, given [to others], made effort, and possessed a repenting mind, had no jealousy, nor any mind of anger." This is what we call "words based on the result." "What are cause-and-result words? This is as when it is stated in a sutra: "O good man! The six sense-organs which beings now possess arose from the cause of touch and are the results of the past. The Tathagata also speaks of this and calls it karma. The causal relations of this karma call forth the results that one has to harvest in the time to come." These are "words based on cause-and-result". "What is a metaphor? For example, "lion-king" refers to me. Such terms as great elephant-king, great naga-king, parijata, ball of seven treasures, great ocean, Mount Sumeru, great earth, great rain, master mariner, guide, best trainer, wrestler, cow-king, Brahmin, sramana, great castle, and tala tree are metaphorical terms. "What are non-accorded words? I say in a sutra: "Heaven and earth come into one; the river does not get into the sea; for the sake of King Prasenajit, mountains come from [all] around." It is as when I spoke to Mrgaramata, such as: "Even the sal trees would gain the bliss of humans and heaven if they received the eight precepts." The case is thus. I may even say that the Bodhisattvas of the ten stages have a retrogressing mind, but never will I say that the Tathagata employs two kinds of words. I might even say that a srotapanna might fall into the three unfortunate realms, but I will never say that the Bodhisattva of the ten stages has a retrogressive mind. These are non-accorded words. "What are the words that apply in the world? These are such as the Buddha uses, such as: man and woman, big and small, to go and to come, to sit and to lie, vehicle and house, pot, clothing, beings, the eternal, bliss, self, and the pure, army, forest, castle-town, phantom, transformed existence, and to become one and to disperse. These are the words that obtain in the world. "What are words that come forth as one wills? This is as when I reproach those who violate the prohibitions and I make them guard against this. I praise those of the srotapanna stage and enable common mortals to gain a good [state of] mind. I praise Bodhisattvas and enable common mortals to aspire to Enlightenment. I speak of the sufferings of the three unfortunate realms and cause people to do good. I say that all gets burnt, addressing those who are addicted to the notion that all things are created things. So does it go with the non-Self. We say that all beings possess the Buddha-Nature. All this is to cause all beings not to be indolent. These are the words that come out of one's free will. "O good man! The Tathagata also possess words which come out of his own free will. There are two kinds [aspects] in the Buddha-Nature of the Tathagata, namely: 1) "is", and 2) "not-is". The "is" refers to: the 32 signs of perfection, 80 minor marks of excellence, ten powers, four fearlessnesses, three remembrances, Great Loving-Kindness and Great Compassion, such innumerable samadhis as the Suramgama Samadhi, etc., such innumerable samadhis as the vajrasamadhi, etc., such innumerable samadhis as of the expedients, etc., and such innumerable samadhis as of the five knowledges. These are all "is". "Not-is" refers to all the Tathagta's good deeds of the past, the non-good, indefinables [i.e. neither good nor bad], karmic causes, karmic results, defilements, the five skandhas, the 12 links of interdependence, etc. These are the "not-is". "O good man! There are the "is" and the "not-is", good and non-good, defiled and non-defiled, mundane and supra-mundane world, holy and non-holy, the created and the non-created, the real and the non-real, quietude and non-quietude, disputation and non-disputation, world and non-world, illusion and non-illusion, cleaving and non-cleaving, prophecy and non-prophecy, existence and non-existence, the Three Times and not the Three Times, time and non-time, Eternal and non-Eternal, the Self and the non-Self, Bliss and non-Bliss, the Pure and the non-Pure, form-feeling-perception-volition-consciousness, and non-form-non-feeling-non-perception-non-volition-non-consciousness, the six sense-organs and non-six sense organs, the six sense-fields and the non-six sense-fields, the 12 links of interdependent arising and the non12 links of interdependent arising. These are the "is" and "not-is" of the Tathagata's Buddha-Nature. And the same applies to the Buddha-Nature of the icchantika. "O good man! I say: "All beings possess the Buddha-Nature." But beings do not understand the words of the Buddha that accord with his own will. As such words cannot even be understood by the Bodhisattva personifying another person. How could the two vehicles and all other Bodhisattvas understand them? "O good man! I, at one time at Grdhrakuta, discussed worldly truths with Maitreya. None of the 500 disciples, including Sariputra, knows of these, still less of the supramundane "Paramarthasatya" [Ultimate Truth]. O good man! There are cases where the Buddha-Nature is with an icchantika and not with a person of virtue, or where it is with a person of virtue but not with an icchantika. Or it can be with both or not with both. O good man! Those of my disciples who know of these four cases should not criticise and say: "Is the Buddha-Nature definitely with an icchantika or not?" When it is stated: "Beings all possess the Buddha-Nature", this is to be called the Tathagata's words of his own will. How could beings understand this at all? "O good man! This is comparable to a situation in which there are seven beings in the river Ganges. These are those who: 1) always get drowned, 2) come up for a time and then sink down again, 3) come up and stay there, 4) come up and look all around, 5) look all around and go [move], 6) get out and stay there again, 7) go [move about] both on land and water. "We speak of one who always sinks. This means that the person undergoes the great evil karmic result of a big fish, so that his body is heavy and the place is deep. Hence, he always sinks. "We speak of one who, for a time, comes up but sinks gain. This means that the person suffers from the evil karma of a big fish, so that his body is heavy and the place shallow, so that, for a time, he sees the light. By means of the light, he comes up for a time, but his body being heavy, he sinks again. "We speak of one who, on coming up, remains there. This refers to the fish called "timi" [a kind of shark]. It lives in shallow waters and enjoys the light. Hence, we say that it comes up and remains [there].

"We speak of one who comes up and looks all around him. This is the case of a shark which looks all around and seeks food. On this account, it looks around. "We speak of one who, having seen, goes off. This means that the fish, having seen some other things far off, soon goes off after them in order to devour them. Hence, having seen, it goes off. "We speak of one who, having gone, stays. This means that the fish goes off, and having eaten what it wanted to have, stays there. This is why we say that it goes off and then stays there. "We speak of one who goes on both land and water. This refers to the tortoise. "O good man! In this all-wonderful river of Nirvana, there live seven living beings. These are the first - always-sinking - up to the seventh. Some sink and some come up. "We speak of one who always sinks. This refers to one who hears this said: "This Great Nirvana Sutra states that the Tathagata is Eternal, does not change, and is the Eternal, Bliss, the Self, and the Pure; that he does not ultimately enter Nirvana; that all beings possess the Buddha-Nature; that the icchantika, the slanderers of the vaiulya sutras, those who have committed the five deadly sins, those guilty of the four grave offences, will all perfect the Way to Enlightenment; that the srotapanna, sakrdagamin, anagamin, arhat, and pratyekabuddha will unfailingly achieve unsurpassed Enlightenment." On hearing this, such a person does not believe, but thinks to himself: "This Nirvana Sutra is one that belongs to the tirthikas and is not a Buddhist sutra." This person then departs from the Way, and does not give ear to Wonderful Dharma. At times, he may happen to hear [Dharma], but he cannot think well. He may think, but cannot think of good. As he does not think of good, he abides in evil. Abiding in evil has six ways, which are: 1) evil, 2) non-good, 3) defiled dharma [state], 4) augmentation of "is", 5) worry in heat [i.e. becoming hellishly hot with worry], 6) receiving evil results. This is to sink. "Why is it to sink? When a person does not have a good [state of] mind, when he always does evil, when he does not practise the Way, we call this "sinking". We say "evil" because a holy person reproaches [him], the mind feels fear, good persons hate [this], and because there is no benefiting of beings. Hence, evil. "We say non-good because innumerable evils come about, because ignorance always binds the person, because he is always intimate with evil people, because he does not practise all the [various] kinds of good, because his mind is always inverted and always goes wrong. Hence, non-good. "We say "defiled dharma" because it always defiles body and mouth, because it defiles pure beings, because it increases non-good actions, because it keeps the person away from good things. Hence, defiled dharma. "We speak of augmenting "is" because what is done by the three persons mentioned above truly increases the

causes for hell, hungry ghosts, and animals. Such a person does not practise Dharma for Emancipation. He does not scorn the actions of body, mouth and mind, and all others. This is to augment "is". "We speak of "worrying heat" because this person minutely [constantly] does such four things and makes the body and mind feel worried over the two things, and there is no time for quietude. This is "heat". This ends in the karmic consequence of hell. Hence, heat. This burns all beings. Hence, heat. This burns all good things. Hence, heat. O good man! This person does not possess faith and coolness. Hence, heat. "We speak of suffering from evil results. This person fully does all the five things stated above, and after death falls into the realms of hell, hungry preta, and animals. "O good man! There are three evil things through which one suffers evil results, namely: 1) the evil of defilement, 2) the evil of karma, 3) the evil of karmic returns. O good man! As this person possesses the above-quoted six things, he cuts himself off from the root of good, commits the five deadly sins, performs the four grave offences, slanders the Three Treasures, uses the things which belong to the Sangha, and does all kinds of non-good. Because of these causal relations, he sinks into Avichi Hell and receives a body 84,000 yojanas wide and broad. The sin of his actions of body, mouth and mind being grave, the person cannot extricate himself from suffering. Why not? Because his mind cannot call forth anything good. Innumerable Buddhas may come into the world, but such a person will not give ear to them or see them. Hence, we say that he forever sinks. This is as with the big fish in the river Ganges. "O good man! I say: "The icchantika is one who eternally sinks, but there are icchantikas who do not fall within the class of those who eternally sink." Who are such? This is as in the case where, for the sake of "is", the person practises giving, sila [morality], and good. This is one who is eternally sunk. "O good man! There are instances where four good things call forth evil results. What are the four? They are: 1) reading and reciting the sutras so as to come above others, 2) upholding the prohibitions and precepts for the sake of profit, 3) giving because one belongs to others, 4) setting one's mind on, and meditating for the sake of gaining, the thoughtlessness-and-non-thoughtlessness state of mind. These four evoke evil results. That is why we say of one who practises and amasses such that he sinks and comes up again. Why do we say he sinks? Because he enjoys the three existences [i.e. the kamadhatu, rupadhatu, and arupadhatu - worlds of desire, form, and non-from]. Why do we say he comes up? Because he sees the light. The light corresponds to his hearing [Dharma], upholding the silas, giving, and sitting in meditation. "Why do we say that the person sinks? Because he gains in evil views and acquires arrogance. Hence, I say in the sutra: "If beings seek all existences And do good and evil deeds for existence, Such persons will lose the way to Nirvana. This is why we say that The person temporarily comes up but sinks again. He sails on the dark ocean of birth and death, He may gain Emancipation And do away with defilement. But the person again suffers from evil returns. This is temporarily coming up Only to sink again." "O good man! This is as in the case of the big fish that comes out of the water for a time when it sees the light, but, as its body is heavy, sinks down again. That is how things also proceed with the two persons mentioned above. "O good man! And there is a person who clings to, and takes pleasure in, the three existences. This is sinking. He hears the Great Nirvana Sutra and gains faith. This is coming up. Why do we say coming up? When the person hears this sutra, he does away with evil and practises good. This is coming up. The person believes, but is not perfect. Why is he not perfect? The person believes in Mahaparinirvana and the Eternal, Bliss, the Self, and the Pure, but says that the Tathagata's body is non-Eternal, non-Bliss, non-Self, and non-Pure. "The Tathagata has two Nirvanas. One is the created, and the other is the uncreated. With created Nirvana, there are no Eternal, Bliss, Self, and the Pure. A person may believe that beings possess the Buddha-Nature, but not that all beings have it. So we say "not perfect in faith". "O good man! There are two kinds [aspects] of faith: one is believing, and the other seeking. Such a person possesses faith, but does not push on and seek. Hence, not perfect in faith. "There are also two phases of faith. One [type of faith] arises from hearing, and the other from thinking. The faith of this person arises from hearing, not from thinking. Hence, not perfect in faith. "Also, there are two kinds. One [kind] believes in the fact that there is Enlightenment, and the other [kind of faith believes that there are] people who have gained it. Hence, not perfect in faith. "Again, there are two kinds. One is belief in what is right, and the other

in what is evil. A person says that there are cause and result and the Buddha, Dharma, and Sangha. This is believing in what is right. A person says that there cannot be any such things as cause and result and that the Three Treasures are different in nature. The person believes in evil words and the Puranas. This is believing in evil. The person believes in the Buddha, Dharma, and Sangha, but does not believe that the Three Treasures are one in nature and characteristics. He believes in cause and result, but does not believe that there is anyone who has gained [Enlightenment]. Hence, not perfect in faith. This person is not perfect in faith and does not observe the prohibitions and the precepts. Why do we say not perfect? Being not perfect, the sila [the moral precepts] which one has received is not perfect. And why does one say not perfect? "Of sila, there are two kinds, namely: 1) sila aimed at deportment and 2) sila for sila's sake [i.e. sila observed not as a matter of form]. The person upholds the sila for deportment, but not the sila for sila's sake. Hence, not perfect in sila. "Also, there are two kinds, which are: 1) one that is purported and 2) one that is not purported. The person may be in accord with sila but has no non-purported sila. Hence, not perfect in sila. "Also, there are two kinds, which are: 1) the person carries on right living in body and mind and 2) the person does not carry on right living in body and mind. This person does not have right living in body and mind. Hence, not perfect in sila. "Also, there are two kinds, namely: 1) seeking sila and 2) abandoned sila. This person upholds the sila that is aimed at "is", but cannot attain the abandoned sila. Hence, not perfect in sila. "Also, there are two kinds, which are: 1) to accord with "is" and 2) to accord with Enlightenment. The person upholds the sila that accords with "is", but not that which accords with Enlightenment. Hence, not perfect in sila. "Also, there are two kinds, namely: 1) good sila and 2) evil sila. When body, mouth, and mind are good, this is good sila. And such silas as of cows and dogs are evil silas. The person believes that these two silas call forth good results. Hence, not perfect in sila. As the person does not possess the two, faith and sila, he is not perfect in his learning. "In what way do we speak of not being perfect in hearing? The person believes only in six of the 12 types of sutra which the Tathagata has delivered and does not believe in the other six. Hence, not perfect in hearing. Or he upholds the six sutras, but cannot recite and expound them to others and no benefit is given. Hence, not perfect in hearing [i.e. in listening to Dharma]. "And also, having received these six sutras, he recites them and speaks about them for discussion, for superceding others, for profit, for all existences. Hence, not perfect in hearing. "O good man! I speak in my sutras about perfect hearing. How is a person perfect? There is a bhiksu who is good in body, mouth, and mind. First of all, he makes offerings to all teachers, personal [i.e. his own] or otherwise, and also to the virtuous. These gain a loving mind towards this bhiksu, and through this causal relationship, they teach him what is stated in the sutras. The man, with the sincerest mind, upholds what is taught him and recites [it]. Upholding and reciting [this], he gains Wisdom. Having gained Wisdom, he thinks well and lives in accordance with Dharma. Thinking well, he gains the right meaning. Gaining the right meaning, his body and mind gain quietude. Gaining quietude in body and mind, joy arises. From the gladdened mind comes dhyana [meditation]. From dhyana comes right knowledge. Because of right knowledge, he abhors existence. This abhorrence of existence calls forth Emancipation. This person has nothing of this kind. Hence, not perfect in hearing. As this person is not perfect in these three things, he does not give. "Of giving, there are two kinds, namely: 1) giving of wealth, and 2) giving of Dharma. This person practises giving of wealth, but seeks "is". Though he practises giving of Dharma, this, too, is not perfect. Why not? He conceals things and does not explain all. Because he fears that others might come above him. Hence, not perfect in giving. "Of the giving of wealth and Dharma, there are two kinds, namely: 1) holy and 2) non-holy. By holy is meant the giving that does not seek any return when [something is] given; by non-holy is meant the giving that cares for [i.e. seeks] a return when giving. What the holy person gives is augmentation of Dharma. What the non-holy gives is augmentation of material things. Such a person gives wealth to augment wealth and gives of Dharma to augment wealth. Hence, not perfect in giving. "Also, next, this person receives the six types of sutra. He gives to people who receive Dharma, but not to those who do not receive it. Hence, not perfect in giving.

"As this person does not possess the four things stated above, whatever Wisdom he practises is not perfect. The nature of Wisdom discriminates the nature well. This person cannot see the Eternal and the non-Eternal of the Tathagata. As to the Tathagata, this Nirvana Sutra says: "The Tathagata is Emancipation, and Emancipation is the Tathagata. The Tathagata is Nirvana, and Nirvana is Emancipation." He cannot discriminate between what is said. Pure action is the Tathagata. The Tathagata is Loving-Kindness, Compassion, Sympathetic Joy, and Equanimity. Loving-Kindness, Compassion, Sympathetic Joy, and Equanimity are Emancipation. Emancipation is Nirvana, and Nirvana is Loving-Kindness, Compassion, Sympathetic Joy, and Equanimity. He cannot gain any discrimination in what is said. Hence, not perfect in Wisdom. "Also, next, he is not clear as to the fact that the Buddha-Nature is the Tathagata. The Tathagata is one that does not exist in all other things. What does not exist in all other things is Emancipation. Emancipation is Nirvana, and Nirvana is something that does not exist in all other things. He cannot gain any discrimination in what is said [i.e. cannot discriminate the meaning of what is said]. Hence, not perfect in Wisdom. "Also, next, he cannot gain any discrimination between the Four Truths of Suffering, the Cause of Suffering, Extinction, and the Way to Extinction. As he does not know the Four Truths, he is unable to know holy action. As he does not know holy action, he cannot know the Tathagata. As he does not know the Tathagata, he cannot know Emancipation. As he does not know Emancipation, he cannot know Nirvana. Hence, not perfect in Wisdom. "He is thus not perfect in five things. Of these, there are two kinds, which are: 1) what increases good and 2) what increases evil. How does he increase evil? This person does not see what is evil in his own self. He says that he is perfect and gains a clinging mind. To those fellow wayfarers of his, he says he is the winner. So, he associates with evil persons, who take his side. Befriending such persons, he further hears about what is imperfect. Having heard [such], he is glad at heart, gains clinging and arrogance, and is indolent. Being indolent, he associates with the laity. "Also, he takes pleasure in hearing about the secular world and keeps at a distance the teaching of renunciation. As a result of this, evil increases. As he grows in evil, he gains evil actions in body, mouth, and mind. These three actions not being pure, the three realms of hell, hungry pretas, and animals increase. This is temporarily coming up and sinking again. Who of my following corresponds to this temporarily coming up and then sinking again? This is Devadatta, Bhiksu Kokalika, Bhiksu Carved-Arm, Bhiksu Sunaksatra, Bhiksu Tisya, Bhiksu Full-Abode, Bhiksuni Compassionate-Soil, Bhiksuni Wilderness, Bhiksuni Squareness, Bhiksuni Arrogance, rich man Pureness, Upasaka Is-Seeking, Sharokushakushu , rich man Elephant, Upasika Fame, Upasika Light, Upasika Nanda, Upasika Army, and Upasika Bell. These persons are those who temporarily come up and sink again. For example, this is as in the case of the big fish which, when it sees the light, comes up but, as its body is heavy, sinks down again. "The second kind of person deeply realises that he is not perfect in action. Being not perfect, he associates with a good teacher of the Way. Associating with a good friend, he is pleased to seek to learn what he has not yet heard. Having heard [it], he is pleased to act in the way he is told. Having received [these instructions], he is pleased to meditate. Having well thought about [it], he lives in accordance with Dharma. As he abides in Dharma, the good increases. As it increases, he does not sink any more. This is "abiding". "Who of the Sangha are those who would answer to this description? They are five such bhiksus as Sariputra, Mahamaudgalyayana, Ajnatakaundinya and the others, the five bhiksus of the group of Yasas, and such others as Aniruddha, Kumarakasyapa, Mahakasyapa, Dasabalakasyapa, Bhiksuni Kisagotami, Bhiksuni Utpala, Bhiksuni Superior, Bhiksuni True-Meaning, Bhiksuni Manas, Bhiksuni Bhadra , Bhiksuni Purity, Bhiksuni Non-Retrogression, King Bimbisara, rich man Ugra, rich man Sudatta, Mahanama, poor man Sudatta, son of rich man Upali, rich man Jo, Upasika Fearless, Upasika Supratistha, Upasika Dharma-Loving, Upasika Valorous, Upasika Heaven-Gained, Upasika Sujata, Upasika Perfect-Body, Upasika Cow-Gained, Upasika Wilderness, Upasika Mahasena. All such bhiksus, bhiksunis, upasakas and upasikas can well be called "abodes" [i.e. those who abide]. "Why do we say "abide"? Because such a person always truly sees the good light. Hence, whether the Buddha has appeared in the world or not, such a person never does evil. That is why we say "abide". This is as in the case in which the fish, "timi", seeks the light and does not sink and hide away. With all such beings things proceed thus. That is why I say in the sutras:

"If a person truly discriminates the meanings,
And with an intensive mind seeks
The fruition of a sramana,
And if a person truly reproaches all existences,
Such a person is one who lives
In accordance with Dharma.
If a person makes offerings to innumerable Buddhas
And practises the Way for innumerable kalpas
And if blessed with worldly pleasures,
Such a person is one who abides in Dharma.
If a person makes friends with a good teacher of the Way
And hears Wonderful Dharma, and
If the person thinks well in his mind,
And lives in accordance with the Way
And seeks the light and practises the Way,
That person attains Emancipation
And lives in peace."

"O good man! Regarding the imperfection of knowledge, there are five things to consider. The person comes to know and seeks to befriend a good friend, who will now come to see which out of greed, anger, ignorance, and sensing is predominant. To a person with a lot of greed, meditation on impurity will be taught. To a person who is prone to anger, loving-kindness is taught. To a person who thinks too much, counting the breath will be taught. To a person who has too much clinging to self, the dissection of the 18 realms is given. By this means, the person, with the best of minds, upholds and practises the Way as shown. Acting as he has been told to act, he, by degrees, gains the meditation of the four remembrances, i.e. the meditation on the four items of body, feeling, mind, and dharma. This meditation completed, that on the 12 links of interdependent arising gradually follows. This done, he next substantiates the world of warming-up ["usmagata": a mental warming-up that one experiences before one gains the Wisdom of "darsana-marga" - the path of seeing, of inner understanding]." Bodhisattva Kasyapa said to the Buddha: "O World-Honoured One! All things have warmingsup. Why so? Just as you, the Buddha, say, three things combine and we get beings. These are: 1) life, 2) warming-up, and 3) consciousness. If this is said, this will entail that all beings must possess the warming-up already. Why does the Tathagata say: "The warming-up comes about by coming into contact with a teacher of the Way?" The Buddha said: "O good man! That kind of warming-up about which you speak is with all beings, down to the icchantika. The warming-up which I now speak about necessarily comes about only by an expedient, which is what originally was not but is now. Hence, it is not that it is with one from the very beginning. So, you should not object and say that all beings have warming-up by birth. O good man! The warming-up spoken of is what belongs to the world of form, not the world of desire. Should you say that all beings must possess it, this would entail your saying that even the beings of the world of desire must also possess it. As it does not exist in the world of desire, we cannot say that all possess it. "O good man! It can be in the world of form, but it is not the case that all possess it. Why not? My

disciples have it, but not the tirthikas. Hence, it is not the case that all beings must possess it.

O good man! All the tirthikas meditate on the six actions [i.e. the six meditations of two groups, made up of: 1) negative, i.e. one of abhorring, and 2) positive, i.e. that of seeking. One of the systems of practice of the Way], and all of my disciples are perfect in the 16 actions [i.e. the 16 categories observed in meditating on the Four Truths]. And all of these 16 are not possessed by all beings." Bodhisattva Kasyapa said to the Buddha: "O World-Honoured One! Why do we say "warming-up"? Is it a warming-up by one's own self, or does it come about caused by others?" The Buddha said: "O good man! Such a warming-up arises out of one's own nature. It does not so come about caused by others." Bodhisattva Kasyapa said: "O World-Honoured One! You said previously that Asvaka and Punarvasu did not possess the warming-up. Why not? When a person does not have faith in the Three Treasures, he does not have it. So we should know that faith is none other than a warming-up." "O good man! Faith is not a warming-up. Why not? Because one gains the warming-up by faith. O good man! The warming-up is at once Wisdom. Why? Because it meditates on the Four Noble Truths. Hence, we call this the "16 actions". This action is Wisdom. O good man! You ask why we say "to warm-up". O good man! Now, warming-up is a phase of fire of the Noble Eightfold Path. That is why we say "to warm-up". O good man! For example, when we make fire, there is the cause of fire beforehand, then we get it, and then smoke arises. It is the same with this undefiled way. To warm-up is none other than the 16 actions. The fire is the fruition of the srotapanna, and the smoke is the practising of the Way and the segregation [i.e. dispelling] of defilement." Bodhisattva Kasyapa said to the Buddha: "O World-Honoured One! Even such a thing as the warming-up is of the class of the "is". It is something created. This thing gains, in return, the five skandhas of the world of form. Hence "is", and also the "created". If it is a thing created, how could it represent the undefiled Way?" The Buddha said: "O good man! It is thus, it is thus! It is as you say. O good man! Although this warming-up belongs to the category of "is", it truly breaks [destroys] the created and the "is". Hence, it represents the undefiled Way. "O good man! A man rides a horse, and he both loves and whips it. It is thus. It is also the same with the mind that warms up. Due to craving, life is gained, and due to abandoning [i.e. renunciation], one meditates. For this reason, it is a thing of the "is". Though a created thing, it does represent the Right Path. Those who gain the warming-up are of the 73 kinds and the 10 of the world of desire. These persons are all clad in defilement. It goes from one tenth up to nine tenths. As in the case of the world of desire, things go from the first dhyana up to the thoughtlessness-and-non-thoughtlessness heaven. We say that there are 73 kinds. Such a person, on gaining the warming-up, never cuts off the root of good, commits the five deadly sins, or performs the four grave offences. "Of this person, there are two types. One associates with a good friend, and the other with a bad friend. The one who associates with a bad friend is up for a time, but sinks again. The one who associates with a good friend looks all around. To look all around refers to the "topmost-height" ["murdhana"; this topmost dharma is a fruition of practice likened to the topmost height of a hill, which is both the topmost point, but is also a turning-point for falling down or retrogressing. A stage of practice in the Hinayana category - K. Yamamoto]. The nature of this stage is as yet of the class of the five skandhas, and yet is related to the Four Truths. Hence, one can see all around. After the stage of the topmost-height, the person attains that of "cognition" [i.e. a stage of practice in which one obtains cognition of the nature of the Four Truths and from which one no more retrogresses. There are several grades of it - K. Yamamoto]. The same is the case with the stage of cognition, too. The nature is of the four skandhas, but is related to the Four Truths. This person next gains the laukikagradharma ["first-of-the-world root of good"], which is of the nature of the five skandhas and has causal relations with the Four Truths. The person, by degrees, gains the "cognition of suffering". The nature of Wisdom actualises the causal relation of the First Truth. Having thus actualised the causal relation of the truth of cognition, the person cuts away defilement and attains [to the level of] srotapanna. This is the fourth stage of seeing all around in the four directions. The four directions are none other than the Four Truths." Bodhisattva Kasyapa said to the Buddha: "O World-Honoured One! You said before: "The srotapanna cuts away defilement as one would 40 ris of water crosswise and lengthwise. What remains is like water a single hair's breadth in extent." By this, you meant the cutting off of the three fetters ["trini-samyojanani"] and calling this the srotapanna. These are: 1) wrong view of the Self, 2) seeing non-cause as cause, and 3) doubt. O World-Honoured One! Why do you say that a person of the srotapanna stage truly sees in [all] four directions, and why is such a person called a srotapanna, and why do you resort to the parable of the timi fish?" The Buddha said: "O good man! The srotapanna truly cuts off innumerable defilements. But these three are of a serious nature. And, also, these include all the defilements which the srotapanna has to cut off. O good man! A great king comes out of his palace and wishes to make an inspection. Even when the four armies are with him, the people of the world but say that the King comes and goes. Why? Because this comes from the fact that the world makes much matter of the King. It is the same with the three defilements, too. Why serious? Because these people are all subject to these. As they are minutely small in size and not cognizable, we say serious. As these three are difficult to remove, and as these three become the cause of all defilements. As these three are the enemies to be subdued, we say: 1) precepts, 2) meditation, and 3) Wisdom. "O good man! When all beings hear that the srotapanna indeed cuts off such countless defilements, they gain a retrogressive mind and say: "How can beings possibly cut off such countless defilements?" Because of this, as an expedient, the Tathagata speaks of three. You ask why I take up the case of the srotapanna and liken it to looking in the four directions. O good man! The srotapanna meditates on the Four Truths and gains four things, which are: 1) sticking unrelentingly to the Way, 2) meditating well, 3) seeing things well in the right way, and 4) truly crushing a great enemy. "We say that we stick unrelentingly to the Way, because nothing can move the sense-organs of the person who has attained the stage of srotapanna. Due to this, we say that we stick unrelentingly to the Way. "We speak of seeing well all around. This means that the person indeed reproaches the defilements within and without. "We say that we see in a true way. This is the knowledge of cognition. "We say that we truly crush a great enemy. This refers to the four inversions. "You ask: "Why do we say srotapanna?" O good man! "Shu" [Jap. "shudaon" = srotapanna, which literally means: srotas = stream + apanna = entered] means "undefiled"; "daon" means "to learn and practise". One practises the undefiled. Hence, "srotapanna". O good man! Shu means stream. Of streams, there are two kinds. One is the ordinary type, and the other that which flows in a counter direction." Bodhisattva Kasyapa said: "O World-Honoured One! If this is so, why are srotapannas, sakrdagamins and arhats not all called srotapannas?" "O good man! Those from the stage of srotapanna up to all Buddhas could well be called srotapanna. If it is not the case that those from the sakrdagamin stage up to the Buddha do not possess the nature of the srotapanna, how could there be such as from sakrdagamin up to the Buddha? All beings have two kinds of name, which are: 1) old, and 2) objective. As a common mortal, one has a name of the secular world. When one has entered the Way, one is called "srotapanna". When this is first gained, one is called srotapanna; gained later, one is called sakrdagamin. Such a person is called srotapanna and sakrdagamin. The same is the case with the Buddha, too. "O good man! There are two kinds of stream, of which one is Emancipation and the other Nirvana. All holy persons possess these, too, and they can be srotapannas and sakrdagamins. The same also applies to the Buddha. O good man! The srotapanna can also be called a Bodhisattva. Why? The Bodhisattva is none other than a person who is perfect in the "knowledge of extinction" [i.e. the knowledge in which defilement is completely extinguished] and the "knowledge of birthlessness" [i.e. the knowledge in which one is awake to the existence which is birthlessness]. The sakrdagamin, too, seeks these two knowledges. Hence, one may know that a person of the srotapanna stage can also be called a Bodhisattva. The sakrdagamin, too, can be called one who is "enlightened". Why? Because he is enlightened regarding the darsanamarga [i.e. the stage of practice in which one first enters the great sea of Truth] and cuts away defilement, because he is correctly enlightened as to the law of causal relations, because he is enlightened in the ways that are "common to all" and those which are "not common to all". The same applies to the sakrdagamin up to arhatship. "O good man! There

are two kinds of this srotapanna. One is sharp and the other dull. Those of the dull category repeat lives in the worlds of humans and the gods seven times. And in this class of the dull, there are five further kinds. There are those who get reborn six more times, five more times, four more times, three more times, and twice more. Those who are sharp-born gain in this present life the fruition of the stages of srotapanna up to arhatship. "O good man! You ask why the srotapanna should be compard to the timi fish. O good man! There are four things characterising the timi, which are: 1) as its bones are small, it is light, 2) as it has fins, it is light, 3) it desires to seek the light, 4) it bites and holds on tightly. With the srotapanna, there are four things. Saying that the bones are small is comparable to the smallness of the amount of defilement. Having fins can be compared to samatha and vipasyana. Saying that it seeks and enjoys the light is comparable to darsanamarga. Saying that it bites and holds on tightly can be compared to the fact that the person hears what the Tathagata says regarding the non-eternal, suffering, non-Self, and the non-pure and that he holds tightly to what he has heard when Mara transforms himself and disguises himself as a Buddha, or when the rich man Sura sees and is wonderstruck, and that Mara, seeing the rich man moved in his heart, says: "What I said before about the Four Truths is not true. I shall now, for your sake, speak about the five truths, six skandhas, 13 spheres, and 19 realms." On hearing this, the rich man examines what is said and sees that there is nothing in it that is true. Hence, an analogy is sought here to explain the immovability of the mind." Bodhisattva Kasyapa said to the Buddha: "Is this srotapanna so called because the person first enters the Way, or is it because he has first gained the fruition? If one is a srotapanna because one has first entered the Way, why is one not so called when one has gained the cognition of suffering, instead of calling one "apatti" [= happening or entering]? If the first fruition is called srotapanna, why do we not call the tirthika a srotapanna who first excises the fetter of defilement and gains the existencelessness mental state, and having practised the Way of the undefiled, attains the stage of anagamin?" "O good man! When the first fruition is gained, we say srotapanna. You ask why it is that the tirthika first cuts away the bond of defilement and gains the existencelessness mental state, and practising the undefiled Way gains the fruition of the anagamin, and not the srotapanna. O good man! Due to the fact that a person gains the first fruition, we say srotapanna. The person, at that time, gains the eight knowledges and the 16 actions." Kasyapa said: "O World-Honoured One! It is the same with one who attains the fruition of the anagamin, too. He also gains the eight knowledges and the 16 actions. Why do we not in fact call such a person a srotapanna?" "O good man! There are two kinds of the 16 defiled actions. One is what is common to all, and the other what is not. There are also two kinds of the undefiled 16 actions. One is what faces towards fruition, and the other is what a person has gained. There are also two kinds of the eight knowledges, too. One is what faces towards fruition, and the other is what the person has gained. A person of the srotapanna stage abandons the 16 actions that are common to all and gains the 16 which are not common to all, and abandoning the eight knowledges that face towards fruition, gains the eight knowledges that are the fruition. With a person of the anagamin stage, things are not thus. That is why the first fruition is called srotapanna. O good man! The srotapanna is concerned with the Four Truths, whereas the anagamin has relations with but one Truth. That is why the first fruition is called srotapanna. Hence, the timi fish is employed as a simile. "We say that the person looks all around and then goes off. This is the sakrdagamin. His mind wholly set on the Way, he practises the Way, and in order to cut out greed, anger, ignorance, and arrogance, he, like the timi, looks around, and then goes off to seek food. "We say that a person goes off and then remains again. This can be compared to the anagamin, who, having partaken of the food, abides there. There are two kinds of this anagamin. One is he who has now attained the fruition of arhatship and, practising the Way still further, gains the further fruition of the arhat [stage]. The other is he who greedily adheres to the samadhi of silence of the world of form and non-form. This person is called an anagamin. He does not gain a body from the world of desire. Of the anagamin, there are five kinds, namely: 1) middle-grade Parinirvana, 2) carnal Parinirvana, 3) action Parinirvana, 4) actionless Parinirvana, and 5) upstream Parinirvana. There are six kinds. Of these, the five are as above, and the sixth is the actual enjoyment of the fruition of Parinirvana. There are also seven

kinds, of which the six are as above and the seventh is the Parinirvana of the world of non-form. "Action Parinirvana possesses ttwo kinds, which may have the two carnal bodies or four carnal bodies. If one possesses two bodies, we call this being one of the sharp-born; if one possesses four bodies, we call this dull-born. Again, there are two kinds. One person makes effort, has no unmolested samadhi, whereas the second is indolent and has unmolestedness. Again, there are two kinds. One person abides in the samadhi of effort, whereas the second does not. "O good man! There are two kinds in [the category of] what is done by the beings of the world of desire. The one is what the person does, and the other is the action gained by birth. "A person of middle-grade Nirvana has works [actions] to do, but not works gained by birth. Because of this, such a person herein enters Parinirvana. He abandons the carnal body of the world of desire, but does not yet attain the world of form. The sharp-born person enters Nirvana herein. With the person of middle-grade Nirvana, there are four minds [mental states], namely: 1) non-learning and not non-learning, 2) learning, 3) non-learning, and 4) the person enters the Nirvana of non-learning and not non-learning. Why middle-grade Nirvana? O good man! Now, of the four minds of this anagamin, two are Nirvana and two are not. Hence, we say middle-grade Nirvana. "There are two kinds of carnal-body Nirvana. One is what one does, while the other is action by birth. This person abandons the body of the world of desire and gains the body of the world of form. With effort, he practises the Way, lives his allotted life-span, and enters Nirvana." Bodhisattva Kasyapa said: "O World-Honoured One! If we say that the person enters Nirvana when his life ends, how can we call it the Nirvana of carnal life?" The Buddha said: "O good man! When the person is born as a human, he cuts off the defilements of the three worlds. Hence, the Parinirvana of carnal life. "We say Parinirvana by action. The person always practises the Way and through the power of the samadhi practised by this created body, the person cuts off defilement and enters Nirvana. Hence, Parinirvana by action. "We say Nirvana by non-action. The person know that he will definitely reach Nirvana. Hence, indolence arises. Also, through the power of the samadhi of the created body, he gains Nirvana when his life ends. This is actionless Parinirvana. "We say up-stream Parinirvana. On gaining the fourth dhyana, the person gains a mind of craving. Because of this, retrogression takes place and he gains a life of the first dhyana. In this, there are two streams. One is the stream of defilement, and the other is the stream of the Way. Because of the stream of the Way, the person gains the craving of the second dhyana, when his life ends. Because of the causal relation of craving, he gains birth in the second dhyana. It is the same with things up to the fourth dhyana. "In the fourth dhyana [state], there are two kinds. One person enters the world of non-form, and the second the Suddhavasa Heaven. Of such two persons, one seeks samadhi and the other Wisdom. The one who seeks Wisdom gains the Suddhavasa heaven, and the one who seeks samadhi gains the world of non-form. Of these two, there are two kinds. With the one who practises the fourth dhyana, there are five different stages of practice. The second person does not practise the Way. What are the five? They are: low, middle, top, middle of the top, and topmost. "The person who practises the Way of the topmost gains birth in Akanistha Heaven. The one who practises the Way of the middle of the top gains birth in Sudarsana Heaven. One who practises the Way of the top gains birth in the heaven where he can see good. One who practises the middle-grade Way gains birth in the heaven where there is no [oppressive] heat. The person who practises the Way of the low-grade gains birth in the heaven of small width [size]. Of these two kinds of person, the one cares for discussion, and the other for quietude. The one who likes quietude gains birth in the world of non-form, and the one who likes discussion gains birth in Suddhavasa Heaven. "And there are two kinds. One person practises the fragrant dhyana, and the other does not. The one who practises the fragrant dhyana enters Suddhavasa Heaven, and the one who does not practise the fragrant dhyana gains birth in the world of non-form, where, when his life ends, he gains Parinirvana. Any person who wishes to enter the world of non-form cannot carry out the five different modes of practice of the fourth dhyana. Any person who has practised the five different modes of dhyana will be critical of the dhyana of the world of non-form." Bodhisattva Kasyapa said to the Buddha: "O World-Honoured One! The person who practises middle-grade Nirvana is one who is sharp-born. If sharp-born, why does he not enter Nirvana in this present life? Why is there in the world of desire middle-grade Nirvana, but it

does not exist in the world of non-form?" The Buddha said: "O good man! The four great elements of this person are weak and emaciated, so that he cannot practise the Way. Even though the four great elements are sound and stubborn, there is a lack of a house to live in, food and drink, clothing, bedding, medical attendance and medicine, and all causal relations do not come to him. Due to this, he cannot gain Nirvana in this present life. "O good man! Once I was dwelling in the vihara [Buddhist monastic residence] of Anathapindada in the state of Sravasti. And there was a bhiksu who came to my place and said: "O World-Honoured One! Although I always practise the Way, I cannot rise from the fruition of srotapanna to that of arhat." Then I said to Ananda: "See now to what this bhiksu needs to have." Then Ananda took this bhiksu to Jetavana and gave him a good house. Then the bhiksu said to Ananda: "O great virtuous one! Please decorate the house for me, have it repaired and make it pure and clean. There should be the seven jewels. Also hang up silken banners!" Ananda said: "A sramana is called the poor of the world. How can I supply what you want to have?" The bhiksu said: "O greatly virtuous one! If you do [as I ask], you do good. If you do not, I shall go back to the World-Honoured One." Then Ananda came to the Buddha and said: "O World-Honoured One! The bhiksu in question desires to have the place variously adorned with gems and banners. This is strange. What am I to do?" Then I said to Ananda: "Go back to the bhiksu and meet his wishes, and decorate the place as he would wish to have it decorated." Then Ananda went back to the house and made things ready for the bhiksu. Having gained what he wanted, he applied himself to the practice of the Way. Before long, he gained the fruition of srotapanna and attained arhatship. "O good man! Innumerable beings, though they must [i.e. are bound to] gain Nirvana, lose their head due to a lack of things. Hence, they fail to gain it. O good man! Also, there are beings who have much desire. Their minds are busily occupied and they cannot meditate well. Hence, they cannot gain Nirvana in this life. "O good man! You ask why there is middle-grade Nirvana to serve the world of desire well to abandon the body , and why there is not such in the world of form. "O good man! This person sees the two causal relations of the world of desire. One is inner and the other is outer. In the world of form, there is not the causal relation of the category of the outer. And in the world of desire, there are again two types of craving mind. One is the craving of desire, and the other the craving for eating. Meditating on these cravings, the person seriously reproaches himself. Reproaching his own mind, he enters Nirvana. "In this world of desire, the person can well reproach the coarse defilements, which are: stinginess, greed, anger, jealousy, non-repentance, and not having a sense of shame. Due to this causal relation, the person indeed gains Nirvana. And also the nature of the way of the world of desire is valorous. Why? Because the person gains the entering and the fruition. Hence, we have in the world of desire middle-grade Nirvana, which one does not find in the world of form. O good man! Middle-grade Nirvana is of three kinds, namely: top, middle, and low. The top-grade gains Nirvana, not abandoning the carnal body and the world of desire. The middle-grade attains Nirvana by first leaving the world of desire and not yet arriving at the world of form. The low gains Nirvana when the person leaves the world of desire and comes near the boundary line of the world of form. For example, this is the case with the timi fish, which, having eaten, stays. It is the same with this person. "Why do we say "stay"? This is said because the person gains life in the world of form and of non-form and there he gains a body. Hence, we speak of "staying". Humans and devas of the world of desire do not gain life in the realms of hell, animals, and hungry ghosts. Hence, we say staying. Having already cut innumerable bonds of defilement, there is little that is left. Hence, to stay. And, also, we say stay because that person nevermore does the things of the world of common mortals. Hence, to stay. He is not afraid and does not cause others to be afraid. Hence, to stay. He is away from the two cravings, stinginess, greed and anger. Hence, to stay. "O good man! Gaining the other shore can be compared to the arhat, pratyekabuddha, Bodhisattva, and the Buddha. This is like the godly tortoise, who can travel both on water and on land. Why do we employ the example of the tortoise? Because he truly shuts in [i.e. pulls in, withdraws] the five things [i.e. limbs and head]. It is the same with the arhat up to the Buddha, who truly shut in the five sense-organs. Hence comparison is drawn with the tortoise. "We say water and land. Water can be compared to the world, and land to getting out of the secular world.

It is the same with these holy people, too. They indeed gain the other shore, as they meditate thoroughly on bad defilements. Hence, comparison is sought with travelling both on water and on land. "O good man! Seven kinds of being in the river Ganges possess the name of tortoise. But they do not part from the water. Thus, in the case of this all-wonderful Great Nirvana, there come about several different names, such as those from icchantika up to all Buddhas. But these do not part from the water of the Buddha-Nature. O good man! With these seven beings, be it that things concern Wonderful Dharma, non-Wonderful Dharma, the means, the Way of Emancipation, the gradual Way, causation or result, all are the Buddha-Nature. They are the words of the Tathagata that come from his own free will." Bodhisattva Kasyapa said: "O World-Honoured One! If there is a cause, there comes about a result. If no cause, there cannot be a result. Nirvana is the result. As it is something that is eternal, there cannot be any cause to speak of. If there is no cause, how can we call it a result? This Nirvana is also called "sramana" and the fruition of the sramana. What is a sramana? And what is the fruition of a sramana?" "O good man! In all worlds, there are seven kinds of fruition, which are those of: 1) through the means, 2) repaying obligations, 3) befriending, 4) that which remains, 5) equality, 6) karma, and 7) segregation. "We say "fruition by means". In autumn, secular people harvest cereal and say to one another that they are gaining the fruition of the means which they have put into effect. The fruition of the means is called the fruition of karmic actions. Such fruition has two causes, namely: 1) near [proximate, immediate] cause, and 2) far-out [indirect] cause. The near cause is the so-called "seed"; the far-out cause is water, dung, human being, and effort. This is fruition [which comes about] from putting the means into effect. We say "fruition by repaying obligations". Secular people make offerings to their parents. All the parents say: "We are now reaping the fruit of what we did when nourishing [our children]." When the child indeed repays [them], we call this the fruition. The case is thus. Such fruition has two causes, namely: 1) the near cause, and 2) the far-out cause. What is near is the pure actions which the parents performed in the past; the far-out refers to the filial child who developed. This is the fruition of repaying obligations. "We say "fruition of befriending".

For example, there is a man who makes friends with a good person [i.e. a good teacher of Buddhism], as a result of which he can gain the fruits of the srotapanna [level] up to arhatship. The person now says: "I now gain the fruition of befriending." The case is thus. Such fruition has two causes, namely: 1) the near cause, and 2) the far-out cause. What is near is faith; what is far-out is the good friend. This is the fruition from befriending. "We say "fruition of that which remains". By non-killing, one lengthens the life span of the third body. This is what obtains. This is the fruition of that which remains. Such fruition has two causes. One is near, the other far-out. By near is meant purity of body, mouth [i.e. speech], and mind; by far-out, the extension of the life span and the enjoying of old age. This is the fruition of that which remains. "By "equal fruition" is meant what is common to the world at large. Such fruition again has two causes: 1) near, and 2) far-out. By near-cause is meant the ten good actions which beings perform; by far-out is meant the so-called three calamities [i.e. of water, fire, and war]. This is what is called "equal fruition". "We speak of "recompense fruition". A person gains a pure carnal body and performs what is pure in body, mouth, and mind. This person says: "I am harvesting the fruition of recompense." Such fruition has two causes, which are: 1) near, and 2) far-out. By the near is meant what is done with body, mouth, and mind; by the far-out cause is meant the purity of body, mouth, and mind in the past. This is what we call the fruition of recompense. "We say "of segregation", which is Nirvana. A person segregates his self from all defilements. All good actions are the cause of Nirvana. Also, there are two kinds, which are: 1) near cause, and 2) far-out cause. By near cause is meant the gate of the three emancipations [i.e. the samadhis of voidness, formlessness, and desirelessness]; by the far-out cause we mean the good actions which the person has practised in innumerable worlds. "O good man! The world speaks of: 1) cause by birth and 2) cause by revealing. The case is thus. It is the same with the fleeing away from the world, too. And we speak at times of cause by birth, and also of cause by revealing. "O good man! The gate of the three emancipations has 37 chapters. These turn out to be - as regards all defilements - the cause of birthless life and the revealing cause for Nirvana. O good man! When one comes away from defilement, one can clearly see Nirvana. Hence, what there is is the revealing cause and not cause by birth. "O good man! You ask what a sramana is and what the samana fruition. O good man! The sramana is the Eightfold Right Path. The fruition of the sramana is that we follow the Way and eternally do away with greed, ill-will, ignorance, etc. This is the sramana and the fruition of the sramana." Bodhisattva Kasyapa said: "Why do we call the Eightfold Right Path sramana?" "O good man! "Srama", the world says, means "to lack", and "na" is "way". Such a way cuts off all that is lacking. That is why we call the Eightfold Right Path "sramana". Since, as a result of this, one gains the fruition, we say "fruition of the sramana". "O good man! And it is also as in the case where there is in the world a person who loves quietude, when we say that such a one is a sramana. Thus is it also with the Way. It causes any who practise the Way to do away with the evil way of life of the body, mouth, and mind, and to gain quietude. That is why we say sramana. "O good man! The low-grade person of the world becomes the top-grade. This is a sramana. With the Way, too, things are thus. As it truly makes the low-grade person into the top, we say sramana. "O good man! If an arhat practises this Way, he gains the fruition of the sramana. And thus he reaches the other shore. The fruition of an arhat is none other than the five-part Dharma body of no-more-learning, which comprises the moral precepts, samadhi, Wisdom, Emancipation, and the intellectual insight [generated] by Emancipation. Through these five [factors], the person reaches the other shore. Hence, the arrival at the other shore. When he gains the other shore, he says to himself: "My life is now completed, pure actions [have already been] performed, what ought to have been done has been done, [and] I now no more gain [i.e. get reborn into] any [samsaric] existence." "O good man! As this arhat has now eternally cut off the causal relations of birth in the Three Times, he says: "My life is now completed." "Also, as he has indeed done away with the body of the five skandhas of the three worlds, he says: "My life is already completed." "And as he now leaves the stage of learning, he says that he is now standing. And as he has now gained what he once desired to arrive at, he says that he has attained all. Having practised the Way and gained the fruition, he says: "Already accomplished". As he has gained the knowledge of all-extinction and the knowledge of birthlessness, he says that he has done away with all bondage. Thus we say that the arhat now attains the other shore. It is the same with the pratyekabuddha, too. As the Bodhisattvas and the Buddha are perfect and accomplished in the six paramitas, they are called those who have "arrived at the other shore". When the Buddha and the Bodhisattvas have attained unsurpassed Enlightenment, we say that they are perfect in the six paramitas. Why? Because they are now harvesting the fruit of the six paramitas. As there is the arriving at the fruition, we say "perfect". "O good man! These seven beings do not adjust their body, do not uphold the precepts, do not cultivate their mind and Wisdom. As they do not uphold well the four things, they commit the five deadly sins, cut off the root of good, commit the five grave offences, and speak ill of the Buddha, Dharma and Sangha. Hence, we say that they sink down deeply. "O good man! If any of the seven beings associates with a good teacher of the Way, and with the sincerest mind gives ear to the Wonderful Dharma of the Tathagata, bethinks well within himself, lives in accordance with Dharma, and practises, with his best efforts, the body, precepts, mind, and Wisdom, such a person can indeed cross the river of birth and death and reach the other shore. "If a person says: "Even the icchantika gains unsurpassed Bodhi" - this is defiled clinging; if he says, "not", this is what is false. "O good man! Of these seven beings, there can be one who possesses the seven qualities in his one person or each of the seven may possess one each. "O good man! If a person thinks and speaks differently in mind and mouth, and says: "The icchantika gains unsurpassed Bodhi", know that such a person slanders the Buddha, Dharma and Sangha. If a person thinks and speaks differently, and says: "The icchantika does not gain unsurpassed Bodhi", such a person also slanders the Buddha, Dharma and Sangha. "O good man! If a person says: "The Noble Eightfold Path is what common mortals gain", such a person, too, slanders the Buddha, Dharma and Sangha. If a person says: "The Noble Eightfold Path is not gained by any common mortal", such a one, too, slanders the Buddha, Dharma and Sangha. O good man! If a person says: "All beings definitely possess or do not possess definitely the Buddha-Nature", such a person also slanders the Buddha, Dharma and Sangha. "O good man! That is why I say in a sutra: "There are two kinds of people who slander the Buddha, Dharma and Sangha." These are: 1) those who do not believe and speak with an angry mind, and 2) those who, though they believe, do not gain the meaning. "O good man! If a person does not possess faith and Wisdom, such a person augments his ignorance. If a person possesses Wisdom, but not faith, such a person increases distorted views. O good man! A person who has no faith says, out of an angry mind: "There cannot be any Buddha, Dharma and Sangha." "If a person should believe, but have no Wisdom, such a person will understand things in an inverted way and cause those who give ear to sermons to slander the Buddha, Dharma and Sangha. O good man! For this reason, I say that one who has no faith and who has an angry mind, and one who has faith but no Wisdom, slanders the Buddha, Dharma and Sangha. Thus do I say. "O good man! If a person says: "The icchantika, not yet having arrived at Wonderful Dharma, attains unsurpassed Bodhi", such a person well slanders the Buddha, Dharma and Sangha. If a person says: "The icchantika abandons the state of the icchantika and attains the unsurpassed body in a different body", such a person, too, may be said to slander the Buddha, Dharma and Sangha. Also a person may say: "The icchantika may well gain the root of good, continue to possess it, and may well attain unsurpassed Bodhi. Hence, the icchantika attains unsurpassed Bodhi." Know that such a person does not slander the Three Treasures. "O good man! A person may say that all definitely have the Buddha-Nature, that the Eternal, Bliss, the Self, and the Pure are not what have been made or what have been born, that only due to defilement, people cannot see [them]. Know that this person slanders the Buddha, Dharma and Sangha. If a person says that all beings do not possess the Buddha-Nature, as in the case of the horns of a hare, that all comes about by expediency, and that they are what was not but now are, or what once was but now are not, know that this person slanders the Buddha, Dharma and Sangha. If a person says: "The Buddha-Nature of beings does not exist like the Void, nor is it something that is not [i.e. something that does not exist], as with the horns of a hare. Why so? For the Void is eternal, and there is no such thing in the world as the horns of a hare. Hence, we can say either "is" or "is-not". As it is an "is", it breaks the horns of the hare [i.e. it cannot be likened to the non-existent horns of a hare], and as it is empty, it indeed breaks the Void." Any person who speaks thus does not slander the Three Treasures. "O good man! The Buddha-Nature is not a thing, not ten things, not 100 things, not 1,000 things, and not 10,000 things. When unsurpassed Bodhi has not yet been attained, all of good and not good, and all that is neutral, can fall into the category of the Buddha-Nature. The Tathagata at times speaks of the fruition in the state of cause or at times of the cause in the state of fruition. This is what we call the Tathagata's words which he speaks following his own will. Because of the things spoken of from the Tathagata's own free will, we call him "Tathagata". Due to the fact that [his words are] spoken from his free will, we say "arhat". Due to the fact that [his words are] spoken from his own free will, we say "samyaksambuddha" [i.e. Fully Awakened One]." Bodhisattva Kasyapa said to the Buddha: "O World-Honoured One! You, the Buddha, say: "The Buddha-Nature of the being is like the Void." Why do you say the "Void"? "O good man! The nature of the Void is not past, future or present. It is the same with the Buddha-Nature, too. O good man! The Void is not the past. Why not? Because it is but what is now. If anything exists in the present, we may well speak of the past. As there is no present to speak of, there cannot be any past to speak of. And also, there is no present to speak of. Why not? Because there is nothing as the future. If there is something as the future, one may well speak of the present. As there is no future, there is no present. And also, there is no future. Why not? For there is nothing as the present or past. If there are the present and past, there can be the future. As there are no past and present, there is no future. Because of this, the nature of the Void does not fall into the category of the Three Times. "O good man! There is no Void. On account of this, there are no Three Times. It is not that as there are the Three Times, there are no Three Times. For the flower of the Void does not exist. This is as in the case in which there are no Three Times. The case is thus. The same is the case with the Void, too. As this is no "is", there cannot be the Three Times. "O good man! If there is nothing, this is the Void. The same is the case with the Buddha-Nature, too. O good man! As the Void is empty, it does not fall into the category of the Three Times. As the Buddha-Nature is Eternal, it is not within the category of the Three Times. "O good man! As the Tathagata

has gained unsurpassed Bodhi, the Buddha-Nature that he possesses and all the Buddhist teachings turn out to be [i.e. come into being], there being no change. Hence, no Three Times. This is as in the case of the Void. "O good man! As the Void is nothing that can be represented, it is neither "in" nor "out". As the Buddha-Nature is Eternal, there is no "in" or "out". That is why I say that the Buddha-Nature is like the Void."

"O good man! In the world, when there is no obstruction, we speak of voidness. As the Tathagata has gained unsurpassed Enlightenment, he sees nothing that obstructs within Buddha-Dharma. That is why I say that the Buddha-Nature is like the Void. For this reason do I say: "The Buddha-Nature is like the Void." "Bodhisattva Kasyapa said to the Buddha: "O World-Honoured One! You say that the Tathagata, the Buddha-Nature, and Nirvana do not fall into the category of the Three Times. And you state that it [i.e. Tathagata, Buddha-Nature and Nirvana] is "is". The Void also does not fall into the category of the Three Times. Why cannot we call it "is"? The Buddha said: "O good man! Due to non-Nirvana, we speak of Nirvana. Due to non-Tathagata, we speak of the Tathagata. Due to non-Buddha-Nature, we speak of the Buddha-Nature. "Why do we say "non-Nirvana"? All defilements are grounded on what is created. To crush out such created things of defilement, we say Nirvana. "Non-Tathagata" refers to the icchantika up to the pratyekabuddha. In order to crush out those from the icchantika up to the pratyekabuddha, we say Tathagata. We say "non-Buddha-Nature". This refers to all bulwarks, gravel, stones, and non-sentient things. One departs from all such non-sentient things. And this is the Buddha-Nature. "O good man! In all the world, there is nothing that competes with the Void which is non-Void." Bodhisattva Kasyapa said to the Buddha: "O World-Honoured One! In the world, we have no negative apposites [opposites, antonyms] of the four great elements. Yet we say that there are the four great elements. Why can we not call the appositelessness of the Void something that exists?" The Buddha said: "O good man! You may say that Nirvana does not fall within the category of the Three Times and so is Void. But this is not so. Why not? "Nirvana is an existence, something visible, that which is veritable, matter, the foot-print, the sentence and the word, that which is, characteristics, by-cause, the refuge which one takes, quietude, light, peace, and the other shore". That is why we can indeed say that it does not come within the category of the Three Times. With the nature of the Void, there is nothing as such [i.e. nothing such as this]. That is why we say "not-is". Should there be anything other than this, we could well say that it falls into the category of the Three Times. If Voidness is a thing of the "is", it cannot be other than be in the category of the Three Times. O good man! The people of the world speak of voidness and speak of it as non-matter, as something that has no apposite [opposite], and is invisible. The case is thus. If it is not matter, something with no apposite, and invisible, it must be caitasika. If the Voidness is of the category of caitasika, it cannot be other than within the category of caitasika. If it is of the category of the Three Times, it cannot be other than the four groups [skandhas]. Therefore, other than the four groups, there can be no Voidness. "Also, next, O good man! All tirthikas say that the Void is light. If light, it is matter. If the Void is matter, it is non-eternal. If non-eternal, it comes within the category of the Three Times. How can the tirthikas say that it is not of the Three Times? If it is of the Three Times, it is not the Void. And how can one say that the Void is non-eternal? "O good man! And some say that the Void is a place where one lives. If it is a place where one lives, it is matter. And all places are non-sentient and fall into the category of the Three Times. How could the Void not be Eternal and not fall into the category of the Three Times? If any place can be spoken of, we may know that there cannot exist the Void [there]. "Also, some people say that the Void is gradual. If gradual, it can be a caitasika. If countable, it falls within the category of the Three Times. If of the Three Times, how can it be Eternal? "O good man! Also, some people say: "Now, the Void is none other than these three things: 1) Void, 2) real, and 3) void-real." If we say that this is the Void, we can know that the Void is non-eternal. Why? Because it has no actual place to exist. If it is said that it really is this, we can know that the Void is non-eternal. Why? Because it is not empty. If we say "void-real", we can know that the Void is non-eternal. Why? Because it is not empty. If we say void-real, we can know that the Void is also non-eternal. Why? Because nothing can exist in two places. Hence, the Void is empty. "O good man! The

people of the world may say: "Anything of the world where there is no hindrance [obstacle] is the Void." A place where there is nothing to hinder is an all-over "is". How can it be any partial existence? If it is an all-over "is", we can know that there is no Void in other places. If partial, this is a thing countable. If countable, it is non-eternal. "O good man! A person may say: "The Void co-exists with the "unobstructed "is". Or someone might say: "The Void exists within a thing. It is like fruit within a vessel." Neither is the case. There are three kinds of co-existence, namely: 1) differently made things become one, as in the case of flying birds which gather together in a tree; 2) two things common to each other become one, as in the case of two sheep which come into contact; 3) co-existing of the two pairs of those that meet to exist in one place. We say "different things meet". Of difference, there are two kinds. One is a "thing", and the other is the Void. If Voidness joins the thing, this Voidness must be non-eternal. If a thing joins with the Void, the thing does not become one-sided. If there is nothing that is one-sided, it again is non-eternal. "A person may say: "The Void is eternal; and its nature is immovable. This joins with what moves." But this is not so. Why not? If the Void is eternal, matter, too, must be eternal. If matter is non-eternal, the Void, too, must be non-eternal. A person may say: "The Void, too, is both eternal and non-eternal." This does not accord with reason. A person may say that things of common lot meet. The case is not so. Why not? The Void is all-pervading. If it joins with what is made, what is made must also become all-pervading. If it pervades, all must be pervading. If all is all-pervading, all can be joined as one. We cannot say that there can exist both joining and non-joining. A person may say: "That which has once joined joins again, as in the case of two fingers that meet." But this is not so. Why not? Joining cannot forego. Joining comes about later. If what did not exist before comes about, this is nothing but what is non-eternal. Hence, we cannot say: "The Void is that which was already joined [and which now] joins." What obtains in the world is that which did not exist before but later comes about. This is as with a thing which has no eternity. If the Void sits on a thing like fruit in a vessel and if it is thus, it must also be non-eternal. A person may say that if the Void sits on a thing, it is like fruit in a vessel. But this is not so. Why not? Where could the Void in question exist, not having the vessel at hand? If there is any place [for it] to exist, the Void would have to be many. If many, how could one say eternal, one, and all-pervading? If the Void exists in places outside of the Void, then a thing could well subsist without the Void. So, one knows that there cannot be such a thing as the Void. "O good man! If a person says: "The place which one can point out is Void", know that the Void is what is non-eternal. Why? We have four directions to point in. If there are the four quarters, know that the Void, too, must possess the four directions. All that is eternal has no direction to point to. To have directions means that the Void, accordingly, is non-eternal. If non-eternal, it is not away from the five skandhas. If one were to say that by all means there is parting from the five skandhas, there is no place to exist. O good man! If anything exists by causal relations, we can know that such a thing is non-eternal. O good man! For example, all beings and trees stand on the ground. As the ground is non-eternal, what stands on the ground is accordingly non-eternal. "O good man! The earth stands on water. As water is non-eternal, the earth, too, is non-eternal. Water hangs on the wind, and as the wind is non-eternal, water, too, is non-eternal. The wind rests on the Void, and as the Void is non-eternal, the wind, too, is non-eternal. If it is non-eternal, how can we say: "The Void is eternal and it fills the Void"? As the Void is empty, it has no past, future or present. As the horns of a hare are no thing, they have no past, future or present. Things are thus. So I say: "As the Buddha-Nature is eternal, it does not come within the category of the Three Times. As the Void is Void, it does not come within the category of the Three Times." "O good man! I never quarrel with the world. Why not? If worldly knowledge says "is", I say "is"; if worldly knowledge says "not-is", I, too, say "not-is"." Bodhisattva Kasyapa said: "O World-Honoured One! How many things does a Bodhisattva-mahasattva require to be perfect, so that he does not quarrel with the world and does not get wetted and defiled by what obtains in the world?" The Buddha said: "The Bodhisattva-mahasattva is perfect in ten things and does not quarrel with the world and does not get wetted and defiled by what obtains in the world. What are the ten? These are: 1) faith, 2) upholding of the precepts, 3) befriending a good friend, 4) bethinking well within one's own self, 5) effort, 6) right remembrance, 7) Wisdom, 8) right words, 9)caring

for Wonderful Dharma, and 10) pitying all beings. O good man! As the Bodhisattvamahasattva is perfect in [these] ten things, he does not quarrel with the world and does not get wetted and defiled by what obtains in the world, as in the case of the utpala." Bodhisattva Kasyapa said to the Buddha: "O World-Honoured One! You, the Buddha, say that one says "is" if worldly knowledge says "is", and if worldly knowledge says "not-is", one says "not-is. But what are the "is" and "not-is" of worldly knowledge?" The Buddha said: "O good man! This is as when the world says: "Matter is non-eternal, suffering, void, and non-Self", and things go thus down to consciousness. O good man! This is what worldly knowledge says is an "is", and I, too, say that this is an "is". O good man! Worldly knowledge says that matter has nothing of the Eternal, Bliss, Self, and the Pure. So does it say about feeling, perception, volition, and consciousness. O good man! This is where worldly knowledge says "not-is". I, too, say "not-is". Bodhisattva Kasyapa said to the Buddha: "O World-Honoured One! Those who are wise are all Bodhisattvas and holy persons. Why is it that when worldly knowledge says that matter is non-eternal, suffering, void, and non-Self, you the Tathagata say that the carnal body of the Buddha is Eternal and Unchanging? What the wise of the world say has no law [nothing of Dharma]. Why does the Tathagta say "is"? And how can you say that you do not quarrel with the world and that you do not get wetted and defiled by worldly things? The Tathagata is already away from the three kinds of inversion, namely the inversions of mental image, mind, and world-views. Where the Buddha should be saying that matter really is non-eternal, you now say it is eternal. How can you say that you part far from the inversions and that you do not quarrel with the world?" The Buddha said: "O good man! The matter [i.e. physical form, "rupa"] of common mortals arises out of defilement. Hence I say that worldly knowledge and matter are non-eternal, suffering, void, and non-Self. The matter of the Tathagata departs from defilement. So, I say Eternal and Unchanging." Bodhisattva Kasyapa said: "O World-Honoured One! How does matter arise out of defilement?" "O good man! There are three kinds of defilement, which are the leakings ["asravas", negative outflows] of: 1) desire, 2) the "is", and 3) ignorance. One who is wise should meditate on the three sins that arise out of these three leakings.

Why? When one realises the sin, one segregates one's self from it. For example, this is as with a doctor who first sees, who first feels the pulse, sees where the illness resides, and then dispenses medicine. O good man! A man takes a blind person into a thorny bush and abandons him there and comes home. Then, the blind person finds it difficult to get out. Even if he gets out, his body will be full of wounds. It is the same with the common mortals of the world, too. If unable to see the ills of the three defilements, the person adapts to them and acts. The ills [once] seen, one segregates one's self from them. The karmic returns seen through, one may well have to suffer from the returns of sins, but one suffers little. "O good man! There are four kinds of people. One is the person who works hard when acting, but light returns come when he has to undergo such. Another is one whose work is light when [he is] doing [it], but the return is heavy. The third is the person who works hard at the time of acting and at the time when the return comes. The fourth is the person whose work is light during the doing and [also] when the return comes. O good man! If one sees through [i.e. realises] the ills of defilement, one's work is light both at the time of its doing and on receiving the karmic return. "O good man! One who has Wisdom thinks: "I must part from such defilements and I must not do such low-grade things that are evil. Why not? Because I cannot [otherwise] remove myself from the karmic returns of hell, hungry ghosts, animals, humans and gods. By practising the Way, I shall, through this power, do away with all such sufferings." Thinking thus, what the person performs is light as regards greed, ill-will, and ignorance. Greed, ill-will and ignorance being light, the person is happy. He thinks further: "I now thus, through the power of practising the Way, part from evil things and can now draw near to Wonderful Dharma. Thus I gain the Right Way. I shall now make effort and increase it." Now, this person makes away with all the innumerable evil defilements and is now removed from the returns of hell, hungry pretas, animals, and those of humans and gods. Hence, I say in my sutras: "One should meditate on all the defilements and on the causes of the defilements." Why? Should any wise person meditate on the defilements, but not on the cause of the defilements, he will not be able to do away with the defilements. Why? Because any wise person can see what will arise from the cause of

the defilements. I am now severed from the cause, and the defilements do not come about. "O good man! This is as in the case of a doctor. Once he removes the cause, illness will not raise its head any more. It is the same with the wise person who extirpates the cause of defilement. One who is wise should first meditate on the cause and, later, on the result. He sees that good results come from a good cause, and evil from what is evil. Meditating on the result which comes about, he does away with the cause. When he has meditated on the result that will come about, he should further meditate on the lightness and heaviness of the defilements. Having meditated on lightness and heaviness, he first does away with what is heavy. When the heavy has been done away with, what is light will go away by itself. "O good man! If the wise person realises the defilements, the cause of the defilements, the result of the defilements, and the lightness and heaviness of the defilements, that person will make effort on the Way, not cease, and not feel remorse. Such a person will associate with a good friend and give ear to Dharma with the sincerest mind. This is all to make away with the defilements. "O good man! When a sick person knows that his illness is slight and that it can easily be cured, he will not feel unhappy when a bitter medicine is prescribed to him, and he will take it. It is the same with the wise man, too. He makes effort, practises the Holy Way, is happy, does not cease and feels no regret. "O good man! If a person comes to know of defilement, the cause of defilement, the result of defilement, the lightness and heaviness of defilement, he will make effort and eliminate defilement and practise the Way; with such a person, "matter" [physical form] does not come about, nor do feeling, perception, volition, and consciousness. If a person does not see defilement, the cause of defilement, the result of defilement, the lightness and heaviness of defilement, and does not make effort and practise the Way, for such a person matter, feeling, perception, volition, and consciousness will come about. "O good man! "He" "who sees defilement, the cause of defilement, the result of defilement, the lightness and heaviness of defilement, and who practises the Way is the Tathagata. Because of this, the body "["rupa"]" of the Tathagata is Eternal. So is it with "[his]" feeling, perception, volition, and consciousness, which are all Eternal.

Chapter Forty-Three: On Bodhisattva Kasyapa 4

[The Buddha said:] "O good man! A person who does not know defilement, the cause of defilement, the result of defilement, the lightness and heaviness of defilement, and who does not practise the Way is a common mortal. So, the material form of the common mortal is non-eternal, and all such as [his] feeling, perception, and consciousness are non-eternal. "O good man! The wise of the world, all holy persons, the Bodhisattvas, and all Buddhas speak of these two significations. I, too, speak thus. That is why I say: "I do not quarrel with the wise of the world. I am not made wet and defiled by what obtains in the world." Bodhisattva Kasyapa said to the Buddha: "O World-Honoured One! The Buddha speaks about the defilements of the three existences. What are the defilements of desire, existence, and ignorance?"

The Buddha said: "O good man! We speak of the defilement of desire, which is the defilement of desire that comes about due to the internal sensing of evil which raises its head, initiated by external causal relations. That is why, in days past, at Rajagriha, I said to Ananda: "Accept now the gatha [verse] which the woman speaks. This gatha is what the Buddhas of the past spoke. For this reason, I say that the sensing of evil within and the causal relations that work upon one from without are desire. This is the defilement of desire." "The defilements are all those evil things that are mental in the worlds of form and non-form and the causal relations that work upon one from without, excepting all the causal relations that work upon one from without and the mental sensings of the world of desire. We call these defilements. "We speak of the defilements of illusion. When one does not know one's own self and what belongs to self, and when one fails to see the difference between things in and out, we say that there are the defilements of ignorance. "O good man! Ignorance is the root of all defilements. Why? All beings, due to the causal relations of ignorance, call forth all imaginings and forms in the field of the five skandhas, the 12 spheres, and the 18 realms [of sense]. These are inverted notions as regards image, mind, and world-view. From these, all defilements arise. Therefore, I state in the 12 types of sutra: "Ignorance is the cause of greed,

the cause of ill-will, and the cause of ignorance." Bodhisattva Kasyapa said: "O World-Honoured One! The Tathagata once said in the 12 types of sutra: "The causal relations of thinking of non-good things evokes greed, ill-will, and ignorance." Why do you now say "ignorance"? "O good man! Such things become the cause and the result to one another and grow. The thinking of non-good calls forth ignorance, and the causal relation of ignorance calls forth the thinking of non-good. O good man! All that increases illusions is the causal relation of illusions. Any action that befriends the causal relation of illusion is called the non-good thinking of ignorance. A seed calls forth a bud. This seed is the near cause; the four great elements are the far cause. The same is the case with illusion." Bodhisattva Kasyapa said to the Buddha: "You the Buddha say that ignorance is a defilement. How can you say that ignorance calls forth all defilements?" The Buddha said: "O good man! I speak of the defilements of ignorance. This refers to internal ignorance. If all defilements come about from ignorance, this is nothing but the cause of "in" and "out". If ignorance is a defilement, this is an internal inversion, which relates to the ignorance of the non-eternal, suffering, voidness, and the non-Self. If ignorance is stated to be the causal relation of all illusions, this will mean that one does not know the self and what belongs to the self, which concern the outer relations. If reference is made to the defilements of ignorance, this is none but beginninglessness and endlessness. From ignorance arise the five skandhas, the 18 realms, and the 12 spheres." Bodhisattva Kasyapa said to the Buddha: "O World-Honoured One! You the Buddha say: "A person who has Wisdom knows the cause of the defilements." How can you say that such a person knows the cause of illusion?" "O good man! One who is wise will meditate and try to know why this illusion comes about, when this illusion comes about, when one lives with whom, at what place one gains this, by seeing what, in whose house, on receiving what bedding, food and drink, clothing, and medicine. Through what causal relations does the low come up to be the middle, the middle to be the top, the low actions to be the middle ones, and the middle ones to be those of the top? When the Bodhisattva-mahasattva thinks in this way, he severs the illusions that he has had from birth. As he thinks in this way, this shuts out the illusions that have not yet arisen and causes them not to arise, and the illusions that have already arisen are annihilated. That is why I say in my sutra: "A person who has Wisdom should meditate on the cause of illusion." Bodhisattva Kasyapa said to the Buddha: "O World-Honoured One! Whatever various kinds of illusion does the single body of a being call forth?" The Buddha said: "O good man! A single container holds within itself various seeds. When water and rain come, each shoots forth buds. It is the same with beings. Due to the causal relations of craving, various kinds of illusion come about." Bodhisattva Kasyapa said: "O World-Honoured One! How does a wise man meditate on the fruition of karma?" "O good man! A person who is wise should think: "The causal relations of all defilements truly call forth [rebirth in the realms of] hell, hungry pretas [ghosts], and animals. The causal relations of this defilement gain a person the body of a human or a god. These are non-eternal, suffering, Void, and non-Self. In this container of the carnal body, we gain three sufferings and three noneternals. The causal relation of this defilement truly causes beings to commit the five deadly sins[i.e. patricide, matricide, killing of an arhat, causing dissension within the Sangha, and causing blood to flow from the Buddha's body.], as a result of which man receives evil returns, and as a result of which man cuts off the seed of good, performs the four grave offences [i.e. killing, stealing, unlawful lust, and lying], and slanders the Three Treasures." A wise person should meditate and think: "I must not gain such a body and call forth such defilements and suffer from such evil consequences." Bodhisattva Kasyapa said: "You say that there are undefiled results, and the wise cut themselves off from karmic results. Does the undefiled fruition lie in what we cut off or not? All those who gain the Way gain the undefiled fruitions. If the wise seek the undefiled fruition, why does the Buddha say that all the wise must segregate themselves from fruitions? If cut off, how could there be all such holy persons?" "O good man! The Tathagata, at times, speaks of the result in the cause. This is as when people of the world say that earth is a pot or a thread is clothing. This is speaking of the result while still in the stage of the cause. We say that the cause is stated at the stage of the result. This is as when a cow arises out of watery grass and a man out of food. I, too, speak of the result in the cause. I have already stated in the sutras: "By my mind, I gain the body of Brahma." This is to speak of the result in the cause. I speak about the result in the cause. I speak of the cause in the stage of the result. This is as in: "These six spheres arise out of past karma." This is where I speak of the cause at the stage of the result. "O good man! All holy persons, truth to tell, have no [sic!] undefiled results. All the results from practising the Way of the holy persons do not call forth any defilements. So we speak of "undefiled results". "O good man! A person who has Wisdom sees things thus, and he ulltimately does away with the results of defilement. O good man! A wise man sees things thus and practises the Holy Way, so as to cut off the results of defilement. The Holy Way is none other than the Void, formlessness, and desirelessness. Having practised this Way, the person indeed cuts off the results of defilement."

Chapter Forty-Four: On Bodhisattva Kasyapa 5

Bodhisattva Kasyapa said to the Buddha: "All beings reap the karmic fruit of defilement. Defilement is evil. The defilement that arises out of evil defilement is [also] evil. If so, there are two kinds. One is the "cause", and the other the "result". As the cause is evil, so the result is evil. As the fruition is evil, the seed is evil. This is as with the nimba fruit. As the seed is bitter, the flower, fruit, stem, and leaves are all bitter. This is as with the seed of a poisonous tree, where as the seed is poisonous, the fruit, too, is poisonous. The cause is the being and the result is the being. The cause is defilement, and the result is also defilement. The cause and the result of defilement are beings, and beings are the cause and result of defilement. If this is indeed the inference, why did the Tathagata employ the parable of the grass in the Himalayas which is poisonous and [also] an all-wonderful medicine"? If we say that defilement is the being and the being defilement, how can we say that there is a wonderful medicine in the body of the being?" The Buddha said: "Well said, well said, O good man! Innumerable beings have the same doubt. You now do well to ask for an answer. I shall make this point clear too. Listen well, listen well! Think well about this. I shall now clearly state and explain this to you. "O good man! I speak of the Himalayas in my parable, alluding therein to beings. The poisonous grass refers to defilement, and the all-wonderful medicine refers to pure deeds. O good man! When beings practise such pure deeds, we say that they possess an all-wonderful medicine within." Bodhisattva Kasyapa said to the Buddha: "O World-Honoured One! How does a being possess pure deeds?" "O good man! In the world, we see that a seed brings forth fruit. Now, there are cases where this seed, at times, becomes the cause of the fruit. Or there are cases where it does not. It can only be called "seed" and "fruit" when things proceed thus. When things do not proceed thus, we only say "fruit", and not "seed". It is the same with beings. All have two kinds [of deed]. With the one, it is the result of defilement, and also the cause of defilement. With the other, it is the fruit of defilement, but not the cause of defilement. When it is the fruit of defilement, but not the cause of defilement, we call this a "pure deed". O good man! Beings meditate on feeling and come to

know that this is the near cause of all defilements. Because of feeling, a person cannot cut off all the defilements that are inside and out. All defilements, too, are unable to get out of the prison house of the three worlds. Beings, due to feeling, adhere to self and what belongs to self and gain the inversions of mind, image, and views of life. Hence, beings must first meditate on feeling. Such feeling becomes the near-cause of all phases of craving. For this reason, the wise, when they desire to extirpate craving, must first meditate on feeling. "O good man! All the good and evil of beings that come forth from the 12 links of interdependence take their rise from feeling. That is why I said to Ananda: "All the good and evil deeds of all beings take their rise at the time of feeling." That is why a person who possesses Wisdom must first meditate on feeling. When this meditation is done, the person then thinks: "Through what causal relations does such a feeling come about? If from causal relations, from what do such causal relations come about? If by non-cause, why is it that such a non-cause does not call forth non-feeling?" He also thinks: "This feeling does not come about through the works of Mahesvara, nor through man, nor by motes, season, image, nature, self, power from without; nor does it come about through the combined working of one's own self and others; nor is it through non-cause. This feeling comes about through combined causal relations. The causal relations are at once craving. It is not that there is craving in this combination, nor is it that there is no craving. It is not that there is no feeling. For this reason, I truly cut off this harmonisation [conjoining]. By cutting off this harmonisation, no feeling comes about." "O good man! The cause [once] thought about, the wise person now meditates on the fruition of karma: "Beings, through feeling, suffer from the innumerable sorrows of hell, hungry pretas, and animals down to the three realms. Because of the causal relations of feeling, there is no Eternal and no Bliss. The person thus extirpates the root of good and through this, the person gains emancipation." When one thus meditates, there exists no cause of feeling. "How can we say that it does not call forth the cause of feeling? This is the discrimination of feeling. What feeling becomes the cause of craving and what craving is the cause of feeling? "O good man! As beings thoroughly meditate on the cause of craving, they truly segregate themselves from self and what belongs to self. O good man! If one thoroughly meditates thus, one will indeed come to see where craving and feeling end. That is to say that one sees craving, and feeling goes off somewhat. Know that there ultimately will be an end. Then, one comes to have faith in Emancipation. As one gains faith, one comes to see from where Emancipation arises. One sees that this arises from the Eightfold Right Path, and one learns to practise. "What is the Eightfold Right Path? In this are the three feelings: 1) suffering, 2) joy, and 3) non-suffering and non-joy. These three increase one's body and mind. Why is there increase? This arises from touch ["sparsa"]. Touch has three phases, which are: 1) touch of ignorance, 2) touch of brightness, and 3) touch of non-brightness and non-ignorance. The touch of brightness is the Eightfold Right Path. The other two touches increase body and mind and the three feelings. That is why I say that one must extirpate the two touches. When one extirpates the touch of the causal relations, one no longer gains the three feelings. "O good man! Such feeling is the cause and also the result. One who is wise must meditate on the cause-result. What is the cause? From feeling one gains craving. This is the cause. What is the result? It arises from touch. Hence, the result. So, this feeling is the cause-result. The wise person thus meditates on feeling and craving. When one harvests the karmic results, this we call craving. A wise person meditates on craving in two ways, namely: 1) mixed eating and 2) non-eating. The craving for mixed eating causes birth, old age, illness, and death, and all other existences. The craving of non-eating cuts off birth, old age, illness, and death, and all other existences, and devours but the undefiled Way. A wise person will think: "Should I gain craving for mixed food, I shall not be able to do away with birth, old age, illness, and death. Though I now devour the undefiled Way, if I do not make away with the cause of feeling, I shall not be able to gain the fruition of the undefiled Way. So I must make away with this touch. Touch once cut off, feeling will die away by itself. Feeling once done away with, craving, too, dies away by itself. This is the Eightfold Right Path." "O good man! If a person meditates thus, there can be the all-wonderful medicine in the body of poison, just as in the

Himalayas there is the all-wonderful medicineal herb, although there is also poisonous grass, too. O good man! One thus receives a karmic result through defilement. But this karmic result does not further become a cause of [subsequent] defilement. This is pure action. "Also, next, O good man! A wise person meditates and reflects on why the pair, feeling and touch, come about, and he sees that they come about through image. How? Beings see material form and do not gain desire. And also at the time of feeling, no desire comes about. If one should gain an inverted image regarding material form and say that material form is the Eternal, Bliss, Self, and the Pure, and that there can be no change, one, through this inversion, will gain greed, ill-will, and ignorance. So the wise must meditate on image. "How does one mediate on image? One should think that all beings have not yet gained the Right Way and that they all have inverted images. What is an inverted image? Being in what is not Eternal, a person has an image of [i.e. sees this as] the Eternal; in non-Bliss, a person has an image of Bliss; being in what is not Pure, he has an image of what is Pure; being in what is empty, he has an image of the Self; being in what is not man or female, big or small, day or night, month or year, clothing, house, or bedding, he has images of man and female, down to bedding. "Of this image, there are three kinds, namely: 1) small, 2) big, and 3) boundless. Through a small causal relation, one gains a small image; through a big causal relation, one gains a big image; through an unbounded causal relation, one gains an unlimited image. Also, there is a small image, which refers to one who has not yet gained samadhi. Also, there is a big image, which relates to one who has already gained samadhi. Also, there is an [unbounded] image, which relates to the ten reciprocal all-enterings ["dasa-krtsnayatana"]. Also, there is a small image, which relates to all the images of the world of desire. Also, there is a big image, which corresponds to all the images of the world of form. Also, there is an unbounded number of images, which refers to all the images of the world of formlessness. When the three phases of image die away, feeling by itself dies away. When the image and feeling go away, we say "Emancipation". Bodhisattva Kasyapa said: "O World-Honoured One! When all phases of things die away, we gain Emancipation. Why do you, Tathagata, say that the extinction of image and feeling is

Emancipation?" The Buddha said: "O good man! The Tathagata, at times, speaks by the being, at which the one listening understands the thing; or, at times, he stands on the thing about the being , and the one listening understands what is said about the being. "What do I mean by saying that when I speak of the being, the person who is listening takes it to refer to a thing? This is as when I once said to Mahakasyapa: "O Kasyapa! When the being dies, Wonderful Dharma dies out too." This is what I mean when I say that when I speak standing on the being, the one listening takes it to refer to a thing. What do I mean by saying that when I speak, standing on dharma, about the being, the listener takes it to have been said about the being? This is as I once said to Ananda: "I do not say that I befriend all things or that I do not. If I befriend the law [Dharma], the good law [Wonderful Dharma] will weaken and the non-good will become luxuriant. One must not befriend such a law. If one befriends the law, the non-good will weaken and the good law augment. One should come near such a law." This is what I say, standing on a thing, about the being, and the one listening takes it as my speaking about a being. "O good man! The Tathagata speaks about the two extinctions of image and feeling. But he has already spoken about all that could be extirpated. When a wise person has meditated on such an image, he must next meditate on the cause of the image. "How do all the innumerable images come about? One comes to know that they come about from touch. And this touch is of two kinds, namely: 1) touch by defilement and 2) touch by Emancipation. If it arises out of ignorance, we call this "touch by defilement". What comes about from "brightness" is called "touch from Emancipation". The touch from ignorance calls forth an inverted image, and that from Emancipation calls forth a non-inverted image. When one has meditated on the cause of the image, one next meditates on the karmic result." Bodhisattva Kasyapa said to the Buddha: "The inverted image comes about from the image of defilement. All holy persons, truth to tell, possess inverted images and yet possess no defilement. How am I to understand this?" The Buddha said: "O good man! In what way does a holy person possess an unverted image?" Bodhisattva Kasyapa said: "O World-Honoured One! All holy ones, on seeing a cow, gain the image of a cow and say that this is a cow. Seeing a horse, they gain the image of a horse and say that this is a horse. The same applies to man, woman, big and small, house, vehicle, going and coming. This is an inversion." "O good man! All beings possess two kinds of image, namely: 1) the image current in the world and 2) the image from clinging. All holy people have only the image current in the world, but do not have any image from clinging. All beings gain the image of clinging, because of the meditation by evil sensing. All holy persons do not gain the image of clinging, because of [their] awakening to good. Hence, all common mortals are classed as of the inverted, whereas the holy persons are not so classed, though they may know. "Having meditated on the cause of the image, a person who is wise next meditates on the karmic results. One suffers such karmic results of the evil image in the realms of hell, hungry ghosts, and animals, and of humans and gods. As I have done away with the image of evil awakening, I have cut off ignorance and touch. So does the image go. When the image is done away with, the person also removes the karmic consequences. To cut off the cause of the image, the wise person practises the Eightfold Right Path. O good man! Any person who thus meditates is called one who practises pure deeds. "O good man! Thus do I say: "In the poisonous body of the being there is an all-wonderful medicine. Though in the Himalayas there is a poisonous [type of] grass, there is [also] an all-wonderful medicine." Also, next, O good man! One who is wise meditates on desire. Desire is colour, sound, smell, taste, and touch. O good man! Thus the Tathagata speaks of the result in the stage of cause. From these five things, desire raises its head. And it is no desire. "O good man! A person who is ignorant greedily seeks to partake of these. In these material forms, the person gains an inverted image. And this gaining of an inverted image extends down to "touch". And from the causal relation of inversion, there arises feeling. That is why I say that from this inverted image the world gains the ten images. "From the causal relation of desire, one harvests evil karmic consequences in the world. The evil is directed to parents, sramanas, and Brahmins. One does what one ought not to do, and one does this wilfully, head and foot. Thus, a person who is wise realises the fact that this causal relation of evil evokes a covetous mind. Having thus realised the cause of evil, the wise person first meditates on the cause of covetousness and then thinks about the karmic results. When there is much desire, there come forth many evil results, such as [the realms of] hell, hungry ghosts, animals, humans and gods. This is what we call realising evil results.

"If one is able to do away with the evil image, no mind of covetousness will arise. When there is no covetous mind, there arises no evil feeling. With no evil feeling, there cannot be any evil result. That is why I first do away with the evil image. The image of evil once done away with, things as such naturally die away. Hence, the wise person practises the Eightfold Right Path, in order to do away with the evil image. This is what we call "pure action". This is why we say that in the poisonous body of the being, there is an all-wonderful medicine, as in the case of the Himalayas, where, though there are poisonous grasses, there is an all-wonderful medicine, too. "Also, next, O good man! Having meditated thoroughly in this way on desire, the wise person next meditates on karma. Why? The wise person thinks: "Feeling, image, touch, and desire are defilements. Defilement truly brings forth living karma, but not harvesting karma. Such a defilement goes along with karma and is made up of two kinds: 1) living karma and 2) harvesting karma. Hence, the wise person must meditate well on karma. This karma is of three kinds: body, mouth, and mind." O good man! The pair, body and mouth, are also called karma and also the karmic result. The mind is called merely "karma", and not "result". As it is the cause of karma, we say "karma". O good man! We call the karmas of body and mouth the external karma, and the mental karma the internal. These three karmas go together with defilement. So we have two karmas, namely: 1) living karma and 2) feeling karma. "O good man! "Right karma" is mental karma. We say "temporal karma". This refers to the karmas of body and mind. Being what appears first, we say "mental karma". What arise from the mental are the bodily and oral karmas. So, what is mental is called "right". Having meditated on karma, a wise person must meditate on the cause of karma. The cause of karma is the touch of ignorance. Due to the touch of ignorance, beings see "existence". The causal relation of existence is "craving". Due to the causal relation of craving, a person performs the three actions of body, mouth, and mind. "O good man! Having meditated on the cause of karma, the wise person meditates on the karmic

result. There are four kinds of karmic result, namely: 1) black-black karmic result, 2) white-white karmic result, 3) mixed-mixed karmic result, and 4) non-black-non-white-non-black-non-white karmic result. "The black-black karmic result is such that it is defiled at the time of the action and the karmic result, too, is defiled. We say white-white karmic result, which is pure when [the deed is] being enacted, and the karmic result too is pure. We speak of a mixed-mixed karmic result, which is one [of a] mixed [nature] during [the deed's] enactment, and the karma, too, is mixed. We say non-white-non-black-non-white-non-black karmic result. This is undefiled karma." Bodhisattva Kasyapa said to the Buddha: "O World-Honoured One! You said before that the undefiled has no karmic result. Why do you now speak about the non-white-non-black of the karmic result?" The Buddha said: "O good man! There are two meanings to this. One is the result and the recompense put together, and the second is the fruition, but not the recompense. The black-black karmic result is the result, and also the recompense. When it arises out of a black cause, it is a "result"; when it becomes a cause, we say "recompense". It is the same with the pure and the mixed. The undefiled result comes out of a defiled cause. Hence, "result". When it does not become the cause of any other thing, we do not say "recompense". Bodhisattva Kasyapa said to the Buddha: "O World-Honoured One! This undefiled karma is not that which is black. Why do you not call it white?" "O good man! As there is no recompense, I do not call it white. When a cure is caused to the black, I say white. I now say: "What receives the karmic result is called black or white. As this undefiled action does not harvest any recompense, I do not call it white. I say "quietude". All such actions are definitely subject to recompense. The ten evil things are definitely subject to the realms of hell, hungry pretas, and animals. The ten good things definitely gain [one] the world of humans and gods. In the ten good things, we have the grades of: top, middle, low. Through the top causal relation, one gains hell, through the middle causal relation the animal [realm], and through the low, life in hell. Also, of a human's ten good deeds there are four kinds, namely: 1) low, 2) middle, 3) top, and 4) topmost. Through the low causal relation, one gains life in Uttarakuru; through that of the middle, Purvavideha; through the top causal relation, Godaniya; and through the topmost causal relation, life in Jambudvipa. "When this meditation is performed, the wise man thinks: "How am I to segregate myself from this karmic result?" He also thinks: "This causal relation arises out of ignorance and touch. If I do away with ignorance and touch, such a karmic result will die out and not come about. Hence, a person who is wise, in order to extirpate the causal relations of ignorance and touch, must practise the Eightfold Right Path. This is pure action." O good man! This is why I say that in the poisonous body of the being there is an all-wonderful medicine. This is as in the instance of the Himalayas, where, though there are poisonous herbs, there is a medicinal herb, too. "Also, next, O good man! Having meditated on karma and defilement, a wise man then meditates on the two karmic results that have been attained. These two karmic results are of suffering. When this suffering is known, one segregates one's self from all beings. The wise person also thinks: "The causal relation of defilement also calls forth defilement. Being the causal relation of karma, it again calls forth defilement. The causal relation of defilement again calls forth karma. The causal relation of karma calls forth suffering, and from the causal relation of suffering comes about defilement. The causal relation of defilement calls forth existence, and the causal relation of existence calls forth suffering. The causal relation of existence calls forth existence. The causal relation of existence calls forth karma, and the causal relation of karma calls forth defilement. The causal relation of defilement calls forth suffering. The causal relation of suffering calls forth suffering." "O good man! If any wise person thus meditates thoroughly, one should know that such a person truly meditates on the suffering of karma. Why? All that is stated above referring to meditation are the causal relations of birth and death of the 12 links of interdependent arising. If a person thus thinks thoroughly about the 12 links of interdependence, one may know that this person no longer creates any new karmas and thoroughly crushes out old sufferings. "O good man! A person who has Wisdom meditates on the suffering of hell. From one hell to 136 places, each hell has various types of suffering. All arise out of the causal relations of the karma of defilement. Thus does one meditate. When the meditation on hell has been completed, this leads to the meditation on the sufferings of the hungry pretas and animals. Having done this meditation, one again thinks of all the sufferings of humans and gods. All such sufferings arise from the karmas of defilement. "O good man! In the life of heaven, we do not have any of this kind of great suffering. The body is soft, delicate and smooth. [But] when one sees the five forebodings of decline, great suffering raises its head. It is as with the suffering of hell, which proceeds in the same way, all equally. "O good man! The wise meditate and think that all the sufferings of the three worlds take their rise from the causal relations of defilement. O good man! For example, a tile that has not yet been passed through heat is easy to break. It is the same with the physical body of a being, too. Gaining the body, this is now a vessel of suffering. For example, the luxuriance of the flowers and fruit of a big tree gets destroyed by birds; and piles of dried grass can easily be burnt up by a small bit of fire. It is the same with the fleshly body of the being, which easily breaks up. "O good man! If a wise person can meditate well on the eight sufferings as in holy actions , know that this person indeed segregates himself from all sufferings. "O good man! A wise person deeply meditates on the eight sufferings, and next on the cause of suffering. The cause of suffering is the ignorance of craving, which is made up of two things: 1) seeking what is bodily and 2) seeking wealth. Seeking what is bodily and seeking wealth are both sources of suffering. So one must know that the ignorance of craving is the cause of suffering. "O good man! There are two kinds of this ignorance of craving, namely: 1) inner and 2) outer. That which is inner truly moulds karma, whereas what is external augments it. Also, that which is internal indeed moulds karma, and what is external moulds the karmic result. If internal craving is done away with, karma can indeed be done away with. If external craving is cut off, the karmic fruit goes away. Internal craving moulds the suffering of the world that is to come, whereas external craving calls forth the suffering of the present life. The wise meditate on the cause of suffering, which is craving. Having meditated on the cause, they do so on the karmic result. The karmic result of suffering is "cleaving" ["upadana" - clinging to existence]. The result of craving is cleaving. The karmic result of craving is cleaving. The causal relation of this cleaving, which is inner and outer craving, calls forth the suffering of craving. "O good man! The wise must meditate and think that craving is causally related to cleaving, and cleaving is causally related to craving. If one truly extirpates this pair, craving and cleaving, there will be no more karmic action; one will no more suffer from any kind of sorrow. Hence, the wise should practise well the Eightfold Right Path and make away with all sufferings. "O good man! If any person meditates thus, this is pure action. This is where we say that beings possess an all-wonderful medicine in their carnal poisonous body and that in the Himalayas, amidst the poisonous grass, there is an all-wonderful medicinal herb." Bodhisattva Kasyapa said to the Buddha: "O World-Honoured One! What is pure action?" The Buddha said: "All things are nothing but pure action." Bodhisattva Kasyapa said: "O World-Honoured One! All things are not fixed in meaning. Why? The Tathagata calls them either good or non-good. At times, he says that such is the meditation of the four remembrances, or at times, the 12 spheres, or the good teacher of the Way, or the 12 links of interdependence, or the being, right view, wrong view, the 12 types of sutra, or the two truths; or the Tathagata now says that all things are pure actions. All in all, what do you mean by "all things"? The Buddha said: "Well said, well said, O good man! The all-wonderful Great Nirvana Sutra is the treasure-house of all dharmas. It is like the great sea, which stores up all treasures. It is the same with this Nirvana Sutra. This is the secret house which contains all the meanings of all words. "O good man! Just as Mount Sumeru is the root source of all medicines, so is this sutra the root source of the Bodhisattva precepts. "O good man! It is as with the Void, wherein rests all that exists. So is it with this sutra, which is the abode of Good Dharma. "O good man! It is like the great wind, which no one can bind or check. So is it with all Bodhisattvas who practise this sutra. No defilement or evil teaching can check or bind [them]. "O good man! It is like the diamond, which no one can destroy. So do matters stand with this sutra, which no tirthikas or men of evil notions can destroy. "O good man! It is like the sand of the river Ganges, which no one can count. So is it with the meaning of this sutra. No one can truly count it out to completion. "O good man! This sutra is the banner of the Dharma of all Buddhas, just as things so obtain with the hanging ensigns of Sakra. "O good man! This sutra is the merchant that journeys nirvana-wards, or the great guide that takes to the great sea with all merchants. "O good man! This sutra is the light of the Dharma of all Bodhisattvas, just as the light of the sun and moon truly destroy the gloom all round. "O good man! This sutra serves as the best [medicine] to all beings who are suffering from illness. It is like the all-wonderful king of medicine of Gandhamadana, which thoroughly cures all illnesses. "O good man! This sutra truly serves as a staff to the icchantika, as in the case of a weak person who can [thereby] easily support himself and stand up. "O good man! This sutra truly serves as a bridge to all evil persons, just as a bridge even allows all the evil persons of the world to pass [over it]. "O good man! This sutra truly serves as a cool shade to all those who carry on their life in the five realms, where they feel hot due to the heat of defilement, serving [them] like a parasol that protects a person well from the heat. "O good man! This sutra is the king of fearlessness, which thoroughly crushes out all the devils of defilement, acting like the lion king, who truly subdues all beasts. "O good man! This sutra is a great charmer that can thoroughly crush out all the devils of defilement, just as a charmer makes away with the mountain elf. "O good man! This sutra is like the unsurpassed frost and hail that crush out all the karmic results of birth and death, just as the hail destroys the fruit trees. "O good man! This sutra is the greatest of medicines to a person who violates sila [the moral precepts], just as the ajata can truly cure pain of the eyes. "O good man! This sutra houses all good dharmas, just like the earth, which serves as the support for all things. "O good man! This sutra is a bright mirror to all beings who violate the precepts, just like a mirror which reflects well all colours and forms. "O good man! This sutra serves as clothing for those who do not feel ashamed of what they do, just like clothing that can well cover and hide the carnal form. "O good man! This sutra serves as a great treasure-house to those who are lacking in good things, just as Gunadevi gives benefit to the poor man. "O good man! This sutra serves as the water of amrta [Immortality] for those who thirst for Dharma, just like the water of the eight tastes, which thoroughly satisfies a thirsty man. "O good man! This sutra serves as a bed of Dharma to those who have the worries of defilement, just like the bed of peace that serves the people of the world. "O good man! By means of this sutra, the Bodhisattva rises from the first stage up to the tenth. It is the cart upon which are laden jewellery, incense, flowers, and all such incense as pasting, powdery, and burning incense, and the cart in which those of pure castes can ride. It truly supercedes [surpasses] the six paramitas. This is a wonderful land of bliss. It is like the parijata tree of Trayastrimsa Heaven. "O good man! This sutra is an adamantine and sharpened hatchet which can indeed fell the great tree of all defilements. This is the sharpened sword that can truly make away with the taint of ill smell. This is the valiant and strong that can thoroughly crush out the adversity [opposition] of Mara. This is the fire of Wisdom, which burns up the fuel of defilement. This is the storehouse of causal relations which gives birth to the pratyekabuddha. This is the storehouse of hearing which gives birth to the sravakas. This is the eye of all gods that serves as the Right Path to all beings. This is a refuge to all animals. This is where the hungry ghosts gain Emancipation, the most holy of hell, and the unsurpassed utensil for all beings of the ten directions. This is the parent of all Buddhas of the ten directions of past, future, and present. O good man! Thus, this sutra holds within itself all dharmas." [The Buddha said:] "As I have already said, this sutra embraces all dharmas. But I have stated that the pure actions about which I speak are none other than the 37 elements assisting towards Bodhi [Enlightenment]. O good man! Separated from the 37 elements of Enlightenment, one cannot attain the fruition of sravaka practice and unsurpassed Enlightenment, and one cannot see the Buddha-Nature, nor the fruition that arises from the Buddha-Nature. This being so, pure action is the 37 Bodhi elements ["bodhipakshikadharma" - the 37 prerequisites for attaining Enlightenment; they include mindfulness, and the Noble Eightfold Path]. How can we say this? Because the 37 elements assisting towards Enlightenment are those factors which, by nature, are not inverted and indeed crush out the inversions. They are, by nature, not evil views, and can truly crush out evil views. They are, by nature, not fears, and they well crush out fear. They are, by nature, pure actions, so that beings ultimately perform pure actions." Bodhisattva Kasyapa said to the Buddha: "O World-Honoured One! Even the defiled can also become a cause of the non-defiled. Why is it that the Tathagata does not say that the defiled, too, is pure action?" "O good man! All defiled things are nothing but inversions [of Truth]. That is why I cannot claim the defiled to be pure action." Bodhisattva Kasyapa said to the Buddha: "Is the first-of-the world root of good ["laukikagradharma" - intellectual penetration and insight] that which is defiled or non-defiled?"

The Buddha said: "It is that which is defiled." "O World-Honoured One! Though defiled, its nature is not inverted. Why do you not call it pure action?" "O good man! The first-of-the-world root of good is the cause of the defiled. So it well resembles it. As it faces the undefiled, we do not call it any inversion. O good man! Pure action takes its rise from the stage of taking one's aspiration [to Buddhahood]. It goes thus and attains the uttermost. The first-of-the-world root of good is none but one mind. That is why we cannot call it pure action." Bodhisattva Kasyapa said to the Buddha: "O World-Honoured One! The five consciousnesses of the being are the defiled, and yet not inversions. Nor are they of one mind. Why do we not say pure actions?" "O good man! The five consciousnesses of the being are not of one mind. They are the defiled and inversions. As defilements increase, we say "defiled". The body is not of true stuff. Due to clinging and the image, they are inversions. Why do we say that the body is not true? Because of clinging and image. Where there is no man or woman, they gain the image of man or woman. So does it go with house, vehicle, pot, clothing, etc. This is an inversion. "O good man! With the 37 factors of Enlightenment, there is no inversion. So we can speak of "pure action". O good man! If any Bodhisattva comes to know of the root, cause, what takes in, what augments, the master, what leads, what is superior, what is true, and the ultimate, such a Bodhisattva is one of pure action." Bodhisattva Kasyapa said to the Buddha: "O World-Honoured One! In what sense do we say that one knows the root up to the ultimate?" The Buddha said: "O good man! Well said, well said! What you, Bodhisattva, speak about concerns two things. One is for your own good, and the other is for knowing by others. You now know, but since innumerable beings do not yet understand, you ask. So I now praise you once again. It is good, it is good. O good man! The root of the 37 elements assisting towards Enlightenment is desire. The cause is the touch of brightness; that which takes in is "feeling"; that which augments is "thinking"; the "master" is "remembrance"; that which leads is dhyana [meditation]; that which is superior is Wisdom;

that which is true is Emancipation; and the ultimate is Great Nirvana. "O good man! All the worries of the world take their rise from craving. All illnesses rest on the food cooked on the preceding day. All segregation arises out of quarrelling and disputation. All evils arise out of falsehood. The situation is thus." Bodhisattva Kasyapa said: "O World-Honoured One! The Tathagata has already in this sutra stated that all good things are grounded on non-indolence. You now say "desire". How am I to understand this?" The Buddha said: "O good man! If the cause is sought relating to [a good thing's] coming about, it is good desire. If the revealing cause [Jap. "ryoin": the cause that reveals what is hidden, like, for example, lamplight that shines and shows what lies hidden when it is dark - K. Yamamoto] is sought, this is non-indolence. We say in the world that the result depends on the seed; and we say that the seed is the cause of the coming about, and the soil is the revealing cause. The same is the case here too." Bodhisattva Kasyapa said: "O World-Honoured One! The Tathagata says in other sutras that the 37 Enlightenment factors constitute the base. What does this imply?" "O good man! The Tathagata said before that beings first come to know of the 37 factors of Enlightenment. The Buddha is the root. To awaken depends on desire." "O World-Honoured One! What do you mean when you say that "bright touch" is the cause?" "O good man! The Tathagata at times speaks about brightness and says that it is Wisdom; and at time he says "faith". O good man! Through the causal relation of faith, one draws near to a good teacher of the Way. This is touch [contact]. The causal relation of befriending leads the person to give ear to Wonderful Dharma. This is "touch". When one listens to Wonderful Dharma, one's body, mouth and mind become pure. This is "touch". Through the purity of the three actions, one gains right living. This is touch. Through right living, one gains the sila that purifies the sense-organs. On account of the sila that purifies the sense-organs, one comes to seek a silent place. In quietude, one thinks of good. By good thinking, one thinks of a life that accords with Dharma. Through right living, one gains the 37 elements of Enlightenment. And one thoroughly crushes out innumerable evil defilements. "O good man! Feeling is called "taking-in". Beings do good or evil at the stage of feeling. Hence, we say that feeling is the taking-in. O good man! Through the

causal relation of feeling, all kinds of defilements come about. The 37 Bodhi elements truly crush these out. Because of this, we call feeling the taking-in. Good thinking well crushes out the defilements. Hence we speak of "augmenting". Why? We make effort and try to learn. And we arrive at these 37 elements of Enlightenment. Meditation truly destroys evil defilements. This always is grounded on exclusive mindfulness. So, to think is the master. In the world, all the four armies move at the will of the head general. It is the same with the 37 elements of Enlightenment. All follow the will of the master, which is the mind. "When one enters dhyana [meditation], the 37 elements of Enlightenment well discriminate all phases of dharma. Hence, meditation is what leads one. We look into the 37 elements of Enlightenment and see that Wisdom is the most superior. Because of this, Wisdom is the most superior. That is why Wisdom is made [stated to be] superior. Thus, Wisdom sees defilement. Through the power of Wisdom, defilement dies. "In the world, the four armies crush out the enemy. There may well be one or two who are valiant and strong and that do well. So is it with the 37 elements assisting towards Enlightenment. Through the power of Wisdom, defilement is done away with. Hence, Wisdom is that which is superior. "O good man! By learning and practising the 37 elements of Enlightenment, one gains the four dhyanas, the miraculous divine powers, and peace. But this is not called "real". When defilement is done away with and Emancipation is reached, we say "real". A person may aspire to learn and practise the 37 elements of Enlightenment and be blessed with worldly bliss, supramundane bliss, the fruition of sramana practice, and Emancipation. Yet, we cannot call this the "Ultimate". When all the practices of the 37 elements of Enlightenment have been done away with, this is Nirvana. That is why I say that the Ultimate is Great Nirvana." "Also, next, O good man! The good-loving mind is desire. Through the good-loving mind, a person associates with a good friend. Hence, "touch". This is "cause". When a person associates with a good friend, we call this love. This is a taking-in. Befriending a good teacher, that person thinks well. Hence, "to augment". Through four dharmas is the Way well augmented, namely: 1) desire, 2) remembrance, 3) meditation, and 4) Wisdom. This is: 1) master, 2) leading, and 3) superior.

Through these three dharmas, the person attains three Emancipations. Cutting off craving, he attains Emancipation of mind. Doing away with ignorance, he attains Emancipation of Wisdom. This is the Real. All such dharmas result in fruition. This is Nirvana. Hence, the "Ultimate". "Also, next, O good man! "Desire" is aspring and renouncing. Touch is the four jnapti-caturtha-karman [one of the rituals in the vinaya = monks' code of monastic living]. This is the cause. Taking-in means receiving the two kinds of precept, namely: 1) pratimoksa and 2) sila that purifies the sense-organs. This is "feeling" and also "taking-in". To augment means to learn and practise the four dhyanas. The Master refers to the fruitions of srotapanna and sakrdagamin. To lead refers to the fruition of the anagamin; "superior", to that of arhatship. The Real refers to the fruition of the pratyekabuddha; the "Ultimate" is unsurpassed Enlightenment. "Also, next, O good man! "Desire" is consciousness. Touch is called the six [sensual] spheres. Taking-in is feeling. Augmenting is ignorance. The master is mind-and-body. To lead in is craving. The superior is cleaving. The real is existence. The ultimate is birth, old-age, illness, and death." Bodhisattva Kasyapa said: "O World-Honoured One! What difference is there between the three items of: 1) root, 2) cause, and 3) augmentation?"

"O good man! The root referred to is that which is to take rise; the cause is that which resembles; augmentation is cutting off resemblance, and yet, calling forth resemblance. Also, next, O good man! The root is to do, the cause fruition, and augmentation is the use. O good man! The world that is to come sees the karmic results. But not yet receiving [them], we call this "cause". When received, that is augmentation. Also, next, O good man! The root is to seek; to gain is the cause, and the use is to augment. O good man! The root spoken of in this sutra is darsanamarga [the path of seeing, leading the person from mere blind trust in the Four Noble Truths to actual comprehension of them, transforming him or her into a "stream-enterer"], the cause is bhavanamarga [the path of self-development through meditation], and to augment is asaiksamarga. Also, next, O good man! The root is the right cause and the cause is the expedient cause. From this right cause comes about the karmic result which one harvests. This is to augment." Bodhisattva Kasyapa said: "O

World-Honoured One! If things are as you the Buddha state, the Ultimate is no less than Nirvana. How can one reach this Nirvana?" "O good man! If the Bodhisattva, bhiksu, bhiksuni, upasaka, or upasika practises well the ten images, know that such a person will well attain Nirvana. What are these ten? They are the images of: 1) non-eternal, 2) suffering, 3) non-Self, 4) abhorring food, 5) the world as having nothing in it to enjoy, 6) death, 7) one's having many sins, 8) parting from [the worldly] and emancipating [oneself], 9) extinction [of defilement], 10) non-craving. "O good man! If any Bodhisattva-mahasattva, bhiksu, bhiksuni, upasaka or upasika practise these ten images, such a person will definitely attain Nirvana. Such a person will not follow what other minds think, but will discriminate the good and the non-good for himself. This is what we call: "Truly according with the Way of a bhiksu [monk] or according with the Way of a bhiksuni [nun] ". Bodhisattva Kasyapa said: "O World-Honoured One! How do those from Bodhisattvamahasattva down to upasika practise the image of the non-eternal?" "O good man! There are two kinds of Bodhisattva, namely: 1) the one who has first aspired to and 2) the one who has finished the practice of the Way. There are two kinds of image of the non-eternal, namely: 1) coarse and 2) fine. The Bodhisattva who has first aspired to Bodhi, when he meditates on the image of the non-eternal, thinks: "There are two kinds of thing which obtain in the world: 1) inner and 2) outer. What is within is non-eternal and changes. When I get born, I see that things obtain differently at such times of life as when I am small, big, in the prime of life, in old-age, and when dying, and I see that at all such times of life, things are not the same. Hence, I have to know that what is with me is non-eternal." "Also, this thought comes to him: "When I look at beings, one is [i.e. I see one person who is] well nourished and fresh, and is perfect in physical strength and in the movements of going and coming, in stepping forward or stopping; and things all proceed unimpededy and without hindrance. Or through illness, [another] person's physical strength is weak and his face fallen and haggered, with nothing of freedom. Or I see that a person's storehouse is full, or that another person is poverty-stricken. Or I see one who is full of all virtues, or I see one full of evil. Thus I definitely know that what is within one is non-eternal. Also, as regards the external world, too, I see things are different one from the other, as, for example, at the times of seed, bud, stem, leaf, flower, and fruit. All that stands [there] in the external world is either perfect or not perfect. And I know that all things are definitely non-eternal." "Having thus seen that things are all non-eternal, one next meditates on what one listens to sermons. "I hear that though the devas [gods, heavenly beings] fully enjoy the best of pleasures, and though they are unimpeded in divine powers, they are subject to the five declining forebodings [intimations of their eventual personal decline from the status of being devas]. Due to this, one knows that what there is is non-eternal." "Also, I hear that at the beginning of the kalpa [aeon, age], there were many beings. Each was garbed in the best of virtues. The light that shone from their bodies was so great that one did not need any more to depend upon the light of the sun and moon. [But] due to the power of the noneternal, the light waned and the virtues lessened. Also, I hear that there lived, in days gone by, a Chakravartin [world emperor] who ruled over the four lands. The seven gems [which he possessed] were perfect, and his power was greatly unconstrained. And yet he could not beat the non-eternal." "Also, he meditates that on the great earth, at one time in the past, innumerable beings were fully stationed in life and enjoyed peace, so that no furrows of the wheel sat one upon the other. Wonderful medicines were ready at hand, and people grew up. Bushes, trees and fruits were full-grown. The beings were [gradually] less blessed and this great earth had little strength. Whatever grew had to waste away. Hence, one can know that all things are non-eternal. That is what we call "coarse" and non-eternal. "The coarse having been meditated upon, the detailed parts are next meditated upon. How do we meditate? The Bodhisattva-mahasattva meditates on all things, both within and without, down to mote existences. Whatever might come about in the future will be non-eternal. Why? Because all things are perfect in the forms of breaking [i.e. are fully subject to dissolution]. If things were not non-eternal in the future, we could not say that there are the differences of the ten kinds of physical form. What are the ten? They are at the times: 1) membrane, 2) foam, 3) pox, 4) ball of flesh, 5) limbs, 6) small infant, 7) child, 8) boyhood, 9) prime of life, 10) tottering old age. The Bodhisattva meditates: "If the membrane is not non-eternal, it cannot become foam. And if the prime of life were

not non-eternal, it could never reach old age. If time were not fleeting by, moment after moment, it could never last long. All would have to grow up at one and the same time and be full in size. Hence, one must definitely know that there are the fine, non-eternal mote existences that have to go on existing thus continuously [i.e. changing from moment to moment]." "Also, we see a person with all his sense-organs perfect, and of a bright and shining mien, [only for] all this to fade away into a weakened state. "Also, he thinks: "There is with this person the non-eternal [i.e. that which is impermanent] going on moment after moment." Also, he meditates on the four great elements and the four deportments. Also, he meditates on the cause of suffering, hunger, and thirst, the cold and heat that exist within and without. Also, he meditates: "If these four things were not non-eternal moment after moment, we could not speak of such four sufferings." If the Bodhisattva well meditates thus, we call this the Bodhisattva's meditating minutely upon the non-eternal." [The Buddha said:] "As with all things that exist within and without, so does it go with what obtains in the mind. Why? Because action obtains in the six spheres. When this obtains in the six spheres, there comes about the happy mind, the angry mind, the craving mind, or the greedy mind. Life goes differently one after the other, and cannot be one. For this reason, one has to know that all that is physical and non-physical is non-eternal. "O good man! If the Bodhisattva can, in the flash of a moment, see the birth and death and non-eternality of all things, this is what we call the Bodhisattva's being perfect in the image of the non-eternal. O good man! The wise man learns and practises the image of the non-eternal, and makes away with the arrogance of the eternal, the inversion [i.e. wrong-headed view] of the eternal, and the inversion of the image. "Next, he practises the image of suffering. Why should there be such suffering? He sees that this suffering is grounded on the non-eternal, that because of the non-eternal, there is the suffering of birth, old age, illness, and death, that because of birth, ageing, illness, and death, there is the non-eternal, that because of the non-eternal, there is internal and external suffering, and such suffering as [that from] hunger, thirst, cold, heat, whipping, beating, abusing, and endurance. He sees that all suffering is based on the non-eternal. "Also, next, the wise man looks deeply into this fleshly body and sees that it is a vessel of the non-eternal, and that this vessel is suffering. And as the vessel is suffering, the things that are put into it are suffering. "O good man! The wise person meditates [thus]: "Suffering is non-eternal. If suffering is non-eternal, how can the wise say that there is the Self [there]? Suffering is not the Self. The same is the case with the non-eternal [i.e. that which is impermanent is not the Self]. Thus, the five skandhas are also the non-eternal of suffering. How could all beings say that there is the Self [there]?" "Also, next, he meditates on all things [thus]: "There is a conjoining of what is different. All things do not come about from a single conjoining. Also, one thing is not the result of the conjoining of all things. The conjoining of all things does not have a Self of its own. Also, there is no single nature and no different natures. Also, there is no nature of material form, and no unmolestedness [freedom to do as one wills; unobstructedness]. If all things possess these aspects of existence, how can the wise say that here is the Self?" "Also, he thinks: "Of all things, there is not one thing that is done by the creator of its own [i.e. nothing creates itself]. If there is not one thing that has that which creates it, the conjoining of all things also cannot come about. All things cannot come about alone and die out alone. Through [the act of] conjoining, they die, and through conjoining, they come about. "When things have come about, beings gain an inverted [view] and say that this is conjoining and that this comes about by conjoining. There is nothing true in the inverted [view] of beings. How could there be any [such view] that is true?" Hence, the wise meditate on the non-Self. "And, also, the wise person clearly thinks: "For what reason do beings speak about the Self? Why is it that beings speak about the Self? If this Self exists, it must be [either] one or many. If it is one, how can there be such as Kshatriyas, Brahmins, Sudras, humans and gods, hell, hungry ghosts, animals, or big and small, or old age or the prime of life? For this reason, I know that the Self is not one. If the Self is many, how can we say that the Self of the being is one and all-pervading, knowing no bounds? Be it one or many, in either case, there is no Self." "Having so meditated that there is no Self, the wise man next meditates on the image of abhorring food, and thinks: "If all things are non-eternal, suffering, and non-Self, how could one, for the sake of food, commit the three evil actions of body, mouth and mind, all that has been in hand

goes along with [the person] and, later, the karmic results visit [him], and no one [else] indeed can share them." O good man! The wise person further meditates [thus]: "All beings, on account of food and drink, suffer from the sorrows of body and mind. If one gains various sorrows from food, why should I gain any greed or clinging? Hence, I do not covet a greedy mind for food." "And, next, the wise person meditates [thus]: "Through food and drink, one gains one's own bodily augmentation [i.e. one perpetuates the process of one's physical embodimentation]. I now practise renunciation and receive sila and practise the Way. All of this is to abandon the carnal body. I now covet this food. How [then] will I be able to abandon this body of mine?" So meditating, even if food is accepted, this is as though he were partaking in the wilderness of the flesh of his own son, in which situation his mind is so hard-pressed that there cannot be any talk of sweetness or pleasure [here]. When food is meditated upon, we see such wrongs [i.e. such ills]. "Next, the person meditates on the touch of food: "It is like an unskinned cow that gets eaten by innumerable worms." "Next, the person thinks of food as being comparable to a great fire-ball, and consciousness of food as being like 300 halberds. When the wise person meditates on the four foods, there cannot be any entertaining of any image of having greed and enjoying food. If the person has any greed for food, he must meditate on the impurities. Why? This is to segregate himself from the love of greed. He must discriminate the images of impurities in all food and realise that all impurities obtain thus. When he meditates thus, and when good or bad food is spread out before his eyes, he feels as though ointment were being applied to his own carbuncles, gaining no thought of craving there any more. "O good man! If any wise person comes to meditate thus, this is accomplishing the renunciation of the image of food." Bodhisattva Kasyapa said to the Buddha: "O World-Honoured One! The wise person meditates on food and gains the image of impurity. Can this be a true meditation or one that is false? If it is true, whatever is partaken of cannot be impure. If this is a false understanding, how can one call this a root of good?" The Buddha said: "Such an image is both true and also a false understanding. If the greed is thoroughly crushed out, it is one that is true. When what is not a worm is seen as a worm, this is a false understanding. O good man! All defilements are false, yet, they can be real. O good man! The mind of a bhiksu starts from begging and thinks: "I shall now beg for food. I pray that I shall gain what is good and not what is coarse and bad; let it be a lot and not a small amount. I pray that I shall gain it at once, that it will not be late in coming." Such a bhiksu is not called one who possesses the image of renunciation. The good things done will diminish day and night. What is evil will by degrees increase. "O good man! If there is any bhiksu who begs for food, he must first pray and say: "I shall satisfy all those who beg for food. This giving of food will bring in immeasurable blessings. If I gain food, I shall heal the poisoned body, and I shall learn and practise what is good and give benefit to the person who gave." After he has vowed thus, the good he practises will increase day and night, and what is bad will hide away [retreat]. O good man! If any bhiksu practises the Way thus, such a one will not meaninglessly partake of what is given. "O good man! The wise who are perfect in the four images will practise an image and think that there is nothing to please them, and they will think to themselves: "In all the world, there is no place where birth, old age, illness, and death do not exist. And there is no place where I do not get born. If there is no place where one finds no birth, old age, illness, and death, how can I be happy with the world? In all the world, one moves onwards and there is no place where one cannot come back. Hence, the world is definitely non-eternal. If it is non-eternal, how can a wise person feel happy? Every being goes around the world and minutely suffers and has joy. One may be blessed with the body of Brahma and attain such as the life of the thoughtlessness-and-non-thoughtlessness heaven. But when life ends, one gains life once again in the three unfortunate realms. One may gain the body of the four guardians of the earth, or that of the Paranirmitavasavartin, but when one's life ends, one falls again into the three unfortunate realms. Or one may get born as a lion, a tiger, a Chinese buffalo, a jackal, a wolf, an elephant, a horse, a cow, or a donkey." "Next, the person meditates [thus]: "The Chakravartin may well reign over the four lands and can be gorgeous and unlimited [in his power]. But when his fortune departs, he will become poor and will feel the want of food and clothing." The wise person indeed deeply meditates thus and gains an image of the world as

not a place where one can be happy. "The wise person also meditates [thus]: "All the things of the world, such as horses, clothing, food and drink, bedding, medicine, incense and flowers, jewellery, the various kinds of music, treasures and gems are sought solely to segregate oneself from sorrow. All such things are based on sorrow. How can one hope to get out of sorrow through sorrow?" O good man! When a wise man thus meditates, he no longer entertains the thought of worldly things and gains [from them] any image of pleasure. O good man! For example, a man who is suffering from a serious illness will not greedily have any feeling for music, beautiful females, flowers and incense, and jewellery. Thus the wise man meditates. "O good man! The wise man thinks deeply about the world. He sees: "It is not a place to take refuge in, to gain Emancipation, quietude, love, and it is not the other shore, and nothing of the Eternal, Bliss, the Self, and the Pure. If I greedily pursue the world, how can I segregate myself from it? This is as with a man who, abhorring the gloom, seeks the light and, yet, turns back again to the gloom. The gloom is the world; the light is the Supramundane. If I adhere to the world, I shall increase the gloom and part from the light. Gloom is ignorance, and light the brightness of Wisdom. The cause of the brightness of Wisdom is the image where one does not feel any sense of wanting to enjoy worldly things. All greed is nothing but the bond of defilement. I shall now avidly seek the light of Wisdom, and not the world." The wise person meditates thus. This is the image where one does not seek for one's own self. O good man! The wise person has already practised the image of not seeking worldly pleasures. Next, he practises the image of death. He sees this life. He sees that it is ever bound to innumerable enmities. Every moment sees a decrease, nothing increasing. It is like a mountain, where the rushing water cannot find any place to rest, or the morning frost that cannot long remain. It ever proceeds to the market-place of the prison house, only leading one to death. It is like taking a cow or sheep to where death awaits them." Bodhisattva Kasyapa said: "O World-Honoured One! How does a wise person meditate on momentary extinction?" "O good man! For example, there are four persons all skilled in archery. They forgather at a place, and each releases an arrow into a [particular] direction. They all think: "We all release arrows together, which will all fall." And one person thinks: "Before the four arrows fall to the ground, I shall catch them with my hand." Thus does he think. O good man! Does this person act speedily or not?" Bodhisattva Kasyapa said: "He does this in a speedy way, O World-Honoured One!" The Buddha said: "O good man! The devil that lives on earth moves more quickly than this person does. There is a flying devil who goes faster than the one on the ground. The four guardians of the earth move still faster than the flying devil. The sun and moon and the heavenly gods move faster than the four guardians of the earth. The gyokenshitsuten [garuda] goes faster than the sun and moon. The life span of a human goes more quickly than the kenshitsuten. O good man! In one breath and in one wink, the life of a being comes about and dies 400 times. If a wise person meditates on human life thus, this is to meditate on momentary extinction. "The wise man meditates [thus] on the life span: "It depends on Yama [ruler of the hells, who sends old age, sickness and death]. If I can get away from Yama, I shall eternally part from the non-eternal." "Also, next, the wise person meditates on life and views it as a great tree standing on a cliff; or he sees it as one [would] who has committed a great deadly sin, whom no one ever pities while he is being punished. Or things are compared to a lion-king who faces a great famine, or a viper that breathes in fiery air, or a thirst-ridden horse who guards and begrudges water; or to the anger of a great devil about to explode. So do things stand with the king of death in relation to beings. O good man! If a wise person meditates thus, this is to learn and practise the image of death." "O good man! The wise person also meditates [thus]: "I now renounce. Even if I only get life for seven days and nights, I shall make effort therein. I shall be true to the moral precepts, and I shall deliver sermons and bestow benefit upon beings." This is how the wise person learns and practises the image of death. "And he makes seven days and nights more than enough. "Or if I gain only six, five, four, three, two days, or one day, or one hour, or one moment in which I breathe in and out, I shall make effort and practise the Way, uphold and protect the precepts, deliver sermons, teach the Way, and bestow benefit upon beings." This is how the wise person meditates on the image of death. "When the wise person is perfect in the six images, this becomes the cause of the seven images. What are the seven? They are: 1) always practising the images, 2) feeling joy in practising? ?the images, 3) the image of non-anger, 4) the image of not being jealous, 5) the image of seeking good, 6) the image of not being proud, and 7) being unmolested [unrestricted] in samadhi. "O good man! If a bhiksu is perfect in these seven images, such a person is a sramana or a Brahmin. This is quietude, purity, and Emancipation. This is one who is wise, and this is the right view. This is arrival at the other shore, and a great doctor, and a great merchant, and this is how we gain the secret bosom of the Tathagata. "Also, this is being versed in the seven kinds of words of all Buddhas, and also cutting off the web of doubt regarding what exists there in the seven kinds of words of right seeing. "O good man! If a person is perfect in the six images stated above, that person truly reproves and renounces, and extinguishes, and does not love the three worlds [of Desire, Form, and Formlessness]. This is how we speak of a wise person who is perfect in the ten images. If a bhiksu is perfect in the ten images, this means that he indeed praises the characteristics of a sramana." Then, Bodhisattva Kasyapa applauded the Buddha in a gatha in his presence:

"The Great Doctor who pities the world is serene in both body and Wisdom.
"In the world of the non-Self, there is the True Self.
Hence, I pay homage to the Unsurpassed One.
The mind that first aspires to [Enlightenment] and the end attained are not separate.
Of these two minds, it is difficult to say which comes first.
The end not yet attained, one saves others first.
That is why I pay homage to the initial aspiration.
From the first, he is the teacher of humans and gods
And is far above sramanas and pratyekabuddhas.
Such an aspiration transcends the three worlds.
That is why he is the most superior.
He seeks to save the world and gains the end.

Unasked, the Tathagata becomes the refuge.
The Buddha follows the world like a calf,
So we call him the greatly compassionate cow.
The virtue of the Tathagata towers above all the world.
Common mortals are low and ignorant and cannot appraise him.
I now praise the compassionate heart,
Which is to thank him for the two actions of body and mouth.
The eternal and bliss of the world obtain only for one's own good.
The Tathagata never does this.
He truly cuts off the karmic results of all beings.
Hence, I give respect to actions that help one's own self and others.
The benefiting of the world follows the grade of befriending,
Calling forth different benefits.
The good works of the Tathagata know of no animosity or befriending.
The thought of the Tathagata does not proceed as with people of the world.
Hence, his heart works equally
And there are not two [i.e. no division within him].
The world speaks variously and its actions differ.
The Tathagata acts as he says and his actions do not differ.
Whatever is practised fully cuts off all [defilements].
Hence, we call him Tathagata.
Before, he is aware of the ills of defilement.
He speaks and acts as he speaks, all for the sake of beings.
It is long since he attained Emancipation in the world,
And he seeks to live amidst birth and death, all for compassion's sake.
He manifests himself in the worlds of humans and gods,
But his compassion follows him like a calf.
The Tathagata is the mother of beings.
His compassionate heart is the little calf.
Himself undergoing pains, he only thinks of the beings.
Working in Compassion, no repentance is there in him.
Overflowing is he with Compassion, and he knows no hardships.
That is why I bow to him, the one who extracts pain.
Innumerable are the works of good which the Tathagata performs,
Yet he is pure in deeds bodily, oral, and mental.
He always acts for the sake of beings, but not for his own sake.
That is why I bow to his pure actions.
The Tathagata suffers from hardships and he feels it not.
He looks upon the pains of the beings as he does the pains of his own son.
He lives in hell for the sake of beings,
But he has no thought of pain or regret.
All beings experience different pains,
All of which are those of his single Self.
Having attained the light, his heart is firm.
Thus does he practise well the unsurpassed Way.
The Buddha has a great compassionate heart of one taste,
And pities beings as though they were his children.
Beings do not know that the Tathagata truly saves.
And they slander the Tathagata, Dharma, and Sangha.
The world is full of defilement, and there are innumerable ills.
But all such fetters of defilement and sins and ills
The Tathagata broke out of at his first stage of aspiration.

Only him, the Buddha, do all Buddhas praise.
Other than the Buddha, there is none who is praised.
I now with one single Dharma praise him.
The so-called compassionate heart travels the world.
The Tathagata is a great ball of Dharma,
And his Compassion also truly saves beings.
This is true Emancipation; Emancipation is Great Nirvana."

Chapter Forty-Five: On Kaundinya 1

Then the World-Honoured One spoke to Kaundinya: "Material form is non-eternal. By doing away with this form, one arrives at the Eternal form of Emancipation. So does it obtain with feeling, perception, volition, and consciousness, too. By doing away with consciousness, one arrives at the Eternal form of Emancipation and Peace. This also pertains to feeling, perception, volition, and consciousness. "O Kaundinya! Form is Void. By doing away with the form that is All-Void, one arrives at the Non-Void form of Emancipation. So does it obtain also with feeling, perception, volition, and consciousness. ""O Kaundinya! Material form ["rupa"] is non-Self. By doing away with such form, one arrives at the form of the True Self of Emancipation. Feeling is non-Self. By doing away with such feeling, one arrives at the feeling of the True Self of Emancipation. Perception is non-Self. By doing away with such perception, one arrives at the perception of the True Self of Emancipation. Volition is non-Self. By doing away with such volition, one arrives at the volition of the True Self of Emancipation. Consciousness is non-Self. By doing away with such consciousness, one arrives at the consciousness of the True Self of Emancipation." "O Kaundinya! Form is the non-Pure. By doing away with this form, one arrives at the Pure Form of Emancipation. So does it obtain also with feeling, perception, volition, and consciousness. "O Kaundinya! Form is what represents birth, old age, illness, and death. By doing away with such form, one arrives at the form of the non-birth, non-old-age, non-illness, and non-death form of Emancipation. So does it also obtain with feeling, perception, volition, and consciousness. "O Kaundinya! Form is the cause of ignorance. By doing away with such form, one arrives at the form of the non-cause of ignorance [characteristic] of Emancipation. So does it also obtain with feeling, perception, volition, and consciousness. "O Kaundinya! Or form is the cause of birth even. By doing away with such form, one arrives at the form of the non-birth cause of Emancipation. So does it also obtain with feeling, perception, volition, and consciousness. "O Kaundinya! Form is the cause of the four inversions. By doing away with inverted form, one arrives at the form of the four non-inverted causes

of Emancipation. So does it also obtain with feeling, perception, volition, and consciousness. "O Kaundinya! Physical form is the cause of innumerable evil things. It is the carnal body of the male, etc. It is the love of the food of lust. It is greed, anger, and jealousy. It is an evil and a grudging mind. It is ordinary food [i.e. food that has flavour, taste, and touch, and which can be cut and eaten], consciousness food [i.e. consciousness serving as food. For example, the mental power that at times checks one's sense of hunger], thought food [i.e. the power of thinking, or the volitional power], and touch food [i.e. the emotional sense that at times serves to check one's sense of hunger]. There is egg-birth, embryo-birth, and transformed birth. There are the five desires and the five overshadowings. All of these are grounded on material form. "By doing away with form, one arrives at the form of Emancipation, which does not contain any such evil things. It is the same with feeling, perception, volition, and consciousness. "O Kaundinya! Form is bondage. By doing away with the form of bondage, one arrives at the form of Emancipation, which is no bondage. It is the same with feeling, perception, volition, and consciousness. "O Kaundinya! Form is a stream. By doing away with the form which is a stream, one arrives at the form of Emancipation, which is not a stream. So is it also with feeling, perception, volition, and consciousness. "O Kaundinya! Form is non-taking-of-refuge. By doing away with form, one arrives at the form of Emancipation, which is the taking of refuge. The same also applies to feeling, perception, volition, and consciousness. "O Kaundinya! Form is the pox and warts. By doing away with form, one arrives at Emancipation, which is not the pox or warts. The same applies to feeling, perception, volition, and consciousness, too. "O Kaundinya! Form is non-quietude. By doing away with this form, one arrives at the form of quietude of Nirvana, which is quiet. So does it also obtain with feeling, perception, volition, and consciousness. "O Kaundinya! If there is any person who can so know things, such a person is a sramana or a Brahmin, and such a one is perfect in the Dharma of the sramana or Brahmin. O Kaundinya! If one parts from Buddha-Dharma, then one is no sramana or Brahmin; nor is there any Dharma of the sramana or Brahmin. All tirthikas speak falsely and cheat. And there is no action that is true [with them]. Also, they pretend to say that there are such two. But this is not true. Why not? If there is no Dharma of the sramana or Brahmin, how can one say that here is a sramana or Brahmin? I always give a lion's roar amidst the congregation. You, too, should do the same amidst this congregation." At that time, many tirthikas were present, who, on hearing this, became angry and said: "Gautama now says that there are no sramanas and Brahmins among us, and that there exists no Dharma of the sramana or Brahmin. What means shall we extensively adopt and address Gautama, to tell him that we too have sramanas and the Dharma of sramanas, and Brahmins and the Dharma of Brahmins?" Then, there was amongst the crowd a Brahmacarin who said: "O all of you! What Gautama says is a thing of madness. There is no difference. What worth is there in taking up this point and worrying about it? All mad people sing, dance, weep, laugh, reprove, and praise. They cannot distinguish between enemies and friends. It is the same with Gautama, who says that he was born in the house of Suddhodana, or that he was not; or that when born, he took seven steps, or not; or that from his childhood he learnt the things of the world, or that he is the All-Knower; or that, at one time, he lived a palatial life, tasted [all] the pleasures and had a son, or that, at another time, he despised and reproved and reviled [sensual pleasures]; or that he, at times, practised penance for six years, or that he condemned the penances of the tirthikas; or that he followed Udrakaramaputra and Aradakalama and was taught what he did not know before, or that there is nothing that he does not know; or that he attained unsurpassed Bodhi [Enlightenment] under the shade of the Bodhi Tree, or that he did not go to the tree, and that he did nothing; or that Nirvana comes when the fleshly body has gone. What Gautama says is what a mad man says, there is no difference. So why should we need to trouble ourselves over it?" All the Brahmins answered and said: "O great one! How can we not but be troubled? Sramana Gautama renounced the world and said that what there was was nothing but the non-eternal, suffering, Void, non-Self, and the Impure, and our disciples heard his words and became frightened. How could we beings be non-eternal, suffering, Void, non-Self, and impure? We do not give ear to him. Now, Gautama is here

again now, in this sal forest, and tells people that there is the Dharma of the Eternal, Bliss, the Self, and the Pure. All of my disciples hear his words, leave me and listen to Gautama's words. For this reason, I am greatly worried." Then there was a Brahmin who said: "All of you! Listen carefully to me, listen carefully to me! Gautama professes to practise compassion. This is a lie. It is not true. If he has compassion, how can he teach my disciples and make them take to his teaching? The fruition of compassion is to follow the will of others. He is going against my wishes. How can we say that he has compassion? If Gautama says that he is not tainted by the eight things of the world, this again is nothing but falsehood. If it is said that Gautama desires little and that he is satisfied with what little he has, how, again, can he deprive us of what is ours? If he says that he is born of a high caste, this again is untrue. Why? Since of old, we have not seen or heard of a great lion-king who has ever caused harm to little rats. If Gautama is of high caste, how can he cause worry to us? If people say that Gautama possesses great power, this is a lie. Why? Since of old, we have never seen a garuda quarrelling with a cow. If he possesses great power, why would he quarrel with us? If it is said that Gautama possesses the power of reading people's minds, this again is a lie. Why so? If he is armed with this knowledge, how is it that he is dark in reading our minds? All of you! Once upon a time, I was with an aged and wise man who said that in 100 years' time, there would appear an apparition. This could well be Gautama. And such an apparition is now about to pass away in this forest of sal trees before long. Do not be worried!" Then, there was a Nirgrantha, who said: "O you brothers! My mind is pained. This is not from the offerings of my disciples. The trouble is that the world is ignorant and eyeless and does not know what is a field of blessings and what is not. For they make offerings to one young, forsaking the aged and wise Brahmins. This is what worries me. Sramana Gautama knows much of sorcery. By this means, he presents one body in numerous forms and numerous forms in one, or he presents himself as a man, woman, cow, sheep, elephant, or horse. I will destroy such sorcery. When Sramana Gautama is gone, you will again enjoy many offerings and be blessed with peace." Then there was a Brahmin who said: "Sramana Gautama is accomplished and perfect in innumerable virtues. So, you should not fight against him." The great crowd said: "O you ignorant one! How dare you say that Sramana Gautama is accomplished in great virtue. Seven days after his birth, his mother died. Is that what you call a family of great blessings?" The Brahmin said: "When reproached, one does not become angry, and when beaten, one does not strike back. Know that this can be none other than the form of great weal. His body is perfect in the 32 signs of perfection and the 80 minor marks of excellence and is armed with innumerable miraculous powers. So you must know that these are all of weal. His mind knows no arrogance. His mind first asks and reflects. What is said is gently spoken. There is no coarseness from the very start. His age and will are both rigorous, yet his mind is not rude. He does not covet any kingdom or wealth. He has abandoned all that, as one would tears and spit. That is why I say that Sramana Gautama is accomplished in innumerable virtues." The great crowd said: "Well said! Sramana Gautama is, as you say, truly perfect in innumerable miraculous powers. How can I not fight with him against this? Sramana Gautama is gentle in feeling and nature. So he cannnot endure penance. Born in the depths of the palace, he is unable to master things. All he does is talk in a low voice. He knows no art, nothing of books and discussion. Let us talk about the essentials of Right Dharma. If he defeats me, I shall serve him; if I win, he serves me." At that time, there were many tirthikas [present]. Gathering together, they went to Magadha, to Ajatasatru. The king saw them and asked: "You are all in the holy teaching. You are those who have renounced the world. You have abandoned wealth and things of the secular life. The people of my land make all offerings to you. They look up to you with respect and do not act against you. Why do you band together and come here in one body and wish to see me? O you! You all belong to different teachings and have different precepts and different circumstances in which you renounced your homes. You each practise the Way following precepts. Why is it that you are all of one mind, as though the wind had driven the fallen leaves all together into one place? What do you intend to speak about by coming here "en masse"? I always protect world-fleeing people [i.e. spiritual questers, renunciates] and am not lagging much behind others in using my body and life [to help them]." Then all the tirthikas said with one voice: "O great King! Listen to us carefully. You are now

the great bridge of Dharma, the great horn, the great scales of Dharma. You are the utensil of all laws. You are the true nature of all virtues. You are the highway of Right Dharma. You are the last field wherein to sow seed. You are the fountainhead of the state. You are the bright mirror of all lands. You are all the forms of all heavens. You are the parent to the people of all lands. O great King! You are the treasure-house of all the virtues of the world. This is the King's body. Why do we say that you are the storehouse of virtue? The King carries on the administration of the state with no thought of partiality or hostility. The King's mind is fair like the earth, water, fire, and wind. That is why we say that the King is the storehouse of virtue. "O great King! The life span of beings in the present age is paltry. But the virtue of the King is like that of kings from days gone by, when man was blessed with long life and peace. The situation is like that of Head-Born, Sudarsana, Forbearance, Nahusa, Yajata, Sibi, and Iksvaku. All such kings were perfect in the Good Dharma. You too, King, are the same. O great King! Due to you, the land is at peace and the people are doing well. That is why all the world-fleeing love this state and uphold the precepts, make effort, and practise the right way. O great King! I state in my sutras that if the world-fleeing observe the precepts and make effort as set forth in the state, the King also shares in the good which is practised. O great King! You have already made away with all robbers, and there is nothing for the world-fleeing to be afraid of. Only, there lives just one evil person - Sramana Gautama. You, King, have not yet tested him. We are all afraid. This person sits on [prides himself on] his high birth and caste and on his bodily accomplishment, and by dint of the past danas he has performed, he is recompensed with many offerings. In all such circumstances, he is arrogant, and because of his sorcery, he is haughty. For this reason, we cannot carry out our penances. He receives soft clothes and bedding. Thus, he is the most evil in all the world. For profit, people go to him, and on becoming members of his hosuehold, they are unable to practise penance. Through sorcery, he vanquished Kasyapa, Sariputra, Maudgalyayana, and others. And now he has come to our place, to the forest of sal trees, and, declaring that this body is the Eternal, Bliss, Self, and the Pure, he lures away our disciples. O great King! Previously Gautama said: non-eternal, non-bliss, non-Self, and non-pure. I well forbore it. Now he says: Eternal, Bliss, Self, and Pure. I cannot stand it. Please, O great King! Allow me to argue the point with Gautama." The king said: "All you great ones! What has stirred you up, so that you now become mad and unsettled like great waves of water, or like circles of flame, or like monkeys who throw themselves across the trees? This is a shame. If the wise hear of this, they will pity you. If the ignorant hear of this, they will laugh at you. What you say is not appropriate for any world-fleeing person. If you are suffering from the illness of wind or from the yellow-water pox, I have medicine for all of this. I shall cure you. If it comes from any illness of a devil, my family man [family doctor], Jivaka [a famous doctor in the royal household of Ajatasatru], will thoroughly do away with it. All of you now intend to srape Mount Sumeru with your hands and nails, or to try to chew and gnaw on a diamond. "O all of you great ones! This is like an ignorant person wanting to awaken a sleeping lion-king at a time when the lion is feeling hungry; or like trying to touch the mouth of a viper with one's finger; or like playing with the embers that lie under the ashes. This is the situation with you now. This is like a wild fox wishing to imitate a lion's roar, or a mosquito competing in speed with a garuda [swift, mythical bird]. It is like a hare desiring to cross the sea and plumb its depths. You, too, are now like this. If you are dreaming of a victory over Gautama, such a dream is one that is fanatical [fantastical]. It is not worth believing in. O you great ones! You now think thus. This is like a flying moth that throws itself into a fire ball. Take my word! Do not say any more! You say that I am fair and am like a pair of scales. But do not let anything like this reach the ears of other persons." Then the tirthikas said: "O great King! The sorcery of Gautama will be such that, when it appears before you, it will make the mind of the great King not doubt the words of these holy ones. O great King! Please do not despise the great ones. O great King! Who gave the knowledge of the waxing and waning of the moon, the saltiness of the water of the great sea, and of Mount Malaya? Is all this not the work of the Brahmins? O great King! Did you not hear that the rishi, Gautama, performed a miracle, so that for 12 long years he transformed himself into the carnal body of the Sakya, and made the body of the Sakya like that of a ram and made 1,000 valvas which were made to remain in the body of the Sakya? O great King! Have you not heard that the sishi, Jatukarna, drank in one day the waters of the four seas, so that the earth all became dry? O great King! Have you not heard that the rishi, Vasu, became a Mahesvara and had three eyes? O great King! Have you not heard that the rishi, Aradakalama, changed Garapu Castle into earth? O great King! The Brahmins have such men of great power. You can easily check the facts. O great King! Why do you so belittle them?" The king said: "All of you! If you do not believe what I tell you, the Tathagata, the Right-Enlightened one, is now in the forest of sal trees. You may go and question or reprove him as you will. The Tathagata too will see you and for your sake will explain things in detail and answer your questions." Then King Ajatasatru went to the Buddha, together with the tirthikas and with his own retinue. He prostrated himself on the ground, and walked around the Buddha three times. Having paid his homage, he drew back and took his seat on one side and said to the Buddha: "These tirthikas desire to put questions to you in their own way. Will you be so good as to answer them?" The Buddha said: "O great King! Wait! I know when I must." Then, amongst those who were present, there was a Brahmin, Jataishuna by name. He said: "O Gautama! Do you state that Nirvana is that which is eternal?" "It is thus, it is thus, O great Brahmin!" The Brahmin said: "You say that Nirvana is eternal. But this is not the case. Why not? What obtains in the world is that from a seed comes about the fruit. This continues, and there is no disruption. This is as with a pot, which comes about from the earth and from thread cloth. You, Gautama, always say: "When one practises the image of the non-eternal, one arrives at Nirvana." You also say, Gautama: "When one makes away with desire and greed, this is Nirvana. When one does away with the greed of the body ["rupa"] and non-body, this is Nirvana. When one has made away with the defilement of ignorance, this is Nirvana." All that goes from desire up to the defilement of ignorance is non-eternal. If the cause is non-eternal, the Nirvana that comes about [from it] must also be non-eternal. You, Gautama, also say: "Through cause comes about birth in heaven; through cause one gains hell, and through cause emancipation. Thus, all things come about from causes." If Emancipation results from a cause, how can one call it eternal? "Also you, Gautama, say: "Form ["rupa"] comes about from causal relations.

Hence, non-eternal. So is it also with feeling, perception, volition, and consciousness." If Emancipation is form, know that what there is [here] is non-eternal. So does it also stand with feeling, perception, volition, and consciousness. If there is any Emancipation away from the five skandhas, that Emancipation is Void. If it is Void, we cannot say that things come from causal relations. Why not? Because eternity is one and pervades everywhere. You, Gautama, also say that what comes about from causation is suffering. If it is suffering, how can we say that Emancipation is Bliss? "O Gautama! And you say that the non-eternal is suffering and that suffering is non-Self. If non-eternal, suffering, and non-Self, what there is is the non-pure. What does not come from cause must be non-eternal, suffering, non-Self, and non-pure. How can we say that Nirvana is the Eternal, Bliss, the Self, and the Pure? O Gautama! If one states: eternal and non-eternal, suffering and bliss, the Self and the non-Self, pure and non-pure - are these not two terms? I once heard from the aged and wise that: "If any Buddha appears in the world, he does not speak any double words." You Gautama now speak of two words and say: "And the Buddha is my own carnal self." What do you mean by this?" The Buddha said: "O Brahmin! I shall now ask you about what you say. Answer just as you think!" The Brahmin said: "Well said, Gautama!" The Buddha said: "Is your nature eternal or non-eternal?" The Brahmin said: "My nature is eternal." "O Brahmin! Does this nature become a cause of things within and without?" "That is so, Gautama." The Buddha said: "O Brahmin! How does it become the cause?" "O Gautama! From nature comes about "great"; from great, arrogance; from arrogance, 16 things, which are: 1) earth, water, fire, wind, and space; 2) the five sense-organs, which are: eye, ear, nose, tongue, and touch; 3) the five acting organs, which are: hand, foot, voice, the two sexual organs of male and female; 4) the all-equal sense-organs of mind. These 16 things come about from five things, which are: colour, sound, smell, taste, and touch. These 21 things have three root qualities, which are: 1) defiling, 2) coarse, and 3) black. The defiling is craving; the coarse is anger; and black is ignorance. O Gautama! These 25 things come about from nature." "O Brahmin! Are these things that are great, etc., eternal or non-eternal?" "O Gautama! The dharma nature that I speak about is eternal. All things, beginning with "great",

are non-eternal." "O Brahmin! From what you say, it seems that according to you the cause is eternal and the fruit non-eternal. Now, what wrong could there be when I say that the cause is non-eternal, but the result is eternal? O Brahmin! Are there two causes in what you speak of?" The reply came back: "Yes! There are." The Buddha said: "What are the two?" The Brahmin said: "One is cause by birth and the other is the revealing cause." The Buddha said: What is cause by birth and what the revealing cause?" The Brahmin said: "The cause by birth may be likened to the earth from which comes about a pot; the revealing cause is like a lamp that shines upon a thing." The Buddha said: "Of these two kinds of cause, is the nature of the cause one? If it is one, cause by birth may well turn out to be the revealing cause, and the revealing cause may turn into cause by birth. Is this not so?" "No, O Gautama!" The Buddha said: "I say that Nirvana is attained from the non-eternal, but it is not non-eternal. O Brahmin! When we gain it through the revealing cause, we gain the Eternal, Bliss, the Self, and the Pure. When we see it from the standpoint of cause by birth, we gain the non-eternal, non-birth, non-Self, and non-Pure. That is why the Tathagata speaks in two ways. There can be no such two words. That is why we say that the Tathagata does not have two words. You say that you once heard from wise people who are now gone that: "The Buddha appears in the world and he does not speak any two words." This is all very well. What is said by all Buddhas of the ten directions and of the Three Times does not differ. That is why we say that the Buddha does not have any two words [i.e. differing statements]. "How do they not differ? What is "is" is declared as "is"; whatever is "is-not" is stated to be "isnot". Hence, one meaning. O Brahmin! The Tathagata-World-Honoured One says two things. This is but to reveal one word. How do two words come to reveal one? It is as in the case of the two words of "eye" and "form", which call forth the one word of "living consciousness". So does it obtain with mind and dharma." The Brahmin said: "O Gautama! You well grasp the meanings of such words. I do not yet gain the meaning that two words are one." Then the World-Honoured One spoke of the Four Truths. "O Brahmin! We speak of the "Truth of Suffering", which is two and also one. This applies all the way down to the Truth of the Way, which again is two and also one." The Brahmin said: "O

World-Honoured One! I now see." The Buddha said: "In what way do you see?" "O World-Honoured One! We say "Truth of Suffering". All common mortals see two things. But with the holy persons, what there is is one. So is it with the Truth of the Way, too." The Buddha said: "Well said! You see well." The Brahmin said: "O World-Honoured One! I have now heard Dharma and gained the right view. I shall now take refuge in the Buddha, Dharma, and Sangha. I pray that you will admit me into your Order." Then the World-Honoured One said to Kaundinya: "You now shave this Jadaishuna and admit him into the Order." Then Kaundinya, by order of the Buddha, shaved [Jadaishuna]. When this was done, there were two fallings: one of hair, and the other of defilement. And at that instant, he attained arhatship. Also, there was a Brahmacarin called Vasistha, who said: "O Gautama! Is the Nirvana you speak of eternal?" "It is so, O Brahmacarin!" Vasistha said: "O Gautama! When there is no defilement, do you not call this Nirvana?" "It is thus, O Brahmacarin!" Vasistha said: "There are four instances where we say "not-is". These are: 1) a thing which has not yet come about. This is a not-is. This is as in the case of a pot when it has not yet come out of the mud. And we say that there is no pot; 2) whatever has gone is called "not-is". This is as in the case of a broken pot. At such a time, we say that there is no pot; 3) whatever does not exist in things that are different in nature, when we say is-not, as in the case of a cow, in which there is nothing of a horse, and in that of a horse, in which there is no cow; 4) when nothing exists in any circumstances whatsoever, as in the case of the hair of a tortoise or the horns of a hare. O good man! If Nirvana is that which is when defilement is done away with, Nirvana is a "not-is". If so, how can we say that there are the Eternal, Bliss, the Self, and the Pure?" The Buddha said: "O good man! Nirvana as such is not like a pot that did not exist when as yet in the mud. Also, it is not like the "not-is" of extinction, or the not-is of a pot that is broken. Also, it is not the not-is if the absolute not-is, as in the case of the hair of a tortoise or the horns of a hare; nor is it the not-is of that which is different by nature. "O good man! You can say that there is no horse in a cow. But you cannot say: "There is no cow." There is no cow in a horse, but you cannot say: "There is no horse." So does it also obtain with Nirvana. There is no Nirvana in defilement, and no

defilement in Nirvana. So, we say that different things do not mutually possess each other." Vasistha said: "O Gautama! If you say that Nirvana is what does not exist in what is other, this will entail your saying that the Eternal, Bliss, Self, and the Pure do not exist in the noneness of a different thing. O Gautama! How can you say that there are the Eternal, Bliss, the Self, and the Pure?" The Buddha said: "There are three nonenesses in what you say. The case of the cow and the horse is what was not before, but what is. This is what was not before. What was, but what is not [any longer], is what comes about when a thing breaks up. The non-is by way of difference is as you say. O good man! We do not find these three kinds of not-is in Nirvana. Therefore, Nirvana is the Eternal, Bliss, Self, and the Pure. This is as as with one who is ill, [where there is either]: 1) fever, 2) illness from wind, or 3) cold. These can well be cured by the three kinds of medicine. A person suffering from fever can be well cured by butter; one suffering from wind can be cured by oil; and a person who is suffering from a cold can indeed be cured by honey. These three kinds of medicine can indeed cure the three kinds of evil illnesses. O good man! In wind, there is no oil, and in oil no wind; or in honey, there is no cold, and in the cold there is no honey. Therefore, a cure indeed results. It is the same with all beings, too. They have three illnesses, which are: 1) greed, 2) ill-will, and 3) ignorance. Three kinds of medicine will cure these three illnesses. Meditation upon impurity will act as a medicine against desire; that on loving-kindness will act as medicine against ill-will; that on the knowledge of causal relations will act against ignorance. "O good man! In order to make away with desire, one meditates on non-desire; to make away with ill-will, the meditation upon non-ill-will is performed; to make away with ignorance, one meditates on non-ignorance. In the three illnesses we do not have the three kinds of medicine, and in the three kinds of medicine we do not have the three kinds of illness. O good man! As there are not the three kinds of medicine in the three kinds of illness, this is the non-eternal, non-Self, non-bliss, and non-pure. In the three kinds of medicine there are not the three types of illness. Hence, the Eternal, Bliss, the Self, and the Pure." Vasistha said: "O World-Honoured One! You, the Tathagata, explain to me about the eternal and the non-eternal. What is the eternal, and what is the non-eternal?" The Buddha said: "O good man! Form is non-eternal, and emancipation from form is the Eternal. And consciousness is non-eternal, and emancipation from consciousness is the Eternal. O good man! If there is any good man or woman who can well see that form down to consciousness are non-eternal, know that such a person can well attain what is Eternal." Vasistha said: "O World-Honoured One! I have now truly come to know the Eternal and the non-eternal." The Buddha said: "O good man! How do you know the Eternal and the non-eternal?" Vasistha said: "I now know that self and form are non-eternal and that Emancipation is Eternal. So is it with [the skandhas] down to consciousness." "O good man! You now well repay to this carnal body what you owe." To Kaundinya, he said: "This Vasistha has now attained the fruition of arhatship. Give him the three clothes [robes] and a bowl." Then Kaundinya gave the clothes as instructed by the Buddha. Then, on receiving the robes and bowl, Vasistha said: "O Kaundinya, greatly virtuous one! I have now gained upon this carnal body of mine a great karmic reward. Please, O greatly virtuous one, condescend to go to the Buddha and report in detail what has transpired with me. This evil body of mine has touched and defiled the Tathagata and now adopts his family name of Gautama. Please report on my behalf and say that I now repent of my evil self. I, also, cannot have this body of mine long in life. I shall now enter Nirvana." Then Kaundinya went to the Buddha and said: "O World-Honoured One! The bhiksu Vasistha repents and says: "Obstinate fool that I was, I touched the body of the Tathagata and am now one of his group [following]. I cannot have this viperous body of mine staying long in the world." He now desires to make away with this body and comes to me and repents." The Buddha said: "O Kaundinya! Vasistha has long amassed virtue at the places of innumerable Buddhas. Having now been taught by me, he is rightly abiding in the Way. Abiding rightly in the Way, he has arrived at the right fruition. You should make offerings to his carnal self." Kaundinya, thus directed by the Buddha, went to where the person lived and made offerings. Then, Vasistha, at the time of his cremation, performed many a divine miracle. All the tirthikas saw this and said aloud: "This Vasistha has acquired sorcery at the place of Sramana Gautama." Then, at that time, there was among the group a Brahmacarin called Senika,

who said: "O Gautama! Is there self?" The Tathagata was silent. He asked a second time, and a third time. The Buddha was silent. Senika said: "O Gautama! All beings possess self, which pervades everywhere, and the creator is one. O Gautama! Why do you sit silently and not answer?" The Buddha said: "O Senika! Do you say that this self pervades everywhere?" Senika answered and said: "It is not I alone who say so, but all the wise have also shown this." The Buddha said: "O good man! If self pervades everywhere, all the beings of the five realms would have to gain the returns of actions performed at one [i.e. the same] time. If all the people of the five realms have [the same] karmic results, why do you avoid all evil actions, so as to evade hell, and do all good things, so as to gain life in heaven?" Senika said: "O Gautama! There are two kinds of self of which I talk, namely: 1) the carnal self and 2) the eternal self. For the sake of the carnal self, we practise the Way and shun evil, so as not to gain hell, and practise all good deeds, so as to gain life in heaven." The Buddha said: "O good man! You say that self pervades all places. It it is in the created self, you may know that such a self is non-eternal. If it is not created, how can you say that it pervades everywhere?" "O Gautama! The self I speak of exists in what is created and yet is what is eternal. O Gautama! A person happens to cause a fire in the house. The master of the house comes out. So we cannot say: "When the house is reduced to ashes, the master of the house is also reduced to ashes." It is the same with what I say. This created body is non-eternal. But when the non-eternal is about to start out [i.e. when the body is about to die], the self goes out. So the self I speak of is all-pervading and eternal." The Buddha said: "O good man! You say: "The self I speak of is all-pervading and eternal." But this is not so. Why not? Of what pervades, there are two kinds. These are: 1) eternal and 2) non-eternal. Again, there are two kinds, namely: 1) form and 2) non-form. Hence, when one says that all exists, this means that it is eternal and non-eternal; it is form and non-form. You may say that the master of the house is out of the house, and that there is no non-eternal to come about. But this is not so. Why? The house is no master and the master no house. That which is different is burnt and what is different is out. Thus goes the logic. The self is not anything as such. Why not? The self is form and form self. Non-form is self and self non-form. How can you say that when form suffers change, the self is out of it? "O good man! You may say that all beings possess the same self. But this is contrary to what obtains in the secular or supramundane world. Why? What obtains in the secular world speaks of father and mother, boy and girl. If we are to say: "The self is one; the father is the son, the son the father; the mother is the girl, and the girl the mother; the enemy is the friend, and the friend the enemy; this is that and that this. Hence, all beings possess the same self" - this is counter to what obtains in the secular or the supramundane world." Senika said: "I, too, do not say that all beings possess one self. I say that each person possesses one self." The Buddha said: "O good man! If it is said that each person has one self, this means none other than that there are many selves. This is not so. Why not? You said before that self pervades. If self goes everywhere, the karmic root of all beings must be the same. When heaven sees, the Buddha sees; when heaven acts, the Buddha acts; when heaven hears, the Buddha hears. All things must be thus. If heaven can see and the Buddha cannot, we cannot say that self extends everywhere. If it is non-pervading, this is nothing other than the non-eternal." Senika said: "O Gautama! The self of all beings pervades everywhere, whereas law [Dharma]: [the following discussion on self is obscure in its details, and difficult to follow - ed.] and non-law do not. By this, the Buddha can act differently and heaven also can act thus. Hence, you, Gautama, should not say: "When the Buddha sees, heaven can see, and when the Buddha can hear, heaven can hear." The Buddha said: "O good man! Is it not the case that law and non-law are what one does?" Senika said: "Such are the works of one's actions." The Buddha said: "If law [dharma, that which exists] and non-law are what one does, this means the same thing. How could they be different? Why? Where the Buddha gains action in hand, heaven gains the self; where heaven gains action in hand, the Buddha gains in hand the self. Hence, when the Buddha can do, heaven can do. Law and non-law must obtain thus. O good man! So, if the law and non-law of beings is thus, there cannot be any other different karmic results. O good man! From the seed comes about the fruit. This seed never thinks: "I shall become the fruit of a Brahmin, not that of a Kshatriya, Vaishya, or Sudra." Why? The seed carried forth the fruit. It concerns [i.e. is concerned with] no caste or

anything as such. It is the same with law and non-law, too. We cannot discriminatingly think: "I shall only attain the fruition of Buddhahood, not of heaven; I shall only attain the fruition of heaven, but not of Buddhahood." Why not? Because karma works fairly."

Senika said: "O Gautama! For example, there are hundreds and thousands of lamps in a room. The wicks may differ, but the light does not differ. The fact that the wicks of the lamps differ can be compared to law and non-law, and the fact that there is no difference in the light can be compared to the self of beings." The Buddha said: "O good man! You take up the case of the light of a lamp and mean [thereby] to explain self. This does not apply well. Why not? The room is different and the lamp is different. The light of the lamp goes around the wick and it also pervades the room. If the self you speak of is thus, self must lie around law and non-law. There must be law and non-law in self. If law and non-law do not exist in self, one cannot say: "It pervades all places." If it [they] go together, how can we employ the analogy of the light of the wick? O good man! If you truly mean to say that the wick and the light are different, why is it that when the number of wicks increases, the light becomes brighter, and when the wick is spent, the light, too, dies out? Hence, we can compare law and non-law to the wick and the light, and the non-difference of light to self. Why? Because the three - law, non-law, and self - are but one." Senika said: "O Gautama! You take up the simile of the lamp. This is unfortunate. Why? If the simile of the lamp is good, I have already employed it before. If it is unfortunate, what more need is there to refer to it again?" "O good man! I employ analogies. But these have nothing to do with what is fortunate or unfortunate. I accord with your will, and in the analogy I say that there is light away from the wick and that there is light along with the wick. Your mind is not fair. You purposely take up the case of the wick and the lamp and compare these to law and non-law, and liken the light to self. That is why I mean to reprove [you on this point]. The wick is the light. Is there any light away from the wick? Dharma is at once [i.e. at the same time] the self; the self is at once Dharma. Non-Dharma is at once self and self at once non-Dharma. Now, you say: "Why does one take up one aspect and not take up the other?" But such a simile is unfortunate for you. That is why I crush you instead. O good man! Such an analogy does not work out [i.e. does not work well as] an analogy. Due to the fact that it does not constitute an analogy, it works favourably on my side and not on yours. O good man! You may think: "If it is unfortunate for me, is it not also so for you?" But this is not so. Why not? In the world we see a person who kills himself with his own sword; whatever is done by one's own hand is made use of by others. The analogy you employ works likewise. Luck is on my side and ill-luck on yours." Senika said: "O Gautama! You reproved me before for the unfairness of my mind. Now, what you say is not fair either. Why not? O Gautama! You now direct [ascribe] luck to yourself and bad luck to me. From this, I conclude and see this unfairness." The Buddha said: "What is not fair on my side truly breaks [destroys? evens out] what is not fair on your side. Because of this, what is fair with you and what is not on my side bespeak luck. What is not fair on my side breaks what is not on your side, and you harvest what is fair. This is the fairness on my side. Why? Because this calls forth what is fair on all holy persons." Senika said: "O Gautama! Self is always fair. How can you say that you crush out the non-fair? All beings possess self all-equally. How can you say that self is not all-equal?" "O good man! You too say that one gains birth in hell, one gains birth in the realm of hungry pretas, one gains birth in the animal realm, and one gains birth in the worlds of humans and gods. If self already pervades the five realms, can one say that one gains life in various realms? You also say that through the harmony [i.e. coming together] of parents, a child comes about. If there is a child beforehand, how can one say that through harmonisation a child comes about? Because of this, one possesses the body of the five realms. If it is the case that these five realms already precede the carnal existence of the body, how can one say that one enacts karma? Hence, unequal. "O good man! You may mean to say that self is that which does. But this is not so. Why not? If self is that which does [i.e. performs actions], why should one do what is pain to oneself? But we actually see beings who are suffering from pain. Thus we may know that self is not that which does. If we are to say that this pain is not what is done [made] by self and that it does not come about from a cause, this must mean that all things, too, do not come about from a cause. On what grounds can you say

that it is the doing of self? "O good man! All the sufferings and happinesses of beings come about from causes and conditions. Thus, suffering and happiness call forth apprehension and joy. When one has apprehension, there is no joy; when there is joy, there is no apprehension. It is either joy or apprehension. How can any wise person call this eternal? "O good man! You state that self is eternal. If it is eternal, how can you say that there are the differences of the ten times [i.e. the stages of growth of the human, from embryo to old age]? With the Eternal, there can never be any kalala [embryo] time, down to the days of old age. The permanent existence of the Void cannot have a single "time". How could there be the ten times? "O good man! Self is no time of kalala or the days of old age. How can you say that there are the differences of the ten times? O good man! If self is something that does, there must be with this self the time of the prime of life and the days of old age. Beings, too, have this prime of life and the days of old age. If self is anything of this sort, how could it be eternal? O good man! If self is that which does, how could there be the differences of sharp and dull to one [i.e. how could there be mental sharpness and dullness amongst people]? O good man! If self is something that acts, this self can certainly perform bodily, oral and mental actions. If this is the work of self, how can one say that there is no self in the mouth? How can one doubt and wonder if it is "is" or "is-not"? "O good man! You may say that there is seeing separate from the eye. But this is not so. Why not? If there is any seeing separate from the eye, what point is there in using the eyes? The same applies to the bodily sense-organs, too. You may say that self always sees with the eyes. But the case is not thus. Why not? This is like saying: "The Sumana bloom reduces a great village to ashes." How does it burn? It burns with fire. The same is the case when you say that self sees." Senika said: "O Gautama! It is like the case of the sickle, with which one can cut grass. The same is the case with self, which can indeed see and hear and touch through the five sense-organs." "O good man! The sickle and the man are different things. Because of this, a person can indeed take up the sickle and do things. Away from the sense-organs, there can be no self. How can one say: "Self can [act] with all the sense-organs?" O good man! If you mean to say that a person can indeed mow when he takes up a sickle, and the same is the case with self - does this self have a hand or not? It it does, why not take it [i.e. why does not self directly pick up the sickle, without the use of physical hands]? If self has no hands, how can we say that self is one that does? O good man! That which cuts the grass is the sickle. It is not self, nor is it man. If self or man can indeed cut, why does one need to depend upon any sickle? "O good man! The man performs two actions, namely: 1) taking the grass and 2) using the sickle. The sickle can truly cut. The same is the case with beings. The eye indeed sees forms. This arises from harmonisation [conjoining of causes and conditions]. If something is seen through the harmonisation of causal relations, how can the wise say that there is self? This is not so. Why not? In the world, we do not see that heaven performs actions and that the Buddha receives the fruit. If you mean to say that it is not that the body does but self receives without having enacted the cause, why should you hope to attain Emancipation through causal relations? If your body were to be born with no cause, after attaining Emancipation you would gain your body without any cause. Just as with the body, so all defilements, too, would thus come about." Senika said: "O Gautama! There are two selves. One knows and the other knows not. The self that knows not truly gains the physical body and the self that abandons one's own self. This is as with an earthen pot, which, when treated in the oven, changes its colour and when there is nothing that is to come about again any more. It is also thus with the defilements of a wise person. There is no more coming about [of them]." The Buddha said: "O good man! You speak of "knowing". Is it the intellect that knows or self that knows? If the intellect can know, why do we say that self knows? If self knows, why do we particularly work out means for knowing? If you mean to say that self knows through the intellect, this is as in the case of the analogy of the flower, which breaks and falls. O good man!

This is as in the case of a tree that has thorns, which prick by nature. We cannot say that the tree takes the thorns and pricks. It is the same with the intellect too. The intellect knows by itself. How can we say that self takes the intellect and knows? O good man! You say in your teaching that self arrives at emancipation. Is it the non-intellectual self or the intellectual self which gains [this]? If it is the non-intellectual self which gains [this], we

can know that it must still possess defilement. If it is the case that the intellect gains [Emancipation], we can know that there are already the five senses and sense-organs. Why? There cannot be any intellect other than the roots. If all the root organs are perfect, how can we say that the person arrives at Emancipation? If the nature of self is pure and is separate from the five roots, how can it pervade, and exist in, the five realms? Why does a person practise all good deeds to arrive at Emancipation? "O good man! For example, it is [like] extracting thorns from the Void. Things go the same with you. If the self is pure, how can we say that a person cuts off all defilements? If you intend to say that the person arrives at Emancipation not being based on causal relations, why is it that all animals do not arrive at it?" Senika said: "O Gautama! If it is selfless, whoever can remember well?" The Buddha said to Senika: "If there is self, why do we forget? O good man! If remembering is self, why do we remember unhappy things, remember what we do not wish to remember, and not remember what we mean to remember?" Senika said: "O Gautama! If there is no self, who sees and who hears?" The Buddha said: "One has six spheres within and six dusts [i.e. the six sense-fields] without. The inner and outer conjoin and one gains the six kinds of consciousness. Now, these six consciousnesses gain their name through causal relations. "For example, a fire comes about from a tree, and we speak of a "tree fire". Grass catches fire, and we speak of "grass fire". Bran catches fire, and we speak of "bran fire". Cow dung catches fire, and we speak of "cow-dung fire". It is the same thing with the consciousness of beings, too. "We gain consciousness by means of the eyes, colour, light, and desire, and we say "eyeconsciousness". O good man! Such eye-consciousness does not exist in the eye, nor in the desire, etc. The four things conjoin and we get this consciousness. It is the same with the consciousness of mind. If things come into being thus, we cannot say that knowing and seeing are self, and that touching is self. "O good man! That is why we say that self is the eye-consciousness down to mental consciousness, and that all things are phantoms. How are they like phantoms? Because of the fact that what originally was not is what now is, and what once was is now no more. O good man! For example, the mixing together of butter, barley, flour, honey, ginger, pepper, pippali [a long pepper], grapes, walnuts, pomegranate, and suishi [a kind of prune] is called "kangigan" [possibly the name of a drug]. Apart from this mixing together, there can be no kangigan. The six spheres of the inner and outer are what we call the being, self, man, or male. Other than the spheres within and without, there can be no being or man." Senika said: "O Gautama! If selfless, why do we say: "I see", "I hear", "I have sorrow", "I feel bliss", "I have apprehension", or "I am glad"? The Buddha said: "O good man! If we say "I see", "I hear", etc., this implies that there is a self. Why does the world say: "The sins of our deeds are not what I see or hear about?" O good man! The coming together of the four armies [i.e. the four constituent parts of an army] is termed an "army". These four are not one, but we say: "Our army is valiant, our army is superior to his." It is the same with what comes about through the conjoining together of the inner and outer spheres, too. Though they are not one, we say: "I do", "I feel", "I see", "I hear", "I have sorrow", "I feel bliss"'. Senika said: "O Gautama! You speak of the "conjoining together of the inner and outer." Who is it that says: "I do", "I feel"? The Buddha said: "O Senika! From the causal relations of the ignorance of craving comes about action, from it existence, from it the innumerable varieties of mental actions, and mental wakefulness in perception. This mental wakefulness in perception causes the wind to rise, and the wind, following the mind, touches the throat, tongue, teeth, and lips. The inverted voice of the image of the being comes out and says: "I do, I feel, I see, and I hear." O good man! The bell on top of a hanging ensign rings due to causal relations. If the wind is strong, the sound is strong; if the wind is weak, the sound is weak. And yet, no one does it. That is how matters stand. When a heated iron is put into water, this engenders various sounds. And yet, there is truly no one who does it [i.e. who makes those sounds]. The case is thus. O good man! The common mortal is unable to think or discriminate such things and says: "There is self, and what belongs to self; I do, I feel, etc." Senika said: "O Gautama! You say that there is no self, and nothing that belongs to self. Then, why do you speak of the Eternal, Bliss, the Self, and the Pure?" "The Buddha said: "Nobly-born One, I have never taught that the six inner and outer ayatanas [sense-spheres] and the six consciousnesses are Eternal, Blissful, the Self, or Pure; but I do declare that the cessation of the six inner and outer ayatanas and the six consciousnesses arising from them is termed the Eternal. Becasue that is Eternal, it is the Self. Because there is Eternity and the Self, it is termed Blissful. Because it is Eternal, the Self and Blissful, it is termed Pure. Nobly-born One, ordinary people abhor suffering and by eliminating the cause of suffering, they may freely/ spontaneously distance themselves from it. This is termed the Self. Therefore, I have spoken of the Eternal, the Self, the Blissful, and the Pure. [alternative rendering into English, by Samuel Beal, of this important passage can be found in the latter's "A Catena of Buddhist Scriptures from the Chinese", "1871, pp.179-180 "Sena asked: "According to Gotama's opinion, then, that there is no 'I', let me ask what can be the meaning of that description he gives of Nirvana, that it is permanent, full of joy, personal, and pure?" Buddha says: "Illustrious youth, I do not say that the six external and internal organs, or the various species of knowledge, are permanent, etc; but what I say is that "that" is permanent, full of joy, personal, and pure, which is left after the six organs and the six objects of sense, and the various kinds of knowledge are all destroyed. Illustrious youth, when the world, weary of sorrow, turns away and separates itself from the cause of all this sorrow, then, by this voluntary rejection of it, there remains that which I call the True Self; and it is of this I plainly declare the formula, that it is permanent, full of joy, personal, and pure."]. "Senika said: "O World-Honoured One! Great Compassionate One! Explain to me, I pray, how I am to attain the Eternal, Bliss, the Self, and the Pure, about which you speak." "The Buddha said: "Nobly-born One, the entire world possesses great pride [mana] from the very beginning, which augments pride and also functions as the cause of [further] pride and proud actions. Therefore, beings now experience the results of pride and are not able to eliminate all the klesas [mental/moral defilements] and attain the Eternal, Blissful, the Self, and the Pure. If beings wish to do away with all defilements, what they need to do is , first of all, to make away with pride." [Note: the Sanskrit word for pride, mana, has a different semantic range from the English "pride/ arrogance". It is derived from the verbal root, man (to think, believe, measure, conceive, deem, value, reagrd as) and also means "measure", "computation", "means of proof". The "pride" sense here implies the process of generating or projecting what are implicitly false mental constructs. It refers to the process described in the earlier chapter in the sutra on the four perverse views. - Stephen Hodge]. Senika said: "O World-Honoured One! It is thus, it is thus! All is as your holy teaching says. I had, from the very start, arrogance; I was grounded on the causal relations of this arrogance. That is why I addressed you by the family name of Gautama. I am now removed from such great arrogance. That

is why, with the sincerest heart, I seek Dharma. How am I to arrive at the Eternal, Bliss, the Self, and the Pure?" The Buddha said: "Listen carefully to me, listen carefully! I shall now explain matters to you in detail. "O good man! If all thoughts of your own self, of others and of beings are done away with, you will segregate yourself from such." Senika said: "O World-Honoured One! I have now understood and gained the right Dharma Eye."

The Buddha said: "In what way have you known, understood, and gained the right Dharma-Eye?" "O World-Honoured One! The physical form ["rupa"] of which we speak is not our own, not another's, nor that of beings." "So does it obtain with all [the skandhas] down to consciousness. Seeing things thus, I have arrived at the right Dharma-Eye. O World-Honoured One! I am now very eager to renounce the world and be admitted into the Order. Be good enough to admit me into the Order!" The Buddha said: "Welcome, O bhiksu!" At once he was perfect in pure actions, and he attained arhatship. Among the tirthikas, there was a Brahmacarin [present] by the name of Kasyapa. He also said: "O Gautama! Is the body life? Or are body and life different things?" The Tathagata said nothing. So he asked a second and a third time. The Brahmacarin again said: "O Gautama! A man dies and does not yet gain his next body. In this in-between state, do we not say that the body is different and the life is different? If they are different, why do you sit silently and not reply?" "O good man! Body and life both arise from causal relations. I say that nothing comes about without causal relations. As with the body and life, so does it proceed with all things." The Brahmacarin further said: "O Gautama! I see things in the world that do not proceed in accordance with causal relations." The Buddha said: "O Brahmacarin! In what way do you see things that do not proceed in accordance with causal relations?" The Brahmacarin said: "I see trees being burnt. The wind blows out the flakes [cinders, sparks] of fire, which fall in different places. Is this not what has nothing to do with causal relations?" The Buddha said: "O good man! I say that this fire, too, comes about from causal relations. It is not the case that it does not accord with any cause." The Brahmacarin said: "O Gautama! When the fire flakes go [i.e. move off], these do not depend upon fuel or charcoal. So

how can we say that these are dependent on causal relations?" The Buddha said: "O good man! Though there is no fuel or charcoal, the wind drives the fire flakes away. Through the causal factor of the wind, the fire does not die out." "O Gautama! A man dies, but does not yet gain his next body. How can we call the life that exists in between one of causal relations?" The Buddha said: "O Brahmacarin! Ignorance and craving are the causal relations. Through the causal relations of ignorance and craving, life is able to be sustained. O good man! Through causal relations, the body can be life, and life the body. Through causal relations, the body is different, and life different. A wise person should not say that the body and life are different all through." The Brahmacarin said: "O World-Honoured One! Please condescend to analyse and explain to me clearly, so that I will truly be able to understand causal relations." The Buddha said: "O Brahmacarin! The cause is the five skandhas and the result too is the five skandhas. The fire not started, there cannot be any smoke." The Brahmacarin said: "O World-Honoured One! I now know and I now have understood." "O good man! In what way have you come to know and in what way have you understood?" "O World-Honoured One! Fire is the defilement, which truly burns in the realms of hell, hungry pretas, animals, humans and the gods. The smoke is the karmic results which a person harvests, which are non-eternal, non-pure and which emit a bad smell and are defiled and to be despised. Hence, "smoke". If beings do not perform any defilement, there cannot be any karmic result of defilement. That is why the Tathagata says that where there is no fire, there is no smoke. O World-Honoured One! I now see correctly. What I wish for is that you will now allow me to renounce the world?" Then the World-Honoured One said to Kaundinya: "Admit this Brahmacarin and allow him to receive the precepts."

By order of the Buddha, he reported the matter to all the members of the Sangha and had him take the upasampada. After five days, the man attained arhatship. Among the tirthikas, there was [present] a Brahmacarin by the name of Purana. He said: "O Gautama! Have you seen the fact that the world is eternal and do you say that it is eternal? Is what is said true or not true? Is it eternal, non-eternal, or eternal and non-eternal, or non-eternal and not non-eternal? Is it something that has a boundary line, is it without a boundary line, is it [both] with and without a boundary line, or is it something which does not have a boundary line or something that has no boundary line? Are the body and life one, or are body and life different? Or after the death of the Tathagata, are you one who has gone, or are you one who is gone and not gone, or one who is not one gone and not one who is not gone?" The Buddha said: "O Purana! I never say that the world where we live is eternal, falsely made, or real; that it is non-eternal, eternal and non-eternal, or non-eternal and not non-eternal; that it has or has not a boundary line, that it is not one that has a boundary line and one that is not one that has not a boundary line; that this is the body, this is life, that the body and life are different, that after the Tathagata's death, he is one gone, one not gone, one gone and not gone, or that he is not one gone, nor one not gone." Purana questioned further: "O Gautama! What wrong do you see in this, that you do not say?" The Buddha said: "O Purana! If any person should say that the world is eternal, and this is real, and that all others are false, this is what is wrongly seen ["drsti": i.e. a faulty view or vision of things]. What this wrong seeing sees is the action of wrong seeing, and this is the karma of wrong seeing, and this is the clinging of wrong seeing, and this is the bondage of wrong seeing, and this is the suffering of wrong seeing, and this is the cleaving of wrong seeing, and this is the fear of wrong seeing, and this is the heat of wrong seeing, and this is the bondage of wrong seeing. O Purana! Common mortals cling to what is wrongly seen, and cannot do away with birth, old age, illness, and death. Repeating lives in the six realms, they suffer from innumerable sorrows. And the same applies to what obtains regarding matters extending to not-gone or not not-gone, also. O Purana! I see in this wrong seeing such a lapse. So I do not cling, and so I do

not speak about it to other persons." "O Gautama! If you see such a lapse, do not cling to it and do not speak about it, O Gautama, what do you now see, cling to, and speak about?" The Buddha said: "O good man! Now, the clinging of wrong seeing is the dharma of life and death. As the Tathagata has done away with life and death, he does not cling. O good man! The Tathagata is one who well sees and who well speaks. But he is not one who clings." "O Gautama! In what way do you well see and well speak?" "O good man! "I well see suffering, the cause of suffering, the extinction [of suffering], and the Way to the extinction of suffering, and discriminate and speak about four such Truths. I see thus. So, I segregate myself from all wrong seeings, all cravings, all streams and arrogances. That is why I am garbed in pure actions, unsurpassed quietude, and the Eternal Body. And this Body also has no east, no west, no south, and no north." "Purana said: "O Gautama! Why does the Eternal body have no east, no west, no south, and no north?" The Buddha said: "O good man! I shall now put a question to you. Answer as you will. Why? It is like making a big fire before you. When it burns, do you know whether or not it is burning?" "That is right. O Gautama!" "When the fire dies, do you know it or not?" "It is thus, it is thus, O Gautama!" "O Purana! When people ask: "From where does the burning come and where does it go to?", how would you reply?" "O Gautama! If there were anyone who were to ask this, I should reply: "This fire starts up from various causal relations. When the original causal relation ends and the new causal relation has not yet come about, the fire dies." "If again there is a person who asks: "When extinguished, where does it go to?", how would you answer?"

"O Gautama! I should answer: "When the causal relations end, it dies. It does not have any direction to turn to." "O good man! It is the same with the Tathagata, too. If there is any non-eternal form down to non-eternal consciousness, there is burning, because it is based on craving. "Burning" means receiving the 25 existences. Thus one can well say, when it burns, this fire has an easterly, westerly, southerly, or northerly direction. If craving now dies out, the fire of the karmic results of the 25 existences also ceases to burn. When it does not burn, we cannot say that there are the directions of east, west, south, or north. O good man! The Tathagata has already extinguished the cause of non-eternal form and non-eternal consciousness. Hence, his Body is Eternal. His Body being Eternal, we cannot speak of east, west, south, or north." Purana said: "I wish to make an analogy. Please condescend to give ear to it." The Buddha said: "Well said, well said! Speak as you will!" "O World-Honoured One! For example, outside a big village, there is a sal forest. There is a tree in it. Before the forest came into being, it was born, and 100 years passed. The owner of the forest gave water to it and spent timely care upon it. The tree is old and rotten, and the bark, branches and leaves all drop off. What there is is quietude and truth. It is the same with the Tathagata. All that is old is gone; what there is is what is true. O World-Honoured One! I now very much desire to renounce the world and practise the Way." The Buddha said: "Welcome, O bhiksu!" When the Buddha had said this, Purana at once entered the Path and, defilement gone, attained arhatship.

Chapter Forty-Six: On Kaundinya 2

Also, there was a Brahmacarin by the name of "Pure", who said: "O Gautama! What do all beings not know as a result of which they do not see the eternal and non-eternal of the world, and also the eternal-non-eternal, not eternal and not non-eternal, down to not-gone and not not-gone?" The Buddha said: "O good man! Not knowing material form down to not knowing consciousness [i.e. the five skandhas], a person does not see the eternal, down to the not-gone and not not-gone of the world." The Brahmacarin said: "O Gautama! What do beings know, so that they do not see the eternal of the world, down to the not-gone and not not-gone?" The Buddha said: "O good man! They know material form down to consciousness, so that they do not see the eternal, down to the not-gone and the not not-gone." The Brahmacarin said: "O World-Honoured One! Please condescend to expound to me the eternal and the non-eternal of the world." The Buddha said: "O good man! If one casts away the old, and does not create new karma, one truly knows the eternal and the non-eternal." The Brahmacarin said: "O World-Honoured One! I now know." The Buddha said: "O good man! In what way do you see and know?" "O World-Honoured One! What is old is ignorance and craving, and the new is cleaving and [phenomenal, samsaric] existence. If one segregates one's self from the eternal and the non-eternal and has no more cleaving and existence, one will know the true nature of the eternal and the non-eternal. I have now acquired the pure eye of Wonderful Dharma, and I take refuge in the Three Treasures. O Tathagata! Admit me into the Order!" The Buddha said to Kaundinya: "Admit this Brahmacarin into the Order and let him receive sila." At these words of the Buddha's, Kaundinya took the man and went to the gathering of monks, and through the ritualistic procedure of karman, the man was admitted into the Order. After 15 days, all his defilements having been eternally extirpated, the man attained arhatship. Also, the Brahmacarin, Vatsiputriya, said: "O Gautama! I now wish to put some questions to you. Will you indeed allow me to do so?" The Tathagata sat silently. At the second and third time, he said nothing.

Vatisiputriya said again: "O Gautama! I have long been on friendly terms with you. We could not be two [i.e. divergent] in our acceptations [understanding] in any way. I desire to ask. Why are you silent?" The World-Honoured One thought: "It is thus, O Brahmacarin! Your nature is gentle and graceful, pure, good, and innocent. You always seek to know. This is not to cause worry to others. I shall answer, to accord with your wish." The Buddha said: "Well said, well said, O Vatsiputriya! I shall answer what you desire to know." Vatsiputriya said: "O Gautama! Is there in the world what may be termed "good"? "It is thus, O Vatsiputriya!" "Is there "non-good"? "Yes, that is so." "O Gautama! Please expound the good and the non-good to me." The Buddha said: "O good man! I shall speak extensively about it. I shall now analyse and explain [matters] to you in a concise way. Desire is non-good; getting emancipated is that which is good. So are anger and ignorance [non-good]. Killing is what is not good; non-killing is what is good. So does it proceed down to the twisted views of life. O good man! I now, for your sake, expound to you the three kinds of what is good and non-good; also the ten kinds of what is good and non-good. If any of my disciples can see the difference between the three kinds of good and non-good, down to the ten kinds of good and non-good, such will indeed do away with all such defilements as desire, anger, and ignorance, and will cut off what is "is" [i.e. samsarically driven, imperfect, ever-changing, phenomenal existence]." The Brahmacarin said: "O Gautama! Is there any single bhiksu among those of the Buddhist Sangha who does away with all such defilements as desire, anger, and ignorance?" The Buddha said: "O good man! There are not only one, two, three or five hundred, but innumerable bhiksus who do away with all such defilements and things of the "is", such as desire, anger, ignorance and all such defilements." "O Gautama! If we exclude the bhiksus, is there any bhiksuni among those of the Buddhist Sangha who has done away with all such defilements and things of the "is", such as desire, anger, and ignorance?" The Buddha said: "There are not only one, two, three, or five hundred such bhiksunis, but innumerable bhiksunis who have done away with all these defilements and things of the "is", such as greed, anger, and ignorance."

Vatsiputriya said: "O Gautama! Let us leave aside the cases of individual bhiksus or bhiksunis. Is there among those of the Buddhist Sangha any upasaka who has been true to sila and made effort, and has been pure in his deeds, has crossed over the waters of doubt, and having cut away the web of doubt, has attained the other shore?" The Buddha said: "O good man! There is not just one, two, three or five hundred, but countless upasakas who have been true to sila, who have made effort, whose deeds have been pure, and who, having rent asunder the web of doubt, have destroyed the five bonds of defilement [i.e. greed (or desire), ill-will, ignorance, jealousy, and stinginess, which cause one to get reborn into the three unfortunate realms of hell, ghosts, and animals], attaining thereby the fruition of the anagamin, and who have gained the other shore beyond doubt, doing away with the web of doubt." Vatsiputriya said: "Let us leave aside the cases of bhiksus, bhiksunis, and upasakas. Is there any upasika among those of the Buddhist Sangha who has been true to sila, who has made effort, who has been pure in her deeds, and who has reached the other shore of doubt, having cut away the web of doubt?" The Buddha said: "Of such there is not only one, two, three or five hundred, but there are countless upasikas who have been true to sila, who have made effort, who have destroyed the five fetters of defilement, who have attained the fruition of the anagamin, and who are now on the yonder shore of doubt, having cut away the web of doubt." Vatsiputriya said: "O Gautama! Let us now leave aside the case of bhiksus or bhiksunis who have eliminated all defilements, and the case of upasakas and upasikas who have observed sila, made effort, and whose deeds have been pure, and who have cut away the web of doubt. Is there any upasaka among those of the Buddhist Sangha who enjoys the pleasures of the five [sensual] desires and who has no doubt in his mind?" "O good man! Of such there is not only one, two, three or five hundred. There are countless people who have destroyed the three bonds, attaining thereby the fruition of the srotapanna and growing less in desire, ill-will, and ignorance, and thus gaining the fruition of the sakrdagamin. It is the same with the upasaka and upasika." "O World-Honoured One! I would like now to draw an analogy."

The Buddha said: "Well said, well said! Speak out what you desire to say." "O World-Honoured One! The naga kings, Nanda and Upananda, both provide us with great rains. So does it obtain with the Tathagata's rain of Dharma. All-equally do you let the rain fall upon the upasakas and upasikas. O World-Honoured One! If any tirthikas were to come [here] and desire [to train under you], I wonder how many months you would keep them on probation?" The Buddha said: "O good man! We test for four months. It is not necessarily to be of one kind [i.e. whatever the type of person who applies]." "O World-Honoured One! If it is not of one kind, please admit me into the Order." Then, the World-Honoured One said to Kaundinya: "See that this Vatsiputriya is admitted into the Order and that he receives sila." At these words of the Buddha, Kaundinya stood up amidst the congregation and carried out the ritual of karman. Fifteen days later, the man attained the fruition of srotapanna. Having attained this fruition, he thought to himself: "If I am to practise the Way with Wisdom, I have now already gained it, and I shall indeed be able to see the Buddha." Then, he went to where the Buddha was, prostrated himself on the ground, and having paid his homage, drew back and seated himself on one side. And he said to the Buddha: "O World-Honoured One! Whatever is to be attained by knowing, I have now attained. Please condescend again to expound [things] to me, so that I might gain the learninglessness knowledge." The Buddha said: "O good man! Make effort and practise two things, namely: 1) samatha [calmness meditation] and 2) vipasyana [insight meditation]. O good man! If any bhiksu wishes to attain the fruition of the srotapanna, such a person should practise these two things. If anyone desires to attain the fruitions of the sakrdagamin, anagamin, and arhatship, such a person too should practise the same. "O good man! Any bhiksus who desire to attain the four dhyanas, the four boundless minds, the six divine powers, the eight emancipations, the eight superior places, the non-disputing knowledge, the top knowledge, the ultimate knowledge, the four unhindered knowledges, the Adamantine Samadhi, the all-extinguished knowledge, and the birthlessness knowledge must all practise these two ways. "O good man! If there is anyone who wishes to attain the ten-abode soil, the birthlessness cognition, the all-wonderfulness cognition, holy actions, pure actions, heavenly actions, Bodhisattva practice, the All-Void samadhi, the jnana-mudra-samadhi, the samadhi of

All-Void, formlessness and non-action, the bhumi-samadhi, the non-retrogression samadhi, the Suramgama Samadhi, the Adamantine Samadhi, and the Buddhist action of unsurpassed Bodhi, such a one must practise these two ways." Vatsiputriya, having heard this, paid homage and left. He practised these two ways in the sal forest, and before long he had attained the fruition of arhatship. At that time, there were innumerable bhiksus who were on the way to where the Buddha was. Vatsiputriya, on seeing them, asked: "O great ones! Where are you intending to go?" All the bhiksus said: "We intend to go to the Buddha." "O great ones! If you go to the Buddha, please tell him: "The Brahmacarin, Vatsiputriya, having practised the two ways, has now attained the learninglessness knowledge. Now, feeling grateful to the Buddha, he enters Nirvana." Then all the bhiksus, on going to the Buddha, said: "O World-Honoured One! The bhiksu, Vatsiputriya, wanted us to report to you that, having now practised the two ways, he has attained the learninglessness knowledge and that, feeling grateful, he will now enter Nirvana." The Buddha said: "The Brahmacarin, Vatsiputriya, has now attained the fruition of arhatship. Go now and make offerings to his remains." Then the bhiksus, at these words of the Buddha, went to where the corpse lay and made great offerings. The Brahmacarin, Kasaya, then said: "O Gautama! You Gautama say that a person does what is good and not good innumerable times, and in the future gains bodies again that are good or not good. This is not so, because, just as you Gautama say, a person gains a body through defilement. If a person gains his body, does the body come first or the defilement come first? If defilement comes about first, who creates it and where does it stay? If the body comes about first, how can we say that the person gains it through defilement? Because of this, if it is said that defilement comes about first, this does not fit well. It is also not good to say that the body comes about first. If it is said that both come about at the same time, this also will not be right. Any such speaking as of "before" and "after", or of "at the same time", is not acceptable. So I say: "Everything has its own nature, not depending on causal relations." "Also, next, O Gautama! Hardness is the nature of the earth; moisture is the nature of water; heat is that of fire; movement is that of the wind; and not being obstructed is that of space. These five natures are existences which do

not depend on causal relations. If there is in the world but one thing that does not depend on causal relations, it must be thus with all other things, too. What is is the existence that is not grounded on causal relations. If it is said that all depend on the single law of causal relations, why is it that the nature of the five elements does not depend on the law of causal relations? "O Gautama! Beings gain emancipation from this body of good and non-good based on their own nature, and not on causal relations. So I say: "Everything exists based on its own nature and not on causal relations." "Also, next, O Gautama! Things of the world have their own places of use. For example one says: "Such and such kinds of wood are for making wheels, and such and such are for making doors and benches." "Also, it is as with the goldsmith, who calls what is worn above the brow a hair adornment, what one puts around one's neck a necklace, what is worn on the arm a bracelet, and what is worn on the finger a ring. As the place of use is fixed, we say that the nature is fixed. So go things with beings, too. There are the natures of the five realms. So we have hell, hungry pretas, animals, humans, and heaven. If things are thus, how can we say that they depend on causal relations? "Also, next, O Gautama! Each being has a nature different from that of others. That is why we say that all things have their own natures. The tortoise is born on land but can easily go into the water; the calf, soon after its birth, easily drinks milk; the fish sees the bait on the hook and spontaneously and greedily bites at it; the viper, as soon as it is born, feeds on the earth. Whoever teaches such things? When a thorn appears, its point is always sharp; the colours of flying birds differ from each other. So is it with the beings of the world. There are those who are sharp-witted and those who are dull, those who are rich and those who are poor; there are those who are good-looking and those who are ugly; there are those who attain emancipation and those who get born into a lowly status. From this we can know that there is a nature to each existence. "Also, next, O Gautama! If you say that desire, ill-will, and ignorance arise out of causal relations and that these three poisons are based on causal relations and the five sense-fields, the situation is not so. Why not? When one sleeps, one is away from the five sense-fields. And yet there come about desire, ill-will, and ignorance. Even in the womb, the same is the case. When one first emerges from it, one cannot feel the good or non-good of the five sense-fields. And yet, there appear desire, ill-will, and ignorance. All rishis and sages live in quiet and silent places, and there exist no five sense-fields. But still there are desire, ill-will, and ignorance. "Also, a person, through the five sense-fields, gains non-desire, non-anger, and non-ignorance. Hence, all things do not necessarily come about due to causal relations, but because of the nature of each thing. "Also, next, O Gautama! We see people in the world who possess great wealth and much freedom, being yet imperfect in the five sense-organs, and those who are poor, mean, and not free, who serve other people, they themselves having perfect sense-organs. If things arise from causal relations, how could matters come about thus? So we say that all things have natures of their own and are not based on causal relations. "Also, next, O Gautama! Children also are not clear as regards the five sense-organs, but they laugh and weep. When laughing, they feel joy, and when weeping sorrow. Because of this, we can know that all things have their own nature. Also, next, O Gautama! There are two kinds of thing in the world, which are: 1) the "is" and 2) the "is-not". The "is" is the Void and the "is-not" is the hairs of a tortoise. Of these, the one does not depend on the causal relations because of "is", and the other does not depend on causal relations because of "is-not". So, all things depend on their own nature and not on causal relations." The Buddha said: "O good man! You say that it is with all things as it is with the natures of the five great elements. But this is not so. Why not? O good man! You say that the five great elements are eternal. Why? All things are not eternal. If what exists in the world is non-eternal, how can these five great elements not be non-eternal? If the five great elements are eternal, all that exists in the world must also be eternal. Therefore, when you say that the five great elements have their own natures, that they do not depend on causal relations, and that the case of all things is like that of the five great elements, this has no basis [of truth] to stand upon. O good man! You say that as there are places where things can be of use, things must have natures of their own. But this is not so. Why not? Because they gain their denominations through causal relations. If a name comes about from a cause, the meaning must come about from a cause. Why do we say that the name comes about through a cause? What is worn on the brow

is called a head ornament, what is on the neck a necklace, what is on the arm a bracelet, and what a cart has is wheels. If fire burns grass and plants, we speak of a grass and plant fire. O good man! A tree, when born, does not possess the nature of the arrow or halberd. Through causal relations, the artisan takes it and makes arrows; through causal relations he makes a halberd out of it. So, we cannot say that things possess natures of their own. "O good man! You say that the tortoise is born on land and that by its own nature it goes into the water; that the calf, when born, drinks milk by its own nature, and that things proceed thus. But this is not so. Why not? If it is not through causal relations that it gets into the water, there is nothing in the world that is based on causal relations. So why is it that it does not go into fire? The calf drinks milk soon after birth. If this is not through causal relations, there cannot be any causal relations to talk about. Why does it not suck on the horn? "O good man! You say that everything has its own-born nature, that there is no need for learning, and that there is no development. But this is not so. Why not? Now, there is teaching, and through this teaching there is growing up [development]. Hence, you must know that there is no nature of its own. "O good man! If everything possessed its own original nature, no Brahmin would need to kill sheep to pray and arrive at a pure body. If a person prays for the sake of his own self, this tells us that he has no original nature of his own. "O good man! There are three ways of speaking, which are: 1) the desire to do something, 2) the time of the doing, and 3) the completed doing. If it is the case that there is a nature of its own, how can there be in the world these three ways of speaking? The fact that there are these three ways of speaking tells us that there is no nature of its own in a thing. "O good man! If you say that everything has its own nature, know that all things must have a fixed nature. If there is a fixed nature, how is it that the single thing, the sugar cane, can become juice, honey, rock candy, liquor, and vinegar? If there is a single nature, how could such things come about? If such things come about from a single thing, know that this indicates that everything cannot be fixedly one and of one nature.

"O good man! If everything has a fixed nature, why do the holy ones not take the juice of the sugar cane, the rock candy, and the molasses at the time of taking the liquor, and later take it when it has been made into vinegar? For this reason, we can know that there is no fixed nature. If there is no fixed nature, how could it be other than by causal relations? "O good man! If everything has a fixed nature, how can there be any ground for analogies? If there are analogies, this tells us: know that there is no fixed nature in any thing. If there were a fixed nature, there could be - you should know - no analogies. All the wise persons of the world employ analogies. Know that there can be no nature of a thing and there is no single nature. "O good man! You ask: "Does the body exist first or defilement?" This cannot obtain. Why not? If I say that the body comes first, you too will reprove me and say that with you too, as with me, the body cannot precede. Why do you reprove thus? "O good man! There can be no before and after in the body of beings. Things happen at the same time. Though of the same time-relations, the body comes about due to defilement; it is not that there is defilement because of the existence of the body. What you make it is that a person gains two eyes at the same time and one is not the cause of the other, that the eye on the left-hand side does not stand on [depend on] the right-hand eye, and that of the right not on that of the left-hand side. Should you say that the situation is the same with defilement and the body, I would have to say that this is not so. Why not? What obtains in the world is that the eye sees that the wick and the light exist in the same time-relations. But the light always depends on the wick, but the wick does not depend on the light. "O good man! You may say that the body does not exist before; that, therefore, there is no cause to speak of. But this is not so. Why not? If you mean that there is no cause to speak of because of the fact that the body came about first and that there are no causal relations, you cannot say that all things depend on causality. You may say that as you do not see, there is no cause to speak of. But now we see a pot that comes about from causal relations. Why cannot we say that the body comes about as in the case of the earthen pot? "O good man! Whether we see or not, all things depend on causal relations and there cannot be any talk of something having its own nature. "O good man! If you say that everything has its own nature and that there are no causal relations, how can you explain the five great elements? These five great elements are nothing but the result of causal relations. "O good man! The five

great causal relations are also thus. But one cannot say that all things are like the five great causal relations. We might say that all world-fleeing people make effort and uphold sila. But candalas also make effort and uphold sila. "O good man! You say that the five great elements definitely have a concrete nature. But this nature changes. So I see that it is not static. "O good man! Butter, wax, and glue must be soil according to your way of thinking. Soil is indefinite. It is like water, or is equal to soil. So, we cannot call them anything concrete. "O good man! Solder, lead, zinc, copper, iron, gold, and silver would have to be fire, according to your way of thinking. Fire has four qualities. When it flows, it has the nature of water; when moving, the nature of wind; when hot, it has the nature of fire; and when hard, it has the nature of earth. How can one state it definitely possesses the nature of fire [alone]? "O good man! The nature of water is that of flowing. Even when water gets frozen, we do not call it earth. If it is called water, why do we not call it the wind when it is moving? If it is still to be called water, why do we not call it wind when moving? If a thing, when moving, is not called wind, we may well call water not water when it is in a frozen state? If these two cases are grounded on causal relations, how can you say that all things are not based on causal relations? "O good man! The five sense-organs by nature see, hear, sense, know, and touch. We may say that these all depend on their nature and not on causal relations. But this is not so. Why not? O good man! What something has by nature cannot be changed. If we say that the sense-organ of the eye can truly see, it must always be able to see. There cannot be any case where it sees and where it does not see. Hence, we can know that it truly sees through causal relations and that this is not through non-causal relations. "O good man! You say that you gain greed from the five dusts [i.e. the five sense-fields] and that a person does not get emancipated. This is not so. Why not? O good man! A person gains desire and gets emancipated. Though this may not arise out of the causal relations of the five dusts, the person gains desire due to the evil sensing of the world, and he gains emancipation through the good sensing of the world. O good man! Through internal causal relations, the person gains desire and emancipation; through external causal relations comes about augmentation [growth]. So, it goes against reason to say that all things have natures of their own and that a person does not gain desire from the five dusts and that the person gains emancipation. "O good man! You say that though perfect in all the sense-organs, a person has little wealth and is not free; and that lacking in all sense-organs, another person has abundant wealth and great freedom. This indicates that to say that a thing has its own nature and that there is no such thing as causal relations to speak of, is not right. Why not? O good man! A person reaps results through karma. There are three kinds of karma result, namely: 1) fruition that comes about in this life, 2) fruition which one reaps in the next life, and 3) fruition that one harvests in later lives. Poverty, great wealth, perfect sense-organs and imperfection of the sense-organs arise from different karmas. If there were any [single] nature of its own, those perfect in the sense-organs would have to be rich, and one who is rich would have to be perfect in all his sense-organs. But things do not obtain thus. So, one can definitely know that there can never be any fixed nature of its own and that all arises out of causal relations. "O good man! You say that a child cannot discriminate the causal relations of the five dusts and yet it weeps and laughs, and that this indicates, you say, that everything has its own nature. But this is not so. Why not? If laughing goes by nature [i.e. if laughing exists based on a fixed nature], one would always have to be laughing; if weeping were based on a nature, one would always have to be weeping. There cannot be laughing at one time and weeping at another. If one laughs at one time and weeps at another, this tells us - we can know - that all is based on causal relations. Hence, you should not say that all things have their own nature and that causal relations have nothing to do with it." The Brahmacarin said: "O World-Honoured One! If all things exist due to causal relations, how can such a body come into being?" The Buddha said: "The causal relations of this carnal body are grounded on defilement and karma." The Brahmacarin said: "If this carnal body is based on defilement and karma, can we extirpate the defilement and karma?" The Buddha said: "It is thus, it is thus!" The Brahmacarin further said: "O World-Honoured One! Please be good enough to analyse and expound to me, so that I can truly hear and immediately cut away the bond." The Buddha said: "O good man! If a person comes to know that the two sides and the in-between are unhindered [unobstructed], such a person indeed segregates [himself from] defilement and karma." "O World-Honoured One! I now know and have gained the right Dharma-Eye." The Buddha said: "In what manner do you know?" "O World-Honoured One! The two sides are "material form" and "emancipation from material form", and the "in-between" is the Eightfold Right Path. So does it also obtain with feeling, perception, volition, and consciousness." The Buddha said: "Well said, well said, O good man! You have now come to know of the two sides and have cut away defilement and karma." "O World-Honoured One! Please admit me into the Order and let me receive sila!" The Buddha said: "Welcome, O bhiksu!" Immediately he extirpated the defilements of the three worlds and arrived at the fruition of arhatship. Then there was a Brahmin, named "Wide-Wide", who said: "O Gautama! Do you know what I have in my mind?" The Buddha said: "O good man! Nirvana is Eternal and what is created is non-eternal. What is twisted is twisted views, and what is straight is the Noble Path." The Brahmin said: "O Gautama! Why do you say so?" "O good man! What you think is that to beg alms is eternal and singly-to-be-invited is non-eternal. What is twisted is to shut one's self in and what is straight is the imperial hanging-ensign. That is why I say: "Nirvana is Eternal; what is twisted is twisted views, and what is straight is the Eightfold Path." It is not as you think." The Brahmin said: "O Gautama! You see well what is in my mind. Does this Noble Eightfold Path enable beings to attain extinction or not?" Then, the World-Honoured One remained silent and did not answer. The Brahmin said: "O Gautama! You see my mind well. Why do you remain silent and not answer me?" Then Kaundinya said: "O great Brahmin! If any person asks about the limitedness or non-limitedness of the world, the Tathagata is silent and does not reply. The Noble Eightfold Path is what is straight, and Nirvana is what is Eternal. When the Noble Eightfold Path is practised, one attains extinction; if not, no such thing results. "O great Brahmin! For example, a great castle has four walls, where there are no apertures, except for a gate. The gate-keeper is wise. He knows whom to let pass and whom to shut out. He may not know the number of those who come and go, but he knows that anyone who enters has to come through the gate. The situation is thus. O good man! It is the same with the Tathagata. The castle is Nirvana, the gate is the Noble Eightfold Path, and the gate-keeper is the Tathagata. O good man! Though the Tathagata does not reply [to questions] about [the world's being] finite or infinite, what ends must needs practise the Noble Eightfold Path." The Brahmin said: "Well said, well said, O greatly virtuous Kaundinya! The Tathagata truly expounds All-Wonderful Dharma. I now know the castle, and the Way to it, and I desire to be the gate-keeper." Kaundinya said: "Well said, well said! You now well aspire to the Great Mind." The Buddha said: "Say not thus, say not thus, O Kaundinya! It is not the case that this Brahmin now aspires for the first time to this Mind. A long, long time ago, far back in the days of countless Buddhas, there was a Buddha called "Tathagata All-Shining", the Alms-Deserving, the All-Enlightened One, the All-Accomplished One, the Well-Gone, the All-Knower, the Unsurpassed One, the Best Trainer, the Teacher of Gods and Humans, the Buddha-World-Honoured One. This person [i.e. the Brahmin] had already aspired to unsurpassed Bodhichitta at the place of this Buddha. He will now attain Buddhahood in this Bhadrakalpa. He has long been versed in Dharma. For the sake of beings, he lives as a tirthika and presents himself as one not versed in Dharma. For this reason, Kaundinya, you should not say: "Well said, well said! You now aspire to the Great Mind." Then, seeing all, the World-Honoured One said to Kaundinya: "Is Ananda present?" Kaundinya said: "O World-Honoured One! Ananda is away from the sal forest, 12 yojanas from this congregation, and is surrounded by 64,000 billion Maras. All these Maras are transforming themselves into the Tathagata. They say that all things arise from causal relations, or that all things do not arise from causal relations; or they say that all causal relations are eternal or that all that arises from causal relations is non-eternal. Or they say that the five skandhas are real, or that they are false. So also with the 18 realms and the 12 spheres. Or they say that there are the 12 links of interdependence or that there are rightly the four causal relations, or that all things are like phantoms or visions, or like mirages in the hot season; or they say that Dharma comes to one through hearing, or that one gains it through thinking; or they speak about the usmagata, murdhana, laukikagradharma, the stages of learning and learninglessness, or about the Bodhisattva's ten stages, from the first up to the tenth; or they speak about the All-Void, formlessness and non-action; or they speak about sutra, geya, vyakarana, gatha, udana, nidana, avadana, itivrttaka, jataka, vaipulya, adbhutadharma, and upadesa; or there are those who speak about the four remembrances, four right efforts, four at-willnesses, five roots, five powers, seven Bodhi elements, Noble Eightfold Path; or they may speak about the internal Void, the external Void, the internal-external Void, the Void of the created, the Void of the non-created, the Void of beginninglessness, the Void of nature, the Void of segregation, the Void of dispersion, the Void of the characteristics of self, the Void of formlessness, the Void of the skandhas, the Void of the [12] spheres, the Void of the [18] realms, the Void of good, the Void of non-good, the Void of indefinables, the Void of Bodhi, the Void of the Path, the Void of Nirvana, the Void of action, the Void of what one has gained, the Void of Ultimate Truth, Void-Void, and Great Void. Or they may display miracles and transformations. Their body emits water and fire; or water comes out from the upper body and fire from down below; or from down below water comes out and from the upper body fire. Or the left armpit is down and the right armpit gives out water; or the right armpit is down and the left armpit gives out water. On [from] one armpit thunder rolls and shakes, and on [from] the other armpit rain falls. Or there may be one who shows the worlds of all Buddhas; or the scene of the Bodhisattva as he first appears in the world and takes seven steps, lives in the depths of the palace, wherein he pursues a life of the five desires, or the scene in which he leaves the palace and performs austerities, or in which he advances towards the Bodhi Tree, sitting thereunder in samadhi, or the scene in which he defeats the army of Maras, or the scene in which he delivers the [first] sermon, or the scene in which he performs great miracles, or where he enters Nirvana. "O World-Honoured One! Ananda, on seeing this, thinks to himself: "I have not seen such miracles. Who is working all of these? Or are these all of Sakyamuni Buddha?" He wishes to stand up, speak out, but the action will not follow his will. This is due to the fact that Ananda has been caught in Mara's traps. He also thinks: "All that these Buddhas say is not the same. Whose words should I now give ear to?" O World-Honoured One! Ananda is now suffering greatly. Although he thinks of the Tathagata, none comes to save him. That is why he is not here amongst the congregated." Then, the Bodhisattva-mahasattva Manjusri said to the Buddha: "O World-Honoured One! Among this great mass of people congregated here, there are many Bodhisattvas who have aspired to unsurpassed Enlightenment in one life or who have aspired to Bodhichitta over the course of innumerable lives. They truly make offerings to innumerable Buddhas. Their mind is firm-set and they practise danaparamita up to prajnaparamita. They have long come to innumerable Buddhas, practised pure actions, and are unretrogressive in their Bodhichitta. They have attained the unretrogressive state of cognition and have arrived at the avinivartaniya and are perfect in right cognition and are in the Suramgama Samadhi. Such people listen to the Mahayana sutras and do not doubt [them]. They understand well and speak about the oneness of the Three Treasures and that their nature and characteristics are Eternal and Unchanging. They hear of miraculous things, but their minds do not become surprised and do not shake. They hear about many kinds of Voidness and their minds are [not] in fear. They clearly grasp all kinds of Dharma-Nature. They uphold well all the 12 types of sutra and they understand their meaning extensively. Also, they uphold the 12 types of sutra of all the innumerable Buddhas. How could one be apprehensive as to their not being able to uphold the Great Nirvana Sutra? Why is it that you ask Kaundinya where Ananda is?" Then, the World-Honoured One said to Manjusri: "Listen carefully, listen carefully! O good man! Since the day when I attained Buddhahood, I have lived for over 30 years in Rajagriha. At that time, I said to all the bhiksus: "Who of all those who are gathered here can uphold the 12 types of sutra of the Tathagata and attend to what one [i.e. the Buddha] may need to have and yet not lose his own profit?" "At that time, Kaundinya was one of those in the congregation, and he came to me and said: "I can well uphold the 12 types of sutra, attend to all that there should be, and yet not lose what I may gain." "I said: "O Kaundinya! You are already far advanced in age. You must use somebody else. How could you expect to serve me?" "Then, Sariputra said: "I can certainly uphold all the words that the Buddha speaks, attend to what he needs to have, and I shall not lose whatever profit I may gain." "I then said: "O Sariputra! You are already too old. Use somebody else. How can you wish to serve me?" "Things proceeded thus with

all 500 arhats. I did not accept [any of them]. Then, Maudgalyayana, being amongst their number, thought: "The Tathagata does not accept the attendance of the 500 arhats. Who might it be that the Buddha desires to have?" Thinking thus, he entered into dhyana and saw that the Tathagata's mind was set upon Ananda, just as when the sun first rises and shines upon a western wall. Having seen this, he got up from his dhyana seat [from his meditation posture] and said to Kaundinya: "O greatly virtuous one! I now see that the Tathagata desires to have Ananda attend him." "Then Kaundinya, along with the 500 arhats, went to Ananda and said: "O Ananda! You should go and serve the Tathagata. Accept this!" "Ananda said: "O all you virtuous ones! I cannot well serve the Tathagata. Why not? The Tathagata is austere, like the king of lions; he is like the dragon and fire. I am as yet defiled and weak. How can I truly serve him?" All the bhiksus said: "You must take our word and serve the Tathagata. You will be blessed with great benefit." This went on for a second and third time. "Ananda said: "All you greatly virtuous ones! I also do not seek any great benefit. Truth to tell, I am not able to serve him." "Then Maudgalyayana said again: "O Ananda! Do you not yet know?" "Ananda said: "O great one! Please tell me of it." "Maudgalyayana said: "The Tathagata desired to have one from among us priests. All the 500 arhats wanted to meet his wish. But the Tathagata would not have it. I then sat in dhyana and saw that the Tathagata wishes you to be the one. Why do you not desire to accept the post?" "On hearing this, Ananda folded his hands, prostrated himself on the ground and said: "O greatly virtuous one! If this actually took place, I shall act as you wish and serve him, as long as the Tathagata will permit me three things." "Maudgalyayana said: "What are the three things?" "Ananda said: "First, that the Tathagata will allow me not to accept - should he wish to give it me - any used clothing; secondly, that the Tathagata will permit me not to follow him when he receives private invitations; and thirdly, that the Tathagata will allow me freedom of movement. If the Tathagata permits me these three things, I am ready to concede to the words of all you priests." "Then Kaundinya and the 500 bhiksus came back to me and said: "We have persuaded Ananda to accept, but in connection with this he desires three things to be permitted. If you will allow them, he will follow the words of the priests [i.e. he will do as they have asked him]." "O Manjusri! I then applauded Ananda and said: "Well said, well said, O bhiksu Ananda! You have Wisdom and seek to foreguard [i.e. guard against future contingencies]. Why so? For people might say that you serve the Tathagata on account of the clothing and food that you might gain. That is why he does not wish to receive the used clothing and why he does not wish to accompany me on the occasion of any private invitations which I may have to accept. O Kaundinya! Ananda has Wisdom. If he should be restrained by time [i.e. if he has a rigid and constricting timetable to follow], he would not have time to give benefit to the four classes of the Buddhist Sangha. That is why he desires that there should be no fixed time for his service. "O Kaundinya! I accede to these three requests for the sake of Ananda." "Then Maudgalyayana went back to Ananda and said: "I entreated the Buddha for the three things you wished to have, and the Tathagata, out of his great pity, has consented." Ananda said: "O greatly virtuous one! If the Buddha has agreed, I shall go and serve him." "O Manjusri! Ananda has served me for over 20 years and possesses eight wonders. What are the eight? These are: 1) for 20 years since he began to serve me, he has never eaten a meal [on the occasion] of any private invitation; 2) he has never once accepted used clothing; 3) since he began serving me, he has never come to me at the wrong hour; 4) since the time when he began serving me, he has had occasion to associate with all [kinds of] kings, Kshatriyas, nobles, and men of great clans, and he has met all [kinds] of females and naga females, and although he has defilements, he has never once yet given himself up to lustful thoughts; 5) since he began serving me, he has upheld the 12 types of sutra, and after having heard something once, he never asks me of it [i.e. to repeat it] a second time [i.e. he remembers whatever teachings the Buddha utters]. It is like shifting the water of [several] pots into one pot, except for one single question. O good man! Prince Vidudabha killed the people of the Sakya clan [i.e. the Buddha's own clan] and demolished the castle [citadel] of Kapilavastu. Ananda, at that time, was of sorrowful mind and wept. Coming to me, he said: "I was born together with you in this castle, and I am of the Sakya tribe. How is it that the Tathagata looks radiant as on ordinary days, and I feel so awearied?" I then replied: "O

Ananda! I practise the samadhi of the Void. So I am not like you." Three years passed by, and he came to me and asked: "O World-Honoured One! In days gone by, I heard at the castle of Kapilavastu that the Tathagata practised the samadhi of the Void. Is this true or not?" I said: "O Ananda! It is thus, it is thus! It is just as you say"; 6) since the day he began to serve me, he has not yet gained the ability to read others' minds, but he always knew the dhyanas I was in; 7) since the day he began serving me, he has not as yet gained the knowledge [which would enable him] to know whatever he wishes to know, [yet] he well knew and would say: "Such and such people came to the Tathagata and such and such people have now gained the four fruitions of sramana and such and such have gained these later, such and such have gained human life, and such and such have gained a heavenly body"; 8) since his [first] day of serving me, he has understood all the unspoken words of the Tathagata. "O good man! Bhiksu Ananda possesses these eight wonders. That is why I call Ananda the storehouse of rich hearing. "O good man! Bhiksu Ananda is perfect in eight things and thus upholds in perfect ways the 12 types of sutra. "What are the eight? They are: 1) his faith is strong, 2) his mind is straight, 3) his body is without illness or pain, 4) he makes effort unremittingly, 5) [he is] perfect in the praying mind, 6) his mind has no arrogance, 7) [he is] perfect in the settled mind, and 8) through hearing [Dharma], knowledge comes about. "O Manjusri! The disciple and attendant of Buddha Vipasyin was called Asoka. He was also perfect in these eight things. The disciple and attendant of Tathagata Sikhin was called Samakara, the disciple and attendant of Buddha Visvabuk was called Upasanta, the disciple and attendant of the great Buddha Krakucchanda was called Bhadrika, the disciple and attendant of Buddha Kanakamuni was called Sotei , and the disciple and attendant of Buddha Kasyapa was called Yobamitta. They all posssessed these virtues. That is why I say that Ananda is a storehouse of rich hearing. "O good man! Just as you say, there are amongst those gathered here innumerable Bodhisattvas. But as these Bodhisattvas have heavy tasks to perform, such as the works of Great Loving-Kindness and Great Compassion, they inevitably have busy hours to work, to train the retinues and to adorn their own bodies. So, after my entering Nirvana, they will not be able to propound the 12 types of sutra. Or there may be Bodhisattvas who may propound them, but people will not believe what they say. O Manjusri! Bhiksu Ananda is my younger brother [Ananda is actually the Buddha's cousin, but is here called his brother to convey a sense of familiarity - K. Yamamoto]. Since the day when he began to serve me, 20 years have now passed. But he remembers what he has heard, like water stored in a pot. Because of this, I look back to [i.e. think of] Ananda and seek to know where he might be. And I desire to entrust this Nirvana Sutra to him. "O good man! When I am gone, what Ananda did not hear will be propounded by "Bodhisattva Wide-Wide"; what Ananda did hear will be promulgated by Ananda himself. "O Manjusri! Ananda is now 12 yojanas distant from this congregation and is surrounded by 64,000 billion Maras. Make haste, go now, and say aloud: "O all you Maras! Listen closely, listen closely! The Tathagata now speaks a great dharani [spell]. All devas, nagas, gandharvas, asuras, garudas, kimnaras, mahoragas, humans, non-humans, mountain-gods, tree-gods, river-gods, sea-gods, and house-gods! Hear this dharani! There is none who does not respect and uphold this. This dharani is what all Buddhas, as many in number as the sands of ten Ganges, propound. This will indeed change the female form and enable one to read one's own fortune. If any person receives [i.e. practises] well the five things, namely: 1) pure actions, and abstention from: 2) meat, 3) alcohol, 4) spices, and 5) happily abides in quietude, and after becoming perfect in these five things, believes in this dharani, recites it, and writes it, know that such a person can indeed discard the 77 billion ill-omened [i.e. inauspicious] bodies." Then, the World-Honoured One spoke thus: "Amarei bimarei nemarei bakyarei keimaranyakappi sanmanabaddai shabatashadanni baramatashadanni manashi asettai hiragi anraraitei baranmi baranmasharei fumi funamanuraitei" [meaning unknown - ed.]. Then, Manjusri, having been entrusted with this dharani, went to where Ananda was and, amidst the Maras, said: "O you Maras and retinues! Hear well the dharani which I have received from the Buddha and which I am now going to pronounce." The Mara King, on hearing this, aspired to unsurpassed Enlightenment and, casting aside evil actions, released Ananda. Manjusri, accompanying Ananda, returned to the Buddha. Ananda, on seeing the Buddha, paid the sincerest homage, stepped back and took his seat

on one side. The Buddha said to Ananda: "In this forest of sal trees, there is a Brahmacarin named Subhadra, who is 120 years old. He possesses the five miraculous powers. But he is not away from [i.e. has not yet overcome] arrogance. He has attained the stage of thoughtlessness-non-thoughtlessness dhyana. He has arrived at All-Knowledge and has a mental image of Nirvana. Go to him and say: "The Buddha's appearance in the world is like that of the udumbara. He will, this [very] midnight, attain Parinirvana. If you wish to act, act immediately. Do not have regret in the days to come!" O Ananda! He will believe what you say. Why? Because, in the course of 500 years, you were once Subhadra's son. The taint of the loving mind has not yet left him. For this reason, he will believe what you say." Then, at these words of the Buddha, Ananda went to Subhadra and said: "Know that the Tathagata appears in the world as rarely as the [blossoming of the] udumbara. This night he will enter Parinirvana. If you wish to act, act meet to the occasion. Do not have any regrets for later days." Subhadra said: "Well said, O Ananda! I shall now go to the place of the Tathagata." Then Ananda went back to the place of the Buddha, accompanied by Subhadra. Then, on arriving, Subhadra spoke thus: "O Gautama! I now wish to ask a question. Answer me as [i.e. in the spirit of how] I mean to ask." The Buddha said: "O Subhadra! It is now time. I shall answer you. I shall employ the means and answer you." "O Gautama! All sramanas and Brahmins say: "Everybody encounters karmic results; they are sad or happy; and all arise out of what they did before. Hence, if one upholds the moral precepts, makes effort, and undergoes bodily and mental pain, this will crush out the original karma. When the primary karma ends, all suffering ends. Suffering ending, Nirvana results." What do you think of this?" "O good man! If there are any such sramanas or Brahmins, I shall feel pity and go to them. On arriving, I shall ask: "Do you speak thus?" If they say: "We do speak this. Why? O Gautama! We see all the people who do all kinds of evil and who [yet] are rich, and act as they will. And people who are very poor, although doing good. Or people who do not seek, and who [yet] somehow gain things. Or there are people who have compasion and do not kill, and yet they die at an untimely hour. Or people who enjoy killing, who gain a long life. Or there are those who perform pure actions, who make effort and uphold sila, and who gain - or do not gain - Emancipation. That is why we say that all people suffer from sorrow or are blessed with happiness due to the primary karma which they have engendered in the past." "O Subhadra! I shall now ask: "Do you see or not the karma of the past? If there is this karma, is it many or few? Does the penance that one undergoes not crush out the suffering in any way? Do we know or not whether this karma has died our or not? Does all end when this karma ends?" Should the person say: "I really do not know", I shall take up a parable. "Suppose, for example, that a man is struck by a poisoned arrow. The people of the house call for a doctor, so as to have the poisoned arrow extracted. Once the arrow has been removed, the [man's] body is at peace. Ten years on, the person still recalls the event very clearly. "This doctor extracted the poisoned arrow for me, treated me with medicine, and I now enjoy peace." You do not know the past karma. How can you know whether the penance you now perform crushes out the karma done in the past?" Or he may well say: "O Gautama! Now, you yourself have karmic results from the past. Why should you reprove me in regard to my past karma? In Gautama's own sutras, this thing is spoken of. You say: "If one sees a rich and noble person, and a person who enjoys freedom, one can indeed know that such a person has made good offerings in past lives]. Do you not say that they are the karmas of the past?" I shall reply: "Any such knowing is a comparative knowing and is not one that is true. In the Buddhist teaching of my house, there is the case of knowing the result from the cause or the cause from the result. In our Buddhist teaching, we speak of the karma of a past life and of this present life. With you it is not like that. What there is [with you] is past karma, but not karma of the present. Your [doctrine] does not handle karma by expediency. With us it is not like that. We see karma through the eyes of expedient means. With you, if you reach the end of karma, suffering comes to an end. But with us, that is not so. When defilement goes, the suffering of karma ends. That is why I criticise the karma of the past about which you speak." If the person says: "O Gautama! Truth to tell, I do not know about this - I got this from my teacher. My teacher says so; I am not to be reproved." Then I shall say: "Who is your teacher?" If he says: "He is Purana", I shall then say: "Why did you not ask each of your teachers whether they know the karma of the past? If your teacher says that he does not know, why should you take his word [i.e. believe what he teaches regarding karma]? If he says that he knows, you should ask whether the causal relations of the lowest grade of suffering call forth the causal relations of the top grade of suffering, or whether or not the causal relations of suffering of the middle grade harvest the suffering of the lowest or top-grade suffering. Or ask if the causal relations of the top grade gain one the suffering of the middle and low grades. If no, you may well ask: "How can you, the teacher, say that the result of bliss or suffering only rests in the past and not in the present? Also you could well ask whether or not the suffering of the present exists in the past? If it is in the past, it must be the case that the karma of the past is now ended. If it is ended, how is it possible for a person to harvest it in this present life? If it is the case that there is no past, but what there is is merely the present, how can one say that the being's suffering and bliss arise from past karma? If you know that penance in the present life can truly crush out the karma of the past life, how can one crush out the penance [suffering] of the present life? If it is not crushed out, suffering must be eternal. If suffering is eternal, how can one say that one attains Emancipation from suffering? If what one does crushes out suffering, then the past is already gone. How can there be any suffering? O you! Does penance cause the karma of bliss to harvest the fruit of suffering? Also, can the karma of suffering cause one to harvest the fruit of bliss? Does the karma of non-suffering and non-bliss become the fruition of non-receiving? Is it possible that whatever result one has to harvest now, becomes one to be harvested in the life to come or not? Is it possible or not that what one is to harvest in the next life can be harvested in this life? Is it possible or not to cause these two karmic returns to be of no-return? Is it possible or not? Is it possible or not to make a karmic return that is definite into one that is indefinite? Is it possible to make an indefinite return one that is definite? "If he says: "O Gautama! It is not possible", I shall again say: "O you! If it is not possible, why should you suffer penance? You should well know that there are cases where past karma forms the causal relations of the present. That is why I say that karma arises out of defilement and that by karma one meets with the recompense. O you! Know that all beings have karma of the past and the cause of the present. Though beings have the past karma of life, they have to depend upon the causal relations of food in the present life. O you! One may say that beings suffer from sorrow and are blessed with bliss, all definitely grounded in the primary karmic causes from the past life. But the situation is not thus. Why not? O you! For example, it is as when a person does away with the enemy of the King, as a result of which he gains treasure and is blessed with bliss in the present life. Such a person generates the cause of bliss in this present life and reaps the recompense of bliss in this present life. For example, this is analogous to the man who kills the King's son and through this loses his life. Such a person engenders the cause of suffering now and harvests the karmic return in this present life. O you! All beings, now in this present life, encounter suffering and bliss from the four great elements, the seasons, the land, and people. That is why I say that all beings do not necessarily harvest suffering and bliss primarily from their past karma. O you! If a person can arrive at Emancipation through the power of the causal relations of cutting off karma, we could say that all sages cannot attain it. Why not? Because the primary karma of beings has no beginning and no end. That is why I say that when one practises the Holy Way, this Way truly makes away with the karma that has no head or tail. O you! If one gained the Path through penance [austerities], all animals would have to attain it. That is why one first subdues the mind and not the body. Hence I say in my sutra that one must cut down the forest but not the tree. Why? From the forest, one gains fear, but not from the tree. If one wishes to adjust the body, one must first adjust the mind. The mind is the forest, and the body is the tree. So may we compare things." The Bhagavat [Blessed One = the Buddha] said, "Noble son, how have you previously trained/ disciplined your mind?" Subhadra replied, "Bhagavat, I reflected intensely upon the fact that the [Realm of] Desire is impermanent, unpleasant, and utterly impure, and realised that the [Realm of] Form is permanent, pleasant, and utterly pure. Having realised thus, I severed the *kleshas* of the Realm of Desire and attained the sphere [*ayatana*] of Form. In that way, I previously trained / disciplined my mind. "Then, when I investigated the [Realm of] Form, I realised that form is impermanent and is like a sore, an ulcer, poison, or a thorn. I saw that the [Realm of] Formlessness is permanent, pure and peaceful. Having realised this, I severed the *kleshas* of the Realm of Form and attained the sphere of Formlessness. In that way, I previously trained / disciplined my mind. "Then, when I investigated ideation [*samjna* = the making of thoughts and ideas in the mind], I realised that it is impermanent and is like a sore, an ulcer, poison, or a thorn, and I attained the *samadhi* of the sphere of neither-ideation-nor-non-ideation [*naivasa-njaanasa-njaa*]. [I realised that] the sphere of neither-ideation-nor-non-ideation is all-knowing awareness [*sarvajna-jnana*], peaceful, pure, irreversible and unchanging. In that way, I previously trained / disciplined my mind." The Bhagavat said, "Noble son, how have you trained / disciplined your mind? What you have attained is the *samadhi* of the sphere of neither-ideation-nor-non-ideation, but that is still ideation. If Nirvana is devoid of ideation, why do you term this 'Nirvana'? Noble son, if you previously disdained coarse ideation, why are you attached to subtle ideation, not knowing that it is inferior? Even that sphere of neither-ideation-nor-non-ideation may be termed 'ideation'. It too is like a sore, an ulcer, poison, or a thorn. Noble son, though your teacher, Udraka-Ramaputra, has acute faculties and is prudent, he worships the sphere of neither-ideation-nor-non-ideation. If he still is embodied in a low-grade body, what need is there to say anything further!" Subhadra asked, "How does one sever all [samsaric] existence?" The Bhagavat replied, "Noble son, if any individual engages in the true / real ideation, all [samsaric] existence will be severed." Subhadra asked, "Bhagavat, how should one know true / real ideation?" "Noble son, the ideation of non-ideation should be known as the true / real ideation." "Bhagavat, how is the ideation of non-ideation to be known?" "Noble son, all phenomena [*dharmas*] are devoid of their own defining [external, distinguishing] attributes / characteristics [*lakshanas*], devoid of the defining attributes [*lakshanas*]of what is another, devoid of both their own and other defining attributes. They are devoid of the defining attribute of being without cause, devoid of the defining attribute of result, devoid of the defining attribute of being experienced, devoid of the defining attribute of being an agent, devoid of the defining attribute of being an experiencer; devoid of the defining attribute of being an entity/ thing [*dharma*] and devoid of the defining attribute of not being an entity / thing. They are devoid of the defining attributes of male or female, devoid of the defining attribute of a human being; they are devoid of the defining attribute of an atom, devoid of the defining attribute of time and season. They are devoid of the defining attribute of having been done for oneself, devoid of the defining attribute of being done for another, devoid of the defining attribute of being done for both oneself and another. They are devoid of the defining attribute of existence and they are devoid of the defining attribute of non-existence; they are devoid of the defining attribute of being a producer and devoid of the defining attribute of being a product. They are devoid of the defining attribute of cause and devoid of the defining attribute of being a secondary cause; they are devoid of the defining attribute of result and devoid of the defining attribute of being a secondary result. They are devoid of the defining attribute of day and night, devoid of the defining attribute of light and darkness. They are devoid of the defining attribute of what is seen and devoid of the defining attribute of being a seer; they are devoid of the defining attribute of what is heard and devoid of the defining attribute of being a hearer; they are devoid of the defining attribute of what is felt and known and devoid of the defining attribute of being a feeler and a knower. They are devoid of the defining attribute of awakening [*bodhi*] and devoid of the defining attribute of being one who attains awakening. They are devoid of the defining attribute of karma and devoid of the defining attribute of being one responsible for karma; they are devoid of the defining attribute of *klesha* [negative mental or behavioural mode] and devoid of the defining attribute of being one who is responsible for *kleshas*. Noble son, wherever *lakshanas* [defining attributes] are extinguished is termed the true / real *lakshana*. "Noble son, all *dharmas* are not veridical. Wherever they are extinguished is termed the True / the Real, the true ideation, the *Dharmadhatu* [all-encompassing realm of Ultimate Reality], the Culmination of Knowing [*nistha-jnana*], Ultimate Truth [*paramartha-satya*], Ultimate Emptiness

[*paramartha-sunyata* = complete Openness and Non-Obstruction by any limitations or limits]. "Noble son, if one engages in the *lakshana* [or "ideation"?], the *Dharmadhatu*, the Culmination of Knowing [*nistha-jnana*], Ultimate Truth, Ultimate Emptiness with inferior insight [*prajna*], one will attain the awakening of the *sravakas*; if with middle-grade insight, [one will attain the awakening of the] *pratyekabuddha*, and if with Top-Grade Insight, one will attain Unsurpassed Awakening." When this Dharma had been delivered, 10,000 Bodhisattvas attained the real mental image of one life, one-million-five-hundred Bodhisattvas attained the two-life Dharmadhatu, two-million-five-hundred Bodhisattvas attained to Ultimate Knowing, and 3,500 Bodhisattvas awoke to Ultimate Truth. This Ultimate Truth is also *Paramartha-Sunyata*, and also the S*uramgama Samadhi*. Forty-five thousand Bodhisattvas attained the All-Emptiness *Samadhi*. This all-Emptiness S*amadhi* is also called the Vast and Great *Samadhi*, and the Knowledge-Impression *Samadhi*. Fifty-five thousand Bodhisattvas attained non-retrogression cognition. This non-retrogression *Samadhi* is Dharma-accorded cognition, and also the Dharma-accorded world. Sixty-five thousand Bodhisattvas attained the dharani. This dharani is also the Great-Praying Mind, and is also Unobstructed Knowledge. And seventy-five thousand Bodhisattvas attained the Lion's Roar *Samadhi*. This Lion's Roar is also called the Adamantine *Samadhi*, and also the Samadhi of Five-Knowledge Impression. Eighty-five thousand Bodhisattvas attained the All-Equal *Samadhi*. This All-Equal *Samadhi* is also called Great Loving-Kindness and Great Compassion. Beings as numerous as the grains of sand of countless Ganges aspired to unsurpassed *Bodhichitta* [Awakened Mind]; beings as numerous as the grains of sand of countless Ganges aspired to the *pratyeka* mind, and beings as numerous as the grains of sand of innumerable Ganges aspired to the *sravaka* mind. Two-million-billion females of the worlds of the humans and the gods discarded their female forms and became males*. Subhadra attained arhatship.

* Note from the new publisher, MahaVajra, of the esoteric Buddhist tradition of Mahajrya: In all the wonderful sutras thought to us by the Buddha, there is a message of unity in all things, and that everyone can attain enlightenment. The Buddha made no disctinction in gender. It is too easy, at the end of a document, to add a little line to indicate a difference in gender, and thus, taint the teachings with a cultural trait, such as disgracing women by telling them they cannot enlighten. I, like many other teachers of Buddhism, affirm that women can attain enlightenment, since it has nothing to do with biological disposition. The female form often was used to describe sensuality, and over thousands of years, might have brought about confusion in multiple translations.

Made in the USA
Middletown, DE
05 January 2024